P9-DEP-686

Frommer's®

England

Here's what the critics say about Frommer's:

"Amazingly easy to use. Very portable, very complete."
—*Booklist*

♦

"The only mainstream guide to list specific prices. The Walter Cronkite of guidebooks—with all that implies."
—*Travel & Leisure*

♦

"Complete, concise, and filled with useful information."
—*New York Daily News*

♦

"Hotel information is close to encyclopedic."
—*Des Moines Sunday Register*

Other Great Guides for Your Trip:

Frommer's London

Frommer's Scotland

Frommer's Britain's Best-Loved Driving Tours

Frommer's London from Day to Day

Frommer's England from $60 a Day

Frommer's Born to Shop London

Frommer's Memorable Walks in London

Frommer's Irreverent Guide to London

Frommer's® 99

England

by Darwin Porter
&
Danforth Prince

MACMILLAN • USA

ABOUT THE AUTHORS

A native of North Carolina, **Darwin Porter** was a bureau chief for the *Miami Herald* when he was 21 and was assigned to write the very first edition of a Frommer guide devoted solely to one European country. Since then, he has written numerous best-selling Frommer guides, notably to France, Italy, and Germany. In 1982, he was joined in his research efforts across England by **Danforth Prince**, formerly of the Paris bureau of *The New York Times,* who has traveled in and written extensively about England. Together, they are also the authors of *Frommer's London, Frommer's England from $60 a Day,* and *Frommer's Scotland.*

MACMILLAN TRAVEL

A Simon & Schuster Macmillan Company
1633 Broadway
New York, NY 10019

Find us online at www.frommers.com

Copyright © 1999 by Simon & Schuster, Inc.
Maps copyright © by Simon & Schuster, Inc.

ISBN 0-02-862307-X
ISSN 1055-5404

Editor: John Rosenthal
Production Editor: Suzanne Snyder
Photo Editor: Richard Fox
Design by Michele Laseau
Digital Cartography by Ortelius Design, Roberta Stockwell, and John DeCamillis
Page Creation by Tammy Ahrens, Jerry Cole, Stephanie Hammett, Bob LaRoche, and David E. W. Pruett

Front Cover Photo: Salisbury Cathedral

SPECIAL SALES

Bulk purchases (10+ copies) of Frommer's and selected Macmillan travel guides are available to corporations, organizations, mail-order catalogs, institutions, and charities at special discounts, and can be customized to suit individual needs. For more information write to Special Sales, Macmillan General Reference, 1633 Broadway, New York, NY 10019.

Manufactured in the United States of America

Contents

List of Maps

An Invitation to the Reader

In researching this book, we discovered many wonderful places—hotels, restaurants, shops, and more. We're sure you'll find others. Please tell us about them, so we can share the information with your fellow travelers in upcoming editions. If you were disappointed with a recommendation, we'd love to know that, too. Please write to:

Frommer's England '99
Macmillan Travel
1633 Broadway
New York, NY 10019

An Additional Note

Please be advised that travel information is subject to change at any time—and this is especially true of prices. We therefore suggest that you write or call ahead for confirmation when making your travel plans. The authors, editors, and publisher cannot be held responsible for the experiences of readers while traveling. Your safety is important to us, however, so we encourage you to stay alert and be aware of your surroundings. Keep a close eye on cameras, purses, and wallets, all favorite targets of thieves and pickpockets.

What the Symbols Mean

✪ Frommer's Favorites

Our favorite places and experiences—outstanding for quality, value, or both.

The following abbreviations are used for credit cards:

AE	American Express	DISC	Discover
CB	Carte Blanche	MC	MasterCard
DC	Diners Club	V	Visa

Find Frommer's Online

Arthur Frommer's Outspoken Encyclopedia of Travel (www.frommers.com) offers more than 6,000 pages of up-to-the-minute travel information—including the latest bargains and candid, personal articles updated daily by Arthur Frommer himself. No other Web site offers such comprehensive and timely coverage of the world of travel.

The Best of England

Planning a trip to England can present you with a bewildering array of choices. We've scoured the country in search of the best places and experiences, and in this chapter we'll share our very personal and opinionated choices. We hope they'll give you some ideas and get you started.

1 The Best Travel Experiences

- **Enjoying a Night at the Theater:** The torch passed down from Shakespeare is still burning brightly. Today, London's theater scene is acknowledged as the finest in the world. There are two major subsidized companies, the Royal Shakespeare Company, performing at the Barbican in London and at Stratford-upon-Avon, and the National Theatre on the South Bank. And fringe theater offers surprisingly good and often innovative productions staged in venues ranging from church cellars to the upstairs rooms of pubs. See chapter 5.
- **Pub Crawling:** The pursuit of the pint takes on cultural significance in England. Ornate taps fill tankards and mugs in pubs that serve as the social heart of every village and town. Quaint signs for such names as the Red Lion, the White Swan, the Bull, and the Royal Oak dot the landscape and beckon you in—not only for the pint but also for the conviviality, and perhaps even the entertainment or the food.
- **Motoring Through the Cotswolds:** If *driving* means going on a determined trip from one place to another, *motoring* is wandering at random, and there's no better place for it than the Cotswolds, less than 100 miles west of London. Its rolling hills and pasturelands are green from nurturing rains, and peppered with ivy-covered inns, stone walls, and honey-colored stone cottages. See chapter 12.
- **Punting on the Cam:** This is Cantabrigian English for gliding along in a flat-bottom boat, a long pole pushed into the River Cam's shallow bed, as you bypass the weeping willows along the banks, watch the strolling students along the graveled walkways, and take in the picture-postcard vistas of green lawns along the water's edge. See chapter 14.
- **Touring Stately Homes:** England has hundreds of mansions open to visitors, some of them centuries old, and we'll tell you about

dozens in the pages that lie ahead. The homes are often surrounded by beautiful gardens—perhaps a landscape by Capability Brown—and when the owners got fanciful, they added splashing fountains and miniature pagodas or temples.

- **Shopping for Antiques:** Whatever old treasure you're looking for can be found somewhere in England. We're talking Steiff teddy bears, a blunderbuss, an 1890 tin-plate toy train, an aircraft propeller from a downed RAF plane, an eggcup allegedly used by Queen Victoria, a first-edition English print from 1700, a theater program from 1926, or the definitive Henry Harper grandfather clock. No one polishes up his antiques and curios quite as brightly as English dealers. From auction houses to quaint shops, from flea markets to country fairs, England, particularly Victorian England, is for sale.

- **Cruising on Lake Windermere:** Inspired by the lyric poetry of Wordsworth, you can board a boat at Windermere or Bowness and sail England's most famous lake. You'll see the Lake District's scenery, its tilled valleys in the shadow of forbidding peaks, as it was meant to be viewed—from the water. A great jaunt is the round-trip from Bowness to Ambleside, at the head of the lake, all the way back around to the village of Lakeside, at the southern tip. See chapter 17.

2 The Best of Literary England

- **Samuel Johnson's House** (London): The backwater at no. 7 Gough Square, situated on the north side of Fleet Street, was Johnson's home from 1749 to 1758. Here he worked on his *Rambler* essays and his *Dictionary,* and here his beloved wife, "Tetty," died in 1752. Before he died in 1784, Johnson listed (for the sake of his future biographers) more than a dozen addresses where he had lived in London. See chapter 5.

- **Keats House** (Hampstead, London): Most of the poet's brief life was spent in London, where he was born in 1795 in a livery stable run by his father. He moved to Hampstead in 1817, and here he met his fiancée, Fanny Brawne. In this house he coughed blood into his handkerchief. "That drop of blood is my death warrant," he said. "I must die." He left to die in Rome a year later, in 1821. See chapter 5.

- **Jane Austen Country:** The author of *Pride and Prejudice* and *Sense and Sensibility* wrote of rural delights and a civilized society—set mainly in her beloved Hampshire. In 1809 she moved with her mother to Chawton, 50 miles south of Bath, where she lived until 1817. Her house is now a museum. Her novels *Persuasion* and *Northanger Abbey* are associated with the city of Bath, where she visited frequently in her youth and lived from 1801 to 1806. In her final year she moved to 8 College St. in Winchester and was buried in Winchester Cathedral. See chapters 8 and 9.

- **Stratford-upon-Avon:** Although the bard remains a mysterious figure, the folks who live in touristy Stratford gleefully peddle his literary legacy. There is Shakespeare's Birthplace, where the son of a glover was born on April 23, 1564. He died in Stratford on the same day, 52 years later. Anne Hathaway's Cottage, in the hamlet of Shottery, is also popular; Shakespeare married Hathaway when he was only 18 years old. See chapter 13.

- **Sherwood Forest:** You won't see Errol Flynn in Technicolor green tights gallivanting through a forest of mighty oaks with his merry band of men. Although most of the forest has been open grassland since the 14th century, it lives on in legend, literature, and lore as the most famous woodland in the world. At the

Sherwood Forest Visitor Centre at Edinstowe, the world of Friar Tuck and Little John live on, along with Maid Marian and Alan-a-Dale. See chapter 15.

- **Grasmere** (The Lake District): William Wordsworth lived here with his sister, Dorothy, who commented on the "domestic slip of mountain" behind their home, Dove Cottage. The cottage itself is now part of the Wordsworth Museum, displaying manuscripts and memorabilia. The poet also lived for a time at nearby Rydal Mount, just north of Ambleside, and one of his descendants still owns the property, where you can see gardens landscaped by the poet himself. Throughout the region, you'll view the landscapes that inspired this giant of English romanticism, including the shores of Ullswater, where Wordsworth saw his famous "host of golden daffodils." See chapter 17.
- **Haworth** (West Yorkshire): England's second major literary pilgrimage site is the home of the Brontë Parsonage Museum. Here the famous Brontë sisters lived and spun their web of romance. Emily wrote *Wuthering Heights,* Charlotte *Jane Eyre* and *Villette,* and even Anne wrote two novels, *The Tenant of Wildfell Hall* and *Agnes Grey,* although neither matches up to her sisters' work. See chapter 18.

3 The Best of Legendary England

- **Stonehenge** (near Salisbury, Wiltshire): The most celebrated prehistoric monument in all of Europe, Stonehenge is some 4,000 years old. Despite the "definitive" books written on the subject, its original purpose remains a mystery. Was it an astronomical observatory for a sun-worshipping cult? The romantic theory that Stonehenge was "constructed by the Druids" is nonsense, since it was completed before the Druids reached Britain in the 3rd century B.C., but legend still persists. See chapter 9.
- **Glastonbury Abbey** (Somerset): One of the great abbeys of England and once a center of culture and learning, Glastonbury quickly fell into a ruin following the Dissolution of the Monasteries. One story about the abbey says that Jesus came here as a child with Joseph of Arimathea. According to another legend, King Arthur was buried at Glastonbury, which was the site of the fabled Avalon. Today the abbey's large ruins are open to the public. See chapter 9.
- **Tintagel** (Cornwall): On the windswept Cornish coast, the castle of Tintagel is said to have been the birthplace of King Arthur. The castle was actually built much later than the Arthurian legend, around 1150. But who wants to stand in the way of a good story? No one in Cornwall, that's for sure. Tintagel merrily goes on its way, touting the King Arthur legend—in town you can order an Excaliburger! See chapter 11.

4 The Best of Ancient & Roman England

Stonehenge is listed in "The Best of Legendary England" category above.

- **Roman Painted House** (Dover, Kent): Called Britain's "buried Pompeii," this 1,800-year-old Roman structure has exceptionally well-preserved walls and even an under-floor heating system used by the Romans. It's best known for its unique bacchic murals. See chapter 7.
- **Avebury** (west of Marlborough, Wiltshire): Although not as famous as Stonehenge, this is one of Europe's leading prehistoric monuments. Its circle of more than 100 stones—some of them weighing in at 50 tons—is arrayed on a 20-acre site. See chapter 9.

- **Roman Baths** (Bath, Avon): Dedicated to the goddess Sulis Minerva, these baths were founded by the Romans in A.D. 75. They are among the finest Roman remains in the country and are still fed by Britain's most famous hot-water spring. The site of the Temple of Sulis has been excavated and is open to view. See chapter 9.
- **Corinium Museum** (Cirencester, in the Cotswolds): This regional museum contains one of the best collections of archaeological remains from the Roman occupation of Britain. You'll see Roman mosaics that have remained in Britain, along with provincial sculpture, such as figures of Minerva and Mercury. See chapter 12.
- **Hadrian's Wall** (north of England): A World Heritage Site, this wall—now in ruins—was ordered built by Hadrian, the Roman emperor, in A.D. 121 to hold back the barbarian invasions from the north. Marking the far northern border of the Roman Empire, the wall stretched 73 miles from Wallsend or Wall's End north of Newcastle upon Tyne in the east all the way to Bowness-on-Solway beyond Carlisle in the west. A small fort (called a "milecastle") was added at every mile along the wall. Garrison forts, some quite large, were constructed behind the wall. A highlight is Vindolanda, with the ruins of eight successive Roman forts. See chapter 18.

5 The Best of Norman & Medieval England

- **Battle** (East Sussex): This is the site of the famous Battle of Hastings (fought on October 14, 1066), in which the Normans defeated King Harold's English army. A great commemorative abbey was built here by William the Conqueror, the high altar of its church erected over the spot where King Harold fell in battle. The abbey was destroyed at the time of the Dissolution of the Monasteries, in 1538. The place where the altar stood is identified by a plaque. Some ruins and buildings remain, about which Tennyson wrote, "O Garden, blossoming out of English blood." See chapter 7.
- **Hastings Castle** (Hastings, on the south coast of England): Now in ruins, this was the first of the Norman castles erected in England (ca. 1067). The fortress was defortified by King John in 1216. An audiovisual presentation of the castle's history—shown on the grounds—includes the famous battle of 1066. See chapter 7.
- **Rye** (Sussex): Near the English Channel and flourishing in the 13th century, this *Antient* Cinque Port was a smuggling center for centuries. Writer Louis Jennings once wrote, "Nothing more recent than a Cavalier's Cloak, Hat and Ruffles should be seen on the streets of Rye." It's one of England's best preserved towns. See chapter 7.
- **Dunster Castle** (in the West Country): This castle was built on the site of a Norman castle granted to William de Mohun of Normandy by William the Conqueror shortly after the conquest of England. A 13th-century gateway remains from the original fortress. In 1376 the castle and its lands were bought by the Luttrell family and remained in their possession until the National Trust took it over in 1976. See chapter 9.
- **Warwick Castle:** This is one of the major sights in the Midlands. Little remains of William the Conqueror's motte-and-bailey castle of 1068, but much of today's external structure remains unchanged from the mid-1300s. Today Warwick Castle is the finest medieval castle in England, lying on a cliff overlooking the Avon. Its most powerful commander was the earl of Warwick in the 1400s, who, during the

War of the Roses, was called the "Kingmaker." One of the best collections of medieval armor and weapons in Europe is enclosed behind its walls. See chapter 13.

- **Fountains Abbey & Studley Royal** (southwest of Ripon, in North Yorkshire): These ruins evoke the monastic life of medieval England. The Cistercian monks constructed "a place remote from all the earth" in 1132. You'll explore the ruins as well as the Studley Royal, whose lavish 18th-century landscaping is one of the few surviving examples of a Georgian green garden. See chapter 18.

6 The Best of Tudor & Georgian England

- **Hampton Court Palace:** This is the most magnificent of a series of grand residences and royal palaces lining the River Thames west of Central London. Surrounded by rolling parkland, Hampton Court was built in grand style for Cardinal Wolsey—until Henry VIII snatched it away. Henry added the great hall in 1532, forcing laborers to toil 24 hours a day in shifts. The sheer size of the palace is amazing, and on its grounds is the world's first indoor tennis court. See chapter 5.
- **Bath:** Much magnificent 18th-century architecture remains exactly as Jane Austen once saw it, despite repeated World War II bombings. At one time Bath was the most fashionable spa in Britain. Architect John Wood (1704–54), among others, helped create a city of harmony and beauty, with landscaped terraces, famous crescents such as the Royal Crescent, and Palladian villas. See chapter 9.
- **Kenilworth Castle** (Warwickshire): Once the abode of Simon de Montfort, this castle was the setting for Sir Walter Scott's romantic novel, *Kenilworth,* first published in 1862, which recounts the supposed murder of Amy Robsart, wife of Robert Dudley, earl of Leicester. Elizabeth I had presented Kenilworth Castle to her favorite earl in 1563. The castle was destroyed after the civil war and is now in ruins. At one time the castle walls enclosed 7 acres. See chapter 13.

7 The Best of Victorian England

- **Albert Memorial** (London): If any statue symbolized an era, this flamboyant tribute to Victoria's consort, her beloved Albert (1819–61), does—it's the epitome of Victorian excess. Romantic and flamboyant, the statue depicts Albert holding a catalogue of the Great Exhibition. He overlooks the South Kensington Culture Centre, his last legacy. The 14-foot-high statue, with the blessing of the queen, went into place in 1876 and was instantly described as an "outsize reliquary casket." See chapter 5.
- **Houses of Parliament** (London): No government building in England symbolizes the Victorian age like the Palace of Westminster, housing Parliament. Replacing a palace destroyed by fire in 1834, it cost £2 million to build, a princely sum at the time. The building was almost completed by 1847 and turned out to be a Gothic fantasy, its facade decorated with rulers ranging from William the Conqueror to Queen Victoria. See chapter 5.
- **Osborne House** (southeast of East Cowes on the Isle of Wight): This was Queen Victoria and Prince Albert's most cherished residence. Constructed at Queen Victoria's own expense, it is imbued with her spirit. The rooms are a perfect period piece of Victoriana, with all their artifacts and stuffy chairs—a cozy clutter best evoked by her sitting room. Grief stricken at the death of Albert in 1861, the Queen requested that the house be kept as it was upon the death of her husband. See chapter 8.

- **Manchester:** A major inland port since 1894, Manchester long had a reputation as a blackened, foggy, and forbidding city, grim and dowdy, the worst of the Midlands. But it's been cleaned up, and today its center is filled with masterpieces of sturdy, solid Victorian architecture, including homes built for the great industrial barons of the 19th century. See chapter 16.
- **National Railway Museum** (York): The first national museum to be built away from London is devoted to the locomotive that changed the face of Victorian England. Set in an original steam locomotive depot, the museum is filled with railway memorabilia left by the Victorians. More than 40 full-size locomotives are on display, along with the century-old Royal Saloon, in which Queen Victoria rode until her death (it's like a small hotel!). See chapter 18.

8 The Best Museums

- **The British Museum** (London): When Sir Hans Sloane died in 1753, he bequeathed to England his vast collection of art and antiquities for only £20,000 ($32,000). This formed the nucleus of the collection that would one day embrace everything from the Rosetta stone to the hotly contested Elgin marbles (Greece wants them back). It's all here—and much, much more—in one of the world's great museums. See chapter 5.
- **The National Gallery** (London): One of the world's greatest collections of Western art dazzles the eye. Every artist from Leonardo da Vinci to Rembrandt to Picasso is represented here. The gallery is especially rich in works by Renaissance artists. See chapter 5.
- **Tate Gallery** (London): Two great national collections—some 10,000 works—call this gallery home. Sir Henry Tate, a sugar producer, started the nucleus of the collection with only 70 or so paintings. But the Tate has grown and grown, and was considerably enlarged when J. M. W. Turner bequeathed some 300 paintings and 19,000 watercolors to England upon his death. The Tate is also a repository of the most avant-garde modern art; its collection is so rich it has to be rotated every year. See chapter 5.
- **The American Museum** (Claverton, 2 miles east of Bath): Housed in a neoclassical country house, this collection presents 2 centuries of American life and styles—including George Washington's mother's recipe for gingerbread. See chapter 9.
- **The Fitzwilliam Museum** (Cambridge): Although London dominates the museum list, there are some outstanding regional museums, including this gem near King's College. Exhibits range from paintings by Leonardo da Vinci and Michelangelo to Chinese, Egyptian, and Greek antiquities. See chapter 14.
- **Walker Art Gallery** (Liverpool): One of the finest collections of European and British paintings in Britain, this gallery deserves to be better known. A nearly complete study of British paintings is displayed here, from Tudor days to the present. The gallery also owns an outstanding collection of pre-Raphaelites. See chapter 16.

9 The Best Cathedrals

- **Westminster Abbey** (London): One of the world's greatest Anglo-French Gothic buildings has witnessed a parade of English history—from the crowning of William the Conqueror on Christmas Day 1066 to the funeral of Princess Diana in 1997. With few exceptions, the kings and queens of England have all been crowned here, and many are buried here as well. See chapter 5.

- **Canterbury Cathedral:** The object of countless pilgrimages, as described in Chaucer's *Canterbury Tales,* this cathedral replaced one that was destroyed by fire in 1067. A new cathedral, dedicated in 1130, was also destroyed by fire in 1174, when the present structure was built. Thomas à Becket, the archbishop of Canterbury, was murdered here, and his shrine was an important site for pilgrims until the Reformation. See chapter 7.
- **Winchester Cathedral:** Dominating this ancient city and capital of old Wessex, Winchester Cathedral began to be built in 1079. In time it became England's longest medieval cathedral, noted for its 12-bay nave. Many famous people are buried here, including Jane Austen. See chapter 8.
- **Salisbury Cathedral:** The most stylistically unified of all cathedrals in England, this edifice was built between 1220 and 1265. Its landmark spire—its most striking feature—was constructed from 1285 to 1320. Salisbury Cathedral epitomizes the early English style of architecture. See chapter 9.
- **Durham Cathedral:** Completed between 1095 and 1133, this cathedral exemplifies Norman architecture on a broad scale. Its nave, a structure of almost majestic power, is its most notable feature. Its outstanding 13th-century Chapel of the Nine Altars was an early English addition. See chapter 18.
- **York Minster:** The largest Gothic cathedral north of the Alps is also among the grandest, with incredible stained glass. In fact, these windows combine to create the largest single surviving collection of medieval stained glass in England. Its unusual octagonal Chapter House has a late 15th-century choir screen by William Hyndeley and a wooden vaulted ceiling. See chapter 18.

10   The Best Castles, Palaces & Historic Homes

- **Woburn Abbey:** A Cistercian abbey for 4 centuries, Woburn Abbey, the seat of the dukes of Bedford, has been visited by everybody from Queen Victoria to Marilyn Monroe (that's quite a stretch!). You'll see Queen Victoria's Bedroom and the Canaletto Room, with 21 perspectives of Venice. The grounds, even more popular than the house, house the Wild Animal Kingdom; the best collection in England after the London Zoo. See chapter 6.
- **Hatfield House** (Hertfordshire): Hatfield was the childhood home of Elizabeth I, who was under an oak tree there when she learned she had become queen of England. Hatfield remains one of England's largest and finest country houses, complete with antiques, tapestries, paintings, and even the red silk stockings Elizabeth I wore. See chapter 6.
- **Windsor Castle:** The largest inhabited stronghold in the world and England's largest castle, Windsor Castle has been a royal abode since William the Conqueror constructed a motte and bailey on the site 4 years after conquering England. Severely damaged by fire in 1992, the castle has now been mainly restored. Its major attraction is the great Perpendicular Chapel of St. George's, begun by Edward IV. The chancel is known for its three-tiered stalls, which abound in misericords and ornate carvings. See chapter 6.
- **Blenheim Palace** (Woodstock): England's answer to Versailles, this extravagant baroque palace was the home of the 11th duke of Marlborough as well as the birthplace of Sir Winston Churchill. The structure was designed by Sir John Vanbrugh, of Castle Howard fame. Sarah, the duchess of Marlborough, battled the architects and builders from the beginning, wanting "a clean sweet house and garden be it ever so small." That she didn't get—the structure measures 850 feet from end to end. Capability Brown designed the gardens. See chapter 6.

- **Knole** (Kent): Begun in 1456 by the archbishop of Canterbury, Knole is celebrated for its 365 rooms (one for each day of the year), its 52 staircases (for each week of the year), and its 7 courts (for each day of the week). Knole, one of England's largest private houses and set in a 1,000-acre deer park, is a splendid example of Tudor architecture. See chapter 7.
- **Penshurst Place** (Kent): One of England's most outstanding country homes, this mansion was the former residence of Elizabethan poet Sir Philip Sidney (1554–86). In its day, the house attracted literati, including Ben Jonson. The original 1346 hall has seen the subsequent addition of Tudor, Jacobean, and neo-Gothic wings. See chapter 7.
- **Hever Castle & Gardens** (Kent): This was the childhood home of Anne Boleyn, second wife of Henry VIII and mother of Queen Elizabeth I. In 1903, William Waldorf Astor, a multimillionaire American and Anglophile, bought the castle, restored it, and landscaped the grounds. From the outside, it still looks like it did in Tudor times, with a moat and drawbridge protecting the castle. See chapter 7.
- **Beaulieu Abbey–Palace House** (Beaulieu, in New Forest): The home of the first Lord Montagu, Palace House blends monastic Gothic architecture from the Middle Ages with Victorian trappings. Yet many visitors consider the National Motor Museum, also on the premises and with a collection of more than 250 antique automobiles, more fascinating than the house. See chapter 8.
- **Harewood House & Bird Garden** (West Yorkshire): Edwin Lascelles began constructing this house in 1759, and his "pile" has been called an essay in Palladian architecture. The grand design involved some of the major talents of the day, including Robert Adam, Thomas Chippendale, and Capability Brown, who developed the grounds. A 4½-acre bird garden features exotic species from all over the world. See chapter 18.
- **Castle Howard** (North Yorkshire): This was Sir John Vanbrugh's grand masterpiece, and also the first building he ever designed. Many people will recognize it as the principal location for "Brideshead Revisited." A gilt-and-painted dome tops the striking entrance, and the park around Castle Howard is one of the most grandiose in Europe. See chapter 18.

11 The Best Gardens

- **Kew Gardens** (near London): A delight in any season. Everything from delicate exotics to commonplace flowers and shrubs bloom in profusion in this 300-acre garden. It's all part of a vast lab dedicated to identifying plants from all parts of the globe and growing some for commercial purposes. An easy trip from London, Kew Gardens embraces the largest herbarium on earth. Fabled landscape architect Capability Brown helped lay out some of the grounds. See chapter 5.
- **Wisley Garden** (Kent): Wisley Garden sprawls across 250 acres, filled with a profusion of flowers and shrubs. Maintained by the Royal Horticultural Society, it ranges from alpinelike meadows to summer carpets of flowers. In early summer, the gardens are brilliant with flowering rhododendrons. The landscaped orchid house alone is worth the trip here. See chapter 7.
- **Sissinghurst Castle Garden** (Kent): That notorious literary couple, Vita Sackville-West and Harold Nicholson, created this garden in sunny Kent. Its flamboyant parentage, unusual landscaping (the grounds were laid between the surviving parts of an Elizabethan mansion), and location just 21 miles northeast of Cranbrook make it the most intriguing garden on London's doorstep. Overrun by tourists in

summer, it's lovely in autumn, when the colors are at their dramatic best. See chapter 7.

- **Stourhead** (near Shaftesbury): Outside of the Greater London area, this is the most famous garden in England. The birthplace of English landscape gardening, Stourhead is still the best executed example of the taste for natural landscaping that swept England in the 1700s. The grounds have been compared to the painting of an old master such as Constable, but in 3-D. A wealth of flowering shrubs, trees, and beds upon beds of multihued blooms. Grottoes, bridges, and temples add to the allure. See chapter 9.
- **Hidcote Manor Garden** (near Chipping Campden, in the Cotswolds): Just outside one of the Cotswolds' most charming towns lies this stunning garden, laid out around a stone-built manor house. It's the largest garden in the Cotswolds, and one of the most intriguing in all of Britain. The garden originally bloomed under Major Lawrence Johnstone, an American horticulturist who created it in 1907. He traveled the world and brought back specimens to plant here. It shows. See chapter 12.

12 The Best Luxury Hotels

- **The Dorchester** (London; ☎ 800/727-9820 or 0171/629-8888): Acclaimed for decades as one of the world's great hotels, this citadel of luxury is owned by the richest man on earth, the sultan of Brunei. With such an owner, the hotel naturally drips with opulence. After a multimillion-pound restoration, "The Dorch" is more splendid than ever. The rooftop suites are dazzling, and the Terrace Restaurant, the Grill Room, and the Oriental Room—London's most exclusive Chinese restaurant—all deserve their acclaim. See chapter 4.
- **The Hempel** (London; ☎ 0171/298-9000): A relative newcomer to the scene, this deluxe hotel caused an overnight sensation when it first opened. Small and intimate, it has an artful, Zen simplicity. Mementos from Asia fill both the public areas and the deliberately understated rooms. The handsome, hip, young staff provides top-drawer service that ranks among London's finest. The hotel's restaurant, I-Thai, links two of the world's greatest cuisines: Italian and Thai. The menu is sparse but innovative, as chic as the guests. See chapter 4.
- **Chewton Glen Hotel** (New Milton, Hampshire; ☎ 01425/275341): On the fringe of New Forest between Lymington and Bournemouth, this hotel/health-and-country club is the best place to stay in southwest England. Service, taste, and quality are its hallmarks. The health club has a stunning design, with a centerpiece swimming pool and 70 acres of manicured grounds. Guest rooms feature period furniture. And the meals served in the Marryat Room Restaurant are prepared with first-rate ingredients. See chapter 8.
- **Ston Easton Park** (near Bath; ☎ 01761/241631): This splendid 1740 Palladian house has been massively and magnificently restored. The hotel's gardens are reason enough to stay here, but the bedrooms, with Chippendale or Hepplewhite four-poster beds, are equally worthy. Check in here for a taste of the *Upstairs, Downstairs* world of the 1700s. See chapter 9.
- **Thornbury Castle** (near Bristol; ☎ 01454/281182): Henry VIII seized this castle for a royal abode, and Mary Tudor lived here for a while. Eventually it was returned to the progeny of its original owner, the duke of Buckingham. This luxurious choice has all the elements associated with English castle living: Tudor portraits, candlelit baronial public rooms, Elizabethan fireplaces, oriel windows,

spiral staircases, four-posters, and stone fireplaces. There's even a garden for croquet. See chapter 9.

- **Gidleigh Park Hotel** (Chagford, Devon; ☎ 01647/432367): Forty acres of grounds in the Teign valley enclose a country-house hotel that is the epitome of gracious living. Every detail suggests the best of rural life: the premier antiques, those big English sofas, fabrics of the highest quality, and floral arrangements from the hotel's gardens. All that and a reputation for fine food unequaled in the area. See chapter 10.
- **Lygon Arms** (Broadway, Cotswolds; ☎ 01386/852255): Dating from 1532, this fabled inn in the Cotswolds has hosted many famous guests—Charles I used to drop in, and even Oliver Cromwell spent a night here, on the eve of the Battle of Worcester. Some of the inn's antiques are listed in *The Dictionary of English Furniture*. Request one of the nine rooms in the Tudor Wing, which have tilted oak floors and wooden beams. Number 20, with its massive canopied bed, is our favorite. See chapter 12.
- **Ettington Park Hotel** (Alderminster, south of Stratford-upon-Avon; ☎ 01789/450123): From the plant-filled conservatory entrance right up to the spacious, antique-filled bedrooms, you know you're getting something special here. The house is refurbished every year, and guests can soak up Old England country-house living in the tasteful Victorian drawing room or the richly paneled library bar. See chapter 13.
- **Sharrow Bay Country House Hotel** (Lake Ullswater, near Penrith; ☎ 01768/486301): This gem in the Lake District is known as much for its cuisine as for its accommodations. The location alone would justify checking in: a 12-acre site with gardens in a national park on bucolic Lake Ullswater, beneath Barton Fell. The lakeside dining room offers panoramic views of the water, and whether it be grilled scallops from the Kyle of Lochalsh or noisettes of English lamb, there is always something delectable on the menu here. See chapter 17.

13 The Best Moderately Priced Hotels

- **Diplomat Hotel** (London; ☎ 0171/235-1544): This hotel, near Sloane Square and Knightsbridge in the heart of Belgravia, provides the seemingly impossible: an affordable accommodation in one of the most expensive and elegant neighborhoods of London. Built in 1882 for one of the most famous architects of the Victorian era, it offers high-ceilinged and comfortable rooms, many of which were renovated in 1996. The overwhelming feeling is Victorian, though there are spick-and-span modern baths. See chapter 4.
- **The Fielding Hotel** (London; ☎ 0171/836-8305): Named after the novelist Henry Fielding, of *Tom Jones* fame, this hotel is one of the most eccentric in London. You'll either love it or hate it. Most guests love its cramped, quirky, quaint aura, and its location at Covent Garden is unbeatable. Everything is old-fashioned and traditional, but if you complain the bedrooms are too small, Smokey, the African Grey parrot, will tell you off! See chapter 4.
- **The Jenkins Hotel** (London; ☎ 0171/387-2067): Hailed by one London publication as 1 of the 10 best hotel values in town, the Jenkins was featured on the PBS *Mystery!* series *Poirot*. Those seeking a good and decent accommodation in Bloomsbury, at an affordable price, have been making their way to this address in Cartwright Gardens ever since Maggie Jenkins opened the place back in the 1920s. Rooms are small but well furnished, and some of the original Georgian charm remains. See chapter 4.

- **Wilbraham Hotel** (London; ☎ **0171/730-8296**): An inexpensive choice for Chelsea, this relatively modest hotel was formed by joining a trio of Victorian town houses. The rooms are small and pristine, but the price is right for expensive London, and the area, right off Sloane Street, is desirable. Have a drink in The Bar and Buttery and wander into the England of yesteryear. See chapter 4.
- **Old Parsonage Hotel** (Oxford; ☎ **01865/310210**): The site dates from the 14th century, and the present building was erected in 1660. Oscar Wilde was once a guest. It's hard to find a more charming hotel with as much character in Oxford today. Good taste, stylish comfort, fine accessories, and a clubby bar make this a winning choice. See chapter 6.
- **Howfield Manor** (west of Canterbury; ☎ **01227/738294**): This former manor house outside the cathedral city retains architectural treasures from its days as part of the Priory of St. Gregory. Bedrooms are divided between the original house and a new one. The manor is filled with character and has lots of details such as solid oak pieces and exposed beams. See chapter 7.
- **Mermaid Inn** (Rye; ☎ **01797/223065**): England's most famous smugglers' inn, the Mermaid sheltered Elizabeth I on her visit to Rye in 1573. At the time of the queen's visit, the inn had already been operating for 150 years. Still going strong, it leans heavily on English romance—old-world furnishings, linen-fold paneling, four-poster beds, and even a secret staircase. From its doorstep, the cobblestone streets of ancient Rye await exploration. See chapter 7.
- **Apsley House Hotel** (Bath; ☎ **01225/336966**): Away from the city center on the road to Bristol, this 1830 house was supposedly constructed for the duke of Wellington. Its owners have restored it and created a period house of character with an ambience of subdued elegance. See chapter 9.
- **The Rising Sun Hotel** (Lynmouth; ☎ **01598/753223**): At the mouth of the Lyn River, at the very end of a quay, this 14th-century thatched inn has uneven floors and crooked ceilings that are part of its charm. Snug, cozy, "under-the-eaves" bedrooms guarantee a good night's sleep; or you can rent Shelley's Cottage, where the poet honeymooned with his underage bride. The inn stakes out part of the river for salmon fishing. See chapter 10.
- **Bickleigh Cottage Country Hotel** (Bickleigh, Devon; ☎ **01884/855230**): This small thatched 17th-century cottage is a virtual cliché of Devonshire country charm. It has a riverside garden leading down to the much-photographed Bickleigh Bridge, where swans and ducks glide by. Inside, the cottage rooms are cozy with oak beams and old fireplaces. See chapter 10.
- **Abbey Hotel** (Penzance; ☎ **01736/366906**): Owned by Jean Shrimpton, former international model, and her husband, Michael Cox, this small-scale hotel is charming and of high quality. Dating from 1660, it occupies the site of a 12th-century abbey overlooking Penzance harbor. See chapter 11.
- **The Old Farmhouse Hotel** (Lower Swell; ☎ **01451/830232**): This was a working farm until the 1960s. A bar-lounge and a restaurant are in the original farmhouse, which dates from the 1500s. Some bedrooms are in converted stables, but the best rooms are in the old coach house. From here, you can rent a mountain bike and go exploring in the Cotswolds. See chapter 12.
- **Dean Court Hotel** (York; ☎ **01904/625082**): This building, dating from 1850, was originally intended to lodge the cathedral clergy of York Minster. Now this privately owned hotel lies right beneath the towers of the minster. It offers light and airy bedrooms; those at the front open onto cathedral views. See chapter 18.

14 The Best Restaurants

- **Le Gavroche** (London; ☎ 0171/408-0881): In this bastion of haute French cuisine, perfection is the rule. For more than a quarter of a century, Le Gavroche has reigned as the apogee of London's great French restaurants by serving classic French cookery with the most luxurious of ingredients—foie gras, truffles, and lobster. Michel Roux, son of Albert Roux (who founded the restaurant with his brother), is the chef today and serves some of the dishes his father made classic as well as his own innovations. See chapter 4.
- **The Oak Room/Marco Pierre White** (London; ☎ 0171/259-5380): Britain's enfant terrible of the kitchen, Marco Pierre White, has been Britain's most talked about chef for the past decade. Although this temperamental chef is spread thin these days (he directs several other properties as well), this is his pride and joy and the showcase of his culinary mastery. Working late into the night, Pierre White often creates his own dishes. They are inspired by the finest cuisine in England and on the Continent, but they are also utterly his own. Fish is his forte—none better than roast fillet of sea bass with olives, artichokes, and tomato butter. Critics hail his food as "more French than the French." See chapter 4.
- **La Tante Claire** (London; ☎ 0171/352-6045): Chef Pierre Koffman's cuisine has been defined as one of "ravishing purity." Although it stems from French roots, this cuisine achieves a style and quality that's rarely encountered—even in France. Koffman manages to bring more flavor to classic Gallic dishes than one might think possible. Beautifully portioned and impeccably prepared, his legendary pig's trotters with morels is just one of his signature dishes. See chapter 4.
- **Le Manoir aux Quat' Saisons** (Great Milton, southeast of Oxford; ☎ 01844/278881): The country-house hotel and restaurant of self-taught chef Raymond Blanc have brought him a TV series, as well as cookbooks and a school of cuisine. Although still showing intensely French loyalties, the celebrated chef now roams the world for inspiration. A new lightness, inspired mainly by Japan and the Mediterranean, is more and more evident in his creations. More meatless dishes appear on the seasonal menu, although the classics remain: sweetbread-stuffed pig's trotters, kidneys, and foie gras, even veal tongue. See chapter 6.
- **Harvey's Restaurant** (Bristol; ☎ 0117/9275034): Chef Daniel Galmiche, who first became known while cooking in Scotland, is a formidable talent. His cuisine is French, yet like many young chefs today, he experiments with ingredients and flavors from other culinary traditions, most notably the Far East and the Mediterranean. The unusual dining room is installed in wine cellars that date from 1796, and the service is amiably informal. See chapter 9.
- **The Carved Angel** (Dartmouth; ☎ 01803/832465): The elegant and airy Devon quay-side setting is ideal for the inspired cuisine of Joyce Molyneux, doyenne of British chefs. Her imaginative and inventive technique is based on strong British tradition, but more and more, the flavors and aromas of Provence, Italy, and even Asia are appearing on the menus. A mandatory stop for foodies. See chapter 10.
- **Le Champignon Sauvage** (Cheltenham; ☎ 01242/573449): David Everitt-Matthias has awakened the sleepy taste buds of Cheltenham. Thoroughly imbued in the French classics, he also adds more modern and lighter touches to his table d'hôte menus, the finest at this old spa. Some dishes reach into the old English repertoire, including stuffed leg of wild rabbit served with black pudding and turnip sauerkraut. His desserts are acclaimed as the most luscious in England. See chapter 12.

9

- **Marsh Goose** (Moreton-in-Marsh; ☎ **01608/652111**): Fans call it the Cotswolds' best-kept secret. Chef Sonya Kidney brings flair and individuality to her four-course dinner menus, with about seven or eight choices per course. All her dishes are flavorful (some evoke the Caribbean), but her roasted Cotswold lamb with eggplant and tomatoes is alone worth the trip. See chapter 12.
- **Le Talbooth** (Dedham; ☎ **01206/323150**): In Constable country, this restaurant dispenses its wares in a half-timbered Tudor building on the banks of the River Stour. In fair weather, you can dine alfresco under canvas parasols. The English/French à la carte menu changes six times a year, and special dishes change daily, reflecting the best produce available at the market. See chapter 14.
- **Miller Howe Hotel** (Windermere; ☎ **015394/45664**): At John Tovey's Edwardian country house above Lake Windermere, the chef is renowned for his English cuisine. What makes his cooking unusual are the unexpected combinations: mashed rutabagas with cider, glazed carrots flavored with Pernod, and most definitely the cardamom ice cream. See chapter 17.

15 The Best Pubs

- **The Salisbury** (London; ☎ **0171/836-5863**): Glittering cut-glass mirrors and old-fashioned banquettes, plus lighting fixtures of veiled bronze girls in flowing togas, recreate the Victorian gin-parlor atmosphere right in the heart of the West End. Theatergoers drop in for a homemade meat pie or a salad buffet before curtain time. See chapter 4.
- **The Grenadier** (London; ☎ **0171/235-3074**): Arguably London's most famous pub, and reputedly haunted, the Grenadier was once frequented by the duke of Wellington's officers on leave from fighting Napoléon. It pours the best Bloody Marys in town, and fillet of beef Wellington is always a specialty. See chapter 4.
- **The Ship Inn** (Exeter; ☎ **01392/272040**): Frequented by Sir Francis Drake and Sir Walter Raleigh, this pub on St. Martin's Lane near Exeter Cathedral is the most celebrated in Devon. It still provides tankards of real ale, the same drink swilled down by the likes of Sir John Hawkins. You can also eat here; portions are large, as in Elizabethan times. See chapter 10.
- **The Cott Inn** (Dartington, near Totnes, Devon; ☎ **01803/863777**): Constructed in 1320, this is believed to be the second-oldest inn in England. It's a low, rambling two-story building of stone, cob, and plaster under a thatched roof. A gathering place for the locals of Dartington, it's a good place for a drink on a windy night, as log fires keep the lounge and bar snug. See chapter 10.
- **The Punch Bowl Inn** (Lanreath, near Looe, Cornwall; ☎ **01503/220218**): Licensed since 1620 as a pub, this was a former rendezvous for smugglers. High-backed settees and old fireplaces evoke the atmosphere of olde England. You can sample drinks in one of the kitchens—they're among the few "kitchens" in England licensed in Britain as bars. See chapter 11.
- **The Turk's Head** (Penzance, Cornwall; ☎ **01736/363093**): Dating from 1233, this durable local favorite is filled with artifacts and timeworn beams. Drinkers take their lagers into a summer garden, or retreat inside to the snug chambers when the wind blows cold. See chapter 11.
- **The Lamb Inn** (Burford; ☎ **01993/823155**): This is our favorite place for a lager in all the Cotswolds. In a mellow old house from 1430 with thick stones and mullioned and leaded windows, it's a good place to spend the night, have a traditional

English meal, or else a beer. Snacks are served in the timeworn bars and lounges or in a garden in summer. See chapter 12.

- **The Black Swan** (Stratford-upon-Avon; ☎ **01789/297312**): This has been a popular hangout for Stratford players since the 18th century, and over the years we've spotted everybody from Peter O'Toole to Lord Laurence Olivier here having a drink. Locals affectionately call it "The Dirty Duck." In cool weather an open fireplace blazes, and you can stick around if you wish and order the chef's specialty: honey-roasted duck. See chapter 13.

Getting to Know England

Traveling in England is like walking through the pages of an illustrated history book—this is, after all, a country where 2,500 eventful years have left their mark. You can ponder the ancient mystery of Stonehenge, stand in the inner courtyard of the Tower of London where Lady Jane Grey was beheaded, walk through Westminster Abbey on the stone grave markers of famous political and literary figures, or visit the homes where Samuel Johnson, Charles Dickens, and Emily Brontë lived and worked.

England is a patchwork quilt of treasures, where you'll find an Elizabethan country estate in Devon, a half-timbered thatched cottage by the sea in Dorset, a regency manor in the Lake District, the great colleges in Cambridge and Oxford. And, of course, there's the exciting, cosmopolitan, colorful city of London, a bastion of tradition but also the hottest, hippest city in the world at the moment.

1 The Regions in Brief

England is a part of the United Kingdom, which is made up of England, Wales, Scotland, and Northern Ireland. Only 50,327 square miles—about the same size as New York State—England has an amazing amount of rural land and natural wilderness and an astonishing regional, physical, and cultural diversity.

London Some seven million Londoners live in this mammoth metropolis, a parcel of land that's more than 609 square miles. The City of London proper is merely 1 square mile but all the rest of the city is made up of separate villages, boroughs, and corporations. London's neighborhoods and outlying areas are described in chapter 4.

The Thames Valley England's most famous river runs westward from Kew to its source in the Cotswolds. A land of meadows, woodlands, attractive villages, small market towns, and rolling hillsides, this is one of England's most scenic areas. Highlights include **Windsor Castle** (Elizabeth II's favorite residence) and nearby **Eton College,** founded by a young Henry VI in 1440. **Henley,** site of the Royal Regatta, remains our favorite Thames-side town; and at the university city of **Oxford,** you can tour the colleges.

The Southeast (Kent, Surrey & Sussex) This is the land of Charles Lamb, Virginia Woolf, Sir Winston Churchill, and Henry James. Here are some of the nation's biggest attractions: **Brighton, Canterbury,**

Dover, and dozens of country homes and castles—not only **Hever and Leeds castles** but also **Chartwell,** the more modest abode where Churchill lived. In small villages, such as Rye and Winchelsea in Sussex, and in interesting towns like Haslemere, you discover the charm of the southeast. Almost all of the Sussex shoreline is built up, and seaside towns, such as Eastbourne and Hastings, are often tacky. In fact, although the area's major attraction is **Canterbury Cathedral,** the **Royal Pavilion at Brighton** rates as an outstanding, extravagant folly. Tea shops, antique shops, pubs, and small inns abound in the area. Surrey is essentially a commuter suburb of London and is easily reached for day trips.

Hampshire & Wiltshire Southwest of London, these two counties possess two of England's greatest **cathedrals** (Winchester and Salisbury) and one of Europe's most significant prehistoric monuments, **Stonehenge.** But there are other reasons for visiting, too. Hampshire is hemmed in by the woodlands and heaths of **New Forest** in its far west. **Portsmouth and Southampton** loom large in naval heritage. You might also want to take a ferry over to the **Isle of Wight,** once Queen Victoria's preferred vacation retreat. In Wiltshire, you encounter the beginning of the **West Country,** with its scenic beauty and monuments—Wilton House, the 17th-century home of the earls of Pembroke, and Old Sarum, the remains of what is believed to have been an Iron Age fortification.

The Southwest (Dorset, Somerset, Devon & Cornwall) These four counties are the great vacation centers and retirement havens of England. Dorset, associated with Thomas Hardy, is a land of rolling downs, rocky headlands, well-kept villages, and rich farmlands. Somerset—the Somerset of King Arthur and Camelot—offers such magical towns as **Glastonbury.** Devon has both **Exmoor and Dartmoor,** and northern and southern coastlines with such famous resorts as Lyme Regis and such villages as Clovelly. In Cornwall, you're never more than 20 miles from the rugged coastline, which ends at **Land's End.** Among the cities worth visiting in these counties are **Bath,** with its impressive Roman baths and Georgian architecture; **Plymouth,** departure point of the *Mayflower;* and **Wells,** site of a great cathedral.

The Cotswolds A wonderful region to tour, this is a bucolic land of honey-colored limestone villages where rural England unfolds before you like a storybook. In the Middle Ages, wool made the Cotswolders prosperous, but now they put out the welcome mat for visitors, with famously lovely inns and pubs. Start at Burford, the traditional gateway to the region, and continue on to Bourton-on-the-Water, Lower and Upper Slaughter, Stow-on-the-Wold, Moreton-in-Marsh, Chipping Campden, and Broadway. Cirencester is the uncrowned capital of the south Cotswolds, and Cheltenham is a still-elegant Regency spa. Our two favorite villages are Painswick, with its minute cottages, and Bibury, with its cluster of former weavers' cottages, Arlington Row.

Stratford & Warwick This is Shakespeare country in the Midlands, which was the birthplace of the Industrial Revolution, which made Britain the first industrialized country in the world. Its foremost tourist town is **Stratford-upon-Avon,** but also drawing visitors are **Warwick Castle,** one of England's great castles, and the ruins of **Kenilworth Castle. Coventry,** heavily bombed in World War II, is visited mainly for its outstanding modern cathedral.

Birmingham & the West Midlands The area known as the West Midlands embraces the so-called "Black Country." **Birmingham,** nicknamed "Brum," is Britain's largest city after London. The sprawling metropolis is still characterized by its overpass jungles and tacky suburbs, as well as great piles of Victorian architecture. Urban renewal is underway. The English marshes cut through the old counties of

Shropshire and **Herefordshire.** Ironbridge Gorge was at the heart of the Industrial Revolution, and the famous **Potteries** are in Staffordshire.

East Anglia (Essex, Cambridgeshire, Norfolk & Suffolk)   East Anglia, a semicircular geographic bulge northeast of London, is the name applied to these four very flat counties. The land of John Constable is still filled with his landscapes. The Fens—that broad expanse of fertile, black soil lying north of Cambridge—remains our favorite district. Go there to see **Ely Cathedral. Cambridge,** with its colleges and river, is the chief attraction. The most important museum is the Fitzwilliam in Cambridge, but visitors also flock to East Anglia for the scenery and its solitary beauty—fens and salt marshes and villages of thatched cottages.

The East Midlands (Derbyshire, Leicestershire, Lincolnshire, Northamptonshire & Nottinghamshire)   This area encompasses some of the worst of industrial England, yet there is great natural beauty to be found, too, as well as stately homes. These include Chatsworth in Derbyshire, the seat of the dukes of Devonshire; Sulgrave Manor in Northamptonshire, the ancestral home of George Washington; and Althorp House, also in Northamptonshire, the childhood home of the princess of Wales. **Lincoln** has one of England's great cathedrals, rebuilt in the 13th and 14th centuries. Bostonians like to visit their namesake, the old seaport town of Boston. **Nottingham** recalls Robin Hood, although the deforested Sherwood Forest is obviously not what it was in the outlaw's heyday.

The Northwest   Stretching from Liverpool to the Scottish border, northwest England can be a bucolic delight if you steer clear of its industrial pockets. Most people come here to follow in the footsteps of such romantic poets as Wordsworth, who wrote of the beauty of the Lake District (see below). But **Chester, Manchester,** and **Liverpool** merit stopovers along the way. The resort of **Blackpool** is big, brash, and a bit tawdry, drawing the working class of the Midlands for Coney Island–style fun by the sea. In contrast, the Roman city of Chester is a well-preserved medieval town, known for its encircling wall. And Liverpool is culturally alive and always intriguing, if only to see where the Beatles came from, but it also has a branch of London's Tate Gallery.

The Lake District   The literary Lakeland evokes memories of the Wordsworths, Samuel Taylor Coleridge, John Ruskin, and Beatrix Potter, among others. **Windermere** makes the best center, but there are many others as well, including **Grasmere and Ambleside.** The lake district contains some of England's most dramatic scenery.

Yorkshire & Northumbria   Yorkshire will be familiar to fans of the Brontës and James Herriot. **York,** with its immense cathedral and medieval streets, is the city to visit, although more and more visitors are calling on the cities of **Leeds and Bradford.** Northumbria comprises **Northumberland, Cleveland, Durham,** and **Tyne** and **Wear** (the area around **Newcastle**). The whole area echoes the ancient border battles between the Scots and English. **Hadrian's Wall,** built by the Romans, is a highlight. The great cathedral at Durham is one of Britain's finest examples of Norman church architecture, and **Fountains Abbey** is among the country's greatest ecclesiastical ruins. Country homes abound; here you find **Harewood House** and **Castle Howard.**

2 History 101

FROM MURKY BEGINNINGS TO ROMAN OCCUPATION   Britain was probably split off from the continent of Europe some 8 millennia ago by continental drift and other natural forces. The early inhabitants, the Iberians, were later to be identified

Dateline
- **54 B.C.** Julius Caesar invades England.
- **A.D. 43** Romans conquer England.

with stories of fairies, brownies, and "little people." These are the people whose ingenuity and enterprise are believed to have created Stonehenge, but despite that great and mysterious monument, little is known about them.

They were replaced by the iron-wielding Celts, whose massive invasions around 500 B.C. drove the Iberians back to the Scottish Highlands and Welsh mountains, where some of their descendants still live today.

In 54 B.C. Julius Caesar invaded England, but the Romans did not become established there until A.D. 43. They went as far as Caledonia (now Scotland), where they gave up, leaving that land to "the painted ones," or the warring Picts. The wall built by Emperor Hadrian across the north of England marked the northernmost reaches of the Roman Empire. During almost 4 centuries of occupation, the Romans built roads, villas, towns, walls, and fortresses; they farmed the land and introduced first their pagan religions, then Christianity. Agriculture and trade flourished.

FROM ANGLO-SAXON RULE TO THE NORMAN CONQUEST When the Roman legions withdrew, around A.D. 410, they left the country open to waves of invasions by Jutes, Angles, and Saxons, who established themselves in small kingdoms throughout the former Roman colony. From the 8th through the 11th centuries, the Anglo-Saxons contended with Danish raiders for control of the land.

By the time of the Norman conquest, the Saxon kingdoms were united under an elected king, Edward the Confessor. His successor was to rule less than a year before the Norman invasion.

The date 1066 is familiar to every English schoolchild. It marked an epic event, the only successful military invasion of Britain in history, and one of England's great turning points. King Harold, the last Anglo-Saxon king, was defeated at the Battle of Hastings, and William of Normandy was crowned as William I.

One of William's first acts was to order a survey of the land he had conquered, assessing all property in the nation for tax purposes. This survey was called the *Domesday Book*, or "Book of Doom," as some pegged it. The resulting document was completed around 1086 and has been a fertile sourcebook for British historians ever since.

Norman rule had an enormous impact on English society. All high offices were held by Normans, and

- **410** Jutes, Angles, and Saxons form small kingdoms in England.
- **500–1066** Anglo-Saxon kingdoms fight off Viking warriors.
- **1066** William, duke of Normandy, invades England, defeats Harold II at the Battle of Hastings.
- **1154** Henry II, first of the Plantagenets, launches their rule (which lasts until 1399).
- **1215** King John signs the Magna Carta at Runnymede.
- **1337** Hundred Years' War between France and England begins.
- **1485** Battle of Bosworth Field ends the War of the Roses between the Houses of York and Lancaster; Henry VII launches the Tudor dynasty.
- **1534** Henry VIII brings the Reformation to England and dissolves the monasteries.
- **1558** The accession of Elizabeth I ushers in an era of exploration and a renaissance in science and learning.
- **1588** Spanish Armada defeated.
- **1603** James VI of Scotland becomes James I of England, thus uniting the crowns of England and Scotland.
- **1620** Pilgrims sail from Plymouth on the Mayflower to found a colony in the New World.
- **1629** Charles I dissolves Parliament, ruling alone.
- **1642–49** Civil War between Royalists and Parliamentarians; the Parliamentarians win.
- **1649** Charles I beheaded, and England is a republic.
- **1653** Oliver Cromwell becomes Lord Protector.
- **1660** Charles II restored to the throne with limited power.
- **1665–66** Great Plague and Great Fire decimate London.

the Norman barons were given great grants of lands, and they built Norman-style castles and strongholds throughout the country. French was the language of the court for centuries—few people realize that heroes such as Richard the Lionheart probably spoke little or no English.

FROM THE RULE OF HENRY II TO THE MAGNA CARTA   In 1154 Henry II, the first of the Plantagenets, was crowned (reigned 1154–89). This remarkable character in English history ruled a vast empire—not only most of Britain but Normandy, Anjou, Brittany, and Aquitaine in France.

Henry was a man of powerful physique, both charming and terrifying. He reformed the courts and introduced the system of common law, which not only still operates in moderated form in England today, but also influenced the American legal system. But Henry is best remembered for ordering the infamous murder of Thomas à Becket, Archbishop of Canterbury. Henry, at odds with his archbishop, exclaimed, "Who will rid me of this turbulent priest?" His knights, overhearing and taking him at his word, murdered Thomas in front of the high altar in Canterbury Cathedral.

Henry's wife, Eleanor of Aquitaine, the most famous woman of her time, was no less of a colorful character. She accompanied her first husband, Louis VII of France, on the Second Crusade, and it was rumored that there she had a romantic affair with the Saracen leader, Saladin. Domestic and political life did not run smoothly, however, and Henry and Eleanor and their sons were often at odds. The pair have been the subject of many plays and films, including *The Lion in Winter, Becket,* and T. S. Eliot's *Murder in the Cathedral.*

Two of their sons were crowned kings of England. Richard the Lionheart actually spent most of his life outside England, on crusades or in France. John was forced by his nobles to sign the Magna Carta at Runnymede, in 1215—another date well known to English schoolchildren.

The Magna Carta guaranteed that the king was subject to the rule of law and gave certain rights to the king's subjects, beginning a process that eventually led to the development of parliamentary democracy as it is known in Britain today, a process that would have enormous influence on the American colonies many years later. The Magna Carta became known as the cornerstone of English liberties, though it only granted liberties to the barons. It took the

- **1688** James II, a Catholic, is deposed, and William and Mary come to the throne, signing a bill of rights.
- **1727** George I, the first of the Hanoverians, assumes the throne.
- **1756–63** In the Seven Years' War, Britain wins Canada from France.
- **1775–83** Britain loses its American colonies.
- **1795–1815** The Napoleonic Wars lead, finally, to the Battle of Waterloo and the defeat of Napoléon.
- **1837** Queen Victoria begins her reign as Britain reaches the zenith of its empire.
- **1901** Victoria dies, and Edward VII becomes king.
- **1914–18** England enters World War I and emerges victorious on the Allied side.
- **1936** Edward VIII abdicates to marry an American divorcée.
- **1939–45** In World War II, Britain stands alone against Hitler from the fall of France in 1940 until America enters the war in 1941. Dunkirk is evacuated in 1940; bombs rattle London during the blitz.
- **1945** Germany surrenders. Churchill is defeated; the Labor government introduces the welfare state and begins to dismantle the empire.
- **1952** Queen Elizabeth II ascends the throne.
- **1973** Britain joins the European Union.
- **1979** Margaret Thatcher becomes prime minister.
- **1982** Britain defeats Argentina in the Falklands War.
- **1990** Thatcher is ousted; John Major becomes prime minister.
- **1991** Britain fights with Allies to defeat Iraq.

rebellion of Simon de Montfort half a century later to introduce the notion that the boroughs and burghers should also have a voice and representation.

THE BLACK DEATH & THE WARS OF THE ROSES
In 1348, half the population died as the Black Death ravaged England. By the end of the century, the population of Britain had fallen from four million to two million.

England also suffered in the Hundred Years' War, which went on intermittently for more than a century. By 1371 England had lost much of its land on French soil. Henry V, immortalized by Shakespeare, revived England's claims to France, and his victory at Agincourt was notable for making obsolete the forms of medieval chivalry and warfare.

After Henry's death in 1422, disputes arose among successors to the crown that resulted in a long period of civil strife, the Wars of the Roses, between the Yorkists, who used a white rose as their symbol, and the Lancastrians with their red rose. The last Yorkist king was Richard III, who got bad press from Shakespeare, but who is defended to this day as a hero by the people of the city of York. Richard was defeated at Bosworth Field, and the victory introduced England to the first Tudor, the shrewd and wily Henry VII.

THE TUDORS TAKE THE THRONE
The Tudors were unlike the kings who had ruled before them. They introduced into England a strong central monarchy with far-reaching powers. The system worked well under the first three strong and capable Tudor monarchs, but began to break down later when the Stuarts came to the throne.

- **1992** Royals jolted by fire at Windsor Castle and marital troubles of their two sons. Britain joins the European Single Market. Deep recession signals the end of the booming 1980s.
- **1994** England is linked to the Continent by rail via the Channel Tunnel or Chunnel. Tony Blair elected Labour party leader.
- **1996** The IRA breaks a 17-month cease-fire with a truck bomb at the Docklands that claims two lives. Her Majesty prompts Charles and Di's divorce. The government concedes a possible link between mad-cow disease and a fatal brain ailment afflicting humans; British beef imports face banishment globally.
- **1997** London swings again. The Labour party ends 18 years of Conservative rule with a landslide election victory. The tragic death of Diana, Princess of Wales, prompts worldwide outpouring of grief.
- **1998** Prime Minister Tony Blair launches "New Britain"—young, stylish, and informal.

Henry VIII is surely the most notorious Tudor. Imperious and flamboyant, a colossus among English royalty, he slammed shut the door on the Middle Ages and introduced the Renaissance to England. He is best known, of course, for his treatment of his six wives and the unfortunate fates that befell five of them.

When his first wife, Catherine of Aragon, failed to produce an heir, and his ambitious mistress, Anne Boleyn, became pregnant, he tried to annul his marriage, but the pope refused, and Catherine contested the action. Defying the power of Rome, Henry had his marriage with Catherine declared invalid and secretly married Anne Boleyn in 1533.

The events that followed had profound consequences and introduced the religious controversy that was to dominate English politics for the next 4 centuries. Henry's break with the Roman Catholic Church and the formation of the Church of England, with himself as supreme head, was a turning point in English history. It led eventually to the Dissolution of the Monasteries, civil unrest, and much social dislocation. The confiscation of the church's land and possessions brought untold wealth into the king's coffers, wealth that was distributed to a new aristocracy that supported the monarch. In one sweeping gesture, Henry destroyed the ecclesiastical culture of the Middle Ages.

Among those who were executed for refusing to cooperate with Henry's changes was Sir Thomas More, humanist, international man of letters, and author of *Utopia*.

Anne Boleyn bore Henry a daughter, the future Elizabeth I, but failed to produce a male heir. She was brought to trial on a trumped-up charge of adultery and beheaded; in 1536, Henry married Jane Seymour, who died giving birth to Edward VI. For his next wife, he looked farther afield and chose Anne of Cleves from a flattering portrait, but she proved disappointing—he called her "The Great Flanders Mare." He divorced her the same year and next picked a pretty young woman from his court, Catherine Howard. She was also beheaded on a charge of adultery, but unlike Anne Boleyn, was probably guilty. Finally, he married an older woman, Catherine Parr, in 1543. She survived him.

Henry's heir, sickly Edward VI (reigned 1547–53), did not live long. He died of consumption—or, as rumor has it, overmedication. He was succeeded by his sister, Mary I (reigned 1553–58), and the trouble Henry had stirred up with the break with Rome came home to roost for the first time. Mary restored the Roman Catholic faith, and her persecution of the adherents of the Church of England earned her the name of "Bloody Mary." Some 300 Protestants were executed, many burned alive at the stake. She made an unpopular and unhappy marriage to Philip of Spain; despite her bloody reputation, her life was a sad one.

Elizabeth I (reigned 1558–1603) came next to the throne, ushering in an era of peace and prosperity, exploration, and a renaissance in science and learning. An entire age was named after her: the Elizabethan age. She was the last great and grand monarch to rule England, and her passion and magnetism were said to match her father's. Through her era marched Drake, Raleigh, Frobisher, Grenville, Shakespeare, Spenser, Byrd, and Hilliard. During her reign, she had to face the appalling precedent of ordering the execution of a fellow sovereign, Mary Queen of Scots. Her diplomatic skills kept war at bay until 1588, when at the apogee of her reign, the Spanish Armada was defeated. She will be forever remembered as "Good Queen Bess."

CIVIL WAR ERUPTS   The Stuarts ascended the throne in 1603, but though they held it through a century of civil war and religious dissension, they were not as capable as the Tudors in walking the line between the demands of a strong centralized monarchy and the rights increasingly demanded by the representatives of the people in Parliament.

Charles I, attracted by the French idea of the divine right of the king, considered himself above the law, a mistake the Tudors had never made (Elizabeth, in particular, was clever and careful in her dealings with Parliament). Charles's position was a fatal response to the Puritans and other Dissenters who sought far more power. In 1629, Charles dissolved Parliament, determined to rule without it.

Civil War followed, and the victory went to the Roundheads under Oliver Cromwell. Charles I was put on trial and was led to his execution, stepping onto the scaffold through the window of his gloriously decorated Banqueting House. His once-proud head rolled on the ground.

Oliver Cromwell, the melancholy, unambitious, clumsy farmer, became England's first and only virtual dictator. He saw his soldiers as God's faithful servants, and promised them rewards in heaven. The English people, however, did not take kindly to this form of government, and after Cromwell's death, Charles II, the dead king's son, returned and was crowned in 1660, but was given greatly limited powers.

FROM THE RESTORATION TO THE NAPOLEONIC WARS   The reign of Charles II was the beginning of a dreadful decade that saw London decimated by the Great Plague and destroyed by the Great Fire.

His successor, James II, attempted to return the country to Catholicism, an attempt that so frightened the powers that be that Catholics were for a long time deprived of their civil rights. James was deposed in the "Glorious Revolution" of 1688 and succeeded by his daughter Mary and her husband, William of Orange, thus securing the Protestant succession that has continued to this day. These tolerant and levelheaded monarchs signed a bill of rights, establishing the principle that the monarch reigns not by divine right but by the will of Parliament.

Queen Anne, Mary's sister, was the last of the Stuarts: She outlived all her children. Her reign (1702–14) saw the full union of England and Scotland.

After her death in 1714, England looked for a Protestant prince to succeed her, and they chose George of Hanover. He was invited to take the throne in 1714 as George I and thus began a 174-year dynasty. He spoke only German and spent as little time as possible in England. He left the running of the government to the English politicians and created the office of prime minister. Under the Hanoverians, the powers of Parliament were extended, and the constitutional monarchy developed into what it is today.

The American colonies were lost under the Hanoverian George III, but British possessions were expanded: Canada was won from the French in the Seven Years' War (1756–63), British control over India was affirmed, and Captain Cook claimed Australia and New Zealand for England. The British became embroiled in the Napoleonic Wars (1795–1815), achieving two of their greatest victories and acquiring two of their greatest heroes: Nelson at Trafalgar and Wellington at Waterloo.

THE INDUSTRIAL REVOLUTION & THE REIGN OF VICTORIA   The mid- to late 18th century saw the beginnings of the Industrial Revolution. This event changed the lives of the laboring class, created a wealthy middle class, and transformed England from a rural, agricultural society into an urban, industrial economy. England was now a world-class financial and military power. Male suffrage was extended, though women were to continue under a series of civil disabilities for the rest of the century.

Queen Victoria's reign (1837–1901) coincided with the height of the Industrial Revolution. When she ascended the throne, the monarchy as an institution was in considerable doubt, but her 64-year reign, the longest in tenure in English history, was an incomparable success.

The Victorian era was shaped by the growing power of the bourgeoisie, the queen and her consort's personal moral stance, and the perceived moral responsibilities of managing a vast empire. During this time, the first trade unions were formed, a public (state) school system was developed, and railroads were built.

Victoria never recovered from the death of her German husband, Albert. He died from typhoid fever in 1861, and the queen never remarried. Although she had many children, she found them tiresome, but was a pillar of family values nonetheless. One historian said her greatest asset was her relative ordinariness.

Middle-class values ruled Victorian England and were embodied by the queen. The racy England of the past went underground. Our present-day view of England is still influenced by the attitudes of the Victorian era, and we tend to forget that English society in earlier centuries was famous for its rowdiness, sexual license, and spicy scandal.

Victoria's son Edward VII (reigned 1901–10) was a playboy who had waited too long in the wings. He is famous for mistresses, especially Lillie Langtry, and his love of elaborate dinners. During his brief reign, he, too, had an era named after him: the Edwardian age. Under Edward, the country entered the 20th century at the height of

The New British Invasion

Nothing in British musical history has equaled the popular enthusiasm that greeted the British revolution of the 1960s. Aided by improvements in acoustical technology and the changing sociology of Britain, music was suddenly the passionate interest of millions of youthful Brits, setting the scene for a cultural invasion of American shores that hadn't been seen since the 18th century.

It began with the Beatles, of course—John, Paul, George, and Ringo, who won the hearts of every schoolgirl in America when they appeared on the *Ed Sullivan Show* in February 1964. They seemed to be in the vanguard of every cultural and musical movement, and as the 1960s progressed, the Beatles didn't simply capitalize on their success or the musical styles that had originally made them popular. Their music evolved with the times and helped shape the cultural and political texture of their era.

The Beatles were only the first of many British bands who found fertile ground and a receptive audience overseas. They were soon followed by The Rolling Stones and The Who.

And today British pop music is undergoing a rebirth, enjoying acclaim from critics around the world for being so thoroughly British, so contemporary, yet so actively retro in mirroring the sights, sounds, and actions of Swinging London of the '60s.

Neo-Brit brats Oasis are the preeminent band to score on MTV. This quintet has sold millions of records, with brothers Liam and Noel Gallagher presiding over hip London, bickering, spitting sarcasm about everyone and everything, and managing to show up at all the right parties and places, looking fashionably like The Who, and as scruffy as any Rolling Stone ever was, while sounding ever so Beatlesesque in melody. They're a product of their times, delivering messages for the nineties.

Other groups, such as Blur, Cast, and Ocean Colour Scene, also acknowledge the influence of the Beatles and the Stones, as well as The Who, The Kinks,

---

its imperial power, whereas at home the advent of the motorcar and the telephone radically changed social life, and the women's suffrage movement began.

World War I marked the end of an era. It had been assumed that peace, progress, prosperity, empire, and even social improvement would continue indefinitely. World War I and the troubled decades of social unrest, political uncertainty, and the rise of Nazism and fascism put an end to these expectations.

THE WINDS OF WAR   World War II began in 1939, and soon thereafter Britain had found a new and inspiring leader, Winston Churchill. Churchill led the nation during its "finest hour." For many months, Britain stood alone against Hitler, from the time the Germans took France until they were joined by their U.S. Allies. The evacuation of Dunkirk in 1940, the blitz of London, and the Battle of Britain were dark hours for the British people, and Churchill is remembered for urging them to hold onto their courage. Once the British forces were joined by their American allies, the tide finally turned, culminating in the D-Day invasion of German-occupied Normandy. These bloody events are still remembered by many with pride, and with nostalgia for the era when Britain was still a great world power.

The years following World War II brought many changes to England. Britain began to lose its grip on an empire (India became independent in 1947), and the Labour

David Bowie, Gary Glitter, T-Rex, The Sex Pistols, The Clash, and Faces. And the cities that gave birth to their talents—London, Liverpool, and Manchester—have exciting club scenes as a result.

Of course, if you agree with Prince Harry, it will be The Spice Girls for you. They are now a quartet (formerly a quintet) of talented beauties destined to conquer the world (until the world moves on to the next big media creation). Singing and dancing in trendy, eye-catching clothes, they're loaded with sex appeal and energy. With names like Baby, Posh, Scary, and Sporty Spice, what else would you expect but frothy fun?

Just wander through the London of today. The youthquake that's hit the capital of Dear Old Blighty pulsates with life and the sound of music. Jazz is alive in the clubs, as is the latest wave of British punk rock. Dancers can groove and trance to all variations of techno. Tricky keeps pushing the limits, reminding the world that he is a leader of all-influence, no-rules hip-hop. Bjork has followed the city's musical lead, and fled from her cold Scandinavian roots to London. Here she is sought out by no less an icon than Madonna for songwriting and inspiration because of her marriage of torch songs, hip-hop, and quirky pop.

But it's unfair to suggest that today's British musicians are simply following in the footsteps of past British invasions. Regardless of influences, they have created their own music, often from the pain and anguish of their own experiences. Today's pop sensations deliver a very identifiable national product to an international market.

At its best, Britpop is inclined to cultural introspection. What gives this latest invasion its identity is the insight young songwriters have gained from the 30 years of cultural, political, and economic turbulence that defined their lives. Listen closely: They are as pragmatic as their predecessors were visionary.

government, which came into power in 1945, established the welfare state and brought profound social change to Britain.

QUEEN ELIZABETH RULES TO THE PRESENT DAY Upon the death of the "wartime king," George VI, Elizabeth II ascended the throne in 1953. Her reign has seen the erosion of Britain's once-mighty industrial power, and, in recent years, a severe recession.

Political power has seesawed back and forth between the Conservative and Labour parties. Margaret Thatcher, who became prime minister in 1979, seriously eroded the welfare state and was ambivalent toward the European Union. Her popularity soared during the successful Falklands War, when Britain seemed to recover some of its military glory for a brief time.

Although the queen has remained steadfast and punctiliously performed her ceremonial duties, rumors about the royal family abounded, and in the year 1992, which Queen Elizabeth labeled an *annus horribilis*, a devastating fire swept through Windsor Castle, the marriages of several of her children crumbled, and the queen agreed to pay taxes for the first time. Prince Charles and Princess Diana agreed to a separation, and there were ominous rumblings about the future of the House of Windsor. By 1994 and 1995, Britain's economy was improving after several glum years, but Conservative prime minister John Major, heir to Margaret Thatcher's legacy, was coming under increasing criticism.

The IRA, reputedly enraged at the slow pace of peace talks, relaunched its reign of terror across London in February 1996, planting a massive bomb that ripped through a building in London's Docklands, injuring more than 100 people and killing two. Shattered, too, was the 17-month cease-fire by the IRA, which brought hope that peace was at least possible. Another bomb went off in Manchester in June.

Headlines about the IRA bombing gave way to another big bomb: the end of the marriage of Princess Diana and Prince Charles. The Wedding of the Century had become the Divorce of the Century. The lurid tabloids had been right all along about this unhappy pair. But details of the $26 million divorce settlement didn't satisfy the curious: Scrutiny of Prince Charles's relationship with Camilla Parker Bowles, as well as gossip about Princess Diana's love life, continued in the press.

But in 1997, everyone's attention shifted to the parliamentary election. John Major's support had been steadily eroding since the early nineties, but the public's confidence in him seemed to hit an all-time low with his handling of the mad-cow disease crisis. Although scientists now claim the epidemic will end naturally by 2001, many British voters blamed Major and the Tories for it.

The political limelight now rested on the young Labour Leader Tony Blair. From his rock-star acquaintances to his "New Labour" rhetoric, which is chock-full of pop-culture buzzwords, he is a stark contrast to the more staid Major. And his media-savvy personality obviously registered with the British electorate. On May 1, 1997, the Labour Party ended 18 years of Conservative rule with a landslide election victory. At age 44, Blair became Britain's youngest prime minister in 185 years, following in the wake of the largest Labour triumph since Winston Churchill was swept out of office at the end of World War II.

Blair's election—which came just at the moment when London was being touted by the international press for its renaissance in art, music, fashion, and dining—had many British entrepreneurs poised and ready to take advantage of what they perceived as enthusiasm for new ideas and ventures. Comparisons to Harold Macmillan and his reign over the Swinging Sixties were inevitable, and insiders agree that something's in the air.

However, events took a shocking turn in August 1997 when Princess Diana was killed—along with her companion, Harrods heir Dodi al-Fayed—in a high-speed car crash in Paris.

"The People's Princess" still continued to dominate many headlines in 1998 with bizarre conspiracy theories about her death. But the royal family isn't the real force in Britain today. The spotlight remains on Tony Blair, who is moving ahead in streamlining the government.

Blair continues to lead Britain on a program of constitutional reform without parallel in this century. Critics fear that Blair will one day preside over a "disunited" Britain, with Scotland breaking away and Northern Ireland forming a self-government.

Of course, the future of the monarchy still remains a hot topic of discussion in Britain. There is little support for doing away with the monarchy in Britain today in spite of wide criticism of the royal family's behavior in the wake of Diana's death. Apparently, if polls are to be believed, some three-quarters of the British populace want the monarchy to continue, despite the fact that Prince William has reportedly announced that he doesn't want to be king. At the very least the monarchy is good for the tourist trade, on which Britain is increasingly dependent. And what would the tabloids do without it?

3 Pies, Pudding & Pints: The Lowdown on British Cuisine

The late British humorist George Mikes wrote that "the Continentals have good food; the English have good table manners." But the British no longer deserve their reputation for soggy cabbage and tasteless dishes. Contemporary London—and the country as a whole—boasts many fine restaurants and sophisticated cuisine.

There's a lot more to British food today than the traditional roast, which has been celebrated since long before the days of Henry VIII. Of course, parsnip soup is still served, but now it's likely to graced with a dollop of walnut salsa verde. In contemporary England, the chef of the 1990s has taken on celebrity status. The man or woman in the kitchen creating breast of Gressingham duck topped with deep-fried seaweed and served with a passion-fruit sauce is honored the way rock stars were in the 1970s. Some restaurants are so popular that they are demanding reservations 2 weeks in advance, if not more.

If you want to see what Britain is eating today, just drop in at Harvey Nichol's Fifth Floor in London's Knightsbridge for its dazzling display of produce from all over the globe.

The new buzzword for British cuisine is *magpie*, meaning borrowing ideas from global travels, taking them home, but improving on the original.

Be aware that many of the trendiest, most innovative restaurants are mind-blowingly expensive, especially in London. We'll point out some innovative but affordable choices in the pages that follow, but if you're really trying to save on dining costs, you'll no doubt find yourself falling back on the traditional pub favorites (or better still, turning to an increasingly good selection of ethnic restaurants).

WHAT YOU'LL FIND ON THE MENU   On any pub menu you're likely to encounter such dishes as the **Cornish pasty** and **shepherd's pie.** The first, traditionally made from Sunday-meal leftovers and taken by West Country fishers for Monday lunch, consists of chopped potatoes, carrots, and onions mixed together with seasoning and put into a pastry envelope. The second is a deep dish of chopped cooked beef mixed with onions and seasoning, covered with a layer of mashed potatoes, and served hot. Another version is cottage pie, which is minced beef covered with potatoes and also served hot. Of course, these beef dishes are subject to availability. In addition to a pasty, Cornwall also gives us "Stargazy Pie"—a deep-dish fish pie with a crisp crust covering a creamy concoction of freshly caught herring and vegetables.

The most common pub meal, though, is the **ploughman's lunch,** traditional farm-worker's fare, consisting of a good chunk of local cheese, a hunk of homemade crusty white or brown bread, some butter, and a pickled onion or two, washed down with ale. You'll now find such variations as pâté and chutney occasionally replacing the onions and cheese. Or you might find **Lancashire hot pot,** a stew of mutton, potatoes, kidneys, and onions (sometimes carrots). This concoction was originally put into a deep dish and set on the edge of the stove to cook slowly while the workers spent the day at the local mill.

Among appetizers, called **"starters"** in England, the most typical are potted shrimp (small buttered shrimp preserved in a jar), prawn cocktail, and smoked salmon. You might also be served pâté or "fish pie," which is very light fish pâté. Most menus will feature a variety of soups, including cock-a-leekie (chicken soup flavored with leeks), perhaps a game soup that has been doused with sherry, and many others.

Among the best-known traditional English meals is **roast beef and Yorkshire pudding** (the pudding is made with a flour base and cooked under the roast, allowing the fat from the meat to drop onto it). The beef could easily be a large sirloin (rolled loin), which, so the story goes, was named by James I when he was a guest at Houghton Tower, Lancashire. "Arise, Sir Loin," he cried, as he knighted the leg of beef before him with his dagger. (Again, because of the mad-cow crisis, beef dishes may not be available or advisable.) Another dish that makes use of a flour base is toad-in-the-hole, in which sausages are cooked in batter. Game, especially pheasant and grouse, is also a staple on British tables.

On any menu, you'll find **fresh seafood:** cod, haddock, herring, plaice, and Dover sole, the aristocrat of flatfish. Cod and haddock are used in making British **fish-and-chips** (chips are fried potatoes or thick french fries), which the true Briton covers with salt and vinegar. If you like **oysters,** try some of the famous Colchester variety. On the west coast, you'll find a not-to-be-missed delicacy: **Morecambe Bay shrimp.** Every region of England has its seafood specialties. In Ely, lying in the marshy fen district of East Anglia, it might be fenland eel pie with a twiggy seaweed as your green vegetable. Amphire also grows here in the salt marshes and along the Norfolk Coast. It's pickled in May and June and appears as a delicacy on many summer menus.

The **East End of London** has quite a few interesting old dishes, among them tripe and onions. In winter, Dr. Johnson's favorite tavern, the Cheshire Cheese on Fleet Street, offers a beefsteak-kidney-mushroom-and-game pudding in a suet case; in summer, there's a pastry case. East Enders can still be seen on Sunday at the Jellied Eel stall by Petticoat Lane, eating eel, cockles (small clams), mussels, whelks, and winkles—all with a touch of vinegar.

The British call desserts "sweets," although some people still refer to any dessert as **"pudding." Trifle** is the most famous English dessert, consisting of sponge cake soaked in brandy or sherry, coated with fruit or jam, and topped with cream custard. A **"fool,"** such as gooseberry fool, is a light cream dessert whipped up from seasonal fruits. Regional sweets include the **northern "flitting" dumpling** (dates, walnuts, and syrup mixed with other ingredients and made into a pudding that is easily sliced and carried along when you're "flitting" from place to place). Similarly, **hasty pudding,** a Newcastle dish, is supposed to have been invented by people in a hurry to avoid the bailiff. It consists of stale bread, to which some dried fruit and milk are added before it is put into the oven.

Cheese is traditionally served after dessert as a savory. There are many regional cheeses, the best known being cheddar, a good, solid, mature cheese. Others are the semismooth Caerphilly, from a beautiful part of Wales, and Stilton, a blue-veined crumbly cheese that's often enriched with a glass of port.

ENGLISH BREAKFASTS & AFTERNOON TEA   Britain is famous for its enormous breakfast of bacon, eggs, grilled tomato, and fried bread. Some places have replaced this cholesterol festival with a continental breakfast, but you'll still find the traditional morning meal available.

Kipper, or smoked herring, is also a popular breakfast dish. The finest come from the Isle of Man, Whitby, or Lock Fyne, in Scotland. The herrings are split open, placed over oak chips, and slowly cooked to produce a nice pale-brown smoked fish.

Many people still enjoy afternoon tea, which may consist of a simple cup of tea or a formal tea that starts with tiny crustless sandwiches filled with cucumber or watercress and proceeds through scones, crumpets with jam, or clotted cream, followed by cakes and tarts—all accompanied by a proper pot of tea. The tea at Brown's, in London, is quintessentially English, whereas the Ritz's tea is an elaborate affair, complete with orchestra and dancing.

In the country, tea shops abound, and in Devon, Cornwall, and the West Country you'll find the best cream teas; they consist of scones spread with jam and thick, clotted Devonshire cream. It's a delicious treat, indeed. People in Britain drink an average of four cups of tea a day, although many younger people prefer coffee.

WHAT TO WASH IT ALL DOWN WITH   English pubs serve a variety of cocktails, but their stock-in-trade is beer: brown beer, or bitter; blond beer, or lager; and very dark beer, or stout. The standard English draft beer is much stronger than American beer and is served "with the chill off," because it doesn't taste good cold. Lager is always chilled, whereas stout can be served either way. Beer is always served straight from the tap, in two sizes: half-pint (8 oz.) and pint (16 oz.).

One of the most significant changes in English drinking habits has been the popularity of wine bars, and you will find many to try, including some that turn into discos late at night. Britain isn't known for its wine, although it does produce some medium-sweet fruity whites. Its cider, though, is famous—and mighty potent in contrast to the American variety.

Whisky (spelled without the *e*) refers to scotch. Canadian and Irish whiskey (spelled with the *e*) are also available, but only the very best-stocked bars have American bourbon and rye.

While you're in England, you may want to try the very English drink called Pimm's, a mixture developed by James Pimm, owner of a popular London oyster house in the 1840s. Although it can be consumed on the rocks, it's usually served as a Pimm's Cup—a drink that will have any number and variety of ingredients, depending on which part of the world (or empire) you're in. Here, just for fun, is a typical recipe: Take a very tall glass and fill it with ice. Add a thin slice of lemon (or orange), a cucumber spike (or a curl of cucumber rind), and 2 ounces of Pimm's liquor. Then finish with a splash of either lemon or club soda, 7-Up, or Tom Collins mix.

The English tend to drink everything at a warmer temperature than Americans are used to. So if you like ice in your soda, be sure to ask for lots of it, or you're likely to end up with a measly, quickly melting cube or two.

3 Planning a Trip to England

In the pages that follow, we've compiled everything you need to know about how to handle the practical details of planning your trip in advance: finding the best airfare, deciding when to go, figuring out British currency, and more.

1 Visitor Information & Entry Requirements

VISITOR INFORMATION Before you go, you can obtain general information from **British Tourist Authority Offices:**

- In the United States: 551 Fifth Ave., Suite 701, New York, NY 10176-0799 (☎ **800/462-2748** or 212/986-2200).
- In Canada: 111 Avenue Rd., Suite 450, Toronto, ON M5R 3J8 (☎ **888/VISIT-UK** in Canada, or 416/925-6326).
- In Australia: University Centre, 8th floor, 210 Clarence St., Sydney NSW 2000 (☎ **02/267-4413**).
- In New Zealand: Suite 305, Dilworth Building, at the corner of Queen and Customs streets, Auckland 1 (☎ **09/303-1446**).

The BTA maintains a Web page at **www.visitbritain.com,** covering special interests, attractions, trip-planning tips, festivals, accommodations, and more.

For a full information pack on London, write to the **London Tourist Board,** Glenn House, Stag Place, London SW1E 6LT (☎ **0171/932-2000**). You can also call the recorded-message service, **Visitorcall** (☎ **01839/123456**), 24 hours a day. Various topics are listed; calls cost 50p (80¢) per minute.

You can usually pick up a copy of *Time Out,* the most up-to-date source for what's happening in London, at any international newsstand. You can also check it out on the Net at **www.timeout.co.uk**.

ENTRY REQUIREMENTS All U.S. citizens, Canadians, Australians, New Zealanders, and South Africans must have a passport with at least 2 months remaining validity. No visa is required. The immigration officer will also want proof of your intention to return to your point of origin (usually a round-trip ticket) and visible means of support while you're in Britain. If you're planning to fly from the United States or Canada to the United Kingdom and then on to a country that requires a visa (India, for example), you should secure that visa before you arrive in Britain.

Your valid driver's license and at least one year of driving experience is required to drive personal or rented cars.

CUSTOMS   For visitors **coming to England,** goods fall into two basic categories: purchases made in a non–European Union (EU) country (or bought tax-free within the EU), and purchases on which tax was paid in the European Union. In the former category, limits on imports by individuals (aged 17 and older) include 200 cigarettes, 50 cigars, or 250 grams (8.8 oz.) of loose tobacco; 2 liters (2.1 qt.) of still table wine, 1 liter of liquor (over 22% alcohol content), or 2 liters of liquor (under 22%); and 2 fluid ounces of perfume. In the latter category—items on which tax was paid in the EU—limits are *much* higher: An individual may import 800 cigarettes, 200 cigars, *and* 1 kilogram (2.2 lb.) of loose tobacco; 90 liters (23.8 gal.) of wine, 10 liters (2.6 gal.) of alcohol (over 22%), *and* 110 liters (29.1 gal.) of beer; plus unlimited amounts of perfume.

Returning U.S. citizens who have been away for 48 hours or more are allowed to bring back, once every 30 days, $400 worth of merchandise duty-free. You'll be charged a flat rate of 10% duty on the next $1,000 worth of purchases. Be sure to have your receipts handy. On gifts, the duty-free limit is $100. For more specific guidance, write to the **U.S. Customs Service,** P.O. Box 7407, Washington, DC 20044 (☎ 202/ 927-6724), requesting the free pamphlet *Know Before You Go.* You can download the pamphlet from the Internet at **www.customs.ustreas.gov/travel/kbygo.htm**.

For a clear summary of **Canadian rules,** write for the booklet *I Declare,* issued by **Revenue Canada,** 2265 St. Laurent Blvd., Ottawa K1G 4KE (☎ 800/461-9999 or 613/993-0534). Canada allows its citizens a $500 exemption, and you are allowed to bring back duty-free 200 cigarettes, 2.2 pounds of tobacco, 40 imperial ounces (1.2 qt.) of liquor, and 50 cigars. In addition, you are allowed to mail gifts to Canada from abroad at the rate of Can$60 a day, provided they are unsolicited and aren't alcohol or tobacco (write on the package: "Unsolicited gift, under $60 value"). All valuables should be declared on the Y-38 Form before departure from Canada, including serial numbers of, for example, expensive foreign cameras that you already own. *Note:* The $500 exemption can be used only once a year and only after an absence of 7 days.

The duty-free allowance in **Australia** is A$400 or, for those under 18, A$200. Personal property mailed back from England should be marked "Australian goods returned" to avoid payment of duty. Upon returning to Australia, citizens can bring in 250 cigarettes or 250 grams of loose tobacco, and 1 liter (1.1 qt.) of alcohol. If you're returning with valuable goods you already own, such as foreign-made cameras, you should file form B263. A helpful brochure, available from Australian consulates or customs offices, is *Customs Information for All Travellers.* For more information, contact **Australian Customs Services,** GPO Box 8, Sydney NSW 2001 (☎ 02/92132000).

The duty-free allowance for **New Zealand** is NZ$700. Citizens over 17 years of age can bring in 200 cigarettes, or 50 cigars, or 250 grams of tobacco (or a mixture of all three if their combined weight doesn't exceed 250 grams); plus 4.5 liters of wine and beer, or 1.125 liters of liquor. New Zealand currency does not carry import or export restrictions. Fill out a certificate of export, listing the valuables you are taking out of the country; that way, you can bring them back without paying duty. Most questions are answered in a free pamphlet available at New Zealand consulates and customs offices: *New Zealand Customs Guide for Travellers,* Notice no. 4. For more information, contact **New Zealand Customs,** 50 Anzac Ave., P.O. Box 29, Auckland (☎ 09/359-66-55).

Ireland allows its citizens to bring in 200 cigarettes or 100 cigarillos or 50 cigars or 250 grams of tobacco, plus 1 liter of liquor exceeding 22% by volume (such as whisky, brandy, gin, rum, or vodka), or 2 liters of distilled beverages and spirits with a wine or alcoholic base of an alcoholic strength not exceeding 22% by volume, plus 2 liters of other wine and 50 grams of perfume. Other allowances include duty-free goods to a value of £73 per person or £36.50 per person for travelers under 15 years of age. For more information, contact **The Revenue Commissioners,** Dublin Castle, Dublin 2 (☎ **01/679-27-77**).

2 Money

The British currency is the pound sterling (£), made up of 100 pence (p), which is used throughout the United Kingdom. Notes are issued in £5, £10, £20, and £50 denominations. (A £1 note also circulates in Scotland.) Coins come in 1p, 2p, 5p, 10p, 50p, and £1.

At this writing, the price conversion in this book have been computed at the rate of $1 equals 63p (or £1 = $1.60). Bear in mind, however, that exchange rates can always fluctuate for a variety of reasons, so it's important to check the latest quotes before your trip so you can budget accordingly.

ATM NETWORKS Plus, Cirrus, and other ATM networks are accessible throughout London and other parts of Britain. When using an ATM abroad, you'll get your money in the local currency; the rate of exchange tends to be as good, if not better, than what you would receive at an airport money counter or a hotel. Note that international withdrawal fees will be higher than domestic fees; ask your bank for specifics. (Also, check to see if your PIN code must be reprogrammed for usage in London. Most ATMs outside the United States require a four-digit PIN.)

To receive a directory of **Cirrus** ATMs, call ☎ **800/424-7787;** for **Plus** locations, call ☎ **800/843-7587.** You can also access the Visa/PLUS International ATM Locator Guide through the Web at **www.visa.com/visa**.

If you have a Citibank Visa or MasterCard, you can call Citibank's offices in London at ☎ **0171/500-5500** for information on where to get cash from automatic tellers.

TRAVELER'S CHECKS Though ATM usage abroad is becoming increasingly easy, many people still prefer the security of carrying traveler's checks, since they know they'll be able to recoup the value of the checks if they're stolen. And most banks will give you a better exchange rate for traveler's checks than cash. Purchase them in pound denominations to make your life easier.

Major issuers of traveler's checks include **American Express** (☎ 800/221-7282); **Citicorp** (☎ **800/645-6556** in the U.S. and Canada, or 813/623-1709 collect from anywhere else in the world); **Thomas Cook** (☎ **800/223-7373** in the U.S. and Canada, or 609/987-7300 collect from other parts of the world); and **Interpayment Services** (☎ **800/221-2426** in the U.S. and Canada, or 212/858-8500 collect from other parts of the world).

Most large banks sell traveler's checks, charging fees that average between 1% and 2% of the value of the checks you buy. If your bank wants more than a 2% commission, you'll be better off calling the traveler's-check issuers yourself and finding the location of an outlet where the commission is more reasonable.

Issuers sometimes have agreements with groups to sell checks commission-free. For example, the American Automobile Association (AAA) sells American Express checks without commission.

The U.S. Dollar & the British Pound

U.S.$	UK £	U.S.$	UK £
0.25	0.16	15	9.45
0.50	0.32	20	12.60
0.75	0.47	25	15.75
1.00	0.63	50	31.50
2.00	1.26	75	47.25
3.00	1.89	100	63.00
4.00	2.52	150	94.50
5.00	3.15	200	126.00
6.00	3.78	250	157.50
7.00	4.41	300	189.00
8.00	5.04	350	220.50
9.00	5.67	400	252.00
10.00	6.30	500	315.00

CREDIT CARDS   The way to get the best rate of exchange is to buy whatever you can with credit cards. They almost always offer a rate of exchange better than any you can get by changing your money, and there's no accompanying service charge. American Express, Visa, and Diners Club are widely accepted. A Eurocard or Access sign displayed at an establishment means that it accepts MasterCard. **Citicorp Visa's** U.S. emergency number is ☎ **800/645-6556. American Express** cardholders and traveler's check holders should call ☎ **800/221-7282** for all money emergencies. **MasterCard** holders should call ☎ **800/307-7309.**

EXCHANGING YOUR MONEY   It's always wise to exchange enough money before you leave home to get you from the airport to your hotel. This way, you avoid delays and the lousy rates at the airport exchange booths.

When exchanging money, you're likely to get a better rate for traveler's checks than for cash.

London banks generally offer the best rates of exchange; they're usually open Monday to Friday from 9:30am to 3:30pm. Many of the "high street" branches are now open until 5pm; a handful of Central London branches are open until noon on Saturday, including **Barclays,** 208 Kensington High St., W8 (☎ **0171/441-3200**).

Money exchange is now also available at competitive rates at major London post offices, with a 1% service charge. Money can be exchanged during off-hours at a variety of bureaux de change throughout the city, found at small shops and in hotels, railway stations (including the international terminal at Waterloo Station), travel agencies, and airports, but their exchange rates are poorer and they charge high service fees. Examine the prices and rates carefully before handing over your dollars, as there's no consumer organization to regulate the activities of privately run bureaux de change.

Time Out recently did a survey of various exchange facilities, and American Express came out on top, with the lowest commission charged on dollar transactions. **American Express** is at 6 Haymarket, SW1 (☎ **800/221-7282** or 0171/930-4411), and other locations throughout the city. American Express charges no commission when cashing travelers checks; however, a flat rate of £2 ($3.20) is charged when exchanging the dollar to the pound. Most other agencies tend to charge a percentage rate commission (usually 2%) with a £2 to £3 ($3.20 to $4.80) minimum charge.

Other reputable firms are **Thomas Cook,** 45 Berkeley St., W1A 1EB (☎ **800/223-7373** or 0171/408-4218), with branches at Victoria Station, Marble Arch, and other city locations; and, for 24-hour foreign exchange, **Chequepoint,** at 548 Oxford Street, W1N 9HJ (☎ **0171/723-1005**), and other locations throughout London (hours will vary). Try not to change money at your hotel; the rates they offer tend to be horrendous.

3 When to Go

THE CLIMATE   Yes, it rains, but you'll rarely get a true downpour. It's heaviest in November (2½ inches on average). British temperatures can range from 30° to 110° Fahrenheit but they rarely drop below 35° or go above 78°. Evenings are cool, even in summer. Note that the British, who consider chilliness wholesome, like to keep the thermostats about 10° below the American comfort level. Hotels have central heating but are usually kept just above the goose bump (in Britspeak, "goose pimple") margin.

London's Average Daytime Temperature & Monthly Rainfall (inches)

	Jan	Feb	Mar	Apr	May	June	July	Aug	Sept	Oct	Nov	Dec
Temp. °F	40	40	44	49	55	61	64	64	59	52	46	42
Rainfall	2.1	1.6	1.5	1.5	1.8	1.8	2.2	2.3	1.9	2.2	2.5	1.9

WHEN YOU'LL FIND BARGAINS   The cheapest time to travel to England is in the off-season: that means November 1 to December 12 and December 25 to March 14. In the last few years, the airlines have been offering irresistible fares during these periods.

Weekday flights are cheaper than weekend fares (often by 10% or more).

Rates generally increase between March 14 to June 5 and in October, then hit their peak in the high travel seasons between June 6 and September 30 and December 13 and 24. July and August are also the months when most Britons take their holidays, so besides the higher prices, you'll have to deal with limited availability of accommodations and crowds.

You can avoid crowds by planning trips for November or January through March. Sure, it may be rainy and cold—but England doesn't shut down when the tourists leave! In fact, the winter season includes some of London's best theater, opera, ballet, and classical music offerings, and gives visitors a more honest view of English life. Additionally, many hotel prices drop by 20%, and cheaper accommodations offer weekly rates (unheard of during peak travel times). By arriving after the winter holidays, you can also take advantage of post-Christmas sales to buy your fill of woolens, china, crystal, silver, fashion clothing, handicrafts, and curios.

In short, spring offers the countryside at its greenest, autumn brings the bright colors of the northern moorlands, and summer's warmer weather gives rise to the many outdoor music and theater festivals. But winter offers savings across the board and a chance to see Britons going about their everyday lives largely unhindered by tourist invasions.

HOLIDAYS   England observes New Year's Day, Good Friday, Easter Monday, May Day (1st Monday in May), spring and summer bank holidays (the last Monday in May and August, respectively), Christmas Day, and Boxing Day (December 26).

ENGLAND CALENDAR OF EVENTS

January

◆ **London International Boat Show.** Europe's largest boat show, held at the Earl's Court Exhibition Centre, Warwick Road. Call ☎ **01784/473377** for details. Early January.

• **Charles I Commemoration,** London. To mark the anniversary of the execution of King Charles I "in the name of freedom and democracy," hundreds of cavaliers march through central London in 17th-century dress, and prayers are said at White-hall's Banqueting House. Last Sunday in January.

• **Chinese New Year,** London. The famous Lion Dancers in Soho perform free on the nearest Sunday to Chinese New Year. Either in late January or early February (based on the lunar calendar).

February

• **Jorvik Festival,** York. This 2-week festival celebrates this historic cathedral city's role as a Viking outpost. For more information, call ☎ **01904/621756.**

March

◆**Crufts Dog Show,** Birmingham. The English, they say, love their pets more than their offspring. Crufts offers an opportunity to observe the nation's pet lovers doting on 8,000 dogs, representing 150 breeds. It's held at the National Exhibition Centre, Birmingham, West Midlands. Tickets can be purchased at the door. For more information, contact **The Kennel Club,** 1-5 Clarges St., Piccadilly, London W1Y 8AB, or call its ticket hot line at ☎ **0171/518-1012.** First week of March.

April

• **Martell Grand National Meeting,** outside Liverpool. England's premier steeple-chase event takes place over a 4-mile course at **Aintree Racecourse,** Aintree (☎ **0151/5232600**). First weekend of April.

◆**The Shakespeare Season,** Stratford-upon-Avon. The Royal Shakespeare Company begins its annual season, presenting works by the Bard in his hometown, at the **Royal Shakespeare Theatre,** Waterside (☎ **01789/295623**). Tickets are available at the box office, or through such agents as Keith Prowse (☎ **800/669-8687** or 212/398-1430) in New York. April to January.

• **London Marathon.** More than 30,000 competitors run from Greenwich Park to Buckingham Palace; call ☎ **0161/703-8161** for information. If you'd like to take the challenge, call from May to June for an application. Mid-April.

• **Devizes to Westminster International Canoe Race.** This 125-mile race runs along the Avon River, the Kennet Canal, and the River Thames. No tickets are needed. Call ☎ **01372/453976** for more information. Three days in mid-April.

• **Easter Parade,** London. A memorable parade of brightly colored floats and marching bands around Battersea Park.

May

• **Chichester Festival Theatre.** Some great classic and modern plays are presented at this West Sussex theater. For tickets and information, contact the **Festival Theatre,** Oaklands Park, West Sussex PO19 4AP (☎ **01243/781312**). The season runs May to October.

• **Brighton Festival.** England's largest arts festival, with some 400 different cultural events. For information, write the Brighton Festival, 21–22 Old Steine, Brighton, Sussex BN1 1EL. Most of May.

- **Royal Windsor Horse Show.** The country's major show-jumping presentation, held at the Home Park, Windsor, Berkshire, is attended by the queen herself. Call ☎ **01753/860633** for more information. Mid-May.

- ✪ **Bath International Music Festival.** One of Europe's most prestigious international festivals of music and the arts features as many as 1,000 performers at various venues in Bath. For information, contact the **Bath Festivals Trust,** 2 Midland Bridge Rd., Bath, Somerset BA2 3EQ (☎ **01225/463362**). Mid-May to early June.

- ✪ **Glyndebourne Festival.** One of England's major cultural events, this festival is centered at the 1,200-seat Glyndebourne Opera House in Sussex, some 54 miles south of London. Tickets, which cost anywhere from £10 to £110 ($16 to $176), are available from **Glyndebourne Festival Opera Box Office,** Lewes, East Sussex BN8 5UU (☎ **01273/813813**). Mid-May to late August.

- **Shakespeare Under the Stars.** The Bard's works are performed at the **Open Air Theatre,** Inner Circle, Regent's Park, NW1, in London. Take the tube to Baker Street. Performances are Monday to Saturday at 8pm; Wednesday, Thursday, and Saturday also at 2:30pm. Call ☎ **0171/486-2431** for more information. Previews begin in late May and last throughout the summer.

- **Chelsea Flower Show,** London. The best of British gardening, with plants and flowers of the season, is displayed at the Chelsea Royal Hospital. Contact the local British Tourist Authority Office to find out which overseas reservations agency is handling ticket sales, or contact the **Chelsea Show Ticket Office,** P.O. Box 1426, London W6 0LQ (☎ **0171/630-7422**). Tickets are also available through London Ticketmaster (☎ **0171/344-4343**). Late May.

June

- **Vodafone Derby Stakes.** This famous horse-racing event (the "Darby," as it's called here) is held at Epsom Downs, Epsom, Surrey. Men wear top hats and women, including the queen, put on silly millinery creations. Grandstand tickets range from £22 to £55 ($35.20 to $88). For more details, call ☎ **01372/463072**). First week of June.

- **Grosvenor House Art and Antique Fair,** London. This very prestigious antique fair is held at Grosvenor House, Park Lane. For information, contact Grosvenor House Art and Antiques Fair, Grosvenor House, 86–90 Park Lane, London W1A 3AA (☎ **0171/495-8743**). Ten days in mid-June.

- **Kenwood Lakeside Concerts.** These annual concerts on the north side of Hampstead Heath have continued a British tradition of outdoor performances for nearly 50 years. Fireworks displays and laser shows enliven the premier musical performances. The audience catches the music as it drifts across the lake from the performance shell. Concerts are held every Saturday from mid-June to early September. For more information call ☎ **0181/348-1286**.

- **Royal Academy's Summer Exhibition,** London. This institution, founded in 1768, has for some 2 centuries held Summer Exhibitions of living painters at Burlington House, Piccadilly Circus. Call ☎ **0171/439-7438** for more information. Early June to mid-August.

- ✪ **Trooping the Colour.** This is the queen's official birthday parade, a quintessential British event, with exquisite pageantry and pomp as she inspects her regiments and takes their salute as they parade their colors before her at the Horse Guards Parade, Whitehall. Tickets for the parade and two reviews, held on preceding Saturdays, are allocated by ballot. Applicants must write between January 1 and the end of February, enclosing a self-addressed stamped envelope or International Reply Coupon to the Ticket Office, HQ Household Division, Horse Guards, Whitehall, London

SW1X 6AA. Exact dates and ticket prices will be supplied later. The ballot is held in mid-March, and only successful applicants are informed in April. Held on a day designated in June (not necessarily the queen's actual birthday).

- **Aldeburgh Festival of Music and the Arts.** The composer Benjamin Britten launched this festival in 1948. For more details on the events, and for the year-round program, write to **Aldeburgh Foundation,** High Street, Aldeburgh, Suffolk IP15 5AX (☎ **01728/452935**). Two weeks from mid- to late June.
- **Royal Ascot Week.** Although Ascot Racecourse is open year-round for guided tours, events, exhibitions, and conferences, there are 24 race days throughout the year, with the feature races being the Royal Meeting in June, Diamond Day in late July, and the Festival at Ascot in late September. For information, contact **Ascot Racecourse,** Ascot, Berkshire SL5 7JN (☎ **01344/622211**).
- ✪**Lawn Tennis Championships,** Wimbledon. Ever since players took to the grass courts at Wimbledon in 1877, this tournament has attracted quite a crowd, and there's still an excited hush at Centre Court and a certain thrill associated with being there. Savor the strawberries and cream that are part of the experience.

  Acquiring tickets and overnight lodgings during the annual tennis competitions at Wimbledon can be difficult to arrange independently. Two outfits that can book both hotel accommodations and tickets to the event include **Steve Furgal's International Tennis Tours,** 11828 Rancho Bernardo Rd., San Diego, CA 92128 (☎ **800/258-3664**), and **Championship Tennis Tours,** 8040 E. Morgan Trail, no. 12, Scottsdale, AZ 85258 (☎ **800/468-3664**). Early bookings for the world's most famous tennis tournament are strongly advised. Tickets for Centre and Number One courts are obtainable through a lottery. Write in from August to December to **A.E.L.T.C.,** P.O. Box 98, Church Road, Wimbledon, London SW19 5AE (☎ **0181/946-2244**). Outside court tickets are available daily, but be prepared to wait in line. Late June through early July.
- **City of London Festival.** This annual art festival is held in venues throughout the city. Call ☎ **0171/377-0540** for information. June and July.
- **Henley Royal Regatta,** Henley, in Oxfordshire. This international rowing competition is the premier event on the English social calendar. For more information, call ☎ **01491/578034** or 01491/572153. Late June to early July.
- **Ludlow Festival.** This is one of England's major arts festivals, complete with an open-air Shakespeare performance within the Inner Bailey of Ludlow Castle. Concerts, lectures, readings, exhibitions, and workshops round out the offerings. From March onward, a schedule can be obtained from the box office. Write to The Ludlow Festival box office, Castle Square, Ludlow, Shropshire SY8 1AY, enclosing a self-addressed stamped envelope, or call ☎ **01584/872150.** The box office is open daily beginning in early May. Late June to early July.

July

- **Royal Tournament,** London. In July, Britain's armed forces put on dazzling displays of athletic and military skills at the Earl's Court Exhibition Centre. For information about performance times and tickets, call ☎ **0171/244-0244.** Ticket prices range from £5 to £25 ($8 to $40).
- **The Proms,** London. A night at "The Proms"—the annual Henry Wood promenade concerts at Royal Albert Hall—attracts music aficionados from around the world. Staged almost daily (except for a few Sundays) these traditional concerts were launched in 1895 and are the principal summer engagements for the BBC Symphony Orchestra. Cheering and clapping, Union Jacks on parade, banners and balloons—it's great summer fun. Mid-July through mid-September.

- **The Exeter Festival.** The town of Exeter hosts more than 150 events celebrating classical music, ranging from concerts and opera to lectures. Festival dates and offerings vary from year to year, and more information is available by contacting the Exeter Festival Office at ☎ **01392/265200;** www.exeter.ac.uk/festival. Three weeks in July.

August

- **Cowes Week,** off the Isle of Wight. This yachting festival takes place in early August. For details, call ☎ **01983/291914.**

- **Notting Hill Carnival,** London. One of the largest annual street festivals in Europe, attracting more than half a million people. There's live reggae and soul music plus great Caribbean food. Two days in late August.

- ✪**International Beatles Week,** Tens of thousands of fans gather in Liverpool to celebrate the music of the Fab Four. There's a whole series of concerts from international cover bands, plus tributes, auctions, and tours. Cavern City Tours, a local company, offers hotel and festival packages that include accommodations and tickets to tours and events, starting around £70 ($120) for two nights. For information contact Cavern City Tours at ☎ **0151/7088838** or the Tourist Information Centre in Liverpool at ☎ **0151/7088854**. Late August through the first couple of days of September.

September

- **International Beatles Week,** Liverpool. Throngs of diehard fans flock to Liverpool for a 7-day celebration highlighted by concerts from cover bands, plus tributes, auctions, and tours. **Cavern City Tours,** a local company, offers hotel and festival packages that include accommodations and tickets to tours and events, starting around £75 ($120) for 2 nights. For information, contact Cavern City Tours at ☎ **0151/7088838** or the Tourist Information Centre in Liverpool at ☎ **0151/7088854.** Last week of August to first few days of September.

- **Burghley Horse Trials,** Lincolnshire. This annual event is staged on the grounds of the largest Elizabethan house in England, Burghley House, Stamford, Lincolnshire (☎ **01780/752451**). Three days in early September.

- **Raising of the Thames Barrier,** Unity Way, SE18. Once a year, usually in September, a full test is done on this miracle of modern engineering; all 10 of the massive steel gates are raised against the low and high tides. Call ☎ **0181/854-1373** for exact date and time.

October

- **Cheltenham Festival of Literature.** This Cotswold event features readings, book exhibitions, and theatrical performances—all in the famed spa town of Gloucestershire. Call ☎ **01242/522878** for more details, or 01242/237377 to receive mailings about the event. Early to mid-October.

- ✪**Opening of Parliament,** London. Ever since the 17th century, when the English beheaded Charles I, British monarchs have been denied the right to enter the House of Commons. Instead, the monarch opens Parliament in the House of Lords, reading an official speech that is in fact written by the government. Queen Elizabeth II rides from Buckingham Palace to Westminster in a royal coach accompanied by the Yeoman of the Guard and the Household Cavalry. The public galleries are open on a first-come, first-served basis. First Monday in October.

- **Quit Rents Ceremony,** London. At the Royal Courts of Justice, the Queen's Remembrancer receives token rents on behalf of the queen. The ceremony includes splitting sticks and counting horseshoes. Call ☎ **0171/936-6131** for more information. Late October.

- **Horse of the Year Show,** Wembley. Riders fly from every continent to join in this festive display of horsemanship (much appreciated by the queen). The British press calls it an "equine extravaganza." It's held at Wembley Arena, outside London. For more information, call ☎ **0181/902-8833.** Early October.

November

- **London–Brighton Veteran Car Run.** This race begins in London's Hyde Park and ends in the seaside resort of Brighton, in East Sussex. Call ☎ **01580/893413** for more details. First Sunday in November.
- **Guy Fawkes Night,** throughout England. This British celebration commemorates the anniversary of the "Gunpowder Plot," an attempt to blow up King James I and parliament. Huge organized bonfires are lit throughout London, and Guy Fawkes, the plot's most famous conspirator, is burned in effigy. Check *Time Out* for locations. Early November.
- ✪**Lord Mayor's Procession and Show,** London. The queen has to ask permission to enter the square mile in London called the City—and the right of refusal has been jealously guarded by London merchants since the 17th century. Suffice to say that the lord mayor is a powerful character, and the procession from the Guildhall to the Royal Courts is appropriately impressive. You can watch the procession from the street; the banquet is by invitation only. Second week in November.

4 Special-Interest Vacations

BIKE TRIPS   If you're planning a bike trip on your own, you can take your two wheels on passenger trains in England if you pay a £3 ($4.80) extra charge.

The **Cyclists Tourist Club,** Cotterell House, 69 Meadrow, Godalming, Surrey GU7 3HS (☎ **01483/417217**), can suggest routes and provide information. Memberships cost £25 ($40) a year for adults, £12.50 ($20) for those 18 and under. A family (three or more members) membership costs £42 ($67.20).

If you'd like to participate in an organized bike trip, in which you do the pedaling but leave the logistics to someone else, consider calling **Backroads,** 801 Cedar St., Berkeley, CA 94710-1800 (☎ **800/462-2848**). Tours last 6 days, 5 nights, and include luxury accommodations in sites of historic or architectural interest, all breakfasts, most dinners, and most lunches. The cost is $2,395 per person double occupancy. Don't have wheels of your own? Backroads can rent you a bike and helmet for the duration of the tour, starting from $140. Each tour has no more than 22 participants and is accompanied by two expert tour leaders who are well versed in local geography. Vans carry luggage and the occasional tired cyclist.

A worthy competitor is **Butterfield & Robinson,** 70 Bond St., Suite 300, Toronto, Ontario M5B 1X3, Canada (☎ **800/678-1147**). It offers a 7-night bicycle trek through the Cotswolds, with lodgings at the very finest accommodations available within the region. Most meals and all guide fees and bike-rental charges are included. They also feature walking trips, a 5-night, 6-day excursion.

Himalayan Travel, 110 Prospect St., Stamford, CT 06901 (☎ **800/225-2380**), best known for its walking tours of England (see below), also offers a roster of roughly equivalent bike tours within England.

Vermont Bicycle Touring, P.O. Box 711, Bristol, VT 05443 (☎ **800/245-3868** or 802/453-4811), also offers tours throughout England geared to different levels of physical ability; extra guidance, assistance, and services are always available. A van transports your luggage.

FISHING   Fly-fishing was born here, and it's considered an art form. An expert in leading programs for fly-fishers eager to experience the cold, clear waters of Britain is **Rod & Reel Adventures,** 566 Thomson Lane, Suite B6, Copperopolis, CA 95228 (☎ 800/356-6982). Don't expect smooth salesmanship at this place, but if you persevere, someone at this company should be able to link you up with a local fishing guide who can lead you to English waters that are well stocked with trout, perch, grayling, sea bream, Atlantic salmon, and such lesser-known species as rudd and roach. Rod & Reel Adventures has contacts in the Lake District, Scotland, and the Norfolk Broads. Such streams as the Wear, the Derwent, the Copuquet, and the Till are especially prolific.

If you prefer to go it alone, contact the **British Salmon & Trout Association,** Fishmonger's Hall, London Bridge, London EC4R 9EL (☎ 0171/283-5838), for information about British fishing regulations.

GOLF   Although the sport originated in Scotland, golf has been around in England since Edward VII first began stamping over the greens of such courses as Royal Lytham & St. Annes, in England's northwest, or Royal St. Georges, near London.

The unyielding reality is that golf in England remains a clubby sport where some of the most prestigious courses are usually reserved exclusively for members. Rules at most English golf courses tend to be stricter in matters of dress code and protocol than their equivalents in the United States.

If, however, your heart is set on enjoying a round or two on the emerald-colored turf of England, **Golf International,** 275 Madison Ave., New York, NY 10016 (☎ 800/833-1389 or 212/986-9176), can open doors for you. Golf packages in England are arranged for anywhere from 7 to 14 days and can include as much or as little golf, on as many different courses, as a participant wants. Weeklong vacations, with hotels, breakfasts, car rentals, and greens fees included, range from $1,800 per person, double occupancy, airfare not included.

Worthy competitors that operate on a less comprehensive scale than Golf International include **Adventures in Golf,** 11 Northeastern Blvd., Suite 360, Nashua, NH 03062 (☎ 603/882-8367); and **Jerry Quinlan's Celtic Golf,** 124 Sunset Blvd., Cape May, NJ 08204 (☎ 800/535-6148). Each of their tours is customized, and usually includes lodging in anything from simple guest houses to five-star deluxe manor houses.

HIKING, WALKING & RAMBLING   In England and Wales alone there are some 100,000 miles of trails and footpaths. The **Ramblers' Association,** 1-5 Wandsworth Rd., London SW8 2XX (☎ 0171/582-6878), publishes an annual yearbook that lists some 2,500 bed-and-breakfasts near the trails; it costs £11 ($17.60). Send a check in sterling for the yearbook if you plan to order before your trip; otherwise the yearbook can be purchased in England for £4.99 ($8).

Alternatively, you can join an organized hiking tour. One of the longest-running tour operators is **Himalayan Travel,** 110 Prospect St., Stamford, CT 06901 (☎ 800/225-2380). Between April and October, they offer hiking tours within seven districts of England, each configured for between 1 and 2 weeks. Participants cover between 8 and 15 miles a day within such regions as the Cotswolds, Dorset, Northumberland, Cornwall, or the Yorkshire Dales, spending the night at small inns en route. Participants should be reasonably fit, but don't have to be marathon runners. All tours include breakfast daily and overnight lodging, as well as some meals. A weeklong tour costs around $900 per person, double occupancy.

Wilderness Travel, Inc., 1102 Ninth St., Berkeley, CA 94710 (☎ 800/368-2794 or 510/558-2488), also specializes in treks and inn-to-inn hiking tours, plus less strenuous walking tours of Cornwall and the Cotswolds that combine transportation with walking sessions of 3 hours or less.

English Lakeland Ramblers, 18 Stuyvesant Oval, Suite 1A, New York, NY 10009 (☎ 800/724-8801 outside New York City, or 212/505-1020 within New York City), offers 7- to 8-day walking tours for the average active person. On its Lake District tour, you'll stay and have your meals in a charming 17th-century country inn near Ambleside and Windermere. A minibus takes hikers and sightseers daily to trails and sightseeing points. Experts tell you about the area's culture and history and highlight its natural wonders. There are also tours of the Cotswolds and Scotland, as well as inn-to-inn tours and privately guided tours.

Other contenders include **Country Walkers,** P.O. Box 180, Waterbury, VT 05676 (☎ 802/244-1387). Their "walking vacations" usually last 7 days and tend to focus on such scenic areas as the Lake District, Cornwall, and the Cotswolds. These packages include overnight accommodations at well-respected but not excessively luxurious three-star hotels, and the occasional manor house; most meals; and a guide who's well versed in local paths, trails, and lore. Four to 12 miles are covered each day. Prices start at $2,050 per person, double occupancy, without airfare.

HORSEBACK RIDING   You can learn to ride or brush up on your skills at **Eastern Equation,** a facility located on the Essex/Suffolk border. British Horse Society–certified instructors teach riders at a facility with a large indoor arena, a jumping course, and 30 horses and ponies of various sizes and abilities. Many trails go directly from the farm to the countryside. You can stay in a room with a private bath at the beautiful 16th-century farmhouse (subject to availability), or find accommodation in a comfortable nearby hotel. Contact **Cross Country International,** P.O. Box 1170, Millbrook, NY 12545 (☎ 800/828-8768).

There are also American companies that offer horseback-riding package tours of England. **Equitour/FITS Equestrian Tours,** P.O. Box 807, Dubois, WY 82513 (☎ 800/545-0019), is one such firm. Formed from the 1996 merger of two well-respected tour operators based in Wyoming and California, this outfit specializes in package tours for riding enthusiasts who want to experience the horsey traditions of the land of foxes and hounds. Two types of tours can be arranged through their auspices: Stationary tours where instruction in jumping and dressage are conducted over a 7-day period at a stable beside the Bristol Channel or on the fields of Dartmoor, and "progressive" tours where treks of from 4 to 10 days are conducted in Exmoor and Wales. Most riders eager to experience as wide a view of England as possible opt for the latter, spending each night at a different B&B or inn, and lodging their mounts at nearby stables. The accommodations are simple, and prices are kept deliberately low. A 4-day horseback excursion in Dartmoor that includes use of a horse and its tack, guide services, overnight accommodations, and all meals costs around $700 per person, double occupancy.

BEER & BREWERY TOURS   A Seattle-based company, **MIR Corporation,** 85 S. Washington St., Suite 210, Seattle, WA 98104 (☎ 800/424-7289), offers 9-day Brew Tasting and Brewery Tours that include visits to such major breweries as Samuel Smith's and Young's, outside of London; the Caledonian brewery, outside of Edinburgh; and a host of lesser-known, family owned breweries, such as Traquair House, scattered throughout the countryside. Included are frequent opportunities to taste local brew at atmospheric pubs en route. Don't expect demure sobriety during the course of this experience. Most participants quaff their first pint at least an hour before lunch and continue sampling the merchandise throughout the course of the day and evening. Prices, without airfare, begin at $1,395 per person, double occupancy. Accommodations are in unpretentious middle-bracket hotels and inns. Each tour is limited to 20 participants, and transport throughout is by train and motor coach.

UNIVERSITY STUDY PROGRAMS   You can study English literature at renowned universities such as Oxford and Cambridge during the week and then take weekend excursions to the countryside of Shakespeare, Austen, Dickens, and Hardy. While doing your course work, you can live in dormitories with other students and dine in elaborate halls or the more intimate Fellows' clubs. Study programs in England are not limited to the liberal arts, or to high-school or college students. There are many programs, some designed specifically for teachers and senior citizens (see "For Seniors" later in this chapter). For more information, contact the organizations listed below or those mentioned in the section "For Students" later in this chapter.

Affiliated with Richmond College, in London, **American Institute For Foreign Study,** 102 Greenwich Ave., Greenwich, CT 06830 (☎ **800/727-2437**), offers both 10- and 60-day traveling programs for high-school students and internships and academic programs for college students. There are also programs leading to the British equivalent of an MBA.

IIE (Institute of International Education), U.S. Student Programs Division, 809 United Nations Plaza, New York, NY 10017-3580 (☎ **212/883-8200**), administers a variety of academic, training, and grant programs for the U.S. Information Agency (USIA), including the Fulbright grants. It is especially helpful in arranging enrollments for U.S. students in summer-school programs.

NRCSA (National Registration Center for Study Abroad), P.O. Box 1393, Milwaukee, WI 53201 (☎ **414/278-0631**), produces a $5 catalog outlining 80 to 90 summer schools in Great Britain that offer courses of from 1 to 4 weeks from July through September. Students, teachers, and interested adults can take one course or combine several in England, Scotland, and Wales. Subjects include theater, history, literature, art, castles, architecture, gardens, economics, current events, crafts, and wildlife. NRCSA will register you at the school of your choice and arrange for room and board. Ask for a free copy of their newsletter, or download the newsletter and catalog from the Web at **www.nrcsa.com**.

University Vacations, 3660 Bougainvillea Rd., Coconut Grove, FL 33133 (☎ **800/792-0100**), offers upmarket liberal-arts programs at Oxford and Cambridge universities. Courses usually last 7 to 12 days and combine lectures and excursions with dining in the intimate Fellows' Dining Rooms. Accommodations are in private rooms with available en-suite facilities in the medieval colleges. There are neither formal academic requirements nor pressure for examinations or written requirements. Its summer headquarters is Brasenose College, Oxford.

5 Health & Insurance

STAYING HEALTHY   You will encounter few health problems while traveling in England. The tap water is safe to drink, the milk is pasteurized, and health services are good.

You may want to stay away from British beef because of the mad-cow crisis. The scare is largely over, but caution is always advised. (For example, it's been suggested that it's safer to eat British beef cut from the bone instead of on the bone.) Other than that, traveling to England doesn't pose any health risks.

If you need a doctor, your hotel can recommend one, or you can contact your embassy or consulate. Outside London, dial ☎ **100** and ask the operator for the local police, who will give you the name, address, and telephone number of a doctor in your area. *Note:* U.S. visitors who become ill while they're in England are only eligible for free *emergency* care. For other treatment, including follow-up care, you will be asked to pay.

Before you leave home, you can obtain a list of English doctors from the **International Association for Medical Assistance to Travelers (IAMAT).** Contact IAMAT in the United States at 417 Center St., Lewiston, NY 14092 (☎ **716/754-4883**); in Canada at 40 Regal Rd., Guelph, Ontario N1K 1B5 (☎ **519/836-0102**).

If you suffer from a chronic illness, talk to your doctor before taking the trip. For such conditions as epilepsy, diabetes, or a heart condition, wear a **Medic Alert Identification Tag,** which will immediately alert any doctor to your condition and provide the number of Medic Alert's 24-hour hot line so that a foreign doctor can obtain your medical records. Membership costs $35. In addition, there is a $15 annual fee, which is waived the first year. Contact the **Medic Alert Foundation,** 2323 Colorado, Turlock, CA 95382 (☎ **800/825-3785**).

INSURANCE   Before going out and spending money on various sorts of travel insurance, check your existing policies to see if they'll cover you while you're traveling. For example, your homeowner's or renter's insurance might cover off-premises theft and loss wherever it occurs. And check that your health insurance will cover you when you're away from home.

Some credit cards offer automatic flight insurance when you purchase an airline ticket with that card. These policies insure against death or dismemberment in case of an airplane crash. If you are traveling on a tour or have prepaid a large chunk of your travel expenses, you might want to ask your travel agent about trip-cancellation insurance.

If you are going to rent a car in England, check to see whether your automobile insurance, automobile club, or credit card covers personal accident insurance (PAI), collision damage waiver (CDW), or other insurance options. You may be able to avoid additional rental charges if you are already covered.

The following companies sell a variety of travel insurance policies: **Access America,** 6600 W. Broad St., Richmond, VA 23230 (☎ **800/284-8300**); **Healthcare Abroad (MEDEX),** c/o Wallach & Co., P.O. Box 480 (107 W. Federal St.), Middleburg, VA 20118-0480 (☎ **800/237-6615**); **Mutual of Omaha** (Tele-Trip Company, Inc.), Mutual of Omaha Plaza, Omaha, NE 68175 (☎ **800/228-9792**); **Travel Guard International,** 1145 Clark St., Stevens Point, WI 54481 (☎ **800/826-1300** or 716/345-0505); and **Travel Insured International, Inc.,** P.O. Box 280568, East Hartford, CT 06128-0568 (☎ **800/243-3174** in the U.S., or 203/528-7663 outside the U.S., between 7:45am and 7pm EST).

If you're buying a package tour or a charter that requires you to pay up front, don't buy your cancellation insurance from the tour operator! Consider buying from one of the agencies recommended above.

6 Tips for Travelers with Special Needs

FOR TRAVELERS WITH DISABILITIES   Before you go, there are many agencies that will provide advice. One is the **Travel Information Service,** Industrial Rehab Program, 1200 W. Tabor Rd., Philadelphia, PA 19141, which provides information to telephone callers only: Call ☎ **215/456-9900** or 215/456-9602 (for TTY) for assistance with your travel needs.

You may also want to consider joining a tour specifically for visitors with disabilities. One such tour operator is **FEDCAP Rehabilitation Services** (formerly known as

the Federation of the Handicapped), 211 W. 14th St., New York, NY 10011. Call
☎ 212/727-4200 or fax 212/727-4374 for information about membership and
summer tours. For names and addresses of other tour operators and additional rele-
vant information, contact the **Society for the Advancement of Travel for the Handicapped,** 347 Fifth Ave., Suite 610, New York, NY 10016 (☎ 212/447-7284; fax
212/725-8253). Yearly membership dues are $45, or $30 for senior citizens and students. Send a self-addressed stamped envelope.

For people who are blind or have visual impairments, the best source is the **American Foundation for the Blind,** 11 Penn Plaza, Suite 300, New York, NY 10001
(☎ 800/232-5463 to order information kits and supplies). It offers information on
traveling with seeing-eye dogs. It also issues identification cards to those who are
legally blind.

One of the best organizations serving the needs of people who use wheelchairs or
walkers is **Flying Wheels Travel,** 143 West Bridge, P.O. Box 382, Owatonna, MN
55060 (☎ 800/525-6790), offering various escorted tours and cruises internationally, and private tours in a minivan with a lift.

For a $25 annual fee, you can join **Mobility International USA,** P.O. Box 10767,
Eugene, OR 97440 (☎ 541/343-1284 voice and TDD; fax 541/343-6182), which
answers questions on various destinations and also offers discounts on videos, publications, and programs that it sponsors.

Many London hotels, museums, restaurants, and sightseeing attractions have
wheelchair ramps. Persons with disabilities are often granted special discounts at
attractions and, in some cases, nightclubs. These are called "concessions" in Britain. It
always pays to ask. Free information and advice is available from **Holiday Care Service,** Imperial Building, 2nd Floor, Victoria Road, Horley, Surrey RH6 7PZ
(☎ 01293/774535; fax 01293/784647).

The **British Tourist Authority** sells *London Made Easy* (£2.50/$4), a booklet
offering advice and describing facilities for travelers with disabilities. Bookstores often
carry *Access in London* (£4/$6.40), an even more helpful publication.

The transport system, cinemas, and theaters are still pretty much off-limits, but
London Transport does publish a leaflet called *Access to the Underground,* which gives
details of elevators and ramps at individual Underground stations; call ☎ 0171/
918-3312. And the London Black Cab is perfectly suited for those in wheelchairs; the
roomy interiors have plenty of room for maneuvering.

In London, the most prominent organization for information about access to theaters, cinemas, galleries, museums, and restaurants is **Artsline,** 54 Chalton St.,
London NW1 1HS (☎ 0171/388-2227; fax 0171/383-2653). It offers free information about wheelchair access, theaters with hearing aids, tourist attractions, and
cinemas. Artsline will mail information to North America, but it's even more helpful
to contact Artsline after your arrival in London. Call between 9:30am and 5:30pm,
Monday to Friday.

Another organization that cooperates closely with Artsline is **Tripscope,**
The Courtyard, 4 Evelyn Rd., London W4 5JL (☎ 0181/994-9294; fax 0181/
994-3618), which offers advice on travel for persons with disabilities in Britain and
elsewhere.

FOR GAY & LESBIAN TRAVELERS   England has one of the most active gay and
lesbian scenes in the world, centered mainly around London. Gay bars, restaurants,
and centers are also found in all large English cities, notably Bath, Birmingham, Manchester, and especially Brighton.

For the gay and lesbian traveler to England, the best guides are *Spartacus Britain
and Ireland* and *London Scene.* For up-to-the-minute activities in Britain, we

recommend *Gay Times (London)*. These books and others are available from **Giovanni's Room,** 1145 Pine St., Philadelphia, PA 19107 (☎ **215/923-2960;** fax 215/923-0813).

Our World magazine, 1104 N. Nova Rd., Suite 251, Daytona Beach, FL 32117 (☎ **904/441-5367;** fax 904/441-5604), covers options and bargains for gay and lesbian travel worldwide. It costs $35 for 10 issues. *Out and About,* 8 W. 19th St., Suite 401, New York, NY 10011 (☎ **800/929-2268** or 212/645-6922; fax 800/929-2215), is another great publication on gay travel that profiles the best gay or gay-friendly hotels, gyms, clubs, and other places worldwide. It costs $49 a year for 10 information-packed issues.

With some 1,200 member agencies, the **International Gay Travel Association (IGTA),** 4331 N. Federal, Suite 304, Ft. Lauderdale, FL 33308 (☎ **800/448-8550** or 954/776-2626), specializes in networking travelers with the appropriate gay-friendly service organization or tour specialist. It offers a quarterly newsletter, marketing mailings, and a membership directory.

Our Family Abroad, 40 W. 57th St., Suite 430, New York, NY 10019 (☎ **800/999-5500** or 212/459-1800), operates escorted tours for gay men and women to points throughout the world, including several to Britain. Tour guides serve on a volunteer basis—a system that tends to assure the absence of homophobic guides.

In London, the **Lesbian and Gay Switchboard** (☎ **0171/837-7324**) is open 24 hours a day, providing information about gay-related London activities or advice in general. The **Bisexual Helpline** (☎ **0181/569-7500**) offers useful information, but only on Tuesday and Wednesday from 7:30 to 9:30pm and Saturday between 9:30am and noon. The best bookstore is **Gay's the Word,** 66 Marchmont St., WC1 (☎ **0171/278-7654;** tube: Russell Square), which is the largest such store in Britain. It is open Monday through Wednesday and Friday and Saturday from 10am to 6pm, Thursday 10am to 7pm, and Sunday 2 to 6pm.

FOR SENIORS   Many discounts are available for seniors. Most of the major U.S. airlines, including American, United, Continental, US Airways, and TWA, offer discount programs for senior travelers—be sure to ask whenever you book a flight. Senior citizens over 60 years old receive special 10% discounts on British Airways through its Privileged Traveler program. They also qualify for reduced restrictions on APEX cancellations. Discounts are also granted for BA tours and for intra-Britain air tickets if booked in North America.

However, in England itself, you often have to be a member of an association to obtain discounts. Public transportation reductions, for example, are available only to holders of British Pension books. Even if discounts aren't posted, you might ask to see if they are available.

If you're a member of **AARP (American Association of Retired Persons),** 601 E St. NW, Washington, DC 20049 (☎ **202/434-AARP**), you may get discounts on car rentals and hotels.

Elderhostel, 75 Federal St., Boston, MA 02110-1941 (☎ **617/426-8056**), offers university-based educational programs for seniors in England and other parts of the world. Most courses last about 3 weeks and are remarkable values—the cost includes airfare, accommodations in student dormitories or modest inns, meals, and tuition. Courses emphasize the liberal arts and include field trips and excursions, and best of all, there's no homework or grades. You must be 55 or older to participate.

SAGA International Holidays, 222 Berkeley St., Boston, MA 02116 (☎ **800/343-0273**), offers inclusive tours and cruises for those 50 and older.

You can write for a helpful publication, ***101 Tips for the Mature Traveler,*** available from Grand Circle Travel, 347 Congress St., Suite 3A, Boston, MA 02210

(☎ **800/221-2610** or 617/350-7500; fax 617/350-6206); this travel agency also offers escorted tours and cruises for seniors.

Information on travel for seniors is also available from the **National Council of Senior Citizens,** 8403 Colesville Rd., Suite 1200, Silver Spring, MD 20910 (☎ **301/ 578-8800**). A nonprofit organization, the council charges a membership fee of $12 per couple for which you receive a magazine six times a year and membership benefits, including discounts on hotel and auto rentals, a discount pharmacy program, and accidental-death insurance.

Mature Outlook, P.O. Box 9390, Des Moines, IA 50306-9519 (☎ **800/ 336-6330;** fax 515/252-7855), is a travel organization for people over 50 years of age. Members are offered discounts at ITC-member hotels and will receive a bimonthly magazine. Annual membership is $14.95 to $19.95, which entitles its members to discounts and in some cases free coupons for discounted merchandise from Sears Roebuck Co.

FOR FAMILIES   On airlines, you must request a special menu for children at least 24 hours in advance. If baby food is required, however, bring your own and ask a flight attendant to warm it to the right temperature.

Arrange ahead of time for such necessities as a crib, bottle warmer, and car seat (in England, small children aren't allowed to ride in the front seat).

If you're staying with friends and can't take advantage of amenities offered by a hotel, you can rent baby equipment from **Chelsea Baby Hire,** 83 Burntwood Lane, London SW17 OAJ (☎ **0181/540-8830**).

The London Black Cab is a lifesaver for families; the roomy interior allows a stroller to be lifted right into the cab without unstrapping baby.

If you want a night out without the kids, you're in luck: London has its own children's hotel, **Pippa Popins,** 430 Fulham Road, SW6 1DU (☎ **0171/385-2458**), which accommodates children overnight in a wonderful nursery filled with lots of toys and caring caregivers. Other recommendable babysitting services in London are: **Babysitters Unlimited** (☎ **0181/892-8888**) and **Childminders** (☎ **0171/935-2049** or 0171/935-3000). Baby-sitters can also be found for you at most hotels.

Family Travel Times is published quarterly by **TWYCH** (Travel With Your Children) and includes a weekly call-in service for subscribers. Subscriptions ($40 a year) can be ordered by mail from TWYCH, 40 Fifth Ave., New York, NY 10011 (☎ **212/ 477-5524;** fax 212/477-5173). An information packet, including a sample newsletter, is available for $2.

Families Welcome!, 4711 Hope Valley Rd., Suite 4B, Durham, NC 27707 (☎ **800/326-0724** or 919/489-2555), a travel company specializing in worry-free vacations for families, offers "City Kids" packages to London, featuring accommodations in family friendly hotels or apartments. Individually designed family packages can include car rentals, train and ferry passes, and special air prices. A welcome kit is available, containing "insider's information" for families traveling in London, such as reliable baby-sitters, where to buy disposable diapers, and a list of family friendly restaurants.

To find out what's on for children while you're in London, pick up the leaflet *Where to Take Children,* published by the London Tourist Board and Convention Bureau. If you have specific questions, ring **Kidsline** (☎ **0171/222-8070**) Monday to Friday between 4 and 6pm and summer holidays between 9am and 4pm, or the **London Tourist Board**'s special children's information lines (☎ **0891/505-456** or 0891/505-460). Both numbers offer listings of special events and places to visit for children. The number is accessible in London only at the cost of 50p (80¢) per call.

7 Getting There

BY PLANE
THE MAJOR AIRLINES

British Airways (☎ **800/AIRWAYS**) offers flights from 18 U.S. cities to Heathrow and Gatwick airports as well as many others to Manchester, Birmingham, and Glasgow. Nearly every flight is nonstop. With more add-on options than any other airline, British Airways can make a visit to Britain cheaper than you might have expected. The 1993 union of some of BA's functions and routings with U.S. Airways opened additional North American gateways to BA, improved services, and reduced some of its fares. Ask about packages that include both airfare and discounted hotel accommodations in Britain.

Known for consistently offering excellent fares, **Virgin Atlantic Airways** (☎ **800/862-8621**) flies daily to either Heathrow or Gatwick from Boston, Newark, New Jersey, New York's JFK, Los Angeles, San Francisco, Washington's Dulles, Miami, and Orlando.

American Airlines (☎ **800/433-7300**) offers daily flights to London's Heathrow from half a dozen U.S. gateways—New York's JFK (six times daily), Chicago's O'Hare and Boston's Logan (twice daily), and Miami International and Los Angeles International (each once daily).

Depending on day and season, **Delta Air Lines** (☎ **800/241-4141**) runs either one or two daily nonstop flights between Atlanta and Gatwick. Delta also offers nonstop daily service from Cincinnati.

Northwest Airlines (☎ **800/447-4747**) flies nonstop from Minneapolis and Detroit to Gatwick, with connections possible from other cities, such as Boston or New York.

Continental Airlines (☎ **800/525-0280**) has daily flights to London from Houston and Newark.

TWA (☎ **800/221-2000**) flies nonstop to Gatwick every day from its hub in St. Louis. Connections are possible through St. Louis from most of North America.

United Airlines (☎ **800/538-2929**) flies nonstop from New York's JFK and Chicago's O'Hare to Heathrow two or three times daily, depending on the season. United also offers nonstop service twice a day from Dulles Airport, near Washington, D.C., plus once-a-day service from Newark, Los Angeles, and San Francisco to Heathrow.

For travelers departing from Canada, **Air Canada** (☎ **800/776-3000**) flies daily to London's Heathrow nonstop from Vancouver, Montréal, and Toronto. There are also frequent direct services from Edmonton, Calgary, Winnipeg, Ottawa, Halifax, and St. John's.

From Canada, **British Airways** (☎ **800/247-9297**) has direct flights from Toronto, Montréal, and Vancouver.

For travelers departing from Australia, **British Airways** (☎ **800/262-1234**) has flights to London from Sydney, Melbourne, Perth, and Brisbane. **Qantas** (☎ **800/AIRWAYS**) offers flights from Australia to London's Heathrow. Direct flights depart from Sydney and Melbourne. Some have the bonus of free stopovers in Bangkok or Singapore.

Departing from New Zealand, **Air New Zealand** (☎ **800/262-1234**) has direct flights to London from Auckland. These flights depart Wednesday, Saturday, and Sunday.

Cyberdeals for Net Surfers

It's possible to get some great deals on airfare, hotels, and car rentals via the Internet. So grab your mouse and start surfing: You could save a bundle on your trip!

Microsoft Expedia (**www.expedia.com**): The best part of this multipurpose travel site is the "Fare Tracker." You fill out a form on the screen indicating that you're interested in cheap flights to London from your hometown, and, once a week, they'll e-mail you the best airfare deals. The site's "Travel Agent" will steer you to bargains on hotels and car rentals, and you can book everything, including flights, right on-line. This site is even useful once you're booked: Before you go, log on to Expedia for oodles of up-to-date travel information, including weather reports and foreign exchange rates.

Travelocity (**www.travelocity.com**):   This is one of the best travel sites out there. In addition to its "Personal Fare Watcher," which notifies you via e-mail of the lowest airfares for up to five different destinations, Travelocity will track the three lowest fares for any routes on any dates in minutes. You can book a flight right then and there, and if you need a rental car or hotel, Travelocity will find you the best deal via the SABRE computer reservations system (a huge database used by travel agents worldwide). Click on "Last Minute Deals" for the latest travel bargains.

Trip.Com (**www.thetrip.com**): This site is really geared toward the business traveler, but vacationers-to-be can also use Trip.Com's valuable fare-finding engine, which will e-mail you every week with the best city-to-city airfare deals on your selected route or routes.

Discount Tickets (**www.discount-tickets.com**): Operated by the ETN (European Travel Network), this site offers discounts on airfares, accommodations, car rentals, and tours.

Short flights from Dublin to London are available through **British Airways** (☎ 800/AIRWAYS), with four flights daily into London's Gatwick airport, and **Aer Lingus** (☎ 800/223-6537), which flies into Heathrow. Short flights from Dublin to London are also available through **Ryan Air** (☎ 0541/569-569) and **British Midland** (☎ 0345/554-554).

Getting the Best Airfare

BUCKET SHOPS & CONSOLIDATORS   You might be able to get a great deal on airfare by calling a bucket shop or consolidator, outfits that act as clearinghouses for blocks of tickets that airlines discount and consign during normally slow periods of air travel. Tickets are usually priced 20% to 35% below the full fare. However, payment terms can vary and you might be assigned a poor seat on the plane at the last minute.

Bucket shops abound from coast to coast. You might try **Travac,** 989 Sixth Ave., New York, NY 10018 (☎ 800/TRAV-800 in the U.S., or 212/563-3303) or 2601 E. Jefferson St., Orlando, FL 32803 (☎ 407/896-0014); **TFI Tours International,** 34 W. 32nd St., 12th Floor, New York, NY 10001 (☎ 800/745-8000 outside N.Y. state, or 212/736-1140); **Unitravel,** 1137 Administration Dr., Suite 120, St. Louis, MO 63146 (☎ 800/325-2222; fax 314/569-2503); **Travel Avenue,** 10 S. Riverside Plaza,

E-Savers Programs: Several major airlines offer a free e-mail service known as E-Savers, via which they'll send you their best bargain airfares on a weekly basis. Here's how it works: Once a week (usually Wednesday), subscribers receive a list of discounted flights to and from various destinations, both international and domestic. Now here's the catch: These fares are only available if you leave the very next Saturday (or sometimes Friday night) and return on the following Monday or Tuesday. It's really a service for the spontaneously inclined and travelers looking for a quick getaway. But the fares are cheap, so it's worth taking a look. If you have a preference for certain airlines (in other words, the ones you fly most frequently), sign up with them first. Another caveat: You'll get frequent-flier miles if you purchase one of these fares, but you can't use miles to buy the ticket.

Here's a list of airlines and their Web sites, where you can not only get on the e-mailing lists, but also book flights directly:

* **Air Canada**: www.aircanada.com
* **American Airlines**: www.americanair.com
* **British Airways:** www.british airways.com
* **Continental Airlines:** www.flycontinental.com
* **Northwest Airlines:** www.nwa.com
* **TWA**: www.twa.com
* **US Airways:** www.usairways.com
* **Virgin Atlantic:** www.fly.virgin.com
* **Epicurious Travel** (travel.epicurious.com), another good travel site, allows you to sign up for all of these airline e-mail lists at once.

Suite 1404, Chicago, IL 60606 (☎ **800/333-3335**), the nation's oldest and largest rebate travel agency. There's also **1-800-FLY-4-LESS,** a nationwide airline reservation and ticketing service that specializes in finding only the lowest fares.

CHARTER FLIGHTS   Strictly speaking, a charter flight occurs on an aircraft reserved months in advance for a one-time-only transit to some predetermined point. Before paying for a charter, check the restrictions on your ticket or contract. You'll pay a stiff penalty (or forfeit the ticket entirely) if you cancel. Charters are sometimes canceled when the plane doesn't fill up.

One reliable charter-flight operator is **Council Charter,** run by the Council on International Educational Exchange, 205 E. 42nd St., New York, NY 10017 (☎ **800/2-COUNCIL** or 212/822-2900), which arranges charter seats on regularly scheduled aircraft. You could also try **Travac,** 989 Sixth Ave., New York, NY 10018 (☎ **800/TRAV-800** or 212/563-3303).

REBATERS   Rebaters pass part of their commission along to the passenger, although many of them assess a fee for their services. Most rebaters offer discounts ranging from 10% to 25% plus a $25 handling charge. They are not the same as travel agents but sometimes offer similar services, including discounted accommodations and car rentals.

Midwest travelers might want to try **Travel Avenue,** 10 S. Riverside Plaza, Suite 1404, Chicago, IL 60606 (☎ **800/333-3335** or 312/876-6866). Another major rebater is **The Smart Traveller,** 3111 SW 27th Ave. (P.O. Box 330010), Miami, FL 33133 (☎ **800/448-3338** or 305/448-3338; fax 305/443-3544). They also offer discounts on packaged tours.

LATE-SAVER FARE   Virgin Atlantic Airways (☎ **800/862-8621**) offers passage from North America to London that can be reserved within 48 hours of the departure time, if seats are available. This type of fare, known as a Late-Saver fare, is available during the off-season when seats are plentiful.

TRAVEL CLUBS   Travel clubs supply an unsold inventory of tickets at discounts of 20% to 60%. You pay an annual fee and are given a hot-line number to find out what discounts are available. Many discounts become available several days in advance of the actual departure, sometimes as long as a month in advance. Of course, you're limited to what's available, so you have to be fairly flexible.

Moment's Notice, 7301 New Utrecht Ave., Brooklyn, NY 11204 (☎ **718/ 234-6295,** www.moments-notice.com) charges $25 per year and offers tours geared for impulse purchases and last-minute getaways. Even nonmembers can call the Moment's Notice hot line (see above) to learn what options are available. Most of the company's best-priced tours depart from the New York metropolitan area.

Travelers Advantage, 3033 S. Parker Rd., Suite 1000, Aurora, CO 80014 (☎ **800/548-1116**), offers a 3-month trial period for $1; the annual membership fee is $49. Benefits include a hotel card, which gets you 50% off the regularly published room rate at more than 3,000 hotels, members-only vacation packages at discounted rates, and a 5% cash bonus on all purchases made through the service (with a copy of your itinerary and any receipts).

BY TRAIN FROM CONTINENTAL EUROPE

Britain's isolation from the rest of Europe led to the development of an independent railway network with different rules and regulations from those observed on the Continent. That's all changing now, but one big difference that may affect you still remains: If you're traveling to Britain from the Continent, *your Eurail pass will not be valid when you get there.*

In 1994, Queen Elizabeth and Pres. François Mitterand officially opened the Channel Tunnel, or Chunnel, and the *Eurostar Express* passenger train began twice-daily service between London and both Paris and Brussels—a 3-hour trip. The $15 billion tunnel, one of the great engineering feats of all time, is the first link between Britain and the Continent since the Ice Age.

So if you're coming to London from say, Rome, your Eurail pass will get you as far as the Chunnel. At that point you can cross the English Channel aboard the *Eurostar,* and you'll receive a discount on your ticket. Once in England, you would either begin using a separate Britrail pass or purchase a direct ticket to continue on to your destination.

Rail Europe (☎ **800/4-EURAIL;** www.raileurope.com) sells direct-service tickets on the *Eurostar* between Paris or Brussels and London. A round-trip fare between Paris and London ranges from $278 to $598 in first class and $170 to $278 in second class. One-way unrestricted fares for passage on the Eurostar between Paris and London cost $199 in first class and $139 in second class. In London, make reservations for **Eurostar** by calling ☎ **0345/300003;** in Paris, call ☎ **01/44-51-06-02;** and in the United States, it's ☎ **800/4-EURAIL.** Eurostar trains arrive and depart from London's Waterloo Station, Paris's Gare du Nord, and Brussels's Central Station.

BY FERRY/HOVERCRAFT FROM CONTINENTAL EUROPE

P & O Channel Lines (☎ 0990/980980) operates car and passenger ferries between Portsmouth and Cherbourg, France (three departures a day; 4¼ hours each way; 7 hours at night); between Portsmouth and Le Havre, France (three a day; 5½ hours each way); and between Dover and Calais, France (25 sailings a day; 75 minutes each way).

P & O's major competitor is **Stena Sealink** (☎ 01233/615455), which carries both passengers and vehicles on its routes. This company is represented in North America by **Continental Rail** (☎ 800/677-8585, 212/575-2667 in New York City, or 800/555-2748 in Canada). It offers conventional ferryboat service between Cherbourg and Southampton (one or two trips a day; 6 to 8 hours, each way) and between Dieppe and Newhaven (four departures daily; 4 hours each way). Its conventional carferries between Calais and Dover are very popular; they depart 20 times a day in both directions and take 90 minutes to make the crossing. Typical fares between France and England are as follows: £25 ($40) for a one-way adult ticket, £22 ($35.20) for seniors, and £12 ($19.20) for children.

By far the most popular route across the English Channel is between Calais and Dover. **Hoverspeed** operates at least 12 hovercraft crossings daily; the trip takes 35 minutes. They also run a SeaCat (a catamaran propelled by jet engines) that takes slightly longer to make the crossing between Boulogne and Folkestone. The SeaCats depart about four times a day on the 55-minute voyage.

Traveling by hovercraft or SeaCat cuts the time of your surface journey from the Continent to the United Kingdom. A hovercraft trip is definitely a fun adventure, since the vessel is technically "flying" over the water. A SeaCat crossing from Folkestone to Boulogne is longer in miles but is covered faster than conventional ferryboats make the Calais-Dover crossing. For reservations and information, call Hoverspeed (☎ 01304/240241). Typical one-way fares are £25 ($40) per person.

BY CAR FROM CONTINENTAL EUROPE

If you plan to transport a rented car between England and France, check in advance with the car-rental company about license and insurance requirements, and additional drop-off charges, before you begin.

The English Channel is crisscrossed with "drive-on, drive-off" car-ferry services, with many operating from Boulogne and Calais in France. From either of those ports, Sealink ferries will carry you, your luggage, and, if you like, your car. The most popular points of arrival along the English coast include Dover and Folkestone.

Taking a car beneath the Channel is more complicated and more expensive. Since the Channel Tunnel's opening, most passengers have opted to ride the train alone, without being accompanied by their car. The *Eurostar* trains, discussed above, carry passengers only; *Le Shuttle* trains carry freight cars, trucks, lorries, and passenger cars.

One-way fares for cars on the Le Shuttle trains vary from £80 to £265 ($128 to $424) according to their size. Frankly, it's a lot cheaper to transport your car across by conventional ferryboat, but if you insist, here's what you'll need to know: You'll negotiate both English and French customs as part of one combined process, usually on the English side of the Channel. You can remain within your vehicle even after you drive it onto a flatbed railway car during the 35-minute crossing. (For 19 minutes of this crossing, you'll actually be underwater; if you want, you can leave the confines of your car and ride within a brightly lit, air-conditioned passenger car.) When the trip is over, you simply drive off the flatbed railway car and drive off toward your destination. Total travel time between the French and English highway system is about 1 hour. As a means of speeding the flow of perishable goods across the Channel, the car and truck service usually operates 24 hours a day, at intervals that vary from 15 minutes to once an hour, depending on the time of day or night. Neither BritRail nor any of the agencies dealing with reservations for passenger trains through the Chunnel will reserve space for your car in advance, and considering the frequency of the traffic on the Chunnel, they're usually not necessary. For information about **Le Shuttle** car-rail service after you reach England, call ☎ **01304/288617** or 0990/353535.

Duty-free stores, restaurants, and service stations are available to travelers on both sides of the Channel. A bilingual staff is on hand to assist travelers at both the British and French terminals.

8 Package & Escorted Tours

PACKAGE TOURS

Package tours are not the same thing as escorted tours. They are simply a way of buying your airfare and accommodations at the same time—and they can save you a ton of money. In many cases, a package that includes airfare, hotel, and transportation to and from the airport will cost you less than just the hotel alone if you booked it yourself. That's because the elements of packages are sold in bulk to tour operators, who resell them to the public.

Some packages offer a better class of hotels than others. Some offer the same hotels for lower prices. Some offer flights on scheduled airlines while others book charters. In some packages, your choices of accommodations and travel days may be limited. Some packages let you choose between escorted vacations and independent vacations; others will allow you to add on just a few excursions or escorted day trips (also at prices lower than if you booked them yourself) without booking an entirely escorted tour. So the time you spend shopping around will be well rewarded.

The best place to start looking is the travel section of your local Sunday newspaper. Also check the ads in the back of national travel magazines. **Liberty Travel** (many locations; check your local directory, since there's not a central 800 number) is one of the biggest packagers in the Northeast, and usually boasts a full-page ad in Sunday papers. You won't get much in the way of service, but you will get a good deal.

Another good resource is the airlines themselves, which often package their flights together with accommodations. When you pick the airline, you can choose one that has frequent service to your home town and the one on which you accumulate frequent flyer miles.

Far and away, you'll find the most options through **British Airways** (☎ **800/ AIRWAYS**). Its offerings within the British Isles are more comprehensive than those of its competitors, and can be tailored to your specific interest and budget. Tours can be as straightforward or as specialized as you need. They might include a 1-day jaunt from London to Canterbury or Brighton (with a return to London in time for a West End play); or they might include excursions from London to the Edinburgh Music Festival (with difficult-to-obtain tickets included as part of the bargain). Many of the tours, such as the 9-day all-inclusive tour through the great houses and gardens of England, include the ongoing services of a guide and lecturer. But if you prefer to travel independently, without following an organized tour, a sales representative can tailor an itinerary specifically for you, with discounted rates in a wide assortment of big-city hotels. If you opt for this, transfers between stopovers would take place within a self-driven rented car or, less frequently, by train. For a free catalog and additional information, call British Airways *before you book your airline ticket,* since some of the company's available options are contingent upon the purchase of a round-trip transatlantic air ticket.

British Airways is not the only airline offering package tours to England. Its main competitors include **Delta Dream Vacations** (☎ 800/872-7786), **TWA Getaway Vacations** (☎ 800/438-2929), **Continental Vacations** (☎ 800/634-5555), and **United Vacations** (☎ 800/328-6877).

ESCORTED TOURS

Before choosing an escorted tour, ask a few simple questions:

1. What is the cancellation policy? Can they cancel the trip if they don't get enough people? Do you get a refund if you cancel? If *they* cancel?
2. How jam-packed is the schedule? Do they try to fit 25 hours into a 24-hour day, or is there ample time for relaxing or shopping? If you don't enjoy getting up at 7am every day and not returning to your hotel until 6 or 7pm at night, certain escorted tours may not be for you.
3. How big is the group? The smaller the group, the more flexible and the less time you'll spend waiting for people to get on and off the bus. Tour operators may be evasive about this, because they may not know the exact size of the group until everybody has made his or her reservations, but they should be able to give you a rough estimate. Some tours have a minimum group size, and may cancel the tour if they don't book enough people.
4. What is included? Don't assume anything. You may have to pay to get yourself to and from the airport. Or a box lunch may be included in an excursion but drinks might cost extra. How much choice do you have? Can you opt out of certain activities, or does the bus leave once a day, with no exceptions? Are all your meals planned in advance? Can you choose your entree at dinner, or does everybody get the same chicken cutlet?

If you choose an escorted tour, think strongly about purchasing travel insurance, especially if the tour operator asks to you pay up front. But don't buy insurance from the tour operator! If they don't fulfill their obligation to provide you with the vacation you've paid for, there's no reason to think they'll fulfill their insurance obligations either. Get travel insurance through an independent agency. See section 5 on travel insurance, earlier in this chapter.

Abercrombie & Kent, 1520 Kensington Rd., Oak Brook, IL 60523 (☎ **800/ 323-7308**), offers extremely upscale escorted tours that are loaded with luxury. Their most unusual conveyance is the *Royal Scotsman* train, which, for 2 nights and 3 days, hauls participants along less frequently used railway spurs of Wiltshire, Somerset, and Devon within vintage railway cars that were fashionable around the turn of the century. Prices begin at $1,500 per person, double occupancy, for lots of local color and spit-and-polish service. Tours emphasize visits to sites of historical interest, and sometimes involve rides on buses that pick up and redeposit passengers at local railway stations.

One of Abercrombie's top rivals is **Travcoa,** Box 2630, Newport Beach, CA 92658 (☎ **800/992-2003**), which offers upscale tours by deluxe motor coach through the countryside of England and Scotland. Tours last from 14 to 24 days, include at least 3 nights in London, usually at such citadels of glamour as The Dorchester, and come with meals and virtually every other aspect of a holiday included in the price. Don't expect cost savings here: Without airfare, rates range from $5,895 to $10,895 per person double occupancy.

Other contenders in the upscale package-tour business include **Maupintour,** 1515 St. Andrews Dr., Lawrence, KS 66047 (☎ **800/255-4266**), whose offerings are roughly equivalent to those at Travcoa, and Maupintour's leading competitor, **Tauck Tours,** Box 5027, 276 Post Rd. W., Westport, CT 06881 (☎ **800/468-2825**).

But not all escorted tours are so pricey. Mostly older, British folks make up a large portion of the clientele of one of the United Kingdom's largest tour operators, **Wallace Arnold Tours,** Gelderd Rd., Leeds LS12 6DH (☎ **0181/686-4962** in the U.K.). Most of the company's tours last between 5 and 10 days, include lodgings at solid but not particularly extravagant hotels, most meals, and are reasonably priced from £183 ($292.80), without airfare.

Trafalgar Tours, 11 E. 26th St., New York, NY 10010 (☎ **800/854-0103**), offers affordable packages with lodgings in unpretentious but comfortable hotels. It's one of Europe's largest tour operators. There may not be a lot of frills, but you can find 8-day itineraries priced from $650 per person, double occupancy, without airfare, that include stopovers in Stratford-upon-Avon and Bath; and hotel packages at first-class hotels in London, with some money-saving coupons thrown in, for $499 per person, double occupancy.

One of Trafalgar's leading competitors, known for offering roughly equivalent moderately priced tours through Britain, is **Globus/Cosmos Tours,** 5301 S. Federal Circle, Littleton, CO 80123-2980 (☎ **800/221-0090**).

Finally, there's **BritainShrinkers Tours.** An affiliate of BritRail, this company operates a number of escorted, full-day tours from May to the end of October to such popular places as Stratford-upon-Avon, Oxford, and the Cotswolds. All tours include transportation and sightseeing by bus. Tours usually include some free time for lunch, shopping, and exploring on your own. Tours return to London in time for dinner or the theater. Rates include entrance fees and value-added tax (VAT), but usually not the price of lunch.

BritainShrinkers offers excellent value for the money. And if you have a BritRail pass or Flexipass, you'll save up to 60% on the cost of each tour you take. Their tours can be purchased from either your travel agent or BritRail in the United States. (See "By Train" in section 9, below, for more details.)

9 Getting Around

BY PLANE
British Airways (☎ **800/AIRWAYS**) flies to more than 20 cities outside London, including Manchester, Glasgow, and Edinburgh. Ask about the British Airways Super Shuttle Saver fares, which can save you up to 50% on travel to certain key British cities. If seats are available on the flight of your choice, no advance reservations are necessary, although to benefit from the lowest prices, passengers must spend a Saturday night away from their point of origin and fly during defined off-peak times. Flights are usually restricted to weekdays between 10am and 3:30pm, whereas most night flights are after 7pm and, in certain cases, on weekends.

For passengers planning on visiting widely scattered destinations within the United Kingdom, perhaps with a side trip to a city on Europe's mainland, British Airways' **Europe Airpass** allows discounted travel in a continuous loop to between 3 and 12 cities anywhere on BA's European and domestic air routes. Passengers must end their journey at the same point they begin it and fly exclusively on BA flights. Such a ticket (for instance, from London to Paris, then to Manchester, and finally to London again) will cut the cost of each segment of the itinerary by about 40% to 50% over individually booked tickets. The pass is available for travel to about a dozen of the most-visited cities and regions of Britain, with discounted add-ons available to most of BA's

destinations in Europe as well. (This Airpass is a good bargain for round-trip travel
between London and Rome, but not very practical for air travel from, say, Rome to
Madrid. You'd be better off traveling between points on the Continent by full-fare airline ticket, or by train, bus, or car.)

BA's Europe Airpass must be booked and paid for at least 7 days before a passenger's
departure from North America. All sectors of the itinerary, including transatlantic passage from North America, must be booked simultaneously. Some changes are permitted in flight dates (but not in destinations) after the ticket is issued. Check with
British Airways for full details and restrictions.

BY TRAIN

As it heads for the millennium, British Rail's infrastructure is being altered, although
the essential rail network remains intact, and, in some cases, is being expanded. To
raise capital and improve service, the government is selling some of its routes to independent operators who agree to maintain the switches, tracks, and rail cars according
to standards set by British Rail's supervisory board, Railtrack. None of these behind-
the-scenes changes currently affect how you'll buy rail passes or individual tickets.

A Eurail pass is not valid in Great Britain, but there are several special passes for
train travel outside London. For railroad information, go to Rail Travel centers in the
main London railway stations (Waterloo, King's Cross, Euston, and Paddington).

Americans can obtain a BritRail passes at **BritRail Travel International,** 500
Mamaroneck Ave., Suite 314, Harrison, NY 10528 (☎ **800/677-8585;** 800/555-
2748 in Canada).

TRAIN TRAVEL FROM LONDON TO PRINCIPAL CITIES

To	From London Station	Typical No. of Trains Per Day	Miles	Travel Time
Bath	Paddington	25	107	1 hr. 11 min.
Birmingham	Euston/Paddington	35	113	1 hr. 37 min.
Bristol	Paddington	46	119	1 hr. 26 min.
Carlisle	Euston	10	299	3 hr. 40 min.
Chester	Euston	16	179	2 hr. 36 min.
Exeter	Paddington	17	174	1 hr. 55 min.
Leeds	King's Cross	19	185	2 hr. 12 min.
Liverpool	Euston	14	193	2 hr. 34 min.
Manchester	Euston	16	180	2 hr. 27 min.
Newcastle	King's Cross	26	268	2 hr. 50 min.
Penzance	Paddington	9	305	5 hr.
Plymouth	Paddington	14	226	2 hr. 35 min.
York	King's Cross	27	188	1 hr. 57 min.

BRITRAIL CLASSIC PASS   This pass allows unlimited rail travel during a set time
period (8 days, 15 days, 22 days, or 1 month). For 8 days, the pass costs $375 in first
class, $259 in "standard" class; for 15 days, $575 in first class, $395 in standard; for
22 days, $740 in first class, $510 in standard; and for 1 month, $860 in first class,
$590 in standard. Senior citizens (60 and over) qualify for discounts, but only in seats

Train Routes in England

Legend

- — Roads
- ⫶⫶⫶ Railroads
- – – – Ferries

Ferry Routes

1. to Larne
2. to Belfast
3. to Douglas
4. to Dublin
5. to Dun Laoghaire
6. to Rosslare
7. to Cork
8. to Isles of Scilly
9. to Guernsey & Jersey
10. to Cherbourg
11. to Dieppe
12. to Boulogne
13. to Calais
14. to Dunkerque
15. to Ostend
16. to Vlissingen
17. to Hook of Holland
18. to Hamburg
19. to Esbjerg
20. to Gothenburg
21. to Kristiansand & Oslo
22. to Zeebrugge
23. to Rotterdam
24. to Esbjerg
25. to Gothenburg
26. to Bergen & Stavanger

2743

within first-class—not standard class—compartments of trains. These cost $319 for 8-day passes, $489 for 15-day passes, $630 for 22-day passes, and $730 for 1 month passes. If a child age 5 to 15 is traveling with a full-fare adult, the fare is half the adult fare. Children under 5 travel free.

BRITRAIL FLEXIPASS   This pass lets you travel anywhere on BritRail, and is particularly good for visitors who want to alternate travel days with blocks of uninterrupted sightseeing time in a particular city or region. Flexipasses can be used for 4 days within any 1-month period and cost $315 in first class and $219 in standard. Seniors pay $269, and youths ages 16 to 25 pay $175 to travel standard class. Also available is a Flexipass that allows 8 days of travel within a month and costs $459 in first class, $315 in standard. A senior pass costs $390, the youth standard class $253.

SOUTHEAST PASS   If you're only planning day trips southeast of London, BritRail's Southeast Pass might make better sense than a more expensive rail pass that's valid in all parts of Britain. This pass allows unlimited travel to accessible destinations throughout BritRail's "Network Southeast," which includes Oxford, Cambridge, Dover, Canterbury, Salisbury, and Portsmouth. Frequent trains—about 41 daily from London to Brighton alone—let you leave early in the morning and return to London in time for the theater or dinner.

A Southeast Pass that's good for 3 days of travel out of any consecutive 8-day period costs $94 in first class, $69 in standard class. A Southeast Pass that's good for 4 days out of any 8-day consecutive period sells for $126 in first class and $94 in standard class. A Southeast Pass that's good for 7 days out of any 8-day consecutive period costs $166 in first class and $126 in standard class. Children under 16 pay $27 and $18 in first and standard class, respectively, for any of the three passes. The Southeast Pass must be purchased either from your travel agent or BritRail Travel International in the United States or Canada (see phone numbers above).

BY COACH

In Britain, a long-distance touring bus is called a "coach," and "buses" are taken for local transportation. There's an efficient and frequent express motor-coach network—run by National Express and other independent operators—that links most of Britain's towns and cities. Destinations off the main route can be easily reached by stopping and transferring to a local bus. Tickets are relatively cheap, often half the price of rail fare, and it's usually cheaper to purchase a round-trip (or "return") ticket than two one-way fares separately.

Victoria Coach Station, on Buckingham Palace Road (☎ **0171/730-3466**), is the departure point for most large coach operators. The coach station is located just two blocks from Victoria Station. For credit-card sales (MasterCard and VISA only), call ☎ **0171/730-3499** Monday to Saturday between 9am and 7pm. For cash purchases, get there at least 30 minutes before the coach departs.

National Express runs luxurious long-distance coaches that are equipped with hostesses, light refreshments, reclining seats, toilets, and no-smoking areas. Details about all coach services can be obtained by phoning ☎ **0990/808080** daily between 8am and 10pm. The National Express ticket office at Victoria Station is open from 8am to 7pm.

You might want to consider National Express's **Tourist Trail Pass,** which offers unlimited travel on their network. (This company's service is most extensive in England and Wales.) A 3-day pass costs £49 ($78.40), a 5-day pass £79 ($126.40), an 8-day pass, £119 ($190.40), and a 15-day pass, £179 ($286.40).

For journeys within a 35-mile radius of London, try the **Green Line** coach service, Lesbourne Rd., Reigate Surrey RH2 7LE (☎ **0181/668-7261**). With a 1-day **Diamond Rover Ticket**, costing £7 ($11.20) for adults and £5 ($8) for children, you can visit many of the attractions of Greater London and the surrounding region, including Windsor Castle and Hampton Court. The pass is valid for 1 day on almost all Green Line coaches and country buses Monday to Friday after 9am and all day on Saturday and Sunday.

Green Line has bus routes called Country Bus Lines that circle through the periphery of London. Although they do not usually go directly into the center of the capital, they do hook up with the routes of the Green Line coaches and red buses that do.

BY CAR

If you want to be on your own, and driving on the left appeals to your sense of adventure, here are some guidelines.

RENTALS   The British car-rental market is among the most competitive in Europe. Nevertheless, car rentals are often relatively expensive, unless you avail yourself of one of the promotional deals that are frequently offered by British Airways and others.

And car-rental rates vary even more than airline fares. The price depends on the size of the car, the length of time you keep it, where and when you pick it up and drop it off, where you take it, and a host of other factors.

Asking a few key questions could save you hundreds of dollars. (For example, weekend rates may be lower than weekday rates. Ask if the rate is the same for pickup Friday morning as it is Thursday night.) If you're keeping the car 5 or more days, a weekly rate may be cheaper than the daily rate. Some companies may assess a drop-off charge if you do not return the car to the same renting location; others do not. Ask if the rate is cheaper if you pick up the car at the airport or a location in town. If you see an advertised price in your local newspaper, be sure to ask for that specific rate; otherwise you may be charged the standard (higher) rate. Don't forget to mention membership in AAA, AARP, frequent-flyer programs, and trade unions. These usually entitle you to discounts ranging from 5% to 30%. Ask your travel agent to check any and all of these rates.

And most car rentals are worth at least 500 miles on your frequent-flyer account!

There are Internet resources that can make comparison shopping easier. For example, Yahoo's partnership with Flifo Global travel agency allows you to look up rental prices for any size car at more than a dozen rental companies in hundreds of cities. Just enter the size car you want, the rental and return dates, and the city where you want to rent, and the server returns a price. It will even make your reservation for you. Point your browser to **http://travel.yahoo.com/travel/** and then choose "Reserve car" from the options listed.

Since cars in Britain travel on the left side of the road, their steering wheels are positioned on the "wrong" side of the vehicle. Also keep in mind that most rental cars are manual, so be prepared to shift with your left hand; you'll pay more for an automatic—and make sure to request one when you reserve.

Most car-rental companies will accept your U.S. driver's license, provided you're 23 years old (21 in rare instances) and have had the license for more than a year. Many rental companies will grant discounts to clients who reserve their cars in advance (usually 48 hours) through the toll-free reservations offices in the renter's home country. Rentals of a week or more are almost always less expensive per day than day rentals.

When you reserve a car, be sure to ask if the price includes the 17.5% value-added tax (VAT), personal accident insurance (PAI), collision-damage waiver (CDW), and any other insurance options. If not, ask what they will cost, because at the end of your rental, they can make a big difference in your bottom line. As in the United States, the CDW and some added insurance are sometimes offered free by certain credit-card companies if you use the card to pay for the rental. Check directly with your credit-card issuer to see if you are covered by your credit card so you can avoid the sometimes unnecessary coverage.

The car-rental companies also offer additional liability insurance (if you harm others in an accident), personal accident insurance (if you harm yourself or your passengers), and personal effects insurance (if your luggage is stolen from your car). If you have insurance on your car at home, you are probably covered for most of these unlikelihoods. If your own insurance doesn't cover you for rentals, or if you don't have auto insurance, you should consider the additional coverages.

Rentals are available through **Avis** (☎ 800/331-2112; www.avis.com), **British Airways** (☎ 800/AIRWAYS; www.british-airways.com), **Budget Rent-a-Car** (☎ 800/472-3325; www.budget.com), and **Hertz** (☎ 800/654-3001; www. hertz.com). **Kemwel Holiday Autos** (☎ 800/678-0678; www.kemwel.com) is among the cheapest and most reliable of the rental agencies. **AutoEurope** (☎ 800/ 223-5555 in the U.S., or 0800/899893 in London; www.autoeurope.com) acts as a wholesale company for rental agencies in Europe.

DRIVING RULES & REQUIREMENTS   In England, *you drive on the left* and pass on the right. Road signs are clear and the international symbols are unmistakable.

You must present your passport and driver's license when you rent a car in Britain. No special British license is needed. It's a good idea to get a copy of the *British Highway Code,* available from almost any gas station or newsstand (called a "news stall" in Britain).

Warning: Pedestrian crossings are marked by striped lines (zebra striping) on the road; flashing lights near the curb indicate that drivers must stop and yield the right of way if a pedestrian has stepped out into the zebra zone to cross the street.

ROAD MAPS   The best road map is *The Ordinance Survey Motor Atlas of Great Britain,* whether you're trying to find the fastest route to Manchester or locate some obscure village. Revised annually, it's published by Temple Press and is available at most bookstores, including **W & G Foyle, Ltd.,** 113 and 119 Charing Cross Rd., London, WC2 HOEB (☎ 0171/439-8501).

BREAKDOWNS   If you are a member of AAA in the U.S., you are automatically eligible for the same roadside services you receive in this country. Be sure to bring your membership card with you on your trip. In an emergency all the Automobile Association of Great Britain's emergency road service (☎0800/887-766). If you are not a member of AAA, you might want to join one of England's two major auto clubs—the Automobile Association (AA) and the Royal Automobile Club (RAC). Membership, which can be obtained through your car-rental agent, entitles you to free legal and technical advice on motoring matters, as well as a whole range of discounts on automobile products and services.

The **AA** is located at Norfolk House, Priestly Road, Basingstoke, Hampshire RG24 9NY (☎ 0990/448866). The **RAC** can be contacted at P.O. Box 700, Bristol, Somerset BS99 1RB (☎ 01454/208000).

If your car breaks down on the highway, you can call for **24-hour breakdown service** from a roadside phone. The 24-hour number to call for AA is ☎ 0800/887766; for RAC it is ☎ 0800/828282. All superhighways (called motorways in Britain) are provided with special emergency phones that are connected to police traffic units, and the police can contact either of the auto clubs on your behalf.

GASOLINE   Called "petrol," gasoline is sold by the liter, with 4.2 liters to a gallon. Prices are much higher than Stateside, and you'll probably have to serve yourself. In some remote areas, stations are few and far between, and many are closed on Sunday.

10 Tips on Accommodations

Reserve your accommodations as far in advance as possible, even in the so-called slow months from November to April. Tourist travel to London peaks from May to October, and during that period, it's hard to come by a moderate or inexpensive hotel room.

CLASSIFICATIONS   Unlike some countries, England doesn't have a rigid hotel-classification system. The tourist board grades hotels by crowns instead of stars. Hotels are judged on their standards, quality, and hospitality, and are rated "approved," "commended," "highly commended," and "deluxe." Five crowns (deluxe) is the highest rating. There is even a classification of "listed," with no crowns, and these accommodations are for the most part very modest.

In a five-crown hotel, all rooms must have a private bath; in a four-crown hotel, only 75% have them. In a one-crown hotel, buildings are required to have hot and cold running water in all the rooms, but in "listed" hotels, hot and cold running water in the rooms is not mandatory. Crown ratings are posted outside the buildings. However, the system is voluntary, and many hotels do not participate.

Many hotels, especially older ones, still lack private bathrooms for all rooms. However, most have hot and cold running water, and many have modern wings with all the amenities (as well as older sections that are less up-to-date). When making reservations, always ask what section of the hotel you'll be staying in if it has extensions.

All hotels used to include a full English breakfast of bacon and eggs in the room price, but today that is true for only some hotels. A continental breakfast is commonly included, but that usually means just tea or coffee and toast.

BED & BREAKFASTS   In towns, cities, and villages throughout England, homeowners take in paying guests. Watch for the familiar bed-and-breakfast (B&B) signs. Generally, these are modest family homes, but sometimes they are like small hotels, with as many as 15 rooms. If they're that big, they are more properly classified as guest houses. B&Bs are the cheapest places you can stay in England and still be comfortable.

Hometours International, P.O. Box 11503, Knoxville, TN 37939 (☎ 800/367-4668 or 423/690-8484), will make bed-and-breakfast reservations in England, Scotland, and Wales. This is the only company to guarantee reservations for more than 400 locations in Britain. Accommodations are paid for in the United States in dollars, and prices start as low as $40 per person per night, although they can go as high as $90 per person in London. The company can also arrange for apartments in London or cottages in Great Britain that begin at $600 per week. In addition, it offers walking tours of Great Britain, with prices starting as low as $560 for 7 days, including meals.

Reservations for bed-and-breakfast accommodations in London can also be made by writing (not calling) the **British Travel Centre,** Rex House, 4-12 Lower Regent St., London SW1 4PQ. Once in London, you can also visit their office (tube: Piccadilly Circus).

In addition, Susan Opperman and Rosemary Lumb run **Bed and Breakfast Nationwide,** P.O. Box 2100, Clacton-on-Sea, Essex CO16 9BW, an agency specializing in privately owned bed-and-breakfasts all over Great Britain. Host homes range from small cottages to large manor houses, as well as working farms, and the prices vary accordingly. One thing you can be sure of is that owners have been specially selected for their wish to entertain visitors from overseas. Remember that these are private homes, so hotel-type services are not available. You will, however, be assured of a warm welcome, a comfortable bed, a hearty breakfast, and a glimpse of British life. Write for a free brochure. For bookings in accommodations outside London, call ☎ **01255/831235** or fax 01255/831437, daily between 9am and 6pm.

FARMHOUSES   In many parts of the country, farmhouses have one, two, even four rooms set aside for paying guests, who usually arrive in the summer months. Farmhouses don't have the facilities of most guest houses, but they have a rustic appeal and charm, especially for motorists, as they tend to lie off the beaten path. Prices are generally lower than bed-and-breakfasts or guest houses, and sometimes you're offered some good country home cooking (at an extra charge) if you make arrangements in advance. The British Tourist Authority will provide a booklet, *Stay on a Farm,* or you can ask at local tourist offices.

The **Farm Holiday Bureau** (☎ **1203/696909**) publishes an annual directory in early December that includes 1,000 farms and bed-and-breakfasts throughout the United Kingdom. The listings include quality ratings, the number of bedrooms, nearby attractions and activities, and prices, as well as line drawings of each property. Also listed are any special details, such as rooms with four-poster beds or activities on the grounds (fishing, for example). Many farms are geared toward children, who can participate in light chores—gathering eggs or just tagging along—for an authentic farm experience. The prices range from £13 to £35 ($20.80 to $56) a night and include an English breakfast and usually private facilities. (The higher prices are for stays at mansions and manor houses.)

Another option is self-catering accommodations, which are usually cottages or converted barns that cost from £150 to £600 ($240 to $960) per week, and include dishwashers and central heating. Each property is inspected every year not only by the Farm Holiday Bureau but also by the English Tourist Board. The majority of the properties, with the exception of those located in the mountains, are open year-round.

For a copy of the directory, contact the **Farm Holiday Bureau,** National Agricultural Centre, Stoneleigh Park, Warwickshire CV8 2LZ (☎ **1203/696909**). It costs £10 ($16) and may be purchased by credit card.

NATIONAL TRUST PROPERTIES   The **National Trust of England, Wales, and Northern Ireland,** 36 Queen Anne's Gate, London SW1H 9AS (☎ **0171/ 222-9251**), is Britain's leading conservation organization. In addition to the many castles, forests, and gardens it maintains, the National Trust owns 235 houses and cottages in some of the most beautiful parts of England, Wales, and Northern Ireland. Some of these properties are in remote and rural locations, some have incomparable views of the coastline, and others stand in the heart of villages and ancient cities.

Most of these comfortable self-catering holiday accommodations are available for rental throughout the year. Examples include a simple former coast guard cottage in Northumbria, a gaslit hideaway on the Isle of Wight, a gem of a country house above the Old Brewhouse at Chastleton, a 15th-century manor house in a hidden corner of the Cotswolds, and a superb choice of cottages in Devon and Cornwall. Houses can be booked for a week or more. Many can be booked for midweek or weekend breaks on short notice, particularly in the autumn and winter months. National Trust properties can sleep from 2 to 12 guests, and range in price from £130 ($208) per week for a small rental in winter to £1,200 ($1,920) per week for a larger property in peak season. Prices include value-added tax.

Although anyone can book rentals in National Trust properties, it's worth mentioning the trust's U.S. affiliate, the **Royal Oak Foundation,** 285 W. Broadway, Suite 400, New York, NY 10013-2299 (☎ **800/913-6565** or 212/966-6565), which publishes a full-color 120-page booklet that describes all National Trust holiday rental properties, their facilities, and prices. Copies cost $5 for members, $7.50 for non-members. Individual annual memberships are $45, and family memberships are $70. Benefits include free admission to all National Trust sites and properties open to the public, plus discounts on reservations at cottages and houses owned by them, and air and train travel.

HOLIDAY COTTAGES & VILLAGES   Throughout England, there are fully furnished studios, houses, cottages, "flats" (apartments), even trailers suitable for families or groups that can be rented by the month. From October to March, rents are sometimes reduced by 50%.

The British Tourist Authority and most tourist offices have lists available. The BTA's free *Apartments in London and Holiday Homes* lists rental agencies such as **At Home Abroad,** 405 E. 56th St., Suite 6H, New York, NY 10022 (☎ **212/421-9165;** fax 212/752-1591). Interested parties should write or fax a description of their needs, and At Home Abroad will send listings at no charge.

British Travel International, P.O. Box 299, Elkton, VA 22827 (☎ **800/327-6097** or 540/298-2232; fax 540/298-2347), represents between 8,000 and 10,000 rental properties in the United Kingdom, with rentals by the week (Saturday to Saturday), and requires a 50% payment at the time of booking. A catalog with pictures of their offerings is available for a $5 fee that is counted toward a deposit. They have everything from honey-colored, thatch-roofed cottages in the Cotswolds to apartments in a British university city. The company represents about 100 hotels in London whose rates are discounted by 5% to 50%, depending on the season and market conditions, and they have listings of some 4,000 bed-and-breakfast establishments. They are also the North American representative of the United Kingdom's largest bus company, National Express.

The **Barclay International Group (BIG),** 150 E. 52nd St., New York, NY 10022 (☎ **800/845-6636** or 212/832-3777), specializes in short-term apartment (flat) rentals in London and cottages in the English countryside. These rentals can be appropriate for families, groups of friends, or businesspeople traveling together, and are sometimes less expensive than equivalent stays in hotels. Apartments, available for stays as short as 1 night (although the company prefers that guests stay a minimum of 3 nights and charges a premium if your stay is shorter), are usually more luxurious than you'd imagine. Furnished with kitchens, they offer a low-cost alternative to restaurant meals. Apartments suitable for one or two occupants begin, during low season, at around $500 a week (including tax) and can go much higher for deluxe accommodations that offer many hotel-like features and amenities. For extended stays in the English countryside, BIG has country cottages in such areas as the Cotswolds, the Lake District, and Oxford, as well as farther afield in Scotland and Wales. The company can also arrange for tickets for sightseeing attractions, BritRail passes, and various other "extras." They have recently established an office in England at 45 Albemarle St., London W1X 3FE. (☎ 0171/4952986; fax 0171/4992312).

At the cheaper end of the spectrum, there's **Hoseasons Holidays,** Sunway House, Lowestoft, NR32 2LW (☎ **01502/500-500**), a reservations agent based in Suffolk (East Anglia). They arrange stopovers in at least 300 vacation villages throughout Britain. Although many are isolated in bucolic regions far from any of the sites covered within this guidebook, others lie within an hour's drive of Stratford upon Avon or Oxford. Don't expect luxury or convenience: Vacation villages in England usually consist of a motley assortment of trailers, uninsulated bungalows, and/or mobile homes perched on cement blocks. They're intended as frugal escapes for claustro-phobic urbanites with children. Such a place might not meet your expectations for a vacation in the English countryside (and a minimum stay of 3 nights is usually required), but it's hard to beat the rate. A 3-day sojourn begins at £45 ($72) per person, double occupancy.

YOUTH HOSTELS   The **Youth Hostels Association** (England and Wales) operates a network of 240 youth hostels in major cities, in the countryside, and along the coast. They can be contacted at Customer Services Department, YHA, Trevelyan House, 8 St. Stephen's Hill, St. Albans, Hertfordshire, AL1 2DY (☎ **01727/855215**), for a free map showing the locations of each youth hostel and full details, including prices.

11 Tips on Shopping

When shopping for the best buys in England, note that British goods, even products from Wales and Scotland, may offer sensational buys even when sold in England. You will also find Irish stores and Irish departments in some stores often selling merchandise at the same good value you'd find on a shopping trip to Ireland itself. Many French brands, it may come as a surprise, are less expensive in the United Kingdom than in France!

This section is an overview of England's shopping scene, including what's hot, where to get it, and how you can save money and secure value-added tax (VAT) refunds. If you're heading to London, check out chapter 5 for coverage of the capital's shopping and the famous sales.

THE BEST BUYS OF BRITAIN

When bargain hunting, focus on those goods that are manufactured in England and are liable to cost much more when exported. These include anything from The Body Shop, Filofax, or Doc Martens; many woolens and some cashmeres; most English brands of bone china; antiques, used silver, and rare books.

ANTIQUES   Whether you're looking for museum-quality antiques or simply fun junk, England has the stores, the resources, the stalls, and the markets. You can shop the fanciest of upmarket antique shops—mostly in London, Bath, and the Cotswolds—or browse through antique shows, markets, fairs, buildings, centers, arcades, warehouses, jumble fairs, fetes, and car boot sales throughout the country. (A car boot sale is the British version of a yard sale. Participants set up tables at an abandoned parking lot or airfield to sell their goods.)

Actually, prices are better once you get outside of London. Entire towns and areas in Britain are known to be treasure troves for those seeking anything from architectural salvage to a piece of the Holy Grail. Whereas the Cotswolds and Bath are known as charming places to shop for antiques, there are warehouses in Suffolk, Merseyside, and in the Greater Manchester (Yorkshire and Lancashire) area that aren't glamorous but offer dealers and those in the know the best buys. Serious shoppers can head directly to the Manchester area, get a car or van and just start shopping. The best hunting grounds are Boughton (right outside Chester), Liverpool, Prestwich, and Stockport. Harrogate and nearby Knaresborough are known for antiques, but offer a far more upscale scene with prices competitive to those in the Cotswolds.

AROMATHERAPY   The British must have invented aromatherapy—just about every store sells gels, creams, lotions, or potions made with the right herbs and essential oils to cure whatever ails you, including jet lag. Whether it works or not is secondary to the fact that most of the British brands are half the U.S. price when bought on home soil. **The Body Shop** becomes the best store in the world at prices like these. Check out drugstore brands as well. Shoppers like the Body Shop knock-offs that **Boots The Chemist** makes, as well as their own line (sold in another part of the store) of healing foot gels. Both of these are national brands available all over the United Kingdom. In addition, some small communities have homemade brands—check out **Woods of Windsor** (in the heart of downtown Windsor) for English flower soaps, lotions, and cures.

BASIC BRIT GEAR   Don't assume any bargains on woolens, cashmeres, tweeds and the like—often British quality is much higher than similar, and less expensive, goods available in the United States. If you want the best and expect it to last forever, you can't beat British-made, especially in gear that has been fine-tuned over the last century for the weather and outdoor lifestyle: from wax coats (**Barbour** is the leading status brand) to raincoats to guns (and English roses). While we can hardly put **Doc Martens** brand of shoes in the traditional Brit category, they do cost a lot less in Britain than in America, as any teen will tell you. The other quintessential English accessory is the **Filofax,** sold in a variety of versions with inserts galore for 30% to 50% less than prices in the United States.

BEAUTY PRODUCTS   Dime-store brands of makeup cost less than they do in the United States. The French line **Bourjois** (made in the same factories that produce Chanel makeup) costs less in London than in Paris and isn't sold in the United States; Boots makes its own Chanel knockoff line, **Number 7.**

BONE CHINA   Savings actually depend on the brand, but can be as much as 50% off U.S. prices. The trick is that shipping and U.S. duties may wipe out any savings; know what you're doing before you buy—and how you plan to get it back. Don't forget that there are factory outlets that sell seconds.

DESIGNER THIS & THAT   Designer clothing from any of the international makers may be less in London than in the United States or Paris, but know your prices. Often the only differential is the VAT refund, which at 15% to 17.5% is substantial. This game is also highly dependent on the value of the dollar.

While you won't get a VAT refund on used designer clothing, London has the best prices on used Chanel (and similar) clothing of any major shopping city.

HATS   "Does anyone still wear a hat?," Elaine Stritch asked archly in the musical *Company.* In England, the answer is yes. *Everyone* wears a hat, including the queen. Hats are sold all over England in department stores and specialty stores. You can buy a hat for $50 or for $5,000. Resale shops are an excellent graveyard for m'lady's discards; used designer hats begin around £25 ($40).

ROYAL SOUVENIRS   Forget about investing in Diana memorabilia; word is that it won't appreciate significantly because there was so much of it. Still, royal collectibles can be cheap kitsch bought in street markets or serious pieces from coronations long past found in specialist's shops. If you're buying new for investment purposes, it must be kept in mint condition.

TAPESTRY & KNITTING   For some reason, the English call needlepoint "tapestry." It's a passion, perhaps the seasonal flip side to gardening. Tapestry kits by the famous English designers, and Welsh queen of needles Elizabeth Bradley, cost a fraction of their U.S. prices when purchased anywhere in England or Wales.

Whereas England is famous for its sweaters (jumpers), what it should be famous for are the sweater kits: do-it-yourself jobs from the major designers that come with yarn, instructions, and a photo. These kits usually sell for about £50 ($80). A finished sweater from one of these designers (knit by someone else) can sell for as much as £300 ($480). English knitter-designers are cult heroes in Britain and do everything but knit autographs.

SHOPPING STRATEGIES

Most English towns feature a main street usually called the High Street. On this one road you'll find a branch of each of what is locally called "the High Street multiples." These are the chain stores that dominate the retail scene.

The leader among them is **Marks & Spencer,** a private label department store with high-quality goods at fair value prices; **Boots The Chemist** (a drugstore); **Laura Ashley** (less expensive in the United Kingdom); **The Body Shop** (the most popular politically correct bath and beauty statement of our times); **Monsoon** (a firm that sells hot fashion made from Far Eastern fabrics for moderate prices; they also have a dress-up division called **Twilight** and an accessories business called **Accessorize**); **Habitat** (sort of the English version of the Pottery Barn); and maybe (if you're lucky) **Past Times,** sort of a museum shop selling reproduction gifts and souvenirs. **Shelly's, Pied a Terre,** and **Hobbs** are all shoe stores selling everything from Doc Martens to expensive-looking cheap shoes. **Knickerbox** is usually found in train stations rather than on High Streets, but it's interesting nonetheless—the store sells fashion underwear at what the English call moderate prices.

ANTIQUES GALORE   Napoléon was wrong, England is not a nation of shopkeepers—it's a nation of antique collectors. Weekends are devoted to fairs and markets; evenings can be spent reading the dozens of newsstand specialty magazines geared to collectors or the plethora of books. Books in Britain are more expensive than in the United States, but the selection of titles on design, home furnishings, do-it-yourself, and collecting is staggering.

There are a number of famous antique fairs held at certain times of the year as well as several annual big-time events that attract several thousand dealers and thousands of shoppers. Among the best outside of London are those held at the **Newark and Nottinghamshire Showgrounds** (six times a year); **Sussex Midweek Fairs,** Ardingly (six times a year); **Newmarket** (four times a year); **Shepton Mallet** (four times a year); **Cardiff International** (twice a year); and **Royal Welsh Showgrounds** (twice a year). For the exact dates of any of these events, contact **County Antiques Fairs** (☎ 01278/784912; fax 01278/792687); or **DMG Antique Fairs, Ltd.** (☎ 01636/702326).

For immediate information on current antique fairs and events, check the magazine section of the *Sunday Times* where you'll find the Antique Buyer's Guide, which lists fairs all over England, not just in London. If you're serious about all this, you might want a subscription to *Antiques Diary*—six issues a year; £22 ($35.20) sent to the United States. Contact Antiques Diary, P.O. Box 30, Twyford, Reading RG10 8DQ, England. This small magazine lists fairs, shows, auctions, some big car boot events and even specialty house sales. You can also pick up the free *Lockson's Guide to Antiques in Britain* from the British Tourist Authority. Send a self-addressed, business-size envelope with 32¢ postage to: 551 Fifth Ave., Suite 701, New York, NY 10176-0799.

There are also continual **car boot sales,** as well as **house sales,** during which entire estates are cleaned out. There are only a few of these each year, and they become sort of voyeuristic social events; people drive for miles in order to attend. Advertisements are usually taken in magazines such as *Country Life.*

Just as house sales have boomed in recent years, the other big trend to come out of the recession is that **resale shops** are springing up all over. No one seems shy about

How to Get Your VAT Refund

To receive back a portion of the tax paid on purchases made in Britain, first ask the store personnel if they do VAT refunds and what their minimum purchase is. Once you've achieved this minimum, ask for the paperwork; the retailer will have to fill out a portion themselves. Several readers have reported that merchants have told them that they can get refund forms at the airport on their way out of the country. *This is not true.* You must get a refund form from the retailer (don't leave the store without one), and it must be completed by the retailer on the spot.

Fill out your portion of the form and then present it, along with the goods, at the customs office in the airport. Allow a half hour to stand in line. *Remember:* You're required to show the goods at your time of departure, so don't pack them in your luggage and check it; put them in your carry-on instead.

Once you have the paperwork stamped by the officials, you have two choices: You can mail the papers and receive your refund in either a British check (no!) or a credit card refund (yes!), or you can go directly to the Cash VAT Refund desk at the airport and get your refund in your hand, in cash. The bad news: If you accept cash other than sterling, you will lose money on the conversion rate. (If you plan on mailing your paperwork, try to remember to bring a stamp with you to the airport; if you forget, you can usually get stamps from stamp machines and/or the convenience stores in the terminal.)

Be advised that many stores charge a flat fee for processing your refund, so £3 to £5 may be automatically deducted from the total refund you receive. But since the VAT in Britain is 17.5%, if you get back 15%, you're doing fine.

Note: If you're traveling to other countries within the European Union, you don't go through any of this in Britain. At your final destination, prior to departure from the European Union, you file for all your VAT refunds at one time.

admitting that her Chanel and Louis Feraud are secondhand. London has a lot of these shops, but many out-of-the-way towns and cities have enormous resale shops as well.

TAXES & SHIPPING   Value added tax is the British version of sales tax, but it is a whopping 17.5% on most goods. This tax is added to the total so that the price on a sales tag already includes VAT. Non–European Union residents can get back all, or most, of this tax if they apply for a VAT refund (see box).

One of the first secrets of shopping in England is that the minimum expenditure needed to qualify for a refund on value-added tax (VAT) is a mere £50 ($80). Not every store honors this minimum (it's £100 ($160) at Harrods; £75 ($120) at Selfridges; £62 ($99.20) at Hermès), but it's far easier to qualify for a tax refund in Britain than almost any other country in the European Union. (See the box above for details on how to get your refund.)

Vendors at flea markets might not be equipped to provide the paperwork for a refund, so if you're contemplating a major purchase and really want that refund, ask before you fall in love. Be suspicious of any dealer who tells you there's no VAT on antiques. There didn't used to be, but there is now. The European Union has now made the British add VAT to antiques. Since dealers still have mixed stock, pricing should reflect this fact. So ask if it's included before you bargain on a price. Get to the price you're comfortable with first, then ask for the VAT refund.

VAT is not charged on goods shipped out of the country, whether you spend £50 ($80) or not. Many London shops will help you beat the VAT by shipping for you.

But watch out: Shipping can double the cost of your purchase. Also expect to pay U.S. duties when the goods reach you at home.

You may want to consider paying for excess baggage (rates vary with the airline), or else have your packages shipped independently. Independent operators are generally less expensive than the airlines. Try **London Baggage,** London Air Terminal, Victoria Place, SW1 (☎ **0171/828-2400;** tube: Victoria), or **Burns International Facilities.** They are found at Heathrow Airport in Terminal 1 (☎ **0181/745-5301**), or at Terminal 4 (☎ **0181/745-7460**).

DUTY-FREE AIRPORT SHOPPING   Shopping at airports is big business, so big business has taken over the management of some of Britain's airports to ensure that passengers in transit are enticed to buy. Terminal 4 at London Heathrow Airport is a virtual shopping mall, but each terminal has a good bit of shopping, with not a lot of crossover between brands.

Prices at the airport for items such as souvenirs and candy bars are actually higher than on the streets of London, but the duty-free prices on luxury goods are usually fair. There are often promotions and coupons that allow for pounds off at the time of the purchase.

Don't save all your shopping until you get to the airport, but do know prices on land and sea so that you know when to pounce.

12 Sightseeing Passes

There are several passes available that can cut down considerably on entrance costs to the country's stately homes and gardens. If you plan to do extensive touring, you'll save a lot of pounds by using one of these passes instead of paying the relatively steep entrance fees on an attraction-by-attraction basis.

Listed below are three organizations that offer passes waiving admission charges to hundreds of historical properties located throughout the United Kingdom. Each is a good deal, as the money you'll save on visitation to just a few of the available sites will pay for the price of the pass.

The British National Trust offers members free entry to some 240 National Trust sites in Britain, and more than 100 properties in Scotland. Focusing on gardens, castles, historic parks, abbeys, and ruins, sites include Chartwell, St. Michael's Mount, and Beatrix Potter's House. The membership fee includes a listing of all properties, maps, and essential information for independent tours, and listings and reservations for holiday cottages located on the protected properties.

Individual memberships cost $45 annually, and family memberships, including up to seven people, run $70, so savings on the admission charges, combined with discounts on holiday cottage reservations and British Air or BritRail travel, make this especially appealing. Visa and MasterCard are accepted.

Contact The British National Trust, 36 Queen Anne's Gate, London SW1H 9AS (☎ **0171/222-9251**), or **The Royal Oak Foundation,** 285 W. Broadway, no. 400, New York, NY 10013-2299 (☎ **800/913-6565** or 212/966-6565).

The **English Heritage** sells 7- and 14-day passes and annual memberships, offering free admission to more than 300 historical sites in England, and half-price admission to more than 100 additional sites in Scotland, Wales, and the Isle of Man. (Admission to these additional sites is free for anyone who renews his or her annual membership after the first year.) Sites include Hadrian's Wall, Stonehenge, and Kenilworth Castle.

Also included is free or reduced admission to 450 historic reenactments and open-air summer concerts, a handbook detailing all properties, a map, and, with the purchase of an annual membership, events and concerts diaries, and *Heritage Today*, a quarterly magazine.

A 7-day Overseas Visitor Pass runs £16 ($25.60) for an adult, £7 ($11.20) for a child, and £35 ($56) for a family of six or less; and a 21-day pass is £20 ($32) for an adult, £10 ($16) for a child, and £45 ($72) for a family. Annual memberships are also available with rates of £20 ($32) for an adult, £13.50 ($21.60) for a youth between the ages of 16 and 21, £9.50 ($15.20) for a youth under 16, and £38.50 ($61.60) for a family. MasterCard and Visa are accepted.

For visitor passes and membership, contact Customer Services, English Heritage, 429 Oxford St., London W1R 2HD (☎ **0171/973-3434**) or join directly at the site.

The Great British Heritage Pass, available through **BritRail,** allows entry to more than 500 public and privately owned historic properties, including Shakespeare's birthplace, Stonehenge, Windsor Castle, and Edinburgh Castle. Included in the price of the pass is the *Great British Heritage Gazetteer,* a brochure that lists the properties with maps and essential information.

A pass gains you entrance into private properties not otherwise approachable. A 7-day pass costs $45, a 15-day pass is available for $69, and a 1-month pass is $90. Passes are nonrefundable, and there is no discounted children's rate. A $2 handling fee is charged additionally for each ticket issued.

To order passes, contact **BritRail Travel International, Inc.,** 500 Mamaroneck Ave., Suite 314, Harrison, NY 10528; visit BritRail's British Travel Shop at 551 Fifth Ave. (at 45th Street), New York, NY 10176; or call ☎ **888/BRITRAIL;** or check them out on the Web at **www.britrail.com/us/ushome.htm.**

FAST FACTS: England

For information on London, refer to "Fast Facts: London," in chapter 4.

Area Codes   The country code for England is **44.** London has two area codes, 0171 and 0181. All the phone numbers given in this book include the local area code. Remember, use the initial zero when you're calling from one part of Britain to another; drop if you're calling from outside Britain. See also "Telephone" below.

Business Hours   With many, many exceptions, business hours are Monday to Friday from 9am to 5pm. In general, stores are open Monday to Saturday from 9am to 5:30pm. In country towns, there is usually an early closing day (often on Wednesday or Thursday), when the shops close at 1pm.

Car Rentals   See "Getting Around," earlier in this chapter.

Climate   See "When to Go," in this chapter.

Currency   See "Money," earlier in this chapter.

Customs   See "Visitor Information & Entry Requirements," earlier in this chapter.

Documents Required   See "Visitor Information & Entry Requirements," earlier in this chapter.

Drugstores   In Britain they're called "chemists." Every police station in the country has a list of emergency chemists. Dial ☎ "0" (zero) and ask the operator for the local police, who will give you the name of the one nearest you.

Electricity   British electricity is 240 volts AC (50 cycles), roughly twice the voltage in North America, which is 115 to 120 volts AC (60 cycles). American plugs don't fit British wall outlets. Always bring suitable transformers and/or adapters—if you plug an American appliance directly into a European electrical outlet without a transformer, you'll destroy your appliance and possibly start a fire. Tape recorders, VCRs, and other devices with motors intended to revolve at a fixed number of revolutions per minute probably won't work properly even with transformers.

Embassies & Consulates   See "Fast Facts: London," in chapter 4.

Emergencies   Dial ☎ **999** for police, fire, or ambulance. Give your name, address, and telephone number and state the nature of the emergency.

Holidays   See "When to Go," earlier in this chapter.

Information   See "Visitor Information & Entry Requirements," earlier in this chapter, and the individual city/regional chapters that follow.

Legal Aid   The American Services section of the U.S. Consulate (see "Embassies & High Commissions" under "Fast Facts: London," in chapter 4) will give advice if you run into trouble abroad. They can advise you of your rights and even provide a list of attorneys (for which you'll have to pay if services are used). But they cannot interfere on your behalf in the legal processes of Great Britain. For questions about American citizens who are arrested abroad, including ways of getting money to them, telephone the **Citizens Emergency Center** of the Office of Special Consulate Services in Washington, D.C. (☎ **202/647-5225**).

Liquor Laws   The legal drinking age is 18. Children under 16 aren't allowed in pubs, except in certain rooms, and then only when accompanied by a parent or guardian. Don't drink and drive. Penalties are stiff.

In England, pubs can legally be open Monday to Saturday from 11am to 11pm and on Sunday from noon to 10:30pm. Restaurants are also allowed to serve liquor during these hours, but only to people who are dining on the premises. The law allows 30 minutes for "drinking-up time." A meal, incidentally, is defined as "substantial refreshment." And you have to eat and drink sitting down. In hotels, liquor may be served from 11am to 11pm to both residents and nonresidents; after 11pm, only residents, according to the law, may be served.

Mail   Post offices and subpost offices are open Monday to Friday from 9am to 5:30pm and Saturday from 9:30am to noon.

Sending an airmail letter to North America costs 43p (70¢) for 10 grams (.35 oz), and postcards require a 35p (55¢) stamp. British mailboxes are painted red and carry a royal coat of arms. All post offices accept parcels for mailing, provided they are properly and securely wrapped.

Pets   It is illegal to bring pets to Great Britain—except with veterinary documents, and then most are subject to an outrageous 6-month quarantine.

Police   Dial ☎ **999** if the matter is serious. Losses, thefts, and other criminal matters should be reported to the police immediately.

Safety   Stay in well-lit areas and out of questionable neighborhoods, especially at night. In Britain, most of the crime perpetrated against tourists is pickpocketing and mugging. These attacks usually occur in such cities as London, Birmingham, or Manchester. Most villages are safe.

Taxes   To encourage energy conservation, the British government levies a 25% tax on gasoline (petrol). There is also a 17.5% national value-added tax (VAT) that is added to all hotel and restaurant bills and will be included in the price of

many items you purchase. This can be refunded if you shop at stores that participate in the Retail Export Scheme (signs are posted in the window). See the
"How to Get Your VAT Refund" box in the "Tips on Shopping" section, above.

In October 1994, Britain imposed a departure tax: either £5 ($8) for flights
within Britain and the European Union or £10 ($16) for passengers flying else-
where, including to the United States.

Telephone   To call England from North America, dial 011 (international code),
44 (Britain's country code), the local area codes (usually three or four digits and
found in every phone number we've given in this book), and the seven-digit local
phone number. The local areas codes found throughout this book all begin with
"0"; you drop the "0" if you're calling from outside Britain, but you need to dial
it along with the area code if you're calling from another city or town within
Britain. For calls within the same city or town, the local number is all you need.

For **directory assistance** in London, dial **142**; for the rest of Britain, **192.**

There are three types of public pay phones: those taking only coins, those
accepting only phonecards (called Cardphones), and those taking both
phonecards and credit cards. At coin-operated phones, insert your coins before
dialing. The minimum charge is 10p (15¢).

Phonecards are available in four values—£2 ($3.20), £4 ($6.40), £10 ($16),
and £20 ($32)—and are reusable until the total value has expired. Cards can be
purchased from newsstands and post offices. Finally, the credit-call pay phone
operates on credit cards—Access (MasterCard), Visa, American Express, and
Diners Club—and is most common at airports and large railway stations.

To make an international call from Britain, dial the international access code
(00), then the country code, then the area code, and finally the local number. Or
call through one of the following long-distance access codes: **AT&T USA Direct**
(☎ 0800/890011), **Canada Direct** (☎ 0800/890016), **Australia** (☎ 0800
/890061), and **New Zealand** (☎ 0800/890064). Common country codes are:
USA and Canada, 1; Australia, 61; New Zealand, 64; South Africa, 27.

If you're calling collect or need the assistance of an international operator, dial
155.

Caller, beware: Some hotels routinely add outrageous surcharges onto phone
calls made from your room. Inquire before you call! It'll be a lot cheaper to use
your own calling card number or find a pay phone.

Time   England follows Greenwich mean time (5 hours ahead of eastern standard time), with British summertime lasting (roughly) from the end of March to
the end of October. Throughout most of the year, including the summer, Britain
is 5 hours ahead of the time observed on the East Coast of the United States.
Because of different daylight-saving-time practices in the two nations, there's a
brief period (about a week) in autumn when Britain is only 4 hours ahead of New
York, and a brief period in spring when it's 6 hours ahead of New York.

Tipping   For cab drivers, add about 10% to 15% to the fare shown on the
meter. However, if the driver personally loads or unloads your luggage, add something extra.

In hotels, porters receive 75p ($1.20) per bag, even if you have only one small
suitcase. Hall porters are tipped only for special services. Maids receive £1
($1.60) per day. In top-ranking hotels, the concierge will often submit a separate
bill showing charges for newspapers and other items; if he or she has been particularly helpful, tip extra.

Hotels often add a service charge of 10% to 15% to most bills. In smaller bed-and-breakfasts, the tip is not likely to be included. Therefore, tip for special services, such as the waiter who serves you breakfast. If several people have served you in a bed-and-breakfast, you may ask that 10% to 15% be added to the bill and divided among the staff.

In both restaurants and nightclubs, a 15% service charge is added to the bill, which is distributed among all the help. To that, add another 3% to 5%, depending on the service. Waiters in deluxe restaurants and nightclubs are accustomed to the extra 5%. Sommeliers (wine stewards) get about £1 ($1.60) per bottle of wine served. Tipping in pubs isn't common, but in wine bars, the server usually gets about 75p ($1.20) per round of drinks.

Barbers and hairdressers expect 10% to 15%. Tour guides expect £2 ($3.20), although it's not mandatory. Gas station attendants are rarely tipped and theater ushers don't expect tips.

Settling Into London 4

Europe's largest city is like a great wheel, with Piccadilly Circus at the hub and dozens of communities branching out from it. Since London is such a conglomeration of neighborhoods, each with its own personality, first-time visitors may be confused until they get the hang of it. You'll probably spend most of your time in the West End, where many attractions are located, except for the historic part of London known as The City, which includes the Tower of London. This chapter will help you get your bearings.

1 Orientation

ARRIVING
BY PLANE

London is served by four airports. The one you'll fly into will depend on your airline's point of departure.

LONDON HEATHROW AIRPORT Heathrow, west of London, in Hounslow (☎ **0181/759-4321**), is divided into four terminals. Terminal 4 handles the long-haul and transatlantic operations of British Airways. Most transatlantic flights of U.S. airlines arrive at Terminal 3. Terminals 1 and 2 receive the intra-European flights of several European airlines.

Getting to Central London from Heathrow There is an Underground (subway) connection from Heathrow Central to the center of London; the trip takes 50 minutes and costs £3.30 ($5.30). The new Heathrow Express, which debuted in the Spring of 1998, is by far the easiest (if more expensive) way to get into Central London. Trains leave every 15 minutes for a 15-minute ride to Paddington Station. (And when you leave London to catch your flight home, you can even check your luggage right at the train station!) Fares are £10 ($16) for a regular ticket, £20 ($32) for first class. For more information, call **Heathrow Express** (☎ **0845/600-1515**). Airbuses will also take you to central London in about an hour; they cost £6 ($9.60) for adults and £4 ($6.40) for children. A taxi will cost £25 to £35 ($40 to $56), maybe more. For more information about train or bus connections, call ☎ **0171/222-1234**.

GATWICK AIRPORT This smaller and more remote airport (☎ **01293/535353** for flight information) lies 25 miles south of London, in West Sussex. Some charter flights as well as many scheduled flights on major airlines arrive here.

Getting to Central London from Gatwick   Trains leave for London every 15 minutes during the day and every hour at night; they cost £9.50 ($15.20) for adults and half price for children ages 5 to 15 (under 5 free). There is also an express Flightline bus (no. 777) from Gatwick to Victoria Station that departs every half hour from 6:30am to 8pm and every hour from 8 to 11pm; it costs £7.50 ($12) per person. For more information about train or bus connections, call ☎ **0171/222-1234.**

It's very expensive to take a taxi from Gatwick into central London. A taxi usually costs £50 to £65 ($80 to $104); however, you must negotiate a fare with the driver before you get into the cab—the meter does not apply since Gatwick lies outside the Metropolitan Police District.

LONDON CITY AIRPORT   Located just 3 miles east of the bustling business community of Canary Wharf and 6 miles east of The City, London City Airport (☎ **0171/474-5555**) is served by 11 airlines (Air Engiadina, Air France, Air Jet, Air UK, Augsburg Airways, CityJet Crossair, Denimair, Lufthansa, Malmö Aviation, Sabena, and VLM) that fly from 18 European destinations—Amsterdam, Antwerp, Augsburg, Bern, Brussels, Cologne/Bonn, Dublin, Düsseldorf, Edinburgh, Eindhoven, Frankfurt, Geneva, Lugano, Malmö, Paris, Rotterdam, Stockholm, and Zurich.

Getting to Central London from London City Airport   A blue-and-white bus charges £3 ($4.80) each way to take you from the airport to the Liverpool Street Station, where you can connect with rail or Underground transportation to almost any destination. The bus runs every 20 minutes Monday through Friday, and every 30 minutes Saturday and Sunday during the hours the airport is open (approximately 7am to 8:30pm).

There's also a shuttle bus to Canary Wharf, where trains from the Dockland Line Railway make frequent 10-minute runs to the heart of London's financial district, known as "The City." Here, passengers can catch the Underground from the Bank tube stop.

In addition, London Transport bus no. 473 goes from the City Airport to East London, where you can board any Underground at the Plaistow tube stop.

LONDON STANSTED AIRPORT   Located about 50 miles northeast of London's West End, Stansted (☎ **01279/680-500**) was originally a U.S. air base during World War II, and was expanded massively in the 1980s. Most of its flights arrive from continental Europe, although it also has an increased number of charter flights from the North American mainland as well.

Getting to Central London from Stansted   Your best bet is the Stansted Express, a train that takes you from the airport to Liverpool Street Rail and Tube Station in 45 minutes. Tickets cost £11 ($17.60) for adults and £7.90 ($12.65) for children. Daily service runs every 30 minutes from 5:30am to 11pm.

If you prefer the relative privacy of a taxi, you'll pay dearly for the privilege. For a ride to London's West End, they'll charge you around £60 ($96) for up to four passengers, and £90 ($144) for five or six passengers. Expect the ride to take around 75 minutes during normal traffic conditions, but beware of Friday afternoons, when dense traffic might require about twice as long. Stick to the Express.

BY TRAIN

Most trains originating in Paris and traveling through the Chunnel arrive at **Waterloo Station.** Visitors from Amsterdam arrive at the **Liverpool Street Station,** and those journeying south by rail from Edinburgh pull in at **King's Cross Station.** Each of these stations is connected to London's vast bus and Underground network, and each has phones, restaurants, pubs, luggage-storage areas, and London Regional Transport Information centers.

BY CAR

If you're taking a car ferry across the Channel, you can quickly connect with a motorway into London. *Remember to drive on the left.* London is encircled by a ring road. Determine which part of the city you wish to enter and follow the signs there.

Once you're in London, we don't recommend driving. Unfortunately, parking is scarce and expensive. Before you arrive in London, call your hotel and ask for advice on where to park your car.

VISITOR INFORMATION

The British Travel Centre, Rex House, 4-12 Lower Regent St., London SW1 4PQ (tube: Piccadilly Circus), caters to walk-in visitors who wait in line for information on all parts of Britain. (Telephone information has been suspended.) On the premises are a British Rail ticket office, a travel agency, a theater-ticket agency, a hotel-booking service, a bookshop, and a souvenir shop. Open Monday through Friday from 9am to 6:30pm, Saturday and Sunday from 10am to 4pm, with extended hours on Saturday from June through September.

Equally useful is the London Tourist Board's **Tourist Information Centre,** forecourt of Victoria Station, SW1 (tube: Victoria). The center deals with accommodations in all size and price categories. It also arranges for travel, tour-ticket sales, and theater reservations, and it has a shop that sells books and souvenirs. Open from Easter to October, daily from 8am to 7pm; November to Easter, Monday to Saturday from 8am to 6pm, Sunday from 9am to 4pm.

The tourist board also maintains offices at Heathrow Airport's Terminals 1, 2, and 3, Underground Concourse, and at the Liverpool Street Railway Station.

The tourist board has a 24-hour recorded information service, **Visitorcall** (☎ **01839/123456**), which, for a fee of 50p (80¢) per minute, will play a recorded message about tourist attractions that change every day.

LONDON'S NEIGHBORHOODS IN BRIEF

THE WEST END NEIGHBORHOODS

Mayfair   Bounded by Piccadilly, Hyde Park, and Oxford and Regent streets, this is the most elegant, fashionable section of London, filled with luxury hotels, Georgian town houses, and swank shops. Grosvenor Square (pronounced *Grov*-nor) is nicknamed "Little America," because it's home to the American embassy and a statue of Franklin D. Roosevelt; Berkeley Square (pronounced *Bark*-ley) was made famous by the song, whose mythical nightingale sang here. At least once you'll want to dip into this exclusive section. One of the curiosities of Mayfair is **Shepherd Market,** a tiny village of pubs, 2-story inns, book and food stalls, and restaurants, all sandwiched between Mayfair's greatness.

Marylebone   All first-time visitors head to Marylebone, to explore Madame Tussaud's waxworks or walk along Baker Street in the make-believe footsteps of Sherlock Holmes. The streets form a near-perfect grid, with the major ones running north-south from Regent's Park toward Oxford Street. Marylebone Lane and High Street still retain some of their former village atmosphere, but this is otherwise a now rather anonymous area. At Regent's Park, you can visit Queen Mary's Gardens or, in summer, see Shakespeare performed in an open-air theater.

London at a Glance

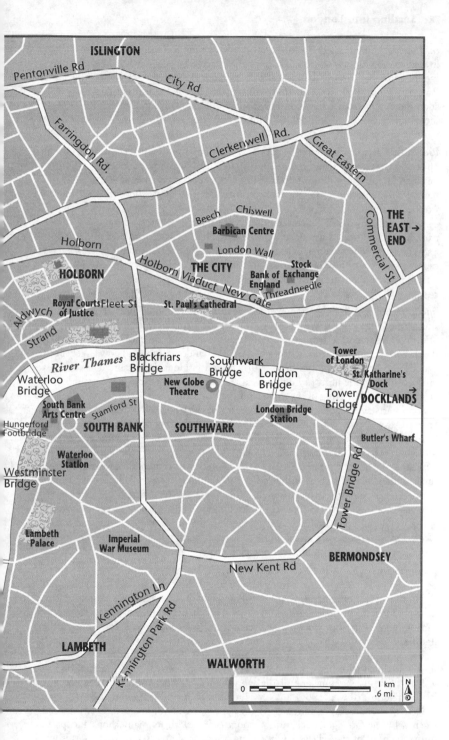

ISLINGTON

Pentonville Rd

City Rd

Farringdon Rd.

Clerkenwell Rd.

Great Eastern

THE EAST →
END

Commercial St

Beech

Chiswell

Barbican Centre

London Wall

Holborn

HOLBORN

Holborn Viaduct New Gate

THE CITY

Stock Exchange

Bank of England

Threadneedle

Royal Courts of Justice

Fleet St

St. Paul's Cathedral

Aldwych

Strand

River Thames

Blackfriars Bridge

Southwark Bridge

London Bridge

Tower of London

St. Katharine's Dock

Waterloo Bridge

New Globe Theatre

DOCKLANDS →

Tower Bridge

South Bank Arts Centre

Stamford St

London Bridge Station

Hungerford Footbridge

SOUTH BANK

SOUTHWARK

Butler's Wharf

Waterloo Station

Tower Bridge Rd

Westminster Bridge

Lambeth Palace

Imperial War Museum

BERMONDSEY

New Kent Rd

Kennington Ln

Kennington Park Rd

LAMBETH

WALWORTH

0   1 km
     .6 mi.

N

St. James's   Often called "Royal London," St. James's is home to Elizabeth II, who lives at its most famous address, Buckingham Palace. The neighborhood begins at Piccadilly Circus and moves southwest, incorporating Pall Mall, The Mall, St. James's Park, and Green Park; it's "frightfully convenient," as the English say, enclosing such addresses as American Express on Haymarket and many of London's leading department stores. Be sure to stop in at Fortnum & Mason, at 181 Piccadilly, the world's most luxurious grocery store.

Piccadilly Circus & Leicester Square   **Piccadilly Circus** is the very heart and soul of London, its gaudy living room. The circus isn't Times Square yet, but its traffic, neon, and jostling crowds don't do anything to make it fashionable. If you want a little more grandeur, retreat to the Regency promenade of exclusive shops, the Burlington Arcade, designed in 1819.

A bit more tawdry is **Leicester Square,** a center of theaters, restaurants, movie palaces, and nightlife. It was once a chic address, but it changed forever in the Victorian era, when four towering entertainment halls were opened (even Queen Victoria came to see a circus here on occasion). In time the old palaces changed from stage to screen; three of them are still showing films.

Soho   Every city has its raunchy area, of course, but in few are the red lights woven into a texture of such richness and variety as in London's Soho. These densely packed streets in the heart of the West End are famous for their gloriously cosmopolitan mix of people and trades. A decade ago, much was heard about the decline of Soho, when the thriving sex industry threatened to engulf it. That destruction has now largely been halted: Respectable businesses have returned, and fashionable restaurants and shops prosper; it's now the heart of London's expanding cafe society. But Soho wouldn't be Soho without a scattering of sex shops and porno theaters.

Soho starts at Piccadilly Circus and spreads out; it's basically bordered by Regent Street, Oxford Street, Charing Cross Road, and the theaters of Shaftesbury Avenue. Carnaby Street, a block from Regent Street, was the center of the universe in the Swinging '60s, but now it's just a schlocky sideshow. Across Shaftesbury Avenue, a busy street lined with theaters, is London's **Chinatown,** centered on Gerrard Street: small, authentic, and packed with excellent restaurants. But Soho's heart—with marvelous French and Italian delicatessens, fine butchers, fish stores, and wine merchants—is farther north, on Brewer, Old Compton, and Berwick streets; Berwick is also a wonderful open-air fresh-food market. To the north of Old Compton Street, Dean, Frith, and Greek streets have fine little restaurants, pubs, and clubs, like Ronnie Scott's for jazz. The British movie industry is centered in Wardour Street.

Bloomsbury   This district, a world within itself, lies northeast of Piccadilly Circus, beyond Soho. It is, among other things, the academic heart of London; here you'll find the University of London, several other colleges, and many bookstores. Despite its student population, this neighborhood is fairly staid. Its reputation has been fanned by such writers as Virginia Woolf, who lived within its bounds and became one of the unofficial leaders of a group of artists and writers known as "the Bloomsbury Group."

The heart of Bloomsbury is **Russell Square,** and the streets jutting off from the square are lined with hotels and B&Bs. Most visitors come to the neighborhood to visit the British Museum, one of the world's greatest repositories of treasures. The British TeleCom Tower (1964) in Cleveland Street is a familiar landmark.

Nearby is **Fitzrovia,** bounded by Great Portland, Oxford, and Gower streets, and reached by the Goodge Street tube. Goodge Street, with its many shops and pubs, forms the heart of the "village." Once a major haunt of artists and writers—this was the stamping ground of Ezra Pound, Wyndham Lewis, and George Orwell, among others—the bottom end of Fitzrovia is a virtual extension of Soho, with a cluster of Greek restaurants.

Holborn   The old borough of Holborn, which abuts The City to the west, takes in the heart of legal London— the city's barristers, solicitors, and law clerks call it home. A 14-year-old Dickens was once employed as a solicitor's clerk at Lincoln's Inn Fields. Old Bailey has stood for English justice down through the years (Fagin went to the gallows from this site in *Oliver Twist*). Everything here seems steeped in history. Even as you're quenching your thirst with a half-pint of bitter at the Viaduct Tavern, 126 Newgate St. (tube: St. Paul's), you learn the pub was built over the notorious Newgate Prison (which specialized in death by pressing) and was named after the Holborn Viaduct, the world's first overpass.

Covent Garden & The Strand   The flower, fruit, and "veg" market is long gone (since 1970), but memories of Professor Higgins and Eliza Doolittle linger on. **Covent Garden** now contains the city's liveliest group of restaurants, pubs, and cafes outside of Soho, as well as some of the city's hippest shops— including the world's only Dr. Marten's Super Store. The restored marketplace with its glass and iron roofs has been called a "magnificent example of urban recycling." Covent Garden is traditionally London's theater area, and Inigo Jones's St. Paul's Covent Garden is known as the actors' church. The Theatre Royal Drury Lane was where Charles II's mistress Nell Gwynne made her debut in 1665.

Beginning at Trafalgar Square, **The Strand** runs east into Fleet Street and borders Covent Garden to the south. It's flanked with theaters, shops, hotels, and restaurants. The Strand runs parallel to the River Thames, and to walk it is to follow in the footsteps of Mark Twain, Henry Fielding, James Boswell, William Thackeray, and Sir Walter Raleigh. The Savoy Theatre helped make Gilbert and Sullivan a household name.

Westminster   Westminster has been the seat of the British government since the days of Edward the Confessor. Dominated by the Houses of Parliament and Westminster Abbey, the area runs along the Thames to the east of St. James's Park. **Trafalgar Square,** at the area's northern end and one of the city's major landmarks, remains a testament to England's victory over Napoléon in 1805, and the paintings in its landmark **National Gallery** will restore your soul. Whitehall is the main thoroughfare, linking Trafalgar Square with Parliament Square. You can visit Churchill's Cabinet War Rooms; and no. 10 Downing Street, the world's most famous street address, is home to Britain's prime minister. No visit is complete without a call at **Westminster Abbey**, one of the greatest Gothic churches in the world.

Westminster also encompasses **Victoria,** an area that takes its unofficial name from bustling Victoria Station, known as "the gateway to the Continent."

THE CITY & ENVIRONS

The City   When Londoners speak of "The City" (EC2, EC3), they don't mean all of London; they mean the original square mile that's now the British version of Wall Street. The buildings of this district are known all over the world: the Bank of England, the London Stock Exchange, and the financially troubled Lloyd's of London. This was the origin of Londinium, as it was called by its Roman conquerors. Despite its age, The City doesn't easily reveal its past; much of it has been swept away by the Great Fire of 1666, the bombs of 1940, the IRA bombs of the early 1990s, and the zeal of modern developers. Still, it retains its medieval character, and landmarks include **St. Paul's Cathedral,** the masterpiece of Sir Christopher Wren, which stood virtually alone among the rubble after the Blitz.

Fleet Street was London's journalistic hub since William Caxton printed the first book in English here. However, most of the London tabloids have recently abandoned Fleet Street for the Docklands development across the river.

The City of London still prefers to function on its own, separate from the rest of the city; in keeping with its independence, it maintains its own **Information Centre** at St. Paul's Churchyard, EC4 (☎ 0171/332-1456).

Docklands   In the last 2 decades, this area—which is bordered roughly by Tower Bridge to the west and London City Airport and the Royal Docks to the east—has undergone an ambitious redevelopment, and has attracted many businesses, including most of the Fleet Street newspapers; Thames-side warehouses have been converted to Manhattan-style lofts; and museums, entertainment complexes, shops, and an ever-growing list of restaurants have popped up at this 21st-century river city in the making.

Canary Wharf, on the Isle of Dogs, is the heart of Docklands; this huge 71-acre site is dominated by an 800-foot-high tower, the tallest building in the United Kingdom, designed by Cesar Pelli. The Piazza is lined with shops and restaurants. Across from the country's largest sports complex, London Arena, is the **Docklands Visitor Centre** (☎ 0171/512-3000). On the south side of the river at Surrey Docks, the Victorian warehouses of **Butler's Wharf** have been converted by Sir Terence Conran into offices, workshops, houses, shops, and restaurants; Butler's Wharf is also home to the Design Museum.

To get to Docklands, take the Underground to Tower Hill and pick up the **Docklands Light Railway** (☎ 0171/363-9500), which operates Monday to Friday from 5:30am to 12:30am, with selected main routes now offering weekend service from 6:30am to 11:30pm.

The East End   Traditionally, this was one of London's poorest districts, and was nearly bombed out of existence by the Nazis. Hitler, in the words of one commentator at the time, created "instant urban renewal." The East End extends from the City Walls east encompassing Stepney, Bow, Poplar, West Ham, Canning Town, and other districts. The East End has always been filled with legend and lore. It's the home of the Cockney, London's most colorful character. To be a true Cockney, it's said that you must have been born "within the sound of Bow Bells," a reference to a church, St. Mary-le-Bow, rebuilt by Sir Christopher Wren in 1670. Many immigrants to London have found a home here.

South Bank   Although not officially a district like Mayfair, South Bank is the setting today for the **South Bank Arts Centre,** now the largest arts center in Western Europe and still growing. Reached by Waterloo Bridge, it lies across the Thames from the Victoria Embankment. Culture buffs flock to its many galleries and halls, including the National Theatre, Queen Elizabeth Hall, Royal Festival Hall, and the Hayward Gallery. It's also the setting of the National Film Theatre and the Museum of the Moving Image (MOMI). Nearby are such neighborhoods as Elephant and Castle and **Southwark,** home to grand Southwark Cathedral. To get here, take the tube to Waterloo Station.

CENTRAL LONDON BEYOND THE WEST END

Knightsbridge   One of London's most fashionable neighborhoods, Knightsbridge is a top residential and shopping district, just south of Hyde Park. **Harrods,** on Brompton Road, is its chief attraction. Right nearby, Beauchamp Place (pronounced *Beech*-am) is one of London's most fashionable shopping streets, a Regency-era boutique-lined little street with a scattering of fashionable restaurants.

Belgravia   South of Knightsbridge, this area has long been the aristocratic quarter of London, rivaling Mayfair in grandness. Although it reached the pinnacle of its prestige during the reign of Queen Victoria, it's still a chic address, the duke and duchess of Westminster, one of England's richest families, still live at Eaton Square. Its centerpiece is Belgrave Square, which was built between 1825 and 1835. When the town houses were built, the aristocrats followed—the duke of Connaught, the earl of Essex, even Queen Victoria's mother, the duchess of Kent. Chopin on holiday in 1837 was appropriately impressed: "And the English! And the houses! And the palaces! And the pomp, and the carriages! Everything from soap to the razors is extraordinary."

Chelsea   This stylish Thames-side district lies south of Belgravia. It begins at Sloane Square, where flower sellers hustle their flamboyant blooms here year-round. The area has always been a favorite of writers and artists, including such names as Oscar Wilde (who was arrested here), George Eliot, James Whistler, J. M. W. Turner, Henry James, and Thomas Carlyle. Mick Jagger and Margaret Thatcher (not together) have been more recent residents, and the late Princess Diana and her "Sloane Rangers" of the 1980s gave it even more fame.

Its major boulevard is **King's Road,** where Mary Quant launched the miniskirt in the '60s and where the English punk look began. King's Road runs the entire length of Chelsea; it's at its liveliest on Saturday. The hip-hop of King's Road isn't typical of otherwise upmarket Chelsea, an elegant village filled with town houses and little mews dwellings that only successful stockbrokers and solicitors can afford to occupy.

On the Chelsea/Fulham border is **Chelsea Harbour,** a luxury development of apartments and restaurants with a private marina. You can spot its tall tower from far away; the golden ball on top moves up and down to indicate tide level.

Kensington   This Royal Borough (W8) lies west of Kensington Gardens and Hyde Park and is traversed by two of London's major shopping streets, Kensington High Street and Kensington Church Street. Since 1689, when asthmatic William III fled Whitehall Palace for Nottingham House (where the air was fresher), the district has enjoyed royal associations. In time, Nottingham House became Kensington Palace, and the royals grabbed a chunk of Hyde Park to plant their roses. Queen Victoria was born here. "KP," as the royals say, was the home of Princess Diana and her two young princes for a time. Kensington Gardens is now open to the public. In 1997, this area became a focal point for the nation's grief over Diana's death, and the area in front of her former palace was blanketed with flowers and tributes.

Southeast of Kensington Gardens and Earl's Court, primarily residential **South Kensington** is often called "museumland" because it's dominated by a complex of museums and colleges—set upon land bought with the proceeds from Prince Albert's Great Exhibition, held in Hyde Park in 1851—that includes the **Natural History Museum, the Victoria and Albert Museum,** and the **Science Museum;** nearby is **Royal Albert Hall.** South Kensington is also home to some fashionable restaurants and town-house hotels. One of the district's chief curiosities is the **Albert Memorial;** for sheer excess, the Victorian monument is unequaled in the world.

Earl's Court   Earl's Court lies below Kensington, bordering the western half of Chelsea. For decades a staid residential district, Earl's Court now attracts a new and younger crowd (often gay), particularly at night, to its pubs, wine bars, and coffeehouses. It's long been a popular base for budget travelers (particularly Australians, for reasons known only to them), thanks to its wealth of B&Bs and budget hotels, and its convenient access to central London: A 15-minute tube ride will take you into the heart of Piccadilly, via either the District or Piccadilly lines.

Once regarded as the boondocks, nearby **West Brompton** is seen today as an extension of central London. It lies directly south of Earl's Court (take the tube to West Brompton) and directly southeast of West Kensington. It also has many good restaurants, pubs, and taverns, as well as some budget hotels.

Notting Hill   Increasingly fashionable Notting Hill is bounded on the north by Bayswater Road and on the east by Kensington. Hemmed in on the north by West Way and on the west by the Shepherd's Bush ramp leading to the M40, it has many turn-of-the-century mansions and small houses sitting on quiet, leafy streets, plus a growing number of hot restaurants and clubs. Gentrified in recent years, it's becoming an extension of central London.

On the north end, across **Notting Hill Gate,** west of Bayswater, is the increasingly hip neighborhood known as Notting Hill Gate; Portobello Road is home to one of London's most famous street markets. The area tube stops are Notting Hill Gate, Holland Park, and Ladbroke Grove.

Nearby **Holland Park** is a chichi residential neighborhood visited chiefly by the chic guests of Halcyon Hotel, one of the grandest of London's small hotels.

Paddington & Bayswater   The Paddington section centers around Paddington Station, north of Kensington Gardens and Hyde Park. It's one of the major centers in London, attracting budget travelers who fill up the B&Bs in Sussex Gardens and Norfolk Square. After the first railway was introduced in London in 1836, it was followed by a circle of sprawling railway termini, including Paddington Station in 1838, which spurred the growth of this middle-class area, which is now blighted in parts.

Just south of Paddington, north of Hyde Park, and abutting more fashionable Notting Hill to the west is **Bayswater,** a sort of unofficial area also filled with a large number of B&Bs attracting budget travelers. Inspired by Marylebone and elegant Mayfair, a relatively prosperous set of Victorian merchants.

FARTHER AFIELD

Greenwich   Some 4 miles to the north of the city, Greenwich—ground zero for use in the reckoning of terrestrial longitudes—enjoyed its heyday under the Tudors. Henry VIII and both of his daughters, Mary I and Elizabeth I, were born here. Greenwich Palace, Henry's favorite, is long gone, though; today's visitors come to this lovely port village for nautical sights along the Thames, including the 1869 tea clipper *Cutty Sark.*

Hampstead   This residential suburb of north London, beloved by Keats and Hogarth, is a favorite spot for weekending Londoners. Everybody from Sigmund Freud to John Le Carré has lived here, and it's still one of the most desirable districts in the Greater London area to call home. Its centerpiece is **Hampstead Heath,** nearly 800 acres of rolling meadows and woodland with panoramic views; it still maintains its rural atmosphere even though engulfed by cityscapes on all sides. The hilltop village is filled with cafes, tearooms, and restaurants, and there are pubs galore, some with historic pedigrees. Take the Northern Line to Hampstead Heath station.

Highgate   Along with Hampstead, Highgate in north London is another choice residential area, particularly on or near Pond Square and along Hampstead High Street. It's long been a desirable place to live, and Londoners used to flock to its taverns and pubs for "exercise and harmless merriment"; some still do. Today, most visitors come to see moody **Highgate Cemetery,** London's most famous cemetery—it's the final resting place of such famous figures as Karl Marx and George Eliot.

2 Getting Around

Remember that cars drive on the left, and vehicles have the right-of-way in London over pedestrians. Wherever you walk, always look both ways before stepping off a curb.

BY PUBLIC TRANSPORTATION

Transportation within London is unusually easy and inexpensive. Both the Underground (subway) and bus systems are operated by **London Transport**—with **Travel Information Centres** in the Underground stations at King's Cross, Hammersmith, Oxford Circus, St. James's Park, Liverpool Street Station, and Piccadilly Circus, as well as in the main line stations at Euston and Victoria and in each of the terminals at Heathrow Airport. They take reservations for London Transport's guided tours and have free Underground and bus maps and other information. A **24-hour telephone information** service is available by calling ☎ **0171/222-1234.**

DISCOUNT PASSES   London Transport, Travel Information Service, 55 Broadway, London SW1H 0BD (☎ **0171/222-5600**) also offers **Travelcards** for use on the bus, Underground, and main line service inside Greater London. Available in a number of combinations for adjacent zones, Travelcards can be purchased for periods of 7 days to a year. A Travelcard allowing travel in two zones for 1 week costs £16.60 ($26.55) for adults and £5.80 ($9.30) for children.

To purchase a Travelcard, you must present a Photocard. If you're 16 years old or older, bring along a passport-type picture of yourself when you buy your Travelcard and the Photocard will be issued free. Child-rate Photocards for Travelcards are issued only at Underground ticket offices or Travel Information Centres; in addition to a passport-type photograph, proof of age is required (a passport or birth certificate). Teenagers (14 or 15) are charged adult fares on all services unless they have one of the cards.

For shorter stays in London, consider the **One-Day Off-Peak Travelcard.** This Travelcard can be used on most bus, Underground, and main-line services throughout Greater London Monday through Friday after 9:30am and at any time on weekends and bank holidays. The Travelcard is available at Underground ticket offices, Travel Information Centres, and some newsstands. For two zones, the cost is £3.50 ($5.60) for adults and £1.80 ($2.90) for children aged 5 to 15. Children 4 and under ride free.

The **Visitor Travelcard** is worthwhile if you plan to travel a lot within Greater London. This card allows unlimited transport within all six zones of Greater London's Underground and bus network. You'll most likely travel within the first two zones of the network's boundaries, but you could travel as far as Heathrow during valid times. However, *you must buy this pass in North America;* it's not available in England. A pass good for 3 consecutive days of travel costs $25 for adults and $11 for children aged 5 to 15; a pass good for 4 consecutive days of travel costs $33 for adults, $13 for children; and a pass good for 7 consecutive days of travel costs $53 for adults, $21 for children. For more information, contact **BritRail Travel International,** 500 Mamaroneck Ave., Suite 314, Harrison, NY 10528 (☎ **800/677-8585**).

You can now buy **Carnet tickets,** a booklet of 10 single Underground tickets valid for 12 months from the issue date. Carnet tickets are valid for travel only in Zone 1 (Central London), and cost £10 ($16) for adults and £4.80 ($7.70) for children (up to 15). A book of Carnet tickets gives you a savings of £2 ($3.20) over the cost of 10 individual tickets. Another pass is the **Family Travelcard,** a 1-day ticket. It's a go-as-you-please card, allowing as many journeys as you wish on the tube, buses (excluding night buses) displaying the London Transport bus sign, and even the Docklands Light Railway or any rail service within the travel zones designated on your ticket. The family card is valid after 9:30am Monday through Friday, all day on weekends, and public holidays. The cost is £3.20 ($5.10) to £4 ($6.40) for adults, or £.50 (80¢) for children. Yet a final discount pass is the **Weekend Travel card** allowing 2 days of weekend transportation on the Underground or buses. The cost ranges from £4.80 ($7.70) to £6 ($9.60) for adults or £2.50 ($4) for children. These passes are available at all Underground stations.

By Underground

Known locally as "the tube," this is the fastest and easiest way to get from place to place. All Underground stations are clearly marked with a red circle and blue crossbar. You descend by stairways, escalators, or huge elevators, depending on the depth. Some Underground stations have complete subterranean shopping arcades and several boast high-tech gadgets such as push-button information machines.

If you have British coins, you can get your ticket at a vending machine. Otherwise, buy it at the ticket office. You can transfer as many times as you like as long as you stay in the Underground. The flat fare for one trip within the Central zone is £1.30 ($2.10). Trips from the Central zone to destinations in the suburbs range from £1.30 to £4.60 ($2.10 to $7.35) in most cases.

Be sure to keep your ticket, as it must be presented when you get off. If you're caught without a valid ticket, you'll be fined £10 ($16) on the spot. If you owe extra money, you'll be asked to pay the difference by the attendant.

Also keep in mind that many trains stop running at midnight (11:30pm on Sunday).

For information on the London tube system, call the London Underground at ☎ **0171/222-1234,** but expect long delays before an actual person comes to the phone. See the full-color Underground map on the inside cover of this guide.

By Bus

The first thing you learn about London buses is that nobody just gets on them. You queue up (that is, form a single-file line) at the bus stop.

The comparably priced bus system is almost as good as the Underground, and you'll have a better view. You can pick up a free bus map at one of London Regional Transport's Travel Information Centres listed above.

London still has some of the old-style Routemaster buses, with both a driver and conductor. Once you're on the bus, a conductor will pass by your seat. You state your destination and pay the fare, receiving a ticket in return. However, this type of bus is being phased out for newer buses with only a driver. On these, you pay the driver as you enter, and exit through one of the rear doors.

As with the Underground, the fares vary according to the distance traveled. Generally, the cost is 50p to £1.20 (80¢ to $1.90), which is less than tube fares. If you travel for two or three stops, the cost is 60p (95¢); longer runs within Zone 1 cost 90p ($1.45). If you want to be warned when to get off, simply ask the conductor.

Call the 24-hour hot line (☎ 0171/222-1234) for schedules and fares.

By Taxi

You can get a cab from a cab station or hail one on the street; if the yellow light on the roof is on, the taxi is accepting passengers. For a radio cab, call ☎ **0171/ 272-0272** or 0171/253-5000.

The minimum fare is £1.40 ($2.25) for the first third of a mile or 1 minute and 51 seconds, with increments of 20p (30¢) thereafter, based on distance or time. Each additional passenger is charged 40p (65¢). Passengers pay 10p (15¢) for each piece of luggage in the driver's compartment and any other item more than 2 feet long. Surcharges are imposed after 8pm and on weekends and public holidays. All these tariffs include value-added tax (VAT). Fares usually increase annually. We recommend tipping 10% to 15% of the fare. All taxis take all major credit cards.

If you call for a cab, the meter starts running when the taxi receives instructions from the dispatcher, so you could find £1.40 ($2.25) or more already on the meter when you step inside.

Cab sharing is permitted in London, and allows cabbies to offer rides for two to five people. The taxis accepting such riders display a sign on yellow plastic with the words shared taxi. Each of two sharing riders is charged 65% of the fare a lone passenger would be charged. Three people pay 55%, four pay 45%, and five (the seating capacity of all new London cabs) pay 40% of the single-passenger fare.

FAST FACTS: London

American Express   The main office is at 6 Haymarket, SW1 (☎ 0171/930-4411; tube: Piccadilly Circus). Full services are available Monday through Friday from 9am to 5:30pm and on Saturday from 9am to 4pm. At other times (Saturday from 9am to 6pm and Sunday from 10am to 5pm), only the foreign-exchange bureau is open.

Area Codes   London has two area codes: **0171** and **0181.** The 0171 area code is for central London within a 4-mile radius of Charing Cross (including the city of London, Knightsbridge, and Oxford Street, and as far south as Brixton). The 0181 area code is for outer London (including Heathrow Airport, Wimbledon, and Greenwich).

Within London, you'll need to dial the area code when calling from one of these sections of the city to the other, but you don't need to dial the area code when you're calling within a section.

If you're calling London from home before your trip, the country code for England is 44. It must precede the London area code. When you're calling London from outside Britain, drop the "0" in front of the local area code.

Baby-Sitters   If your hotel won't recommend a sitter, call **Childminders,** 9 Paddington St. (☎ 0171/935-3000; tube: Baker Street). The rates are £5.50 ($8.80) per hour during the day and £3.70 to £4.70 ($5.90 to $7.50) per hour at night. There is a 4-hour minimum, and hotel guests pay a £5 ($8) booking fee each time they use a sitter.

Currency Exchange   In general, banks in London provide the best exchange rates, and you're likely to get a better rate for traveler's checks than for cash. At London's airports, there are branch offices of the main banks, but these charge a small fee. There are also *bureaux de change* at the airports, with offices around London; they charge a fee for cashing traveler's checks and personal U.K. checks and for changing foreign currency into pounds sterling. Some travel agencies, such as American Express and Thomas Cook, also have currency-exchange services (see "Money," in chapter 3).

Dentists   For dental emergencies, call **Eastman Dental Hospital** (☎ 0171/915-1000; tube: King's Cross).

Doctors   In an emergency, contact **Doctor's Call** (☎ 07000/372255). Some hotels also have doctors on call. **Medical Express,** 117A Harley St. (☎ 0171/499-1991; tube: Regent's Park), is a private British clinic. If you need a prescription filled, stop by, but to fill the British equivalent of a U.S. prescription, there is sometimes a surcharge of £20 ($32) in addition to the cost of the medication. The clinic is open Monday through Friday from 9am to 6pm and on Saturday from 9:30am to 2:30pm.

Embassies & High Commissions   The **U.S. Embassy** is at 24 Grosvenor Sq., W1 (☎ 0171/499-9000; tube: Bond Street). However, for passport and visa information, go to the **U.S. Passport and Citizenship Unit,** 55-56 Upper Brook St., London, W1 (☎ 0171/499-9000, ext. 2563 or 2564; tube: Marble Arch or Bond Street). Hours are Monday through Friday from 8:30am to noon and from 2 to 4pm; on Tuesday, the office closes at noon.

The **Canadian High Commission,** MacDonald House, 38 Grosvenor Sq., W1 (☎ 0171/258-6600; tube: Bond Street), handles visas for Canada. Hours are Monday through Friday from 8 to 11am only.

The **Australian High Commission** is at Australia House, The Strand, WC2 (☎ 0171/379-4334; tube: Charing Cross or Aldwych). Hours are Monday through Friday from 10am to 4pm.

The **New Zealand High Commission** is at New Zealand House, 80 Haymarket at Pall Mall, SW1 (☎ 0171/930-8422; tube: Charing Cross or Piccadilly Circus). Hours are Monday through Friday from 9am to 5pm.

The **Irish Embassy** is at 17 Grosvenor Place, SW1 (☎ 0171/235-2171; tube: Hyde Park Corner). Hours are Monday through Friday from 9:30am to 1pm and 2:15 to 5pm.

Emergencies   In London, for police, fire, or an ambulance, dial ☎ 999.

Hospitals   The following offer emergency care in London, 24 hours a day, with the first treatment free under the National Health Service: **Royal Free Hospital,** Pond Street (☎ 0171/794-0500; tube: Belsize Park), and **University College Hospital,** Gower Street (☎ 0171/387-9300; tube: Warren Street). Many other London hospitals also have accident and emergency departments.

Hot Lines   If you're in some sort of legal emergency, call **Release** at ☎ 0171/729-9904, 24 hours a day. The **Rape Crisis Line** (☎ 0171/837-1600), accepts calls after 6pm. **Samaritans,** 46 Marshall St. (☎ 0171/734-2800), maintains a crisis hot line that helps with all kinds of trouble, even threatened suicides, from 9am to 9pm. **Alcoholics Anonymous** (☎ 0171/352-3001) answers its hot line daily from 10am to 10pm.

Information   See "Visitor Information" earlier in this chapter.

Maps   If you plan on exploring London in any depth, you'll need a detailed street map with an index, not one of those superficial overviews given away at many hotels and tourist offices. The best ones are published by Falk, and they're available at most newsstands and nearly all bookstores. And no Londoner is without a *London A to Z,* the ultimate street-by-street reference, available at bookstores and newsstands everywhere. One good source for maps is **W & G Foyle, Ltd.,** 113-119 Charing Cross Rd., WC2 (☎ 0171/439-8501; tube: Leicester Square).

Police   In an emergency, dial ☎ 999 (no coins are needed).

Telephone   For **directory assistance** for London, dial ☎ 142; for the rest of Britain, dial ☎ 192. See also "Area Codes," above.

Transit Information   Call ☎ 0171/222-1234, 24 hours daily.

3 Accommodations

The best place to stay is Buckingham Palace, but unlike the Lincoln Bedroom at the White House, it's a bit more exclusive. After a spate of openings in the mid-1990s, the London hotel scene has cooled considerably. There have been some new ones launched, but often they are sterile modern—and not the hotels of character we'd like to include in this guide. The Metropolitan (see below) has generated the most excitement.

The good news is that to meet increasing competition, many hotels have redecorated and refurbished, emerging with at least an attempt at that Laura Ashley look, although the late Ms. Ashley might turn over in her grave at some failed attempts to achieve her famous style. Even some hotels that seemed to have changed little since the days of Charles Dickens are freshening and brightening up. More and more showers are being added to private rooms. Regrettably, these rooms weren't designed for private showers, so space is invariably cramped.

But the big problem with London hotels is that there are too many expensive ones and not enough of the moderately priced choices so typical of other European capitals. You'll have to pay more for a good hotel room in London than you probably would in many other world-class cities.

Most hotels add a service charge ranging from 10% to 15% to the bill. The British government also imposes a value-added tax (VAT) that adds 17.5% to your bill. However, you'll usually get breakfast (either continental or a full English spread) included in most hotels.

It's harder to get a hotel room, particularly an inexpensive one, during July and August. Inexpensive hotels are also tight in June, September, and October. If you arrive without a reservation, begin looking for a room as early in the day as possible. Many West End hotels have vacancies, even in peak season, between 9 and 11am, but by noon they are often booked.

MAYFAIR
VERY EXPENSIVE

✪ Brown's Hotel. 29-34 Albemarle St., London W1X 4BP. ☎ **800/225-5843** or 0171/493-6020. Fax 0171/493-9381. 114 units. A/C MINIBAR TV TEL. £235–£265 ($376–$424) double; from £385 ($616) suite. Children 12 and under stay free in parents' room. AE, DC, MC, V. Tube: Green Park.

Among the top traditional choices, Brown's is the quintessential town-house hotel. This upper-crust establishment opened in 1837, the creation of James Brown, a former manservant of Lord Byron. Today, Brown's Hotel occupies some 14 historic houses on two streets in Mayfair, just off Berkeley Square. Here you'll find old-fashioned comfort dispensed with courtesy in a dignified, clubby atmosphere. A liveried doorman ushers you to an antique reception desk. The rooms vary considerably but all have been decorated in a restrained, tasteful style, usually with well-chosen antiques.

Dining: Afternoon tea is served in the Albemarle Room. The dining room, with unmatched service, offers mainly à la carte meals, as well as a set luncheon menu and a fixed-price dinner. The lounges on the street floor are inviting, including the Roosevelt Room, the Rudyard Kipling Room, and the paneled St. George's Bar. Men are required to wear jackets and ties for teas and for dining.

Amenities: 24-hour room service; laundry and dry cleaning; baby-sitting; maid service; secretarial services; valet; men's hairdresser; tour desk; business center.

Central London Accommodations

Academy Hotel **29**	Hart House Hotel **6**
Adare House **3**	Hotel La Place **8**
Astors Hotel **16**	Hotel 22 Jermyn
Blooms Hotel **28**	Street **22**
Brown's Hotel **20**	Ivanhoe Suite Hotel **11**
Cartref House **16**	James House **16**
Caswell Hotel **18**	The Jenkins **30**
Central Club **27**	Lime Tree Hotel **16**
Covent Garden Hotel **26**	Metropolitan **13**
Crescent Hotel **30**	Mornington Hotel **1**
Darlington Hyde Park **4**	Oak House **17**
The Dorchester **12**	Park Lane Hotel **14**
Dorset Square Hotel **7**	Regency Hotel **9**
Dukes Hotel **19**	Regent Palace Hotel **21**
Durrants Hotel **10**	Royal Adelphi Hotel **23**
Edward Lear House **4**	Ruskin Hotel **28**
The Fielding Hotel **25**	The Savoy **24**
The Gate House **2**	Thanet Hotel **28**
Goring Hotel **15**	Tophams Belgravia **16**

✪ The Dorchester. 53 Park Lane, London, W1A 2HJ. ☎ **800/727-9820** or 0171/ 629-8888. Fax 0171/409-0114. 244 units. A/C MINIBAR TV TEL. £285–£315 ($456–$504) double; from £400 ($640) suite. AE, DC, MC, V. Tube: Hyde Park Corner or Marble Arch.

The Dorchester is London's best hotel, without the elitism of Claridge's or the snob-bishness of the Connaught. It's owned by The Audley Group, Ltd., and has benefited from a $192 million makeover in recent years. Opulence is the order of the day here, including luxurious bathrooms stylishly done in Italian marble. Bedrooms feature linen sheets, electronic gadgets, and double- and triple-glazed windows to keep the noise out. Furniture includes plump armchairs and cherry-wood pieces, and, in many cases, four-poster beds. The best rooms open onto views of Hyde Park.

Dining: The Grill, one of London's finest restaurants, remains largely the same today as when "The Dorch" opened in 1931. Although the decor is Spanish in style, the menu reflects traditional English cooking using the freshest ingredients. The hotel's Asian restaurant, The Oriental, London's most exclusive and expensive Chinese restaurant, has been awarded Michelin stars for 4 years running. The Dorchester Bar is a legendary rendezvous spot, and the marble pillared Promenade is a great place for tea.

Amenities: 24-hour room service; laundry; dry cleaning; medical service; the Dorchester Spa, one of London's best-outfitted health clubs; barbershop; hairdresser.

✪ The Metropolitan. 19 Old Park Lane, London W1Y 4LB. ☎ **1071/447-1000.** Fax 0171/447-1100. 155 units. A/C MINIBAR TV TEL. £245–£285 ($392–$456) double; from £305 ($488) and *way* up for various suites. AE, DC, DISC, MC, V. Tube: Hyde Park Corner. Bus: 2, 16, 36, 73.

Our choice for best newcomer of the year, the Metropolitan, smack dab between the Hilton and the Four Seasons, is the first hotel to open on Park Lane since the heady '80s. Unlike some of its opulent neighbors, minimalism is the word here. Designer Keith Hobbs believes in understatement, a style he perfected at Dublin's Clarence Hotel. His staff uniforms have nothing to do with the top hats and tails seen at some of the posh nests nearby.

The Metropolitan is graced with hardwood floors, simple marbles, and natural fab-rics. Simplistic elegance is the hallmark of the bedrooms, the most desirable of which open onto views of Hyde Park. Bedrooms have moleskin covers and cushions in soothing pastels, fax machines, modem ports, VCRs available on request, and simple wood furnishings—spare, functional, yet luxurious in a way. The clientele is the young and well heeled, patrons who value style and a chic, cool atmosphere. The place is a relaxing retreat, with its wood and leather sofas, its carved stone clock in the pale marble lobby, and its cool blue patterned rugs.

Dining/Diversions: An all-white skylit breakfast room, open to residents only, sets the tone for the day. The Japanese restaurant and sushi bar, a twin to New York's Nobu, is one of the most chic restaurants in London. A late-night bar and club has a 1950s aura with frosted glass and metal tables.

Amenities: 24-hour room service; concierge; dry cleaning/laundry; massage; baby-sitting; secretarial services; express checkout.

✪ Park Lane Hotel. Piccadilly, London W1Y 8BX. ☎ **800/223-5652** or 0171/ 499-6321. Fax 0171/499-1965. 340 units. MINIBAR TV TEL. £275 ($440) double; from £345 ($552) suite. AE, DC, MC, V. Parking £16 ($25.60). Tube: Hyde Park Corner or Green Park.

The most traditional of the Park Lane mansions, and once the lone holdout against chain management, was sold in 1996 (at least 95%) to the Sheraton Corporation, which is upgrading but maintaining the Park Lane's quintessential British character. Its silver entrance remains an art deco marvel. Designed in a U-shape, with a view overlooking Green Park, the Park Lane Hotel offers luxurious and spacious accommodations, with double-glazed windows. Many suites have marble fireplaces and the original marble-sheathed bathrooms.

Dining/Diversions: The Hotel has an award-winning restaurant, Bracewells. Less expensive but still very charming is the Brasserie, serving French cuisine. Bracewells Bar is one of London's most popular cocktail bars, with a talented evening pianist. A harpist plays in the Palm Court Lounge every Sunday.

Amenities: Concierge; 24-hour room service; laundry and dry cleaning; babysitting; valet; secretarial services; fitness center; business center; gift and newspaper shop; barbershop and women's hairdresser; Daniel Ryman Aromatherapy Shop.

INEXPENSIVE

Ivanhoe Suite Hotel. 1 St. Christophers Place, Barrett St. Piazza, London W1M 5HB. ☎ **0171/935-1047.** Fax 0171/224-0563. 8 units. MINIBAR TV TEL. £74 ($118.40) double. Rates include continental breakfast. AE, DC, MC, V. Tube: Bond Street.

This hidden treasure is located above a restaurant on a pedestrian lane of boutiques and restaurants just off Oxford Street—a perfect location for serious shoppers, as it's also near New and Old Bond Streets. A town-house hotel, it has attractively furnished rooms with sitting areas. Rooms have style, with their own entry security video, a fridge/bar, plus a wide selection of videotapes. You're also close to the shop-flanked New and Old Bond streets. Breakfast is served in the restaurant downstairs, and you can stop off for a nightcap at the corner pub, a real neighborhood locale. The hotel offers a number of perks including room service, baby-sitting, secretarial services, and laundry.

MARYLEBONE
EXPENSIVE

✪ **Dorset Square Hotel.** 39-40 Dorset Sq., London NW1 6QN. ☎ **800/553-6674** or 0171/723-7874. Fax 0171/724-3328. 38 units. MINIBAR TV TEL. £125–£185 ($200–$296) double; £195 ($312) junior suite. AE, MC, V. Tube: Baker Street or Marylebone.

A grand English country house, the Dorset Square is made up of two Georgian Regency town houses on the small square near Regent's Park. Hotelier Tim Kemp and his wife, Kit, both interior decorators known for their bold and often daring taste, have created a space that resembles an elegant private home. The decor is personal, yet extravagantly beautiful. The luxurious bedrooms are decorated in chintz or printed materials that complement the furniture, a mix of antiques and reproductions. Half the rooms are air-conditioned. The Kemps attract a sophisticated, well-traveled crowd who also gravitate to their newer Covent Garden Hotel (see below).

Dining: The Potting Shed provides simple, well-prepared dishes at reasonable prices.

Amenities: 24-hour room service; laundry; baby-sitting.

Durrants Hotel. George St., London W1H 6BJ. ☎ 0171/935-8131. Fax 0171/487-3510. 99 units. TV TEL. £135–£140 ($216–$224) double; from £250 ($400) suite. AE, MC, V. Tube: Bond Street.

Established in 1789 off Manchester Square, this historic hotel is a snug, cozy, and traditional—almost like a more affordable Brown's. In some ways, we find it one of the most quintessentially English of all London hotels, and a soothing retreat on a cold, rainy day. During the 100 years it has been owned by the Miller family, several neighboring houses have been incorporated into the original structure, making a walk through the pine-and-mahogany-paneled public rooms a tour through another century.

You'll find such 18th-century niceties as a letter-writing room sheathed with old paneling and a popular neighborhood pub with Windsor chairs, an open fireplace, and a decor that probably hasn't changed very much in 200 years. The oldest bedrooms face the front and have slightly higher ceilings than the newer ones. Even the most recent accommodations, however, have elaborate cove moldings, comfortable furnishings, and a solid feeling of well-being, although the overall effect is rather bland. Some even have air-conditioning.

Dining: The restaurant serves full afternoon teas and a satisfying French or traditional English cuisine in a beautiful Georgian room. The less formal breakfast room is ringed with 19th-century political cartoons by a noted Victorian artist.

Amenities: Laundry; baby-sitting; 24-hour room service.

MODERATE

Hotel La Place. 17 Nottingham Place, London W1M 3FB. ☎ **0171/486-2323.** Fax 0171/486-4335. 28 units. MINIBAR TV TEL. £98–£150 ($156.80–$240) double; from £120 ($192) suite. Rates include English breakfast. AE, CB, DC, MC, V. Parking £8.50 ($13.60). Tube: Baker Street.

This elegantly furnished West End Hotel is known as a safe haven for women travelers. Actually, it's a good bet for anyone. One of the most desirable hotels north of Oxford Street, near Madame Tussaud's, it is a Victorian-era building with a red brick facade. It's been completely refurbished inside, and is now one of London's better B&Bs for the price. "Discreet and lovely," is how one guest described it, and we agree. Bedrooms are done in the Laura Ashley country-house style, with traditional furnishings. Tall windows are opulently swagged and draped. Rooms are moderate in size but not cramped, and each contains a beverage-maker, an orthopedic mattresses, and a hair dryer. For such a small hotel, a remarkable number of services are provided, including a concierge, room service, dry cleaning/laundry, in-room massage, baby-sitting, and a business center. There's also Jardin, an intimate wine bar and restaurant, cozy and chic with an indoor/outdoor atmosphere and good food and drink.

INEXPENSIVE

Edward Lear Hotel. 28-30 Seymour St., London W1H 5WD. ☎ **0171/402-5401.** Fax 0171/706-3766. 35 units, 12 with bathroom. TV TEL. £60 ($96) double without bathroom, £79.50 ($127.20) double with bathroom; £85 ($136) suite. Rates include English breakfast. MC, V. Tube: Marble Arch.

The Edward Lear is a popular affordable option, 1 block from Marble Arch in a pair of brick town-houses, both of which date from 1780. The western house was the London home of the 19th-century artist and poet Edward Lear, whose illustrated limericks adorn the walls of one sitting room. Steep stairs lead up to the bedrooms. The cozy units are fairly small but have all the usual amenities. One major drawback is that this is an extremely noisy part of London (rooms in the rear are quieter).

Hart House Hotel. 51 Gloucester Place, Portman Sq., London W1H 3PE. ☎ **0171/ 935-2288.** Fax 0171/935-8516. 16 units, 10 with bathroom. TV TEL. £75 ($120) double without bathroom, £93 ($148.80) double with bathroom; £98 ($156.80) triple without bathroom, £110 ($176) triple with bathroom; £130 ($208) quad with bathroom. Rates include English breakfast. AE, MC, V. Tube: Marble Arch or Baker Street.

This has been a longtime favorite with Frommer's readers. It's a well-preserved historic building, part of a group of Georgian mansions that were occupied by French nobility living in exile during the French Revolution. It's within easy walking distance of many theaters, as well as shopping and public parks. The rooms are spick-and-span, each one with a different character. Favorites include no. 7, a triple with a big bath and shower. On the top floor, ask for no. 11 if you'd like a brightly lit aerie. The bedrooms have a variety of furnishings, ranging from Portobello antique to modern.

The Regency Hotel. 19 Nottingham Place, London W1M 3FF. ☎ **0171/486-5347.** Fax 0171/224-6057. 20 units. MINIBAR TV TEL. £85 ($136) double; £99 ($158.40) family room. AE, DC, MC, V. Tube: Baker Street or Regent's Park.

This centrally located hotel was originally built, along with most of its neighbors, in the late 1800s. Although it has functioned as a hotel since the 1940s, in 1991 it was gutted, upgraded, and tastefully renovated. One of the better choices on the street, it offers simple, conservatively modern bedrooms scattered over four floors, and a breakfast room set in what used to be the cellar. Each room has a hair dryer, trouser press, and ironing board. Room service is available. Marble Arch, Regent's Park, and Baker Street all lie within a 12-minute walk. Laundry and dry cleaning service, room service, and massage are available.

ST. JAMES'S

✪ **Dukes Hotel.** 35 St. James's Place, London SW1A 1NY. ☎ **800/381-4702** or 0171/491-4840. Fax 0171/493-1264. 76 units. A/C TV TEL. £190–£255 ($304–$408) double; from £250 ($400) suite. AE, DC, MC, V. Parking £35 ($56). Tube: Green Park.

Dukes provides elegance without ostentation and, along with its nearest competitors, The Stafford and 22 Jermyn Street, attracts those looking for a hotel with charm, style, and tradition. It stands in a quiet courtyard off St. James's Street, within walking distance of Buckingham Palace, the Houses of Parliament, and the shopping areas of Bond Street and Piccadilly. Renovated most recently in 1994, each of the well-furnished and centrally heated bedrooms is decorated in the style of a particular English period, ranging from Regency to Edwardian. Each room has a marble bathroom and a private bar.

Dining: Dukes' Restaurant is small, tasteful, and elegant, combining both classic British and continental cuisine. The hotel also has a clublike bar that is known for its rare collection of vintage ports, Armagnacs, and cognacs.

Amenities: 24-hour room service; butler, valet, housekeeping, secretarial services; travel reservations; theater-booking service; baby-sitting; laundry/dry cleaning.

The Stafford. 16-18 St. James's Place, London SW1A 1NJ. ☎ **800/525-4800** or 0171/493-0111. Fax 0171/493-7121. 80 units. AC TV TEL. £220–£260 ($352–$416) double; from £330 ($528) suite. AE, DC, MC, V. Tube: Green Park.

Famous for its discretion, the American Bar, and the warmth of its Edwardian decor, the clubby Stafford was built late in the 19th century as a private home on a cul-de-sac. It can be entered via St. James's Place or a cobble-covered courtyard, originally designed as a mews (living quarters adapted from stables) and known today as the Blue Ball Yard. The recently refurbished Stafford retains a homelike, country-house atmosphere with touches of antique charm amid the modern amenities. Bedrooms and suites are individually decorated and come in varying shapes and sizes. You'll have to walk across the cobblestones of the mews yard to reach the newer and plusher accommodations in a restored stable mews.

Dining: The elegant Stafford Restaurant serves classic international dishes made from fresh, select ingredients. The American Bar, which resembles a memento-packed library of an English country house, is quite cozy.

Amenities: Concierge; 24-hour room service; laundry; baby-sitting; secretarial services; massage.

PICCADILLY CIRCUS
VERY EXPENSIVE
✪ **Hotel 22 Jermyn Street.** 22 Jermyn St., London SW1Y 6HL. ☎ **800/682-7808** or 0171/734-2353. Fax 0171/734-0750. 18 units. MINIBAR TV TEL. £185 ($296) double; from £240 ($384) suite. AE, DC, MC, V. Valet parking £25 ($40). Tube: Piccadilly Circus.

This is London's premier town-house hotel, a gem of elegance and discretion. Set behind a facade of gray stone with neoclassical embellishments, it was originally built in 1870 as an apartment house for English gentlemen doing business in London. Since 1915, it has been administered by three generations of the Togna family, who closed it for a radical restoration in 1990 and redecorated again in 1996. Now reveling in its new role as a chic and upscale hotel, 22 Jermyn Street has beautiful guest rooms, decorated in traditional English style, with masses of fresh flowers. It doesn't have the bar or restaurant facilities of The Stafford or Dukes, but its rooms are even more richly appointed, with modern touches such as dual phone lines.

Amenities: Concierge; 24-hour room service; laundry/dry cleaning; baby-sitting; secretarial services; weekly newsletter detailing London events; free use of Dictaphones, videophones, and fax; video library; a CD-ROM library with access to the Internet; nearby health club.

MODERATE
Regent Palace Hotel. 12 Sherwood St., near Piccadilly Circus, London W1A 4BZ. ☎ **0171/734-7000.** Fax 0171/734-6435. 950 units, none with bathroom. TV TEL. £103 ($164.80) double without breakfast. For stays of 2 or more nights, £72–£88 ($115.20–$140.80) per person, including English breakfast. AE, DC, MC, V. Tube: Piccadilly Circus.

Built in 1915 at the edge of Piccadilly Circus, this is one of Europe's largest hotels, well located if you want to be near the bright lights and neon of London's "Broadway." The decor is pretty standard stuff. Shared bathrooms in the hallways are adequate and kept spick-and-span, and each room has a sink with hot and cold running water.

The Hotel's Original Carvery makes for good, inexpensive dining and The Dome bistro is open for pretheater meals. Drinks are served in the Half Sovereign and the Planters bars. Coffee, sandwiches, and snacks are available in Antonio's Coffee Bar. There are souvenir and gift shops, an exchange bureau, and a theater-booking agent.

SOHO
✪ **Hazlitts 1718.** 6 Frith St., Soho Sq., London W1V 5TZ. ☎ **0171/434-1771.** Fax 0171/439-1524. 24 units. £148 ($236.80) double; £205–£245 ($328–$392) suite. AE, DC, MC, V. Tube: Leicester Square or Tottenham Court Road.

This is one of London's best small hotels. Tucked away in Soho Square, it was once home to the poet Mary Barker, a friend of Jonathan Swift. Yet it is named after another famous person, William Hazlitt, who died here in 1830. He was the founder of the Unitarian Church in America and an early biographer of Napoléon.

Since 1986, the hotel has occupied three historic homes with no elevators. Rooms are often booked by artists, journalists, actors, and models. Some find the Georgian decor—mostly collectibles picked up at estate auctions—a bit spartan, but the 2,000 original prints hanging on the walls brighten it considerably. Many rooms have four-poster beds, and some bathrooms have their original claw-footed bathtubs from the 1800s. Only one unit has a shower. Some floors dip and sway, but that's part of the charm. Swinging Soho is at your doorstep, and the young, hip staff can point you to the restaurants and clubs of the moment.

BLOOMSBURY
EXPENSIVE

Academy Hotel. 17-21 Gower St., London WC1E 6HG. ☎ **800/678-3096** in the U.S., or 0171/631-4115. Fax 0171/636-3442. 45 units. A/C TV TEL. £115 ($184) double; £150 ($240) suite. AE, DC, MC, V. Tube: Tottenham Court Road, Goodge Street, or Russell Square.

Right in the heart of London's publishing district stands the Academy. Although tacky modern style rears its ugly head here and there, many of the original architectural details were preserved when these three 1776 Georgian row houses were joined. The hotel was substantially upgraded in the 1990s, with a private bathroom added to every unit (whether there was space or not). Grace notes include the glass panels, colonnades, and the intricate plasterwork on the front of the building. Rooms are decorated in an inoffensive neutral style and they are well cared for. The location is within walking distance of the theater section, Covent Garden, and other spots in the West End. Facilities include an elegant bar, a library room, a secluded patio garden, and a restaurant serving modern European food that often attracts businesspeople who entertain their clients here.

Blooms Hotel. 7 Montague St., London WC1B 5BP. ☎ **0171/323-1717.** Fax 0171/ 636-6498. 27 units. TV TEL. £140–£180 ($224–$288) double. Extra person £40 ($64). Rates include English breakfast. AE, DC, MC, V. Tube: Russell Square.

This exquisitely restored town house has a pedigree: It stands in what was formerly the grounds of Montague House (now the British Museum). It's had a distinguished if eccentric list of former occupants, including Dr. John Cumming, who firmly believed he'd witness the end of the world. On long winter nights, his ghostly presence has been spotted. Even though it's situated in the heart of London, the house has the ambience of an English country home. The decor is a reproduction of the original, as exemplified by the lounge with fireplace and period art. Guests take morning coffee in a walled garden overlooking the British Museum. In summer, light meals are served here. Bedrooms are individually designed with traditional elegance in beautifully muted tones. Room service is available 24 hours a day, as well as laundry, dry cleaning, and concierge.

INEXPENSIVE

Crescent Hotel. 49-50 Cartwright Gardens, London WC1H 9EL. ☎ **0171/387-1515.** Fax 0171/383-2054. 24 units, 15 with bathroom (some with shower only, some with tub only). TV TEL. £50 ($80) double without bathroom; £68 ($108.80) double with bathroom. Rates include English breakfast. MC, V. Tube: Russell Square.

The Crescent stands in the heart of intellectual London; the private square is owned by the City Guild of Skinners and guarded by the University of London, whose student residential halls are just across the street. You have access to the gardens, with their private tennis courts. Mrs. Bessolo and Mrs. Cockle, the managers, are the kindest hosts along the street. They view the Crescent as an extension of their home and welcome you to its comfortably elegant Georgian surroundings, which date from 1810. Some guests have been returning here for decades, enjoying a range of rooms, including small singles with shared bathrooms (although a few have private plumbing). Standard doubles with modest furnishings are rented, as are some spacious twin and double rooms. Thoughtful extras include alarm clocks, beverage-makers, and hair dryers. The good ladies will even let you do your ironing so you'll look sharp for an evening out.

✪ **The Jenkins Hotel.** 45 Cartwright Gardens, Russell Sq., London WC1H 9EH. ☎ **0171/387-2067.** Fax 0171/383-3139. 15 units, 6 with bathroom. MINIBAR TV TEL.

£55 ($88) double without bathroom, £65 ($104) double with bathroom; £76 ($121.60) triple with bathroom. MC, V. Rates include English breakfast. Tube: Euston Station.

Followers of the TV series *Poirot* might recognize this Cartwright Gardens residence. Back in the 1920s one Maggie Jenkins converted the former residence into a hotel, and so it remains today. Guests who stay here are surrounded by the British Museum, London University, theaters, and antiquarian bookshops. E. M. Forster used to drop in here for tea. The antiques are gone, the rooms are small, but some of the original charm of the Georgian house remains—enough so that the *London Mail on Sunday* recently proclaimed it one of the "ten best hotel values" in the city. There are some drawbacks (no elevator, no reception or sitting room), but it's still a place where you can settle in and feel at home.

Ruskin Hotel. 23-24 Montague St., London WC1B 5BH. ☎ **0171/636-7388.** Fax 0171/323-1662. 32 units, 6 with bathroom. £60 ($96) double without bathroom, £74 ($118.40) double with bathroom; £75 ($120) triple without bathroom, £85 ($136) triple with bathroom. Rates include English breakfast. AE, DC, MC, V. Tube: Russell Square or Holborn.

This hotel has been managed for 2 decades by a hard-working family that enjoys a repeat clientele. They keep the place very tidy, even though the hotel doesn't have much decorative flair and the furnishings, though well polished, are worn. Double-glazed windows in the front rooms block out noise, but we prefer the cozily old-fashioned units in the rear that open onto a park. Note that there's no elevator. The plantings in the cellar-level breakfast room provide a grace note, and the breakfast is big enough to fortify you for a full day at the British Museum next door.

Insider's tip: Although you'd probably want a private bathroom in most cases, they're ridiculously small here, while the shared bathrooms in the hall are generous and well maintained. Do yourself a favor and opt for a room with no bathroom.

Thanet Hotel. 8 Bedford Place, Russell Sq., London WC1B 5JA. ☎ **0171/636-2869.** Fax 0171/323-6676. 16 units. TV TEL. £75 ($120) double; £90 ($144) triple; £99 ($158.40) quad. Rates include English breakfast. AE, MC, V. Tube: Russell Square.

The myriad hotels around Russell Square become peas in a pod at some point, but the Thanet stands out. It no longer charges the same rates it did when it first appeared in *England on $5 a Day*, but it continues to be a winning choice nonetheless—still affordable, and close to the British Museum, theaters, and Covent Garden. The building, which has landmark status, stands on a quiet Georgian terrace between Russell and Bloomsbury squares. The Orchard family, the hotel's operators, are third-generation hoteliers. They offer small, comfortably furnished rooms in subdued colors, with beverage-makers and radios.

COVENT GARDEN
VERY EXPENSIVE

Covent Garden Hotel. 10 Monmouth St., London WC2H 9HB. ☎ **0171/806-1000.** Fax 0171/806-1100. 50 units. A/C MINIBAR TV TEL. £200–£295 ($320–$472) double; £375–£550 ($600–$880) suite. AE, MC, V. Tube: Leicester Square or Covent Garden.

Originally built as a French hospital around 1850, the premises of this hotel lay derelict and empty for many years. Then, in 1996, the talented Tim and Kit Kemp of the Firmdale Group reconfigured them into one of the most charming boutique hotels in London. Across from Neal's Yard and behind a bottle-green facade that evokes a 19th-century storefront, the site contains two charming restaurants, plus a paneled lobby outfitted with elaborate marquetry furniture and sweeping draperies. Upstairs, above a dramatic stone staircase, soundproof rooms are lushly outfitted in the English style with Asian fabrics, many of which are elaborately adorned with hand-embroidered designs, sometimes in crewel work. In an outrageous touch, each room contains a clothier's mannequin draped in the same fabric used in the room's decor. All rooms also have VCRs, CD players, two phone lines with voice mail, and marble-sheathed bathrooms with double vanities. Many afford glimpses of the original ceiling beams, and in some cases, views over the surrounding rooftops of Covent Garden.

Dining: Max's Brasserie is an upscale French-English bistro that harks back to the 19th century in its style. With its high stools at the bar and its crisp table linens, it's a chic place for lunch.

Amenities: Concierge; 24-hour room service; valet; business services; and a small health club/gym.

MODERATE

✪ **The Fielding Hotel.** 4 Broad Ct., Bow St., London WC2B 5QZ. ☎ **0171/ 836-8305.** Fax 0171/497-0064. 26 units. £88–£98 ($140.80–$156.80) double; £140 ($224) triple; £185 ($296) suite for 4. AE, DC, MC, V. Tube: Covent Garden.

One of London's more eccentric hotels, and an excellent buy, the Fielding is cramped, quirky, and quaint, but an enduring favorite nonetheless. Next to the Bow Street Magistrates Court, and almost opposite the Royal Opera House, the hotel lies on a pedestrian-only street still retaining its 1800s gas lamps. Covent Garden, with its pubs, shops, markets, restaurants, and street entertainment, is just outside your door. The entrance is framed by flower boxes. Upon entering the bar, be sure to introduce yourself to Smokey, the African Grey parrot, the hotel's oldest resident.

Rooms are a little less than small, and few have a view. Their floors dip and sway, and the furnishings have seen better days. If such quirkiness doesn't bother you (it can make a nice respite from sterile modern hotels), it's hard to beat the central London location. Breakfast is served.

Royal Adelphi Hotel. 21 Villiers St., London WC2N 6ND. ☎ **0171/930-8764.** Fax 0171/930-8735. 49 units, 35 with bathroom. TV TEL. £60 ($96) double without bathroom; £78 ($124.80) double with bathroom; £105 ($168) triple with bathroom. Extra bed £15 ($24). Rates include continental breakfast. AE, DC, MC, V. Tube: Charing Cross, Embankment.

If you care most about location, consider the Royal Adelphi. Close to Covent Garden, theaterland, and Trafalgar Square, it's an unorthodox choice but it's away from the typical B&B stamping grounds. The hotel is upstairs above an Italian restaurant. Though the bedrooms quickly call to mind London's swinging 1960s heyday, accommodations are decently maintained and comfortable. Plumbing, however, is a bit creaky. The higher up you go, the better the view. London has far better B&Bs, but not in this part of town, where you can walk to the Victoria Embankment Garden.

THE STRAND

The Savoy. The Strand, London WC2R 0EU. ☎ **800/63-SAVOY** or 0171/836-4343. Fax 0171/240-6040. 202 units. A/C MINIBAR TV TEL. £295–£305 ($472–$488) double; from £365 ($584) suite. AE, CB, DC, MC, V. Parking £23 ($36.80). Tube: Charing Cross; Covent Garden.

The Savoy is a London landmark. Although not as swank as the Dorchester, it is the premier address in The Strand and Covent Garden area. With eight stories of opulence and a facade of light terra-cotta glazed tiles, the Savoy literally and figuratively dwarfs all of its nearby competition. Forty-eight of the Hotel's rooms have their own sitting rooms. Each has a different decor, and all have comfortable chairs, solid furniture, and large closets. Suites overlooking the river are the most sought after.

Dining/Diversions: The world-famous Savoy Grill has long been popular with theater types. The even more elegant River Restaurant has tables overlooking the Thames;

a four-person band plays in the evening for dancing. Also here is Upstairs, specializing in champagne, Chablis, and seafood.

Amenities: 24-hour room service; same-day laundry and dry cleaning; nightly turndown; room service; secretarial services; hairdresser; news kiosk; and a unique Health Club, built on top of the historic Savoy Theatre. Guests are also granted temporary membership in the exclusive Wentworth Club, a golf and country club in the outskirts of London (proof of handicap required to play golf).

WESTMINSTER & VICTORIA
VERY EXPENSIVE

✪ **Goring Hotel.** 15 Beeston Place, Grosvenor Gardens, London SW1W 0JW. ☎ **0171/396-9000.** Fax 0171/834-4393. 76 units. A/C TV TEL. £185–£225 ($296–$360) double; from £250–£275 ($400–$440) suite. AE, DC, MC, V. Parking £17.50 ($28). Tube: Victoria.

Built in 1910, this was the first hotel in the world to have central heating and a private bath in every room. It's located just behind Buckingham Palace, within easy reach of Victoria Station, Westminster Abbey, and the Houses of Parliament. For tradition and location, it's a terrific choice. Not only does the hotel offer top-quality service, but all the well-furnished rooms have been refurbished with marble baths. Some units are air-conditioned.

Dining: Your three-course luncheon or dinner might feature one of the chef's specialties: duckling pâté, calves' liver with bacon and fried onions, venison, or roast boned best end of lamb.

Amenities: 24-hour room service, beauty salon, laundry/dry cleaning, valet, free use of local health club, concierge.

MODERATE

Lime Tree Hotel. 135-137 Ebury St., London SW1W 9RA. ☎ **0171/730-8191.** Fax 0171/730-7865. 26 units. TV TEL. £100–£110 ($160–$176) double. Rates include breakfast. AE, MC, V. Tube: Victoria.

Longtime veterans of London's B&B business, the Wales-born Davies family transformed what had been a rundown guest house into an affordable but cozy hotel with reasonable rates. Scattered over four floors of a brick-fronted town house that's almost next door to a popular bistro (Ebury Wine Bar), its rooms have small balconies overlooking Ebury Street. Rooms in the back don't have balconies, but are quieter and sport views over the hotel's small rear garden. Each of the simply furnished rooms has recently refitted curtains, cupboards, and upholsteries. Accommodations tend to be larger than those in similarly priced hotels, and breakfasts are served in generous portions. Buckingham Palace, Westminster Abbey, and the House of Parliament are within easy reach, as is Harrods.

Tophams Belgravia. 28 Ebury St., London SW1W 0LU. ☎ **0171/730-8147.** Fax 0171/823-5966. 43 units, 24 with bathroom. TV TEL. £95 ($152) double without bathroom, £115–£135 ($184–$216) double with bathroom; £230 ($368) suite. AE, CB, DC, MC, V. Tube: Victoria.

Tophams came into being in 1937, when five small row houses were connected; with its flower-filled window boxes, the place still has a country-house flavor. It was completely renovated in 1997. The little, informal reception rooms are decorated with flowery chintzes and nice antiques. All rooms have tea- and coffeemakers and hair dryers; the best of the bunch are comfortably appointed with private bathrooms and four-poster beds. And the location is great, especially if you're planning to cover a lot of ground by tube or train: It's only a 3-minute walk from Victoria Station.

Tophams Restaurant offers both traditional and modern English cooking for lunch and dinner in a dining room that's decorated with family heirloom paintings.

INEXPENSIVE

Astors Hotel. 110-112 Ebury St., London SW1W 9QD. ☎ **0171/730-3811.** Fax 0171/823-6728. 22 units, 12 with bathroom. TV. £55 ($88) double without bathroom, £64 ($102.40) double with bathroom; £84 ($134.40) triple with bathroom. Rates include English breakfast. MC, V. Tube: Victoria.

If you'd like a convenient location from which to walk over and have tea with the queen, this might be your choice. You're not only close to Buckingham Palace, but you're just 5 minutes from the tube stations of Victoria. The brick-fronted, Victorian building attracts frugal travelers looking for a decent, affordable address in pricey London. Rooms are more functional than glamorous, but are well maintained. Space and furnishings vary greatly, so ask to see a room before committing yourself to a night's stay. But get here early—the hotel books up quickly.

Caswell Hotel. 25 Gloucester St., London SW1V 2DB. ☎ **0171/834-6345.** 18 units, 7 with bathroom. MINIBAR TV. £54 ($86.40) double without bathroom, £75 ($120) double with bathroom. Rates include English breakfast. MC, V. Tube: Victoria.

Among the traffic-clogged streets near Victoria Station, this hotel, situated on a cul-de-sac, stands out as a calm oasis in an otherwise busy area. Run with consideration and thoughtfulness by Mr. and Mrs. Hare, the hotel contains four floors of well-furnished if not spectacular rooms, each with a hair dryer and beverage-maker. The decor is understated, and sometimes you can meet intriguing guests in the chintz-filled lobby.

✪ **James House/Cartref House.** 108 Ebury St. and 129 Ebury St., London, SW1W 9QD. ☎ **0171/730-7338** for James House, **0171/730-6176** for Cartref House. Fax 0171/730-7338. 21 units, 9 with bathroom. TV. £65 ($104) double without bathroom, £75 ($120) double with bathroom; £105 ($168) quad with bathroom. MC, V. Tube: Victoria.

Hailed by many publications, including the *Los Angeles Times*, as one of the top 10 B&Bs in London, James House and Cartref House (across the street) deserve their accolades. Derek and Sharon James run both properties, and seem to have real dedication to their work. They are the finest hosts in the area around Victoria Station. They are constantly refurbishing, so everything looks state of the art. Each room is individually designed, and some of the large rooms have bunk beds suitable for families. The generous English breakfast means you might skip lunch. There's no elevator, but few people complain about any inconveniences at this winning entry. Don't worry about which house you're assigned. Each is as good as the other.

✪ **Oak House Hotel.** 29 Hugh St., London SW1V 1QJ. ☎ **0171/834-7151.** 6 units. TV. £34 ($54.40) double. No credit cards. Tube: Victoria Station.

This little jewel of a hotel, perhaps the smallest in the area, is a real find for London, with lots of homespun charm. The Symingtons from Scotland bring the hospitality from the north of Britain to their home in the Victoria Station area. When Mr. Symington isn't putting on his kilt to do the Scottish war dance, he's out driving a London taxi. Mrs. Symington is here to welcome you to her tidily maintained bed rooms, which are small yet handsomely furnished and appointed. Half of the rooms have double beds; the others are twins. Each has a beverage-maker and a hair dryer. The closets aren't big enough, so be prepared to hang your garments on hooks and store your other items on shelves. Bathrooms are adequate and spotlessly maintained. Rooms are reserved only for 5 or more consecutive days.

KNIGHTSBRIDGE
VERY EXPENSIVE

Basil Street Hotel. 8 Basil St., London SW3 1AH. ☎ **0171/581-3311.** Fax 0171/ 581-3693. 87 units, 71 with bathroom. TV TEL. £170 ($272) double without bathroom, £188 ($300.80) double with bathroom; £240 ($384) family room. AE, DC, MC, V. Parking £22–£27 ($35.20–$43.20) at 24-hour lot nearby. Tube: Knightsbridge.

The Basil, an Edwardian charmer, has long been a favorite among older British matrons making their annual pilgrimage to Harrods, "Just 191 steps away," and the Chelsea Flower Show. Harvey Nichols is also nearby. Filled with nooks and crannies, it offers several spacious lounges appropriately furnished with 18th- and 19th-century decorative accessories. Off the many rambling corridors are smaller sitting rooms. Rooms are well maintained, but furnished in a rather standard way; a few rooms don't have private bathrooms, and some accommodations are air-conditioned.

Dining: In the hotel's restaurant, candlelight and piano music re-create the atmosphere of a bygone era. The Parrot Club, a rendezvous reserved only for women, is ideal for afternoon tea. There's also 24-hour room service.

✪ **The Beaufort.** 33 Beaufort Gardens, London SW3 1PP. ☎ **800/888-1199** in the U.S. and Canada, or 0171/584-5252. Fax 0171/589-2834. 28 units. TV TEL. £150–£260 ($240–$416) double; £295 ($472) junior suite for 2. Rates include breakfast and afternoon tea. AE, DC, MC, V. Free overnight parking on street. Tube: Knightsbridge.

If you'd like to stay in one of London's finest boutique hotels, try the Beaufort. Located only 200 yards from Harrods, it sits behind two Victorian porticoes and an iron fence that was added when the buildings were constructed in the 1870s. The owner combined a pair of adjacent houses, ripped out the old decor, and created an updated ambience of merit and charm. One added advantage of this place is the helpful staff and the direction of its owner, Diana Wallis, a television producer. She created the feeling of a private house in the heart of London, putting earphone radios, hair dryers, flowers, and a selection of books in each beautifully decorated room.

Dining: Light meals are available from room service; a 24-hour honor bar is also available.

Amenities: Theater tickets; car rental; baby-sitting; massage; room service; access to nearby health club at a nominal charge.

Hyatt Carlton Tower. 2 Cadogan Place, London SW1 X9PY. ☎ **800/233-1234** or 0171/235-1234. Fax 0171/235-9129. 224 units. A/C MINIBAR TV TEL. £255 ($408) double; from £425 ($680) suite. AE, DC, MC, V. Parking £30 ($48). Tube: Knightsbridge.

Its location and towering height made this luxurious hotel a landmark even before Hyatt's decorators, painters, and antique dealers transformed it into the chain's European flagship. It's one of the most plushly decorated and best-maintained hotels in London. And the setting is lovely—it overlooks one of the city's most civilized gardens, and is surrounded by Regency-era town houses. The comfortable and conservatively modern guest rooms feature marble baths and artwork; many open onto panoramic views over the rooftops of the neighborhood.

Dining: After the publicity it received as "Britain's Tea Place of the Year," the hotel has remained one of the most fashionable spots to enjoy a midafternoon pick-me-up. The hotel has a new northern Italian restaurant, Grissini London, a sibling restaurant to the Grissini at the Grand Hyatt Hong Kong. The newer Grissini serves specialties such as ravioli stuffed with lobster and fried lemon-bread monkfish medallions.

Amenities: 24-hour room service; valet; laundry; beauty salon; baby-sitting; express checkout; secretarial services; health club with exercise equipment; aerobics studio; massage; sauna; solariums; tennis courts; Jacuzzi; shopping arcade.

EXPENSIVE

✪ **Claverley Hotel.** 13-14 Beaufort Gardens, London SW3 1PS. ☎ **800/747-0398** in the U.S., or 0171/589-0541. Fax 0171/584-3410. **25** units, 23 with bathroom. MINIBAR TV TEL. £120–£160 ($192–$256) double with bathroom; from £160 ($256) suite. Rates include English breakfast. AE, DC, MC, V. Tube: Knightsbridge.

Located on a quiet cul-de-sac, this tasteful hotel, just a few blocks from Harrods, is one of the very best choices in the neighborhood. It's a small, cozy place accented with Georgian-era accessories. In the beautiful and comfortable lounge, the hotel serves complimentary tea, coffee, hot chocolate, and cookies 24 hours a day. Most rooms have Victorian-inspired wallpaper, wall-to-wall carpeting, and comfortably uphol-stered armchairs. Two singles are without private bathroom.

Knightsbridge Green Hotel. 159 Knightsbridge, London SW1X 7PD. ☎ **0171/584-6274.** Fax 0171/225-1635. 27 units. A/C MINIBAR TV TEL. £135 ($216) double; £155 ($248) suite. AE, DC, MC, V. Tube: Knightsbridge.

This unusual choice was constructed a block from Harrods in the 1890s. In 1966, when it was converted into a hotel, the developers retained the wide baseboards, cove molding, high ceilings, and spacious proportions of the dignified old structure. Though none of the accommodations have a kitchen, the result comes close to apartment-style living. Many of the doubles or twins are well-furnished suites, each with access to the second-floor "club room," where coffee and pastries are avail-able throughout the day. Rooms each contain a trouser press and hair dryer. However, the amenities and decor here don't measure up to the nearby Claverley Hotel (see above).

BELGRAVIA

✪ **Diplomat Hotel.** 2 Chesham St., London SW1X 8DT. ☎ **0171/235-1544.** Fax 0171/259-6153. 27 units. TV TEL. £120–£150 ($192–$240) double. Rates include English breakfast buffet. AE, CB, DC, MC, V. Tube: Sloane Square or Knightsbridge.

The Diplomat Hotel is a small, relatively reasonably priced hotel in an otherwise quite expensive neighborhood. It was originally built in 1882 by one of the neighborhood's most famous architects, Thomas Cubitt, on a wedge-shaped corner near the site of today's Belgravia Sheraton. Each of the comfortable high-ceilinged rooms (many of which were renovated in 1996) boasts well-chosen wallpaper in Victorian-inspired colors, as well as a modern bathroom equipped with a hair dryer. The staff is very helpful. Some readers have commented that the hotel is not exactly state-of-the-art. If you're expecting regal accommodations, remember that this is a moderately priced choice for pricey London.

CHELSEA

Blair House Hotel. 34 Draycott Place, London SW3 2SA. ☎ **0171/581-2323.** Fax 0171/823-7752. 11 units. TV TEL. £110–£117 ($176–$187.20) double. Extra bed £8 ($12.80). Rates include continental breakfast. AE, DC, MC, V. Tube: Sloane Square.

This comfortable B&B-style hotel near Sloane Square, is a good alternative if you're trying to avoid the high prices of Chelsea's tonier hotels. An older building of some architectural interest, it's been completely refurbished inside. Rooms are individually decorated, but may have too many flowery prints for most tastes. Although most sin-gles are small, some accommodations are spacious enough to accommodate a family of four. Reached by an elevator, rooms contain beverage-makers, hair dryers, and trouser presses. Baby-sitting and laundry can be arranged, and breakfast is served. If you're bothered by noise, ask for one of the quieter rooms in the back.

Hotels & Dining from Knightsbridge to Kensington

Church ✝   Information ⓘ   Post Office ✉   Tube Station ⊖

Accommodations

Abbey House **2**
Aster House Hotel **8**
Aston's Budget Studios & Designer Studios & Suites **10**
Basil Street Hotel **29**
The Beaufort **26**
Blair House Hotel **18**

Blake's **12**
Claverley Hotel **26**
The Cranley **11**
Diplomat Hotel **24**
Five Summer Place **8**
The Gore **4**
Hotel 167 **9**
Hyatt Carlton Tower **28**

Knightsbridge Green Hotel **30**
Number Sixteen **8**
Pelham Hotel **20**
The Regency Hotel **6**
Vicarage Private Hotel **2**
Wilbraham Hotel **16**

3-0580

Dining

Aubergine **13**
Bibendum/The Oyster Bar **19**
Bill Bentley's **25**
Bombay Brasserie **5**
English Garden **12**
English House **23**

The Enterprise **22**
Grenadier **31**
Hilaire **7**
Joe's **21**
La Tante Claire **15**
The Orangery **1**
San Lorenzo **27**

Star Tavern **33**
The Tearoom at
  Chelsea Physic
  Garden **14**
Vong **32**
Wodka **4**

103

⊙ **Wilbraham Hotel.** 1-5 Wilbraham Place (off Sloane St.), London SW1X 9AE.
☎ **0171/730-8296.** Fax 0171/730-6815. 59 units. TV TEL. £97 ($155.20) double;
from £99 ($158.40) suite. No credit cards. Nearby parking £17.50 ($28). Tube: Sloane
Square.

This is a dyed-in-the-wool British hotel set on a quiet residential street just a few hundred yards from Sloane Square. It occupies three Victorian town houses that have been
joined together. Sure, it's faded a bit, but the rooms are furnished in a traditional style
and are well maintained, with a fireplace, leaded-glass windows, and wood paneling.
The best double, certainly the most spacious, is no. 1. Even the towel racks are heated
in the bathroom, a lovely comfort on a cold gray London morning. On the premises
is an attractive and old-fashioned lounge, the Victorian-style Bar and Buttery, where
you can order drinks, simple lunches, and veddy English dinners.

KENSINGTON
VERY EXPENSIVE

⊙ **Blake's Hotel.** 33 Roland Gardens, London SW7 3PF. ☎ **800/926-3173** or 0171/
370-6701. Fax 0171/373-0442. 51 units. MINIBAR TV TEL. £155–£300 ($248–$480) double;
from £476–£695 ($761.60–$1,112) suite. AE, DC, MC, V. Parking £30 ($48). Tube: South
Kensington or Gloucester Road.

This is one of the best small hotels of London. The opulent and highly individual creation of actress Anouska Hempel Weinberg, Blake's was created by converting a row
of Victorian town houses, with seemingly no expense spared. Here you'll find everything from the Empress Josephine's daybed to swagged draperies, Venetian glassware,
walls covered with cloth wallpaper, draped curtains, and sumptuous bedrooms. The
hotel's richly appointed lobby boasts British Raj-era furniture from India. The guest
rooms are individually decorated, some with antiques. Many are quite small, however;
go for a deluxe room if you can manage it. No-smoking rooms are available upon
request.

Dining: The hotel's stylish restaurant is one of the best in town. Neville Campbell's
cuisine blends the best of East and West, ranging from baked sea bass with a crispy
fennel skin to chicken and crab shaped like a large delectable Fabergé egg. With cuisine this fabulous, it's no wonder that reservations are strictly required.

Amenities: A concierge who can arrange anything; 24-hour room service; laundry;
baby-sitting.

INEXPENSIVE

⊙ **Abbey House.** 11 Vicarage Gate, London W8 4AG. ☎ **0171/727-2594.** 16 units, none
with bathroom. TV. £65 ($104) double; £78 ($124.80) triple; £90 ($144) quad. Rates include
English breakfast. No credit cards. Tube: Kensington High Street.

Some hotel critics have rated this the best B&B in London. Considering how well run
and well maintained it is, we give it top marks for value in this neighborhood. Thanks
to renovations, this hotel, which was built in about 1860 on a typical Victorian square,
is modern, although many of the original features have been retained. It's a family run
business, and the owners display a keen sense of dedication and hospitality. The spacious rooms have central heating, electrical outlets for shavers, vanity lights, and sinks.
The hotel offers shared baths, one for every two lodging units. The rooms are refurbished annually, although the decor may be too frilly for some.

Vicarage Private Hotel. 10 Vicarage Gate, London W8 4AG. ☎ **0171/229-4030.** Fax
0171/792-5989. 18 units, none with bathroom. £63 ($100.80) double; £80 ($128) triple; £88
($140.80) family room for 4. No credit cards. Rates include English breakfast. Tube: High
Street Kensington or Notting Hill Gate.

Eileen and Martin Diviney have a host of admirers on all continents. Their hotel is tops for old-fashioned English charm, affordable prices, and hospitality. This Victorian town house retains many of its original features, and lies on a residential garden square close to the shopping bargains of High Street Kensington, Knightsbridge, and Portobello Market. Furnished individually in a homey, English country-house style, rooms are suitable for singles, couples, or families up to four. Guests meet in a cozy sitting room for conversation or to watch the telly. In the morning a hearty English breakfast will await you. As a thoughtful extra, hot drinks are available 24 hours a day. If you want a hideaway, opt for the top floor aerie (no. 19).

SOUTH KENSINGTON
VERY EXPENSIVE

✪ **The Gore.** 189 Queen's Gate, London SW7 5EX. ☎ **800/637-7200** or 0171/584-6601. Fax 0171/589-8127. 54 units. MINIBAR TV TEL. £175–£255 ($280–$408) double; £280 ($448) the Tudor Room. AE, DC, MC, V. Tube: Gloucester Road.

Once owned by the marquess of Queensberry's family, The Gore has been a hotel since 1892. It's always been one of our favorites. Would-be Victorians feel at home here amid all the walnut and mahogany, antique English prints (there are some 4,000), and Oriental carpets. Yet the hotel's eccentricity is what draws most guests: The Venus Room, for example, has a bed once owned by Judy Garland. Every room is different, so find one that suits your personality. The dark-paneled Tudor Room is the most fascinating, with its gallery and wood-burning fireplace. A comfortable room here no longer costs the 50p it used to, that's for sure.

Dining: The Gore is also known for its Bistro 190, where renowned chef Antony Worrall Thompson crafts excellent meals. The fish dishes alone are worth the trip across town—try the marinated squid, the roast cod with twice-baked endive, or the steamed mussels with green curry.

The Pelham Hotel. 15 Cromwell Place, London, SW7 2LA. ☎ **0171/589-8288.** Fax 0171/584-8444. 52 units. A/C MINIBAR TV TEL. £175–£225 ($280–$360) double; from £350 ($560) suite. AE, MC, V. Tube: South Kensington.

This small, privately owned hotel is sure to please discerning travelers, and its location is ideal, close to the Victoria and Albert Museum, Hyde Park, and Harrods. Kit and Tim Kemp, hoteliers extraordinaire, preside over this stunningly decorated setting, formed from a row of early 19th-century terrace houses with a white portico facade. Returning guests are welcomed here like part of an extended family. In the drawing room, 18th-century paneling, high ceilings, and fine moldings create a suitable backdrop for a collection of antiques and Victorian art; needlepoint rugs and cushions evoke a homelike warmth, and an honor bar system completes the clublike atmosphere. The sumptuously decorated rooms are outfitted with eiderdown duvets, Oriental carpets, and unique oils—even the smallest room will have a handsome desk.

Dining: Kemps is one of the finest restaurants in South Kensington.

Amenities: Concierge; 24-hour room service.

EXPENSIVE

The Cranley. 10-12 Bina Gardens, London SW5 0LA. ☎ **800/553-2582** in the U.S., or 0171/373-0123. Fax 0171/373-9497. 39 units. A/C MINIBAR TV TEL. £140–£160 ($224–$256) double; £180–£220 ($288–$352) suite. AE, DC, MC, V. Tube: Gloucester Road.

This trio of adjacent 1875 town houses comprises one of the most charming hotels in South Kensington. The high-ceilinged guest rooms have enormous windows, much of the original plasterwork, a scattering of antiques, and plush upholstery; it all adds up to an old-fashioned ambience that feels like a private residence, not a hotel. The public rooms are like a stage set for an English country house. Ground-floor suites open onto a private terrace and have Jacuzzis. All but one of the guest rooms have tiny kitchenettes.

Dining: Light meals are served in a small café, and room service is available daily from 7am to 11pm.

Amenities: Guests are granted access to a nearby health club.

Number Sixteen. 16 Sumner Place, London SW7 3EG. ☎ **800/592-5387** or 0171/589-5232. Fax 0171/584-8615. 36 units, 34 with bathroom. MINIBAR TV TEL. £110.25 ($176.40) double without bathroom, £157.50–£189 ($252–$302.40) double with bathroom; £200 ($320) triple with bathroom. Rates include continental breakfast. AE, DC, MC, V. Parking £20 ($32). Tube: South Kensington.

This is an elegant and luxurious pension, composed of four early Victorian town houses linked to form a dramatically organized whole. The lovely front and rear gardens of each of the four houses are scrupulously maintained, making them one of the most idyllic spots on the street. The rooms are decorated with an eclectic mix of English antiques and modern paintings, although some look a little faded.

Amenities: There's an honor-system bar in the library. On chilly days, a fire roars in the flowery drawing room's fireplace, and guests linger there or in the library. Breakfast is served in the privacy of your room, and tea and coffee service is available from 7am to 10:30pm. You can also order breakfast in the conservatory or garden, with its burbling fountain and fish pond. Guests are also granted access to a nearby health club with a pool.

The Regency Hotel. 100 Queen's Gate, London SW7 5AG. ☎ **800/328-9898** or 0171/370-4595. Fax 0171/370-5555. 209 units. A/C MINIBAR TV TEL. £139 ($222.40) double; from £199–£235 ($318.40–$376) luxury suite for 2. AE, DC, MC, V. Tube: South Kensington.

The Regency, located close to museums, Kensington, and Knightsbridge, is actually six Victorian terrace houses that were converted into one stylish, seamless whole by an army of construction engineers and decorators. One of the building's main stairwells has what could be London's most unusual lighting fixture: five Empire chandeliers suspended vertically, one on top of the other. The modernized guest rooms are tasteful and elegant.

Dining: The Hotel's Pavilion Restaurant serves moderately priced international dishes.

Amenities: Services include 24-hour room service, laundry, and baby-sitting. At your disposal are the Regency Health Club (with steam rooms, minigym, saunas, and a sensory-deprivation tank) and a business center.

MODERATE

✪ **Aster House Hotel.** 3 Sumner Place, London SW7 3EE. ☎ **0171/581-5888.** Fax 0171/584-4925. 12 units. A/C MINIBAR TV TEL. £115–£145 ($184–$232) double. Rates include continental breakfast. MC, V. Tube: South Kensington.

The place is a charmer, especially for the price—you'd pay almost twice this much at other London choices for similar amenities. At the end of an early Victorian terrace built in 1848, Aster House is the epitome of discretion. There's not even a sign outside to indicate this is a hotel. Ring the bell and traverse a pink marble floor where you'll be welcomed by the staff. The owners, Rachel and Peter Carapiet, will give you your own front-door key. By now they've won so many awards they've lost count; prizes range from The Spencer Trophy for the best B&B in London to the London in Bloom Trophy for the floral displays in their garden in back (the only place you're allowed to smoke). Each room is individually decorated in the English country-house style, and, although many other properties do this better, the effect is warm, cozy, and inviting. The minuscule showers are a bit *too* cozy, however. Many rooms have four-poster, half-canopied beds along with silk wallpaper. A buffet is served in the glassed-in garden conservatory, L'Orangerie, where breakfasts are more health conscious than the usual hotel offering.

5 Sumner Place. 5 Sumner Place, London SW7 3EE. ☎ **0171/584-7586.** Fax 0171/823-9962. 14 units. MINIBAR TV TEL. £116–£130 ($185.60–$208) double. Rates include English breakfast. AE, MC, V. Tube: South Kensington.

This little charmer is an excellent choice. Completely restored to be classically English and elegant, it was a Victorian terrace house (ca. 1848), and today enjoys landmark status. The hotel has successfully recreated the flavor of its bygone era. An elevator services the five floors. After you register, you're given your own front-door key, and London is yours. The well-maintained rooms are tasteful, with traditional period furnishings, and a few have refrigerators. The staff has a certain grace, which is especially evident when they serve you breakfast in a Victorian-style conservatory.

Hotel 167. 167 Old Brompton Rd., London SW5 0AN. ☎ **0171/373-0672.** Fax 0171/373-3360. 19 units. MINIBAR TV TEL. £90–£99 ($148–$163.35) double. Rates include continental breakfast. AE, DC, MC, V. Tube: South Kensington or Gloucester Road.

Hotel 167 is one of the more fashionable guest houses in the area, attracting travelers in their 20s and 30s. It occupies a 3-story Victorian town house. The decor is quite stylish, with Scandinavian modern and Japanese accents. Each room is a comfortable medley of contemporary, antique, and art deco, with large modern paintings decorating the walls. The basement rooms have big windows. Guests who are at first unsure about being assigned a room in the basement often end up requesting the same room when they return because of its cozy feeling. The hotel attracts lots of businesspeople and journalists because of its central location. Owner-manager Frank Cheevers is helpful and friendly and is a font of information about London.

INEXPENSIVE

Aston's Budget Studios & Aston's Designer Studios & Suites. 39 Rosary Gardens, London SW7 4NQ. ☎ **800/525-2810** in the U.S., or 0171/370-0737. Fax 0171/835-1419. 76 studios and apts, 54 with bathroom. A/C TV TEL. Budget studios £76 ($121.60) double; £95 ($152) triple; £115 ($184) quad. Designer studios £105 ($168) double. Weekly rentals are preferred, but daily rentals are also accepted. MC, V. Tube: Gloucester Road.

An excellent buy! This carefully restored row of interconnected Victorian town-houses offers comfortably furnished studios and suites. Heavy oak doors and 18th-century hunting pictures give Aston's foyer a rich traditional atmosphere. Accommodations range in size from budget to designer suites. Regardless of its price, however, each unit has a compact but complete kitchenette concealed behind doors. The budget studios have fully serviced baths that you'll share with only a handful of other guests. The air-conditioned designer studios and two-room designer suites are decorated with rich fabrics and furnishings and contain marble bathrooms with private showers. Services include laundry, secretarial services, private message lines, fax machines, catering on request, car and limousine, and daily maid service in the designer studios and suites.

NOTTING HILL GATE
EXPENSIVE

The Abbey Court. 20 Pembridge Gardens, London W2 4DU. ☎ **0171/221-7518.** Fax 0171/792-0858. 25 units. TV TEL. £130–£145 ($208–$232) double or twin; £175 ($280) suite with 4-poster bed. AE, CB, MC, V. Tube: Notting Hill Gate.

The Abbey Court is a small and rather luxurious choice. Situated in a white-fronted mid-Victorian town house, it has a flowery patio in front and a conservatory in back where breakfast is served. You'll find fresh flowers in the reception area and the hallways. Each room offers carefully coordinated fabrics and fine antique furnishings. Italian-marbled bathrooms are equipped with Jacuzzi, shower, and heated towel rails. Light snacks and drinks are available from room service 24 hours a day. Kensington Gardens is a short walk away, as are the antique stores along Portobello Road.

The Portobello Hotel. 22 Stanley Gardens, London W11 2NG. ☎ **0171/727-2777.** Fax 0171/792-9641. 25 units. TV TEL. £135–£140 ($216–$224) double; £175–£210 ($280–$336) suite. Rates include continental breakfast. AE, DC, DISC, MC, V. Tube: Notting Hill Gate.

At this privately owned hotel on an elegant Victorian Terrace in Kensington, you can relive the Upstairs-Downstairs era. Mixing an eclectic medley of styles, two six-floor town houses from 1850 near the Portobello antique market were converted to form this quirky property, which doesn't please everybody, but has its fans. Frankly, we remember these rooms when they looked better, but even though they might be tattered here and there, they still have plenty of character. Whimsy and flamboyance went into their design. An elevator will take you to the third floor; after that, it's the stairs. Some of the cheaper accommodations are so tiny they're like top-floor garrets (some visitors find this romantic). Who knows what will show up in what nook? Perhaps a Chippendale, and most definitely a multinozzle claw-foot tub. You and your significant other might encounter a round bed tucked under a gauze canopy. Try for no. 16 with a full-tester bed facing the garden. Some rooms are air-conditioned. Service could be better.

   Amenities: A 24-hour bar and restaurant in the basement is a favorite on the night-owl circuit and also provides hotel room service. Laundry and secretarial services are available.

INEXPENSIVE

The Gate Hotel. 6 Portobello Rd., London W11 3DG. ☎ **0171/221-2403.** Fax 0171/221-9128. 6 units. MINIBAR TV. £65–£72 ($104–$115.20) double. Rates include continental breakfast. AE, DC, MC, V. Tube: Notting Hill Gate.

Perfect for antique hunters, this is the only hotel along the entire length of Portobello Road, and because of rigid zoning restrictions, it will probably remain the only hotel for many years to come. It has two cramped but cozy bedrooms on each of its three floors, plus a renovated breakfast room in the cellar. Bedrooms are color coordinated, with a bit of style, and have such amenities as a full-length mirror and a built-in wardrobe. Especially intriguing are the wall paintings that show what the Portobello Road market was like in its early days, when every character looked as if he or she came straight from the pages of a Dickens novel. Of course, be prepared for some very steep English stairs. The manager can direct you to the nearby antique markets and the attractions of Notting Hill Gate and Kensington Gardens, both of which lie within a 5-minute walk.

PADDINGTON & BAYSWATER
VERY EXPENSIVE

✪ **The Hempel.** Hempel Sq., 31-35 Craven Hill Gardens, London W2 3EA. ☎ **0171/298-9000.** Fax 0171/402-4666. 42 units. A/C MINIBAR TV TEL. £200–£225 ($320–$360) double; from £370 ($592) suite. AE, CB, DC, DISC, MC, V. Tube: Lancaster Gate.

This interconnected trio of nearly identical 19th-century row houses is the newest statement of flamboyant interior designer Anouska Hempel. Don't expect the swags, tassels, and labyrinthine elegance of her better-established hotel, Blake's; the feeling at The Hempel is radically different. It manages to combine a grand Italian sense of proportion with artful Zen simplicity—all designed for capitalists rich enough to afford it. The Hempel definitely caters to business travelers from around the world, most of whom appreciate the tactful service and undeniably snobbish overtones. Soothing monochromatic tones produced in both plaster and stone prevail. Throughout the hotel are carefully positioned mementos from Asia, including Thai bullocks carts that double as coffee tables. Enter a deliberately underfurnished lobby flanked by symmetrical fireplaces. Bedrooms continue with the consciously simple and elegantly spare motif, except for their carefully concealed battery of electronic gadgets: VCRs, CD players, twin phone lines, and modem hookups for laptops.

Dining: In the cellar is an innovative restaurant, I-Thai.

EXPENSIVE

Pembridge Court Hotel. 34 Pembridge Gardens, London W2 4DX. ☎ **0171/229-9977.** Fax 0171/724-4982. 20 units. TV TEL. £135–£175 ($216–$280) double. Rates include English breakfast. AE, DC, MC, V. Tube: Notting Hill Gate.

In an 1852 private Victorian home, this hotel presents an elegant cream-colored neoclassical facade to a residential Notting Hill Gate neighborhood that has grown increasingly fashionable. Avid antique hunters like its proximity to Portobello Road and its markets. Most guest rooms contain at least one antique, as well as 19th-century engravings and plenty of warm-toned floral fabrics. Some of the largest and most stylish rooms are on the top floor, with baths tiled in Italian marble. Three air-conditioned deluxe rooms, all with VCRs, overlook Portobello Road. Spencer and Churchill are the resident pair of ginger cats, two of the most adorable in London. Churchill likes the pop stars who stay at the hotel; Spencer tries to avoid them.

Dining: In the hotel's brick-lined restaurant, good French, Thai, and English food and drink, along with a well-chosen array of wines, is served. It's open for residents only, in the evening from 4 to 11pm.

Amenities: 24-hour room service; laundry; same-day dry cleaning; baby-sitting; car-rental agency; day membership in a nearby health club available.

MODERATE

Darlington Hyde Park. 111-117 Sussex Gardens, London W2 2RU. ☎ **0171/460-8800.** Fax 0171/460-8828. 45 units. TV TEL. £100 ($160) double; £110–£120 ($176–$192) suite. Rates include continental breakfast. AE, DC, MC, V. Tube: Paddington Station. Bus: 15.

It may not have a lot of flashy frills and services, but the price is right. This winning choice is a good value for central London. Rooms are in an updated Victorian style, tasteful and neatly decorated, albeit a bit short of flair. The maintenance is good, however, and a happy blend of business people and vacationers check in here. Five bedrooms are no-smoking. The hotel "restaurant" really isn't, serving breakfast only. A continental breakfast is generally the order of the day, although a full English breakfast, featuring the works, is also served. There is no bar, but guests are invited to BYOB and drink in the lounge. La Cuisine, a nearby modern European restaurant, provides room service. Laundry and dry cleaning are available, and a health club lies nearby.

Mornington Hotel. 12 Lancaster Gate, London W2 3LG. ☎ **800/528-1234** in the U.S., or 0171/262-7361. Fax 0171/706-1028. 66 units. TV TEL. £99–£140 ($158.40–$224) double. Rates include Scandinavian buffet breakfast. AE, CB, DC, MC, V. Tube: Lancaster Gate.

Affiliated with Best Western, the Mornington brings a touch of northern European hospitality to the center of London. Just north of Hyde Park and Kensington Gardens, the Hotel has a Victorian exterior and a Scandinavian-inspired decor. The hotel is close to Marble Arch, Oxford Street shopping, and the ethnic restaurants of Queensway. It's also convenient for strolling or jogging in Hyde Park. The recently renovated guest rooms are tastefully conceived and comfortable. You can wind down in the library, and order snacks or afternoon tea from the well-stocked bar. The staff is extremely helpful. Guest services include baby-sitting, dry cleaning, and laundry service.

INEXPENSIVE

Adare House. 153 Sussex Gardens, London W2 2RY. ☎ **0171/262-0633.** Fax 0171/ 706-1859. 16 units (10 with shower). TV. £58 ($92.80) double with shower. Rates include full English breakfast. No credit cards. Tube: Paddington.

This place still has a little soul, whereas so many of its neighbors along Sussex Gardens have lost theirs. You're welcomed by Anne O'Neill, who runs a good ship, and has done so exceedingly well for 25 years. The Adare still remains one of the best inexpensive choices in the host of B&Bs along Sussex Gardens. The property is well maintained and has been gradually improved over the years with the addition of private baths in admittedly cramped space. The public areas, although relatively modest, still have a touch of class, especially with their smart Regency-era striped wallpaper and red carpeting. Rooms, many quite small, are nevertheless spick-and-span and comfortably furnished, even if they're more down-home than glamorous. Accommodations contain beverage-makers, and those with private baths also have hair dryers.

NEAR HEATHROW

Sheraton Skyline. Bath Rd. A4, Hayes, Middlesex UB3 5BP. ☎ **800/325-3535** in the U.S., or 0181/759-2535. Fax 0181/750-9150. 356 units. A/C MINIBAR TV TEL. £180 ($288) double; from £400 ($640) suite. AE, DC, MC, V. Parking £4 ($6.40) per day for hotel guests. Bus: 111 or 285 from the airport.

The Sheraton Skyline, something of a miniature village, has consistently been voted the world's best airport hotel. It's designed around an atrium where tropical plants and towering palms thrive beneath a translucent roof. The foundations of a cabana bar are set into the temperature-controlled waters of a pool. Each guest room sports a color TV with in-house pay-per-view and free movie channels and a massage-style shower.

Dining: A fireplace flickers late into the night in the Edwardian Colony Bar and in the adjacent well-upholstered restaurant, the Colony Room, where well-prepared food is served beneath massive ceiling timbers and heavy brass chandeliers. A French cafe offers light meals and full buffet breakfasts. The Sports Bar serves drinks in a casual atmosphere.

Amenities: 24-hour room service; shuttle service to and from four terminals at Heathrow (running every 5 minutes between 6am and 11pm), and confirmation of flight departures; baby-sitting; dry cleaning/laundry; concierge; secretarial services; fitness center; heated pool; business center.

The Swan. The Hythe, Staines, Middlesex TW18 3JB. ☎ **0178/445-2494.** Fax 0178/ 446-1593. 12 units, 6 with bathroom. TV TEL. £59 ($94.40) double without bathroom, £81 ($129.60) double with bathroom; £90 ($144) suite. Rates include English breakfast. AE, DC, MC, V. Tube: Heathrow, then taxi.

Dating back beyond the days of Samuel Pepys, The Swan is on the south bank of the Thames, beside Staines Bridge, and is within easy access of Heathrow (15 min.). Rooms have central heating and beverage-makers. The attractive old inn also has a reputation for good food ranging from bar snacks to traditional English "fayre." The food is served in a gazebo-style dining room, featuring wholesome cooking. If you're

just arriving in London, this preservation area might be a good introduction to the city's history before you go into the center. The Hythe was in existence by the late 7th century, established as a port on a curve of the river. A bridge in time linked it to the town of Staines across the river. Staines was an important Roman settlement, and many surviving buildings in the area date from the 17th century.

NEAR GATWICK

Brooklyn Manor Hotel. Bonnetts Lane, Ifield, Crawley, W. Sussex RH11 0NY. ☎ **01293/546024.** Fax 01293/510366. 11 units, 4 with bathroom. £35 ($56) double without bathroom, £45 ($72) double with bathroom. AE, MC, V. Bus C5 (Crawley/Ifield).

Brooklyn Manor is an old, well-cared-for Victorian house set on 5 acres of English countryside, only 5 minutes from Gatwick. The hotel provides free transportation to and from the airport—just call when you arrive and someone will come and fetch you. Martin Davis rents rooms with full central heating and beverage-makers. Breakfast costs extra, and you can order a light snack in the evening. In addition, a free courtesy service takes guests to and from a nearby restaurant, and there are two pubs within about a 10-minute walk, both of which serve inexpensive meals. The hotel doesn't have a bar, but it is licensed, so you can have drinks in the lounge if you wish.

Gatwick Hilton International Hotel. South Terminal, Gatwick Airport, Gatwick, W. Sussex RH6 0LL. ☎ **800/HILTONS** in the U.S., or 01293/518080. Fax 01293/528980. 567 units. A/C TV TEL. £195–£217 ($312–$347.20) double; from £250 ($400) suite. AE, DC, MC, V. Parking £4.95 ($7.90).

This deluxe five-floor hotel is linked to the airport terminal by a covered walkway; an electric buggy service transports people back and forth. The most impressive part of the hotel is the first-floor lobby; its glass-covered portico rises four floors and contains a scale replica of the de Havilland Gipsy Moth airplane *Jason*, used by Amy Johnson on her solo flight from England to Australia in 1930. The reception desk is nearby, in an area with a lobby bar and lots of greenery. Well-furnished rooms are equipped with soundproofing, triple-glazed windows, and tea- and coffeemakers. Recently, 123 of the rooms were refurbished, in addition to the executive floor and all of their junior suites. Three hundred of the rooms now have minibars, stocked upon request.

Dining/Diversions: The American-themed restaurant, Amy's, serves buffet breakfasts, lunches, and dinners. The Garden Restaurant, outfitted in a formal English garden theme, offers drinks and full meals. There's also the Lobby Bar, open 24 hours a day, plus a watering hole with a polo-playing theme, aptly named the Jockey Bar.

Amenities: 24-hour room service; same-day laundry/dry cleaning; up-to-date flight information channel; hairdresser; bank; concierge; newspapers; baby-sitting; secretarial services; health club (with sauna, steam room, massage room, swimming pool, gymnasium); Jacuzzi; business center; shopping arcade.

4 Dining

"You don't go to London for the cuisine," said a character in a forgotten 1937 novel. Another author, W. Somerset Maugham, claimed, "If you want to eat well in England, have three breakfasts a day." But that's no longer true.

London has been swept by a restaurant revolution. Some critics are now claiming you can dine better in today's London than in Paris, although that point is arguable. Even the once-lowly pub, notorious for its "pub grub," has entered the culinary sweepstakes. Believe the unthinkable: At certain pubs, you can now dine better than in many standard restaurants.

Central London Dining

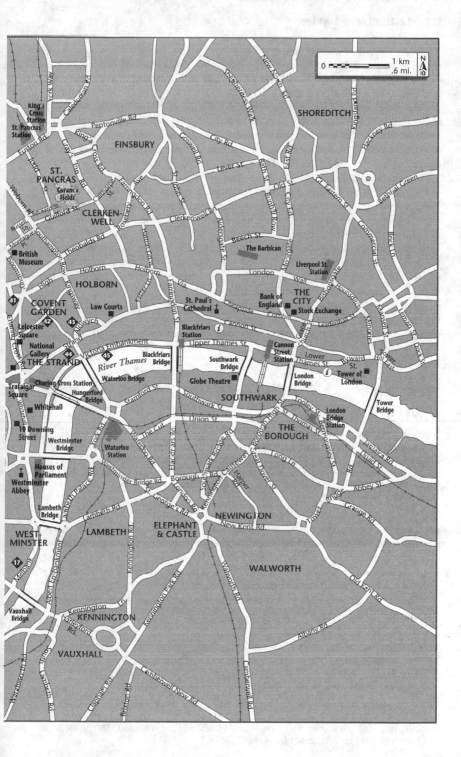

0 — 1 km
.6 mi.

N

King's Cross Station
St. Pancras Station

SHOREDITCH

York Way
Caledonian Rd.
Pentonville Rd.
King's Cross Rd.
Euston Rd.
Gray's Inn Rd.
Grays Inn Rd.
City Rd.
Goswell Rd.

FINSBURY

ST. PANCRAS

Coram's Fields
Lever St.

Woburn Pl.
Bernard St.
Clifford St.
Russell Sq.
Montague Pl.
Southampton Row
Theobalds Rd.

Catherine St.
Farringdon Rd.

CLERKEN-WELL

Clerkenwell Rd.

Bath St.
East Rd.
New North Rd.

Gt. Eastern St.

Hackney Rd.

Bethnal Green

Kingsland Rd.
Commercial St.
Brick Ln.

British Museum

HOLBORN

Holborn
Holborn Via.

London Wall

Beech St.

The Barbican

Aldersgate St.
Moorgate

Liverpool St. Station

Bloomsbury
High
Kingsway
Gray's Inn Rd.

COVENT GARDEN

Law Courts

St. Paul's Cathedral

THE CITY

Bank of England

Bishopsgate
Houndsditch
Leadenhall
Minories
Fenchurch St.
Dock St.

Leicester Square

National Gallery

THE STRAND

Aldwych
Strand

Victoria Embankment

Fleet St.
Farringdon St.

Cheapside
Cornhill

Blackfriars Station

Cannon St.

Stock Exchange

Cannon Street Station

Upper Thames St.
Lower Thames St.

Byward St.

Tower Hill East

Trafalgar Square

Charing Cross Station

Hungerford Bridge

Blackfriars Bridge

River Thames

Waterloo Bridge

Southwark Bridge

Globe Theatre

London Bridge

Tower of London

Tower Hill

Whitehall

Stamford St.

Southwark St.

SOUTHWARK

London Bridge Station

Tower Bridge

10 Downing Street

Westminster Bridge

The Cut

Union St.

THE BOROUGH

Tooley St.
St. Thomas St.

Jamaica Rd.
Druid St.

Waterloo Station

Blackfriars Rd.

Borough High St.
Great Dover St.
Long Ln.

Abbey St.

Houses of Parliament

Westminster Abbey

Borough Rd.

London Rd.

Harper

Tower Bridge Rd.

Grange Rd.

Lambeth Bridge

Westminster Bridge Rd.

Lambeth Palace Rd.

St. George's Rd.

Kennington Rd.

NEWINGTON

New Kent Rd.

Old Kent Rd.

WEST MINSTER

LAMBETH

ELEPHANT & CASTLE

WALWORTH

Millbank

Kennington Park Rd.
Kennington Rd.

Walworth Rd.

Vauxhall Bridge

Kennington

Hereford Rd.

KENNINGTON

Albert Embankment

Albany Rd.

Camberwell New Rd.

VAUXHALL

Clapham Rd.
Brixton Rd.

Camberwell Rd.

113

Culinary peacocks like Sir Terence Conran and Marco Pierre White now enjoy a status once the privilege of film stars. The restaurant scene is hip and happening, but we've also tried to strike a balance between the chic and celebrated and the undiscovered bistro serving good food at reasonable prices.

On a darker note, many personality chefs spend a lot more time writing cookbooks and making TV appearances than they do cooking in their own kitchens. Many of the more celebrated chefs seem to open a restaurant only for the publicity these days. As soon as the newspaper and magazine feeding frenzy at one place is over, they are off to another enterprise—and more publicity. That chef you've read about in *Condé Nast Traveler* or *Travel & Leisure* may not be around when you get here. But never fear: He or she may have been replaced with an up-and-coming star who's even better, or at least spends more time shopping and preparing ingredients than demonstrating how to cook on the telly. And many restaurants are becoming so mammoth that the identity of the chef is irrelevant anyway.

Despite this ongoing game of culinary musical chairs, London has become one of the great food capitals of the world. Chefs have pioneered the new style of cooking called "Modern British," as they prepare remarkable and inventive English dishes by making use of the very fresh produce available in the country.

If you want to splurge in a big way, the very top restaurants in London rank among the best anywhere. But you'll also find many more moderately priced and inexpensive choices. Among these are pubs, which we've listed separately below (there are even more choices listed in chapter 5).

Important note: The prices below include a 17.5% value-added tax (VAT). Most restaurants add a 10% to 15% service charge to your bill. Look at your check to make sure of that. If nothing has been added, leave a 12% to 15% tip.

MAYFAIR
VERY EXPENSIVE

✪ **Chez Nico at Ninety Park Lane.** 90 Park Lane, W1. ☎ **0171/409-1290.** Reservations required (2 days in advance for lunch, 7 days for dinner). Fixed-price lunch £32 ($51.20) for 3 courses; à la carte dinner £50 ($80) for 2 courses, £62 ($99.20) for 3 courses. AE, DC, MC, V. Mon–Fri noon–2pm; Mon–Sat 7–11pm. Closed 10 days around Christmas/New Year's. Tube: Marble Arch. FRENCH.

The setting is as opulent as the cuisine, but nothing takes precedence over the food produced by one of London's supreme culinary artists, the temperamental but always amusing Chef Nico Ladenis. This former oil-company executive, self-taught cook, and economist remains one of the most talked about chefs of Great Britain, and his food is always impressive, always stylish. In fact, he constantly seems to be reinventing dishes we thought he had already perfected.

Who can top his quail salad with sweetbreads, flavored with an almond vinaigrette? Another intriguing appetizer is a paupiette of marinated salmon accompanied by salmon mousse and lightly coated with a gazpacho sauce. The main courses continue to be a tour de force of culinary skill. With great mastery of technique, Nico's chefs dazzle with ever-changing offerings that always include the signature prawn ravioli. The cookery remains in the best postnouvelle tradition, in which the tenets of classical cuisine are creatively and flexibly adapted to local fresh ingredients.

✪ **Le Gavroche.** 43 Upper Brook St., W1. ☎ **0171/408-0881.** Reservations required, as far in advance as possible. Main courses £27.50–£70 ($44–$112); fixed-price lunch £40 ($64); *menu exceptionnel* (tasting menu) for entire party £85 ($136) per person. AE, MC, V. Mon–Fri noon–2pm and 7–11pm. Tube: Marble Arch. FRENCH.

Le Gavroche has long stood for quality French cuisine. We think it might be England's finest (although Michelin gives it only two stars). Service is faultless, and the ambience is chic and formal without being stuffy.

The menu changes constantly, depending on what fresh produce is available and the current inspiration of the chef. But it remains classically French, although we don't agree that it's the "essentially old-fashioned bourgeois repertoire" that some critics suggest. But there are signature dishes that have been honed over years of unswerving practice. Try, if featured, the soufflé Suissesse, *papillote* of smoked salmon, or *tournedos gratinés aux poivres.* Desserts are sublime, ranging from a *sablé* of pears and chocolate to an omelette Rothschild. The wine cellar is among the most interesting in London.

The fixed-price menu has been recently replaced with the *menu exceptionnel,* a tasting menu for everyone at the table. The menu usually consists of four to five smaller courses, followed by one or two desserts and coffee. At £85 ($136) per person, this may be a smarter way to go than ordering à la carte.

✪ **Nobu.** In the Metropolitan Hotel, 19 Old Park Lane, W1. ☎ **0171447-4747.** Reservations required. Main courses £14.50–£27.50 ($23.20–$44); sushi and sashimi £2.75–£4.75 ($4.40–$7.60) per piece; fixed-price menu £60 ($96). AE, DC, MC, V. Mon–Fri noon–2:15pm, Mon–Sat 6–10:30pm. Tube: Hyde Park or Green Park. JAPANESE.

Robert de Niro and his restaurant gang of Nobu Matsuhisa and Drew Nieporent have taken their trendy New York hot spot to London, where they offer wildly innovative cuisine. With a beauty like Isabella Rossellini claiming that eating at Nobu keeps her lean and mean, how can you go wrong here?

The kitchen staff is brilliant and as finely tuned as their New York cousins. Those on the see-and-be-seen circuit don't seem to mind the high prices that go with these gastronomic pyrotechnics. Where else but at Nobu can you find a good sea urchin tempura? Salmon tartare with caviar is a brilliant appetizer (Madonna agrees). Follow with a perfectly done fillet of sea bass in a sour bean paste or soft-shell crab rolls. The squid pasta is sublime, as is the black cod with miso. Cold sake arrives in a green bamboo pitcher.

✪ **The Oak Room/Marco Pierre White.** In Le Meridien Piccadilly, 21 Piccadilly, W1. ☎ **0171/734-8000.** Reservations required as far in advance as possible. Fixed-price lunch £29.50 ($47.20); fixed-price menu gourmand £75 ($120). AE, MC, V. Mon–Fri noon–2:15pm; Mon–Sat 7–11:15pm. Closed Christmas. Tube: Piccadilly Circus. MODERN BRITISH.

Put simply, Marco Pierre White is the best chef in London. He no longer operates out of the Hyde Park Hotel, but has moved to the more glamorous surroundings of Le Meridien. You not only get some of London's finest cuisine here, but the setting alone is almost worth the trip—this is one of the city's most beautiful dining rooms, and it's been restored to its original oak and gilt splendor. Not only that, but Monsieur White has filled the room with art, including works by Cocteau and Chagall.

Creative, sophisticated, and bold, this daring young chef claims he never apprenticed in France, other than 2 weeks of eating in Paris restaurants. Lavish and luxurious in his choice of ingredients, White explores the depths of flavor in food. As you peruse the dozen or so appetizers, you'll note that most of them feature foie gras, caviar, and truffles. After those tantalizing appetizers, you can proceed to such main courses as Bressole of Bresse pigeon (with foie gras again), or braised pig's trotter inspired by Pierre Koffmann's masterpiece at La Tante Claire in Chelsea. Platters sometimes appear with brilliant colors, including a gratinée of brill with a soft herb crust, young spinach, and a sabayon of chives. In spite of all this fancy fare, Marco Pierre White makes the world's greatest mashed potatoes. One diner hailed their virtuosity and technical accomplishment, declaring they've been "sieved, pureed, and squeezed through silk stockings." White vies with Chef Nico Ladenis as the most temperamental in London, but he's clearly a magician. If you can afford it, try to catch his show.

EXPENSIVE

Quaglino's. 16 Bury St., SW1. ☎ **0171/930-6767.** Reservations recommended. Main courses £12–£26 ($19.20–$41.60). Fixed-price 3-course menu (available only at lunch and pretheater dinner between 5:30 and 6:30pm) £15.50 ($24.80) for 2 courses, £19.50 ($31.20) for 3 courses. AE, DC, MC, V. Daily noon–3pm; Mon–Thurs 5:30pm–midnight, Fri–Sat 5:30pm–1am, Sun 5:30pm–11pm. Tube: Green Park. MODERN EUROPEAN.

It's vast, it's convivial, and it's definitely fun. Sir Terence Conran, noted design guru, worked his magic with the funky decor—eight different artists decorated the octet of massive columns that support the soaring ceiling. There's a mezzanine with a bar featuring live jazz every Friday and Saturday night, and a pianist the rest of the week. The place attracts yuppies, an occasional royal head, and glitterati from the performing arts. An "altar" at the restaurant's back is devoted to an impressive display of crustaceans and shellfish.

Dishes have been criticized for their quick and standard preparation. Everything seems to be served in bowls. But considering how busy it is, the marvel is that the place functions as well as it does. So come for fun, not for culinary finesse. Dishes include goat cheese and caramelized onion tart; tartlet of crab with saffron; seared salmon with potato pancakes; and grilled rabbit with herb jus, roast cod and ox cheek, and charcoal-grilled vegetables.

MODERATE

The Greenhouse. 27A Hays Mews, W1. ☎ **0771/499-3331.** Reservations required. Main courses £9.50–£18.50 ($15.20–$29.60). AE, DC, MC, V. Mon–Fri noon–2:30pm, Sun 12:30–2:30pm; Mon–Sat 6:30–11pm, Sun 6:30–10:30pm. Closed Christmas, bank holidays. Tube: Green Park. MODERN BRITISH.

A covered walkway provides entrance to this comfortably appointed room, with prints and dried flowers enhancing the decor. The kitchen uses the finest of fresh ingredients. Chef Graham Grafton isn't afraid to offer that Brit favorite, deep-fried cod-and-chips, although the version here is far more exciting than what you'd find at any local chippie. If his poached skate is any example, we're sure he has a winning way with fish. But you may prefer his lip-smacking fare from the heart of England, especially a roast breast of pheasant that would have kept Henry VIII from beheading the chef, and most definitely grilled farmhouse pork or warm smoked eel with bacon and new potatoes. Some of the delightfully sticky desserts would have pleased your Midlands grandma: a moist bread-and-butter pudding or else a ginger pudding with orange marmalade.

Kai Mayfair. 65 S. Audley St., W1. ☎ **0171/493-8988.** Reservations recommended. Main courses £9–£12 ($14.40–$19.20). AE, DC, MC, V. Mon–Fri noon–2:15pm, Sat–Sun 12:30–3pm; Mon–Sat 6:30–10:45pm, Sun 6:30–10:30pm. Tube: Marble Arch or Hyde Park Corner. CHINESE.

London is filled with sterile Chinese eateries, using recipes that didn't transport well from the Far East. Not this winning dining room, one of the glitziest Chinese restaurants in town, lying near the American Embassy. The menu promises dishes that have such fanciful categories as "The Whims and Fancies of the Empress" or "Buddha Jumps Over the Wall." The tried-and-true Chinese dishes are here, but many other dishes show more imagination and flair, especially shark's fin and abalone. Some of the fish dishes, especially the Dover sole, lobster noodles, and turbot, are award winning.

Bang-bang chicken in a nut sauce packs a powerful taste punch. Children are especially catered to, with dishes prepared just for them.

INEXPENSIVE

Hard Rock Cafe. 150 Old Park Lane, W1. ☎ **0171/629-0382.** Reservations not accepted. Main dishes £8.50–£15 ($13.60–$24). AE, MC, V. Sun–Thurs 11:30am–12:30am, Fri–Sat 11:30am–1am. Closed Dec 25–26. Tube: Green Park or Hyde Park Corner. AMERICAN.

There's always a line at this outpost of the popular rock 'n' roll restaurant chain. This down-home American roadside-style diner serves pretty good food at reasonable prices. Portions are generous; service is friendly. The tempting dessert menu includes homemade apple pie and thick, cold shakes.

Zen Central. 20-22 Queen St., W1. ☎ **0171/629-8103.** Reservations recommended. Daily 12:15–2:30pm; Mon–Sat 6:30–11:30pm, Sun 6:30–11pm. Main courses £10–£15.50 ($16–$24.80). AE, DC, MC, V. Tube: Green Park. SZECHUAN.

Movie stars always seem to have an advance scouting party informing them of the best places to dine when they visit a foreign city. When we heard that Tom Cruise was heading here for Szechuan cuisine, we followed in his footsteps. And whoever sent him was right. We didn't spot any stars, but found a designer chic Mayfair restaurant with a cool decor in minimalist black and white. Mirrors cover much of the place (maybe that's why movie stars like it). Served by a competent staff, the cuisine is first rate. Start with the coriander and crab meat croquettes, or the soft-shell crabs tenderly cooked in a crust of salt. The steamed sea bass is perfectly cooked and, for extra flavor, served with a black bean sauce. Pork chops with lemon grass has a Thai flavor, and the baked lobster with crushed roast garlic and livers of tangerine peel is worth the walk across Mayfair.

ST. JAMES'S

Suntory. 72-73 St. James's St., SW1. ☎ **0171/409-0201.** Reservations required. Main courses £18.20–£40.30 ($29.10–$64.50); set lunch £13.50–£38 ($21.60–$60.80), fixed-price dinner £49.80–£69.40 ($79.70–$111.05). AE, DC, MC, V. Mon–Sat noon–2pm and 6–10pm. Tube: Green Park. JAPANESE.

Owned and operated by the Japanese distiller and brewer, Suntory is one of London's most elite, expensive, and best Japanese restaurants. Most first-time visitors prefer the Teppanyaki Dining Room downstairs, where iron grills are set in each table and you watch the masterful skills of the high-hatted chef, who is quite comfortable with a knife. You can also dine in other rooms on sukiyaki, tempura, or sushi. Waitresses in traditional dress serve you. Appetizers are artful and delicate, and even the tea is superior.

PICCADILLY & LEICESTER SQUARE
VERY EXPENSIVE

L'Odeon. 65 Regent St., W1. ☎ **0171/287-1400.** Reservations required. Main courses £14.50–£26 ($23.20–$41.60). AE, DC, MC, V. Daily noon–2:30pm; Mon–Sat 5:30–11:30pm. Tube: Piccadilly Circus. CONTINENTAL.

One of London's fancier brasseries is done up like a chic 1930s restaurant. When the Michelin-starred chef Bruno Loubet opened this place, headlines read "Loubet cooks for the masses." The sous-chef, Anthony Demetre, now carries on in Loubet's tradition, following his departure. But the menu remains rooted in the Loubet repertoire, with innovative new additions. Many diners opt for a table opening onto Regent Street with its bright red double-deckers heading for Piccadilly Circus. In all, some 220 diners can pack this place (and often do).

The white linens and place settings are kept very simple, but not the food. The chef roams the world for inspiration—a bit of the continent here, a bow to California here, a touch of the Far East, and so on. Starters include roast scallops on black pudding with mashed potatoes and a garlic coulis. For a main course, try the roast Hereford duck breast with beetroot and rhubarb marmalade or the firm red mullet with cannelloni, which is bliss on a plate. The hot apple tart with an "alcoholic" Calvados ice cream is a creamy treat.

Wiltons. 55 Jermyn St., SW1. ☎ **0171/629-9955.** Reservations required. Jacket and tie required for men. Main courses £15–£25 ($24–$40). AE, DC, MC, V. Sun–Fri 12:30–2:30pm and 6–10:30pm. Tube: Green Park or Piccadilly Circus. BRITISH.

Wiltons is as thoroughly British as a nanny. Its menu is known for fish and game. You might begin with an oyster cocktail and follow with Dover sole, plaice, salmon, or lobster, prepared in any number of ways. In season (beginning mid-August), you can enjoy such delights as roast partridge, roast pheasant, or roast grouse. The chef might ask you if you want them "blue" or "black," a reference to roasting times. Game is often accompanied by bread sauce (made of milk thickened with bread crumbs). To finish, order a savory such as Welsh rarebit or soft roes or even anchovies, but if that's too much, try the sherry trifle or syllabub.

The restaurant has what we consistently find to be the most sensitive serving staff in the West End. Since this is a bastion of old-school ties and the like, don your oldest suit and look like you believe the Empire still exists.

EXPENSIVE TO MODERATE

Atlantic Bar & Grill. 20 Glasshouse St., W1. ☎ **0171/734-4888.** Reservations required. Main courses £10.50–£18 ($16.80–$28.80); fixed-price lunch £14.90 ($23.85), including 2 glasses of wine. AE, MC, V. Mon–Fri noon–3pm; Mon–Sat 6pm–3am, Sun 6–10:30pm. Tube: Piccadilly Circus. MODERN BRITISH/MODERN EUROPEAN.

A titanic place installed in a former art deco ballroom off Piccadilly Circus, this 160-set restaurant was white-hot when it opened in 1994 as "restaurant of the year." It's not that trendy anymore, but that's because of the fickle whims of London foodies more than the quality of the food, which we still find to be quite good.

The original chef, Richard Sawyer, is serving his second tour of duty here, in hopes of regaining the restaurant's former buzz. Even American cuisine comes into focus here, with such dishes as grilled tuna on mashed black beans with seared tomatoes, spiced avocado, and corn chips—the best this side of Santa Fe. The menu changes every 2 months, but is always strong on seafood. The panfried skate wing stuffed with black olive puree is a delight worth keeping on the menu. The desserts are nursery room favorites perhaps best left there. (Remember rice pudding?)

If you're rushed, you can drop into Dick's Bar for a quick dinner; it serves everything from lamb burgers sparked with yogurt and fresh mint to Cashel blue cheese and pumpkin seeds on ciabatta bread.

Coast. 26B Albemarle St., W1X 3FA. ☎ **0171/495-5999.** Reservations required. Main courses £10.50–£21.50 ($16.80–$34.40). AE, MC, V. Mon–Sat noon–3pm and 6pm–midnight, Sun noon–3:30pm and 6–11pm. Tube: Piccadilly Circus. MODERN INTERNATIONAL.

It's so cutting-edge that perhaps it struggles and strains a bit to maintain its superhip image. Set within a former automobile showroom, with lots of parquet woodwork, it's painted in spring green with lighting fixtures that protrude like aliens' bug-eyes from their settings. The main decorative feature is an electronic sculpture by fashionable artist Angela Bulloch. Using motion-sensitive lasers, this drawing machine uses a robot-style metallic arm to scribble graphs on an electronic screen that's periodically wiped clean. It's just another accessory that keeps the restaurant's publicity machines coasting along.

The food is as eclectic and international as you'd expect. Chef Stephen Terry is an original, truly innovative (some say too innovative). Textures are well handled, and flavor is paramount, especially in the lightness of the cuisine and the fish dishes. To get you going, Terry tempts with his pressed terrine of quail, panfried foie gras, celeriac, and prunes, or else his papardelle pasta with roasted chestnut velouté and Perigord truffles. Then it's on to monkfish tail osso buco with dried orange zest and roasted mirepoix, or else roast duck breast on Asian greens with pappadom and Thai red curry.

The Criterion Brasserie–Marco Pierre White. 224 Piccadilly, W1. ☎ **0171/930-0488.** Main courses £11.50–£15 ($18.40–$24); £14.95 ($23.90) fixed-price 2-course lunch, £17.95 ($28.70) fixed-price 3-course lunch. AE, MC, V. Daily noon–2:30pm and 6pm–midnight. Tube: Piccadilly Circus. MODERN BRITISH.

The bad boy of British cookery, Michelin-starred Marco Pierre White runs what he calls his "junior" restaurant here. Before he took over, the Criterion was already a London legend, having been designed by Thomas Verity in the 1870s. It knew its greatest fame in World War II when it was the site of tea dances. Now this palatial neo-Byzantine mirrored marble hall is now a glamorous backdrop for the master chef's cuisine, served under a golden ceiling, with peacock-blue theater-size draperies.

The menu is wide-ranging, served by a mainly French staff. The cuisine ranges from Paris brasserie food to "nouvelle-classical." The food is excellent, even if it doesn't soar to the sublime. Start with squid-ink risotto with roast calamari before going on to such dishes as escalope of cod with a soft parsley crust, a chive sabayon, and buttered noodles. The roast skate wing with deep-fried snails is especially delectable, as is the roast saddle of lamb stuffed with mushrooms and spinach.

Greens Restaurant and Oyster Bar. 36 Duke St., SW1. ☎ **0171/930-4566.** Reservations recommended for dinner. Main courses £9.50–£35 ($15.20–$56). AE, DC, MC, V. Restaurant daily 12:30–3pm; Mon–Sat 6–11pm. Oyster bar Mon–Sat 11:30am–3pm and 5:30–11pm, Sun noon–3pm. Tube: Piccadilly Circus or Green Park. SEAFOOD.

The excellent menu, charming staff, and central location make this a good, if traditional, choice. It's a tried-and-true favorite. This busy place has a cluttered entrance leading to a crowded bar where you can stand at what the English call "rat-cat counters," to sip fine wines and, from September through April, enjoy oysters.

In the dining room, you can select from a long menu ranging from fish cakes with roast pepper and tomato sauce to whole Scottish lobster. For zesty starters, try either the smoked eel filets if you're going Cockney, or the avocado and bacon salad with baby leaf spinach if you're dining more trendy.

Momo. 25 Heddon St., W1. ☎ **0171/434-4040.** Reservations required 2 weeks in advance. Main courses £10.50–£15.50 ($16.80–$24.80); 2-course fixed-price lunch £12.50 ($20); 3-course fixed-price lunch £15.50 ($24.80). AE, DC, MC, V. Tube: Piccadilly Circus. MOROCCAN/NORTH AFRICAN.

You'll be greeted by a friendly and casual staff member clad in black and white T-shirts and fatigue pants. The setting is like something in Marrakech, with stucco walls, a wood and stone floor, patterned wood window shades, burning candles, and cozy banquettes. You can practically fill up on the freshly baked bread the waiter brings along with complimentary hors d'oeuvres such as garlicky marinated olives and pickled carrots spiced with pepper and cumin. Among the tantalizing appetizers are the *briouants*, paper-thin and very crisp triangular packets of puffed pastry filled with saffron-flavored chicken and other treats.

A Moroccan salad appears, a medley of highly spiced onions, cubed peppers, toma-toes, and cucumbers. One of the chef's finest specialties is pastilla au pigeon, a tradi-tional poultry pie with almonds. Lamb with artichokes is another winning selection. Tagine comes with chunks of lamb, dates, and prunes—all the flavors of the Sahara. Many diners visit only for the couscous, and it's among the best in London. The cous-cous maison comes in a decorative pot on which the lid is lifted to tantalize you with various aromas. This dish of raisins, meats (including merguez sausage), chicken, lamb, and chickpeas is given added flavor with that powerful hot sauce of the Middle East, marissa.

SOHO
VERY EXPENSIVE

Gay Hussar. 2 Greek St., W1. ☎ **0171/437-0973.** Reservations recommended. Main courses £20–£25 ($32–$40); fixed-price lunch £16 ($25.60). AE, DC, MC, V. Mon–Sat 12:15–2:30pm and 5:30–10:45pm. Tube: Tottenham Court Road. HUNGARIAN.

The Gay Hussar has been called the best Hungarian restaurant in the world. It's an intimate place, where diners can begin with a chilled wild-cherry soup or smoked Hungarian sausage. Gutsy main courses might include cabbage stuffed with minced veal and rice, half a perfectly done chicken in mild paprika sauce with cucumber salad and noodles, excellent roast duck with red cabbage and Hungarian-style caraway pota-toes, and, of course, veal goulash with egg dumplings. Expect gigantic portions. The dishes remain undeniably authentic, the sort of cookery you'd expect if grandma came from Budapest. Everything tastes better when washed down with Hungarian Bull's Blood.

Quo Vadis. 26-29 Dean St., W1. ☎ **0171/437-9585.** Reservations required. Main courses £13–£26 ($20.80–$41.60); set lunches £14.95–£17.95 ($23.90–$28.70). AE, MC, V. Mon–Fri noon–3pm; Mon–Sat 6–11pm, Sun 6–10:30pm. Tube: Leicester Square or Tottenham Court Road. MODERN BRITISH.

This hyper-trendy restaurant occupies the former apartment house where Communist patriarch Karl Marx lived between 1851 and 1856. He'd never recognize this stylish ode to cutting-edge art today. Many rubberneckers bypass the restaurant altogether and head upstairs to the bar. Here the controversial Damien Hirst, the same artist whose cow carcasses in formaldehyde wowed the London art scene in the early 1990s, has positioned a severed cow's head and a severed bull's head in separate aquariums filled with preservatives. A satirical ode to the destructive effects of mad-cow disease? A tongue-in-cheek commentary on the upscale meat-market atmosphere of the bar itself? Whatever the piece's intended meaning, it's certainly a conversation starter. And downstairs in the street-level dining room, dozens of avant-garde paintings donated either by Damien Hirst or his artistic cohorts are showcased.

Although the restaurant is associated with culinary superstar Marco Pierre White, don't expect this temperamental chef to personally garnish your plate. He's only a con-sultant to the executive chef; Tim Payne and Lawrence Keyo have day-to-day respon-sibility for the kitchen. Also, the harassed and overburdened staff may not have the time to pamper you or your ego. Be assured of one thing, though: This is one of the flashiest restaurants of the moment in London. The food? Not nearly as artful or inno-vative as the floods of recent publicity might lead you to believe. Although competent and highly appealing, the cuisine is only secondary to the hip decor and clientele. Begin with a mussel-and-saffron soup before proceeding to the sage-scented roast rabbit with a tomato confit and ratatouille.

EXPENSIVE

✪ Alastair Little. 49 Frith St., W1. ☎ **0171/734-5183.** Reservations recommended. Fixed-price dinner £30 ($48); fixed-price lunch £25 ($40). AE, MC, V. Mon–Fri noon–3pm; Mon–Sat 6–11pm. Tube: Leicester Square or Tottenham Court Road. BRITISH.

In a circa-1830 brick-fronted town house (which supposedly housed John Constable's art studio for a brief period), this pleasant restaurant is an informal and cozy place. Some loyal fans claim that Alastair Little is still the best chef in London, though he's been buried under the avalanche of new talent of late. (Actually, he's not here a lot, as he divides his time between his other enterprises and a cooking school in Umbria.) The talented Jonathan Ricketts is in charge, and he believes in keeping dishes simple but flavorful, with exceptional tastes and textures. The menu, which changes twice a day, reflects whatever is available that day from the market and takes its inspiration from Japan and Thailand, from France and Italy. You might enjoy a full-flavored baked sea trout with herb-dressed sorrel, a tender rack of lamb with rosemary, and a Mediterranean-inspired black mushroom risotto.

Mezzo/Mezzonine. 100 Wardour St., W1. ☎ **0171/314-4000.** Reservations required for Mezzonine. Mezzonine main courses £15–£20 ($24–$32); 3-course dinner £25–£30 ($40–$48); Mezzo 3-course dinner £35–£40 ($56–$64). £5 ($8) cover at Mezzo Wed after 10pm. AE, DC, MC, V. Mezzo daily noon–2:30pm; Mon–Thurs 6pm–midnight, Fri–Sat 6pm–3am; Mezzonine daily noon–2:30pm, Sun–Thurs 5:30pm–1am, Fri–Sat 5:30pm–3am. Tube: Tottenham Court Road. MODERN EUROPEAN/INTERNATIONAL.

This all-out blockbuster, the latest creation of entrepreneur Sir Terence Conran, is a 750-seat Soho eatery, dubbed the biggest restaurant in Europe. The mammoth space has been split into several separate restaurants, including the Mezzonine upstairs, serving Thai/Asian cuisine with a European flair. Downstairs is the swankier Mezzo, which can seat 400 at a time in an atmosphere that evokes Hollywood in the 1930s. There's even a Mezzo Café, stocked with sandwiches and drinks.

Mezzonine serves up dishes such as marinated salmon with ginger, star anise, and shallots, or else roast marinated lamb with yogurt and cumin on flat bread. In the basement the cuisine is more ambitious, with a view of 100 chefs working behind glass. Here a modern British menu includes seared tuna with coconut and lime dressing for an appetizer, followed by a spicy pork and crab roll. For a main course, opt for the shoulder of lamb slow-roasted and enlivened with lemon zest and anchovies. The roast cod is crisp-skinned and cooked to perfection, whereas the eggplant ravioli disappoints—the food here tends to be uneven. But the place is dining as theater, and it's amazing how this many people are fed at all, considering the size. For dessert, you can't beat the butterscotch ice cream with a pitcher of hot fudge.

A live jazz band entertains after 10:30pm on Thursday and Friday, and the London world of Marlene Dietrich and Noël Coward comes alive again.

MODERATE

Bahn Thai. 21-A Frith St., W1. ☎ **0171/437-8504.** Reservations recommended. Fixed-price dinner for 2, £37–£51 ($59.20–$81.60). AE, DC, MC, V. Mon–Sat noon–2:45pm and 6–11:15pm; Sun 12:30–10:30pm. Tube: Leicester Square. THAI/SOUTHEAST ASIAN.

Located in the heart of Soho, this trendy but somewhat threadbare establishment continues to entertain London diners with a vast menu and dining environment options. Certainly one of the first decisions you'll have to make is where you would like to eat: in the upstairs dining room, or downstairs in the casual café, which has more of a Bangkok bistro feel. Perusing the encyclopedic menu is enough work to make you hungry. Bear in mind that if the menu says a particular dish is spicy, they're not kidding. Nothing's been cooled down for British palates. Curry comes in four different types, including our favorite, Penang, an aromatic blend of ground peanuts, coconut cream, anise-scented basil, and kaffir lime. The staff is accommodating, and the cuisine is excellent, helping maintain Bahn Tahi's reputation as one of the finest Thai restaurants in the city.

Dell'Ugo. 56 Frith St., W1. ☎ **0171/734-8300.** Reservations required. Main courses £6.25–£13.25 ($10–$21.20). AE, DC, MC, V. Mon–Fri noon–3pm; Mon–Sat 7pm–midnight. Tube: Tottenham Court Road. MEDITERRANEAN.

One of Soho's finest affordable choices, this multistory restaurant is immensely popular. Legions of young bloods in suits stake it out as their favorite. In a noisy atmosphere with modern designer styling, the landmark doesn't please everybody. Critics claim there's too long a wait between courses and dishes are overly contrived. However, we've found the robust Mediterranean dishes to be packed with flavor and based on the finest of ingredients. It's not the spot for quiet romance, but is immensely appealing. The ground floor "caff" offers bar snacks throughout the day, from tapas to meze. Both the restaurant and bistro in separate sections change their à la carte choices frequently. Try the linguine with langoustine or the rosemary-skewered lamb with charred eggplant. Fish dishes, delectably seasoned and not allowed to dry out on the grill, range from monkfish to sea bass. Some main courses, admittedly, are tough (especially the duck), and lack spice. The crème brûlée for dessert is excellent.

The Ivy. 1-5 West St., WC2. ☎ **0171/836-4751.** Reservations required. Main courses £8.50–£16 ($13.60–$25.60); Sat–Sun lunch £15.50 ($24.80). AE, DC, MC, V. Daily noon–3pm and 5:30pm–midnight (last order). Tube: Leicester Square. ENGLISH/FRENCH.

Effervescent and sophisticated, The Ivy has been intimately associated with the West End theater district since it opened in 1911. Renovated in the early 1990s, the place, with its ersatz 1930s look, is fun, humming, and throbbing with glamorous energy. The menu may seem simple, but the dishes mask a solid appreciation for fresh ingredients and skillful preparation. They include white asparagus with sea kale and truffle butter; seared scallops with spinach, sorrel, and bacon; and salmon fish cakes. You can also order Mediterranean fish soup, a great mixed grill, salads, and such English desserts as sticky toffee and caramelized bread-and-butter pudding. Meals are served quite late to accommodate a post-theater crowd.

INEXPENSIVE

Ming. 35-36 Greek St., W1. ☎ **0171/734-2721.** Main courses £7.50–£15 ($12–$24); 2-course fixed-price dinner £15 ($24); 3-course fixed-price dinner £20 ($32). AE, DC, MC, V. Mon–Sat noon–11:45pm. Tube: Tottenham Court Road. CANTONESE/PEKINESE.

This winning choice lies on Shaftesbury Avenue behind the Palace Theatre. The chefs in the kitchen, Mr. Bib and Mr. Bun (we're not making this up), welcome you to their Far East outpost, which is gaily decorated in green and pink. This is no chop suey and chow mein menu joint. Many of the recipes have real flair. One is fancifully described on the menu as from an 18th-century recipe from the Emperor Qian Long's head chef. What dazzled the emperor? Lean pieces of tender lamb with a slightly sweetened soy sauce. Fish, especially prawns and squid, are prepared in delectable ways, as are a number of tofu combinations. Cauliflower, sautéed in batter and flavored with bits of chiles and slivers of spring onions, is an unusual appetizer. You might follow with spiced and peppered duck breast, or chicken with fresh coriander and lemon zest. Mussels in black bean sauce are worthy of a return visit, as is a whole sea bass cooked Thai style. But we couldn't work up the nerve to order the "Chiu Yim sliced eel and sea spice shredded pork"!

BLOOMSBURY

EXPENSIVE

Nico Central. 35 Great Portland St., W1. ☎ **0171/436-8846.** Reservations required. Fixed-price 2-course lunch £22 ($35.20); fixed-price 3-course dinner £27 ($43.20). AE, DC, MC, V. Mon–Fri noon–2:45pm; Mon–Sat 7–11pm. Tube: Oxford Circus. FRENCH/ANGLO.

This light and modern brasserie, founded by London's most legendary chef, Nico Ladenis, serves earthy French cuisine that's been described as "haute but not haughty." It's a terrific value, for such technically well-executed cooking. Everything is handled with considerable sophistication and skill.

Guests sit on bentwood chairs at linen-covered tables. Nearly a dozen starters, the pride of the chef, will tempt you. The menu changes seasonally but might include grilled duck served with risotto with cepes (flap mushrooms) and Parmesan; panfried foie gras served with brioche and a caramelized orange; or baked fillet of brill with assorted vegetables. Save room for the divine desserts, such as a caramelized lemon tart.

MODERATE

Museum Street Café. 47 Museum St., W1. ☎ **0171/405-3211.** Reservations required. Lunch £13.50 ($21.60) for 2 courses, £16.50 ($26.40) for 3 courses; dinner £18.50 ($29.60) for 2 courses, £22.50 ($36) for 3 courses. AE, MC, V. Mon–Fri 12:30–2:15pm (last order); Tues–Fri 6:30–9:15pm (last order). Tube: Tottenham Court Road. MODERN BRITISH.

A 2-minute walk from the British Museum, this informal restaurant has been transformed from a greasy spoon to a charming dining room that offers great value. It's proven so popular in London that it's doubled in size. You can sample creative, up-to-date dishes impeccably prepared with fresh ingredients, with appetizers such as salmon and coconut soup with lime, chile, and coriander, or a dill and leek tart with smoked salmon. Follow with charcoal-grilled quails with a Muscat sauce, or perhaps crispy polenta with wilted spinach, baked mushrooms, and pomegranate balsamic vinaigrette (another winning combination). Who can resist the blood-orange sorbet? There aren't many frills here, but the standard of cooking is quite high.

CLERKENWELL

✪ **Maison Novelli.** 29-31A Clerkenwell Green, EC1. ☎ **0171/251-6606.** Reservations required. Main courses in restaurant £13–£21 ($20.80–$33.60); main courses in brasserie £9–£14 ($14.40–$22.40). AE, MC, V. Mon–Fri noon–3pm; Mon–Sat 5–11:30pm. Closed 2 weeks in July–Aug. Tube: Farringdon. CONTINENTAL.

You often have to abandon the heart of London these days to experience the city's finest and most imaginative cooking. High rents have driven such stellar chefs as Jean-Christophe Novelli to this up-and-coming area of the city. The cuisine is worth the trouble to get here. Novelli, who oversees the entire operation, is aided by the capable Richard Guest, a devotee of bold flavors, the freshest of ingredients, and imaginative culinary twists.

The ground floor is a brasserie, with seats outside when the weather's fair. More formal service and a more expensive menu are found upstairs. Set side by side, the brasserie and the more formal restaurant share a blue-violet decor that's lined with modern art. When the weather's fine, chairs are set on the pavement outside. The brasserie serves such hearty fare as a mackerel and lemon grass kebab or braised onion filled with cubed lamb. But it is in their restaurant upstairs that Guest and Novelli truly shine. The signature dish is a cassoulet terrine that we could dine on every day of the week. But that's only the beginning. Opt for the baby squid and scallop nage, followed by the sublime grilled John Dory (St-Pierre to the French diners). It comes with a sliver of foie gras and a green pea pod emulsion. Stuffed pig's trotters are stunningly rich and appear with mashed almonds with an exquisite flavor.

St. John. 26 St. John St., EC1. ☎ **0171/251-0848.** Reservations required. Main courses £8.20–£13.50 ($13.10–$21.60). AE, DC, MC, V. Mon–Fri noon–11:30pm; daily 6–11pm. Closed Christmas and bank holidays. Tube: Farringdon. MODERN BRITISH.

Located in a former smokehouse, just north of Smithfield Market, this canteenlike dining room is the place for carnivores. This dining oddity is a showcase for the talents of owner-chef Fergus Henderson. He doesn't use just part of the animal; he uses it all, and we're talking neck, trotter, tail, liver, heart—the works. There is a straightforward earthiness and simplicity to this cuisine that's unequaled in London.

Henderson makes the best lambs' brains on toast in London, and his grilled ox heart with rocket and pickled shallots, and duck neck and gizzard terrine cannot be beat. Roast bone marrow appears with a parsley salad, and pork chops are called pig chops here. It's getting hard these days to find an eel, bacon, and clam stew, but it's on the menu here. The food is excellent, with flavor-packed ingredients. Those French wines help to wash it all down. The breads served here may be purchased in an on-site bakery.

COVENT GARDEN & THE STRAND
VERY EXPENSIVE

Simpson's-in-the-Strand. 100 The Strand, WC2. ☎ **0171/836-9112.** Reservations required. Jacket and tie required for men. Main courses £17.50–£25 ($28–$40); fixed-price 2-course lunch and pretheater dinner £12.50 ($20); set breakfasts £11.50 ($18.40). AE, DC, MC, V. Mon–Fri 7am–noon; daily noon–2:30pm and 6–11pm. Tube: Charing Cross or Embankment. BRITISH.

Simpson's, next to the Savoy Hotel, is more of an institution than a restaurant—it's been in business since 1828. All this very Victorian place needs is an empire. It has everything else: Adam paneling, crystal, and an army of grandly formal waiters. Nouvelle cuisine here means anything after Henry VIII. However, most diners agree that Simpson's serves the best roasts in London. The classic dishes are roast sirloin of beef, roast saddle of mutton with red-currant jelly, roast Aylesbury duckling, and steak, kidney, and mushroom pie. (Remember to tip the tailcoated carver.) For a pudding, you might order the treacle roll and custard or Stilton with vintage port.

Taking advantage of the recent surge in popularity for traditional British cooking, Simpson's recently started serving the "trad British brekky," including "the great British breakfast." But one of their most popular breakfasts is the curiously named "10 deadly sins," which features a plate of sausage, a fried egg, streaky and back bacon, black pudding, lamb's kidneys, fried bread, bubble and squeak, baked beans, lamb's liver, and fried mushrooms and tomatoes. That will certainly fortify you for the day.

The unthinkable has happened in this bastion of tradition: Simpson's now features late-night jazz.

EXPENSIVE

Rules. 35 Maiden Lane, WC2. ☎ **0171/836-5314.** Reservations recommended. Main courses £13.95–£16.95 ($22.30–$27.10). AE, DC, MC, V. Daily noon–11:30pm. Tube: Covent Garden. ENGLISH.

If you're looking for London's most quintessentially British restaurant, eat here or at Wiltons or Simpson's. This is the site of London's oldest restaurant (an oyster bar established in 1798), and today it rambles through a series of Edwardian dining rooms just dripping in nationalistic nostalgia. You can order such classic dishes as Irish or Scottish oysters, jugged hare, and a bowl of mussels. Game is offered from mid-August to February or March. There's also wild Scottish salmon or wild sea trout, wild Highland red deer, and grouse, snipe, partridge, pheasant, and woodcock. For a finale, their puddings continue to impress, decade after decade.

MODERATE

Belgo Centraal. 50 Earlham St., WC2. ☎ **0171/813-2233.** Reservations required for the restaurant. Main courses £7.95–£19 ($12.70–$30.40); set menus £7–£14 ($11.20–$22.40). AE, DC, MC, V. Mon–Sat noon–11:30pm, Sun noon–10:30pm. Closed Christmas. Tube: Covent Garden. BELGIAN.

Chaos reigns supreme in this audacious and cavernous basement where mussels *marinière* (cooked in gravy with onions) with frites and 100 Belgian beers are the stars of the menu. Take a freight elevator down past the busy kitchen and into a converted cellar that has been divided into two large eating areas. One is a beer hall seating about 250. The menu here is the same as in the restaurant, but reservations aren't needed. Reservations are required for the restaurant, which has three nightly seatings: 5:30, 7:30, and 10pm.

Although mussels are the big attraction here, you can also opt for fresh Scottish salmon, roast chicken, a perfectly done steak, or one of the vegetarian specialties. Gargantuan plates of wild-boar sausages arrive with *stoemp*, a Belgian version of mashed spuds and cabbage. Belgian stews called waerzooï are also served. Unfailingly amusing waiters dressed in maroon monk's habits with black aprons bark orders into headset microphones.

Joe Allen. 13 Exeter St., WC2. ☎ **0171/836-0651.** Reservations required. Main courses £6.50–£13.50 ($10.40–$21.60); pretheater dinner £12–£14 ($19.20–$22.40); Sun brunch £13.50–£15.50 ($21.60–$24.80). AE, MC, V. Mon–Fri noon–1am, Sat 11:30am–1am, Sun 11:30am–midnight. Tube: Covent Garden or Embankment. AMERICAN.

This fashionable American restaurant, near the Savoy, attracts primarily theater crowds. The decor is inspired by the New York branch—it's decorated with theater posters. The menu has grown increasingly sophisticated and might include dishes such as grilled corn-fed chicken with sunflower-seed pesto, marinated sweet peppers, and garlic roast new potatoes, as well as such specialties as black-bean soup and pecan pie. The Sunday brunch served here is one of the best in London. You get main dishes like a mixed grill with lamb chop, calf's liver, and Cumberland sausage, with your choice of a Bloody Mary, Bucks Fizz, or a glass of champagne.

Porter's English Restaurant. 17 Henrietta St., WC2. ☎ **0171/836-6466.** Reservations recommended. Main courses £7.95–£10.95 ($12.70–$17.50); fixed-price menu £16.50 ($26.40). AE, DC, MC, V. Mon–Sat noon–11:30pm, Sun noon–10:30pm. Tube: Covent Garden or Charing Cross. ENGLISH.

In 1979 the 7th earl of Bradford opened this restaurant, stating "it would serve real English food at affordable prices." He has succeeded admirably (not just because Lady Bradford turned over her carefully guarded recipe for banana and ginger steamed pudding). This place has a friendly, informal, and lively atmosphere in comfortable surroundings on two floors. Porter's specializes in classic English pies, and of course, bangers and mash. Main courses have generous portions, and are served with vegetables and side dishes, so you hardly need to order an appetizer. With whipped cream or custard, the puddings come hot or cold, including bread-and-butter pudding or steamed syrup sponge. The bar does quite a few exotic cocktails, as well as beer, wine, or traditional English mead. A traditional English tea is also served for £3.50 ($5.60).

WESTMINSTER & VICTORIA

The Atrium. 4 Millbank, SW1. ☎ **0171/233-0032.** Reservations recommended for lunch, not needed for dinner. 2 courses for £17.95 ($28.70); 3 courses for £20.95 ($33.50). AE, DC, MC, V. Mon–Fri noon–3pm and 6–11pm. Tube: Westminster. BRITISH/IRISH.

In a soaring six-story atrium in a Westminster office building, this restaurant is surviving the departure of fabled restaurateur Antony Worall Thompson, and seems to be doing quite well without him. The media has been unkind, ranting against the bland cookery and the terrible venue. However, it's still a solid choice in a neighborhood where the pickings are otherwise slim. You might begin with a warm onion tart with a green tomato pickle. There's always a meat pie or a roast of the day—leg of lamb or beef and Guinness pie. Other mains are likely to include dill-flavored salmon fish cakes, pot roast, or even vegetable dishes. A rib of beef with mashed potatoes and fresh vegetables is regularly featured, followed by such desserts as apple charlotte or tipsy trifle. The restaurant also has a good selection of British and Irish cheese, and a decent wine list. A pianist entertains in the evening.

Simply Nico. 48A Rochester Row, SW1. ☎ **0171/630-8061.** Reservations required. 2-course set lunch £22 ($35.20); 3-course set lunch £25 ($40); 3-course fixed-price dinner £27 ($43.20). AE, DC, MC, V. Mon–Fri 12:30–2pm; Mon–Sat 7–11pm. Tube: Victoria or St. James's. FRENCH.

This place was created by Nico Ladenis, the owner of a grander and more expensive restaurant, Chez Nico at Ninety Park Lane. Run by his sous-chef, Simply Nico is, in the words of Nico, cheap and cheerful. Wood floors seem to reverberate with the din of contented diners, who pack in here daily at snug tables. The food is often simply prepared and invariably French-inspired. The fixed-price menu might include poached egg tartlet with hollandaise sauce and marinated pureed mushrooms followed by crispy duck with plum sauce.

THE CITY

Poons in The City. 2 Minster Pavement, Minster Ct., Mincing Lane, EC3. ☎ **0171/626-0126.** Reservations recommended for lunch. Set lunches £5.15–£22.50 ($8.25–$36) per person; main courses £26.80–£42 ($42.90–$67.20). AE, DC, MC, V. Mon–Fri noon–10:30pm. Tube: Tower Hill. CHINESE.

Poons is less than a 5-minute walk from the Tower of London. It is modeled on the Luk Yew Tree House in Hong Kong. Poons' famous Lap Yuk Soom has finely chopped wind-dried bacon. Main courses feature crispy, aromatic duck, prawns with cashew nuts, and barbecued pork. Special dishes can be ordered on 24-hour notice. At the end of the L-shaped restaurant is an 80-seat fast-food area and take-out counter that's accessible from Mark Lane. The menu changes every 2 weeks.

Ship Hispaniola. River Thames, Victoria Embankment, Charing Cross, WC2. ☎ **0171/839-3011.** Reservations recommended. Main courses £9.50–£19.50 ($15.20–$31.20). AE, DC, MC, V. Mon–Fri noon–2pm; Mon–Sat 6–10:30pm (last order). Closed Dec 24–Jan 4. £15 ($24) minimum per person. Tube: Embankment. BRITISH/FRENCH.

This large, comfortably outfitted ship was originally built in 1953 to haul passengers around the islands of Scotland. Stripped of its engine in 1976, the ship is permanently moored to a quay beside the Thames, a few steps from the Embankment underground station. Good food and views of the passing river traffic are part of the waterborne experience. The menu changes frequently and might include flambéed Mediterranean prawns with garlic, fried fish cake with tartar sauce, poached halibut on a bed of creamed spinach, Dover sole meunière, rack of lamb flavored with rosemary and shallots, and several vegetarian dishes. On most nights there is live music.

Ye Olde Cheshire Cheese. Wine Office Ct., 145 Fleet St., EC4. ☎ **0171/353-6170.** Main courses £6.95–£14.95 ($11.10–$23.90). AE, DC, MC, V. Mon–Sat noon–9:30pm; Sun noon–2:30pm and 6–9:30pm. Drinks and bar snacks available daily 11:30am–11pm. Tube: St. Paul's or Blackfriars. ENGLISH.

In a recently remodeled, carefully preserved building whose foundation was originally laid in the 13th century, you'll find this most famous of the old city's chophouses and pubs. It was established in 1667 and claims to be the spot where Dr. Samuel Johnson entertained his admirers with his acerbic wit. Later, many ink-stained journalists and scandalmongers of 19th- and early 20th-century Fleet Street made its four-story premises their "local." Charles Dickens and other literary lions also patronized the place.

Within, there are six bars and two dining rooms. The house specialties include "ye famous pudding"—steak, kidney, mushrooms, and game—and Scottish roast beef, with Yorkshire pudding and horseradish sauce. Sandwiches, salads, and such standby favorites as steak-and-kidney pie are also available.

SOUTH BANK

Oxo Tower Restaurant. Barge House St., South Bank, SE1. ☎ **0171/803-3888.** Main courses £25–£35 ($40–$56); set lunch £24.50 ($39.20). AE, DC, MC, V. Daily noon–3:30pm; Mon–Sat 6–11pm, Sun 6–10:30pm. Tube: Waterloo. MEDITERRANEAN/CONTINENTAL/ASIAN.

In the South Bank shopping complex, on the eighth floor of the art deco Oxo Tower Wharf, this is London's latest dining sensation. It's called "the other tower," and is operated by the Knightsbridge department store, Harvey Nichols. Just down the street from the newly rebuilt Globe Theatre, this 140-seat restaurant has been long awaited. Despite a stunning building (with structural waves and curves designed to suggest the ebb and flow of the mighty Thames itself), a stylish 1930s-style decor, and an impressive panoramic view of London, the cuisine isn't that exciting. It's respectable, and menu items change based on the season and market conditions, but for these prices, we were disappointed. Count on a modern interpretation of British cookery. The fish is fresh, and you can order such English classics as a mixed grill. The chicken with orange sauce has a certain zest, and even vegetarians can feel safe here. A pretheater three-course meal here costs only £18.50 ($29.60), although the average main course is £25 ($40).

KNIGHTSBRIDGE & BELGRAVIA

San Lorenzo. 22 Beauchamp Place, SW3. ☎ **0171/584-1074.** Reservations required. Main courses £14.50–£20 ($23.20–$32). No credit cards. Mon–Sat 12:30–3pm and 7:30–11:30pm. Tube: Knightsbridge. ITALIAN.

This fashionable restaurant, once a favorite of the late Princess Diana, specializes in regional cuisines from Tuscany and the Piedmont region. Frequently mentioned in the London tabloids because of its high-profile clients, it is the domain of its effervescent owners, Lorenzo and Mara Berni. Reliability is the keynote of the seasonal cuisine, which often includes homemade fettuccine with salmon, carpaccio risotto with fresh asparagus, *bollito misto*, fried calamari, veal piccata, grouse, and partridge in white-wine sauce. Regional offerings might include salt cod with polenta. The food remains really good after all these years, although the service could be better and more gracious. Nevertheless, it remains the most fabled trattoria of Knightsbridge, especially if you're engaging in some trendy shopping along Beauchamp Place.

❂ **Vong.** In the Berkeley Hotel, Wilton Place, SW1. ☎ **0171/235-1010.** Reservations required 7 days in advance. Main courses £12.75–£26.75 ($20.40–$42.80); vegetarian main courses £9–£11 ($14.40–$17.60); tasting menu £45 ($72); 2-course fixed-price dinner £27 ($43.20); 3-course fixed-price dinner £36.50 ($58.40); pre- and post-theater dinner £17.50 ($28). AE, DC, MC, V. Mon–Sat noon–2:30pm and 6–11:30pm. Pre- and post-theater dinner available 6–7pm and 10:30–11:30pm. Tube: Knightsbridge. FRENCH/THAI.

Just 600 yards from Harrods, this restaurant on three levels with a strikingly modern decor is one of the chic new spots. In 1997 it was the most talked-about newcomer in the city. Jean-Georges Vongerichten is the darling of the New York restaurant scene, winning four coveted stars from *The New York Times* for his new restaurant Jean-Georges. Now he's brought a version of his award-winning French/Thai menu from Vong in New York to London. The chef boldly states that the more superior Thai ingredients available in London will make the offspring better than the parent. The results here are innovative and inspired with the most incredible flavor combinations. Subtle use is made of fresh herbs and spices.

In a minimalist setting, you can partake of the "black plate," featuring samples of six starters, if you'd like a taste of everything. Other options are a perfectly done roast halibut or a lobster and daikon roll, the latter with a rosemary and ginger sauce. You can virtually eat everything on the menu and be filled with a wonder and admiration, especially by the crab spring roll with a vinegary tamarind dipping sauce. The sautéed foie gras with ginger and mango literally melts in the mouth. Desserts are equally exotic, especially the salad of banana and passion fruit with white-pepper ice cream (yes, you read right).

CHELSEA
VERY EXPENSIVE
✪ **Aubergine.** 11 Park Walk, SW10. ☎ **0171/352-3449.** Reservations required 2 months in advance. 2-course fixed-price lunch £24 ($38.40); fixed-price dinner £45 ($72); menu prestige £60 ($96). AE, DC, MC, V. Mon–Fri noon–2:15pm; Mon–Sat 7–10:30pm. Tube: South Kensington. FRENCH.

The "Eggplant" is luring savvy diners down to the lower reaches of Chelsea, where Gordon Ramsay, the owner and chef, continues to create excitement and deliver what some food critics, including the producer Andrew Lloyd Webber (a true gourmet), claim is the best food in London. Ramsay trained with some of Europe's greatest chefs, including Marco Pierre White and Joël Robuchon, but he forges ahead with his own creative statement. Celebrities don't seem to impress him, whether it's Princess Margaret complaining that the air-conditioning is too cold (he lent her his cardigan) or Madonna calling for late-night bookings (Evita was turned down). There are only 14 tables, so reservations are imperative.

Quality dishes, not quantity, emerge from the lair of this talented chef. Ramsay is a perfectionist, but not pretentious. He's celebrated for his cappuccino of white beans with grated truffle. But the fish and the lighter, Mediterranean-style dishes are stunning achievements as well. Subtlety and delicacy of cuisine are always achieved here, without any sacrifice of the food's natural essence.

✪ **La Tante Claire.** 68-69 Royal Hospital Rd., SW3. ☎ **0171/352-6045.** Reservations required at least 2 weeks in advance. Main courses £26.50–£30 ($42.40–$48); 3-course fixed-price lunch £28 ($44.80); minimum charge £50 ($80) per person. AE, CB, DC, MC, V. Mon–Fri 12:30–2pm and 7–11pm. Closed Dec 24 and Jan 3. Tube: Sloane Square. FRENCH.

Prepare yourself for one of London's finest dining experiences. The quality of its cuisine is so legendary that this "Aunt Claire" is one of London's best French restaurants, even though the setting is far from grand. The ring of a doorbell set discreetly into the facade of Aegean blue and white prompts an employee to usher you politely inside.

Pierre Koffman is the celebrated chef, creating such culinary fireworks as ravioli langoustine or pig's trotters stuffed with morels. Who would think that the lowly pig trotter could be turned into such a faultless, terrific, sublime creation as that served here? For dessert, try a caramelized ice-cream soufflé with hazelnuts and a coulis of raspberries or the pistachio soufflé. Year after year, Tante Claire maintains its consistency, as the chef is far more interested in turning out food of the highest order than he is in creating a media frenzy.

MODERATE

English Garden. 10 Lincoln St., SW3. ☎ **0171/584-7272.** Reservations required. Main courses £9.25–£17.75 ($14.80–$28.40); fixed-price set lunch £17.75 ($28.40). AE, DC, MC, V. Mon–Sat 12:30–2:30pm and 7:30–11:30pm, Sun 12:30–2pm and 7–10:30pm. Closed Dec 25–26. Tube: Sloane Square. ENGLISH.

This is a metropolitan restaurant par excellence. The decor is pretty and light-hearted in this historic Chelsea town house: The Garden Room is whitewashed brick, with panels of large stylish flowers, and attractive pelmets, in vivid florals, contrast with stark-white curtains; rattan chairs in a Gothic theme and candy-pink napery complete the scene. With the domed conservatory roof and banks of plants, the relaxing atmosphere is complete. Every component of a meal here is chopped or cooked to the right degree and well proportioned. Start out with a caramelized red onion and cheddar cheesecake or cream of Jerusalem artichoke soup. For a main course, opt for such delights as roast partridge with beetroot and juniper or else roast saddle of hare with black currants. Some of these dishes sound as if they were created from an English cookbook of the Middle Ages—and are they ever good. Desserts would have pleased Miss Marple, especially the rhubarb and cinnamon ice cream or the candied orange tart with orange syrup.

The English House. 3 Milner St., SW3. ☎ **0171/584-3002.** Reservations required. Main courses £8–£17 ($12.80–$27.20); fixed-price set lunch £15.25 ($24.40); set dinner (Sun only) £20.75 ($33.20). AE, DC, MC, V. Mon–Sat 12:30–2:30pm and 7:30–11:15pm, Sun 12:30–2pm and 7:30–9:45pm. Closed Dec 26. Tube: Sloane Square. BRITISH.

The English House, another design creation of Roger Wren, who did the English Garden, is a tiny restaurant where you'll feel like you're a guest in an elegant Victorian house with a cozy atmosphere. The food is British, the menu seasonal, and each dish is given a subtle, modern treatment. The menu isn't trendy, but year after year we've gotten letters from readers who found it immensely satisfying. Begin with a pumpkin-and-rosemary soup, which sounds almost medieval, or else grilled pigeon breast with a bean compote. For a main dish, try either the roast chump of lamb with bubble and squeak (cabbage and potatoes) or else a braised ham hock with corn and mashed apples. Game is available in season, as is fresh fish of the day. Summer berries in season predominate on the pudding menu, including a bowl of fresh berries laced with elder-flower syrup. Other offerings include a "Phrase of Apples," the chef's adaptation of a 17th-century recipe for a delectable apple pancake.

KENSINGTON

Joe's. 126 Draycott Ave., SW3. ☎ **0171/225-2217.** Reservations required. Main courses £10–£15.50 ($16–$24.80); Sun brunch £12 ($19.20). AE, DC, MC, V. Mon–Sat noon–3pm and 7–11pm; Sun 10am–5pm. Tube: South Kensington. MODERN BRITISH.

This is one of three London restaurants established by fashion designer Joseph Ettedgui; partly because of its sense of glamour and fun, it is often filled with well-known names from the British fashion, music, and entertainment industries. You can enjoy spiced venison strips and vegetables, roast cod in a champagne crab sauce, char-grilled swordfish with cracked wheat and salsa *verde* (green sauce), or fresh lobster lasagna. No one will mind if your meal is composed exclusively of appetizers. There's a bar near the entrance, a cluster of tables for quick meals near the door, and more leisurely (and gossipy) dining available in an area a few steps up from the bar and entrance level. Brunch is served on Sunday, which is the cheapest way to enjoy this place. The atmosphere remains laid-back and unstuffy, just like trendsetters in South Ken prefer it. With a name like Joe's, what else could it be?

Wodka. 12 St. Albans Grove, W8. ☎ **0171/937-6513.** Main courses £9.50–£12.50 ($15.20–$20); fixed-price lunch £9.95 ($15.90). AE, MC, V. Mon–Fri 11am–11pm, Sat–Sun 6–11pm. Tube: High Street Kensington. POLISH.

This London restaurant has done a lot to change attitudes about Polish cuisine, which is viewed as typically heavy, overcooked, and sauce-laden. Here there is a lighter and more delicate touch in the kitchen. Young Poles who have moved west have been picking up the culinary challenge of London and have made their cuisine more appealing to today's young tastes. Although the place has a bohemian charm, it's the food, not the decor, that packs people in. Young Poles living in London come here to debate the merits of various vodkas that are flavored with everything from pineapple to rose petals. (You can opt for a Polish beer as well.)

After sampling one of the crisp, vinegary pickles placed on the table, begin with Chlodnik, a chilled beet soup that's magenta in color and has a sharp peppery flavor. It's on to delicate little blinis with marinated herring or a roast pepper salad. Devotees go for *leniwe,* light dumplings with herbs and cheese accompanied by a sun-dried tomato sauce. The traditional favorite is *golabki,* stuffed cabbage (with pork), served with wild rice. For dessert, finish perhaps with the crêpe stuffed with cheese, nuts and raisins, with a raspberry sauce drizzled on.

SOUTH KENSINGTON
VERY EXPENSIVE

Bibendum/The Oyster Bar. 81 Fulham Rd., SW3. ☎ **0171/581-5817.** Reservations required in Bibendum; not accepted in Oyster Bar. Main courses £17–£23 ($27.20–$36.80); 3-course fixed-price lunch £28 ($44.80); cold seafood platter in Oyster Bar £22 ($35.20) per person. AE, DC, MC, V. Bibendum Mon–Fri noon–2:30pm and 7–11:15pm, Sat 12:30–3pm and 7–11:15pm, Sun 12:30–3pm and 7–10:15pm. Oyster Bar Mon–Sat noon–11:30pm, Sun noon–3pm and 7–10:30pm. Tube: South Kensington. MODERN FRENCH/MEDITERRANEAN.

In the environs of trendy Brompton Cross, this still rather fashionable spot occupies two floors of a garage that is an art deco masterpiece. Its heyday was in the early nineties, but it's still going strong. Bibendum is located one floor above street level in a white-tiled, art deco–inspired room whose stained-glass windows, streaming sunlight, and chic clientele make meals extremely pleasant. Menu choices are carefully planned interpretations of seasonal ingredients, known for their freshness and simplicity. The chefs prepare a fabulously eclectic haute cuisine. Dishes might include roast quail flavored with marsala and thyme, braised oxtail with prunes and almonds, and *ris de veau* (sweetbreads) with black butter and capers. Some of the best dishes are for dining *a deux:* Bresse pullet flavored with fresh tarragon or roast best end of lamb with a soubise (white onion sauce) and onion rings.

Simpler meals and cocktails are available on the building's street level, in the Oyster Bar. The bar-style menu and 1930s-style decor stress fresh shellfish presented in the traditional French style on ice-covered platters occasionally adorned with strands of seaweed. It's a crustacean lover's lair. Here's your chance to try those old Cockney favorites, winkles and whelks.

EXPENSIVE

✪ **Bombay Brasserie.** Courtfield Close, adjoining Bailey's Hotel, SW7. ☎ **0171/ 370-4040.** Reservations required. Main courses £12.50–£20.95 ($20–$33.50); buffet lunch £15.95 ($25.50). DC, MC, V. Buffet daily 12:30–3pm. Mon-Sat 7:30pm–midnight, Sun 7:30–11:30pm. Closed Dec 25–26. Tube: Gloucester Road. INDIAN.

This was London's best, most popular, and most talked-about Indian restaurant in the early 1990s. It's still an impressive place, if a bit frayed here and there, and most visitors still find the cuisine fabulous. The wait staff is professional and accommodating, willing to advise you on the spicy delicacies. Before heading in to dinner, you might enjoy a mango Bellini amid the wicker chairs of the pink-and-white bar.

One look at the menu and you're launched on a grand culinary tour of the subcontinent: tandoori trout, fish with mint chutney, chicken tikka, and vegetarian meals. Part of the menu is reserved for Goan cookery, representing a part of India seized from Portugal in 1961. Mughlai specialties include chicken biryani, the famous Muslim pilaf dish. Under the category "Some Like It Hot," you'll find such main courses as lamb korma, Kashmiri-style.

Hilaire. 68 Old Brompton Rd., SW7. ☎ **0171/584-8993.** Reservations recommended. 2-course fixed-price lunch £19.50 ($31.20); 3 courses £24 ($38.40); 3-course fixed-price dinner £30 ($48); 4-course fixed-price dinner £36 ($57.60); dinner main courses £14.50–£19.50 ($23.20–$31.20). AE, DC, MC, V. Mon–Fri 12:15–2:30pm; Mon–Sat 6:30–11:30pm. Closed bank holidays. Tube: South Kensington. CONTINENTAL.

After this former Victorian storefront was refurbished following a fire, it became one classy joint, like an elegant restaurant you might find in a provincial French town. With its large vases of flowers and shiny mirrors, it's a fitting ambience to enjoy some of South Ken's finest food. Chef Bryan Webb prepares a mixture of classical French and *cuisine moderne,* and does so exceedingly well, always following his own creative impulses and good culinary sense and style. The cookery is direct, with an intent on finding the maximum flavor in every ingredient used. The menu always reflects the best of the season's offerings. A typical lunch might begin with a red-wine risotto with radicchio and sun-dried tomato pesto, followed with sautéed scallops with creamed chicory, and ending with rhubarb sorbet. Dinner main courses might include rack of lamb with tapenade and wild garlic, saddle of rabbit, or grilled tuna with Provençal vegetables.

NOTTING HILL GATE

Mondola. 139 Westbourne Grove, W11. ☎ **0171/229-4734.** Reservations recommended. Fixed-price meals £6.95–£10 ($11.10–$16), vegetarian fixed-price meals £3.50–£8 ($5.60–$12.80). No credit cards. Daily 11am–11:30pm. Tube: Notting Hill Gate. SUDANESE.

Of all the African restaurants of London, this presumably is the only one that specializes in the spicy, unique cuisine of the Sudan. Very small and intimate, on the fringe of trendy Notting Hill, this bohemian hangout doesn't have a liquor license, although you'll be free to brown bag it.

The food is a blend of various cuisines, like Sudanese food itself. The chefs borrow from various kitchens of North Africa, Ethiopia, and even the Middle East. The fare is eclectic and inexpensive. Begin with the classic soup of the region, made with meat and peanuts. Although the menu is limited, the dishes are tasty and well prepared with fresh ingredients. Opt for one of the lamb dishes, as they are the best offerings, including tasty chops marinated in African spices. Ground red chiles add zest to any dish that tastes a bit bland. Lentils with caramelized garlic is another tasty treat, and there's also a raw salad bar, costing £7.50 ($12) for two persons, that's almost a meal unto itself. Skip the treacly desserts and perhaps settle for a traditional African coffee.

✪ **Sugar Club.** 33A All Saints Rd., W11. ☎ **0171/221-3844.** Reservations required. Main courses £10–£15 ($16–$24). AE, DC, MC, V. Daily 12:30–3pm and 6:30–10:30pm. Closed Christmas and New Year's. Tube: Westbourne Park. PACIFIC RIM.

Homesick Aussies head here for the grilled loin of kangaroo, but New Zealand–born chef Peter Gordon is far more versatile than that. Savvy foodies make their way to this Notting Hill Gate bistro, with its open kitchen and cramped basement dining room, for "Southern Hemisphere Pacific Rim Modern Mediterranean Cosmopolitan British cookery." The aforementioned national symbol of Australia doesn't have a gamy flavor but is very tender with a deep rich taste. It's best with a piquant salsa. The menu changes daily and might include duck leg braised in tamarind and star anise with coconut rice or panfried turbot with spinach and sweet potato, along with a red-curry sauce and onion raita. Many of the starters are vegetarian and can be upgraded to a main course. There are also several fresh fish dishes. For dessert, the blood-orange curd tart with crème fraîche is drop-dead good.

HAMMERSMITH

The River Café. Thames Wharf, Rainville Rd., W6. ☎ **0171/381-6217.** Reservations required. Main courses £16–£25 ($25.60–$40). AE, DC, MC, V. Mon–Fri 12:30–3pm, Sat–Sun 1–2:45pm; Mon–Thurs 7:30–11pm, Fri–Sat 7:30–11:30pm. Closed bank holidays and for 10 days at Christmas and New Year's. Tube: Hammersmith. ITALIAN.

For some of the best Italian fare in London today, head down to Hammersmith to a Thames-side bistro operated by Ruth Rogers and Rose Gray. This charmingly contemporary venue with a highly polished steel bar was designed by Ruth's husband, Richard, who also designed the Pompidou Center in Paris.

Ruth and Rose have succeeded in their aim of serving food similar to what they'd enjoyed in private homes in the Italian countryside. The best dishes are either slowly roasted or quickly seared. Some chefs can be seen shopping in London's markets. But not the chefs here. The market comes to them—first spring asparagus harvested in Andalusia and served on their tables within a day, live scallops and langoustines rescued by divers in the icy North Sea, and, of course, a daily shipment of the finest harvest of Italy, ranging from radicchio to artichokes. Even tiny bulbs of fennel are zipped across the Channel from France. Britain's own rich bounty appears in pheasant and wild salmon.

5 Afternoon Tea

Everyone should indulge in a formal afternoon tea at least once while in London. This relaxing, drawn-out, civilized affair usually consists of three courses, all elegantly served on delicate china: first, dainty finger sandwiches (with the crusts cut off, of course); then fresh-baked scones served with jam and deliciously decadent clotted cream (also known as Devonshire cream); and, lastly, an array of bite-sized sweets. All the while, an indulgent server keeps the pot of tea of your choice fresh at hand. Sometimes, ports and apéritifs are on offer to accompany your final course. It's a quintessential British experience; we've listed our favorite places for tea below.

But if high tea isn't your style, consider dropping in to one of the tea shops in the alleys around Shepherd's Market or Covent Garden. Cafes and tea shops rise and fall as regularly as the seasons here, but you can always find a charming one to pop in for a pot of tea and a scone any afternoon between 2 and 5:30pm. We've also included a handful of less formal alternatives here.

MAYFAIR

✪ **Brown's Hotel.** 29-34 Albemarle St., W1. ☎ **0171/493-6020.** Reservations not accepted. Afternoon tea £16.95 ($27.10). AE, DC, MC, V. Daily 3–5:45pm. Tube: Green Park.

Along with the Ritz, Brown's ranks as one of the most chic spots for tea in London. It's served in the drawing room, decorated with English antiques, wall panels, oil paintings, and floral chintz. Give your name to the concierge when you arrive; he'll seat you at one of the clusters of sofas and settees or at low tables. There's a choice of 10 teas, plus sandwiches, scones, and pastries (all made right in the Hotel kitchens) that are rolled around on a trolley for your selection.

Claridge's. Brook St., W1. ☎ **0171/629-8860.** Reservations recommended. Jacket and tie required for men. High tea £17.50 ($28). AE, DC, MC, V. Daily 3–5pm. Tube: Bond Street.

Claridge's teatime rituals have lived on through the years with as much pomp and circumstance as the British Empire itself. It's never stuffy, though; you'll feel very welcome. Tea is served in The Reading Room, where a portrait of Lady Claridge gazes benevolently from above as a choice of 17 kinds of tea is served ever so politely. The various courses are served consecutively, including finger sandwiches with cheese savories, apple and raisin scones, and yummy pastries.

✪ **Goode's.** 19 South Audley St., Mayfair Sq., W1. ☎ **0171/409-7242.** Fixed-price lunch £30 ($48) for 2 courses, £37.50 ($60) for 3. Afternoon pot of tea £3 ($4.80); high tea £16 ($25.60); high tea with glass of champagne £23.50 ($37.60). AE, DC, MC, V. Mon–Fri noon–3pm, and 4–6pm (tea). Tube: Bond Street or Green Park.

Few other places so thoroughly capture the charm and verve of the Edwardian age. The high-ceilinged gold and blue salon is housed on the premises of a prestigious British emporium of fine porcelain, Thomas Goode. A hostess and battalion of formally dressed butlers in tails present their fare on Thomas Goode porcelain at lunch (Versailles) and teatime (Pink Carousel).

During teatime, any overt reference to the ever-so-polite commerce in the adjoining china shop is swept under the rug. You won't find the staid cucumber-with-wilted-lettuce sandwiches you'd expect. You'll enjoy about half a dozen types of tea, sandwiches made of poached chicken with red onion and compote of pear, or tuna with sweet corn and rocket; and scones with gingered rhubarb preserves and clotted cream.

Palm Court Lounge. In the Park Lane Hotel, Piccadilly, W1. ☎ **0171/836-2400.** Afternoon tea £14 ($22.40). AE, DC, MC, V. Daily 3:30–6:30pm. Tube: Hyde Park Corner or Green Park.

This is one of the great London favorites for tea. The Palm Court Lounge has an atmosphere straight from 1927. Restored to its former charm, the lounge has a yellow-and-white domed ceiling, torchères, and palms in Compton stoneware jardinieres. A delightful afternoon tea with many different types of tea is served daily. Many guests come here after the theater for a sandwich and a drink, as hot food is served 24 hours a day. During the week a pianist plays every afternoon.

ST. JAMES'S

✪ **Ritz Palm Court.** In the Ritz Hotel, Piccadilly, W1. ☎ **0171/493-8181.** Reservations required at least 8 weeks in advance. Jacket and tie required for men. Afternoon tea £23.50 ($37.60). AE, DC, MC, V. Daily 2–6pm. Tube: Green Park.

This is the most fashionable place in London to order afternoon tea—and the hardest to get into without reserving way in advance. Its spectacular setting is straight out of *The Great Gatsby*, complete with marble steps and columns and a baroque fountain. You have your choice of a long list of teas, served with delectable sandwiches and luscious pastries.

St. James Restaurant/The Fountain Restaurant. In Fortnum & Mason, 181 Piccadilly, W1. ☎ **0171/734-8040.** In the St. James, full tea £10.50–£12.25 ($16.80–$19.60). In The Fountain, full tea £6.95–£9.95 ($11.10–$15.90). AE, DC, MC, V. Mon–Sat 3–5:30pm (St. James); Mon–Sat 3–6pm (The Fountain). Tube: Piccadilly Circus.

This pair of tea salons function as a culinary showplace for London's most prestigious grocery store, Fortnum & Mason, making for a pretty spiffy tea-drinking ritual. The more formal of the two venues, the St. James, lies on the venerable store's fourth floor, within a pale green and beige homage to formal Edwardian taste.

Less formal and better-tuned to the hectic pace of London shoppers and commuters is the Fountain Restaurant on the store's street level, where a sense of tradition and urban manners is very much a part of the teatime experience, but in a less opulent setting. The quantities of food served in either place are usually ample enough to be full-fledged early suppers for most theatergoers.

PICCADILLY CIRCUS & LEICESTER SQUARE

The Living Room. 3 Bateman St., W1. ☎ **0171/437-4827.** Tea £1 ($1.60) a cup; cakes and pastries 60p–£2.40 (95¢–$3.85); sandwiches £3–£3.70 ($4.80–$5.90). No credit cards. Mon–Sat 8am–midnight; Sun 9am–11pm. Tube: Leicester Square.

In contrast to the grande dame tearooms mentioned above, this is a cozy, somewhat eccentric enclave lined with the artworks of some of its regular patrons, battered sofas that might have come out of a college dorm, and a gathering of likable and irreverent urban hipsters. You can enjoy dozens of varieties of tea, including herbals, served in steaming mugfuls. Lots of arty and eccentric types gather here during the late afternoon, emulating some of the rituals of the old-fashioned tea service but with absolutely none of the haughtiness.

Oak Room Lounge. In Le Méridien London, 21 Piccadilly, W1. ☎ **0171/734-8000.** Reservations not accepted. Afternoon tea £13.50–£19.50 ($21.60–$31.20). AE, DC, MC, V. Daily 3:30–6pm. Tube: Piccadilly Circus or Green Park.

Restored to its former Edwardian glory, the Oak Room Lounge is a wonderful place to experience a very traditional afternoon tea. The soothing elegance of this formal but unstuffy oak-paneled room is augmented by comfortable armchairs and background music by a resident harpist. A complete tea includes a selection of sandwiches and tarts, and the menu lists a tempting array of exotic teas.

COVENT GARDEN & THE STRAND

MJ Bradley's. 9 King St., WC2. ☎ **0171/240-5178.** Cups of tea 95p ($1.50) each; sandwiches £1.85–£3.50 ($2.95–$5.60) each. No credit cards. Mon–Fri 8am–8:30pm, Sat–Sun 11am–8:30pm. Tube: Covent Garden or Charing Cross.

Although this is more of a coffeehouse, many of its fans resolutely drop in for a cup of as many as 20 different kinds of tea, including Earl Grey, Assam, and peppermint. It's outfitted like a brasserie that combines old-time nostalgia with modern wall sculptures. You can also order imaginative sandwiches with fillings of herb-flavored cream cheese with sun-dried tomatoes.

The Waldorf Meridien. In the Waldorf Hotel, Aldwych, WC2. ☎ **0171/836-2400.** Reservations required. Jacket and tie required for men at tea dance. Afternoon tea £17–£20 ($27.20–$32); tea dance £24–£27 ($38.40–$43.20). AE, DC, MC, V. Afternoon tea Mon–Fri 3:30–6pm; tea dance Sat 2:30–5:30pm; Sun 4–6:30pm. Tube: Covent Garden.

This Hotel's Palm Court combines afternoon tea with afternoon dancing (such as the fox-trot, quickstep, and the waltz). The Palm Court is aptly compared to a 1920s movie set, which is in fact what it's been several times in its long life. You can order tea on a terrace or in a pavilion the size of a ballroom that's lit by skylights. On tea-dancing days, the orchestra leader will conduct such favorites as "Ain't She Sweet" and "Yes, Sir, That's My Baby," as a butler in a cutaway inquires if you want a cucumber sandwich.

KNIGHTSBRIDGE

✪ **The Georgian Restaurant.** On the 4th floor of Harrods department store, 87-135 Brompton Rd., SW1. ☎ **0171/225-6800.** High tea £15.50 ($24.80) per person. Teatime Mon–Sat 3:45–5:30pm (last order). AE, DC, MC, V. Tube: Knightsbridge.

As long as anyone can remember, teatime at Harrods has been a special feature of Europe's most famous department store. A flood of shoppers and visitors is somehow gracefully herded into a high-volume but nevertheless elegant room. The staff hauls silver pots and trolleys laden with pastries and sandwiches through the dining room. (Harrods' famous teatime buffets were eliminated in favor of tableside service.) The list of teas available (at least 50) is sometimes so esoteric that choosing one might remind you of selecting between the vintages of a sophisticated wine cellar.

Richoux. 86 Brompton Rd. (opposite Harrods department store), Knightsbridge, SW3. ☎ **0171/584-8300.** Full tea (a minimeal) £12.50 ($20), English tea £7.50 ($12). AE, MC. Open Jan to mid-May, Mon–Sat 8:30am–8pm, Sun 10am–9:30pm; mid-May to Dec Mon–Sat 8:30am–9pm, Sun 10am–9:30pm. Tube: Knightsbridge.

Richoux has an old-fashioned atmosphere. You can order four hot scones with strawberry jam and whipped cream or choose from the patisserie that are displayed. A full menu, with fresh salads, sandwiches, burgers, and more, is available all day long.

There are three other locations: a branch at the bottom of Bond Street, 172 Piccadilly (☎ **0171/493-2204;** tube: Piccadilly Circus or Green Park), one at 41A S. Audley St. (☎ **0171/629-5228;** tube: Green Park or Hyde Park Corner), and one at St. John's Wood, 3 Circus Rd. (☎ **0171/483-4001;** tube: St. John's Wood). The branches are open Monday through Saturday from 8:30am to 11pm, Sunday from 10am to 11:30pm.

BELGRAVIA

The Lanesborough. Hyde Park Corner, SW1. ☎ **0171/259-5599.** Reservations required. High tea £18.50 ($29.60); high tea with strawberries and champagne £22.50 ($36). Cup of tea £3.50 ($5.60). AE, DC, MC, V. Daily 3:30–6pm (last order). AE, DC, MC, V. Tube: Hyde Park Corner.

You'll suspect that many people sipping exotic teas here have dropped in to see the public areas of one of London's most expensive hotels. For tea, you'll sit in the Conservatory, a glass-roofed Edwardian fantasy loaded with potted plants and a majestic sense of the British Empire. There's a selection of seven teas, including the Lanesborough special blend and such herbal esoteria as Rose Cayou. The finger sandwiches, scones, and sweets are all appropriately lavish and completely correct.

CHELSEA

The Tearoom at the Chelsea Physic Garden. 66 Royal Hospital Rd., SW3. ☎ **0171/352-5646.** Tea with cake £3.50 ($5.60). No credit cards. Wed noon–5pm, Sun 2–6pm. Closed Nov–Mar. Tube: Sloane Square.

The Chelsea Physic Garden encompasses 3½ acres crisscrossed with gravel paths and ringed with a high brick wall that shuts out the roaring traffic of Royal Hospital Road. But this small space manages to create an almost Mediterranean microclimate. Founded in 1673 as a botanical education center, its list of successes include the exportation of rubber from South America to Malaya and tea from China to India. The tearoom is only open 2 days a week, and it's likely to be filled with botanical enthusiasts merrily sipping cups of tea as fortification for their treks within the garden. The setting is a rather banal-looking Edwardian building. Since the tearoom is only an adjunct to the glories of the garden itself, don't expect the lavish rituals of other places to take tea. But you can carry your cakes and cups of tea outside, admiring a garden that despite meticulous care, always looks a bit unkempt. (Herbaceous plants within its hallowed precincts are left untrimmed to encourage bird life and seed production.)

KENSINGTON

✪ **The Orangery.** In the gardens of Kensington Palace, W8. ☎ **0171/376-0239.** Reservations not accepted. Pot of tea £1.60 ($2.55); summer cakes and puddings £1.90–£3.85 ($3.05–$6.15). MC, V. Apr–Sept 10am–6pm; Oct–Mar 10am–4:30pm. Tube: High Street Kensington or Queensway.

This is one of the most amazing places for afternoon tea in the world. This long and narrow garden pavilion, about 50 yards north of Kensington Palace, was built in 1704 by Queen Anne as a site for her tea parties. In homage to that monarch's original intentions, rows of potted orange trees bask in sunlight from soaring windows, and tea is still served amid Corinthian columns, ruddy-colored bricks, and a pair of Grinling Gibbons woodcarvings. There are even some urns and statuary that the royal family brought to the site from Windsor Castle. Tea is served in high style, and you can also order lunchtime soups and sandwiches.

NOTTING HILL

The Garden Café. London Lighthouse, 111-117 Lancaster Rd., W11. ☎ **0171/792-1200.** Cups of tea 40p (65¢); platters of food £2.50–£4 ($4–$6.40). No credit cards. Mon–Fri 9am–7:30pm, Sat–Sun noon–2:30pm. Tube: Ladbroke Grove.

This is the most unusual of the places we recommend, and the most worthwhile. The Garden Café is in The Lighthouse, the largest center in Europe for people with HIV and AIDS. The late Princess Diana made the organization one of her projects and even stopped in for tea in person. The cafeteria is open to the public and is less institutional looking than you might have expected. French doors open onto a spectacular garden with fountains and summertime tables. Tea is available throughout the day, although the midafternoon, between 3:30 and 5:30pm, seems to be the most convivial time. Its Notting Hill location is only a short walk from Portobello Road.

6 Pubs & Wine Bars

ST. JAMES'S

Red Lion. 2 Duke of York St., off Jermyn St., SW1. ☎ **0171/930-2030.** Mon–Sat noon–11pm. Tube: Piccadilly Circus. BRITISH.

This little Victorian pub with its early 1900s decorations and 150-year-old mirrors offers premade sandwiches, but once they're gone you're out of luck. On Friday and Saturday, homemade fish-and-chips are also served. Wash down your meal with Ind Coope's fine ales, or the house's special beer, Burton's, an unusual brew made from springwater from the Midlands town of Burton-upon-Trent.

LEICESTER SQUARE

Cork & Bottle Wine Bar. 44-46 Cranbourn St., WC2. ☎ **0171/734-7807.** Mon–Sat 11am–midnight, Sun noon–10:30pm. Tube: Leicester Square.

Don Hewitson, a connoisseur of fine wines, has presided here for more than a quarter of a century. The wine list features an excellent selection of Beaujolais wines from Alsace, 30 selections from Down Under, 30 champagnes, and a good selection of California labels. And if you want something to munch, the most successful dish is a raised cheese-and-ham pie. The kitchen also offers a chicken and apple salad, Lancashire sausage hot pot, Mediterranean prawns with garlic and asparagus, tandoori chicken, and lamb in ale.

☉ The Salisbury. 90 St. Martin's Lane, WC2. **☎ 0171/836-5863.** Mon–Sat 11am–11pm, Sun noon–10:30pm. Tube: Leicester Square.

Salisbury's glittering cut-glass mirrors reflect the faces of English stage stars (and hopefuls) sitting around the curved buffet-style bar. You can also sit at an old-fashioned wall banquette with copper-top tables and art nouveau decor. The pub's specialty is home-cooked pies set out on a buffet cabinet with salads; it's really quite good and inexpensive. Hot food is served from noon until 7:30pm, cold sandwiches from noon to 10pm.

COVENT GARDEN

Bow Wine Vaults. 10 Bow Churchyard, EC4. **☎ 0171/248-1121.** The Restaurant and Grill Bar, Mon–Fri 11am–10pm. Pub, Mon–Fri 11am–11pm. Tube: Bank Street or St. Paul's.

One of the most famous (and surprisingly affordable) wine bars of London beckons diners and drinkers belowground to its vaulted cellars. Menu choices in the Cellar Grill bar, as it's called, include such traditional fare as deep-fried Camembert, chicken Kiev, and a mixed grill, along with fish. More elegant meals, served in the street-level dining room, called The Restaurant, include mussels in cider sauce, English wild mushrooms in puffy pastry, beef Wellington, and steak with brown-butter sauce. Adjacent to the restaurant is a cocktail bar, open weekdays from 11:30am to 8pm, that's popular with City employees after work.

The Jamaica Wine House. St. Michael's Alley, off Cornhill, EC3. **☎ 0171/626-9496.** Mon–Fri 11am–9:30pm. Tube: Bank Street.

The Jamaica Wine House is one of the first coffeehouses to be opened in England, and, reputedly, in the Western world. For years, London merchants and daring sea captains came here to lace deals with rum and coffee. Nowadays, the two-level house dispenses beer, ale, lager, and fine wines, among them ports. The street level oak-paneled bar attracts a jacket-and-tie crowd of investment bankers, whereas the basement bar is an even cozier retreat. You can order toasted sandwiches and a ploughman's lunch.

The Nag's Head. 10 James St., WC2. **☎ 0171/836-4678.** Mon–Sat 11am–11pm, Sun noon–10:30pm. Tube: Covent Garden.

The Nag's Head is one of the most famous Edwardian pubs of London. Lunch is typical pub grub—sandwiches, salads, pork cooked in cider, and garlic prawns—and snacks are available in the afternoon.

Olde Wine Shades. 6 Martin Lane, Cannon St., EC4. **☎ 0171/626-6876.** Jacket and tie required for men. Mon–Fri 11:30am–3pm and 5–8pm. Closed bank holidays. Tube: Cannon Street.

Dating from 1663, the Olde Wine Shades is The City's oldest wine house. Near the Monument, it survived the Great Fire of 1666 and Hitler's bombs. It's also one of the many London bars that Dickens used to patronize. There is a restaurant downstairs, and you can order light meals upstairs, say, jacket potatoes filled with cheese or venison pie.

VICTORIA

Ebury Wine Bar. 139 Ebury St., SW1. **☎ 0171/730-5447.** Mon–Sat 11am–10:30pm, Sun 6–10pm. Tube: Victoria or Sloane Square.

The Revolution: Haute Cuisine Comes to the Neighborhood Pub

After decades—nay, centuries—of enduring some of the worst food in England, pub-goers still can't believe what has happened to their neighborhood locals: They've become foodie havens. More and more pubs are offering food you can actually eat, not just canned beans on stale toast. Believe it or not, some of the chefs cooking in pubs today could even hold court in top restaurants.

What's brought about such a transformation in the lowly pub? Many up-and-coming chefs simply can't afford the price tag of opening a restaurant, so they've turned to the pub as an alternative venue. They've cleaned up the decades-old beer and nicotine stains and thrown out the smoke-scented draperies hung when Edward VII was on the throne, and lo! The place becomes light and airy. A modern kitchen and a new menu follows, and suddenly grandpa's local is a hot new dining destination.

You don't have to be a young fashion victim to enjoy the superb fare served at **The Cow,** 89 Westbourne Park Rd., W2 (☎ 0171/221-0021; tube: Westbourne Grove). Tom Conran (son of restaurateur/entrepreneur Sir Terence Conran) holds forth nightly in this increasingly hip Notting Hill watering hole, which looks like an Irish pub. With a pint of Fuller's or London Pride firmly in hand, you can linger over the modern European menu, which changes daily, but is likely to include mussels in curry and cream or steak with onion rings. The seafood selections are especially delectable. "The Cow Special"—half a dozen Irish rock oysters with a pint of Guinness or a glass of wine for £8 ($12.80)—is the star of the show. A raw bar downstairs serves an array of fresh choices in addition to oysters. To finish, skip the filtered coffee served upstairs (it's wretched), and opt for an espresso downstairs. Main courses run £8 to £14 ($12.80 to $22.40); 2-course fixed-price dinner £35 ($56). Open Monday through Saturday from 7 to 11:30pm and Sunday from 12:30 to 3:30pm; bar open daily from 11:30am to 11:30pm; MC, V accepted.

Another of our favorites is **The Engineer,** 65 Gloucester Ave., NW1 (☎ 0171/722-0950; tube: Chalk Farm or Camden Town), a stylishly converted North London pub owned by Abigail Osborne and Tamsin Olivier, daughter of Sir Laurence (or "Larry's daughter," as she's called locally). The pub is divided into a bar, a dining room, and a garden area that welcomes diners on warm days. The decor is light and modern, enhanced by regular exhibits by local artists. The cuisine relies on seasonal produce and organic meat and eggs. Choices include Moroccan-style chicken tagine with couscous and a warm salad of shiitake

---

Older professional people who don't mind smoke and the smell of sizzling steaks close to their tables gravitate here. It's one of the most popular and enduring wine bars in the area—all dark and woodsy. In addition to those steaks, the wine-bar menu is surprisingly varied. Some dishes have a Pacific Rim influence, including Thai fish balls. Others are more typically English, as exemplified by roast pork with a crackling and apple sauce.

KNIGHTSBRIDGE

Bill Bentley's. 31 Beauchamp Place, SW3. ☎ 0171/589-5080. Mon–Sat noon–2:30pm and 6–10:30pm. Tube: Knightsbridge.

mushrooms with celeriac and red-onion confit. A tantalizing appetizer is the deep fried Camembert with kiwi fruit relish. Main courses run £8.50 to £12 ($13.60 to $19.20). Open daily from noon to midnight, with the bar closing at 11pm. Reservations are required to dine; MC, V accepted.

The poshest pub conversion in town is **The Enterprise,** 35 Walton St., SW3 (☎ **0171/584-3148;** tube: South Kensington). Its proximity to Harrods attracts both regulars and out-of-towners loaded down with packages from the swank department store. Although the joint is cruisy at night (whatever your preference), during the day it attracts the ladies-who-lunch crowd with banquettes, white linen, and fresh flowers on the tables. The kitchen serves very respectable traditional English fare prepared with fresh ingredients; featured dishes include fried salmon cakes with perfectly done fries, and grilled sole with new potatoes. The salads are freshly made, especially the crab and prawn stuffed into a pappadam. Main courses cost £8.50 to £8.50 to £12.50 ($13.60 to $20). Open daily from noon to 2:30pm, Monday through Friday 7 to 11pm, and Saturday and Sunday 7 to 10:30pm (the bar is open all day). Reservations are accepted for lunch but not for dinner; AE, MC, V accepted.

The offbeat **Prince Bonaparte,** 80 Chepstow Rd., W2 (☎ **0171/229-5912;** tube: Notting Hill Gate or Westbourne Park), serves great grub in what was a grungy pub in the days before Notting Hill Gate became fashionable. Now pretty young things show up, spilling out onto the sidewalk when the evenings are warm. The pub is filled with mismatched furniture from schools and churches; jazz and lazy blues fill the air, competing with the babble. It may seem at first that the staff doesn't have its act together, but once the food arrives, you won't care one way or the other: It's very good. The menu roams the world for inspiration: Moroccan chicken with couscous is as good or better than any you'll find in Marrakech; the seared salmon teriyaki with basmati rice is perfectly prepared. Start with hummus and feta cheese on a grilled slab of grainy bread. Roast lamb, tender and juicy, appears on the traditional Sunday menu. Main courses run £6.50 to £7 ($10.40 to $11.20). Open Monday, Wednesday, Thursday, and Friday from noon to 11pm, Tuesday 5 to 11pm, and Sunday noon to 10:30pm. No credit cards.

If this nouvelle trend's got you down, don't worry: You still can dig into traditional pub grub in dozens of pubs that slept through the revolution. We've recommended a handful of our favorites in these pages.

This wine bar stands right on this fashionable restaurant- and boutique-lined block. Its varied and reasonably priced wine list includes a good selection of Bordeaux. In summer, you can sit on a garden patio. The wine-bar menu includes half a dozen oysters, plus Bill Bentley's famous fish cakes. In the more formal restaurant, the menu has been simplified and is rather less expensive than before. Our favorite main dishes include the chef's leek-and-ham hot pot, salmon fish cakes, and, when we're feeling festive, Dover sole meunière.

✪ **The Grenadier.** 18 Wilton Row, SW1. ☎ **0171/235-3074.** Daily noon–3pm; Mon–Sat 6–10pm, Sun noon–3:30pm and 7–10:30pm. Closed Dec 25–26 and Jan 1. Tube: Hyde Park Corner.

Tucked away in a back street, Grenadier is one of London's numerous reputedly haunted pubs. The basement also houses the original bar and skittles alley used by the duke of Wellington's officers on leave from fighting Napoléon. The scarlet front door of the one-time officers' mess is guarded by a scarlet sentry box and shaded by a vine. The bar is nearly always crowded. Lunch and dinner are offered daily—on Sunday, it is traditional to drink Bloody Marys. In the stalls along the side, you can order good-tasting (surprisingly pricey) fare based on seasonal ingredients. Tempting dishes include venison, pheasant, salmon in puff pastry with dill butter, and everybody's favorite: Duke of Wellington steak. Snacks, such as fish-and-chips, are available at the bar.

Star Tavern. 6 Belgrave Mews W., SW1. ☎ **0171/235-3019.** Restaurant Mon–Fri noon–2:30pm and 6:30–8:45pm. Pub Mon–Sat noon–11pm, Sun noon–3pm and 7–10:30pm. Closed Dec 25–26. Tube: Knightsbridge or Hyde Park Corner.

In a Georgian mews, the Star Tavern is one of the West End's most colorful pubs, with a picture-postcard facade. And it's quite cozy in winter with two fireplaces going. Groups of office workers descend after work. The place is attractive inside, with Victorian walls and banquettes beneath 19th-century Victorian moldings. You can order such affordable dishes as baby spring chicken, sirloin steak (if available), or vegetable quiche. Place your order at the bar.

Exploring London 5

London is more eclectic and electric than it's been in years. Some even think it's surpassed New York for sheer energy, outrageous fashion, trendy restaurants, and a nightlife that's second to none.

But we don't want to mislead. Although London is more open and dynamic than it's been since 1969, it's not one giant house party. There are problems here, as elsewhere, that all the trendy restaurants and pricey boutiques in the world cannot obliterate. The gulf between rich and poor continues to widen, and violent crime, once relatively rare, is on the rise.

And although the cool youth culture is grabbing headlines, it's not all there is to London these days. What makes the city so fascinating is its cultural diversity. It seems that half the world is flocking there, not just from the far-flung former colonies of the once great British Empire, but also from Algeria, Argentina, China, and Senegal. And these recent transplants are transforming a city once maligned as a drab, stuffy metropolis with their talent and new ideas. In the London of today, where everything's changing, only the queen appears the same. (After she's gone, even the House of Windsor may be in for a shake-up.)

In this chapter, we can explore only a fraction of what's exciting in London. We went in search of what's causing the hottest buzz in shopping and nightlife, but we also provide plenty of detail about London's time-tested treasures: ancient monuments, literary shrines, walking tours, Parliament debates, royal castles, waxworks, palaces, cathedrals, and royal parks.

Note: As a rule, and unless otherwise stated on the listings below, children's prices at London attractions apply to those aged 16 and under. You must be 60 years of age or older to obtain available senior-citizen discounts at some attractions. For students to get available discounted admissions they must have a valid student ID card.

SUGGESTED ITINERARIES

For the first time visitor, the question is never what to do, but what to do first.

If You Have 1 Day

Make sure to see Westminster Abbey, with its Poets' Corner inside. After you've visited the abbey, walk over to see Big Ben and the Houses

Central London Sights

142

of Parliament. Also witness the Changing of the Guard at Buckingham Palace, if it's being held, and then walk over to 10 Downing St., home of the prime minister. For dinner, try a Covent Garden restaurant, such as Porter's English Restaurant. For a nightcap, head over to the Red Lion, 2 Duke of York St., in Mayfair, where you can enjoy a lager in the ultimate Victorian pub.

If You Have 2 Days

Spend your first day as above. Devote a good part of the second day to exploring the British Museum, one of the world's biggest and best museums. Spend the afternoon visiting the Tower of London and seeing the collection of crown jewels (expect slow-moving lines). For dinner, go to one of London's landmark restaurants such as Simpson's-in-the-Strand, 100 The Strand, where your favorite roast will be carved at your table.

If You Have 3 Days

Spend days 1 and 2 as above. On the third day, go to the National Gallery, facing Trafalgar Square, in the morning. Then enjoy the afternoon at Madame Tussaud's Waxworks. It's also worthwhile to walk around St. James's. In the evening, try to catch a performance at the South Bank Centre, site of the Royal Festival Hall.

If You Have 4 Days

Spend the first 3 days as above. On the morning of the fourth day, head for The City, the financial district of London in the East End, where you can explore Sir Christopher Wren's St. Paul's Cathedral. Spend a few hours strolling The City and visit a few of its many metropolitan attractions. In the late afternoon, head down King's Road in Chelsea to check out the boutiques, followed by dinner at a Chelsea restaurant.

If You Have 5 Days

On the fifth day, explore the Victoria and Albert Museum in the morning, or perhaps the Tate Gallery (you can plan to have lunch at its restaurant). Spend the rest of the afternoon wandering through the gallery enjoying its masterpieces. Finally, see where history was made during the dark days of World War II by visiting the Cabinet War Rooms at Clive Steps, where Churchill directed the British operations against the Nazis. If you haven't already crammed in as many West End shows as you can on the first 4 nights, attend the theater this final evening.

1 The Top Attractions

✪　**The Tower of London.** Tower Hill, on the north bank of the Thames, EC3. ☎ **0171/709-0765.** Admission £8.50 ($13.60) adults, £6.40 ($10.25) students and senior citizens, £5.60 ($8.95) children; free for children under 5. Family ticket for 5 (but no more than 2 adults), £25.40 ($40.65). Mar–Oct Mon–Sat 9am–5pm, Sun 10am–5pm; Nov–Feb Tues–Sat 9am–4pm, Sun–Mon 10am–4pm. Closed Dec 24–26, Jan 1. Tube: Tower Hill. Boats: From Westminster Pier.

This ancient fortress continues to pack in visitors because of its macabre associations with all the legendary figures who were imprisoned and/or executed here. James Street once wrote, "There are more spooks to the square foot than in any other building in the whole of haunted Britain. Headless bodies, bodiless heads, phantom soldiers, icy blasts, clanking chains—you name them, the Tower's got them." Plan on spending a lot of time here.

One-hour tours are given by the Yeoman Warders at frequent intervals, starting at 9:30am from the Middle Tower near the main entrance. The tour includes the Chapel

Beauchamp Tower ⑪
Bell Tower ③
Bloody Tower ⑦
Bowyer Tower (torture chamber) ⑭
Brick Tower ⑮
Broad Arrow Tower ⑱
Byward Tower ②
Chapel Royal of St. Peter ad Vincula ⑧
Constable Tower ⑰
Cradle Tower ㉑
Develin Tower ㉓
Devereux Tower ⑫

Flint Tower ⑬
Jewel House (entrance) ⑨
Lanthorn Tower ⑳
Martin Tower ⑯
Middle Tower ①
Salt Tower ⑲
Site of Scaffold ⑩
St. Thomas's Tower ⑤
Traitor's Gate ④
Wakefield Tower ⑥
Well Tower ㉒

Royal of St. Peter and Vincula (St. Peter in Chains). The last guided walk starts at around 3:30pm in summer, 2:30pm in winter.

Insider's tip: The secret to avoiding the notoriously long lines here is to come early. The hordes descend in the afternoon. Arrive the moment the gates open. And try to avoid Sundays, when crowds are awful.

The fortress is actually a compound, in which the oldest and finest structure is the White Tower, begun by William the Conqueror. Here you can view the Armouries, which date from the reign of Henry VIII. A display of instruments of torture and execution recalls some of the most ghastly moments in the Tower's history. At the Bloody Tower, the Little Princes (Edward V and the duke of York) were allegedly murdered by their uncle, Richard III. Through Traitors' Gate passed such ill-fated but romantic figures as Robert Devereux, known as the second earl of Essex, a favorite of Elizabeth I. At Tower Green, Anne Boleyn and Catherine Howard, two wives of Henry VIII, lost their lives. Many other notable figures have lost their lives at the tower, including Sir Thomas More and the 4-day queen, Lady Jane Grey, who was executed at Tower Green.

To see the **Jewel House,** where the Crown Jewels are kept, go early in the day during summer because long lines often form. Since it's on the ground level, there's easy access for wheelchairs. Ask one of the Yeoman Warders (Beefeaters) in Tudor uniform to tell you how Colonel Blood almost made off with the crown and regalia in the late 17th century. Of the three English crowns, the Imperial State Crown is the most important—in fact, it's the most famous crown on earth. Made for Victoria in 1837, it is worn today by Queen Elizabeth when she opens Parliament. Studded with some 3,000 jewels (principally diamonds), it includes the Black Prince's Ruby, worn by Henry V at Agincourt (the 1415 battle where the English defeated the French). The 530-carat Star of Africa is a cut diamond on the Royal Sceptre with Cross.

The Tower of London has an evening ritual called the **Ceremony of the Keys,** the locking up of the Tower. The Yeoman Warder will explain to guests the ceremony's significance. For free tickets, write to the Ceremony of the Key, Waterloo Block, Tower of London, London EC3N 4AB, and request a specific date, but also list alternative dates. At least 6 weeks' notice is required. All requests must be accompanied by a stamped, self-addressed stamped envelope (British stamps only) or two International Reply Coupons. With ticket in hand, you'll be admitted by a Yeoman Warder at 9:35pm.

Then there are the ravens. Six of them, plus two spares, are all registered as official Tower residents and each is fed exactly 6 ounces of rations per day. According to a legend, the Tower of London will stand as long as those black, ominous birds remain in the Tower (to be on the safe side, one of the wings of each raven is clipped).

A palace once inhabited by King Edward I in the late 1200s was opened to visitors for the first time in 1993. Above Traitor's Gate, it is the only surviving medieval palace in Britain. Guides are dressed in period costumes. Reproductions of furniture and fittings, including Edward's throne, evoke the era, along with burning incense and candles. Admission to the palace is included in the standard ticket price.

✪ **Westminster Abbey.** Broad Sanctuary, SW1. ☎ **0171/222-7110.** Admission £5 ($8) adults, £3 ($4.80) students and seniors; £1.50 ($2.40) children 11–18; free for children ages 10 and under. Mon–Fri 9am–3:45pm, Sat 9:15am–1:45pm and 4–4:45pm. Tube: Westminster or St. James's Park.

Nearly every figure in English history has left his or her mark on Westminster Abbey. In 1065 the Saxon king, Edward the Confessor, founded the Benedictine abbey and rebuilt the old minster church on this spot, overlooking Parliament Square. The first English king crowned in the abbey was Harold in 1066, before he was killed at the Battle of Hastings later that same year. The man who defeated him, Edward's cousin, William the Conqueror, was also crowned at the abbey; the coronation tradition has continued to the present day, broken only twice (Edward V and Edward VIII). Most recently, in September 1997, the abbey served as the setting for the funeral of Diana, Princess of Wales.

Built on the site of the ancient lady chapel in the early 16th century, the Henry VII Chapel is one of the loveliest in Europe, with its fan vaulting, Knights of Bath banners, and Torrigiani-designed tomb of the king himself. Also here are the feuding half-sisters, ironically buried in the same tomb, Catholic Mary I and Protestant Elizabeth I (whose archrival, Mary Queen of Scots, is entombed on the other side of the Henry VII Chapel). In one end of the chapel, you can stand on Cromwell's memorial stone and view the RAF chapel and its Battle of Britain memorial stained-glass window, unveiled in 1947 to honor the RAF.

You can also visit the most hallowed spot in the abbey, the shrine of Edward the Confessor (canonized in the 12th century). In the saint's chapel is the Coronation Chair, made at the command of Edward I in 1300 to display the Stone of Scone. Scottish kings were once crowned on this stone. The stone has since been returned to Scotland.

Another noted spot in the abbey is the **Poets' Corner,** to the right of the entrance to the Royal Chapel, with monuments to everybody—Chaucer, Shakespeare, "O Rare Ben Johnson" (his name misspelled), Samuel Johnson, the Brontë sisters, Thackeray,

Bookshop **16**

Chapel of St. John the Baptist **6**

Chapel of St. John the Evangelist **5**

Chapter House **14**

Henry V's Chantry **8**

Poets' Corner **13**

Royal Air Force Chapel **11**

St. Andrew's Chapel **3**

St. Edward's Chapel
(Coronation Chair) **7**

St. George's Chapel **1**

St. Michael's Chapel **4**

Tomb of Mary I &
Elizabeth I **9**

Tomb of Henry VII **10**

Tomb of Mary,
Queen of Scots **12**

Tomb of the Unknown Warrior/
Memorial to Churchill **2**

Undercroft Museum **15**

Dickens, Tennyson, Kipling, even the American Longfellow. The most stylized monument is Sir Jacob Epstein's sculptured bust of William Blake. A more recent tablet commemorates poet Dylan Thomas.

Statesmen and men of science, such as Disraeli, Newton, Charles Darwin, are also interred in the abbey or honored by monuments. Near the west door is the 1965 memorial to Sir Winston Churchill. Near this memorial is the tomb of the Unknown Soldier, commemorating the British dead in World War I. Some totally obscure personages are also buried in the abbey, including an abbey plumber.

Off the Cloisters, the College Garden is the oldest garden in England, under cultivation for more than 900 years. Surrounded by high walls, flowering trees dot the lawns and park benches provide comfort where you can hardly hear the roar of passing traffic. It is open only on Tuesday and Thursday. In the Cloisters, you can make a rubbing at the **Brass Rubbing Center** (☎ **0171/222-2085**).

The only time photography is allowed in the abbey is Wednesday evening from 6 to 7:45pm. On Sunday, the Royal Chapels are closed, but the rest of the church is open, unless a service is being conducted. For times of services, phone the **Chapter Office** (☎ **0171/222-5152**). Up to six supertours of the abbey are conducted by the vergers Monday through Saturday, beginning at 10am and costing £7 ($11.20) per person.

Insider's tip: Far removed from the pomp and glory of this edifice is the **Abbey Treasure Museum,** with a bag of oddities. They're displayed in the undercroft or crypt, part of the monastic buildings erected between 1066 and 1100. Here are royal effigies that were used instead of the real corpses for lying-in-state ceremonies. You'll see the almost lifelike effigy of Admiral Nelson (his mistress arranged his hair) and even the effigy of Edward III, his lip warped by the stroke that felled him. Other treats include everything from a Middle English lease to Chaucer, the much-used sword of Henry VI, and the Essex Ring Elizabeth I gave to her favorite earl (when she was feeling good about him and didn't want his head).

✪ **Houses of Parliament.** Westminster Palace, Old Palace Yard, SW1. ☎ **0171/ 219-4272** for the House of Commons, or **0171/219-3107** for the House of Lords. Free admission. House of Lords, open to public Mon–Wed from 2:30pm, Thurs from 3pm; also some Fridays (check by phone). House of Commons, open to public Mon, Tues, and Thurs 2:30–10pm, Wed and Fri from 9:30am–3:30pm. Join line at St. Stephen's entrance. Tube: Westminster.

These are the stronghold of Britain's democracy, the assemblies that effectively trimmed the sails of royal power. Both Houses (Commons and Lords) are situated in the former royal Palace of Westminster, the king's residence until Henry VIII moved to Whitehall.

The debates are often lively and controversial in the House of Commons (seats are at a premium during crises). Your chance of getting into the House of Lords when it's in session is generally better than for the more popular House of Commons, where even the queen isn't allowed. The old guard of the palace informs us that the peerage speak their minds more freely and are less likely to adhere to the party line than their counterparts in the Commons.

The present Houses of Parliament were built in 1840, but the Commons chamber was bombed and destroyed by the Luftwaffe in 1941. The 320-foot tower that houses **Big Ben,** however, remained standing and the "symbol of London" continues to strike its chimes. (Big Ben, incidentally, was named after Sir Benjamin Hall, a cabinet minister distinguished only by his long-windedness.)

To be admitted to the Strangers' Galleries, join the public line outside the St. Stephen's entrance; often there is a delay before the line is admitted. The line for the House of Commons forms on the left, or on the right for the Lords. You might speed matters up by applying at the American Embassy or the Canadian High Commission for a special pass. However, the embassy has only four tickets for daily distribution, so you might as well stand in line. To arrange a tour before you leave home, you can write House of Commons Information Office, 1 Derby Gate, Westminster, London SW1A 2DG. Tours are usually conducted on Fridays.

✪ **The British Museum.** Great Russell St., WC1. ☎ **0171/323-8299,** or 0171/ 636-1555 for a recording. Free admission. Mon–Sat 10am–5pm, Sun 2:30–6pm (the galleries start to close 10 min. earlier). Closed Jan 1, Good Friday, early May, Dec 24–26. Tube: Holborn, Tottenham Court Road, or Russell Square.

The British Museum shelters one of the most comprehensive collections of art and artifacts in the world, including countless treasures of ancient and modern civilizations. Even on a cursory first visit, you'll want to see the Asian collections (the finest assembly of Islamic pottery outside the Islamic world), the Chinese porcelain, the Indian sculpture, and the Prehistoric and Romano-British collections.

Here's our advice: The museum is so vast, so overwhelming (with 2½ miles of galleries) that it's best to take a 1½-hour tour for £6 ($9.60) on your first visit. They're offered Monday through Saturday at 10:45am, 11:15am, 1:45pm, and 2:15pm, or Sunday at 3pm, 3:20pm, and 3:45pm. Later you can come back and examine more closely what interested you. If you have only minutes to spare for the museum, concentrate on the Greek and Rome rooms (nos. 1 through 15). They contain all the booty bought or stolen from the Empire's once far-flung colonies.

(world wonder)

Exploring lost cultures? Take along an **AT&T Direct**® **Service** wallet guide. It's a list of access numbers you need to call home fast and clear from around the world, using an AT&T Calling Card or credit card. What an amazing planet we live on.

For a list of AT&T Access Numbers, take the attached wallet guide.

It's all within your reach. **AT&T**

For Travelers
who want more than
the Official Line

For Travelers Who Want More Than the Official Line

the
Unofficial
Guide® to
New Orleans

The Guides with More Than 2.5 Million Copies in Print!

the
Unofficial
Guide® to
Walt Disney World®

The Series with More Than 2.5 Million Copies Sold!

For Travelers Who Want More Than the Official Line

the
Unofficial
Guide® to
Las Vegas

The Series with More Than 2.5 Million Copies Sold!

♦ Save Time & Money
♦ Hotels & Restaurants
Candidly Rated & Ranked
♦ Insider Tips & Warnings

Steve Zibart with Bob Sehlinger

♦ Tips & Warnings
♦ Save Money & Time
♦ All Attractions Ranked & Rated
♦ Plus Disney's New Animal Kingdom

Bob Sehlinger

♦ Save Time & Money
♦ Insider Gambling Tips
♦ Casinos & Hotels
Candidly Rated & Ranked

Bob Sehlinger

Macmillan Publishing USA

Also Available:

- The Unofficial Guide to Branson
- The Unofficial Guide to Chicago
- The Unofficial Guide to Cruises
- The Unofficial Disney Companion
- The Unofficial Guide to Disneyland
- The Unofficial Guide to the Great Smoky & Blue Ridge Mountains
- The Unofficial Guide to Miami & the Keys
- Mini-Mickey: The Pocket-Sized Unofficial Guide to Walt Disney World
- The Unofficial Guide to New York City
- The Unofficial Guide to San Francisco
- The Unofficial Guide to Skiing in the West
- The Unofficial Guide to Washington, D.C.

The British Museum

HIGHLIGHTS

Assyrian Transept **1**
Black Obelisk of
  Shalmaneser III **3**
Caryatid from the
  Erechtheum **5**
Elgin Marbles **4**
King's Library **12**
Manuscript Room **11**
Mausoleum of
  Halicarnassus **6**
Mummies **8**
Portland Vase **7**
Rosetta Stone **2**
Standard of Ur **9**
Sutton-Hoo
  Anglo-Saxon
  burial ship **10**

UPPER FLOOR

94 93 92
Lift
91 90

66
60 **8** 61 62 63 64
59 58 57 **9** 56 55 54 53
73 52
72 51
71 50
70 49
7
36 Lift **10**
35 40 41 42
69a 69 68 37 38 39 47 46
48
Montague Place
Entrance 34

KING EDWARD VII GALLERY
33a
33
33b

LOWER FLOOR
Lift
33c
23 22
10 **12** 24
9 **6**
5 21 25B
14 **12**
4 7 **READING**
8 20 25 **ROOM** 32
6 **16** 25
5 **3** 19 **2**
17 **1** Lift
4 **11**
3 26 29 30
2 1 27 31
30a
Cafeteria
28 **Great Russell Street**

DUVEEN GALLERY
HALL OF EGYPTIAN SCULPTURE
KING'S LIBRARY

3-04-35

149

As you enter the front hall, you may want to head first to the Assyrian Transept on the ground floor, where you'll find the winged and human-headed bulls and lions that once guarded the gateways to the palaces of Assyrian kings. Nearby is the **Black Obelisk of Shalmaneser III** (858-824 B.C.) depicting Jehu, king of Israel, paying tribute. From here you can continue into the angular hall of Egyptian sculpture to see the **Rosetta stone,** whose discovery led to the deciphering of hieroglyphs.

Also on the ground floor is the Duveen Gallery, housing the **Elgin marbles,** consisting chiefly of sculptures from the Parthenon, on the Acropolis in Athens.

The classical sculpture galleries house a caryatid from the Erechtheum, also on the Acropolis, a temple started in 421 B.C. and dedicated to Athena and Poseidon. Displayed here, too, are sculptures from the Mausoleum at Halicarnassus (ca. 350 B.C.).

The Department of Medieval and Later Antiquities has its galleries on the first floor (second floor to Americans), reached by the main staircase. Of its exhibitions, the Sutton Hoo Anglo-Saxon burial ship, discovered in Suffolk, is, in the words of an expert, "the richest treasure ever dug from English soil"; it held gold jewelry, armor, weapons, bronze bowls and cauldrons, silverware, and the inevitable drinking horn of the Norse culture.

The featured attractions of the upper floor are the Egyptian Galleries, especially the **mummies.** Egyptian Room 63 is extraordinary, resembling the props for *Cleopatra*, with its cosmetics, domestic utensils, toys, tools, and other work. Items of Sumerian art, unearthed from the Royal Cemetery at Ur (southern Iraq), lie in a room beyond, some dating from around 2500 B.C. In the Iranian room rests "The Treasure of the Oxus," a hoard of riches, perhaps a temple deposit, dating from the 6th to the 3rd century B.C. See also the galleries of the City of Rome and its Empire, which include exhibitions of art before the Romans.

The year 2000 will see changes to the historic museum. Dubbed the "Great Court" project, the inner courtyard will be canopied by a lightweight, transparent roof transforming the area into a covered square, housing a Centre for Education, exhibition space, bookshops, and restaurants. The center of the Great Court will feature the Round Reading Room restored to its original decorative scheme. The hallowed reading room itself has moved across town to 96 Euston Rd. (☎ **0171/412-7111**). The fabled reading room at the British Museum, where Karl Marx meditated, as did Virginia Woolf, closed forever in the autumn of 1997.

✪ **Buckingham Palace.** At the end of The Mall (the street running from Trafalgar Sq.). ☎ **0171/930-9625.** Palace tours £9 ($14.40) adults to age 60, £6.50 ($10.40) adults over 60, £5 ($8) children under 17. Changing of the Guard free (call Visitorcall at ☎ 01839/123-411 for up-to-date information; toll charges 39p–49p (60ce–80ce) per min.). Queen's Gallery: £3.60 ($5.75) adults, £2.50 ($4) seniors, £2 ($3.20) children 5–17. Daily 9:30am–4:30pm. Royal Mews: £3.60 ($5.75) adults, £2.50 ($4) seniors, £2 ($3.20) children 5–17. Usually Apr–July Tues–Thurs noon–4pm; Aug–Sept Mon–Thurs noon–4pm; Oct–Mar Wed only; times are very tentative so call ahead. Tube: St. James's Park, Green Park, or Victoria.

This massively graceful building is the official residence of the queen, and you can tell whether Her Majesty is at home by the Royal Standard flying at the masthead. During most of the year, you can't visit the palace unless you're officially invited, but you can do what thousands of others do: Peep through the railings into the front yard.

However, in the spring of 1993, Queen Elizabeth II agreed to allow visitors to tour her state apartments and picture galleries, at least until 2000. The palace will be open to the public for 8 weeks in August and September, when the royal family is away on vacation. The queen decided on these Buckingham Palace tours to help defray the massive cost of fire damage at Windsor Castle.

You can avoid the long lines by purchasing tickets through **Edwards & Edwards,** 1270 Avenue of the Americas, Suite 2414, New York, NY 10020 (☎ **800/223-6108** or 212/332-2435), before your trip. Visitors with disabilities can reserve tickets directly through the palace by calling ☎ **0171/930-5526.**

The tours include not only the state apartments, but a number of other rooms used by King George IV and designed by John Nash in the 1800s, including the Throne Room and the grand staircase. The queen's picture gallery has some masterpieces that are rarely if ever seen by the public, including Van Dyck's celebrated equestrian portrait of Charles I.

The redbrick palace was built as a country house for the notoriously rakish duke of Buckingham. In 1762 it was bought by King George III, who (if nothing else) was prolific; he needed room for his 15 children. From then on, the building was expanded, remodeled, faced with Portland limestone, and twice bombed (during the Blitz). Today in a 40-acre garden, it stands 360 feet long and has 600 rooms.

Buckingham Palace's most famous spectacle is the **Changing of the Guard.** This ceremony begins (if it begins) at 11:30am and lasts for half an hour. It's perhaps the finest example of military pageantry you'll ever see. The new guard, marching behind a band, comes from either the Wellington or Chelsea barracks and takes over from the old guard in the forecourt of the palace. The time at which this martial ceremony occurs is the subject of mass confusion, and you should always check locally to see if one of the world's most famous military rituals is likely to be staged at the time of your visit. This ceremony has been dropped at the last minute and on short notice, leaving thousands of tourists confused, baffled, and a little angry, feeling they have missed out on a London must-see.

Any schedule announced here is not written in stone. Officials of the ceremony never announce their plans a year in advance (which poses a dilemma for guidebook writers!). In theory at least, the guard is changed daily from about April to mid-July, at which time it goes on its "winter" schedule—that is, changing every other day. The cutback is said to be because of budget constraints. The ceremony might also be abruptly canceled during "uncertain" weather conditions. Check tourist information offices or local publications for schedules.

In the **Queen's Gallery,** you can see a sampling of the royal family's art collection. We can't predict what exhibition you're likely to see, as they change yearly, but we can tell you that the queen's collection contains an unsurpassed range of royal portraits.

The **Royal Mews,** also on Buckingham Palace Road, is one of the finest working stables in the world today. Housed here are the gilded and polished state carriages—such as the gold State Coach used at every coronation since 1831—along with the horses that draw them.

Madame Tussaud's. Marylebone Rd., NW1. ☎ **0171/935-6861.** Admission £8.95 ($14.30) adults, £6.75 ($10.80) seniors, £5.90 ($9.45) children under 16. Combination tickets, including the new planetarium, cost £11.20 ($17.90) adults and £7.10 ($11.35) children under 16. Mon–Sat 10am–5:30pm. Tube: Baker Street.

In 1770, an exhibition of life-size wax figures was opened in Paris by Dr. Curtius. He was soon joined by his niece, Strasbourg-born Marie Tussaud, who learned the secret of making lifelike replicas of the famous and the infamous. During the French Revolution, the head of almost every distinguished victim of the guillotine was molded by Madame Tussaud or her uncle.

Whereas some of the figures on display today come from molds taken by Madame Tussaud, who continued to make portraits until she was 81, the exhibition also introduces new images of whoever is au courant. An enlarged Grand Hall continues to house years of royalty and old favorites, as well as many of today's heads of state and political leaders. In the Chamber of Horrors, you can have the vicarious thrill of walking through a Victorian London street where special effects include the shadow terror of Jack the Ripper. The instruments and victims of death penalties contrast with present-day criminals portrayed within the confines of prison. You are invited to mingle with the more current stars in the garden party, "meeting" everyone from Arnold Schwarzenegger to Elizabeth Taylor.

"Super Stars" offers the latest technologies in sound, light, and special effects combined with new figures from the fields of film and sports.

One of the latest attractions to open here is called "The Spirit of London," a musical show that depicts 400 years of London's history, using special effects that include audio-animatronic figures that move and speak. Visitors take "time-taxis" that allow them to see and hear "Shakespeare" as he writes and speaks lines, to be received by Queen Elizabeth I, and to feel and smell the great fire that started in Pudding Lane in 1666.

✪ **Tate Gallery.** Beside the Thames on Millbank, SW1. ☎ **0171/887-8000.** Free admission, except special exhibitions varying from £5 ($8) to £7 ($11.20). Daily 10am–5:50pm. Closed Dec 24–26. Tube: Pimlico. Bus: 77A, 36, C10, or 88.

The Tate houses the best groupings of British paintings from the 16th century on, as well as England's finest collection of modern art (the works of British artists born after 1860), together with foreign art from the impressionists onward. The number of paintings is staggering. Try to schedule at least two visits—the first to see the classic English works, the second to take in the modern collection. Since only a portion of the collections can be displayed at any one time, the works on view change from time to time.

The first giant among English painters, William Hogarth (1697–1764), is well represented, particularly by his satirical *O the Roast Beef of Old England* (known as *Calais Gate*). Two other famous 18th-century British painters are Sir Joshua Reynolds (1723–92) and Thomas Gainsborough (1727–88).

In the art of J. M. W. Turner (1775–1851), the Tate possesses its largest collection of the works of a single artist. Most of the paintings and watercolors exhibited here were willed to the nation by Turner. In 1987, a new wing at the Tate, called the Clore Gallery, was opened so that the artist's entire bequest can be seen.

In a nation of landscape painters, John Constable (1776–1837) stands out. American-born Sir Jacob Epstein became one of England's greatest sculptors, and some of his bronzes are owned and occasionally displayed by the Tate.

The Tate also has the works of many major painters from both the 19th and 20th centuries, including Paul Nash. The drawings of William Blake (1757–1827), the incomparable mystical poet and illustrator of such works as *The Book of Job, The Divine Comedy,* and *Paradise Lost,* attract the most attention.

In the modern collections, the Tate houses works by Matisse, Dalí, Modigliani, Munch, Bonnard, and Picasso. Truly remarkable is the room devoted to several enormous, somber, but rich abstract canvases by Mark Rothko; the group of paintings and sculptures by Giacometti (1901–66); and the paintings of one of England's best-known modern artists, the late Francis Bacon. Sculptures by Henry Moore and Barbara Hepworth are also occasionally displayed.

Insider's tip: Spare a little time for the Art Now Gallery, housing the most recent works of both new and established artists, some of whom are the most controversial in England. There's always something new, different, and on the cutting edge of the art world here.

The average traveler may find it difficult to obtain tickets to a popular exhibit. If you know of an exhibit you'll want to see, we suggest calling **First Call** (☎ **0171/ 420-0002;** fax 0171/420-0055; P.O. Box 92, London WC2H 9SU), the agency responsible for distributing tickets to said events. A call before your trip, or a call while in London, will save you a good bit of time and trouble.

Downstairs is the internationally renowned gallery restaurant, with murals by Rex Whistler as well as a coffee shop.

Plans call for the Tate Gallery to split into two separate galleries, the original to be known as the Tate Gallery of British Art. A modern international collection will move across the Thames and will become the new Tate Gallery of Modern Art. The galleries will be linked by a pedestrian bridge across the river. Dates of this transfer and split will be announced further along.

✪ **The National Gallery.** On the north side of Trafalgar Sq., WC2. ☎ **0171/ 737-2885.** Free admission. Mon–Tues 10am–6pm, Wed 10am–8pm, Thurs–Sat 10am–6pm, Sun noon–6pm. Closed Jan 1, Good Friday, Dec 24–26. Tube: Charing Cross, Embankment, or Leicester Square.

In an impressive neoclassical building, the National Gallery houses one of the most comprehensive collections of Western paintings, representing all the major schools from the late 13th to the early 20th centuries. The largest part of the collection is devoted to the Italians, including the Sienese, Venetian, and Florentine masters, now housed in the Sainsbury Wing.

Insider's tip: The National Gallery has a computer information center in the Sainsbury Wing where visitors can design a personal tour map. The computer room, located in the Micro Gallery, includes 12 computer workstations open to the public. The system offers 2,200 paintings to select from, with supporting text for each one. The program includes four indexes that are cross-referenced for your convenience. Using a touch-screen computer, you can design your own personalized tour by selecting a maximum of 10 paintings that you would like to view. Once you have made your choices, you print a free personal tour map that shows your selections. There's a small charge, usually about £1 ($1.60), for printouts.

Of the early Gothic works, the *Wilton Diptych* (French or English school, late 14th century) is the rarest treasure; it depicts Richard II being introduced to the Madonna and Child by John the Baptist and the Saxon king, Edward the Confessor.

A Florentine gem by Masaccio is displayed, as well as notable works by Piero della Francesca, Leonardo da Vinci, Michelangelo, and Raphael.

Among the 16th-century Venetian masters, the most notable works include a rare *Adoration of the Kings* by Giorgione, *Bacchus and Ariadne* by Titian, *The Origin of the Milky Way* by Tintoretto, and *The Family of Darius Before Alexander* by Veronese.

A number of satellite rooms are filled with works by major Italian masters of the 15th century, such as Andrea Mantegna of Padua, Giovanni Bellini, and Botticelli.

The painters of northern Europe are well represented. For example, there is Jan van Eyck's portrait of G. Arnolfini and his bride, plus Pieter Brueghel the Elder's Bosch-influenced *Adoration.*

One of the National's big drawing cards is its collection of Rembrandts. His *Self-Portrait at the Age of 34* shows him at the pinnacle of his life; his *Self-Portrait at the Age of 63* is deeply moving and revealing.

Five of the greatest of the homegrown artists—Constable, Turner, Reynolds, Gainsborough, and Hogarth—have masterpieces here, as do three giants of Spanish painting. Velázquez's portrait of the sunken-faced Philip IV, El Greco's *Christ Driving the Traders from the Temple,* and Goya's portrait of the duke of Wellington (once stolen) and his mantilla-wearing *Doña Isabel de Porcel* are on display.

Other rooms are devoted to early 19th-century French painters, such as Delacroix and Ingres; the later 19th-century French impressionists, such as Manet, Monet, Renoir, and Degas; and postimpressionists such as Cézanne, Seurat, and van Gogh.

Kensington Palace. The Broad Walk, Kensington Gardens, W8. ☎ **0171/937-9561.** Admission £7 ($11.20) adults, £4.70 ($7.50) children, £5.75 ($9.20) students and senior citizens. Summer daily 10am–6pm by guided tour; winter 10am–4pm. Tube: Queensway or Bayswater on the north side of the gardens or High Street Kensington on the south side; then you'll have a long walk.

The palace is located at the far western end of Kensington Gardens; the entrance is from the Broad Walk. Kensington Palace was acquired by William III in 1689 and was remodeled by Sir Christopher Wren. George II, who died in 1760, was the last king to use it as a royal residence. You can tour parts of the palace, but many rooms are private. Princess Diana used this as her London residence, and the area in front of the palace drew tens of thousands of mourners after her death. A sea of flowers and tributes stood testament to a nation's grief.

The most interesting chamber to visit is Queen Victoria's bedroom. Here, on the morning of June 20, 1837, she was aroused from her sleep with the news that she had succeeded to the throne, following the death of her uncle, William IV. As you wander through the apartments, you'll see many fine paintings from the Royal Collection.

A special attraction is the Royal Ceremonial Dress Collection, which shows restored rooms from the 19th century, including Queen Victoria's birth room and a series of room settings with the appropriate court dress of the day.

The palace gardens adjoin Hyde Park and are open to the public for daily strolls around Round Pond, near the heart of Kensington Gardens. Also in Kensington Gardens is the **Albert Memorial,** honoring Queen Victoria's consort. Facing Royal Albert Hall, the statue reflects the ostentation of the Victorian era.

✪ **St. Paul's Cathedral.** St. Paul's Churchyard, EC4. ☎ **0171/248-8348** or 0171/ 236-4128. Cathedral £4.50 ($7.20) adults, £2 ($3.20) children 6–16; free for children 5 and under. Galleries £3.50 ($5.60) adults, £1.50 ($2.40) children. Guided tours £3.50 ($5.60), recorded tours £3 ($4.80). Sightseeing Mon–Sat 8:30am–4pm; galleries Mon–Sat 10am–4:15pm. No sightseeing Sun (services only). Tube: St. Paul's.

During World War II, newsreel footage reaching America showed the dome of St. Paul's Cathedral lit by fires caused by bombings all around it. That it survived at all is a miracle, since it was badly hit twice during the early years of the Nazi bombardment of London. But St. Paul's is accustomed to calamity, having been burned down three times and destroyed once by invading Norsemen. It was during the Great Fire of 1666 that the old St. Paul's was razed, making way for a new Renaissance structure designed (after many mishaps and rejections) by Sir Christopher Wren and built between 1675 and 1710.

The classical dome of St. Paul's dominates The City's square mile. Inside, the cathedral is laid out like a Greek cross; it houses few art treasures (Grinling Gibbons's choir stalls are an exception) but many monuments, including one to the "Iron Duke" and a memorial chapel to American service personnel who lost their lives in World War II while stationed in the United Kingdom. Encircling the dome is the Whispering Gallery, so be careful what you say. In the crypt lie not only Wren but also the duke of Wellington and Lord Nelson. A fascinating Diocesan Treasury was opened in 1981. You can climb to the very top of the dome for a spectacular 360° view of London.

Guided tours last 1½ hours and include parts of the cathedral not open to the general public. They take place Monday through Saturday at 11am, 11:30am, 1:30pm, and 2pm. Recorded tours lasting 45 minutes are available throughout the day.

All Souls' Chapel **2**
American Memorial Chapter **8**
Anglican Martyr's Chapel **6**
Chapel of St. Michael
  & St. George **14**
Dean's Staircase **15**
Entrance to Crypt
  (Wren's grave) **11**
Font **5**

High Altar **7**
Lady Chapel **9**
Nelson Monument **12**
Pulpit **10**
St. Dunstan's Chapel **3**
Staircase to Library,
  Whispering Gallery & Dome **13**
Wellington Monument **4**
West Doorway **1**

St. Paul's is an Anglican cathedral with daily services at the following times: Matins Monday through Friday at 7:30am, Saturday at 10am, Holy Communion Monday through Saturday at 8am and 12:30pm, and Evensong Monday through Saturday at 5pm. On Sunday, there is Holy Communion at 8 and again at 11am, Matins at 8:45am, and Evensong at 3:15pm. Admission charges do not apply if visitors are attending services.

Insider's tip: One of the loveliest things you can do during a spring visit to London is to saunter through the free gardens of St. Paul's when the roses are in bloom.

Victoria and Albert Museum. Cromwell Rd., SW7. ☎ **0171/938-8500.** £5 ($8) for adults, £3 ($4.80) for students and seniors. Free for children under 18 and persons with disabilities. Mon noon–5.50pm, Tues–Sun 10am–5.50pm. Tube: South Kensington. Bus C1, 14, or 74.

Located in South Kensington, this museum is one of the liveliest and most imaginative in London. It's named after the queen and her consort but not run in their spirit. The general theme here is the fine and decorative arts, but adhered to in a pleasantly relaxed fashion.

The medieval holdings include many treasures, such as the Eltenberg Reliquary (Rhenish, second half of the 12th century); the Early English Gloucester Candlestick; the Byzantine Veroli Casket, with its ivory panels based on Greek plays; and the Syon Cope, a highly valued embroidery made in England in the early 14th century. The Gothic tapestries, including the Devonshire ones depicting hunting scenes, are

✪   Frommer's Favorite London Experiences

Cruising London's Waterways. In addition to the Thames, London is riddled with an antique canal system, complete with towpath walks, bridges, and wharves. Replaced by the railroad, the canal system remained forgotten until recently, when it was rediscovered by a new generation. Now, an urban renewal effort has restored the system, with bridges painted and repaired, and towpaths cleaned up. See "Organized Tours," below.

Viewing the Turners at the Tate. Upon his death in 1851, J. M. W. Turner bequeathed his personal collection of 19,000 watercolors and some 300 paintings to the people of Britain. He wanted his finished works, some 100 paintings, displayed under one roof. Today at the Tate, you get not only Turner, but glimpses of the Thames through the museum's windows. How appropriate—the artist lived and died on its banks in Chelsea, and painted the river in its many changing moods.

Enjoying a Traditional Afternoon Tea. Nothing is more typically British and it's a great way to spend an afternoon. We've suggested our favorite places for tea in chapter 4.

Shopping Harrods. Regardless of how many times you visit London, it's hard to resist a visit to this vast Knightsbridge emporium. Spread across 15 acres, Harrods proclaims as its motto *Omnia Omnibus Ubique* or "everything for everyone, everywhere." They mean it, too: Someone didn't believe the claim, and in 1975 called Harrods at midnight and ordered a baby elephant to be delivered to the home of the governor of California, Ronald Reagan, and his wife in Sacramento. The animal arrived safely, albeit a bit bewildered. (Nancy even sent a thank-you note.) The Food Hall is our favorite, with some 500 different cheeses and some 163 brands of whisky among zillions of other goodies. At Christmas, Harrods sells an estimated 100 tons of Christmas puddings.

displayed in another gallery. An area devoted to Islamic art houses the Ardabil carpet from 16th-century Persia (320 knots per square inch).

The Victoria and Albert houses the largest collection of Renaissance sculpture outside Italy, including a Donatello marble relief, *The Ascension;* a small terra-cotta statue of the Madonna and Child by Antonio Rossellino; a marble group, *Samson and a Philistine,* by Giovanni Bologna; and a wax model of a slave by Michelangelo. The highlight of 16th-century art from the Continent is the marble group *Neptune with Triton* by Bernini. The cartoons by Raphael, which were conceived as designs for tapestries for the Sistine Chapel, are owned by the queen and can also be seen here.

A most unusual, huge, and impressive exhibit is the Cast Courts, life-size plaster models of ancient and medieval statuary and architecture.

The museum has the greatest collection of Indian art outside India. It has Chinese and Japanese galleries as well. In complete contrast are suites of English furniture, metalwork, and ceramics dating beyond the 16th century, and a superb collection of portrait miniatures, including the one Hans Holbein the Younger made of Anne of Cleves for the benefit of Henry VIII, who was again casting around for a suitable wife.

In a major redevelopment plan, the entire run of the British Galleries won't be fully open until 2001. But the museum has a lively program of changing exhibitions and displays, so there's always something new to see. The year 1999 and the turn of the century will see the hosting of *A Grand Design: The Art of the Victoria and Albert Museum,* a celebration of the last 2,000 years of art.

Rowing on the Serpentine. When the weather is right, we like to head to this 41-acre artificial lake dating from 1730. A stream was dammed to create the artificial lake, whose name derives from its winding, snakelike shape. At the Boathouse, you can rent a boat by the hour. With the right companion, it's one of the most idyllic ways to spend a sunny London afternoon. Renoir must have agreed; he depicted the custom on canvas.

Wandering Through Covent Garden. George Bernard Shaw got his inspiration for *Pygmalion* here, where the character of Eliza Doolittle sold violets to wealthy operagoers and became a household name around the world. The old fruit and vegetable market, with its Cockney cauliflower peddlers and butchers in blood-soaked aprons, is long gone. But what's left is just as interesting: Covent Garden today is London's best example of urban renewal. There's an antique market in the piazza on Monday, and a crafts market Tuesday through Saturday. When you're thirsty, plenty of pubs in the area will quench your thirst.

Watching the Sunset at Waterloo Bridge. Waterloo Bridge is the best place in London to watch the sun set over Westminster. From here, you can also see the last rays of sunlight bounce off The City spires in the East End.

Spending a Night at the West End Theater. London is the theatrical capital of the world. The live stage offers a unique combination of variety, accessibility, and economy—and a look at next year's Broadway hit.

Crawling the London Pubs. With some 5,000 pubs within the city limits, you would be crawling indeed if you tried to have a drink in each of them. Enough traditional ones remain, especially in central London, to make it worthwhile to go on a crawl, perhaps fortifying yourself with a ploughman's lunch or a plate of shepherd's pie.

A restaurant serves snacks and meals, and two museum shops sell wonderful gifts, posters, cards, and books.

Insider's tip: As incongruous as it sounds, the museum hosts a jazz brunch on Sunday mornings from 11am to 3pm for only £8 ($12.80). Also, check out the museum's most bizarre gallery, "Fakes and Forgeries." The art impostors in this gallery are amazingly authentic—in fact, we'd judge some of them better than the old masters themselves.

Trafalgar Square. Tube: Charing Cross.

One of the landmark squares of London, Trafalgar Square honors one of England's great military heroes, Horatio, Viscount Nelson (1758–1805), who died at the Battle of Trafalgar. Although he suffered from seasickness all his life, he went to sea at the age of 12 and was an admiral at the age of 39. Lord Nelson was a hero of the Battle of Calvi in 1794 where he lost an eye, the Battle of Santa Cruz in 1797 where he lost an arm, and the Battle of Trafalgar in 1805 where he lost his life.

The square today is dominated by a 145-foot granite column, the work of E. H. Baily in 1843. The column looks down Whitehall toward the Old Admiralty, where Lord Nelson's body lay in state. The figure of the naval hero towers 17 feet high, not bad for a man who stood 5 feet 4 inches in real life. The capital is of bronze cast from cannons recovered from the wreck of the *Royal George.* Queen Victoria's favorite animal painter, Sir Edward Landseer, added the four lions at the base of the column in 1868. The pools and fountains were not added until 1939, the last work of Sir Edwin Lutyens.

Political demonstrations still take place at the square and around the column, which has the most aggressive pigeons in London. These birds will even land on your head or perform less desirable stunts. Actually, the birds are part of a long feathery tradition, for this site was once used by Edward I (1239–1307) to keep his birds of prey. Called "Longshanks," he came here often before he died of dysentery in 1307. Richard II, who ruled from 1377 to 1399, kept goshawks and falcons here too. By the time of Henry VII, who ruled from 1485 to 1509, the square was used as the site of the royal stables. Sir Charles Barry, who designed the Houses of Parliament, created the present square in the 1830s.

Much of the world focuses on the square via TV cameras on New Year's Eve. It's a wild and raucous time with revelers jumping into the chilly waters of the fountains. The giant Christmas tree that is installed here every December is an annual gift from Norway to the British people, in appreciation for sheltering their royal family during World War II. Today, street performers, now officially licensed, will entertain you and hope for a token of appreciation for their efforts.

To the southeast of the square, at 36 Craven St., stands a house once occupied by Benjamin Franklin when he was a general of the Philadelphia Academy (1757–74). On the north side of the square rises the National Gallery, constructed in the 1830s. In front of the building is a copy of a statue of George Washington by J. A. Houdon.

To the left of St. Martin's Place is the National Portrait Gallery, a collection of British greats (and not-so-greats)—everyone from Chaucer and Shakespeare to Captain Hook and Nell Gwyn. Also on the square is the landmark St. Martin-in-the-Fields by James Gibbs, with its towering steeple, a resting place of such figures as Sir Joshua Reynolds, William Hogarth, and Thomas Chippendale.

2 More Attractions

OFFICIAL LONDON

Whitehall, the seat of the British government, grew up on the grounds of Whitehall Palace and was turned into a royal residence by Henry VIII, who snatched it from its former occupant, Cardinal Wolsey. Whitehall extends south from Trafalgar Square to Parliament Square. Along it you'll find the Home Office, the Old Admiralty Building, and the Ministry of Defence.

Visitors today can see the **Cabinet War Rooms,** the bombproof bunker suite of rooms, just as they were when abandoned by Winston Churchill and the British government at the end of World War II. You can see the Map Room with its huge wall maps, the Atlantic map a mass of pinholes (each hole represents at least one convoy). Next door is Churchill's bedroom-cum-office, which has a bed and a desk with two BBC microphones on it for his famous speech broadcasts that stirred the nation.

The Transatlantic Telephone Room, its full title, is little more than a broom closet, but it housed the Bell Telephone Company's special scrambler phone, called Sig-Saly, and it was where Churchill conferred with Roosevelt. Visitors are provided with a step-by-step personal sound guide, providing a detailed account of each room's function and history.

The entrance to the War Rooms is by Clive Steps at the end of King Charles Street, SW1 (☎ 0171/930-6961; tube: Westminster or St. James's), off Whitehall near Big Ben. Admission is £4.60 ($7.35) for adults, £2.30 ($3.70) for children, and £3.40 ($5.45) students and seniors. The rooms are open from April to September daily, 9:30am to 6pm (last admission 5:15); and October through March daily, 10am to 5:30pm; they're closed during Christmas holidays.

Official London: Westminster & Whitehall

0   .2 km
    .12 mi
N

Piccadilly Circus

St. Martin-In-the-Fields

Charing Cross Rd.

Strand

Charing Cross Station

Trafalgar Square

Northumberland Ave.

Dover St.

Stratton St.

Piccadilly St.

Duke of York St.

Jermyn St.

Lower Regent St.

Haymarket

King St.

Pall Mall

St. James's Sq.

St. James's St.

Carlton House Terr.

The Mall

Horse Guards Rd.

Whitehall Pl.

Whitehall

Horse Guards Ave.

Green Park

Marlborough Rd.

St. James's Park

Downing St.

Parliament St.

Constitution Hill

The Mall

St. James's Park Lake

King Charles St.

Queen Victoria Memorial

The Spur

Birdcage Walk

Queen Anne's Gate

Old Queen St.

Gt. George St.

Westminster

Bridge St

Parliament Square

Big ben

Guildhall

Buckingham Palace Gardens

Buckingham Palace Rd.

Palace St.

Wilfred St.

Castle La.

Petty France

Tothill St.

St. James's Park

Broad Sanctuary

Houses of Parliament

Stag Pl.

Bressenden Pl.

Caxton St.

Victoria St.

Millbank St.

Victoria

Victoria St.

Great Peter St.

Smith Sq.

Victoria Station

Wilton Rd.

Vauxhall Bridge Rd.

Carlisle Pl.

Francis St.

Ambrosden Ave.

Howick Pl.

Greencoat Pl.

Monck St.

Horseferry Rd.

Wilton Rd.

Tube Station ⊖   Information ⓘ

Banqueting House/ Whitehall Palace **7**		National Gallery **4**	
Buckingham Palace **1**		National Portrait Gallery **5**	
Cabinet War Rooms **8**		Nelson's Column **3**	
Duke of York Steps **2**		Queen's Gallery **1**	
Home Office **11**		Tate Gallery **13**	
Horse Guards Parade **6**		Westminster Abbey **10**	
Houses of Parliament **9**		Westminster Cathedral **12**	

3-0433

159

At the Cenotaph (honoring the dead from two world wars), turn down unpretentious **Downing Street** to the modest little town house at no. 10, flanked by two bobbies. Walpole was the first prime minister to live here, Churchill the most famous. But Margaret Thatcher was around longer than any of them.

Nearby, north of Downing Street, is the **Horse Guards Building**, Whitehall (☎ **0171/414-2396**; tube: Westminster), now the headquarters of the horse guards of the Household Division and London District. There has been a guard change here since 1649, when the site was the entrance to the old Palace of Whitehall. You can watch the Queen's Life Guards ceremony at 11am Monday through Saturday (10am on Sunday). You can also see the hourly smaller change of the guard, when mounted troopers are changed. And at 4pm you can watch the evening inspection, when 10 unmounted troopers and two mounted troopers assemble in the courtyard.

Across the street is Inigo Jones's **Banqueting House,** Palace of Whitehall, Horse Guards Avenue (☎ **0171/930-4179**; tube: Westminster), site of the execution of Charles I. William and Mary accepted the crown of England here, but they preferred to live at Kensington Palace. The Banqueting House was part of Whitehall Palace, which burned to the ground in 1698, but the ceremonial hall escaped razing. Its most notable feature today is an allegorical ceiling painted by Peter Paul Rubens. Admission to the Banqueting House is £3.25 ($5.20) for adults, £2.15 ($3.45) for children, £2.50 ($4) for senior citizens and students. It's open Monday through Saturday from 10am to 5pm (last admission 4:30pm).

Finally, stroll to Parliament Square for a view of **Big Ben** (tube: Westminster), the world's most famous timepiece and the symbol of the heart and soul of England. Big Ben is actually the name of the deepest and loudest bell, but it's become the common name for this clock tower on the Houses of Parliament. Opposite, in the gardens of Parliament Square, stands the statue of Churchill by Oscar Nemon.

LEGAL LONDON

The smallest borough in London, bustling Holborn (pronounced *Ho*-burn) is often referred to as Legal London, home of the city's barristers, solicitors, and law clerks. It also embraces the university district of Bloomsbury. Holborn, which houses the ancient **Inns of Courts**—Gray's Inn, Lincoln's Inn, Middle Temple, and Inner Temple—was severely damaged during World War II bombing raids. The razed buildings were replaced with modern offices, but the borough still retains pockets of its former days.

At the 60 or more **Law Courts** presently in use, on The Strand, all civil and some criminal cases are heard. Designed by G. E. Street, the neo-Gothic buildings (1874–82) contain more than 1,000 rooms and 3.5 miles of corridors. Sculptures of Christ, King Solomon, and King Alfred grace the front door; Moses is depicted at the back entrance. Admission is free, and the courts are open during sessions Monday to Friday from 10am to 4:30pm. No cameras, tape recorders, video cameras, or cellular phones are allowed during sessions. Tube: Holborn or Temple.

The court known as the **Old Bailey,** on Newgate Street, EC4 (☎ **0171/ 248-3277**), replaced the infamous Newgate Prison, once the scene of public hangings and other forms of "public entertainment." It's fascinating to watch the bewigged barristers presenting their cases to the high court judges. Entry is strictly on a first-arrival basis, and guests line up outside. Courts 1 to 4, 17, and 18, are entered from Newgate Street, and the balance from Old Bailey (the street). To get here, take the Tube to Temple, Chancery Lane, or St. Paul's. Travel east on Fleet Street, which along the way becomes Ludgate Hill. Cross Ludgate Circus and turn left to the Old Bailey, a domed structure with the figure of Justice standing atop it. Admission is free; children under

Albert Memorial ❷
Brompton Oratory ❼
Chelsea Barracks ❿
Chelsea Embankment ⓬
Earl's Court Exhibition Centre ⓭
Harrods ❽
Kensington Palace ❶
King's Road ❾
National Army Museum ⓫
Natural History Museum ❹
Royal Albert Hall ❸
Science Museum ❺
Victoria & Albert Museum ❻

† Church
▪ Tube Station
ⓘ Information

14 are not admitted, and ages 14 to 16 must be accompanied by adult. No cameras or tape recorders are allowed. Hours are Monday to Friday 10:30am to 1pm and 2 to 4pm.

MORE MUSEUMS

Apsley House. The Wellington Museum, 149 Piccadilly, Hyde Park Corner, W1. ☎ 0171/499-5676. Admission £4 ($6.40) adults, £3 ($4.80) seniors and children 12–17, under 12 free. Tues–Sun 11am–5pm. Closed Jan 1, May Day, Dec 24–26. Tube: Hyde Park Corner.

This is the former town house of the Iron Duke, the British general (1769–1852) who defeated Napoléon at the Battle of Waterloo and later became prime minister. The building was designed by Robert Adam and was constructed in the late 18th century. Wellington once had to retreat behind the walls of Apsley House, fearing an attack from Englishmen outraged by his autocratic opposition to reform. In the vestibule, you'll find a colossal marble statue of Napoléon by Canova—ironic, to say the least; it was presented to the duke by King George IV.

In addition to the famous *Waterseller of Seville* by Velázquez, the Wellington collection includes works by Correggio, Jan Steen, and Pieter de Hooch.

Insider's tip: Apsley House seems an unlikely place for silver and porcelain collectors, but Wellington's former house has some of the finest pieces in Europe. Grateful to Wellington for saving their thrones, European monarchs endowed him with treasures. Head for the Plate and China Room on the ground floor first. The Sèvres Egyptian service was intended as a divorce present from Napoléon to Josephine, but she refused it—foolish woman. Eventually, Louis XVIII of France presented it to Wellington. The Portuguese Silver Service in the dining room was created between 1812 and 1816: It's been hailed as the single greatest artifact of Portuguese neoclassical silver.

The British Library. 96 Euston Rd., NW1. ☎ 0171/412-7000. Free admission. Mon–Sat 10am–5pm, Sun 2:30–6pm. Tube: King's Cross (St. Pancras.)

One of the world's greatest libraries is no longer at the British Museum but has moved to St. Pancras, and, although it has reopened in parts, the entire library may not be fully functioning until the dawn of the millennium. The move began in December 1996, and will continue for some 2½ years. During this period, the library will move some 12 million books, manuscripts, and other items. The library has installed special phone lines to provide information on the whereabouts of specific exhibitions or manuscripts in the meantime.

Most people visit the library to view its rare books. The moving of these books began in the summer of 1997. These rare books include items of historical and literary interest, featuring two of the four surviving copies of King John's Magna Carta (1215). Almost every major author—Dickens, Jane Austen, Charlotte Brontë, Keats, and hundreds of others—is represented in the section devoted to English literature. Also on display are Nelson's last letter to Lady Hamilton and the journals of Captain Cook.

The history of the book is illustrated by notable specimens of early printing, including the Diamond Sutra of 868, the first dated example of printing, as well as the Gutenberg Bible, the first book ever printed from movable type, 1455. Beneath Roubiliac's 1758 statue of Shakespeare stands a case of documents relating to the Bard, including a mortgage bearing his signature and a copy of the First Folio of 1623.

Courtauld Gallery. Somerset House, The Strand, WC2. ☎ 0171/873-2526. Admission £4 ($6.40) adults, £2 ($3.20) children under 18. Mon–Sat 10am–6pm; Sun 2–6pm. Last admission 5:30pm. Tube: Temple, Covent Garden, or Embankment.

This gallery, slated to reopen in autumn 1998, displays a wealth of paintings: the great collection of French impressionist and postimpressionist paintings (masterpieces by Monet, Manet, Degas, Renoir, Cézanne, van Gogh, Gauguin) brought together by the late textile industrialist Samuel Courtauld; the Princes Gate collection of superb old-master paintings and drawings, especially those by Rubens, Michelangelo, and Tiepolo; the Gambier-Parry collection of early Italian paintings, ivories, majolica, and other works of art; the Lee collection of old masters; the Roger Fry collection of early 20th-century English and French painting; and the Hunter collection of 20th-century British painting.

Insider's tip: Although it's a surprisingly little-known fact, this gallery contains one of the world's greatest collections of impressionist paintings outside Paris. It's the equivalent of the Frick Collection in New York, a display of superb works of art in a jewel-like setting. We always come here at least once every season to revisit one painting: Manet's *A Bar at the Folies-Bergère.* It's exquisite.

Design Museum. Butler's Wharf, Shad Thomas, SE1. ☎ **0171/403-6933.** £5.50 ($8.80) adults, £3.75 ($6) students and children. Family ticket £12 ($19.20). Weekdays 11:30am–6pm; weekends noon–6pm. Tube: Tower Hill (then walk over the bridge) or London Bridge (then walk along Tooley St.). Docklands Light Railway: Tower Gateway (then walk over the bridge). Bus: 15, 78, 47, 42, or 188.

Part of the new Docklands development, this museum, located at Butler's Wharf, displays all kinds of manufactured products that have won love and acclaim for their design. It's the only museum in Europe that explains why and how mass-produced objects work and look the way they do. You'll see cars, furniture, appliances, graphics, and ceramics, including the Volkswagen Bug and the anglepoise lamp. The museum shop has everything from designer socks to sleek alarm clocks.

Hayward Gallery. On the South Bank, SE1. ☎ **0171/928-3144** or 0171/261-0127 for recorded information. Admission £5 ($8) adults, £3.50 ($5.60) children, students, and senior citizens, under 12 free with adult; family ticket £12 ($19.20). Fees can vary according to exhibitions. Mon and Thurs–Sun 10am–6pm; Tues–Wed 10am–8pm. Tube: Waterloo or Embankment.

This gallery, part of the South Bank Centre, presents a changing program of major contemporary and historical exhibitions. The gallery is closed between exhibitions, so check before crossing the Thames.

Imperial War Museum. Lambeth Rd., SE1. ☎ **0171/416-5000.** Admission £5 ($8) adults, £4 ($6.40) senior citizens and students, £2.50 ($4) children; free daily 4:30–6pm. Daily 10am–6pm. Closed Dec 24–26. Tube: Lambeth North or Elephant & Castle.

Built around 1815, this large, domed building, the former Bethlehem Royal Hospital for the Insane (or Bedlam), houses the museum's collections relating to the two world wars and other military operations since 1914. There are four floors of exhibitions, including the Large Exhibits Gallery, a vast area showing historical displays, two floors of art galleries, and a dramatic re-creation of London at war during the Blitz. You can see a Battle of Britain Spitfire, the rifle carried by Lawrence of Arabia, and Hitler's political testament, as well as models, decorations, uniforms, photographs, and paintings.

London Transport Museum. The Piazza, Covent Garden, WC2. ☎ **0171/379-6344.** Admission £4.95 ($7.90) adults, £2.95 ($4.70) seniors and children, £12.85 ($20.55) family ticket. Sat–Thurs 10am–6pm, Fri 11am–6pm. Closed Dec 24–26. Tube: Covent Garden or Charing Cross.

This splendidly restored Victorian building once housed the flower market. Now it's home to horse buses, motor buses, trams, trolleybuses, railway vehicles, models, maps, posters, photographs, and audiovisual displays that trace 200 years of London transport history. The story is enlivened by several interactive video exhibits—you can put yourself in the driver's seat of a bus or tube train. The fabulous gift shops sells a variety of London Transport souvenirs. Much to the glee of parents, the museum has added "kidzones"—interactive programs for children so parents can enjoy the museum without having to entertain the kids.

✪ **Museum of London.** 150 London Wall, EC2. ☎ **0171/600-3699.** Admission £4 ($6.40) adults, £2 ($3.20) children, students, and seniors, £9.50 ($15.20) family ticket. Tues–Sat 10am–5:50pm, Sun noon–5:50pm. Tube: St. Paul's, Barbican, Bank, or Moorgate.

In the Barbican district near St. Paul's Cathedral, the Museum of London allows visitors to trace the city's history from prehistoric times to the postmodern era through relics, costumes, household effects, maps, and models. Anglo-Saxons, Vikings, Normans—they're all here, displayed on two floors around a central courtyard. The exhibits are arranged so that visitors can begin and end their chronological stroll through 250,000 years at the museum's main entrance, and exhibits have quick labels for museum sprinters, more extensive ones for those who want to study, and still more detail for scholars. It's an enriching experience for everybody—allow at least an hour for a full (but still quick) visit.

You'll see the death mask of Oliver Cromwell; the Great Fire of London in living color and sound; reconstructed Roman dining rooms with kitchen and utensils; cell doors from Newgate Prison, made famous by Charles Dickens; and an amazing shop counter with pre–World War II prices on the items. But the pièce de résistance is the lord mayor's coach, built in 1757 and weighing 3 tons. Still used each November in the Lord Mayor's Procession, this gilt-and-red horse-drawn vehicle is like a fairy-tale coach.

Free lectures on London's history are often given during lunch hours; ask at the entrance hall if one will be given the day you're here. You can reach the museum, which overlooks London's Roman and medieval walls, by going up to the elevated pedestrian precinct at the corner of London Wall and Aldersgate, 5 minutes from St. Paul's.

National Army Museum. Royal Hospital Rd., SW3. ☎ **0171/730-0717.** Free admission. Daily 10am–5:30pm. Closed Jan 1, Good Friday, May bank holiday, Dec 24–26. Tube: Sloane Square.

Located in Chelsea, this museum traces the history of the British land forces, the Indian army, and colonial land forces. The collection starts with 1485, the date that the Yeomen of the Guard was formed. The saga of the forces of the East India Company is also traced, from its beginning in 1602 to Indian independence in 1947. The gory and glory are all here—everything from Florence Nightingale's lamp to the cloak wrapped around the dying Gen. James Wolfe at Québec in 1759. There are also "cases of the heroes," mementos of such outstanding men as the duke of Marlborough and the duke of Wellington. But the field soldier isn't neglected either: The Nation in Arms Gallery tells the soldier's story in two world wars, including an exhibit of the British Army in the Far East from 1941 to 1945.

National Portrait Gallery. St. Martin's Place, WC2. ☎ **0171/306-0055.** Free admission, except for special exhibitions. Mon–Sat 10am–5:45pm, Sun noon–5:45pm. Tube: Charing Cross or Leicester Square.

The National Portrait Gallery was founded in 1856 to collect the likenesses of famous British men and women. Today the collection is the most comprehensive of its kind in the world and constitutes a unique record of the men and women who created the history and culture of the nation. A few paintings tower over the rest, including Sir Joshua Reynold's portrait of Samuel Johnson ("a man of most dreadful appearance"). Among the best are Nicholas Hilliard's miniature of a handsome Sir Walter Raleigh and a full-length Elizabeth I, along with the Holbein cartoon of Henry VIII (sketched for a family portrait that hung, before it was burned, in the Privy Chamber in White-hall Palace). You'll also see a portrait of William Shakespeare (with gold earring, no less), which is claimed to be the most "authentic contemporary likeness" of its subject of any work yet known. One of the most unusual pictures in the gallery is a group of the three Brontë sisters painted by their brother Branwell. Famous people of today, including the Baroness Thatcher, are celebrated in two floors of the most recent galleries. The portrait of Diana, the late Princess of Wales, is on the Royal Landing.

Insider's tip: The galleries of Victorian and early 20th-century portraits were radically redesigned. Occupying the whole of the first floor, they display portraits from 1837 up through the beginning of the 1960s—a remarkable span of British history. Some of the more flamboyant personalities of the age, from the pre-Raphaelites to the Bloomsbury Group, are on show, including our two favorites—G. F. Watts's famous portrait of his great actress wife, Ellen Terry, and Vanessa Bell's portrait of her sister, Virginia Woolf.

National Postal Museum. King Edward Building, King Edward St., EC1. ☎ **0171/776-3636.** Free admission. Mon–Fri 9:30am–4:30pm. Closed all bank holidays. Tube: St. Paul's or Barbican.

In 1840, Britain introduced the world's first postage stamp, the Penny Black, but for 200 years before that a postal service of sorts was operating. In the main gallery, all the stamps of Britain are on display. Also displayed are valentines and other greeting cards; scales and hand stamps; and letter boxes, which were introduced by the Post Office surveyor and novelist Anthony Trollope in 1852.

Natural History Museum. Cromwell Rd., S. Kensington, SW7. ☎ **0171/938-9123.** Admission £6 ($9.60) adults, £3.20 ($5.10) seniors and students, £3 ($4.80) children 5–17, free for children 4 and under; family ticket £16 ($25.60). Mon–Sat 10am–5:50pm, Sun 11am–5:50pm. Closed Dec 23–26. Tube: South Kensington.

With towers, spires, and a huge navelike hall, this terra-cotta building is a wonder in itself. The core of the collection came from Sir Hans Sloane. Today, only a fraction of the museum's natural treasures—fossils, animal- and plant-life exhibits, and minerals—can be displayed. Among the highlights are the dinosaurs in the main hall, the Human Biology exhibit that features many interactive displays, and an ecology exhibit. There's also an earthquake simulator and an insect display.

Royal Academy of Arts. Burlington House, Piccadilly, W1. ☎ **0171/300-8000.** Admission varies, depending on the exhibition. Daily 10am–6pm. Closed Dec 25, Good Friday. Tube: Piccadilly Circus or Green Park.

Established in 1768, the academy included Sir Joshua Reynolds, Thomas Gainsborough, and Benjamin West among its founding members. Since its beginning, each academician had to donate a work of art, so over the years the academy has built up a sizable collection. The annual summer exhibition has been held for more than 200 years.

Saatchi Gallery. 98A Boundary Rd., NW8. ☎ **0171/624-8299.** Admission £4 ($6.40), children under 12 free; free Thurs for all. Thurs–Sun noon–6pm. Tube: St. John's Wood or Swiss Cottage.

In the world of contemporary art, this collection is unparalleled (except perhaps by New York's MOMA.) Charles Saatchi is one of Britain's greatest private collectors, and this personal museum features rotating displays from his vast holdings. Enter through the unmarked metal gateway of a former paint warehouse. The aim, as set forth by Saatchi, is to introduce new art, or art largely unseen in the United Kingdom, to a wider audience. The collection comprises more than 1,000 paintings and sculptures. Works that are not on display at the gallery are frequently on loan to museums around the world.

The main focus is on young British arts including controversial ones, such as Damien Hirst's 14-foot tiger shark preserved in a formaldehyde-filled tank. Also on occasional exhibit is Marc Quinn's frozen "head" cast from nine pints of blood taken from the artist over several months. Art critics were shocked at Richard Wilson's art when it was introduced: 2,500 gallons of used sump oil that flooded through an entire gallery. Jenny Saville was commissioned to paint a series of paintings, which debated obesity and challenged the accepted perceptions of female beauty.

Young American and European artists are also represented, their work often controversial as well. Regardless of the exhibition on display at the time of your visit, it's almost guaranteed to be fascinating. And if you've ever wondered what many British people think American tourists look like, catch Duane Hanson's *Tourists II* (1988). It's devastating!

Science Museum. Exhibition Rd., SW7. ☎ **0171/938-8000.** Admission £5.95 ($9.50) adults, £3.20 ($5.10) seniors and children 5–17, free for children 4 and under. Daily 10am–6pm. Closed Dec 24–26. Tube: South Kensington.

Among the most notable exhibits here are naval models; the Puffing Billy (1813), one of the oldest locomotives still in existence; Arkwright's spinning machine; Wheatstone's electric telegraph; Fox Talbot's first camera; Edison's original phonograph; the Vickers "Vimy" aircraft, which made the first Atlantic crossing in 1919; and Sir Frank Whittle's turbojet engine.

Three new galleries are designed to appeal to children. The Garden provides water, construction, sound-and-light shows, and games for 3- to 6-year-olds. The other two galleries appeal to 7- to 12-year-olds, with interactive exhibits and networked computer terminals that they can play on.

Sir John Soane's Museum. 13 Lincoln's Inn Fields, WC2. ☎ **0171/430-0175.** Free admission. Tues–Sat 10am–5pm; 1st Tues of each month 6–9pm. Tours given Sat at 2:30pm (£3/$4.80); tickets distributed at 2pm, first come, first served—groups by appointment only; call ☎ 0171/405-2107. Closed bank holidays. Tube: Chancery Lane or Holborn.

This is the former home of Sir John Soane (1753–1837), an architect who rebuilt the Bank of England (not the present structure). With his multilevels, fool-the-eye mirrors, flying arches, and domes, Soane was a master of perspective and a genius of interior space (his picture gallery, for example, is filled with three times the number of paintings a room of similar dimensions would be likely to hold). William Hogarth's satirical series, *The Rake's Progress,* includes his much-reproduced *Orgy* and *The Election,* a satire on mid–18th-century politics. Soane also filled his house with paintings and classical sculpture. On display is the sarcophagus of Pharaoh Seti I, found in a burial chamber in the Valley of the Kings. Also exhibited are architectural drawings from the collection of 30,000 in the Sloane Gallery.

The Wallace Collection. Hertford House, Manchester Sq., off Wigmore St., W1. ☎ **0171/935-0687.** Free admission. Mon–Sat 10am–5pm, Sun 2–5pm. Apr–Sept Sun 11am–5pm. Closed Jan 1, Good Friday, 1st Mon in May, Dec 24–26. Tube: Bond Street.

This outstanding collection of artworks, bequeathed to the nation by Lady Wallace in 1897, is still displayed in the house of its founders. The works of art (mostly French) include important pictures by artists of all European schools. There's also sculpture,

Bloomsbury

British Museum **4**
Courtauld Institute
  Galleries **10**
Dickens's House **3**
Gray's Inn **5**
Hayward Gallery **14**
Inner Temple **12**
Inns of Court
  & Chancery **8**
London Transport
  Museum **7**
Middle Temple **9**
Royal Academy of
  Dramatic Arts **2**
Royal National
  Theatre **13**
Sir John Soane's
  Museum **6**
Somerset House **10**
University College **1**

Church ✝
Tube Station ⊖

0   .25 mi
0   .4 km

N

furniture, goldsmiths' work, and Sèvres porcelain, along with valuable collections of majolica and European and Asian arms and armor. Frans Hals's *Laughing Cavalier* is the most celebrated painting in the collection, but Pieter de Hooch's *A Boy Bringing Pomegranates* and Watteau's *The Music Party* are also well known.

LITERARY LANDMARKS

See the discussion of Hampstead Village in section 4, "Sights on the Outskirts," for details on Keats House. See section 1, "The Top Attractions," for details on Poet's Corner in Westminster Abbey.

Born in London in 1882, the author Virginia Woolf lived and worked in **Bloomsbury,** and set many of her works in London. Virginia spent her formative years at 22 Hyde Park Gate, off Kensington High Street, west of Royal Albert Hall. After the death of her father, the family left Kensington for Bloomsbury and settled in the area around the British Museum (upper-class Victorians at that time, however, didn't view Bloomsbury as "respectable"). From 1905, they lived first at 46 Gordon Sq., east of Gower Street and University College. It was here that the nucleus of the soon-to-be celebrated Bloomsbury Group was created, which would in time embrace Clive Bell (husband of Vanessa) and Leonard Woolf, who was to become Virginia's husband. Later, Virginia went to live at 29 Fitzroy Sq., west of Tottenham Court Road, in a house once occupied by George Bernard Shaw. During the next 2 decades, Virginia resided at several more addresses in Bloomsbury, including on Brunswick Square, Tavistock Square, and Mecklenburg Square; these homes have either disappeared or else been altered beyond recognition. During this time, the Bloomsbury Group reached out to include the artists Roger Fry and Duncan Grant, and Virginia became friends with the economist Maynard Keynes and the author E. M. Forster. At Tavistock Square (from 1924 to 1939) and at Mecklenburg Square (from 1939 to 1940) she operated Hogarth Press with Leonard. She published her own early work here, as well as T. S. Eliot's *The Waste Land.*

To escape from urban life, Leonard and Virginia purchased Monk's House in the village of Rodmell between Lewes and Newhaven in Sussex. Here, they lived until 1941 when Virginia drowned herself in the nearby Ouse. Her ashes were buried in the garden at Monk's House.

Carlyle's House. 24 Cheyne Row, SW3. ☎ 0171/352-7087. Admission £3.20 ($5.10) adults, £1.60 ($2.55) children. Easter through Oct Wed–Sun 11am–4:30pm. Tube: Sloane Square. Bus: 11, 19, 22, or 239.

From 1834 to 1881, Thomas Carlyle, author of *The French Revolution,* and Jane Baillie Welsh Carlyle, his noted letter-writing wife, resided in this modest 1708 terraced house. Furnished essentially as it was in Carlyle's day, the house is located about three-quarters of a block from the Thames, near the Chelsea Embankment along King's Road. It was described by his wife as being "of most antique physiognomy, quite to our humour; all wainscoted, carved and queer-looking, roomy, substantial, commodious, with closets to satisfy any Bluebeard." The most interesting room is the not-so-soundproof "soundproof" study in the skylit attic. Filled with Carlyle memorabilia—his books, a letter from Disraeli, personal effects, a writing chair, even his death mask.

Dickens's House. 48 Doughty St., WC1. ☎ 0171/405-2127. Admission £3.50 ($5.60) adults, £2.50 ($4) students, £1.50 ($2.40) children, £7 ($11.20) families. Mon–Sat 10am–5pm. Closed Christmas and some bank holidays. Tube: Russell Square.

In Bloomsbury stands the simple abode in which Charles Dickens wrote *Oliver Twist* and finished *The Pickwick Papers* (his American readers actually waited at the dock for the ship that brought in each new installment). The place is almost a shrine for a Dickens fan; it contains his study, manuscripts, and personal relics, as well as reconstructed interiors.

Samuel Johnson's House. 17 Gough Sq., EC4. ☎ 0171/353-3745. Admission £3 ($4.80) adults, £2 ($3.20) students and seniors, £1 ($1.60) children 11-16, free for children 10 and under. May–Sept Mon–Sat 11am–5:30pm; Oct–Apr Mon–Sat 11am–5pm. Tube: Blackfriars. Walk up New Bridge St. and turn left onto Fleet. Gough Sq. is tiny and hidden, north of Fleet.

Dr. Johnson and his copyists compiled a famous dictionary in this Queen Anne house, where the lexicographer, poet, essayist, and fiction writer lived from 1748 to 1759. Although Johnson also lived at Staple Inn in Holborn and at a number of other places, the Gough Square house is the only one of his residences remaining in London. The 17th-century building has been painstakingly restored, and it's well worth a visit.

✪ **Shakespeare's Globe Theatre & Exhibition.** New Globe Walk, Bankside, SE1. ☎ 0171/902-1500. Exhibition and tour admission £6 ($9.60) adults, £4 ($6.40) children 15 and under, £5 ($8) seniors and students. Daily 10am–5pm (guided tours every 30 min or so). Tube: Mansion House.

This is a re-creation of what was probably the most important public theater ever built—on the exact site where many of Shakespeare's plays were originally staged in the 16th century. The late American filmmaker, Sam Wanamaker, worked for some 20 years to raise funds to re-create the theater as it existed in Elizabethan times, thatched roof and all. A fascinating exhibit tells the story of the Globe's re-creation in modern times, using the material (including goat's hair in the plaster), techniques, and craftsmanship of 400 years ago. The new Globe isn't actually an exact replica: It seats 1,500 patrons, not the 3,000 that regularly squeezed in during the early 1600s; and this thatched roof has been specially treated with a fire retardant. Guided tours of the facility are offered throughout the day.

In May 1997, the Globe's company staged its first slate of plays. See section 9, "London After Dark," later in this chapter, for details on attending a play here.

Plans also call for an archival library, shops, an auditorium, and an exhibition gallery, but the full complex may not be fully operational until September 1999.

Ye Olde Cheshire Cheese. Wine Office Court, 145 Fleet St., EC4. ☎ 0171/353-6170. Tube: St. Paul's or Blackfriars.

The burly literary figure of G. K. Chesterton, author of What's Wrong with the World (1910) and The Superstition of Divorce (1920), was a familiar patron at the pub Cheshire Cheese. Flamboyant in manner, he usually swept into the place encased in a cloak. That, along with his sword stick, became his trademarks. Earlier, it's said that Oliver Goldsmith, playwright of She Stoops to Conquer (1773), patronized the Cheshire Cheese. Dr. Johnson, who lived at 17 Gough Sq., off Fleet Street, where he completed his dictionary, was also a frequent visitor. He must have had some lean nights at the pub, because by the time he had compiled his dictionary, he'd already spent his advance of 1,500 guineas.

LANDMARK CHURCHES

Many of the churches listed below offer free **lunchtime concerts**—it's customary to leave a small donation. A full list of churches offering lunchtime concerts is available from the London Tourist Board.

✪ **St. Martin-in-the-Fields,** overlooking Trafalgar Square, WC2 (☎ 0171/930-0089; tube: Charing Cross), is the Royal Parish Church. The first known church on the site dates from the 13th century, but the present classically inspired church, with its famous steeple, dates from 1726. From St. Martin's vantage position in the theater district, it has drawn many actors to its door—none more notable than Nell Gwyn, the mistress of Charles II. On her death in 1687, she was buried in the crypt. Throughout the war, many Londoners rode out uneasy nights in the crypt, while Blitz bombs rained down overhead. One, in 1940, blasted out all the windows. Today the crypt has a pleasant restaurant, a bookshop, and a gallery. It is home to London's original **Brass Rubbing Centre** (☎ 0171/930-9306).

St. Bride's Church, on Fleet Street (☎ 0171/353-1301; tube: Blackfriars), is known as the church of the press. It's also a remarkable landmark: The current church is the eighth one that's stood here. Its spire has four octagonal tiers capped by an obelisk that's topped off with a ball and vane. This soaring confection (234 feet tall) inspired the wedding cakes of a pastry cook who lived in Fleet Street in the late 17th century, it's said. The crypts are now a museum.

Done in the Italian Renaissance style, **Brompton Oratory,** Brompton Road (☎ 0171/589-4811; tube: South Kensington), is famous for its **musical services.** Its organ has nearly 4,000 pipes. After Westminster Cathedral and York Minster, this is the widest nave in England.

St. Etheldreda's, Britain's oldest Roman Catholic church, lies on Ely Place, Holborn Circus, EC1 (☎ 0171/405-1061; tube: Farringdon or Chancery Lane), leading off Charterhouse Street at Holborn Circus. Built in 1251, it was mentioned by the Bard in both *Richard II* and *Richard III.* One of the survivors of the Great Fire of 1666, the church was built by and was the property of the diocese of Ely. Until this century, the landlord of Ye Olde Mitre public house near Ely Place had to obtain his license from the Justices of Cambridgeshire rather than in London, and today Ely Place is still a private road, with impressive iron gates and a lodge for the gatekeeper, all administered by six elected commissioners. The church has a distinguished musical tradition, with an 11am Latin mass on Sunday.

The spectacular brick-and-stone **Westminster Cathedral,** Ashley Place (☎ 0171/798-9055; tube: Victoria), is the headquarters of the Roman Catholic church in Britain. Done in high Byzantine style, it's massive. One hundred different marbles compose the richly decorated interior. Mosaics emblazon the chapels and the vaulting of the sanctuary. If you climb to the top of the 273-foot-tall campanile, you'll be rewarded with a sweeping view over Victoria and Westminster.

ALONG THE THAMES

All of London's history and development is linked to this winding ribbon of water—which connects the city with the sea—from which London drew its wealth and its power. For centuries the river was London's highway and main street, and today there is a row of fascinating attractions lying on, across, and alongside the River Thames.

Some of the bridges that span the Thames are household words. **London Bridge,** which, contrary to the nursery rhyme, has never "fallen down," was dismantled and shipped to Arizona in 1971 and was immediately replaced by a new London Bridge; it ran from the Monument (a tall pillar commemorating the Great Fire of 1666) to Southwark Cathedral, parts of which date from 1207.

Its neighbor to the east is ✪ **Tower Bridge,** SE1 (☎ 0171/403-3761; tube: Tower Hill), one of the city's most celebrated landmarks and the most photographed and painted bridge on earth. The Tower Bridge was built between 1886 and 1894 with two towers 200 feet apart, joined by footbridges that provide glass-covered walkways for the public. Exhibitions housed in the bridge's towers utilize advanced technology, including animatronic characters, video, and computers to illustrate the history of the Tower Bridge. The bridge is a photographer's dream, with interesting views of St. Paul's, the Tower of London, and in the distance, part of the Houses of Parliament.

You can visit the main engine room with Victorian boilers and steam-pumping engines, which used to raise and lower the roadway across the river. One model shows how the 1,000-ton arms of the bridge can be raised in 1½ minutes to allow ships' passage. Nowadays, electric power is used to raise the bridge, an occurrence that usually happens about once a day, more often in summer. Admission to the **Tower Bridge Experience** (☎ 0171/403-3761) is £5.95 ($9.50) for adults and £3.95 ($6.30) for children 5 to 15, students, and senior citizens. It's free for children 4 and under. From April through October, hours are daily from 10am to 6:30pm; off-season daily 9:30am to 6pm. Last entry is 1¼ hours before closing. It's closed Good Friday, December 24 through 26, and January 1 through 28.

3 London's Parks & Gardens

London has the greatest system of parklands of any large city on the globe. Not as rigidly laid out as the parks of Paris, London's are maintained with a loving care and lavish artistry that puts their American equivalents to shame.

Largest of them—and one of the world's biggest—is **Hyde Park,** W2. With the adjoining Kensington Gardens, it covers 636 acres of central London with velvety lawn interspersed with ponds, flower beds, and trees. Hyde Park was once a favorite deer-hunting ground of Henry VIII. Running through the width is a 41-acre lake known as the Serpentine. Rotten Row, a 1½-mile sand track, is reserved for horseback riding and on Sunday attracts some skilled equestrians.

At the north-eastern corner of Hyde Park, near Marble Arch, is **Speaker's Corner,** where anyone can get up and speak. The only rules: You can't blaspheme, be obscene, or incite a riot. The tradition began in 1855—before the legal right to assembly was guaranteed in 1872—when a mob of 150,000 gathered to attack a proposed Sunday Trading Bill. Orators from all over Britain have been taking advantage of it in this spot ever since.

Lovely ✪ **Kensington Gardens,** W2, blending with Hyde Park, border on the grounds of Kensington Palace. These gardens are home to the celebrated statue of Peter Pan, with the bronze rabbits that toddlers are always trying to kidnap. The Albert Memorial is also here, and you'll recall the sea of flowers and tributes left here after the death of Diana, Princess of Wales.

East of Hyde Park, across Piccadilly, stretch **Green Park** and **St. James's Park,** W1, forming an almost-unbroken chain of landscaped beauty. This is an ideal area for picnics, and one that you'll find hard to believe was once a festering piece of swamp near the leper hospital. There is a romantic lake, stocked with a variety of ducks and pelicans, descendants of the pair that the Russian ambassador presented to Charles II in 1662.

Regent's Park, NW1, covers most of the district by that name, north of Baker Street and Marylebone Road. Designed by the 18th-century genius John Nash to surround a palace of the prince regent that never materialized, this is the most classically beautiful of London's parks. The core is a rose garden planted around a small lake alive with waterfowl and spanned by humped Japanese bridges. The open-air theater and the **London Zoo** are here, and, as in all the local parks, there are hundreds of deck chairs on the lawns in which to sunbathe. The deck-chair attendants, who collect a small fee, are mostly college students on vacation.

The **London Zoo** (☎ 0171/722-3333) is more than 150 years old. Run by the Zoological Society of London, the 36-acre garden houses some 8,000 animals, including some of the rarest species on earth. It waned in popularity in recent years, but a recent campaign won the zoo corporate sponsorship that is funding a modernization program. Zoo admission is £8.50 ($13.60) for adults, £6 ($9.60) for children 4 to 14, and free for children under 4. The zoo is open daily from 10am to 5:30pm (closes at 4pm from October through February). You can watch the penguins or the denizens of the aquarium being fed their lunch daily at 2:30pm. Take the tube to Camden Town or bus no. 274 or Z2 in summer only.

Battersea Park, SW11 (☎ 0181/871-7530), is a vast patch of woodland, lakes, and lawns on the south bank of the Thames, opposite Chelsea Embankment between Albert Bridge and Chelsea Bridge. Formerly known as Battersea Fields, the present park was laid out between 1852 and 1858 on an old dueling ground. The park, which measures ¾ mile on each of its four sides, has a lake for boating, a fenced-in deer park with wild birds, and fields for tennis and football (soccer). There's even a children's zoo. The park's architectural highlight is the Peace Pagoda, built of stone and wood.

The park, open May through September daily from 7:30am until dusk, is not well serviced by public transportation. The nearest tube is in Chelsea on the right bank (Sloane Square); from here it's a brisk 15-minute walk. If you prefer to ride the bus, take no. 137 from the Sloane Square station, exiting at the first stop after the bus crosses the Thames.

See "Sights on the Outskirts," below, for details on Hampstead Heath and Kew Gardens.

4 Sights on the Outskirts

HAMPSTEAD HEATH & VILLAGE

Located about 4 miles north of the center of London, **Hampstead Heath,** an 800-acre expanse of high heath entirely surrounded by London, is a chain of continuous park, wood, and grassland. On a clear day you can see St. Paul's Cathedral and even the hills of Kent south of the Thames from here. For years, Londoners have come here to fly kites, sun worship, fish the ponds, swim, picnic, or jog. In good weather, it's also the site of big 1-day fairs. At the shore of Kenwood Lake, in the northern section, is a concert platform devoted to symphony performances on summer evenings. In the northeast corner, in Waterlow Park, ballets, operas, and comedies are staged at the Grass Theatre in June and July.

When the Underground came to **Hampstead Village** (tube: Hampstead) in 1907, its attraction as a place to live became widely known, and writers, artists, architects, musicians, and scientists—some from The City—came to join earlier residents. D. H. Lawrence, Rabindranath Tagore, Shelley, and Robert Louis Stevenson all once lived here, and Kingsley Amis and John Le Carré still do.

The Regency and Georgian houses in this village are just 20 minutes by tube from Piccadilly Circus. There's a palatable mix of historic pubs, toy shops, and chic boutiques along Flask Walk, a pedestrian mall. The original village, on the side of a hill, still has old roads, alleys, steps, courts, and groves to be strolled through.

✪ **Keats House.** Wentworth Place, Keats Grove, Hampstead, NW3. ☎ 0171/ 435-2062. Admission free, but donations welcome. Apr–Oct Mon–Fri 10am–1pm and 2–6pm, Sat 10am–1pm and 2–5pm, Sun 2–5pm. Nov–Mar Mon–Fri 1–5pm, Sat 10am–1pm and 2–5pm, Sun 2–5pm. Tube: Belsize Park or Hampstead. Bus: 24 from Trafalgar Square.

The poet lived here for only 2 years, but that was something like two-fifths of his creative life, because he died in Rome of tuberculosis at the age of 25 (in 1821). In Hampstead, Keats wrote some of his most celebrated odes, including "Ode on a Grecian Urn" and "Ode to a Nightingale." His Regency house possesses the manuscripts of his last sonnet ("Bright star, would I were steadfast as thou art") and a portrait of him on his deathbed in a house on the Spanish Steps in Rome.

Kenwood House. Hampstead Lane, NW3. ☎ **0181/348-1286.** Admission free. Apr–Oct daily 10am–6pm, Nov–Mar daily 10am–4pm. Closed Dec 24–25.

Kenwood House was built as a gentleman's country home and was later enlarged and decorated by the famous Scottish architect Robert Adam, starting in 1764. The house contains period furniture and paintings by Turner, Frans Hals, Gainsborough, Reynolds, and more.

Fenton House. Windmill Hill, NW3. ☎ **0171/435-3471.** Admission £4 ($6.40) adults, £2 ($3.20) children; family ticket £10 ($16). Apr–Oct Wed–Fri 2–5:30pm, Sat–Sun 11am–5:30pm; Mar Sat–Sun 2–5pm. Closed Good Friday and Nov–Feb. Tube: Hampstead.

This National Trust property is on the west side of Hampstead Grove, just north of Hampstead Village. You pass through beautiful wrought-iron gates to reach the red-brick house in a walled garden. Built in 1693, it's one of the earliest, largest, and finest houses in the Hampstead section, and contains the outstanding Benton-Fletcher collection of early keyboard musical instruments, dating from 1540 to 1805. Occasional concerts are given.

Freud Museum. 20 Maresfield Gardens, NW3. ☎ **0171/435-2002.** Admission £3 ($4.80) adults, free for children under 12, £1.50 ($2.40) for full-time students. Wed–Sun noon 5pm. Tube: Finchley Road.

After he and his family left Nazi-occupied Vienna as refugees, Sigmund Freud lived, worked, and died in this spacious three-story redbrick house in northern London. In view are rooms with original furniture, letters, photographs, paintings, and personal effects of Freud and his daughter, Anna. In the study and library, you can see the famous couch and Freud's large collection of Egyptian, Roman, and Asian antiquities.

✪ **Highgate Cemetery.** Entered from Swain's Lane, N6. ☎ **0181/340-1834.** Admission to east side £1 ($1.60); west side £3 ($4.80), including a guided tour. £1 ($1.60) fee for a camera pass. Apr–Sept daily 10am–5pm, Oct–Mar daily 10am–4pm. Tube: Archway, then walk through Waterlow Park.

A stone's throw east of Hampstead Heath, Highgate Village has a number of 16th- and 17th-century mansions, as well as small cottages, lining three sides of the now-pond-less Pond Square. Its most outstanding feature, however, is this beautiful cemetery, laid out around a huge, 300-year-old cedar tree and laced with serpentine pathways. The cemetery was so popular and fashionable in the Victorian era that it was extended on the other side of Swain's Lane in 1857. The most famous grave is that of Karl Marx, who died in Hampstead in 1883; his grave, marked by a gargantuan bust, is in the eastern cemetery. In the old western cemetery—only accessible if you take a guided tour, given hourly in summer— are scientist Michael Faraday and poet Christina Rossetti.

Tours are given at noon, 2, and 4pm weekdays, and every hour on Saturday and Sunday, but call ahead and make an appointment before trekking out to Highgate.

HAMPTON COURT

✪ **Hampton Court Palace.** On the north side of the Thames, 13 miles west of London in East Molesey, Surrey. ☎ **0181/781-9500.** Admission to all attractions £9.25 ($14.80) adults, £7 ($11.20) students and seniors, £6.10 ($9.75) children 5–15; free for children under 5. Cloisters, courtyards, state apartments, Great Kitchen, cellars, and Hampton Court exhibition mid-Mar to mid-Oct daily 9:30am–6pm, mid-Oct to mid-Mar Mon 10:15am–6pm, Tues–Sun 9:30am–6pm. Tudor tennis court and banqueting house are open the same hours as above, but only from mid-Mar to mid-Oct. You can get to

Hampton Court by train, bus, boat, or car. Frequent trains from Waterloo Station (Network Southeast) go to Hampton Court Station. London Transport buses no. 111, 131, 216, 267, and 461 make the trip, as do Green Line Coaches (ask at the nearest London Country Bus office for routes 715, 716, 718, and 726). Boat service is offered to and from Kingston, Richmond, and Westminster. If you're driving from London, take A308 to the junction with A309 on the north side of Kingston Bridge over the Thames.

The 16th-century palace of Cardinal Wolsey can teach us a lesson: Don't try to outdo your boss, particularly if he happens to be Henry VIII. The rich cardinal did just that, and he eventually lost his fortune, power, and prestige and ended up giving his lavish palace to the Tudor monarch. Henry took over, even outdoing the Wolsey embellishments. The Tudor additions included the Anne Boleyn gateway, with its 16th-century astronomical clock that even tells the high-water mark at London Bridge. From Clock Court, you can see one of Henry's major contributions, the aptly named Great Hall, with its hammer-beam ceiling. Also added by Henry were the tiltyard, a tennis court, and kitchen.

To judge from the movie *A Man for All Seasons,* Hampton Court had quite a retinue to feed. Cooking was done in the Great Kitchen. Henry cavorted through the various apartments with his wife of the moment—everybody from Anne Boleyn to Catherine Parr (the latter reversed things and lived to bury her erstwhile spouse). Charles I was imprisoned here at one time and temporarily managed to escape his jailers.

Although the palace enjoyed prestige and pomp in Elizabethan days, it owes much of its present look to William and Mary—or rather to Sir Christopher Wren, who designed and had built the Northern or Lion Gates, intended to be the main entrance to the new parts of the palace. The fine wrought-iron screen at the south end of the south gardens was made by Jean Tijou around 1694 for William and Mary. You can parade through the apartments today, filled as they are with porcelain, furniture, paintings, and tapestries. The King's Dressing Room is graced with some of the best art, mainly paintings by old masters on loan from Queen Elizabeth II. Finally, be sure to inspect the royal chapel (Wolsey wouldn't recognize it). To confound yourself totally, you may want to get lost in the serpentine **shrubbery maze** in the garden, also the work of Sir Christopher Wren.

The **gardens**—including the Great Vine, King's Privy Garden, Great Fountain Gardens, Tudor and Elizabethan Knot Gardens, Board Walk, Tiltyard, and Wilderness—are open daily year-round from 7am until dusk (but not later than 9pm) and can be visited free except for the Privy Garden for which admission is £2 ($3.20), unless you pay for a palace ticket. A garden cafe and restaurant is in the Tiltyard Gardens.

KEW

✪ **Kew Gardens.** 9 miles southwest of central London at Kew, near Richmond. ☎ **0181/940-1171.** Admission £4.50 ($7.20) adults, £3 ($4.80) students and seniors, £2.50 ($4) children; family ticket £12 ($19.20). Apr–Oct Mon–Sat 9:30am–6:30pm, Sun and public holidays 9:30am–8pm; Nov–Mar Mon–Sat 9:30am–3:30pm. Closed New Year's Day and Christmas.

The Royal Botanic Gardens, better known as Kew Gardens, are among the best-known botanic gardens in Europe and offer thousands of varieties of plants. But Kew is no mere pleasure garden—it's essentially a vast scientific research center that happens to be beautiful. A pagoda, erected from 1761 to 1762, represents the "flowering" of chinoiserie. The Visitor Centre at Victoria Gate houses an exhibit telling the story of Kew, as well as a bookshop where guides to the garden are available.

The least expensive and most convenient way to visit the gardens is to take the District line tube to Kew Gardens on the south bank of the Thames. The most romantic way to come in summer is via a steamer from Westminster Bridge to Kew Pier.

The gardens, on a 300-acre site, encompass lakes, greenhouses, walks, garden pavilions, and museums, together with fine examples of the architecture of Sir William Chambers. No matter what season you visit Kew, there's always something to see, beginning with the first spring flowers and lasting through the winter, when the Heath Garden is at its best. Among the 50,000 plant species are notable collections of arum lilies, ferns, orchids, aquatic plants, cacti, mountain plants, palms, and tropical water lilies.

Much interest focuses on the redbrick **Kew Palace** (dubbed the Dutch House), a former residence of King George III and Queen Charlotte. Regrettably, it will be closed for restoration until spring 1999.

GREENWICH

Greenwich mean time is the basis of standard time throughout most of the world, the zero point used in the reckoning of terrestrial longitudes since 1884. But Greenwich is also home of the Royal Naval College, the National Maritime Museum, and the Old Royal Observatory. In dry dock at Greenwich Pier is the clipper ship *Cutty Sark*.

Greenwich will be the site of Britain's **Millennium Dome,** which has been billed as "the most spectacular event on earth." At least it will be the largest on earth: a multimedia extravaganza that will mix education and entertainment. A recent poll showed that four out of five Brits oppose the whole project, but work goes on. It's still not known what the dome will contain, only a vague theme called Time. A live show of some sort will run in the dome's central arena, with a series of themed exhibitions around the edge. A few of the features have already been announced, including a 150-foot androgynous human figure with working arteries and veins. Most of the project's cost, estimated at more than $1 billion, will come from national lottery revenues.

Part of the fun of going to Greenwich, about 4 miles from The City, is getting here. The most appealing way to take one of the frequent ferryboats that cruise along the Thames every half hour (in summer) to every 45 minutes (in winter). Boats that depart from Westminster Pier (tube: Westminster) are maintained by **Westminster Passenger Services, Ltd. (☎ 0171/930-4097)**. Boats that depart from the Charing Cross Pier (tube: Embankment) and the Tower Pier (tube: Tower Hill) are run by **Catamaran Cruises, Ltd. (☎ 0171/987-1185)**. Depending on the tides and the carrier you select, travel time varies from 50 to 75 minutes each way. Passage for adults costs from £6.70 to £7.20 ($10.70 to $11.50) round-trip; £3.70 to £4.20 ($5.90 to $6.70) children ages 5 to 12. It's free for children under 5.

You can also take the train from Charing Cross Station, which, frankly, is a lot more prosaic than the ride along the Thames described above. Rail Europe trains take about 15 minutes to reach Greenwich, charging between £2.10 and £3 ($3.35 and $4.80) round-trip, depending on the time of day you travel. A commuter train that runs independently from British Rail (and is something of a tourist attraction in its own right) is the Docklands Light Railway, a narrow-gauge railway whose blue-and-white cars are supported on stilts high above the Docklands. Passengers board the train at Tower Gate (tube: Tower Hill), passing above the Isle of Dogs before arriving at the train's final stop at Island Gardens, in the Docklands. From here, walk through a pedestrian tunnel that extends below a branch of the Thames to a point in Greenwich a few steps from the *Cutty Sark*. One-way fare is £1.60 ($2.55).

A final option, least desirable of all, is taking a bus, although the trip takes much longer. Bus no. 188 goes from Euston Station through Waterloo to Greenwich. One-way fare is £1.70 ($2.70).

The **Greenwich Tourist Information Centre** is at 46 Greenwich Church St., London SE10 9BL (☎ 0181/858-6376); April to October, it's open daily from 10am to 5pm. From November to March, hours are Monday to Thursday 11:15am to 4:30pm, Friday to Sunday from 10am to 5pm.

The Tourist Information Centre conducts **walking tours** that visit each of Greenwich's major sights. The tours, which cost £4 ($6.40) each, depart daily at 12:15 and 2:15pm and last 1½ to 2 hours. Advance reservations are not required, but although the tours are a stable and ongoing service provided by the tourist office, it's nonetheless a good idea to phone in advance to find out if there have been any last-minute changes. Participation in any walking tour, incidentally, includes a 50% reduction in the entrance price to the National Maritime Museum.

Designed by Inigo Jones, **Queen's House** (1616), on Romney Road (☎ 0181/858-4422), is a fine example of this architect's innovative style. It's most famous for the cantilevered tulip staircase, the first of its kind. Carefully restored, the house contains a collection of royal and marine paintings and other objets d'art.

Adjoining the Queen's House, the **National Maritime Museum** (☎ 0181/858-4422) displays many priceless items associated with Horatio Nelson, including the coat showing the hole made by the bullet that killed him. The 20th-century gallery shows modern naval warfare illustrated with videos, paintings, and ship models both merchant and military. Look for some bizarre oddities here—everything from a simulated breakfast at sea long ago (rats, moldy biscuits, stale water), to the dreaded cat-o'-nine-tails used to flog sailors until 1879.

Located high on a hill overlooking the Thames, the **Old Royal Observatory,** Flamsteed House, Greenwich Park (☎ 0181/858-4422), is the original home of Greenwich mean time. The observatory has the largest refracting telescope in the United Kingdom and a collection of historic timekeepers and astronomical instruments. You can stand astride the meridian and set your watch precisely by the falling time-ball. Wren designed the Octagon Room. Here the first royal astronomer, Flamsteed, made his 30,000 observations that formed the basis of his *Historia Coelestis Britannica.* Edmond Halley, who discovered Halley's Comet, succeeded him. In 1833, the ball on the tower was hung to enable shipmasters to set their chrono-meters accurately. Many galleries will be closed intermittently through 1999 to allow for massive renovations.

Admission to all three attractions is £5 ($8) for adults, £4 ($6.40) for seniors, and £2.50 ($4) for children 5 to 16 (4 and under free).

The **Royal Naval College,** King William Walk, off Romney Road (☎ 0181/858-2154), a complex designed by Sir Christopher Wren in 1696, occupies 4 blocks named after King Charles, Queen Anne, King William, and Queen Mary. Formerly, Greenwich Palace stood here from 1422 to 1640. See the magnificent Painted Hall by Thornhill, where the body of Nelson lay in state in 1805, and also the Georgian chapel of St. Peter and St. Paul. Admission is free.

On weekends is the fun **Greenwich Antiques Market,** Greenwich High Road (opposite St. Alfeges Church). This market has everything—books, furniture, crafts, and all kinds of bric-a-brac.

5 Especially for Kids

Kids of all ages will enjoy these attractions. For more information about what to do with children in London, call **Kidsline** (☎ 0171/222-8070), computerized information about current events that might interest kids. The line is open from 4 to 6pm during school-term time, and from 9am to 4pm on holidays. (However, it's almost impossible to get through.)

London Dungeon. 28-34 Tooley St., SE1. ☎ **0171/403-0606.** Admission £8.95 ($14.30) adults, £7.95 ($12.70) students and seniors, £6.50 ($10.40) children under 15. Apr–Sept daily 10am–5:30pm; Oct–Mar daily 10am–4:30pm. Closed Christmas. Tube: London Bridge.

Situated under the arches of London Bridge Station, the dungeon is a series of tableaux, more grizzly than Madame Tussaud's, that faithfully reproduce the ghoulish conditions of the Middle Ages. The rumble of trains overhead adds to the spine-chilling horror of the place. Dripping water and live rats (caged!) make for even more atmosphere. The heads of executed criminals were stuck on spikes for onlookers to observe through glasses hired for the occasion. The murder of Thomas à Becket in Canterbury Cathedral is also depicted. There's a burning at the stake, as well as a torture chamber with racking, branding, and fingernail extraction. The Great Fire of London is brought to crackling life by a computer-controlled spectacular that re-creates Pudding Lane, where the fire started.

Bethnal Green Museum of Childhood. Cambridge Heath Rd., E2. ☎ **0181/980-2415.** Free admission. Mon–Thurs and Sat 10am–5:50pm; Sun 2:30–5:50pm. Tube: Bethnal Green.

Here you'll find displays of toys past and present. The variety of dolls alone is staggering. The dollhouses range from simple cottages to miniature mansions, complete with fireplaces, grand pianos, carriages, furniture, kitchen utensils, and household pets. In addition, the museum displays optical toys, toy theaters, marionettes, puppets, and soldiers and battle toys of both world wars. There is also a display of children's clothing and furniture.

6 Organized Tours

BUS TOURS   If you're a first-time visitor and you'd like an overview, one popular choice is **The Original London Sightseeing Tour.** This 1½-hour tour on a traditional double-decker bus includes live commentary by a guide. The tour costs £12 ($19.20) for adults, £6 ($9.60) for children under 16, free for those under 5. You can hop on or hop off the bus at any point in the tour at no extra charge. The tour plus Madame Tussaud's costs from £21 ($33.60) for adults and £12 ($19.20) for children. You can buy tickets on the bus or from any London Transport or London Tourist Board Information Centre where you can receive a discount. Most hotel concierges also sell these tickets. You depart from various convenient points within the city, which you can decide upon when you purchase your ticket. For information or ticket purchases by phone, call ☎ **0181/877-1722.**

An air-conditioned double-decker coach in the distinctive green-and-gold livery of **Harrods** takes sightseeing tours around London's attractions. The first departure from door no. 8 of Harrods on Brompton Road is at 10:30am, and there are also tours at 1:30 and 4pm. Tea, coffee, and orange juice are served on board. The 2-hour tour costs £18 ($28.80) for adults, £10 ($16) for children ages 5 to 14, free for children under 5. Half-day tours to Windsor are also available. You can purchase tickets at Harrods Coach Tours, lower ground floor (☎ **0171/581-3603;** tube: Knightsbridge).

The Big Bus Company Ltd., Waterside Way, London SW17 (☎ **0181/ 944-7810**), is another alternative. It operates a 2-hour tour in summer, daily from 9am to 6pm, with departures every 5 to 15 minutes (in winter, tours run daily from 9am to 6pm with departures every 10 to 15 minutes). Narrated tours pass by 18 sights, including all the highlights. Departure points are Marble Arch by Speakers Corner, Green Park by the Ritz Hotel, and Victoria Station (Buckingham Palace Road by the Royal Westminster Hotel). It costs £12 ($19.20) for adults, £6 ($9.60) for children. A 1-hour tour follows the same route, but only goes by 13 sights. Tickets are valid all day and you can hop on and off the bus as you wish.

BOAT TRIPS ON THE THAMES   Touring boats operate on the Thames all year and can take you to various places within Greater London. Main embarkation points are Westminster Pier, Charing Cross Pier, and Tower Pier, so, for example, you can take a "water taxi" from the Tower of London to Westminster Abbey.

The **Westminster-Greenwich Thames Passenger Boat Service** concerns itself only with downriver traffic from Westminster Pier to such destinations as Greenwich. From April through October, the most popular excursion departs for Greenwich (a 50-min. ride) at half-hour intervals between 10am and 4pm, and from June to August between 10am and 5pm. From November to March, boats depart from Westminster Pier at 40-minute intervals, daily between 10:40am and 3:20pm. One-way fares are £5.80 ($9.30) for adults, £3.10 ($4.95) for children under 16. Round-trip fares are £7 ($11.20) for adults and £3.60 ($5.75) for children. A family ticket for two adults and up to three children under 15 costs £15.70 ($25.10) one way, £18.60 ($29.75) round-trip. For information and ticket sales, contact the Westminster-Greenwich Thames Passenger Boat Service, Westminster Pier, Victoria Embankment, SW1 (☎ **0171/930-4097**; tube: Westminster).

Westminster Passenger Association (Upriver) Ltd., Westminster Pier, Victoria Embankment, SW1 (☎ **0171/930-2062/4721**), offers the only riverboat service upstream from Westminster Bridge to Kew, Richmond, and Hampton Court. There are regular daily sailings from the Monday before Easter until the end of October, on traditional riverboats, all with licensed bars. Trip time, one way, can be as little as 1½ hours to Kew and between 2½ and 4 hours to Hampton Court depending on the tide. Cruises from Westminster Pier to Hampton Court via Kew Gardens leave daily at 10:30am, 11:15am, and noon. Round-trip tickets are £8 to £12 ($12.80 to $19.20) adults, £6 to £10 ($9.60 to $16) senior citizens, and £4 to £7 ($6.40 to $11.20) for children 4 to 14. One child under 4 accompanied by an adult cruises free. Evening cruises from May to September are also available, departing Westminster Pier at 7:30pm and 8:30pm (9:30pm on demand) for £5 ($8) for adults and £3.50 ($5.60) for children.

Pool of London allows travelers to visit sites along the Thames River between London Bridge and St. Katharine's Dock by taking a hop-on, hop-off ferry. For only £2 ($3.20) for a single fare, a passenger can use the ferry as often as one likes within a day. The ferry stops at five piers, including Tower Pier, London Bridge Pier, H.M.S. Belfast, Butlers Wharf, and St. Katherine's Dock. The ferry runs between 11am and 5pm until the end of October. From then until the end of March, it operates only on Saturday and Sunday, running every half hour. Beginning in April again, daily service resumes. Tickets are sold on board. For more information, call ☎ **0171/488-0344.**

CANAL CRUISES   The London canals were once major highways, and now some of the traditional painted canal boats have been resurrected for Venetian-style trips through these waterways. One of them is *Jason,* which takes you on a 90-minute trip from Blomfield Road in Little Venice through the long Maida Hill tunnel under Edgware Road, through Regent's Park, passing the mosque, the London Zoo, Lord Snowdon's Aviary, past the Pirate's Castle to Camden Lock, and returns to Little Venice. Passengers making the 45-minute one-way journey disembark at Camden Lock.

The season begins on March 28 and lasts through October. The boat runs at 10:30am, 12:30pm, and 2:30pm. In June, July, and August, there is an additional trip on weekends and bank holidays at 4:30pm.

There is a canal-side restaurant/cafe at Jason's moorings where lunches, dinners, and teas are freshly made to order and food can also be ordered for the boat trips. The round-trip fare is £5.95 ($9.50) for adults and £4.50 ($7.20) for children. One-way fares are £4.95 ($7.90) for adults and £3.75 ($6) for children. For reservations, contact **Jason's Trip,** Jason's Wharf opposite 60 Blomfield Rd., Little Venice, London W9 (☎ 0171/286-3428; tube: Warwick Avenue).

WALKING TOURS   John Wittrich, of **J.W. Promotions,** 88 Woodlawn St., Whitstable, Kent CT5 1H (☎ 0122/777-2619), is a Freeman of the city of London and a member of two ancient London guilds, as well as the author of several books on London walks. He runs personal walking tours for families and groups who have booked in advance. A walking tour of 1½ to 2 hours costs £20 ($32) for one or two adults, with £12.50 ($20) per hour assessed for extended walks. A whole-day guided tour costs £75 ($120).

The best regularly scheduled public walks are offered by **The Original London Walks.** The oldest established walking-tour company in London, it's run by an Anglo-American couple, David and Mary Tucker, "off their kitchen table": 87 Messina Ave., London NW6 4LW (☎ 0171/624-3978). Their hallmarks are a variety of routes, reliability, reasonably sized groups, and, above all, superb guides. The guides include the renowned crime historian Donald Rumbelow ("internationally recognized as the leading authority on Jack the Ripper"), the foremost authority on the Regent's Canal, several prominent actors and actresses, and the like. More than 100 walks a week are offered year-round. Their repertory ranges from Greenwich to Ghost Walks, Beatles to Bloomsbury, Dickens to Docklands, Hampstead to Hidden London, and more. Walks cost £4.50 ($7.20) for adults or £3.50 ($5.60) for students and senior citizens. Children go free. No reservations are needed.

7 Active Pursuits & Spectator Sports

Questions about any spectator or participatory sport will be answered free by **Sportsline** (☎ 0171/222-8000), Monday through Friday from 10am to 6pm.

ACTIVITIES

BOATING   You can rent a paddleboat or a rowboat from the boathouse on the north side of **Hyde Park's Serpentine.** The boathouse is open from March to October. Rowboats and sailing dinghies are also available for rent in **Regent's Park** (☎ 0171/486-4759) and at the **Royal Victoria Dock Project,** Royal Victoria Dock, Tidal Basin Rd., E16 (☎ 0171/511-2326).

HORSEBACK RIDING   The **Ross Nye Riding School,** 8 Bathurst Mews W2 (☎ 0171/262-3791; tube: Lancaster Gate), is one of two public stables in Hyde Park. The school has 16 horses that are reliable and not easily disturbed by traffic or other disruptions. Go early in the morning to avoid crowds in the park. The stable opens at 7am with rides leaving each hour during the week until dark, except on Monday when it is closed. On the weekend, scheduled rides are at 10am, 11am, 2pm, and 3pm on Saturday, and 10am, 11am, 1:30pm, and 2:30pm on Sunday. A group lesson costs £25 ($40), a private lesson £30 ($48).

The **Stag Lodge Stables,** Robin Hood Gate, Richmond Park, SW15 (☎ 0181/974-6066), provides a more pastoral setting. They also have a pony club, the Red Riders, for children, which meets on Saturday.

SPECTATOR SPORTS

CRICKET   In summer, the nation's passion turns to cricket, played either at **Lord's,** St. John's Wood Road, NW8 (☎ 0171/289-1611; tube: St. John's Wood), in north

London; or at the somewhat less prestigious **Oval Cricket Ground,** The Oval, Kennington, London SE11 (☎ **0171/582-6660;** tube: The Oval), in south London. During the international test, matches between Britain and Australia, the West Indies, India, or New Zealand (equivalent in importance to the World Series in the United States), the country goes into a collective trance, with everyone glued to the nearest radio or TV describing the event.

FOOTBALL (SOCCER)   England's soccer ("football") season runs from August to April and attracts fiercely loyal fans. Games usually start at 3pm and are great to watch, but the stands can get very rowdy, so think about splurging for seats. Centrally located first-division football clubs include: **Arsenal,** Arsenal Stadium, Avenell Road, N5 (☎ **0171/704-4000,** box office 0171/704-4040; tube to Arsenal); **Tottenham Hotspur,** 748 High Rd., N17 (☎ **0181/365-5000,** box office 0171/420-0234; tube to Seven Sisters); and **Chelsea,** Stamford Bridge, Fulham Road, SW6 (☎ **0171/ 385-5545,** box office 0891/121011; tube to Fulham Broadway). Tickets cost £22 to £50 ($35.20 to $80), and games are usually played on Saturday.

HORSE-RACING   Within easy reach of central London, there are horse-racing tracks at Kempton Park, Sandown Park, and the most famous of them all, Epsom, where the Derby is the main feature of the meeting in early June. Racing takes place both midweek and on weekends, but not continuously. Sometimes during the summer there are evening race meets, so you should contact **United Racecourses Ltd.,** The Grandstand, Epsom, Surrey (☎ **01372/470047**), for information on the next races at Epsom, Sandown Park, or Kempton Park.

THE ROYAL TOURNAMENT   It's hard to find a comprehensive tag for the Royal Tournament, which some viewers describe as a series of indoor parades paying homage to the traditions and majesty of the British armed forces. Performed every year in late July, usually for a 2½-week run, this long-running spectacle attracts an enthusiastic audience. The show includes massed bands presenting stirring music, the Royal Navy field-gun competition, the Royal Air Force with their dogs, the Royal Marines in action, the King's Troop Royal Horse Artillery, the Household Cavalry, and a series of visiting military-style exhibitions from throughout the British Commonwealth. There are two performances Tuesday through Saturday, at 2:30 and 7:30pm, at the Earl's Court Exhibition Centre, Warwick Road, SW5. Seats cost from £5 to £25 ($8 to $40), with discounts of around 20% for children 5 to 14 and senior citizens over 65. For tickets and other information, write to the Royal Tournament Exhibition Centre, Warwick Road, London SW5 9TA (tube: Earl's Court Station). You can also contact the Royal Tournament, Warwick Road, London SW5 9TA (☎ **0171/370-8206;** tube: Victoria).

TENNIS   Fans from around the world focus on ✪ **Wimbledon** for 2 weeks (beginning around late June). At the All England Lawn Tennis & Croquet Club, you'll see some of the world's greatest tennis players in action, while enjoying the traditional snack of strawberries and cream. The famous annual championships in 1999 take place from June 21 to July 4, with matches lasting from about 2pm till dark. (The gates open at 10:30am.) Most tickets range in price from a low of £8 to £54 ($12.80 to $86.40). Center court seats are sold by lottery. Tickets for the outside courts are usually available at the gate. For information during the tournament, call ☎ **0181/ 944-2244** for recorded information. For details, send a self-addressed stamped envelope (only from September through December) to the All England Lawn Tennis & Croquet Club, P.O. Box 98, Church Road, Wimbledon, SW19 5AE, or call ☎ **0181/ 946-2244.** To reach Wimbledon, take the tube to Southfields.

8 Shopping

THE TOP SHOPPING STREETS & NEIGHBORHOODS

There are several key streets that offer some of London's best retail stores—or simply one of everything—compactly located in a niche or neighborhood, so you can just stroll and shop.

THE WEST END   The West End includes the tony Mayfair district and is home to the core of London's big-name shopping. Most of the department stores, designer shops, and multiples (chain stores) have their flagships in this area.

The key streets are **Oxford Street** for affordable shopping (start at Marble Arch tube station if you're ambitious, or Bond Street station if you just want to see some of it), and **Regent Street,** which intersects Oxford Street at Oxford Circus (tube: Oxford Circus).

While there are several branches of the private label department store **Marks & Spencer,** their Marble Arch store (on Oxford Street) is the flagship, and worth shopping for their high-quality goods. There's a grocery store in the basement and a home furnishings department upstairs.

Regent Street has fancier shops—more upscale department stores (including the famed **Liberty of London**), multiples (**Laura Ashley**), and specialty dealers—and leads all the way to Piccadilly.

In between the two, parallel to Regent Street, is **Bond Street.** Divided into New and Old, Bond Street (tube: Bond Street) also connects Piccadilly with Oxford Street and is synonymous with the luxury trade. Bond Street has had a recent revival and is the hot address for all the international designers; **Donna Karan** has not one but two shops here. A slew of international hotshots have their digs surrounding hers, from **Chanel** and **Ferragamo** to **Versace.**

Burlington Arcade (tube: Piccadilly Circus), the famous glass-roofed, Regency-style passage leading off Piccadilly, looks like a period exhibition and is lined with intriguing shops and boutiques. The small, smart stores specialize in fashion, jewelry, Irish linen, cashmere, and more. If you linger in the arcade until 5:30pm, you can watch the beadles, those ever-present attendants in their black-and-yellow livery and top hats, ceremoniously put in place the iron grills that block off the arcade until 9am the next morning, at which time they just as ceremoniously remove them to mark the start of a new business day. Also at 5:30pm, a hand bell called the Burlington Bell is sounded, signaling the end of trading.

Just off Regent Street (actually tucked right behind it) is **Carnaby Street** (tube: Oxford Circus), which is also having a comeback. While it no longer dominates the world of pacesetting fashion as it did in the 1960s, it's still fun to visit for teens who may need cheap souvenirs, a purple wig, or a little something in leather. There's also a convenient branch of **Boots The Chemist** here.

For a total contrast, check out **Jermyn Street,** on the far side of Piccadilly, a tiny 2-block-long street devoted to high-end men's haberdashers and toiletries shops; many have been doing business for centuries. Several hold royal warrants, including **Turnball & Asser,** where HRH Prince Charles has his pj's made.

The West End leads to the theater district, so there's two more shopping areas: the still-not-ready-for-prime-time **Soho,** where the sex shops are slowly being turned into cutting-edge designer shops; and **Covent Garden,** which is a masterpiece unto itself. The original marketplace has overflowed its boundaries and eaten up the surrounding neighborhood so that even though the streets run a little higgledy-piggledy and you can easily get lost, it's fun to just wander and shop. Covent Garden is especially mobbed on Sundays.

KNIGHTSBRIDGE & CHELSEA This is the second-most famous of London's retail districts and the home of **Harrods** (tube: Knightsbridge). A small street nearby, **Sloane Street,** is chockablock with designer shops; and another street in the opposite direction, **Cheval Place,** is also lined with designer resale shops.

Walk toward Museum Row and you'll soon find **Beauchamp Place** (pronounced *Bee*-cham) (tube: Knightsbridge). The street is only 1 block long, but it features the kinds of shops where young British aristos buy their clothing.

Head out at the **Harvey Nichols** end of Knightsbridge, away from Harrods, and shop your way through the designer stores on Sloane Street (**Hermès, Armani, Prada,** and the like), then walk past Sloane Square and you're in an altogether different neighborhood: King's Road.

King's Road (tube: Sloane Square), the main street of Chelsea, which starts at Sloane Square, will forever remain a symbol of London in the Swinging Sixties. Today, the street is still frequented by young people, but there are fewer Mohican haircuts, "Bovver boots," and Edwardian ball gowns than before. More and more in the 1990s, King's Road is a lineup of markets and "multistores," large or small conglomerations of indoor stands, stalls, and booths within one building or enclosure.

Chelsea doesn't begin and end with King's Road. If you choose to walk the other direction from Harrods, you connect to a part of Chelsea called **Brompton Cross,** another hip and hot area for designer shops made popular when Michelin House was rehabbed by Sir Terence Conran for **The Conran Shop.**

Also seek out **Walton Street,** a tiny little snake of a street running from Brompton Cross back toward the museums. About 2 blocks of this 3-block street are devoted to fairy-tale shops for m'lady where you can buy aromatherapy from **Jo Malone,** needlepoint, costume jewelry, or meet with your interior designer, who runs a small shop of objets d'art.

Finally, don't forget all those museums right there in the corner of the shopping streets. They all have great gift shops.

KENSINGTON & NOTTING HILL **Kensington High Street** is the new hangout of the classier breed of teen, who has graduated from Carnaby Street and is ready for street chic. While there are a few staples of basic British fashion on this strip, most of the stores feature items that stretch, are very, very short, or very, very tight. The tube station here is High Street Kensington.

From Kensington High Street, you can walk up **Kensington Church Street,** which, like Portobello Road, is one of the city's main shopping avenues for antiques. Kensington Church Street dead-ends into the Notting Hill Gate tube station, which is where you would arrive for shopping in **Portobello Road.** The dealers and the weekend market are two blocks beyond.

MARKETS

THE WEST END The most famous market in all of England, **Covent Garden Market** (☎ **0171/836-9136;** tube: Covent Garden), offers several different markets daily from 9am to 5pm (we think it's most fun to come on Sunday). It can be a little confusing, until you are here exploring it all. **Apple Market** is the fun, bustling market in the courtyard, where traders sell, well, everything. Many of the items are what the English call collectible nostalgia; they include a wide array of glassware and ceramics, leather goods, toys, clothes, hats, and jewelry. Some of the merchandise is truly unusual. Many items are handmade, with some of the craftspeople selling their own wares—except on Mondays, when the craftspeople are replaced by antique dealers. Meanwhile, out back is **Jubilee Market** (☎ **0171/836-2139**), which is also an antique market on Mondays. Every other day of the week, it's sort of a fancy

Shipping It Home

Many shoppers opt to have their goods shipped straight from London to their homes (no schlepping!). **Mail + Pack,** 343-453 Latimer Rd., London, W10 6RA (☎ **0181/964-2410;** tube: Latimer Road) specializes in packing small to medium-size consignments, although they can also arrange for the shipment of antiques and a wide range of collectibles. Their rates include all packing charges, customs documentation, and home delivery; excluding duties and taxes. It's usually less expensive if you carry the goods directly to the company's headquarters. However, the company can also arrange to pick up your goods, for a surcharge, at your London hotel or at the place where you made the original purchase.

hippie-ish market with cheap clothes and books. Out front there are a few tents of cheap stuff, except again on Monday, when antique dealers take over here, too.

The market itself (in the superbly restored hall) offers one of the best shopping opportunities in London. The specialty shops that fill the building sell fashions and herbs, gifts and toys, books and personalized dollhouses, hand-rolled cigars, automata, and much, much more. There are bookshops and branches of famous stores (**Hamley's, The Body Shop**), and prices are kept moderate.

St. Martin-in-the-Fields Market (tube: Charing Cross) is good for teens and hipsters who don't want to trek all the way to Camden Market (see below) and can make do with imports from India and South America, crafts, and some local football souvenirs. It's located near Trafalgar Square and Covent Garden; hours are Monday through Saturday from 11am to 5pm, and Sundays noon to 5pm.

NOTTING HILL   Whatever you collect, you'll find it at the **Portobello Market** (tube: Notting Hill Gate). It's mainly a Saturday happening, from 6am to 5pm. You needn't be here at the crack of dawn; 9am is fine. You just want to beat the motor-coach crowd. Once known mainly for fruit and vegetables (still sold here throughout the week), Portobello in the past 4 decades has become synonymous with antiques. But don't take the stall-holder's word for it that the fiddle he's holding is a genuine Stradivarius left to him in the will of his Italian great-uncle; it might just as well have been nicked from an East End pawnshop.

The market is divided into three major sections. The most crowded is the antique section, running between Colville Road and Chepstow Villas to the south. (Warning: There's a great concentration of pickpockets in this area.) The second section (and the oldest part) is the "fruit and veg" market, lying between Westway and Colville Road. In the third and final section there's a flea market, where Londoners sell bric-a-brac and lots of secondhand goods they didn't really want in the first place. But looking around still makes for interesting fun.

The serious collector can pick up a copy of a helpful official guide, *Saturday Antique Market: Portobello Road & Westbourne Grove,* published by the Portobello Antique Dealers Association. It lists where to find what, ranging from music boxes to militaria, lace to 19th-century photographs.

Note: Some 90 antique and art shops along Portobello Road are open during the week when the street market is closed. This is actually a better time for the serious collector to shop because you'll get more attention from dealers. And you won't be distracted by the organ grinder.

NORTH LONDON   If it's Wednesday, it's time for **Camden Passage** (☎ **0171/359-9969;** tube: Angel) in Islington, where each Wednesday and Saturday there's a very upscale antique market. It starts in Camden Passage and then sprawls into the streets behind. It's on Wednesdays from 7am to 2pm and Saturdays from 9am to 3:30pm.

Don't confuse Camden Passage with **Camden Market** (very, very downtown). Camden Market (tube: Camden Town) is for teens and others into body piercing, blue hair (yes, still), and vintage clothing. Serious collectors of vintage may want to explore during the week, when the teen scene isn't quite so overwhelming. Market hours are 9:30am to 5:30pm daily, with some parts opening at 10am.

THE DEPARTMENT STORES

✪ **Fortnum & Mason, Ltd.** 181 Piccadilly, W1. ☎ **0171/734-8040.** Tube: Piccadilly Circus.

The world's most elegant grocery store is a British tradition dating from 1707. Down the street from the Ritz, it draws the carriage trade, those from Mayfair or Belgravia who come seeking such tinned treasures as pâté de foie gras or a boar's head. Enter the doors and be transported to another world of deep-red carpets, crystal chandeliers, spiraling wooden staircases, and unobtrusive, tailcoated assistants.

The grocery department is renowned for its impressive selection of the finest foods from around the world—the best champagne, the most scrumptious Belgian chocolates, and succulent Scottish smoked salmon. You can wander through the four floors and inspect the bone china and crystal cut glass, perhaps find the perfect present in the leather or stationery departments, or browse the furniture, paintings, and ornaments in the antiques department.

✪ **Harrods.** 87-135 Brompton Rd., Knightsbridge, SW1. ☎ **0171/730-1234.** Tube: Knightsbridge.

As firmly entrenched in English life as Buckingham Palace and the Ascot Races, Harrods is an elaborate emporium, as fascinating as a museum. The store has returned to the elegance it knew in the 1920s and 1930s. Some of the goods displayed for sale are works of art, and so are the 300 departments displaying them. The sheer range, variety, and quality of merchandise is dazzling.

The whole fifth floor is devoted to sports and leisure, with a wide range of equipment and attire. Toy Kingdom is on the fourth floor, along with children's wear. The Egyptian Hall, on the ground floor, sells crystal from Lalique and Baccarat, plus porcelain. Along with the bounty, check out the architectural touches. When you're ready for a break, you have a choice of 18 restaurants and bars. Best of all is the Food Halls, stocked with a huge variety of foods and several cafes (Harrods began as a grocer in 1849 and it's still the heart of the business). In the basement you'll find a bank, a theater-booking service, a travel bureau, and Harrods Shop for logo gifts.

Harvey Nichols. 109-125 Knightsbridge, SW1. ☎ **0171/235-5000.** Tube: Knightsbridge.

Locals call it Harvey Nicks. It has its own gourmet-food hall and fancy restaurant, The Fifth Floor, and a huge store crammed with the best designer home furnishings, gifts, and fashions for all, although women's clothing is the largest segment of its business. The store does carry a lot of American designer brands; avoid them, as they're more expensive in London.

✪ **Liberty PLC.** 214-220 Regent St. ☎ **0171/734-1234.** Tube: Oxford Circus.

This is the flagship of the major British department store, which has branches all over the United Kingdom. It is celebrated for its Liberty prints. The front part of the store on Regent Street is sort of normal-looking, but don't be fooled: Outside and around back, Liberty is restored to its original Tudor splendor—whitewashed and half-timbered outside, galleries of wooden paneled salons inside. There are six floors of fashion, china, and home furnishings, as well as the famous Liberty Print fashion fabrics, upholstery fabrics, scarves, ties, luggage, and gifts.

Marks & Spencer. 458 Oxford St., W1. ☎ **0171/935-7954.**

They call it M & S or sometimes Marks & Sparks; it's the most beloved of English institutions, ranking right up there with tea and scones and the Queen Mother. Their fortune has been made in selling high quality, private label (St. Michael) clothing for all, plus home furnishings and groceries at slightly less-than-regular retail prices.

Despite the fact that the store offers value, it's not considered down-market—simply good British common sense. Members of the aristocracy wouldn't shop anywhere else; many businessmen buy their suits here. M & S is also famous for its cotton-knit underwear, which 7 out of every 10 women in London are wearing right now as you read this.

SOME CLASSIC LONDON FAVORITES

ANTIQUES   See also "Street & Flea Markets," above. Portobello Road is really the prime hunting ground.

At the **Antiquarius Antiques Centre,** 131-141 King's Rd., SW3 (☎ **0171/ 351-5353;** tube: Sloane Square), more than 120 dealers offer specialized merchandise, such as antique and period jewelry, silver, first-edition books, boxes, clocks, prints, and paintings, with an occasional piece of antique furniture. You'll find a lot of items from the 1950s. Closed Sunday.

Alfie's Antique Market, 13-25 Church St., NW8 (☎ **0171/723-6066;** tube: Marylebone or Edgware Road), is the biggest and one of the best-stocked conglomerates of antique dealers in London, all crammed into the premises of what was built before 1880 as a department store. It contains more than 370 stalls, showrooms, and workshops scattered over 35,000 square feet of floor space. Closed Sunday and Monday. A whole antique district has grown up around Alfie's along Church Street.

BATH & BODY   There are branches of **The Body Shop** seemingly everywhere. Check out the one at 375 Oxford St., W1 (☎ **0171/409-7868;** tube: Bond Street). Prices are drastically lower in the United Kingdom than they are in the United States.

Boots The Chemist has a million branches; we like the one across the street from Harrods for its convenience and size. It's at 72 Brompton Rd., SW3 (☎ **0171/ 589-6557;** tube: Knightsbridge). The house brands of beauty products are usually the best, be they Boots' products (try the cucumber facial scrub), Boots' versions of The Body Shop (two lines, Global and Naturalistic), or Boots' versions of Chanel makeup (called No. 7).

Stock up on essential oils, or perhaps dream pillows, candles, sachets of letters of the alphabet, and aromatherapy fans at **Culpeper the Herbalist,** 8 The Market, Covent Garden, WC2 (☎ **0171/379-6698**). There's another branch in Mayfair at 21 Bruton St., W1 (☎ **0171/629-4559**).

Floris, 89 Jermyn St., SW1 (☎ **0171/930-2885;** tube: Piccadilly Circus), stocks a variety of toilet articles and fragrances in floor-to-ceiling mahogany cabinets, which are architectural curiosities in their own right, dating from the Great Exhibition of 1851.

Czech & Speake, 39C Jermyn St. SW1 (☎ **0171/439-0216;** tube: Piccadilly Circus), has over the past 15 years introduced seven fragrance lines, including a best-selling perfume, 88, an elixir of sandalwood, vetiver, and cassie.

Neal's Yard Remedies, 15 Neal's Yard, WC2 (☎ **0171/379-7222;** tube: Covent Garden), is noted the world over for their cobalt-blue bottles. These homemade-style bath, beauty, and aromatherapy products are chichi must-haves for those who pooh-pooh The Body Shop as too common. Prices are much higher in the United States.

The Victorian perfumery called **Penhaligon's**, 41 Wellington St., WC2 (☎ 0171/836-2150; tube: Covent Garden), offers a large selection of perfumes, aftershaves, soaps, and bath oils for women and men. Gifts include antique-silver scent bottles and leather traveling requisites.

FASHION, PART I: THE TRUE BRIT Every internationally known designer worth his or her weight in shantung has a boutique in London, but the best buys are on the sturdy English styles that last forever.

The name ✪ **Burberry,** 18-22 Haymarket, SW1 (☎ 0171/930-3343; tube: Piccadilly Circus), has been synonymous with raincoats ever since Edward VII publicly ordered his valet to "bring my Burberry" when the skies threatened. An impeccably trained staff sells the famous raincoats, along with excellent men's shirts, sportswear, knitwear, and accessories. Raincoats are available in women's sizes and styles as well. Prices are high, but you get quality and prestige.

The finest name in men's shirts, ✪ **Hilditch & Key,** 37 and 73 Jermyn St., SW1 (☎ 0171/734-4707; tube: Piccadilly Circus or Green Park), has been in business since 1899. The two shops on this street both offer men's clothing (including a bespoke shirt service) and women's ready-made shirts. Hilditch also has an outstanding tie collection. Shirts go for half price during the twice-yearly sales. Men fly in from all over the world for them.

Next, 20 Long Acre, WC2 (☎ 0171/836-1516; tube: Covent Garden), a chain of "affordable fashion" stores knew its heyday when it became celebrated in the 1980s for its high street-fashion revolution. No longer at its peak (except for its mail order division), it still merits a stopover. The look is still very contemporary, with a continental flair worn not only by men and women but kids, too.

Westaway & Westaway, 62-65 and 92-93 Great Russell St., WC1 (☎ 0171/405-4479; tube: Tottenham Court Road), opposite the British Museum, is a substitute for a shopping trip to Scotland. Here you'll find kilts, scarves, waistcoats, capes, dressing gowns, and rugs in authentic clan tartans. They also sell cashmere, camel-hair, and Shetland knitwear, along with Harris tweed jackets, Burberry raincoats, and cashmere overcoats for men.

FASHION, PART II: THE CUTTING EDGE No one in the British fashion scene is hotter than the unstoppable ✪ **Vivienne Westwood,** 6 Davies St., W1 (☎ 0171/629-3757; tube: Bond Street). While it's possible to go to more than 550 stores worldwide and purchase select Westwood pieces, her U.K. shops are the best place to find her full range of fashion designs. The flagship store at Davies Street concentrates on her couture line, or The Gold Label, as it's known. Using a wide range of uniquely British resources, Westwood creates jackets, skirts, trousers, blouses, dresses, and evening dresses. Her line features taffeta ball gowns for fall wear, made-to-measure tailored shirts, and even some Highland plaids.

The World's End branch on King's Road carries casual designs, including T-shirts, jeans, and other sportswear, and the sale shop at Conduit Street has a bit of everything: The Gold Label, her second women's line, The Red Label, and The Man Label, her menswear collection. Accessories available include women's and men's shoes, belts, and jewelry. Branches: World's End, 430 King's Rd., SW3 (☎ 0171/352-6551; tube: Sloane Square); Vivienne Westwood, 43 Conduit St., W1 (☎ 0171/439-1109; tube: Oxford Circus).

Another of the British big-name designers, **Katharine Hamnett,** 20 Sloane St., SW1 (☎ 0171/823-1002; tube: Knightsbridge), is best known for her slogan

T-shirts. Her late '90s collections are getting mixed reviews. You can judge for yourself while browsing through her complete line of men's and women's day and evening wear. Hamnett's so-called "slut dresses" earned her the title of the bad girl of Brit fashion. She's also a strong environmental activist and is known for using "nature friendly" fabrics.

Egg, 36 Kinnerton St., SW1 (☎ **0171/235-9315;** tube: Hyde Park Corner or Knightsbridge), is hot, hot, hot with fashion setters, featuring imaginatively designed, contemporary clothing by Indian textile designer Asha Sarabhai and knitwear by Eskandar. Designs created from handmade textiles from a workshop in India range from everyday dresses and coats to hand-embroidered silk coats. A line of crafts and ceramics is also available.

FASHION, PART III: VINTAGE & SECONDHAND CLOTHING Note that there's no value-added tax (VAT) refund on used clothing.

A London institution since the 1940s, ✪ **Pandora,** 16-22 Cheval Place, SW7 (☎ **0171/589-5289;** tube: Knightsbridge), stands in fashionable Knightsbridge, a stone's throw from Harrods. Several times a week, chauffeurs will drive up with bundles packed anonymously by the gentry of England. One woman voted best dressed at Ascot several years ago was wearing a secondhand dress acquired here. Prices are generally one-third to one-half the retail value. Outfits are usually no more than two seasons old.

For the best in original street wear from the '50s, the '60s, and the '70s, **Pop Boutique,** 6 Monmouth St., WC2 (☎ **0171/497-5262;** tube: Covent Garden), is tops. Right next to the chic Covent Garden Hotel, it has fabulous vintage wear at affordable prices—leather jackets for £40 ($64), for example, the equivalent selling for $300 in New York.

FILOFAX All major department stores sell Filofax supplies, but the full range is carried in their own stores. Go to the main West End branch, **The Filofax Centre,** at 21 Conduit St., W1 (☎ **0171/499-0457;** tube: Oxford Circus); it's larger and fancier than the Covent Garden branch at 69 Neal St. (☎ **0171/836-1977),** with the entire range of inserts and books, and prices that will floor you: at least half the U.S. going rate. They also have good sales; calendars for the next year go on sale very early the previous year (about 10 months in advance).

HOME DESIGN & HOUSEWARES At the **Conran Shop,** Michelin House, 81 Fulham Rd., SW3 (☎ **0171/589-7401;** tube: South Kensington), you'll find high style at reasonable prices from the man who invented it all for Britain: Sir Terence Conran. It's great for gifts, home furnishings, and table top—or just for gawking.

MUSEUM SHOPS Not only are the museums worth going to but so are their shops. Particularly wonderful is the **London Transport Museum** Shop, adjacent to Covent Garden Marketplace, WC2 (☎ **0171/379-6344;** tube: Covent Garden), which carries reasonably priced retro and antique travel posters as well as tons of fun gifts and souvenirs. The London Underground maps in their original size as seen at every tube station can be purchased here.

And the best museum shop in London is the **Victoria and Albert Gift Shop,** Cromwell Road, SW7 (☎ **0171/938-8500;** tube: South Kensington). It sells cards, books, and the usual items, along with reproductions from the museum archives.

MUSIC The biggies in town are **Tower Records,** 1 Piccadilly Circus, W1 (☎ **0171/439-2500;** tube: Piccadilly Circus), one of the largest tape, record, and CD stores in Europe; and its major rival, the **Virgin Megastore,** 14-16 Oxford St., W1 (☎ **0171/631-1234;** tube: Tottenham Court Road). You'll find whatever you're looking for at either one. Another Megastore is at 527 Oxford St., W1 (☎ 0171/491-8582).

SHOES　Dr. Marten makes a brand of shoe that has become so popular that now there's an entire department store selling accessories, gifts, and even clothes: **Dr. Marten's Department Store,** 1-4 King St., WC2 (☎ 0171/497-1460; tube: Covent Garden). Teens come to worship here because ugly is beautiful, and because the prices are far better than they are in the United States, or elsewhere in Europe.

　Shelly's, 266 Regent St., W1 (☎ 0171/287-0939; tube: Oxford Circus), is the flagship of the mother of all London shoe shops, which sells hip shoes and boots for everyone from tots to grown-ups. They're famous for their Doc Martens, but there's much more—and none of it traditional.

TEAS　The Tea House, 15A Neal St., WC2 (☎ 0171/240-7539; tube: Covent Garden), sells everything associated with tea, tea drinking, and teatime. It boasts more than 70 quality teas and tisanes, including the best of China, India, Japan, and Sri Lanka, plus such longtime favorite English blended teas as Earl Grey. The shop also offers novelty teapots and mugs, among other items.

TOYS　Hamleys, 188-196 Regent St., W1 (☎ 0171/734-3161; tube: Oxford Circus), is the finest toy shop in the world—more than 35,000 toys and games on 7 floors of fun and magic. A huge selection is offered, including soft, cuddly stuffed animals, as well as dolls, radio-controlled cars, train sets, model kits, board games, outdoor toys, and computer games. There's also a small branch at Covent Garden, and another at Heathrow Airport.

TRAVEL SERVICES　The retail flagship of British Airways, **British Airways Travel Department Store,** 156 Regent St., W1 (☎ 0171/434-4700; tube: Piccadilly Circus or Oxford Circus), housed on three floors, offers not only worldwide travel and ticketing, but also a wide range of services and shops, including a clinic for immunizations, a pharmacy, a bureau de change, a passport and visa service, and a theater-booking desk. The ground floor sells luggage, guidebooks, maps, and other goods.

9　London After Dark

Weekly publications such as *Time Out* and *Where* carry full entertainment listings, including information on restaurants and nightclubs. You'll also find listings in daily newspapers, notably the *Times* and the *Telegraph*.

THE THEATER

In London, you'll have a chance to see the world-renowned English theater on its home ground. Matinees are on Wednesday (Thursday at some theaters) and on Saturday. Theaters are closed on Sunday. It's impossible to describe all of London's theaters in this space, so below are listed just a few from the treasure trove. The biggest theater excitement in London today is being stirred up by the new Globe Theatre. Since this is also a sightseeing attraction, it's previewed above in section 2.

GETTING TICKETS

If you want to see specific shows, especially hit ones, purchase your tickets in advance. The best way is to buy your ticket from the theater's box office, which you can do over the phone using a credit card. You'll pay the theater price and pick up the tickets the day of the show. You can also go to a reliable ticket agent (the greatest cluster is in Covent Garden), but you'll pay a fee, which varies depending on the show.

Central London Theaters

THEATERS

Adelphi **13**	Old & Young Vic **11**
Albery **29**	Palace **27**
Aldwych **19**	Peacock **7**
Almeida **5**	Phoenix **25**
Apollo **40**	Piccadilly **42**
Apollo Victoria **46**	The Playhouse **12**
Arts **28**	Prince Edward **26**
Barbican **6**	Prince of Wales **37**
Cambridge **23**	Queen's **38**
Comedy **36**	Royal Court Downstairs **3**
Criterion **43**	Royal National **9**
Dominion **2**	St. Martin's **24**
Donmar Warehouse **22**	Savoy **15**
Duchess **17**	Shaftesbury **3**
Fortune **21**	Strand **18**
Garrick **32**	Theatre Royal Drury Lane **20**
Gielgud **39**	Theatre Royal Haymarket **35**
Globe **10**	Vaudeville **14**
Her Majesty's **34**	Victoria Palace **45**
London Palladium **1**	Whitehall **33**
Lyceum **16**	Wyndhams **30**
Lyric **41**	
Lyric Hammersmith **44**	
Mermaid **8**	
New London **4**	

189

You can also make theater reservations through ticket agents. In the case of hit shows, only brokers may be able to get you a seat, but you'll pay for the privilege.

With offices in London and the United States, **Keith Prowse/First Call** can reserve tickets for hit shows weeks or even months in advance. In the United States, contact them at Suite 1000, 234 W. 44th St. New York, NY 10036 (☎ **800/669-8687** or 212/398-1430; fax 212/302-4251). In London, their number is (☎ **0171/ 836-9001.** The fee for booking a ticket in the United States is 35%; in London, it's 25%.

For tickets and information to just about any show and entertainment in London, Edwards & Edwards has a New York office, if you'd like to arrange tickets before you go, at 1270 Avenue of the Americas, Suite 2414, New York, NY 10020 (☎ **800/ 223-6108** or 914/328-2150; fax 914/328-2752). They also have offices in London: **Edwards & Edwards** at the Palace Theatre, Shaftesbury Avenue, W1 8AY (☎ **0171/734-4555**) or at **Harrods'** ticket desk. A personal visit is not necessary; they'll mail tickets to your home, fax confirmation, or leave tickets at the box office if you are in a hurry. Instant confirmations are available with special "overseas" rates for most shows. There is a booking and handling fee of up to 20% added to the ticket price.

Another option is **Theatre Direct International (TDI)** (☎ **800/334-8457**), which specializes in providing London theater and Fringe production tickets. Their immediate confirmation lets you arrive in London with your tickets, or else tickets will be held for you at the box office.

London theater tickets are priced quite reasonably when compared with those in the United States. Prices vary greatly depending on the seat—from £15 to £52 ($24 to $83.20). Sometimes gallery seats (the cheapest) are sold only on the day of the performance, so you'll have to head to the box office early in the day and return an hour before the performance to queue up, since they're not reserved seats.

Many of the major theaters offer reduced-price tickets to students on a stand-by basis, but not to the general public. When available, these tickets are sold 30 minutes prior to curtain. Line up early for popular shows, as standby tickets go fast and furious. Of course, you must have a valid student ID.

Warning: Beware of scalpers who hang out in front of theaters with hit shows. There are many reports of scalpers selling forged tickets, and their prices are outrageous.

THE MAJOR COMPANIES & THEATERS

The Old Vic. Waterloo Rd., SE1. ☎ **0171/928-7616** or 0171/928-2651 (box office). Plays £7–£24 ($11.20–$38.40). Tube: Waterloo.

The Old Vic, a repertory theater, is a 180-year-old theater whose facade and much of the interior have been restored to their original early 19th-century style, but most of the modernization is behind the scenes. The proscenium arch has been moved back, the stage has tripled in size, and more seats and stage boxes have been added. This fabled theater was where Sir John Gielgud made his debut in 1921 and Lord Olivier directed the National Theatre. But it was announced in 1997 that the theater would be put up for sale. What will eventually happen to this theater seems to be anybody's guess. According to London city codes, it could even be turned into a disco.

Open Air. Inner Circle, Regent's Park, NW1. ☎ **0171/935-5884.** Tickets £8–£20 ($12.80–$32). Tube: Baker Street.

This outdoor theater is right in the center of Regent's Park. The setting is idyllic. Presentations are mainly Shakespeare, usually in period costume, and both seating and acoustics are excellent. If it rains, you're given tickets for another performance. The

Discount Tickets

The **Society of London Theatre** (☎ 0171/577-6700) operates a **Half-Price Ticket Booth** in Leicester Square, where tickets for many shows are available at half price, plus a £2 ($3.20) service charge. Tickets are sold only on the day of performance, and there is a limit of four per person. You cannot return tickets, and no credit cards are accepted. Hours are daily from 12:30 to 6:30pm, except on days when there are matinees. Then the booth opens from noon to 6:30pm.

---

season runs from the end of May through mid-September, Monday through Saturday at 8pm, plus Wednesday, Thursday, and Saturday matinees at 2:30pm.

○ **The Royal National Theatre.** South Bank, SE1. ☎ 0171/452-3540. Tickets £10–£25 ($16–$40); midweek matinees, Sat matinees, and previews cost less. Mon–Sat 10am–11pm. Tube: Waterloo, Embankment, or Charing Cross.

This is the flagship of British theater. Home to one of the world's greatest stage companies, the National houses not one but three theaters. The largest, named after Lord Laurence Olivier, is the Olivier, with 1,200 seats and a style reminiscent of the Greek amphitheater with its fan-shaped open stage. The more traditional proscenium-arch auditorium, the Lyttelton, seats 900 people, whereas the Cottesloe is a small box-shaped studio theater with flexible seating and staging, with space for up to 400 people. Across its three stages the National presents a repertoire of the finest theater in the world from classic drama to award-winning new plays, and from comedy to musicals to shows for young people.

○ **The Royal Shakespeare Company (RSC).** Barbican Centre, Silk St., Barbican, EC2. ☎ 0171/638-8891 (box office). Barbican Theatre £5–£26 ($8–$41.60); The Pit £12–£18 ($19.20–$28.80) matinees and evening performances. Tube: Barbican or Moorgate.

One of the world's finest theater companies is based in Stratford-upon-Avon and here at the Barbican Centre. The central core of the company's work remains Shakespeare, but it also presents a wide-ranging program of three different productions each week in the Barbican Theatre—the 1,200-seat main auditorium, which has excellent sight lines throughout, thanks to a raked orchestra—and The Pit, the small studio space where much of the company's new writing is presented. The troupe is in residence during the winter months.

○ **Shakespeare's Globe Theatre.** New Globe Walk, Bankside, SE1. ☎ 0171/928-6406, or box office 0171/401-9919. Tickets £5 ($8) for groundlings, £5–£20 ($8–$32) for gallery seats. Tube: Mansion House.

In May 1997, the new Globe Theatre—a replica of the Elizabethan original, thatched roof and all—staged its first slate of plays (*Henry V* and *A Winter's Tale*) on the exact site of the 16th-century theater where the Bard originally staged his work.

Productions vary in style and setting; not all are performed in Elizabethan costume. In keeping with the historic setting, there's no lighting focused just on the stage, but floodlighting is used during evening performances to replicate daylight in theater. Theatergoers sit on wooden benches of yore—in thatch-roofed galleries, no less—but these days you can rent a cushion to make yourself more comfortable. About 500 "groundlings" can stand in the uncovered yard around the stage, just as they did when the bard himself was here. Mark Rylane, the artistic director of the Globe, told the press he'd be delighted if the audience threw fruit at the actors, as they did in Shakespeare's time. A spokesperson coyly told us that they wish for the theatergoing experience to be "as authentic as possible."

From May through October, the company holds performances Tuesday through Saturday at 2pm and 7:30pm, and Sunday at 4pm. There will be a limited winter schedule. In any season, the schedule may be affected by the weather, since this is an outdoor theater. Performances last 2½ to 4 hours, depending on the play.

Also in the works is a second theater, the **Inigo Jones Theatre,** based on the architect's designs from the 1600s, where plays will be staged year-round. For details on the exhibition that tells the story of the painstaking re-creation of the Globe, as well as guided tours of the theater, see section 2, earlier in this chapter.

THE REST OF THE PERFORMING ARTS SCENE

The nation's most elite opera company **(The Royal Opera)** and leading ballet company **(The Royal Ballet)** have been temporarily dislodged from the Royal Opera House, their Covent Garden home, because of its ongoing renovation. They'll be back on their home stage in the autumn of 1999. In the meantime, they will be appearing at a number of venues within London and abroad, including the Barbican, Royal Albert Hall, and a West End theater. The Royal Ballet also has seasons at the Labatts Apollo in Hammersmith, the Royal Festival Hall, and the London Coliseum. Performances of the Royal Opera are usually sung in the original language, but supertitles are projected, translating the libretto for the audience. The Royal Ballet performs a repertory with a tilt toward the classics, including works by its earlier choreographer-directors Sir Frederick Ashton and Sir Kenneth MacMillan. For information on Royal Opera and Royal Ballet performances in other venues, call ☎ **0171/212-9123.**

Barbican Centre. Silk St., The Barbican, EC2. ☎ **0171/638-8891.** Tickets £6–£30 ($9.60–$48). Tube: Barbican, Moorgate, St. Paul's, Liverpool Street, or Bank.

The largest art and exhibition center in western Europe, the Barbican was created to make a perfect setting to enjoy good music and theater from comfortable, roomy seating. The Barbican *Theatre* is the London home of the **Royal Shakespeare Company** (see above), and the Barbican *Hall* is the permanent home address of the **London Symphony Orchestra** and host to visiting orchestras and performers, from classical to jazz, folk, and world music.

In addition to the hall and theater, the Barbican Centre has The Pit, a studio theater; the Barbican Art Gallery; the Concourse Gallery and foyer exhibition spaces; Cinemas One and Two; a general lending library that also places a strong emphasis on the arts; and three restaurants, as well as cafes and bars. The box office is open daily from 9am to 8pm.

English National Opera. Performing in the London Coliseum, St. Martin's Lane, WC2. ☎ **0171/632-8300.** Tickets £5–£10 ($8–$16) balcony, £12.50–£55 ($20–$88) upper dress circle or stalls; about 100 discount balcony tickets sold on the day of performance from 10am on during the season. Tube: Charing Cross or Leicester Square.

The London Coliseum, built in 1904 as a variety theater and converted into an opera house in 1968, is London's largest theater. The English National Opera is one of the two national opera companies and performs a wide range of works, from great classics to Gilbert and Sullivan to new and experimental works, staged with flair and imagination—and every performance is in English. A repertory of 18 to 20 productions is presented 5 or 6 nights a week for 11 months of the year (dark in July). Although the balcony seats are cheaper, many visitors prefer the Upper Circle or Dress Circle.

Kenwood Lakeside Concerts. Kenwood, Hampstead Lane, Hampstead Heath, London NW3 7JR. ☎ **0181/348-1286.** Tickets for adults £9–£12 ($14.40–$19.20) for seats on the grass lawn, £11–£16 ($17.60–$25.60) for reserved deck chairs. Reductions of 25% for students and persons over 60. Every summer Sat at 7:30pm from mid-June to early Sept. Tube: Golders Green or Archway, then bus no. 210.

Presented on the north side of Hampstead Heath, these band and orchestral concerts have been a British tradition for some 50 years. In recent years, laser shows and fireworks have added to a repertoire that includes everything from rousing versions of the *1812 Overture* to jazz, and such operas as *Carmen.* The final concert of the season always features some of the Pomp and Circumstance Marches of Sir Edward Elgar, everyone's favorite imperial composer. Music drifts across the lake from the performance amphitheater above a verdant scene that encourages wine-and-cheese parties on the grass.

London Palladium. Argyll St., W1. ☎ **0171/494-5020.** Tickets £10–£32 ($16–$51.20) depending on show. Closed Sun. Tube: Oxford Circus.

It's hard to encapsulate the prestige of this show-business legend in a paragraph. Performers from Britain, Europe, and America know they've arrived when they've appeared here. The season's highlight is the Royal Command Performance, held before the queen, which includes an introduction of the artists to Her Majesty.

Royal Albert Hall. Kensington Gore, SW7. ☎ **0171/589-8212,** or 01891/500252 for 24-hour events information and ticket availability. Tickets £8–£130 ($12.80–$208) depending on the event. Tube: South Kensington, High Street Kensington, or Knightsbridge.

Opened in 1871 and dedicated to the memory of Queen Victoria's consort, Prince Albert, this building encircles one of the world's most famous auditoriums with a seating capacity of 5,200. Since 1941, the hall has been the setting for the BBC **Henry Wood Promenade Concerts** ("The Proms"), a concert series that lasts for 8 weeks between mid-July and mid-September. Although most of the audience occupies reserved seats, true aficionados usually opt for standing room in the orchestra pit for close-up views of the musicians performing on stage. The programs are outstanding and often present newly commissioned works for the first time. The last night of The Proms is the most traditional, as such rousing favorites as "Jerusalem" or "Land of Hope and Glory" echo through the hall. For tickets, call Ticketmaster at ☎ **0171/379-4444,** rather than calling Royal Albert Hall directly, ☎ **0189/500252.**

✪ **Royal Festival Hall.** On the South Bank, SE1. ☎ **0171/960-4242.** Tickets £5–£90 ($8–$144); credit cards accepted. Box office 10am–9pm. Tube: Waterloo or Embankment.

In the aftermath of World War II, three of the most comfortable and acoustically perfect concert halls in the world arose out of the industrial wastelands on the south side of the Thames, across Waterloo Bridge. They include Royal Festival Hall, Queen Elizabeth Hall, and the Purcell Room. Within their precincts, more than 1,200 performances a year are presented, including classical music, ballet, jazz, popular classics, pop, and contemporary dance. The center also accommodates the inter-nationally famous Hayward Gallery whose exhibitions include both contemporary and historical art.

The Royal Festival Hall is open from 10am every day. There are free exhibitions in the foyers and free lunchtime music from 12:30pm. The Poetry Library is open from 11am to 8pm, and there are shops selling books, records, and crafts.

Sadler's Wells Theatre. Rosebery Ave., Islington, EC1. ☎ **0171/314-8800.** Tickets £7.50–£35 ($12–$56). Tube: Angel.

This is London's premier venue for dance. It occupies the site of a theater that was built in 1683, on the site of a well that was once prized for the healing powers of its water. In the early 1990s, the old-fashioned, turn-of-the-century theater that had evolved from the original 17th-century core was demolished, and construction began on an innovative new design that was scheduled for completion sometime during the lifetime of this edition, in late 1998 or perhaps 1999. In the interim, performances are being presented in a rented circa 1960 theater, the Peacock on Portugal Street, WC2 (same phone; tube: Holborn).

For the new theater, look for something akin to a phoenix rising from the ashes that will offer both traditional and experimental dance within two theaters. They will include the new, state-of-the-art theater on Sadler Wells original site (Rosebery Avenue, in Islington) as well as offshoot productions within the above-mentioned Peacock, which the Sadlers Wells Trust, Ltd. will continue to rent until sometime after the millennium.

THE CLUB & MUSIC SCENE
CABARET & COMEDY

The Comedy Store. 1A Oxendon St., off Piccadilly Circus, SW1. ☎ **01426/914433** for a recorded message. Cover £10 ($16) Tues–Thurs; £12 ($19.20) Fri–Sat. Tube: Leicester Square or Piccadilly Circus.

This is London's most visible showcase for both established and emerging comic talent. Many big TV personalities got their start here. You must be over 18 to see a show. There's no particular dress code. Reservations are accepted through **Ticket-master** at ☎ **0171/344-4444,** and the club opens 1½ hours before each show. Go on Tuesday when the humor is more cutting-edge—the riffs are right out of the week's headlines.

Tiddy Dols. 55 Shepherd Market, Mayfair, W1. ☎ **0171/499-2357.** Tube: Green Park.

Tiddy Dols is housed in nine small Georgian houses that were built around 1741. Here you can enjoy dishes such as jugged hare, cock-a-leekie, plum pudding, and gingerbread while being entertained with madrigals, Noël Coward, Gilbert and Sullivan operettas, vaudeville, and music-hall songs. In summer, there is a large pavement cafe with parasols; in winter, open fires crackle. Main courses range in price from £11.50 to £15.25 ($18.40 to $24.40).

ROCK

The Bull & Gate. 389 Kentish Town Rd., NW5. ☎ **0171/485-5358.** Cover £2–£4 ($3.20–$6.40). Tube: Kentish Town.

Smaller, cheaper, and less touristy than many of its competitors, the Bull & Gate is the unofficial headquarters of London's pub-rock scene. Usually relatively unknown rock bands are often served up back-to-back by the half dozen within a woodsy, somewhat battered Victorian pub setting where everyone seems to spill beer on the floor and no one cares. This is off-the-beaten-track London at its most authentic, and requires real curiosity and love of rock music for anyone to make the trek up from the West End. Blur, Madness, and Pulp all played here before they hit the big time, and may drop in again from time to time. There's music nightly from 8 to 11:30pm.

The Rock Garden. 6-7 The Piazza, Covent Garden, WC2. ☎ **0171/836-4052.** Cover for The Venue £5–£12 ($8–$19.20); diners enter free. Tube: Covent Garden.

The Rock Garden has a restaurant at street level, and a bar and stage in the cellar known as The Venue. Dire Straits, the Police, and U2 all played here in the early days. You may see tomorrow's Oasis here, or just a bunch of blokes you'll never hear from ever again.

Wag Club. 35 Wardour St., WI. ☎ **0171/437-5534.** Cover £3–£10 ($4.80–$16). Tube: Piccadilly Circus or Leicester Square.

This popular dance club covers two floors, one decorated with Celtic designs in gold with colorful renditions of medieval tarot cards, the other in bright primary colors, with huge black-and-white canvasses. White-fur fabric sculptures adorn the walls and advanced modern lighting illuminates a floor of dancers. The music—live bands, recorded music, whatever—changes every night.

TRADITIONAL ENGLISH MUSIC

Cecil Sharp House. 2 Regent's Park Rd., NW1. ☎ **0171/485-2206.** No cover. Tube: Camden Town.

CSH was the focal point of the folk revival in the '60s and continues to treasure, document, and nurture this music. Here you will find a whole range of traditional English music and dancing performed. Call to see what's happening and when.

JAZZ & BLUES

Ain't Nothing But Blues Bar. 20 Kingly St., W1. ☎ **0171/287-0514.** Cover Fri–Sat £3–£5 ($4.80–$8), free before 9:30pm. Tube: Oxford Circus.

Featuring mostly local acts, the club also books American bands on tour, and bills itself as the only true blues place in town. On weekends, prepare to queue. From the Oxford Circus tube exit, walk south on Regent Street, turn left on Great Marlborough Street, and then take a quick right on Kingly Street.

The Blue Note. 1 Hoxton Sq., N1. ☎ **0171/729-8440.** Cover £5–£12 ($8–$19.20). Tube: Old Street.

Owned by the Acid Jazz Record label, this is a cafe-bar by day, and a live-music club at night. It became famous on the London nightlife circuit when it was known as the Bass Clef. The Acid Jazz Record people took it over and saved the building from demolition. It features bands playing styles ranging from jazz to funk to soul. Sunday features soul music upstairs and jazz in the basement.

100 Club. 100 Oxford St., W1. ☎ **0171/636-0933.** Cover Fri £8 ($12.80) for everybody; Sat £8 ($12.80) members, £9 ($14.40) nonmembers; Sun £6 ($9.60). Tube: Tottenham Court Road or Oxford Circus.

The less plush and less expensive 100 Club is a serious rival of the city's many jazz clubs. Its cavalcade of bands includes the best British jazz musicians, as well as many touring Americans. Rock, R&B, and blues are also on tap.

Pizza Express. 10 Dean St., W1. ☎ **0171/439-8722.** Cover £8–£15 ($12.80–$24). Tube: Tottenham Court Road.

Yes, it's a restaurant, but it also serves up some of the best jazz in London presented by mainstream artists. The darkly lit club offers jazz that's cool and pies that are hot (you must order food). Make reservations, as this place fills up quickly.

✪ **Ronnie Scott's.** 47 Frith St., W1. ☎ **0171/439-0747.** Cover nonmembers £15 ($24); members £4–£8 ($6.40–$12.80). Tube: Tottenham Court Road, Leicester Square, or Piccadilly Circus.

Mention the word *jazz* in London and people immediately think of Ronnie Scott's, long the citadel of modern jazz in Europe. Featured on almost every bill is an American band, often with a top-notch singer. The club's in the heart of Soho, a 10-minute walk from Piccadilly Circus via Shaftesbury Avenue. There are three separate areas: the Main Room, the Upstairs Room, and the Downstairs Bar. You don't have to be a member, although you can join if you wish. If you have a student ID, your cover from Monday through Thursday costs £8 ($12.80). In the Main Room you can either stand at the bar to watch the show or sit at a table, where you can order dinner. The more intimate Downstairs Bar is a quiet rendezvous where you can meet and talk with the regulars, often some of the world's most talented musicians. On weekends, the separate Upstairs Room has a disco called the Club Latino.

DANCE CLUBS

Bar Rumba. 26 Shaftesbury Ave., W1. ☎ **0171/287-2715.** Cover £3–£12 ($4.80–$19.20). Tube: Piccadilly Circus.

A secret address among Latinophiles, Bar Rumba leans toward radical jazz fusion on some nights, phat funk on other occasions. Boasting two full bars, it has a different musical theme every night, and Tuesday and Wednesday are the only nights you probably won't have to line up at the door. Monday showcases jazz, hip-hop, and drum and bass; Fridays feature soul, R&B, and swing. Saturday is the most popular night, featuring a mix of house and garage.

The Cross. The Arches, King's Cross Goods Yard, York Way, N1. ☎ **0171/837-0828.** Cover £10–£15 ($16–$24). Tube: King's Cross.

In the backwaters of King's Cross, this club has been hot since 1993. A hip crowd comes here to dance, and the building's warm brick-lined vaults create a stylish interior with a good vibe. Call to find out who's performing.

Equinox. Leicester Sq., WC2. ☎ **0171/437-1446.** Cover £5–£12 ($8–$19.20). Tube: Leicester Square.

The Equinox was built in 1992 on the site of a dance emporium (the London Empire) that witnessed the changing styles of social dancing since the 1700s. Amazingly, its popularity continues. It has nine bars, the city's largest dance floor, and a restaurant styled after a 1950s American diner. Virtually every kind of dance music is featured here. The setting is lavishly illuminated with one of Europe's largest lighting rigs, and the crowd is as varied as London itself. The Equinox has been quite busy lately, hosting some of the United Kingdom's hottest talents. Most recently, the Equinox featured those international sex symbols, the Spice Girls. Summer visitors can enjoy their theme nights, which are geared to entertaining a world-wide audience, including a once a week "Ibiza" foam party—you'll actually boogie the night away on a foam covered dance floor. Happy hour drinks are £1 ($1.60) from 5 to 7pm.

Hanover Grand. 6 Hanover St., W1. ☎ **0171/499-7977.** Cover £5–£15 ($8–$24). Tube: Oxford Circus.

Thursdays are funky, attracting dancers in whatever they happened to have at the front of their closets. Friday and Saturday the crowd gets more stylish. Dance floors are always busy here, as crowds surge up and down the stairs interconnecting the two levels. Who knows if it'll still be popular when you're here.

Hippodrome. Leicester Sq., WC2. ☎ **0171/437-4311.** Cover £4–£12 ($6.40–$19.20). Tube: Leicester Square.

Here is one of London's greatest discos, an enormous place where light and sound beam in from all directions. Think of it as the Studio 54 of London. Revolving speakers even descend from the roof to deafen you in patches, and you can watch yourself on closed-circuit video.

Limelight. 136 Shaftesbury Ave., WC2. ☎ **0171/434-0572.** Cover £4–£8 ($6.40–$12.80) before 10pm, £8–£12 ($12.80–$19.20) thereafter. Tube: Leicester Square.

Although it opened in 1985, this large dance club, located inside a former Welsh chapel dating from 1754, has only recently realized its potential. In addition to several dance floors and bars, there are plenty of Gothic nooks and crannies. The DJs spin a good selection of house music.

Ministry of Sound. 103 Gaunt St., SE1. ☎ **0171/378-6528.** Cover £12–£20 ($19.20–$32). Tube: Elephant & Castle.

Because it's removed from the city center, this club-of-the-minute is popular with the local sweat set and relatively devoid of tourists. It has a big bar and an even bigger sound system that blasts garage and house music to enthusiastic and energetic crowds who fill the two dance floors or relax in the cinema room. Be forewarned that entrance to this place is not particularly cheap and the door policy is selective.

Stringfellows. 16-19 Upper St. Martin's Lane, WC2. ☎ **0171/240-5534.** Cover £10–£15 ($16–$24). Reservations recommended. Tube: Leicester Square.

This is one of the relatively elegant longtime staples on London's nighttime landscape, with a widely varied clientele and lots of velvet and glossy accessories. In theory, it's a members-only club, but, at the management's discretion, nonmembers may be admitted. Its disco has a glass dance floor and a dazzling sound-and-light system.

Subterania. 12 Acklam Rd., W10. ☎ **0181/960-4590.** Cover £8–£10 ($12.80–$16). Tube: Ladbroke Grove.

This unpretentious, informal club changes its style during the week to reflect the live bands it books. You'll have to call to find out who's playing and what the vibe will be like. The place contains a busy dance floor on its street level, and a mezzanine-style bar upstairs. Energy levels are perked up by a collection of orange, purple, and blue sofas upholstered in faux leopard skin. Friday night features soul, funk, hip-hop, and swing; Saturday night, house and garage.

Velvet Room (formerly The Velvet Underground). 143 Charing Cross Rd., WC2. ☎ **0171/439-4655.** Cover £4–£10 ($6.40–$16). Mon–Thurs 10pm–3am, Fri–Sat 10:30pm–4am. Tube: Tottenham Court Road.

The Velvet Underground was a London staple for years. Times changed and the clientele grew up—hence the Velvet Room, a more mature setting designed to convey a luxurious bar with the stuffiness. Classy vibrancy is the catch phrase now. DJs Carl Cox and others spin favorite dance hits—more laid back to better represent the new theme. We think this place has grown with the times and made a smooth transition from the laid-back to the upbeat without sacrificing one shred of cool, setting a standard for the next generation of Soho bar life.

Venom Club/The Zoo Bar. 13-18 Bear St., WC2. ☎ **0171/839-4188.** Zoo Bar daily 4pm–2am; Venom Club daily 9:30pm–3am. Entrance to both venues free before 10pm, cover £3–£5 ($4.80–$8) thereafter. Tube: Leicester Square.

Its developers spent millions of pounds to create the slickest, glossiest, flashiest, and most psychedelic decor in London. Everyone on the staff seems to be gorgeous. The decor of the hyper-trendy Zoo Bar (upstairs) focuses on a menagerie of real and mythical animals, meticulously depicted in mosaics beneath a glassed-in ceiling dome. Downstairs, in the Venom Club, no one will care if you can't think of anything witty to say, because you can't be heard over the music anyway. The crowd is over 18, but something less than 35-ish and holding, and beyond gender designation anyway. If you're gay and a fan of Boy George, the first Wednesday of every month is devoted to that singer's groupies. They flock here en masse, in clothing inspired by the wardrobe of the master himself (who, incidentally, usually shows up sometime during the evening).

LATIN RHYTHMS

Cuba. 11 Kensington High St., W8. ☎ **0171/938-4137.** Cover £3–£5 ($4.80–$8) after 10pm. Tube: High Street Kensington.

This is a Spanish/Cuban-style bar-restaurant upstairs and a music club downstairs. The crowd is an odd mix of diners, after-work drinkers, Latinophile music aficionados, and dancers, here to eat, drink, and check out live musical acts from Cuba, Brazil, Spain, and other Latin countries.

Salsa. 96 Charing Cross Rd., WC2. ☎ **0171/379-3277.** Cover Fri–Sat £7 ($11.20) after 9pm. Tube: Leicester Square.

This lively bar-restaurant and music club for Latinophiles features musical acts from Central and South America. Dance lessons are available nightly starting at 6:30pm; live music starts at 9pm. Some of the best Latin dancers in London show up here.

THE GAY & LESBIAN SCENE

The most reliable source of information on gay clubs and activities is the **Gay Switchboard** (☎ **0171/837-7324**). The staff runs a 24-hour service for information on places and activities.

The Box. 32-34 Monmouth St. (at Seven Dials), WC2. ☎ **0171/240-5828.** Tube: Covent Garden.

This is a cheerful, popular rendezvous for London's gay and counterculture communities. Set adjacent to one of Covent Garden's best-known traffic junctions, Seven Dials, this Mediterranean-style bar caters to lesbians, especially on Sunday nights, when it's "Girl Bar at the Box"—reserved for women only. The rest of the time, gay men may slightly outnumber gay women, though everyone is pretty blasé about sexual definitions. Daily, from noon on, the place does most of its business as a restaurant, serving meal-sized salads, club sandwiches, and soups. Food service ends abruptly at 5:30pm.

The Edge. 11 Soho Sq., W1. ☎ **0171/439-1313.** Tube: Tottenham Court Road.

Tolerance, humor, and sophistication lead to conviviality and a full house at The Edge. When the late-night dance music is playing, two lower floors tend to be the most high-energy, animated, and crowded. If you want quiet conversation, keep climbing for the upper floors.

First Out. 52 St. Giles High St., WC2. ☎ **0171/240-8042.** Tube: Tottenham Court Road.

First Out prides itself on being the first (est. 1986) all-gay coffee shop in London. Set within a 19th-century building whose venerable wood panels have been painted all colors of the liberationist rainbow, it maintains two floors of intimate (read: not particularly cruisy) space where menu items are exclusively vegetarian, and priced at only £3.25 ($5.20). Cappuccino and whisky are the preferred drinks; curry dishes, potted pies in phyllo pastries, and salads are the foods of choice. Don't expect raucousness—some people have brought their grandmothers here. Look for the bulletin board, where the leaflets and business cards of gay and gay-friendly entrepreneurs are posted.

Halfway to Heaven. 7 Duncannon St., WC2. ☎ **0171/321-2791.** Tube: Charing Cross or Embankment.

Housed within a century-old structure with a beamed ceiling, this is the least frenetic gay bar in the Trafalgar Square neighborhood. The quiet, snug downstairs saloon and the upstairs bar attract a young, cruisy clientele.

Heaven. The Arches, Craven St., WC2. ☎ **0171/930-2020.** Cover £5–£8 ($8–$12.80). Tube: Charing Cross or Embankment.

This landmark club sits within the vaulted cellars of Charing Cross Railway Station. Painted black inside, and reminiscent of a very large air-raid shelter, Heaven is one of England's biggest gay clubs. It's divided into at least four distinctly different areas, each connected by a labyrinth of catwalks, stairs, and hallways. Heaven features different theme nights; call to check the schedule before you go.

Madame Jo Jo's. 8 Brewer St., W1. ☎ **0171/734-2473.** Cover £12.50–£22.50 ($20–$36). Tube: Piccadilly Circus.

This is London's most popular drag show. The decadent art-nouveau interior has attracted the eye of many a film director, including Stanley Kubrick, who came here to film *Eyes Wide Shut* with Tom Cruise. Many celebrities, such as Hugh Grant and Mick Jagger have come here to see the cabaret. Drag shows are presented Thursday through Saturday nights, with outside promoters organizing entertainment on other nights. Call to see what's up.

THE BAR & PUB SCENE
For additional pub listings, see chapter 4.

OUR FAVORITE BARS

The American Bar. In The Savoy, The Strand, WC2. ☎ **0171/836-4343.** Tube: Charing Cross or Embankment.

At the American Bar, still one of the most sophisticated gathering places in London, the bartender is known for such special concoctions as the "Savoy Affair" and the "Prince of Wales," as well as for making the best martini in town. Monday through Saturday evenings from 7 to 11pm, jazz piano music is featured. The location, near so many West End theaters, is ideal for a pre- or post-theater drink. Men should wear jackets.

Bracewells Bar. In the Park Lane Hotel, Piccadilly, W1. ☎ **0171/499-6321.** Tube: Green Park or Hyde Park.

Chic, nostalgic, and elegant, it's the kind of bar where Edward VII and his stylish companion, Ms. Langtry, might have felt very much at home. Its ambience is like that of an elegant private club. Complimentary hors d'oeuvres are offered in the evenings. The bar adjoins Bracewells, one of London's finest hotel restaurants.

The Dorchester Bar. In the Dorchester, Park Lane, W1. ☎ **0171/629-8888.** Tube: Hyde Park Corner.

This is a fun and sophisticated modern hideaway on the lobby level of one of the world's most lavishly decorated hotels. You can order upscale Italian snacks, lunches, and suppers throughout the day and evening. Otherwise, the bartender can make any drink ever conceived on the planet Earth. A pianist plays suitable background music every evening after 7pm; he is joined by a jazz trio Wednesday through Saturday.

Lillie Langtry Bar. In the Cadogan Hotel, Sloane St., SW1. ☎ **0171/235-7141.** Tube: Sloane Square.

This spot epitomizes some of the charm and elegance of the Edwardian era. Lillie Langtry, actress and society beauty at the turn of the century (notorious as the mistress of Edward VII), used to live here. Oscar Wilde was arrested here on charges of sodomy, but that unfortunate event is long forgotten and the playwright today is honored on the drink menu with Hock & Seltzer, his favorite drink, a kind of white-wine spritzer. The bar, next to Langtry's Restaurant, exudes a 1920s aura. An international menu is also served in the adjoining restaurant.

OUR FAVORITE PUBS

There's no better way to determine the character of the different villages that make up London than to drop into the local pub for a pint. Eavesdrop to hear the accents, slang, and topics that differentiate upper-crust Kensington from blue-collar Wapping. Identify the village lush, catch up on local gossip—and while you're at it, enjoy some of the finest ciders, ales, stouts, and malt whiskies in the world.

The Heart of the City

Central London is chock-full of wonderful old pubs with histories almost as rich and varied as the city itself.

The Black Friar. 174 Queen Victoria St., EC4. ☎ **0171/236-5650.** Tube: Blackfriars.

This place will shift you into the Edwardian era, with its fabulous marble and bronze art-nouveau decor, featuring bas-reliefs of mad monks, a low-vaulted mosaic ceiling, and seating built into golden marble recesses. It's especially popular with an after-work crowd, and offers Adnams, Wadworth 6X, Tetleys, and Brakspears on tap.

The Cittie of Yorke. 22 High Holborn, WC1. ☎ **0171/242-7670.** Tube: Holborn Chancery Lane.

This place boasts the longest bar in all of Britain, rafters ascending to the heavens, and a long row of immense wine vats, giving it the air of a medieval Great Hall—which seems appropriate since a pub has been in service at this location since 1430. Samuel Smiths OB is on tap, and the bar also offers such novelties as chocolate-orange fla-vored vodka.

The Lamb & Flag. 33 Rose St., off Garrick St., WC2. ☎ **0171/497-9504.** Tube: Leicester Square.

Dickens's description of the clientele may seem dated now, but the room itself is little changed from when he prowled this neighborhood. The pub has a scandalous history: Dryden was almost killed by a band of thugs outside its doors in December 1679, and it was nicknamed the "Bucket of Blood" during the Regency period (1811 to 1820) because of the bare-knuckled prizefights it hosted. Courage Best and Directors, Mor-lands Old Speckled Hen, John Smiths, and Wadworth 6X are on tap.

Olde Mitre. Ely Place, EC1. ☎ **0171/405-4751.** Tube: Chancery Lane.

This is the namesake of a working-class inn built here in 1547, when the Bishops of Ely controlled the district. It's a small pub with an odd mix of customers. Friary Meux, Ind Coope Burton, and Tetleys are on tap.

Seven Stars. 53 Carey St., WC2. ☎ **0171/242-8521.** Tube: Holborn.

This place is tiny and plain except for its collection of toby mugs and law-related art. The art is an obvious tribute to the pub's location at the back of the Law Courts, and its large clientele of barristers, who fill the place. A great place to have a listen and learn some British legal slang. Courage Best and Directors on tap, as well as a selection of malt whiskies.

West London

The Churchill Arms. 119 Kensington Church St., W8. ☎ **0171/727-4242.** Tube: Notting Hill Gate or High Street Kensington.

Loaded with Churchill memorabilia, this place offers a week of celebration leading up to his birthday on November 30. Show up then and you may get recruited to help dec-orate the place, as visitors are often welcomed like old regulars here. Decorations and festivities surround Halloween, Christmas, and St. Patrick's Day as well, helping to create as much of a homey, village feel as you're likely to find.

The Dove. 19 Upper Mall, W6. ☎ **0181/748-5405.** Tube: Ravenscourt Park.

Relax by the Thames at the pub where James Thomson composed "Rule Britannia," and part of his lesser-known "The Seasons." For toasting the old empire, you can hoist a Fullers London Pride or ESB, among the offerings on tap.

Ladbroke Arms. 54 Ladbroke Rd., W11. ☎ **0171/727-6648.** Tube: Holland Park.

This place is known for its food, a secondary consideration to ales in most pubs, and has been honored as London's Dining Pub of the Year. A changing menu includes such dishes as chicken breast stuffed with avocado or garlic steak in pink peppercorn sauce. This is served in combination with background jazz and rotating art prints. The place may stray from the traditional pub feel, but it makes for a pleasant stop and a good meal. Eldridge Pope Royal Oak, John Smiths, Courage Best and Directors are among the offerings on tap, and there are several malt whiskies as well.

6 The Thames Valley

The historic Thames Valley and Chiltern Hills lie so close to London that they can easily be reached by car, train, or Green Line coach. In fact, you can explore this area during the day and return to London in time to see a West End show.

The most visited historic site in England is Windsor Castle, 21 miles west of London. Going to Windsor Castle is the most popular day trip for visitors venturing outside of London for the first time. If you base yourself in Windsor, you can spend another day exploring some of the sights on its periphery, including Eton (which adjoins Windsor), Runnymede, and Savill Garden.

If your visit coincides with the spring social sporting season, you can head to Ascot or Henley-on-Thames for the famous social sporting events: Ascot and the Royal Regatta. Be sure to wear a hat!

There are also some great historic homes and gardens in the area, including Woburn Abbey, Hatfield House, Hughenden Manor, the Mapledurham House, and the Wellington Ducal Estate. If your time is severely limited, the two most important country mansions to visit are Woburn Abbey and Hatfield House. Woburn Abbey could consume an entire day, whereas Hatfield can be visited in a morning or afternoon.

It's not just the historic homes that make the Home Counties intriguing to visit; the land of river valleys and gentle hills makes for wonderful drives. The beech-clad Chilterns are at their most beautiful in spring and autumn. This 40-mile chalk ridge extends in an arc from the Thames Valley to the old Roman city of St. Albans in Hertfordshire. The whole region is popular for boating holidays on its 200-mile network of canals.

Certainly your principal reason for visiting Oxfordshire is to explore the university city of Oxford, about an hour's ride from London by car or train. It's not a good day trip, though, because there's too much to see and do. Plan to spend the night, and the following morning you can visit Blenheim Palace, England's answer to Versailles. And Oxfordshire is a land of great mansions, old churches of widely varying architectural styles, and rolling farmland.

The Thames Valley

Ascot Racecourse **11**
Blenheim Palace **1**
Cliveden **6**
Eton College **7**
Hatfield House **13**
Hughenden Manor **5**
Mapledurham House **3**
Oxford University **2**
Runnymede **10**
Savill Garden **9**
Wellington Ducal Estate **4**
Windsor Castle **8**
Woburn Abbey **12**

0 [====] 10 mi
16.6 km

1 Windsor & Eton

21 miles W of London

Were it not for the castle, Windsor might still be a charming Thames town to visit. But because it is the home of the best-known asset the royal family possesses, it is virtually overrun in summer by tourists who all but obscure the town's charm.

The good news is that after the disastrous fire of 1992, Windsor Castle is restored, even though some of the new designs for Windsor Castle have been called a "Gothic shocker" or "ghastly." Actually, in spite of some media criticism, a remarkable activity in restoration went on, as young woodcarvers used ancient draw knives to smooth the 1,200-pound unseasoned oak beams that descended on the town. They followed the same techniques as did their predecessors in the Middle Ages. Gilders applied gold leaf, and plasterers formed little flowers by hand. This was virtually the same work done 9 centuries ago when William the Conqueror started to build the castle. Queen Elizabeth in November 1997 opened the state apartments following a $62 million project that returned most of the ruined part of the castle to its original condition. Other work will go on some time until late 1999. The restoration was completed in time for the celebration of the queen's 50th wedding anniversary. The work was revealed to the world by a producer on British television, Edward Windsor—yes, the queen's youngest son. Even Charles came on camera (Edward has powerful connections) to discuss everything from fabricating the new roof to reinstalling the stained-glass windows. *Windsor Restored,* a documentary, has been shown around the world.

Fire, restoration, or whatever, Windsor Castle remains Britain's second-most-visited historic building, behind the Tower of London, attracting 1.2 million visitors a year.

ESSENTIALS

GETTING THERE The train from Waterloo or Paddington Station in London makes the trip in 30 minutes (you'll have to transfer at Slough to the Slough-Windsor shuttle train). There are more than a dozen trains per day, and the cost is £6.20 ($9.90). Call **Thames Trains, Ltd.,** at ☎ **0178/908-3678** for more information.

Green Line coaches (☎ **0181/668-7261**) no. 700 and 702 from Hyde Park Corner in London take about 1½ hours. A same-day round-trip costs £4.35 to £5.50 ($6.95 to $8.80). The bus will drop you near the parish church, across the street from the castle.

If you're driving from London, take M4 west.

VISITOR INFORMATION A **Tourist Information Centre** is located across from Windsor Castle on High Street (☎ **01753/743900**). There's also an information booth in the Tourist Centre at Windsor Coach Park. Both are open Monday to Friday from 9am to 5pm, Saturday and Sunday 10am to 5pm. They also book walking tours for the Oxford guild of guides.

CASTLE HILL SIGHTS

✪ **Windsor Castle.** ☎ **01753/868286** for information. Admission £8.80 ($14.10) adults, £6.20 ($9.90) students and seniors, £4.60 ($7.35) children 16 and under; £22.50 ($36) for a family of four. Mar–Oct daily 10am–4pm; Nov–Feb daily 10am–3pm. Last admission 1 hour before closing. Closed for periods in Apr, June, and Dec when the royal family is in residence. Call ahead and check what's open before visiting.

William the Conqueror first ordered a castle built on this spot, and since his day it's been a fateful spot for English sovereigns: King John cooled his heels at Windsor while waiting to put his signature on the Magna Carta at nearby Runnymede; Charles I was imprisoned here before losing his head; Queen Bess did some renovations; Victoria mourned her beloved Albert, who died at the castle in 1861; the royal family rode out much of World War II behind its sheltering walls; and when Queen Elizabeth II is in residence, the royal standard flies. With 1,000 rooms, Windsor is the world's largest inhabited castle.

The apartments display many works of art, porcelain, armor, furniture, three Verrio ceilings, and several 17th-century Gibbons carvings. Several works by Rubens adorn the King's Drawing Room and in the relatively small King's Dressing Room is a Dürer, along with Rembrandt's portrait of his mother, and Van Dyck's triple portrait of Charles I. Of the apartments, the grand reception room, with its Gobelin tapestries, is the most spectacular.

In November 1992, a fire swept through part of Windsor Castle, severely damaging it. The castle has since reopened, and all the rooms that were once open to the public should be available for viewing in 1999. However, St. George's Hall and the Grand Reception Room are now currently open.

We think that the Windsor ✪ **Changing of the Guard** is a much more exciting and moving experience than the London exercises. In Windsor, the guard marches through town when the queen is in residence, stopping the traffic as it wheels into the castle to the tune of a full regimental band; when the queen is not here, a drum-and-pipe band is mustered. From May to August, the ceremony takes place Monday through Saturday at 11am. In winter, the guard is changed every 48 hours Monday through Saturday. It's best to call ☎ **01753/868286** to find out which days the ceremony will take place.

Queen Mary's Doll's House. Castle Hill. ☎ **01753/831118.** Windsor Castle tickets include admission here for an additional £1 ($1.60) per person. Combined ticket to Queen Mary's Doll's House and St. George's chapel without Windsor Castle £6 ($9.60) adults, £4.50 ($7.20) students and seniors, £3 ($4.80) ages 16 and under. Mar–Oct daily 10am–4pm; Nov–Feb daily 10am–3pm.

A palace in perfect miniature, the Doll's House was given to Queen Mary in 1923 as a symbol of national goodwill. The house, designed by Sir Edwin Lutyens, was created on a scale of 1 to 12. It took 3 years to complete and involved the work of 1,500 tradesmen and artists. Every item is a miniature masterpiece; each room is exquisitely furnished and every item is made exactly to scale. Working elevators stop on every floor, and there is running water in all five bathrooms.

✪ **St. George's Chapel.** Castle Hill. Admission is included in admission to Windsor Castle. Combined ticket to Queen Mary's Doll's House and St. George's chapel without Windsor Castle £6 ($9.60) adults, £4.50 ($7.20) students and seniors, £3 ($4.80) ages 16 and under. Mon–Sat 10am–4pm, Sun 2–3:45 or 4pm. Closed during services, Jan, and a few days in mid-June.

A gem of the Perpendicular style, this chapel shares the distinction with Westminster Abbey of being a pantheon of English monarchs (Victoria is a notable exception). The present St. George's was founded in the late 15th century by Edward IV on the site of the original Chapel of the Order of the Garter (Edward III, 1348). You first enter the nave, which has fan vaulting (a remarkable achievement in English architecture) and contains the tomb of George V and Queen Mary, designed by Sir William Reid Dick. Off the nave in the Urswick Chapel, the Princess Charlotte memorial provides an ironic touch; if she had survived childbirth in 1817, she, and not her cousin Victoria, would have ruled the British Empire. In the aisle are tombs of George VI and Edward IV. The Edward IV "Quire," with its imaginatively carved 15th-century choir stalls (crowned by lacy canopies and Knights of the Garter banners), evokes the pomp and pageantry of medieval days. In the center is a flat tomb, containing the vault of the beheaded Charles I, along with Henry VIII and his third wife, Jane Seymour. Finally, you may want to inspect the Prince Albert Memorial Chapel, reflecting the opulent tastes of the Victorian era.

NEARBY ETON COLLEGE

Eton is home of what is arguably the most famous public school (Americans would call it a private school) in the world. From Windsor Castle's ramparts, you can look down on the river and on the famous playing fields of Eton.

You can take a train from Paddington Station, go by car, or take the Green Line bus to Windsor. By car, take the M4 motorway to Exit 5 to go straight to Eton. Insider's tip: Parking is likely to be a problem, so we advise turning off M4 at Exit 6 to Windsor; you can park here and take an easy stroll past Windsor Castle and across the Thames bridge. Follow Eton High Street to the college.

Eton College (☎ **01753/671177**) was founded by 18-year-old Henry VI in 1440. Some of England's greatest men, notably the duke of Wellington, have played on these fields. Twenty prime ministers were educated here, as well as such literary figures as George Orwell, Aldous Huxley, Ian Fleming, and Percy Bysshe Shelley, who, during his years at Eton (from 1804 to 1810), was called "Mad Shelley" or "Shelley the Atheist" by his fellow pupils. Prince William, second in line to the throne, is currently a student here. If it's open, take a look at the Perpendicular chapel, with its 15th-century paintings and reconstructed fan vaulting.

The history of Eton College since its inception in 1440 is depicted in the **Museum of Eton Life,** Eton College (☎ **01753/671177**), located in vaulted wine cellars under College Hall, which were originally the storehouse for use of the college's masters. The displays, ranging from formal to extremely informal, include a turn-of-the-century boy's room, schoolbooks, canes used by senior boys to apply punishment they felt needful to their juniors, and birch sticks used by masters for the same purpose.

Admission to the school and museum costs £2.50 ($4) for adults. You can also take guided tours for £3.70 ($5.90). Eton College is open from March 22 to April 16 and June 28 to September 2, daily from 10:30am to 4:30pm; April 17 to June 27 and September 3 to October 5, daily from 2 to 4:30pm. However, it may close for special occasions.

MORE TO SEE & DO IN & AROUND WINDSOR

The town of Windsor is largely Victorian, with lots of brick buildings and a few remnants of Georgian architecture. In and around the castle are two cobblestone streets, Church and Market, which have antique shops, silversmiths, and pubs. One shop on Church Street was supposedly occupied by Nell Gwynne, who needed to be within call of Charles II's chambers. After lunch or tea, you may want to stroll along the 3-mile, aptly named **Long Walk.**

On Sunday, there are often **polo matches** in Windsor Great Park, and at Ham Common, and you may see Prince Charles playing and Prince Philip serving as umpire while the queen watches. The park is the site of the queen's occasional equestrian jaunts. On Sunday she attends a little church near the Royal Lodge. Traditionally, she prefers to drive herself here, later returning to the castle for Sunday lunch. For more information, call the Tourist Information Centre (see above).

Savill Garden, Wick Lane, Englefield Green, Egham, and Surrey (☎ **01753/860222**) are all in **Windsor Great Park,** which is signposted from Windsor, Egham, and Ascot. Started in 1932, the 35-acre garden is one of the finest of its type in the northern hemisphere. The display starts in spring with rhododendrons, camellias, and daffodils beneath the trees; then throughout the summer there are spectacular displays of flowers and shrubs presented in a natural and wild state. It's open daily year-round (except at Christmas) from 10am to 6pm (to 4pm in winter); admission is £3.50 ($5.60) for adults, free for children 15 and under. It's 5 miles from Windsor along A30; turn off at Wick Road and follow the signs to the gardens. The nearest rail station is at Egham; from here you'll need to take a taxi a distance of 3 miles. There's a licensed, self-service restaurant on the premises.

Adjoining the Savill Garden are the **Valley Gardens,** full of shrubs and trees in a series of wooded natural valleys running down to the water. It's open daily throughout the year. Entrance to the gardens is free, although parking your car costs £3 ($4.80) per vehicle.

Queen Victoria died on January 22, 1901, and was buried beside her beloved Prince Albert in a mausoleum at **Frogmore** (a private estate), a mile from Windsor. The prince consort died in December 1861. The house, gardens, and mausoleum are only open a few days out of the year, usually in May and August, from around 10am to 6pm. The cost for adults is £9.80 ($15.70); seniors pay £7.20 ($11.50). Call ☎ **01753/868286,** ext. 2235, for more details.

On the B3022 Bracknell/Ascot Road, outside Windsor, **Legoland,** a 150-acre theme park, opened in 1996. Although a bit corny, it's fun for the entire family. Attractions, spread across five main activity centers, include the Duplo Gardens, offering a boat ride, puppet theater, and water works, plus a Miniland, showing

European cities or villages re-created in minute detail from millions of Lego bricks. The "Enchanted Forest" has treasure trails, a castle, and animals created from Lego bricks. For reservations and information, call ☎ 0990/040404. The park is open daily from March through October. Admission costs £15 ($24) for adults, £12 ($19.20) for children 3 to 15, and is free for children 2 and under.

Three miles south of Windsor is **Runnymede,** the 188-acre meadow on the south side of the Thames, in Surrey, where it's believed that King John put his seal on the Great Charter after intense pressure from his feudal barons and lords. Today, Runnymede is also the site of the John F. Kennedy Memorial, an acre of English ground given to the United States by the people of Britain. The memorial, a large block of white stone, is hard to see from the road but is clearly signposted and reached after a short walk. The pagoda that shelters it was placed here by the American Bar Association to acknowledge the fact that American law stems from the English system.

The historic site, to which there is free access all year, lies beside the Thames, half a mile west of the hamlet of Old Windsor on the south side of the A308. If you're driving on the M25, exit at Junction 13. The nearest rail connection is at Egham, half a mile away. Trains depart from London's Waterloo Station, and take about 25 minutes.

BUS & BOAT TOURS, HORSE RIDES & GUIDED WALKS OF WINDSOR

The tourist office can put you in touch with a Blue Badge (official) guide to lead you on a **walking tour** of town. These trained local guides cost £45 ($72) per hour—get together a group to split the cost. Advance booking is essential.

You can also take a 30-minute **carriage ride** up the sycamore-lined length of Windsor Castle's Long Walk. Horses with their carriages and drivers line up beside the castle waiting for fares, charging about £20 ($32) for up to four passengers.

Boat tours depart from Windsor's main embarkation point along Windsor Promenade, Barry Avenue, for a 35-minute round-trip to Boveney Lock. The cost is £3.20 ($5.10) for adults, half price for children. You can also take a 2-hour tour through the Boveney Lock and up past stately private riverside homes, the Bray Film Studios, Queens Eyot, and Monkey Island, for £5.40 ($8.65) for adults, half price for children. There's also a 45-minute tour from Runnymede on board the *Lucy Fisher*, a replica of a Victorian paddle steamer. You pass Magna Carta Island, among other sights. This tour costs £2.90 ($4.65) for adults, half price for children. In addition, longer tours between Maidenhead and Hampton Court are offered. The boats offer light refreshments and have a well-stocked bar, plus the decks are covered in case of an unexpected shower. Tours are operated by **French Brothers, Ltd.,** Clewer Boathouse, Clewer Court Road, Windsor (☎ 01753/851900).

SHOPPING

A colorful traditional English perfumery, **Woods of Windsor,** Queen Charlotte Street (☎ 01753/868125), dates from 1770. It offers soaps, shampoos, scented drawer liners, and hand and body lotions, all prettily packaged in pastel-flower and bright old-fashioned wraps.

The Token House, High Street (☎ 01753/863263), is the largest gathering of everyone's favorite china and crystal. Place settings in Wedgwood, Royal Albert, Minton, and Spode, plus Portmeirion bowls, Royal Dalton figurines, Waterford crystal stemware and collector plates, bowls, and vases are stacked through the airy, bright shop, along with silver-plated and stainless-steel cutlery. **The Reject China**

Shop across the street has items that sell for less, but there is no connection to The Token House.

At **Billings & Edmonds,** 132 High St., Eton (☎ 01753/861348), you may think you've blundered into a time warp. This distinctive clothing store offers excellent traditional tailoring, suits made to order, and a complete line of cufflinks, shirts, ties, and accessories.

Asquith's Teddy Bear Shop, 33 High St., Eton (☎ 01753/831200), appeals to your inner child with every bear imaginable, including Winnie and Paddington. Bear clothes from dungarees to Eton College uniforms mix with tinware and hatboxes covered in teddy-bear prints.

WHERE TO STAY IN THE WINDSOR AREA

During the Ascot races and Windsor Horse Show, reservations are necessary far in advance.

The Castle Hotel. 18 High St., Windsor, Berkshire SL4 1LJ. ☎ 800/225-5843 in the U.S. and Canada, or 01753/851011. Fax 01753/830244. 106 units. TV TEL. £140–£180 ($224–$288) double; £200 ($320) suite. Children 15 and under stay free in parents' room. AE, DC, MC, V.

In the shadow of Windsor Castle, on the main street, is this solid choice with a dignified Georgian facade. It was originally built in the 15th century to shelter the workers laboring on the town's foundations and royal buildings. More recently, Princess Anne has dropped in for breakfast. Centuries ago, the grounds behind the hotel served as the stable yard for Windsor Castle, but now they contain a modern wing, where the bedrooms are much more sterile than those in the main building. The restaurant's food has improved a lot recently.

Fairlight Lodge. 41 Frances Rd., Windsor, Berkshire SL4 3AQ. ☎ 01753/861207. Fax 01753/865963. 10 units. TV TEL. £69–£79 ($110.40–$126.40) double; £90 ($144) family room for 2 adults and 2 children. Rates include English breakfast. AE, MC, V.

Built in 1885 as the home of the mayor of Windsor, this highly rated B&B in a residential section is only a few minutes' walk south of Windsor Castle. It offers comfortable rooms with coffeemakers; two have large four-poster beds. There's a fully licensed Garden Restaurant, which serves affordable dinners, and caters to vegetarians and special dietary needs.

✪ The Oakley Court Hotel. Windsor Rd., Water Oakley, Windsor, Berkshire SL4 5UR. ☎ 01753/609988. Fax 01628/637011. 125 units. MINIBAR TV TEL. Mon–Thurs £185 ($296) double, £295 ($472) suite; Fri–Sun £140 ($224) double, £200 ($320) suite. Weekend rates include breakfast. AE, DC, MC, V. Take the river road, A308, 3 miles from Windsor toward Maidenhead.

Built beside the Thames (only a 20-minute drive from Heathrow) by a Victorian industrialist, the Oakley Court has quite a sense of tradition. Today it's affiliated with the Queen's Moat House hotel chain. The building's jutting gables and bristling turrets have lent themselves to the filming of several horror movies, including the *Rocky Horror Picture Show* and *Dracula.* Recently renovated, the hotel, with all the requisite oak paneling, is a comfortable place to stay—far superior to your choices in the heart of Windsor. Although the grandest public areas are in the main house, most rooms are in a pair of well-accessorized modern wings that ramble through the estate's 35 acres of well-tended parks and gardens

Dining: The hotel is home to a relatively new branch of venerable restaurant based since the 1920s in London, Le Boulestin (reviewed below). Less formal is Boaters

Brasserie, which opens for lunch Monday through Saturday from 12:30 to 1:45pm, and from 7:30 to 9:45pm.

Amenities: You can rent a boat for punting on the Thames, stroll through the extensive gardens, or order room service 24 hours a day. Recently installed facilities include a leisure club with a pool and Jacuzzi, plus a gym with sauna and steam room.

Royal Adelaide Hotel. 46 King's Rd., Windsor, Berkshire SL4 2AG. ☎ **01753/863916.** Fax 01753/830682. 40 units. TV TEL. £95 ($152) double. Rates include English breakfast. AE, DC, MC, V.

This interesting Georgian building is opposite the famous Long Walk leading to Windsor Castle, 5 minutes away. It was named for Queen Adelaide, who visited the premises during her reign, thereby dubbing it "royal." All the well-furnished rooms, which vary in size, have trouser presses, hair dryers, alarm clocks, and hot-beverage makers. A fixed-priced dinner is available, but arrangements should be made in advance. The cuisine is both English and French.

Sir Christopher Wren's House Hotel. Thames St., Windsor, Berkshire SL4 1PX. ☎ **01753/861354.** Fax 01753/860172. 60 units. TV TEL. Mon–Thurs £145 ($232) double; £210 ($336) suite. Fri–Sun (including breakfast) £98.50–£210 ($157.60–$336). AE, DC, MC, V. Free parking.

Designed by Christopher Wren in 1676 as his own home, this former town house occupies a prime position on the Thames, its gardens overlooking swans and boats. It's between Eton and Windsor, just a 3-minute walk from the castle. The impressive central hall features a Queen Anne black-marble refectory table. Wren's oak-paneled former study is equipped with his Empire desk, a fireplace, and shield-back Hepplewhite chairs. The bay-windowed main drawing room opens onto a garden and a riverside flagstone terrace for after-dinner coffee and drinks. Some rooms have fine old furniture, and all are equipped with trouser presses. Several overlook the river. Room 2, which was Sir Christopher Wren's bedroom, is said to be haunted.

Dining: The hotel's restaurant, The Orangerie, is recommended below.

Amenities: Room service, concierge, dry cleaning/laundry, newspaper delivery, secretarial services, access to a nearby health club, business center.

Ye Harte & Garter Hotel. 31 High St., Windsor, Berkshire SL4 1PH. ☎ **01753/863426.** Fax 01753/830527. 39 units. TV TEL. £90–£180 ($144–$288) double. AE, DC, MC, V.

On Castle Hill opposite Windsor Castle, the old Garter Inn, named for the Knights of the Garter, was the setting for scenes in Shakespeare's *Merry Wives of Windsor.* The Garter burned down in the 1800s and was rebuilt as part of one hostelry that included the Harte. From the front rooms, you can watch the guards marching up High Street every morning on their way to change the guard at the castle. The recently renovated rooms are most comfortable, and rather functionally furnished, although they vary greatly in size and shape. More expensive are the Windsor rooms, which have front views and Jacuzzis.

Dining: The hotel operates a carvery, plus a separate fish-and-chips restaurant and a bistro/cafe bar.

WHERE TO DINE IN WINDSOR & ETON

Many visitors prefer to dine in Eton; most of the restaurants and fast-food places along the main street of Windsor, in front of the castle, serve dreary food.

Antico. 42 High St., Eton. ☎ **01753/863977.** Reservations strongly recommended. Main courses £9.50–£16 ($15.20–$25.60). AE, DC, MC, V. Mon–Fri 12:30–2:30pm; Mon–Sat 7–10:30pm. Closed bank holidays. ITALIAN.

Eton's finest Italian restaurant, Antico serves Mediterranean food in a formal setting. People have been dining here for 200 years, although not from an Italian menu. On your way to the tiny bar you pass a cold table, displaying hors d'oeuvres, fresh fish, and cold meats. There are many fish dishes, such as grilled fresh sardines, Dover sole, or calamari. The food is substantial and filling—a good value, but rarely exciting.

Eton Wine Bar. 82–83 High St., Eton. ☎ **01753/854921.** Reservations recommended. Main courses £8.50–£12.50 ($13.60–$20). AE, DC, MC, V. Mon–Fri noon–2:30pm and 6–11pm, Sat–Sun 11am–11pm. MODERN BRITISH/CONTINENTAL.

Just across the bridge from Windsor, this charming place is located on Eton's main street, among the antique shops. It is furnished with pinewood tables and old church pews and chairs, and there's a glassed-in conservatory out back. A brigade of seven chefs turns out quite good modern British dishes. Begin with one of the well-prepared soups, or a smoked-salmon-and-artichoke tart. Main dishes include pine-nut-and-spinach risotto topped with pecorino cheese, and rack of lamb with an herb crust served with Boulangère potatoes and vegetables. For dessert, try the pecan pie with cinnamon ice cream or the white and dark chocolate terrine with raspberry coulis.

House on the Bridge. 71 High St., Eton. ☎ **01753/860914.** Reservations recommended. Main courses from £12.95 ($20.70); fixed-price meal £19.95 ($31.90) at lunch, £29.95 ($47.90) at dinner. AE, DC, MC, V. Mon–Sat noon–2:30pm and 6–11pm, Sun noon–3:30pm and 6–10:30pm. ENGLISH/INTERNATIONAL.

This restaurant is in a charming redbrick and terra-cotta Victorian building, adjacent to the bridge and beside the river at the edge of Eton. Near the handful of outdoor tables is an almost vertical garden whose plants cascade into the Thames. Among the well-prepared main dishes are crispy duckling with calvados and Seville oranges, chicken supreme flavored with tarragon and served with mushrooms, and chateaubriand. Good ingredients go into the dishes, and the food, although traditionally based, has many modern touches.

۞ Le Boulestin at the Oakley Court Hotel. Windsor Rd., Water Oakley, Windsor. ☎ **01753/609988.** Reservations recommended. Jacket and tie required for men. Table d'hôte lunch £23.50 ($37.60); table d'hôte dinner £28 ($44.80). AE, DC, MC, V. Daily 12:30–2pm and 7–10pm. INTERNATIONAL.

In the mid-'90s, this chic London restaurant, known for its delectable food and sophisticated clientele, moved from central London to this new setting beside the Thames. Today, under the supervision of chef Murdo MacSween, the reincarnated Le Boulestin serves a modern cuisine that might include a parfait of duck livers with a confit of red onions and mandarin oranges; and a pavé of Scottish salmon with creamed leeks served with broad beans and a red-wine shallot sauce, or a cheddar and parmesan souffle. Even more unusual, and somewhat experimental, is a saltimbocca of red mullet with ratatouille, saffron, and black olive butter sauce.

The Orangerie. In Sir Christopher Wren's House Hotel, Thames St., Windsor. ☎ **01753/861354.** Main courses £10.95–£18 ($17.50–$28.80). AE, DC, MC, V. Daily 12:30–2:30pm and 6:30–10pm. CONTINENTAL.

This restaurant near the castle is Windsor's most elegant and charming, with garden terraces and a conservatory. The dining room is designed a bit like a greenhouse. Although it has a good range of starters, including blue-cheese beignets, main courses are limited. Count on competently prepared English dishes such as lemon sole, Welsh lamb, and venison steak. A traditional roast half duckling, served with a light orange and brandy sauce, is quite delectable. At dinner, a pianist entertains.

SIDE TRIPS FROM WINDSOR

If you have time to spare in the Windsor area, you can take any number of fascinating excursions. But if you can squeeze in only one, make it Hughenden Manor (see below).

HUGHENDEN MANOR: DISRAELI CALLED IT HOME

✪ **Hughenden Manor.** High Wycombe. ☎ **01494/532580.** Admission £4 ($6.40) adults, £2 ($3.20) children; £10 ($16) family ticket. Garden only, £1 ($1.60) adults, 50p (80¢) for children. Apr–Oct Wed–Sun 1–5pm; Mar Sat–Sun only 1–5pm. Closed Nov–Feb; Good Friday. From Windsor take the M4 (toward Reading), then A404 to A40. Continue north of High Wycombe on the A4128 for about 1½ miles. From London, catch coach no. 711 to High Wycombe, then board a Beeline bus (High Wycombe-Aylesbury no. 323 or 324).

This country manor not only gives us insight into the age of Victoria but also acquaints us with a remarkable man. In Benjamin Disraeli, we meet one of the most enigmatic figures of 19th-century England. At age 21, Dizzy published anonymously his five-volume novel *Vivian Grey.* Then he went on to other things and in 1839 married an older widow for her money, although they apparently developed a most harmonious relationship. He entered politics in 1837 and continued writing novels; his later ones met with more acclaim.

In 1848, Disraeli acquired Hughenden Manor, a country house that befitted his fast-rising political and social position. He served briefly as prime minister in 1868, but his political fame rests on his stewardship as prime minister from 1874 to 1880. He became Queen Victoria's friend, and in 1877 she paid him a rare honor by visiting him at Hughenden. In 1876, Disraeli became the earl of Beaconsfield: he had arrived, but his wife had died, and he was to die in 1881. Instead of being buried at Westminster Abbey, he preferred the simple little graveyard of Hughenden Church.

Today, Hughenden houses an odd assortment of memorabilia, including a lock of Disraeli's hair, letters from Victoria, autographed books, and a portrait of Lord Byron.

WEST WYCOMBE

Snuggled in the Chiltern Hills 30 miles west of London and 15 miles northwest of Windsor, the village of West Wycombe still has an atmosphere of the early 18th century. The thatched roofs have been replaced by tiles, and some of the buildings have been replaced, but the village is still 2 centuries removed from the present day.

From Windsor, take the M4 (toward Reading), then A404 to A40. Signs to follow en route include Maidenhead, Marlow, and Oxford. If you previously visited Hughenden Manor, the village of West Wycombe lies immediately to the west.

A visit to West Wycombe wouldn't be complete without a tour of **West Wycombe Park,** seat of the Dashwood family. Now owned by the National Trust, it's of both historical and architectural interest. The house is one of the best examples of Palladian-style architecture in England. The interior is lavishly decorated with paintings and antiques from the 18th century.

In the mid–18th century, Sir Francis Dashwood began an ambitious building program at West Wycombe. His strong interest in architecture and design led Sir Frances to undertake a series of monuments and parks that are still among the finest in the country.

Sir Francis also commissioned the excavation of a cave on the estate. Its primary purpose was to serve as a meeting place for "The Knights of St. Francis of Wycombe," later known as the notorious Hellfire Club, which spent its time partying, drinking, and ravishing innocent virgins. It seems that some satanic rites also took place here—not so much to invoke Satan as to inspire the general debauchery. The cave is about a half mile long, filled with stalactites and stalagmites, and dotted with statues of Sir Francis, his friend Lord Sandwich, and even Ben Franklin.

The house and grounds are open June through August, Sunday through Thursday from 2 to 6pm. Admission is £4 ($6.40) for adults or £10 ($16) for a family ticket. If you wish to visit only the grounds, the cost is £2.50 ($4). The caves are open daily from March through October from 11am to 5:30pm; off-season hours are only on Saturday and Sunday from 11am to 5:30pm. Admission is £3 ($4.80) for adults, or £1.50 ($2.40) for seniors and children. The cave tour includes stops for talks about former Hellfire members; it lasts 20 to 30 minutes. For more information, call the West Wycombe Estate Office at West Wycombe ☎ **01494/524411,** the caves at **01494/533739,** or the grounds at **01628/488675.**

Other sights at West Wycombe include the **Church of St. Lawrence,** perched on West Wycombe Hill and topped by a huge golden ball. Parts of the church date from the 13th century; its richly decorated interior was copied from a 3rd-century Syrian sun temple. The view from the hill is worth the trek up. Near the church stands the **Dashwood mausoleum,** built in a style derived from Constantine's Arch in Rome.

After your tour of the park, head for **George & Dragon,** High Street (☎ **01494/464414**), for a pint or a good, inexpensive lunch. In a building that dates back to 1720, this was a former coaching inn with a cheerful log fire, a comfortable-sized bar (that nevertheless gets crowded on weekends), and an impressive oak staircase with its own ghost. There is a separate no-smoking room open to children, a children's play area, and a garden for dining outside. If you like West Wycombe and want to stay over, there are eight cozily furnished rooms with private bath, phone, and TV, costing £62 ($99.20) for a double, including breakfast.

CLIVEDEN: FORMER HOME OF LADY ASTOR

Cliveden House. 10 miles northwest of Windsor. Admission to grounds £4.50 ($7.20); family ticket £11 ($17.60). Admission to house £1 ($1.60) extra. Grounds Mar 22–Nov 2 daily 11am–6pm; off-season daily 11am–4pm. Apr–Oct Thurs and Sun 3–6pm, 3 rooms of the mansion are open to the public, as is the Octagon Temple, with its rich mosaic interior. From Windsor, follow the M4 toward Reading to the junction at No. 7 (direction Slough West). At the roundabout, turn left onto the A4 signposted Maidenhead. At the next roundabout, turn right signposted Burnham. Follow the road for 2½ miles to a T junction with B476. The main gates to Cliveden are directly opposite.

Now a National Trust property, Cliveden House, former home of Lady Astor, stands on a constructed terrace of mature gardens high above the Thames. The estate's original mansion and the vast sweep of the lawns were created by William Winde in 1666 for the second duke of Buckingham. Later the father of King George III reared his sons here. After a fire in 1795, the house was redesigned by Sir Charles Barry, the architect of the House of Parliament, into its present gracefully symmetrical form. A soaring clock tower was added to one side as a later Victorian folly. When the house was sold by the duke of Southerland to the Astors in 1893, Queen Victoria lamented the passage. The house remained part of the Astor legacy until 1966, a repository of a notable collection of paintings and antiques.

The surrounding **gardens** have a distinguished variety of plantings, ranging from Renaissance-style topiary to meandering forest paths with vistas of statuary and flowering shrubs. Garden features are a rose garden, a magnificent parterre, and an amphitheater where "Rule Britannia" was played for the first time. There are 375 acres of garden and woodland to explore.

The manor also accepts paying guests, and it's a spectacular place to stay, as we've described below.

Where to Stay & Dine

✪ **Cliveden House**, Cliveden, Taplow, Maidenhead, Berkshire SL6 0JF. ☎ **01628/ 668561**. Fax 01628/661837. 38 units. TV TEL. £245–£685 ($392–$1,096) double. AE, DC, MC, V.

Lady Astor's former estate is one of the most beautiful and luxurious hotels in England. Often acclaimed as "hotel of the year" by various rating services in England, this majestic property was home to a Prince of Wales and a scattering of dukes before the Astors moved in. It was also a setting for the infamous Profumo scandal of the 1960s, which shook the Empire.

Nothing (except perhaps renting Lady Astor's bedroom itself) is more elegant here than walking down to the river and boarding a hotel boat for a champagne cruise before dinner. In the morning you can go horseback riding on the 376-acre estate along the riverbank. Inside, pause to admire the splendid Great Hall with its carved wood and stone fireplace. A traditional English breakfast is served in the paneled French rococo dining room. Rooms are sumptuous, each stylishly furnished and decorated in impeccable taste. The baths are among the finest we've ever seen in England. Less preferred are the recently added rooms in the Clutton Wing.

Dining: The main drawing room of the house is now the Terrace Dining Room, with panoramic views. Classical French and modern and traditional English cuisine are served here. The wild mushrooms and grilled leeks in a truffle sauce would surely have pleased Lady Astor herself. You can also dine at Waldo's, a showcase for a talented chef, Ron Maxfield, who specializes in a contemporary British cuisine that's innovative. Men can pay a trip to the "gents," where they'll see drawings of Mandy Rice-Davies and Christine Keeler by Dr. Stephen Ward, all legends from the Profumo scandal that led to the collapse of the Conservative government in 1964. There's also a conservatory dining room in the original walled garden.

Amenities: A luxurious Pavilion Spa with separate steam rooms for men and women, plus indoor and outdoor pools, a gym, and a beauty treatment room.

THE COTTAGE WHERE MILTON WROTE *PARADISE LOST*

The modern residential town of **Gerrards Cross** is often called the Beverly Hills of England, as it attracts many wealthy Londoners, among others. To the north of it is **Chalfont St. Giles,** where the poet John Milton lived during the Great Plague in 1665. To reach it, take the A355 north from Windsor bypassing Beaconsfield until you come to the signposted cutoff for Chalfont St. Giles to the east.

Chalfont St. Giles is today a typical English village, although its history goes back to Roman times. The charm of the village is in its center, with shops, pubs, and cafes clustered around the green and the village pond.

The 16th-century **John Milton's Cottage,** Chalfont St. Giles (☎ **01494/872313**), is not only the site where the great poet completed *Paradise Lost*—he also started *Paradise Regained* here. Its four rooms contain many relics and exhibits devoted to Milton. It is open March through October, Tuesday through Sunday from 10am to 1pm and 2 to 6pm, charging adults £2 ($3.20) and children 60p (95¢).

2 Ascot

28 miles W of London

While following the royal buck hounds through Windsor Forest, Queen Anne decided to have a racecourse on Ascot Heath. The first race meeting at Ascot, which is directly south of Windsor at the southern end of Windsor Great Park, was held in 1711. Since then, the Ascot Racecourse has been a symbol of high society as pictures of the royal family, including the queen and Prince Philip, have been flashed around the world. Nowadays, it is Princess Anne, an avid horsewoman herself, who provides curious onlookers with royal conversation topics. Ladies: Be sure to wear a hat.

GETTING THERE

Trains travel between Waterloo in London and Ascot Station, which is about 10 minutes from the racecourse. The trip takes 30 minutes, and service is about every 30 minutes during the day. For rail information, call ☎ **0345/484950** in the U.K., or 01603/764776 in the U.S.

Buses frequently depart from London's Victoria Coach Station. Call ☎ **0990/ 808080** for more information.

If you're driving from Windsor, take A332 west.

THE ASCOT RACECOURSE

The **Ascot Racecourse,** High Street (☎ **01344/622211**), England's largest and most prestigious course, is open throughout the year, although no races are heldduring March. The facility hosts 24 days of racing yearly. The highlight of the Ascot social season is the above-mentioned **Royal Meeting (or Royal Week),** when many women wear fancy hats and white gloves. There is also excellent racing on De Beers Diamond Day (4th Saturday in July) and during the Festival at Ascot (last Saturday and Sunday in September), when the prize money usually exceeds £1 million per event.

You can buy tickets for one of three distinctly different observation areas, known locally as "enclosures." These include the Members' Enclosure, which during the Royal Meeting (4 days in June) is known as the Royal Enclosure. Also available are Tattersall's Enclosure, largest of the three; and the Silver Ring, which does not enjoy direct access to the paddocks and has traditionally been the site of most of Ascot's budget seating. Except during the Royal Meeting, newcomers can usually secure viewing space in the Member's Enclosure, but only if they call ahead to confirm that space is available. Tickets cost £12 to £23 ($19.20 to $36.80) for seats in the Member's Enclosure, £8 to £15 ($12.80 to $24) in the Grandstand and Paddock, and £5 to £7 ($8 to $11.20) in the Silver Ring. Prices depend on the race and the season. Children 16 and under are admitted free if accompanied by an adult, and there is free supervised daycare for children under 8.

Advance bookings for guaranteed seating in the most desirable areas during the most popular races can be arranged beginning January 1 every year. Write for tickets to the Secretary's Office, Ascot Racecourse, Ascot, Berkshire SL5 7JN. For admission to the Royal Enclosure, write to Her Majesty's Representative, Ascot Office, St. James's Palace, London SW1. First-timers usually have difficulty being admitted to the Royal Enclosure, since their application must be endorsed by someone who has been admitted to the Royal Enclosure at least eight times before. Credit cards are accepted by calling ☎ **01344/876456.** Car parking is free except on June 22, July 27, and the Festival Meeting in September.

WHERE TO STAY & DINE

Berystede Country House Hotel. Bagshot Rd., Sunninghill Ascot, Berkshire SL5 9JH. ☎ **01344/623311.** Fax 01344/872301. 91 units. TV TEL. £150 ($240) double; from £190 ($304) suite. AE, DC, MC, V. Free parking. Take the A330 1½ miles south of Ascot.

This hotel just south of Ascot is a Victorian fantasy of medieval towers, half-timbering, steeply pitched roofs, and a landscaped garden. Drawing race-goers and businesspeople, it also caters to conferences (at which time it's best avoided). The entrance hall incorporates a huge stone fireplace, which might be blazing if the weather's cool enough. The rooms, with their high ceilings and chintz, evoke a private country house. The suite boasts mahogany reproductions of 18th-century antiques. The best rooms are in the main building. However, most of the accommodations are in the less desirable and more sterile modern extension.

Brockenhurst. Brockenhurst Rd., S. Ascot, Berkshire SL5 9HA. ☎ **01344/621912.** Fax 01344/873252. 11 units. TV TEL. £79–£100 ($126.40–$160) double. Rates include continental breakfast. AE, DC, MC, V.

A small, tastefully refurbished 1905 Edwardian hotel of charm and distinction, Brockenhurst is conveniently situated near shops and the train station. The most expensive rooms are called "executive" and include whirlpool baths, trouser presses, and hair dryers. The hotel has a bar and offers a room-service menu. The owners serve mainly traditional and Thai cuisine, and, if given 24 hours' notice, will try to prepare a meal of your choice. This is a very good alternative to the pricey Royal Berkshire or Berystede.

The Royal Berkshire. London Rd., Sunninghill, Ascot, Berkshire SL5 OPP. ☎ **01344/623322.** Fax 01344/627100. 63 units. TV TEL. £176 ($281.60) double; from £220 ($352) suite. AE, DC, MC, V. Free parking. Take A322 2 miles northeast of Ascot.

This is a prestigious and elegant hotel with a rich history. Built of russet-colored bricks in Queen Anne style in 1705, it housed the Churchill family for many years. Harmonious color schemes and well-chosen furnishings set a stylish tone in the rooms, which are divided between the main house and an annex. The annex rooms are furnished well, but aren't the equal of those in the main building.

   Dining: Many people visit only for a meal in the Stateroom Restaurant, which overlooks the hotel lawns and gardens. The food, some of the finest in the area, is prepared with quality ingredients and often with artistic flair. The menu changes frequently and offers contemporary English dishes.

3 Henley-on-Thames & the Royal Regatta

35 miles W of London

At the eastern edge of Oxfordshire, Henley-on-Thames, a small town and resort on the river at the foothills of the Chilterns, is the headquarters of the ♦ **Royal Regatta,** held annually in late June and early July. Henley, which lies on a stretch of the Thames that's known for its calm waters, unobstructed bottom, and predictable currents, is a rowers' mecca. The regatta, which dates back to the first years of Victoria's reign, is the major competition among international oarspeople who find it both challenging and entertaining.

   The Elizabethan buildings, the tearooms, and the inns along the town's High Street will live up to your preconception of an English country town. Henley-on-Thames is an excellent (though pricey) stopover en route to Oxford; its fashionable inns are far from cheap.

ESSENTIALS

GETTING THERE   Trains depart from London's Paddington Station but require a change at the junction in Twyford. More than 20 trains make the journey daily; the trip takes about an hour. For rail information, call ☎ **0345/484950** in the U.K. or 01603/764776 in the U.S.

   About 10 buses depart every day from London's Victoria Coach Station for Henley. Because the bus makes multiple stops, the trip takes about 1¼ hours. There is no Sunday service in winter. Call ☎ **0990/808080** for more information.

If you're driving from London, take M4 toward Reading to Junction 819, then head northwest on A4130.

VISITOR INFORMATION   The **Tourist Information Centre** is at Town Hall, Market Place (☎ **01491/578034**). It's open daily from 10am to 7pm; in winter, the center closes at 4pm.

THE HENLEY ROYAL REGATTA

The Henley Royal Regatta, held the first week in July, is one of the country's premier racing events. If you want a close-up view from the Stewards' Enclosure, you'll need a guest badge, which is only obtainable through a member. In other words, you have to know someone to obtain special privileges, but admission to the Regatta Enclosure is open to all. Information is available from the Secretary, Henley Royal Regatta, Henley-on-Thames, Oxfordshire RG9 2LY (☎ **01491/572153**).

During the annual 5-day event, up to 100 races will be organized each day, with starts scheduled as frequently as every 5 minutes. This event is open only to all-male crews of up to nine at a time. In late June, rowing events for women are held at the 3-day Henley Women's Regatta.

If you want to float on the waters of the Thames yourself, stop by the town's largest and oldest outfitter, **Hobbs & Sons, Ltd.,** Station Road Boathouse (☎ **01491/572035**), established in 1870. Their armada of watercraft includes rowboats that rent for between £6.50 to £9 ($10.40 to $14.40) per hour. Motorboats can be rented for £17 to £32 ($27.20 to $51.20) per hour. On the premises, a chandlery shop sells virtually anything a boat crew could need, as well as souvenir items like straw boater's hats and commemorative T-shirts.

WHERE TO STAY & DINE IN THE AREA

It's impossible to find a room during the Royal Regatta, unless you've made reservations months in advance.

Red Lion Hotel. Hart St., Henley-on-Thames, Oxfordshire RG9 2AR. ☎ **01491/572161.** Fax 01491/410039. 26 units, 23 with bathroom (some with tub only, some with shower only). TV TEL. £115 ($184) double. AE, MC, V.

This ivy-covered, redbrick coaching inn (ca. 1531) near Henley Bridge used to keep a bedchamber ready for the duke of Marlborough, who would stop here on his way to Blenheim. The guest list reads like a hall of fame—Johnson and Boswell, and even George IV, who, it is said, consumed 14 mutton chops one night. Charles I stayed here in 1632 on his way from London to Oxford. If you're an admirer of the late Princess Grace, you can book the room in which she stayed when her brother Jack was competing in the Royal Regatta in 1947. Most of the well-furnished rooms overlook the Thames. The hotel also offers laundry service.

Dining: The last dinner is served at 10pm, but 24-hour room service is provided. Guests congregate in the low-beamed bar and take meals in the Regatta Brasserie. The international menu has a Mediterranean influence. New chef selects local produce each morning to prepare a "market-fresh" repertoire.

Stonor Arms. Stonor, by A4130 on B480 near Henley-on-Thames, Oxfordshire RG9 6HE. ☎ **01491/638866.** Fax 01491/638863. 10 units. TV TEL. £105 ($168) double. Rates include breakfast. AE, MC, V.

For the area's finest dining and accommodations, head to the village of Stonor, 4 miles north of Henley. The village pub dates from the 1700s. New chef Stephen Morris, backed up by a hardworking and talented staff, prepares such fine food that he often attracts Londoners. For those who wish to stay over, a wing of rooms is handsomely furnished, often with antiques. Cots for children can be added to most rooms.

Dining: Open daily for lunch and dinner, the Stonor Restaurant offers a fixed-price menu for £25 ($40). The cuisine is mainly English, but with some French and Italian influences. Main dishes change nightly but might include panfried breast of duckling with an apple puree or lamb shanks with leek polenta. Fresh produce is used whenever possible, and the fish is brought in from Cornwall. You can dine outdoors in summer.

SIDE TRIPS FROM HENLEY
A ROMANTIC BOAT TRIP TO A HISTORIC HOME

Mapledurham House. ☎ 01189/723350. Admission to house and mill £4 ($6.40) adults, £2 ($3.20) children 5–14, free for children 4 and under. Easter–Sept Sat–Sun and holidays 2:30–5pm; the mill opens at 1pm. Closed Oct–Easter. From Henley-on-Thames, head south along A4155 toward Reading. At the junction with A329 head west. Mapledurham is signposted from this road. Or take the boat trip described below.

The Blount family mansion lies beside the Thames in the unspoiled village of Mapledurham. In the house, you'll see the Elizabethan ceilings and the great oak staircase, as well as the portraits of the two beautiful sisters with whom the poet Alexander Pope, a frequent visitor here, fell in love. The family chapel, built in 1789, is a fine example of modern gothic architecture. Cream teas with homemade cakes are available at the house. On the grounds, the last working water mill on the Thames still produces flour.

The most romantic way to reach this lovely old house is to take the boat that leaves the promenade next to Caversham Bridge at 2pm on Saturday, Sunday, and bank holidays from Easter to September. The journey upstream takes about 45 minutes, and the boat leaves Mapledurham again at 5pm for the return trip to Caversham. This gives you plenty of time to walk through the house. The round-trip boat ride from Caversham costs £3.85 ($6.15) for adults and £2.75 ($4.40) for children. Further details about the boat can be obtained from **Thames Rivercruises Ltd.,** Pipers Island, Bridge Street, Caversham Bridge, Reading (☎ **01189/481088**).

THE WELLINGTON DUCAL ESTATE

Stratford Saye House. 1 mile west of Reading, beside the A33 to Basingstoke. ☎ **01256/882882.** Admission £5 ($8) adults, £2.50 ($4) children 5–16; free for children under 5. Combined ticket for Stratford Saye and Wellington Country Park £7 ($11.20) adults, £3.25 ($5.20) children. May and Sept Sat–Sun and holidays noon–4pm; June–Aug Sat–Thurs noon–4pm. Closed Oct–Apr. From Henly, head south along A1455.

Tangible evidence of the fortune of the duke of Wellington and his descendants is obvious in this combined house and country park. The complex's centerpiece is the Stratford Saye House. This has been the home of the dukes of Wellington since 1817, when the 17th-century house was bought for the Iron Duke to celebrate his victory over Napoléon at the Battle of Waterloo. A grateful Parliament granted a large sum of money for its purchase. Many memories of the first duke remain in the house, including his billiard table, battle spoils, and pictures. The funeral carriage that once rested in St. Paul's Cathedral crypt is on display. In the gardens is the grave of Copenhagen, the charger ridden to battle at Waterloo by the first duke. There are also extensive landscaped grounds, together with a tearoom and gift shop.

Although extensive parks and gardens surround Stratford Saye, all except those immediately adjacent to the house are closed to the public. If you're looking for greenery and lovely landscaping, you'll find it 3 miles away, on the opposite side of the A33 highway, at the **Wellington Country Park.**

Wellington Country Park. Riseley, Reading, Berkshire RG7 1SP. ☎ **01189/326444.** Admission £3.70 ($5.90) adults, £1.90 ($3.05) children 5–16; free for children under 5. Combined ticket for Stratford Saye and Wellington Country Park £7 ($11.20) adults, £3.25 ($5.20) children. Park and exhibits Mar 1–Oct 31 daily 10am–5:30pm.

Under the same administration as Stratford Saye, this is a favorite place for the locals to picnic and stroll, since it has a nice lake that attracts waterfowl and miles of well-maintained walking paths. But there's a handful of attractions inside as well: The park contains the National Dairy Museum (where you can see the relics of 150 years of dairying), a riding school, a miniature steam railway, a deer park, and the Thames Valley Time Trail, a walk-through series of exhibits related to the geology of the region and the dinosaurs that once inhabited it.

MARLOW: RETREAT OF *THE COMPLEAT ANGLER*

This Thames-side town, 35 miles northwest of London and 8 miles east of Henley-on-Thames, is a miniature version of the better-known Henley. To reach it from Henley, take route 4155 and just follow the signs. Many prefer its more pastoral look to the larger Henley.

The town stands on a great loop of the riverbank between Maidenhead and Oxford. Here, along this middle reach of the Thames, is some of the most beautiful rural scenery in England, a land of green fields and deep woods, of stately mansions and parks. It was in these surroundings that Izaak Walton wrote his immortal work on fishing, *The Compleat Angler*, which was published in 1655. On the south bank of the river facing Marlow itself stood the inn in which he stayed. That inn still stands and is named after his work.

Where to Stay & Dine

✪ **The Compleat Angler Hotel.** Marlow Bridge, Bisham Rd., Marlow, Buckinghamshire S17 IRG. ☎ **01628/484444.** Fax 01628/486388. 62 units. TV TEL. £165–£205 ($264–$328) double; from £350 ($560) suite. AE, DC, MC, V.

This hotel of charm and character blends architectural eras, including Queen Anne, Regency, Georgian, and Victorian. It occupies an emerald swath of lawns stretching down to the banks of the Thames. It's had a long and distinguished list of guests, including Percy Shelley and his wife, Mary, along with Dame Nellie Melba (for whom the peach dessert was named), J. M. Barrie (author of *Peter Pan*), F. Scott Fitzgerald (what was he doing here?), and Noël Coward. Behind its reddish brick facade, the hotel is a well-organized and impeccably polite center of English chintz, mahogany and oak antiques, plush carpeting, predictably elegant bars, and very fine dining. Each of the rooms is outfitted a lot like those in an elegant, private country home, with antiques or reproductions and plush, comfortable beds and armchairs. The more expensive rooms look out on the Thames.

4 Oxford: The City of Dreaming Spires

54 miles NW of London; 54 miles SE of Coventry

A walk down the long sweep of The High, one of the most striking streets in England; a mug of cider in one of the old student pubs; the sound of May Day dawn when choristers sing in Latin from Magdalen Tower; students in traditional gowns whizzing past on rickety bikes; towers and spires rising majestically; nude swimming at Parson's Pleasure; the roar of a cannon launching the bumping races; a tiny, dusty bookstall where you can pick up a valuable first edition—all that is Oxford, home of one of the greatest universities in the world.

Romantic Oxford is still here, but to get to it, you'll also have to experience the bustling and crowded city that is also Oxford. You may be surprised by the never-ending stream of polluting buses and the fast-flowing pedestrian traffic—the city core feels more like London than once-sleepy Oxford. Surrounding the university are suburbs that keep growing, and not in a particularly attractive manner.

At any time of the year, you can enjoy a tour of the colleges, many of which represent a peak in England's architectural history, as well as a valley of Victorian contributions. The Oxford Tourist Information Centre (see below) offers guided walking tours daily throughout the year. Just don't mention the other place (Cambridge) and you shouldn't have any trouble. Comparisons between the two universities are inevitable: Oxford is better known for the arts, Cambridge more for the sciences.

The city predates the university—in fact, it was a Saxon town in the early part of the 10th century. By the 12th century, Oxford was growing in reputation as a seat of learning, at the expense of Paris, and the first colleges were founded in the 13th century. The story of Oxford is filled with conflicts too complex and detailed to elaborate here. Suffice it to say, the relationship between town and gown wasn't as peaceful as it is today. Riots often flared, and both sides were guilty of abuses. Nowadays, the young people of Oxford take out their aggressiveness in sporting competitions.

Ultimately, the test of a great university lies in the caliber of the people it turns out. Oxford can name-drop a mouthful: Roger Bacon, Sir Walter Raleigh, John Donne, Sir Christopher Wren, Samuel Johnson, Edward Gibbon, William Penn, John Wesley, William Pitt, Matthew Arnold, Lewis Carroll, Arnold Toynbee, Harold Macmillan, Graham Greene, A. E. Housman, T. E. Lawrence, and many others.

ESSENTIALS

GETTING THERE   Trains from Paddington Station reach Oxford in 1¼ hours. Service is every hour. A cheap, same-day round-trip ticket costs £12.40 ($19.85). For more information, call ☎ 0171/930-2150.

Oxford CityLink provides coach service from London's Victoria Station (☎ 0171/824-0056) to the Oxford Bus Station. Coaches usually depart about every 20 minutes during the day; the trip takes approximately 1¾ hours. A same-day round-trip ticket costs £6.50 ($10.40).

If you're driving, take M40 west from London and just follow the signs. Traffic and parking are a disaster in Oxford, and not just during rush hours. However, there are four large park-and-ride parking lots on the north, south, east, and west of the city's ring road, all well marked. Parking is free at all times, but from 9:30am on and all day Saturday, you pay 70p ($1.10) for a bus ride into the city, which drops you off at St. Aldate's Cornmarket or Queen Street to see the city center. The buses run every 8 to 10 minutes in each direction. There is no service on Sunday. The parking lots are on the Woodstock road near the Peartree traffic circle, on the Botley road toward Farringdon, on the Abingdon road in the southeast, and on A40 toward London.

VISITOR INFORMATION   The **Oxford Tourist Information Centre** is at Gloucester Green, opposite the bus station (☎ 01865/726871). The center sells a comprehensive range of maps, brochures, and souvenir items, as well as the famous Oxford University T-shirt. It provides hotel booking services for £2.50 ($4). Guided walking tours leave from the center daily (see below). Open Monday through Saturday from 9:30am to 5pm and Sunday and bank holidays in summer from 10am to 3:30pm.

GETTING AROUND   Competition thrives in Oxford transportation, and the public benefits with swift, clean service by two companies. The **Oxford Bus Company,** 395 Cowley Rd. (☎ 01865/785400), has green Park and Ride buses that leave from four car parks in the city using the north-south or east-west routes. A round-trip costs £1.10 ($1.75). Their CityLink buses are blue and travel to London, Heathrow, and Gatwick. The company's red CityLink buses cover 15 routes in all suburbs, with a day pass allowing unlimited travel for £1.50 ($2.40). Weekly and monthly passes are available. The competition, **Thames Transit,** Unit 4, Horsepath, Cowley (☎ **01865/772250**), uses blue-and-cream minibuses and red-and-gray coaches. City buses leave from Cornmarket Street in Oxford center. Day passes cost £1.50 ($2.40). Abington Road buses are marked "Red Bridge" and Iffley Road buses are labeled "Rose Hill."

TOURS OF OXFORD

The best way to get a running commentary on the important sights is to take a 2-hour **walking tour** through the city and the major colleges. The tours leave daily from the Oxford Information Centre at 11am and 2pm. Tours costs £4 ($6.40) for adults and £2.50 ($4) for children; the tours do not include New College or Christ Church.

The **Oxford Story,** 6 Broad St. (☎ **01865/790055**), is a concise and entertaining audiovisual ride through the campus. It explains the structure of the colleges and high-lights architectural and historical features. Visitors are also filled in on the general background of the colleges and the antics of some of the famous people who have passed through the University's portals. The audiovisual presentation is given daily between 10am and 4:30pm. Admission is £4.95 ($7.90) for adults, £4.25 ($6.80) for students, and £3.95 ($6.30) for children. A family ticket for two adults and two children is £14 ($22.40).

For a good orientation, hour-long, open-top bus tours around Oxford are available from **Guide Friday,** whose office is at the railway station (☎ **01865/790522**). Buses leave every 20 minutes daily; in summer, buses leave every 5 minutes. Tickets are good for the day. Tours begin at 9:30am on winter weekends, 10:10am Monday through Friday. In summer, tours begin at 9:10am. The cost is £8 ($12.80) adults, £6.50 ($10.40) students and seniors, and £2.50 ($4) children. Tickets can be purchased from the driver.

Spires & Shires (☎ **01235/212345**) has tours beginning in March, including a Ghost Tour of 15 sites in the country around Oxford. Another Oxford ghost tour is offered by the **Tourist Information Centre,** Old School Building, Gloucester Green (☎ **01865/726871**). The office has a number of walking tours, with the ghost tour available Friday and Saturday evenings from July through October. It begins at 7pm, ends at 8:30pm, and covers the dark alleyways around the ancient schools. The cost is £4 ($6.40) for adults and children; tickets are available at the office during the day. Day tours begin at 11am and 2pm daily, including Christmas, even for one person.

EXPLORING OXFORD UNIVERSITY

Many Americans arriving at Oxford ask, "Where's the campus?" If a local looks amused when answering, it's because Oxford University is, in fact, made up of 35 colleges sprinkled throughout the town. To tour all of these would be a formidable task. It's best to focus on just a handful of the better-known colleges.

Our favorite pastime here is to take **Addison's Walk** through the water meadows. The stroll is named after a former Oxford alumnus, Joseph Addison, the 18th-century essayist and playwright noted for his contributions to *The Spectator* and *The Tatler.*

A word of warning: The main business of a university, is, of course, to educate—and this function at Oxford has been severely hampered by the number of visitors who disturb the academic work of the university. So visiting is restricted to certain hours and small groups of six or fewer. Furthermore, there are areas where visitors are not allowed at all, but the tourist office will be happy to advise you when and where you may take in the sights of this great institution.

Oxford

All Souls College ❶
Ashmolean Museum ㉕
Balliol College ㉒
Brasenose College ⓴
Carfax Tower ⑯
Christ Church College ⑫
Corpus Christi College ⑪
Exeter College ㉑
Hertford College ❷
Jesus College ⑱
Keble College ㉘
Lincoln College ⑲

Magdalen College ❻
Manchester College ㉝
Mansfield College ㉛
Merton College ❽
Museum of Modern Art ⑮
New College ❸
Oriel College ⑩
Pembroke College ⑭
Queen's College ❹
Regent's Park College ㉖
Rhodes House ㉚
Sheldonian Theatre ㉞

Somerville College ㉗
St. Catherine's
   College ❺
St. Hilda's College ❼
St. John's College ㉔
St. Peter's College ⑰
Town Hall ㉟
Trinity College ㉓
University College ❾
University Museum ㉙
Wadham College ㉜
Worcester College ⑬

3-043

AN OVERVIEW　For a bird's-eye view of the city and colleges, climb **Carfax Tower,** located in the center of the city. This structure is distinguished by the clock and figures that strike the quarter hours. Carfax Tower is all that remains from St. Martin's Church, where William Shakespeare once stood as godfather for William Davenant, who also became a successful playwright. A church stood on this site from 1032 until 1896. The tower used to be higher, but after 1340 it was lowered, following complaints from the university to Edward III that townspeople threw stones and fired arrows at students during town-and-gown disputes. Admission is £1.20 ($1.90) for adults, 60p (95¢) for children. The tower is open year-round. From April through October, hours are daily from 10am to 5:30pm. Off-season hours are Monday through Saturday from 10am to 3:30pm. The tower is closed from Christmas Eve until January 2. For information, call ☎ **01865/792653.**

✪ **CHRIST CHURCH**　Begun by Cardinal Wolsey as Cardinal College in 1525, Christ Church (☎ **01865/276492**), known as the House, was founded by Henry VIII in 1546. Facing St. Aldate's Street, Christ Church has the largest quadrangle of any college in Oxford. Tom Tower houses Great Tom, the 18,000-pound bell referred to earlier. It rings at 9:05pm nightly, signaling the closing of the college gates. The 101 times it peals originally signified the number of students in residence at the time the college was founded. Although the student body has grown significantly, Oxford traditions live on forever. There are some interesting portraits in the 16th-century Great Hall, including works by Gainsborough and Reynolds. Prime ministers are pictured, since Christ Church was the training ground for 13 prime ministers. There's a separate portrait gallery.

The college chapel was constructed over a period of centuries, beginning in the 12th century. (Incidentally, it's not only the college chapel, but also the cathedral of the diocese of Oxford.) The cathedral's most distinguishing features are its Norman pillars and the vaulting of the choir, dating from the 15th century. In the center of the great quadrangle is a statue of Mercury mounted in the center of a fishpond. The college and cathedral can be visited between 9am and 5:30pm. The entrance fee is £3 ($4.80) for adults and £2 ($3.20) for children.

MAGDALEN COLLEGE　Pronounced *Maud*-lin, Magdalen College, High Street (☎ **01865/276000**), was founded in 1458 by William of Waynflete, bishop of Winchester and later chancellor of England. Its alumni range from Wolsey to Wilde. Opposite the botanic garden, the oldest in England, is the bell tower, where the choristers sing in Latin at dawn on May Day. The reflection of the 15th-century tower is cast in the waters of the Cherwell below. On a not-so-happy day, Charles I, his days numbered, watched the oncoming Roundheads from this tower. Visit the 15th-century chapel, in spite of many of its latter-day trappings. Ask when the hall and other places of special interest are open. The grounds of Magdalen are the most extensive of any Oxford college; there's even a deer park. You can visit from Easter to September, daily between noon and 6pm; off-season, daily between 2 and 6pm. Admission is £2 ($3.20), but it's charged only from Easter to September.

MERTON COLLEGE　Founded in 1264, Merton College, Merton Street (☎ **01865/276310**), is among the three oldest colleges at the university. It stands near Corpus Christi College on Merton Street, the sole survivor of Oxford's medieval cobbled streets. Merton College is noted for its library, built between 1371 and 1379 and said to be the oldest college library in England. There was once a tradition of keeping some of its most valuable books chained. Now only one book is so secured to illustrate that historical custom. One of the library's treasures is an astrolabe (an astronomical instrument used for measuring the altitude of the sun and stars) thought to have belonged to Chaucer. You pay £1 ($1.60) to visit the ancient library as well as the Max Beerbohm Room (the satirical English caricaturist who died in 1956). The library and college are open Monday through Friday from 2 to 4pm and Saturday and Sunday from 10am to 4pm. It's closed for 1 week at Easter and at Christmas.

UNIVERSITY COLLEGE University College, High Street (☎ **01865/276602**), is the oldest one at Oxford and dates from 1249, when money was donated by an ecclesiastic, William of Durham (the old claim that the real founder was Alfred the Great is more fanciful). The original structures have all disappeared, and what remains today represents essentially the architecture of the 17th century, with subsequent additions in Victoria's day as well as in more recent times. For example, the Goodhart Quadrangle was added as late as 1962. The college's most famous alumnus, Shelley, was "sent down" for his part in collaborating on a pamphlet on atheism. However, all is forgiven today, as the romantic poet is honored by a memorial erected in 1894. The hall and chapel of University College can be visited daily during vacations from 2 to 4pm for a charge of £1.50 ($2.40) for adults, 60p (95¢) for children. Chapel services are held daily at 4 and 6pm.

NEW COLLEGE New College, New College Lane, off Queen's Lane (☎ **01865/279555**), was founded in 1379 by William of Wykeham, bishop of Winchester and later lord chancellor of England. His college at Winchester supplied a constant stream of students. The first quadrangle, dating from before the end of the 14th century, was the initial quadrangle to be built in Oxford and formed the architectural design for the other colleges. In the antechapel is Sir Jacob Epstein's remarkable modern sculpture of Lazarus and a fine El Greco painting of St. James. One of the treasures of the college is a crosier (pastoral staff of a bishop) belonging to the founding father. In the garden, you can stroll among the remains of the old city wall and the mound. The college (entered at New College Lane) can be visited Easter to September, daily between 11am and 5pm; off-season, daily between 2 and 4pm. Admission is £1 ($1.60) from Easter to September and free off-season.

PUNTING

Punting on the River Cherwell remains the favorite outdoor pastime in Oxford. At Punt Station, **Cherwell Boathouse,** Bardwell Road (☎ **01865/515978**), you can rent a punt (flat-bottom boat maneuvered by a long pole and a small oar) for £8 to £10 ($12.80 to $16) per hour, plus a £40 to £50 ($64 to $80) deposit. Similar charges are made for punt rentals at Magdalen Bridge Boathouse. Punts are rented from March to mid-June and late August to October, daily from 10am until dusk; from mid-June to late August, when a larger inventory of punts is available, daily from 10am to 10pm. However, hours of operation seem to be rather informal; you're not always guaranteed that someone will be here to rent you a boat, even if the punt itself is available.

SHOPPING

Golden Cross, an arcade of first-class shops and boutiques, lies between Cornmarket Street and the Covered Market (or between High Street and Market Street). Parts of the colorful gallery date from the 12th century. Many buildings remain from the medieval era, along with some 15th- and 17th-century structures. The market also has a reputation as the Covent Garden of Oxford, where live entertainment, from dancing in Radcliffe Square to melodious presentations by the Magdalen College Choir from high atop Magdalen Tower, takes place on Saturday mornings in summer. In the arcade shops you'll find a diverse selection of merchandise, including handmade

Belgian chocolates, specialty gifts, clothing for both women and men, and luxury leather goods.

In its way, **Alice's Shop,** 83 St. Aldate's (☎ **01865/723793**), played an important role in English literature. Set within a 15th-century building that has housed some kind of shop since 1820, it functioned as a general store (selling brooms, hardware, and the like) during the period that Lewis Carroll, at the time a professor of mathematics at Christ Church College, was composing *Alice in Wonderland.* It is believed to have been the model for important settings within the book. Today, the place is a favorite stopover of Lewis Carroll fans from as far away as Japan, who gobble up commemorative pencils, chess sets, party favors, bookmarks, and in rare cases, original editions of some of Carroll's works.

The **Bodleian Library Shop,** Old School's Quadrangle, Radcliffe Square, Broad Street (☎ **01865/277216**), specializes in Oxford souvenirs, from books and paperweights to Oxford banners and coffee mugs.

Castell & Son (The Varsity Shop), 13 Broad St. (☎ **01865/244000**), is the best outlet in Oxford for clothing emblazoned with the Oxford logo or heraldic symbol. Choices include both whimsical and dead-on-serious neckties, hats, T-shirts, sweatshirts, pens, bookmarks, beer and coffee mugs, and cuff links. It's commercialized Oxford, but it's still got a sense of relative dignity and style.

WHERE TO STAY IN & AROUND OXFORD

Accommodations in Oxford are limited, although recently, motels have sprouted on the outskirts—good for those who want modern amenities. In addition, if you've got a car, you may want to consider country houses or small B&Bs on the outskirts of town; they're the best choices in the area if you don't mind commuting.

Bedrooms, albeit expensive ones, are also provided at the Bath Place Hotel and Le Manoir aux Quat' Saisons (reviewed under "Where to Dine," below).

The **Oxford Tourist Information Centre,** Gloucester Green, behind the bus bays (☎ **01865/726871**), operates a year-round room-booking service for a £2.50 ($4) fee, plus a 10% refundable deposit. If you'd like to seek lodgings on your own, the center has a list of accommodations, maps, and guidebooks.

VERY EXPENSIVE

✪ **Old Parsonage Hotel.** 1 Banbury Rd., Oxford OX2 6NN. ☎ **01865/310210.** Fax 01865/311262. 30 units. MINIBAR TV TEL. £165 ($264) double; £205 ($328) suite. Rates include English breakfast. AE, DC, MC, V. Bus: 7.

This extensively renovated hotel, near St. Giles Church and Keble College, is so old (1660) it looks like an extension of one of the ancient colleges. Originally a 13th-century hospital, it was restored in the early 17th century. Oscar Wilde once lived here for a time and is famed for the remark, "Either this wallpaper goes, or I do." In the 20th century a modern wing was added, and in 1991 it was completely renovated and made into a first-rate hotel. The rooms are individually designed but not large, with such amenities as satellite TV and hair dryers. The marble rooms are air-conditioned; all the suites and some rooms have sofa beds. The rooms open onto the private gardens, and 10 of them are on the ground floor.

Dining: The Parsonage Bar serves everything from cappuccino to mixed drinks, and you can order from a well-prepared menu of continental and English food from 7am until late at night. There's also 24-hour room service.

The Randolph. Beaumont St., Oxford, Oxfordshire OX1 2LN. ☎ **800/225-5843** in the U.S. and Canada, or 01865/247481. Fax 01865/791678. 109 units. TV TEL. £135–£175 ($216–$280) double; from £225 ($360) suite. AE, DC, MC, V. Parking £9 ($14.40). Bus: 7.

Since 1864, the Randolph has overlooked St. Giles, the Ashmolean Museum, and the Cornmarket. Its arched stone entrance is striking. The hotel is an example of how historic surroundings can be combined with modern conveniences to make for elegant accommodations. The lounges, although modernized, are cavernous enough for dozens of separate and intimate conversational groupings. The furnishings are traditional, and all rooms have hair dryers and hot beverage-makers. Some rooms are quite large; others are a bit cramped. The double glazing on the windows seems inadequate to keep out the noise of midtown traffic. In this price range, we'd opt first for the Old Parsonage before checking in here.

Dining: The hotel's Spires Restaurant presents both a time-tested English and a modern cuisine in a high-ceilinged Victorian dining room. There's also a wine bar with an entrance off the street. The Chapters Bar has a tradition-laden atmosphere.

Studley Priory Hotel. Main St., Horton-cum-Studley, Oxfordshire OX33 1AZ. ☎ **800/437-2687** in the U.S. and Canada, or 01865/351203. Fax 01865/351613. 19 units. TV TEL. £130–£245 ($208–$392) double; £250 ($400) suite. Rates include English breakfast. AE, DC, MC, V. From Oxford, drive to the end of Banbury Rd. At the traffic circle, take the 3rd exit (toward London). Go approximately 3½ miles. At the next traffic circle, take the 1st exit (signposted Horton-cum-Studley) and travel 4½ miles. Go through the estate and stay on the same road until you come to "staggered crossroads." Go straight across, signposted Horton-cum-Studley, 2½ miles. This road will bring you right into the village; the hotel is at the top of the hill on the right-hand side.

The Studley Priory Hotel, the best country house hotel in Oxford, may be remembered by those who saw the movie *A Man for All Seasons*. The former Benedictine priory, a hotel since 1961, was used in background shots as the private residence of Sir Thomas More. It's a stunning example of Elizabethan architecture, although it originally dates from the 12th century. Located on 13 acres of wooded grounds and occupied for around 300 years by the Croke family, the manor is 7 miles from Oxford. It's built of stone in the manorial style, with large halls, long bedroom wings, and gables with mullioned windows. The rooms are very large and the furnishings tasteful. Room service is provided all day. Even if you're not staying over, you may want to visit for lunch or dinner. Getting here is a bit complicated, so be armed with a good map when you strike out from Oxford.

EXPENSIVE

Eastgate Hotel. 23 Merton St., The High, Oxford, Oxfordshire, OX1 4BE. ☎ **01865/248244.** Fax 01865/791681. 62 units. TV TEL. £110 ($176) double; £130 ($208) suite. AE, DC, MC, V. Bus: 7.

The Eastgate, built on the site of a 1600s structure, stands opposite the ancient Examination Halls, next to Magdalen Bridge, within walking distance of Oxford College and the city center. Recently refurbished, it offers modern facilities while retaining somewhat the atmosphere of an English country house. All of the comfortably furnished rooms contain beverage-makers. The Shires Restaurant offers roasts and traditional English fare, complemented by a choice of wines. Many undergraduates frequent the bar.

Weston Manor. Weston-on-the-Green, Oxfordshire OX6 8QL. ☎ **01869/350621.** Fax 01869/350901. 39 units. TV TEL. £125 ($200) double; £199 ($318.40) suite. Rates include English breakfast. AE, DC, MC, V. Drive 6 miles north of Oxford on A34.

Ideal as a center for touring the district (Blenheim Palace is only 5 miles away), this 13-acre manor, owned and run by the Osborn family, has existed since the 11th century; portions of the present building date from the 14th and 16th centuries. The estate is the ancestral home of the earls of Abingdon and Berkshire. It was also an abbey until the abbeys were abolished by Henry VIII, who became the owner of this property. Of course, there are ghosts: Mad Maude, the naughty nun who was burned at the stake for her "indecent and immoral" behavior, returns to haunt the Oak rooms. Prince Rupert, during the English Civil War, hid from Cromwell's soldiers in one of the fireplaces, eventually escaping in drag as the "maiden of the milk bucket."

The reception lounge is dominated by a Tudor fireplace and a long refectory table. Most of the rooms are spacious and furnished with antiques (often four-poster beds), old dressing tables, and chests.

Dining: The Great Hall is one of the most beautiful dining rooms in England, with an open-rafter and beamed ceiling, a minstrels' gallery, and a large wrought-iron chandelier. The English food is first-rate and the selection of classic wines diverse.

Amenities: In warm weather, you can enjoy an outdoor heated swimming pool surrounded by gardens, a squash court, and a croquet lawn.

MODERATE

Oxford Moat House. Godstow Rd., Wolvercote Roundabout, Oxford, Oxfordshire OX2 8AL. ☎ **01865/489988.** Fax 01865/310259. 155 units. TV TEL. £98–£140 ($156.80–$224) double. AE, DC, MC, V. Closed Dec 24–Jan 2. Bus: 60.

This is a good choice if you have a car; it's 2 miles north of the city center, and hidden from traffic at the junction of A40 and A34. It attracts a lot of business travelers, but also tourists. It's a good base for exploring not only Oxford but the Cotswolds, which are within easy reach. The M40 motorway is just an 8-mile drive away. Rooms are motel-like, with standard furnishings that are nothing special but are comfortable and spacious. Each has pay-per-view movies, a trouser press, and a kettle. The moat house also has some of the best facilities in the area, including a fully equipped gym, heated indoor swimming pool, squash courts, a sauna, solarium, and billiards table. The Oxford Blue Restaurant has a full carvery, which is one of the better food values in the area, plus an à la carte menu. There's also a sports bar serving food.

INEXPENSIVE

Dial House. 25 London Rd., Headington, Oxford, Oxfordshire OX3 7RE. ☎ **01865/ 769944.** 8 units. TV. £55–£60 ($88–$96) double. No credit cards. Bus: 7, 7A, 20, 21, or 22.

Two miles east of the heart of Oxford, beside the main highway leading to London, is this country-style house originally built between 1924 and 1927. Graced with mock Tudor half-timbering and a prominent blue-faced sundial (from which it derives its name), it has cozy and recently renovated rooms, each equipped with tea-maker and hair dryer. The owners, the Morris family, serve only breakfast in their bright dining room. No smoking.

River Hotel. 17 Botley Rd., Oxford OX2 OAA. ☎ **01865/243475.** Fax 01865/724306. 21 units, 19 with bathroom. TV TEL. £67.50 ($108) double with bath. Rates include breakfast. MC, V. Bus: 4C or 52.

This hotel lies within a quarter mile west of Oxford's commercial core, and charges less than many of its competitors that are just a bit more central. It was originally built around 1900 by a respected local craftsman whose casement windows and flower boxes are still in place. About a quarter of the accommodations lie across the street, within a comfortable stone-sided annex, whose architectural details more or less match those of the main house. There's a bar on the premises, a simple restaurant, and cozy furnishings within the bedrooms. Three singles without bath rent for £45 ($72). Each contains a tea-maker.

Tilbury Lodge Private Hotel. 5 Tilbury Lane, Eynsham Rd., Botley, Oxford, Oxfordshire OX2 9NB. ☎ **01865/862138.** Fax 01865/863700. 9 units. TV TEL. £56–£66

($89.60–$105.60) double, £75–£82 ($120–$131.20) double with 4-poster bed. Rates include English breakfast. MC, V. Bus: 42, 45, 45A, 45B, or 109.

On a quiet country lane about 2 miles west of the center of Oxford, this small hotel is less than a mile from the railway station, where hotel staff will pick you up to save you the walk. Eddie and Eileen Trafford accommodate guests in their well-furnished and comfortable rooms. The most expensive room has a four-poster bed. The guest house also has a Jacuzzi and welcomes children.

Welcome Lodge. Peartree Roundabout, Woodstock Rd., Oxford, Oxfordshire OX2 8JZ. ☎ **800/225-5843** in the U.S. and Canada, or 01865/554301. Fax 01865/513474. 98 units. TV TEL. Mon–Thurs £46.95 ($75.10) double, Fri–Sun £49.95 ($79.90) double. Rates include English breakfast. AE, MC, V. Park and Ride bus, with frequent trips from downtown Oxford to a public parking lot nearby.

Located 3 miles north of Oxford, near the beginning of the A34 highway leading away from town, this large commercial hotel is suitable if you have a car. Situated near a large bus stop, the hotel is easy to spot because of the international flags fluttering in the breezes. Its lower-level rooms open onto private terraces. The furnishings are in the typical motel style, with compact, built-in necessities. Each room has a picture-window wall, individually controlled heating, and tea-maker. Dining choices include the Lodgekeepers Restaurant and Bar, the Little Chef Grill, the Granary Self-Service Restaurant, and a family shop.

WHERE TO DINE
VERY EXPENSIVE
Bath Place Hotel. 4–5 Bath Place (at Holywell St.), Oxford. ☎ **01865/791812.** Reservations recommended. Main courses £15–£22 ($24–$35.20). AE, MC, V. Wed–Sat noon–2pm, Sun 12:30–2:30pm; Sun–Thurs 7–10pm, Fri–Sat 7–10:30pm. Bus: 7. MEDITERRANEAN.

Composed of four 17th-century cottages that were joined together, this place is known for sophisticated cuisine. Since it also houses 12 cozy bedrooms upstairs, it operates something like a French restaurant *avec chambres,* where diners can head directly upstairs after an evening meal, thus avoiding the need to drive after enjoying their food and wine. The menu, which changes about every month and also includes vegetarian selections, reflects a pleasing mixture of Mediterranean cuisines, with heavy emphasis on French. Dishes might include salmon and scallop ravioli served on a bed of braised endive with grilled scallops and an olive-oil emulsion of basil, saffron, olives, and tomatoes; grilled fillet of Cornish sea bass with charcoal-grilled Provençal vegetables and a saffron-butter sauce; and seafood tagliatelle, lightly grilled and served with homemade pasta and beurre blanc sauce.

The rooms upstairs go for £95 to £135 ($152 to $216) double, including continental breakfast. No smoking.

✪ Le Manoir aux Quat' Saisons. Great Milton, Oxfordshire. ☎ **01844/278881.** Reservations required. Main courses £30–£33 ($48–$52.80); lunch menu du jour £32 ($51.20); lunch or dinner menu gourmand £69 ($110.40). AE, DC, MC, V. Daily noon–2:15pm and 7:15–10:15pm. Take Exit 7 off M40 and head along A329 toward Wallingford; look for signs for Great American Milton Manor about a mile after. FRENCH.

Some 12 miles southeast of Oxford, Le Manoir aux Quat' Saisons offers the finest cuisine in the Midlands. The gray- and honey-colored stone manor house was originally built by a Norman nobleman in the early 1300s, and over the years attracted many famous visitors. The connection with France has been masterfully revived by the Gallic owner and chef, Raymond Blanc. His reputation for comfort and cuisine attracts guests from as far away as London.

The main focus is a pair of beamed-ceiling dining rooms whose mullioned windows offer views of the garden. You can enjoy such highly creative specialties as quail eggs; spinach, Parmesan, and black truffle ravioli in a truffle-and-rosemary jus; light crab bisque with ginger and lemongrass and crab ravioli; or roasted breast of Barbary duck in honey and lemon, with a cherry, clove, and cinnamon-scented sauce. Each dish is an exercise in studied perfection.

Accommodations are also available here. The gabled house was built in the 1500s and improved and enlarged in 1908. An outdoor swimming pool, still in use, was added much later. Each very pricey room—rates are £195 to £425 ($312 to $680) double—is decorated boudoir-style with lots of flowery draperies and ruffled canopies and high-quality antique reproductions.

EXPENSIVE

Cherwell Boathouse Restaurant. Bardwell Rd. ☎ **01865/552746.** Reservations recommended. Main courses £10–£14 ($16–$22.40); fixed-price dinner from £19.50 ($31.20); Sun lunch £17.50 ($28). AE, DC, MC, V. Tues 6–11:30pm, Wed–Sat noon–2pm and 6–11:30pm, Sun noon–2pm. Closed Dec 24–30. Bus: Banbury Road. FRENCH.

This Oxford landmark on the River Cherwell is owned by Anthony Verdin, who is assisted by a young crew. A fixed-price menu is offered, and the cooks change the fare every 2 weeks to take advantage of the availability of fresh vegetables, fish, and meat. There is a very reasonable, even exciting, wine list. Children are charged half price. In summer, the restaurant also serves on the terrace. The menu is always intriguing. On any given night you might find starters such as game terrine with Cumberland sauce or a warm salad of black pudding and bacon with a damson dressing. For a main course, you might opt for breast of guinea fowl with tapenade or, for vegetarians, an eggplant gratin with saffron custard and a mixed bean ragout. For dessert, who can resist the fallen chocolate soufflé with drunken prunes and sour cream?

Elizabeth. 82 St. Aldate's St. ☎ **01865/242230.** Reservations recommended. Main courses £13.25–£18.75 ($21.20–$30); lunch £15 ($24). AE, DC, MC, V. Tues–Sat 12:30–2:30pm and 6:30–11pm, Sun 7–10:30pm. Closed Easter weekend and Christmas week. Bus: 7. FRENCH/CONTINENTAL.

Despite the portraits of Elizabeth II that hang near the entrance, this restaurant is named after its original owner, a matriarch who founded this stone-sided house opposite Christ Church College in the 1930s. Today, you're likely to find a well-trained staff from Spain, serving beautifully presented dishes in the French style. The larger of the two dining rooms displays reproductions of paintings by Goya and Velázquez and exudes a restrained kind of dignity; the smaller room is devoted to Alice in Wonderland designs inspired by Lewis Carroll. Dishes that show the kitchen at its best include chicken royale; a range of Scottish steaks; grilled salmon, Dover sole, and sea bass, served in white-wine or lemon-butter sauce; duck with orange sauce; and roast rack of lamb with *gratin dauphinois*.

MODERATE

۞ Le Petit Blanc. 71–72 Walton St. ☎ **01865/510999.** Reservations recommended. Main courses £8–£15 ($12.80–$24); fixed-price lunch £15 ($24). AE, DC, MC, V. Daily noon–3:30pm and 6:30–11pm. CONTINENTAL.

The biggest culinary news in Oxford has been the return of Raymond Blanc (of Le Manoir aux Quat' Saisons fame; see above) with another Le Petit Blanc. (A previous one proved disappointing.) However, Monsieur Blanc is a more wizened restaurateur now, and this buzzing brasserie is up and running—and doing just fine. A former piano shop has been converted into a stylish place offering a menu that promises something for every palate. Here you can get a taste of the famous chef's creations without the high prices of his famed Le Manoir aux Quat' Saisons, though here he keeps the menu simple and fairly straightforward, with a great emphasis on fresh ingredients.

An open kitchen with a spit roast allows you to learn chef's secrets. The terrine of duck liver, and fennel, accompanied by a beetroot dressing, will get you going if you didn't opt for the cream of butternut squash soup, declared absolutely divine by the English lady at the table next to us. The crab ravioli or the morel risotto with crisp Parmesan wafers prove delightful, and the desserts are first rate, especially the raspberry soufflé.

INEXPENSIVE

Al-Shami. 25 Walton Crescent. ☎ **01865/310066.** Reservations recommended. Main courses £7.50–£12 ($12–$19.20); fixed-price menu £15 ($24). MC, V. Daily noon–midnight. Bus: 7. LEBANESE.

Ideal for meals all afternoon and late into the evening, this Lebanese restaurant has awakened the sleepy taste buds of Oxford. Before it opened, the only ethnic restaurants open after the theaters got out were Chinese and Indian. Many diners don't go beyond the appetizers, since they comprise more than 35 delectable hot and cold selections—everything from falafel to a salad made with lamb's brains. Charcoal-grilled chopped lamb, chicken, or beef constitute most of the main-dish selections. In between, guests nibble on raw vegetables. Desserts are chosen from the trolley, and vegetarian meals are also available.

Munchy Munchy. 6 Park End St. ☎ **01865/245710.** Reservations recommended. Main courses £5.50–£9.75 ($8.80–$15.60). MC, V. Tues–Sat noon–2pm and 5:30–10pm. Closed 2 weeks in Sept and 3 weeks in Dec. Bus: 52. SOUTHEAST ASIAN/INDONESIAN.

Some Oxford students, who frequent this restaurant near the station, claim that it offers the best value in the city. Ethel Ow, the chef, is adept at herbs and seasoning, and often uses fresh fruit creatively, as reflected in such dishes as king prawns sautéed with turmeric, coriander, and a puree of apricots, or a spicy lamb with eggplant, Szechuan red pepper, star anise, and crushed yellow-bean sauce. Indonesian and Malaysian dishes are popular. Sometimes long lines form at the door, especially on Friday and Saturday. Children 5 and under are not permitted on Friday and Saturday evenings.

OXFORD AFTER DARK
THE PERFORMING ARTS

Highly acclaimed orchestras playing in truly lovely settings mark the Music at Oxford series at the **Oxford Playhouse Theatre,** Beaumont Street (☎ **01865/798600**). The autumn season runs from mid-September to December, the spring-summer season from January to early July. Tickets range from £10 to £27 ($16 to $43.20). Classical music is performed by outstanding groups such as the European Union Chamber Orchestra, the National Symphony of the Ukraine, the Canterbury Musical Society, the Bournmouth Symphony, and the Guild Hall String Ensemble of London. All performances are held in the Sheldonian Theatre, a particularly attractive site, designed by Sir Christopher Wren, with paintings on the ceiling.

Blackwell's Music Shop, Holywell Street (☎ **01865/261384**), sells tickets for chamber music in the Oxford Coffee Concerts. Ensembles such as the Schubert Chamber Players and the Adderbury Ensemble perform baroque and classical repertoires on Sunday at 11:15am in the Holywell Music Room on Holywell Street, a hall dating from 1748. Ticket prices are £6 ($9.60) adults, £5 ($8) students, seniors, and children under 16. The seasons generally run in 3-month increments ending just before the Christmas holidays and picking up again in January. Coffee is served at the King's Arms or the Turf Tavern from 10:30am and after the concert upon presentation of your ticket.

The **Apollo,** George Street (☎ 01865/244544), is Oxford's primary theater. Tickets are £14.50 to £23.50 ($23.20 to $37.60). A continuous run of comedy, ballet, drama, opera, and even rock contributes to the variety. The Welsh National Opera often performs, and The Glyndebourne Touring Opera appears regularly. Advance booking is recommended, although some shows may have tickets the week of the performance. Don't try for tickets for popular shows on the same day.

At the **Oxford Stage Company,** Beaumont Street (☎ 01865/798600), performances at the Oxford Playhouse range from Shakespeare to modern comedy and drama. Tickets are £6 to £14 ($9.60 to $22.40). They are open most nights year-round, except Sundays and after Christmas for a week.

Insider's tip: For some of the best productions in England, with some of the most talented actors, ask at the tourist office about summer performances in some of the college gardens. These used to be student productions, but increasingly are being taken over by professional companies. There are two Shakespeare troupes as well as other groups. Tickets usually cost from £8 to £10 ($12.80 to $16).

THE CLUBS: BLUES, JAZZ & "CELTIC ROCK"

As a sign of the times, **Freud,** Walton Street at Great Clarendon Street (☎ 01865/311171), has turned a 19th-century church, stained-glass windows and all, into a jazz and folk club with an expansive array of drink choices. The cover charge is £3 ($4.80) after 10pm on Saturday and Sunday.

The **Old Fire Station,** 40 George St. (☎ 01865/794494), covers all the bases, including live entertainment, a bar, theater, art museum, and a new science museum called Curiosity, with a light show and other exhibits. The restaurant, open daily at 8am, serves breakfast until 6pm, with free coffee, tea, and toast. Music cover charges begin at 9pm and are £6.50 ($10.40) nightly. Offerings change nightly but include 1970s disco, blues, jazz, and local bands.

The **Zodiac,** 190 Crowley Rd. (☎ 01865/726336), presents everything from easy listening to "Celtic Rock." Cover varies from £3 to £12 ($4.80 to $19.20) depending on the group featured. It's open usually from about 7:30pm to 2am Monday through Saturday; closed Sunday. Club ownership is shared by some major English bands, and local and big-name bands are featured along with DJs, so call ahead to be sure of what you're getting.

THE PUB SCENE

These places are all good choices for affordable meals, too.

The **Head of the River,** Abingdon Road at Folly Bridge, near the Westgate Centre Mall (☎ 01865/721600), is operated by Fuller Smith and Turner, a family brewery. It's a lively place, with barbecues, snooker games, and bucking-bronco contests, but they offer true traditional ales and lagers, along with very good sturdy fare and home-made desserts. In summer, guests sit by the river and can rent a punt or a boat with an engine. Three rooms, all with bath and overlooking the river, are available for £60 ($96) in summer, including breakfast, newspaper, and parking.

Jolly Farmers, 20 Paradise St. (☎ 01865/7973759), offers real ale, several lagers, and stout, year-round, including Stella, Bass, and Murphy's. There's occasional entertainment.

Pubs with a Pedigree

Every college town the world over has a fair number of bars, but few can boast local watering holes with such atmosphere and history as Oxford.

A short block from The High, overlooking the north side of Christ Church College, **The Bear Inn**, on Alfred Street (☎ **01865/721783**), is an Oxford landmark, built in the 13th century and mentioned time and time again in English literature. The Bear brings together a wide variety of people in a relaxed way. You might talk with a raja from India, a university don, or a titled gentleman who's the latest in a line of owners that goes back more than 700 years. Some former owners developed an astonishing habit: clipping neckties. Around the lounge bar you'll see the remains of thousands of ties, which have been labeled with their owners' names.

Even older than the Bear is **The Turf Tavern,** 4 Bath Place (off Holywell Street; ☎ **01865/243235**), on a very narrow passageway near the Bodleian Library. The pub is reached via St. Helen's Passage, which stretches between Holywell Street and New College Lane. (You'll probably get lost, but any student worth his beer can direct you.) Thomas Hardy used the place as the setting for *Jude the Obscure*. It was "the local" of Burton and Taylor when they were in Oxford many years ago making a film, and today's patrons include a healthy sampling of the university's students and faculty. During his student days at Oxford, the future U.S. president, Bill Clinton, was a frequent visitor here. At night, the nearby old tower of New College and part of the old city wall are floodlit, and during warm weather you can choose a table in any of the three separate gardens that radiate outward from the pub's central core. For wintertime warmth, braziers are lighted in the courtyard and in the gardens. A separate food counter, set behind a glass case, displays the day's fare—salads, soups, sandwiches, and platters of chili con carne, and so on. Local ales (including one named Headbanger, with a relatively high alcohol content) are served, as well as a range of wines.

Just outside of town, hidden away some 2½ miles north of Oxford, **the Trout Inn,** 195 Godstow Rd., Wolvercote (☎ **01865/302071**), is a private world where you can get ale and beer and standard fare. Have your drink in one of the historic rooms, with their settles, brass, and old prints, or go out in sunny weather to sit on a stone wall. On the grounds are peacocks, ducks, swans, and herons that live in and around the river and an adjacent weir pool; they'll join you if you're handing out crumbs. Take an arched stone bridge, stone terraces, architecture with wildly pitched roofs and gables, add the Thames River, and you have the Trout. The Stable Bar, the original 12th-century part, complements the inn's relatively "new" 16th-century bars. Daily specials are featured, and there's a cold-snack bar. Hot meals are served all day in the restaurant; salads are featured in summer, and there are grills in winter. On your way there and back, look for the view of Oxford from the bridge. Take bus 520 or 521 to Wolvercote, then walk half a mile; it's also fun to bike here from Oxford.

At **The Eagle and Child,** 49 St. Giles St. (☎ **01865/310154**), literary history suffuses the dim, paneled alcoves and sedates the atmosphere. For at least a quarter of a century, it was frequented by the likes of C. S. Lewis and J. R. R. Tolkien. In fact, *The Chronicles of Narnia* and *The Hobbit* were first read aloud at this pub. Known as the

"Bird and Baby," this hallowed ground still welcomes the local dons, and the food is good. It's a settled, quiet place to read the newspapers and listen to classical music on CDs.

The King's Arms, 40 Holywell St. (☎ **01865/242369**), rocks a mix of students, gays, and professors. One of the best places in town to strike up a conversation, the pub, owned by Young's Brewery, features six of the company's ales along with visiting lagers and bitters that change periodically.

5 Woodstock & Blenheim Palace

62 miles NW of London; 8 miles NW of Oxford

The small country town of Woodstock, the birthplace in 1330 of the Black Prince, ill-fated son of King Edward III, lies on the edge of the Cotswolds. Some of the stone houses here were constructed when Woodstock was the site of a royal palace. This palace had so suffered the ravages of time that its remains were demolished when Blenheim Palace was built. Woodstock was once the seat of a flourishing glove industry.

ESSENTIALS

GETTING THERE   Take the train to Oxford (see above). The Gloucester Green bus (no. 20) leaves Oxford about every 30 minutes during the day. The trip takes just over a half hour. Call **Thames Transit** at ☎ **01865/772250** for details. If you're driving, take A44 from Oxford.

VISITOR INFORMATION   The **Tourist Information Centre** is on Hensington Road (☎ **01993/811038**), open Monday through Saturday in summer from 9:30am to 1pm and 2 to 5:30pm; November through February, 10am to noon and 1 to 3pm.

ONE OF ENGLAND'S MOST MAGNIFICENT PALACES

✪ Blenheim Palace. ☎ **01993/811325.** Admission £7.80 ($12.50) adults, £5.75 ($9.20) seniors and children 16–17, £3.80 ($6.10) children 5–15; free for children under 5. Family ticket £20 ($32). Daily 10:30am–4:45pm. Closed Nov to mid-Mar.

The extravagantly baroque Blenheim Palace is England's answer to Versailles. Blenheim is the home of the 11th duke of Marlborough, a descendant of John Churchill, the first duke, who was an on-again, off-again favorite of Queen Anne's. In his day (1650–1722), the first duke became the supreme military figure in Europe. Fighting on the Danube near a village named Blenheim, Churchill defeated the forces of Louis XIV, and the lavish palace of Blenheim was built for the duke as a gift from the queen. It was designed by Sir John Vanbrugh, who was also the architect of Castle Howard; the landscaping was created by Capability Brown. The palace is loaded with riches: antiques, porcelain, oil paintings, tapestries, and chinoiserie.

North Americans know Blenheim as the birthplace of Sir Winston Churchill. The room in which he was born is included in the palace tour, as is the Churchill exhibition, four rooms of letters, books, photographs, and other relics. Today the former prime minister lies buried in Bladon Churchyard, near the palace.

Insider's tip: The **Marlborough Maze,** 600 yards from the palace, is the largest symbolic hedge maze on earth, with an herb and lavender garden, a butterfly house, and inflatable castles for children. Also, be sure to look for the Castle's gift shops, tucked away in an old palace dairy. Here you can purchase a wide range of souvenirs, handicrafts, and even locally made preserves.

WHERE TO STAY & DINE

The Bear Hotel. Park St., Woodstock, Oxfordshire OX20 1SZ. ☎ **800/225-5843** in the U.S. and Canada, or 01993/811511. Fax 01993/813380. 47 units. TV TEL. ƒ115–£135 ($184–$216) double; £180 ($288) suite. AE, DC, MC, V.

The Bear Hotel is one of the six oldest coaching inns in England, dating from the 16th century. The half-stone structure is located in the center of Woodstock. Look for the signs in front with the picture of a huge brown bear. Richard Burton and Elizabeth Taylor stayed in the Marlboro suite, an attractively decorated sitting room with a minibar, plus a bedroom and bath. According to legend, one of the chambers of the hotel is haunted. Modern amenities are combined with antiques in the rooms, which have hair dryers and trouser presses. Blazing hearth fires are found throughout the hotel when the days and nights are cool.

Dining: You can relax in the big, black-beamed bar or enjoy a drink in the comfortable lounge. Traditional English dishes are served in the dining room, where table d'hôte meals are reasonably priced.

✪ **Feathers.** Market St., Woodstock, Oxfordshire OX20 1SX. ☎ **01993/812291.** Fax 01993/813158. 17 units. TV TEL. £105–£169 ($168–$270.40) double; £215–£260 ($344–$416) suite. Rates include continental breakfast. AE, DC, MC, V.

Just a short walk from Blenheim Palace, Feathers dates from the 17th century and has been an inn since the 18th century. The bedrooms in this beautifully furnished hotel are individually decorated. The two lounges have wood fires. One boasts fine china and valuable old books; the other is oak-paneled with sturdy beams. A multitude of stuffed birds (from which the house took its name) adorns the bar; from here you can go into the delightful garden in the courtyard.

Dining: The modern British cuisine at Feathers is the best in the area, even better than that served at the Bear. Whether you're here for lunch or for a candlelit dinner, you're sure to enjoy the well-prepared dishes. In summer, you can have a light lunch or afternoon tea in the courtyard garden. Moderately priced set menus are served daily at lunch and dinner.

TWO FAVORITE LOCAL PUBS

The **Star Inn** (☎ 01993/811373) has three locally brewed real ales from which to choose: Tetleys, Wadworth 6X, and Marston's Pedigree. You can enjoy the requisite bar munchies as well as full dinners. The management boasts that its half-shoulder of lamb is the tenderest around because of the slow cooking process. You can also pick and choose from a cold buffet that features salads and sandwich fixings.

The **King's Head** is tucked away at 11 Park Lane (☎ 01993/812164) in Woodstock. Tourists seem to like the "potato pub," as the locals call it, though it's a bit hard to find. The name comes from the wide variety of stuffed potato skins that the pub serves. Enjoy these with a real ale; the owners are sure to have a different specialty ale every month. If you come for dinner, a three-course meal, which may include fish, ribs, or homemade lasagna, costs about £12 ($19.20).

6 Aylesbury

46 miles NW of London; 22 miles E of Oxford

Aylesbury has retained much of its ancient charm and character, especially along the narrow Tudor alleyways and in the 17th-century architecture of the houses in the town center. Among the more interesting structures is St. Mary's Church, which dates from the 13th century and features an unusual spirelet. The 15th-century King's Head

Public House, a National Trust property, has seen many famous faces in its time, including Henry VIII, who was a frequent guest while he was courting Anne Boleyn.

The market, which has been an integral part of the town since the 13th century, is still a thriving force in Aylesbury life, with markets held on Wednesday, Friday, and Saturday, and a flea market on Tuesday. During the 18th and 19th centuries, ducks were the most famous commodity of the Aylesbury market. The pure white ducks were a delicacy for the rich and famous of London and were much desired for their dinner tables. The demand for the Aylesbury duck declined in the 20th century, although not before the breed became threatened with extinction. Today, however, most ducks found on restaurant menus are raised elsewhere and the threat to the Aylesbury duck has subsided. The ivory fowl are now enjoyed more for their beauty than their flavor.

ESSENTIALS

GETTING THERE   Aylesbury is 1 hour by train from London's Marylebone Station, or 25 minutes off the M25 via A41. For rail information, call ☎ 0345/484950 in the U.K. or 01603/764776 in the U.S.

VISITOR INFORMATION   The **Aylesbury Tourist Information Centre,** 8 Bourbon St. (☎ 01296/330559), is open April to October from 9:30am to 5pm Monday through Saturday. From November to March, hours are Monday through Saturday from 10am to 4:30pm.

SEEING THE SIGHTS

Aylesbury is blessed with an abundance of interesting architecture. If you aren't busy spending money at the market, you may want to stroll through the town to see the houses and buildings that line the streets. **Hickman's Almshouses** and the **Prebendal Houses** are structures that date from the 17th century; you can walk by after enjoying tea at St. Mary's Church, which is just down the road.

Buckinghamshire County Museum. Church St. ☎ 01296/331441. Admission to main museum free; Children's Gallery £2.50 ($4) adults, £2 ($3.20) children. Mon–Sat 10am–5pm, Sun 2–5pm.

This museum is located in two buildings, a house and grammar school both dating from the 18th century. The newest addition to the recently refurbished museum is the Roald Dahl Children's Gallery. Dahl's children's books, especially *Charlie and the Chocolate Factory* and *James and the Giant Peach,* come to life as visitors ride in the Great Glass Elevator or crawl inside the Giant Peach. The hands-on exhibits don't stop upon entering the main museum, however. Innovative displays focusing on the cultural heritage of Buckinghamshire are interactive and touchable. Advance arrangements are necessary for the Children's Gallery because of the large number of school groups that visit.

Oak Farms Rare Breeds Park. Off the A41 on the way to Broughton. ☎ 01296/415709. Admission £2 ($3.20) adults, £1 ($1.60) ages 16 and under. Wed–Sun 10am–5pm. Closed Nov–Mar 27.

While you're in the area, you'll of course want to see those famous **Aylesbury ducks,** and this is the best place to catch sight of the once-threatened species. The traditional working farm is home to a variety of animals, from sheep to pigs, many of which are rare breeds. Guests can hand-feed special food to the animals and take a picnic of their own to enjoy. There's also a nature trail.

Waddeson Manor. Bicester Rd. ☎ 01296/65182. Admission to house and grounds £9 ($14.40) adults, £7.50 ($12) children; grounds only, £3 ($4.80) adults, £1.50 ($2.40) children. House open Apr 2–Nov 1 Thurs–Sun and bank holidays 11am–4pm; also Wed 11am–4pm in July–Aug. Grounds and aviary Mar 1–Dec 21 Wed–Sun and bank holidays 10am–5pm.

Built by Baron Ferdinand de Rothschild in the 1870s, the manor features French Renaissance architecture and a variety of French furniture, carpets, and porcelain. Eighteenth-century artwork by several famous English and Dutch painters is exhibited, and there are, of course, wine cellars. In the surrounding gardens, an aviary houses exotic birds. On the premises is a restaurant and gift shop, both featuring a vast assortment of Rothschild wines.

WHERE TO STAY

Bell Inn. Aston Clinton, near Aylesbury, Buckinghamshire HP22 5HP. ☎ **01296/630252.** Fax 01296/631250. 20 units. TV TEL. £60–£90 ($96–$144) double. AE, MC, V.

This near legendary stopover is a former coaching inn believed to have been built at the end of the 18th century. Under the guidance of the Harris family, the inn is acclaimed for its cuisine (see below). Advertised by a large bell instead of an inn sign, it stands unobtrusively by the road, 4 miles from Aylesbury, off the A41 leading south to London. A mossy brick structure with a Georgian portico, it is coolly elegant, with polished wood and an ancient bar with an inglenook fireplace ablaze on a cold wintry night. Former stables around a flower-filled courtyard have been turned into a block of rooms, with luxuriously appointed baths, plus sitting areas, generous space, and a blend of antique and reproduction furniture. Some rooms have four-poster beds.

✪ **Hartwell House.** Oxford Rd., Aylesbury, Buckinghamshire HP17 8NL. ☎ **01296/747444.** Fax 01296/747450. 47 units. TV TEL. £170–£280 ($272–$448) double; £550 ($880) suite. AE, MC, V.

One of London's great showcase country estates and a member of Relais & Châteaux, Hartwell House lies just 2 miles southwest of Aylesbury (the nearest rail station) on A418, near the village of Stone, and about 20 miles from Oxford or an hour's drive from Heathrow. It stands on 90 acres of landscaped parkland. As you enter the house, you're transported back to another era, and can enjoy a medley of architectural styles, part Georgian, part Jacobean, ranging from the 16th through the 18th centuries. The home was built for the Hampden and Lee families, ancestors of the Confederacy's Gen. Robert E. Lee. You can wander from the morning room with its rococo ceiling to the oak-paneled bar, pausing in the library where a former tenant, the exiled Louis XVIII (of gargantuan girth), signed the document returning him to the throne of France. This property stands on in the Vale of Aylesbury.

Rooms are as regal as the prices. The stellar accommodations literally ooze with comfort, charm, and character, even those recently built in a converted stable block. Many of the rooms have garden views.

Dining: The chef cooks with an international flair, using fresh regional ingredients, backed up by a supreme wine list. It's worth the trip here just to try the roast breast of Aylesbury duck with a duck confit flavored with cumin.

Amenities: The Hartwell Spa, modeled on an orangery inspired by Sir John Soane, the early 19th-century architect, is set in landscaped gardens, with a large swimming pool and a fitness center, along with a beauty salon and solarium. The house also has two all-weather tennis courts.

WHERE TO DINE

✪ **Bell Inn.** Aston Clinton. ☎ **01296/630252.** Reservations required. Main courses £9.50–£21.50 ($15.20–$34.40); fixed-price menus £13 ($20.80) for 2 courses, £16 ($25.60) for 3 courses. AE, MC, V. Daily noon–1:30pm; Mon–Sat 7–9:45pm, Sun 7–9pm. CONTINENTAL/ENGLISH.

The county's finest restaurant is a delightful dining experience. The seasonally adjusted menu is always carefully calibrated to serve what's fresh and best at all times. The room sparkles with its polished wood and shiny glass and silver. We almost always come here for the "duck menu," which is centered around roast Aylesbury duck flambé (doused with brandy) with a chartreuse of leg confit, and Perigourdine sauce. The food has remained consistently good over the years, preferring time-tested recipes to innovation. Try, for example, such classics as grilled salmon with ratatouille or pan-fried guinea fowl with mushrooms. One dish we particularly enjoy, when featured, is roast quails stuffed with snails and flavored with fresh tarragon, accompanied by foie gras. You'd have to go back to London to find a wine list as fine as this one, with more than 300 selections available by the glass.

AYLESBURY AFTER DARK

The **Hobgoblin,** Kingsbury Square (☎ **01296/6415100**), has been in service as a pub for only a couple of years, but this structure was built in 1742. Among the on-tap offerings are house ales, Hobgoblin and Wychwood, as well as John Smith's, and there is also a full bar. Snack food is available, as are such distractions as pool tables, TVs, and video games. Sunday nights there's live jazz (no cover). On weekends, the second floor opens as a dance club called **Merlin's.** Hours are Friday and Saturday from 10pm to 2:30am, and Sunday from 10pm to 12:30am, with a cover charge of £4 ($6.40).

7 St. Albans

27 miles NW of London; 41 miles SW of Cambridge

Dating back 2,000 years, today's cathedral city of St. Albans was named after a Roman soldier who was the first Christian martyr in England. Medieval pilgrims made the trek to visit the shrine of St. Alban, and visitors today still find the ancient cathedral city and the surrounding countryside inspiring.

Peter Rabbit was created in this county by Beatrix Potter, and George Bernard Shaw found inspiration in the view from his countryside home near Ayot St. Lawrence. As you explore St. Albans and its nearby attractions, you'll be treading in the footsteps of the Good Queen Bess and Henry VIII, who passed through before you.

Although today industry has crept in and Greater London keeps getting greater and greater, St. Albans is situated at the center of what was known as "the market basket of England." The 1,000-year-old tradition of the street market continues as merchants of every kind set up colorful stalls to display their goods. The market is held on Wednesday and Sunday, and is one of the largest in the southeast.

Tourism has also become very important to the town, since it is near the M25 and the M1 and on the way to many historic homes and attractions. St. Albans itself is home to several museums, well-preserved Roman ruins, and beautiful gardens.

ESSENTIALS

GETTING THERE   St. Albans is easily reached from London. North London Railways leaves from London's Euston Station every 40 minutes Monday through Saturday and hourly on Sunday. The rail connection, ThamesLink, takes you from London to St. Albans in just 17 minutes. From London, Green Line coach no. 724 also runs to St. Albans frequently. For rail information, call ☎ **0345/484950** in the U.K. or **01603/764776** in the U.S. For bus information, dial ☎ **0990/808080.**

If you're driving, take M25 Junction 21A or 22; M1 Junctions 6, 7, or 9; and A1(M) Junction 3.

VISITOR INFORMATION   The **Tourist Information Centre** is at the Town Hall, Market Place (☎ **01727/864511**). From April through October, its hours are Monday through Saturday from 9:30am to 5:30pm; off-season hours are Monday through Saturday from 10am to 4pm. From the end of July until mid-September, the office is also open Sunday from 10:30am to 4:30pm.

EXPLORING THE TOWN

The Association of Honorary Guides, a trained group of local volunteers, provides **guided walks.** These include a tour of the Roman Verulamium and the Medieval Town, a ghost walk, and a coaching-inn walking tour. In addition to prebooked tours, free public guided walks are available on Sunday; the tour begins at 3pm at the clock tower. Guides are also available on Sunday at the Verulamium Museum and Roman Theatre to give short talks on a number of topics concerning the Romans and their time in the area. Full details can be obtained from the Tourist Information Centre (see above) or from the **Tours Secretary** (☎ **01727/833001**).

The **Cathedral of St. Albans,** Holywell Hill and High Street (☎ **01727/860780**) is still known as "The Abbey" to the locals, even though Henry VIII dissolved it as such in 1539. Construction of the cathedral was launched in 1077, making it one of the early Norman churches of England. The bricks, especially visible in the tower, came from the old Roman city of Verulamium, located at the foot of the hill. The nave and west front date from 1235.

The new chapter house, the first modern building beside a great medieval cathedral in the country, was opened by the queen in 1982. The structure houses an information desk, gift shop, and restaurant. There is also a video detailing the history of the cathedral that you can view for £1.50 ($2.40).

St. Albans Cathedral and the chapter house are generally open daily from 9am to 4:30pm, closing at 5:45pm in winter. In addition to church services, there are often organ recitals which are open to the public. The church's choir can sometimes be heard rehearsing, if they're not on tour.

The **Verulamium Museum at St. Michael's** (☎ **01727/819339**) stands on the site of the ancient Roman city of the same name. Here you'll view some of the finest Roman mosaics in Britain as well as re-created Roman rooms. Part of the Roman town hall, a hypocaust, and the outline of houses and shops are still visible in the park that surrounds the museum. The museum is open year-round Monday through Saturday from 10am to 5pm and Sunday from 1 to 5pm. Admission is £2.80 ($4.50) for adults, £1.60 ($2.55) for children, and £7 ($11.20) for a family ticket. By car, Verulamium is a 10-minute drive from Junction 21A on M25; it is also accessible from Junctions 9, 7, or 6 on M1; follow the signs for St. Albans and the Roman Verulamium. Taking a train to St. Albans City Station will put you within 2 miles of the museum.

Just a short distance from Verulamium is the **Roman Theatre** (☎ **01727/835035**). The structure is the only theater of the period that is open to visitors in Britain. You can tour the site daily between 10am and 5pm (4pm in winter).

Museum of St. Albans, Hatfield Road (☎ **01727/819340**), details the history of St. Albans from the departure of the Romans to the present day. The Museum of St. Albans is open Monday through Saturday from 10am to 5pm and Sundays from 2 to 5pm. Admission is £1.50 ($2.40) adults, £1 ($1.60) seniors, 50p (80¢). It is located in the city center on A1057 Hatfield Road and is a 5-minute walk from St. Albans City Station.

From St. Albans you can visit **Gorhambury,** a classic mansion built in 1777. The private home, owned by the earl and countess of Verulam, contains 16th-century enameled glass and historic portraits. It's open May to September from 2 to 5pm on

Thursday only. Admission for adults is £4 ($6.40), £2.50 ($4) for children, and £2 ($3.20) for seniors. Gorhambury is located 2½ miles west of St. Albans near the A5. From the Verulamium Museum, cross Bluehouse Hill Road; the house is about a mile up a private drive.

Batchwood's 18-hole golf course is one of the finest public courses in the country. The Batchwood Indoor Tennis Centre, which has four indoor courts plus outdoor courts, has professional coaches available for all play levels. Both the golf and the tennis center are located on the grounds of the Batchwood Hall mansion on **Batchwood Drive** (☎ 01727/854051).

SHOPPING

The twice-weekly **street market,** held every Wednesday and Saturday on St. Peters Street, is defined by its frantic pace. In contrast, modern off-street precincts and small specialty shops in St. Albans combine to create a unique, laid-back atmosphere the rest of the week.

Jesters, Christopher Place (☎ **01727/851162**), carries an assortment of wooden toys and games such as trains, cars, and juggling equipment. Visit **Whittard's of Chelsea,** 25 Market Place (☎ **01727/867092**), for teas and coffees as well as mugs, teapots, biscuits, and chocolates. **The Past Times Shop,** 33 Market St. (☎ **01727/812817**), sells items that cover 12 historic eras. Here you'll find books on historic places, jewelry, clothes such as Victorian-style nightdresses, and CDs featuring music from a variety of time periods.

For antiques, visit **By George,** 23 George St. (☎ **01727/853032**). St. Albans' largest antique center, the building also houses a tearoom and crafts arcade. **Forget-Me-Not Antiques,** 27 High St. (☎ **01727/848907**), specializes in jewelry, especially Victorian name brooches. At **St. Albans Antique Centre,** 9 George St. (☎ **01727/844233**), up to 20 dealers gather to sell their goods. You can browse through the furniture and collectibles, then have a light snack in the tearoom or tour the gardens.

WHERE TO STAY

The Black Lion Inn. St. Michael's Village, Fishpool St., St. Albans, Hertfordshire AL3 4SB. ☎ **01727/851786.** Fax 01727/859243. 16 units, 14 with bathroom. Sun–Thurs £56 ($89.60) double without bathroom, £65 ($104) double with bathroom; Fri–Sat £48 ($76.80) double without bathroom, £55 ($88) double with bathroom. Rates include English breakfast. AE, MC, V.

This is the best pub hotel—and one of the best bargains. A former bakery built in 1837, it lies in the most colorful part of town, St. Michael's Village, where bustling coaches from London once arrived. Bedrooms are utterly simple and plain and, although a bit cramped, are well maintained. Owners Barry, Tony, and Royal Scott, all brothers, also welcome you to their Giovanni's Italian Restaurant, which is known locally for wishing you a *buon appetito* with its robust Italian cuisine made with fresh ingredients.

✪ **The Manor.** St. Michael's Village, Fishpool St., St. Albans, Hertfordshire AL3 4RY. ☎ **01727/864444.** Fax 01727/848909. 23 units. TV TEL. £120–£130 ($192–$208) double; £165 ($264) suite. Special weekend rate of £145 ($232) per day (minimum of 2 nights), with half board. AE, DC, MC, V.

Set on 5 acres of beautifully maintained lakeside gardens, The Manor was built in 1586 but was recently upgraded and refurbished. Constructed on medieval fortifications, the hotel stands in award-winning gardens with an abundance of wildlife. It's hard to imagine you're in a city. To the original structure, a William and Mary bow-fronted center section was added, along with a Georgian-style extension. The rooms are individually decorated with fine antique pieces. Each one has a certain charm; there's no bad choice among them. Furnishings are a mixture of antique and reproduction pieces, and the rooms are well stocked with everything from mineral water to a teddy bear to sleep with.

Dining: The Manor also has a superb restaurant, the Terrace Room, with an ornate Victorian conservatory overlooking the floodlit lawns, that offers the very best seasonally prepared regional English cooking. There's also 24-hour room service.

Sopwell House. Cottonmill Lane, St. Albans, Hertfordshire AL1 2HQ. ☎ **01727/864477.** Fax 01727/844741. 92 units. TV TEL. £136–£165 ($217.60–$264) double; £165 ($264) suite. Reduced weekend rates of £99.75–£109.75 ($159.60–$175.60) double; £165 ($264) suite. Child £10 ($16) extra. AE, DC, MC, V.

This place is in a neck-to-neck competition with The Manor (see above), although Sopwell has more facilities. A private mansion from the days of George III, it once belonged to Lord Louis Mountbatten and has seen its share of royal heads. Now converted into a hotel of taste, charm, and character, it occupies nearly a dozen acres 2 miles southeast of the city center. Avoid it if it's hosting a conference, but at other times you can enjoy the grace of an English country house. From the drawing room to the library, public rooms are elegant, cozy, and comfy. Some of the bedrooms are equipped with four-poster beds and have a traditional feel, whereas others are more contemporary. Regardless, the decor is tasteful, rather chic, and handsomely coordinated. All rooms are accompanied by amenity-filled marble baths with "power showers." For a review of the hotel's restaurant, see below.

Amenities: Indoor swimming pool, Jacuzzi, gym, sauna, spa with sun beds, hair salon.

WHERE TO DINE

Magnolia Conservatory. In the Sopwell House Hotel, Cottonmill Lane. ☎ **01727/864477.** Reservations recommended. Fixed-price lunches £17.95–£24.50 ($28.70–$39.20); fixed-price dinner £24.50 ($39.20); main courses £13–£16 ($20.80–$25.60). AE, DC, MC, V. Sun–Fri 12:30–2:30pm; Mon–Sat 7:30–10pm. FRENCH/ENGLISH.

Consistently serving the best food in the area, this restaurant lies beneath a glass roof that's pierced with a trio of magnolias whose leaves gracefully arch into the open air outside. The ambience is light, elegant, upscale, and inviting, partly because of its formal and well-trained staff, and partly because the food is more sophisticated, and prepared with more flair, than anywhere else in town. You might begin with a casserole of fresh *langoustines* (crayfish) and white beans scented with essence of truffles; or sample an award-winning version of seared scallops with polenta, served with a marmalade of fresh cherry tomatoes and angel-hair pasta. Main courses change with new chef Warren Jones' inspiration, but we enjoyed the supreme of guinea fowl filled with a mousseline of wild mushrooms and served on a rösti of parsnips. Dessert anyone? With your significant other (it's served only for two), sample the Sopwell Symphony, a degustation of half a dozen of the chef's favorite desserts, arranged on the same platter.

Also on the premises is an upscale pub (they call it a brasserie) that's open daily from 11:30am to 10pm. The food it serves is a lot more down-home, but also a lot cheaper.

THEATER PERFORMANCES

St. Albans' nightlife is centered around its theaters. The Company of Ten, which has its base at the **Abbey Theatre,** Westminster Lodge, Holywell Hill (☎ 01727/

857861), is one of the leading amateur dramatic companies in Britain. The troupe presents 10 productions each season in either the well-equipped main auditorium or a smaller studio. Performances begin at 8pm; tickets cost from £4 to £6 ($6.40 to $9.60). **The Maltings Arts Theatre,** in the Maltings Shopping Center (☎ 01727/844222), presents performances based on literature—from Shakespeare to modern novels. Plays are presented only once and begin at 8pm on Thursday, Friday, and Saturday. Tickets are £6 to £7.50 ($9.60 to $12).

SIDE TRIPS FROM ST. ALBANS

✪ Hatfield House. 6 miles east of St. Albans on A414. ☎ **01707/262823** for information. Admission £5.50 ($8.80) adults, £3.40 ($5.45) children. Mar 25–2nd Sun in Oct, Tues–Sat noon–4pm, Sun 1–4:30pm, and bank holiday Mondays 11am–4:30pm. Closed Good Friday. From St. Albans, take A414 east and follow the brown signs that lead you directly to the estate. By bus, take the University bus from St. Albans City Station. Hatfield House is directly across from Hatfield Station.

Hatfield was much a part of the lives of both Henry VIII and his daughter Elizabeth I. In the old palace, built in the 15th century, Elizabeth romped and played as a child. Although Henry was married to her mother, Anne Boleyn, at the time of Elizabeth's birth, the marriage was later nullified (Anne lost her head and Elizabeth her legitimacy). Henry also used to stash away his oldest daughter, Mary Tudor, at Hatfield. But when Mary became queen of England and set about earning the dubious distinction of "Bloody Mary," she found Elizabeth to be a problem. For a while she kept her in the Tower of London, but eventually let her return to Hatfield. In 1558, while at Hatfield, Elizabeth learned of her succession to the throne of England.

Only the banqueting hall of the original Tudor palace remains; the rest of the house is Jacobean. The structure that exists today has much antique furniture and many tapestries and paintings, as well as three often-reproduced portraits, including the ermine and rainbow portraits of Elizabeth I. The Great Hall is suitably medieval, complete with a minstrel's gallery. One of the rarest exhibits is a pair of silk stockings, said to have been worn by Elizabeth herself, the first woman in England to don such apparel. The park and the gardens are also worth exploring. Luncheons and teas are available from 11am to 5pm in the converted coach house in the Old Palace yard.

Elizabethan banquets are staged in the banqueting hall of the Old Palace Tuesday and Thursday through Saturday, with much gaiety and music. Guests are invited to drink in an anteroom, then join the long tables for a feast of five courses with continuous entertainment from a group of Elizabethan players, minstrels, and jesters. Wine is included in the cost of the meal, but you're expected to pay for your before-dinner drinks yourself. The best way to get here from London for the feast is to book a coach tour for an inclusive fee starting at £44 ($70.40). The Evan Evans agency has tours leaving from Mount Royal Hotel, Cockspur Street, and Herbrand Street in London. The coach returns to London after midnight. If you get here under your own steam, the cost is £29.50 ($47.20) on Tuesday, £31 ($49.60) on Friday, and £33 ($52.80) on Saturday. For private reservations, call ☎ 01707/262055.

Shaw's Corner. In the village of Ayot St. Lawrence. ☎ **01438/820307.** Admission £3.10 ($4.95) adults, £1.50 ($2.40) children. Apr–Oct Wed–Sun and bank holidays 2–6pm. From St. Albans, take B651 to Wheathampstead. Pass through the village, go right at the roundabout, and take the first left turn. A mile up on the left is Brides Hall Lane, which leads to the house.

George Bernard Shaw lived here from 1906 to 1950. The utilitarian house, with its harsh brickwork and rather comfortless interior, is practically as he left it at his death. In the hall, for example, his hats are still hanging, as if ready for him to don one. Shaw wrote 6 to 8 hours a day, even when he'd reached his 90s—he is said to have muttered,

"This damned energy will not let me stop." Evidence of his longtime relationship with the written word is obvious throughout the house; one of his old typewriters is even still in position. Shaw, of course, was famous for his eccentricities, his vegetarianism, and his longevity. And, of course, for his vast literary output, the most famous of which remains *Pygmalion*, on which the musical *My Fair Lady* was based.

Mosquito Aircraft Museum. On the grounds of Salisbury Hall, just off the main M25 London–St. Albans rd. ☎ **01727/822051.** Admission £3 ($4.80) adults; £1 ($1.60) children 5–16, seniors, and students with identification; free for children under 5. Mar–Oct Tues, Thurs, and Sat 2–5:30pm; Sun and bank holidays 10:30am–5:30pm. Take M25 Junction 22 at London Colney about 5 miles south of St. Albans. The museum is on the B556.

This is the oldest aircraft museum in Britain. The hall where the de Havilland Aircraft Company developed the "Mosquito," known as the most versatile aircraft of World War II, is no longer open to the public. However, the museum displays more than 20 types of aircraft, including modern military and civil jets, along with aircraft engines and other memorabilia. Several of the displays are hands-on exhibits. There is also an active restoration program; visitors are encouraged to get an up-close look at the refurbishment process.

8 Woburn Abbey: England's Great Georgian Manor

44 miles N of London

Aside from Windsor Castle, the most visited attraction in the Home Counties is Woburn Abbey, which is so spectacular you should try to visit even if you have to miss all the other historic homes described in this chapter. The great 18th-century Georgian mansion has been the traditional seat of the dukes of Bedford for more than 3 centuries.

TOURING THE ESTATE

✪ **Woburn Abbey.** ½ mile from the village of Woburn, which is 13 miles southwest of Bedford. ☎ **01525/290666.** Admission £7.50 ($12) adults, £6.50 ($10.40) seniors, £3 ($4.80) children. House Mar 22–Nov 2 Mon–Sat 10am–4:30pm, Sun 10am–4:45pm; Jan 1–Mar 22 Sat–Sun and bank holidays 11am–5pm. Park Mon–Sat 10am–4:30pm, Sun 10am–4:45pm. In summer, travel agents can book you on organized coach tours out of London. Otherwise, if you're driving, take the M1 (motorway) north to Junction 12 or 13, where Woburn Abbey directions are signposted.

In the 1950s the present duke of Bedford opened Woburn Abbey to the public to pay off his debt of millions of pounds in inheritance taxes. In 1974, he turned the estate over to his son and daughter-in-law, the marquess and marchioness of Tavistock, who reluctantly took on the business of running the 75-room mansion. And what a business it is, drawing hundreds of thousands of visitors a year and employing more than 300 people to staff the shops and grounds.

Its state apartments are rich in furniture, porcelain, tapestries, silver, and a valuable art collection, including paintings by Van Dyck, Holbein, Rembrandt, Gainsborough, and Reynolds. A series of paintings by Canaletto, showing his continuing views of Venice, grace the walls of the Venetian Room, an intimate dining room. (Prince Philip said the duke's collection was superior to the Canalettos at Windsor, but Her Royal Highness quickly corrected him.) Of all the paintings, one of the most notable is the Armada Portrait of Elizabeth I. Her hand rests on the globe, as Philip's invincible armada perishes in the background.

Queen Victoria and Prince Albert visited Woburn Abbey in 1841; Victoria's Dressing Room displays a fine collection of 17th-century paintings from the Netherlands.

Among the oddities and treasures at Woburn Abbey are a Grotto of Shells, a Sèvres dinner service (gift of Louis XV), and a chamber devoted to memorabilia of "The Flying Duchess." Wife of the 11th duke of Bedford, she was a remarkable woman who disappeared on a solo flight in 1937 (the same year as Amelia Earhart). The duchess, however, was 72 years old at the time.

Today, Woburn Abbey is surrounded by a 3,000-acre deer park that includes the famous Père David deer herd, originally from China and saved from extinction at Woburn. The **Woburn Safari Park** has lions, tigers, giraffes, camels, monkeys, Przewalski's horses, bongos, elephants, and other animals.

NEARBY SHOPPING & AFTERNOON TEA

In a wonderful old building, **Town Hall Antiques,** Market Place (☎ 01525/ 290950), is a treasure trove of collectibles and antiques, including some early English porcelain and pieces from the 1940s. Some unusual commemorative items are also sold, such as an array of Victorian, Georgian, and Edwardian memorabilia. There's something here to suit a wide range of pocketbooks, including clocks, Victorian jewelry, brass, copper, and "kitchenalia."

When it's teatime, head to **Copperfields,** Woburn (☎ 01525/290464), located inside a B&B with low-beamed ceilings that add to its intimacy and charm. There is no set tea, but a pot of tea with clotted cream and a cake is £3.25 ($5.20). Baked goods include scones, and chocolate, lemon, Victoria sponge, carrot, coffee, and fruit cakes, as well as daily specials. The tearoom is open daily, but it's a good idea to call on weekends between January and Easter, since it might be closed if business is slow.

WHERE TO STAY

Bedford Arms. 1 George St., Woburn, Bedfordshire MK17 9PX. ☎ **01525/290441.** Fax 01525/290432. 53 units. MINIBAR TV TEL. £108 ($172.80) double; £170 ($272) suite. Children stay free in parents' room. AE, DC, MC, V.

After visiting the abbey, head here for food and lodging at the gates of the estate. This is a Georgian coaching inn with a checkered history that blends the old and new. Tastefully modernized, it preserves a certain mellow charm. Guests are housed in one of several well-furnished and beautifully maintained rooms, which were refurbished in 1995. A more recent block provides "executive bedrooms," which don't have the charm of the older units but are more up-to-date and comfortable.

Dining/Diversions: The 75-seat Georgian dining room was designed by Henry Holland, architect of Woburn Abbey. Adjacent to the restaurant is the Tavistock Bar, a good place for a pint, with its exposed old beams as well as its inglenook fireplace. There is also a more elegant and modern cocktail bar.

WHERE TO DINE

Paris House. Woburn Park (2¼ miles southeast of Woburn on A4012). ☎ **01525/290692.** Reservations required. Fixed-price dinner £43–£47 ($68.80–$75.20); set lunch £26–£43 ($41.60–$68.80). AE, DC, MC, V. Tues–Sat noon–2pm and 7–10pm, Sun noon–2pm. Closed Feb. CONTINENTAL.

This reconstructed timbered house stands in a park where you can see deer grazing. The black-and-white timbered building originally stood in Paris where it was constructed for the Great Exhibition 1878, but it was torn down and transplanted, timber by timber, to Woburn. Since 1983, it has been the domain of Bedfordshire's finest chef, Peter Chandler, who was the first English apprentice of the legendary Roux brothers. Chandler not only learned his lesson well, but has brought his own innovative touch to the dishes served here. He still regularly visits France for new ideas, and is known for his use of the freshest of seasonal ingredients. Try his delectable marinated Cajun prawns, delicately spiced savory, or his duck breast in a fig and muscat sauce. The palpably fresh fillet of halibut in a champagne sauce had just the right touch. The chef is rightly known for his *tulipe en fantaisie,* a sugar-fairy fantasy with fruit and ice cream.

7 Kent, Surrey & Sussex

Lying to the south and southeast of London are the shires (counties) of Kent, Surrey, and Sussex—fascinating areas within easy commuting distance of the capital.

In **Kent,** Canterbury is the major highlight and makes the best base for exploring the area. Dover, which is Britain's historic gateway to the Continent, is famed for its white cliffs, and is another convenient option. This county is on the fringes of London yet is far removed in spirit and scenery. Since the days of the Tudors, cherry blossoms have enlivened the fertile landscape. Orchards and hop fields abound, earning Kent the title of "the garden of England"—and in England, the competition's tough. Kent suffered severe destruction during World War II, since it was the alley over which the *Luftwaffe* flew in its blitz of London. But despite much devastation, it's still filled with interesting old towns and castles.

In fact, Kent boasts some of Europe's grandest mansions. If your time is limited, seek out the big four: **Knole,** one of the largest private houses of England, a great example of Tudor architecture; **Hever Castle,** dating from the end of the 13th century, a gift from Henry VIII to the "great Flanders mare," Anne of Cleves; **Penhurst Place,** a magnificent English Gothic mansion, one of the outstanding country houses of Britain; and lovely **Leeds Castle,** near Maidstone, dating from A.D. 857. Although it doesn't compare with these grand castles, Chartwell House also merits a visit because of the man who used to call it home: Sir Winston Churchill. For more advice on how to tour these homes, refer to "Kent's Country Houses, Castles & Gardens," below.

With the continuing expansion of London's borders, it's a wonder that the tiny county of **Surrey** hasn't been gobbled up and turned into a sprawling suburb. Yet its countryside remains unspoiled, even though many people commute from homes here to jobs in London (you're only about 45 minutes to an hour away).

If King Harold hadn't loved **Sussex** so much, the course of English history might have been changed forever. Had the brave Saxon waited longer in the north, he could have marshaled more adequate reinforcements before striking south to meet the Normans. But Duke William's soldiers were ravaging the countryside he knew so well, and Harold rushed down to counter them.

Harold's enthusiasm for Sussex is understandable. The landscape rises and falls like waves. The county is known for its woodlands, from

Kent, Surrey & Sussex

KENT & SURREY

Canterbury Cathedral ❷
Charwell House ❸
Dover Castle ❶
Down House ❶
Heve Castle ❶
Ightham Mote ❾
Knole ❿
Leeds Castle ❸
Loseley House ㉒
Penshurst Place ❽
Polesden Lacey ⓴
Squerryes Court ⓬
Wisley Garden ㉑

SUSSEX

Aruncel Castle ㉓
Bateman's ❼
Battle Abbey ❻
Bluebell Railway ⓱
Glyndebourne
Opera House ⓰
Hastings Castle ❺
House on Pooh Corner ⓯
Monk House ⓱
The Royal Pavilion ⓲
Smallythe Place ❹

3-0582

which came the timbers to build England's mighty fleet in days gone by. The shires lie south of London and Surrey, bordering Kent in the east, Hampshire in the west, and opening directly onto the English Channel, where the coast is dotted with seaside towns.

Like the other sections in the vulnerable south of England, Sussex was the setting of some of the most significant events in English history. Apart from the Norman landings at Hastings, the most life-changing transformation occurred in the 19th century, as middle-class Victorians flocked to the seashore, pumping new spirit into Brighton and even old Hastings.

The old towns and villages of Sussex, particularly Rye and Winchelsea, are far more intriguing than the seaside resorts. No Sussex village is lovelier than Alfriston (and the innkeepers know it, too); Arundel is noted for its castle; and the cathedral city of Chichester is a mecca for theater buffs. The old market town of Battle was the setting for the Battle of Hastings in 1066.

Where to base yourself in Sussex? The best option is Brighton, since it has a wide choice of hotels, restaurants, and nightclubs. There's more excitement here at "London by the Sea" than at Hastings. If you're seeking old-English charm and village life, head instead to Alfriston or Rye.

1 Canterbury

56 miles SE of London

Under the arch of the ancient West Gate journeyed Chaucer's knight, solicitor, nun, squire, parson, merchant, miller, and others—spinning tales. They were bound for the shrine of Thomas à Becket, archbishop of Canterbury, who was slain by four knights of Henry II on December 29, 1170. (The king later walked barefoot from Harbledown to the tomb of his former friend, where he allowed himself to be flogged in penance.) The shrine was finally torn down in 1538 by Henry VIII, as part of his campaign to destroy the monasteries and graven images. But Canterbury, by then, had already become an attraction.

The medieval Kentish city on the River Stour is the ecclesiastical capital of England. The city was once completely walled, and many traces of its old fortifications remain. Canterbury was inhabited centuries before the birth of Jesus Christ. Although its most famous incident was the murder of Becket, the medieval city witnessed other major events in English history, including Bloody Mary's order to burn nearly 40 victims at the stake. Richard the Lion-Hearted returned this way from crusading, and Charles II passed through on the way to claim his crown.

Canterbury pilgrims still continue to arrive today, except now they're called daytrippers and they overrun the city and its monuments. It's amazing that the central core of the city is as interesting and picture-perfect as it is, considering the enormous damage caused by the Nazi blitz of 1941. The city has an active university life—mainly students from Kent—and an enormous number of pubs. And its High Street is filled with shoppers in from the country. We suggest exploring Canterbury in the early morning or the early evening, after the busloads have departed.

ESSENTIALS

GETTING THERE   There is frequent train service from Victoria, Charing Cross, Waterloo, and London Bridge stations. The journey takes 1½ hours. For rail information, call ☎ **0345/484950** in the U.K. or 01603/764776 in the U.S.

The bus from Victoria Coach Station takes 2 to 3 hours and leaves twice daily. For schedules call ☎ **0990/808080.**

Canterbury

St. Martin's Rd.
College Rd.
Edith Rd.
St. Gregory's Rd.
North Holmes Rd.

Havelock St.
Old Ruttington Ln.

Military Rd.
Broad St.

Broad St.

Monastery St.
Langport
Ivy Lane
Lower Chantry Lane
New Dover Rd.
Upper Chantry Lane
St. George's Place

Lower Bridge St.

St. George's St.
Dover St.
Vernon Pl.
Old Dover Rd.

St. Mary Magdalene's Tower
St. George's Tower
Canterbury Lane
Burgate
Upper Bridge St.
Bus Station

Christ Church Gate
St. George's St.

Knott Lane
Palace St.
King St.
Mill Lane
Blackfriars
The Borough

St. Margaret's St.
Gravel Walk
Ross Lane

Watling St.

St. Radigund's St.
High St.
Eastbridge Hospital
Hawks Lane
Beer Cart Lane
St. John's Lane
Castle St.
St. Mary's St.

St. Peter's Lane
Greyfriars
St. Peter's Grove
Black Griffin Lane
St. Peter's St.
Pound Lane
River Stour

Castle Row
Pin Hill

Rail Station West
St. Dunstan's St.
Whitehall Rd.

Rheims Way

Rail Station East

Rheims Way

N

Canterbury Cathedral ⑥
Canterbury Heritage Museum ②
Canterbury Roman Museum ⑤
The Canterbury Tales ④
St. Augustine's Abbey ⑦
The Weaver's House ③
West Gate Museum ①

If you're driving from London, take A2, then M2. Canterbury is signposted all the way. The city center is closed to cars, but it's only a short walk from several parking areas to the cathedral.

VISITOR INFORMATION   A few doors away from St. Margaret's Church, the **Canterbury Tourist Information Centre,** 34 St. Margaret's St., Canterbury CT1 2TG (☎ **01227/766567**), sells a useful guidebook, *North Downs Way,* for £2.95 ($4.70). It's open daily from 9:30am to 5:30pm April through October, and daily 9:30am to 5pm November through March.

GETTING AROUND BY BIKE   Ten-speed and mountain bikes are a terrific way to tour Canterbury. **Canterbury Cycle Mart,** 19 Lower Bridge St., Canterbury (☎ **01227/761488**), rents 15-speeds for £10 ($16) per day. You will need a credit-card number or £50 ($80) cash deposit. Dutch touring bikes, small, folding bikes, and mountain bikes can be rented at the **House of Agnes Hotel,** 71 St. Dunstan's St., Canterbury (☎ **01227/472185**). A simple map comes with each bike, and an Ordinance Survey map of East Kent is offered for £4.95 ($7.90). A credit card or £100 ($160) deposit is required for city bikes and £100 ($160) for mountain bikes.

WHAT TO SEE & DO
✪ **Canterbury Cathedral.** 11 The Precincts. ☎ **01227/762862.** Admission £2.50 ($4) adults, £1.50 ($2.40) children. Guided tours, based on demand, £3 ($4.80) adults, £2 ($3.20) children. Mon–Sat 9am–5pm, Sun 12:30–2:30pm and 4:30–5:30pm.

The foundation of this splendid cathedral dates from A.D. 597, but the earliest part of the present building is the great Romanesque crypt built around A.D. 1100. The monastic "quire" erected on top of this at the same time was destroyed by fire in 1174, only 4 years after the murder of Thomas à Becket on a dark December evening in the northwest transept, which is still one of the most famous places of pilgrimage in Europe. The destroyed "quire" was immediately replaced by a magnificent early Gothic one, the first major expression of that architectural style in England.

The cathedral is noteworthy for its medieval tombs of royal personages, such as King Henry IV and Edward the Black Prince, as well as numerous archbishops. To the later Middle Ages belong the great 14th-century nave and the famous central "Bell Harry Tower." The cathedral stands on spacious precincts amid the remains of the buildings of the monastery—cloisters, chapter house, and Norman water tower—which have survived intact from Henry VIII's dissolution to the present day.

Becket's shrine was destroyed by the Tudor king, but the site of that tomb is in Trinity Chapel, near the high altar. The saint is said to have worked miracles, and the cathedral has some rare stained glass depicting those feats.

But the most miraculous event is that the windows escaped Henry VIII's agents of destruction as well as Hitler's bombs. The windows were removed as a precaution at the beginning of the war. During the war, a large area of Canterbury was flattened, but the main body of the church was unharmed. However, the cathedral library was damaged during a German air raid in 1942. The replacement windows of the cathedral were blown in, which proved the wisdom of having the medieval glass safely stored away.

OTHER ATTRACTIONS
The Canterbury Tales. 23 St. Margaret's St. (off High St., near the cathedral). ☎ **01227/454888.** Admission £4.95 ($7.90) adults, £4.25 ($6.80) seniors and students, £3.95 ($6.30) children 5–16; free for children 4 and under. Family ticket £14 ($22.40). Mar–June and Sept–Oct daily 9:30am–5:30pm; July–Aug daily 9am–6pm; Nov–Feb Sun–Fri 10am–4:30pm, Sat 9:30am–5:30pm.

One of the most visited museums in town re-creates the pilgrimages of Chaucerian England through a series of medieval tableaux. Visitors are handed headsets with earphones, which give oral recitations of five of Chaucer's *Canterbury Tales* and the murder of St. Thomas à Becket. Audiovisual aids bring famous characters to life, and stories of jealousy, pride, avarice, and love are recounted. A tour of all exhibits takes about 45 minutes.

Canterbury Heritage Museum of the City. Stour St. ☎ **01227/452747.** Admission £2.20 ($3.50) adults, £1.45 ($2.30) students and seniors, £1.10 ($1.75) children. Year-round Mon–Sat 10:30am–5pm; June–Oct Sun 1:30–5pm. Last entry time is 4pm. Closed Christmas week and Good Friday.

Set in the ancient Poor Priests' Hospital with its medieval interiors and soaring oak roofs, the museum features award-winning displays to showcase the best of the city's treasures and lead the visitor through crucial moments that have shaped Canterbury's history. State-of-the-art video, computer, and hologram technology transports the visitor back in time to such events as the Viking raids and the wartime Blitz. Collections include a huge display of pilgrim badges from medieval souvenir shops and the Rupert Bear Gallery.

Canterbury Roman Museum. Butchery Lane. ☎ **01227/785575.** Admission £2.20 ($3.50) adults, £1.45 ($2.30) students and seniors, £1.10 ($1.75) children. Year-round Mon–Sat 10am–5pm; June–Oct Sun 1:30–5pm. Last entry time is 4pm. Closed Christmas week and Good Friday.

The museum is located beneath street level and is constructed around actual archaeological excavations. Interactive computer shows and actual handling of Roman artifacts bring the past to life for all ages. The Roman town of Durovernum Cantiacorum was established shortly after Emperor Claudius's invasion of the area in A.D. 43 and continued to flourish for nearly 400 years. Visitors can follow the archaeologists' detective work through an excavated Roman house site with patterned mosaics that was discovered after the wartime bombing.

St. Augustine's Abbey. Corner of Lower Chantry Lane and Longport Rd. ☎ **01227/767345.** Admission £2.50 ($4) adults, £1.90 ($3.05) students and seniors, £1.30 ($2.10) children. Apr–Sept daily 10am–6pm; Oct–Mar daily 10am–4pm.

This is one of the most historic religious centers in the country, of which only the ruins remain, mostly at ground level. Augustine was buried here, along with other archbishops and Anglo-Saxon kings. Adjacent to the remains are the abbey buildings that were converted into a royal palace by Henry VIII and used briefly by several monarchs, including Elizabeth I and Charles I.

In an attempt to convert the Saxons, Pope Gregory I sent Augustine to England in 597. Ethelbert, the Saxon King, allowed Augustine and his followers to build a church outside the city walls, and it endured until Henry VIII tore it down. In its day, the abbey church rivaled the cathedral in size, and enough of the ruins remain to conjure the whole of the cloister, church, and refectory.

WALKING & BOAT TOURS

From Easter to early November, daily guided tours of Canterbury are organized by the **Guild of Guides** (☎ **01227/459779**), costing £3.50 ($5.60) for adults, £3 ($4.80) for students and children over 14, and £8.50 ($13.60) for a family ticket. Meet at the Tourist Information Centre at 34 St. Margaret's St., in a pedestrian area near the cathedral, daily (including Sunday) at 2pm from the end of March to the end of October. From the beginning of July to the end of August there's also a tour at 11am Monday through Saturday.

From just below the Weavers House, boats leave for half-hour **trips on the river** with a commentary on the history of the buildings you pass. Umbrellas are provided to protect you against inclement weather.

HORSEBACK RIDING

The **Bursted Manor Riding Centre** in Pett Bottom (☎ **01227/830568**) is open from 9am to dusk Tuesday through Sunday. The last lesson is at 7pm on weekdays and 5pm on Saturday and Sunday. Ex-competition and riding-school mounts are available at £15 ($24) for a 1-hour group lesson or hack ride, or a half-hour private lesson. A Boxing Day hunt is open to the public.

SHOPPING

Handmade pottery (vases, mugs, and teapots in earth colors of blues, greens, and browns) is sold at **Canterbury Pottery,** 38 Burgate, just before Mercury Lane (☎ **01227/452608**). It is sturdy fare that wears well, including house number plates that take 2 weeks to complete, but can be mailed to your home.

English tradition holds firm at the **English Teddy Bear Company,** 4 St. Peter's St. (☎ **01227/784640**), which is stuffed with hundreds of teddy bears with embroidered noses, humps in their backs, silk feet, and long arms and legs. Famous bears don't hang out here—no Rupert, no Winnie, and no Paddington. Additional items include bearish T-shirts and sweatshirts, jams and marmalades, and clothes for the bears.

Put on your tweed jacket and grab your pipe for a trip to a secondhand **Chaucer Bookstop,** 6 Beer Cart Lane (☎ **01227/453912**), with first editions (both old and modern), out-of-print books, special leather-bound editions, and a large selection of local history books. The **Albion Bookstop,** 13 Mercery Lane (☎ **01227/768631**), is the place to find good local folding maps. At the **Chaucer Centre,** 22 St. Peter's St. (☎ **01227/470379**), *The Canterbury Tales* in book and tape formats join all things Chaucerian, including *Canterbury Tales* T-shirts, St. Justin jewelry from Cornwall, Ellesmere cards, and balls and plates for juggling.

WHERE TO STAY

In spite of all its fame as a tourist destination, Canterbury still lacks a really first-class hotel. What you get isn't bad, but it's not state-of-the-art.

MODERATE

The Chaucer Hotel. 63 Ivy Lane (off Lower Bridge St.), Canterbury, Kent CT1 1TU. ☎ **800/ 225-5843** in the U.S. and Canada, or 01227/464427. Fax 01227/450397. 42 units. TV TEL. £90 ($144) double. AE, DC, MC, V.

Located on a historic street, The Chaucer Hotel, a member of the Forte chain, lies in a Georgian house that stands a few minutes' walk from the cathedral and the Micawber house made famous in *David Copperfield.* Your comfortably furnished room will lie at the end of a labyrinth of stairs, narrow hallways, and doors. (The hotel staff will carry your luggage and park your car.) The best rooms, with views over the rooftops of Canterbury and the cathedral, are nos. 60, 61, and 65. All rooms, however, are named in a wonderfully quirky way that honors former archbishops as well as some of Chaucer's racier pilgrims. The hotel offers limited services, including babysitting (prebooked), dry cleaning/laundry, and secretarial services.

You can have a drink in the Pilgrim's Bar, with its Regency mantelpieces and French windows that open to outdoor terraces in summer. The hotel also has a good restaurant, the Geoffrey Chaucer, serving English meals until 9:30pm, and it provides room service.

County Hotel. High St., Canterbury, Kent CT1 2RX. ☎ **01227/766266.** Fax 01227/451512. 73 units. TV TEL. £102.50 ($164) double; £180 ($288) suite. AE, DC, MC, V. Parking £2.50 ($4).

This is the leading hotel in Canterbury itself. It's been around since the closing years of Victoria's reign, with a recorded history going back to the end of the 12th century. The time-mellowed atmosphere is exemplified by the residents' lounge on the second floor, with its old timbers and carved antiques. The hotel is constantly refurbished. Its sumptuous suite is the best room in Canterbury. There are also a dozen period rooms with either Georgian or Tudor four-poster beds; opt for these if available.

For fine dining, go to Sully's restaurant, the hotel's air-conditioned dining room (reviewed below). For snacks, vegetarian specialties, salads, and hot dishes, the coffee shop may be your best bet. There's also the Tudor Bar for cocktails.

Falstaff Hotel. 8–10 St. Dunstan's St., Canterbury, Kent CT2 8AF. ☎ **01227/462138.** Fax 01227/463525. 24 units. TV TEL. £105–£120 ($168–$192) double. AE, DC, MC, V.

Located 400 yards from the West Station, this is a classic Canterbury choice, complete with a flagstone-covered courtyard that retains its sense of history. Next to the Westgate Tower, it has its own parking lot, and easy access to the M2 and M20.

Rooms are small, but cozy, well maintained, and neatly organized. Their baths have recently been upgraded. Public rooms are as cozy as the bedrooms, and even if you aren't staying here, you might want to drop in for a drink at The Falstaff Tap, an ale and cider house on the grounds. There is also a comfortable lounge and a good, no-smoking restaurant offering standard English fare prepared with fresh ingredients. The Falstaff's high tea is one of the best in Canterbury.

✪ **Howfield Manor.** Chartham Hatch (2 miles from Canterbury along the A28 Ashford Rd.), Canterbury, Kent CT4 7HQ. ☎ **01227/738294.** Fax 01227/731535. 16 units. TV TEL. £97.50 ($156) double; £105 ($168) suite. Rates include English breakfast. AE, MC, V. Take the A28 2¼ miles from Canterbury.

Once part of the estate of the Priory of St. Gregory, this is one of the most charming country manors near Canterbury. It's not plush and Laura Ashley–style chintzy, but it's a good and reliable choice, with enough beams and private nooks to please the traditionalist.

Set on 5 acres of rolling meadows, the house offers tastefully furnished rooms with alarm clocks, trouser presses, and hair dryers. They are decorated attractively, not grandly, and each is snug and cozy. Rooms in the original house have more character (exposed beams), whereas rooms in the new wing are larger and furnished with solid oak pieces. For a recommendation of the manor's restaurant, Old Well, see below.

Slatters. St. Margaret's St., Canterbury, Kent CT1 2TR. ☎ **01227/463271.** Fax 01227/764117. 29 units. TV TEL. £75 ($120) standard double, £85 ($136) executive double. Rates include English breakfast. AE, DC, MC, V.

In the heart of Canterbury, 200 yards from the cathedral, this building is historic but the rooms are motel-like. Most of them convert into sitting areas with armchairs during the day. Each is furnished with a trouser press and hair dryer, and a welcome tray with everything you need to make tea or coffee. The fully licensed French restaurant serves a table d'hôte dinner. Bar snacks are also available at lunchtime.

INEXPENSIVE

Cathedral Gate Hotel. 36 Burgate, Canterbury, Kent CT1 2HA. ☎ **01227/464381.** Fax 01227/462800. 24 units, 12 with bathroom. TV TEL. £45–£55 ($72–$88) double without bathroom, £58–£77.50 ($92.80–$124) double with bathroom. Rates include continental breakfast. AE, DC, MC, V. Parking £2 ($3.20).

For those who want to stay close to the cathedral and perhaps have a view of it, there is no better choice. Built in 1438, adjoining Christchurch Gate and overlooking the Buttermarket, this former hospice became one of the earliest of the fashionable coffeehouses and teahouses of England in the early 1600s, and the interior reveals many little architectural details of that century. The rooms are comfortably but modestly furnished, with sloping floors and massive oak beams.

Lunchtime bar snacks and dinner are served. The menu is a deliciously sinful throwback to the 1960s—Lancashire hot pot, Cornish pasties, steak and kidney pie, and treacle sponge with custard and cream for dessert. An in-house bar is licensed to serve residents. A courtyard garden with cathedral views is available for guests. The hotel is a 10-minute walk from the train station.

Ebury Hotel. 65-67 New Dover Rd., Canterbury, Kent CT1 3DX. ☎ **01227/768433.** Fax 01227/459187. 15 units. TV TEL. £65–£72 ($104–$115.20) double; £79 ($126.40) triple; £89 ($142.40) quad. Rates include English breakfast. AE, MC, V. Closed Dec 14 to Jan 16. Follow the signs to A2, Dover Rd., on left-hand side south of the city.

One of the finest B&Bs in Canterbury, this gabled Victorian house stands on 2 acres of gardens at the edge of the city, within easy walking distance of the city center. It's important to reserve in advance. Built in 1850, it's composed of two separate houses that were joined several years ago; the management also rent flats on a weekly basis. The accommodations are well furnished, roomy, and pleasantly decorated. The hotel has a heated, indoor swimming pool and spa, as well as a spacious lounge and a licensed restaurant serving good English meals prepared with fresh vegetables. Charcoal-grills and dishes based on family recipes are especially good.

Three Tuns Inn. 24 Watling St. (just off Castle St.), Canterbury, Kent CT1 2UD. ☎ **01227/767371.** Fax 01227/785962. 6 units. TV TEL. £42.50–£50 ($68–$80) double. AE, DC, MC, V.

In the center of town, this old-fashioned inn derives most of its business from its exceptionally busy pub. Upstairs are a handful of antique bedrooms, which impart a feeling of old-world charm. The inn occupies a fine 15th-century building on the site of an ancient Roman theater. William and Mary, who later became king and queen of England, stopped here in 1679. You can even stay in the room they stayed in—it's attractively furnished and has a four-poster bed. The pub downstairs serves a buffet-style "tavern fare" lunch daily. The spillover from the pub gravitates into a side room, the Chapel Restaurant, where illegal Catholic masses were held during the civil war. It still has the entrance to a secret passageway that allowed the worshippers to leave quickly in case of danger.

A NEARBY PLACE TO STAY

The Old Coach House. Dover Rd., Barham, Kent. ☎ **01227/831218.** Fax 01227/831932. 7 units. TV TEL. £50 ($80) double. MC, V.

The inn stands halfway between Canterbury and Dover on the A2 (southbound), which makes it ideal for exploring, shopping, country walking, or horse riding. The Old Coach House provides a distinctly French flavor. A coaching inn in the 19th century, it is now run as a relaxed French country auberge by chef-patron Jean-Claude Rozard and his English wife, Angela.

The award-winning restaurant offers a wide range of dishes from local game in season to fresh fish, such as turbot, bass, grilled lobster, and Dover sole. Jean-Claude is a Frenchman with a real culinary flair and offers an imaginative and quite extensive wine cellar. You truly feel you have crossed the Channel here when you sip French Chardonnay, eat French bread spread with butter from little brown pots, and partake of *moules à la marinière* (mussels cooked in gravy with onions).

WHERE TO DINE

Duck Inn. Pett Bottom, near Bridge. ☎ **01227/830354.** Reservations recommended. Main courses £6.95–£12.95 ($11.10–$20.70); 2-course fixed-price lunch (Mon–Fri) £7.50 ($12); 3-course fixed-price dinner £10 ($16). AE, MC, V. Drive 5 miles outside Canterbury near the village of Bridge on the road to Dover. ENGLISH.

Once called the Woodsmen Arms, this restaurant became known as the Duck Inn because of its low door. (As you entered the establishment, the clientele would shout "Duck!") Set in the Pett Bottom valley in a 16th-century structure, it offers traditional English fare. Although there are bar and restaurant areas, diners can sit outdoors in the English country garden during the summer. The menu posted on two chalkboards changes weekly, although a few standard English favorites remain on a permanent basis. For your main course, the menu may include game pies (in season) or mussels marinara, and some duck preparation is always on the menu. James Bond fans will appreciate this place's location; according to the film *You Only Live Twice*, 007 grew up next door to the Duck Inn.

Old Well Restaurant. At Howfield Manor, Chartham Hatch. ☎ **01227/738294.** Reservations recommended. Main courses £11.95–£16.95 ($19.10–$27.10). AE, MC, V. Daily noon–2pm and 7:30–9pm. CONTINENTAL.

At this country manor (see Howfield Manor above), nonresidents and guests can enjoy a cuisine served in the chapel part of the manor, dating from 1181. The old well can still be seen; monks drew their water here. Head chef Andrew Leach and his brigade create a market-fresh cuisine that's prepared daily. The excellent food is backed up by a homelike atmosphere, friendly service, and a well-chosen wine list. You might start with a phyllo pastry basket filled with chicken livers in a wild-mushroom-and-port-wine sauce, and proceed on to guinea fowl with apple and calvados or a confit of duck surrounded by a sauce of black currants and pink peppercorns. Arrive early to enjoy a drink in the Priory Bar, with its trompe l'oeil murals and a real "priesthole" (the bar staff will be delighted to explain what that means, just to get the conversation rolling).

Sully's. In the County Hotel, High St. ☎ **01227/766266.** Reservations recommended. Fixed-price lunch £17 ($27.20) for 2 courses, £18 ($28.80) for 3 courses; set dinner £21–£27.50 ($33.60–$44). AE, DC, MC, V. Daily 12:30–2:20pm and 7–10pm. ENGLISH/CONTINENTAL.

The most distinguished restaurant in Canterbury is located in its most distinguished hotel. Although the place is without windows and the decor is a bit dated (ca. 1965), the seating and comfort level are first-rate. Considering the quality of the ingredients, the menu offers good value. You can always count on a selection of plain, traditional English dishes, but try one of the more imaginatively conceived platters instead. A typical menu might begin with fresh rock oysters glazed with a lime sabayon and follow with a roast from the carving trolley, perhaps a fillet of pork with rösti (hash-brown potatoes) and a Madeira sauce. We recommend the boned Dover sole with a white-wine-and-chive sauce or pot-roasted guinea fowl served with a puree of parsnip.

Tuo e Mio. 16 The Borough. ☎ **01227/761471.** Reservations recommended, especially at lunch; call ☎ 01227/472362. Main courses £7.70–£13.50 ($12.30–$21.60); fixed-price lunch £13.50 ($21.60). AE, DC, MC, V. Tues 7–10:45pm, Wed–Sun noon–2:30pm and 7–10:45pm. Closed Mon, the last 2 weeks in Aug, and the last 2 weeks in Feb. ITALIAN.

Tuo e Mio is a bastion of zesty Italian cookery. Signor R. P. M. Greggio, known locally as "Raphael," sets the style and plans the menu at his casual and long-standing bistro. Some dishes are standard, including the pastas, beef, and veal found on most Italian menus, but the daily specials have a certain flair, based on the freshest ingredients available on any given day. Try the fish dishes, including skate, which is regularly featured. A selection of reasonably priced Italian wines accompanies your meal. The white-walled dining room has time-blackened ceiling beams.

CANTERBURY AFTER DARK

The **Gulbenkian Theatre,** University of Kent, Giles Lane (☎ 01227/769075), is open during school terms (except Cricket Week, the first week in August) and offers a potpourri of jazz and classical productions, dance, drama, comedy, and a mix of new and student productions. Check newspapers for schedules; tickets cost £5 to £12 ($8 to $19.20).

The **Marlowe,** The Friars (☎ 01227/787787), is Canterbury's only commercial playhouse. It's open year-round and offers drama, jazz and classical concerts, and contemporary and classical ballet. Tickets cost from £10 to £12 ($16 to $19.20).

The **Penny Theatre,** 30-31 Northgate (☎ 01227/470512), with a cover charge of £2 to £6 ($3.20 to $9.60), is a locally well-regarded spot for an eclectic mix of live music—everything from jazz and reggae to indie rock. The music plays every day, except Sunday, from noon to midnight, and the bands are well known, both locally and internationally.

A favorite local pub, **Alberry's Wine & Food Bar,** 38A St. Margaret's St. (☎ 01227/452378), offers live music, mostly jazz, played by local and student groups. In winter, there's a gig at least once a month; in summer, acts play several times a week. Cover charges depend on the group. The menu offers affordable daily specials and light snacks at lunch and dinner.

A laid-back student hangout, **The Cherry Tree,** 10 White Horse Lane (☎ 01227/451266), offers a wide selection of beers, including Bass Ale on draft, Cherry Tree ale, three traditional lagers, and four bitters. The atmosphere is clubby, filled with casual conversation. If you visit for lunch, you'll find a 32-item menu—the best pub menu in town—plus three types of ploughman's lunch.

Another good choice on your Canterbury pub crawl is **The Flying Horse,** 1 Dover St. (☎ 01227/463803), which attracts a garrulous mix of young and old. This 16th-century pub bridges generations with oldsters and the hip student crowd. A weekly quiz night stirs the conversation.

2 The White Cliffs of Dover

76 miles SE of London; 84 miles NE of Brighton

In Victoria's day, Dover basked in popularity as a seaside resort, but today it's known as a port for cross-Channel car and passenger traffic between England and France (notably Calais). Dover was one of England's most vulnerable and easy-to-hit targets during World War II; repeated bombings destroyed much of its harbor. Dover has become more important since the opening of the Channel Tunnel (Chunnel) in 1994.

Unless you're on your way to France or want to use Dover as a base for exploring the surrounding countryside, you can skip a visit here. Dover has always been rather dull except for those white cliffs. Even its hotels are second-rate; many people prefer to stay in Folkestone, about 10 miles to the southwest.

ESSENTIALS

GETTING THERE   Frequent trains run between Victoria Station or Charing Cross Station in London and Dover daily from 5am to 10pm. You arrive in Dover at Priory Station, off Folkestone Road. During the day, two trains per hour depart Canterbury

East Station heading for Dover. For rail information, call ☎ **0345/484950** in the U.K., or 01603/764776 in the U.S.

Frequent buses leave throughout the day—daily 7:30am to 11pm—from London's Victoria Coach Station bound for Dover. Call ☎ **0990/808080** for schedules. The local bus station is on Pencester Road (☎ **01304/240024**). Stagecoach East Kent provides daily bus service between Canterbury and Dover.

If you're driving from London, head first to Canterbury (see above), then continue along A2 southeast until you reach Dover, on the coast.

VISITOR INFORMATION The **Tourist Information Centre** is on Townwall Street (☎ **01304/205108**). It's open daily from 9am to 6pm.

EXPLORING DOVER

You'll get your best view of the famous ✪ **white cliffs** if you're arriving at Dover by ferry or hovercraft from Calais. Otherwise, you could walk out to the end of the town's Prince of Wales pier, the largest of the town's western docks. The cliffs loom above you. Or you could drive 5 miles east of Dover to the pebble-covered beaches of the fishing hamlet of Deal. Here, a local fisher might take you on an informal boat ride.

Dover Castle. Castle Hill. ☎ **01304/211067** or 01304/201628. Admission £7 ($11.20) adults, £3.50 ($5.60) children under 16, £5.50 ($8.80) seniors and students, £17.50 ($28) family. Apr–Oct daily 10am–6pm (last tour at 5pm); Nov–Mar daily 10am–4pm (last tour at 3pm). Bus: no. 90 bound for Deal.

Rising nearly 400 feet above the port is one of the oldest and best-known castles in England. Its keep was built at the command of Becket's fair-weather friend, Henry II, in the 12th century. The ancient castle was called back to active duty as late as World War II. The "Pharos" on the grounds is a lighthouse built by the Romans in the first half of the 1st century. The Romans first landed at nearby Deal in 54 B.C., but after 6 months they departed and didn't return until nearly 100 years later, in A.D. 43, when they stayed and occupied the country for 400 years. The castle houses a military museum and a film center, plus "Live and Let's Spy," an exhibition of World War II spying equipment.

Secret War Time Tunnels. Dover Castle, Castle Hill. ☎ **01304/211067** or 01304/201628. Admission free with castle admission. Open same days and hours as the castle. Last tour leaves 1 hr. before castle closing time. Bus: no. 90 bound for Deal.

These secret tunnels, used during the evacuation of Dunkirk in 1940 and the Battle of Britain, can now be explored on a guided tour. The tunnels were originally excavated to house cannons to be used (if necessary) against an invasion by Napoléon. Some 200 feet belowground, they were the headquarters of Operation Dynamo, when more than 300,000 troops from Dunkirk were evacuated. Once forbidden ground to all but those with the strongest security clearance, the networks of tunnels can now be toured. You can stand in the very room where Ramsey issued orders; experience the trauma of life in an underground operating theater; and look out over the English Channel from the hidden, cliff-top balcony, just as Churchill did during the Battle of Britain.

✪ **Roman Painted House.** New St. ☎ **01304/203279.** Admission £2 ($3.20) adults, 80p ($1.30) children 15 and under. Apr–Sept Tues–Sun 10am–5:30pm.

This 1,800-year-old Roman structure, called Britain's "buried Pompeii," has exceptionally well preserved walls and an under-floor heating system. It's famous for its unique bacchic murals and has won four national awards for presentation. Brass-rubbing is also offered. You'll find it in the town center near Market Square.

Deal Castle. On the seafront. ☎ **01304/372762.** Admission £2.80 ($4.50) adults, £2.10 ($3.35) seniors, £1.40 ($2.25) children. Apr–Sept daily 10am–6pm; Oct–Mar Wed–Sun 10am–4pm.

Deal Castle is just a mile north of Walmer Castle and is a quarter mile south of the Deal town center, 5 miles from Dover. A defensive fort built around 1540, it's the most spectacular example of the low, squat forts constructed by Henry VIII. Its 119 gun positions made it the most powerful of his defense forts. Centered around a circular keep surrounded by two rings of semicircle bastions, the castle was protected by an outer moat. The entrance was approached by a drawbridge with a portcullis. The castle was damaged by bombs during World War II but has been restored to its early form. A free videotape of the castle is included in the admission charge.

WHERE TO STAY
The Churchill. Waterloo Crescent, Dover, Kent CT17 9BP. ☎ **01304/203633.** Fax 01304/216320. 68 units. TV TEL. £75 ($120) double; £90 ($144) triple or quad. AE, DC, MC, V.

Dover's most consistently reliable hotel is composed of an interconnected row of town houses built to overlook the English Channel in the 1830s. After World War I, the premises were transformed into a hotel, and in 1994 it was completely refurbished after being acquired by the Henley Lodge hotel chain. There's a rambling seafront balcony, a glass-enclosed front veranda, and rooms that are comfortable and tranquil, each with beverage-maker. The restaurant, Winston's, serves an international menu at lunch and dinner daily. The hotel lies close to the eastern and western docks and the Hoverport for travel to and from France and Belgium.

The County Hotel. Townwall St., Dover, Kent CT16 1SZ. ☎ **01304/509955.** Fax 01304/213230. 79 units. TV TEL. £74.50–£95 ($119.20–$152) double. AE, DC, MC, V. Parking £3.50 ($5.60).

In the center of town, just a few minutes away from the train station, the seafront, and the international ferry terminal and Hoverport, this hotel is a bit dull but features rooms with queen-size beds, in-house movies, hair dryers, and beverage-makers. On the premises are an indoor heated swimming pool and Braid's Restaurant, with a carvery and salad bar, plus coffee-shop facilities and an English-style bar. Room service from 7am to 10pm, laundry, and fax services are available.

Wallett's Court. West Cliffe, St. Margaret's at Cliffe, Dover, Kent CT15 6EW. ☎ **01304/852424.** Fax 01304/853430. 14 units. TV TEL. £65–£120 ($104–$192) double. Rates include breakfast. AE, DC, MC, V. Closed 2 weeks at Christmas. Follow A258 for 1½ miles east from the center of Dover (signposted Deal). Wallett's Court is signposted off the A258.

Surrounded by fields and gardens, within a tiny hamlet that's 1½ miles east of Dover, this property was rebuilt in the Jacobean style in the 1400s, on a foundation that dated from the time of the Norman conquest of England. Since then, it has belonged to or has been lived in by Bishop Odo of Bayeux, Queen Eleanor of Castile, Edward Gibbon, William Pitt, and various admirals of the British navy. In 1975, in seriously dilapidated condition, it was bought and restored by members of the Oakley family. The setting, near clifftops overlooking the English Channel, is savored by bird watchers and hill climbers. Each of the carefully restored bedrooms feature a different decorative theme, with the more expensive ones containing four-poster beds. Some lie within a barn that was comfortably converted into living quarters. Richly accessorized, each has a vivid Edwardian country house motif and lots of mementos. There's a restaurant on the premises that's separately recommended in "Where to Dine," below, with breakfasts that feature all the wholesomeness of local eggs, bacon, and bread.

WHERE TO DINE

Britannia. 41 Townwall St. ☎ **01304/203248.** Main courses £5.50–£10.95 ($8.80–$17.50). MC, V. Restaurant daily noon–2:30pm and 5:30–10pm. Pub Mon–Sat 11am–11pm, Sun noon–10:30pm. INTERNATIONAL.

If you gravitate to typically English, pub-style meals, try this restaurant, whose windows overlook the ferry terminal and the many ships arriving from Calais and Boulogne. Its well-maintained facade has a bow window with lots of gilt and brass nautical accents. The popular pub is on the ground floor and the restaurant on the upper level. The fare is very standard, typical of what you'd get if you stopped to eat along a motorway in England. Try a prawn cocktail or a pâté to start, followed by rump steak or a mixed grill. There's a selection of vegetarian dishes. Dover sole is a specialty, available at market prices. Three TVs in the pub will keep sports fans at bay.

Topo Gigio. 1-2 King St. ☎ **01304/201048.** Reservations recommended. Pizzas £4–£6.35 ($6.40–$10.15); main courses £5.75–£14 ($9.20–$22.40). AE, DC, MC, V. Winter daily noon–2:30pm; Mon–Thurs 6:30–10:30pm, Fri–Sat 6:30–11pm. Summer daily noon–10:30pm. ITALIAN.

Established by an Italian entrepreneur from Vicenza, this restaurant was named after the most famous cartoon character in Italy, Topo Gigio, a Mickey Mouse look-alike. Located a short walk from Dover's market square, in a setting accented with brick arches and a wood-burning pizza oven, it serves 15 types of pastas, 16 types of pizzas, and steak, chicken, veal, and fish dishes prepared Italian-style or any way you request. The restaurant's staff and clientele tend to be animated and energetic, which makes an outing here lighthearted and fun. The food's not gourmet, but it's satisfying and filling.

Wallett's Court. West Cliffe, St. Margaret's at Cliffe. ☎ **01304/852424.** Reservations recommended. Main courses £15–£23 ($24–$36.80); three-course fixed-price dinner £23.50 ($37.60). AE, DC, MC, V. Daily 7–10pm. Closed 2 weeks at Christmas. BRITISH/INTERNATIONAL.

One of the most appealing restaurants in the district lies within a half-timbered Jacobean-era manor house, grandly restored over 15 years by Chris Oakley and his family. Within a dining room that's exemplary for its carved beams and sense of history, you can enjoy dishes such as leek and potato soup, a Kentish huntsman's platter (terrine of game served with apple jelly), salmon with a champagne and shallot sauce; fricassee of monkfish with a lobster-flavored shrimp sauce; or Scottish Angus beef with a wine and tarragon sauce. The menu changes every month, but meals are always relatively formal, well-prepared, and in most cases, very appealing.

3 The Ancient Seaport of Rye

62 miles SE of London

"Nothing more recent than a Cavalier's Cloak, Hat and Ruffles should be seen in the streets of Rye," said Louis Jennings. This ancient town, formerly an island, flourished in the 13th century. In its early days, Rye was a smuggling center, its residents sneaking in contraband from the marshes to stash away in little nooks.

But the sea receded from Rye, leaving it perched like a giant whale out of water, 2 miles from the Channel. Attacked several times by French fleets, Rye was practically razed in 1377. But it rebuilt itself successfully, in full Elizabethan panoply. When Queen Elizabeth I visited in 1573, she was so impressed that she bestowed upon the town the distinction of Royal Rye. This has long been considered a special place and over the years has attracted famous people, such as novelist Henry James.

Its narrow cobblestone streets twist and turn like a labyrinth, and jumbled along them are buildings whose sagging roofs and crooked chimneys indicate the town's medieval origins. The town overflows with sites of architectural interest.

Neighboring Winchelsea has also witnessed the water's ebb. It traces its history from Edward I and has experienced many dramatic moments, such as sacking by the French. In the words of one 19th-century writer, Winchelsea is "a sunny dream of centuries ago." The finest sight of this dignified residential town is a badly damaged 14th-century church containing a number of remarkable tombs.

ESSENTIALS

GETTING THERE   From London, the Southern Region Line offers trains south from Charing Cross or Cannon Street Station, with a change at Ashford, before continuing on to Rye. You can also go via Tunbridge Wells with a change in Hastings. Trains run every hour during the day, arriving at the Rye Train Station off Cinque Ports Street. The trip takes 1½ to 2 hours. Call ☎ **01424/429325** for schedules and information.

You need to take the train to get to Rye, but once you're here you'll find buses departing every hour on the hour for many destinations, including Hastings. Various bus schedules are posted on signs in the parking lot. For bus information on connections in the surrounding area, call ☎ **0891/910910.**

If you're driving from London, take M25, M26, and M20 east to Maidstone, going southeast along A20 to Ashford. At Ashford, continue south on A2070.

VISITOR INFORMATION   The **Rye Tourist Office** is in the Heritage Centre on the Strand Quay (☎ **01797/226696**). It's open daily from mid-March to the end of October from 9am to 5:30pm; November until mid-March, weekdays from 10am to 3pm and Saturday and Sunday from 10am to 4pm. The Heritage Centre houses a free exhibition and is also home to Rye Town Model, a sound-and-light show depicting more than 700 years of Rye's history. Adults pay £2 ($3.20), seniors and students £1.50 ($2.40), and children £1 ($1.60).

EXPLORING THE AREA

In Rye, the old town's entrance is **Land Gate,** where a single lane of traffic passes between massive, 40-foot-high stone towers. The parapet of the gate has holes through which boiling oil used to be poured on unwelcome visitors, such as French raiding parties.

Rye has had potteries for centuries and today is no exception, with a number of outlets in town. The best potteries include the **Rye Pottery,** Ferry Road (☎ **01797/223038**); **Rye Tiles,** Wishward Street (☎ **01797/223038**); **David Sharp Ceramics,** The Mint (☎ **01797/222620**); **Iden Pottery,** Conduit Hill (☎ **01797/226920**); and the **Cinque Ports Pottery,** Conduit Hill (☎ **01797/222033**), where you can see the potters at work during the week. The town also abounds in antique and collectible shops and new and used bookstores.

St. Mary's Parish Church. Church Square. ☎ **01797/224935.** Admission to tower £2 ($3.20) adults, £1 ($1.60) children. Contributions appreciated to enter the church. June–Aug daily 9am–7pm; off-season daily 9am–4pm.

One notable historical site is the mid-12th-century with its 16th-century clock flanked by two gilded cherubs (known as Quarter Boys because of their striking of the bells on the quarter hour). The church is often referred to as "the Cathedral of East Sussex" because of its expansive size and ornate beauty. If you're brave, you can climb a set of wooden stairs and ladders to the bell tower of the church for an impressive view.

Lamb House. West St. (at the top of Mermaid St.). ☎ **01797/224982.** Admission £2.50 ($4) adults, £1.25 ($2) children. Wed and Sat 2–6pm. Closed Nov–Mar.

Henry James lived at Lamb House from 1898 to 1916. Many James mementos are scattered throughout the house, which is set in a walled garden. Its previous owner rushed off to join the gold rush in North America but perished in the Klondike, and James was able to buy the freehold for a modest £2,000 ($3,200). Some of his well-known books were written here. In *English Hours,* James wrote: "There is not much room in the pavilion, but there is room for the hard-pressed table and tilted chair—there is room for a novelist and his friends."

Rye Castle Museum. Gungarden. ☎ **01797/226728.** Admission £1.50 ($2.40) adults, £1 ($1.60) students and senior citizens, 50p (80¢) children. Apr–Oct daily 10:30am–5:30pm; Nov–Mar Sat–Sun 10:30am–4pm.

This stone fortification was constructed around 1250 by King Henry III to defend the coast against attack by the French. For 300 years it was the town jail but has long since been converted into a museum. In 1996, the Medieval Tower was restored.

Smallhythe Place. Smallhythe (on B2082 near Tenterden, about 6 miles north of Rye). ☎ **01580/762334.** Admission £3 ($4.80) adults; £1.50 ($2.40) children; £7.50 ($12) family ticket. Apr–Oct Sat–Wed 1–5:30pm. Take bus no. 312 from Tenterden or Rye.

On the outskirts of Winchelsea, this was for 30 years the country house of Dame Ellen Terry, the English actress acclaimed for her Shakespearean roles, and who had a long theatrical association with Sir Henry Irving; she died in the house in 1928. This timber-framed structure, known as a "continuous-jetty house," was built in the first half of the 16th century and is filled with Terry memorabilia—playbills, props, makeup, and a striking display of costumes. An Elizabethan barn, adapted as a theater in 1929, is open to view on most days.

WHERE TO STAY

Some of the best rooms in Rye are at the Benson Hotel on East Street; see "Where to Dine," below for a review of its restaurant.

Durrant House Hotel. Market St. (off High St.), Rye, E. Sussex TN31 3LA. ☎ **01797/223182.** 17 units, 9 with washbasins, 8 with shower. TV. £45 ($72) double without shower, £58 ($92.80) double with shower; £80 ($128) suite. Rates include English breakfast. MC, V.

This beautiful Georgian house is set on a quiet residential street at the end of Market Street. The hotel's charm and character are enhanced by a cozy lounge with an arched, brick fireplace and, across the hall, a residents' bar. The renowned artist Paul Nash lived next door until his death in 1946; in fact, his celebrated view, as seen in his painting *View of the Rother,* can be enjoyed from the River Room, a four-poster bedroom suite. At one time the house was used as a relay station for carrier pigeons; these birds brought news of the victory at Waterloo.

The George. High St., Rye, E. Sussex TN31 7JP. ☎ **01797/222114.** Fax 01797/224065. 22 units. TV TEL. Mon–Thurs £95 ($152) double. Fri–Sun (minimum of 2 nights required) £65 ($104) per person daily, including full board. AE, DC, MC, V.

This coaching inn has a long history dating from 1575. In the 18th century it drew a diverse clientele: some traveling by horse-drawn carriage, others by boat between London and France. The half-timbered architecture charms a visitor like no other small inn in the region (except the Mermaid, which has even more of an antique atmosphere). Some of the timbers may be from the wreck of an English ship broken up in Rye Harbour after the defeat of the Spanish Armada. Bedrooms are snug and cozy, furnished with traditional English country-house styling. The Georgian ball-room is complete with a minstrel's gallery. The hotel's two blazing fireplaces warm chilled winter visitors. You can enjoy moderately priced meals in its old-fashioned restaurant.

Hope Anchor Hotel. Watchbell St., Rye, E. Sussex TN31 7HA. ☎ **01797/222216.** Fax 01797/223796. 13 units, 7 with bathroom. TV. £25 ($40) double without bathroom, £60 ($96) double with bathroom. Rates include English breakfast. MC, V.

At the end of a cobblestone street, on a hill dominating the town, stands this 17th-century hostelry, which enjoys panoramic views of the surrounding countryside and overlooks the Strand Quay, where impressive yachts can be seen at their moorings. Oak beams and open fires in winter make this a most inviting place to spend a few days. The comfortable bedrooms all have beverage-makers; two feature four-poster beds and have recently been refurbished.

Bar meals are served at lunch and in the evening, and the Hope Anchor Restaurant serves a standard English cuisine, featuring fresh fish caught locally.

✪ Mermaid Inn. Mermaid St. (between West St. and The Strand), Rye, E. Sussex TN31 7EU. ☎ **01797/223065.** Fax 01797/225069. 31 units, 29 with private bathroom. TV TEL. £100–£120 ($160–$192) double. Rates include English breakfast. AE, DC, MC, V.

When Elizabeth came to Rye and the Mermaid in 1573, the inn had already been operating for nearly 150 years. The Mermaid Inn is one of the most famous of the old smugglers' inns of England, known to that band of cut-throats, the real-life Hawkhurst Gang, as well as to Russell Thorndike's fictional character, Dr. Syn. (One of the present rooms, in fact, is called Dr. Syn's Bedchamber, and is connected by a secret staircase, stowed away in the thickness of the wall, to the bar.) This place remains one of the most romantic, old-world inns in Sussex, with its Elizabethan asso-ciations and its traditional touches. A covered carriageway leads to the parking area. In the center of the hotel is a courtyard, with a pedestal fountain with water flowing down onto water lilies. The most sought-after rooms are in the building overlooking the cobblestone street. Five units have four-poster beds.

Dining: The hotel restaurants specialize in attractively priced, fresh food—freshly caught local fish, Marsh lamb, Sussex beef, and an abundance of locally grown veg-etables. Traditional beers are also on tap.

White Vine House. High St., Rye, E. Sussex TN31 7JF. ☎ **01797/224748.** 6 units. TV. £64–£110 ($102.40–$176) double. 2-night booking required on weekends. Rates include English breakfast. AE, DC, MC, V.

Winner of several awards for the beauty of its small front garden and the quality of its restoration, this charming house was originally built in 1568. Restored from an almost derelict shell in 1987 and recently refurbished by its new owners, the creeper-clad inn carefully maintains the Georgian detailing of the formal public rooms and the Tudor-style wall and ceiling beams of the antique bedrooms.

Dining: An in-house restaurant, strictly for nonsmokers, serves reasonably priced dinners. The cuisine is healthy and home-styled, with a reduced-fat content. Every-thing is prepared from the finest local ingredients, from meat to dairy. Even the fish, when possible, comes from Rye boats.

WHERE TO DINE

Our preferred spot for teatime is the **Swan Cottage Team Rooms,** 41 The Mint, High St. (☎ 01797/222423), dating from 1420 and situated on the main street. This black and white half-timbered building is one of the most historic in town. We gravitate to the room in the rear because of its big brick fireplace. Delectable pastries and freshly made cakes await you along with a selection of teas, including Darjeeling, Earl Grey, Pure Assam, and others.

Benson Hotel Restaurant. East St., ☎ **01797/225131.** Fax 01797/22512. Reservations recommended on weekends. Main courses £15–£20 ($24–$32). MC, V. Daily 7–9pm. Closed 2 weeks in Nov. FRENCH/INTERNATIONAL.

Once the Georgian vicarage for St. Mary's Church, this charming spot off High Street was converted into a French-style *restaurant avec chambres* in 1979. Although the owners, Sarah and Bill Foster, maintain four beautifully decorated rooms upstairs, they're best known for their elegant restaurant. Guests are seated near a carved fireplace, they enjoy classic French and international dishes. The menu changes monthly to make the most of local fish and meat. A typical menu might include homemade onion soup, fish bisque, puff pastry stuffed with pine nuts and spinach with a homemade tomato sauce, or steak-and-mushroom pie, followed by unusual homemade desserts.

The rooms, with breakfast included, are £35 to £42 ($56 to $67.20) daily per person. Units feature private baths, TVs, phones, and a carefully assembled kind of panache.

✪ Flushing Inn. 4–5 Market St., ☎ **01797/223292.** Reservations required. Fixed-price meal from £14.50 ($23.20) at lunch, from £25.50 ($40.80) at dinner AF, DC, MC, V. Wed–Mon noon–2pm; Wed–Sun 6:45–9pm. Closed 1st 2 weeks in Jan. SEAFOOD/ENGLISH.

This is the best restaurant in Rye. In a 16th-century inn on a cobblestone street near Rye Parish Church, the Flushing Inn has preserved the finest of the past, including a wall-size fresco dating from 1544 that depicts a menagerie of birds and heraldic beasts. A rear dining room overlooks a flower garden. A special feature is the Sea Food Lounge Bar, where sandwiches and plates of seafood are available.

You'll begin with the justifiably praised hors d'oeuvres—a fine selection of smoked fish and shellfish. Main dishes might range from locally caught Rye Bay plaice to an old-fashioned loin of English lamb prepared with honey and lavender or scented with rosemary.

Besides these lunches and dinners, gastronomic evenings are held at regular intervals between October and April. One of these specialty meals costs £50 ($80) per person, including your aperitif, wine, and after-dinner brandy. Fine-wine evenings cost £50 to £70 ($80 to $112) per person. The property next door was recently acquired by the Flushing Inn and seats more diners.

In addition, the owners have constructed a luxurious accommodation known as the John Lester Suite within the 15th-century building. It costs £170 ($272) for two persons per night, which includes dinner and a full English champagne breakfast.

The Landgate Bistro. 5-6 Landgate. ☎ **01797/222829.** Reservations required on weekends. Main courses £9–£14 ($14.40–$22.40); fixed-price menu (Tues–Thurs) £15.90 ($25.45). AE, DC, MC, V. Tues–Fri 7–9:30pm, Sat 7–10pm (closing time may vary). MODERN BRITISH.

People come from miles around to dine in this pair of interconnected Georgian shops whose exteriors are covered with "mathematical tiles" (18th-century simulated brick, applied over stucco facades to save money). Inside, Toni Ferguson-Lees and her partner, Nick Parkin, offer savory modern British cuisine that changes with the seasons. Skillfully prepared dishes might include braised squid with white wine, tomatoes, and garlic; grilled Dover sole; and noisettes of English lamb with tomato-basil sauce.

4 1066 & All That: Hastings & Battle

Hastings: 45 miles SW of Dover; 63 miles SE of London
Battle: 34 miles NE of Brighton; 55 miles SE of London

The world has seen bigger skirmishes, but few are as well remembered as the Battle of Hastings in 1066. When William, duke of Normandy, landed on the Sussex coast and lured King Harold (already fighting Vikings in Yorkshire) southward to defeat, the destiny of the English-speaking people was changed forever.

The actual battle occurred at what is now Battle Abbey (8 miles away), but the Norman duke used Hastings as his base of operations. You can visit the abbey, and then have a cup of tea in Battle's main square, and then you can be off, as the rich countryside of Sussex is much more intriguing than this sleepy market town.

Hastings today is a little seedy and run-down. If you're seeking an English seaside resort, head for Brighton instead.

ESSENTIALS

GETTING THERE   Daily trains run hourly from London's Victoria Station or Charing Cross to Hastings. The trip takes 1½ to 2 hours. The train station at Battle is a stop on the London-Hastings rail link. For rail information, call ☎ **0345/484950** in the U.K., or 01603/764776 in the U.S.

Hastings is linked by bus to Maidstone, Folkestone, and Eastbourne, which has direct service with scheduled departures. **National Express** operates regular daily service from London's Victoria Coach Station. If you're in Rye or Hastings in summer, several frequent buses run to Battle. For information and schedules, call ☎ **0990/808080.**

If you're driving from the M25 ring road around London, head southeast to the coast and Hastings on A21. To get to Battle, cut south to Sevenoaks and continue along A21 to Battle via A2100.

VISITOR INFORMATION   In Hastings, the **Hastings Information Centre** is at Queen's Square, Priory Meadow (☎ **01424/781111**). It's open Monday through Friday from 10am to 5pm and on Saturday from 10am to 1pm and 2 to 5pm.

In Battle, the **Tourist Information Centre** is at 88 High St. (☎ **01424/773721**), and is open April through September daily from 10am to 6pm; off-season, Monday through Saturday from 10am to 4pm and on Sunday from 1 to 4pm.

EXPLORING THE HISTORIC SITES

Battle Abbey. At the south end of Battle High St. (a 5-minute walk from the train station). ☎ **01424/773792.** Admission £4 ($6.40) adults, £2 ($3.20) children, £3 ($4.80) seniors and students. Apr–Sept daily 10am–6pm; Oct–Mar daily 10am–4pm.

King Harold, last of the Saxon kings, fought bravely here, not only for his kingdom but for his life. As legend has it, he was killed by an arrow through the eye, and his body was dismembered. To commemorate the victory, William the Conqueror founded Battle Abbey; some of the construction stone was shipped from his own lands at Caen in northern France.

During the Dissolution of the Monasteries from 1538 to 1539 by King Henry VIII, the church of the abbey was largely destroyed. Some buildings and ruins, however, remain in what Tennyson called "O Garden, blossoming out of English blood." The principal building still standing is the Abbot's House, which is leased to a private school for boys and girls and is open to the general public only during summer holidays. Of architectural interest is the gatehouse, which has octagonal towers and stands at the top of Market Square. All of the north Precinct Mall is still standing, and one of the most interesting sights of the ruins is the ancient Dorter Range, where the monks once slept.

The town of Battle flourished around the abbey; even though it has remained a medieval market town, many of the old half-timbered buildings have regrettably lost much of their original character because of stucco plastering carried out by past generations.

Insider's tip: This is a great place for the kids. There's not only a themed play area here, but at the gate a daily activity sheet is distributed. You can relax with a picnic or stroll in the parkland that once formed the monastery grounds.

✪ **Hastings Castle.** Castle Hill Rd., West Hill. ☎ 01424/781112. Admission £2.90 ($4.65) adults, £2.30 ($3.70) seniors and students, £1.90 ($3.05) children. Easter–Sept daily 10am–5pm; Oct–Easter daily 11am–3:30pm. Take the West Hill Cliff Railway from George St. to the castle for 70p ($1.10), 40p (65¢) for children.

In ruins now, the first of the Norman castles built in England sprouted on a western hill overlooking Hastings, around 1067. Precious little is left to remind us of the days when proud knights, imbued with a spirit of pomp and spectacle, wore bonnets and girdles. The fortress was defortified by King John in 1216 and was later used as a church. Owned by the Pelham dynasty from the latter 16th century to modern times, the ruins have been turned over to Hastings. There is now an audiovisual presentation of the castle's history, including the famous battle of 1066. From the mount, you'll have a good view of the coast and promenade.

✪ **The Hastings Embroidery.** The Sussex Hall, White Rock Theatre, White Rock Rd. ☎ 01424/781111. Admission £1.50 ($2.40) adults, £1 ($1.60) children and senior citizens. May–Sept Mon–Fri 10am–4:30pm; Oct–Apr Mon–Fri 11:30am–3pm.

A commemorative work, the Hastings Embroidery is a remarkable achievement that traces 900 years of English history through needlework. First exhibited in 1966, the 27 panels, 243 feet in length, depict 81 historic scenes, including some of the nation's greatest moments and legends: the murder of Thomas à Becket, King John signing the Magna Carta, the Black Plague, Chaucer's pilgrims going to Canterbury, the Battle of Agincourt with the victorious Henry V, the War of the Roses, the Little Princess in the Tower, Bloody Mary's reign, Drake's *Golden Hind,* the arrival of Philip II's ill-fated armada, Guy Fawkes's Gunpowder Plot, the sailing of the *Mayflower,* the disastrous plague of 1665, the great London fire of 1666, Nelson at Trafalgar, the Battle of Waterloo, the Battle of Britain, and the D-day landings at Normandy. Also exhibited is a scale model of the battlefield at Battle, with William's inch-high men doing-in Harold's model soldiers.

SEASIDE AMUSEMENTS

Linked by a 3-mile promenade along the sea, Hastings and St. Leonards were given a considerable boost in the 19th century by Queen Victoria, who visited several times. Neither town enjoys such royal patronage today; rather, they do a thriving business with English families on vacation. Hastings and St. Leonards have the usual shops and English sea-resort amusements.

Smugglers Adventure. St. Clements Caves, West Hill. ☎ 01424/422964. Admission £4.40 ($7.05) adults, £2.70 ($4.30) children, £12.95 ($20.70) family. Apr–Sept daily 10am–5:30pm; Oct–Mar daily 11am–4:30pm. Take the West Cliff Railway from George St. to West Hill for 70p ($1.10) adults, 40p (65¢) for children.

Here you can descend into the once-secret underground haunts of the smugglers of Hastings. In these chambers, where the smugglers stashed their booty away from customs authorities, you can see an exhibition and museum, a video in a theater, and take a subterranean adventure walk with 50 life-size figures, along with dramatic sound and lighting effects.

WHERE TO STAY
IN HASTINGS

Beauport Park Hotel. Battle Rd. (A2100), Hastings, E. Sussex TN38 8EA. ☎ 01424/851222. Fax 01424/852465. 23 units. TV TEL. £100–£110 ($160–$176) double; £130 ($208) suite. Rates include English breakfast. AE, DC, MC, V. Bus: 4 or 5 from Hastings. Head 3½ miles northwest of Hastings, to the junction of A2100 and B2159.

This hotel has a cozy country-house aura, and is more intimate and hospitable than The Royal Victoria (reviewed below). Originally the private estate of General Murray, former governor of Québec, the building was destroyed by fire in 1923 and rebuilt in the old style. It's surrounded by beautiful gardens; the Italian-style grounds in the rear feature statuary and flowering shrubbery. The self-contained Forest Lodge is equipped with a double, twin, children's room, living area, and kitchen, and is available for £130 ($208).

Dining: The hotel offers well-prepared and handsomely arranged meals. Some of the produce comes from the hotel's own gardens. There's a fixed-price lunch and dinner.

Amenities: The parklike grounds offer an outdoor pool, putting green, and tennis, badminton, and croquet.

The Royal Victoria. Marina, St. Leonards, Hastings, E. Sussex TN38 OBD. ☎ 01424/ 445544. Fax 01424/721995. 50 units. TV TEL. £89 ($142.40) double. Children 15 and under stay free in parents' room. Rates include English breakfast. AE, DC, MC, V.

This seafront hotel, constructed in 1828, has the most impressive architecture in town and offers the best accommodations in Hastings or St. Leonards. It has welcomed many famous visitors, including its namesake, Queen Victoria herself. It's attractively furnished and decorated. Many of the elegant and comfortably appointed rooms have separate lounge areas and views of the English Channel and Beachy Head.

Dining: The hotel restaurant serves a fine cuisine; even if you're not staying here, reserve a table. Bar snacks are served from Monday to Saturday. Both traditional and international cuisine are offered, and the all-you-can-eat Sunday carvery is well attended, with its choice of succulent English roasts.

IN BATTLE

The George Hotel. 23 High St., Battle, E. Sussex TN33 OEA. ☎ 01424/774466. Fax 01424/774853. 20 units. TV TEL. Mon–Thurs £65 ($104) double, Fri–Sun £28 ($44.80) per person double. Rates include breakfast. AE, DC, MC, V.

Although there has been some kind of inn on this site for more than 600 years, the hotel that stands here today dates from 1739. Much renovated since then, the George combines modern comfort with a historic building. The owners offer well-furnished, although rather nondescript, rooms with hot-beverage facilities. The hotel has a comfortable bar, with a full menu. Open log fires make the place cozy in winter.

✪ **Netherfield Place.** Netherfield Rd., Battle, E. Sussex TN33 9PU. ☎ 800/828-5572 in the U.S., or 01424/774455. Fax 01424/774024. 14 units. TV TEL. £115–£160 ($184–$256) double. Rates include English breakfast. AE, DC, MC, V. Closed Dec 15–Jan 15. Take the A2100 1¾ miles northwest of Battle.

Built in 1924 on 30 acres of parkland, this is by far the best place to stay in Battle. The symmetrical wings of this brick-fronted neo-Georgian mansion extend toward flowering gardens on all sides. Once you pass beneath the cornices of the entrance, you'll discover a world of plush upholstery, comfortable bedrooms, and sunny panoramas, as well as a freshly redecorated hall and stairway. The Pomeroy Room, with a four-poster bed, is the most desirable accommodation.

Dining: You can enjoy tea or a drink in the glassed-in lounge overlooking the trees outside. The international cuisine is both good and carefully served, prepared with fresh, wholesome produce. Fresh fruit and vegetables come from the hotel's garden.

WHERE TO DINE

When the wind and rain blow in from the Channel, head for **The Willow Tea Room,** 84 All Saint's St., Old Town in Hastings (☎ 01424/430656), a favorite spot for afternoon tea—one of their Indian, Ceylon, China, or fruit teas, each served with an assortment of sandwiches, scones, chunky jam, fresh cream, or a slice of cake. A full tea with all the trimmings costs £4.50 ($7.20).

Röser's. 64 Eversfield Place, Hastings. ☎ **01424/712218.** Reservations required. Main courses £14.95–£19 ($23.90–$30.40); fixed-price dinner £23.95 ($38.30) Tues–Fri. AE, DC, MC, V. Tues–Fri noon–2pm; Tues–Sat 7–10pm. Closed last 2 weeks in Jan. FRENCH.

This is a pleasant culinary surprise in the gastronomic wasteland of southern England. The restaurant, in a brick-fronted Victorian row house, is a showcase for chef Gerald Röser, the best chef in East Sussex. Menu choices, which change about every 3 weeks, might include seared Scottish scallops with saffron sauce and charcoal-grilled vegetables; fresh, locally caught sea bass served Mediterranean-style with olive oil, lemon juice, and capers; and, in season, wild-boar chop with lentil sauce. Service is first-rate, as is the wine list.

5 Royal Tunbridge Wells

36 miles SE of London; 33 miles NE of Brighton

Dudley Lord North, courtier to James I, is credited with the accidental discovery in 1606 of the mineral spring that led to the creation of a fashionable resort. Over the years, the "Chalybeate Spring" became known for its curative properties and was the answer for everything from too many days of wine and roses to failing sexual prowess. It's still possible to take the waters today.

The spa resort reached its peak in the mid–18th century under the foppish patronage of Beau Nash (1674–1761), a dandy and final arbiter on how to act, what to say, and even what to wear (for example, he got men to remove their boots in favor of stockings). Tunbridge Wells continued to enjoy a prime spa reputation up through the reign of Queen Victoria, who used to vacation here as a child, and in 1909 Tunbridge Wells received its Royal status.

Today the spa is long past its zenith. But the town is a pleasant place to stay—it can be used as a base for exploring the many historic homes in Kent (see below); it's very easy, for example, to tour Sissinghurst and Chartwell from here.

The most remarkable feature of the town itself is **The Pantiles,** a colonnaded walkway for shoppers, tea drinkers, and diners, built near the wells. If you walk around town, you'll see many other interesting and charming spots. Entertainment is presented at the Assembly Hall and Trinity Arts Centre.

ESSENTIALS

GETTING THERE   Two to three trains per hour leave London's Charing Cross Station during the day bound for Hastings, but going via the town center of Royal Tunbridge Wells. The trip takes 50 minutes. For rail information, call ☎ 0345/484950 in the U.K., or 01603/764776 in the U.S.

There are no direct bus links with Gatwick Airport or London. However, there is hourly service during the day between Brighton and Royal Tunbridge Wells (call ☎ 0345/696996 for the bus schedule). You can purchase tickets aboard the bus.

If you're driving from London, after reaching the ring road around London, continue east along M25, cutting southeast at the exit for A21 to Hastings.

VISITOR INFORMATION   The **Tourist Information Centre,** Old Fish Market, The Pantiles (☎ 01892/515675), provides a full accommodations list and offers a room-reservations service. Open from 9am to 5pm Monday through Saturday (9am–6pm in summer), and 10am to 4pm Sunday.

WHERE TO STAY

The Russell. 80 London Rd., Royal Tunbridge Wells, Kent TN1 1DZ. ☎ **01892/544833.** Fax 01892/515846. 24 units. TV TEL. £84 ($134.40) double; £90 ($144) suite. Rates include English breakfast. Discounts usually offered during slow periods. AE, DC, MC, V.

One of the best-recommended hotels at the spa is the Russell, which is composed of three row houses (each built in 1875) that were joined and transformed into a hotel in 1920. Owned and managed by tactful members of the Wilkinson family, the hotel overlooks Tunbridge Wells's Common (central square), a short walk from the main shopping district. Beverage-makers are available in the rooms. The in-house restaurant features mostly regional dishes and boasts an extensive wine list.

The Spa Hotel. Mt. Ephraim, Royal Tunbridge Wells, Kent TN4 8XJ. ☎ **800/528-1234** in the U.S., or 01892/520331. Fax 01892/510575. 74 units. TV TEL. £89–£135 ($142.40–$216) double. Children 13 and under stay free in parents' room. AE, DC, MC, V. From The Pantiles, take Major Yorks Rd.

Standing on 15 acres, this building dates from 1766; once a private home, it was converted to a hotel in 1880, and remains the town's leading hotel to this day. This is the kind of old-fashioned place where many guests check in for long stays. They find bedrooms of various sizes and shapes, as was the custom of buildings like this in the 19th century.

Dining/Diversions: The Chandelier Restaurant serves a combination of English and French cuisine. The hotel's most impressive feature is its large lounge with dark paneling and Corinthian columns, although the Equestrian Bar is a cozier retreat.

Amenities: Beauty salon, dance studio, a half-mile jogging track, a sauna, a solarium, tennis courts, and an indoor swimming pool.

WHERE TO DINE

✪ **Thackeray's House.** 85 London Rd. (at the corner of Mt. Ephraim Rd.). ☎ **01892/ 511921.** Reservations required. Main courses £13.90–£19.85 ($22.25–$31.75); fixed-price midweek dinner (Tues–Thurs) £24.50 ($39.20); 4-course dinner £45 ($72); 2-course lunch £13.50–£19.50 ($21.60–$31.20). MC, V. Tues–Sun noon–2pm; Tues–Sat 7–10pm. ENGLISH/FRENCH.

Thackeray's serves the finest food in town. You get a little history here as well, since this old house was once inhabited by novelist William Makepeace Thackeray, who wrote *Tunbridge Toys* here. The house dates from about 1660. Bruce Wass, the owner-chef, worked at one of our favorite restaurants in London, Odin's, before coming here to set up his own place. He has created an elegant atmosphere, backed by attentive service, for his specialties.

Care goes into all his dishes, and many have flair, including an occasional salad of preserved duck with quail's eggs. He reaches perfection with roast monkfish with saffron, tomatoes, and capers, or peppered fillet of venison with port sauce.

6 Kent's Country Houses, Castles & Gardens

Many of England's finest country houses, castles, and gardens are in Kent. This is where you'll find the palace of Knole, a premier example of English Tudor-style architecture; Hever Castle, once the childhood home of Anne Boleyn, and later the home of William Waldorf Astor; Leeds Castle, a spectacular castle with ties to America; and Penshurst Place, a stately home which was a literary salon of sorts during the first half of the 17th century. It is said to have inspired Ben Jonson to write one of his greatest poems. Kent also has a bevy of homes that once belonged to famous men but have since been turned into intriguing museums, such as Chartwell, where Sir Winston Churchill lived for many years, and Down House, where Charles Darwin wrote his still-controversial book *On the Origin of Species*. Here you can amble down the same path the naturalist trod every evening.

It would take at least a week to see all of these historic properties—more time than most visitors have. When you make your choices, keep in mind that Knole, Hever, Penshurst, Leeds, and Chartwell are the most deserving of your attention.

We have found the guided tours to some of Kent's more popular stately homes too rushed and too expensive to recommend. Each attraction can be toured far more reasonably on your own. Because public transportation into and around Kent can be awkward, we advise driving from London, especially if you plan to visit more than one place in a day. Accordingly, this section is organized as you might drive it from London. However, if it's possible to get to an attraction via public transportation, we've included that information in the individual listings below.

If you only have a day, you might want to confine your time to Chartwell, former home of Winston Churchill; and Knole, one of England's largest private estates with a vast complex of courtyards and buildings.

An entire second day is needed to visit Leeds Castle and Hever Castle. Note that Leeds allows morning visits. (Most castles and country homes in Kent can only be visited in the afternoon.) That means that you can see Leeds in the morning, then tour Hever Castle that afternoon.

If you have more time for castle-hopping, visit Canterbury Cathedral in the morning of your third day (when most castles are closed), then tour Penshurst Place in the afternoon. (See section 1 of this chapter for details on Canterbury.) Penshurst is one of the finest Elizabethan houses in England, and its Baron's Hall is one of the greatest interiors to have survived from the Middle Ages.

Two other notable attractions are Sissinghurst Castle Garden and Ightham Mote, a National Trust property dating from 1340. They are open afternoons during the week, and mornings Saturday and Sunday.

✪ **Chartwell.** Near the town of Edenbridge. ☎ **01732/868381.** Admission to house only £5.20 ($8.30); house and gardens, £7.80 ($12.50). Children enter for half price; family tickets are £13 ($20.80). Wed–Sun 11am–5pm (last admission at 4:40pm). Closed Dec to mid-Apr. If you're driving from London, head east along M25, taking the exit to Westerham. Drive 2 miles south of Westerham on B2026 and follow the signs.

This was the late prime minister's home from 1922 until his death. Although not as grand as his birthplace (Blenheim Palace), Chartwell has preserved its rooms as the Conservative politician left them—maps, documents, photographs, pictures, personal mementos, and all. Two rooms display gifts that the prime minister received from people all over the world. There is also a selection of many of his well-known uniforms, including his famous "siren-suits" and hats. Terraced gardens descend toward the lake, where you'll find black swans swimming. Many of Churchill's paintings are displayed in a garden studio. You can see the garden walls that the prime minister built with his own hands and the pond where he sat to feed the Golden Orfe. A restaurant on the grounds serves from 10:30am to 5pm on days when the house is open.

Québec House. At the junction of Edenbridge and Sevenoaks rds. (A25 and B2026). ☎ **01959/562206.** Admission £2.50 ($4) adults, £1.25 ($2) children. Apr–Oct Sun and Tues only, 3–6pm.

This square, redbrick gabled house was the boyhood home of Gen. James Wolfe, who led the English in their victory over the French in the battle for Québec. Wolfe was born in Westerham on January 2, 1727, and lived here until he was 11 years old. A National Trust property, Québec House contains an exhibition about the capture of Québec and memorabilia associated with the military hero. See, for example, Wolfe's traveling canteen which comes complete with a griddle, frying pans, and decanters, evoking the life of an 18th-century officer on a campaign. At the rear of the walled garden are the former stables, dating from Tudor times.

Squerryes Court. ½ mile west of the center of Westerham (10 minutes from Exit 6 or Exit 5 on the M25). ☎ **01959/562345.** Admission to house and grounds £3.70 ($5.90) adults, £3.40 ($5.45) seniors and students, £1.80 ($2.90) children under 14. Grounds only £2.20 ($3.50) adults, £2 ($3.20) seniors, £1.20 ($1.90) children under 14. End of Mar–Sept Wed and Sat–Sun, grounds are open noon–5:30pm, house 1:30–5:30pm. Take A25 just west of Westerham and follow the signs.

Built in 1681 and owned by the Warde family for 250 years, this still-occupied manor house has—in addition to a fine collection of paintings, tapestries, and furniture—pictures and relics of General Wolfe's family. In 1216 a house on this site was occupied by the de Squerie family until the mid–15th century. The family restored the formal gardens, dotting the banks surrounding the lake with spring bulbs, azaleas, herbaceous borders, and old roses to retain its beauty year-round, and returned the rooms to their original uses. You can enjoy the fine collection of old-master paintings from the Italian, 17th-century Dutch, and 18th-century English schools, along with antiques, porcelain, and tapestries, all acquired or commissioned by the family in the 18th century. The military hero received his commission on the grounds of the house—the spot is marked by a cenotaph.

Down House. On Luxted Rd., in Downe. ☎ **01689/859119.** Admission £5 ($8) adults, £3.80 ($6.10) students and seniors, £2.50 ($4) children. Apr–Oct daily 10am–6pm; Nov–Mar daily 10am–4pm. Closed Dec. 24–25, and 26. From Westerham, get on A233 and drive 5½ miles south of Bromley to the village of Downe. Down House is ¼ mile southeast of the village. From London's Victorian Station, take a train (available daily) to Bromley South, then go by bus no. 146 (Monday to Saturday only) to Downe or to Orpington by bus no. R2.

Here stands the final residence of the famous naturalist Charles Darwin. In 1842, upon moving in, he wrote, "House ugly, looks neither old nor new." Nevertheless, he lived there "in happy contentment" until his death in 1882. The drawing room, dining room, billiard room, and old study have been restored to the way they were when Darwin was working on his famous, and still controversial, book *On the Origin of Species,* first published in 1859. The museum also includes collections and memorabilia from Darwin's voyage on the HMS *Beagle.* The garden retains its original landscaping and a glass house, beyond which lies the Sand Walk or "Thinking Path," where Darwin took his daily solitary walk.

✪ **Knole.** 5 miles north of Tonbridge, at the Tonbridge end of the town of Sevenoaks. ☎ **01732/462100.** Admission to house £5 ($8) adults, £2.50 ($4) children; family pass £12.50 ($20). Admission to gardens £1 ($1.60) adults, 50p (80¢) children. House Wed and Fri–Sat noon–4pm, Sun and bank holiday Mon. 11am–5pm, Thurs 2–5pm. Gardens open only first Wed of the month in May–Sept; last admission at 3pm. Park is open daily to pedestrians and open to cars only when the house is. Closed Nov 1–Easter. To reach Knole from Chartwell, drive north to Westerham, pick up A25, and head east for 8 miles. Frequent train service is available from London (about every 30 minutes) to Sevenoaks, and then you can take the connecting hourly bus service, a taxi, or walk the remaining 1½ miles to Knole.

Begun in the mid–15th century by Thomas Bourchier, archbishop of Canterbury, and set in a 1,000-acre deer park, Knole is one of the largest private houses in England and is one of the finest examples of pure English Tudor-style architecture.

Henry VIII liberated the former archbishop's palace from the church in 1537. He spent considerable sums of money on Knole, but there is little record of his spending much time here after extracting the place from the reluctant Archbishop Cranmer; history records one visit in 1541. It was then a royal palace until Queen Elizabeth I granted it to Thomas Sackville, first earl of Dorset, whose descendants have lived here ever since. (Virginia Woolf, often a guest of the Sackvilles, used Knole as the setting for her novel *Orlando*.)

The house covers 7 acres and has 365 rooms, 52 staircases, and 7 courts. The elaborate paneling and plasterwork provide a background for the 17th- and 18th-century tapestries and rugs, Elizabethan and Jacobean furniture, and the collection of family portraits. The building was given to the National Trust in 1946.

Insider's tip: If you want to see a bed that's to die for, check out the state bed of James II in the King's Bedroom. And, although most people don't know this, you can actually take afternoon tea at Knole. From the early 17th century the tearooms here were used as a brew house where beer and ale were brewed regularly. Today you can enjoy a pot of tea with scones, jam, and cream, or else devour one of their gâteaux such as carrot-and-walnut sponge topped with a cream-cheese-and-lemon-juice icing.

Ightham Mote. ☎ **01732/810378.** Admission £4 ($6.40) adults, £2 ($3.20) children; free for children under 5. Mon and Wed–Fri noon–5:30pm, Sun and bank holiday Mon. 11am–5:30pm; last admission at 5pm. Closed Nov–Mar. Drive 6 miles east of Sevenoaks on A25 to the small village of Ivy Hatch; the estate is 2½ miles south of Ightham; it's also signposted from A227.

Dating from 1340, Ightham Mote was extensively remodeled in the early 16th century, and remodeling is still going on. The chapel with its painted ceiling, timbered outer wall, and ornate chimneys reflects the Tudor period. You'll cross a stone bridge over a moat to its central courtyard. From the Great Hall, known for its magnificent windows, a Jacobean staircase leads to the old chapel on the first floor, where you go through the solarium, which has an oriel window, to the Tudor chapel.

Unlike many other ancient houses in England that have been occupied by the same family for centuries, Ightham Mote passed from owner to owner, with each family leaving its mark on the place. When the last private owner, an American who was responsible for a lot of the restoration, died, he bequeathed the house to the National Trust, which chose to keep the Robinson Library laid out as it was in a 1960 edition of *Homes & Gardens*.

☼ Penshurst Place. 6 miles west of Tonbridge. ☎ **01892/870307.** Admission to house and grounds £5.70 ($9.10) adults, £3.20 ($5.10) children ages 5–16. Grounds only £4.20 ($6.70) adults, £2.80 ($4.50) children ages 5–16. Children 4 and under enter free. Apr–Oct daily, house noon–5:30pm, grounds 11am–6pm; Mar Sat Sun only, house noon 5:30pm, grounds 11am 6pm. Closed Nov–Feb. From M25 junction follow A21 to Tonbridge, leaving at the Tonbridge (North) exit; then follow the brown tourist signs. The nearest mainline station is Tonbridge.

Stately Penshurst Place is one of the outstanding country houses in Britain. It is also one of England's greatest defended manor houses, standing in a peaceful rural setting that has changed little over the centuries. In 1338, Sir John de Pulteney, four times

Touring Leeds Castle: "The Loveliest in the World"

Once described by Lord Conway as the loveliest castle in the world, Leeds Castle (☎ **01622/765400**) dates from A.D. 857. Originally constructed of wood, it was rebuilt in 1119 in its present stone structure on two small islands in the middle of the lake; it was an almost impregnable fortress before the importation of gunpowder. Henry VIII converted it to a royal palace.

The castle has strong links with America through the sixth Lord Fairfax who, as well as owning the castle, owned 5 million acres in Virginia and was a close friend and mentor of the young George Washington. The last private owner, the Hon. Lady Baillie, who restored the castle with a superb collection of fine art, furniture, and tapestries, bequeathed it to the Leeds Castle Foundation. Since then, royal apartments, known as *Les Chambres de la Reine* (the queen's chambers), in the Gloriette, the oldest part of the castle, have been open to the public. The Gloriette, the last stronghold against attack, dates from Norman and Plantagenet times, with later additions by Henry VIII.

Within the surrounding parkland is a wildwood garden and duckery where rare swans, geese, and ducks abound. The redesigned aviaries contain a superb collection of birds, including parakeets and cockatoos. Dog lovers will enjoy the Dog Collar Museum at the gate house, with a unique collection of collars dating from the Middle Ages. A 9-hole golf course is open to the public. The Culpepper Garden is a delightful English country flower garden. Beyond are the castle greenhouses, with the maze centered on a beautiful underground grotto and the vineyard recorded in the *Domesday Book*. It is once again producing Leeds Castle English white wine.

Insider's tip: Hurried visitors overlook the Aviary, but it's really special. Opened by Princess Alexandra in 1988, it houses a collection of more than 100 rare species of birds. It aims not only at conservation, but also at successful breeding—to reintroduce endangered species into their original habitats.

From March to October, the park is open daily from 10am to 5pm; the castle, daily from 11am to 5:30pm. From November to February, the park is open daily from 10am to 3pm; the castle, daily from 10:15am to 3:30pm. The castle and grounds are closed on the last Saturday in June and the first Saturday in July before open-air concerts. Admission to the castle and grounds is £8.80 ($14.10) for adults and £4.80 ($7.70) for children. Students and senior citizens pay £5.60

lord mayor of London, built the manor house whose Great Hall still forms the heart of Penshurst—after more than 600 years. The boy king, Edward VI, presented the house to Sir William Sidney, and it has remained in that family ever since. It was the birthplace in 1554 of Sir Philip Sidney, the soldier-poet. In the first half of the 17th century, Penshurst was known as a center of literature and attracted such personages as Ben Jonson, who was inspired by the estate to write one of his greatest poems.

The Nether Gallery, below the Long Gallery, which has a suite of ebony-and-ivory furniture from Goa, houses the Sidney family collection of armor. You can also see the splendid state dining room. In the Stable Wing is an interesting toy museum, with dolls, toy soldiers, dollhouses, and many other playthings from past generations. On the grounds are nature and farm trails plus an adventure playground for children.

($8.95). For the grounds only, it's £6.80 ($10.90) adults, £5.30 ($8.50) senior citizens and students, and £4.30 ($6.90) children. Car parking is free, with a free ride on a fully accessible minibus available for those who cannot manage the half-mile or so walk from the parking area to the castle.

Trains run frequently from London's Victoria Station to Maidstone. Buses run weekdays from London's Victoria Coach Station to Maidstone, 36 miles to the southeast. If you're driving, from London's ring road, continue east along M26 and M20. The castle is 4 miles east of Maidstone at the junction of the A20 and the M20 London–Folkestone roads.

Snacks, salads, cream teas, and hot meals are offered daily at a number of places on the estate, including Fairfax Hall, a restored 17th-century tithe barn, and the Terrace Restaurant, which provides a full range of hot and cold meals.

Kentish Evenings are presented in Fairfax Hall on the first Saturday of the month throughout the year (except in August), starting at 7pm with a cocktail reception, then a private guided tour of the castle. Guests feast on smoked salmon mousse, followed by broth and roast beef carved at the table, plus seasonal vegetables. A half bottle of wine is included in the overall price of £42 ($67.20) per person. During the meal, musicians play appropriate music for the surroundings and the occasion. Advance reservations are required, made by calling the castle. Kentish Evenings finish at 12:30am, so it's best to stay overnight nearby.

Instead of driving back late at night, you can spend the night at **Grangemoor/Grange Park,** 4–8 St. Michael's Rd. (off Tonbridge Road), Maidstone, Kent ME16 8B5 (☎ 01622/677623; fax 01622/679246), which are two buildings facing each other across the street. Grangemoor is the main accommodation, with 38 well-furnished rooms, each with private bath, phone, and TV. The cost is £52 ($83.20) for a double, Monday through Thursday, and £48 ($76.80) on other nights, including an English breakfast. Across the street, Grange Park has only 12 rooms but is similarly furnished, renting for £46 ($73.60) a night, including an English breakfast. Both places are located in a tranquil residential area that's close to the center of Maidstone. There is also a Tudor-style bar and restaurant, offering a three-course meal for £12.50 ($20). Children are welcome in both the bar and restaurant area.

✿ **Hever Castle & Gardens.** ☎ 01732/865224. Admission to castle and gardens £7 ($11.20) adults, £6 ($9.60) seniors and students, £3.80 ($6.10) children ages 5–16. Family ticket (2 adults, 2 children) £17.80 ($28.50). Garden only £5.50 ($8.80) adults, £4.70 ($7.50) seniors and students, £3.60 ($5.75) children ages 5–16. Family ticket £14.60 ($23.35). Children 4 and under enter free. Gardens daily 11am–6pm; castle daily noon–6pm. Closed Dec–Feb. To get here, follow the signs northwest of Royal Tonbridge Wells; it's 3 miles southeast of Edenbridge, midway between Sevenoaks and East Grinstead, and 30 minutes from Exit 6 of M25.

Hever Castle dates from 1270, when the massive gate house, the outer walls, and the moat were first constructed. Some 200 years later, the Bullen (or Boleyn) family added a comfortable Tudor dwelling house inside the walls. Hever Castle was the childhood home of Anne Boleyn, the second wife of Henry VIII and mother of Queen Elizabeth I.

In 1903, William Waldorf Astor acquired the estate and invested time, money, and imagination in restoring the castle, building the "Tudor Village," and creating the gardens and lakes. The Astor family's contribution to Hever's rich history can be appreciated through the castle's collections of furniture, paintings, and objets d'art, as well as the quality of its workmanship, particularly in the wood carving and plasterwork.

The gardens at Hever Castle were created between 1904 and 1908. They have now reached their maturity and are ablaze with color throughout most of the year. The spectacular Italian Garden contains statuary and sculpture dating from Roman to Renaissance times, which William Waldorf Astor acquired in Italy. The formal gardens include a walled Rose Garden, fine topiary work, and a maze. There's a 35-acre lake and many streams, cascades, and fountains.

Sissinghurst Castle Garden. ☎ **01580/712850.** Admission £6 ($9.60) adults, £3 ($4.80) children. Apr to mid-Oct Tues–Fri 1–6:30pm, Sat–Sun and Good Friday 10am–5:30pm. The garden is 53 miles southeast of London and 15 miles south of Maidstone. It's most often approached from Leeds Castle, which is 4 miles east of Maidstone at the junction of the A20 and the M20 London–Folkestone roads. From this junction, head south on B2163 and A274 through Headcorn. Follow the signposts to Sissinghurst.

These spectacular gardens, which are situated between surviving parts of an Elizabethan mansion, were created by one of England's most famous and dedicated gardeners, Bloomsbury writer Vita Sackville-West, and her husband, Harold Nicolson. In spring, the garden is resplendent with flowering bulbs and daffodils in the orchard.

The white garden reaches its peak in June. The large herb garden, a skillful montage that reflects her profound plant knowledge, has something to show all summer long, and the cottage garden, with its flowering bulbs, is at its finest in the fall. Meals are available in the Granary Restaurant. The garden area is flat, so it is wheelchair accessible; however, only two wheelchairs are allowed at a time.

7 Historic Mansions & Gardens in Dorking & Guildford

Dorking, birthplace of Lord Laurence Olivier, lies on the Mole River at the foot of the North Downs. Within easy reach are some of the most scenic spots in the shire, including Silent Pool, Box Hill, and Leith Hill.

The guildhall in Guildford, a country town on the Wey River, has an ornamental projecting clock that dates from 1683. Charles Dickens claimed that High Street, which slopes to the river, was one of the most beautiful in England.

ESSENTIALS
GETTING THERE   Frequent daily train service takes 35 minutes from London's Victoria Station to Dorking. The train to Guildford departs from London's Waterloo Station and takes 40 minutes. For rail information, call ☎ **0345/484950** in the U.K., or 01603/764776 in the U.S.

Green Line buses (no. 714) leave from London's Victoria Coach Station daily, heading for Kingston with a stop at Dorking. The trip takes 1 hour. National Express operates buses from London's Victoria Coach Station daily, with a stopover at Guildford on its runs from London to Portsmouth. For schedules call ☎ **0990/808080.** It's usually more convenient to take the train.

If you're driving to Dorking, take A24 south from London. If you're driving to Guildford from London, head south along A3.

VISITOR INFORMATION The **Guildford Tourist Information Centre** is at 14 Tunsgate (☎ **01483/444333**). It's open October through April, Monday through Saturday from 9:30am to 5:30pm, and from May through September, Monday through Saturday from 9am to 6pm and 10am to 5pm on Sunday.

THE TOP SIGHTS

✪ **Wisley Garden.** Wisley (near Ripley, just off M25, Junction 10, on the A3 London–Portsmouth road). ☎ **01483/224234.** Admission £5 ($8) adults, £2 ($3.20) children 6–16; free for children 5 and under. Mon–Fri 10am–4:30pm; Sat 9am–4:30pm.

This is one of the great gardens of England. Every season of the year, this 250-acre garden has a profusion of flowers and shrubs, ranging from the alpine meadow carpeted with wild daffodils in spring, Battleston Hill brilliant with rhododendrons in early summer, the heather garden's colorful foliage in the fall, and a riot of exotic plants in the greenhouses in winter. Recent developments include model gardens and a landscaped orchid house. This garden is the site of a laboratory where botanists, plant pathologists, and entomologists experiment and assist amateur gardeners. A large gift shop stocks a wide range of gardening books.

Polesden Lacey. A few miles from Great Bookham, off the A246 Leatherhead–Guildford road. ☎ **01372/452048.** Admission £3 ($4.80) adults; £1.50 ($2.40) children ages 6–17; free for children 5; family ticket £7.50 ($12). Grounds daily 11am–dusk. House March Sat–Sun 1:30–5:30pm; Apr–Oct Wed–Sun 1:30–5:30pm, except on bank holiday Mon, when hours are 11am–5:30pm.

This former Regency villa was built in 1824. It houses the Greville collection of antiques, paintings, and tapestries. In the early part of this century it was enlarged to become a comfortable Edwardian country house when it was the home of a celebrated hostess, Mrs. Ronald Greville, who frequently entertained royalty from 1906 to 1939. The estate consists of 1,400 acres. Stroll the 18th-century garden, lined with herbaceous borders and featuring a rose garden and beech trees.

Loseley House. Loseley Park (2½ miles southwest of Guildford). ☎ **01483/304440.** Admission £4.50 ($7.20) adults; £3.75 ($6) students and, seniors; £2.75 ($4.40) children. June–Aug Wed–Sat 2–5pm.

This beautiful and historic Elizabethan mansion visited by Queen Elizabeth I, James I, and Queen Mary has been featured on TV and in numerous films. Its works of art include paneling from Henry VIII's Nonsuch Palace, period furniture, a unique carved chalk chimneypiece, magnificent ceilings, and cushions made by the first Queen Elizabeth. Lunches and teas are served in the Courtyard Restaurant from 11am to 5pm.

WHERE TO STAY & DINE
IN DORKING

Burford Bridge Hotel. Box Hill, Dorking, Surrey RH5 6BX. ☎ **01306/884561.** Fax 01306/880386. 48 units. TV TEL. Mon–Thurs £110 ($176) double, Fri–Sun £85 ($136) double. AE, DC, MC, V. Take the A24 1½ miles north of Dorking.

The Burford Bridge Hotel is the best in Dorking, offering stylish living in a rural town. At the foot of beautiful Box Hill, the hotel has many historical associations. Lord Nelson was a frequent patron, and Keats completed "Endymion" here in 1817. Wordsworth and Robert Louis Stevenson also visited the hotel occasionally. You get the best of both the old and the new, including a tithe barn (ca. 1600), as well as a large bedroom. The restaurant serves good English food, and a bar opens onto a flowered patio with a fountain. In summer, you can enjoy the garden swimming pool and frequent barbecues.

White Horse Hotel. High St., Dorking, Surrey, RH4 1BE. ☎ **800/225-5843** in the U.S. and Canada, or ☎ and fax 01306/881138. 68 units. TV TEL. Mon–Thurs £95 ($152) double, Fri–Sun £65 ($104) double. B&B rates £53 ($84.80) per person Mon–Thurs, £50 ($80) per person Fri–Sun. AE, MC, V.

This member of the Forte chain, just 10 miles from Gatwick Airport, is supposed to have been the home of the "Marquis of Granby" in the *Pickwick Papers.* At least Dickens was known to have frequented the bar parlor. All the well-furnished rooms have beverage-makers; some units are in a rather sterile modern annex. Called "the most interesting house in Dorking," the inn has a restaurant, as well as the Pickwick Bar that offers a moderately priced table d'hôte dinner. The hotel also has a rose garden and can arrange a temporary membership in a nearby sports club with its own swimming pool.

IN GUILDFORD

Forte Posthouse Hotel. Egerton Rd., Guildford, Surrey GU2 5XZ. ☎ **01483/574444**. Fax 01483/302690. 111 units. MINIBAR TV TEL. £109 ($174.40) double; £149 ($238.40) suite. 2-night weekend packages available from £40 ($64) per person double per night, including 3-course dinner and full English breakfast. AE, MC, V. Head about 2 miles southwest of the center of Guildford, just off A3.

It's only been around for a decade, but a feeling of heritage is conveyed by natural red-elm joinery, polished brass fittings, marble floors, and landscaped grounds. The bedrooms incorporate both living and sleeping areas, and all are equipped with beverage-makers. The needs of guests with disabilities have been taken into consideration. The hotel has an in-house restaurant called Jules that serves modern cuisine in a relaxed, informal setting. There's also a health and fitness club with an indoor heated swimming pool and a sun terrace.

Inn on the Lake. Ockford Rd., Godalming, Surrey GU7 1RH. ☎ **01483/415575**. Fax 01483/860445. 21 units. TV TEL. £85–£95 ($136–$152) double. Rates include English breakfast. AE, DC, MC, V. From Guildford, take A3100 south for 3 miles.

This haven of landscaped gardens with ducks drowsing on pools beside the lake is only 3 miles from Guildford. The rooms are decorated with pretty country prints and simple furniture, all with tea- and coffeemakers. Excellent snacks are served in a real old-world bar, where some of the timbers date from Tudor times. In summer, barbecues are held in the garden. More substantial dinners (fixed-price menus for Sunday lunch only) are offered, plus à la carte with a varied selection of grills, English favorites, and continental dishes. Room service is available. The house, listed in the *Domesday Book,* has Tudor, Georgian, and Victorian associations. A postwar addition blends more or less gracefully into the complex.

WHERE TO SHARE A PINT

The Jolly Farmer, Millford (☎ 01483/538779), is a riverside pub, rebuilt in 1913, with a large conservatory and a terraced garden along the River Wey. It offers traditional pub food with homemade specials served daily at lunch and dinner; bar snacks are available all day. A variety of real ales are on tap. Children are welcome until 9pm.

   The White House, 8 High St. (☎ 01483/302006), is another riverside pub, with a conservatory overlooking a lovely waterside garden. Pub grub is available at lunch and dinner; sandwiches are offered all day. They serve traditional London ales aged in barrels.

   The **Forger and Firkin,** 55 Woodbridge Rd. (☎ 1483/578999), is Guildford's only brew pub, producing five ales and offering brewery tours. They also have traditional dishes and in summer serve breakfast. Saturday nights feature free live music.

8 Haslemere

42 miles SW of London; 37 miles NW of Brighton

In this quiet, sleepy town, early English musical instruments are made by hand and an annual music festival is the town's main drawing card. Over the years, the Dolmetsch family has been responsible for the acclaim that has come to this otherwise unheralded little Surrey town, which lies in the midst of some of the shire's finest scenery.

GETTING THERE

Haslemere is an hour's train ride from Waterloo Station in London. For rail information, call ☎ 0345/484950 in the U.K., or 01603/764776 in the U.S.

There is no bus service from London to Haslemere because the train service is so excellent. Once in Haslemere, local buses connect the town to such nearby villages as Farnham and Grayshott.

If you're driving, from Guildford (see above), continue south on A3100, going via Godalming and branching onto A286.

THE HASLEMERE FESTIVAL

In the center of Haslemere rises one of Surrey's most prominent theaters, **Haslemere Hall,** Bridge Road, Haslemere, Surrey GU27 2AS (☎ 01428/642161). Throughout the year, it presents concerts, musical comedies, and serious dramas, the programs of which change about every month. Throughout the year, someone will usually be on hand to sell tickets and answer questions Monday through Friday from 9am to 1pm and Saturday from 9am to noon.

One of Surrey's musical highlights occurs for 6 days in mid-July, when the Haslemere Festival attracts music aficionados from throughout Europe. At that time, a world-famous musicologist, Dr. Carl Dolmetsch, accompanied by three generations of his family and friends, presents a program of 16th-, 17th-, and 18th-century chamber music. The music, including obscure pieces culled from the extensive family archives, is produced on harpsichords, violas da gamba, recorders, violins, and lutes that either date from those centuries or are reproductions faithfully crafted by the Dolmetsch family in their Haslemere workshops. During the festival, there is a Saturday matinee beginning at 3:15pm; evening performances start at 7:30pm. Tickets range from £5.50 to £9.50 ($8.80 to $15.20), depending on seat location and event.

Well-intentioned musicians and music lovers are allowed to visit the **Dolmetsch workshops,** set on the village outskirts, by phoning ahead for a mutually convenient time of arrival. Don't think of it as an outing to a museum; it's a visit to an arts-conscious factory of international renown where musical instruments are manufactured to centuries-old standards. For information, contact **Dolmetsch Musical Instruments,** Unit 1B Unicorn Trading Estate, Weydown Road, Haslemere, Surrey, GU27 1DN (☎ 01428/643235).

WHERE TO STAY

✪ **Lythe Hill Hotel.** Petworth Rd., Haslemere, Surrey GU27 3BQ. ☎ 800/323-5463 in the U.S., or 01428/651251. Fax 01428/644131. 40 units. TV TEL. £115 ($184) double; £135–£175 ($216–$280) suite. AE, DC, MC, V. Take B2131 1½ miles east from Haslemere.

This former farmhouse on the outskirts of Haslemere, with parts dating from 1475, is situated on 20 acres of parkland overlooking National Trust woodlands—just an hour from London, Heathrow, and Gatwick. Across the courtyard is the main hotel, with luxuriously appointed bedrooms and suites, as well as an English restaurant. In the black-and-white-timbered farmhouse are five elegant period units with marble-tile baths. One has a four-poster bed from 1614.

Dining: Downstairs in the farmhouse is the renowned, oak-beamed and paneled Auberge de France Restaurant, offering a classic French cuisine served by candlelight on polished oak tables. Specialties include turbot, fresh Scottish salmon, *tournedos de bœuf* (small fillet of beef), and a cellar of fine wines.

WHERE TO DINE

✪ **Fleur de Sel.** 23-27 Lower St. ☎ **01428/651462.** Reservations required. Fixed-price lunch £9.50 ($15.20) for 2 courses, £12.50–£16.50 ($20–$26.40) for 3 courses; fixed-price dinner £21 ($33.60) for 2 courses, £26 ($41.60) for 3 courses. AE, MC, V. Tues–Fri and Sun noon–2pm; Tues–Sat 7–10pm. FRENCH.

This main-street restaurant, created from a row of terraced cottages, is bright and furnished in modern overtones. The menu changes seasonally, and there are nightly specials, but classic French fare is always the order of the day. The food is consistently of high quality, prepared with only the freshest and most well chosen of ingredients. Starters might include a puff pastry case filled with asparagus in a creamy tomato sauce or pasta parcels filled with lobster. The main courses may feature roast crispy duck in a honey-and-ginger sauce or fillets of Scottish salmon with a tomato-and-basil sauce.

9 Chichester

31 miles W of Brighton; 69 miles SW of London

Chichester might have been just a market town if the Chichester Festival Theatre had not been born here. One of the oldest Roman cities in England, Chichester draws a crowd from all over the world for its theater presentations. Other than the theater, there's not much else to see. But the town does make a good base for exploring a history-rich part of southern England.

ESSENTIALS

GETTING THERE   Trains depart for Chichester from London's Victoria Station once every hour during the day. The trip takes 1½ hours. However, if you visit Chichester to attend the theater, plan to stay over—the last train back to London is at 9pm. For rail information, call ☎ **0345/484950** in the U.K., or **01603/764776** in the U.S.

Buses leave from London's Victoria Coach Station four times per day. For schedules call ☎ **0990/808080.**

If you're driving from London's ring road, head south on A3, turning onto A286 for Chichester.

VISITOR INFORMATION   The **Tourist Information Centre,** 29A South St. (☎ **01243/775888**), is open Monday through Saturday from 9:15am to 5:15pm, and in summer, Sunday from 10am to 4pm.

THE CHICHESTER FESTIVAL THEATRE

Only a 5-minute walk from the Chichester Cathedral and the old Market Cross, the 1,400-seat theater, with its apron stage, stands on the edge of Oaklands Park. It opened in 1962, and its first director was none other than Lord Laurence Olivier. Its reputation has grown steadily, pumping new vigor and life into the former walled city, although originally many irate locals felt the city money could have been better spent on a swimming pool instead of a theater.

The ✪ **Chichester Festival Theatre,** built in the 1960s, offers plays and musicals during the summer season, from May to September, and in the winter and spring months, orchestras, jazz, opera, theater, ballet, and a Christmas show for the entire family.

The **Minerva,** built in the late 1980s, is a multifunctional cultural center that includes a theater plus dining and drinking facilities. The Minerva Studio Theatre and the Chichester Festival Theatre are managed by the same board of governors but show different programs and different plays.

Theater reservations made over the telephone will be held for a maximum of 4 days (call ☎ **01243/781312**). It's better to mail inquiries and checks to the Box Office, Chichester Festival Theatre, Oaklands Park, Chichester, West Sussex PO19 4AP. MasterCard, Visa, and American Express are accepted. Season ticket prices range from £9.50 to £22.50 ($15.20 to $36). Unreserved seats, sold only on the day of performance, cost £6.50 to £7.50 ($10.40 to $12).

SEEING THE SIGHTS NEARBY

In addition to the sights listed below, you might want to stop in nearby **Bosham,** which is primarily a sailing resort and one of the most charming villages in West Sussex. It's 4 miles west of Chichester on A259, and there's good bus service between the two towns. Bosham was the site where Christianity was first established on the Sussex coast. The Danish king, Canute, made it one of the seats of his North Sea empire, and it was the home of a manor (now gone) of the last of England's Saxon kings, Harold, who sailed from here to France on a journey that finally culminated in the invasion of England by William the Conqueror in 1066.

Bosham's little **church** was depicted in the Bayeux Tapestry. Its graveyard overlooks the boats, and the church is filled with ship models and relics, showing the villagers' link to the sea. A daughter of King Canute is buried inside. Near the harbor, it is reached by a narrow lane.

Roman Palace. North of A259, off Salthill Rd. (signposted from Fishbourne; 1½ miles from Chichester). ☎ **01243/785859.** Admission £4 ($6.40) adults, £2.20 ($3.50) children, £10.50 ($16.80) family ticket. Apr–Oct daily 10am–5pm (to 6pm in Aug); mid-Feb and Nov daily 10am–4pm; Dec to mid-Feb Sun only 10am–4pm. Buses stop regularly at the bottom of Salthill Rd., and the museum is within a 5-minute walk of British Rail's station at Fishbourne.

This is what remains of the largest Roman residence yet discovered in Britain. Built around A.D. 75 in villa style, it has many mosaic-floored rooms and even an underfloor heating system. The gardens have been restored to their original 1st-century plan. The story of the site is told both by an audiovisual program and by text in the museum. Guided tours are offered twice a day. (See what an archaeological dig from July 1996 unearthed.)

Weald & the Downland Open Air Museum. At Singleton, 6 miles north of Chichester on A286 (the London rd.). ☎ **01243/811348.** Admission £4.90 ($7.85) adults, £2.50 ($4) children; family ticket £12 ($19.20). Mar–Oct daily 10:30am–6pm; Nov Feb Wed and Sat–Sun 10:30am–4pm. Bus no. 60 from Chichester.

In the beautiful Sussex countryside, historic buildings, saved from destruction, are reconstructed on a 40-acre downland site. The structures show the development of traditional building from medieval times to the 19th century, in the weald and downland area of southeast England.

Exhibits include a Tudor market hall, a medieval farmstead and other houses, dating from the 14th to the 17th century, a working water mill producing stoneground flour, a blacksmith's forge, plumbers' and carpenters' workshops, a toll cottage, a 17th-century tread wheel, agricultural buildings including thatched barns and an 18th-century granary, a charcoal burner's camp, and a 19th-century village school. A "new" reception area with shops and offices is set in Longport House, a 16th-century building rescued from the site of the Channel Tunnel.

WHERE TO STAY IN THE AREA

Marriott Goodwood Park Hotel & Country Club. Goodwood, Chichester PO18 0QB. ☎ **01243/775537.** Fax 01243/520120. 94 units. TV TEL. £70–£140 ($112–$224) double. Rates include breakfast. AE, DC, MC, V.

Goodwood House was the home to the dukes of Richmond for more than 300 years. The hotel now located on these grounds is aesthetically built in the 1786 style of the original Goodwood House. The well-furnished rooms have hair dryers and beverage-makers, and easily qualify as the best in the area.

Dining: The restaurant serves a fixed-price lunch for £15.95 ($25.50) and a fixed-price dinner for £21.95 ($35.10). The cuisine is of a high international standard, with the use of fresh, local ingredients when possible. It is closed for lunch on Saturday.

Amenities: There are many leisure activities available, from horseshoes to golf on an 18-hole course.

✪ **Millstream Hotel.** Bosham Lane, Bosham, Chichester, W. Sussex PO18 8HL. ☎ **01243/573234.** Fax 01243/573459. 33 units. TV TEL. £109 ($174.40) double; rates include English breakfast. Double room and half board available for £146 ($233.60). AE, DC, MC, V. Bus: Bosham bus from Chichester. Take the road to the village of Bosham and its harbor, off A27.

The Millstream was originally built in the 1700s to provide food and accommodation for the people and horses who traveled through Sussex from other parts of England. Located 5 miles south of Chichester, the hotel is in the hamlet of Bosham, with its beautiful harbor. Behind a facade of weathered yellow bricks, the hotel features blazing fireplaces, a sense of history, and recently redecorated and upgraded bedrooms, each with floral-patterned wallpaper and conservative furniture.

Dining/Diversions: There's a cocktail bar and an adjacent restaurant, where you can order such dishes as moules marinière (mussels cooked in gravy with onions) and roast Sussex lamb with fresh herbs or Selsey crab.

Ship Hotel. North St., Chichester, W. Sussex PO19 1NH. ☎ **01243/778000.** Fax 01243/788000. 34 units. TV TEL. £115 ($184) double. Rates include English breakfast. AE, DC, MC, V.

One of the classic Georgian buildings of the city, the Ship is only a few minutes' walk from the cathedral, the Chichester Festival Theatre, and many fine antique shops. It was built as a private house in 1790 for Adm. Sir George Murray (one of Nelson's commanders) and still retains an air of elegance and comfort. A grand Adam staircase leads from the main entrance to the bedrooms, which are all named after historic ships.

Dining/Diversions: Hornblower's Lounge, relatively formal with its own fireplace and rows of books, is an elegant place for a drink. Murray's Restaurant offers good value for the money and features a three-course dinner menu for £17.50 ($28) every evening.

✪ **The Spread Eagle Hotel.** South St., Midhurst, W. Sussex GU29 9NH. ☎ **01730/816911.** Fax 01730/815668. 39 units. TV TEL. £110–£120 ($176–$192) double; £195 ($312) suite. Rates include English breakfast. AE, DC, MC, V. Midhurst bus from Chichester.

The 1430 inn and the market town of Midhurst are so steeped in history that the room you sleep in and the pavement you walk on have a thousand tales to tell. The rooms here have beams, small mullioned windows, and unexpected corners, and five of them are equipped with four-poster beds. The eagle in the lounge is the actual one from the back of Hermann Göring's chair in the Reichstag. It was acquired for its apt illustration of the hotel's name.

Dining/Diversions: The dining hall is lit by candles that flicker on the gleaming tables. In the winter, log fires blaze. The lounge, with its timbered ceiling, is where Elizabeth I and her court might have sat to watch festivities in the Market Square outside.

Amenities: The old has been enhanced by the new with the addition of a health, beauty, and leisure club.

WHERE TO DINE IN THE AREA

Comme ça. 67 Broyle Rd. (a 5-minute walk from the town center). ☎ 01243/788724. Reservations required. Tues–Sat main courses £10.25–£29.75 ($16.40–$47.60), 2-course lunch £14.75 ($23.60), 3-course lunch £17.75 ($28.40); Sun 3-course lunch £15.75 ($25.20). MC, V. Tues–Sun 12:15–2pm; Tues–Sat 6–10pm. FRENCH.

This is the best French restaurant in town—in fact, the best restaurant, period. The unpretentious decor has a certain French provincial quality. The decor blends old Victorian and Edwardian prints with objets d'art. The theme continues in the new garden room leading through French doors to an enclosed patio and garden. In summer you'll want to dine out here, although in winter a log fire in the inglenook fireplace welcomes you to the bar.

Try such delights of the field, river, and forest as baked fresh Scottish salmon, pan-fried breast of guinea fowl with a black-currant sauce, or calves' liver sautéed in sage butter and served with bacon. Only the finest-quality ingredients are used. All menus have vegetarian dishes, and special dietary requirements can also be catered to.

White Horse. 1 High St., Chilgrove. ☎ 01243/535219. Reservations required on weekends. Main courses £11.50–£17.50 ($18.40–$28); 2-course lunch £17.50 ($28); 3-course lunch £19.75 ($31.60); 4-course dinner £24.50 ($39.20) with a £4 ($6.40) reduction if no appetizer is ordered. AE, MC, V. Tues–Sat noon–3pm and 6–10pm. Closed Feb, the last week in Oct, and Dec 25–26. Head 6½ miles north of Chichester on B2141 to Petersfield. ENGLISH/FRENCH.

The wine cellar at this informally elegant country restaurant is one of the most comprehensive in Britain. This is partly because of the careful attention the owners pay to the details of their 18th-century inn, whose patina has been burnished every day since it was first built in 1765. The trio of dining rooms features old beams and lots of hardwood. The menu is heavy on local game in season, bought from people known by the owners. Menu choices include roast breast of pheasant on a bed of celeriac puree, cold lobster, and roast lamb in a reduced sauce.

A bed-and-breakfast is now available at the adjoining **Forge Cottage,** Chilgrove, Chichester, West Sussex, PO18 QHX (☎ 01243/535333; fax 01243/535363).

10 Arundel Castle

21 miles W of Brighton; 58 miles SW of London

The small town of Arundel in West Sussex nestles at the foot of one of England's most spectacular castles. Without the castle, it would be just another English market town. The town was once an Arun River port, and its residents enjoyed the prosperity of considerable trade and commerce. However, today the harbor traffic has been replaced with buses filled with tourists.

ESSENTIALS

GETTING THERE   Trains leave hourly during the day from London's Victoria Station. The trip takes 1¼ hours. For rail information, call ☎ **0345/484950** in the U.K., or 01603/764776 in the U.S.

Most bus connections are through Littlehampton, opening onto the English Channel west of Brighton. From Littlehampton, you can leave the coastal road by taking bus no. 11, which runs between Littlehampton and Arundel hourly during the day. If you're dependent on public transportation, the tourist office (see below) keeps an update on the possibilities.

If you're driving from London, follow the signs to Gatwick Airport and from there head south toward the coast along A29.

VISITOR INFORMATION   The **Tourist Information Centre**, 61 High St. (☎ **01903/882268**), is open from April through October, Monday through Friday from 9am to 5pm and on weekends from 10am to 5pm; off-season, Monday through Friday from 10am to 3pm and weekends from 10am to 3pm.

GETTING AROUND   One of the best ways to explore Arundel and the area around it is by bike rented from **Arundel Cycle Hire**, 4 School Lane (☎ **01903/883712**), costing £10 ($16) per day, plus a deposit. Hours are March through October, Friday through Wednesday from 9am to 6pm.

SEEING THE SIGHTS

✪ **Arundel Castle.** On Mill Rd. ☎ **01903/883136.** Admission £5.70 ($9.10) adults, £4.20 ($6.70) children 5–15, free for children 4 and under. Family ticket £15.50 ($24.80). Apr–Oct Sun–Fri noon–5pm. Closed Nov–Mar.

The ancestral home of the dukes of Norfolk, Arundel Castle is a much-restored mansion of considerable importance. Its legend is associated with some of the great families of England—the Fitzalans and the powerful Howards of Norfolk. This castle received worldwide exposure when it was chosen as the backdrop for *The Madness of King George* (it was "pretending" to be Windsor Castle in the film). Nigel Hawthorne came here to play George III, running around the Arundel courtyard in a mad frenzy, chased by actress Helen Mirren.

Arundel Castle has suffered destruction over the years, particularly during the civil war, when Cromwell's troops stormed its walls, perhaps in retaliation for the 14th earl of Arundel's (Thomas Howard) sizable contribution to Charles I. In the early 18th century, the castle had to be virtually rebuilt, and in late Victorian times it was remodeled and extensively restored again. Today it's filled with a valuable collection of antiques, along with an assortment of paintings by old masters, such as Van Dyck and Gainsborough.

Surrounding the castle, in the center off High Street, is a 1,100-acre park whose scenic highlight is Swanbourne Lake.

Arundel Cathedral. London Rd. ☎ **01903/882297.** Free admission, but donations appreciated. June–Sept daily 9am–6pm; Oct–May daily 9am–dusk. From the town center, continue west from High St.

A Roman Catholic cathedral, the Cathedral of Our Lady and St. Philip Howard stands at the highest point in town. It was constructed for the 15th duke of Norfolk by A. J. Hansom, who invented the Hansom taxi. However, it was not consecrated as a cathedral until 1965. The interior includes the shrine of St. Philip Howard, featuring Sussex wrought-iron work.

Arundel Toy and Military Museum. At "Doll's House," 23 High St. ☎ **01903/882908.** Admission £1.25 ($2) adults, £1 ($1.60) children and seniors, £4 ($6.40) family. May–Sept daily 11am–5pm; Oct–Apr Sat–Sun 10:45am–5pm.

In a Georgian cottage in the heart of historic Arundel, this museum displays a vast and intriguing family collection spanning many generations of old toys and games, small militaria, dolls, dollhouses, tin toys, musical toys, famous stuffed bears, Britain's animals and model soldiers, arks, boats, rocking horses, crested military models, an eggcup collection, and other curiosities. The museum is opposite Treasure House Antiques and Collectors Market.

Brass Rubbing Centre/Heritage of Arundel Museum. 61 High St. ☎ **01903/882268.** Free admission. Mon–Sat 10:30am–4:30 or 5pm. Closed mid-Oct to Apr.

Both attractions are located in the same stone-sided house as the town's tourist office. The Brass Rubbing Centre is in the cellar, where a collection of movable plaques and gravestones, each of historic and artistic interest, awaits the chalk and heavy paper of those who would like to trace their forms. You're charged according to the stone you choose to copy, usually about £2.50 ($4) per item.

On the street level, adjacent to the rooms housing the tourist information office, is the **Heritage of Arundel Museum.** It displays postcards, memorabilia, antique costumes, and historic documents relating to the history of Arundel and its famous castle.

WHERE TO STAY IN THE AREA

✪ **Amberley Castle Hotel.** Amberley, near Arundel, W. Sussex BN18 9ND. ☎ **800/ 525-4800** in the U.S., or 01798/831992. Fax 01798/831998. 15 units. TV TEL. £145– £300 ($232–$480) double. Rates include English breakfast. AE, DC, MC, V. Take B2139 north of Arundel; the hotel is 1½ miles southwest of Amberley.

The best place for food and lodging is near the village of Amberley. Joy and Martin Cummings offer accommodations in a 14th-century castle with sections dating from the 12th century. From the battlements, you'll have views of weald and downland. Elizabeth I herself held the lease on this castle from 1588 to 1603, and Cromwell's forces attacked it during the civil war. Charles II visited the castle on two occasions. Each of the sumptuous and individually designed and furnished rooms, all doubles, is named after a castle in Sussex, and each has a private Jacuzzi bath as well as a video library.

Dining: You don't have to stay here to dine in the 12th-century Queen's Room Restaurant, the area's finest dining room (reserve ahead). The cuisine is classic French and traditional English. Service is daily from 7 to 10pm.

Norfolk Arms. 22 High St., Arundel, W. Sussex BN18 9AD. ☎ **01903/882101.** Fax 01903/884275. 34 units. TV TEL. £95 ($152) double. Rates include breakfast. AE, DC, MC, V.

A former coaching inn, the Norfolk Arms is on the main street just a short walk from the castle. It's the best place to stay if you want to be in the market town itself. The lounges and dining room are in the typically English country inn style—not ostentatious but unquestionably comfortable. The hotel has been restored with many modern amenities blending with the old architecture. The bedrooms are handsomely maintained and furnished, each with personal touches.

Dining: In the restaurant, you can order good but standard English food. When available, fresh local produce is offered. You can also order set dinners, which include many traditional English dishes.

Portreeves Acre. 2 Causeway, Arundel, W. Sussex BN18 9JJ. ☎ **01903/883277.** 3 units. TV. £36–£42 ($57.60–$67.20) double. Rates include English breakfast. No credit cards.

When this modern, 2-story house was built by a local architect within a stone's throw of the ancient castle and rail station, it caused much local comment. Today the glass-and-brick edifice is the property of Charles and Pat Rogers. Double guest rooms are on the ground floor and have views of the flowering acre in back. The property is bordered on one side by the River Arun.

WHERE TO DINE

China Palace. 67 High St. ☎ **01903/883702.** Reservations recommended on weekends. Main courses £6–£9 ($9.60–$14.40); fixed-price 3-course dinner for 2 £33 ($52.80). AE, MC, V. Daily noon–2:15pm and 6pm–midnight. BEIJING/SZECHUAN.

The most prominent Chinese restaurant in the region has an elaborately carved 17th-century ceiling, imported by a former owner long ago from a palace in Italy. The interior decorations include the artfully draped sails from a Chinese junk. It's located across the road from the crenellated fortifications surrounding Arundel's castle. The Beijing and Szechuan cuisine includes such classic dishes as Peking duck, crispy lamb, king prawns Kung Po, and lobster with fresh ginger and spring onions.

✪ **Queens Room Restaurant.** In the Amberley Castle hotel, Amberley, near Arundel. ☎ **01798/831992.** Reservations required. 5-course fixed-price dinner £35 ($56); 2-course lunch £12.50 ($20). AE, DC, MC, V. Daily noon–2pm and 7–9:30pm. ENGLISH/CONTINENTAL.

There is no contest. The best cuisine in the Arundel area is served at this previously recommended hotel. Although the joint is elegant, the prices aren't as staggering as you might have feared. This 12th-century-styled room is named after the medieval painted panels of "Nine Virtuous Ladies" that once adorned the walls. Its barrel vaulted ceiling and lancet windows provide a medieval-like setting for the chef's inspired cuisine.

The chef has raided England's culinary past for inspiration, but has given his dishes modern interpretations. We especially admire his use of natural ingredients found in the area—wild Southdown rabbit, lavender, lemon thyme, and nettles. The menu changes frequently, though the special menu of the day is always alluring. The gourmet Castle Cuisine menu is worth driving across Sussex to enjoy. One recent menu contained not only poached freshwater fish but a wild-rabbit-and-bacon stew. The intermediate course was a quince-and-gin water-rice (where else can you find that these days?). Desserts such as a warm gratin of orange and dark chocolate with Grand Marnier sabayon make a perfect finish. The staff is attentive, friendly, yet warmly informal, and there's a well-chosen wine list.

11 Brighton: London by the Sea

52 miles S of London

Brighton was one of the first of the great seaside resorts of Europe. The Prince of Wales, the original swinger who was to shape so much of its destiny, arrived in 1783; his presence and patronage gave immediate status to the seaside town.

Fashionable dandies from London, including Beau Brummell, turned up. The construction business boomed as Brighton blossomed with charming and attractive town houses and well-planned squares and crescents. From the Prince Regent's title came the voguish word *Regency,* which was to characterize an era, but more specifically refers to the period between 1811 and 1820. Under Victoria, and despite the fact that she cut off her presence, Brighton continued to flourish.

But earlier in this century, as the English began to discover more glamorous spots on the Continent, Brighton lost much of its old joie de vivre. People began to call it "tatty," and it began to feature the usual run of fun-fair-type English seaside amusements. However, that state of affairs long ago changed, owing largely to the huge numbers of Londoners who moved in (some of whom now commute); the invasion has made Brighton increasingly lighthearted and sophisticated today. It now attracts a fair number of gay vacationers, and a beach east of town has been set aside for nude bathers (Britain's first such venture).

ESSENTIALS

GETTING THERE   Fast trains (41 a day) leave from Victoria or London Bridge Station and make the trip from London in 55 minutes. For rail information, call ☎ 0345/484950 in the U.K., or 01603/764776 in the U.S. Buses from London's Victoria Coach Station take around 2 hours.

If you're driving, M23 (signposted from central London) leads to A23, which takes you into Brighton.

VISITOR INFORMATION   At the **Tourist Information Centre,** 10 Bartholomew Sq. (☎ 01273/292599), opposite the town hall, you can make hotel reservations, reserve tickets for National Express coaches, and pick up a list of current events. It's open June to mid-July, Monday through Friday from 9am to 6pm, Saturday 10am to 5pm, and Sunday 10am to 4pm; mid-July through August, Monday through Friday from 9am to 6pm and Saturday and Sunday from 10am to 6pm. Off-season hours are Monday through Friday from 9am to 5pm, Saturday from 10am to 5pm, and Sunday 10am to 4pm.

GETTING AROUND   The **Brighton Borough Transport** serves both Brighton and Hove with frequent and efficient service. Local fares are only 60p (95¢), and free maps giving the company's routes are available at the Tourist Information Centre (see above). You can also call the company directly at ☎ 01273/886200.

SPECIAL EVENTS   If you're here in May, the international **Brighton Festival** (☎ 01273/676926), the largest arts festival in England, features drama, literature, visual art, dance, and concerts ranging from classical to rock. A festival program is available annually in February for those who want to plan ahead.

THE ROYAL PAVILION

✪ **The Royal Pavilion at Brighton. ☎ 01273/290900.** Admission is £4.10 ($6.55) adults, £3 ($4.80) seniors and students, £2.50 ($4) children ages 5–15; free for children 4 and under. Apr–Sept daily 10am–6pm; Oct–Mar daily 10am–5pm. Closed Dec 25–26.

Among the royal residences of Europe, the Royal Pavilion at Brighton, a John Nash version of an Indian Moghul's palace, is unique. Ornate and exotic, it has been subjected over the years to the most devastating wit of English satirists and pundits, but today we can examine it more objectively as one of the outstanding examples of the orientalizing tendencies of the romantic movement in England.

Originally a farmhouse, a neoclassical villa was built on the site in 1787 by Henry Holland, but it no more resembled its present appearance than a caterpillar does a butterfly. By the time Nash had transformed it from a simple classical villa into an orientalist fantasy, the prince regent had become King George IV, and the king and one of his mistresses, Lady Conyngham, lived in the palace until 1827.

A decade passed before Victoria, then queen, arrived in Brighton. Although she was to bring Albert and the children on a number of occasions, the monarch and Brighton just didn't mix. The very air of the resort seemed too flippant for her. By 1845, Victoria began packing, and the royal furniture was carted off. Its royal owners gone, the Pavilion was in serious peril of being torn down, but by a narrow vote, Brightonians

Brighton

agreed to purchase it. Gradually it was restored to its former splendor, enhanced in no small part by the return of much of its original furniture, including many items on loan from her majesty the queen. A new exhibit tours the Royal Pavilion Gardens.

Of exceptional interest is the domed **Banqueting Room,** with a chandelier of bronze dragons supporting lilylike glass globes. In the Great Kitchen, with its old revolving spits, is a collection of Wellington's pots and pans from his town house at Hyde Park Corner. In the **State Apartments,** particularly the domed salon, dragons wink at you, serpents entwine, lacquered doors shine. The Music Room, with its scalloped ceiling, is a fantasy of water lilies, flying dragons, reptilian paintings, bamboo, silk, and satin.

In the first-floor gallery, look for Nash's views of the Pavilion in its elegant heyday. Other attractions include **Queen Victoria's Apartments,** beautifully re-created, and the impressively restored **South Galleries,** breakfast rooms for George IV's guests. Refreshments are available in the Queen Adelaide Tea Room, which has a balcony overlooking the Royal Pavilion Gardens.

SEASIDE AMUSEMENTS & ACTIVE PURSUITS

The beaches at Brighton aren't sandy; they're pebbly, and unfortunately, the waters are polluted. So, instead of swimming, most visitors to Brighton sunbathe, promenade along the boardwalk, play video arcade games, drink in local pubs and "caffs," and generally enjoy the sea air. Beachfront areas are more for the promenade crowd, which often consists of gay men and women.

Brighton is also the site of Britain's first officially designed clothing-optional beach, located a short walk west of the Brighton Marina. Local signs refer to it as simply "Nudist Beach." Telescombe Beach, mostly frequented by gay men and lesbians, lies 4½ miles to the east of the Palace Pier.

And you can't miss the **Palace Pier,** a somewhat battered late Victorian iron structure jutting seaward toward France. Built between 1889 and 1899 and renovated during the early 1990s, it's lined with somewhat tacky concessions and a late-night crowd that's a bit more sinister than the one that frequents it during the day. The older West Pier is a rusting, abandoned hulk, a solitary reminder of forgotten steam-age pleasures and seafront holidays, with a beach in front that's sometimes used as a rendezvous point for gay men.

If you want to rent or charter a boat, stop by the Brighton Marina, at the intersection of A259 and King's Cliff Parade (☎ **01273/693636**). There's good fishing at the marina as well, but the breakwaters near Hove may be better because there aren't as many boats or swimmers in that area.

One of the best and most challenging 18-hole golf courses around is the **East Brighton Golf Club,** Roedean Road (☎ **01273/604838**). A less challenging 18-hole course is the **Hollingbury Park Golf Club,** Ditching Road (☎ **01273/552010**). Buses from the **Old Steine** are available to both courses.

An indoor pool, diving pool, learner's pool, solarium, and water slide are all available daily at the **Prince Regent Swimming Complex,** Church St. (☎ **01273/ 685692**).

If you enjoy wagering on the horses, the **Brighton Races** are held frequently between April and October at the **Brighton Racecourse,** Race Hill (☎ **01273/ 603580**). An admission fee is charged.

SHOPPING

Mall rats head for **Churchill Square,** Brighton's spacious shopping center, which has major chain stores, including **Habitat.** The shopping center runs from Western Road to North Street (about 2 miles long) and offers many inexpensive shops and stalls with great buys on everything from antiques to woolens. On Saturdays, there are many more antique exhibits and sidewalk stalls.

Regent Arcade, which is located between East Street, Bartholomew Square, and Market Street, sells artwork, jewelry, and other gift items, as well as high-fashion clothing.

Everyone raves about the shopping on **The Lanes,** although you may find them too quaint. The Lanes are a closely knit section of alleyways off North Street in Brighton's Old Town; many of the present shops were formerly fishers' cottages. The shopping is mostly for tourists, and, while you may fall for a few photo ops, you'll find that the nearby **North Lanes**—between The Lanes and the train station—is the area for up-and-coming talent and for alternative retail. Just wander along a street called Kensington Gardens to get the whole effect. There are innumerable shops located in The Lanes with antique books and jewelry, and many boutiques are found in converted backyards on Duke Lane just off Ship Street. In the center of The Lanes is Brighton Square, which is ideal for relaxing or for people-watching near the fountain on one of the benches or from a cafe bar.

On Sunday, Brighton has a good **flea market** in the parking lot of the train station. On the first Tuesday of each month there's the **Brighton Racecourse Antiques and Collectors Fair** (9am to 3pm) with about 300 stalls.

While browsing around the **Brighton Marina,** bargain hunters can find brand-name goods at discount prices at **Merchants Quay Factory Outlet Shopping**

(☎ 01273/818590), with everything from pottery to books, and designer clothes to perfumes. There are many stores to visit at the Brighton Marina. One is **Edinburgh Crystal** (☎ 01273/818702) where you can find cut-glass decanters, vases, glasses, canteens of cutlery, and more. Another is **Leave It to Jeeves** (☎ 01273/818585). Here they have old photographs of the local area, illustrations, prints, and a complete framing service.

In addition to its malls and shopping complexes, Brighton also abounds in specialty shops. The ones below caught our eye.

Bears and Friends of Brighton, 41 Meeting House Lane (☎ 01273/208940), attracts teddy-bear buffs.

Culpeper, 12D Meeting House Lane (☎ 01273/327939), is the place for bath salts, fine English soap, herbal medicines, herbs, natural plant oils, potpourri, and spices.

Le Jazz Hot, 14 Prince Albert St. (☎ 01273/206091), offers a fine selection of art deco and art nouveau ceramics, plus collections of Bakelite jewelry, deco chrome, and period furniture.

Pecksniff's Bespoke Perfumery, 45–46 Meeting House Lane (☎ 01273/328904), creates a fragrance just for you. They hand-blend flowers, herbs, and natural oils to make traditional English scents, and will keep your formula on file for when you need a refill.

The Pavilion Shop, The Royal Pavilion, East Street, Brighton (☎ 01273/603005), next door to The Royal Pavilion, is the finest gift shop in Brighton. Here you can purchase many gift and home-furnishing items in the style of the design schools that created the look (from Regency to Victorian) at The Royal Pavilion. Also available are books, jams, needlepoint kits, notebooks, pencils, stencil kits, and other souvenirs.

WHERE TO STAY

Gay travelers should refer to "Brighton's Gay Scene," later in this section, for a selection of gay-friendly accommodations.

VERY EXPENSIVE

Brighton Metropole. 106 King's Rd., Brighton, E. Sussex BN1 2FU. ☎ 01273/775432. Fax 01273/207764. 338 units. TV TEL. £185 ($296) double; £220–£520 ($352–$832) suite. Weekend breaks £120 ($192) double. Rates include English breakfast. AE, DC, MC, V. Parking free. Bus: 1, 2, or 3.

Originally built in 1889, with a handful of its rooms housed in a postwar addition, the Brighton Metropole is the largest hotel in Brighton and one of the city's top three or four hotels (although it's not as grand as the Grand). This hotel, with a central seafront location, often hosts big conferences. The recently refurbished rooms are comfortable, with movies, hair dryers, trouser presses, and beverage-makers.

Dining: There's an array of dining and drinking choices, among them the Arundel and Windsor restaurants.

Amenities: On the premises is a leisure club, including an indoor swimming pool.

Brighton Thistle Hotel. King's Rd., Brighton, E. Sussex BN1 2GS. ☎ 800/44-UTELL in the U.S., or 01273/206700. Fax 01273/820692. 204 units. A/C MINIBAR TV TEL. Mon–Thurs £164 ($262.40) double; £295 ($472) suite. Fri–Sun £110 ($176) double; £210 ($336) suite. Children under 17 stay free in parents' room. AE, DC, MC, V. Bus: 1, 2, or 3.

This relatively modern hotel is one of the finest accommodations in the south of England, topped in Brighton only by the Grand. Rising from the seafront, just minutes from the Royal Pavilion, it has been stylishly and rather luxuriously designed for maximum comfort. Guests wander at leisure through tastefully furnished public rooms.

Dining: Its restaurant, La Noblesse, is outstanding and merits a separate recommendation (see below). The Promenade restaurant, overlooking the sea, has an imaginative and well-planned menu. Guests and nonresidents can enjoy lunch or dinner here daily. There's also a coffee shop and a bar.

Amenities: 24-hour room service, laundry, baby-sitting, valet parking. The hotel has the best athletic facilities in town—a gym, indoor heated swimming pool, solarium, and sauna.

✪ **The Grand.** King's Rd., Brighton, E. Sussex BN2 1FW. ☎ **01273/321188.** Fax 01273/202694. 200 units. A/C TV TEL. £180–£270 ($288–$432 double; from £550 ($880) suite. Rates include English breakfast. AE, CB, DC, MC, V. Parking £10.20 ($16.30). Bus: 1, 2, or 3.

This is Brighton's premier hotel. The original Grand was constructed in 1864 and entertained some of the most eminent Victorians and Edwardians. This landmark was massively damaged in a 1984 terrorist attack on Margaret Thatcher and key figures in the British government. Several colleagues were killed, Mrs. Thatcher narrowly escaped, and entire sections of the hotel looked as if they had been hit by an air raid. That gave its present owners, De Vere Hotels, the challenge to create a new Grand, and frankly, the new one is better than the old. It's the most elegant Georgian recreation in town.

You enter via a glassed-in conservatory and register in a grandiose public room, with soaring ceilings and elaborate moldings. The hotel has plushly comfortable furniture in traditional tastes with well-chosen accessories. The rooms, of a very high standard, are generally spacious with many amenities, including hospitality trays, trouser presses, and hair dryers. The sea-view rooms have minibars and new beds and furniture. There are also "romantic rooms" with double whirlpool baths and some rooms equipped with additional facilities for travelers with disabilities. All standard rooms have been refurbished with new bathrooms, beds, and soft furnishings.

Dining/Diversions: Both British and continental cuisine are served in the King's Restaurant. The kitchen uses superb ingredients. The restaurant serves set menus throughout the week, followed by a Saturday-night dinner-dance with live music. The Victoria Bar is an elegant rendezvous, and Midnight Blues is the most sophisticated club at the resort.

Amenities: Hobden's Health Spa (complete with spa pool, steam room, sauna, solarium, and massage and exercise arena), hair salon, beautician, 24-hour room service, laundry, baby-sitting.

MODERATE

Old Ship Hotel. King's Rd., Brighton, E. Sussex BN1 1NR. ☎ **01273/329001.** Fax 01273/820718. 156 units. TV TEL. For 1 night from £80–£95 ($128–$152) double; from £250 ($400) suite. For 2–4 nights from £90 ($144) double; from £130 ($208) suite. Children under 12 stay free in parents' rooms. Rates include English breakfast. AE, DC, MC, V. Parking £10 ($16). Bus: 1, 2, or 3.

First used as an inn in 1559, this hotel, a favorite among conference groups, is the largest and best of Brighton's middle-priced choices. (Try to stay for more than 1 night; prices drop dramatically if you do.) Most of what you'll see today dates from the 1880s, and despite many subsequent modernizations, there's still a sense of its old-time late Victorian origins. Nearly two-thirds of the accommodations are well furnished, with modern bathrooms; the rest are still somewhat dowdy. The east wing has the most smartly furnished rooms.

There are comfortable sea-view lounges, an oak-trimmed bar, and a spacious sea-facing restaurant, the Royal Escape, that naturally specializes in seafood. Meals are nicely prepared and copious.

Topps Hotel. 17 Regency Sq., Brighton, E. Sussex BN1 2FG. ☎ **01273/729334.** Fax 01273/203679. 15 units. MINIBAR TV TEL. £84–£129 ($134.40–$206.40) double. Rates include English breakfast. AE, CB, DC, MC, V. Parking £9.20 ($14.70). Bus: 1, 2, 3, 5, or 6.

Flower boxes fill the windows of this cream-colored town house, whose owners, Paul and Pauline Collins, have devoted years to upgrading it. The hotel enjoys a diagonal view of the sea from its position beside the sloping lawn of Regency Square. Each of the differently shaped and individually furnished accommodations has a radio and a trouser press.

INEXPENSIVE

Paskins Hotel. 19 Charlotte St., Brighton, E. Sussex BN2 1AG. ☎ **01273/601203.** Fax 01273/621973. 19 units, 16 with shower. TV TEL. £35 ($56) double without shower, £48 ($76.80) double with shower; £60 ($96) double with 4-poster bed. Children 10 and under sharing with 2 adults are charged £10 ($16). Rates include English breakfast. AE, DC, MC, V. Bus: 7 or 52.

This well-run small hotel is only a short walk from the Palace Pier and Royal Pavilion. The rates depend on the plumbing and furnishings; the most expensive units are fitted with four-poster beds. Bedrooms are individually decorated with contemporary styling. Recent upgrading has made this one of the more charming B&B properties in Brighton. A friendly, informal atmosphere prevails, and the freshly cooked English breakfast, served in a cozy room, is one of the best in town. For a special rendezvous with someone, retreat to the snug little bar.

Regency Hotel. 28 Regency Sq., Brighton, E. Sussex BN1 2FH. ☎ **01273/202690.** Fax 01273/220438. 13 units, 9 with shower, 1 suite with bathroom. TV TEL. £60 ($96) double without shower, £70 ($112) double with shower; £100 ($160) Regency suite with bath. Rates include English breakfast. AE, DC, MC, V. Parking £9.50 ($15.20). Bus: 1, 2, 3, 5, or 6.

This typical Regency town house was built in 1820 with bow windows, a canopied balcony, and a porticoed entrance. The property was once the home of Jane, dowager duchess of Marlborough, and great-grandmother of Sir Winston Churchill. This landmark building features fine cornices, paneled doors, and a fireplace. It was skillfully converted into a family managed hotel with a licensed bar and modern comforts. Each bedroom has a hair dryer and beverage-maker, and many rooms enjoy window views across the square and out to the sea. The Regency Suite has a half-tester bed (1840) and antique furniture, along with a huge bow window dressed with ceiling-to-floor swagged curtains and a balcony facing the sea and West Pier. The Regency is only a few minutes' walk from the Conference Center and only 30 minutes by train or car from Gatwick Airport.

✪ Twenty-One Hotel. 21 Charlotte St., Marine Parade, Brighton, E. Sussex BN2 1AG. ☎ **01273/686450.** Fax 01273/695560. 7 units. TV TEL. £45–£60 ($72–$96) double; £60–£85 ($96–$136) suite. Rates include English breakfast. AE, DC, MC, V. Bus: 7 or 52.

The most sophisticated of Brighton's smaller hotels, this early Victorian white house is a block from the sea. The owner, Mr. Jung, has completely renovated it. All individually designed rooms now have handmade four-poster beds, and there is new carpeting everywhere, including the bathrooms. The best rooms are the "classics," including a twin green room with two single four-poster beds, a double champagne room decorated in blue and gold with light pine furnishings, and a double oak room in rich, deep colors of green and red with a floral design. In addition to the usual amenities (beverage-maker, hair dryers), there are toiletries, crackers, sweets, and mineral water in the rooms. Some rooms even have a small fridge. Mr. Jung is well on his way to reaching his goal of owning the best B&B in Brighton.

Dinner is available, with a minimum notice of 24 hours. Possible main courses are breast of duck with cherry brandy and orange sauce, or breast of chicken with a mustard-and-cream sauce.

IN NEARBY HOVE

Courtlands Hotel. 21-27 The Drive, Hove, E. Sussex BN3 3JE. ☎ **01273/731055.** Fax 01273/328295. 64 units. TV TEL. £75 ($120) double; £85–£95 ($136–$152) executive rooms. Rates include English breakfast. AE, DC, MC, V. Bus: 52.

Courtlands, a mile west of the center, is 400 yards from the sea, opening onto the wide thoroughfare known as "The Drive." This comfortable Victorian building has been recently modernized. In the complex are five particularly agreeable rooms in a pair of outlying cottages. The bedrooms are spacious and harmonious. For dining, there's the Golden Dolphin lounge bar and a dining room opening onto gardens. Good cuisine, both international and English, is served. There's also a solarium and a heated swimming pool.

The Dudley. Lansdowns Place, Hove, Brighton, E. Sussex BN3 1HQ. ☎ **01273/736266.** Fax 01273/729802. 71 units. TV TEL. £99 ($158.40) double. AE, DC, MC, V. Bus: 52.

Near the seafront in Hove, the Dudley—completely redecorated in 1995—is just a few blocks from the resort's bronze statue of Queen Victoria. Going up marble steps, you register within view of 18th-century antiques and oil portraits of Edwardian-era debutantes. The large, high-ceilinged public rooms emphasize the deeply comfortable chairs, the thick cove moldings, and the chandeliers. The bedrooms offer coffeemakers, tall windows, and conservatively stylish furniture.

You must pass through a bar to reach the entrance to the dining room, which offers traditional and modern British cuisine. The hotel also offers laundry, baby-sitting, and 24-hour room service.

Sackville Hotel. 189 Kingsway, Hove, Brighton, E. Sussex BN3 4GU. ☎ **01273/736292.** Fax 01273/205759. 45 units. TV TEL. Mon–Thurs £70 ($112) double, Fri–Sun £60 ($96) double (minimum 3 nights); suite (daily) £85 ($136). Rates include English breakfast. AE, DC, MC, V. Bus: 52.

Its lime- and cream-colored neobaroque facade was built across the road from the beach in 1902. Today, in a comfortably updated form, the Sackville welcomes visitors with high-ceilinged bedrooms featuring big windows, sea views, and Queen Anne furnishings. All units have terraces.

A large ground-floor dining room offers a warm, masculine formality, with views of the sea and good service and food. An adjacent bar, Winston's, is filled with photographs of Churchill in war and peace.

WHERE TO DINE

The **Mock Turtle Restaurant,** 4 Pool Valley (☎ 01273/327380), is a small but busy tearoom that has many locals stopping by to gossip and take their tea. They offer only a few sandwiches, but the varieties of cakes, flapjacks, tea breads, and light, fluffy scones with homemade preserves are dead-on. Everything is made fresh daily. The most popular item is the scones with strawberry preserves or whipped cream. They also serve a wide variety of good teas.

EXPENSIVE

China Garden. 88 Preston St. (in the town center off Western Rd.). ☎ **01273/325124.** Reservations recommended. Main courses £10–£20 ($16–$32); fixed-price menu from £18 ($28.80). AE, DC, MC, V. Daily noon–11:30pm. Closed Dec 25–26. BEIJING/CANTONESE.

The menu at the China Garden is large and satisfying. It may not be ready for London, and it's certainly pricey, but it's the brightest in town, with many classic dishes deftly handled by the kitchen staff. Dim sum (a popular luncheon choice) is offered only until 4pm. Try chicken with lemon sauce, crispy sliced pork Szechuan-style, or Peking roast duck with pancakes.

La Marinade. 77 St. George's Rd., Kemp Town (off King's Cliff along the seafront). ☎ **01273/600992.** Reservations recommended. Main courses £17–£25 ($27.20–$40); fixed-price lunch £12.80–£18.50 ($20.50–$29.60). AE, DC, MC, V. Tues–Fri and Sun noon–2pm; Mon–Sat 7–10pm. FRENCH.

The cuisine, inspired by Normandy and Brittany, shows a certain subtle preparation. You get a nice range of sensitively cooked dishes; care has been taken to preserve natural flavors. A particularly good starter is a combination of snails and quails in a fricassee in the style of Provence. The white-butter sauce on our fish dish was just as good as that served in the Loire Valley. You might prefer the roast pigeon with honey.

✪ **La Noblesse.** In the Brighton Thistle Hotel, King's Rd. ☎ **01273/206700.** Reservations required. 3-course fixed-price meal £18.50 ($29.60) at lunch, £28.50 ($45.60) at dinner. AE, DC, MC, V. Tues–Fri noon–2pm; Tues–Sat 7–9:30pm. CLASSIC CONTINENTAL.

The most elegant dining room in Brighton is the flagship restaurant of this previously recommended hotel. It serves the finest food in town. The chefs are in fine form, and the continental staff is perfectly trained, serving such dishes as broiled fillet of beef topped with wild mushrooms and a tarragon-and-cream sauce or braised oxtail stuffed with fresh herbs and celeriac and served with potato puree, tomatoes, and basil. The sauces are excellent, cooked to bring out natural flavors. Vegetarian meals are also available, including ratatouille on a bed of fresh spinach pasta.

Old Ship Hotel Restaurant. In the Old Ship Hotel, King's Rd. ☎ **01273/329001.** Reservations recommended. Main courses £12–£18 ($19.20–$28.80); fixed-price 3-course meal £10.50 ($16.80) at lunch, £12–£18 ($19.20–$28.80) at dinner. AE, DC, MC, V. Daily 12:30–2:30pm and 7–9:30pm. Bus: 1, 2, or 3. ENGLISH.

A longtime favorite, the Old Ship Restaurant, in the center of town, enjoys an ideal location on the waterfront. Whenever possible, locally caught fish appears on the menu, from Dover sole to panfried red bream fillet. Try such dishes as panfried pork loin with saffron rice or grilled fillet of turbot with a lemon-and-butter sauce. Vegetables, which accompany the main dishes, are always fresh and cooked "new style." Sometimes local dishes such as turkey from Sussex appear on the menu, but with a French sauce. The wine list is excellent. Stop in the adjoining pub for a before- or after-dinner drink. On Saturday night, there is a traditional dinner-dance with a four-course fixed-price dinner for £19.90 ($31.85).

One Paston Place. 1 Paston Place (near the waterfront off King's Cliff). ☎ **01273/606933.** Reservations required. Main courses £14.50–£17.50 ($23.20–$28); fixed-price 2-course lunch £14.50 ($23.20); fixed-price 3-course lunch £16.50 ($26.40). AE, DC, MC, V. Tues–Sat 12:30–2pm and 7:30–10pm. Closed 2 weeks in Jan and 2 weeks in Aug. FRENCH.

Mark (the chef) and Nicole Emmerson offer a wisely limited menu based on the freshest of ingredients available at the market. You might begin with roast quail, soft polenta, and wild mushrooms, then move on to a turbot with lentils and crispy leeks plus *pommes Fondates* with caraway. Vegetarian dishes are also available. One sumptuous dessert is coconut crème brûlée flavored with crispy pineapple.

MODERATE

English's Oyster Bar and Seafood Restaurant. 29-31 East St. ☎ **01273/327980.** Reservations recommended. Main courses £8.50–£25.95 ($13.60–$41.50); fixed-price menus

£6.75–£11.95 ($10.80–$19.10). AE, DC, MC, V. Mon–Sat noon–10:15pm, Sun 12:30–9:30pm. SEAFOOD.

This popular seafood restaurant occupies a trio of very old fisher's cottages and was founded at the turn of the century. Owned and operated by the same family since the end of World War II, it sits behind a nostalgic brass-trimmed facade in the center of town, near Brighton's bus station. For years, diners have enjoyed native oysters on the half shell, hot seafood en croûte with lobster sauce, fried Dover sole, and fresh, locally caught plaice. The newly refurbished upstairs dining area incorporates murals, painted by two local art students, depicting Edwardian dinner and theater scenes. In summer, guests can dine alfresco on the terrace.

BRIGHTON AFTER DARK

Brighton offers lots of entertainment options. You can find out what's happening by picking up the local entertainment monthly, the *Punter*, and by looking for *What's On*, a single sheet of weekly events posted throughout the town.

There are two theaters that offer drama throughout the year: the **Theatre Royal,** New Road (☎ 01273/328488), which has pre-London shows, and the **Gardner Arts Center** (☎ 01273/685861), a modern theater-in-the-round, located on the campus of Sussex University, a few miles northeast of town in Falmer. Bigger concerts in all genres are held at **The Dome,** 29 New Rd. (☎ 01273/674357), and **Brighton Centre,** Russell Road (☎ 01273/202881), a 5,000-seat facility featuring mainly pop-music shows.

Nightclubs also abound. Cover charges range from free admission (most often on early or midweek nights) to £7 ($11.20), so call the clubs to see about admission fees and updates in their nightly schedules, which often vary from week to week or season to season.

The smartly dressed can find their groove at **Steamers,** King's Road (☎ 01273/775432), located in the Metropole Hotel, which does have a dress code. The **Paradox,** West Street (☎ 01273/321628), is a popular club that features Gay Night on Monday, and **The Escape Club,** 10 Marine Parade (☎ 01273/606906), home to both gay and straight dancers, has two floors for dancing, and offers different music styles on different nights of the week.

One of the best hunting grounds for dance clubs is **Kingswest,** a King's Road complex that houses two clubs featuring a blend of techno, house, and disco. **Event II** (☎ 01273/732627) sports more than $1 million worth of lighting and dance-floor gadgetry.

Gloucester, Gloucester Plaza (☎ 01273/699068), has a variety of music through the week, from 1960s to 1980s music to alternative and groove. For a change of pace, visit **Casablanca,** Middle Street (☎ 01273/321817), which features jazz with an international flavor.

Pubs are a good place to kick off the evening, especially the **Colonnade Bar,** New Road (☎ 01273/328728), which has been serving drinks for more than 100 years. The pub gets a lot of theater business because of its proximity to the Theatre Royal. **Cricketers,** Black Lion Street (☎ 01273/329472), is worth a stop because it's Brighton's oldest pub, parts of which date from 1549. The **Squid and Starfish,** 77 Middle St. (☎ 01273/727114), is a good place to meet fellow travelers from the neighboring Backpacker's Hostel; and beachside drinking lures them to **Cuba,** 160 King's Rd. (☎ 01273/770505), and also to **Fortune of War,** 157 King's Rd. (☎ 01273/205065), which attracts those who don't want to do their drinking at Cuba.

H. J. O'Neils, 27 Ship St. (☎ 01273/748339), is an authentic Irish pub located at the top of The Lanes. A stop here will fortify you with traditional Irish pub grub, a creamy pint of Guinness, and a sound track of folk music. Of course, they make the best Irish stew in town.

BRIGHTON'S GAY SCENE

After London, Brighton has the most active gay scene in England. Aside from vacationers, it's home to gay retirees and gay executives who commute into central London by train. The town has always had a reputation for tolerance and humor, and according to jaded owners of some of the town's 20 or so gay bars, there are more drag queens living within the local Regency town houses than virtually anywhere else in England.

But the gay scene here is a lot less glittery than in London. And don't assume that the south of England is as chic as the south of France. Its international reputation is growing, but despite that, gay Brighton remains thoroughly English, and at times, even a bit dowdy.

GAY-FRIENDLY PLACES TO STAY

Brighton Court Craven Hotel. 2 Atlingworth St., Brighton BN2 1PL. ☎ **01273/607710.** 11 units, all with shower but without toilet. TV. Mon–Thurs £40 ($64) double, Fri–Sun £38 ($60.80) double. Rates include breakfast. No credit cards.

This 3-story hotel isn't particularly exciting and doesn't have many facilities, but it's the cheapest option we recommend, and it has an atmosphere of casual permissiveness. It's proud of a clientele that's almost 100% gay, and mostly male. Breakfasts are served communally, with all the traditional English accompaniments, and there's a bar. A highlight here is the chance to chat with owner David Raven, one of Brighton's leading AIDS activists, and a well-known star on the drag circuit who performs under the stage name of Maizie Trollette.

Coward's Guest House. 12 Upper Rock Gardens, Brighton BN2 1QE. ☎ **01273/692677.** 6 units, 2 with shower, all with toilet. £45–£55 ($72–$88) double. MC, V.

Originally built in 1807, this 5-story Regency-era house is extremely well maintained. Inside, Jerry and his partner, Cyril (who's a cousin of the late playwright and bon vivant Noël Coward), welcome only gay men of all degrees of flamboyance. Don't expect any frills in the rooms—they're conservative, standard rooms you might find in any modern hotel across Britain. Although there are very few amenities, a number of gay bars and watering holes lie nearby.

New Europe. 31–32 Marine Parade, Brighton BN2 1TR. ☎ **01273/624462.** Fax 01273/624575. 33 units. TV TEL. £45–£50 ($72–$80) double. AE, DC, MC, V.

Hands-down, this is the largest, busiest, and most fun gay hotel in Brighton. First, it's a bona fide hotel, not a B&B as most of Brighton's other gay-friendly lodgings are. Unlike many of its competitors, it welcomes women, even though very few of them tend to be comfortable (there are two very loud, very male bars on the premises). Because of the high-jinx and raucousness that sometimes float up from the bars below, rooms can sometimes be noisy, but are nonetheless comfortable, clean, and unfrilly. If you want the staff to camp it up for you before your arrival (adding balloons, champagne, flowers, and streamers), someone on the staff will, for a fee, be happy to comply.

GAY-FRIENDLY RESTAURANTS

Every restaurant in town grew used to gay clients long, long ago, but one spot actively caters to them.

Jesters. 87 St. James St. (near the New Europe Hotel). ☎ **01273/624233.** Main courses £5.50–£9 ($8.80–$14.40). AE, MC, V. Mon–Fri 5:30–11pm, Sat–Sun noon–11pm.

Large and busy, Jesters is refreshingly unpretentious. Everything about the place, including the alert attentions of a kindly matriarch directing the traffic flow near the entrance, evokes a traditional and very busy English restaurant, with one important exception: Its clientele is almost exclusively gay. You'll find mostly English food (trout, salmon, pork, beef, and vegetarian items) and a few Italian dishes like lasagna, spaghetti Bolognese, and cannelloni.

GAY NIGHTLIFE

A complete, up-to-date roster of the local gay bars is available in any copy of *G-Scene* magazine (☎ 01273/749947), distributed free in gay hotels and bars throughout the south of England.

See also "Brighton After Dark," above, for a few popular dance clubs.

Doctor Brighton's Bar, 16 Kings Rd., The Seafront (☎ 01273/328765), is the largest and most consistently reliable choice. The staff expends great energy on welcoming all members of the gay community into its premises. In their words, "We get everyone from 18-year-old designer queens to 50-year-old leather queens, and they, along with all their friends and relatives, are welcome." Originally built around 1750, with a checkered past that includes stints as a smuggler's haven and abortion clinic, it also has more history, and more of the feel of an old-time Victorian pub, than any of its competitors. It's open Monday to Saturday from 11am to 11pm, Sunday from noon to 10:30pm. Since there's no real lesbian bar in town, gay women tend to congregate at Doctor Brighton's.

Two of the town's busiest and most flamboyant gay bars, **Legends** and **Schwarz,** lie within the previously recommended New Europe Hotel. The one with the longer hours is Legends, a pubby, clubby, woodsy-looking bar with a view of the sea that's open to the public daily from noon to 11pm, and to residents of the New Europe Hotel and their guests till 5am. Legends features cross-dressing cabarets three times a week (Tuesday and Thursday at 9pm, Sunday afternoons at 2:30pm), when tweedy-looking English matrons and diaphanous Edwardian vamps are portrayed with bucket loads of tongue-in-cheek satire and humor. Schwarz is a cellar-level denim and leather joint that does everything it can to encourage its patrons to wear some kind of uniform. Schwarz is open only Friday and Saturday from 10pm to 2am, and charges a £2 ($3.20) cover.

The Marlborough, 4 Princes St. (☎ 01273/570028), has been a staple on the scene for years. Set across from the Royal Pavilion, this is a woodsy-looking Victorian-style pub with a cabaret theater on its second floor. It remains popular with the gay and, to a lesser degree, straight community. A changing roster of lesbian performance art and both gay and straight cabaret within the second-floor theater is presented.

Wanna go dancing? The largest and usually most frenetic gay disco in the south of England is **Club Revenge,** 32-34 Old Steine (☎ 01273/606064). Combining architectural elements from the Victorian, art deco, and postdisco eras, with a sweeping view over the amusement arcades of the Palace Pier, it has two floors, multiple bars, an interior color scheme of turquoise, blue, and red, and a clientele that includes every conceivable subculture within the gay world. Open Monday to Saturday from 9pm to 2am, it charges a £3 to £5.50 ($4.80 to $8.80) cover.

A SIDE TRIP FROM BRIGHTON TO KIPLING'S HOMETOWN

"Heaven looked after it in the dissolute times of mid-Victorian restoration and caused the vicar to send his bailiff to live in it for 40 years, and he lived in peaceful filth and left everything as he found it," wrote Rudyard Kipling.

He was writing of **Bateman's,** the 17th-century ironmaster's house in the village of Burwash, on A265, the Lewes-Etchingham road, some 27 miles northeast of Brighton,

Winnie-the-Pooh & a Scandalous Death, Too

In an East Sussex farmhouse on the edge of the Ashdown Forest, the legacies of two of England's most popular cultural icons collide in an intriguing coincidence.

Cotchford Farm, a quaint old English house in the wooded countryside near Hartfield village, is the original "House at Pooh Corner," where A. A. Milne penned his famous Winnie-the-Pooh stories in the 1920s, the house where the real Christopher Robin grew up with a stuffed bear named Winnie in constant tow. It's also here (well, in the swimming pool out back, specifically) that Brian Jones, one of the original guitarists of the legendary Rolling Stones, met his untimely death by drowning in 1969.

The Milnes discovered the property in the early 1920s and began spending their vacations here; over the years, they grew quite attached to the house and surrounding woods and moved here permanently from London, only leaving for good after A. A. Milne's death in 1956. (Christopher Robin, incidentally, died in 1996 at age 75.) Though the house itself is not open to the public, Pooh fans can explore the forest where Christopher Robin played, find the bridge where Pooh invented the game of Poohsticks, visit the sandy pit where Kanga's son Roo used to play, buy "bull's-eyes" from the very shop where Christopher Robin bought his sweets (now a souvenir and sweet shop called Pooh Corner, on High Street in Hartfield), and see many other sites that gained fame through Milne's books.

Stones fans might instead choose to mourn Brian Jones with a few reflective moments in the woods. Jones's involvement with Cotchford Farm is somewhat mysterious. A founding member of the Rolling Stones, Jones was known for his penchant for weird instrumentation, and perhaps enjoyed his best musical moment as lead guitarist on the Stones classic "Ruby Tuesday," before his drug troubles became a disruptive influence on the band and his life. Jones was dismissed from the Stones in 1969, a few weeks before his death. Perhaps he retired to the Hartfield farmhouse to reflect on his ejection from what was to become one of the most popular bands in history. Or maybe he was a closet Pooh fan who sought to recapture his youth and set his life straight in Milne's Hundred Acre Wood. Whatever his reasons for moving to the House at Pooh Corner, Jones was eventually found dead in the Cotchford Farm swimming pool. The coroner's report called it "death by misadventure." "They're funny things, Accidents. You never have them till you're having them," Eeyore might have said.

To get to Cotchford Farm, take a train from London to East Grinstead and drive from there. Or you can drive all the way (East Sussex is about an hour from London); from Heathrow, take M25 south to the A22 (Exit 6), and take the A22 south to East Grinstead. Then follow A264 east to the B2026, which will take you south to Hartfield. Once in Hartfield, just ask for Winnie-the-Pooh.

—Philippe Wamba

close to the border with Kent. Born in Bombay, India, in 1865, Kipling loved the countryside of Sussex, and the book that best expressed his feelings for the shire is *Puck of Pook's Hill* (1906). The following year he was to win the Nobel Prize for literature. He lived at Bateman from 1902 until his death in 1936. His widow was to die 3 years later at the dawn of World War II, and she left the house to the National Trust.

Kipling is known mainly for his adventure stories, such as *The Jungle Book* (1894) and *Captains Courageous* (1897). He is also remembered for his tales concerning India, including *Kim* (1901). He lived in America after his marriage to Caroline Balestier in 1892. But by 1896, he had returned to the south of England, occupying a house at Rottingdean, a little village on the Sussex Downs, 4 miles east of Brighton. Here he wrote the famous line: "What should they know of England who only England know?" In a steam-driven motorcar, Kipling and Caroline set out to explore Sussex, of which they were especially fond. Although the population of Rottingdean was only that of a small village, they decided at some point that it had become too crowded. In their motorcar one day they spotted Bateman's, which was to become a final home for both of them. "It is a good and peaceable place standing in terraced lawns nigh to a walled garden of old red brick, and two fat-headed oasthouses with red brick stomachs, and an aged silver-grey dovecot on top," Kipling wrote.

The Burwash city fathers invited Kipling to unveil a memorial to the slain of World War I, and he agreed. It's in the center of town at the church. Kipling said that visitors should "remember the sacrifice." Both the church and an inn across the way appear in the section of *Puck of Pook's Hill* called "Hal o' the Draft." The famed writer and son of Anglo-Indian parents died in London, and was given an impressive funeral before burial in the Poets' Corner at Westminster Abbey.

The interior of Bateman's is filled with Asian rugs, antique bronzes, and other mementos the writer collected in India and elsewhere. Kipling's library is quite interesting. The house and gardens are open April through October, Saturday through Wednesday from 11am to 5pm. Admission is £4.50 ($7.20) for adults, £2.25 ($3.60) for children.

12 Alfriston & Lewes

60 miles S of London

Nestled on the Cuckmere River, Alfriston is one of the most beautiful villages of England. It lies northeast of Seaford on the English Channel, near the resort of Eastbourne and the modern port of Newhaven. During the day, Alfriston is overrun by coach tours (it's that lovely, and that popular). The High Street, with its old market cross, looks just like what you'd always imagined a traditional English village to be. Some of the old houses still have hidden chambers where smugglers stored their loot (alas, the loot is gone). There are also several old inns.

Only about a dozen miles away along A27 toward Brighton, is the rather somber market town of Lewes. (Thomas Paine lived at Bull House on High Street, in what is now a restaurant.) Since the home of the Glyndebourne Opera is only 5 miles to the east, it's hard to find a place to stay even in Lewes during the renowned annual opera festival.

ESSENTIALS

GETTING THERE Trains leave from London's Victoria Station and London Bridge Station for Lewes. One train per hour makes the 1¼-hour trip daily. Trains are more frequent during rush hours. For rail information, call ☎ 0345/484950 in the U.K., or 01603/764776 in the U.S. There is no rail service to Alfriston.

Buses run daily to Lewes from London's Victoria Coach Station, although the 3-hour trip has so many stops that it's better to take the train. Call ☎ 0990/808080 for schedules.

A bus runs from Lewes to Alfriston every 30 minutes. It's operated by **R.D.H. Services** and is called Local Rider no. 125. For bus information and schedules in the area, call ☎ 01273/474747. The bus station at Lewes is on East Gate Street in the center of town.

If you're driving, head east along M25 (the London ring road), cutting south on A26 via East Grinstead to Lewes. Once at Lewes, follow A27 east to the signposted turnoff for the village of Alfriston.

VISITOR INFORMATION   The **Tourist Information Centre** is in Lewes at 187 High St. (☎ **01273/483448**). In season, from Easter until the end of October, hours are Monday through Friday from 9am to 5pm, Saturday 10am to 5pm, and Sunday 10am to 2pm. Off-season hours are Monday through Friday only, from 10am to 2pm.

THE GLYNDEBOURNE OPERA FESTIVAL

In 1934, a group of local opera enthusiasts established an opera company based in the hamlet of Glyndebourne, which is 1½ miles east of Lewes and 5 miles northwest of Alfriston. The festival has been running ever since, and now is one of the best regional opera companies in Britain.

In 1994, the original auditorium was demolished, and a dramatic modern glass, brick, and steel structure, designed by noted English architect Michael Hopkins, was built adjacent to some remaining (mostly ornamental) vestiges of the original building. The new auditorium is known for its acoustics.

Operas are presented here only between mid-May and late August, and the productions tend to be unusual works.

For information, contact the **Glyndebourne Festival,** P.O. Box 2624, Glyndebourne (Lewes), E. Sussex BN8 5UW (☎ **01273/812321**). You can call the box office at ☎ **01273/813813.** Tickets range from £10 to £118 ($16 to $188.80). You usually can get last-minute tickets because of cancellations by season ticket holders. But if you want to see a specific show, it's a good idea to buy a ticket several months in advance. And it's fun to pack your own champagne picnic to enjoy before the performance; you can stock up from shops in Lewes.

To get to the theater from Lewes, take the A26 to the B2192, following the signs to Glynde and Glyndebourne. From Alfriston, follow the hamlet's main street north of town in the direction of highway A27, then turn left following signs first to Glynde, then to Glyndebourne.

EXPLORING THE TWO TOWNS

Lewes has a particularly impressive range of specialty shops, galleries, and craft centers. Our favorite is the **Old Stables Craft Center,** Market Lane (☎ **01273/475433**).

Drusilla's Park. About 1 mile outside Alfriston, off A27. ☎ **01323/870656.** Admission £6.25 ($10) adults, £4.50 ($7.20) seniors, £5.25 ($8.40) children 3–12. Daily 10am–6pm (until 4pm in winter). Closed Dec 24–26.

This fascinating but not-too-large park has a flamingo lake, Japanese garden, and unusual breeds of some domestic animals, among other attractions. Grey Owl Cabin is a replica of a cabin inhabited by a Hastings native living in the Canadian woods in the 1930s; he was a pioneer conservationist who sought to stop the trapping of beaver and the destruction of the Canadian woods. Children particularly like the playland, which now includes a water-play area.

Anne of Cleves House. 52 Southover High St., Lewes. ☎ **01273/474610.** Admission £2.25 ($3.60) adults, £2 ($3.20) students, £1.10 ($1.75) children. Apr–Nov Mon–Sat 10am–5:30pm, Sun noon–5:30pm. Dec–Mar Tues, Thurs, and Sat 10am–5:30pm. Bus no. 123.

This half-timbered house was part of Anne of Cleves's divorce settlement from Henry VIII, but Anne never lived in the house and there's no proof that she ever visited Lewes. Today it's a museum of local history, cared for by the Sussex Archaeological

Society. The museum has a furnished bedroom and kitchen and displays of furniture, local history of the Wealden iron industry, and other crafts.

Museum of Sussex Archaeology. 169 High St., Lewes. ☎ **01273/486290.** Joint admission ticket to both castle and museum £3.40 ($5.45) adults, £1.80 ($2.90) children, £2.90 ($4.65) students and seniors; family ticket £9.50 ($15.20). Both sites Mon–Sat 10am–5pm, Sun 11am–5pm. Closed Christmas Day and Boxing Day. Bus: no. 27, 28, 121, 122, 166, 728, or 729.

Lewes, of course, matured in the shadow of its **Norman castle.** Adjacent to the castle is this museum, where a 20-minute audiovisual show is available by advance request. Audio tours of the castle are also available.

WHERE TO STAY
IN ALFRISTON

The Star Inn. High St., Alfriston, E. Sussex BN26 5TA. ☎ **01323/870495.** Fax 01323/870922. 34 units. TV TEL. £92.50 ($148) double. AE, DC, MC, V.

The Star Inn—the premier place to stay—occupies a building dating from 1450, although it was originally founded in the 1200s to house pilgrims en route to Chichester and the shrine of St. Richard. In the center of the village, its carved front still unchanged, it boasts an overhanging second story of black-and-white timbers and bay windows. The lounges are on several levels, a forest of old timbers. We infinitely prefer the rooms in the main building, which have far more character even though they've been altered and renovated over the years. Out back is a more sterile motel wing, with studio rooms.

White Lodge Country House Hotel. Sloe Lane (a 5-minute walk from the town center off A27), Alfriston, E. Sussex BN26 5UR. ☎ **01323/870265.** Fax 01323/870284. 17 units. TV TEL. £90–£125 ($144–$200) double. Rates include English breakfast. AE, MC, V. Bus: Southdown no. 712.

This converted private home is opulently furnished and situated amid 5 acres of gardens. The public rooms are outfitted like French salons, with carved 18th- and 19th-century antiques, many of them gilded. Bronze statues inspired by classical Greek myths are placed about. Each of the beautifully furnished rooms has a trouser press, hair dryer, tasseled curtains, and countryside views.

Dining: The daytime dining room is French, with Louis XV furniture centered around a chiseled fireplace of violet-tinged marble. Dinner is served below the reception area in an Edwardian room. Four-course lunches and dinners are offered daily. Menu specialties include smoked salmon, grilled lemon sole, and, in season, marinated venison. The cooking is sturdy and reliable, almost home-style.

IN LEWES

Shelleys Hotel. High St., Lewes, E. Sussex BN7 1XS. ☎ **01273/472361.** Fax 01273/483152. 19 units. TV TEL. £149–£204 ($238.40–$326.40) double; £204–£220 ($326.40–$352) suite. AE, DC, MC, V.

This 1526 manor house was first owned by the earl of Dorset before it was sold to the Shelley family, wealthy Sussex landowners (who were kin to the poet Percy Bysshe Shelley). Radical changes were made to the architecture in the 18th century. A complete refurbishment in 1994 turned the hotel into a rather luxurious country-house retreat. There are traditional details throughout, such as the family coat of arms in the central hall. Nowadays, the standards of the management are reflected in the fine antiques, the bowls of flowers, the paintings and prints, the well-kept gardens, and most important, the helpful staff. The bedrooms are personal, individually furnished, usually spacious, and most comfortable. Room 11 has a 16th-century frieze of bacchanalian figures and a design of entwining grapes and flowers.

Dining: The chef often manages to surprise and delight, with, perhaps, a salad of wood pigeon and braised quails (laced with a tarragon and truffle vinaigrette), followed by steamed sea bass with oranges and lemons in white wine or braised guinea fowl served with a burgundy sauce. In the rear is a sun terrace and lawn for tea and drinks; horse chestnuts and copper beech shade the grounds. There's also a lounge with its blazing fireplace.

WHERE TO DINE
IN ALFRISTON

Around teatime, head for **The Tudor House,** on Alfriston's High Street (☎ 01323/870891). The well-lit interior has two tearooms with oak paneling and brass that provide a calm setting for afternoon tea. Cheese, ham-and-cheese, and egg-salad sandwiches and muffins, Danish, scones, and a variety of cakes are served. Afternoon tea costs £2.75 to £4.25 ($4.40 to $6.80), sandwiches £1.50 to £2.75 ($2.40 to $4.40), and cakes and pastries 70p to £2 ($1.10 to $3.20). Hours are daily from 10am to 5:30pm.

Moonrakers. High St. ☎ 01323/870472. Reservations essential on weekends. Main courses £8.50–£14.50 ($13.60–$23.20); fixed-price menus £12.95 and £15.95 ($20.70 and $25.50). AE, MC, V. Mon–Sat 7–10pm. Closed first 2 weeks in Jan. ENGLISH.

The welcome is warm at this charming 16th-century restaurant with old beams, an inglenook fireplace, and a convenient location in the heart of town. The cuisine is well prepared, with market-fresh ingredients. Dishes might include salmon in puff pastry with prawn and creamy vermouth stuffing; roast lamb with a garlic-and-herb crust; and a dessert specialty of sticky toffee pudding. The restaurant has a comprehensive wine list and a polite staff. Logs burn brightly in the fireplace in winter, and in summer there's a flowering patio for outside dining. The two dining rooms are reserved, respectively, for smokers and nonsmokers.

IN LEWES

Pailin. 20 Station St. ☎ 01273/473906. Reservations recommended. Main courses £5.50–£7.50 ($8.80–$12); fixed-price lunch or dinner £13 ($20.80). AE, DC, MC, V. Mon–Sat noon–2:30pm; daily 6:30–10:30pm. Closed Nov 5 and Dec 25–26. THAI.

Spicy hot Thai food has come to Lewes, though some of the fiery hot dishes have been toned down for English taste buds. Begin perhaps with the lemon chicken soup with lemongrass, followed by a crab-and-prawn "hot pot." A special favorite with locals is the barbecued marinated chicken, which is served with a spicy but delectable sweet-and-sour plum sauce. Vegetarian meals are served, and children are welcome and given small portions at reduced prices.

A SIDE TRIP FROM LEWES:
VIRGINIA WOOLF'S HOME & THE BLUEBELL RAILWAY

The small downland village of **Rodmell** lies midway between Lewes and the port of Newhaven on C7. It's known for **Monks House,** a National Trust property that was bought by Virginia and Leonard Woolf in 1919 and was their home until his death in 1969. Virginia wrote of the profusion of fruit and vegetables produced by the garden and of the open-water meadows looking out on the downs. Much of the house was furnished and decorated by Virginia's sister, Vanessa Bell, and the artist Duncan Grant.

The house has extremely limited visiting hours: from the first Saturday in April until the last Wednesday in October, and then only on Wednesday and Saturday from 2 to 5:30pm. Admission is £2.20 ($3.50) adults, £1.10 ($1.75) children 5 and up, and free for children 4 and under. More information is available by calling the headquarters of the **National Trust** in East Sussex (☎ **01892/890651**).

Rodmell also has a 12th-century church, a working farm, and a tiny Victorian school still in use. Take Southdown bus no. 123 from the Lewes rail station.

The all-steam **Bluebell Railway** starts at Sheffield Park Station near Uckfield in East Sussex (☎ **01825/722370**), on A275 between East Grinstead and Lewes. The name is taken from the spring flowers that grow alongside the track, running from Sheffield Park to Kingscote. It's a delight for railway buffs, with locomotives dating from the 1870s through the 1950s, when British Railways ended steam operations. You can visit locomotive sheds and a small museum, then later patronize the bookshop or have lunch in a large buffet, bar, and restaurant complex. The round-trip is 1½ hours as the train wanders through a typical English countryside. It cost £7.20 ($11.50) for adults, £3.60 ($5.75) for children, with a family ticket going for £19.50 ($31.20). Trains run daily from May to September, and Saturday and Sunday the rest of the year.

8 Hampshire & Dorset: Austen & Hardy Country

This countryside is reminiscent of scenes from Burke's *Landed Gentry*, from fireplaces where stacks slowly deplete as logs burn, to wicker baskets of apples freshly picked from a nearby orchard. Old village houses, now hotels, have a charming quality. Beyond the pear trees, on the crest of a hill, you'll find the ruins of a Roman camp. A village pub, with two rows of kegs filled with varieties of cider, is where the hunt gathers.

You're in Hampshire and Dorset, two shires jealously guarded by the English as special rural treasures. Everybody knows of Southampton and Bournemouth, but less known is the hilly countryside farther inland. You can travel through endless lanes and discover tiny villages and thatched cottages untouched by the industrial invasion.

Jane Austen wrote of Hampshire's firmly middle-class inhabitants, all doggedly convinced that Hampshire was the greatest place on earth. Her six novels, including *Pride and Prejudice* and *Sense and Sensibility,* earned her a permanent place among the pantheon of 19th-century writers and unexpected popularity among 1990s film directors and producers. Her books provide an insight into the manners and mores of the English who soon established a powerful empire. Although the details of the life she described have now largely faded, the general mood and spirit of the Hampshire she depicted remains intact. You can visit her grave in Winchester Cathedral and the house where she lived, Chawton Cottage.

Hampshire encompasses the South Downs, the Isle of Wight (Victoria's favorite retreat), and the naval city of Portsmouth. More than 90,000 acres of the New Forest were preserved by William the Conqueror as a private hunting ground, and even today this vast woodland and heath is ideal for walking and exploring. Although Hampshire is filled with many places of interest, for our purposes we've concentrated on two major areas: Southampton, for convenience, and Winchester, for history.

Dorset is Thomas Hardy country. Some of its towns and villages, although altered considerably, are still recognizable from his descriptions. "The last of the great Victorians," as he was called, died in 1928 at age 88. His tomb occupies a position of honor in Westminster Abbey.

One of England's smallest shires, Dorset encompasses the old seaport of Poole in the east and Lyme Regis (known to Jane Austen) in the west. Dorset is a southwestern county and borders the English

Hampshire & Dorset

3-0583

ENGLAND

Hampshire & Dorset

London

Athelhampton House & Gardens ❶
Beaulieu Abbey ❹
Broadlands ❸
Carisbrooke Castle ❼
Chawton Cottage ❶
Chesil Beach ❶❹
Clouds Hill ❶❶
Hardy's Cottage ❶❷
Kingston Lacy ❽
Maritime Museum in Buckler's Hard ❺
Osborne House ❻
Sherborne Castle & Abbey ❶❸
Tank Museum ❾
Winchester Cathedral ❷

301

Channel. It's known for its cows, and Dorset butter is served at many an afternoon tea. This is mainly a land of farms and pastures, with plenty of sandy heaths and chalky downs.

The most prominent tourist center of Dorset is the Victorian seaside resort of Bournemouth. If you don't stay here, you might try a number of Dorset's other seaports, villages, and country towns; we mostly stick to the areas along the impressive coastline. And Dorset, as the frugal English might tell you, is full of bargains.

Where to stay? You'll find the most hotels, but not the greatest charm, at the seaside resort of Bournemouth. (More intriguing than Bournemouth is the much smaller Lyme Regis, with its famed seaside promenade, the Cobb, a favorite of Jane Austen and a setting for *The French Lieutenant's Woman*.) If you're interested in things maritime, opt for Portsmouth, the premier port of the south and the home of HMS *Victory*, Nelson's flagship. For the history buff and Jane Austen fans, it's Winchester, the ancient capital of England, with a cathedral built by William the Conqueror. Winchester also makes a good base for exploring the countryside.

The best beaches are at Bournemouth, set among pines with sandy beaches and fine coastal views, and Chesil Beach, a 20-mile-long bank of shingle running from Abbottsbury to the Isle of Portland—great for beachcombing. There is no doubt: The most natural spectacle is New Forest itself, 145 square miles of heath and woodland, once the hunting ground of Norman kings.

1 Winchester

72 miles SW of London; 12 miles N of Southampton

The most historic city in all of Hampshire, Winchester is big on legends, since it's associated with King Arthur and the Knights of the Round Table. In the Great Hall, which is all that remains of Winchester Castle, a round oak table, with space for King Arthur and his 24 knights, is attached to the wall—but all that spells is undocumented romance. What is known, however, is that when the Saxons ruled the ancient kingdom of Wessex, Winchester was the capital.

The city is also linked with King Alfred, who is believed to have been crowned here and is honored today by a statue. The Danish conqueror Canute came this way too, as did the king he ousted, Ethelred the Unready (Canute got his wife, Emma, in the bargain).

Of course, Winchester is a mecca for Jane Austen fans. You can visit her grave in Winchester Cathedral (Emma Thompson did, while working on her adapted screenplay of *Sense and Sensibility*), as well as Chawton Cottage, Jane Austen's house, which is 15 miles east of Winchester.

Its past glory but a memory, Winchester is essentially a market town today, lying on the downs along the Itchen River. Although Winchester hypes its ancient past, the modern world has arrived, as evidenced by the fast food, reggae music, and the cheap retail-clothing stores that mar its otherwise perfect High Street.

ESSENTIALS

GETTING THERE   From London's Waterloo Station there is frequent daily train service to Winchester. The trip takes 1 hour. For rail information, call ☎ 0345/ 484950 in the U.K., or ☎ 01603/764776 in the U.S. Arrivals are at Winchester Station, Station Hill (☎ 01703/229393).

National Express buses leaving from London's Victoria Coach Station depart every 2 hours for Winchester during the day. The trip takes 2 hours. Call ☎ 0990/808080 for schedules and information.

Winchester

If you're driving, from Southampton drive north on A335; from London, take the M3 motorway southwest.

VISITOR INFORMATION   The **Tourist Information Centre,** at the Winchester Guildhall, The Broadway (☎ **01962/840500**), is open from 10am to 5pm Monday through Saturday. Beginning in May and lasting through October, guided walking tours are conducted for £2 ($3.20) per person, departing from this tourist center. Hours are Monday through Saturday at 10am and 2:30pm, with only one tour offered Sunday, at 1:30pm.

EXPLORING THE AREA

For a day of rambling through the countryside, try strolling part of **South Downs Way,** a 99-mile trail from Winchester to Eastbourne; **Clarendon Way,** a 24-mile path from Winchester to Salisbury; or **Itchen Way,** a beautiful riverside trail from near Cheriton to Southampton.

Winchester and the surrounding area is by far one of the best places to fish in all of England, especially for trout. Try your hand at any of the many nearby rivers including the Rivers Itchen, Test, Meon, Dever, and Avon. The Tourist Information Centre (see above) will provide complete details on the best spots.

Fill up those empty suitcases you brought over at **Cadogan,** 30–31 The Square (☎ **01962/877399**). They've got an upscale and stylish selection of British clothing for both men and women. For a unique piece of jewelry by one of the most acclaimed designers of today, stroll into **Carol Darby Jewellery,** 23 Little Minster St. (☎ **01962/867671**).

From Hampshire to Hollywood: The Oh-So-Popular Jane Austen

Jane Austen, one of the most read and reread English authors, has enjoyed an unprecedented stardom on the silver screen. Cinematic versions of her works first appeared in the 1940s; the most famous of the early films was Laurence Olivier and Greer Garson's *Pride and Prejudice,* the first of at least four productions of that novel alone. Since then, film versions have been made (and sometimes remade) of all six of Austen's major novels.

But 1995 was definitely Jane Austen's cinematic heyday. That year witnessed a BBC production of *Persuasion* (with Amanda Root and Ciaran Hinds), a BBC/A&E remake of *Pride and Prejudice* (with Colin Firth and Jennifer Ehle), and a Columbia Tri-Star production of *Sense and Sensibility* starring the endlessly charming Emma Thompson and Kate Winslet. Even *Clueless,* with Alicia Silverstone, was a modern-day version of *Emma.* In 1996, along came a film of *Emma,* which caused a media feeding frenzy for Gwyneth Paltrow, the actress who plays the title character.

Why this surge of passion for this long-deceased author? Savvy Hollywood types realized long ago that Ms. Austen's novels provide the stylish and socially acceptable skeletons for producers whose scenery resembles a painting by John Constable. Interiors focus on salons from the most spectacular country houses in England, and warehouses of historically accurate costumes can be designed with taste and materials that are probably much, much better than their originals. This, coupled with psychologically intriguing characters who never, *never* dip into the profane or even the controversial, gives Austen's works proven box office clout. (They've even found popularity in the East, as well, especially in Japan.)

Austen continued to make headlines in 1997 with the release of *Jane Austen, A Biography* by the English writer Claire Tomalin, which, contrary to many previous portraits, paints "the shy, retiring daughter of a country clergyman" as remarkably cosmopolitan. Another biography came out the same year: *Jane Austen: Obstinate Heart* by Valerie Grosvenor Myer. One reviewer found that Myer's portrait of Austen was of a "highly complex woman, by turn frivolous and

---

If you have ever dreamed of rummaging through the shelves and stacks of an authentic old English bookstore, stop by **Gilbert's Bookshop,** 19 The Square (☎ **01962/852832**). Their wide selection of stock runs the spectrum from rare gems to hot-off-the-press best-sellers. You can browse forever here.

✪ **Winchester Cathedral.** The Square. ☎ **01962/853137.** Free admission to the cathedral, but £2.50 ($4) donation requested. Admission to library and Triforium Gallery £1 ($1.60) adults, 50p (80¢) children. Free guided tours Apr–Oct Mon–Sat 10am–3pm hourly. Crypt is flooded during winter, but part may be seen from a viewing platform. When it's not flooded, there are regular tours Mon–Sat at 11am and 2pm. Library and Triforium Gallery Easter–Oct Mon 2–4:30pm, Tues–Sat 10:30am–1pm and 2–4:30pm; Nov–Easter Sat 10:30am–4pm.

For centuries, this has been one of the great churches of England. The present building, the longest medieval cathedral in Britain, dates from 1079, and its Norman heritage is still in evidence. When a Saxon church stood on this spot, St. Swithun, bishop of Winchester and tutor to young King Alfred, suggested modestly that he be buried outside. Following his subsequent indoor burial, it rained for 40 days. The legend lives on: Just ask a resident of Winchester what will happen if it rains on St. Swithun's Day, July 15, and you'll get a prediction of rain for 40 days.

poker-stiff, affectionate and spiteful, generous and filled with envy, earthy and refined, in short, as rich in character shadings as the world of her fiction suggests."

Austen's posthumous catapult to fame has brought a flood of visitors to her house, **Chawton Cottage,** in Chawton, 1 mile southwest of Alton off A31 and B3006 (☎ **01420/83262**), 15 miles east of Winchester.

Born in 1775, Jane Austen was the daughter of the Oxford-educated rector, the Rev. Mr. George Austen, a typical Hampshire country gentleman, who had lots of charm but little money. In keeping with a custom of the time, the Austens gave their third son, Edward, to a wealthy, childless family connection, Thomas Knight. As Knight's heir, it was Edward who let his mother and sisters live in the house.

You can see where the novelist spent the last 7½ years of her life, her most productive period. In the unpretentious but pleasant cottage is the table on which she penned new versions of three of her books and wrote three more, including *Emma.* You can also see the rector's George III mahogany bookcase and a silhouette likeness of the Reverend Austen presenting his son to the Knights. It was in this cottage that Jane Austen became ill in 1816 with what would have been diagnosed by the middle of the 19th century as Addison's disease. She died in July 1817.

Chawton Cottage is open from 11am to 4:30pm daily from March through December, and Saturday and Sunday in January and February. Admission is £2.50 ($4) for adults, 50p (80¢) for children 8 to 18. It's closed Christmas Day and Boxing Day (December 26). There's an attractive garden where you can picnic and an old bake house with Austen's donkey cart. A bookshop stocks new and secondhand books.

Across the road from Jane Austen's house is an idyllic place for tea. **Cassandra's Cup,** Chawton (☎ **01420/83144**), is known for its home baking, especially its delectable scones. Freshly made sandwiches and good-tasting cakes and pastries are also sold. Take your tea, such as Darjeeling or Earl Grey, in a traditional setting decorated in green and white, with lace curtains and tablecloths. Later you can browse in their shops for souvenirs, perhaps old porcelain.

In the present building, the nave, with its two aisles, is most impressive, as are the chantries, the reredos (late 15th century), and the elaborately carved choir stalls. Jane Austen is buried here; her grave is marked with a commemorative plaque. There are also chests containing the bones of many Saxon kings and the remains of the Viking conqueror Canute and his wife, Emma, in the presbytery. The son of William the Conqueror, William Rufus (who reigned as William II), was also buried at the cathedral.

The library houses Bishop Morley's 17th-century book collection, and an exhibition room contains the 12th-century Winchester Bible. The Triforium shows sculpture, woodwork, and metalwork from 11 centuries and affords magnificent views over the rest of the cathedral.

WHERE TO STAY

✪ **Lainston House.** Sparsholt, Winchester, Hampshire SO21 2LT. ☎ **01962/863588.** Fax 01962/776672. 41 units. MINIBAR TV TEL. £140–£285 ($224–$456) double; £265–£285 ($424–$456) suite. AE, DC, MC, V. Take A272 3½ miles northwest of Winchester.

The beauty of this fine, restored William and Mary redbrick manor house strikes visitors as they approach via a long, curving, tree-lined drive. It's situated on 63 acres of rolling land and linked with the name Lainston in the *Domesday Book* of 1086. Inside the stately house, elegance is the keynote, with Delft-tile fireplaces, oak-and-cedar paneling, molding, and cornices of the original owners preserved, set off with period pieces. The largest and most elegant rooms are in the main house, with traditional English furnishings and color-coordinated decors. Other rooms, less spacious but also comfortable and harmoniously furnished, are in a nearby annex built in 1990.

Dining: In either of the two dining rooms, you can order such French and English specialties as roast partridge or roast loin of lamb rolled with an herb stuffing.

Royal Hotel. St. Peter St., Winchester, Hampshire SO23 8BS. ☎ **800/528-1234** in the U.S., or 01962/840840. Fax 01962/841582. 78 units. TV TEL. £85 ($136) double; £105 ($168) suite. AE, DC, MC, V.

This fine old hotel, a comfortable choice, was built at the end of the 17th century as a private house. It was used by nuns from Brussels as a convent for 50 years before being turned into a hotel and quickly becoming the center of the city's social life. It's only a few minutes' walk from the cathedral, yet it still enjoys a secluded position. A modern extension overlooks gardens, and all rooms have traditional English styling. Best of all is the garden hidden behind high walls. Meals are served in a small, formal dining room with a view of the private garden. Amenities include shoe cleaning, valet service, and 24-hour room service.

Stratton House. Stratton Rd., St. Giles Hill, Winchester, Hampshire SO23 0JQ. ☎ **01962/863919.** Fax 01962/842095. 10 units, 7 with bathroom. TV. £48–£52 ($76.80–$83.20) double with bathroom. Rates include English breakfast. MC, V. Closed Dec 24–27. Free pickup available from the train or bus station.

This lovely old Victorian house (ca. 1890) is situated on an acre of St. Giles Hill, overlooking the city. It's about a 5- to 10-minute walk from the city center. All the comfortably furnished rooms have beverage-makers. A three-course evening meal can be arranged. There is ample parking in a private courtyard.

✪ **Wykeham Arms.** 75 Kingsgate St., Winchester, Hampshire SO23 9PE. ☎ **01962/853834.** Fax 01962/854411. 13 units. MINIBAR TV TEL. £79.50 ($127.20) double in original building, £89.50 ($143.20) double in extension, £115 ($184) suite. Rates include English breakfast. AE, CB, DC, MC, V.

This is one of our longtime favorites in Winchester, known to almost everyone in town for its food and bar facilities. It lies behind a 200-year-old brick facade in the historic center of town, near the cathedral. The rooms are comfortably and traditionally furnished with antiques or reproductions and such lighthearted touches as fresh flowers and baskets of potpourri. Five rooms were recently added in a 16th-century building that faces the original hotel. A large suite with a cozy fire-warmed sitting room and upstairs bedroom is also available. These rooms overlook the Winchester College Chapel, and have the same amenities as the original rooms. A filling breakfast, complete with fresh-squeezed orange juice, is served in a charming dining area in the main house.

The Wykeham Arms is especially known for its paneled pub and restaurant, where carefully flavored food is served in historic surroundings. Lunches are informal affairs with pub snacks and platters. Evening meals are more elaborate, with main courses starting at £10 ($16).

WHERE TO DINE

Elizabethan Restaurant. 18 Jewry St. ☎ **01962/853566.** Reservations recommended. Main courses £8.50–£15.95 ($13.60–$25.50); fixed-price lunch and early evening menu

£12.50 ($20). AE, DC, MC, V. Mon–Sun noon–2:30pm; Mon–Sat 6–10:30pm, Sun 6:30–10:30pm. ENGLISH/FRENCH.

In an old-fashioned atmosphere, you can dine under hand-hewn beams by candlelight. The street-level bar is for drinks and lunch snacks, whereas the more formal dining room is one floor above. The restaurant sits in the upper reaches of the village, just north of the center of town, in a building originally dating from 1509. The well-run kitchen offers an excellent English cuisine with many French-inspired dishes. Try poached salmon with a white-wine and cream sauce, chicken Dijonnaise, or veal marsala.

✪ **Hotel du Vin & Bistro.** 14 Southgate St., Winchester, Hampshire SO23 9EF. ☎ **01962/841414.** Reservations recommended. Main courses £7.50–£15 ($12–$24). AE, DC, MC, V. Daily noon–2pm and 7–9:30pm. ENGLISH/CONTINENTAL.

A touch of chic has come to sleepy Winchester with the opening of a bistro in this town-house hotel that dates from 1715 and has a walled garden. Gerard Basset and Robin Hutson learned their lessons well at the exclusive Chewton Glen (see below) before embarking on their own enterprise. They wisely hired James Martin as chef, and he delivers the finest food served in Winchester today. The bistro food is excellent and a good value. The menu always features regional ingredients: Try the lamb with honey-roasted parsnips or charcoal-grilled sea bass with eggplant and olive tomato rue. The sommelier (Basset himself) has collected the finest wine list in the county.

You can also stay overnight in one of the 23 rooms decorated with a wine theme. The quite comfortable rooms have good beds, antiques, TVs, and state-of-the-art bathrooms. It costs from £79 to £110 ($126.40 to $176) per person for the B&B.

Nine The Square. 9 Great Minster St. ☎ **01962/864004.** Reservations recommended. Main courses £7.50–£16.50 ($12–$26.40). AE, DC, MC, V. Mon–Sat noon–2pm and 7–10pm. ITALIAN.

Winchester's long-reigning best restaurant, now seriously challenged by the Hotel du Vin & Bistro, has an enviable view of the cathedral. Diners may either head upstairs to the comfortably formal restaurant or sit at street level, where dining tables are scattered near the sometimes-crowded stand-up bar. The food is beautifully prepared and served with fresh ingredients. A typical starter is bruschetta with goat cheese and sun-dried tomatoes. Mussels and clams with green and pink peppercorns may be a starter or a main course, or perhaps you'll prefer roast Gressingham duck with fig and strawberries and Italian fish casserole.

WINCHESTER AFTER DARK

The place to go is **The Porthouse,** Upper Brook Street (☎ **01962/869397**), a pub-cum-nightclub, sprawling across three floors. Different nights have different themes, from karaoke (yikes!) to retro music from the 1960s through the 1980s. On Friday the 25-plus crowd takes over. The only cover, ranging from £3 to £5 ($4.80 to $8), is charged on Thursday, Friday, and Saturday nights from 8:30 to 10:30pm. There's a ground-floor pub where lunch is served.

2 Portsmouth & Southsea

75 miles SW of London; 19 miles SE of Southampton

Virginia, New Hampshire, and even Ohio may have a Portsmouth, but the forerunner of them all is the old port and naval base on the Hampshire coast, seat of the British navy for 500 years. German bombers in World War II leveled the city, hitting about nine-tenths of its buildings. But the seaport was rebuilt admirably and now aggressively promotes its military attractions. It draws visitors interested in the nautical history of England as well as World War II buffs.

Its maritime associations are known around the world. From Sally Port, the most interesting district in the Old Town, countless naval heroes have embarked to fight England's battles. That was certainly true on June 6, 1944, when Allied troops set sail to invade occupied France.

Southsea, adjoining Portsmouth, is a popular seaside resort with fine sands, lush gardens, bright lights, and a host of vacation attractions. Many historic monuments can be seen along the stretches of open space, where you can walk on the Clarence Esplanade, look out on the Solent Channel, and view the busy shipping activities of Portsmouth Harbour.

ESSENTIALS

GETTING THERE   Trains from London's Waterloo Station stop at Portsmouth and Southsea Station frequently throughout the day. The trip takes 2 hours. Call ☎ **0345/484950** in the U.K., or 01603/764776 for rail information.

National Express coaches operating out of London's Victoria Coach Station make the run to Portsmouth and Southsea every 2 hours during the day. The trip takes 2 hours and 20 minutes. Call ☎ **0990/808080** for information and schedules.

If you're driving from London's ring road, drive south on A3.

VISITOR INFORMATION   The **Tourist Information Centre,** at The Hard in Portsmouth (☎ **01705/826722**), is open daily April to September from 9:30am to 5:45pm, and October to March daily from 9:30am to 5:15pm.

EXPLORING PORTSMOUTH & SOUTHSEA

You might want to begin your tour on the Southsea front, where you can see a number of **naval monuments.** These include the big anchor from Nelson's ship *Victory,* plus a commemoration of the officers and men of HMS *Shannon* for heroism in the Indian Mutiny. An obelisk with a naval crown honors the memory of the crew of HMS *Chesapeake,* and a massive column, the Royal Naval Memorial, honors those lost at sea in the two world wars. A shaft is also dedicated to men killed in the Crimean War. There are also commemorations of those who fell victim to yellow fever in Queen Victoria's service in Sierra Leone and Jamaica.

Southsea Common, between the coast and houses of the area, known in the 13th century as Froddington Heath and used for army bivouacs, is a picnic and play area today. Walks can be taken along Ladies' Mile if you tend to shy away from the common's tennis courts, skateboard and roller-skating rinks, and other activities.

MARITIME ATTRACTIONS IN PORTSMOUTH

You can buy a ticket that admits you to the HMS *Victory,* the *Mary Rose,* the HMS *Warrior 1860,* and the Royal Naval Museum. It costs £11 ($17.60) for adults, £9.50 ($15.20) for senior citizens, and £8 ($12.80) for children.

✪ **The *Mary Rose* Ship Hall and Exhibition.** College Rd., Portsmouth Naval Base. ☎ **01705/750521.** Admission £5.50 ($8.80) adults, £4.75 ($7.60) seniors, £4 ($6.40) children and students. Daily 10am–5:30pm. Closed Dec 25. Use the entrance to the Portsmouth Naval Base through Victory Gate and follow the signs.

The *Mary Rose,* flagship of the fleet of King Henry VIII's wooden men-of-war, sank in the Solent Channel in 1545 in full view of the king. In 1982, Prince Charles watched the *Mary Rose* break the water's surface after more than 4 centuries on the ocean floor, not exactly shipshape but surprisingly well preserved nonetheless. Now the remains are on view, but the hull must be kept permanently wet.

The hull and the more than 20,000 items brought up by divers constitute one of England's major archaeological discoveries. On display are the almost-complete equipment of the ship's barber-surgeon, with cabin saws, knives, ointments, and plaster all ready for use; long bows and arrows, some still in shooting order; carpenters' tools; leather jackets; and some fine lace and silk. Close to the Ship Hall is the *Mary Rose* Exhibition, where artifacts recovered from the ship are stored. It features an audiovisual theater and a spectacular two-deck reconstruction of a segment of the ship, including the original guns. A display with sound effects recalls the sinking of the vessel.

HMS *Victory*. No. 2 Dry Dock, in Portsmouth Naval Base. ☎ **01705/723549.** Admission £5.50 ($8.80) adults, £4.75 ($7.60) seniors, £4 ($6.40) children. Mar–Oct daily 10am–5:30pm; Nov–Feb daily 10am–5pm. Closed Dec 24–25. Use the entrance to the Portsmouth Naval Base through Victory Gate.

Of major interest is Lord Nelson's flagship, a 104-gun, first-rate ship that is the oldest commissioned warship in the world, launched May 7, 1765. It earned its fame on October 21, 1805, in the Battle of Trafalgar, when the English scored a victory over the combined Spanish and French fleets. It was in this battle that Lord Nelson lost his life. The flagship, after being taken to Gibraltar for repairs, returned to Portsmouth with Nelson's body on board (he was later buried at St. Paul's in London).

Royal Naval Museum. In the dockyard, Portsmouth Naval Base. ☎ **01705/727562.** Free admission with ticket for HMS *Victory*; otherwise £3 ($4.80) adults, £2.50 ($4) seniors, £2 ($3.20) children. Summer daily 10am–5:30pm; off-season daily 10am–4:30pm.

The museum is next to Nelson's flagship, HMS *Victory,* and the *Mary Rose,* in the heart of Portsmouth's historic naval dockyard. The only museum in Britain devoted exclusively to the general history of the Royal Navy, it houses relics of Nelson and his associates, together with unique collections of ship models, naval ceramics, figureheads, medals, uniforms, weapons, and other memorabilia. Special displays feature "The Rise of the Royal Navy" and "HMS *Victory* and the Campaign of Trafalgar."

Royal Navy Submarine Museum. Haslar Jetty Rd., Gosport. ☎ **01705/529217.** Admission £3.50 ($5.60) adults, £2.50 ($4) children and seniors, £9.50 ($15.20) family. Apr–Oct daily 10am–4:30pm; Nov–Mar daily 10am–3:30pm. Last tour 1 hour before closing. Closed Christmas week. Bus: 19. Ferry: From The Hard in Portsmouth to Gosport.

Cross Portsmouth Harbour by one of the ferries that bustles back and forth all day to Gosport. Some departures go directly from the station pontoon to HMS *Alliance* for a visit to the submarine museum, which traces the history of underwater warfare and life from the earliest days to the present nuclear age and contains excellent models, dioramas, medals, and displays from all ages. There's also as much about submariners themselves as about the steel tubes in which they make their homes.

Within the refurbished historical and nuclear galleries, the principal exhibit is HMS *Alliance,* and after a brief audiovisual presentation, visitors are guided through the boat by ex-submariners. Midget submarines, not all of them English, including an X-craft, can be seen outside the museum.

MORE ATTRACTIONS

Charles Dickens's Birthplace Museum. 393 Old Commercial Rd. (near the center of Portsmouth, off Mile End Rd./M275 and off Kingston Rd.). ☎ **01705/827261.** Admission £2 ($3.20) adults, £1.50 ($2.40) seniors, £1.20 ($1.90) students; free for children 12 and under. Daily 10am–5:30pm. Closed Nov–Mar.

The small terrace house of 1804 in which the famous novelist was born on February 7, 1812, and lived for a short time, has been restored and furnished to illustrate the middle-class taste of the southwestern counties of the early 19th century.

Southsea Castle. Clarence Esplanade, Southsea. ☎ **01705/827261.** Admission £1.70 ($2.70) adults, £1.40 ($2.25) seniors, £1 ($1.60) students and ages 13–18; free for children 12 and under. Apr–Oct daily 10am–5:30pm; Nov–Mar Sat–Sun 10am–4:30pm. Closed Dec 24–26.

A fortress built of stones from Beaulieu Abbey in 1545 as part of King Henry VIII's coastal defense plan, the castle is now a museum. Exhibits trace the development of Portsmouth as a military stronghold, as well as the naval history and the archaeology of the area. The castle is in the center of Southsea near the D-Day Museum.

D-Day Museum. Clarence Esplanade (on the seafront), Southsea. ☎ **01705/827261.** Admission £4.75 ($7.60) adults, £3 ($4.80) seniors, £2.40 ($3.85) children and students, £12.35 ($19.75) family of 4, children under 5 free. Daily 10am–5pm. Closed Dec 24–26.

Right next door to Southsea Castle, this museum, devoted to the Normandy landings, displays the Overlord Embroidery, which shows the complete story of Operation Overlord. The appliquéd embroidery, believed to be the largest of its kind (272 ft. long and 3 ft. high), was designed by Sandra Lawrence and took 20 women of the Royal School of Needlework 5 years to complete. There's a special audiovisual program with displays, including reconstructions of various stages of the mission with models and maps. You'll see a Sherman tank in working order, jeeps, field guns, and even a DUKW (popularly called a Duck), an incredibly useful amphibious truck that operates on land and sea.

Portchester Castle. On the south side of Portchester off A27 (between Portsmouth and Southampton, near Fareham). ☎ **01705/378291.** Admission £2.50 ($4) adults, £1.90 ($3.05) seniors, £1.30 ($2.10) children 5–15; free for children 4 and under. Apr–Sept daily 10am–6pm; Oct–Mar daily 10am–4pm.

On a spit of land on the northern side of Portsmouth Harbour are the remains of this castle, plus a Norman church. Built in the late 12th century by King Henry II, the castle is set inside the impressive walls of a 3rd-century Roman fort built as a defense against Saxon pirates when this was the northwestern frontier of the declining Roman Empire. By the end of the 14th century, Richard II had modernized the castle and had made it a secure small palace. Among the ruins are the hall, kitchen, and great chamber of this palace.

WHERE TO STAY

Hospitality Inn. South Parade, Southsea, Portsmouth, Hampshire PO4 0RN. ☎ 01705/731281. Fax 01705/817572. 117 units. TV TEL. £88 ($140.80) double; £165 ($264) suite. Rates include English breakfast. AF, DC, MC, V.

The balconied Victorian facade of this hotel, directly east of Southside Common, rises above the boulevard running beside the sea. Restored by its owners, the hotel's interior decor ranges from contemporary to full-curtained traditional, depending on the room. However, it doesn't stack up with the nearby Marriott. Each of the bedrooms has been renovated with built-in furniture and equipped with such extras as a trouser press and tea-making equipment. Twenty rooms are set aside for nonsmokers.

Portsmouth Marriott. North Harbour, Cosham (2 miles southeast of Portsmouth's center, at the junction of A3 and M27), Portsmouth, Hampshire PO6 4SH. ☎ **800/228-9290** in the U.S. and Canada, or 01705/383151. Fax 01705/388701. 170 units. TV TEL. £69–£79 ($110.40–$126.40) double; £125 ($200) suite. AE, DC, MC, V. Take the bus marked Cosham from Portsmouth's center.

Located a short walk from the ferryboat terminal for ships arriving from Le Havre and Cherbourg in France, this 7-story building towers above everything in its district. Originally built as a Holiday Inn in 1980, it was acquired by Marriott in 1992 and refurbished in 1997. Some of the public areas are sheltered by a steel-and-glass greenhouse-style dome with big windows. The bedrooms are clean, comfortable, and modern. There's a cocktail lounge and a restaurant that serves breakfast, lunch, and dinner. Facilities include an atrium style swimming pool, gym equipment, a sauna, spa bath, children's playroom, and solarium.

IN NEARBY WICKHAM

✪ **The Old House Hotel.** The Square, Wickham, Fareham, Hampshire PO17 5JG. ☎ **01329/833049.** Fax 01329/833672. 12 units. TV TEL. £90 ($144) double. AE, CB, DC, MC, V. Bus: 69 from Fareham. Head 9 miles west from Portsmouth on the M27 motorway; exit at number 10. The village is 2 miles north of the junction of B2177 and A32.

A handsome early Georgian (1715) structure, the Old House is surrounded by low, medieval timber structures around the square. The paneled Georgian rooms on the ground and first floors of the hotel contrast with the beamed bedrooms on the upper floors, once the servants' quarters. All nine bedrooms have period furniture, many pieces original antiques; an additional three rooms, in a cottage 50 yards from the main property in a building dating from the 16th century, enjoy all the facilities of the main hotel.

The restaurant occupies what was once a timber-frame outbuilding with stables, adjacent to a garden overlooking the Meon River; it serves French provincial cuisine.

WHERE TO DINE

Bistro Montparnasse. 103 Palmerston Rd., Southsea. ☎ **01705/816754.** Reservations required Sat. Main courses £11.25–£15.20 ($18–$24.30); 2-course dinner £12.50 ($20); 3-course dinner £14.90 ($23.85). AE, MC, V. Tues–Sat 7–10pm. Closed 2 weeks in Jan (dates vary). Southsea bus. Follow the signs to the D-Day Museum, and at the museum turn left and go to the next intersection; the restaurant is on the right. BRITISH/FRENCH.

Serving the best food in the area, this bistro offers a welcoming atmosphere and background music to get you in the mood. Fresh produce is delicately prepared in the well-rounded selection of dishes here. The cooking is familiar fare but well executed. Although the menu changes, you might try confit of duck with oranges and Grand Marnier sauce, fillet of Scotch beef with wild mushrooms and grain mustard sauce, or salmon in pastry with ginger and currants in a shallot butter sauce. Homemade breads and fresh fish, caught locally, are the specialties.

3 Southampton

87 miles SW of London; 161 miles E of Plymouth

To many North Americans, England's number-one passenger port, home base for the *QE2*, is the gateway to Britain. Southampton is a city of sterile wide boulevards, parks, and dreary shopping centers. During World War II, some 31.5 million men set out from here (in World War I, more than twice that number), and Southampton was repeatedly bombed, which destroyed its old character. Today, the rather shoddy downtown section represents what happens when the architectural focus is timeliness rather than grace. There's not much to see in the city itself but there's a lot on the outskirts. If you're spending time in Southampton between ships, you may want to explore some of the major sights of Hampshire nearby (New Forest, Winchester, the Isle of Wight, and Bournemouth, in neighboring Dorset).

Its supremacy as a port dates from Saxon times when the Danish conqueror Canute was proclaimed king here in 1017. Southampton was especially important to the Normans and helped them keep in touch with their homeland. Its denizens were responsible for bringing in the bubonic plague, which wiped out a quarter of the English population in the mid–14th century. On the Western Esplanade is a memorial tower to the Pilgrims, who set out on their voyage to the New World from Southampton on August 15, 1620. Both the *Mayflower* and the *Speedwell* sailed from here but were forced by storm damages to put in at Plymouth, where the *Speedwell* was abandoned.

In the spring of 1912, the "unsinkable" White Star liner, the 46,000-ton *Titanic*, sailed from Southampton on its maiden voyage. Shortly before midnight on April 14, while steaming at 22 knots, the great ship collided with an iceberg and sank to the bottom of the icy Atlantic. The sinking of the *Titanic*, subject of the Oscar-winning box office smash of 1997, became one of the greatest disasters in maritime history, as 1,513 people perished.

ESSENTIALS

GETTING THERE   Trains depart from London's Waterloo Station several times daily. The trip takes just over an hour. Call ☎ **0345/484950** in the U.K., or 01603/764776 for information and schedules.

National Express operates hourly departures from London's Victoria Coach Station. The trip takes 2½ hours. Call ☎ **0990/808080** for information and schedules.

If you're driving, take M3 southwest from London.

VISITOR INFORMATION   The **Tourist Information Centre,** 9 Civic Centre Rd. (☎ **01703/221106**), is open Monday to Wednesday and Friday and Saturday from

9am to 5pm, and Thursday from 10am to 5pm; closed Good Friday and Easter Monday, Christmas, December 26, and New Year's Day.

EXPLORING SOUTHAMPTON

Ocean Village and the town quay on Southampton's waterfront are bustling with activity and are filled with shops, restaurants, and entertainment possibilities.

West Quay Retail Park, the first phase of Southampton's £250 million ($400 million) Esplanade development, recently opened and has become a major hub for shoppers. The central shopping area is pedestrian-only, and tree- and shrub-filled planters provide a backdrop for summer flowers and hanging baskets. You can sit and listen to the buskers or perhaps watch the world parade by from one of the nearby restaurants or pavement cafes. For a vast array of shops, try the **Town Quay** (☎ **01703/228353**), the **Canutes Pavilion** at Ocean Village (☎ **01703/228353**), or **Kingsland Market** (☎ **01703/221736**).

The most intriguing shopping on the outskirts is at the **Whitchurch Silk Mill,** 28 Winchester St., Whitchurch (☎ **01256/892065**). Visitors flock to this working mill in colorful surroundings on the River Test. Historic looms weave silk here as in olden days, and visitors can observe water-wheel–powered machinery, warping, and winding. The gift shop sells silk on the roll, ties, scarves, handkerchiefs, jewelry, and souvenirs. Hours are Tuesday to Sunday from 10:30am to 5pm, although looms don't operate on Sunday.

City tour guides offer a wide range of **free guided walks** and regular **city bus tours.** Free guided walks of the town are offered throughout the year on Sunday and Monday at 10:30am and June to September twice daily at 10:30am and 2:30pm. Tours start at Bargate. For details of various boat or bus trips that might be offered at the time of your visit, check with the tourist office.

Museum of Archaeology. God's House Tower, Winkle St. ☎ **01703/635904.** Free admission. Tues–Fri 10am–noon and 1–4pm, Sat 10am–noon and 1–4pm, Sun 2–5pm. Bus: 2, 6, 8, or 13.

The museum, housed in part of the town's 15th-century defenses, traces the history and portrays the daily life of the Roman, Saxon, and medieval eras.

Southampton Maritime Museum. The Wool House, Town Quay. ☎ **01703/223941.** Free admission. Tues–Sat 10am–4pm, Sun 2–5pm. Closed bank holiday Mondays, Christmas, and Boxing Day. Bus: 2, 6, 8, or 13.

This museum is housed in an impressive 14th-century stone warehouse with a magnificent timber ceiling. Its exhibits trace the history of Southampton, including a model of the docks as they looked at their peak in the 1930s. Also displayed are artifacts from some of the great ocean liners whose home port was Southampton.

The most famous of these was the fabled *Titanic*, which was partially built in Southampton and sailed from this port of its fateful, fatal voyage. James Cameron's box office smash, which retells the story of the ship's sinking, has also increased traffic to the relatively small *Titanic* exhibit at the museum as well. It features photographs of the crew (many of whom were from Southampton) and passengers, as well as letters from passengers, Capt. Edward Smith's sword, and a video with a dated interview with the fallen captain plus modern interviews with survivors, including elderly Southampton resident Milvien Deen.

WHERE TO STAY

Finding a place to stay right in Southampton isn't as important as it used to be. Very few ships now arrive, and the places to stay just outside the city are generally better. For more choices in the area, refer to "Where to Stay Around New Forest," below.

County Hotel–Southampton. 119 Highfield Lane, Portswood (off Portswood Rd.), Southampton, Hampshire SO17 1AQ. ☎ **01703/359955.** Fax 01703/583910. 66 units. TV TEL. Sun–Thurs £70 ($112) double; Fri–Sat £52.50 ($84) double. AE, DC, MC, V. Bus: 11 or 13.

In a residential area on the northern outskirts of the city, this modern hotel, a member of Queen's Moat House hotel group, offers comfortable but lackluster accommodations and efficient service. Its restaurant, Hamilton's, serves a standard à la carte menu complemented by a comprehensive wine list.

✪ De Vere Grand Harbour Hotel. W. Quay Rd., Southampton, Hampshire SO15 1AG. ☎ **01703/633033.** Fax 01703/633066. 176 units. MINIBAR TV TEL. £135–£165 ($216–$264) double; £225–£385 ($360–$616) suite. Rates include breakfast. AE, DC, MC, V.

If you must stay in town, this is the most comfortable place to be, if you can afford it. Completed in 1994, the 5-story structure, sheathed in granite and with a dramatically tilted glass facade, is the most exciting hotel to be built in Southampton since World War II. The dramatic public areas include an atrium furnished in wicker and a reception area that's almost entirely done in marble and paneling. Some 30 of the brightly painted bedrooms have air-conditioning. Bathrooms are filled with amenities, including separate walk-in showers and granite vanities. About nine of them are equipped for persons with disabilities.

Dining: The more formal of the hotel's two restaurants is Allerton's, with somewhat mediocre food. More boisterous is Brewster's, an informal bistro.

Amenities: 24-hour room service, laundry, baby-sitting, indoor swimming pool with a separate indoor pool for children, gym, spa bath, steam room, sauna.

The Dolphin. 35 High St., Southampton, Hampshire SO14 2HN. ☎ **01703/339955.** Fax 01703/333650. 73 units. TV TEL. £85 ($136) double; £105 ($168) suite. AE, DC, MC, V. Bus: 2, 6, or 8.

This bow-windowed Georgian coaching house on the main street, dating back to the 13th century, was Jane Austen's choice, and Thackeray's, too. Even Queen Victoria visited via her horse-drawn carriage. If you want tradition, this is your best bet. It's in the center of the city, approached through an arched entrance over which rests a coat of arms of William IV and Queen Adelaide. The rooms vary widely in size, but are generally spacious and well furnished. English meals at the Thackeray Restaurant are quite good, and drinks are served in the Nelson Bar. The hotel has health and fitness facilities.

Forte Post House. Herbert Walker Ave., Southampton, Hampshire SO15 1HJ. ☎ **800/ 225-5843** in the U.S. and Canada, or 01703/330777. Fax 01703/332510. 128 units. TV TEL. £59–£99 ($94.40–$158.40) double. AE, DC, MC, V. Bus: 2, 6, or 8.

This 10-floor high-rise across from Mayflower Park was built near the new docks to overlook the harbor, but is only 5 minutes away from the city center. You can unload your luggage under a sheltered drive and walk into the reception area. The rooms are standard but generally spacious, with built-in furniture and picture-window walls. Among the facilities of the hotel are an indoor swimming pool, a Jacuzzi, a full gym, and a lounge. The Trader Bar adjacent to the restaurant offers an intimate atmosphere.

Polygon Hotel. Cumberland Place, Southampton, Hampshire SO15 4WQ. ☎ **800/ 225-5843** in the U.S. and Canada, or 01703/330055. Fax 01703/332435. 95 units. TV TEL. £60 ($96) double; £80 ($128) suite. AE, DC, MC, V. Bus: 2, 6, or 8.

Close to the Civic Center, this is the oldest and most historic hotel in Southampton, bearing the name of the Polygon district in which it sits. Originally built during the 17th century, it was expanded first by the Victorians, and then by its owners just before World War II. The present hotel retains many of its Victorian details, despite many refurbishments. Some bedrooms were renovated a few years ago. All accommodations feature traditional furniture, country house–style curtains, and beverage-makers, and 11 are set aside for nonsmokers. Many offer views over Watts Park and Southampton's Civic Centre. There's a plush bar and a dignified restaurant called Chandlers.

WHERE TO DINE

Ennios. Town Quay Rd. ☎ **01703/221159.** Reservations recommended. Main courses £10–£22 ($16–$35.20). AE, DC, MC, V. Mon–Sat noon–3pm and 6:30–10pm (last order). Bus: 2, 6, or 8. ITALIAN.

The best restaurant in Southampton, Ennios was designed by Scottish-born architect John Geddes as a warehouse and boatyard. At the time, the sea came up to its foundations and boats could unload their cargoes directly into its cavernous interior. Today, although the exterior is rustic and weathered, its interior is stylish. The restaurant's wine cellar, with 600-year-old walls, once part of the medieval wall that ringed Southampton, has an extensive list of Italian wines as well as some French and New World labels. Meals feature typical pastas, as well as shrimp scampi or veal piccata. Freshly caught fish is listed daily on a blackboard. The restaurant, informal wine bar, and brasserie are much favored by local businesspeople at lunch and by relatively informal diners in the evening.

La Margherita. 4–6 Commercial Rd. ☎ **01703/333390.** Main courses £6.50–£12.95 ($10.40–$20.70); pastas and pizzas £5.50–£6.90 ($8.80–$11.05). AE, MC, V. Mon–Sat noon–2pm and 6:30–11pm, Sun 6–11pm. Bus: 7, 9, or 10. ITALIAN.

Popular with families, this restaurant offers pizza and pasta, as well as veal, poultry, beef, and fish dishes—nothing special, but not bad, either. It has one of the most extensive menus in town, beginning with a wide selection of appetizers, ranging from antipasti to Parma ham and melon. Look for the catch of the day, which might be shark steak prepared Sicilian style, or red mullet. Several vegetarian dishes are offered, even veggie burgers. You can order wine by the glass and end your meal with a strong espresso.

A SIDE TRIP TO BROADLANDS:
HOME OF THE LATE EARL OF MOUNTBATTEN

Broadlands. 8 miles northwest of Southampton in Romsey, on A31. ☎ **01794/517888.** Admission £5 ($8) adults, £4.25 ($6.80) students and seniors, £3.50 ($5.60) children 12–16; free for children 11 and under. Noon–5:30pm. Open daily from June 13 to Sept 6. Closed early Sept to early June.

Broadlands was the home of the late Earl Mountbatten of Burma, who was assassinated in 1979. Lord Mountbatten, who has been called "the last war hero," lent the house to his nephew, Prince Philip, and Princess Elizabeth as a honeymoon haven in 1947, and in 1981 Prince Charles and Princess Diana spent the first nights of their honeymoon here.

Broadlands is now owned by Lord Romsey, Lord Mountbatten's eldest grandson, who has created a fine exhibition and audiovisual show that depicts the highlights of his grandfather's brilliant career as a sailor and statesman. The house, originally linked to Romsey Abbey, was transformed into an elegant Palladian mansion by Capability Brown and Henry Holland. Brown landscaped the parkland and grounds.

4 The New Forest

95 miles SW of London; 10 miles W of Southampton

Encompassing about 92,000 acres, the New Forest is a large tract created by William the Conqueror, who laid out the limits of this then-private hunting preserve. Successful poachers faced the executioner if they were caught, and those who hunted but missed had their hands severed. Henry VIII loved to hunt deer in the New Forest, but he also saw an opportunity to build up the British naval fleet by supplying oak and other hard timbers to the boatyards at Buckler's Hard on the Beaulieu River.

Today you can visit the old shipyards and also the museum, with its fine models of men-of-war, pictures of the old yard, and dioramas showing the building of these ships, their construction, and their launching. It took 2,000 trees to construct one man-of-war. A motorway cuts through the area, and the once-thick forest has groves of oak trees separated by wide tracts of common land that's grazed by ponies and cows, hummocked with heather and gorse, and frequented by rabbits. But away from the main roads, where signs warn of wild ponies and deer, you'll find a private world of peace and quiet.

ESSENTIALS

GETTING THERE   On the train, go to Southampton (see above), where rail connections can be made to a few centers in the New Forest. Where the train leaves off, bus connections can be made to all the towns and many villages.

Southampton and Lymington have the best bus connections to New Forest villages. If you're driving, head west from Southampton on A35.

VISITOR INFORMATION   The information office is at the **New Forest Visitor Centre,** Main Car Park, Lyndhurst (☎ **01703/282269**), which is open daily from 10am to 6pm April to September, and daily from 10am to 5pm from October to March.

SEEING THE SIGHTS

✪ **Beaulieu Abbey–Palace House.** Beaulieu, on B3056 in the New Forest (5 miles southeast of Lyndhurst and 14 miles west of Southampton). ☎ **01590/612345.** Admission £9 ($14.40) adults, £7 ($11.20) seniors and students, £6.25 ($10) children 4–16; free for children 3 and under, £30 ($48) family (2 adults and up to 4 children). Easter–Sept daily 10am–6pm; Oct–Easter daily 10am–5pm. Closed Dec 25. Buses run from the Lymington bus station Mon–Sat; Sun you'll need a taxi or car.

The abbey and house, as well as the National Motor Museum, are on the property of Lord Montagu of Beaulieu (pronounced *Bew*-ley). A Cistercian abbey was founded on this spot in 1204, and the ruins can be explored today. The Palace House was the great gatehouse of the abbey before it was converted into a private residence in 1538. It is surrounded by gardens.

The **National Motor Museum,** one of the best and most comprehensive automotive museums in the world, with more than 250 vehicles, is on the grounds and is open to the public. Famous autos include four land-speed record holders, among them Donald Campbell's Bluebird. The collection was built around Lord Montagu's family collection of vintage cars. A special feature is called "Wheels." In a darkened environment, visitors can travel in specially designed "pods" that carry up to two adults and one child along a silent electric track. They move at a predetermined but variable speed, and each pod is capable of rotating almost 360°. Seated in these, you'll view displays (with sound and visual effects) spanning 100 years of motor development without the fatigue of standing in line. For further information, contact the visitor reception manager at the John Montagu Building (☎ 01590/612345).

Maritime Museum. Buckler's Hard. ☎ 01590/616203. Admission £3 ($4.80) adults, £2.50 ($4) students and seniors, £2 ($3.20) children, £8.30 ($13.30) family. Mar–May daily 10am–6pm, June–Sept daily 10am–9pm, Oct–Feb daily 10am–4:30pm.

Buckler's Hard, a historic 18th-century village 2½ miles from Beaulieu on the banks of the River Beaulieu, is where ships for Nelson's fleet were built, including the admiral's favorite, *Agamemnon*, as well as *Eurylus* and *Swiftsure*. The Maritime Museum highlights the village's shipbuilding history as well as Henry Adams, master shipbuilder; Nelson's favorite ship; Buckler's Hard and Trafalgar; and models of Sir Francis Chichester's yachts and items of his equipment. The cottage exhibits re-create 18th-century life in Buckler's Hard—you can stroll through the New Inn of 1793 and a shipwright's cottage of the same period or look in on the family of a poor laborer at home.

The walk back to Beaulieu, 2½ miles along the riverbank, is well marked through the woodlands. During the summer, you can take a half-hour cruise on the River Beaulieu in the present *Swiftsure*, an all-weather catamaran cruiser.

WHERE TO STAY AROUND NEW FOREST

Balmer Lawn Hotel. Lyndhurst Rd., Brockenhurst, Hampshire SO42 7ZB. ☎ 01590/ 623116. Fax 01590/623864. 55 units. TV TEL. £115 ($184) double. Rates include English breakfast. AE, DC, MC, V. Take A337 (Lyndhurst–Lymington road) about half a mile outside Brockenhurst.

This hotel, about a 10-minute walk from Brockenhurst's center in a woodland location, was originally built as a modest private home during the 17th century and was later enlarged into an imposing hunting lodge. During World War II, it was a military hospital. (Within the past decade, significant numbers of overnight guests here have spotted the ghost of one of the white-coated doctors with his stethoscope, still roaming the hotel's first floor.) The hotel has a pleasant and humorous staff (which refers to the ghost as "Dr. Eric").

Dining: There's a newly refurbished bar and lounge, where informal bar snacks are offered at lunchtime. More formal, well-prepared meals are available in the restaurant at night.

Amenities: Two swimming pools (one indoor, one outdoor), gym, sauna, Jacuzzi, two indoor squash courts, and an all-weather tennis court.

Carey's Manor. Lyndhurst Rd., Brockenhurst, Hampshire SO42 7RH. ☎ 01590/623551. Fax 01590/622799. 79 units, some with shower only, some with tub only. TV TEL. £129 ($206.40) double; £179 ($286.40) suite. Rates include English breakfast. AE, DC, MC, V. From the town center, head toward Lyndhurst on A337.

This manor house dates from Charles II, who used to come here when Carey's was a hunting lodge. Greatly expanded in 1888, the building became a country hotel in the 1930s. It's about a 90-minute drive from London. Much improved in recent years, it's better than ever now. The old house is still filled with character, with mellow, time-worn paneling and carved oak staircase. Each bedroom, whether in the restored main building or in the garden wing, has tub or shower, hair dryer, and trouser press.

Dining: The hotel serves good food—modern British and French cuisine.

Amenities: Carey's is ideal as a resort, with an indoor swimming pool, gym, solarium, and sauna, all on 5 acres of landscaped grounds.

✪ **Chewton Glen Hotel.** Christchurch Rd., New Milton, Hampshire BH25 6QS. ☎ 01425/275341. Fax 01425/272310. 53 units. TV TEL. £210–£450 ($336–$720) double;

£400 ($640) suite. AE, DC, MC, V. After leaving the village of Walkford, follow signs off A35 (New Milton–Christchurch rd.), through parkland.

A gracious country house on the fringe of the New Forest, Chewton Glen, within easy reach of Southampton and Bournemouth, is the finest place to stay in southwest England (with princely rates to match). In the old house, the magnificent staircase leads to well-furnished double rooms opening onto views over the spacious grounds. In the new wing, you will find yourself on the ground level with French doors opening onto your own private patio. Log fires burn and fresh flowers add fragrance; the garden sweeps down to a stream and then to rhododendron woods.

Dining: In the dining room, the standards of cooking and presentation are high. Particular emphasis is placed on fresh ingredients. The chef favors a modern cuisine, complemented by excellent sauces and velvety smooth desserts.

Amenities: Open-air heated swimming pool and an indoor swimming pool, two indoor tennis courts, 9-hole golf course, health club, sauna, Jacuzzi, 24-hour room service, valet and laundry service.

Country House Hotel New Park Manor. Lyndhurst Rd., Brockenhurst, Hampshire SO42 7QH. ☎ **01590/623467.** Fax 01590/622268. 24 units. TV TEL. £130 ($208) double; £150–£160 ($240–$256) suite for 2. Rates include breakfast. AE, CB, DC, MC, V. Head 2 miles north off A337 (Lyndhurst–Brockenhurst rd.) toward the New Forest Show Ground.

This former royal hunting lodge, dating from the days of William the Conqueror and a favorite of Charles II, is the only hotel in the New Forest itself. Although it's now a modern country hotel, the original rooms have been preserved, including such features as beams and open log fires. Each room is comfortable and well kept.

Dining: The candlelit restaurant, with its log fire, specializes in flambés. The chef often uses fresh garden produce, which is complemented by a good wine list.

Amenities: There's a swimming pool in a sheltered corner of the garden (heated in summer) and a hard tennis court. Horseback-riding from the hotel's stables is available.

The Crown Hotel. 9 High St., Lyndhurst, Hampshire SO43 7NF. ☎ **01703/282922.** Fax 01703/282751. 40 units. MINIBAR TV TEL. £99 ($158.40) double; £131 ($209.60) suite. Rates include English breakfast. AE, DC, MC, V. Bus: 56 or 56A. Exit the M27 motorway at Junction 1 and drive 3 miles due south.

Although the present building is only 100 years old, there has been a hostelry here on the main street of the New Forest village of Lyndhurst, opposite the church with its tall spire, for centuries. The comfortable rooms are traditionally furnished.

Dining: Much local produce, including venison, is used in the dining room, where the food is not only good but reasonable in price. Locals flock here for Sunday lunch. The hotel also does substantial bar meals.

Lyndhurst Park Hotel. High St., Lyndhurst, Hampshire SO43 7NL. ☎ **01703/283923.** Fax 01703/283019. 59 units. TV TEL. £90 ($144) double. Rates include English breakfast. AE, DC, MC, V. Bus: 56, 56A or X1.

This is a large Georgian country house set on 5 acres of beautiful gardens. The bedrooms all have tea- and coffeemakers, hair dryers, and trouser presses.

Dining: There is a bar, plus an oak-paneled restaurant, where a wide selection is offered at lunch and dinner.

Amenities: Outdoor heated swimming pool, all-weather tennis court.

Master Builders House Hotel. Buckler's Hard, Beaulieu, Hampshire SO42 7XB. ☎ **01590/616253.** Fax 01590/616297. 23 units. TV TEL. Summer £110 ($176) double; winter £80 ($128) double. Rates include breakfast. Half board £134 ($214.40) double in summer, £90 ($144) double in winter (2-night minimum for half board). AE, MC, V.

About 2½ miles south of Beaulieu, in the historic maritime village of Buckler's Hard, this 17th-century redbrick building was once the home of master shipbuilder Henry Adams, who incorporated many of his shipbuilding techniques into the construction of this lovely old house. Views from some of the bedrooms overlook the grass-covered slipways that, centuries ago, were used to ease newly built ocean vessels into the calm waters of the nearby river.

Most of the hotel's comfortable and conservatively decorated accommodations are in a modern wing, built after World War II. The hotel's historic core is devoted to the Yachtsman Buffet Bar and to the restaurant. Here, wide windows overlook the busy river.

Montagu Arms. Palace Lane, Beaulieu, Hampshire, SO42 7ZL. ☎ **01590/612324.** Fax 01590/612188. 24 units. TV TEL. £119.90–£129.90 ($191.85–$207.85) double; £159–£195.90 ($254.40–$313.45) suite. Rates include English breakfast. AE, DC, MC, V.

The core of this historic coaching inn was built in the 1700s to supply food and drink to the teams of laborers who hauled salt from the nearby marshes to other parts of England. The garden walls were built with stones salvaged from Beaulieu Abbey after it was demolished by Henry VIII. Equally important is the hexagonal column supporting a fountain in the hotel's central courtyard—one of six salvaged, according to legend, from the ruined abbey's nave. On the premises is an oak-beamed and paneled dining room, serving traditional English food. The rooms are immaculate and modernized, with comfortable furnishings.

Dining: Today, the oldest part of the inn is its pub, which continues to serve food and ale to visitors who appreciate its well-oiled patina and sense of history.

WHERE TO DINE

Le Poussin. The Courtyard, at the rear of 49–55 Brookley Rd., Brockenhurst. ☎ **01590/623063.** Reservations recommended 1 month in advance. 2-course lunch £15 ($24), 3-course lunch £20 ($32); 2-course dinner £22.50 ($36), 3-course dinner £27.50 ($44). MC, V. Wed–Sun noon–2pm; Wed–Sat 7–10pm. GAME/FISH.

Serving the best food in the area, Le Poussin is located in what was originally a 19th-century stable and workshop. To reach it, pass beneath the arched alleyway (located midway between nos. 49 and 55 Brookley Rd.) and enter the stylishly simple premises directed by English-born chef Alexander Aitken and his wife, Caroline.

Amid a decor accented with framed 19th century poems and illustrations celebrating the pleasures of poultry, the staff will offer fish and game dishes whose ingredients usually come fresh from the nearby New Forest. In season, you'll find venison (try the "Fruits of the New Forest"—individually cooked portions of pigeon, wild rabbit, hare, and venison, encased in puff pastry and served with game sauce). Your meal might begin with a *pithivier* of lobster (a dome-shaped puff pastry filled with chunks of lobster encased in a lobster mousse). Dessert choices change seasonally but usually include a festival of wild strawberries served with an elder-flower sorbet.

5 The Isle of Wight

91 miles SW of London; 4 miles S of Southampton

The Isle of Wight is known for its sandy beaches and its ports, long favored by the yachting set. The island has attracted such literary figures as Alfred, Lord Tennyson, and Charles Dickens. Tennyson wrote his beloved poem "Crossing the Bar" en route across the Solent from Lymington to Yarmouth. A vacation on the island sounds a bit dated, although many British families come here just to relax and enjoy the natural beauty. You may want to come just for the day. Some parts are rather tacky, especially

Sandown and Shanklin, although other areas out on the island still are tranquil and quite beautiful.

The Isle of Wight is compact in size, measuring 23 miles from east to west, 13 miles from north to south. **Ryde** is the railhead for the island's transportation system. **Yarmouth** is something else—a busy little harbor providing a mooring for yachts and also for one of the lifeboats in the Solent area.

Cowes is the premier port for yachting in Britain. Henry VIII ordered the castle built here, but it's now the headquarters of the Royal Yacht Squadron. The seafront, the Prince's Green, and the high cliff road are worth exploring. Hovercraft are built in the town, which is also the home and birthplace of the well-known maritime photographer Beken of Cowes. In winter, everyone wears oilskins and wellies, leaving a wet trail behind them.

Newport, a bustling market town in the heart of the island, is the capital and has long been a favorite of British royalty. Along the southeast coast are the twin resorts of **Sandown,** with its new pier complex and theater, and **Shanklin,** at the southern end of Sandown Bay, which has held the British annual sunshine record more times than any other resort. Keats once lived in Shanklin's Old Village. Farther along the coast, **Ventnor** is called the "Madeira of England" because it rises from the sea in a series of steep hills.

On the west coast are the many-colored sand cliffs of **Alum Bay.** The Needles, three giant chalk rocks, and the Needles Lighthouse, are the farther features of interest at this end of the island. If you want to stay at the western end of Wight, consider **Freshwater Bay.**

ESSENTIALS

GETTING THERE A direct train from London's Waterloo Station to Portsmouth deposits travelers directly at the pier for a ferry crossing to the Isle of Wight; ferries are timed to meet train arrivals. Travel time from London to the arrival point of Ryde on the Isle of Wight (including ferry-crossing time) is 2 hours. One train per hour departs during the day from London to Portsmouth. For rail information, call ☎ **0345/484950** in the U.K., or 01603/764776 in the U.S.

Drive to Southampton (see above) and take the ferry, or leave Southampton and head west along A35, cutting south on A337 toward Lymington on the coast, where the ferry crossing to Yarmouth (Isle of Wight) is shorter than the trip from Southampton.

Red Funnel operates a vehicle ferry service from Terminal 1 in Southampton to East Cowes; the trip takes 55 minutes. An inclusive round-trip fare (valid for 5 days) costs from £36 to £55 ($57.60 to $88) for four persons, depending on the season. More popular with train travelers from Waterloo Station in London is a Hi-Speed passenger-only catamaran operating from the Town Quay Terminal 2 in Southampton, going to West Cowes; the trip takes 22 minutes. A day return fare costs £9.30 ($14.90) for adults and £4.65 ($7.45) for children. For ferry departure times, call ☎ **01703/334010.**

The White Line ferry operates between Portsmouth and Ryde, taking 20 minutes and costing £6.20 ($9.90) for adults and £3.10 ($4.95) for children, round-trip. Daytime departures are every 30 minutes in summer and every 60 minutes in winter. A final option involves a Hovercraft that travels from Southsea (Portsmouth's neighbor) to Ryde, charging £7.90 ($12.65) for adults and £3.95 ($6.30) for children. For information on departure times and schedules, call ☎ **0800/343333** for car-ferries, 01983/811000 for the Hovercraft, or 01705/827744 for the White Line passenger ferries.

GETTING AROUND   Visitors can explore the Isle of Wight just for the day on the Island Explorer bus service. Tickets may be purchased on the bus, and you can board or leave the bus at any stop on the island. The price of a Day Rover is £6.25 ($10) for adults and £3.15 ($5.05) for children. It also entitles you to passage on the island's only railway, which runs from the dock at Ryde to the center of Shanklin, a distance of 8 miles. For further information, call **Southern Vectis** at ☎ **01983/827005.**

VISITOR INFORMATION   The **information office** is at 67 High St., Shanklin (☎ **01983/862942**). It's open Monday to Saturday, March through mid-July and September through October from 9am to 6pm, mid-July through August from 9am to 8:45pm, and November through March from 9:30am to 5pm. It's best to call first, as these hours are subject to change.

QUEEN VICTORIA'S FAVORITE RESIDENCE & A MEDIEVAL CASTLE

✪ **Osborne House.** A mile southeast of East Cowes. ☎ **01983/200022.** House and grounds £6.50 ($10.40) adults, £4.90 ($7.85) seniors, £3.30 ($5.30) children. Admission to grounds only £3.50 ($5.60). Apr–Sept daily 10am–6pm (house closes at 5pm); Oct daily 10am–5pm. Closed Nov–Mar. Bus: 4 or 5.

Queen Victoria's most cherished residence was built at her own expense. Prince Albert, with his characteristic thoroughness, contributed to many aspects of the design of the Italian-inspired mansion, which stands amid lush gardens, right outside the village of Whippingham. The rooms have remained as Victoria knew them, right down to the French piano she used to play and all the cozy clutter of her sitting room. Grief-stricken at the death of Albert in 1861, she asked that Osborne House be kept as it was, and so it has been. Even the turquoise scent bottles he gave her, decorated with cupids and cherubs, are still in place. It was in her bedroom at Osborne House that the queen died on January 22, 1901.

Carisbrooke Castle. Carisbrooke, 1¼ miles southwest of Newport. ☎ **01983/522107.** Castle and museum £4 ($6.40) adults, £3 ($4.80) seniors and students, £2 ($3.20) children. Apr–Oct daily 10am–6pm; Nov–Mar daily 10am–4pm. Bus: 91A.

This fine medieval castle lies in the center of the Isle of Wight. During one of the most turbulent periods of English history, Charles I was imprisoned here, far from his former seat of power in London, by Cromwell's Roundheads in 1647. On the castle premises is the 16th-century Well House, where during periods of siege, donkeys took turns treading a large wooden wheel connected to a rope that hauled up buckets of water from a well. Accessible from the castle's courtyard is a **museum** (☎ **01983/523112**) with exhibits pertaining to the social history of the Isle of Wight and the history of Charles I's imprisonment.

WHERE TO STAY

Biskra House Beach Hotel. 17 St. Thomas's St., Ryde, Isle of Wight PO33 2DC. ☎ **01983/567913.** Fax 01983/616976. 9 units. MINIBAR TV TEL. £47.50–£57.50 ($76–$92) double. Rates include English breakfast. MC, V.

You'll find some of the best dining on the island at Biskra House, which also offers rooms. The rooms are furnished in a comfortable, slightly old-fashioned way, with tea- or coffeemakers and hair dryers. The most expensive double in the house has a private balcony with sunset views over the Solent.

   Giuseppe's Cellar Restaurant serves full Italian meals nightly; the Clipper Bar Restaurant opens onto gardens fronting the beach and serves lunch daily.

Bourne Hall Country Hotel. Luccombe Rd., Shanklin, Isle of Wight PO37 6RR. ☎ **01983/862820.** Fax 01983/865138. 30 units. TV TEL. £65–£82 ($104–$131.20) double. Rates include English breakfast. AE, DC, MC, V. Bus: 12A.

Many visitors prefer to base themselves at Shanklin because of its old village with its thatched cottages and the Chine, two of the island's leading attractions. At Bourne Hall, they receive a warm welcome from the owners, who have one of the area's best-equipped hotels, complete with two swimming pools, a sauna, a solarium, and a Jacuzzi. The hotel stands on its own grounds of nearly three acres adjoining open farmland. Bedrooms are furnished in a delightful English country-house style, and the hotel is noted for its generous and varied cuisine, using local produce whenever possible.

Clarendon Hotel and Wight Mouse Inn. Newport Rd. (B3399; 50 yd. off Military Rd.), Chale, Isle of Wight PO38 2HA. ☎ and fax **01983/730431.** 12 units. TV. £74 ($118.40) double; £114 ($182.40) suite for 2. Children ages 10–16 stay with parents for £24.50 ($39.20), ages 4–9 £12 ($19.20), children 3 and under free. Rates include English breakfast. DC, MC, V.

The Clarendon is a cheerful place to spend the night. This old coaching inn lies on the most southerly part of the island, where the vegetation is almost tropical. From here, you can see over the Channel to the mainland coast. Some rooms are beautifully furnished with antiques, and all have tea- and coffeemakers. Children are welcome here.

The meals are ample, with many fresh ingredients. The pub, the Wight Mouse Inn, is open all day every day for hot meals and drinks; they serve a large selection of beers, real ales, and 365 scotch whiskies, including their own famous Wight Mouse whisky. Live entertainment is provided nightly year-round. Traditional English dishes are served in the more formal Clarendon Restaurant.

Hotel Ryde Castle. The Esplanade, Ryde, Isle of Wight PO33 1JA. ☎ **01983/563755.** Fax 01983/566906. 22 units. TV TEL. £60–£80 ($96–$128) double. Rates include English breakfast. AE, DC, MC, V. Bus: 1 or 1A.

This historic seafront castle looking out on the Solent makes a fine base for exploring the island. The castle, dating from the 16th century, has been added to over the centuries. Field Marshall Montgomery stayed here before the D-day landings. With its crenellated ivy-clad exterior and its well-kept public rooms, the hotel attracts families as well as single visitors. The comfortable suites contain hair dryers and tea- or coffeemakers; double suites have four-poster beds. Kids can hang around at the children's play area.

The hotel dining room makes full use of locally caught fresh fish and island farm products. The family bar/lounge offers inexpensive snacks for lunch.

Luccombe Chine House. Luccombe Chine, Shanklin, Isle of Wight PO37 6RH. ☎ **01983/ 862037.** 6 units. TV. £38 ($60.80) per person. Rates include English breakfast. MC, V. Closed Dec–Jan. Bus: 12A. Take A3055 (Shanklin-Ventnor rd.) to the signposted private driveway. Children not accepted.

Luccombe Chine House is situated on some 10 acres of grounds opening onto Luccombe Bay. Each room is immaculately kept and well furnished, with beverage-maker and a hair dryer; all have four-poster beds. The lounge is comfortable and homelike, with an inglenook fireplace and a well-stocked honor bar. There is a small brook that cascades through the gardens down to the sea. It's a good base from which to explore the Isle of Wight.

St. Catherine's Hotel. 1 Winchester Park Rd., Sandown, Isle of Wight PO36 8HJ. ☎ **01983/402392.** Fax 01983/402392. 20 units. TV TEL. £69 ($110.40) double. Rates include English breakfast. MC, V. Bus: 1 or 1A from Ryde.

Just a few minutes' walk from Sandown's sandy beach, leisure center, and pier complex, with its sun lounges and theater and Sandown railway station, St. Catherine's was built in 1860 of creamy Purbeck stone and white trim for the dean of Winchester College. A modern extension was added for streamlined and sunny bedrooms, which have duvets, white furniture, and built-in headboards. The brightly redecorated lounge has matching draperies at the wide bay windows. There are card tables and a small library of books. Adjacent to the library is a cozy, fully stocked bar and a spacious, comfortable dining room, serving high-quality, well-priced English food.

WHERE TO DINE

The Cottage. 8 Eastcliff Rd., Shanklin Old Village. ☎ **01983/862504.** Reservations recommended. Main courses £13.95 ($22.30); fixed-price lunch £9.85 ($15.75). AE, DC, MC, V. Tues–Sat noon–2pm and 7:30–9:45pm. Closed Feb to mid-Mar and Oct to mid-Nov. ENGLISH/FRENCH.

This restaurant is in a 200-year-old stone-sided cottage that's set among thatch-covered buildings in the center of Shanklin. Inside, two floors of pink and blue dining rooms are accented by lace tablecloths and heavy oak beams. Fixed-price lunches feature chicken sautéed in cream or a roast of the day served with new potatoes and two vegetables. Although most lunch guests opt for the fixed-price menu, tempting à la carte dishes are available at both lunch and dinner, such as sea trout poached and served in a mousseline sauce with wild rice cooked in Darjeeling tea. Two lounges accommodate smokers. The garden and courtyard are open in summer for drinks.

6 Bournemouth

104 miles SW of London; 15 miles W of the Isle of Wight

The south-coast resort at the doorstep of the New Forest didn't just happen: It was carefully planned and executed—a true city in a garden. Flower-filled, park-dotted Bournemouth is filled with an abundance of architecture inherited from those arbiters of taste, Victoria and her son, Edward. (The resort was discovered back in Victoria's day, when sea bathing became an institution.) Bournemouth's most distinguished feature is its chines (narrow, shrub-filled, steep-sided ravines) along the coastline.

Bournemouth, along with neighboring Poole and Christchurch, forms the largest urban area in the south of England. It makes a good base for exploring a historically rich part of England; on its outskirts are the New Forest, Salisbury, Winchester, and the Isle of Wight.

ESSENTIALS

GETTING THERE   An express train from London's Waterloo Station takes 2 hours, with frequent service throughout the day. For schedules and information, call ☎ 0345/484950 in the U.K., 01603/764776 outside the U.K. Arrivals are at the Bournemouth Rail Station, on Holden Surst Road.

Buses leave London's Waterloo Station every 2 hours during the day, heading for Bournemouth. The trip takes 2½ hours. Call ☎ **0990/808080** for information and schedules.

If you're driving, take M3 southwest from London to Winchester, then A31 and A338 south to Bournemouth.

VISITOR INFORMATION   The **information office** is at Westover Road (☎ 01202/451700). From May 4 through September 13, it's open Monday through Saturday from 9:30am to 7pm, Sunday from 10:30am to 5pm; from September 14 through May 3, hours are Monday through Saturday from 9:30am to 5:30pm.

EXPLORING THE AREA

Of Bournemouth's nearly 12,000 acres, about one-sixth consists of green parks and flower beds such as the **Pavilion Rock Garden,** which is perfect for a stroll. The total effect, especially in spring, is striking and helps explain Bournemouth's continuing popularity with the garden-loving English.

The resort's amusements are varied. At the **Pavilion Theatre,** you can see West End–type productions from London. The **Bournemouth Symphony Orchestra** is justly famous in Europe. And there's the usual run of golf courses, band concerts, variety shows, and dancing.

And of course, this seaside resort has a spectacular beach—7 miles of uninterrupted sand stretching from Hengistbury Head to Alum Chine. Most of it is known simply as **Bournemouth Beach,** although its western edge, when it crosses over into the municipality of Poole, is called **Sandbanks Beach.** Beach access is free, and you can swim where a pair of blue flags indicate that the water's fine. The flags also signify the highest standards of cleanliness, management, and facilities. A health-conscious, no-smoking zone now exists at Durley Chine, East Beach, and Fisherman's Walk. Four-teen full-time lifeguards patrol on the shore and the water and are helped by three volunteer corps during the busiest summer months. The promenade is traffic-free during the summer. There are two piers, one at Boscombe and the other at Bournemouth.

Amenities at the beach include beach bungalows, freshwater showers, seafront bistros and cafes, boat trips, row boats, pedalos, jet-skis, and Windsurfers. Cruises run in the summer from Bournemouth Pier to the Isle of Wight.

The traffic-free town center with its wide avenues is elegant but by no means stuffy. Entertainers perform on the corners of streets that are lined with boutiques, cafes, street furniture, and plenty of meeting places. Specialized shopping is found mainly in the suburbs—Pokesdown for antiques and collectibles, Westbourne for individual designer fashion and home accessories. Victorian shopping arcades can be found in both Westbourne and Boscombe.

Two of the better gift shops include **Gifts of Distinction at Peter Stebbin Ltd.,** 7 Post Office Rd. (☎ **01202/552587**), and **Dorset Craft Galleries,** 93 Belle Vue Rd., Southbourne Crossroads (☎ **01202/429644**), with its locally handmade crafts and demonstrations.

Russell-Cotes Art Gallery and Museum. East Cliff. ☎ **01202/451800.** Free admission. Tues–Sun 10am–5pm.

Based in a remarkable Victorian house (1897), the Russell-Cotes boasts an out-standing collection of Victorian fine art and sculpture, ethnography, and modern British art. A new museum extension and relandscaped gardens are the site for an extension program of contemporary craft and sculpture commissions.

The Shelley Rooms. Beechwood Ave., Boscombe. ☎ **01202/303571.** Free admission. Tues–Sun 2–5pm.

True romantics and die-hard fans of Percy Bysshe Shelley should take time to see this small museum and study room, housed in Boscombe Manor, the one-time home of Shelley's son, Sir Percy Florence Shelley. The rooms are devoted to the works of the great poet and his circle. Collections are built primarily around works written during the last few months of Shelley's life when he lived in San Terenzo, Italy.

EXPLORING NEARBY WAREHAM

This historic little town on the Frome River 2 miles west of Bournemouth is an excel-lent center for touring the South Dorset coast and the Purbeck Hills. See the remains of early Anglo-Saxon and Roman town walls, plus the Saxon church of St. Martin, with its effigy of T. E. Lawrence (Lawrence of Arabia), who died in a motorcycle crash in 1935. His former home, **Clouds Hill** (☎ **01929/405616**), lies 7 miles west of

Wareham (1 mile north of Bovington Camp) and is extremely small. It's open only April to October, on Wednesday, Thursday, Friday, and Sunday from noon to 5pm, and bank holiday Mondays from noon to 5pm. Admission is £2.20 ($3.50); free for children 4 and under.

Tank Museum. In the village and army base of Bovington Camp. ☎ **01929/403463.** Admission £5 ($8) adults, £3 ($4.80) children 5–16. Daily 10am–4:30pm (last admission).

Aficionados of military history should head to this installation maintained by the British military. Among the dozens of rare and historic armed vehicles are exhibitions and memorabilia on the life of T. E. Lawrence.

POOLE & CHRISTCHURCH

True history buffs usually head 5 miles west to Poole, or 5 miles east to Christchurch, both of which predated Bournemouth by thousands of years. Both have large but shallow harbors, which were favored by the ancient Romans.

Waterfront Museum. High St., Poole. ☎ **01202/683138.** July–Aug admission £2.50 ($4) adults, £1.75 ($2.80) children ages 5–16; free for children under 5. Apr–June and Sept–Oct admission £1.95 ($3.10) adults, £1.25 ($2) children. Apr–Oct daily 10am–5pm. Call for off-season details.

This museum celebrates the nautical influences that made the region great, with exhibits about the effects of seafaring commerce since the days of the ancient Romans.

Priority Church. Quay Rd., Christchurch. Year-round Mon–Sat 9am–5pm, Sun 2:15–5pm.

The present monastic church was begun in 1094 on a site where there has been a church since A.D. 700. It is famous for the "Miraculous Beam," Norman nave and Turreet, monks' quire with its Jesse reredos and misericords, Lady Chapel, chantries, 15th-century bell tower, and St. Michael's loft, once a school but now a museum.

Red House Museum. Quay Rd., Christchurch. ☎ **01202/482860.** Admission £1.60 ($2.55). Tues–Sat 10am–5pm, Sun 2–5pm.

This museum occupies a redbrick building originally constructed in 1764 as a workhouse. In 1951, a civic-minded resident donated his extensive collection of archaeological and cultural artifacts to form the basis of the town's most visible public monument. An art gallery on the premises sells paintings, and exhibits showcase the region's cultural and social history.

WHERE TO STAY
VERY EXPENSIVE

Carlton Hotel. Meyrick Rd., E. Overcliff, Bournemouth, Dorset BH1 3DN. ☎ **01202/ 552011.** Fax 01202/299573. 70 units. TV TEL. £180 ($288) double; from £250 ($400) suite. Rates include English breakfast. AE, DC, MC, V.

This is more of a resort than an ordinary hotel. The Carlton sits atop a seaside cliff lined with private homes and other hotels. This Edwardian pile, opening onto panoramic views, is the best place to stay in Bournemouth. It exudes a 1920s aura, with rather opulent public rooms. Many of the better rooms are quite spacious, with king size beds, armchairs, writing desks, and contemporary bathrooms.

   Dining: The Carlton boasts a luxury restaurant and cocktail bar, and elegant lounges.

   Amenities: 24-hour room service, laundry. There's a boutique and a swimming pool. Trained staff run a health and beauty spa, featuring a sudsy whirlpool, a gymnasium, sauna, Jacuzzi, and tanning beds.

Norfolk Royale Hotel. Richmond Hill, Bournemouth, Dorset BH2 6EN. ☎ **01202/ 551521.** Fax 01202/299729. 95 units. MINIBAR TV TEL. £125 ($200) double; £175 ($280) suite. AE, MC, V.

One of the oldest and most prestigious hotels in town, located a few blocks from the seafront and the central shopping area, recently underwent a major £5 million ($8 million) renovation program, restoring it to its former Edwardian elegance, with a two-tier cast-iron veranda. Nevertheless, we think it still plays second fiddle to both the Carlton and the Royal Bath. It's like a country estate, with a formal entrance and a rear garden and fountain shaded by trees. The rooms and suites have been luxuriously appointed with the traditional styles of the Edwardian period blending with modern comforts.

Amenities: Among the hotel's special features are the swimming pool covered with a glass dome and the Orangery restaurant set in the terraced gardens.

✪ Royal Bath Hotel. Bath Rd., Bournemouth, Dorset BH1 2EW. ☎ **01202/555555.** Fax 01202/554158. 131 units. TV TEL. £150–£170 ($240–$272) double; £240 ($384) junior suite; £305 ($488) twin/double suite. Rates include English breakfast. AE, DC, MC, V. Parking £7.50 ($12).

This early Victorian version of a French château, with towers and bay windows looking out over the bay and Purbeck Hill, opened on June 28, 1838, the very day of Victoria's coronation. After the adolescent Prince of Wales (later Edward VII) stayed here, the hotel added "Royal" to its name. Over the years it has attracted everybody from Oscar Wilde to Rudolf Nureyev and the great prime minister Disraeli. In amenities and style, it is in a neck-and-neck race with the Carlton. It's located in a 3-acre garden where cliff-top panoramas open onto the sea. Bedrooms are luxuriously furnished, and the larger rooms have sitting areas.

Dining: The hotel has two restaurants: the Garden Restaurant and Oscar's (reviewed below). The resident band plays for a dinner-dance most Saturday evenings.

Amenities: There's a sauna, as well as Swedish massages and special diets. In its cliff-top gardens is a heated kidney-shaped swimming pool.

Swallow Highcliff Hotel. 105 St. Michael's Rd., W. Cliff, Bournemouth, Dorset BH2 5DU. ☎ **01202/557702.** Fax 01202/292734. 157 units. MINIBAR TV TEL. £135–£155 ($216–$248) double; £230 ($368) suite. Rates include English breakfast. AE, DC, MC, V.

This 1888 cliff-side hotel is one of the best in Bournemouth, rivaled only by the Carlton and Royal Bath. The high-ceilinged interior has been tastefully renovated, retaining most of the elegant ceiling moldings but replacing the antiques with modern counterparts. A funicular elevator takes guests from the hotel to the seaside promenade. Many of the bedrooms have beautiful views of the sea. Each is well furnished and maintained, and is either in the main building or in coast-guard cottages built in 1912.

Dining: An elegant restaurant serves well-prepared food in a grand manner, with formal service.

Amenities: The leisure club offers a heated swimming pool, tennis court, sauna, solarium, putting green, and game room.

EXPENSIVE

✪ Langtry Manor Hotel. 26 Derby Rd. (north of Christchurch Rd., A35), E. Cliff, Bournemouth, Dorset BH1 3QB. ☎ **01202/553887.** Fax 01202/290550. 26 units. MINIBAR TV TEL. £109.50 ($175.20) double; £149.50 ($239.20) suite for 2. Rates include English breakfast. AE, DC, MC, V.

This is a much more atmospheric choice and more personally run than either the Carlton or Norfolk Royale. The Red House, as it was originally called, was built in

1877 for Lillie Langtry, as a gift from Edward VII to his favorite mistress. The house contains all sorts of reminders of its illustrious inhabitants, including initials scratched on a windowpane and carvings on a beam of the entrance hall. On the half-landing is the peephole through which the prince could scrutinize the assembled company before coming down to dine, and one of the fireplaces bears his initials. The bedrooms, each a double, range from ordinary twins to the Lillie Langtry Suite, Lillie's own room, with a four-poster bed and a double heart-shaped bathtub; or you can rent the Edward VII Suite, furnished as it was when His Royal Highness lived in this spacious room. The huge carved-oak fireplace has hand-painted tiles depicting scenes from Shakespeare. The four poster bed is genuine Jacobean. The owner has furnished the hotel in the Edwardian style.

Dining: For meals, there is no menu; the dishes are just produced for inspection. A three-course dinner is served Sunday through Friday. On Saturday night, staff in period dress present an Edwardian banquet.

The Mansion House. 7–11 Thames St., Poole (4 miles west of Bournemouth), Dorset BH15 1JN. ☎ 01202/685666. Fax 01202/665709. 28 units. TV TEL. Mon–Thurs £115 ($184) double; £150 ($240) suite. Fri–Sun £98 ($156.80) double; £138 ($220.80) suite. Rates include English breakfast. AE, DC, MC, V.

In nearby Poole, The Mansion House was built more than 200 years ago by an English entrepreneur. The neoclassical detailing and fan-shaped windows are the pride and well-maintained joy of the owners.

A pair of bars are decorated with formal and rustic themes. An upstairs lounge and the graciously furnished bedrooms provide plenty of quiet, well-decorated corners for relaxation. Excellent modern English cuisine is served.

✪ **The Priory Hotel.** Church Green, Wareham, Dorset BH20 4ND. ☎ 01929/551666. Fax 01929/554519. 19 units. TV TEL. £105–£185 ($168–$296) double; £215 ($344) suite. Rates include English breakfast. AE, DC, MC, V.

This hotel, 2 miles west of Bournemouth in Wareham, beside the River Frame and near the village church, has a well-tended garden adorned by graceful trees. Inside, a paneled bar and a lounge filled with antiques open onto views of the lawn. The rooms are tastefully furnished with antiques and complementary textiles and have many extras. The hotel's restaurant is a gem. Dishes are cooked to order, and every effort is made to use the abundant local produce.

INEXPENSIVE

Sea-Dene Hotel. 10 Burnaby Rd., Bournemouth, Dorset BH4 8JF. ☎ 01202/761372. 6 units. TV. £30–£48 ($48–$76.80) double. Rates include English breakfast. No credit cards. Bus: 17.

Set about a mile west of Bournemouth's center, this house was built in 1906 by an Edwardian industrialist for his mistress. As you climb the building's stairs, notice the hearts carved into the balustrade, symbols that the genteel owner, Liz Jones, attributes to the building's original motif of love. The hotel lies a short walk uphill from the sea, and has attractively furnished rooms and a dining room where breakfast is served and evening meals can be prepared, if advance notice is given, for around £6 ($9.60). Two of the building's top-floor bedrooms offer views of the sea.

Sunnydene. 11 Spencer Rd., Bournemouth, Dorset BH1 3TE. ☎ 01202/552281 or 01202/552269. 11 units, 2 with bathroom. £34 ($54.40) double without bathroom, £40 ($64) double with bathroom. Rates include breakfast. No credit cards. Bus: 121 or 124.

This Victorian private hotel is in a substantial gabled house on a tree-lined road between the Central Station and Bournemouth Bay. The rooms are carpeted and centrally heated, with hot and cold running water; some contain TVs. The hotel is licensed, and drinks and other refreshments are served in the sun lounge.

Westcliff Hotel. 27 Chine Crescent, W. Cliff, Bournemouth, Dorset BH2 5LB. ☎ **01202/ 551062.** 30 units. TV. £56–£62 ($89.60–$99.20) double. Rates include English breakfast. Half board £35–£45 ($56–$72) per person. MC, V. Bus: 25 or 34.

This hotel, a 5-minute walk from the town center, near Durley Chine, was once the luxurious south-coast home of the duke of Westminster, who had it built in 1876. Now run by the Blissert family, the hotel draws lots of repeat business. All the comfortably furnished and well-maintained rooms have beverage-makers. You can order bar snacks or complete dinners at the hotel's art deco restaurant. There's a large garden and a parking area, and facilities include a sauna, Jacuzzi, and solarium.

WHERE TO DINE

Oscar's. In the Royal Bath Hotel, Bath Rd. ☎ **01202/555555.** Reservations required. Main courses £16–£28 ($25.60–$44.80); fixed-price meal £15.50 ($24.80) at lunch, £26 ($41.60) at dinner. AE, DC, MC, V. Daily 12:30–2:15pm; Mon–Sat 7:30–10:15pm. FRENCH.

Sporting Oscar Wilde mementos, this restaurant is located cliff-side, offering panoramic views of the sea. The French chef, Gérard Puigdellivol, presents à la carte dishes as well as fixed-price menus. The appetizers might include cured salmon, thinly sliced and marinated with fresh coriander, olive oil, and lime dressing enhanced with chile and presented on rocket leaves. Excellent main courses might be pan-fried sea bass fillet served on a bed of tomato sauce enhanced with anise, basil, lemon, and garlic or roast breast of duck served fanned with a honey-and-spice sauce.

✪ Sophisticats. 43 Charminster Rd. ☎ **01202/291019.** Reservations recommended. Main courses £9.95–£12.95 ($15.90–$20.70). No credit cards. Tues–Sat 7–10pm. Closed 2 weeks in Feb and 2 weeks in Nov. FRENCH/INTERNATIONAL.

Among the leading restaurants in town is this longtime favorite. Located in a shopping area about 1½ miles north of Bournemouth, Sophisticats tempts its diners with its excellent fresh fish, and you can order any number of veal and beef dishes (sometimes the latter will be prepared in the Indonesian style). Also served are game in season and fresh farm duckling with sauces. Appetizers are filled with flavor and texture, and a highly desirable finish to a meal is a dessert soufflé (but let the waiter know in time).

BOURNEMOUTH AFTER DARK

A choice of major art venues offers great performances throughout the year. **International Centre's Windsor Hall** hosts leading performers from London, the **Pavilion** puts on West End musicals as well as dancing with live music, and the **Winter Gardens,** the original home and favorite performance space of the world-famous Bournemouth Symphony Orchestra, offer regular concerts. Program and ticket information for all three of these venues is available by calling ☎ **01202/456456.**

EN ROUTE TO DORCHESTER: A 17TH-CENTURY MANSION

Kingston Lacy. At Wimborne Minster, on B3082 (Wimborne–Blandford road), 1½ miles west of Wimborne. ☎ **01202/883402.** Admission to the house, garden, and park £5.60 ($8.95) adults, £2.80 ($4.50) children. Garden only £2.30 ($3.70) adults, £1.20 ($1.90) children. Sat–Wed noon–5:30pm; park 11:30am–6pm. Closed Nov–Mar.

An imposing 17th-century mansion set on 250 acres of wooded park, Kingston Lacy was the home for more than 300 years of the Bankes family. They entertained such distinguished guests as King Edward VII, Kaiser Wilhelm, Thomas Hardy, George V, and Wellington. The house displays a magnificent collection of artworks by Rubens,

Titian, and Van Dyck. There's also an important collection of Egyptian artifacts.

The present structure was built to replace Corfe Castle, the Bankes family's home that was destroyed in the civil war. During her husband's absence while performing duties as chief justice to King Charles I, Lady Bankes led the defense of the castle, withstanding two sieges before being forced to surrender to Cromwell's forces in 1646 because of the actions of a treacherous follower. The keys of Corfe Castle hang in the library at Kingston Lacy.

7 Dorchester: Hardy's Home

120 miles SW of London; 27 miles W of Bournemouth

Thomas Hardy, in his 1886 novel *The Mayor of Casterbridge,* gave Dorchester literary fame. Actually, Dorchester was notable even in Roman times, when Maumbury Rings, the best Roman amphitheater in Britain, was filled with the sounds of 12,000 spectators screaming for the blood of the gladiators. Today it's a sleepy market town that seems to go to bed right after dinner.

ESSENTIALS

GETTING THERE   Trains run from London's Waterloo Station each hour during the day. The trip takes 2½ hours. For rail information, call ☎ **0345/484950** in the U.K. or 01603/764776 in the U.S. Dorchester has two train stations, the South Station at Station Approach and the West Station on Great Western Road. For information about both, call ☎ **01202/292474.**

Several **National Express** coaches a day depart from London's Waterloo Station heading for Dorchester. The trip takes 3 hours. Call ☎ **0990/808080** for information and schedules.

If you're driving from London, take M3 southwest, but near the end take A30 toward Salisbury where you connect with A354 for the final approach to Dorchester.

VISITOR INFORMATION   The **Tourist Information Centre** is at Unit 11, Antelope Walk (☎ **01305/267992**). It's open April to October, Monday through Saturday from 9am to 5pm; May to September, Sunday from 10am to 3pm; and November to March, Monday through Saturday from 9am to 4pm.

SEEING THE SIGHTS

One mile east of Dorchester is **Stinsford Church,** where Hardy's heart is buried. His two wives are buried there as well. To get to the church, officially called the Church of St. Michael, follow the signs from Dorchester for the Kingston Maurward Agricultural College, then just before the entrance gates to the college, turn right, following the signs toward the Stinsford Church.

The best place for tea in this bustling market town is the **Potter Inn,** 19 Durngate St. (☎ **01305/260312**), with a blue and white interior, and also a small herb-and-flower garden out back with several tables. Many guests stop in for some of the delectable ice creams such as butter pecan, but a proper sit-down tea is served for £4.50 ($7.20). You can also order freshly made sandwiches, cakes, scones, and pastries.

✪ **Athelhampton House & Gardens.** On A35, 5 miles east of Dorchester. ☎ **01305/848363.** Admission £4.80 ($7.70) adults, £1.50 ($2.40) children. Mar–Oct daily 10:30am–5pm; Nov–Feb Sun only 10:30am–5pm. Take the Dorchester–Bournemouth rd. (A35) east of Dorchester for 5 miles.

This is one of England's great medieval houses, the most beautiful and historic in the south, lying a mile east of Puddletown. Thomas Hardy mentioned the place in some of his writings but called it Athelhall. It was begun during the reign of Edward IV on the legendary site of King Athelstan's palace. A family home for more than 500 years, it's noted for its 15th-century Great Hall, Tudor great chamber, state bedroom, and King's Room.

In 1992, a dozen of the house's rooms were damaged by an accidental fire caused by faulty wiring in the attic. However, skilled craftspeople restored all the magnificent interiors.

Insider's tip: Although many visitors come to see the house, the gardens are even more inspiring. Dating from 1891, they are full of vistas, and their beauty is enhanced by the River Piddle flowing through and by fountains. These walled gardens contain the famous topiary pyramids and two pavilions designed by Inigo Jones. You'll see fine collections of tulips and magnolias, roses, clematis, and lilies, and also a 15th-century dovecote. Yes, they were visited often by Thomas Hardy.

Dorset County Museum. High West St. (next to St. Peter's Church). ☎ **01305/262735.** Admission £3 ($4.80) adults, £1.50 ($2.40) children 5–16, £2 ($3.20) seniors, £7.50 ($12) family; free for children 4 and under. July–Aug daily 10am–5pm; Sept–June Mon–Sat 10am–5pm. Closed New Year's Day.

This museum has a gallery devoted to memorabilia of Thomas Hardy's life. In addition, you'll find an archaeological gallery with displays and finds from Maiden Castle, Britain's largest Iron Age hill fort, plus galleries on the geology, local history, and natural history of Dorset.

Hardy's Cottage. Higher Bockhampton (3 miles northeast of Dorchester and half a mile south of Blandford Road/A35. ☎ **01305/262366.** Admission £2.60 ($4.15). Sun–Thurs 11am–5pm. Closed Nov–Mar.

Thomas Hardy was born in 1840 at Higher Bockhampton. His home, now a National Trust property, may be visited by appointment. Approach the cottage on foot—it's a 10-minute walk—after parking your vehicle in the space provided in the woods. Write in advance to Hardy's Cottage, Higher Bockhampton, Dorchester, Dorset DT2 8QJ, England, or call the number above.

WHERE TO STAY & DINE IN & AROUND DORCHESTER

Kings Arms Hotel. 30 High East St., Dorchester, Dorset DT1 1HF. ☎ **01305/265353.** Fax 01305/260269. 33 units. TV TEL. £45 ($72) double; £99 ($158.40) suite. AE, MC, V.

In business for more than 3 centuries, the Kings Arms has great bow windows above the porch and a swinging sign hanging over the road, a legacy of its days as a coaching inn. It's still the best place to stay within Dorchester's center, although there are superior lodgings on the outskirts. An archway leads to the courtyard and parking area at the back of the hotel. All the comfortably furnished rooms have been refurbished and have beverage-makers. Henry's Table, a premier pub restaurant, is also on the premises.

✪ **Summer Lodge.** Summer Lane, Evershot, Dorset DT2 0JR. ☎ **01935/83424.** Fax 01935/83005. 17 units. TV TEL. £235–£305 ($376–$488) double. Rates include English breakfast, afternoon tea, and 5-course dinner and newspaper. AE, DC, MC, V. Head north from Dorchester on A37.

In this country-house hotel 15 miles north of Dorchester, the resident owners, Nigel and Margaret Corbett, provide care, courtesy, and comfort. Once home to the heirs of the earls of Ilchester, the country house, in the village of Evershot, stands on 4 acres of secluded gardens. Evershot appears as Evershed in *Tess of the D'Urbervilles,* and author Thomas Hardy (that name again) designed a wing of the house. More recently, Summer Lodge hosted many of the stars of the locally filmed *Sense and Sensibility,* including Emma Thompson.

In this relaxed, informal atmosphere, the bedrooms have views either of the garden or over the village rooftops to the fields beyond. The hotel is regularly redecorated and recarpeted, and a new kitchen has been added. Although centrally heated, the hotel offers log fires in winter. Guests sit around the fire getting to know each other in a convivial atmosphere.

Dining: The chefs specialize in properly prepared traditional English dishes, emphasizing homegrown and local produce. In addition to the dining room, with its French windows opening onto a terrace, the Corbetts have a bar.

Amenities: Heated outdoor pool, an all-weather tennis court, and a croquet lawn.

Yalbury Cottage Country House Hotel and Restaurant. Lower Bockhampton, near Dorchester, Dorset DT2 8PZ. ☎ **01305/262382.** Fax 01305/266412. 8 units. TV TEL. £117 ($187.20) double. Rates include half board. MC, V. Head 2 miles east of Dorchester (A35) and watch for signs to Lower Bockhampton.

This thatch-roofed cottage with inglenooks and beamed ceilings is in a small country village within walking distance of Thomas Hardy's cottage and Stinsford Church. The cottage is some 300 years old and was once home to a local shepherd and the keeper of the water meadows. A mile to the north is Thorncombe Wood (home to badgers, deer, and many species of birds), which offers a pleasant stroll and a chance to see Hardy's birthplace, which is tucked in under the edge of the woods. The comfortably furnished and equipped bedrooms overlook the English country garden beyond, reflecting a mood of tranquillity. The bedrooms have all pinewood furniture in the English cottage style. Each has beverage-maker, hair dryer, and other small touches for guests' added comfort.

Dining: The restaurant is open in the evenings only and non-residents are welcome. Well-flavored sauces and lightly cooked fresh vegetables enhance traditional English and continental dishes.

8 Dorset's Coastal Towns: Chideock, Charmouth & Lyme Regis

Chideock & Charmouth: 157 miles SW of London; 1 mile W of Bridport
Lyme Regis: 160 miles SW of London; 25 miles W of Dorchester

Chideock is a charming village hamlet of thatched houses with a dairy farm in the center. About a mile from the coast, it's a gem of a place for overnight stopovers, and even better for longer stays. You may be tempted to explore the countryside and the rolling hills.

On Lyme Bay, Charmouth, like Chideock, is another winner. A village of Georgian houses and thatched cottages, Charmouth provides some of the most dramatic coastal scenery in West Dorset. The village is west of Golden Cap, which, according to adventurers who measure such things, is the highest cliff along the coast of southern England.

Also on Lyme Bay near the Devonshire border, the resort of Lyme Regis is one of the most attractive centers along the south coast. For those who shun big, commercial resorts, Lyme Regis is ideal—it's the true English coastal town, but with a mild climate. Seagulls fly overhead, the streets are steep and winding, and walks along Cobb Beach are brisk. The views, particularly of the craft in the harbor, are so photogenic that John Fowles, a longtime resident of the town, selected it as the site for the 1980 filming of his novel *The French Lieutenant's Woman*.

During its heyday, the town was a major seaport. Later, Lyme developed into a small spa, including among its visitors Jane Austen. She wrote her final novel, *Persuasion* (published posthumously and based partly on the town's life), after staying here in 1803 and 1804.

ESSENTIALS

GETTING THERE   The nearest train connection to Chideock and Charmouth is Dorchester (see above). Buses run frequently throughout the day, west from both Dorchester and Bridport.

To get to Lyme Regis, take the London-Exeter train, getting off at Axminster and continuing the rest of the way by bus. For rail information, call ☎ **0345/484950** in the U.K., or 01603/764776 in the U.S. Bus no. 31 runs from Axminster to Lyme Regis (one coach per hour during the day). There's also **National Express** bus service (no. 705) that runs daily in summer at 9:50am from Exeter to Lyme Regis, taking 1¾ hours. Call ☎ **0990/808080** for schedules and information.

If you're driving to Chideock and Charmouth from Bridport, continue west along A35. To get to Lyme Regis from Bridport, continue west along A35, cutting south to the coast at the junction with A3070.

VISITOR INFORMATION   In Lyme Regis, the **Tourist Information Centre,** at Guildhall Cottage, Church Street (☎ **01297/442138**), is open November through March, Monday through Friday from 10am to 4pm and Saturday from 10am to 2pm; in April, Monday through Saturday from 10am to 5pm; May through September, Monday through Friday from 10am to 6pm and Saturday and Sunday from 10am to 5pm; and October, daily from 10am to 5pm.

EXPLORING THE TOWNS

Chideock and Charmouth are the most beautiful villages in Dorset. It's fun to stroll through them to see the well-kept cottages, well-manicured gardens, and an occasional 18th- or 19th-century church. Charmouth, more than Chideock, boasts a small-scale collection of unusual antique shops. Both villages are less than a mile from the western edge of **Chesil Beach,** one of the Hampshire coast's most famous (and longest) beaches. Although it's covered with shingle (sharp rocks), and hard on your feet if you go bathing, the beach nonetheless provides 5 miles of sweeping views toward France.

Today in Lyme Regis, one of the town's most visible characters is ✪ **Richard J. Fox,** three-time world champion Town Crier who, although retired, still does **guided walks.** Famed for his declamatory delivery of official (and sometimes irreverent) proclamations, he followed a 1,000-year-old tradition of newscasting. Dressed as Thomas Payne, a dragoon who died in Lyme Regis in 1644 during the civil war, Mr. Fox leads visitors on a 1½-hour walk around the town every Tuesday at 3pm, beginning at Guildhall (mentioned below). No reservations are necessary, and the price is £2 ($3.20) for adults and £1.50 ($2.40) for children. He can be reached on the premises of **Country Stocks,** 53 Broad St. (☎ **01297/443568**). This shop sells such wares as sweets, antiques, and gifts and is open daily from 10am to 5pm.

Another famous building is **The Guildhall,** Bridge Street (call the tourist office for information), whose Mary and John Wing (built in 1620) houses the completed sections of an enormous tapestry woven by local women. Depicting Britain's colonization of North America, it's composed of a series of 11-by-4-foot sections, each of which took a team of local women 11 months to weave. Admission is free, but if anyone wants to add a stitch to the final tapestry as a kind of charitable donation, it costs £1 ($1.60). It's open Monday through Friday from 10am to 4pm, but only if someone is working on the tapestry.

The surrounding area is a fascinating place for botanists and zoologists because of the predominance of blue Lias, a sedimentary rock well suited to the formation of fossils. In 1810, Mary Anning (at the age of 11) discovered one of the first articulated ichthyosaur skeletons. She went on to become one of the first professional fossilists in England. Books outlining walks in the area and the regions where fossils can be studied are available at the local Information bureau.

WHERE TO STAY & DINE
IN CHIDEOCK & CHARMOUTH

✪ **Chideock House Hotel.** Main St., Chideock, Dorset DT6 6JN. ☎ **01297/489242.** 9 units, 8 with bathroom. TV. £50–£60 ($80–$96) double with bathroom. Rates include English breakfast. AE, MC, V. Bus: 31 from Bridport.

In a village of winners, this 15th-century thatched house is the prettiest. The house was used by the Roundheads in 1645, and the ghosts of the village martyrs still haunt the house since their trial was held here. Located near the road, with a protective stone wall, the house has a garden in back, and a driveway leads to a large parking area. The beamed lounge, recently face-lifted, has two fireplaces, one an Adam fireplace with a wood-burning blaze on cool days. All the bedrooms have beverage-makers, and superior rooms have a hair dryer, dressing gowns, and toiletries.

The restaurant, serving both French and English cuisine, offers dinner nightly; lunch is also served in season. There's even homemade ice cream.

White House. 2 Hillside, The Street, Charmouth, Dorset DT6 6PJ. ☎ **01297/560411.** Fax 01297/560702. 10 units. TV TEL. £90–£110 ($144–$176) double. Rates include English breakfast and 5-course table d'hôte. AE, DC, MC, V. Closed Nov–Jan, but open for Christmas and New Year's Day. Bus: 31 from Bridport.

The White House is the best place to stay in Charmouth. This Regency home, with its period architecture and bow doors, is well preserved and tastefully furnished. Chris Poole and Joel Kassirer took this place, constructed in 1827, and made it comfortable, with touches such as electric kettles in their handsomely furnished bedrooms.

Bar lunches are available during the day; at night home-cooked dishes, with a selection of carefully chosen wines, are offered. West Country regional dishes are featured, including, for example, Dorset honeyed duckling. Five-course dinners begin at £18.50 ($29.60).

IN LYME REGIS

Alexandra Hotel. Pound St., Lyme Regis, Dorset DT7 3HZ. ☎ **01297/442010.** Fax 01297/443229. 27 units. TV TEL. £80–£112 ($128–$179.20) double. Rates include English breakfast. AE, DC, MC, V.

Built in 1735, this hotel is situated on a hill about 5 minutes from the center of Lyme Regis. Today it has the best bedrooms and amenities of any inn in town, although it lacks the personal charm of Kersbrook (reviewed below). It's been discreetly modernized around its original character. Both table d'hôte and à la carte meals are offered in the hotel's excellent dining room, with dinner costing from £18.50 ($29.60). The bar has been entirely renovated.

Kersbrook Hotel and Restaurant. Pound Rd., Lyme Regis, Dorset DT7 3HX. ☎ and fax **01297/442596.** 10 units. TV. £84.50–£104.50 ($135.20–$167.20) double. Rates include breakfast and dinner. AE, MC, V. Closed Dec–Jan.

Built of stone in 1790 and crowned by a thatch roof, the Kersbrook sits on a ledge above the village (which provides a panoramic view of the coast), on 1½ acres of gardens landscaped according to the original 18th-century plans. The public rooms have been refurnished with antique furniture, re-creating old-world charm with modern facilities.

The hotel is justifiably proud of its pink, candlelit restaurant, serving dinner nightly and offering an extensive wine list. The chef is an artist in the kitchen. Traditional English and French cuisine is served, with dinner costing £16.50 ($26.40).

Royal Lion. Broad St., Lyme Regis, Dorset DT7 3QF. ☎ **01297/445622.** Fax 01297/445859. 30 units. TV TEL. £56 ($89.60) double with breakfast; £86 ($137.60) double with breakfast and dinner. AE, DC, MC, V.

This hotel was built in 1610 as a coaching inn, growing throughout the years to incorporate oak-paneled bars, lounges, and comfortably up-to-date bedrooms. Situated in the center of town on a hillside climbing up from the sea, the hotel features country-inspired furnishings and such venerable antiques as the canopied bed that was used regularly by Edward VII when he was Prince of Wales.

On the premises is an indoor heated swimming pool, a Jacuzzi, a sauna, a minigym, a game room, a cocktail lounge, and a pub. Bar snacks are dispensed daily at lunch; dinner is available nightly in the restaurant.

9 Sherborne

128 miles SW of London; 19 miles NW of Dorchester

A little gem of a town with well-preserved medieval, Tudor, Stuart, and Georgian buildings still standing, Sherborne is in the heart of Dorset, surrounded by wooded hills, valleys, and chalk downs. It was here that Sir Walter Raleigh lived before his fall from fortune.

ESSENTIALS

GETTING THERE   Frequent trains depart from London's Waterloo Station throughout the day. The trip takes 2 hours. For rail information, call ☎ **0345/ 484950** in the U.K., or 01603/764776 in the U.S.

There is one **National Express** coach departure daily from London's Victoria Coach Station. Call ☎ **0990/808080** for information and schedules.

If you're driving, take M3 west from London, continuing southwest on 303 and B3145.

VISITOR INFORMATION   The **Tourist Information Centre,** on Digby Road (☎ **01935/815341**), is open mid-March to mid-October, Monday to Saturday from 9:30am to 5:30pm, and mid-October to mid-March, Monday to Saturday from 10am to 3pm.

EXPLORING SHERBORNE

In addition to the attractions listed below, you can go to **Cerne Abbas,** a village south of Sherborne, to see the Pitchmarket, where Thomas and Maria Washington, uncle and aunt of American president George Washington, once lived.

Sherborne Old Castle. Castleton, off A30, half a mile east of Sherborne. ☎ **01935/ 812730.** Admission £1.50 ($2.40) adults, £1.10 ($1.75) seniors and students, 80p ($1.30) children 5–16, free for children 4 and under. Apr–Oct daily 10am–6pm; Nov–Mar Wed–Sun 10am–4pm. Follow the signs 1 mile east from the town center.

The castle was built in the early 12th century by the powerful Bishop Roger de Caen, but it was seized by the crown at about the time of King Henry I's death in 1135 and Stephen's troubled accession to the throne. The castle was given to Sir Walter Raleigh by Queen Elizabeth I. The gallant knight built Sherborne Lodge in the deer park close by (now privately owned). The buildings were mostly destroyed in the Civil War, but you can still see a gate house, some graceful arcades, and decorative windows.

Sherborne Castle. Cheap St. (off New Rd. a mile east of the center). ☎ **01935/813182.** Castle and grounds £4.80 ($7.70) adults, £2.40 ($3.85) children, £4 ($6.40) seniors, £12 ($19.20) family ticket (2 adults, 2 children); grounds only £2.40 ($3.85) adults, £1.20 ($1.90) children. Easter Sat to last Sat in Sept, Thurs, Sat–Sun, and bank holidays 12:30 5pm. Last admission 4:30pm.

Sir Walter Raleigh built this castle in 1594, when he decided that it would not be feasible to restore the old castle to suit his needs. This Elizabethan residence was a square mansion, to which later owners added four Jacobean wings to make it more palatial. After King James I had Raleigh imprisoned in the Tower of London, the monarch gave the castle to a favorite Scot, Robert Carr, and banished the Raleighs from their home. In 1617, it became the property of Sir John Digby, first earl of Bristol, and has been the Digby family home ever since. The mansion was enlarged by Sir John in 1625, and in the 18th century the formal Elizabethan gardens and fountains of the Raleighs were altered by Capability Brown, who created a serpentine lake between the two castles. The 20 acres of lawns and pleasure grounds around the 50-acre lake are open to the public. In the house are fine furniture, china, and paintings by Gainsborough, Lely, Reynolds, Kneller, and Van Dyck, among others.

○ **Sherborne Abbey.** Abbey Close. ☎ **01935/812452.** Free admission but donations for upkeep welcomed. Apr–Sept daily 9am–6pm; Oct–Mar daily 9am–4pm.

One of the great churches of England, this abbey was founded in A.D. 705 as the Cathedral of the Saxon Bishops of Wessex. In the late 10th century, it became a Benedictine monastery, and since the Reformation it has been a parish church. It's famous for its fan-vaulted roof, added by Abbot Ramsam at the end of the 15th century; this was the first fan vault of wide span erected in England. Inside are many fine monuments, including Purbeck marble effigies of medieval abbots as well as Elizabethan "four-poster" and canopied tombs. The baroque statue of the earl of Bristol stands between his two wives and dates from 1698. A public school occupies the abbey's surviving medieval monastic buildings and was the setting for the classic film *Good-bye, Mr. Chips,* starring Robert Donat.

WHERE TO STAY & DINE

Eastbury Hotel. Long St., Sherborne, Dorset DT9 3BY. ☎ **01935/813131.** Fax 01935/817296. 15 units. TV TEL. £65–£80 ($104–$128) double. Rates include English breakfast. AE, MC, V.

This Georgian town-house hotel, Sherborne's best, is situated in its own walled garden near the 8th-century abbey and the two castles. Built in 1740 during the reign of George II, it has a traditional ambience, with its own library of antiquarian books. Beautifully restored, it still retains its 18th-century character. Bedrooms are named after flowers and are handsomely maintained and well decorated. After a restful night's sleep, you can sit outside and enjoy the well-kept garden. The best fresh English produce is served in the dining room, which has an extensive wine list.

Sherborne Hotel. Horsecastles Lane (near the A30 rd. and about a mile west of Sherborne's center), Sherborne, Dorset DT9 6BB. ☎ **01935/813191.** Fax 01935/816493. 59 units. TV TEL. Sun–Thurs £59.50 ($95.20) double, Fri–Sun £49.50 ($79.20) double. AE, DC, MC, V.

Built of red brick in 1969, this 2-story hotel lies near a school and a scattering of factories and houses. Although popular with business travelers, It's more elegant than a typical roadside hotel, with more amenities than might be expected and easy access to Sherborne's historic center. The bedrooms are conservatively modern. There's a bar on the premises, and Castles Restaurant, where fixed-price three-course dinners cost £18.95 ($30.30), and affordable lunches are also served. The staff is efficient and helpful.

10 Shaftesbury

100 miles SW of London; 29 miles NE of Dorchester

The origins of this typical Dorsetshire market town date from the 9th century when King Alfred founded the abbey and made his daughter the first abbess. King Edward the Martyr was buried here, and King Canute died in the abbey but was buried in Winchester. Little now remains of the abbey, but the ruins are beautifully laid out. The museum adjoining St. Peter's Church at the top of Gold Hill provides a good idea of what the ancient Saxon hilltop town was like.

Today, ancient cottages with thatched roofs and tiny paned windows line the steep cobbled streets, and modern stores compete with the outdoor market on High Street and the cattle market off Christy's Lane. The town is an excellent center from which to visit Hardy Country (it appears as Shaston in *Jude the Obscure*), Stourhead Gardens, and Longleat House. (The gardens and house are covered in chapter 9.)

Much of Shaftesbury's charm hearkens back to the agrarian days of bucolic old England. A promenade on **Gold Hill,** a steep cobbled hill, is lined on one side with those thatched cottages so evocative of British wholesomeness. Traffic is prohibited on the road, except for residents of the houses near the top.

Equally nostalgic are the ruins of **Shaftesbury Abbey,** Park Walk, whose boundaries flank one edge of Gold Hill. Founded in A.D. 888 by King Alfred—who appointed his daughter, Aethlgeofu, as its first abbess—it was closed during the Dissolution of the Monasteries in 1539 by Henry VIII and later fell into ruin. Over the centuries, its stones were used widely for other building projects throughout the town, including those houses on Gold Hill. Excavations of the site continue to this day, but during warm weather, from April 1 to October 30, you can visit the abbey daily from 10am to 5pm. Admission is £1 ($1.60) for adults, 75p ($1.20) for students.

ESSENTIALS

GETTING THERE   There is no direct train access, so you'll have to take the Exeter train leaving from London's Waterloo Station to Gillingham in Dorset, where a 4-mile bus or taxi ride to Shaftesbury awaits you. Trains from London run every 2 hours. For rail information, call ☎ **0345/484950** in the U.K., or 01603/764776 in the U.S.

Bus connections are possible from London's Victoria Coach Station once a day. There are also two or three daily connections from Bristol, Bath, Bournemouth, and Salisbury. The tourist office (see below) keeps up-to-date transportation hookups in the area.

If you're driving, head west from London on M3, continuing along A303 until the final approach by A350.

VISITOR INFORMATION   The **Tourist Information Centre,** 8 Bell St. (☎ **01747/853514**), is open daily April through October from 10am to 5pm; from November through March hours are 10am to 1pm from Monday through Friday and 10am to 5pm on Saturday.

WHERE TO STAY & DINE IN & AROUND SHAFTESBURY

King Alfred's Kitchen, 15 High St. (☎ **01747/852147**), is the best place in town for tea, lying in an antique house with low ceiling beams. At the top of Gold Hill, this building with its fireplaces and old settle dates from the 15th century. Afternoon tea costs £4.50 ($7.20), and you can also order a selection of sandwiches, cakes, scones, and pastries.

Shaftesbury   337

☼ Plumber Manor. Hazelbury Bryan Rd. (off A357), Sturminster Newton, Dorset DT10 2AF. ☎ **01258/891265.** Fax 01258/473370. 16 units. TV TEL. £90–£130 ($144–$208) superior double. Rates include English breakfast. AE, DC, MC, V. Closed Feb.

This Jacobean manor house on 600 acres of farmland has been the home of the Prideaux-Brune family since the early 17th century. The present inhabitants, Richard Prideaux-Brune and his wife, Alison, are the hosts in this lovely old place, treating everyone as a houseguest and creating a family atmosphere. Downstairs, a large hall from which the staircase rises is decorated with family portraits. A comfortable lounge is furnished with antiques. Upstairs, a gallery leads to some of the bedrooms, opening onto views over the gardens and the countryside. The others, in a long, low stone barn across the courtyard from the stable block (large umbrellas are provided to make the crossing if necessary), are well designed, with wide window seats, views over the gardens, and well-chosen furnishings.

Dining: There's a bar to serve the restaurant, made up of three connecting dining rooms, where guests can sample the excellent cooking of Brian Prideaux-Brune, Richard's brother. Three-course dinners range from £17.50 to £25 ($28 to $40). Try the English lamb or roast pheasant in port sauce. All main courses are served with fresh vegetables.

Royal Chase Hotel. Royal Chase Roundabout (at the junction of A30 and A350), Shaftesbury, Dorset SP7 8DB. ☎ **01747/853355.** Fax 01747/851969. 34 units. TV TEL. £90–£100 ($144–$160) double. AE, DC, MC, V.

This was once a button-making factory and later a monastery, but now it's a delightfully informal hotel. It's your best choice within the town of Shaftesbury. Early morning tea is complimentary. The bedrooms are comfortably furnished and well equipped.

Dining/Diversions: A meal in the elegant Byzant Restaurant, which begins at £17 ($27.20), includes several regional dishes such as local trout, seasonal game, and venison marinated in sherry. Dinner is served nightly. A more informal restaurant, the Country Restaurant, serves light meals, snacks, and children's favorites throughout the day. They serve Thomas Hardy's Ale, featured in the *Guinness Book of Records* as the strongest beer available in a bottle. Even for less fanatical drinkers, the bar, dominated by an open-kitchen range and decorated with Dorsetshire bygones, is an attraction. There are traditional bar games, shove ha'penny, and table skittles at which to pitch your skill.

Amenities: Indoor swimming pool, Turkish steam room.

9 Wiltshire & Somerset

For our final look at the "West Countree," we move now into Wiltshire and Somerset, two of the most historic shires of England. Once you reach this area of pastoral woodland, London seems far removed.

Most people agree that the West Country, a loose geographical term, begins at **Salisbury,** with its early English cathedral that has a 404-foot pinnacle. Nearby is **Stonehenge,** England's oldest prehistoric monument. (Both Stonehenge and Salisbury are in Wiltshire.) When you cross into Wiltshire, you'll be entering a country of chalky, grassy uplands and rolling plains. Much of the shire is agricultural, and a large part is pastureland.

Somerset has some of the most beautiful scenery in England. The undulating limestone hills of Mendip and the irresistible Quantocks are especially lovely in spring and fall. Somerset opens onto the Bristol Channel, with Minehead serving as its chief resort. The shire is rich in legend and history, with particularly fanciful associations with King Arthur and Queen Guinevere, Camelot, and Alfred the Great. Its villages are noted for the tall towers of their parish churches.

You may find yourself in a vine-covered pub, talking with the regulars and sampling Somerset's famous cider, or perhaps you'll stroll through a large estate in the woods surrounded by bridle paths and sheep walks (Somerset was once a great wool center). Or maybe you'll settle down in a 16th-century thatched stone farmhouse set in the midst of orchards in a vale.

Somerset also encompasses the territory around the old port of **Bristol** and the old Roman city of **Bath,** known for its abbey and spa water, lying beside the river Somerset.

The two best places to base yourself while you explore the area are Bath and Salisbury. From Salisbury you can visit Stonehenge and **Old Sarum,** the two most fabled ancient monuments in the West Country. Yet some say visiting the stones at **Avebury** is a much more personal experience. And **Glastonbury,** with its once-great abbey that now is a ruined sanctuary, may be one of Britain's oldest inhabited sites. The greatest natural spectacle in the area is **Exmoor National Park,** once an English royal hunting preserve, stretching for 265 square miles on the north coast of Devon and Somerset. There are also many terrific country houses and palaces in this region, including **Wilton House,** the site of 17th-century staterooms designed by Inigo Jones. The other

Wiltshire, Somerset & Avon

Avebury **1**
Bristol Cathedral **10**
The Caves of
Mendip **11**
Coleridge Cottage **14**
Combe
Sydenham Hall **15**
Dunster Castle **6**
Glastonbury Abbey **13**
Longleat House **7**
Nether Wallop **2**
Old Sarum **4**
Salisbury Cathedral **5**
Stonehenge **3**
Stourhead **8**
Thornbury Castle **9**
Wells Cathedral **12**
Wilton House **6**

339

two major attractions, **Longleat House** and the fabled gardens at **Stourhead,** can be visited in a busy day while you're based at Bath.

1 Salisbury

90 miles SW of London; 53 miles SE of Bristol

Long before you've even entered Salisbury, the spire of its cathedral will come into view—just as John Constable captured it on canvas. The 404-foot pinnacle of the early English and Gothic cathedral is the tallest in England.

Salisbury, or New Sarum, lies in the valley of the Avon River. Filled with Tudor inns and tearooms, it is the only true city in Wiltshire. It's an excellent base for visitors anxious to explore Stonehenge or Avebury, and, unfortunately, they tend to visit the cathedral and then rush on their way. But the old market town is an interesting destination in its own right, and if you choose to linger here for a day or two, you'll find that its pub-to-citizen ratio is perhaps the highest in the country.

ESSENTIALS

GETTING THERE   **Network Express trains** depart for Salisbury hourly from Waterloo Station in London; the trip takes 2 hours. Sprinter trains offer fast, efficient service every hour from Portsmouth, Bristol, and South Wales. There is also direct rail service from Exeter, Plymouth, Brighton, and Reading. For rail information, call ☎ **0345/484950** in the U.K., or 01603/764776 in the U.S.

If you're driving from London, head west on M3 to the end of the run, continuing the rest of the way on A30.

Five **National Express** buses per day run from London, Monday through Friday. On Saturday and Sunday, four buses depart Victoria Coach Station for Salisbury. The trip takes 2½ hours. Call ☎ **0990/808080** for schedules and information.

VISITOR INFORMATION   The **Tourist Information Centre** is at Fish Row (☎ **01722/334956**), and is open October through April, Monday through Saturday from 9:30am to 5pm; in May, Monday through Saturday from 9:30am to 5pm and Sunday 10:30am to 4:30pm; in June and September, Monday through Saturday from 9:30am to 6pm and Sunday 10:30am to 4:30pm; and in July and August, Monday through Saturday from 9:30am to 7pm and on Sunday from 10:30am to 5pm.

GETTING AROUND   If you'd like to bike out to Stonehenge, go to **Hayball's Cycle Shop,** 26-30 Winchester St. (☎ **01722/411378**), which rents mountain bikes for £7.50 ($12) per day. For an extra £2.50 ($4) you can keep the bike overnight. A £25 ($40) deposit is required. A 7-day rental is £45 ($72).

SPECIAL EVENTS   The **Salisbury St. George's Spring Festival** in April is a traditional medieval celebration of the city's patron saint. You can witness St. George slaying the dragon in the Wiltshire mummers play and see acrobats and fireworks.

With spring comes the annual **Salisbury Festival** (☎ **01722/323883,** or 01722/320333 for the box office). The city drapes itself in banners, and street theater—traditional and unexpected—is offered everywhere. There are also symphony and chamber-music concerts in Salisbury Cathedral, children's events, and much more. It takes place from the end of May through the beginning of June.

At the end of July, you can see **The Salisbury Garden and Flower Show,** Hudson's Field (☎ **01635/867904**). This is a treat for gardening enthusiasts: There's a floral marquee packed with Chelsea exhibits, as well as display gardens created especially for the event. But there's plenty more for the rest of the family, including specialty food tastings, antique and crafts sales, and a vintage and classic car show.

EXPLORING SALISBURY

Many shops in Salisbury are set in beautiful medieval timber-framed buildings. As you wander through the colorful market or walk the ancient streets, you'll find everything from touristy gift shops to unique specialty stores.

The Mitre House, 37 High St. (☎ **01722/333705**), housed in what is reputed to be the oldest structure in Salisbury, is a high-quality gift shop owned by the cathedral.

Hard-core shoppers and locals also gravitate to **The Old George Mall Shopping Centre,** 23B High St. (☎ **01722/333500**), a short walk from the cathedral. It has more than 40 individual shops and High Street stores where you can find the latest fashions in knitwear, sportswear, and baby wear, as well as household appliances, CDs, toiletries, and greeting cards.

Another place of note, situated within a 14th century building with hammered beams and some original windows, is **Watsons,** 8–9 Queen St. (☎ **01722/320311**). This elegant store carries bone china from Wedgwood, Royal Doulton, and Aynsley, Dartington glassware, and a fine line of paperweights.

You can easily see Salisbury by foot, either on your own or by taking a guided daytime or evening walk sponsored by the **Salisbury Tourist Information Centre** (see above). Tickets are £2 ($3.20) for adults and £1 ($1.60) for children.

✪ **Salisbury Cathedral. ☎ 01722/323279.** Suggested donation £2.50 ($4); admission 30p (50¢) for the chapter house. May–Aug daily 8:30am–8:30pm; Sept–Apr daily 8am–6:30pm.

You can search all of England, but you'll find no better example of the early English, or pointed, architectural style than Salisbury Cathedral. Construction on this magnificent building was begun as early as 1220 and took 38 years to complete—rather fast for a cathedral. (Most of Europe's grandest cathedrals took 3 centuries to build.) Salisbury Cathedral is one of the most homogenous of all the great European cathedrals.

The cathedral's 13th-century octagonal chapter house (note the fine sculpture), which is especially attractive, possesses one of the four surviving original texts of the Magna Carta, along with treasures from the diocese of Salisbury and manuscripts and artifacts belonging to the cathedral. The cloisters enhance the cathedral's beauty, along with an exceptionally large close. There are at least 75 buildings in the compound, some from the early 18th century and others from much earlier.

Insider's tip: The 404-foot spire was one of the tallest structures in the world when it was constructed toward the end of the 13th century. In its day, this was far more advanced technology than the world's tallest skyscrapers. Amazingly, the spire was not part of the original design and was conceived and added some 30 years after the rest. The name of the master mason is lost to history. Sir Christopher Wren in 1668 expressed alarm at the tilt of the spire, but no further shift has since been measured. The whole ensemble is still standing and can actually be visited. If you trust towering architecture from 700 years ago, you can explore the tower on guided visits Monday through Saturday from 11am to 2pm (extra tours in summer depending on demand). The cost of the tour is £2.55 ($4.10).

In the cathedral cloisters is a **brass rubbing center** (☎ **01722/323279**), open mid-June through September, Monday to Saturday from 10am to 6pm and Sunday 11:15am to 4pm. Here you can choose from a variety of exact replicas molded perfectly from the original brasses: local medieval and Tudor knights and ladies, famous historical faces, even Celtic designs. A helpful staff will guide you. Most rubbings cost £3 ($4.80) and include materials and instruction.

Mompesson House. Cathedral Close. ☎ **01722/335659.** Admission £3.20 ($5.10) adults, £1.60 ($2.55) children. Apr–Oct Sat Wed noon–5pm.

This is one of the most distinguished houses in the area. Built by Charles Mompesson in 1701, while he was a member of Parliament for Old Sarum, it is a beautiful example of the Queen Anne style, and is well known for its fine plasterwork ceilings and paneling. There is also a collection of 18th-century drinking glasses. Visitors can wander through a garden and later order a snack in the garden tearoom.

The Royal Gloucestershire, Berkshire, and Wiltshire Regiment (Salisbury) Museum—Redcoats in the Wardrobe. The Wardrobe, 58 The Close, Salisbury, Wiltshire. ☎ **01722/414536.** Admission £2.20 ($3.50) adults, £2 ($3.20) senior citizens, 60p (95¢) children. Feb–Mar and Nov Mon–Fri 10am–4:30pm; Apr–Oct daily 10am–4:30pm.

The elegant house in which the museum's collections are displayed dates from 1254 and contains exhibits covering 3 centuries of military history. Visitors can relax in the garden leading to the River Somerset (with views made famous by Constable) and enjoy homemade fare from the Redcoats Tea Rooms.

SIGHTS NEARBY

✪ **Old Sarum.** 2 miles north of Salisbury off A345 on Castle Rd. ☎ **01722/335398.** Admission £1.90 ($3.05) adults, £1.40 ($2.25) seniors, £1 ($1.60) children. Apr–Sept daily 10am–6pm; Oct–Mar daily 10am–4pm. Bus nos. 3, 5, 6, 7, 8, and 9 run every 20 minutes during the day from the Salisbury bus station.

Believed to have been an Iron Age fortification, Old Sarum was again used much later by the Saxons, and flourished as a walled town into the Middle Ages. The Normans built a cathedral and a castle here; parts of the old cathedral were taken down to build the city of New Sarum (Salisbury).

✪ **Wilton House.** 3 miles west of Salisbury on A30. ☎ **01722/746729.** Admission £6.75 ($10.80) adults, £4 ($6.40) children 5–15; free for children under 5. Price inclusive of grounds. Easter–Oct daily 11am–6pm (last entrance at 5pm).

In the town of Wilton is the home of the earls of Pembroke. It dates from the 16th century, but has undergone numerous alterations, most recently in Victoria's day. It is noted for its 17th-century staterooms by the celebrated architect Inigo Jones. (Guides assist in the principal staterooms.) Many famous people have either lived at or visited Wilton, and it is also believed that Shakespeare's troupe entertained here. Preparations for the D-day landings at Normandy were laid out here by Eisenhower and his advisers, with only the Van Dyck paintings in the Double Cube room as silent witnesses.

The house is filled with beautifully maintained furnishings and displays world-class art, including paintings by Sir Anthony Van Dyck, Rubens, Brueghel, and Reynolds. A dynamic film, introduced and narrated by Anna Massey, brings to life the history of the family since 1544, the year they were granted the land by Henry VIII. You then visit a reconstructed Tudor kitchen and Victorian laundry plus "The Wareham Bears," a unique collection of some 200 miniature dressed teddy bears.

Growing on the 21-acre estate are giant cedars of Lebanon trees, the oldest of which were planted in 1630. The Palladian Bridge was built in 1737 by the ninth earl of Pembroke and Roger Morris. There are rose and water gardens, riverside and woodland walks, and a huge adventure playground for children.

WHERE TO STAY
EXPENSIVE

Grasmere House. 70 Harnham Rd., Salisbury, Wiltshire SP2 8JN. ☎ **01722/338388.** Fax 01722/333710. 20 units. TV TEL. £95–£125 ($152–$200) double. Rates include English breakfast. AE, CB, DC, MC, V. Take A3094 1½ miles from the center of town.

Grasmere House stands near the confluence of the Nadder and Somerset Rivers on 1½ acres of grounds. Constructed in 1896 for Salisbury merchants, the house still suggests a family home. The original architectural features were retained as much as possible, including a "calling box" for servants in the dining room. A new conservatory bar overlooks the cathedral, as do three luxurious rooms. Four rooms are in the original house, with the remainder in a new wing. Two accommodations are suitable for guests with disabilities. All rooms have a trouser press and hair dryer.

Dining: The house also operates a good restaurant, popular with locals and residents alike. Steaks are a specialty, served in any number of ways, ranging from flambéed to *au poivre* (with pepper).

Red Lion Hotel. 4 Milford St., Salisbury, Wiltshire SP1 2AN. ☎ **800/528-1234** in the U.S., or 01722/323334. Fax 01722/325756. 56 units. TV TEL. £99–£120 ($158.40–$192) double; £115–£125 ($184–$200) suite. AE, DC, MC, V.

Since the 1300s the Red Lion has been accommodating wayfarers from London on their way to the West Country. This Best Western–affiliated hotel no longer reigns supreme in town (we prefer the White Hart and The Rose and Crown), but it's a fine choice and somewhat more affordable than those two. Cross under its arch into a courtyard with a hanging, much-photographed creeper, a red lion, and a half-timbered facade, and you'll be transported back to an earlier era.

This antique-filled hotel is noted for its unique clock collection, which includes a skeleton organ clock in the reception hall. Guests take a recently installed elevator or the stairs to the comfortable rooms, which feature beverage-makers and hair dryers. The most expensive rooms have four-poster beds.

Dining: Many locals know the hotel for its restaurant, which serves continental and English cuisine daily at lunch and dinner. It has a wattle-and-daub wall that dates from 1230.

☼ **The Rose and Crown.** Harnham Rd., Salisbury, Wiltshire SP2 8JQ. ☎ **01722/399955.** Fax 01722/339816. 28 units. TV TEL. £115–£130 ($184–$208) double; £158.75 ($254) suite. AE, DC, MC, V. Take A3094 1½ miles from the center of town.

This half-timbered, 13th-century gem stands with its feet almost in the River Avon, and beyond the water you can see the tall spire of the cathedral. Because of its tranquil location, it's our top choice. You can easily walk over the arched stone bridge to the center of Salisbury from here in 10 minutes or so. The lawns and gardens between the inn and the river are shaded by old trees, and chairs are set out so you can enjoy the view and count the swans. The inn, part of the Queen's Moat House hotel chain, has both a new and an old wing. The new wing is modern, but the old wing is more appealing, with its sloping ceilings and antique fireplaces and furniture. Each room has a beverage-maker, a hair dryer, and a trouser press.

Dining/Diversions: You can dine on fine English fare while overlooking the river. Across the courtyard are two taverns with oak beams and log fires.

Amenities: Room service, laundry.

White Hart. 1 St. John St., Salisbury, Wiltshire SP1 2SD. ☎ **01722/327476.** Fax 01722/412761. 68 units. TV TEL. £110–£140 ($176–$224) double. AE, DC, MC, V.

Combining the best of old and new, the White Hart has been a Salisbury landmark since Georgian times. Its classic facade is intact, with tall columns crowning a life-size hart. The older accommodations are traditional, and a new section has been added in the rear, opening onto a large parking area—like a motel. New-wing units are tastefully conceived and decorated. The hotel was completely refurbished in 1995.

Dining: You can enjoy a before-dinner drink, followed by a meal of standard international fare, in the White Hart Restaurant.

MODERATE

The Kings Arms Hotel. 7A-11 St. Johns St., Salisbury, Wiltshire SP1 2SB. ☎ **01722/ 327629.** Fax 01722/414246. 17 units. TV TEL. £60–£78 ($96–$124.80) double. Rates include continental breakfast. AE, DC, MC, V.

You'll recognize this former coaching inn, which is in the black-and-white Tudor style, by its lead-glass windows, old pub sign out front, covered entrance for alighting coach passengers, and royalty theme throughout. A special feature is the William-and-Mary four-poster room. The other rooms are cozy and well kept, with traditional styling. No one seems to know the age of the inn, although it's generally acknowledged to be older than the cathedral. Conspirators helping Charles II flee to France were thought to have met here in the mid–17th century.

The hotel features a good restaurant, Pippins, which serves Anglo-French meals, as well as such delightfully old architectural details as oak beams, original ironwork, a priest's hiding hole, and an Elizabethan fireplace. Warm yourself in front of the open fire in winter, or enjoy a pint of ale in the oak-beamed pub anytime.

INEXPENSIVE

The Beadles. Middleton, Middle Winterslow, near Salisbury, Wiltshire SP5 1QS. ☎ **01980/ 862922.** Fax 1980/862922. 3 units. TV. £25–£27.50 ($40–$444) per person double. Rates include English breakfast. MC, V. Turn off A30 at Pheasant Inn to Middle Winterslow. Enter the village, make the first right into the "Flood," turn right again, and it's the first right after "Trevano."

A traditional modern Georgian house with antique furnishings and a view of the cathedral, The Beadles has unobstructed views of the beautiful Wiltshire countryside from its 1-acre gardens. It's situated in a small, unspoiled English village, 8 miles from Salisbury, that offers excellent access to Stonehenge, Wilton House, the New Forest, and the rambling moors of Thomas Hardy. Even the road to Winchester is an ancient Roman byway.

Early morning tea and late-night beverages can be ordered through room service, and children are welcome in the 12-seat dining room. Writing materials, hair dryers, and picnic hampers (including vegetarian and special menus) are provided upon request. Warm-weather meals are served on the patio or in the conservatory, and a predinner drink is free. Owners David and Anne Yuille-Baddeley delight in providing information on the area. No smoking.

The New Inn & Old House. 39-47 New St., Wiltshire SP1 2PH. ☎ **01722/327679.** 8 units. TV. £49.50–£69.50 ($79.20–$111.20) double. Rates include continental breakfast. AE, CB, DC, DISC, MC, V.

This upscale B&B is one of the finest in Salisbury, but, despite its name, it isn't new at all. It's a 15th-century building whose walled garden backs up to the cathedral-close wall. The rooms are well appointed, oak-beamed, and evocative of an earlier century. All have tea- and coffeemakers. The center of the inn is the serving bar, which is a common center for three outer rooms: one, a tiny sitting area; another, a tavern with high-backed settles and a fireplace; and a third, a lounge. Food and drink are available to nonresidents all day for reasonable prices. No smoking.

Wyndham Park Lodge. 51 Wyndham Rd., Salisbury, Wiltshire SP1 3AB. ☎ and fax **01722/328851.** 4 units. TV. £32–£36 ($51.20–$57.60) double; £45–£50 ($72–$80) family room for 3. Rates include English breakfast. No credit cards.

From this appealing Victorian 1880 house, it's an easy walk to the heart of Salisbury and its cathedral, and about a 5-minute walk to a swimming pool and the bus station. The rooms are comfortably furnished with Victorian and Edwardian antiques and matching floral curtains and wallpaper. They have either one double or two twin beds, and contain beverage-makers. Reservations are needed.

A NEARBY PLACE TO STAY FOR AGATHA CHRISTIE FANS

Eight miles east of Salisbury is the little village of **Nether Wallop** (not to be confused with Over Wallop or Middle Wallop, also in the same vicinity). Agatha Christie fans should note that it's the fictitious town of St. Mary Mead, Miss Marple's home, in PBS's *Miss Marple* mysteries. It's 12 miles from Stonehenge and 10 miles from Winchester, on a country road between A343 and A30.

If you'd like to stay over—and perhaps solve a murder if one occurs during your visit—consider the following choice.

The Great Barn. In the nearby village of Stockbridge. ☎ **01264/782142**. 2 units. TV. £26 ($41.60) single; £38 ($60.80) double. Rates include breakfast. No credit cards.

There are only two rooms, one a single, the other a double, both with private bath. Set in the heart of the village, within a walled garden (a 2-minute walk from the village pub), this is a highly unusual 2-story private home. In 1990, it was converted from the premises of a 16th-century barn. Accommodations are simple but tidy, and the hospitality is quite warm.

A CHOICE IN NEARBY DINTON

✪ **Howard's House.** Teffont Evias, near Salisbury, Wiltshire SP3 5RJ. ☎ **01722/716392**. Fax 01722/716820. 9 units. TV TEL. £115–£135 ($184–$216) double. Rates include English breakfast. AE, DC, MC, V. Take A36 and A30 west of Salisbury for 10½ miles; it's on B3089.

On a lane opposite the Black Horse, this partial 17th-century dower house, one of the most appealing small hotels and restaurants in the area, stands in a medieval hamlet. The Ford and Firmin families combined their talent and money to convert this building into an exceptional accommodation. The rooms are carefully furnished, and much care is lavished on the decor and on thoughtful touches such as providing lots of towels and placing fresh flowers in every public room and bedroom. The hotel has attractive gardens, and on chilly nights log fires burn.

Dining: Even if you don't stay here, consider stopping by for a three-course dinner (call to reserve a table first). There are ample choices on the fixed-price menu, such as grilled sirloin steak with a pepper ragout and horseradish Béarnaise. Chilled mango mousse with marinated strawberries makes a splendid dessert. Lunch is also served on Sunday.

WHERE TO DINE

The best restaurants are not in Salisbury itself but on the outskirts—at either the Silver Plough at Pitton (see below for details) or Howard's House at Teffont Evias (see above). See also "Salisbury After Dark," (below,) for a selection of pubs offering affordable fare.

Foodies should step into **David Brown Food Hall & Tea Rooms,** 31 Catherine St. (☎ 01722/329363). They carry the finest fresh foods—meats, cheeses, breads, and other baked goods—making it a terrific place to put together a picnic.

Harper's Restaurant, 7–9 Ox Row, Market Sq. ☎ 01722/333118. Reservations recommended. Main courses £5.50–£12.50 ($8.80–$20), 3-course fixed-price meal £8.50 ($13.60) at lunch and dinner. AE, DC, MC, V. Mon–Sat noon–2pm; daily 6–9:30pm. Closed Sun in Oct–May. ENGLISH/INTERNATIONAL.

The chef-owner of this place prides himself on specializing in "real food"— homemade, simple, and wholesome. The pleasantly decorated restaurant is on the second floor of a redbrick building at the back side of Salisbury's largest parking lot, in the center of town. Within the same all-purpose dining room, you can order from two different menus, one featuring affordable bistro-style platters, including beefsteak casserole with "herbey dumplings." A longer menu, listing items that take a bit more time to prepare, includes all-vegetarian pasta diavolo or spareribs with french fries and rice.

Salisbury Haunch of Venison. 1 Minster St. ☎ **01722/322024.** Main courses £8.95–£12.95 ($14.30–$20.70); bar platters for lunches, light suppers, and snacks £3.95–£5.95 ($6.30–$9.50). AE, DC, MC, V. Daily noon–3pm; Mon–Sat 7–9:30pm. Pub Mon–Sat 11am–11pm, Sun noon–3pm and 7–11pm. Closed Christmas and Easter. ENGLISH.

Right in the heart of Salisbury, this creaky-timbered, 1320 chophouse serves excellent dishes, especially English roasts and grills. Stick to its specialties and you'll rarely go wrong. Begin perhaps with a tasty warm salad of venison sausages with garlic croutons, then follow with the time-honored roast haunch of venison with garlic and juniper berries. Many other classic English dishes are served as well, including a medley of fish and shellfish or grilled Barnsley lamb chops with "bubble and squeak" (cabbage and potatoes).

The centuries have given a gleam to the oak furnishings, and years of polishing have worn down the brass. Twisting steps lead to tiny, cozy rooms (there is one small room with space for about four to sit). Two windows of the restaurant overlook St. Thomas's cloisters.

IN NEARBY PITTON

Silver Plough. White Hill, Pitton, near Salisbury. ☎ **01722/712266.** Reservations recommended. Main courses £8–£13 ($12.80–$20.80); bar platters £3.50–£8 ($5.60–$12.80). AE, DC, MC, V. Restaurant, daily noon–2:30pm; Mon–Sat 7–10pm, Sun 7–9pm. Pub, Mon–Sat 11am–3pm and 6–11pm, Sun noon–3pm and 7–10:30pm. Closed on Dec 25–26 and Jan 1. Take A30 5 miles east of Salisbury; it's at the southern end of the village of Pitton. ENGLISH.

Built as a stone-sided farmhouse 150 years ago, the Silver Plough is now a charming and accommodating country pub with an attached restaurant specializing in fish and game dishes. It contains heavily beamed ceilings hung with tankards, coach horns, and other country memorabilia. Snacks are available in the bar. In the somewhat more formal dining room, the chef prepares such dishes as fresh Dorset mussels in a white-wine, garlic, and cream sauce; sliced breast of duck in cracked-pepper or orange sauce; and roast guinea fowl in a sharp strawberry sauce. The management makes its guests feel at home.

SALISBURY AFTER DARK

The Salisbury Playhouse, Malthouse Lane (☎ **01722/320117,** or 01722/320333 for the box office), produces some of the finest theater in the region. Food and drink are available from the bar and restaurant to complete your evening's entertainment.

The City Hall, Malthouse Lane (☎ **01722/334432,** or 01722/327676 for the box office), has a program of events to suit most tastes and ages in comfortable surroundings. A thriving entertainment center, it attracts many of the national touring shows in addition to local amateur events, exhibitions, and sales, thus providing good entertainment at a reasonable price.

The Salisbury Arts Center, Bedwin Street (☎ **01722/321744**), housed within the former St. Edmund's Church, offers a wide range of performing and visual arts. A typical program will contain a broad mix of music, contemporary and classic theater, and dance performances, plus cabaret, comedy, and family shows. Regular workshops are available for all ages in arts, crafts, theater, and dance. The lively cafe-bar is a pleasant meeting place.

Many a Salisbury pub crawl begins at the **Coach & Horses** on Winchester Street (☎ **01722/336254**), which is said to be Salisbury's oldest pub. (The building dates from 1482.) If you stick around for dinner, a three course evening meal is served. Another good pub is **The Pheasant** on Salt Lane, near the bus station (☎ **01722/ 320675**), which attracts locals as well as visitors on their way to Stonehenge. Snacks, ploughman's lunches, and hot pub grub, including meat pies, are served all day. It's all washed down with a goodly assortment of ales. To cap the night, head for the **Avon Brewery Inn,** 75 Castle St. (☎ **01722/327280**), which is decorated like a Victorian saloon from the gay 1890s, and has an idyllic garden setting overlooking the River Avon. It offers some of the tastiest and most affordable food in town.

2 Prehistoric Britain: Stonehenge & Avebury

✪ **Stonehenge.** At the junction of A303 and A344/A360. ☎ **01980/623108** for information. Admission £3.90 ($6.25) adults, £2.90 ($4.65) seniors and students, £2 ($3.20) children. June–Aug daily 9am–7pm; Mar 16–May and Sept–Oct 15 daily 9:30am–6pm; Oct 16–Mar 15 daily 9:30am–4pm. If you're driving, head north on Castle Rd. from the center of Salisbury. At the first roundabout (traffic circle), take the exit toward Amesbury (A345) and Old Sarum. Continue along this road for 8 miles and then turn left onto A303 in the direction of Exeter. You'll see signs for Stonehenge, leading you up A344 to the right. It's 2 miles west of Amesbury.

This huge circle of lintels and megalithic pillars, believed to be anywhere from 3,500 to 5,000 years old, is the most important prehistoric monument in Britain.

Some visitors are disappointed when they see that Stonehenge is nothing more than concentric circles of stones. But perhaps they don't understand that Stonehenge represents an amazing engineering feat, since many of the boulders, the bluestones in particular, were moved many miles (perhaps from southern Wales) to this site.

The widely held view of 18th- and 19th-century romantics that Stonehenge was the work of the Druids is without foundation. The boulders, many weighing several tons, are believed to have predated the arrival in Britain of the Celtic cult. Recent excavations continue to bring new evidence to bear on the origin and purpose of Stonehenge. Controversy surrounds the prehistoric site, especially since the publication of *Stonehenge Decoded* by Gerald S. Hawkins and John B. White, which maintains that Stonehenge was an astronomical observatory—that is, a Neolithic "computing machine" capable of predicting eclipses.

Your ticket permits you to go inside the fence surrounding the site that protects the stones from vandals and souvenir hunters. You can go all the way up to a short rope barrier, about 50 feet from the stones.

In spring 1996, a full circular tour around Stonehenge was started. A modular walkway has been introduced to cross the archaeologically important avenue, the area that runs between the Heel Stone and the main circle of stones. This enables visitors to complete a full circuit of the stones and to see one of the best views of a completed section of Stonehenge as they pass by. This is an excellent addition to the informative audio tour.

Wilts & Dorset (☎ **01722/336855**) runs several buses daily (depending on demand) from Salisbury to Stonehenge, as well as buses from the Salisbury train station to Stonehenge. The bus trip to Stonehenge takes a half hour, and a round-trip ticket costs £4.40 ($7.05) for adults and £2.20 ($3.50) for children under 14.

Avebury. On A361 between Swindon and Devizes (1 mile from the A4 London–Bath road). The closest rail station is at Swindon, 12 miles away, which is served by the main rail line from London to Bath. For rail information, call ☎ **0345/484950** in the U.K. or 01603/764776 in the U.S. A limited bus service (no. 49) runs from Swindon to Devizes through Avebury.

One of the largest prehistoric sites in Europe, Avebury lies on the Kennet River, 7 miles west of Marlborough and 20 miles north of Stonehenge. Some visitors say visiting Avebury, in contrast to Stonehenge, is a more organic experience—you can walk right up and around the stones, as there's no fence keeping you away. Also, the site isn't mobbed with tour buses.

Visitors can walk around the 28-acre site at Avebury, winding in and out of the circle of more than 100 stones, some weighing up to 50 tons. The stones are made of sarsen, a sandstone found in Wiltshire. Inside this large circle are two smaller ones, each with about 30 stones standing upright. Native Neolithic tribes are believed to have built these circles.

Wilts & Dorset (☎ **01722/336855**) has two buses (nos. 5 and 6) that run between the bus station and Avebury, three times a day from Monday through Saturday and twice daily on Sunday. The one-way trip takes 1½ hours. Round-trip tickets are £4.40 ($7.05) adults and £2.20 ($3.50) children under 14.

Also here is the **Alexander Keiller Museum** (☎ **01672/539250**), which houses one of Britain's most important archaeological collections, including material from excavations at Windmill Hill and Avebury, and artifacts from other prehistoric digs at West Kennet, Long Barrow, Silbury Hill, West Kennet Avenue, and the Sanctuary. The museum is open April to October daily from 10am to 6pm, November to March from 10am to 4pm. Admission is £1.60 ($2.55) for adults and 80p ($1.30) for children.

WHERE TO DINE NEAR AVEBURY

Stones Restaurant. High St. near the Great Barn Museum. ☎ **01672/539514**. Main courses £2.95–£5.95 ($4.70–$9.50), hot buffet lunch £5.95 ($9.50). MC, V. Apr–Oct daily 10am–6pm (serving hot food noon–2:30pm); Nov–Mar Sat–Sun 10am–5pm.

This restaurant has been a hit ever since it was opened within a converted Victorian stable block by two archaeologists, Dr. Hilary Howard and her husband, Michael Pitts. They specialize in organically grown food prepared in original ways and sold at reasonable prices. Their hot lunch platters, which change daily, might include spiced chili with fried peppers served with a mixture of wild, tamargue, and white rice; or the mason's lunch (two cheeses, hand-churned butter, an apple, and homemade bread, pickles, and crackers). Pastries, coffee, fruit juices, bottled beer, cold quiche, snacks, and Welsh and English cheeses are available throughout the day. Especially attractive is the midafternoon cream tea served with whole-wheat scones and clotted cream imported from Cornwall. The owners travel abroad every winter, bringing back their culinary inspirations from Asia and the Pacific.

3 Bath: Britain's Most Historic Spa Town

115 miles W of London; 13 miles SE of Bristol

In 1702, Queen Anne made the trek from London to the mineral springs of Bath, thereby launching a fad that was to make the city the most celebrated spa in England.

The most famous name connected with Bath was the 18th-century dandy Beau Nash, who cut a striking figure as he made his way across the city, with all the plumage of a bird of paradise. This polished arbiter of taste and manners made dueling déclassé. While dispensing (at a price) trinkets to the courtiers and aspirant gentlemen of his day, Beau was carted around in a sedan chair.

The 18th-century architects John Wood the Elder and his son provided a proper backdrop for Nash's considerable social talents. These architects designed a city of

Bath

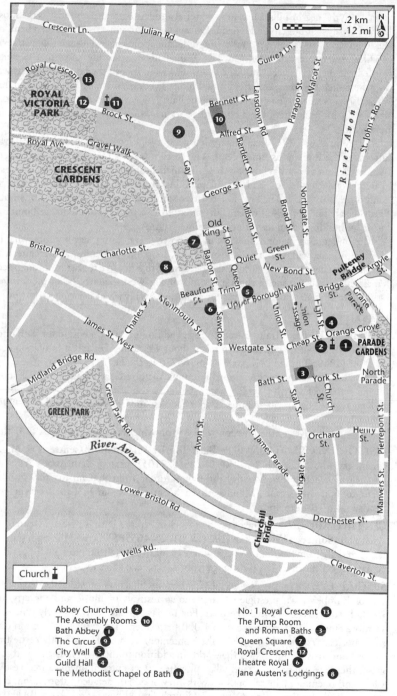

0   .2 km
  .12 mi

N

Crescent Ln.
Julian Rd
Guinea Ln.
Royal Crescent 13
ROYAL VICTORIA PARK
12 † 11
Brock St.
Bennett St.
Lansdown Rd
Paragon St.
Walcot St.
Alfred St. 10
9
Royal Ave.
Gravel Walk
CRESCENT GARDENS
River Avon
St. John's Rd.
George St.
Gay St.
Milsom St.
Broad St.
Northgate St.
Old King St.
7
Charlotte St.
Bristol Rd.
8
John St.
Barton St.
Quiet
Green St.
New Bond St.
Pulteney Bridge
Argyle St.
Beaufort St.
Trim 5
Upper Borough Walls
Bridge St.
Grand Parade
6
Sawclose
Union St.
High St.
Passage
4
Orange Grove
PARADE GARDENS
James St. West
Charles St.
Monmouth St.
Westgate St.
Cheap St.
2 † 1
North Parade
Midland Bridge Rd.
Bath St.
3
York St.
Church St.
GREEN PARK
Green Park Rd.
Avon St.
Stall St.
Orchard St.
Henry St.
Pierrepont St.
River Avon
St. James Parade
Southgate St.
Manvers St.
Lower Bristol Rd.
Dorchester St.
Churchill Bridge
Wells Rd.
Claverton St.

Church †

Abbey Churchyard 2
The Assembly Rooms 10
Bath Abbey 1
The Circus 9
City Wall 5
Guild Hall 4
The Methodist Chapel of Bath 11

No. 1 Royal Crescent 13
The Pump Room and Roman Baths 3
Queen Square 7
Royal Crescent 12
Theatre Royal 6
Jane Austen's Lodgings 8

3-0598

349

stone from the nearby hills, a feat so substantial and lasting that Bath today is the most harmoniously laid-out city in England. During Georgian times, this city, on a bend of the Avon River, was to attract a following of leading political and literary figures, such as Dickens, Thackeray, Nelson, and Pitt. Canadians may already know that General Wolfe lived on Trim Street, and Australians may want to visit the house at 19 Bennett St., where their founding father, Admiral Phillip, lived. Even Henry Fielding came this way, observing in *Tom Jones* that the ladies of Bath "endeavour to appear as ugly as possible in the morning, in order to set off that beauty which they intend to show you in the evening."

And even before its Queen Anne, Georgian, and Victorian popularity, Bath was known to the Romans as Aquae Sulis. The foreign legions founded their baths here (which you can visit today) to ease their rheumatism in the curative mineral springs.

Remarkable restoration and careful planning have ensured that Bath retains its handsome look today. The city suffered devastating destruction from the infamous Baedeker air raids of 1942, when Luftwaffe pilots seemed more intent on bombing historical buildings than in hitting any military target.

After undergoing major restoration in the postwar era, Bath today has somewhat of a museum look, with the attendant gift shops. Its parks, museums, and architecture continue to draw hordes of visitors, and because of this massive tourist invasion, prices remain high. But it's one of the high points of the West Country (a lot more interesting than Bristol) and a good base for exploring Avebury.

ESSENTIALS

GETTING THERE   Trains leave London's Paddington Station bound for Bath once every hour during the day. The trip takes about 1½ hours. For rail information, call ☎ 0345/484950 in the U.K., or 01603/764776 in the U.S.

One **National Express** coach leaves London's Victoria Coach Station every 2 hours during the day. The trip takes 2½ hours. Coaches also leave Bristol bound for Bath, and make the trip in 50 minutes. For schedules and information, call ☎ 0990/808080.

Drive west on M4 to the junction with A4, on which you continue west to Bath.

VISITOR INFORMATION   The **Bath Tourist Information Centre** is at Abbey Chambers, Abbey Church Yard (☎ 01225/477101), next to Bath Abbey. It's open June through September, Monday through Saturday from 9:30am to 7pm, Sunday 10am to 6pm; off-season, Monday through Saturday from 9:30am to 5pm and Sunday from 10am to 4pm.

GETTING AROUND   One of the best ways to explore Bath is by bike. Rentals are available at **Somerset Valley Bike Hire** (☎ 01225/465188), behind the train station. It's open daily from 9am to 6pm, charging £10.50 to £23 ($16.80 to $36.80) per day, depending on the bike. Deposits range from £20 to £75 ($32 to $120).

SPECIAL EVENTS   Bath's graceful Georgian architecture provides the setting for one of Europe's most prestigious international festivals of music and the arts, the ✪ **Bath International Music Festival.** For 17 days in late May and early June each year, the city is filled with more than 1,000 performers. The festival focuses on classical music, jazz, new music, and the contemporary visual arts, with orchestras, soloists, and artists from all over the world. In addition to the main music and art program, there are walks, tours, and talks, plus free street entertainment, a free Festival Club, and opening night celebrations with fireworks. For detailed information, contact the **Bath Festivals Box Office,** 2 Church St., Abbey Green, Bath BA1 1NL (☎ 01225/463362).

SEEING THE SIGHTS

You'll want to stroll around to see some of the buildings, crescents, and squares in town. The **North Parade** (where Goldsmith lived) and the **South Parade** (where English novelist and diarist Frances Burney once resided) represent harmony, and are the work of John Wood the Elder. He also designed beautiful **Queen Square,** where both Jane Austen and Wordsworth once lived. Also of interest is **The Circus,** built in 1754, as well as the shop-lined **Pulteney Bridge,** designed by Robert Adam and often compared to the Ponte Vecchio of Florence.

The younger John Wood designed the **Royal Crescent,** an elegant half-moon row of town houses (copied by Astor architects for their colonnade in New York City in the 1830s). At **No. 1 Royal Crescent** (☎ 01225/428126), the interior has been redecorated and furnished by the Bath Preservation Trust to look as it might have toward the end of the 18th century. The house is located at one end of Bath's most magnificent crescent, west of the Circus. Admission is £3.80 ($6.10) for adults and £3 ($4.80) for children, seniors, and students; a family ticket is £8 ($12.80). Open March to October, Tuesday to Sunday from 10:30am to 5pm, and November to December 1, Tuesday to Sunday from 10:30am to 4pm (last admission 30 min. before closing); closed Good Friday.

Free 1¾-hour walking tours are conducted throughout the year by **The Mayor's Honorary Society** (☎ 01225/477786). Tours depart from outside the Roman Baths Monday through Friday at 10:30am and 2pm, Sunday at 2:30pm, and Tuesday, Friday, and Saturday at 7pm. A slightly different tour led by **Bath Parade Tours,** costing £3 ($4.80) per person, leaves Saturday at 2:30pm from outside the Roman Baths. Reservations aren't needed for either tour.

Jane Austen Tours take you in the footsteps of the author and her characters. Conducted only once a week, tours begin at Abbey Lace Shop, York Street (☎ 01225/436030). The cost is £3 ($4.80) per person, and departures are every Saturday. You'll be told the time to meet for the tour when you make your reservations.

To tour Bath by bus, you can choose among several tour companies. Among the best are **Patrick Driscoll/Beau Nash Guides,** Elmsleigh, Bathampton (☎ 01225/462010), with tours that are more personalized than most.

Avon river boat cruises depart from a pier adjacent to the Pulteney Bridge (directly across the water from the Parade Gardens). Cruises last 50 minutes and are priced £4 ($6.40) for adults, and £2 ($3.20) for children. They're offered from Easter to October via two boats maintained by **The Boating Station** (☎ 01225/466407).

✪ **Bath Abbey.** Orange Grove. ☎ **01225/422462.** £2 ($3.20) donation requested. Admission to the Heritage Vaults, £2 ($3.20) adults, £1 ($1.60) students, children, and seniors. Abbey, Apr–Oct Mon–Sat 9am–6pm; Nov–Mar Mon–Sat 9am–4:30pm; year-round Sun 1–2:30pm and 4:30–5:30pm. The Heritage Vaults, Mon–Sat 10am–4pm.

Built on the site of a much larger Norman cathedral, the present-day abbey is a fine example of the late Perpendicular style. When Queen Elizabeth I came to Bath in 1574, she ordered a national fund to be set up to restore the abbey. The west front is the sculptural embodiment of a Jacob's Ladder dream of a 15th-century bishop. When you go inside and see its many windows, you'll understand why the abbey is called the "Lantern of the West." Note the superb fan vaulting, with its scalloped effect. Beau Nash was buried in the nave and is honored by a simple monument totally out of keeping with his flamboyant character. In 1994 the Bath Abbey Heritage Vaults opened on the south side of the abbey. This subterranean exhibition traces the history of Christianity at the abbey site since Saxon times.

✪ **The Pump Room & Roman Baths.** In the Bath Abbey churchyard. ☎ **01225/ 477785.** Admission £6.30 ($10.10) adults, £5.60 ($8.95) seniors, £3.80 ($6.10) children. Apr–Sept daily 9am–6pm; Oct–Mar Mon–Sat 9:30am–5pm, Sun 10:30am–5pm; Aug evenings 8–10pm.

Founded in A.D. 75 by the Romans, the baths were dedicated to the goddess Sulis Minerva; in their day, they were an engineering feat. Even today they're among the finest Roman remains in the country, and are still fed by Britain's most famous hot-spring water. After centuries of decay, the original baths were rediscovered during Queen Victoria's reign. The site of the Temple of Sulis Minerva has been excavated and is now open to view. The museum displays many interesting objects from Victorian and recent digs (look for the head of Minerva).

Coffee, lunch, and tea, usually with music from the Pump Room Trio, can be enjoyed in the 18th-century pump room, overlooking the hot springs. There's also a drinking fountain with hot mineral water that tastes horrible.

Theatre Royal. Sawclose. ☎ **01225/448844.** Tickets £9–£23 ($14.40–$36.80). Box office Mon–Sat 10am–8pm. Shows Mon–Wed at 7:30pm, Thurs–Sat at 8pm; Wed and Sat matinees at 2:30pm.

The Theatre Royal, located next to the new Seven Dials development, was restored in 1982 and refurbished with plush seats, red carpets, and a painted proscenium arch and ceiling; it is now the most beautiful theater in Britain. It has 940 seats, with a small pit and grand tiers rising to the upper circle. Despite all the work done, Theatre Royal has no company, depending upon touring shows to fill the house during the 8-week theater season each summer. Beneath the theater, reached from the back of the stalls or by a side door, are the theater vaults, where you will find a bar in one with stone walls. The next vault has a restaurant, serving an array of dishes from soup to light à la carte meals.

A studio theater at the rear of the main building opened in 1996. The theater publishes a list of forthcoming events; its repertoire includes West End shows, among other offerings.

✪ **The American Museum.** Claverton Manor, Bathwick Hill. ☎ **01225/460503.** Admission £5 ($8) adults, £4.50 ($7.20) students and seniors, £3 ($4.80) children 5–16, 4 and under free. Late Mar to beginning of Nov Tues–Sun 2–5pm for the museum, and 1–6pm for the garden. Bus: 18.

Some 2½ miles outside Bath, you can get an idea of what life was like in America prior to the mid-1800s. This was the first American museum established outside the United States. In a Greek Revival house (Claverton Manor), the museum sits proudly on extensive grounds high above the Somerset Valley. Among the authentic exhibits shipped over from the States are a New Mexico room, a Conestoga wagon, an Early American beehive oven (try gingerbread baked from the recipe of George Washington's mother), the dining room of a New York town house of the early 19th century, and (on the grounds) a copy of Washington's flower garden at Mount Vernon. Throughout the summer, the museum hosts various special events, from displays of Native American dancing and 1700s military drills to very realistic reenactments of the French and Indian War and the Civil War.

OUTDOOR PURSUITS

GOLF   The 18-hole **Bath Golf Club,** at North Road (☎ 01225/463834), charges £25 ($40) per round on weekdays and £30 ($48) on Saturday and Sunday. There are no golf carts and no clubs for rent. The club is open to visitors with established handicap certificates or letters of introduction from their own club. Before playing, call

☎ 01225/466953 for the best tee times. To get to Bath Golf Club, take A36 (Warminster Road) out of Bath. Turn right onto North Road, signposted Golf Club, University, and American Museum.

Another 18-hole course is the **Lansdown Golf Club,** Lansdown (☎ 01225/422138), with greens fees of £18 ($28.80) daily. Visitors are accepted only with a handicap certificate from their own club. Call ☎ 01225/422138 to book tee times in advance. To get to Lansdown Golf Club, take Lansdown Road out of Bath toward the racecourse and Lansdown Park-and-Ride. At the edge of the city, pass the Park-and-Ride and the Blathway Arms; the Golf Club is on the left-hand side.

A 9-hole public course is the **Entry Hill Golf Course,** Entry Hill (☎ 01225/834248), with greens fees of £5.50 ($8.80) per round on weekdays and £6.20 ($9.90) on Saturday and Sunday. The cost for 18 holes is £8.50 ($13.60) on weekdays and £9.95 ($15.90) on weekends. Golfers need proper golf shoes or trainers. Club rentals are available. Call ☎ 01225/834248 to reserve tee times. To get to Entry Hill Golf Course, take A367 south of Bath along Wellsway. Turn left at the sign for Entry Hill Golf Course.

HORSEBACK RIDING   The Wellow Trekking Centre, in Wellow, near Bath (☎ 01225/834376), is open daily. One-hour rides cost £12 ($19.20), 2-hour rides are £20 ($32), and a half-day pub ride from 10am to 2pm is available for £25 ($40).

TENNIS   There are public outdoor hard courts at **Royal Victoria Park, Sydney Gardens,** and **Alice Park.** Courts are open year-round till sunset; rates are £2.50 ($4) per person per hour. All courts are centrally located and marked on the city map available from the Tourist Information Centre at Abbey Chambers. For racquet and ball rentals or more information, contact **Excel Tennis** (☎ 01225/425066).

SHOPPING

Bath is loaded with markets and fairs, antique centers, and small shops. There are literally hundreds of opportunities to buy (and ship) anything you want (including the famous spa waters, which are for sale by the bottle). Prices are traditionally less than in London but more than in the British boonies.

The whole city is basically one long, slightly uphill shopping area. It's not defined by one High Street, as are so many British towns—if you arrive by train, don't be put off by the lack of scenery. Within 2 blocks are several shopping streets. The single best day to visit, if you are a serious shopper intent on hitting the flea markets, is Wednesday.

The Bartlett Street Antiques Centre, Bartlett Street (☎ 01225/466689), encompasses 60 dealers and 160 showcases displaying furniture, silver, antique jewelry, paintings, clocks, toys, military items, and collectibles. Another option is the **Great Western Antiques Centre,** Bartlett Street (☎ 01225/424243), with 30 dealers. Here you can find costumes, costume jewelry, trains, and other railway items, lace and linens, porcelain and glass, silver, music boxes, canes, and much more.

Walcot Reclamation, 108 Walcot St. (☎ 01225/444404), is Bath's salvage yard. This sprawling and appealingly dusty storeroom of 19th-century architectural remnants is set a quarter-mile northeast of the town center. Its 20,000-square-foot warehouse offers pieces from demolished homes, schools, hospitals, and factories throughout south England. Mantelpieces, panels, columns, and architectural ornaments are each departmentalized into historical eras. Items range from a complete, dismantled 1937 Georgian library crafted from Honduran mahogany to objects costing around £5 ($8) each. Anything can be shipped or altered on site by a battery of artisans who are trained in adapting antique fittings for modern homes.

The largest purveyor of antique coins and stamps in Bath, **The Bath Stamp & Coin Shop,** 12–13 Pulteney Bridge (☎ **01225/463073**), offers hundreds of odd and unusual numismatics. Part of the inventory is devoted to Roman coins, some of which were unearthed in archaeological excavations at Roman sites near Bath.

Near Bath Abbey, the **Beaux Arts Gallery,** 13 York St. (☎ **01225/464850**), is the largest and most important gallery of contemporary art in Bath, specializing in well-known British artists including Ray Richardson, John Bellany, and Nicola Bealing. Closely linked to the London art scene, the gallery occupies a pair of interconnected, stone-fronted Georgian houses. Its half dozen showrooms exhibit objects beginning at £20 ($32).

Poppy & Scorpio, 16 Northgate (☎ **01225/465320**), offers elegant and conservatively stylish women's clothing, mostly from such German and Continental names as Betty Barclay, Basler, Bianca, Lucia, Hucke, Jobis, and Tru.

The very upscale **Rossiter's,** 38–41 Broad St. (☎ **01225/462227**), sells very traditional English tableware and home decor items. They'll ship anywhere in the world. Look especially for the display of Moorcraft ginger jars, vases, and clocks, as well as the Floris perfumes.

Whittard of Chelsea, 10 Union Passage (☎ **01225/447787**), is the most charming and unusual tea emporium in Bath. Inside, you'll find strainers, traditional table and tea services (plus a large selection of offbeat teapot designs), tea biscuits, tea cozies, tea caddies, and teas from all parts of what used to be the Empire. Looking for a fabulously exotic tea to wow your friends with back home? How about monkey-picked oolong—a Chinese tea made from plants so inaccessible their leaves can only be gathered by trained monkeys!

WHERE TO STAY
VERY EXPENSIVE

✪ **Bath Spa Hotel.** Sydney Rd. (east of the city, off A36), Bath, Sunset BA2 6JF. ☎ **01225/444424.** Fax 01225/444006. 98 units. MINIBAR TV TEL. Sun–Thurs £169–£199 ($270.40–$318.40) double; £229–£289 ($366.40–$462.40) suite for 2. Fri–Sat £249–£369 ($398.40–$590.40) double; £289–£369 ($462.40–$590.40) suite for 2. AE, DC, MC, V.

This stunning restored 19th-century mansion is a 10-minute walk from the center of Bath. Behind a facade of Bath stone, it lies at the end of a tree-lined drive on 7 acres of landscaped grounds, with a Victorian grotto and a Grecian temple. Winston Churchill visited when it was the headquarters of the Admiralty in World War II. In its long history, it had served many purposes (once a hostel for nurses) before being returned to its original grandeur. The drawing room of what was once an English general's house is today restored. The hotel uses log fireplaces, elaborate moldings, oak paneling, and staircases to create country-house charm. The rooms are handsomely furnished with the best of English furniture and well-chosen and coordinated fabrics. Most of them are spacious.

Dining: Vellore, the hotel restaurant, offers continental cuisine. You're given immaculate service and superb food and wine with a fixed-price dinner or Sunday lunch. A second venue, the Alfresco Restaurant, offers a Mediterranean-style menu. In summer, guests can dine outside in an informal garden with a fountain.

Amenities: 24-hour room service, valet and laundry service, beauty treatments, hairdressing salon, indoor swimming pool, gymnasium, tennis court, sauna and whirlpool bath, croquet lawn, children's nursery, beauty treatment rooms, healthy-snack cafe, health and leisure spa.

Fountain House. 9-11 Fountain Buildings, Lansdown Rd., Bath, Somerset BA1 5DV. ☎ **01225/338622.** Fax 01225/445855. 14 units. MINIBAR TV TEL. £140–£200 ($224–$320) 1-bedroom suite; £200–£236 ($320–$377.60) 2-bedroom suite. Rates include continental breakfast. AE, DC, MC, V. Parking £12 ($19.20).

On the northern edge of the city center, the three buildings that comprise this hotel are a trio of Georgian neoclassic, natural stone-fronted structures dating from 1735. The hotel stands within 100 yards of Milsom Street, the city's main shopping and historic thoroughfare.

British entrepreneur Robin Bryan created an all-suite hotel that can hold its own with any other in England. Each suite is decorated with original or reproduction antiques, lots of color-coordinated chintz, at least one bedroom, a sitting room, and all the electronic equipment you'd expect in such an elegant hotel. There's no formal breakfast; the fixings are delivered to your door in a basket so you can prepare your own breakfast at your own pace.

The Priory Hotel. Weston Rd., Bath, Somerset BA1 2XT. ☎ **01225/331922.** Fax 01225/448276. 28 units. TV TEL. £180 ($288) standard double; £240–£270 ($384–$432) deluxe room. Rates include English breakfast. AE, DC, MC, V.

Converted from one of Bath's Georgian houses in 1969, the Priory is situated on 2 acres of formal and award-winning gardens with manicured lawns and flower beds. The hotel reopened in the spring of 1997, vastly refurbished and improved. If anything, it is now more inviting than ever. The rooms are individually decorated and furnished with antiques; our personal favorite is Clivia (all rooms are named after flowers or shrubs), a nicely appointed duplex in a circular turret.

Dining: The restaurant consists of three separate dining rooms, one in a small salon in the original building; the others have views over the garden. The menu is varied and reflects seasonal availability. Grouse, partridge, hare, and venison are served in season in several recipes, as is the succulent lamb, roasted with herb-flavored bread crumbs. Sunday brings traditional roasted meats. The menu is always full of surprises—perhaps braised quail with foie gras and wild mushrooms.

Amenities: Swimming pool, croquet lawn, health club, Jacuzzi, sauna, car-rental desk, concierge, room service, dry cleaning/laundry, baby-sitting, courtesy car.

✪ **The Queensberry Hotel.** Russell St., Bath, Somerset BA1 2QF. ☎ **800/323-5463** in the U.S., or 01225/447928. Fax 01225/446065. 30 units. TV TEL. £135–£190 ($216–$304) double. Rates include continental breakfast. MC, V. Parking 50p (80¢) per hour.

A gem of a hotel and better than ever, lying only a short walk from the Assembly Rooms, this town house has been beautifully restored by Stephen and Penny Ross. In our view, it is now among the finest places to stay in a city where the competition for restored town house hotels is fierce. The marquis of Queensberry commissioned John Wood the Younger to build this house in 1772. Each of three interconnected town houses that form this hotel was constructed in the early Georgian era. Today each room has antique furniture and carefully chosen upholstery, in keeping with the character of the house.

Dining: At the hotel you can dine at the exceptional Olive Tree, offering a contemporary English cuisine. See "Where to Dine," below.

✪ **Royal Crescent Hotel.** 16 Royal Crescent, Bath, Somerset BA1 2LS. ☎ **800/457-6000** in the U.S., or 01225/739950. Fax 01225/339401. 57 units. A/C TV TEL. £170–£260 ($272–$416) double; £450–£675 ($720–$1,080) suite. DC, MC, V.

This is a special place, standing proudly in the center of the famed Royal Crescent, the Georgian colonnade of town houses was designed by John Wood the Younger in 1767.

Long regarded as Bath's premier hotel (before the arrival of the even better Bath Spa), it has attracted the rich and famous. Crystal chandeliers, period furniture, and paintings add to the rich adornment. The bedrooms, including the Jane Austen Suite, are lavishly furnished with such amenities as four-poster beds and Jacuzzi baths. Each room is not only individually designed, but also offers such comforts as a trouser press, a hair dryer, bathrobes, bottled mineral water, fruit plates, and other special touches.

Dining: Excellent English cuisine is served in the Dower House Restaurant (reservations are essential), which offers fixed-price lunches and dinners daily. The continental cuisine is imaginative, with ever-so-polite and formal service.

Amenities: Health club, steam room, Jacuzzi, car-rental desk, beauty salon, concierge, room service, dry cleaning/laundry, baby-sitting, courtesy car.

EXPENSIVE

Francis Hotel. Queen Sq., Bath, Somerset BA1 2HH. ☎ **800/225-5843** in the U.S. and Canada, or 01225/424257. Fax 01225/319715. 94 units. TV TEL. £109–£119 ($174.40–$190.40) double; £159–£179 ($254.40–$286.40) triple; £169–£189 ($270.40–$302.40) suite. AE, DC, MC, V.

An integral part of Queen Square, the Francis is an example of 18th-century taste and style, but we find it too commercial and touristy. Originally consisting of six private residences dating from 1729, the Francis was opened as a private hotel by Emily Francis in 1884 and has offered guests first-class service for more than 100 years. Many of the well-furnished and traditionally styled bedrooms overlook Queen Square, named in honor of George II's consort, Caroline. The public rooms feature shell-shaped niches, moldings, and some 18th-century antiques.

Dining/Diversions: There's a cocktail bar and the Edgar Restaurant, which offers a wide array of both British and international food.

MODERATE

Pratt's Hotel. S. Parade, Bath, Somerset BA2 4AB. ☎ **01225/460441.** Fax 01225/448807. 46 units. TV TEL. £95 ($152) double. Children under 15 sharing a room with 2 adults stay free. Rates include English breakfast. AE, DC, MC, V. Parking £8.50 ($13.60).

Once the home of Sir Walter Scott, Pratt's was built in the heady days of Beau Nash. Functioning as a hotel since 1791, it's become part of the legend and lore of Bath. Several elegant terraced Georgian town houses were joined together to form this complex with a very traditional British atmosphere. You can still see the bowed landing on the staircase, designed to enable "chairmen" to take clients back to their rooms in sedan chairs following their treatments in the spa baths. Rooms are individually designed and equipped with amenities such as hair dryers and trouser presses. The hotel is also known for offering good food, a range of English and French dishes.

INEXPENSIVE

✪ **Apsley House Hotel.** 141 Newbridge Hill, Bath, Somerset BA1 3PT. ☎ **01225/336966.** Fax 01225/425462. 7 units. TV TEL. £65 ($104) double; £75–£85 ($120–$136) suite. Rates include English breakfast. DC, MC, V. Take A4 to Upper Bristol Rd. fork right at the traffic signals into Newbridge Hill, and turn left at Apsley Rd.

This charming and stately building, just a mile west of the center of Bath, dates from 1830, during the reign of William IV. It's set in its own gardens, with a square tower, arched windows, and a walled garden with south views. In 1994 new owners refurbished the hotel, filling it with country-house chintzes and a collection of antiques borrowed from the showrooms of an antique store they own. (Some of the furniture in the hotel is for sale; inquire further about the details.) The rooms are comfortably furnished and filled with fine fabrics and attractive accessories.

✪ **Badminton Villa.** 10 Upper Oldfield Park, Bath, Somerset BA2 3JZ. ☎ **01225/ 426347.** Fax 01225/420393. 5 units. TV. £52–£60 ($83.20–$96) double. Rates include English breakfast. MC, V. Bus: 14.

Located about half a mile south of the city center, this house was built in 1883 as part of a suburban development that is now an extremely desirable place to live. Constructed of honey-colored blocks of Bath stone, it lies on a hillside with sweeping views over the world-famous architecture of Bath. When it was acquired in 1992 by John and Sue Burton, the villa had fallen into derelict disrepair. With zest and style, the couple gracefully transformed it into a B&B, one of the most charming small hotels in Bath. Furnishings are an eclectic but unpretentious mix of objects gathered by the Burtons during their travels. The rooms contain tea-makers and hair dryers. There's also a three-tiered garden with patio.

✪ **Bath Tasburgh Hotel.** Warminster Rd., Bathampton, Bath, Somerset BA2 6SH. ☎ **01225/425096.** Fax 01225/463842. 12 units. TV TEL. £65–£83 ($104–$132.80) double; £95 ($152) triple. Rates include English breakfast. AE, MC, V. Bus: 4.

Set about a mile east of Bath center, amid 7 acres of parks and gardens, this spacious Victorian country house was built in 1890 and was once occupied by one of the royal family's official photographers. The redbrick structure contains a glassed-in conservatory, a lounge, original marble fireplaces, stained-glass windows, antiques, and individually decorated rooms, most of which have sweeping panoramic views. Each contains a beverage-maker, and four rooms have four poster beds. The Avon and Kennet Canal runs along the rear of the property, and guests enjoy summer walks along the adjacent towpath.

Dukes' Hotel. 53-54 Great Pulteney St., Bath, Somerset BA2 4DN. ☎ **01225/463512.** Fax 01225/483733. 23 units. TV TEL. £65–£95 ($104–$152) double; £75–£115 ($120–$184) family room. Rates include English breakfast. AE, CB, DC, MC, V. Bus: 18.

A short walk from the heart of Bath, this building dates from 1780 but has been completely restored and rather elegantly furnished and modernized, both in its public rooms and its bedrooms. Many of the original Georgian features, including cornices and moldings, have been retained. Amenities include electric trouser presses and hair dryers. Guests can relax in a refined drawing room or patronize the cozy bar. A traditional English menu is also offered.

Laura Place Hotel. 3 Laura Place, Great Pulteney St., Bath, Somerset BA2 4BH. ☎ **01225/ 463815.** Fax 01225/310222. 8 units. TV TEL. £66–£88 ($105.60–$140.80) double; £70–£100 ($112–$160) family suite. Rates include English breakfast. AE, MC, V. Bus: 18 or 19.

Built in 1789, this hotel has won a civic award for the restoration of its stone facade. Set on a corner of a residential street overlooking a public fountain, it lies within a 2-minute walk of the Roman Baths and Bath Abbey. This very formal hotel has been skillfully decorated with antique furniture and fabrics evocative of the 18th century.

Number Ninety Three. 93 Wells Rd., Bath, Somerset BA2 3AN. ☎ **01225/317977.** 4 units. TV. £38–£55 ($60.80–$88) double; £60–£75 ($96–$120) triple. Rates include English breakfast. AE, MC, V. Bus: 3, 13, 14, 17, or 23; ask for Lower Wells Rd. stop.

This well-run guest house is a traditional B&B, British style: small, but immaculately kept and well maintained. Bedrooms are well furnished, and the owners undertake a continuing program of maintenance and redecoration in the slower or winter months. Its owner is a mine of local information. The elegant Victorian house serves a traditional English breakfast, and it is within easy walking distance from the city center and the rail and National Bus stations. Evening meals are available by prior arrangement. No smoking.

Sydney Gardens Hotel. Sydney Rd., Bath, Somerset BA2 6NT. ☎ and fax **01225/464818.** 6 units. TV TEL. £69 ($110.40) double. Rates include English breakfast. MC, V.

This spot is reminiscent of the letters of Jane Austen, who wrote to friends about the long walks she enjoyed in Sydney Gardens, a public park just outside the city center. In 1852 an Italianate Victorian villa was constructed here of gray stone on a lot immediately adjacent to the gardens. Three rooms have twin beds and the other three have 5-foot-wide double beds. Each accommodation is individually decorated with an English country-house charm. Amenities include hair dryers and beverage-makers. No meals except breakfast are served, since the center of town and many restaurants are nearby. There's a footpath running beside a canal for leisurely strolls. No smoking.

In Nearby Hinton Charterhouse

Homewood Park. Hinton Charterhouse, Bath, Somerset BA3 6BB. ☎ **01225/723731.** Fax 01225/723820. 21 units. £135–£210 ($216–$336) double; £245 ($392) suite. Rates include English breakfast. AE, CB, DC, MC, V. Take A36 (Bath-Warminster rd.) 6 miles south of Bath.

This small, family-run hotel, set on 10 acres of grounds, was built in the 18th century and enlarged in the 19th. Overlooking the Limpley Stoke Valley, it's a large Victorian house with grounds adjoining the 13th-century ruin of Hinton Priory. You can play tennis and croquet in the garden. Riding and golfing are available nearby, and beautiful walks in the Limpley Stoke Valley lure guests. Each of the rooms is luxuriously decorated, with exceptional fabrics, and each is furnished with taste and charm. Most overlook the gardens and grounds or offer views of the valley.

Dining: Visitors come here for the cuisine, served in a dining room facing south, overlooking the gardens. The French and English cooking is prepared with skill and flair.

In Nearby Ston Easton

✪ **Ston Easton Park.** Ston Easton, Somerset BA3 4DF. ☎ **01761/241631.** Fax 01761/241377. 19 units, 1 cottage suite, 6 state rooms. TV. £175–£245 ($280–$392) double; £285 ($456) cottage suite; £275–£360 ($440–$576) state room. Children under 7 not accepted. AE, DC, MC, V.

This is one of the great country hotels of England. From the moment you pass a group of stone outbuildings and the century-old beeches of the 30-acre park—just up the road from Farrington Gurney—you know you've come to a very special place. The mansion was created in the mid-1700s from the shell of an existing Elizabethan house, and in 1793 Sir Humphry Repton designed the landscape. In 1977, after many years of neglect, Peter and Christine Smedley acquired the property and poured money, love, and labor into its restoration. A pair of carved mahogany staircases ringed with ornate plaster detailing are works of sculpture. The sheer volume of antiques filling the place is staggering.

The tasteful rooms are filled with flowers, plus upholstery and antiques. A gardener's cottage was artfully upgraded from a utilitarian building to contain a pair of intensely decorated and very glamorous suites. In addition to the cottage suite, plus the "standard and deluxe" rooms of the main house, there are half a dozen "state rooms," four of which have four-poster beds, and all of which contain lavish but genteel decor.

Dining: A grand formal dining room displays museum-quality oil portraits and exquisite attention to detail. The chef prepares superb food, offering imaginative menus.

In Nearby Hunstrete

Hunstrete House. Hunstrete, Chelwood, near Bristol, Somerset BS18 4NS. ☎ **01761/490490.** Fax 01761/490732. 23 units. TV TEL. £120–£180 ($192–$288) double; £230

($368) superior double; £250 ($400) suite. Half board £210–£230 ($336–$368) double; £280 ($448) suite for 2. Rates include English breakfast. AE, DC, MC, V. Take A4 about 4 miles west of Bath, then A368 another 4½ miles toward Weston-super-Mare.

This fine Georgian house, a member of Relais & Châteaux, is situated on 92 acres of private parkland. Six units are in the Courtyard House, attached to the main structure and overlooking a paved courtyard with its Italian fountain and flower-filled tubs. Swallow Cottage, which adjoins the main house, has its own private sitting room, double bedroom, and bath. Units in the main house are individually decorated and furnished in attractive colors. There is a heated swimming pool in a sheltered corner of the walled garden. Part of the pleasure of staying at Hunstrete is the contemporary and classic cuisine.

WHERE TO DINE

The best place for afternoon tea is **The Pump Room & Roman Baths** (see above). Another choice, just a 1-minute walk from the Abbey Church and Roman Baths, is **Sally Lunn's House,** 4 North Parade Passage (☎ 01225/461634), where visitors have been eating for more than 1,700 years. For £4.78 ($7.65) you can get the Fantastic Sally Lunn Cream Tea, which includes toasted and buttered scones served with strawberry jam and clotted cream, along with your choice of tea or coffee.

At **The Canary,** 3 Queen St. (☎ 01225/424846), you can order a cream tea with scones and strawberry jam, or a cream tea with a sandwich for £5.95 ($9.50). They make all of their own cakes and scones, and have 30 to 40 teas from which to choose.

The Café Retro, Orange Grove (☎ 01225/339347), serves a variety of teas and coffees. You can order a pot of tea for 80p ($1.30), or a large cappuccino for £1.40 ($2.25), and add a tea cake, scone, or crumpet for £1 ($1.60).

Beaujolais. 5 Chapel Row, Queen Sq. ☎ 01225/423417. Reservations recommended. 2-course lunch £7.50–£8.50 ($12–$13.60); 3-course dinner £18.50 ($29.60). AE, MC, V. Daily noon–2:30pm and 7–11pm. FRENCH.

This is the best-known bistro in Bath, maintaining its old regulars but also attracting new admirers every year. Diners are drawn to the honest fare and good value. The house wines are modestly priced. Begin perhaps with grilled monkfish served with a creamy white sauce, then followed with a salmon steak prepared with a ginger dressing. Also served is the widest variety of vegetarian dishes, one of which is a mushroom and spinach combination.

One area of the restaurant is reserved for nonsmokers. Persons with disabilities will appreciate the wheelchair access, and parents can order special helpings for children.

The Hole in the Wall. 16 George St. ☎ 01225/425242. Reservations recommended for weekdays and required Sat. Main courses £15 ($24); 2-course lunch £9 ($14.40); 3-course dinner £16.50 ($26.40). AE, MC, V. Mon–Sat noon–2pm and 6–11pm. MODERN ENGLISH/FRENCH.

This much-renovated Georgian town house is owned by Gunna and Christopher Chown, whose successful restaurant in Wales has already received critical acclaim. The pair of interconnected dining rooms is accented with polished copper pots, darkened ceiling beams, whitewashed walls, and a large fireplace.

The menu choices change frequently, according to the inspiration of the chef and the availability of ingredients. Begin with such delights as a foie gras and duck-liver terrine with pistachio and red-onion marmalade, or bouillabaisse. Proceed into a taste sensation with roast pheasant with grain mustard mash and a blueberry sauce; or red mullet with garlic butter, rosemary, and thyme dressing. Desserts are often a surprise—say, rhubarb parfait with a confit of ginger.

The Moon and Sixpence. 6A Broad St. ☎ **01225/460962.** Reservations recommended. Main courses £8.75–£13 ($14–$20.80); fixed-price dinner £16.95–£20.95 ($27.10–$33.50); fixed-price lunch £6.25 ($10); 2-course lunch buffet in the wine bar £5.50 ($8.80). AE, MC, V. Daily noon–2:30pm; Sun–Thurs 5:30–10:30pm, Fri–Sat 5:30–11pm. INTERNATIONAL.

One of the leading restaurants and wine bars of Bath, The Moon and Sixpence occupies a stone structure east of Queen Square, with an extended conservatory and sheltered patio. It has a cobbled passageway that leads you past a fountain into its courtyard.

The food may not be as good as that served at more acclaimed choices, including The Hole in the Wall, but the value is unbeatable. At lunch, a large cold buffet with a selection of hot dishes is featured in the wine bar section. In the upstairs restaurant overlooking the bar, full service is offered. Main courses are likely to include fillet of lamb with caramelized garlic or medaillons of beef fillet with a bacon, red-wine, and shallot sauce. Look for the daily specials on the continental menu.

The Olive Tree. In the Queensberry Hotel, Russell St. ☎ **01225/447928.** Reservations highly recommended. Main courses £11–£16 ($17.60–$25.60); 3-course fixed-price lunch £13.50 ($21.60); 3-course fixed-price dinner £21 ($33.60). MC, V. Mon–Sat noon–2pm and 7–10pm, Sun 7–9pm. MODERN ENGLISH/MEDITERRANEAN.

Stephen and Penny Ross operate one of the most sophisticated little restaurants in Bath, with a white-tile floor and black wood chairs. Stephen uses the best local produce, with an emphasis on freshness. The menu is changed to reflect the season, with game and fish being the specialties. You might begin with a Provençale fish soup with rouille and croutons or eggplant-and-mozzarella fritters with a sweet red-pepper sauce (unless the grilled scallops with noodles and pine nuts tempts you instead). Then you could go on to Gressingham duck breast, lightly grilled with shallots and kumquats, or else loin of venison with wild rice and morels, delicately flavored with a tarragon sauce. Stephen is also known for his desserts, which are likely to include such treats as a hot chocolate soufflé or an apricot and almond tart.

Popjoy's Restaurant. Sawclose. ☎ **01225/460494.** Reservations recommended. Main courses £12–£15 ($19.20–$24); 3-course fixed-price lunch £10.50 ($16.80). AE, DC, MC, V. Tues–Sat noon–2pm; Tues–Wed 6–11pm, Thurs–Sat 6–10pm. MODERN BRITISH.

Owned by Tomi and Nany Gretener, these two dining rooms are located on separate floors of the Georgian home (ca. 1720) where Beau Nash and his mistress, Julianna Popjoy, once entertained their friends and set the fashions of the day. Inventiveness and a solid technique go into many of the dishes. The food is unpretentious and generally quite satisfying. Menu choices may include a terrine of duck and chicken liver wrapped in bacon with a tomato coulis, watercress and potato soup, sautéed lamb kidneys with crispy smoked bacon, braised lamb shoulder with a sage and garlic stuffing, and tagliatelle with leeks and cream sauce.

Woods. 9–13 Alfred St. ☎ **01225/314812.** Reservations recommended. Main courses £8–£14.95 ($12.80–$23.90); fixed-price lunches £7 ($11.20); fixed-price dinners £8–£14.50 ($12.80–$23.20); main courses £11–£13.50 ($17.60–$21.60). MC, V. Mon–Sat noon–3pm and 6–11pm. ENGLISH/FRENCH/ORIENTAL.

Named after John Wood the Younger, architect of Bath's famous Assembly Room, which lies across the street, this restaurant is run by horse-racing enthusiast David Price and his French-born wife, Claude. A fixed-price menu is printed on paper, whereas the seasonal array of à la carte items are chalked onto a frequently changing blackboard. Good bets might include pear and parsnip soup, spit-roasted or grilled chicken with mustard sauce, sirloin steak with mushrooms, and guinea fowl with whatever sauce the chef is inspired to make at the time.

BATH AFTER DARK

To gain a very different perspective of Bath, you might want to take the **Bizarre Bath Walking Tour** (☎ 01225/335124), an hour-and-15-minute improvisational tour of the streets during which the tour guides pull pranks, tell jokes, and behave in a humorously annoying manner toward tour-goers and unsuspecting residents alike. It's a seasonal affair, running nightly at 8pm from March 24 through the end of summer. No reservations are necessary; just show up, ready for anything, at the Huntsman Inn at North Parade Passage. The cost of the tour is £3 ($4.80); £2.50 ($4) for students.

After your walk, you may need a drink, or want to check out the local club and music scene. At **The Bell,** 103 Walcot St. (☎ 01225/460426), music ranges from jazz and country to reggae and blues on Monday and Wednesday nights and Sunday at lunch. It's a long, narrow 400-year-old room covered in postcards from around the world. On music nights, the band performs in the center of the room.

The 2-story **Hat and Feather,** 14 London St. (☎ 01225/425672), has live musicians or DJs playing funk, reggae, or dance music nightly and all day Sunday. **The Hush,** The Paragon (☎ 01225/446288), offers music at the cutting edge of the English scene Monday through Saturday nights, with a cover of £3 ($4.80).

SIDE TRIPS FROM BATH
LACOCK: AN 18TH-CENTURY VILLAGE

From Bath, take the A4 about 12 miles to the A350, then head south to Lacock, a National Trust village showcasing English architecture from the 13th through the 18th centuries.

Unlike many villages that disappeared or were absorbed into bigger communities, Lacock remained largely unchanged because of a single family, the Talbots, who owned most of it and preferred to keep their traditional village traditional. Turned over to the National Trust in 1944, it's now one of the best preserved villages in all of England with many 16th-century homes, gardens, and churches. Notable is **St. Cyriac Church,** Church Street, a Perpendicular-style church built by wealthy wool merchants between the 14th and 17th centuries.

Lacock Abbey, High Street (☎ 01249/730227), founded in 1232 for Augustinian canonesses, was updated and turned into a private home in the 16th century. It fell victim to Henry VIII's Dissolution, when, upon establishing the Church of England, he seized existing church properties to bolster his own wealth. Admission for all church properties is £5.50 ($8.80) for adults and £3 ($4.80) for children, family ticket £15 ($24). Open April through October, daily from 11am to 5pm; November to March, Wednesday to Monday 11am to 5pm.

While on the grounds, stop by the medieval barn, home to the **Fox Talbot Museum** (☎ 01249/730459). It was here that William Henry Fox Talbot carried out his early experiments with photography, making the first known photographic prints in 1833. In his honor, the barn is now a photography museum featuring some of those early prints. Open daily, March through October from 11am to 5pm. Admission is £3.50 ($5.60) for adults, £2 ($3.20) children.

Where to Stay
The **George Inn** (see below) also rents rooms.

At the Sign of the Angel. Church St., Lacock, Chippenham, Wiltshire SN15 2LA. ☎ 01249/730230. Fax 01249/730527. 9 units. TV. £80–£95 ($128–$152) double. Rates include English breakfast. AE, V.

This ancient inn was built in the 14th century by a wool merchant. It has plenty of character with its sloping floors, low oak-beamed ceilings, and very large fireplaces in the public rooms. The rooms at the inn are quiet and split between the main building and a 17th-century garden cottage. Each of the rooms is decorated differently with a host of antiques. One of the rooms even has a magnificently carved Spanish bed that is said to have belonged to Isambard Kingdom Brunel, the famous railway and canal builder.

Dining: The inn's restaurant offers good, moderately priced meals in an atmosphere where you expect to see Shakespeare walk through the door at any moment. Guests are served under a heavily oak-beamed ceiling, and a fire is built whenever there is a chill in the air.

Where to Dine

The George Inn. 4 West St., Lacock, Wiltshire SN15 2LH. ☎ **01249/730263.** Main courses £4.95–£10.25 ($7.90–$16.40). AE, MC, V. Easter–Oct daily 11am–11pm; Nov–Easter daily 10am–3pm and 5:15pm–11pm. ENGLISH.

Housed in a building that has been used as a pub since 1361, The George Inn has been equipped with some modern conveniences since then, and is today run by John Glass. It still maintains many of its vestiges from the past—uneven floors, a large open fireplace with its very own dog-wheel once used for spit roasting—and has an extensive garden used as a dining area in the summer. There's even a children's playground. About 30 daily specials are chalked onto a blackboard in addition to a regular menu of fish, meat, and vegetarian dishes. Examples of meat dishes include kangaroo, ostrich, and beef steaks. Two of the most popular desserts are bread-and-butter pudding and sticky toffee pudding.

John Glass's wife, Judy, runs a B&B out of the family farmhouse. **The Lower Home Farm** (☎ **01225/790045**) has three double rooms, each with a private bath, that start at £35 ($56) per night, including English breakfast. The grounds are made up of 100 acres of gardens, with plenty of walks and even a lake. It all adds up to a peaceful and serene setting. No credit cards are accepted at the farm, but rates include taxi service to the George Inn, from which guests can walk to all the attractions in this National Trust village.

CASTLE COMBE

Once voted England's prettiest village, this was the site where the financially disastrous *Dr. Doolittle* was filmed, and the 15th-century Upper Manor House, used as Rex Harrison's residence in the movie, is its most famous site. The entire village, though, can just about be absorbed in a glance. Consisting of one street lined with cottages (known simply as "The Street"), it is the quintessential sleepy village. It's easily explored in a morning or afternoon, before moving on to your next destination. Located 10 miles northeast of Bath, take A46 north 9.5 kilometers (6 miles) to A420, then head east to Ford, following the signs north to Castle Combe. From Lacock, take A350 north to Chippenham, then get on A420 west and follow the signs.

Where to Stay & Dine

Manor House Hotel & Golf Club. Castle Combe, Wiltshire SN14 7HR. ☎ **01249/ 782206.** Fax 01249/782159. 45 units. TV TEL. £120–£350 ($192–$560) double. AE, DC, MC, V.

The house and accompanying estate date from the 14th-century and served at one time as the baronial seat in Castle Combe. The main building and its accompanying cottages sit regally on 47 acres of gardens, with wooded trails, a lake, and an 18-hole golf course. South of the manor flows the trout-stocked River Bybrook, where fishing is permitted. The rooms are individually decorated with tasteful furnishings and antiques, and some have four-poster beds. Tea- and coffeemakers complete each guest room. The public rooms are oak paneled and are appointed with period pieces, including an 18th-century frieze of Shakespeare's Falstaff in the main lounge.

Dining/Amenities: Restaurant (formal attire for dinner), bar, swimming pool, and tennis courts.

4 Bristol

120 miles W of London; 13 miles NW of Bath

Bristol, the largest city in the West Country, is just across the Bristol Channel from Wales and is a good place to base yourself for touring western Britain. This historic inland port is linked to the sea by 7 miles of the navigable Somerset River. Bristol has long been rich in seafaring traditions and has many links with the early colonization of America. In fact, some claim that the new continent was named after a Bristol town clerk, Richard Ameryke. In 1497, John Cabot sailed from Bristol, and pioneered the discovery of the northern half of the New World.

Bath is more elegant and pretentious, while Bristol has a working class that definitely votes Labour. Even so, Bristol has some limited attractions, like a colorful harbor life, that make it at least a good overnight stop in your exploration of the West Country.

ESSENTIALS

GETTING THERE   Bristol Airport (☎ **01275/474444**) is conveniently situated beside the main A38 road, just over 7 miles from the city center.

Rail services to and from the area are among the fastest and most efficient in Britain. **British Rail** runs very frequent services from London's Paddington Station to each of Bristol's two main stations: Temple Meads in the center of Bristol, and Parkway on the city's northern outskirts. The trip takes 1½ hours. For rail information, call ☎ **0345/484950** in the U.K., or 01603/764776 in the U.S.

National Express buses depart every hour during the day from London's Victoria Coach Station, making the trip in 2½ hours. For more information and schedules, call ☎ **0990/808080**.

If you're driving, head west from London on the M4.

VISITOR INFORMATION   The **Tourist Information Centre** is at St. Nicholas Church, St. Nicholas Street (☎ **0117/9260767**). In winter, it's open Monday through Saturday from 9:30am to 5:30pm and Sunday 11am to 4pm; 9:30am to 5:30pm in summer.

EXPLORING THE TOWN

Guided **walking tours** are conducted in summer and last about 1½ hours. They depart from Neptune's Statue on Saturday at 2:30pm and on Thursday at 7pm. Guided tours are also conducted through Clifton, a suburb of Bristol, which has more Georgian houses than Bath. Consult the tourist office (see above) for more information.

SS Great Britain. City Docks, Great Western Dock. ☎ **0117/9260680.** Admission £4.95 ($7.90) adults, £3.85 ($6.15) senior citizens, £3.30 ($5.30) children. Apr–Oct daily 10am–5:30pm; Nov–Mar daily 10am–4:30pm. Bus: 511 from city center, a rather long haul.

In Bristol, the world's first iron steamship and luxury liner has been partially restored to its 1843 appearance, although it's still a long way from earning its old title of a "floating palace." This vessel, which weighs 3,443 tons, was designed by Isambard Brunel, a Victorian engineer.

Incidentally, in 1831 (at the age of 25), Brunel began a Bristol landmark, Suspension Bridge, over the 250-foot-deep Somerset Gorge at Clifton.

Bristol Cathedral. College Green. ☎ **0117/9264879.** Free admission; £2 ($3.20) donation requested. Daily 8am–6pm. Bus: 8 or 9.

Construction of the cathedral, once an Augustinian abbey, was begun in the 12th century, and the central tower was added in 1466. The chapter house and gatehouse are good examples of late Norman architecture. The cathedral's interior was singled out for praise by Sir John Betjeman, the late poet laureate.

In 1539, the abbey was closed and the incomplete nave was demolished. The building was turned into the Cathedral Church of the Holy and Undivided Trinity in 1542. In 1868, plans were drawn up to complete the name to its medieval design. The architect, G. E. Street, found the original pillar bases, so that the cathedral is much as it would have been when it was still the abbey church. J. L. Pearson added the two towers at the west end and further reordered the interior.

The eastern end of the cathedral, especially the choir, gives the structure a unique place in the development of British and European architecture. The nave, choir, and aisles are all of the same height, making a large hall. Bristol Cathedral is the major example of a "hall church" in Great Britain and one of the finest anywhere in the world.

St. Mary Redcliffe Church. 10 Redcliffe Way. ☎ **0117/9291487.** Free admission. June–Aug daily 8am–8pm; Sept–May daily 8am–5pm.

The parish church of St. Mary Redcliffe is one of the finest examples of Gothic architecture in England. Queen Elizabeth I, on her visit in 1574, is reported to have described it as "the fairest, goodliest and most famous parish church in England," and Thomas Chatterton, the boy poet, called it "the pride of Bristol and the western land." The American Chapel houses the tomb and armor of Adm. Sir William Penn, father of Pennsylvania's founder.

Theatre Royal. King St. ☎ **0117/9493993.** Box office 0117/9877877. Tickets £4.50–£18.50 ($7.20–$29.60). Any City Centre bus.

Built in 1766, this is now the oldest working playhouse in the United Kingdom. It is the home of the Bristol Old Vic. Backstage tours leave from the foyer. Tours are run Friday and Saturday at 12:30pm and cost £2 ($3.20) for adults and £1.50 ($2.40) for children and students under 19. Call the box office for the current schedule.

SHOPPING

Many major shops are now open on Sunday.

The biggest shopping complex is **Broadmead,** mainly pedestrianized with branches of all High Street stores, plus cafes and restaurants. Many specialty shops are found at **Clifton Village,** in a Georgian setting where houses are interspaced with parks and gardens. Here you'll find a wide array of shops selling antiques, arts and crafts, and designer clothing. Opened in 1991, the **Galleries** is a totally enclosed mall, providing three levels of shopping and restaurants. The **St. Nicholas Markets** opened in 1745, and are still going strong, selling antiques, memorabilia, handcrafted gifts, jewelry, and haberdashery. The **West End** is another major shopping area, taking in Park Street, Queen's Road, and Whiteladies Road. These streets are known for their clothing outlets, bookstores, and unusual gift items from around the world, as well as wine bars and restaurants.

The best antique markets are **The Bristol Antique Centre,** Brunel Rooms, Broad Plain, **Clifton Antiques Market** and **New Antiques Centre,** the Mall in Clifton, and **Clifton Arcade,** Boyces Avenue, also in Clifton. Both Clifton outlets are closed on Monday but The Bristol Antique Centre is open daily, including Sunday.

Spending the Night in a Tudor Castle

Twelve miles north of Bristol, Thornbury is known for its genuine Tudor castle, which is now a hotel. Many of the crenellations and towers were built in 1511. It was the last defensive castle ever constructed in England, and its owner was beheaded by Henry VIII for certain words spoken in haste. Henry confiscated the lands and, to celebrate, stayed here for 10 days with Anne Boleyn in 1535. Later, Mary Tudor spent 3 years of her adolescence here.

Today, you can stay at ✪ **Thornbury Castle** (☎ **01454/281182;** fax 01454/416188) and step back into history. The castle is surrounded by thick stone walls, trees, vineyards, and gardens. After you check in, you reach the 17 bedrooms and 1 suite by way of stone and spiral staircases. Every room is filled with character, and is superbly fitted with fine furniture and many amenities, including televisions and telephones; eight have four-posters. At night the baronial public rooms are lit by candle. The main public lounge has a splendid stone fireplace, along with Tudor and Elizabethan portraits on the walls and high mullioned windows.

Rates, which include continental breakfast, are £120 to £245 ($192 to $392) for a double; £155 to £335 ($248 to $536) for the suite. American Express, Diners Club, Master Card, and Visa are accepted. To get there from Bristol, take the B4061; continue downhill to the monumental water pump, bear left, and continue for 300 yards.

We also recommend Thornbury for its cuisine. French and English dishes highlight the menus at the hotel's three dining rooms. Chef Steven Black changes the menu daily and uses only the best and freshest ingredients to prepare his innovative meals. Dishes might include boned wood pigeon with mangold, a dark green-leaf vegetable of the mangrel-wurzel plant, which many consider superior to spinach. He also takes care to create some very English desserts, such as treacle tart with Cornish clotted cream. The good wine list is especially strong on Bordeaux and Burgundy. You can even sample Thornbury Castle's own wine, made from the Muller-Thurgau vines in the castle's vineyards.

Even if you're not staying at the hotel, you can call for reservations in the dining room. The two-course main menu, available daily from noon to 2pm, costs £19 to £23 ($30.40 to $36.80). Dinner goes for £35 to £39 ($56 to $62.40) per person and is served from 7 to 9:30pm daily.

WHERE TO STAY
EXPENSIVE

Bristol Marriott. Lower Castle St., Bristol, Somerset BS1 3AD. ☎ **800/228-9290** in the U.S. and Canada, or 0117/9294281. Fax 0117/9225838. 297 units. A/C TV TEL. Mon–Thurs £97–£125 ($155.20–$200) double; £160 ($256) suite. Fri–Sun from £65 ($104) double. AE, DC, MC, V. Bus: 9.

In the heart of town at the edge of Castle Park, this modern 11-story hotel is one of Bristol's tallest buildings, and it's far superior to the Hilton in amenities, style, and comfort. Many improvements have been undertaken, since this place used to be a rather ordinary Holiday Inn. It attracts many business travelers as well as foreign tourists. The comfortable rooms are conservatively modern, and public areas are stylish and spacious—all in the upscale traditions of the Marriott chain.

Dining: The more elegant of the hotel's two restaurants is the Château. Less formal is the Brasserie, where platters of British and continental food are served.

Amenities: Heated indoor swimming pool, fully equipped health club.

Grand Hotel. Broad St., Bristol, Somerset BS1 2EL. ☎ **0117/9291645.** Fax 0117/9227619. 194 units. TV TEL. £110 ($176) double; £165–£195 ($264–$312) suite. Discount (minimum of 2 consecutive nights Fri–Sun): £84 ($134.40) double, including half board. AE, DC, MC, V. Bus: 8 or 9.

This Victorian grand hotel sits in the commercial heart of town, adorned with rows of fan-shaped windows and intricate exterior cornices. Inside there are lavishly ornate crystal chandeliers and a good many Victorian details. The rooms, traditionally furnished and well maintained, are more conservative and modern than the public areas.

Dining/Diversions: There are two bars (one with a nautical theme), and a pair of comfortable restaurants, including The Brass Nails, which serves good fixed-price dinners (the White Lion is less formal and less expensive).

Hilton National Bristol. Redcliffe Way, Bristol, Somerset BS1 6NJ. ☎ **800/445-8667** in the U.S. and Canada, or 0117/9260041. Fax 0117/9230089. 201 units. TV TEL. £105 ($168) double; £150 ($240) suite. AE, DC, MC, V. Bus: 1 or 2.

Situated conveniently amid the commercial bustle of the center of town, this modern hotel offers a good, safe haven for the night (though some readers have complained that the pealing bells of St. Mary Redcliffe, next door, kept them awake). The 6-story Hilton is designed in a rather bland international style. Rooms have tea- and coffeemakers.

Dining: Its split-level restaurant, The Kiln, is located inside the brick-lined walls of a former 16th-century glass kiln refurbished in the style of a French brasserie, and serves English and French specialties.

INEXPENSIVE

Alandale Hotel. 4 Tyndall's Park Rd., Clifton, Bristol, Somerset BS8 1PG. ☎ **0117/ 9735407.** Fax 0117/9237965. 11 units. TV TEL. £55 ($88) double. Rates include English breakfast. MC, V. Bus: 8 or 9.

This elegant early Victorian house retains many of its original features, including a marble fireplace and ornate plasterwork. Note the fine staircase in the imposing entrance hall. The hotel is under the supervision of Mr. Burgess, who still observes the old traditions of personal service. Afternoon tea is available, as are sandwiches, drinks, and snacks in the lounge (up to 11:15pm). A continental breakfast is served in your room until 10am, unless you'd prefer the full English breakfast in the dining room. All the plainly furnished rooms have beverage-makers and hair dryers.

Oakfield Hotel. 52–54 Oakfield Rd., Clifton, Bristol, Somerset BS8 2BG. ☎ **0117/ 9733643.** Fax 0117/9744141. 27 units, none with private bathroom. TV. £37 ($59.20) double. Rates include English breakfast. No credit cards. Bus: 8 or 9.

Instead of finding lodging in the center of Bristol, many visitors head for the leafy Georgian suburb of Clifton, 1 mile north, near the famous Suspension Bridge. This impressive guest house from the 1840s, with an Italian facade, would be called a town house in New York. It's on a quiet street, and everything is kept spick-and-span under the watchful eye of Mrs. P. Hurley. Each room has hot and cold running water and central heating, although the furnishings are modest. For another £6.50 ($10.40) you can enjoy a simple dinner.

WHERE TO DINE

✪ Harvey's Restaurant. 12 Denmark St. ☎ **0117/9275034.** Reservations required. Main courses £17–£20 ($27.20–$32); fixed-price lunch £14.95–£17.95 ($23.90 $28.70); fixed-price dinner £32.95–£39.95 ($52.70–$63.90). AE, DC, MC, V. Mon–Fri noon 1:15pm; Mon Sat 7 10:15pm. BRITISH.

This restaurant is one of the finest in this part of England. It's located in medieval cellars that have belonged to Harvey's of Bristol, famous for Harvey's Bristol Cream sherry, since 1796. Chef-manager Daniel Galmiche serves modern classic French cuisine under continuing and award-winning standards.

Look out for touches of the Far East and Mediterranean, too. Try zesty and flavorful creations such as panfried foie gras with apple and raisins for a starter, followed by panfried fillet of turbot with a celeriac puree, or roast farm pigeon with sautéed potatoes and an herb and sherry vinegar sauce. A special dessert is the gratinated pink grapefruit with saffron-and-honey ice cream. The menu is complemented by an extensive wine list, with the red wines of Bordeaux a particular specialty.

The adjoining historic cellars accommodate Harvey's Wine Museum, with collections of English 18th-century drinking glasses, antique decanters, corkscrews, bottles, silverware, and furniture. The museum is open daily, and there are regular guided tours with tutored tastings. Restaurant patrons can usually browse in the museum before their meal.

Michael's. 129 Hotwell Rd. ☎ **0117/9276190.** Reservations required for Sat dinner, and recommended at other times. 2-course fixed-price menus £14.95 ($23.90) at Sun lunch, £21.95 ($35.10) at dinner. AE, DC, MC, V. Sun noon–3pm; Mon–Sat 7–11pm. From city center, take Anchor Rd., left lane becomes Hotwell Rd. FRENCH/MODERN ENGLISH.

This charming and popular restaurant is near Clifton on a highway leading toward the Somerset Gorge. In its pleasant bar, decorated like an Edwardian parlor, an open fire burns. The dining room is also bright and inviting. The fixed-price menus are imaginative and change according to the seasonal produce. The restaurant also caters to vegans; the vegetarian meals offer a selection of four to five dishes. The service is informal and enthusiastic. If you want a cigarette, stick to the bar.

BRISTOL AFTER DARK

Bath may be more stiff and formal, but Bristol clubs and pubs are more laid-back, drawing more working-class Brits than yuppies.

Some of the best pubs are along King Street, especially **Llandoger Trow,** 5 King St. (☎ **0117/926-0783**), with its mellow West Country ambience. If you'd like to meet up with some students, their favorite watering hole is the **Hobgoblin,** 2 Bryon Place (☎ **0117/929-9322**).

Lakota, 6 Upper York St. (☎ **0117/942-6193**), off Stokes Croft, is a club known for its all-night "groove parties," with a funk soundtrack. However, the cover is a bit steep, ranging from £7 to £12 ($11.20 to $19.20), depending on what's featured that night.

In a converted freight steamer moored on the Grove, **Thelka** (☎ **0117/929-3301**) is a venue where acid jazz rains down. The other leading venues for jazz are **The Old Duke,** King Street (☎ **0117/929-7137**), and the **Bebop Club** at The Bear, Hatwell Road (☎ **0117/987-7796**). The leading comedy club is **Jester's,** Watershed, Cherdeham Road (☎ **0117/909-6655**).

The premier gay club is **Just,** 1 Fiennes St. (☎ **0117/9304675**), charging only a £1 ($1.60) cover. They bill themselves as England's first 24-hour gay club.

5 Wells & the Caves of Mendip

123 miles SW of London; 21 miles SW of Bath

To the south of the Mendip Hills, the cathedral town of Wells is a medieval gem. Wells was a vital link in the Saxon kingdom of Wessex—important long before the arrival of William the Conqueror. Once the seat of a bishopric, it was eventually toppled from its ecclesiastical hegemony by the rival city of Bath. But the subsequent loss of prestige has paid off handsomely for Wells today: After experiencing the pinnacle of prestige, it fell into a slumber—and much of its old look was preserved.

Many visitors come only for the afternoon or morning, look at the cathedral, then press on to Bath for the evening. But though it's rather sleepy, Wells makes a tranquil stopover in one of its old inns.

ESSENTIALS

GETTING THERE   Wells has good bus connections with its surrounding towns and cities. Take the train to Bath (see section 3 of this chapter) and continue the rest of the way by Badgerline bus no. 175. Departures are every hour Monday through Saturday and every 2 hours on Sunday. Both no. 376 and 378 buses run between Bristol and Glastonbury every hour Monday through Saturday and every 2 hours on Sunday. Call ☎ 01179/553231 for bus schedules and information.

If you're driving, take M4 west from London, cutting south on A4 toward Bath and continuing along A39 into Wells.

VISITOR INFORMATION   The **Tourist Information Centre** is at the Town Hall, Market Place (☎ 01749/672552), and is open daily November to March from 10am to 4pm and April to October from 9:30am to 5:30pm.

SEEING THE SIGHTS

After a visit to the cathedral, walk along its cloisters to the moat-surrounded **Bishop's Palace.** The Great Hall, built in the 13th century, is in ruins. Finally, the street known as the **Vicars' Close** is one of the most beautifully preserved streets in Europe.

Easily reached by heading west out of Wells, the Caves of Mendip are two exciting natural attractions: the great caves of Cheddar and Wookey Hole; see below.

✪ **Wells Cathedral.** In the center of town. ☎ 01749/674483. Admission free, but donations of £3 ($4.80) adults, £2 ($3.20) seniors, £1 ($1.60) students and children appreciated. Daily 7:15am–6pm or dusk in summer.

Begun in the 12th century, this is a well-preserved example of early English architecture. The medieval sculpture (six tiers of hundreds of statues recently restored) of its west front is without equal. The western facade was completed in the mid–13th century. The landmark central tower was erected in the 14th century, with the fan-vaulting attached later. The inverted arches were added to strengthen the top-heavy structure.

Much of the stained glass dates from the 14th century. The fan-vaulted lady chapel, also from the 14th century, is in the decorated style. To the north is the vaulted chapter house, built in the 13th century and recently restored. Look also for a medieval astronomical clock in the north transept.

Wookey Hole Caves & Paper Mill. Wookey Hole, near Wells. ☎ 01749/672243. 2-hour tour £6.50 ($10.40) adults, £3.50 ($5.60) children 16 and under, £18 ($28.80) family ticket. Apr–Oct daily 9:30am–5:30pm; Nov–Mar daily 10:30am–4:30pm. Closed Dec 17–25. Follow the signs from the center of Wells for 2 miles. Bus: 172 from Wells.

Just 2 miles from Wells, you'll first come to the source of the Axe River. In the first chamber of the caves, as legend has it, is the Witch of Wookey turned to stone. These caves are believed to have been inhabited by prehistoric people at least 60,000 years ago. A tunnel, opened in 1975, leads to the chambers unknown in early times and previously accessible only to divers.

Leaving the caves, you follow a canal path to the mill, where paper has been made by hand since the 17th century. Here, the best-quality handmade paper is made by skilled workers according to the tradition of their ancient craft. Also in the mill are "hands-on vats," where visitors can try their hand at making a sheet of paper, and an Edwardian Penny Pier Arcade where new pennies can be exchanged for old ones with which to play the original machines. Other attractions include the Magical Mirror Maze, an enclosed passage of multiple image mirrors, and Movie Mania, celebrating a century of films.

Cheddar Showcaves & Gorge. Cheddar, Somerset. ☎ **01934/742343.** Admission £6.90 ($11.05) adults, £4 ($6.40) children 5–15, 4 and under free. Easter–Sept daily 10am–5pm; Oct–Easter daily 10:30am–4:30pm. Closed Dec 24–25. From A38 or M5, cut onto A371 to Cheddar village.

A short distance from Bath, Bristol, and Wells is the village of Cheddar, home of cheddar cheese. It lies at the foot of Cheddar Gorge, within which are the Cheddar Caves, underground caverns with impressive formations. The caves are more than a million years old, including Gough's Cave, with its cathedral-like caverns, and Cox's Cave, with its calcite sculptures and brilliant colors. The Crystal Quest is a dark walk "fantasy adventure" taking you deep underground, and in the Cheddar Gorge Heritage Centre is displayed a 9,000-year-old skeleton. You can also climb Jacob's Ladder for cliff-top walks and Pavey's Lookout Tower for views over Somerset—on a clear day you may even see Wales.

Adults and children over 12 years of age can book an Adventure Caving expedition for £7.50 ($12), which includes overalls, helmets, and lamps. Other attractions include local craftspeople at work, ranging from the glassblower to the sweets maker, plus the Cheddar Cheese & Cider Depot.

Chewton Cheese Dairy. Priory Farm, Chewton Mendip. ☎ **01761/241666.** Admission free. Guided tour £2.50 ($4) adults, £2 ($3.20) senior citizens, £1.50 ($2.40) children 4–14, 3 and under free. General admission free. Daily 9am–4:30pm. Head 6 miles north of Wells on the A39 Bristol–Wells rd.

The dairy is owned by Lord Chewton, and visitors are welcome to watch through the viewing window in the restaurant as the traditional cheese-making process is carried out most mornings. A video presentation is featured in a spacious screening room. Guided tours are offered daily April to October at 11:30am, 12:15pm, 1pm, and 1:45pm. Although the dairy is open on Sunday and Thursday, there are no cheese-making demonstrations then. You can purchase a "truckle" (or wheel) of mature cheddar to send home. The restaurant offers coffee, snacks, farmhouse lunches, and cream teas.

WHERE TO STAY

✪ **Star Hotel.** 18 High St., Wells, Somerset BA5 2SQ. ☎ **01749/670500.** Fax 01749/672654. 12 units. TV. £68 ($108.80) double. Rates include English breakfast. AE, DC, MC, V.

The Star had its origins sometime in the 16th century but is most closely associated with the great coaching era, though the hotel front was restored in the Georgian period. The cobbled carriageway, still preserved, leads to the dining room—once the stables. The simply furnished rooms have been modernized, yet retain their old charm. Copper and brass are extensively used for decoration, and several original stone walls and timbers have been exposed.

The inn has a good reputation for traditional British fare. Seasonal à la carte dishes are presented, plus a full selection of wines.

The Swan Hotel. 11 Sadler St., Wells, Somerset BA5 2RX. ☎ **800/528-1234** in the U.S. and Canada, or 01749/678877. Fax 01749/677647. 38 units. TV TEL. £89.50–£97.50 ($143.20–$156) double. Rates include English breakfast. AE, DC, MC, V.

Set behind a stucco facade on one of the town's main streets, this place was originally built in the 15th century as a coaching inn. Today, facing the west front of Wells Cathedral, it is the best of the inns within the town's central core. Several of the well-furnished bedrooms are equipped with four-poster beds. The spacious and elegant public rooms stretch out to the left and right of the entrance as you enter. Both ends have a blazing and baronial fireplace, beamed ceilings, and paneling.

WHERE TO DINE

Market Place Hotel Restaurant. Market Place. Wells, Somerset BA5 2RW. ☎ **01749/ 672616.** Lunch £4.50–£7.25 ($7.20–$11.60); main courses £9–£11 ($14.40–$17.60). AE, MC, V. Daily noon–2pm and 7:30–9:30pm. BRITISH.

This is one of the top places to dine in Wells. The menu is limited but usually well chosen. Starters might include Maryland crab cakes with leeks and sliced or home-cured salmon basted in a citrus dressing. Main courses run the gamut—everything from panfried fillet of sea bass with "crushed" potatoes to roast pork fillet with black pudding, glazed apples, and calvados.

The hotel also rents 34 rooms, each furnished in a contemporary style, with private bath. Rates range from £89.50 to £97.50 ($143.20 to $156) for a double, including an English breakfast.

6 Glastonbury Abbey

136 miles SW of London; 26 miles S of Bristol; 6 miles SW of Wells

Glastonbury may be one of the oldest inhabited sites in Britain. Excavations have revealed Iron Age lakeside villages on its periphery (some of the discoveries that were dug up can be seen in a little museum on High Street). After the destruction of its once-great abbey, the town lost prestige; today it is just a market town with a rich history. The ancient gatehouse entry to the abbey is a museum, and its principal exhibit is a scale model of the abbey and its community buildings as they stood in 1539, at the time of the dissolution.

Where Arthurian myth once held sway, there's now a subculture of mystics, spiritualists, and hippies, all drawn to the kooky legends whirling around the town. Glastonbury is England's New Age center, where Christian spirituality blends with druidic beliefs. The average visitor arrives just to see the ruins and the monuments, but the streets are often filled with people trying to track down Jesus, if not Arthur and Lancelot.

ESSENTIALS

GETTING THERE Go to Taunton, which is on the London-Penzance line that leaves frequently from London's Paddington Station. For rail information, call ☎ **0345/484950** in the U.K. or 01603/764776 in the U.S. From Taunton, you'll have to take a bus the rest of the way. Take the Southern National bus (no. 17) to

Glastonbury, between Monday and Saturday. There are one to three departures per day, and the trip takes 1 hour. Call **Southern National** at ☎ **01823/272033** for details.

You could also leave London's Paddington Station for Bristol Temple Meads, and go the rest of the way by Badgerline bus no. 376. It runs from Bristol via Wells to Glastonbury every hour Monday through Saturday; on Sunday, the schedule is reduced to every 2 hours. The trip takes 1½ hours. For information about Badgerline bus service, call ☎ **01179/553231.**

One **National Express** bus a day (no. 402) leaves London's Victoria Coach Station at 6:30pm and arrives in Glastonbury at 9:55pm. For more information and schedules, call ☎ **0990/808080.**

If you're driving, take M4 west from London, then cut south on A4 via Bath to Glastonbury.

VISITOR INFORMATION   The **Tourist Information Centre** is at The Tribunal, 9 High St. (☎ **01458/832954**). It's open Easter through September, Sunday to Thursday from 10am to 5pm, Friday and Saturday from 10am to 5:30pm; off-season, daily from 10am to 4pm.

SEEING THE SIGHTS

✪ **Glastonbury Abbey.** ☎ **01458/832267** for information. Admission £2.50 ($4) adults, £2 ($3.20) students and seniors, £1 ($1.60) children under 16, £5.50 ($8.80) family ticket. Daily 9:30am–6pm or dusk.

Though it's no more than a ruined sanctuary today, Glastonbury Abbey was once one of the wealthiest and most prestigious monasteries in England. It provides Glastonbury's claim to historical greatness, an assertion augmented by legendary links to such figures as Joseph of Arimathea, King Arthur, Queen Guinevere, and St. Patrick.

It is said that Joseph of Arimathea journeyed to what was then the Isle of Avalon, with the Holy Grail in his possession. According to tradition, he buried the chalice at the foot of the conical Glastonbury Tor, and a stream of blood burst forth. You can scale this more than 500-foot-high hill today, on which rests a 15th-century tower.

Joseph, so it goes, erected a church of wattle in Glastonbury. (The town, in fact, may have had the oldest church in England, as excavations have shown.) And at one point, the saint is said to have leaned against his staff, which was immediately transformed into a fully blossoming tree; a cutting alleged to have survived from the Holy Thorn can be seen on the abbey grounds today—it blooms at Christmastime. Some historians have traced this particular story back to Tudor times.

Another famous chapter in the story, popularized by Tennyson in the Victorian era, holds that King Arthur and Queen Guinevere were buried on the abbey grounds. In 1191 the monks dug up the skeletons of two bodies on the south side of the lady chapel, said to be those of the king and queen. In 1278, in the presence of Edward I, the bodies were removed and transferred to a black marble tomb in the choir. Both the burial spot and the shrine are marked today.

A large Benedictine Abbey of St. Mary grew out of the early wattle church. St. Dunstan, who was born nearby, was the abbot in the 10th century and later became archbishop of Canterbury. Edmund, Edgar, and Edmund "Ironside," three early English kings, were buried at the abbey.

In 1184 a fire destroyed most of the abbey and its vast treasures. It was eventually rebuilt, after much difficulty, only to be dissolved by Henry VIII. Its last abbot, Richard Whiting, was hanged at Glastonbury Tor. Like the Roman forum, the abbey was used as a stone quarry for years.

Today you can visit the ruins of the chapel, linked by an early English "Galilee" to the nave of the abbey. The best-preserved building on the grounds is a 14th-century octagonal Abbot's Kitchen, where oxen were once roasted whole to feed the wealthier pilgrims.

Somerset Rural Life Museum. On the Abbey Farm on Chilkwell St. ☎ **01458/831197.** Admission £2.20 ($3.50) adults; £1.65 ($2.65) students; 50p (80¢) children and seniors; family ticket £5 ($8). Apr–Oct Tues–Fri 10am–5pm, Sat–Sun 2–6pm; Nov–Mar Tues–Fri 10am–5pm, Sat 11am–4pm.

The history of the Somerset countryside since the early 19th century is chronicled here. Its centerpiece is the abbey barn, built around 1370. The magnificent timbered room, stone tiles, and sculptural details (including the head of Edward III) make it special. There is also a Victorian farmhouse comprising exhibits that illustrate farming in Somerset during the "horse age" as well as domestic and social life in Victorian times. In summer, there are demonstrations of butter making, weaving, basketwork, and many other traditional craft and farming activities, which are rapidly disappearing.

WHERE TO STAY

The George & Pilgrims. 1 High St., Glastonbury, Somerset BA6 9DP. ☎ **01458/831146.** Fax 01458/832252. 13 units. TV TEL. £68–£78 ($108.80–$124.80) double. Rates include English breakfast. AE, DC, MC, V.

One of the few pre-Reformation hostelries still left in England, this inn in the center of town once offered hospitality to Glastonbury pilgrims. Its facade looks like a medieval castle, with stone-mullioned windows with leaded glass. Some of the rooms were formerly monks' cells; others have four-poster beds, veritable carved monuments of oak. You may be given the Henry VIII Room, from which the king watched the burning of the abbey in 1539.

The building's original kitchen now functions as a bar, where you can enjoy a pint beneath the span of old oak beams. Nearby is a brasserie, specializing in English and continental food (see "Where to Dine," below).

Number 3 Hotel. 3 Magdalene St., Glastonbury, Somerset BA6 9EW. ☎ **01458/832129.** 5 units (with tub or shower). TV TEL. £70 ($112) double. Rates include continental breakfast. MC, V. Closed Dec–Jan.

John and Ann Tynan have operated this small family property, adjoining the Glastonbury ruins, since the mid-1980s. The couple closed the on-site restaurant so Mrs. Tynan, a chiropractor, could devote her time to administering sports-therapy massage and aromatherapy to guests. Housed in a Georgian structure, the double rooms are all tastefully and individually decorated and have beverage-makers.

WHERE TO DINE

The Brasserie. In the George & Pilgrims Hotel, 1 High St. ☎ **01458/831146.** Reservations recommended. Main courses £5.25–£9.25 ($8.40–$14.80); fixed-price 3-course meal £10.50 ($16.80). Fixed-price meal for guests of The George & Pilgrims Hotel only. AE, MC, V. Daily noon–2:30pm; Sun–Thurs 7–9:30pm, Fri–Sat 7–10pm. ENGLISH/CONTINENTAL.

This is a solid, reliable choice in a town not known for its dining. There's a daily fixed-price menu for hotel guests, as well as a set menu for nonguests and an à la carte menu with the chef's special of the day posted on blackboards. À la carte dishes may include peppered soup, warm avocado and walnuts in a light Stilton sauce, and vegetarian choices such as broccoli-and-cream-cheese bake or vegetable Stroganoff with a timbale of saffron and wild rice.

7 Longleat House & Stourhead Gardens

If you're driving, you can visit both Longleat and Stourhead in one busy day. Follow the directions to Longleat given below, then drive 6 miles down B3092 to Stourton, a village just off the highway, 3 miles northwest of Mere (A303), to reach Stourhead.

✪ **Longleat House and Safari Park.** ☎ **01985/844400.** Admission to Longleat House £5 ($8) adults, £4 ($6.40) children. Safari Park £5.50 ($8.80) adults, £4.50 ($7.20) children. Special exhibitions and rides require separate admission tickets. Passport tickets for all of Longleat's attractions £12 ($19.20) adults, £10 ($16) children. House open mid-Mar to Sept daily 10am–6pm, Oct–Easter daily 10am–4pm. Park open mid-Mar to Nov 1 daily 10am–6pm (last cars admitted at 5:30pm or sunset). From Bath or Salisbury, take the train or bus to Warminster; then take a taxi or Davron Coach no. 53, the local bus, to Longleat (about 10 min.). You'll have to walk the last 2 miles from the bus stop up the road to Longleat House. Driving from Bath, take A36 south to Warminster; then follow the signposts to Longleat House. From Salisbury, take A36 north to Warminster, following the signposts to Longleat House.

A magnificent Elizabethan house built in the early Renaissance style, Longleat House was owned by the seventh marquess of Bath. On first glimpse it's romantic enough, but once you've been inside, it's hard not to be dazzled by the lofty rooms and their exquisite paintings and furnishings.

From the Elizabethan Great Hall and the library to the State Rooms and the grand staircase, the house is filled with all manner of beautiful things. The walls of the State Dining Room are adorned with fine tapestries and paintings, whereas the room itself has displays of silver and plate. The library represents the finest private collection in the country. The Victorian kitchens are open, offering a glimpse of life "below the stairs" in a well-ordered country home. Various exhibitions are mounted in the stable yard.

Adjoining Longleat House is **Longleat Safari Park.** The park hosts several species of magnificent and endangered wild animals, including rhinoceros and elephants, which are free to roam these bucolic surroundings. Here you can walk among giraffes, zebras, camels, and llamas, and view lions and tigers, as well as England's only white tiger, from your car. You can also ride on a safari boat around the park's lake to see gorillas and feed sea lions. You can see the park by train for a railway adventure, or visit the tropical butterfly garden.

The park provides plenty of theme-parklike thrills as well, including an Adventure Castle, Doctor Who exhibition, and the world's longest maze, **The Maze of Love.** Commissioned by the marquess of Bath and designed by Graham Burgess, the maze was inspired by the Garden of Love in Villandry, France, and Botticelli's painting *Primavera.* It lies between Longleat House and the Orangery, and at first appears to be a traditional parterre with gravel paths and small leafed box hedging; it's only on closer examination that its amorous shapes become apparent. The most obvious ones are the four giant hearts and a pair of women's lips, but there are many more. Love's symbolic flower, the rose, has been planted in the beds, and climbing roses trail over the heart-shaped arches. More than 1,300 rose bushes have been planted with names that enhance the symbolic story: First Kiss, Eve, Seduction, and more. The Maze of Love will not open to the public until Valentine's Day, 2000, but visitors can view it from either end in the meantime, enjoying the scent of its roses in summer.

While you're here take a ride in the **Airborne I,** a giant passenger balloon. This ride for visitors of all ages takes you up in a balloon gondola to a height of some 400 feet, from which you can enjoy panoramic views over Longleat House and its gardens, the Maze, and the Safari Park, as well as the wider Wiltshire and Somerset countryside. There are also facilities for access by travelers in wheelchairs.

⭘ **Stourhead.** ☎ **01747/841152.** Mar–Oct, admission £4.40 ($7.05) adults, £2.40 ($3.85) children; off-season, £3.40 ($5.45) adults, £1.50 ($2.40) children. Daily 9am–7pm (or until dusk). Take the Gillingham-bound train from Bath. In Gillingham, switch to Southern National bus no. 58 or no. 58A, both of which go directly to Stourhead, about a 20-minute trip. There's a direct bus from Bath, but it only runs on the first Sat of each month. The return journey is via Frome. From Salisbury, bus service is very limited; however, you can take bus no. 26 to Hindon or Tewesbury, where you'll have to change buses to Stourton.

In a country of superlative gardens and gardeners, Stourhead is the most fabled of all. It's certainly the most celebrated example of 18th-century English landscape gardening. But more than that, it's a delightful place to wander—among its trees, flowers, and colorful shrubs, bridges, grottoes, and temples are tucked away, almost-hidden. Although Stourhead is a garden for all seasons, it is at its most idyllic in summer when the rhododendrons are in full bloom.

A Palladian house, Stourhead was built in the 18th century by the Hoare banking family, which created 100 acres of prime 18th-century landscaped gardens, complete with classical temples, lakes, and grottos. Henry Hoare II (1705–85), known as "Henry the Magnificent," contributed greatly to the development of the landscape of this magnificent estate.

The Temple of Flora was the first building in the garden, designed by the architect Henry Flitcroft in 1744. The wooden seats are copies of those placed near the altar where images of pagan gods were laid. Marble busts of Marcus Aurelius and Alexander the Great can be seen in the niches on the wall.

The Grotto, constructed in 1748, is lined with tufa, a water-worn limestone deposit. The springs of the Stour flow through the cold bath where a lead copy of the sleeping Ariadne lies. In a cave beyond her, the white lead statue of the River God is seen dispensing justice to the waves and to the nymphs who inhabit his stream.

The Pantheon was built in 1753 to house Rysbrack's statues of Hercules and Flora and other classical figures. The temple was originally heated through brass grilles. The nearby Iron Bridge replaced a wooden one in 1860.

In 1765 Flitcroft built the Temple of Apollo, the route to which takes the visitor over the public road via a rock-work bridge constructed in the 1760s. The Apollo Temple is copied from a round temple excavated at Baalbec: The statues that used to be in the niches are now on the roof of Stourhead House. The Turf Bridge was copied from Palladio's bridge in Vicenza.

The Bristol High Cross dates from the early 15th century and commemorates the monarchs who benefited the city of Bristol. It was removed from Bristol and set up by Henry Hoare at Stourhead in 1765.

The house at Stourhead, designed by Colen Campbell, a leader in the Palladian revival, was built for Henry Hoare I between 1721 and 1725. It closely resembles the villas Palladio built for wealthy Venetians. The magnificent interior hosts an outstanding library and picture gallery and a wealth of paintings, art treasures, and Chippendale furniture.

The three fine redbrick walled terraces were built in the early 19th century to supply cut flowers, fresh fruit, salads, and vegetables to the mansion house. They were in use up to the deaths of Sir Henry and Lady Alda Hoare in 1947.

The lower was an herbaceous garden together with a peach and vine house. The pool was part of an irrigation system fed by rainwater from the greenhouses and stable yard.

Henry Hoare II's 18th-century redbrick folly, **Alfred's Tower,** is another feature at Stourhead. It sits 160 feet above the borders of Wiltshire, Somerset, and Dorset and has 221 steps. **The Obelisk** was built between 1839 and 1840 of Bath stone, and replaced the original of Chilmark stone constructed by William Privet for Henry Hoare in 1746.

The plant center is situated near the entrance to the main parking lot in part of the Old Glebe Farm—a small estate dairy farm. This was a working farm until the early 1970s. Now it's a place where visitors can buy plants they've just seen in the garden.

Lunches and suppers are served at the **Spread Eagle Inn,** near the entrance to the garden. Boxes are available to order for picnics in the grounds and garden. The Spread Eagle is noted for dinner in the evening and for its Sunday lunches in the autumn, winter, and spring. A self-service buffet is available in the Village Hall tearoom.

8 Dunster & Exmoor National Park

184 miles W of London; 3 miles SE of Minehead

The village of Dunster, in Somerset, lies near the eastern edge of Exmoor National Park. It grew up around the original Dunster Castle, constructed as a fortress for the de Mohun family, whose progenitor came to England with William the Conqueror. The village, about 4 miles from the Cistercian monastery at Cleeve, has an ancient priory church and dovecote, a 17th-century gabled yarn market, and little cobbled streets dotted with whitewashed cottages.

ESSENTIALS

GETTING THERE   The best rail link is to travel to Minehead via Taunton, which is easily reached on the main London–Penzance line from Paddington Station in London. For rail information, call ☎ **0345/484950** in the U.K., or 01603/764776 in the U.S. From Minehead you have to take a taxi or bus to reach Dunster.

At Taunton, you can take one of the seven **Southern National** coaches (no. 28) (☎ **01823/272033**), leaving hourly Monday through Saturday; there is only one bus on Sunday. Trip time is 1 hour and 10 minutes. Buses (no. 38 or 39) from Minehead stop in Dunster Village at the rate of one per hour, but only from June to September. Off-season visitors must take a taxi.

If you're driving from London, head west along M4, cutting south at the junction with M5 until you reach the junction with A39, going west to Minehead. Before your final approach to Minehead, cut south to Dunster along A396.

VISITOR INFORMATION   Dunster doesn't have an official tourist office, but **Exmoor National Park Visitor Centre** is found at Dunster Steep (☎ **01643/ 821835**), 2 miles east of Minehead. It's open April to October daily from 10am to 5pm, plus limited hours in winter.

EXPLORING THE AREA

✪ **Dunster Castle.** On A396 (just off A39). ☎ **01643/821314.** Admission to castle and grounds £5.20 ($8.30) adults, £2.70 ($4.30) children, family ticket £13.40 ($21.45); to grounds only £2.80 ($4.50) adults, £1.30 ($2.10) children, family ticket £6.70 ($10.70). Castle Apr–Sept Sat–Wed 11am–5pm, Oct Sat–Wed 11am–4pm. Grounds Feb–Mar and Oct–Dec daily 11am–4pm, Apr–Sept daily 10am–5pm. Take bus no. 38 or 39 from Minehead.

Dunster Castle is on a tor (high hill), from which you can see Bristol Channel. It stands on the site of a Norman castle granted to William de Mohun of Normandy by William the Conqueror shortly after the conquest of England. The 13th-century gateway, built by the de Mohuns, is all that remains of the original fortress. In 1376 the castle and its lands were bought by Lady Elizabeth Luttrell; her family owned it until it was given to the National Trust in 1976, together with 30 acres of surrounding parkland.

The first castle was largely demolished during the civil war. The present Dunster Castle is a Jacobean house constructed in the lower ward of the original fortifications in 1620, then rebuilt in 1870 to look like a castle. From the terraced walks and gardens, you'll have good views of Exmoor and the Quantock Hills.

Some of the outstanding artifacts within are the 17th-century panels of embossed painted and gilded leather depicting the story of Antony and Cleopatra, and a remarkable allegorical 16th-century portrait of Sir John Luttrell (shown wading naked through the sea with a female figure of peace and a wrecked ship in the background). The 17th-century plasterwork ceilings of the dining room and the finely carved staircase balustrade of cavorting huntsmen, hounds, and stags are also noteworthy.

EXMOOR NATIONAL PARK

Between Somerset and Devon, along the northern coast of England's southwest peninsula, is Exmoor National Park, an unspoiled plateau of lonely moors. One of the most cherished national parks in Britain, it includes the wooded valleys of the rivers Exe and Barle, the Brendon Hills, a sweeping stretch of rocky coastline, and such sleepy but charming villages as **Culbone, Selworthy, Parracombe,** and **Allerford.** Bisected by a network of heavily eroded channels for brooks and streams, the park is distinctive for its lichen-covered trees, gray-green grasses, gorse, and heather. The moors reach their highest point at Dunkery Beacon, 1,707 feet above sea level.

Although it's one of the smallest national parks in Britain, it contains one of the most beautiful coastlines in England. Softly contoured, without the dramatic peaks and valleys of other national parks, the terrain is composed mostly of primeval layering of sandstone slate. Although noteworthy for its scarcity of trees, the terrain encompasses a limited handful of very old oak groves which are studied by forestry experts for their growth patterns.

On clear days, the coast of South Wales, 20 miles away, can be spotted across the estuary of the Bristol Channel. The wildlife that thrives on the park's rain-soaked terrain includes a breed of wild pony (the Exmoor pony), whose bloodlines can be traced from ancient species.

Although there are more than 700 miles of walking paths in the park, most visitors stay on the **coastal trail** that winds around the bays and inlets of England's southwestern peninsula or along some of the shorter **riverside trails.**

The park's administrative headquarters is located within a 19th-century workhouse in the village of Dulverton, in Somerset, near the park's southern edge. A program of walking tours is offered at least five times a week, to anyone who's interested. Themes include Woodland Walks, Moorland Walks, Bird Watching Excursions, and Deer Spottings. Most of the tours last from 4 to 6 hours, and all are free, with an invitation to donate. Wear sturdy shoes and rain gear.

For the *Exmoor Visitor* brochure, which lists events, guided walks, and visitor information, contact the **Exmoor National Park Visitor Centre,** Dulverton, Somerset TA22 9EX (☎ **01398/323841**). It's open daily between Easter and the end of October from 10am to 5pm, and 10:30am to 2:30pm through the winter.

NEARBY SIGHTS

Combe Sydenham Hall. Monksilver. ☎ **01984/656284.** Admission £4 ($6.40) adults, £2 ($3.20) children. Country Park, Easter–Oct Sun–Fri 10am–5pm; courtroom and gardens, May–Sept at 2pm for guided tours only, Mon and Thurs–Fri. From Dunster, drive on A39, following signs pointing to Watchet and/or Bridgwater. On the right, you'll see a minor zoo, Tropiquaria, at which you turn right and follow the signs pointing to Combe Sydenham.

This hall was the home of Elizabeth Sydenham, wife of Sir Francis Drake, and it stands on the ruins of monastic buildings that were associated with nearby Cleeve Abbey. Here you can see a cannonball that legend says halted the wedding of Lady Elizabeth to a rival suitor in 1585. The gardens include Lady Elizabeth's Walk, which circles ponds originally laid out when the knight was courting his bride-to-be. The valley ponds fed by springwater are full of rainbow trout (ask about getting fly-fishing lessons). You can also take a woodland walk to Long Meadow, with its host of wild-flowers. Also to be seen are a deserted hamlet, whose population reputedly was wiped out by the black death, and a historic corn mill. In the hall's tearoom, smoked trout and pâté are produced on oak chips, as in days of yore, and there is a shop, working bakery, and car park.

Coleridge Cottage. 35 Lime St., Nether Stowey, near Bridgwater. ☎ **01278/732662.** Admission £1.70 ($2.70) adults, 80p ($1.30) children. Apr 1 Oct 1 Tues–Thurs and Sun 2–5pm. From Minehead, follow A39 east about 30 miles, following the signs to Bridgwater. About 8 miles from Bridgwater, turn right, following signs to Nether Stowey.

The hamlet of Nether Stowey is on A39, north of Taunton, across the Quantock Hills to the east of Exmoor. The cottage is at the west end of Nether Stowey on the south side of A39.

Here you can visit the home of Samuel Taylor Coleridge, where he penned "The Rime of the Ancient Mariner." During his 1797-to-1800 sojourn here, he and his friends, William Wordsworth and sister Dorothy, enjoyed exploring the Quantock woods. The parlor and reading room of his National Trust property are open to visitors.

WHERE TO STAY & DINE IN THE AREA

Curdon Mill. Vellow, Williton, Somerset, TA4 4LS. ☎ **01984/656522.** Fax 01984/656197. 6 units (with tub or shower). TV. £60–£90 ($96–$144) double. Rates include English break-fast. AE, MC, V.

Situated on a 200-acre farm 5 miles northeast of Dunster, this guest house, a former mill, sports a 100-year-old water wheel made by the local ironworks. Daphne and Richard Criddle own this place, offering home-style food and accommodations. The individually decorated rooms are equipped with tea and coffee makers. Mrs. Criddle serves English fare, including venison, roast lamb, and pheasant. All the food is home-made and may include a few French-style dishes "when the inspiration strikes."

Luttrell Arms. 32–36 High St., Dunster, Somerset TA24 6SG. ☎ **01643/821555.** Fax 01643/821567. 27 units. TV TEL. £75–£95 ($120–$152) double. Dinner, bed-and-breakfast rates, Mar–June and Sept–Oct £55 ($88) per person per night; July–Aug £60 ($96) per person per night; Nov–Feb £50 ($80) per person per night. 2-night minimum stay required for this rate. AE, DC, MC, V.

This is simply the best choice around. There has been a hostelry for weary travelers on this site for more than 600 years. This hotel is the outgrowth of a guest house the Cis-tercian abbots at Cleeve had built in the village of Dunster. It was named for the Lut-trell lords of the manor, who bought Dunster Castle and the property attached to it in the 14th century. It has, of course, been updated with modern amenities, but from its stone porch to the 15th-century Gothic hall with hammer-beam roof, it still retains a feeling of antiquity. The bedrooms are comfortably appointed and attractively deco-rated in keeping with the hotel's long history; four of them have four-poster beds.

Dining/Diversions: A lounge is upstairs, whereas downstairs you can enjoy a drink in the timbered Tudor bar, with its large inglenook fireplace (this was once the kitchen). The dining room offers a varied menu; depending on the season, you might choose guinea fowl or baked sugared ham with Somerset cider sauce. Bar food is also offered.

10 | Devon

The great patchwork-quilt area of southwest England, part of the "West Countree," abounds in cliff-side farms, rolling hills, foreboding moors, semitropical plants, and fishing villages that provide some of the finest scenery in England. You can pony trek across moor and woodland, past streams and sheep-dotted fields, or relax at a local pub to soak up atmosphere and ale.

The British approach sunny Devon with the same kind of excitement normally reserved for hopping over to the Continent. Especially along the coastline—the English Riviera—the names of the seaports, villages, and resorts are synonymous with holidays in the sun: Torquay, Clovelly, Lynton-Lynmouth. Devon is a land of jagged coasts—the red cliffs in the south face the English Channel. In South Devon, the coast from which Drake and Raleigh set sail, tranquility prevails, and on the bay-studded coastline of North Devon, pirates and smugglers found haven.

Almost every village is geared to accommodate visitors. But many small towns and fishing villages don't allow cars to enter; these towns have parking areas on the outskirts, and then it's a long walk to reach the center of the harbor area. From mid-July to mid-September the most popular villages are quite crowded, so make reservations for a place to stay well in advance.

Along the south coast, the best bases from which you can explore the region are Exeter, Plymouth, and Torquay. Along the north coast, we suggest Lynton-Lynmouth. The area's most charming village (with very limited accommodations) is Clovelly. The greatest natural spectacle is the Dartmoor National Park, northeast of Plymouth, a landscape of gorges and moors filled with gorse and purple heather—home of the Dartmoor pony.

If you're taking the bus around Devon, Stagecoach Devon and Western National bus lines combine to offer a discounted **"Key West Ticket."** Adults can enjoy unlimited use of the lines at these rates: £13.40 ($21.45) for 3 days, £22.65 ($36.25) for 7 days, or £83.50 ($133.60) for 1 month. For families (two adults and two children 5 to 15 years old), there's only a 3-day ticket at £26.80 ($42.90) or a 7-day ticket at £38.20 ($61.10). You can plan your journeys from the maps and timetables available at any **Western National/Devon General** office when you purchase your ticket (☎ **01752/222666**). For further information, contact **Stagecoach Devon Ltd.,** Paris Street, Exeter Devon FX1 2JP (☎ **01392/427711**).

Devon

Bristol Channel

Bristol Channel

Lyme Bay

ENGLAND

London

Devon

EXMOOR NATIONAL PARK

DARTMOOR NATIONAL PARK

DEVON

CORNWALL

Buckland Abbey
(Sir Francis
Drake's House) 5

Castle Drogo 6

Cathedral
of the Moor 7

Exeter Cathedral 2

Lynton/Lynmouth
Railway 1

Museum of
Dartmoor Life 8

Plymouth Barbican 10

Powderham Castle 3

Royal Naval College 6

Torre Abbey 4

3-0584

379

1 Exeter

201 miles SW of London; 46 miles NE of Plymouth

Exeter was a Roman city founded in the 1st century A.D. on the banks of the River Exe. Two centuries later it was encircled by a mighty stone wall, traces of which remain today. Conquerors and would-be conquerors, especially Vikings, stormed the fortress in later centuries; none was more notable than William the Conqueror, who brought Exeter to its knees on short notice.

Under the Tudors, the city grew and prospered. Sir Walter Raleigh and Sir Francis Drake were two of the striking figures who strolled through Exeter's streets. In May 1942, the Germans bombed Exeter, destroying many of its architectural treasures. The town was rebuilt, but the new, impersonal-looking shops and offices can't replace the Georgian crescents and the black-and-white-timbered buildings with their plastered walls. Fortunately, much was spared, and Exeter still has its Gothic cathedral, a renowned university, some museums, and several historic houses.

Exeter is a good base for exploring both Dartmoor and Exmoor national parks, two of the finest England has to offer. (Exmoor National Park is covered in chapter 9.) It's also a good place to spend a day—there's a lot to do in what's left of the city's old core.

ESSENTIALS

GETTING THERE **Exeter Airport** (☎ 01392/367433) serves the southwest, offering both charter and scheduled flights. Lying 5 miles east of the historic center of Exeter, it has scheduled flights to and from Belfast, Jersey, Dublin, and the Isles of Scilly, but no direct flights from London.

Trains from London's Paddington Station depart every hour during the day. The trip takes 2½ hours. For rail information, call ☎ 0345/484950 in the U.K., or 01603/764776 in the U.S. Trains also run once an hour during the day between Exeter and Plymouth; the trip takes 1¼ hours. Trains often arrive at Exeter Central Station on Queen Street, next to Northernhay Gardens, or else at Exeter St. David's Station at St. David's Hill. Since neither station has a direct line, you have to call the **Plymouth station** at ☎ 0345/484950 for information.

A **National Express** coach departs from London's Victoria Coach Station every 2 hours during the day; the trip takes 4 hours. You can also take bus no. 38 or 39 between Plymouth and Exeter. During the day two coaches depart per hour for the 1-hour trip. For information and schedules call ☎ 0990/808080.

If you're driving from London, take M4 west, cutting south to Exeter on M5 (junction near Bristol).

VISITOR INFORMATION The **Tourist Information Centre** is at the Civic Centre, Paris Street (☎ 01392/265700). It's open Monday through Friday from 9am to 5pm, and Saturday from 9am to 1pm and 2 to 5pm.

SPECIAL EVENTS A classical music lover's dream, the **Exeter Festival,** held for 3 weeks in July, includes more than 150 events, ranging from concerts and opera to lectures. Festival dates and offerings vary from year to year, and more information is available by contacting the **Exeter Festival Office,** Civic Center (☎ 01392/265200; www.exeter.ac.uk/festival).

EXPLORING EXETER

Just off "The High," at the top of Castle Street, stands an impressive **Norman Gatehouse** from William the Conqueror's castle. Although only the house and walls survive, the view from here and the surrounding gardens is panoramic.

✪ **Exeter Cathedral.** 1 The Cloisters. ☎ **01392/255573.** Free admission, though a donation of £2 ($3.20) is requested of adults. Mon–Fri 7:30am–6:15pm, Sat 7:30am–6:30pm, Sun 8am–7:30pm.

The Roman II Augusta Legion made its camp on the site where the Cathedral Church of Saint Peter now stands in Exeter. It has been occupied by Britons, Saxons, Danes, and Normans. The English Saint Boniface, who converted northern Germany to Christianity, was trained here in A.D. 690. The present cathedral structure was begún around 1112, and the twin Norman towers still stand. Between the towers runs the longest uninterrupted true Gothic vault in the world, at a height of 66 feet and a length of 300 feet. It was completed in 1369 and is the finest existing example of decorated Gothic architecture. The Puritans destroyed the cathedral cloisters in 1655, and a German bomb finished off the twin Chapels of St. James and St. Thomas in May 1942. Now restored, it's one of the prettiest churches anywhere. Its famous choir sings evensong every day except Wednesday during school term. On school holidays, visiting choirs perform.

Exeter Guildhall. High St. ☎ **01392/265500.** Free admission. Mon–Fri 10:30am–1pm and 2–4pm. It's best to call before visiting.

This colonnaded building on the main street is the oldest municipal building in the kingdom—the earliest reference to the guildhall is in a deed from 1160. The Tudor front that straddles the pavement was added in 1593. Inside you'll find a fine display of silver, plus a number of paintings. The ancient hall is paneled in oak.

St. Nicholas Priory. The Mint, off Fore St. ☎ **01392/265858.** Free admission. Call for opening arrangements.

This is the guest wing of a Benedictine priory founded in 1070. You'll see fine plaster ceilings and period furniture. A recent summer exhibit featured Russian ceramics and crafts.

Underground Passages. Boots Corner, off High St. ☎ **01392/265887.** Admission £2.50 ($4) adults, £1.50 ($2.40) children, £6 ($9.60) family ticket July–Aug £3.50 ($5.60) adults, £2.25 ($3.60) children, £9.50 ($15.20) family ticket. July–Sept Mon–Sat 10am–4:45pm; Oct–May Tues–Fri 2–5pm, Sat 10am–5pm.

The Underground Passages, accessible from High Street, were built to carry the medieval water supply into the city. By entering the new underground interpretation center, visitors can view a video and exhibition before taking a guided tour.

Powderham Castle. In Powderham, Kenton. ☎ **01626/890243.** Admission £4.95 ($7.90) adults, £4.45 ($7.10) seniors, £2.85 ($4.55) children 5–17; free for children 4 and under. Easter–Oct Sun–Fri 10am–5:30pm. Take the A379 Dawlish rd. 8 miles south of Exeter; the castle is signposted.

This private house is occupied by the countess and earl of Devon, who let Ismail Merchant and James Ivory use their home as a setting for *Remains of the Day,* starring Anthony Hopkins and Emma Thompson. It was built in the late 14th century by Sir Philip Courtenay, sixth son of the second earl of Devon, and his wife, Margaret, granddaughter of Edward I. Their magnificent tomb is in the south transept of Exeter Cathedral.

The castle has many family portraits and fine furniture, including a remarkable clock that plays full tunes at 4pm, 8pm, and midnight, some 17th-century tapestries, and a chair used by William III for his first council of state at Newton Abbot. The staircase hall contains some remarkable plasterwork that's more than 2 centuries old, as well as a detailed pedigree of the Courtenay family, a document more than 12 feet high. The chapel dates from the 15th century, with hand-hewn roof timbers and carved pew ends.

SHOPPING

Exeter has long been famous for its silver. If you seek, ye shall find old Exeter silver, especially spoons, still sold in local stores. The best merchant for this is **William Burford,** 1 Bedford St. (☎ **01392/254901**). You can find spoons dating from before the 19th century; look for the three-castle mark of Exeter to be sure you're getting the real thing.

David Trivett Jewelry, 13A Guildhall Precinct (☎ **01392/276224**), carries antique jewelry as well as secondhand designer jewelry. They also carry original designs by artisans who work in the store, or can create a piece that you have designed.

There are a number of antique dealers in Exeter. At least six are on the Quay off Western Way. **The Quay Gallery Antiques Emporium** (☎ **01392/213283**) houses 10 dealers who sell furniture, porcelain, metalware, and other collectibles. **The Antique Centre on the Quay** (☎ **01392/214180**) has 20 dealers.

The **Edinburgh Woolen Mill,** 23 Cathedral Yard (☎ **01392/412318**), carries a large selection of woolen goods, including kilts, Aran jumpers, tartan travel rugs, and quality wool suits for women.

There is also a daily market on Sidwell Street, Exeter's version of an American flea market.

WHERE TO STAY
EXPENSIVE

Rougemont Thistle. Queen St. (opposite the central train station), Exeter, Devon EX4 3SP. ☎ **01392/254982.** Fax 01392/420928. 94 units. TV TEL. £99 ($158.40) double; £160–£180 ($256–$288) suite. Rates include English breakfast. AE, DC, MC, V.

Although its history is far less impressive than that of the Royal Clarence, this great, old-fashioned, rambling Victorian hotel (which was renovated fairly recently) is also a traditional choice for those who want to stay in the center of town. Its neoclassical architecture is a background for contemporary furnishings. Bedrooms are very comfortable and tasteful.

Dining/Diversions: Guests gather in the Adam-style Drake's Bar for drinks. A good stock of wine comes from the cellar, which, incidentally, was once a debtors' prison.

Royal Clarence Hotel. Cathedral Yard, Exeter, Devon EX1 1HD. ☎ **01392/319955.** Fax 01392/439423. 56 units. TV TEL. £99–£129 ($158.40–$206.40) double; from £139 ($222.40) suite. Rates include English breakfast if stay is longer than 1 night. AE, DC, MC, V.

We think the Royal Clarence has far more tradition and style than the sometimes better rated and more recently built Forte Crest at Southernhay East or Rougemont Thistle on Queen Street. It dates from 1769 and escaped the Nazi blitz. Just a step away from the cathedral, it offers individually furnished rooms in Tudor, Georgian, or Victorian styling. Each has such amenities as movies, hair dryer, trouser press, and tea- or coffeemaker. Gilt-framed mirrors, oak paneling, and cove molding add to the rich ambiance.

Dining: The Raleigh Restaurant, with its gilded mirrors and lace-covered tables, serves excellent West Country fare such as sautéed breast of pheasant or the chef's nightly roast.

Amenities: 24-hour room service.

MODERATE

Buckerell Lodge Hotel. Topsham Rd., Exeter, Devon EX2 4SQ. ☎ **800/528-1234** in the U.S. and Canada, or 01392/221111. Fax 01392/491111. 52 units. TV TEL. £75 ($120) double. AE, DC, MC, V. Bus: K, T, or R. Take B3182 1 mile southeast, off Junction 30 of M5.

In Search of the Traditional Devonshire Cream Tea

Cream teas will always be associated with Devon. How did they come about? Think back to the traditional Devonshire farmer's wife laboring away on a far-away grange (though today the clotted cream you find alongside your scones probably came from a high-tech dairy using ultrapasteurized processes). These matriarchs perfected the medieval process of simmering at very low temperatures a batch of whole cow's milk, sometimes for a day or two, to create the region's famous Devonshire clotted cream. Silken-textured and rich, with just enough acidity to perk up the taste buds, it isn't clotted at all. It's a very English, very urbane, and very perishable version of what the French call crème fraîche.

What should accompany your clots of cream? A scone, but not just any scone—preferably one that's just come out of the oven and, it is hoped, one made without baking soda. The resulting, slightly bitter, slightly sour taste seems to go better with the tangy cream. Preserves? Don't even think of asking for anything except strawberry preserves.

The tea itself seems to be less crucial than the above-mentioned items that accompany it. Most Devonites opt for strong, simple Indian tea, eschewing the more delicate Chinese blends as something too fancy to muck about with.

Here are our favorite spots to pause and take your afternoon tea with clotted cream while you're exploring the byways and primrose paths of Devon.

Our all-time favorite (and the most convenient, as it lies between Exeter and Plymouth) is **Buckfast Abbey** at Buckfastleigh (☎ **01364/643301**), which is also an easy drive from Torquay and Dartmoor. The specialty here is a Buckfast wine cake. Prices for a one-scone tea here are £2 ($3.20), rising to £2.90 ($4.65) for two scones. These prices are typical for all the other tearooms as well.

Or head for **The Kettle,** 15 Fore St. (☎ **01297/20428**), east of Exeter. You'll know you're at the right place when you see the wooden sign out front of an old lady holding a kettle. The atmosphere is mellow inside this 4-centuries-old building. It's just a short drive from Exeter along the A376 and A3052.

While visiting the coastal towns of Devon, dart inland to **Honeybees,** High Street (☎ **01404/43392**), in the town of Honiton, long famous for its lace made a century ago. The brick-fronted tearoom with a large bay window is known for its cream teas and "squidgy cakes." From Exeter take A30 straight into Honiton.

Southeast of Exeter, follow the A376 through Exmouth to **The Cozy Teapot,** Fore Street (☎ **01395/444016**), in Budleigh Salterton. A cozy brick building, this tearoom is tucked away just past a small bridge with running water. It serves the best Devon cream tea in the area. You get bone china, lace cloths on the tables, young women in flowery pinafores, and homemade cakes, too.

Our favorite name for a tearoom is **Four and Twenty Blackbirds,** 43 Gold St., Tiverton (☎ **01884/257055**), reached by following the Old Road (now called A396) from Exeter straight into Tiverton to the north. The black-and-white-timbered tearoom stands in a sunken square. Fresh flowers, mismatched furniture, and an assortment of set teas and tea breads and homemade cakes await you.

Finally, there's the **Georgian Tea Room,** High Street (☎ **01392/873465**), in Topsham, reached from Exeter by going along the Polsol Road to A376 (southeast of Exeter). If Aunt Pittipat had been from Devon instead of Atlanta, this is the type of place she'd patronize. Homemade jams accompany the piping-hot scones fresh from the oven.

The house originated in the 12th century, but it has been altered and changed beyond recognition over the years. The exterior is a symmetrical and severely dignified building with a Regency feel; it's pierced with bay windows. Often hosting business travelers, it's also a tourist favorite, especially in summer. The bedrooms, in a range of styles and sizes, are well decorated and nicely equipped. The best rooms are the executive accommodations in the main house, although most bedrooms are in a more sterile modern addition.

Raffles Restaurant is one of the area's finer dining choices, specializing in fresh fish, game, steaks, and poultry; there's always something for the vegetarian. The menu always has an interesting dish or two—perhaps sautéed wild rabbit with a wild thyme jus.

Gipsy Hill. Gipsy Hill Lane, via Pinn Lane, Monkerton, Exeter, Devon EX1 3RN. ☎ **01392/465252.** Fax 01392/464302. 37 units. TV TEL. £85 ($136) double. Rates include English breakfast. AE, MC, V. Bus: E.

This late Victorian country house stands in gardens on the eastern edge of the city and is close to the airport. (It's especially convenient if you're driving, as it's within easy reach of M5 Junction 30.) Family operated, the house has been modernized and offers well-appointed rooms, some of which have four-poster beds. A restaurant on the premises serves both British and continental dishes, with meals beginning at £17 ($27.20).

✪ St. Olaves Court Hotel. Mary Arches St. (off High St.), Exeter, Devon EX4 3AZ. ☎ **800/544-9993** in the U.S., or 01392/217736. Fax 01392/413054. 15 units. TV TEL. Mon–Thurs £85–£95 ($136–$152) double; Fri–Sun £65–£75 ($104–$120) double. Rates include continental breakfast. AE, DC, MC, V.

This is our favorite. The location is ideal, within a short walk of the cathedral—you can hear the church bells. A Georgian mansion, it was constructed in 1827 by a rich merchant as a home. The house has been discreetly furnished, in part with antiques. Each of the bedrooms has been individually decorated in keeping with the Georgian style and has a beverage-maker, trouser press, hair dryer, and what the English call a "hospitality tray." Some units have Jacuzzis. The hotel features excellent English cuisine in its Golsworthy Restaurant (see below for a full review).

White Hart Hotel. 65–66 South St., Exeter, Devon EX1 1EE. ☎ **01392/279897.** Fax 01392/250159. 50 units. TV TEL. Mon–Thurs £78 ($124.80) double. Fri–Sun £49.50 ($79.20) double. Rates include English breakfast. AE, DC, MC, V.

The White Hart Hotel, in the center of town, was a coaching inn in the 17th and 18th centuries and is one of the oldest inns in the city. It is said that Cromwell stabled his horses here. The hotel is a mass of polished wood, slate floors, oak beams, and gleaming brass and copper. The rooms, which combine old and new, have been upgraded with new curtains, bedspreads, tea- and coffeemaker, prints, and light fittings. Guests are housed in either the old wing or a more impersonal modern one. Some units are deluxe.

Hostler's Dining Room, the hotel's main restaurant, serves breakfast and dinner only, plus a Sunday lunch with all the trimmings. The hotel has a wine cellar, which supplies the Ale & Port House (a bar with waiter service where you can feast on traditional English fare), plus the well-known Bottlescreu Bills wine bar, which offers beefsteak-and-oyster pie or, in summer, barbecued steak in the wine garden. You may want to stop by the bar even if you're not a guest.

INEXPENSIVE

Claremont. 36 Wonford Rd., Exeter, Devon EX21 4LD. ☎ **01392/274699.** 3 units. TV. £40 ($64) double; £72 ($115.20) suite for 4. Rates include English breakfast. No credit cards. Bus: H.

This Regency-style 1840 town house is in a quiet residential part of the city, close to the center. The rooms are well kept and have beverage-makers. Geoff and Jacqueline Self, who run the property, assist visitors in many ways. Nonsmokers only, please.

Lea Dene. 34 Alphington Rd. (A3777), St. Thomas, Exeter, Devon EX2 8HN. ☎ 01392/ 57257. 11 units, none with bathroom. TV. £32–£34 ($51.20–$54.40) double. Rates include English breakfast. No credit cards. Blue minibus D from the center.

This Victorian-style guest house was built of red brick before 1930. Set in a southern suburb of Exeter, a 10- to 15-minute walk from the town center, it contains many original details. The rooms are simply but comfortably furnished. Owners Mr. and Mrs. Colin Foster offer a hearty breakfast.

Park View Hotel. 8 Howell Rd., Exeter, Devon EX4 4LG. ☎ 01392/271772. Fax 01392/253047. 15 units, 10 with bathroom. TV TEL. £38 ($60.80) double without bathroom, £43 ($68.80) double with bathroom. Rates include English breakfast. AE, MC, V.

This hotel lies near the heart of town and the train station. A landmark Georgian house, it offers comfortably but plainly furnished rooms. Guests take their breakfast in a cozy room opening onto the hotel's garden. Breakfast is the only meal served, but the staff will prepare a packed lunch for touring.

IN NEARBY BICKLEIGH

Perhaps the finest way to enjoy the cathedral city of Exeter, especially if you have a car, is to stay on the outskirts, 10 to 19 miles from the heart of the city. In the Exe Valley, 4 miles south of Tiverton and 10 miles north of Exeter, lies Bickleigh, a hamlet with a river, an arched stone bridge, a millpond, and thatch-roofed cottages—the epitome of English charm and one of the finest spots in all of Devon.

✪ **Bickleigh Cottage Country Hotel.** Bickleigh Bridge, Bickleigh, Devon EX16 8RJ. ☎ 01884/855230. 9 units. £45 ($72) double. Rates include English breakfast. MC, V. Closed Nov–Mar. Bus: 55 from Exeter.

This thatched, 17th-century hotel has a riverside garden that leads down to the lovely Bickleigh Bridge, where swans and ducks glide by. Inside, the rooms are small with oak beams and old fireplaces. Everything is comfortably cozy—like visiting your great-aunt. Mr. and Mrs. Stuart Cochrane, the owners, provide good and nourishing meals. The raspberries and gooseberries come fresh from the garden and are topped with generous portions of Devonshire cream.

WHERE TO DINE

Golsworthy Restaurant. In the St. Olaves Court Hotel, Mary Arches St. ☎ 01392/ 217736. Reservations recommended. Main courses £13.50–£18.50 ($21.60–$29.60); fixed-price "light lunch" £11.50 ($18.40); fixed-price lunch or dinner £14.50 ($23.20). AE, DC, MC, V. Mon–Fri noon–2pm; daily 6:30–9:30pm. CONTINENTAL.

This is Exeter's finest restaurant. Guests enjoy a before-dinner drink in a paneled bar that overlooks a verdant garden. The cuisine, which reflects the sophisticated palate of the congenial owners, might include breast of wood pigeon served on a puree of lentils and a port-scented jus; pantried fillet of sea trout with herbed nut brown butter and fresh lemon; or salmon soufflé with mixed salad greens and a lemon-and-chive oil. Any of these might be followed by a salad of Stilton cheese with walnuts or a dark-chocolate tort with vanilla crème anglaise (custard sauce) and orange salad.

Lamb's. 15 Lower North St. ☎ 01392/254269. Reservations recommended. Main courses £10.50–£16.50 ($16.80–$26.40); fixed-price lunch £13 ($20.80); fixed-price dinner (Tues–Fri only) £17 ($27.20). AE, MC, V. Tues–Fri noon–2pm; Tues–Sat 7–10pm. BRITISH.

The only serious challenger to Golsworthy in recent years is this winning candidate, with a creative chef named Carolyn Seath. Housed on two floors of a town house from the 1700s, the restaurant exudes a warm, friendly welcome. The cookery is innovative but not flashy, with dishes prepared in ways that bring out the natural flavor without too much sauce. Only quality ingredients go into the dishes, which include monkfish served with a fennel-and-saffron sauce. From the fields of Dartmoor come such succulent offerings as wild-beef rump steak. The desserts are sometimes memorable. The wine list is reasonably balanced, and not at all overpriced.

○ **The Ship Inn.** St. Martin's Lane. ☎ **01392/272040.** Reservations recommended. Restaurant main courses £6–£12 ($9.60–$19.20). Pub platters £3–£6 ($4.80–$9.60). MC, V. Restaurant Wed–Sat noon–3pm and 6–9:30pm. Pub Mon–Sat 11am–3pm, Sun noon–2pm (drinks, Mon–Sat 11am-3pm, Sun noon–10:30pm). ENGLISH.

The Ship Inn was often visited by Sir Francis Drake, Sir Walter Raleigh, and Sir John Hawkins, and even today, it still provides tankards of real ale, lager, and stout. A large selection of snacks is offered in the bar every day, whereas the restaurant upstairs provides more substantial English fare. At either lunch or dinner, you can order French onion soup, whole grilled lemon sole, five different steaks, and more. Portions are large, as in Elizabethan times.

EXETER AFTER DARK

Exeter is a lively university town offering an abundance of classical concerts and theater productions, as well as clubs and pubs. If you need information concerning cultural events and theaters, the **Exeter Arts Booking and Information Centre,** Princesshay (☎ **01392/211080**), open daily from 9:30am to 5pm, provides a monthly brochure of upcoming events and sells tickets.

An abundance of concerts, opera, dance, and film can be found year-round at the **Exeter & Devon Arts Centre,** Bradninch Place, Gandy St. (☎ **01392/421111**), and Exeter University's **Northcott Theatre,** Stocker Road (☎ **01392/26182**), which is also home to a professional theater company.

On the club scene, head to **Volts,** The Quay (☎ **01392/211347;** info line 01392/435820), a 2-story club featuring funk, soul, dance, and alternative tunes on the first floor, and The Hot House, playing classic pop music on the second floor. The crowd here is young, and there's a full bar and fast food available. The cover charge varies from £1 to £3 ($1.60 to $4.80).

Attracting a more diverse crowd, **The Warehouse/Boxes Disco,** Commercial Road (☎ **01392/29292**), is another split club, with different music styles featured throughout the week. Admission of £3 ($4.80) before 10:30pm, and £5 ($8) afterward gets you into both clubs.

Catering to Exeter's gay scene, **Liberty's,** Bartholomew Street (☎ **01392/275623**), hosts a Women's Social Group (no men allowed) on the first and third Wednesday of each month, a mixed gay and straight crowd for '70s and '80s dance music on Fridays, and a largely gay crowd for dancing on Saturdays. Cover is £2 ($3.20).

Pubs vary from the ancient and haunted to haunts of folk-music fans, with the **Turks Head,** High Street (☎ **01392/256680**), offering a bit of local color, since it's housed in a 600-year-old dungeon allegedly haunted by the Turks who were tortured and killed here. The first two floors are unchanged from that bygone era, but the top three floors were turned into the existing pub more than 450 years ago. It was a favorite hangout and scribbling spot of Charles Dickens, whose favorite chair is still on display. Today, it's a lively pub with a computerized juke box and a fast-food menu.

The **Well House Tavern,** Cathedral Close (☎ 01392/319953), is part of the Royal Clarence Hotel. It's housed in a building believed to have been constructed in the 14th century, although the Roman well in the basement predates that estimate. It, too, is said to be haunted—only the ghost here, affectionately called Alice, is said to be good-spirited when she appears in her flowing white dress. Join Alice and the other regulars for a pint or a light meal.

Featuring a great view of the canal, **Double Locks,** Canal Banks (☎ 01392/256947), welcomes a varied crowd, largely students. It features live music with no cover charge 2 or 3 evenings a week, and you can get traditional pub grub to go with your pint. Although spaciously spread through a Georgian mansion, the **Imperial Pub,** New North Road (☎ 01392/434050), is friendly to frugal travelers, with the cheapest brand-name beer in town, starting at 85p ($1.35), and a fast-food menu.

Bring your instrument to **The Mill on the Exe,** Bonhay Road (☎ 01392/214464), for Tuesday evening's Exeter Folk Club, when you are encouraged to sit in with the three-piece house band. This place also has a reputation for pretty good food.

2 Dartmoor National Park

213 miles SW of London; 13 miles W of Exeter

This national park lies northeast of Plymouth, stretching from Tavistock and Oke-hampton on the west to near Exeter in the east, a granite mass that sometimes rises to a height of 2,000 feet above sea level. The landscape offers vistas of gorges with rushing water, gorse, and purple heather ranged over by Dartmoor ponies—a foreboding landscape for the experienced walker only.

In Dartmoor, you'll find 500 miles of foot- and bridle paths and more than 90,000 acres of common land with public access. The country is rough, and on the high moor you should always make sure you have good maps, a compass, and suitable clothing and shoes.

ESSENTIALS

GETTING THERE   Take the train down from London to Exeter (see above), then use local buses to connect you with the various villages of Dartmoor.

Transmoor Link, a public transport bus service, usually operates throughout the summer and is an ideal way to get onto the moor. Information on the Transmoor Link and on the bus link between various towns and villages on Dartmoor is available from the **Transport Coordination Centre** (☎ 01392/382800).

If you're driving, Exeter is the most easily reached gateway. From here, continue west on B3212 to such centers of Dartmoor as Easton, Chagford, Moretonhampstead, and North Bovey. From these smaller towns, tiny roads—often not really big enough for two cars—cut deeper into the moor.

VISITOR INFORMATION   The main source of information is the **Dartmoor National Park Tourist Information Centre,** Town Hall, Bedford Square, Tavistock (☎ 01822/612938). It will book accommodations within a 15-mile radius for £3 to £3.50 ($4.80 to $5.60). It's open April through October Monday, Tuesday, Friday, and Saturday from 10am to 4pm and in summer on Sunday also from 10am to 5pm.

EXPLORING THE MOORS

This region is as rich in myth and legend as anywhere else in Britain. Crisscrossed with about 500 miles of bridle paths and hiking trails and covering about 360 square miles

(180 of which comprise the Dartmoor National Park), the moors rest on a granite base with numerous rocky outcroppings.

The Dartmoor National Park Authority (DNPA) runs **guided walks** of varying difficulty, ranging from 1½ to 6 hours for a trek of some 9 to 12 miles. All you have to do is turn up suitably clad at your selected starting point. Details are available from DNP information centers or from the **Dartmoor National Park Authority,** High Moorland Visitor Centre, Tavistock Road, Princetown (near Yelverton) PL20 6QF (☎ **01822/890414**). Guided tours cost £2 ($3.20) for a 2-hour walk, £3 ($4.80) for a 3-hour walk, £3.50 ($5.60) for a 4-hour walk, and £4 ($6.40) for a 6-hour walk. These prices are subsidized by the national parks services.

Throughout the area are stables where you can arrange for a day's trek across the moors. For **horseback riding** on Dartmoor, there are too many establishments to list. All are licensed, and you are accompanied by an experienced rider/guide. The moor can be dangerous since sudden fogs descend on treacherous marshlands without warning. Prices are around £6 ($9.60) per hour, £13 ($20.80) for a half day, and £22 ($35.20) for a full day. Most riding stables are listed in a useful free publication, *The Dartmoor Visitor,* which also provides details on guided walks, places to go, accommodations, local events, and articles about the national park. *The Dartmoor Visitor* is obtainable from DNP information centers and tourist information centers or by mail. Send an International Reply Coupon to the DNPA headquarters (address above).

CAMPING IN THE PARK

A few official campsites exist, but many campers prefer the open moor for the night. Since the moor is privately owned land, seek permission before camping. Only 1 night in a single spot is permitted. Campsites include **Ashburton Caravan Park,** Waterleat, Ashburton (☎ **01364/652552**); **River Dart Country Park,** Holne Park, Ashburton (☎ **01364/652511**); and **Yertiz Caravan and Camping Park,** Exeter Road, Okehampton (☎ **01837/52281**). Most sites are open from April through September, and charges begin at £3 ($4.80) per person.

CHAGFORD: A GOOD BASE FOR EXPLORING THE PARK

218 miles SW of London; 13 miles W of Exeter; 20 miles NW of Torquay

Six hundred feet above sea level, Chagford is an ancient town; with moors all around, it's a good base from which to explore north Dartmoor. Chagford overlooks the Teign River in its deep valley and is itself overlooked by the high granite tors. There's good fishing in the Teign. From Chagford, the most popular excursion is to Postbridge, a village with a prehistoric clapper bridge.

Surrounded by moors, romantic Chagford is one of the best bases for exploring the often forlorn but romantic north Dartmoor, following in the footsteps of the fictional Lorna Doone. It's also Sir Francis Drake country.

To get here, take a train to Exeter (see above), and then catch a local bus to Chagford (Transmoor Link National Express bus no. 82). If you're driving from Exeter, drive west on A30, then south on A382 to Chagford.

EXPLORING THE TOWN

When it's tea time, drop in at **Whiddons,** High Street (☎ **01647/433406**), which is decorated with fresh flowers in summer. They not only have freshly baked scones, they also have those delectable cucumber sandwiches. After tea, drop in at the Church of St. Michael nearby, where a spurned lover killed Mary Whiddon on her wedding day (later fictionalized in R. D. Blackmore's classic *Lorna Doone*).

✪ **Sir Francis Drake's House.** Buckland Abbey, Yelverton. ☎ **01822/853607.** Admission £4.30 ($6.90) adults, £2.10 ($3.35) children. Apr–Oct Fri–Wed 10:30am–5:30pm; Nov–Mar Sat–Sun 2–5pm. Last admission 45 min. before closing. Go 3 miles west of Yelverton off A386.

Constructed in 1278, Sir Francis Drake's House was originally a Cistercian monastery. The monastery was dissolved in 1539 and became the country seat of sailors Sir Richard Grenville and, later, Sir Francis Drake. The house remained in the Drake family until 1946, when the abbey and grounds were given to the National Trust. The abbey is now a museum and houses exhibits including Drake's drum, banners, and other artifacts.

Castle Drogo. 4 miles northeast of Chagford and 6 miles south of the Exeter-Okehampton rd. (A30). ☎ **01647/433306.** Admission (castle and grounds) £5.20 ($8.30) adults, £2.60 ($4.15) children; (grounds only) £2.40 ($3.85) adults, £1.20 ($1.90) children. Apr–Oct Sat–Thurs 11am–5pm; grounds daily 10:30am–5pm. Take A30 and follow the signs.

This massive granite castle, in the hamlet of Drewsteignton some 17 miles west of Exeter, was designed and built between 1910 and 1930 by the architect Sir Edwin Lutyens, then at the height of his powers, for his client, Julius Drewe. It was the last private country house built in the United Kingdom on a grand scale. Even though constructed of granite and castellated and turreted like a medieval castle from the age of chivalry, it was never intended to be a military stronghold. The castle occupies a bleak but dramatic position high above the River Teign, with views sweeping out over the moors.

The tour covers an elegant series of formal rooms designed in the best tradition of the Edwardian age, including drawing rooms, dining rooms, salons, and a gun room. There are two restaurants on the premises, both with waitress service, and a tearoom where tea, pastries, and snacks are served buffet-style.

Insider's tip: The castle is so overpowering it's easy to forget the secluded gardens. But they are wonderful, including a sunken lawn enclosed by raised walkways, a circular croquet lawn (sets are available for rent), geometrically shaped yew hedges, and a kiddies playroom based on a 1930s residence.

WHERE TO STAY & DINE

Easton Court Hotel. Easton Cross, Chagford, Devon TQ13 8JL. ☎ **01647/433469.** Fax 01647/433654. 8 units. TV TEL. £95 ($152) double. Rates include English breakfast. AE, MC, V. Closed Jan. Take A382 1½ miles northeast of Chagford. Bus: 359 from Exeter.

Ever since it was established as a hotel in the 1920s, this Tudor house has drawn many literary and theatrical celebrities. It's best known as the place where Evelyn Waugh wrote *Brideshead Revisited.* The guest book reads like a who's who of yesteryear: Robert Donat, Margaret Mead, Ralph Richardson, C. P. Snow, Richard Widmark, John Steinbeck. The atmosphere here is very English country house: an ancient stone house with a thatched roof, heavy oak beams, an inglenook where log fires burn in cold weather, and a high-walled flower garden. The bedrooms are snug and comfortable.

Dining: British and international dishes are served, including coq au vin, steak-and-mushroom pie, and curried prawns. Meals, available to nonresidents who reserve, cost £22 ($35.20) and up.

✪ **Gidleigh Park Hotel** Gidleigh Rd. (2 miles outside town), Chagford, Devon TQ13 8HH. ☎ **01647/432367.** Fax 01647/432574. 14 units, 1 cottage. TV TEL. £350–£450 ($560–$720) double; £470 ($752) cottage for 2, £600 ($960) cottage for 4. Rates include English breakfast, morning tea, newspaper, dinner, service, and tax. AE, DC, MC, V. To get here from Chagford Sq., turn right onto Mill St. at Lloyds Bank. After 200 yds, turn right and go down the hill to the crossroads. Cross straight over onto Holy St., following the lane passing Holy St. Manor on your right and shifting into low gear to negotiate 2 sharp bends on a steep hill. Over Leigh Bridge, make a sharp right turn into Gidleigh Park. A half-mile drive will bring you to the hotel.

This Tudor-style hotel, a Relais & Châteaux, is the country house supreme, the finest and most elegant place to stay in the Dartmoor area. The hotel lies in the Teign Valley, opening onto panoramic vistas of the Meldon and Nattadon Hills. Its American owners, Kay and Paul Henderson, have renovated and refurnished the house with flair and imagination. In a park of 40 acres, large beech and oak trees abound.

Inside, the oak-paneled public rooms and the open log fires invite a return to yesteryear. Most of the bedrooms are on the second floor and are reached by a grand staircase. The hotel has a three-room thatched cottage with two bathrooms across the river, 350 yards from the hotel, that's available for two, three, or four people.

Dining: Excellent meals are served in the comfortable dining room. The menu changes daily, and the kitchen only uses the best and freshest products. Dining here is a memorable experience. In fact, this restaurant is one of the best in the West Country, and its wine list has received numerous awards.

Great Tree Hotel. Sandy Park, Chagford, Devon TQ13 8JS. ☎ **01647/432491.** Fax 01647/432562. 10 units. TV TEL. £79–£98 ($126.40–$156.80) double. Rates include English breakfast. AE, DC, MC, V. Take A30 to the traffic circle at Whiddon Down and drive 2½ miles south on A382.

Formerly an old hunting lodge, the Great Tree Hotel is a comfortable country house located on 25 acres of private grounds. The bedrooms are country style, with tea- and coffeemakers.

Beverly and Nigel Eaton-Gray, the proprietors, offer a five-course dinner prepared with homegrown produce; the cost is £21 ($33.60). English and continental meals are served in their Whitewater Restaurant. There are bar snacks at lunch and Devonshire cream teas on the terrace, or by the log fire in winter.

OTHER TOWNS IN & AROUND DARTMOOR

Some 13 miles west of Exeter, the peaceful little town of **Moretonhampstead** is perched on the edge of Dartmoor. Moretonhampstead contains an old market cross and several 17th-century colonnaded almshouses.

The much-visited Dartmoor village of **Widecombe-in-the-Moor** is only 7 miles from Moretonhampstead. The fame of the village of Widecombe-in-the-Moor stems from an old folk song about Tom Pearce and his gray mare, listing the men who were supposed to be on their way to Widecombe Fair when they met with disaster. Widecombe also has a parish church worth visiting. Called the **Cathedral of the Moor,** with a roster of vicars beginning in 1253, the house of worship in a green valley is surrounded by legends. When the building was restored, a wall plate was found bearing the badge of Richard II (1377–99), the figure of a white hart. The town is very disappointing, tacky, and unkempt in spite of its fame.

The market town of **Okehampton** owes its existence to the Norman castle built by Baldwin de Bryonis, sheriff of Devon, under orders from his uncle, William the Conqueror, in 1068, just 2 years after the conquest. The Courtenay family lived here for many generations until Henry VIII beheaded one of them and dismantled the castle in 1538.

The **Museum of Dartmoor Life,** at the Dartmoor Centre, 3 West St., Okehampton (☎ 01837/52295), is housed in an old mill with a water wheel and is part of the Dartmoor Centre, a group of attractions around an old courtyard. Also here are working craft studios, a Victorian Cottage Tearoom, and a Dartmoor National Park information center. Museum displays cover all aspects of Dartmoor's history from prehistoric times, including some old vehicles—a Devon box wagon of 1875, a 1922 Bullnose Morris motorcar, a 1937 motorcycle. There's a reconstructed cider press, a blacksmith, and a tourist information center. The museum is open October to Easter, Monday through Friday from 10am to 5pm, and from Easter to October, Monday through Saturday from 10am to 5pm. It also opens on Sunday from June through September. Admission is £1.60 ($2.55) for adults, £1.30 ($2.10) for seniors, 80p ($1.30) for children, and £4.50 ($7.20) for a family ticket (two adults, two children).

Let yourself drift back in time to the days when craftspeople were the lifeblood of thriving communities. Basket weavers, wood turners, and potters are among the traditional crafters that can still be seen throughout the area. Indulge yourself with some genuine Devon pieces of craftsmanship. In the Dartmoor National Park in West Devon, you'll find that **The Yelverton Paperweight Centre,** Leg O'Mutton (☎ **01822/854250**), presents an impressive display of more than 800 glass paperweights for sale along with paintings of Dartmoor scenes.

For an interesting outdoor shop, **The Kountry Kit,** 22–23 West St., Tavistock (☎ **01822/613089**), carries all the best names in gear and outerwear. It also is a clearinghouse of name-brand seconds. **Green Genie Recycled Crafts,** Mearsdon Manor, Moretonhampstead (☎ **01647/440483**), is a treasure trove of wonderful objects and crafts creatively fashioned from "waste" materials.

WHERE TO STAY & DINE IN THE AREA

The Castle Inn. Lydford, near Okehampton (1 mile off A386), Devon EX20 4BH. ☎ **01822/820241.** Fax 01822/820454. 10 units, 8 with bathroom. £46 ($73.60) double without bathroom, £59 ($94.40) double with bathroom; £60 ($96) superior room. Special Country Breaks (any 2 nights): £89.20–£200.30 ($142.70–$320.50), including half board. AE, DC, MC, V.

The Castle Inn is a 16th-century structure next to Lydford Castle, midway between Okehampton and Tavistock. The inn, with its pink facade and row of rose trellises, is the hub of the village. The owners have maintained the character of the commodious old rustic lounge. One room, called the "Snug," has a group of high-backed oak settles arranged in a circle. The bedrooms are not large but are well planned and attractively furnished, often with mahogany and marble Victorian pieces.

The Foresters' Bar serves a standard lunch and dinner daily, as well as bar snacks. The fixed-price dinner is an especially good buy.

Cherrybrook Hotel. On B3212 between Postbridge and Two Bridges, Yelverton, Devon PL20 6SP. ☎ and fax **01822/880260.** 7 units, all with shower only. TV. £52 ($83.20) double. Rates include English breakfast. No credit cards. Closed Dec 22–Jan 2.

The Cherrybrook Hotel is a small family run hotel in the center of the Dartmoor National Park, on the high moor but within easy driving distance of Exeter and Plymouth. It was built in the early 19th century by a friend of the prince regent who received permission to enclose a large area of the Dartmoor forest for farming. The lounge and bar with their beamed ceilings and slate floors are a reminder of those times. Andy and Margaret Duncan rent comfortably furnished and well-maintained rooms. You can also dine here, paying £15 ($24) for a four-course dinner and coffee.

Holne Chase Hotel. Two Bridges Rd., Ashburton, near Newton Abbot (off the main Ashburton-Princetown rd., between the Holne Bridge and New Bridge), Devon TQ13 7NS. ☎ **01364/631471.** Fax 01364/631453. 18 units. TV TEL. £115–£130 ($184–$208) double; £140 ($224) suite. Rates include continental breakfast. Discount packages available. AE, DC, MC, V.

The Holne Chase Hotel is a white-gabled country house, 3 miles northwest of the center of town, within sight of trout- and salmon-fishing waters. You can catch your lunch and take it back to the kitchen to be cooked. Although the mood of the moor predominates, Holne Chase is surrounded by trees, lawns, and pastures—a perfect setting for walks along the Dart. The house is furnished in period style; a stable block has been converted into four sporting lodges.

Dining: The cooking combines the best of English fare with specialty dishes that are made all the better whenever produce from the gardens or fresh fish from the Dart River and Torquay are used. Devon beef and lamb are also featured. The old cellars hold a nice selection of wine.

3 Torquay: The English Riviera

223 miles SW of London; 23 miles SE of Exeter

In 1968, the towns of Torquay, Paignton, and Brixham joined to form "The English Riviera" as part of a plan to turn the area into one of the super three-in-one resorts of Europe. The area today—the birthplace of mystery writer Agatha Christie—opens onto 22 miles of coastline and 18 beaches. Palm trees even grow here!

Fans of the British comedy *Fawlty Towers,* the television series that made Torquay and the English Riviera known the world over, might be disappointed to learn that it wasn't filmed in Torquay at all, but rather in one of the Home Counties closer to London. (The hotel that served as the comedy's set has since burned down.) Regardless, Torquay continues to be identified with the series, which was inspired by John Cleese's sojourn in Torquay during one of his tours of duty with the Monty Python team.

Torquay is set against a backdrop of the red cliffs of Devon, with many sheltered pebbly coves. With its parks and gardens, including numerous subtropical plants, it's often compared to the Mediterranean. At night, concerts, productions from the West End, vaudeville shows, and ballroom dancing keep the vacationers and many honeymooners entertained.

ESSENTIALS

GETTING THERE The nearest connection is Exeter Airport (see above), 40 minutes away. Frequent trains run throughout the day from London's Paddington Station to Torquay, whose station is at the town center on the seafront. The trip takes 2½ hours. For rail information, call ☎ **0345/484950** in the U.K. or 01603/764776 in the U.S.

National Express coach links from London's Victoria Coach Station leave every 2 hours during the day for Torquay. For information and schedules, call ☎ **0990/808080.**

If you're driving, from Exeter, head west on A38, veering south at the junction with A380.

VISITOR INFORMATION The **Tourist Information Centre** is at Vaughan Parade (☎ **01803/297428**); open Monday through Saturday from 9am to 5pm.

PALM TREES & AGATHA CHRISTIE

This resort is known for offering one of the balmiest climates in Britain. It's so temperate, because of its exposure to the Gulf Stream, that subtropical plants such as palm trees and succulents thrive.

Torre Abbey. Kings Dr. (¼ mile east of Torquay's center). ☎ **01803/293593.** Admission £2.75 ($4.40) adults, £1.50 ($2.40) children. Easter or Apr 1 (whichever is earlier) to Oct 31 daily.

Originally built as a monastery in 1196, then converted into a private home in the 16th century, it has long been associated with Torquay's leading citizens. Today the Torquay Town Council maintains it as a museum. The museum features a room outfitted in a close approximation of **Agatha Christie's private study.** After the mystery writer's death, her family donated for display her Remington typewriter, many of her original manuscripts, an oil portrait of Ms. Christie as a young woman, family photographs, and more.

Oldway Mansion. Torbay Rd., in Preston, near Paignton (a short drive south of the center of Torquay on the main Paignton–Torquay rd.). ☎ **01803/296244.** Tours available May–Sept between 10am and 1pm for £1 ($1.60). Admission free without guided tour. Year-round Mon–Fri 9am–5pm; Apr–Oct also Sat–Sun 9am–5pm.

You'll see the conspicuous consumption of England's gilded age here. The mansion was built in 1874 by Isaac Merritt Singer, founder of the sewing machine empire, and his son Paris then enhanced its decor, massive Ionic portico, and 17 acres of Italianate gardens. The mansion's eclectic decor includes a scaled-down version of the Hall of Mirrors in the Palace of Versailles. During its Jazz Age heyday, Oldway served as a rehearsal space and performance venue for Isadora Duncan, who was having a not terribly discreet affair with Paris.

WHERE TO STAY
EXPENSIVE

✪ **The Imperial.** Park Hill Rd., Torquay, Devon TQ1 2DG. ☎ **800/225-5843** in the U.S. and Canada, or 01803/294301. Fax 01803/298293. 184 units. TV TEL. £108–£150 ($172.80–$240) double; from £200 ($320) suite. Rates include English breakfast, use of sporting facilities, and dancing in the ballroom Mon–Sat. AE, DC, MC, V. Garage parking £5 ($8); free parking lot.

This leading five-star hotel in the West Country dates from the 1860s, but a major refurbishing has kept it abreast of the times and way ahead of all its competition. It sits on 5½ acres of subtropical gardens opening onto rocky cliffs, with views of the Channel. You'll be following the example of some of the characters of Agatha Christie if you check in here. She called it the Esplanade in *The Rajah's Emerald*, the Castle in *Partners in Crime*, and the Majestic in *Peril at End House.* (Who fired that shot in the hotel garden? Ask Poirot.) On the Imperial terrace, Miss Marple has figured out whodunit. Inside is a world of soaring ceilings, marble columns, and ornate plasterwork—enough to make a former visitor, Edward VII, feel at home. Each bedroom has lots of well-ordered space and traditional furniture; many have private balconies suspended high above a view that encompasses offshore islands with black rocks and sheer sides.

Dining: The elegant Regatta Restaurant serves British and international dishes, supplemented by a fine wine list, at lunch and dinner daily (reserve for dinner).

Orestone Manor. Rockhouse Lane, Maidencombe, Torquay, Devon TQ1 4SX. ☎ **01803/328098.** Fax 01803/328336. 18 units. TV TEL. £100–£140 ($160–$224) double. Rates include English breakfast. Winter discounts available. AC, MC, V. Closed Jan. Drive 3½ miles north of Torquay on B3199.

Sometimes the best way to enjoy a bustling seaside resort is from afar, nestling in a country home. Orestone Manor is in nearby Maidencombe, a small village north of Torquay. In one of the loveliest valleys in South Devon, this gabled manor house, constructed in the early 19th century as a private home, enjoys a tranquil rural setting, situated on 2 acres of well-landscaped gardens. The bedrooms are handsomely and comfortably furnished and offer beverage-makers.

Dining: Tasty bar lunches are provided Monday through Saturday, and the fixed-price dinner is always well prepared using only fresh ingredients.

Palace Hotel. Babbacombe Rd., Babbacombe, Torquay, Devon TQ1 3TG. ☎ **01803/ 200200.** Fax 01803/299899. 141 units. TV TEL. £130–£150 ($208–$240) double; £210–£250 ($336–$400) suite for 2. Rates include English breakfast. AE, DC, MC, V. Parking £5 ($8) for garage spaces. From the town center take B3199 east. Bus: 32.

This 1921 hotel was built when life was experienced on a grand scale, an attitude that's reflected by the spacious public rooms with their molded ceilings and columns. With all its many improvements in recent years, the hotel should be able to enter the next century in a premier position. It's luxurious through and through. All its bedrooms are well furnished. The hotel occupies 25 choice acres of real estate in Torquay, sweeping down to Anstey's Cove.

Amenities: Both indoor and outdoor swimming pools along with indoor and outdoor tennis courts, two indoor squash courts, a 9-hole golf course.

INEXPENSIVE

Colindale. 20 Rathmore Rd., Chelston, Torquay, Devon TQ2 6NY. ☎ **01803/293947.** 8 units, 4 with bathroom. £38 ($60.80) double without bathroom, £40 ($64) double with bathroom. Rates include English breakfast. AE, DC, MC, V.

This hotel is a good choice, and it's about as central as you'd want: It opens onto King's Garden, within a 5-minute walk of Corbyn Beach and a 3-minute walk from the railway station. There's a cocktail bar and a residents' lounge and dining room offering a fixed-price dinner for £8.50 ($13.60). Rooms are comfortably and cozily furnished. Colindale is one of a row of attached brick Victorian houses, with gables and chimneys. It's set back from the road, with a parking lot in front.

Craig Court Hotel. 10 Ash Hill Rd., Castle Circus, Torquay, Devon TQ1 3HZ. ☎ **01803/ 294400.** 10 units, 9 with bathroom. TV. £33–£39 ($52.80–$62.40) double without bathroom, £39–£45 ($62.40–$72) double with bathroom. Rates include English breakfast. No credit cards. Take St. Marychurch Rd. (signposted St. Marychurch, Babbacombe) from Castle Circus (the town hall), make the first right onto Ash Hill Rd., go 200 yds, and the hotel is on the right.

This hotel is in a large Victorian mansion with southern exposure that lies a short walk form the heart of town. Owner Ann Box offers excellent value with modernized rooms, many with private facilities. In addition to enjoying the good, wholesome food served here, guests can also make use of a well-appointed lounge or an intimate bar opening onto the grounds. A four-course dinner costs £10 ($16).

Homers. Warren Rd., Torquay, Devon TQ2 5TN. ☎ **01803/213456.** Fax 01803/213458. 15 units. TV TEL. May–Oct £60 ($96) double; £98 ($156.80) suite. Nov–Apr £50 ($80) double; £80 ($128) suite. Rates include English breakfast. AE, DC, MC, V. Turn left from the Sea Front along the front (inside lane) straight up the hill; Warren Rd. is on the right (it's a very tight turn by St. Luke's Church).

The solid Victorian walls of this house were originally built in the 1850s as the summer vacation home of a mining magnate. In 1994, new owners Gerald Clarke and Guy Mansell began a gradual renovation of each bedroom, leaving many family antiques in place along with old-fashioned homey touches. Set near the top of steeply inclined gardens overlooking Tor Bay, the hotel has a restaurant, Les Ambassadeurs. Here, evening meals are prepared only with fresh ingredients, and the chef caters to people with special dietary needs, including vegetarians.

Palm Court Hotel. Sea Front, Torquay, Devon TQ2 5HD. ☎ **01803/294881.** Fax 01803/211199. 37 units. TV TEL. £32–£66 ($51.20–$105.60) double. Suites from £120 ($192). Rates include English breakfast. Half board £30–£35 ($48–$56) per person. DC, MC, V. Parking £3 ($4.80).

The Palm Court Hotel, facing south onto the esplanade overlooking Torquay, offers style and good living. The original row of Regency-era houses were joined together to form a hotel in the 1920s. Two lounges are wood-paneled with leaded-glass windows. In the dining room is a minstrels' gallery. There are two up-to-date bars and the Sands Restaurant, open all day. All rooms have been modernized and are equipped with beverage-makers and central heating. With garden chairs and tables on the sun terrace outside the restaurant, the Palm Court becomes a social center. At night, the colored floodlighting around the bay evokes a Riviera atmosphere.

WHERE TO DINE

Mulberry Room. 1 Scarborough Rd., Torquay, Devon TQ2 5UJ. ☎ **01803/213639.** Reservations required for dinner. Main courses £5.50–£8.50 ($8.80–$13.60); 2-course lunch £5.95 ($9.50), 3-course lunch £7.95 ($12.70). No credit cards. Wed–Sun noon–2pm and 7:30–9:30pm. From the Sea Front, turn up Belgrave Rd.; Scarborough Rd. is the first right. Bus: 32. ENGLISH.

Lesley Cooper is an inspired cook, and she'll feed you well in her little dining room, seating some two dozen diners at midday. The restaurant is situated in one of Torquay's Victorian villas, facing a patio of plants and flowers, with outside tables for summer lunches and afternoon teas. The vegetarian will find comfort here, and others can feast on Lesley's baked lamb, honey-roasted chicken, or grilled natural fried fillets of sole with tartar sauce. Traditional roasts draw the Sunday crowds. The choice is wisely limited so that everything served will be fresh.

You can even stay here in one of three bedrooms, each comfortably furnished and well kept, with private bath. B&B charges range from £21 to £25 ($33.60 to $40) per person daily, making it one of the best bargains of the whole area.

Remy's. 3 Croft Rd. ☎ **01803/292359.** Reservations required. Fixed-price menu £17.85 ($28.55). MC, V. Tues–Sat 7:15–9:30pm. From the Sea Front, head north on Shedden Hill. Bus: 32. FRENCH.

The finest nonhotel restaurant in Torquay, Remy's serves good food at reasonable prices, offering a fixed-price three-course menu that changes daily. French owner and chef Remy Bopp sets great store by his ingredients, whether they be fresh fish from a local fishmonger or vegetables from the market. Everything is homemade, including bread, ice cream, sorbet, and pastries. Guests can also enjoy his carefully selected group of French wines. The food is straightforward and rarely overdone, beginning with the pâté of the chef (garlic, herbs, and pork), and going on to such main dishes as roast chicken in an orange sauce or saddle of lamb in a cream-and-tarragon sauce.

TORQUAY AFTER DARK

There are seven theaters in town, all open year-round, offering everything from Gilbert and Sullivan and tributes to Sinatra and Nat King Cole, to Marine Band concerts and comedy shows. Among the most active of the theaters are the **Palace Avenue Theatre,** Palace Avenue, Paignton (☎ **01803/355-8367**); the **Princess Theatre,** Torbay Road (☎ **01803/329-9992**); and the **Festival Theatre,** The Esplanade, Paignton (☎ **01803/355-8641**).

Fifteen area nightclubs cater to everyone from teenyboppers to the gay scene, but dancing rules the town, and there's virtually nowhere to catch live club acts. Among the better dance clubs are **Claires,** Torwood Street (☎ 01803/329-2079), for its Friday- and Saturday-night house music, with a cover charge varying from £2 to £5 ($3.20 to $8), depending on the DJ; and **Monroes,** Victoria Road (☎ **01803/329-1149**), with a £2 ($3.20) cover on Thursday and Friday, and Saturday before 10pm (afterwards it's £4/$6.40). For a later night and a serious dance groove, try the

Monastery, Torwood Gardens Road (☎ 01803/329-2929), on Saturday, the only night this club opens its doors. You can definitely get your fill of hip-hop and electronica here as the dancing starts at midnight and doesn't end until 7am.

The Pleasure Dome/Judy G's, Belgrave Road (☎ 01803/321-1131), has the Juicy Fruit Club, a gay dance night, once a month on Wednesday, and **Double Two,** Rock Road (☎ 01803/329-2279), is all gay, all the time, with a £2 ($3.20) cover at the door.

4 Totnes

224 miles SW of London; 12 miles NW of Dartmouth

One of the oldest towns in the West Country, the ancient borough of Totnes rests quietly in the past, seemingly content to let the Torquay area remain in the vanguard of the building boom. On the River Dart, upstream from Dartmouth, Totnes is so totally removed in character from Torquay that the two towns could be in different countries. Totnes has several historic buildings, notably the ruins of a Norman castle, an ancient guildhall, and the 15th-century Church of St. Mary, constructed of red sandstone. In the Middle Ages the town was encircled by walls; the North Gate serves as a reminder of that period.

ESSENTIALS
GETTING THERE   Totnes is on the main London-Plymouth line. Trains leave London's Paddington Station frequently throughout the day. For rail information, call ☎ 0345/484950 in the U.K. or 01603/764776 in the U.S.

Totnes is served locally by the Western National and Devon General bus companies (☎ 01752/222555 in Plymouth for information about individual routings).

If you're driving from Torquay, head west on A385.

Many visitors approach Totnes by river steamer from Dartmouth. Contact **Dart Pleasure Craft,** River Link (☎ 01803/834488), for information.

VISITOR INFORMATION   The **Tourist Information Centre** is at the Plains (☎ 01803/863168). It's open daily from 9:30am to 12:30pm and 1:30 to 5pm (closed on Sunday off-season).

EXPLORING TOTNES
Totnes is known for its colorful **markets,** staged year-round in the center of town at Civic Square, on Friday mornings and early afternoons. On Tuesdays from May through September, many vendors are in Elizabethan costumes. You may want to wander throughout the town enjoying its old bookstores, antique shops, and retailers hawking handcrafted goods, lace, clothes, knits, and handmade shoes and toys, plus a myriad of other gifts.

The Elizabethan Museum. Fore St. ☎ 01803/863821. Admission £1.50 ($2.40) adults, 80p ($1.30) seniors, 50p (80¢) children. Easter–Oct Mon–Fri 10:30am–5pm, Sat 2–5pm.

This 16th-century home of a wealthy merchant houses furniture, costumes, documents, and farm implements of the Elizabethan age. One room is devoted to local resident Charles Babbage (1792–1871), a mathematician and inventor. He invented a calculating machine that used cards perforated with a coded series of holes and whose memory capacities categorized it as an early version of the computer. His other inventions included the ophthalmoscope, a speedometer, and the cowcatchers later used to fend cows off the tracks of railways around the world.

Totnes Castle. Castle St. ☎ **01803/864406.** Admission £2.20 ($3.50). Apr–Oct daily 10am–6pm; off-season, daily 10am–4pm.

Crowning the hilltop at the northern end of High Street, this castle was built by the Normans shortly after their conquest of England. It's one of the best examples of motte-and-bailey construction remaining in the United Kingdom. Although the outer walls survived, the interior is mostly in ruins.

Totnes Guildhall. Ramparts Walk. ☎ **01803/862147.** Admission 75p ($1.20) adults, 25p (40¢) children. Easter–Sept Mon–Sat 10:30am–1pm and 2–4:30pm.

This is the symbol of Totnes. Originally built as a priory (monastery) in 1553, it contains an old gaol (jail), a collection of civic memorabilia, and the table Oliver Cromwell used to sign documents during his visit to Totnes in 1646.

WHERE TO STAY IN THE TOTNES AREA

✿ **The Cott Inn.** Dartington, near Totnes (on the old Ashburton–Totnes turnpike), S. Devon TQ9 6HE. ☎ **01803/863777.** Fax 01803/866629. 6 units. TV TEL. £65 ($104) double. Rates 10% lower Oct–Easter. Extra person £15 ($24) per night. AE, MC, V. Bus: X80 travels from Totnes to Dartington, but most people take a taxi for the 1½-mile journey.

Built in 1320, this hotel is the second-oldest inn in England. It's a low, rambling 2-story building of stone, cob, and plaster, with a thatched roof and 3-foot-thick walls. The owners rent low-ceilinged double rooms upstairs, with modern conveniences, including hot and cold running water. The inn is a gathering place for the people of Dartington, and you'll feel the pulse of English country life.

In winter, log fires keep the lounge and bar snug. You'll surely be intrigued with the tavern, where you can also order a meal. A buffet is laid out at lunchtime, priced according to your choice of dish. Dinner features local produce prepared in interesting ways; scallops, duck, steak, or fresh salmon may be available. Even if you're not staying over, you might want to drop by the pub (five beers are on draft). They offer a dining plan for guests at the hotel dining room, which includes a full English breakfast and dinner, starting at £42.50 ($68) per person.

Gabriel Court Hotel. Stoke Gabriel, near Totnes, S. Devon TQ9 6SF. ☎ **01803/782206.** Fax 01803/782333. 22 units. TV TEL. £77 ($123.20) double; £105 ($168) family room for 3. Rates include English breakfast. AE, DC, MC, V. Exit the A38 at Buckfastleigh, taking A384 to Totnes, then A385 to Paignton; approximately 1 mile out of Totnes, turn right at the sign to Stoke Gabriel.

In nearby Stoke Gabriel, the Gabriel Court is a manor house that was owned by the same family from 1487 to 1928, when it was converted into a hotel. Michael and Eryl Beacom, the proprietors, offer good value and hospitality. The hotel, overlooking a pretty village on the banks of the River Dart, stands in a terraced Elizabethan garden, with a heated swimming pool and a lawn tennis court. The 3-acre site is the setting for the white-painted house, which offers well-furnished, comfortable bedrooms. Each of these is in a modern extension that was converted from a hayloft.

The Gabriel Court enjoys a reputation for its well-cooked English food, enhanced by fruit and vegetables from its own garden, as well as trout and salmon from the Dart. The hotel has a bar, and in winter log fires make the restful lounges cozy retreats.

Royal Seven Stars Hotel. The Plains, Totnes, S. Devon TQ9 5DD. ☎ **01803/862125.** Fax 01803/867925. 17 units, 12 with bathroom. TV TEL. £54 ($86.40) double without bath, £62–£72 ($99.20–$115.20) double with bath. Children under 16 £12.50 ($20). Rates include English breakfast. AE, DC, MC, V.

A historic former coaching inn in the center of Totnes, the Royal Seven Stars largely dates from 1660. The hotel has an interesting porch over its entrance and overlooks a square in the town center, near the banks of the River Dart. The interior courtyard, once used for horses and carriages, is now enclosed in glass, with an old pine staircase. With antiques and paintings, the hotel's own heraldic shield, hand-carved chests, and a grandfather clock, the courtyard forms an inviting entrance to the inn. The bedrooms, each with a comfortable bed and a hot beverage maker, have been modernized and have built-in furniture. Two have four-poster beds.

WHERE TO DINE

When it's teatime, **Greys Dining Room,** 96 High St. (☎ **01803/866369**), sets out its fine silver and china to welcome you in an atmosphere of wood paneling and antiques. About 40 different teas along with homemade cakes and scones will invite you to extend the afternoon.

Brutus Room. In the Royal Seven Stars Hotel. ☎ **01803/862125.** Reservations recommended. Main courses £5.50–£14 ($8.80–$22.40); 4-course table d'hôte with coffee and value-added tax (VAT) £16.50 ($26.40); lunch buffet £4–£6 ($6.40–$9.60). DC, MC, V. Daily noon–2:15pm and 7–9pm. ENGLISH.

For the kind of cuisine that pleased Grandpa, this 1660 old coaching inn delivers quite well. Just when it appeared that the world had gone postnouvelle, you find a place like this serving the kind of respectable cuisine Sir Winston might have enjoyed. You can stick with the four-course table d'hôte menu or order à la carte. Begin with smoked fillet of Brixham mackerel or the soup of the day. Main dishes always two-fisted selections such as a grilled sirloin, grilled lemon sole, or a respectable halibut steak. Vegetables of the day are fresh and well prepared. Finish in the British manner with blue Stilton cheese or perhaps a fruit tart—homemade, of course. At last, a place that still serves belle Hélène, an old-fashioned pear dessert. The adjoining Saddle Room bar has a wide range of ales, wine, and spirits.

5 Dartmouth

236 miles SW of London; 35 miles SE of Exeter

At the mouth of the Dart River, this ancient seaport is the home of the Royal Naval College. Traditionally linked to England's maritime greatness, Dartmouth sent out the young midshipmen who saw to it that "Britannia ruled the waves." You can take a river steamer up the Dart to Totnes (book at the kiosk at the harbor); the scenery along the way is panoramic, as the Dart is Devon's most beautiful river. Dartmouth's 15th-century castle was built during the reign of Edward IV. The town's most noted architectural feature is the Butter Walk, which lies below Tudor houses. The Flemish influence in some of the houses is pronounced.

ESSENTIALS

GETTING THERE   Dartmouth is not easily reached by public transport. Trains run to Totnes (see above) and Paignton. There is one bus a day from Totnes to Dartmouth. Call ☎ 01752/222666 for schedules.

If you're driving from Exeter, take A38 southwest, cutting southeast to Totnes on A381; then follow A381 to the junction with B3207.

Riverboats make the 10-mile run from Totnes to Dartmouth, but these trips depend on the tide and operate only from Easter to the end of October. See Totnes, above, for details on obtaining boat schedules.

VISITOR INFORMATION The **Tourist Information Centre** is at the Engine House, Mayors Avenue (☎ **01803/834224**), and is open April to October, Monday to Saturday from 9:30am to 5:30pm and Sunday from 10am to 4pm (off-season Monday to Saturday from 10am to 4pm).

EXPLORING DARTMOUTH

Many visitors come to Dartmouth for the bracing salt air and a chance to explore the surrounding marshlands, which are rich in bird life and natural beauty. The historic monuments here are steeped in much of the legend and lore of Channel life and historic Devon.

The town's most historic and interesting church is **St. Petrox,** on Castle Road, a 17th-century Anglican monument with an ivy-draped graveyard whose tombstones evoke the sorrows of Dartmouth's maritime past. The church is open daily from 7am to dusk.

It's also worth walking through the waterfront neighborhood known as **Bayard's Cove,** a cobbled, half-timbered neighborhood that's quite charming. Set near the end of Lower Street, it prospered during the 1600s thanks to its ship-repair services. In 1620 its quays were the site for repairs of the Pilgrims' historic ships, the *Speedwell* and the *Mayflower,* just after their departure from Plymouth.

Dartmouth Castle. Castle Rd. (½ mile south of the town center). ☎ 01803/833588. Admission £2.40 ($3.85) adults, £1.20 ($1.90) children. Apr–Oct daily 10am–6pm; Nov–Mar Wed–Sun 10am–4pm.

Originally built during the 15th century, the castle was later outfitted with artillery and employed by the Victorians as a coastal defense station. A tour of its bulky ramparts and somber interiors provides insight into the changing nature of warfare throughout the centuries, and you'll see sweeping views of the surrounding coast and flatlands.

Dartmouth Museum. In the Butter Walk. ☎ **01803/832923.** Admission £1 ($1.60) adults, 40p (65¢) children. Mar–Nov Mon–Sat 11am–5pm; rest of the year Mon–Sat noon–3pm.

This is the region's most interesting maritime museum, focusing on the British Empire's military might of the 18th century. Built between 1635 and 1640, it's set amid an interconnected row of 17th-century buildings—The Butter Walk—whose overhanging, stilt-supported facade was originally designed to provide shade for the butter, milk, and cream sold there by local milkmaids. Today the complex houses the museum, as well as shops selling wines, baked goods, and more.

WHERE TO STAY

Dart Marina Hotel. Sandquay, Dartmouth, Devon TQ6 9PH. ☎ **01803/832580.** Fax 01803/835040. 50 units. TV TEL. £113–£158 ($180.80–$252.80) double; £158–£198 ($252.80–$316.80) suite for 2. Rates include half board. AE, DC, MC, V.

This hotel sits at the edge of its own marina, within a 3-minute walk from the center of town. It was originally built as a clubhouse for local yachties late in the 19th century and was then enlarged and transformed into a hotel just before World War II. It does not have as much charm or character as the Royal Castle. The bar, the new riverside terrace, and each bedroom afford a view of yachts bobbing at anchor in the Dart River; about 14 bedrooms have private balconies. The comfortable bedrooms have coffee makers.

Royal Castle Hotel. 11 The Quay, Dartmouth, Devon TQ6 9PS. ☎ **01803/833033.** Fax 01803/835445. 25 units. TV TEL. £90–£145 ($144–$232) double. Rates include English breakfast. AE, MC, V.

A coaching inn on the town quay since 1639, the Royal Castle Hotel has hosted Sir Francis Drake, Queen Victoria, Charles II, and Edward VII. Horse-drawn carriages (as late as 1910) dispatched passengers in a carriageway, now an enclosed reception hall. The glassed-in courtyard, with its winding wooden staircase, has the original coaching horn and a set of 20 antique spring bells connected to the bedrooms. Many rooms open off the covered courtyard and the rambling corridors display antiques. River-view rooms are the most sought after. All units have been recently restored and have central heating. Some are air-conditioned and six units offer a Jacuzzi.

Dining/Diversions: The meals, taken in the restaurant under a beautiful Adam ceiling, are excellent, in the best English tradition. A favorite place to settle in is the Galleon Bar, once two old kitchens, with double fireplaces and large hand-hewn beams said to have been salvaged from Spanish Armada ships. There's another pub-style bar, with settles (benches), that's popular with the locals. Guests lounge on the second floor in a room with a bay window overlooking the harbor.

WHERE TO DINE

✪ **The Carved Angel.** 2 S. Embankment. ☎ **01803/832465.** Reservations recommended. Main courses £21–£24.50 ($33.60–$39.20); 3-course fixed-price meals £15–£29 ($24–$46.40) at lunch, £48.75 ($78) at dinner. MC, V. Tues–Sun 12:30–2:30pm; Tues–Sat 7:30–9:30pm. Closed Jan 1–Feb 15. CONTINENTAL.

The best restaurant in town, the stylishly simple Carved Angel is on the riverfront. The building's half-timbered, heavily carved facade rises opposite the harbor. Inside, there's a statue of a carved angel (hence the name).

The cooking is both innovative and interesting, more akin to the creative cuisine of the continent than to the traditional cookery of England. Appetizers range from Dartmouth smoked salmon with lime couscous to puff of duck and goose livers with grapes and Madeira. Main dishes include roast loin of lamb with ratatouille, deep-fried garlic, and rosemary sauce, and pheasant in pastry with pâté and mushrooms. It's worth saving room for the cranberry tart with crème anglaise or the hot apple-and-cinnamon soufflé with calvados ice cream.

Horn of Plenty. In the Tamar View House, Gulworthy, Tavistock, Devon PL19 8JD. ☎ **01822/832528.** Reservations required. £10.50–£18.50 ($16.80–$29.60) fixed-price lunch; £22.50 ($36) potluck menu Mon; £32.50 ($52) fixed-price dinner (Tues–Sun). AE, MC, V. Tues–Sun noon–2:30pm; daily 7–9pm. Closed Dec 25. Drive 3 miles west of Tavistock on A390. INTERNATIONAL.

As you drive from Tavistock to Callington, you'll see a small sign pointing north along a leafy drive to the solid Regency house where the owners operate what the French call a *restaurant avec chambres.* It was built by the duke of Bedford in the early 1800s as a private home. After a day of touring the country, guests enjoy well-prepared dinners, which might include terrine of duck foie de gras with sweet-and-sour leeks as an appetizer, followed by the fresh fish of the day or roast squab pigeon perfectly done, served with foie gras on a shallot potato cake. Even though all meals are fixed-price arrangements, there is a choice in each category.

You can stay in one of the spacious, warm, and elegant bedrooms (seven in all) that have been installed over the old stables of the house. With a continental breakfast included, doubles go for £88 to £98 ($140.80 to $156.80). All accommodations have TVs, beverage-maker, phones, and well-stocked minibars.

A FAVORITE LOCAL PUB

Just a 2-minute walk from Bayard's Cove is one of our favorite pubs, **The Cherub,** 13 Higher St. (☎ **01803/832571**). It was originally built in 1380 as the harbormaster's house. Today this charming pub is a great place to drink and dine on simple traditional British platters and bar snacks. There's a more formal dining room upstairs that serves a number of fish dishes, steaks, lamb, and duck.

6 Plymouth

242 miles SW of London; 161 miles SW of Southampton

The historic seaport of Plymouth is more romantic in legend than in reality. But this was not always so—during World War II, greater Plymouth lost at least 75,000 buildings to Nazi bombs. The heart of present-day Plymouth, including the municipal civic center on the Royal Parade, has been entirely rebuilt; however, the way it was rebuilt is the subject of much controversy.

For the old part of town, you must go to the Elizabethan section, known as **The Barbican,** and walk along the quay in the footsteps of Sir Francis Drake (once the mayor of Plymouth). From here, in 1577, Drake set sail on his round-the-world voyage. The Barbican also holds special interest for visitors from the United States: it was the final departure point of the Pilgrims in 1620. The two ships, *Mayflower* and *Speedwell,* that sailed from Southampton in August of that year put into Plymouth after they suffered storm damage. Here, the *Speedwell* was abandoned as unseaworthy and the *Mayflower* made the trip to the New World alone.

ESSENTIALS
GETTING THERE   Plymouth Airport lies 4 miles from the center of the city. **Brymon Airways** (☎ **01752/772752**) has direct service from the London airports, Heathrow and Gatwick, to Plymouth.

Frequent trains run from London's Paddington Station to Plymouth in 3 to 3½ hours. For rail information, call ☎ **0345/484950** in the U.K. or 01603/764776 in the U.S. The **Plymouth Train Station** (☎ **0345/484950**) lies on North Road, north of the Plymouth Center. Western National Bus no. 83/84 runs from the station to the heart of Plymouth.

National Express has frequent daily bus service between London's Victoria Coach Station and Plymouth. The trip takes 4½ hours. Call ☎ **0990/808080** for schedules and information.

If you're driving from London, take M4 west to the junction with M5 going south to Exeter. From Exeter, head southwest on A38 to Plymouth.

VISITOR INFORMATION   The **Tourist Information Centre** is at the Island House, The Barbican (☎ **01752/264849**). A second information center, **Plymouth Discovery Centre,** is at Crabtree Marsh Mills, Plymouth (☎ **01752/266030**). Both are open Monday through Saturday from 9am to 5pm and Sunday from 10am to 4pm.

SEEING THE SIGHTS
To commemorate the spot from which the *Mayflower* sailed for the New World, a white archway, erected in 1934 and capped with the flags of Great Britain and the United States, stands at the base of Plymouth's West Pier, on The Barbican. Incorporating a granite monument that was erected in 1891, the site is referred to as both the **Mayflower Steps** and the **Memorial Gateway.**

The **Barbican** is a mass of narrow streets, old houses, and quay-side shops selling antiques, brass work, old prints, and books. It's a perfect place for strolling and browsing through shops at your leisure.

Fishing boats still unload their catch at the wharves, and passenger-carrying ferry-boats run short harbor cruises. A trip includes views of Drake's Island in the sound, the dockyards, naval vessels, and The Hoe from the water. A cruise of Plymouth Harbour costs £3.50 ($5.60) for adults and £1.75 ($2.80) for children. Departures are February through November, with cruises leaving every half hour from 10:30am to 3pm daily. These **Plymouth Boat Cruises** are booked at 8 Anderto Rise, Millbrook, Torpoint (☎ 01752/822797).

White Lane Gallery. 1 White Lane, The Barbican. ☎ **01752/221450.** Free admission. Mon noon–4pm, Tues–Sat 10am–5pm. Bus: 39.

This gallery specializes in contemporary art and crafts, with changing exhibitions of paintings and ceramics. It also has three resident craftspeople, including a potter, furniture maker, and silk painter. It's a 5-minute walk from the town center in Plymouth's historic Barbican, near the *Mayflower* Steps.

Plymouth Gin Distillery. Black Friars Distillery, 60 Southside St. ☎ **01752/667062.** Admission £2.75 ($4.40) adults, £2.25 ($3.60) children 10–18, free for children 9 and under. Mon–Sat 10:30am–4pm. Closed Nov–Easter. Bus: 54.

These premises, one of Plymouth's oldest surviving buildings, were where the Pilgrims met before sailing for the New World. Plymouth Gin has been produced here for 200 years on a historic site that dates from a Dominican monastery built in 1425. There are public guided tours. A Plymouth Gin Shop is on the premises.

Prysten House. Finewell St. ☎ **01752/661414.** Admission 75p ($1.20) adults, 30p (50¢) children. Mon–Sat 10am–4pm.

Built in 1490 as a town house close to St. Andrew's Church, this is now a church house and working museum. Reconstructed in the 1930s with American help, it displays a model of Plymouth in 1620 and tapestries depicting the colonization of America. At the entrance is the gravestone of the captain of the U.S. brig *Argus*, who died on August 15, 1813, after a battle in the English Channel.

WHERE TO STAY

Astor Hotel. 14–22 Elliott St., The Hoe, Plymouth, Devon PL1 2PS. ☎ **01752/225511.** Fax 01752/251994. 55 units. TV TEL. Mar–Oct £72 ($115.20) double; Nov–Feb £45 ($72) double. Rates include English breakfast. AE, DC, MC, V. Free parking overnight, £2.25 ($3.60) permit parking nearby.

The hotel building was originally constructed during the Victorian era as the private home of a prosperous sea captain. In 1987, it underwent a major restoration, and today it has comfortable bedrooms, each with a coffeemaker. The hotel is situated near The Hoe on a street lined with 19th-century buildings. On the premises are well-decorated public lounges and a cozy and accommodating bar—open to guests and the public alike—separated from the reception desk by a fan-shaped trio of glass doors. The hotel's restaurant serves fixed-price menus at lunch and dinner.

Duke of Cornwall Hotel. Millbay Rd., Plymouth, Devon PL1 3LG. ☎ **01752/266256.** Fax 01752/600062. 70 units. TV TEL. £84.50 ($135.20) double. Rates include English breakfast. AE, DC, MC, V.

The Duke of Cornwall Hotel is a Victorian Gothic building that survived World War II bombings. Constructed in 1863, it was regarded by Sir John Betjeman as the finest example of Victorian architecture in Plymouth. The refurbished bedrooms all have hair dryers, trouser presses, and coffeemakers. Some rooms contain antique four-poster beds.

The hotel dining room is of an elegant contemporary style, with a circular ceiling supporting a fine chandelier. Rather standard British and continental selections are featured.

Forte Posthouse. Cliff Rd., The Hoe, Plymouth, Devon PL1 3DL. ☎ **01752/662828.** Fax 01752/660974. 106 units. MINIBAR TV TEL. £69–£76.50 ($110.40–$122.40) double. Weekend break rates (including dinner and breakfast) £45–£53 ($72–$84.80) per person. AE, DC, MC, V.

This 9-story hotel, built in 1970, is situated on a hilltop above the bay and hosts half tourists and half business travelers. The hotel has well-furnished rooms, all but a dozen of which face the sea. Each unit has an iron and a coffeemaker. On the premises is a pub, the Traders Bar, with a separate entrance, along with a free-form, heated outdoor pool (open daily May to September), and the Trader's Restaurant with wide-angle views of the sea.

Plymouth Moat House Hotel. Armada Way, Plymouth, Devon PL1 2HJ. ☎ **01752/639988.** Fax 01752/673816. 221 units. A/C TV TEL. Sun–Thurs £110 ($176) double, Fri–Sat £79 ($126.40) double; suite £130 ($208) all week. AE, DC, MC, V. Parking £2.50 ($4) for duration of stay.

One of the most distinguished hotels in the West Country, overlooking the harbor and The Hoe, the Plymouth Moat House rises like a midget high-rise. The good-sized rooms are well furnished with long double beds and have wide picture windows and tea- and coffeemakers, trouser presses, and hair dryers. Baby-sitting is available. A covered swimming pool is on the grounds, and there's a sauna and sun terrace, with garden tables set up for poolside refreshments.

In the Blue Riband Restaurant, with its panoramic sea views, both à la carte and a table d'hôte menu are served. Seafood is a specialty, some of the catch brought fresh each day from The Barbican.

Novotel Plymouth. Marsh Mills, Plymouth, Devon PL6 8NH. ☎ **800/221-4542** in the U.S., or 01752/221422. Fax 01752/223922. 100 units. A/C TV TEL. £59–£63 ($94.40–$100.80) double. Children 16 or under stay free in parents' room. AE, DC, MC, V. Bus: 21 or 22.

Novotel Plymouth, a 10-minute drive from the town center beside the A38, is convenient if you're driving, and also if you're traveling with children. With landscaped gardens and plenty of parking, it offers an ample number of soundproofed rooms. Two children under 16 sharing a room with their parents also receive free breakfast. There's a swimming pool and a children's play area. A grill restaurant is open daily from 6am to midnight.

WHERE TO DINE

The **Plymouth Arts Centre Restaurant,** 38 Looe St. (☎ **01752/660060**), offers one of the most filling and down-home vegetarian meals in town. Prices range from £2 to £5 ($3.20 to $8), and it's also ideal for a snack. You can even see a movie downstairs if you'd like. Food is served Monday from 10am to 2pm and Tuesday through Saturday from 10am to 8pm.

✪ **Chez Nous.** 13 Frankfort Gate. ☎ **01752/266793.** Reservations required. Fixed-price lunch and dinner £32 ($51.20). AE, DC, V. Tues–Sat 12:30–2pm and 7–10:30pm. Closed 1st 3 weeks in Feb and Sept. FRENCH.

The most distinguished restaurant in Plymouth is Chez Nous, situated directly off Western Approach. This quite pretty and cozy restaurant is in a shopping complex, decorated all in Gallic red, white, and blue. Owner and chef Jacques Marchal borrows heavily from the past, but also expresses his creative talent. His type of cooking is called *la cuisine spontanée*—using fresh produce that changes with the seasons. Look for the specials of the day on the chalkboard menu. Accompanied by a classic and rather elegant and predominantly French wine list, the food is likely to include scallops steamed with ginger, bouillabaisse, and duck breast on a bed of lentils. Fish, generally, is the preferred main dish to order here. Fresh, quality ingredients are a hallmark of the cuisine.

Green Lanterns. 31 New St., The Barbican. ☎ **01752/201313.** Reservations recommended for dinner. Main courses £5.25–£6.50 ($8.40–$10.40) at lunch, £11.45–£15.55 ($18.30–$24.90) at dinner. AE, MC, V. Mon–Sat noon–2pm and 6:30–10:45pm. Bus: 54. ENGLISH/INTERNATIONAL.

A 16th-century eating house on a Tudor street, the Green Lanterns lies 200 yards from the Mayflower Steps and is near the municipally owned Elizabethan House. The family-owned Green Lanterns is run by Ian Cuss, who knows that visitors like the Elizabethan atmosphere, traditional English fare, and personal service. The lunch menu offers a selection of grills, chicken, and fish, all served with vegetables. The kitchen also features chalkboard specials such as Lancashire hot pot. Several unusual dishes are presented on the dinner menu, including goose breast in bread crumbs, wild duck (teal), and venison in red wine. Chicken, beef, turkey, plaice, and mackerel are also available, all served with fresh vegetables.

7 Clovelly

240 miles SW of London; 11 miles SW of Bideford

This is the most charming of all Devon villages and one of the main attractions of the West Country. Starting at a great height, the village cascades down the mountainside. Its narrow, cobblestone High Street makes driving impossible. You park your car at the top and make the trip on foot; supplies are carried down by donkeys. Every step of the way provides views of tiny cottages, with their terraces of flowers lining the main street. The village fleet is sheltered at the stone quay at the bottom.

The major sight of Clovelly is Clovelly itself. Charles Kingsley once wrote ". . . it is as if the place had stood still while all the world had been rushing and rumbling past it." The price of entry to the village (see below) includes a guided tour of a fisherman's cottage as it would have been at the end of the 1800s. For the same price, you can also visit the **Kingsley Exhibition.** Author of *Westward Ho!* and *Water Babies,* Kingsley lived in Clovelly while his father was curate at the church. This exhibition traces the story of his life.

Right down below the Kingsley Exhibition—and our shopping note for the town— is a **Craft Gallery** where you have a chance to see and buy a wide variety of works by local artists and craftspeople. Once you've reached the end, you can sit and relax on the quay, taking in the views and absorbing Clovelly's unique atmosphere from this tiny, beautifully restored 14th-century quay.

Once you've worked your way to the bottom, how are you supposed to get back up? Those in good shape will climb all the way back up these impossibly steep cobbled streets to the top and the parking lot. For those who can't make the climb up the slippery incline, go to the rear of the Red Lion Inn and queue up for a Land Rover. In summer, the line is often long, but considering the alternative, it's worth the wait.

To avoid the tourist crowd, stay out of Clovelly from around 11am until teatime. Visit nearby villages such as Bucks Mills (3 miles to the east) and Hartland Quay (4 miles to the west) during the middle of the day, when the congestion here is at its height.

ESSENTIALS

GETTING THERE   From London's Paddington Station, trains depart for Exeter (see above) frequently. At Exeter, passengers transfer to a train headed for the end destination of Barnstaple. Travel time from Exeter to Barnstaple is 1¼ hours. From Barnstaple, passengers transfer to Clovelly by bus.

From Barnstaple, about one bus per hour, operated by either the Red Bus Company or the Filers Bus Company, goes to Bideford. The trip takes 40 minutes. At Bideford, connecting buses (with no more than a 10-minute wait between the arrival and the departure) continue on for the 30-minute drive to Clovelly. Two Land Rovers make continuous round-trips to the Red Lion Inn from the top of the hill. The visitor center (see below) maintains up-to-the-minute transportation information about how to get to Clovelly, depending on where you are.

If you're driving, from London, head west on M4, cutting south at the junction with M5. At the junction near Bridgwater, continue west along A39 toward Lynton. A39 runs all the way to the signposted turnoff for Clovelly.

VISITOR INFORMATION   Go to the **Clovelly Visitor Centre** (☎ 01237/ 431781), where you'll pay £2.25 ($3.60) for the cost of parking, use of facilities, entrance to the village, and an audiovisual theater admission, offering a multiprojector show tracing the story of Clovelly back to 2,000 B.C. Also included in the price is a tour of a fisherman's cottage and admission to the Kingsley Exhibition (see above). Open Monday through Saturday from 9:30am to 5:15pm April through June, Monday through Saturday 10am to 4:30pm October through March, and daily from 9am to 6pm July through September.

WHERE TO STAY & DINE

New Inn. High St., Clovelly, N. Devon EX39 5TQ. ☎ **01237/431303.** Fax 01237/431636. 21 units, 8 with bathroom. £35–£42.50 ($56–$68) double without bathroom; £65.50–£77 ($104.80–$123.20) double with bathroom. Rates include English breakfast. MC, V.

About halfway down High Street is the village pub, a good meeting place at sundown. It offers the best lodgings in the village, in two buildings on opposite sides of the steep street (but only a 12-foot leap between their balconies). Eight rooms have TVs and phones. If you're driving, you can park in the lot at the entrance to the town. It's advisable to pack a smaller overnight bag, since your luggage will have to be carried down (but is returned to the top by donkey).

This little country inn is also recommended for meals in the oak-beamed dining room. The local fare, including Devonshire cream, is featured whenever possible. Locally caught lobsters are also prepared by the chef.

Red Lion. The Quay, Clovelly, Devon EX39 5TF. ☎ **01237/431237.** Fax 01237/431044. 11 units. TV £83 ($132.80) double. Rates include English breakfast. MC, V.

At the bottom of the steep cobbled street, right on the stone seawall of the little harbor, Red Lion occupies the prime position in the village. Rising 3 stories with gables and a courtyard, it's actually an unspoiled country inn, where life centers around an antique pub and village inhabitants, including sea captains, who gather to satisfy their thirsts over pints of ale. Most rooms look out directly to the sea and all have hot and cold running water and adequate furnishings.

Dinner is available in the sea view dining room with a choice of main dishes, some of which always include fresh local fish, and then a selection from the dessert trolley.

EN ROUTE TO LYNTON-LYNMOUTH: A STAY ON A WORKING FARM

Halmpstone Manor. Chittlehampton Rd., Bishop's Tawton, Barnstaple, N. Devon EX32 0EA. ☎ **01271/830321.** Fax 01271/830826. 5 units. TV TEL. £100–£140 ($160–$224) double.

Rates include English breakfast. AE, DC, MC, V. From Clovelly, take the A39 east for 30 to 45 minutes, turning off the A39 when you see signs for Chittlehampton. About 2 miles after the turnoff, you'll see signs pointing to Halmpstone Manor.

In the countryside, this working farm is operated by Charles and Jane Stanbury. Originally built in the 11th century as a manor house with 22 rooms, the structure has diminished in size because of two fires that occurred in the 15th and 16th centuries. The edifice was rebuilt in 1701 in its present form with 15th-century paneling located in the dining room and high ceilings in the four-poster bedrooms. Family heirlooms are scattered throughout, and all the rooms have beverage-makers and trouser presses.

Dining: Mrs. Stanbury once worked at the prestigious restaurant Le Gavroche in London, and she brings some of that experience to her dining table. She offers a menu based on French and modern English fare made with fresh local ingredients, including dishes such as fillet of Devonshire beef in red-wine sauce with caramelized shallots and spring lamb encased in an herb-brioche crust glazed with port. For dessert, try the sticky toffee pudding with butterscotch sauce. A six-course dinner costs £25 ($40) for guests and £30 ($48) for everyone else.

8 Lynton-Lynmouth

206 miles W of London; 59 miles NW of Exeter

The north coast of Devon is particularly dramatic in Lynton, a village some 500 feet high, which is a good center for exploring the Doone Valley and that part of Exmoor that overflows into the shire from neighboring Somerset. The Valley of the Rocks, west of Lynton, offers the most panoramic scenery.

ESSENTIALS

GETTING THERE   The town is rather remote, and the local tourist office recommends that you rent a car to get here. However, local daily trains from Exeter arrive at Barnstaple. For rail information, call ☎ **0345/484950** in the U.K., or 01603/764776 in the U.S.

From Barnstaple, bus service is provided to Lynton at a frequency of one about every 2 hours. Call ☎ **01598/752225** for schedules.

If you're driving, take M4 west from London to the junction with M5, then head south to the junction with A39. Continue west on A39 to Lynton-Lynmouth.

VISITOR INFORMATION   The **Tourist Information Centre** is at the Town Hall, Lee Road (☎ **01598/752225**), and is open March through October daily from 8:30am to 6pm and from November through February from 9:30am to 1pm Monday through Saturday.

SEEING THE SIGHTS

Lynton is linked to its twin, Lynmouth, about 500 feet below, near the edge of the sea, by one of the most celebrated **railways** in Devon. The century-old train uses no electricity and no power. Instead, the railway covers the differences in distance and altitude by means of a complicated network of cables and pulleys, allowing cars to travel up and down the face of the rocky cliff. The length of the track is 862 feet with a gradient of 1 inch, which gives a vertical height of approximately 500 feet. The two passenger cars are linked together with two steel cables, and the operation of the lift is on the counterbalance system, which is simply explained as a pair of scales where one side, when weighted by water ballast, pulls the other up. The train carries about 40 passengers at a time for 50p (80¢) adults, 30p (50¢) children. Trains depart daily from April to October, at 2- to 5-minute intervals, from 8am to 7pm. From November through March, the train is shut down.

The East Lyn and West Lyn rivers meet in Lynmouth, a popular resort with the British. For a **panoramic view** of the rugged coastline, you can walk on a path halfway between the towns that runs along the cliff. From Lynton, or rather from Hollerday Hill, you can look out onto Lynmouth Bay, Countisbury Foreland, and Woody Bays in the west. From Hollerday Hill, the view encompasses the Valley of Rocks, formed during the Ice Age by towering rock formations with names such as "The Devil's Cheesewring," and its centerpiece, Castle Rock, which is renowned for its resident herd of wild goats.

From Lynmouth harbor there are regular boat trips along what the English have dubbed "The Heritage Coast" of North Devon. You can cruise past nesting colonies of razorbills, guillemots, dunlin, and kittiwakes, with the gulls soaring in the thermals by the highest sea cliffs in England.

Other activities in the locale include fishing, putting, bowls, tennis, pony trekking, and golf courses lying within a 20-mile radius. The visitor center (see above) also keeps abreast of the various outdoor pursuits (which change seasonally) available at the time of your visit.

WHERE TO STAY & DINE

Bath Hotel. Sea Front, Lynmouth, N. Devon EX35 6EL. ☎ 01598/752238. 24 units. TV TEL. £57–£77 ($91.20–$123.20) double. Rates include English breakfast. AE, DC, MC, V. Closed Nov–Feb and weekdays in Mar.

Despite this hotel's functional appearance, its small, almost-obliterated core dates from the 16th century. Most of what a visitor will see, however, is a solidly built, peach-colored structure that dates from the 1880s, set in a prominent position between the busy coastal road and the towering cliffs. All but a few of the comfortably furnished bedrooms offer views over the water, and each has an adjoining private bath. Well-prepared fixed-price meals are served in the hotel's restaurant.

Hewitt's Hotel and Restaurant. The Hoe, N. Walk, Lynton, Devon EX35 6HJ. ☎ 01598/752293. Fax 01598/752489. 8 units. TV TEL. £100–£120 ($160–$192) double. Rates include English breakfast, gourmet dinner, and traditional Devonshire afternoon tea. MC, V.

Hewitt's Hotel and Restaurant is named for Sir Thomas Hewitt, who helped construct the funicular railway that links the twin resorts. In the 1860s, he also built a home for himself, and that place today is one of the most successful small hotels in Lynton. Situated on some 27 acres, it opens onto the beautiful vistas of Lynmouth Bay (best enjoyed while seated on a sunny terrace). The old house is filled with architectural character, as exemplified by its grand staircase, time-mellowed paneling, antiques, and stained-glass windows. All rooms are well furnished and comfortably appointed; some have private balconies. The hotel is "for all seasons" and has a country-house atmosphere. It's a perfect Agatha Christie set.

Dining: The quality of the bar lunches is far above average, and dinner is among the best served at the resort. In fact, since only guests can dine, it's reason enough to stay here. You won't be overcharged either; meals begin at £16.50 ($26.40). A medley of British and continental dishes is served.

✪ **The Rising Sun Hotel.** The Harbour, Lynmouth, N. Devon EX35 6EQ. ☎ 01598/753223. Fax 01598/753480. 16 units, 1 cottage. TV TEL. £98–£130 ($156.80–$208) double; £140 ($224) Shelley's Cottage for 2. Rates include English breakfast. AE, DC, MC, V.

The Rising Sun Hotel is a thatched inn right at the end of the quay at the mouth of the Lyn River. You can bask in the wonder and warmth of an inn that has been in business for more than 600 years. All the rooms, with crazy levels and sloping ceilings, offer views of the water, the changing tides, and bobbing boats. It's a lovely old place. The ceilings are low and the floorboards creak. Behind the inn, halfway up the cliff, is a tiny garden bright with flowers in summer. The owner has refurbished the place and added more rooms by joining two adjacent properties, and he has rooms available nearby in Shelley's Cottage, where the poet honeymooned in 1812. R. D. Blackmore wrote part of *Lorna Doone* while staying at the hotel. Two rooms have four-poster beds.

Dining: It's a delight to dine at the Rising Sun since everything is 101% British in the dining room, with its deeply set window and fireplace. See the original 14th-century fireplace in the bar.

Tors Hotel. Lynmouth, Lynton, N. Devon EX35 6NA. ☎ **01598/753236.** Fax 01598/752544. 35 units. TV TEL. £64–£94 ($102.40–$150.40) double. Rates include English breakfast. AE, DC, MC, V. Closed Jan–Feb.

Set high on a cliff, the Tors Hotel opens onto a view of the coastline and the bay. It was built in 1895 in the fashion of a Swiss château, with more than 40 gables, Tyrolean balconies jutting out to capture the sun (or the moon), black-and-white-timbered wings, and some 30 chimneys. The interior has been modernized, and much attention has been lavished on the comfortable bedrooms. There's a heated swimming pool.

WHERE TO DINE

The Greenhouse Restaurant. 6 Lee Rd., Lynton. ☎ **01598/753358.** Reservations required. Main courses £6.50–£15.95 ($10.40–$25.50). AE, MC, V. Mar–May daily 9am–10pm; June–Sept daily 9am–10:30pm; Oct daily 9am–10pm. Closed Nov–Feb. INTERNATIONAL.

Established in 1890 as a tearoom, this pink-and-gray Victorian restaurant perched atop a 500-foot cliff offers a panoramic view of the Bristol Channel through its all-glass front. A nautical theme carries through the restaurant, and the bar actually has a water wheel built into it. Owners Chris and Anjali Peters serve a large menu that's about as varied as you're likely to find anywhere—a result, they say, of the fact that he's part Indian and she's part Chinese. Whatever the reason, offerings range from British to American, Chinese, Indian, Italian, and beyond. Locals and tourists alike appreciate the results and flock in to dine on main courses like the popular prawn jalsrezi (succulent shrimp in a spicy, medium-hot curry sauce); fresh local trout with almonds and herbs; a slab of steaming spinach-and-mushroom lasagna; or a 12-ounce chicken breast in cheese-and-ham sauce. Many dishes are made with fresh local seafood, and there are more than a dozen vegetarian choices. If you're in the mood for something lighter, you can choose from several salads, soups, and sandwiches.

Cornwall 11

The ancient duchy of Cornwall is in the extreme southwestern part of England, often called "the toe." This peninsula is a virtual island—culturally if not geographically. Encircled by coastline, it abounds in rugged cliffs, hidden bays, fishing villages, sandy beaches, and sheltered coves where smuggling was once rampant. Although many of the little seaports with hillside cottages resemble towns along the Mediterranean, Cornwall retains its own distinctive flavor.

The ancient land had its own language until about 250 years ago, and some of the old words (*pol* for pool, *tre* for house) still survive. The Cornish dialect is more easily understood by the Welsh than by those who speak the queen's English.

We suggest basing yourself at one of the smaller fishing villages, such as East or West Looe, Polperro, Mousehole, or Portloe, where you'll experience the true charm of the duchy. Many of the villages, such as St. Ives, are artists' colonies. Except for St. Ives and Port Isaac, some of the most interesting places lie on the southern coast, often called the Cornish Riviera. However, the north coast has its own peculiar charm as well. The majestic coastline is studded with fishing villages and hidden coves for swimming, with Penzance and St. Ives serving as the major meccas. A little further west is Land's End, where England actually comes to an end. There are also the Isles of Scilly, 27 miles off the Cornish coast, with only five islands inhabited out of more than 100. Here you'll find the Abbey Gardens of Tresco, 735 acres with 5,000 species of plants.

1 The Fishing Villages of Looe & Polperro

Looe: 264 miles SW of London; 20 miles W of Plymouth
Polperro: 271 miles SW of London; 6 miles SW of Looe; 26 miles W of Plymouth

The ancient twin towns of East and West Looe are connected by a seven-arched stone bridge that spans the river. Houses on the hills are stacked one on top of the other in terrace fashion. In each fishing village you can find good accommodations.

The old fishing village of Polperro is reached by a steep descent from the top of a hill from the main road leading to Polperro. You can take the 4½-mile cliff walk from Looe to Polperro, but the less adventurous will want to drive. However, in July and August you're not allowed to take cars into town unless you have a hotel reservation, in order to prevent traffic bottlenecks. There's a large parking area, which charges according to the length of your stay. For those unable to walk, a horse-drawn bus will take visitors to the town center.

Fishing and sailing are two of the major sports in the area, and the sandy coves, as well as **East Looe Beach,** are spots for sea bathing. Beyond the towns are cliff paths and chalky downs worth a ramble. Looe is noted for its shark fishing, but you may prefer simply walking the narrow, crooked medieval streets of East Looe, with its old harbor and 17th-century guildhall.

Polperro is one of the handsomest villages in Cornwall, and parts of it hark back to the 17th century. The village is surrounded by cliffs.

ESSENTIALS

GETTING THERE   Daily trains run from Plymouth to Looe, and rail connections can also be made from Exeter (Devon) and Bristol (Avon). Most visitors drive to Polperro, but the nearest main-line station is at Liskeard, less than 4 hours from London's Paddington Station, with a branch line to Looe. Taxis meet incoming trains to take visitors to the various little villages in the area. For rail information in the area, call ☎ **0345/484950** (in the U.K. only), 01603/764776, or 01793/499458.

Local bus companies have various routings from Plymouth into Looe. Ask at the tourist office in Plymouth for a schedule (see chapter 10). You can take a local bus to Polperro from Liskeard or Looe.

If you're driving to Looe from Plymouth, take A38 west, then B3253. To get to Polperro, follow A387 southwest from Looe.

VISITOR INFORMATION   The **Tourist Information Centre** is at the Guildhall, Fore Street (☎ **01503/262072**), and is open in summer only, daily from 10am to 2pm.

WHERE TO STAY & DINE IN & AROUND LOOE

Commonwood Manor Hotel. St. Martin's Rd. (the main Plymouth–Looe rd., B3253), E. Looe, Cornwall PL13 1LP. ☎ **01503/262929.** Fax 01503/262632. 11 units, 8 cottages. TV TEL. £64–£75 ($102.40–$120) double; £82–£132 ($131.20–$211.20) cottage. Rates include English breakfast. AE, MC, V. Closed Christmas.

A family operated, country-house hotel on the edge of town at the entrance to Looe, about a 5-minute walk from the harbor and the center of the resort, Commonwood Manor stands on a wooded hillside surrounded by 6 acres of private woodlands overlooking the Looe River Valley. Guests are shown to one of the well-furnished and comfortably appointed bedrooms; next, they might enjoy a dip in the heated swimming pool. The meals are good, prepared with fresh ingredients.

Fieldhead Hotel. Portuan Rd., Hannafore, W. Looe, Cornwall PL13 2DR. ☎ **01503/ 262689.** Fax 01503/264114. 14 units. MINIBAR TV TEL. £78 ($124.80) double. Rates include English breakfast. AE, MC, V. Closed Jan.

The Fieldhead, originally built in 1896 as a private home, is now one of the area's best hotels. Commanding a view of the sea, it is situated on 2 acres of gardens, with a heated outdoor swimming pool. The rooms have a high standard of traditional furnishings and are continually maintained, with beverage-makers in every room. Most also open onto views of Looe Bay. You'll also find views of the bay possible from the hotel's restaurant, where flowers and candles on the tables add a festive note for the home-cooked English and continental cuisine.

Hannafore Point Hotel. Marine Dr., W. Looe, Cornwall PL13 2DG. ☎ **01503/263273.** Fax 01503/263272. 37 units. TV TEL. £90–£110 ($144–$176) double. Rates include half board. DC, MC, V.

Cornwall

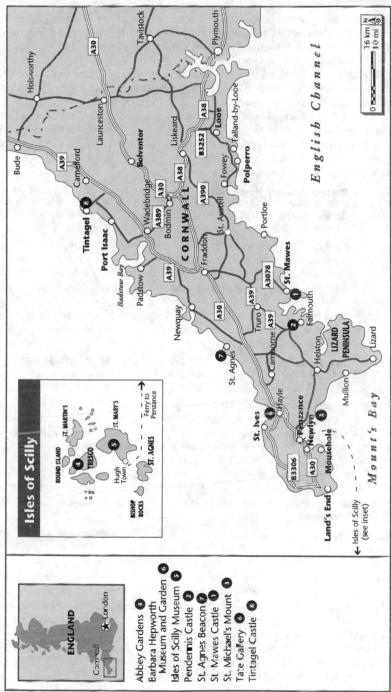

16 km
10 mi

English Channel

Mount's Bay

CORNWALL

LIZARD PENINSULA

Isles of Scilly

ROUND ISLAND
ST. MARTIN'S
TRESCO
ST. MARY'S
Hugh Town
ST. AGNES
BISHOP ROCKS

Ferry to Penzance

Isles of Scilly (see inset)

ENGLAND
London
Cornwall

Abbey Gardens ④
Barbara Hepworth Museum and Garden ⑤
Isles of Scilly Museum ②
Pendennis Castle ⑦
St Agnes Beacon ①
St Mawes Castle ③
St. Michael's Mount ⑥
Tate Gallery ⑧
Tintagel Castle

Plymouth
Tavistock
Holsworthy
Launceston
Dobwalter
Liskeard
Looe
Talland-by-Looe
Polperro
Fowey
Bude
Camelford
Wadebridge
Bodmin
St. Austell
Portloe
Tintagel
Port Isaac
Padstow
Fraddon
St. Mawes
Newquay
Truro
Falmouth
St. Agnes
Camborne
Helston
Lizard
St. Ives
Hayle
Penzance
Newlyn
Mullion
Mousehole
Land's End

Badstow Bay

A30 A39 A389 A30 A38 A38 A390 A39 A39 A3078 B3252 B3306

3-0565

411

This rambling, gabled structure commands a fine view of the harbor—you can see miles of Cornish coastline and one of the most beautiful bays in England. Hannafore Point is in the main center for shark and deep-sea fishing and is ideal for exploring either Cornwall or parts of Devon.

In addition to the older bay-windowed rooms, newer sections have picture windows for viewing the harbor and St. George's Island. Most of the front bedrooms have balconies, and each has a beverage-maker.

Dining: The panoramic view adds to the pleasure of dining in the Headland Restaurant, where fresh ingredients are used in the fine Cornish and French cuisine. The hotel entrance opens onto several levels of comfortable lounges and bars, with cantilever stairs and balconies.

Amenities: Health club with a sauna, indoor pool.

The Old Rectory Country House Hotel. Duloe Rd., St. Keyne, near Liskeard, Cornwall PL14 4RL. ☎ **01579/342617.** Fax 01579/342293. 8 units. TV. £55–£70 ($88–$112) double. Rates include English breakfast. MC, V. From Liskeard, take B3254 to St. Keyne, go through St. Keyne, and make a left turn at the sign for the hotel.

Peacefully secluded 5 miles from Looe in the beautiful countryside of southeast Cornwall, the hotel overlooks 3 acres of gardens with views across the valley. The owners' high standards complement the original architecture with paneled doors, marble fireplaces, Persian rugs, velvet sofas, and crystal. All the comfortably furnished bedrooms have beverage-makers.

English and continental cuisine is served on Wedgwood china in the elegant dining room where home-prepared meals and a selection of table wines are offered. The restaurant is open only to hotel guests.

Talland Bay Hotel. Talland-by-Looe, Cornwall PL13 2JB. ☎ **01503/272667.** Fax 01503/272940. 20 units. TV TEL. £88–£158 ($140.80–$252.80) double. Rates include English breakfast. AE, DC, MC, V. Closed Jan. Take A387 4 miles southwest of Looe.

A country house dating from the 16th century, situated on 2½ acres, this hotel is the domain of Barry and Annie Rosier, who will direct you to local beaches and the croquet lawn. Its rectangular swimming pool is ringed with flagstones and a semitropical garden. Views from the tastefully furnished bedrooms—refurbished in 1995—include the sea and rocky coastline. Some bedrooms are in an annex.

Dining: The food is the area's best, featuring skillfully prepared seafood. Even if you aren't staying here, you may want to reserve a table. A popular buffet lunch is served on the patio by the pool in summer. The restaurant is open for lunch, bar snacks, and dinner daily.

☼ Well House. St. Keyne, Liskeard, Cornwall PL14 4RN. ☎ **01579/342001.** Fax 01579/343891. 9 units. TV TEL. £95–£155 ($152–$248) double. Rates include English breakfast. MC, V. From Liskeard, take B3254 to St. Keyne, 3 miles away.

Well House is another of those *restaurants avec chambres* found occasionally in the West Country, and it's one of the best. Located 3 miles from Liskeard, it has 5 acres of gardens opening onto vistas of the Looe Valley. It offers beautifully furnished bedrooms, with many thoughtful extras, such as fresh flowers. There are two beautiful terrace rooms at the garden level.

Dining: Guests flock here mainly for the fine cuisine. Set menus are offered at both lunch and dinner; the price depends on how many courses you order.

Amenities: Swimming pool, all-weather tennis court.

WHERE TO STAY IN POLPERRO

In and around Polperro, you'll find a number of colorful cottages, houses, small hotels, and inns that accommodate guests.

Lanhael House, Langreek Rd., Polperro, Cornwall PL13 2PW. ☎ **01503/272428.** Fax 01503/273077. 5 units, 3 with bathroom. TV. £38 ($60.80) double without bathroom, £40 ($64) double with bathroom. Rates include English breakfast. No credit cards. Closed mid-Oct to Apr.

One of the best inexpensive accommodations in the area, Lanhael House, which is situated off the road to Fowey, dates from the 17th century. Today it has many amenities, including a swimming pool and a terrace to capture the sun off the Cornish coast. The comfortable rooms are attractively furnished, each with tea- or coffeemaker. An evening meal can be provided if arrangements are made in advance.

WHERE TO STAY IN NEARBY PELYNT & LANREATH

If you want to get away from the busy activity of the two little harbors of Looe and Polperro, the pace of the nearby communities of Pelynt and Lanreath may be just right. The sleepy little village of Pelynt is just 3 miles north of Polperro. Peaceful Lanreath lies just 6 miles away from Polperro off the road to West Looe. Most visitors take a car or taxi from the Looe train station. The two places listed here rank among England's major inns of character.

Jubilee Inn. Jubilee Hill, Pelynt (4 miles from Looe, 3 miles from Polperro), Cornwall PL13 2JZ. ☎ **01503/220312.** Fax 01503/220920. 9 units. TV TEL. £59 ($94.40) double. Rates include English breakfast. V.

Built in the 16th century, this inn takes its name from Queen Victoria's Jubilee celebration, when it underwent restoration. It's a comment on, rather than a monument to, the past. The lounge has a hooded fireplace with a raised hearth, Windsor armchairs, antique porcelain, and copper bowls filled with flowers cut from the garden behind the building. A glass-enclosed circular staircase takes you to the bedrooms. Fitting onto the outside, the winding stairway has been built to serve as a combined tower and hothouse. All but the three newest rooms have excellent 19th-century furnishings.

   The dining room is elegantly Victorian, with mahogany chairs and tables. Vegetables come fresh from the inn's own garden. Both lunch and dinner are served in the bar or in the dignified dining room.

✪ **The Punch Bowl Inn.** Lanreath, near Looe, Cornwall PL13 2NX. ☎ **01503/ 220218.** Fax 01503/220788. 18 units. TV. £40–£60 ($64–$96) double. Rates include English breakfast. MC, V. From Polperro, take B3359 north.

First licensed in 1620, the Punch Bowl has since served as a courthouse, coaching inn, and rendezvous for smugglers. Today its old fireplaces and high-backed settles, as well as its bedrooms (some with four-posters), provide hospitality. There's a modern lounge, a TV room, and an air-conditioned cocktail bar.

   Even if you're not stopping over, you may sample the fare or drinks in one of the kitchens (actually bars—they're among the few "kitchens" licensed in Britain as "bars"). In the Stable Restaurant, with its Tudor beams and fireplace, you order dinner from a menu that includes everything from a bowl of soup to steak.

WHERE TO DINE IN POLPERRO

The Kitchen. Fish na Bridge. ☎ **01503/72780.** Reservations required. Main courses £10.90–£15 ($17.45–$24). MC, V. Tues–Sat 7–9:30pm. Closed Nov–Easter. SEAFOOD.

This pink cottage about halfway down to the harbor from the parking area was once a wagon-builder's shop; it's now a restaurant run by Vanessa and Ian Bateson (Vanessa makes all the desserts and bakes the bread). It offers good English cooking, with everything homemade from the best fresh ingredients available. The menu changes seasonally and prominently features local fresh fish. Typical dishes include Fowey sea trout with lemon-and-herb butter and breast of duckling with blueberry-and-Drambuie sauce. Many vegetarian dishes are offered as main courses.

Nelson's Restaurant. Saxon Bridge. ☎ **01503/272366.** Reservations advised. Main courses £11.95–£16.95 ($19.10–$27.10); 3-course table d'hôte lunch or dinner £11.95 ($19.10); gourmet table d'hôte £24.95 ($39.90). AE, MC, V. Wed–Fri and Sun noon–1:45pm; Tues–Sun 7–9:45pm. Closed mid-Jan to mid-Feb. SEAFOOD.

Situated in the lower reaches of Polperro, near the spot where the local river meets the sea, this is the only structure in town specifically built as a restaurant. Established in 1937, with a recent reincarnation complete with nautical decor from Peter and Betty Nelson, it features succulent preparations of regional fish that arrive fresh from local fishing boats. The menu specialties change with the availability of local ingredients, but usually include a rich casserole of venison, chicken sautéed with plums and ginger, and steamed crab and scallops. A fillet of fresh halibut is dressed with herb butter and vermouth. There's also a lower deck featuring a cafe-bar and bistro. A comprehensive wine list boasts some fine vintages.

2 St. Mawes

300 miles SW of London; 2 miles E of Falmouth; 18 miles S of Truro

Overlooking the mouth of the Fal River, St. Mawes seems like a port on the French Riviera: It's sheltered from northern winds, and subtropical plants can grow here. From the town quay, you can take a boat to Frenchman's Creek and Helford River, as well as other places. St. Mawes is noted for its sailing, boating, fishing, and yachting, and half a dozen sandy coves lie within a 15-minute drive from the port. The town, built on the Roseland Peninsula, makes for interesting walks because of its colorful cottages and sheltered harbor.

GETTING THERE

Trains leave London's Paddington Station for Truro several times a day. The trip takes 4½ hours. For rail schedules and information, call ☎ **0345/484950** (in the U.K. only) or 01603/764776. Passengers transfer at Truro to one of the two buses that make the 45-minute bus trip from Truro to St. Mawes. It's much easier to take a taxi from either Truro or, even better, from the village of St. Austell, which is the train stop before Truro.

Buses depart from London's Victoria Coach Station several times a day for Truro. The bus takes 6 hours. For bus schedules and more information, call ☎ **0990/808080.**

If you're driving, to reach St. Mawes, turn left off A390 (the main road along the southern coast of Cornwall), at a junction 4 miles past St. Austell, onto the Tregony road, which will take you into St. Mawes.

A ferry travels to St. Mawes from both Falmouth and Truro, but schedules are erratic, varying with the tides and the weather conditions.

WHERE TO STAY & DINE

The Idle Rocks. Tredenham Rd., St. Mawes, Cornwall TR2 5AN. ☎ **01326/270771.** Fax 01326/270062. 24 units (with tub or shower only). TV TEL. June–Sept £138–£178 ($220.80–$284.80) double; Apr–May and Oct £128–£168 ($204.80–$268.80) double; Nov–Mar £112–£146 ($179.20–$233.60). Rates include half board. AE, MC, V. Parking available in the town parking lot; cost will be refunded.

The best place to stay is this solid old building, right on the seawall, sporting gaily colored umbrellas and tables all along the terrace. Water laps at the wall, and the site

Trekking the Cornish Coast

Much of Cornwall is an evocatively barren landscape, composed of gray rocks, weathered headlands jutting seaward, and very few trees. The weather alternates between bright sunshine and the impenetrable fogs for which the English Channel is famous.

The land and seascapes provide a scenic backdrop for hiking around the Cornish peninsula's coastline. The government maintains a clearly signposted coastal path more than 600 miles long that skirts the edge of the sea, following the tortured coastline from Minehead (in Somerset, near Dunster) to Poole (in Dorset, near Bournemouth). En route, the path crosses some of the least developed regions of southern England, including hundreds of acres of privately owned land as well as the northern border of the Exmoor National Park. Throughout, there is a sense of ancient Celtic mysticism and existential loneliness. Low-lying gorse, lichens, and heathers characterize the vegetation. In marked contrast to the windblown uplands, verdant subtropical vegetation grows in the tidal estuaries of the Fowey, Fal, Helford, and Tamar rivers.

Your options for exploring the coasts of Cornwall, Devon, and Dorset are numerous. It's a full 4 to 6 weeks of hard trekking to do the whole thing, though most people just pick a short section for a day hike. Although the route is sometimes arduous, no special equipment other than sturdy shoes, good stamina, and waterproof clothing is required.

You might also want to pick up a locally researched and annually revised book: The South West Way Association's *The Complete Guide to the South West Coast Path—Great Britain's Longest Trail.* This book divides the 600-mile coast path into manageable segments, rates them for degrees of difficulty, and contains a comprehensive accommodations section with addresses of pubs, bed-and-breakfasts, inns, hotels, and campsites en route. The book can be ordered from the **South West Way Association,** 1 Orchard Dr., Kingskerswell, Newton Abbot, Devon, England TQ12 5DG (☎ and fax **0183/873061**), or at **Windlestraw,** Penquit, Ermington, Devon, England PL21 0LU (☎ **01752/896237**), at a cost of £4.99 ($8) for postage.

The loneliness of the Cornish moors might be marred by hundreds of other people with exactly the same idea during Britain's school holidays. If possible, schedule your visit for relatively quiet periods, and remember that the weather between late October and early May is rainy, foggy, and windy—romantic, but no fun for hiking.

opens onto views over the river and the constant traffic of sailing boats and dinghies. Most rooms have sea or river views, and they're equipped with central heating, beverage-makers, and intercoms. The 17 units in the main hotel building charge higher rates. Four rooms tout balconies and four-poster beds; other accommodations are in the less desirable, relatively modern, stone-sided annex.

Dining/Diversions: The bar serves tasty lunch snacks, including fresh seafood caught locally.

Amenities: Golf is available at the Truro Golf Club at reduced greens fees. There's also room service, concierge, laundry, baby-sitting, and a courtesy car available.

The Rising Sun. The Square, St. Mawes, Cornwall TR2 5DJ. ☎ **01326/270233.** Fax 01326/270198. 9 units. TV TEL. From £59-£90 ($94.40-$144) double. Rates include English breakfast. AE, MC, V.

Converted from four 17th-century fishing cottages, with a flower-draped flagstone terrace out front, this colorful seafront inn in the center of town exudes charm. Known as one of Cornwall's best inns, it offers recently refurbished bedrooms that are functional and cozy, each with tea- and coffee maker.

Dining/Diversions: Owned by the St. Austell Breweries, the inn houses one of St. Mawes's busiest pubs on its ground floor. This is a rustically appealing place with stone accents, a fireplace, and bar snacks. The inn's restaurant—a dignified room adjacent to the pub—has a reputation for good food, and you might want to try it even if you don't stay at the hotel.

EN ROUTE TO PENZANCE: THE LIZARD PENINSULA

The southernmost point in England is the Lizard, a remarkable spot with jagged rocks reaching out into the sea where cormorants and gulls fish. The Lizard is the lesser known of Cornwall's two peninsulas—most people are more familiar with Land's End. The Lizard has great beaches, small villages, coastal walks, and craft studios. Some of the best beaches are at the coves at Poldhu and Kynance.

Some folks claim that the Lizard is "the most Cornish place" in Cornwall. It was the last place where the Cornish language was spoken before the language was modernized. Most of the places to stay and eat are in the village of Mullion.

To get here, driving from Falmouth, take A395 west to the junction with A3083, which you take south to Lizard Point.

3 Penzance

280 miles SW of London; 77 miles SW of Plymouth

This little harbor town, which Gilbert and Sullivan made famous, is at the end of the Cornish Riviera. It's noted for its moderate climate (it's one of the first towns in England to blossom with spring flowers), and for the summer throngs that descend for fishing, sailing, and swimming. Overlooking Mount's Bay, Penzance is graced in places with subtropical plants including palm trees.

Those characters in *The Pirates of Penzance* were not entirely fictional. The town was raided by Barbary pirates, destroyed in part by Cromwell's troops, sacked and burned by the Spaniards, and bombed by the Germans. In spite of its turbulent past, it offers tranquil resort living today.

The most westerly town in England, Penzance makes a good base for exploring Land's End, the Lizard peninsula, St. Michael's Mount, the old fishing ports and artists' colonies of St. Ives, Newlyn, Mousehole, and even the Isles of Scilly.

ESSENTIALS

GETTING THERE   Ten express trains depart daily from Paddington Station in London for Penzance. The trip takes 5½ hours. Call ☎ **0345/484950** (in the U.K. only) or 01603/764776 for information and schedules.

The **Rapide,** run by National Express from Victoria Coach Station in London (☎ **0990/808080**), costs £33.50 ($53.60) for the one-way trip from London, which takes about 8 hours. The buses have toilets and reclining seats, and a hostess dispenses coffee, tea, and sandwiches.

Drive southwest across Cornwall on A30 all the way to Penzance.

VISITOR INFORMATION   The **Tourist Information Centre** is on Station Road (☎ **01736/362207**). It's open from the end of May to the end of August, Monday to Friday from 9am to 5pm, Saturday from 9am to 4pm, and Sunday from 10am to

1pm; from the end of August to the end of May, hours are Monday to Friday from 9am to 5pm and Saturday from 10am to 1pm.

SEEING THE SIGHTS AROUND PENZANCE

○ **Castle on St. Michael's Mount.** On St. Michael's Mount, Mount's Bay. ☎ **01736/ 710507.** Admission £3.90 ($6.25) adults, £1.95 ($3.10) children. Apr–Oct Mon–Fri 10:30am–4:45pm (open weekends in summer); Nov–Mar Mon, Wed, and Fri by conducted tour only, which leaves at 11am, noon, 2, and 3pm, weather and tide permitting. Bus: 20, 21, or 22 from Penzance to Marazion, the town opposite St. Michael's Mount. Parking £1 ($1.60).

Rising about 250 feet from the sea, St. Michael's Mount is topped by a part medieval, part 17th-century castle; it's 3 miles east of Penzance and is reached at low tide by a causeway. At high tide the mount becomes an island, reached only by motor launch from Marazion. In winter, you can go over only when the causeway is dry.

A Benedictine monastery, the gift of Edward the Confessor, stood on this spot in the 11th century. The castle now has a collection of armor and antique furniture. There's a tea garden on the island, as well as a National Trust restaurant, both open in summer. The steps up to the castle are steep and rough, so wear sturdy shoes. To avoid disappointment, call the number listed above to check on the tides, especially during winter.

Minack Theatre. Porthcurno. ☎ **01736/810694.** Theater tickets £6 ($9.60); tour tickets £2 ($3.20). Exhibition hall, Easter to Dec 31 daily 10am–5:30pm. Performances, end of May to mid-Sept, matinees Wed and Fri at 2pm, evening shows Mon–Fri at 8pm. Leave Penzance on A30 heading toward Land's End; after 3 miles, bear left onto B3283 and follow the signs to Porthcurno.

One of the most unusual theaters in southern England, this open-air amphitheater was cut from the side of a rocky Cornish hill near the village of Porthcurno, 9 miles southwest of Penzance. Its by-now-legendary creator was Rowena Cade, an arts enthusiast and noted eccentric, who began the theater after World War I by physically carting off much of the granite from her chosen hillside. On the premises, an exhibition hall showcases her life and accomplishments. She died a very old woman in the 1980s, confident of the enduring appeal of her theater to visitors from around the world.

Up to 750 visitors at a time can sit directly on grass- or rock-covered ledges, sometimes on cushions if they're available, within sight lines of both the actors and a sweeping view out over the ocean. Experienced theatergoers sometimes bring raincoats for protection against the occasional drizzle. Theatrical events are staged by repertory theater companies that travel throughout Britain, and are likely to include everything from Shakespeare to musical comedy.

WHERE TO STAY

○ **Abbey Hotel.** Abbey St., Penzance, Cornwall TR18 4AR. ☎ **01736/366906.** Fax 01736/351163. 8 units. TV. £85–£130 ($136–$208) double; £135–£185 ($216–$296) suite. Rates include English breakfast. AE, MC, V.

Penzance has never had a first-class hotel, but until one comes along, the Abbey does just fine. This charming, small-scale hotel occupies a stone-sided house that was erected in 1660 on the site of a 12th-century abbey that was demolished by Henry VIII. It's located on a narrow side street on raised terraces that overlook the panorama of Penzance Harbour. Behind the hotel is a medieval walled garden that was part of the original abbey. The bedrooms are stylishly furnished with English country-house flair. The owners, Michael and Jean Cox, bring vitality, style, and charm to the hotel business. Mrs. Cox is the former international model Jean Shrimpton.

On the premises is a restaurant, where herbs from the garden flavor some of the food. Sample dinner dishes include homemade soups, mackerel pâté, fresh local fish, and roast joint. Everything is fresh and delicately cooked.

The Georgian House. 20 Chapel St., Penzance, Cornwall TR18 4AW. ☎ and fax **01736/365664.** 11 units, 9 with bathroom. TV TEL. £38 ($60.80) double without bathroom, £46 ($73.60) double with bathroom. Rates include English breakfast. AE, MC, V.

This former home of the mayors of Penzance, reputedly haunted by the ghost of a Mrs. Baines who owned it hundreds of years ago, has been completely renovated into an intimate hotel. The bright, cozy rooms all have hot- and cold-water basins, hair dryers, and tea- and coffeemakers. The Abbey is better, but this one is quite good too. The house is centrally heated, with a comfortable reading lounge, a licensed bar with a nautical motif, and an intimate dining room, where good Cornish meals are served from April through October.

Tarbert Hotel. 11–12 Clarence St., Penzance, Cornwall TR18 2NU. ☎ **01736/363758.** Fax 01736/331336. 12 units. TV TEL. £56–£64 ($89.60–$102.40) double. Rates include English breakfast. AE, MC, V. Closed Dec 23–Jan 26.

This dignified granite-and-stucco house lies about a 2-minute walk northwest of the town center. Some rooms retain their original high ceilings and elaborate cove moldings, and each is equipped with a tea-making facility and comfortable furniture. Recent improvements include a new reception area, a completely refurbished bar and lounge, and a sun patio.

A restaurant, specializing in fresh seafood brought in by local fishing boats, serves fixed-price evening meals every night. During the day, bar lunches are served to residents, and there's also a licensed bar with an extensive wine list and draft beer. Menu choices might include salmon steak in a white-wine sauce with cucumbers and prawns or duckling breast with an apricot-and-brandy sauce.

WHERE TO DINE

The Nelson Bar, in the Union Hotel on Chapel Street in Penzance (☎ 01736/ 362319), is known for its robust pub grub and collection of Nelsoniana. It's the spot where the admiral's death at Trafalgar was first revealed to the English people. Lunch and dinner are served daily.

Harris's Restaurant. 46 New St. ☎ **01736/364408.** Reservations recommended. Main courses £10.50–£15.50 ($16.80–$24.80). AE, MC, V. Tues–Sat noon–1:45pm; Mon–Sat 7–10pm. Closed 2 weeks in Nov. FRENCH/ENGLISH.

Down a narrow cobblestone street off Market Jew Street, opposite Lloyds Bank, this warm, candlelit place has a relaxed atmosphere and is your best bet for a meal. A beacon of light against the culinary bleakness of Penzance, Harris's offers dining in two small rooms—one upstairs, the other downstairs. The seasonally adjusted menu emphasizes local produce, including seafood and game. Dishes might include crab Florentine, a smoked duck breast salad with walnut oil dressing, or fresh salmon pancakes on an inviting bed of spinach.

✪ **The Turk's Head.** 49 Chapel St. ☎ **01736/363093.** Main courses £4.50–£10 ($7.20–$16); bar snacks from £1.75 ($2.80). AE, MC, V. Mon–Sat 11am–2:30pm and 6–10pm, Sun noon–2:30pm and 6–10pm (bar Mon–Sat 11am–3pm and 5:30–11pm, Sun noon–3pm and 5:30–10:30pm). From the rail station, turn left just past Lloyd's Bank. ENGLISH.

Dating from 1233, this inn is reputed to be the oldest in Penzance. It serves the finest food of any pub in town, far superior to its chief rival, the nearby Admiral Benbow.

In summer, drinkers overflow into the garden. Inside, the inn is decorated in a mellow style, as befits its age, with flatirons and other artifacts hanging from its timeworn beams. Meals include fishermen's pie, local seafood, and chicken curry, and prime quality steaks including rib eye. See the chalkboards for the daily specials.

Ward's Brasserie. 12–13 Chapel St. ☎ **01736/36540.** Reservations recommended. Main courses £5.75–£9.95 ($9.20–$15.90). AE, MC, V. Apr–Oct Mon–Sat 10am–4pm and 7–9pm; off-season Mon–Sat 10am–3pm, Thurs–Sat 7–9pm. Closed 2 weeks in Jan–Feb. BRITISH/SEAFOOD.

Chef/owner Alan Ward serves some of the finest cuisine of the region in a relaxed, informal brasserie in the heart of town. He successfully blends modern techniques with great respect for robust, traditional fare. Only the freshest of fish is used, and it's ordered in small quantities to ensure freshness, so some dishes may sell out quickly. Among the varied appetizers are a confit of quail on a summer leaf salad with balsamic dressing, or a terrine of local fish wrapped in toasted seaweed. Our favorite entrees are a tasty local mackerel scented with wild herbs and baked in paper, or an array of grilled seafood surrounding a timbale of red rice. For carnivores, the saddle of local lamb with herb filling in a red currant sauce is extremely tender and perfectly balanced in flavor.

4 The Isles of Scilly

27 miles WSW of Land's End

Several miles off the Cornish coast, the ✪ **Scilly Isles** are warmed by the Gulf Stream to the point where semitropical plants thrive. In some winters they never see signs of frost. They're the first landfall most oceangoing passengers see on journeys from North America.

There are five inhabited and more than 100 uninhabited islands in the group. Some are only a few square miles, whereas others, such as the largest, St. Mary's, encompass some 30 square miles. Three of these islands—Tresco, St. Mary's, and St. Agnes—attract visitors from the mainland. Early flowers are the main export and tourism is the main industry.

The Isles of Scilly figured prominently in the myths and legends of the ancient Greeks and Romans, and in Celtic legend they were inhabited entirely by holy men. There are more ancient burial mounds on these islands than anywhere else in southern England, and artifacts have clearly established that people lived here more than 4,000 years ago. Today there's little left of this long history for the visitor to see.

St. Mary's is the capital, with about seven-eighths of the total population of all the islands, and it's here that the ship from the mainland docks at Hugh Town. However, if you'd like to make this a day visit, we recommend the helicopter flight from Penzance to Tresco, the neighboring island, where you can enjoy a day's walk through 735 acres, mostly occupied by the Abbey Gardens.

ESSENTIALS

GETTING THERE   You can fly by plane or helicopter. **Isles of Scilly Skybus Ltd.** (☎ **01736/785220**) operates two to eight flights per day, depending on the season, between Penzance's Land's End Airport and Hugh Town on St. Mary's Island. Flight time on the eight-passenger fixed-wing planes is 20 minutes each way. The round-trip fare is £53 ($84.80) for same-day return, and £55 ($88) if you plan to stay overnight.

There's also a helicopter service maintained by **British International Heli -copters** at the Penzance Heliport Eastern Green (☎ **01736/363871** for recorded information), which operates, weather permitting, up to 12 helicopter flights,

Monday through Saturday, between Penzance, St. Mary's, and Tresco. Flight time is 20 minutes from Penzance to either island. A same-day round-trip fare is £58 ($92.80), rising to £89 ($142.40) if you spend a night or more on the island. A bus, whose timing coincides with the departure of each helicopter flight, runs to the heliport from the railway station in Penzance for a cost of £1 ($1.60) per person each way.

The rail line ends in Penzance (see "Getting There" in section 3, above).

Slower but more romantic is a ship leaving from the **Isles of Scilly Travel Centre,** on Quay Street in Penzance (☎ **01736/362009;** fax 01736/351223), which offers daily runs from April to October. The trip from Penzance to Hugh Town, St. Mary's, takes approximately 2 hours 40 minutes, with continuing service on to Tresco. The ship departs Monday through Friday at 9:15am, returning from St. Mary's at 4:30pm. Saturday schedules vary according to the time of year, sometimes with two sailings a day. In winter, service is much more limited. A same-day round-trip ticket from Penzance to St. Mary's costs £32 ($51.20) for adults and £16 ($25.60) for children 15 and under. An onward ticket from St. Mary's to Tresco costs an additional £8 ($12.80) for adults and £4 ($6.40) for children under 14.

VISITOR INFORMATION   **St. Mary's Tourist Information Office** is at Porthcressa Bank, St. Mary's (☎ **01720/422536**). It's open April through October daily from 8:30am to 5pm; November through March, Monday to Thursday from 8:30am to 5pm and Friday from 8:30am to 4:30pm.

For information about Tresco's boat schedules, possible changes in hours and prices at the Abbey Gardens, and other matters, call ☎ **01720/422849.**

TRESCO

No cars or motorbikes are allowed on Tresco, but bikes can be rented by the day; the hotels use a special wagon towed by a farm tractor to transport guests and luggage from the harbor.

For the best selections of island crafts, visit **Phoenix,** Portmellon Ind Est, St. Mary's (☎ **01720/422900**). At this studio, you can watch original artifacts being made into stained glass. The shops also sell a wide assortment of gifts, including jewelry and leaded weights.

The Isles of Scilly Perfumery, Porthloo Studios, St. Mary's (☎ **01720/423304**), a 10-minute walk from the center of Hugh Town, is packed with intriguing gifts made from plants grown on the isles—everything from a delicate shell-shaped soap to fine fragrances, cosmetics, potpourri, and other accessories.

✪ **Abbey Gardens.** ☎ **01720/422849.** Admission £5 ($8) adults; free for children 13 and under. Daily 10am–4pm.

The gardens are the most outstanding feature of Tresco, started by Augustus Smith in the mid-1830s. When he began his work, the area was a barren hillside, a fact visitors now find hard to believe.

The gardens are a nature-lover's dream, with more than 5,000 species of plants from 100 different countries. The old abbey, or priory, now in ruins, is said to have been founded by Benedictine monks in the 11th century, although some historians date it from A.D. 964. Of special interest in the gardens is Valhalla, a collection of nearly 60 figureheads from ships wrecked around the islands; the gaily painted figures from the past have a rather eerie quality, each one a ghost with a different story to tell.

After a visit to the gardens, take a walk through the fields, along paths, and across dunes thick with heather. Flowers, birds, shells, and fish are abundant. Birds are so unafraid that they land within a foot or so of you and feed happily.

WHERE TO STAY & DINE

✪ **Island Hotel Tresco.** Old Grimsby, Tresco, Isles of Scilly, Cornwall TR24 0PU. ☎ **01720/422883.** Fax 01720/423008. 40 units. TV TEL. £80–£175 ($128–$280) per person double; £125–£195 ($200–$312) per person suite. Rates include breakfast and dinner. AE, MC, V. Closed late Oct to early Mar.

This is the finest hotel in the Scillies, located at Old Grimsby near the northeastern shore of Tresco. It was established in 1960 when a late 19th-century stone cottage was enlarged with conservatory-style windows and a series of long and low extensions. Today the plant-filled interior, with water views, feels almost Caribbean. Some rooms overlook the sea, others face inland. All are comfortably furnished with easy chairs and storage spaces. The hotel is noted for its subtropical garden.

Dining: Nonguests can drop by for dinner; expect to spend about £30 ($48) for a five-course evening meal.

New Inn. Tresco, Isles of Scilly, Cornwall TR24 0QQ. ☎ **01720/422844.** Fax 01720/423200. 17 units. TV TEL. £52–£75 ($83.20–$120) per person double. Rates include half board. DC, MC, V.

Composed of an interconnected row of 19th-century fisher's cottages and shops, the New Inn is situated at the center of the island, beside its unnamed main road. The rooms are tastefully decorated in a modern style in blue and creamy yellow hues; each features matching twin or double beds, tea- and coffeemakers, and well-maintained bathrooms. The more expensive units offer sea views.

Dining/Diversions: The place is known for its pub; it offers an outdoor area for those who'd like to picnic or drink a glass of ale alfresco. Inside, the bar is a meeting place for locals and visitors alike. Lunch snacks are available, as are fixed-price dinners served nightly for £18.50 ($29.60). The pictures in the bar show many of the ships that sank or foundered around the islands in the past, as well as some of the gigs used in pilotage, rescue, smuggling, and pillage.

Amenities: Heated outdoor swimming pool.

ST. MARY'S

To get around St. Mary's, cars are available but hardly necessary. The **Island Bus Service** charges £2 ($3.20) from one island point to another; children ride for half fare.

Bicycles are one of the most practical means of transport. **Buccabu Bicycle Rentals,** Porthcressa, St. Mary's (☎ and fax **01720/422289**), is the only bike-rental outfit. They stock "shopper's cycles" with three speeds, "hybrid" bikes with 6 to 12 speeds, and 18-speed mountain bikes. All are available at prices that range from £4 to £5 ($6.40 to $8) daily. A sum of £10 ($16) is required for a deposit.

The **Isles of Scilly Museum,** on Church Street in St. Mary's (☎ **01720/422337**), illustrates the history of the Scillies from 2500 B.C., with drawings, artifacts from wrecked ships, and assorted relics discovered on the islands. A locally themed exhibit changes annually. It's open April to October, daily from 10am to noon and 1:30 to 4:30pm, and May to September, also daily from 7:30 to 9pm; off-season, only on Wednesday from 2 to 4pm. Admission is £1 ($1.60) for adults and 10p (15¢) for children.

WHERE TO STAY

Carnwethers Country House. Pelistry Bay, St. Mary's, Isles of Scilly, Cornwall TR21 0NX. ☎ and fax **01720/422415.** 10 units. £42–£52 ($67.20–$83.20) per person. Rates include English breakfast and dinner. No credit cards. Closed Nov–Apr.

Pelistry Bay, a secluded part of St. Mary's Island northeast of the airport, has a well-sheltered sandy beach, and this modernized farmhouse stands here on top of a hill looking out to fields, beach, and the sea. You can walk at low tide across to the nearby uninhabited island of Tolls. The guest-house rooms are spotless, warm, and comfortable, with many amenities. The main lounge is in two parts, one for conversation and reading, the other with a library filled with books about the island.

Dining/Diversions: Dinner, served at 6:30pm, includes fresh local produce and homegrown vegetables; a limited choice of traditional English fare is offered. Breakfast is a substantial meal, the marmalade being a particular pride of the house. There's also a well-stocked bar.

Amenities: The house has its own grounds with a croquet lawn, and a heated outdoor swimming pool operates from May through September. A sauna and a game room are also available.

Star Castle Hotel. The Garrison, St. Mary's, Isles of Scilly TR21 0JA. ☎ **01720/422317.** Fax 01720/422343. 34 units. TV TEL. £55–£100 ($88–$160) per person. Rates include half board. DC, MC, V (accepted only with 3% surcharge). Closed mid-Oct to mid-Mar.

This hotel was originally built as a castle in 1593, in the shape of an eight-pointed star, to defend the Isles of Scilly against Spanish attacks in retaliation for the 1588 defeat of the armada. The hotel has views out to sea as well as over the town and the harbor. The great kitchen has a huge fireplace where a whole ox could be roasted. A young Prince of Wales (later King Charles II) took shelter here in 1643 when he was being hunted by Cromwell and his parliamentary forces. In 1933 another Prince of Wales officiated at the opening of the castle as a hotel—the man who succeeded to the throne as King Edward VIII but was never crowned. The 18 rooms in the garden annex are extralarge units opening directly onto the gardens. Eight double rooms and five single rooms are in the castle.

Dining: Lunches tend to be simple pub-style platters, and orders are accepted in the cellar bar. Dinners are more elaborate, with most of the vegetables coming from the hotel's large gardens.

Amenities: There's a glass-covered, heated swimming pool, and the garden has many sheltered places for you to relax.

ST. AGNES

St. Agnes lies farther southwest than any other community in Britain and, luckily, remains relatively undiscovered. Much of the area is preserved by the Nature Conservancy Council. Since the main industries are flower farming and fishing, there is little pollution and visitors can enjoy crystal-clear waters ideal for snorkeling and diving. Little traffic moves on the single-track lanes crossing the island, and the curving sandbar between St. Agnes and its neighbor, the island of Gugh, is one of the best beaches in the archipelago. The coastline is diverse and a walker's paradise. A simple trail leads to any number of sandy coves, granite outcroppings, flower-studded heaths and meadows, even a freshwater pool. Sunsets are always romantic and are followed by a brilliant showcase of night stars. This is a place of endless natural wonderment that is truly soothing.

A boat departs from the quay at St. Mary's every day at 10:15am and 12:15pm, requiring a 15- to 20-minute transfer to St. Agnes, for a round-trip charge of about £4 ($6.40). Boats return on a schedule determined by the tides, usually at 2:15 and again at 3pm. The day's transportation schedule is chalked onto a blackboard on the quay at St. Mary's daily. Schedules generally allow you to visit St. Agnes for the day. The boats are operated by two family run companies: **Briar Boating** (☎ **01720/422886**) and **Hicks Boating** (☎ **01720/422541**).

WHERE TO STAY

Coastguards. St. Agnes, Isles of Scilly, Cornwall TR22 0PL. ☎ **01720/422373.** 3 units. £29–£32 ($46.40–$51.20) per person. Rates include half board. No credit cards. Closed the last 2 weeks in Dec.

The home of Danny and Wendy Hick has excellent sea views from its location near St. Warna's Cove. Charles, the Prince of Wales (who is the duke of Cornwall as well), is the landlord, and he makes regular visits to Scilly, which he regards as a jewel in the duchy of Cornwall's crown. One of their double rooms has two beds, and there are beverage-makers in the rooms. There's no choice on the daily menu, but special diets are catered to if advance notice is given. The price of half board depends on whether you order a two- or four-course evening meal.

WHERE TO DINE

The Turks Head. St. Agnes, Isles of Scilly, Cornwall TR22 0PL. ☎ **01720/422434.** Main courses £4–£8.35 ($6.40–$13.35). MC, V. Daily 10:30am–11pm. Pub Mon–Sat 11am–11pm, Sun noon–3pm and 7–10:30pm. Nov–Mar call for times. ENGLISH.

In a solid-looking building that was originally constructed in the 1890s as a boathouse, this is the only pub on the island. Prominently located a few steps from the pier, it's run by John and Pauline Dart, who serve pub snacks and also more solid fare, which includes steaks and platters of local fish. The pub is the second building after the arrival point of the ferryboats from St. Mary's. There's also a twin-bedded room with shower for rent here, costing £22 ($35.20) per person.

5 Newlyn, Mousehole & Land's End

Newlyn: 1 mile S of Penzance; Mousehole: 3 miles S of Penzance, 2 miles S of Newlyn; Land's End: 9 miles W of Penzance

Reached by traveling through some of Cornwall's most beautiful countryside, Land's End is literally the end of Britain. The natural grandeur of the place has been somewhat marred by theme-park-type amusements, but the view of the sea crashing against rocks remains undiminished. If you want to stay in the area, you can find accommodations in either Newlyn or Mousehole, two lovely Cornish fishing villages. If you visit in July and August, you'll need reservations far in advance, as neither Newlyn nor Mousehole has enough bedrooms to accommodate the summer hordes.

GETTING THERE

From London, journey first to Penzance (see above), then take a local bus for the rest of the journey (Bus A to Mousehole and Bus no. 1 to Land's End). There is frequent service throughout the day.

If you're driving from Penzance, take the B3315 south.

NEWLYN

From Penzance, a promenade leads to Newlyn, another fishing village of infinite charm on Mount's Bay. In fact, its much-painted harbor seems to have more fishing craft than that of Penzance. The late Stanhope Forbes founded an art school in Newlyn, and in the past few years the village has achieved a growing reputation for its artists' colony, attracting both serious painters and Sunday sketchers. From Penzance, the old fishing cottages and crooked lanes of Newlyn are reached by bus.

WHERE TO STAY & DINE

Higher Faugan Hotel. Chywoone Hill, Newlyn, Penzance, Cornwall TR18 5NS. ☎ **01736/362076.** Fax 01736/351648. 11 units. TV TEL. £83–£103 ($132.80–$164.80) double. Rates include English breakfast. Children under 12 stay free in parents' room. AE, DC, MC, V. Take B3315 ¾ mile south of Penzance.

The structure was built in 1904 by painter Alexander Stanhope Forbes, whose work is now in demand, as is that of his wife, Elizabeth Adela Forbes, and many other artists from the "Newlyn" school. The spacious building's granite walls, big windows, and steep roofs are surrounded by 10 acres of lawn, garden, and woodland, all of which can be covered on foot by adventurous visitors. The rooms are traditionally furnished and well maintained.

Amenities include a heated outdoor swimming pool, a putting green, a hard tennis court, a billiards room, and a dining room serving beautifully prepared English and continental specialties.

MOUSEHOLE

The Cornish fishing village of Mousehole (pronounced *Mou*-sel) attracts hordes of tourists, who, fortunately, haven't changed it too much. The cottages still sit close to the harbor wall; the fishers still bring in the day's catch; the salts sit around smoking tobacco, talking about the good old days; and the lanes are as narrow as ever. About the most exciting thing to happen here was the arrival in the late 16th century of the Spanish galleons, whose sailors sacked and burned the village. In a sheltered cove of Mount's Bay, Mousehole today has developed as the nucleus of an artists' colony.

WHERE TO STAY & DINE IN THE AREA

Carn Du Hotel. Raginnis Hill, Mousehole, Cornwall TR19 6SS. ☎ and fax **01736/731233.** 7 units. TV. £50–£65 ($80–$104) double. Rates include English breakfast. AE, MC, V. Take B3315 from Newlyn past the village of Sheffield (1½ miles) and bear left toward Castallack; after a few hundred yards, turn left to Mousehole, which is signposted; coming down the hill, the Carn Du is on the left facing the sea.

Twin bay windows gaze over the top of the village onto the harbor with its bobbing fishing vessels. The hotel's rooms (all doubles or twins) offer radios and much comfort. The owners will arrange sporting options for active vacationers but won't mind if you prefer to sit and relax.

Moderately priced meals are straightforward and fresh, usually accompanied by a bottle of wine from the cellars. You can have a drink in one of the lounges.

Lamorna Cove Hotel. Lamorna Cove, Penzance, Cornwall TR19 6XH. ☎ **01736/731411.** 12 units. TV TEL. £34.50 ($55.20) per person. Rates include English breakfast. £49.50 ($79.20) per person with breakfast and dinner. AE, MC, V. Take a taxi from Penzance.

Situated near one of the most perfect coves in Cornwall, only 5 miles south of Penzance but seemingly inaccessible down a winding, narrow road, this hotel was skillfully terraced, after months of blasting, into a series of rocky ledges that drop down to the sea. The hotel offers a rocky garden that clings to the cliff sides and surrounds a small swimming pool and a sun terrace overlooking the sea. The comfortable and cozy bedrooms have sea views. No smoking.

Dining: The dining room is in the old chapel, and a public lounge is furnished with comfortable chairs, centered around a wintertime log fire, with many pictures and antiques. Even if you don't stay at the hotel, stop in for one of its well-recommended, affordable meals or bar snacks.

The Lobster Pot Hotel and Restaurant. Mousehole, Cornwall TR19 6QX. ☎ **01736/731251.** Fax 01736/731140. 25 units, 22 with bathroom. TV TEL. June–Sept £26 ($41.60) per person double without bathroom, £44.25–£53.50 ($70.80–$85.60) per person double with bathroom. Feb–May and Oct–Dec £22 ($35.20) per person double without bathroom, £36.75–£47.25 ($58.80–$75.60) double with bathroom. Rates include English breakfast. MC, V. Closed Jan. Open weekends only in Feb.

Tasteful, nostalgic, and charming, this little hotel is housed in four adjacent former fishers' cottages near the water's edge of Mousehole. In addition to the main hotel, guests are housed in Clipper House, Gull's Cry, or Harbour's Edge. Seven rooms open onto sea views across the harbor and Mount's Bay beyond. The bedrooms are comfortably furnished, with such amenities as tea- or coffeemakers, trouser presses, hair dryers, and razor points. Families are especially welcomed.

Dining: Even if you don't stay here, The Lobster Pot is one of the best dining choices in town. A fixed-price dinner costs £15.50 ($24.80), or you can order à la carte, especially if you want to partake of the chef's specialty, freshly caught lobster (when available). It can be prepared virtually any way you want: steamed, grilled, Newburg, or Thermidor. Crab, sole, and salmon are also featured.

The Ship Inn. S. Cliff, Mousehole, Penzance, Cornwall TR19 6QX. ☎ **01736/731234.** 3 units. TV. £36 ($57.60) double without sea view, £46–£50 ($73.60–$80) double with sea view. Rates include English breakfast. No credit cards.

This charming pub is located on the harbor in this fishing village. The exterior has a stone facade and the interior has retained much of the original rustic charm with its black beams and paneling, granite floors, built-in wall benches, and, of course, a nautical motif decorating the bars. The rooms, offering views of the harbor and the bay, have window seats. Although the rooms are simply furnished with floral chintz fabrics, they all have hair dryers and beverage-makers. Bar snacks are served during the day, and there's an affordable dinner menu.

LAND'S END

Craggy Land's End is where England comes to an end. America's coast is 3,291 miles west of the rugged rocks that tumble into the sea beneath Land's End. Some enjoyable cliff walks and panoramic views are available here.

WHERE TO STAY & DINE

Land's End Hotel. Land's End, Sennen, Cornwall TR19 7AA. ☎ **01736/871844.** Fax 01736/871599. 33 units. TV TEL. £40–£60 ($64–$96) per person. Rates include dinner and breakfast. AE, MC, V.

Situated behind a white facade in a complex of buildings rising from the rugged landscape at the very tip of England, at the end of the main A30 road, this hotel has a panoramic cliff-top position, exposed to the wind and sea spray. The rooms are attractively furnished and well maintained.

Dining: Much of the hotel's business comes from the many day visitors who stop by for a snack or cup of coffee in one of the three restaurants. Bar meals are served daily from noon to 2pm, and a cafeteria remains open all day. In the evening, more formal meals are served, mostly to hotel guests.

6 The Artists' Colony of St. Ives

319 miles SW of London; 21 miles NE of Land's End; 10 miles NE of Penzance

This north-coast fishing village, with its sandy beaches, narrow streets, and well-kept cottages, is England's most famous artists' colony. The artists settled in many years ago and have integrated with the fishers and their families. They've been here long enough to have developed several schools or "splits," and they almost never overlap—except in the pubs. The old battle continues between the followers of the representational and the devotees of the abstract in art, with each group recruiting young artists all the time. In addition, there are the potters, weavers, and other craftspeople—all working, exhibiting, and selling in this area.

St. Ives becomes virtually impossible to visit in August, when you're likely to be trampled underfoot by busloads of tourists, mostly the English themselves. However, in spring and early fall the pace is much more relaxed.

ESSENTIALS

GETTING THERE   There is frequent service throughout the day betweenLondon's Paddington Station and the rail terminal at St. Ives. The trip takes 5½ hours. Call ☎ **0345/484950** (in the U.K. only) or 01603/764776 for schedules and information.

Several coaches a day run from London's Victoria Coach Station to St. Ives. The trip takes 7 hours. Call ☎ **0990/808080** for schedules and information.

If you're driving, take A30 across Cornwall, heading northwest at the junction with B3306, heading to St. Ives on the coast. During the summer, many streets in the center of town are closed to vehicles. You may want to leave your car in the Lelant Salt-ings Car Park, 3 miles from St. Ives on A3074, and take the regular train service into town, an 11-minute journey. Departures are every half hour. It's free to all car passen-gers and drivers, and the parking charge is £6 to £8 ($9.60 to $12.80) per day. You can also use the large Trenwith Car Park, close to the town center, for £1.50 ($2.40) and then walk down to the shops and harbor or take a bus that costs 35p (55¢) per person.

VISITOR INFORMATION   The **Tourist Information Centre** is at the Guildhall, Street-an-Pol (☎ **01736/796297**). From January to mid-May and from late Sep-tember through December, hours are Monday through Thursday from 9:30am to 5:30pm and Friday from 9:30am to 5pm. From mid-May to June, hours are Monday through Saturday from 9:30am to 5:30pm and Sunday from 10am to 1pm. In July and August, hours are Monday through Saturday from 9:30am to 6pm and Sunday from 10am to 1pm. For the first 3 weeks of September, hours are Monday through Saturday from 9:30am to 5:30pm.

SEEING THE SIGHTS

✪ **Tate Gallery St. Ives.** Porthmear Beach. ☎ **01736/796226.** Admission £3.50 ($5.60) per adult, including 1 child under 16; £2 ($3.20) seniors and students 16 or older. Apr–Sept Tues–Sun 10:30am–5:30pm, bank holidays 10:30am–5pm; Oct–Mar Tues–Sun 10:30am–5pm. Closed Dec 24–25 and Mon in July and Aug.

This branch of London's famous Tate Gallery exhibits changing groups of work from the Tate Gallery's preeminent collection of St. Ives painting and sculpture, dating from about 1925 to 1975. The gallery is administered jointly with the Barbara Hepworth Museum (see below). The collection includes works by artists associated with St. Ives, including Alfred Wallis, Ben Nicholson, Barbara Hepworth, Naum Gabo, Peter Lanyon, Terry Frost, Patrick Heron, and Roger Hilton. All the artists whose works are shown here had a decisive effect on the development of painting in the United Kingdom in the second half of the 20th century. About 100 works are on display at all times.

Boasting dramatic sea views, the museum occupies a spectacular site overlooking Porthmear Beach, close to the home of Alfred Wallis and to the studios used by many of the St. Ives artists.

✪ **Barbara Hepworth Museum and Garden.** Barnoon Hill. ☎ **01736/796226.** Admis-sion £2.50 ($4) adults, £1.25 ($2) children. Apr–Sept Tues–Sun 10:30am–6pm, bank holidays 10:30am–5pm; Oct–Mar Tues–Sun 10:30am–5pm. Closed Dec 24–25.

Dame Barbara Hepworth lived at Trewyn from 1949 until her death in 1975 at the age of 72. In her will she asked that her working studio be turned into a museum where future visitors could see where she lived and created her world-famed sculpture.

Today the museum and garden are virtually just as she left them. On display are about 47 sculptures and drawings, covering the period from 1928 to 1974, as well as photographs, documents, and other Hepworth memorabilia. You can also visit her workshops, housing a selection of tools and some unfinished carvings.

WHERE TO STAY

Garrack Hotel and Restaurant. Burthallan Lane, Higher Ayr, St. Ives, Cornwall TR26 3AA. ☎ **01736/796199.** Fax 01736/798955. 18 units. TV TEL. £46–£68 ($73.60–$108.80) per person. Rates include English breakfast. AE, DC, MC, V. Take B3306 to the outskirts of St. Ives; after passing a gas station on the left, take the 3rd road left toward Portmeor Beach and Ayr (there's a red telephone kiosk at the fork) and after 200 yd. look for the hotel sign. Frequent minibus service.

This vine-covered hotel, once a private home, commands a panoramic view of St. Ives and Porthmear Beach from its 2-acre knoll at the head of a narrow lane. It's one of the friendliest and most efficiently run small, medium-priced hotels on the entire coast, with every room furnished in a warm, homey manner. The living room, with a log-burning fireplace, antiques, and comfortable chairs, has an inviting atmosphere.
Amenities: In addition to the swimming pool and its whirlpool spa, there is a sauna, solarium, changing rooms, exercise equipment, and a patio for sunbathing. A small bar overlooks the bay. There is a launderette.

Pedn-Olva Hotel. The Warren, St. Ives, Cornwall TR26 2EA. ☎ **01736/796222.** Fax 01736/797710. 35 units. From £40 ($64) per person double. Rates include English breakfast. Half board from £51 ($81.60) per person. MC, V. Parking £2.50 ($4).

The panoramic view of the bay afforded from the restaurant and lounges is the outstanding feature of this establishment. It was originally built in the 1870s as the home of the paymaster for the local mines, before being transformed into a hotel in the 1930s. The rooms are well furnished and maintained in a modern style. There are sun terraces with lounges and umbrellas and a swimming pool for those who don't want to walk down the rocky path to Porthminster Beach. If you crave solitude, however, scramble down the rocks to sunbathe just above the gentle rise and fall of the sea.

Porthminster Hotel. The Terrace, St. Ives, Cornwall TR26 2BN. ☎ **01736/795221.** Fax 01736/797043. 47 units. TV TEL. £118–£137 ($188.80–$219.20) double. Rates include half board. AE, DC, V.

This leading Cornish Riviera resort, the town's best address, stands on the main road into town amid a beautiful garden and within easy walking distance of Porthminster Beach. Large and imposing, the Porthminster is a traditional choice for visitors to St. Ives. With its Victorian architecture dating from 1894, it's warm and inviting. The spacious rooms are well furnished, although with a bland decor.
   Amenities: Facilities include a sun lounge, a solarium, and a sauna, as well as a swimming pool that's open from June to September.

WHERE TO DINE

Garrack Hotel and Restaurant. In the Garrack Hotel, Burthallan Lane, Higher Ayr. ☎ **01736/796199.** Reservations recommended. Fixed-price dinner £18.50 ($29.60). AE, DC, MC, V. Daily 7–8:30pm. Frequent minibus service. ENGLISH/INTERNATIONAL.

The dining room at the Garrack Hotel produces excellent cuisine and, whenever possible, uses fresh ingredients from their own garden. The hotel dining room, which is open to nonguests, offers a set dinner, plus a cold buffet or snacks at the bar. The menu features some of the best English dishes, such as roast shoulder of lamb with mint sauce and John Dory fillets with cucumber relish, plus a wide sampling of continental fare, such as filet of salmon hollandaise and pork medallions with a French mustard sauce. Live lobsters swim in the seawater tank—until they're removed for preparation and cooked to order. Of course, if you order cold lobster salad, a little prior notice is required. Cheese and dessert trolleys are at your service.

EN ROUTE TO PORT ISAAC

The stretch of coastline between St. Ives and Port Isaac doesn't have the charm of Cornwall's eastern coast. The fastest way to get to Port Isaac is to take the A30 northeast. However the B3301, hugging close to the Atlantic Ocean, is the more scenic route.

Heading north along B3301, your first stop will be the estuary town of **Hayle,** once known for its tin and copper mines, but now a beach resort with miles of sand fronting the often wind-tossed Atlantic. Going north from here, the first attraction is **St. Agnes Beacon** (it's signposted). This is the most panoramic belvedere along this wild stretch of north Cornish coastline. At 628 feet, you can see all the way from Trevose Head in the northeast to St. Michael's Mount in the southwest—that is, if the weather's clear. It's often rainy and cloudy.

The first town of any importance is **Newquay,** a resort with sandy beaches at the foot of the cliffs, opening onto a sheltered bay. Taking its name from the new quay built in 1439, it attracts everyone from young surfers to elderly ladies who check into the B&Bs along the harbor for long stays. Newquay is a rather commercial town, lacking the charm of St. Ives or Port Isaac, but its beaches attract families in summer. At night, its pubs fill up with rowdy surfers ready to party.

If you'd like to stay over in Newquay, we recommend the **Bristol Hotel,** Narrow-cliff (☎ **01637/875181;** fax 01637/879347). This redbrick hotel overlooking the beach has 76 well-furnished rooms that cost £88 to £98 ($140.80 to $156.80) per night, including English breakfast. This friendly and inviting place is popular with families. Facilities include an indoor swimming pool, sauna, and solarium; American Express, Diners Club, Master Card, and Visa are accepted.

Back on the road again, you'll reach the next important stop, **Padstow.** This town has a long and ancient history. It reached its heyday in the 19th century when it was an important port. Unfortunately, ships became too big to pass the sand bar (called "The Doom Bar") at the estuary mouth. Walk along its quay-lined harbor and explore its narrow streets. At the end of the quay stands **St. Petroc's Church** and **Prideaux Place,** a Tudor house with 18th-century battlements.

Try to arrive in Padstow in time for lunch, because a restaurant—simply called **"Seafood,"** at Riverside (☎ **01841/532485**)—offers the best cuisine along this stretch of coastline. Here, Rick Stein selects the best "fruits of the sea," which he crafts into French-influenced dishes such as grillade of monkfish and Dover sole with a *sauce vierge* of garlic, sun-dried tomatoes, and herbs. Stein also rents 26 rooms above the restaurant, the bistro, and the coffee shop for £75 to £130 ($120 to $208) double per night; two have private balconies opening onto harbor views. The bar is open all day; lunch is served from noon to 1:30pm; and dinner is served from 7 to 10pm daily, except Sunday when they are closed; Master Card and Visa accepted.

7 Port Isaac

266 miles SW of London; 14 miles SW of Tintagel; 9 miles N of Wadebridge

Port Isaac remains the most unspoiled fishing village on the north Cornish coastline, in spite of large numbers of summer visitors. By all means, wander through its winding, narrow lanes, gazing at the whitewashed fishing cottages with their rainbow trims.

ESSENTIALS

GETTING THERE   Bodmin is the nearest railway station. It lies on the main line from London (Paddington Station) to Penzance (about a 4- or 4½-hour trip). Call ☎ 0345/484950 (in the U.K. only) or 01793/499458 for schedules. Many hotels will send a car to pick up guests at the Bodmin station or you can take a taxi. If you take a bus from Bodmin, you'll have to change buses at Wadebridge, and connections are not good. Driving time from Bodmin to Port Isaac is 40 minutes.

A bus to Wadebridge goes to Port Isaac about six times a day. It's maintained by the Prout Brothers Bus Co. Wadebridge is a local bus junction to many other places in the rest of England.

If you're driving from London, take M4 west, then drive south on M5. Head west again at the junction with A39, continuing to the junction with B3267, which you follow until you reach the signposted cutoff for Port Isaac.

WHERE TO STAY & DINE

✪ **Port Gaverne Hotel.** Port Gaverne, Port Isaac, Cornwall PL29 3SQ. ☎ **01208/880244.** Fax 01208/880151. 17 units. TV TEL. Summer £103 ($164.80) double, winter £100 ($160) double. Rates include English breakfast. AE, DC, MC, V. Closed early Jan to mid-Feb.

Built in the 17th century as a coastal inn for fishermen who needed a rest from their seagoing labors, Port Gaverne, half a mile east of Port Isaac, today caters to vacationing families and couples. It's the port's best bet for food and lodgings. The bedrooms are well furnished with traditional styling. The hotel boasts a sheltered cove for boating and swimming and can arrange shark fishing, pony trekking, golf, and country hikes. Its painted facade is draped with vines, and inside you'll find a duo of comfortably atmospheric bars for relaxing beside a fireplace (one of them is a modified baking oven). Clusters of antiques, stained glass, and early photographs of Cornwall add sometimes bittersweet touches.

Dining: Dinners are served by candlelight and include locally caught lobster, fish, or crab in season, as well as locally raised lamb and beef. Bar snacks are also available.

Slipway Hotel. The Harbour Front, Port Isaac, Cornwall PL29 3RH. ☎ **01208/880264.** 10 units, 5 with bathroom. TEL. £40–£50 ($64–$80) double without bathroom, £54–£68 ($86.40–$108.80) double with bathroom. Rates include English breakfast. AE, DC, MC, V. Closed Feb.

Originally built in 1527, with major additions in the early 1700s, this waterside building has seen more uses than any other structure in town, serving as everything from fishing cottages to the headquarters of the first bank here. The building was once a lifeboat station for rescuing sailors stranded on stormy seas. The bedrooms are comfortable and cozy.

Dining/Diversions: This hotel is best known for its restaurant, where ultrafresh seafood is a constant favorite. Its main dining room contains a minstrel's gallery and lies adjacent to a popular bar known to virtually everyone in town. At lunch, only bar snacks are served. Dinner is more elaborate, featuring fish imported directly from the nets of local fishers. Menu choices include grilled fillets of turbot served with miniature shrimp and *portugaise* sauce and one of the most elaborate seafood platters in town.

8 Tintagel Castle: King Arthur's Legendary Lair

264 miles SW of London; 49 miles NW of Plymouth

On a wild stretch of the Atlantic coast, Tintagel is forever linked with the legends of King Arthur, Lancelot, and Merlin. So compelling was this legend that medieval writers treated it as a tale of chivalry, even though the real Arthur, if he lived, probably did so around the time of the Roman or Saxon invasions. (Some scholars have speculated that if Arthur existed at all, he might have been not a king but a warlord; his reign might have lasted 3 decades, leading native Britons who were fighting off the Saxon invasion.)

Despite its universal adoption throughout Europe, it was in Wales and southern England that the legend initially developed and blossomed. The story was polished and given a literary form for the first time by Geoffrey of Monmouth around 1135. Combining Celtic myth and Christian and classical symbolism (usually without crediting his sources), Geoffrey forged a fictional history of Britain whose form, shape, and elevated values were centered around the mythical King Arthur. Dozens of other storytellers embellished the written and oral versions of the tale.

The Arthurian legend has captured the imagination of the British people like no other. Arthur himself is supposed to still lie sleeping, ready to arise and save Britain in its greatest need. The version of the legend by Sir Thomas Malory has become the classic, but there were many others: Edmund Spenser's in the Tudor period; John Milton's in the 17th century; Tennyson's, William Morris's, and Swinburne's in the Victorian age; and T. H. White's and C. S. Lewis's in the 20th century, not to mention the many film treatments.

The 13th-century ruins of a castle that stand here—built on the foundations of a Celtic monastery from the 6th century—are popularly known as King Arthur's Castle. They stand 300 feet above the sea on a rocky promontory, and to get to them you must take a long, steep, tortuous walk from the parking lot. In summer, many visitors make the ascent to Arthur's Lair, up 100 rock-cut steps. You can also visit Merlin's Cave at low tide.

The castle is half a mile northwest of Tintagel. It's open April to September daily from 10am to 6pm; November to March daily from 10am to 4pm. Admission is £2.80 ($4.50) for adults, £2.20 ($3.50) for students and senior citizens, and £1.60 ($2.55) for children. For information, call ☎ 01840/770328.

ESSENTIALS

GETTING THERE   The nearest railway station is in Bodmin, which lies on the main rail line from London to Penzance. From Bodmin, you'll have to drive or take a taxi for 30 minutes to get to Tintagel (there's no bus service from Bodmin to Tintagel). For railway inquiries, call ☎ 0345/484950 (in the U.K. only) or 01603/764776.

If you want to take a bus, you'll travel from London to Plymouth. One bus a day travels from Plymouth to Tintagel, at 4:20pm, but it takes twice the time (2 hours) required for a private car (which only takes about 50 minutes), since the bus stops at dozens of small hamlets along the way. For bus schedule information, call ☎ 01209/719988.

If you're driving, from Exeter, head across Cornwall on A30, continuing west at the junction with A395. From this highway, various secondary roads lead to Tintagel.

VISITOR INFORMATION   Tourist information is available at the **Municipal Building,** Boscawen Street, in Truro (☎ 01872/274555); from Easter to November, hours are Monday through Friday from 9am to 6pm and Saturday from 9am to 5pm; from November to Easter it's Monday through Friday from 9am to 5pm.

WHERE TO STAY & DINE IN TINTAGEL

Bossiney House Hotel. Bossiney Rd., Bossiney, Tintagel, Cornwall PL34 0AX. ☎ 01840/770240. Fax 01840/770501. 20 units. TV. £60–£64 ($96–$102.40) double. Rates include

English breakfast. AE, DC, MC, V. Closed Dec–Jan. Take B3263 a half mile northeast of Tintagel.

The hotel, in its inviting location, is comfortable, but not as tranquil or idyllic as the accommodations at somewhat more expensive Trebrea Lodge (see below). The rooms have hair dryers and beverage-makers, and there is a well-stocked bar/lounge with a fine view of the surrounding meadows marching right up to the top of the cliff, as well as the wide expanse of lawn with a putting green. A big English breakfast and other well-prepared, affordable meals are served in the dining room, which offers a panoramic view out over the lawns. On the grounds is a Scandinavian log chalet with a heated swimming pool, a sauna, and a solarium. The rooms have streamlined modern styling.

Old Borough House. Bossiney, Tintagel, Cornwall PL34 0AY. ☎ **01840/770475.** 6 units, 2 with shower, 1 with private bathroom. £38 ($60.80) double without bathroom, £44 ($70.40) double with bathroom. Rates include English breakfast. No credit cards. Walk north from the ruins of Tintagel Castle for 10 min.

Run by the Rayner family, this Cornish house has thick stone walls, small windows, low ceiling beams, and an illustrious history dating back to 1558. Most of what stands today was completed in the late 1600s, when it served as the residence for the mayor of Bossiney, the hamlet in which it's situated. (Bossiney was the seat from which Sir Francis Drake was elected for a brief period to the English Parliament.) The accommodations are cozy, low-ceilinged, antique, and very comfortable. There's a sitting room with a TV for guests' use, and, if you request in advance, affordable evening meals are available.

Trebrea Lodge. Trenale, near Tintagel, Cornwall PL34 0HR. ☎ **01840/770410.** Fax 01840/770092. 7 units, with tub or shower. TV TEL. £80–£90 ($128–$144) double. Rates include English breakfast. MC, V. From Tintagel, take the Boscastle rd. and turn right at the Roman Catholic church; make another right at the top of the lane.

Although its more than 600 years old, Trebrea Lodge reflects the charm of a small Cornish manor house of the Georgian period. Although not elaborate or fancy in any way, it is the best choice in Tintagel. The public rooms are all furnished with antiques, as are the rooms, one of which boasts a grand four-poster bed. All bedrooms have tea- or coffeemakers. The rooms open onto uninterrupted views over the countryside to the Atlantic Ocean.

A fixed-price menu, costing £21 ($33.60), is served in an oak-paneled dining room where all the food is prepared by Sean Devlin, one of the owners, using fresh local ingredients to produce both traditional English and continental dishes.

12 The Cotswolds

Lying between Oxford and the River Severn, about a 2-hour drive west of London, the pastoral Cotswolds occupy a stretch of grassy limestone hills, deep ravines, and barren plateaus known as *wolds*, Old English for "God's high open land." Ancient villages with names like Stow-on-the-Wold, Wotton-under-Edge, and Moreton-in-Marsh dot this bucolic area, most of which is in Gloucestershire, with portions in Oxfordshire, Wiltshire, and Worcestershire.

Made rich by wool from their sheep, the landowners here invested in some of the finest domestic architecture in Europe, distinctively built of honey-brown Cotswold stone. The gentry didn't neglect their spiritual duties, for some of the simplest Cotswold hamlets have churches that, in style and architectural detail, seem far beyond their modest means.

You'll also see some thatched cottages in the Cotswolds, which are fiercely protected by local bylaws yet are endlessly impractical because of their need for frequent repair, maintenance, and replacement. (They also cost a fortune to insure against fire!) More common are the Cotswolds roof shingles fashioned from split slabs of stone, which required massive buttressing from medieval carpenters as a means of supporting the weight of the roof. Buildings erected since the 1700s, however, usually have slate roofs.

You'll really want to rent a car and drive through the Cotswolds at your own pace. This way, you can spend hours viewing the land of winding goat paths, rolling hills, and sleepy hamlets. One of the reasons to visit the Cotswolds is to take advantage of its natural beauty. Play a round of golf on a scenic course, go fishing, or better yet, take a ramble across a meadow where sheep graze or alongside a fast-flowing stream.

Mobbed by tourists, Broadway, with its 16th-century stone houses and cottages, is justifiably the most popular base for touring this area, but we suggest you also head for Bibury, Painswick, or other small villages to capture the true charm of the Cotswolds. You'll find the widest range of hotels and facilities in Cheltenham, once one of England's most fashionable spas, with a wealth of Regency architecture. And families might head to Birdland, in Bourton-on-the-Water, where you can see some 1,200 birds of 361 different species.

BIKING & HIKING THROUGH THE COTSWOLDS

Biking the country roads of the Cotswolds is one of the best ways to experience the quiet beauty of the area. **Country Lanes,** 9 Shaftesbury

The Cotswolds

433

St., Fordingbridge, Hampshire SP6 1JF (☎ **01425/655022**), offers visitors that opportunity.

The company rents 21-speed bicycles fully equipped with mudguards, a water bottle, lock and key, a rear carrier rack, and, of course, safety helmets.

Their recommended day trips are self-guided, so you can ride at your own pace. You'll get an easy-to-follow route sheet. As you explore, you'll pass manor farms and pretty cottages of honey-colored stone. Several villages are also along the path, and the Hidcote Manor Garden is a perfect spot to relax if your legs tire of pedaling. The 10-, 20-, or 28-mile trips all end at the Manor House Hotel, a former 16th-century coaching inn at Moreton-in-Marsh. Here, you'll be served afternoon tea in the garden. The £25 ($40) price includes everything mentioned above and a souvenir T-shirt. Advanced booking is essential; call ☎ **01608/650065** to reserve by credit card.

This is also one of the most famous regions of England for hiking. With such a large area in which to ramble, it's a good idea to know where you are (and aren't) welcome. The **Cotswold Wardens,** c/o County Planning Department, Shire Hall, Gloucester (☎ **01452/425000,** ext. 7542), offers free brochures highlighting trails and paths. Other sources of information include the *Cotswold Way Handbook* by the **Rambler's Association,** c/o R. A. Long, 27 Lambert Ave., Shurdington, Cheltenham (☎ **01242/862594**); *The Cotswold Way: A Walker's Guide* by Mark Richards (Thornhill Press); and *A Guide to the Cotswold Way* by Richard Sale (Constable).

The **Wayfarers,** 172 Bellevue Ave., Newport, RI 02840 (☎ **800/249-4620**), sponsors about 10 Cotswold walks a year from April through October. The cost of most tours is $3,120 per person, including snacks, meals during the walk, and admission to attractions. Two other appealing companies offering similar walking tours are **Hiking Holidays,** Box 711, Bristol, Vermont 05443 (☎ **802/453-4816**), and **Greenscape U.K.,** Milkaway Lane, Croyde, Devon, England EX33 ING (☎ **800/873-7144** in the U.S. for more information).

If you'd like to walk and explore on your own without a guide, you can get data from the Cheltenham Tourist Information Center (☎ **01242/522878**). The center sells a Cotswold Way map.

1 Tetbury

113 miles W of London; 27 miles NE of Bristol

In the rolling Cotswolds, Tetbury was out of the tourist mainstream until the heir to the British throne and his beautiful bride took up residence at the Macmillan Place, a Georgian building on nearly 350 nearby acres. Then crowds from all over the world came here to catch a glimpse of Prince Charles riding horses and Princess Di shopping in the village. (Today, of course, folks keep an eye out for Charles and Camilla Parker-Bowles. They don't frequent any of the local establishments anymore because of the press, but locals often spot them driving by en route to their homes.) Although it cannot be seen from the road, the nine-bedroom Windsor mansion, **Highgrove,** is 1½ miles southwest of Tetbury on the way to Westonbirt Arboretum.

Tetbury itself has a 17th-century market hall and a number of antique shops and boutiques. The town's inns weren't cheap before royalty moved in, and the prices certainly have not dropped since then.

ESSENTIALS

GETTING THERE   Frequent daily trains run from London's Paddington Station to Kemble, 7 miles east of Tetbury. For more information and schedules, call ☎ **0345/484950** (in the U.K. only) or 01603/764776. You can then take a bus from there to Tetbury.

National Express buses leave from London's Victoria Coach Station with direct service to Cirencester, 10 miles northeast of Tetbury. For more information and schedules, call ☎ **0990/808080.** Several buses a day connect Cirencester to Tetbury

If you're driving from London, take the M40 northwest to Oxford, continuing along A40 to the junction with A429. Drive south to Cirencester, where you connect with A433 southwest into Tetbury.

VISITOR INFORMATION The **Tourist Information Centre,** 33 Church St. (☎ **01666/503552**), is open March through October, Monday to Saturday from 9:30am to 4:30pm, and November through February, Monday to Saturday from 11am to 2pm.

EXPLORING THE TOWN

Everything in Tetbury is conveniently located in the center of the village; you can easily spend a morning wandering in and out of the many antique shops and gazing up at the old houses.

The **Parish Church of St. Mary the Virgin,** built between 1777 and 1781, has been hailed as the best Georgian Gothic church in the country. Extensive restoration work has returned the interior to its original 18th-century appearance, and the spire is among England's tallest. For more information, call ☎ **01666/502333;** it's more than likely the vicar himself will come on the line.

One of the finest examples of a Cotswold-pillared market house is the 1655 **Market House of Tetbury.** It's still in use, hosting one of the most interesting markets in the Cotswolds, in the antique stalls of its oak-beamed meeting hall. Try to schedule a Wednesday visit here. Who knows? Some of that bric-a-brac you're sifting through could have come from Camilla's house!

After the market, head for **Chipping Steps.** The Chipping (market) was for centuries the site of "mop fairs," where farmhands and domestic staff offered themselves for employment. Many of the surrounding buildings have medieval origins. In the northeast corner, the steep cobbled steps and weavers' cottages retain a delightful medieval atmosphere.

Another place to explore is **Gumstoll Hill,** one of Tetbury's most ancient streets and now famous for its annual Woolsack Races. Legend has it that at the bottom of the hill, there was a pool where scolding wives and other miscreants were tied to a ducking stool and plunged underwater for punishment.

The **Police Bygones Museum,** Old Court House, 63 Long St., situated in the former police station and magistrates court, is worth a peek. The old cells house a collection of relics from centuries of Cotswold law enforcement. The location and hours are the same as the Tourist Information Centre (see above).

Chavenage House. 2 miles northwest of Tetbury. ☎ **01666/502329.** Admission £3 ($4.80) adults, £1.50 ($2.40) children. May–Sept Thurs and Sun 2–5pm; also open on Easter and bank holiday Mondays.

Aside from its fine Cromwell-era tapestries, furniture, and artifacts, this Elizabethan country house is worth a visit for its rich history and legends.

The drama started with Col. Nathaniel Stephens, who owned the house during the English civil war and met with an unfortunate demise while living here. It seems he was persuaded by Cromwell, who was a relative by marriage, to vote for the impeachment of King Charles. This angered Stephens's daughter to the point that she cursed him. Soon after, Stephens died, and it is rumored that his ghostly form was seen as it was driven away from Chavenage by a headless coachman wearing royal vestments. The house has been used as a location shoot for several BBC television productions, including Agatha Christie's *Hercule Poirot* and *Grace and Favour.*

ANTIQUE SHOPS & GALLERIES

As in so many English villages, Tetbury's shopping centers around antiques and collectibles.

Day Antiques, 5 New Church St. (☎ **01666/502413**), specializes in oak and country furniture and also has a collection of early pottery and metalware.

Most of the other antique dealers are located on Long Street in the city center. These include several shops that specialize in furniture, such as **Breakspeare Antiques,** 36 Long St. (☎ **01666/503122**), which carries mahogany pieces from the 18th and early 19th centuries and walnut pieces from as far back as the 17th century. **Country Homes,** 30 Long St. (☎ **01666/502342**), sells restored pine furniture from England, Ireland, and Europe, and **Gales Antiques,** 52 Long St. (☎ **01666/502686**), features English and French provincial furnishings. For good quality porcelain, try **Dolphin Antiques,** 48 Long St. (☎ **01666/504242**). The **Antiques Emporium,** at the Old Chape, Long Street (☎ **01666/505281**), gathers stock from 40 dealers in 1,750 square feet of showrooms; you're almost guaranteed to find something you like.

There are also several art galleries in Tetbury. **The Connoisseurs Gallery,** 2 Chipping Court Shopping Mall (☎ **01666/503155**), has prints, sculpture, blown glass, and other works created exclusively by artists in residence. **Natural Wood Framing,** Eight Bells Gallery, 14 Church St. (☎ **01666/505070**), specializes in sporting art, and **Tetbury Gallery,** 18 Market Place (☎ **01666/503412**), carries Victorian watercolors and oils and limited-edition prints.

WHERE TO STAY

✪ **Calcot Manor.** Calcot, near Tetbury, Gloucestershire GL8 8YJ. ☎ **800/987-7433** in the U.S., or 01666/890391. Fax 01666/890394. 25 units. TV TEL. £97–£160 ($155.20–$256) double. Rates include early morning tea and continental breakfast. AE, DC, MC, V. Take A4135 3½ miles west of Tetbury.

Although The Close in town has a more refined atmosphere (see below), this inn is the finest place on the outskirts. A 14th-century tithe barn on the grounds of this former farmhouse is among the oldest in Britain. The thick stone walls of the main house shelter a flowering terrace where tea and drinks are served in good weather. Tastefully decorated public rooms mix touches of modernism with clusters of flowers and English antiques. The rooms are furnished with antiques as well as rich fabrics. They all have modern conveniences; four are equipped with whirlpool baths, and one has a four-poster bed. Accommodations for families are located in a refurbished granary near the main house. The building has indoor and outdoor play areas for children in addition to child monitors in each room. Views from many of the rooms encompass a sweep of lawn and the Cotswold countryside.

Dining: The hotel restaurant serves some of the area's finest meals, with continental touches gathered from the proprietors' catering experience in Switzerland and France.

Amenities: Baby-sitting, open-air swimming pool.

✪ **The Close.** 8 Long St., Tetbury, Gloucestershire GL8 8AQ. ☎ **01666/502272.** Fax 01666/504401. 15 units. TV TEL. £165–£245 ($264–$392) double. Rates include English breakfast. AE, DC, MC, V.

The Close, which dates from 1596 and takes its name from a Cistercian monastery that was on this site, is the town's premier inn. Once the home of a wealthy Cotswold wool merchant, the house was built of honey-brown Cotswold stone, with gables and stone-mullioned windows. The ecclesiastical windows in the rear overlook a garden with a reflecting pool, a haven for doves. Most rooms are spacious and handsomely furnished with antiques.

Antiquing the 'Wolds

If ever there were an English fantasy, it's to drive the country back roads of the Cotswolds, to stay in a manor-house hotel, and spend your days browsing the villages, ignoring the touristy teddy-bear shops and concentrating on the antique shops densely packed into these old market towns.

There aren't many bargains in these towns, but it makes for lovely browsing, for days spent strolling, searching, studying, and munching ice-cream cones. Few stores sell inexpensive or junky antiques, although there are some great rummage sales on the weekends (ask your hotel for directions to the nearest and the best if you are into cheap thrills).

For the most part, antiques in the Cotswolds are about patina and provenance—really serious stuff. Most of the dealers are members of Britain's leading antiques associations (like the British Antiques Dealers Association— BADA) so that stores displaying this logo in their window have reputations to safeguard and will only sell you the best merchandise. Naturally, the best is pricey.

There is also the **Cotswold Antique Dealer's Association** (CADA), which publishes a free brochure of members and will happily guide you toward shippers and even hotels. Write to the Secretary, CADA, Barcheston Manor, Shipston-on-Stour, Warwickshire CV36 5AY, England (☎ **01608/661268**).

Each of the Cotswolds' villages usually has an antique center in the heart of town, with a variety of dealers. There's usually also a cafe here or a place for tea, and clean bathrooms. They do not charge an entrance fee and are often open on Sundays. Bigger towns, such as Burford, have several antique centers.

Most of the towns are laid out in traditional style, with retail centered on the High Street. Unlike the rest of England, most of the Cotswolds' towns are not overrun with multiples on their High Streets. The most expensive stores are clustered in the center of the High Street. The further from this center, the less the rent and the more likely the possibility of finding affordable antique shops.

The best town in the Cotswolds, especially for antique shoppers, is **Stow-on-the-Wold;** there's far more to it than a High Street, and it's charming as can be. **Moreton-in-Marsh** is an unusual town; its High Street is Roman and unusually wide. You'll have quite a hike if you shop your way through town on both sides of the street to take in all the shops.

Some of the Cotswolds towns have been turned into tourist traps over the years; many shops in the area sell an artful mix of reproductions, foreign imports, and Asian junk. Buyer beware.

Dining: Before-dinner drinks are served in the Georgian room with a domed ceiling (it once was an open courtyard). Dining is in one of two rooms. Candlelight on winter evenings, floral arrangements, and sparkling silver and glass are the perfect background for the fine food. The cooking is superb, and an à la carte menu offers specialty dishes (see below).

Amenities: Access to nearby health club, car-rental desk, concierge, room service, dry cleaning/laundry, baby-sitting.

The Snooty Fox. Market Place, Tetbury, Gloucestershire GL8 8DD. ☎ **01666/502436.** Fax 01666/503479. 12 units. TV TEL. £90–£120 ($144–$192) double. Rates Include English breakfast. AE, DC, MC, V.

This desirable hotel in the commercial heart of Tetbury was originally a 16th-century coaching inn. Despite its name, it's a lot less snooty than The Close and is a popular local rendezvous. The Victorians added a high front porch under which flowers grow in what used to be watering troughs for horses. A stone-walled lounge, with comfortable chairs and a Gothic fireplace, opens off the reception area. Three rooms have antique beds with canopies, and the rest are comfortably and tastefully furnished in a more modern style. Each room is equipped with radio, hair dryer, trouser press, and beverage-makers.

Dining/Diversions: There's a popular bar inside, with an amusing caricature of a Snooty Fox in full riding regalia. The restaurant is one of the most elegant in town. In warm weather, tables are set at the edge of the market square beneath the 19th-century iron overhang.

WHERE TO DINE

✪ **The Close Restaurant.** In The Close, 8 Long St. ☎ **01666/502272.** Reservations required. Main courses £14.95–£23.45 ($23.90–$37.50); fixed-price menu £29.50 ($47.20). AE, DC, MC, V. Daily noon–2pm and 7–10pm. ENGLISH.

This is a dining room of distinction, set with exquisite porcelain, silver, and glass that reflects the sumptuous but discreet atmosphere and friendly service. While sipping champagne on the terrace, take time to peruse the imaginative menu, which is complemented by the town's best wine list.

The à la carte menu is seasonally adjusted to take advantage of the best market-fresh ingredients. Starters, and main courses, too, reach out for the finest catch or harvest in England's fields and streams. Examples include pressed terrine of foie gras and Bathurst pigeon with a paprika biscuit and shallot marmalade, or hot smoked Cockleford trout with a baby leek and sun-dried sweet-pepper risotto. Main courses are likely to feature local venison, panfried sea bream, or fillet of Scottish salmon. Desserts sometimes reach back in England's culinary attic for inspiration, such as a parsnip-and-Cotswold-honey soufflé with whisky and lime ice.

2 Cirencester

89 miles W of London; 16 miles S of Cheltenham; 17 miles SE of Gloucester; 36 miles W of Oxford

Cirencester is the unofficial capital of the Cotswolds, a throwback to the Middle Ages, when it flourished as the center of the great Cotswold wool industry. Then known as Corinium, five roads converged here during the Roman occupation. In size, it ranked second only to London. Today it is chiefly a market town and a good base for touring. (And don't worry about how to pronounce *Cirencester*. There's disagreement even among the English. Say *Siren*-cess-ter and you won't be too far off.)

ESSENTIALS

GETTING THERE Cirencester has no railway station, but trains depart several times a day from London's Paddington Station for the 80-minute trip to Kemble, which is 4 miles southwest of Cirencester. You may have to transfer trains at Swindon. For schedules and information, call ☎ **0345/484950** (in the U.K. only) or 01603/764776. From Kemble, a bus travels to Cirencester four to five times a day.

National Express buses leave from London's Victoria Coach Station with direct service to Cirencester. For schedules and information, call ☎ **0990/808080.**

If you're driving from London, take the M40 northwest to Oxford, continuing along A40 to the junction with the A429, which you'll take south to Cirencester.

VISITOR INFORMATION The **Tourist Information Centre** is at Corn Hall, Market Place (☎ **01285/654180**). It's open April through October, Monday from

9:45am to 5:30pm and Tuesday to Saturday from 9:30am to 5:30pm. From November through March it closes at 5pm.

EXPLORING CIRENCESTER

Cirencester has some of the greatest walks and scenic views of any town in the Cotswolds. And you don't have to go miles out of town to enjoy these strolls—they are easily reached from the center at Market Place. On the grounds of the Cirencester Parish Church (see below), attractive trees and shrubs evoke a well-manicured landscape. You can see swans and wild fowl on the River Churn and the lake, even remnants of the town's Roman walls. For a great stroll, take the riverside walk alongside the Churn from Barton Lane to the Abbey Grounds. If you want more, head west from Market Place until you reach **Cirencester Park,** 3,000 acres of parkland with woodland walks. The park is open daily for horseback riding and walking. Pedestrian access is from Cecily Hill (no vehicles).

Brewery Arts Centre. Brewery Ct. ☎ **01285/657181.** Free admission. Year-round Mon–Sat 10am–5pm.

The living heart of this arts complex is the workshop area of 15 resident craft workers who produce everything from baskets to chandeliers. Other components of the center include three galleries with exhibitions in both crafts and fine art, a theater, education classes, a shop selling the best in British craft work, a cafe-bar, and a coffeehouse.

✪ **Corinium Museum.** Park St. ☎ **01285/655611.** Admission £2.50 ($4) adults, £1 ($1.60) students, 80p ($1.30) children. Mon–Sat 10am–5pm, Sun 2–5pm. Closed Mon in winter.

The museum houses one of the finest collections of archaeological remains from the Roman occupation, found locally in and around Cirencester. Mosaic pavements excavated on Dyer Street in 1849 and other mosaics are the most important exhibits. Provincial Roman sculpture, including such figures as Minerva and Mercury, pottery, and artifacts salvaged from long-decayed buildings, provide a link with the remote civilization that once flourished here. The museum has been completely modernized to include full-scale reconstructions and special exhibitions on local history and conservation.

Cirencester Parish Church. Market Place. ☎ **01285/653142.** Free admission; donations invited. Mon–Fri 9:30am–4:30pm; Sun 12:30–5:30pm in summer, 2:15–5:30pm in winter.

A church may have stood on this spot in Saxon times, but the present building overlooking the Market Place in the town center dates from Norman times and Henry I. In size, it appears more like a cathedral than a mere parish church, with a variety of styles, largely Perpendicular, as in the early 15th-century tower. Among the treasures inside are a 15th-century "wineglass" pulpit and a silver-gilt cup given to Queen Anne Boleyn 2 years before her execution. In the Trinity Chapel, you can rub some great 15th-century brasses.

SHOPPING

For antiques in Cirencester, try **William H. Stokes,** The Cloisters, 6/8 Dollar St. (☎ **01285/653907**), which specializes in furniture, tapestries, and other items from the 16th and 17th centuries. **Rankine Taylor Antiques,** 34 Dollar St. (☎ **01285/652529**), sells items from the 17th, 18th, and early 19th centuries, including silver, glass, and furniture.

The arts complex known as the **Brewery Arts,** Brewery Court (☎ **01285/657181**), has 15 independent workshops of area craftspeople ranging from jewelers and weavers to basket makers. There are three galleries and a craft shop recognized by the Crafts Council that sells many of the artists' wares.

WHERE TO STAY & DINE IN & AROUND CIRENCESTER

Tatyan's, 27 Castle St. in Cirencester (☎ 01285/653529), is a great place to dine. It serves Peking, Hunan, and Szechuan specialties, with nearly a dozen prawn dishes on the large menu. For a pint, head for the town favorite, the **Slug & Lettuce,** 17 West Market Place (☎ 01285/653206), a friendly pub enjoyed by locals and students alike, with out-of-towners predominating in summer. It has the most convivial after-dark scene in town.

The Jarvis Fleece Hotel. Market Place, Cirencester, Gloucestershire GL7 2NZ. ☎ 01285/658507. Fax 01285/651017. 32 units. TV TEL. Sun–Thurs £89 ($142.40) double; £99 ($158.40) suite. Fri–Sat (including English breakfast) £42.50 ($68) double; £74 ($118.40) suite. AE, DC, MC, V.

The half-timbered facade here hints at origins as an Elizabethan coaching inn, but it was enlarged by the Georgians and today has had many modernizations. When it's chilly, a handful of open fireplaces warm the beamed interior. The comfortably modern rooms feature old-fashioned hints of yesteryear, including quilts and conveniences such as radios and coffeemakers.

Dining: The staff prepares modern English dinners served in a formal dining room. À la carte lunches are offered in the Shepherd's Bar. A flowering courtyard offers a pleasant place to dine on warm days.

The Pear Tree at Purton. Church End, Purton, near Swindon, Wiltshire SN5 9ED. ☎ 01793/772100. Fax 01793/772369. 18 units. TV TEL. £90 ($144) double; £110 ($176.00) four-poster room or suite. Rates include English breakfast. AE, DC, MC, V. Closed Dec 26–30. It's 8 miles southeast of Cirencester, 3 miles from Junction 16 of the M4, and 5 miles from Swindon. To get here from Cirencester, follow route B419 in the direction of Swindown. Turn left when signs point to Cricklade, and from here, follow the signs to Purton.

This English country hotel/restaurant, set in 7½ acres, offers well-furnished, individually decorated rooms equipped with hair dryers, trouser presses, and free sherry and mineral water. All accommodations (three with four-poster beds) have views of the traditional Victorian garden and countryside. The Cotswold stone house was formerly the vicarage for the twin-towered parish Church of St. Mary.

Dining: The owners, Francis and Anne Young, run the best restaurant in the area. The cuisine is inspired by France, although the recipes and cooking are distinctly English. The best seasonal produce is featured, including local lamb and pork. Seafood is brought fresh from Devon, and many of the herbs used to flavor the dishes come from the establishment's own garden. Dining is in an attractive conservatory, with service daily from noon to 2pm and 7 to 9:15pm. Lunch is not served on Saturday. Reservations are required.

Stratton House Hotel. Gloucester Rd., Cirencester, Gloucestershire GL7 2LE. ☎ 01285/651761. Fax 01285/640024. 41 units. TV TEL. £95–£105 ($152–$168) double. Rates include English breakfast. AE, DC, MC, V. Take A417 1¼ miles northwest of Cirencester.

Built in several stages throughout the 18th century, with a modern wing added in the 1990s, this inviting and comfortable country house has a design that is part Jacobean and part Georgian. It's a more atmospheric choice than the Jarvis Fleece if you have a car and don't mind the short commute. It is surrounded by beautiful grounds with a walled garden and herbaceous borders. The large and well-furnished rooms have hair dryers, beverage-makers, and trouser presses. Two-thirds of the rooms are in the modern wing—designer-decorated, with coordinated colors and an aura evoking a traditional private English country house.

Dining: The dining and drawing rooms have some fine antique furniture and oil paintings. At dinner, there is a choice of traditional British dishes, and in winter, log fires blaze in the main hall and in a timbered beam bar.

3 Painswick

4 miles N of Stroud; 107 miles W of London; 10 miles SW of Cheltenham; 15 miles NW of Cirencester

The sleepy, enchanting little town of Painswick is so well preserved today that it affords an escape from the often dull English market towns. Although erected at different periods, its houses blend harmoniously because the builders used only Cotswold stone. The one distinctive feature on the Painswick skyline is the spire of its 15th-century parish church. It's also known for its annual Clipping Feast, when the congregation joins hands and circles around the church as if it were a maypole, singing hymns as they do. Ancient tombstones dot the churchyard.

ESSENTIALS

GETTING THERE   Trains depart from London's Paddington Station several times a day for Stroud, the nearest railway station, 3 miles away. The trip takes from 1½ to 2 hours, and you may have to change trains at Swindon. For rail information, call ☎ 0345/484950 in the U.K., or 01603/764776 in the U.S. From Stroud, buses run to Painswick, some as frequently as once every hour. Many taxis also wait at the Stroud railway station.

Buses depart from Bath heading toward Cheltenham on Wednesday and Saturday, stopping in Painswick (and many other small towns) along the way. For schedules, call ☎ 0990/808080.

If you're driving from Cirencester, continue west along A419 to Stroud, then head north on A46 to Cheltenham and Painswick.

VISITOR INFORMATION   The Painswick **Tourist Information Centre** is at the Painswick Library, Stroud Road (☎ 01452/813552), and is open April through September, Monday to Saturday from 10am to 6pm, and October through March, Monday to Saturday from 10am to 5pm.

SPECIAL EVENTS   The ✪ **Clipping Feast** of Painswick, also referred to as the Clipping Ceremony, is an unusual, early medieval ceremony that anthropologists suspect might have been inspired in the dim Celtic prehistory of Britain. Every September, a month that coincides with the harvest ceremonies of the pagans, adults and as many children as can be mustered hold hands in a circle around St. Mary's Anglican Church. The circle moves first one way, then the other, and the participants sing hymns and pray out loud in a celebration of thanksgiving. Participants and observers come from all over the region to take part in this important rite.

EXPLORING PAINSWICK

Most of Painswick's charm derives from its Cotswold architecture. Most of New Street dates from 1450.

A specific attraction, which is regrettably only open by appointment, is **Painswick House,** Gloucester Street, Highway B4073, Painswick Stroud (☎ 01452/813204); it's about a half mile west of the town center. This 18th-century Georgian and Palladian mansion, built by Charles Hyett in 1734 and enlarged in 1830, has been home to eight generations of the same family. Today it's the home of Lord and Lady Dickinson. The building's rococo gardens are open between February 1 and November 30 every Wednesday to Sunday from 11am to 5pm. Admission is £3 ($4.80) for adults, £1.60 ($2.55) children, £2.70 ($4.30) seniors and students; no appointment is necessary for the gardens.

If you have an itch to shop, stop by **Dennis French** on New Street (☎ 01452/ 883054). They sell woodcrafts influenced by William Morris designs.

St. Mary's Church, the centerpiece of the village, was originally built between 1377 and 1399, and reconstructed into its present form in 1480. Its churchyard contains 99 massive yew trees, each of which is at least 200 years old. Local legend states that no matter how hard well-meaning gardeners have tried, they've never been able to grow more than 99 of them.

WHERE TO STAY

✪ **Painswick Hotel.** Kemps Lane, Painswick, Gloucestershire GL6 6YB. ☎ 01452/ 812160. Fax 01452/814059. 20 units. TV TEL. £105–£150 ($168–$240) double. Rates include Cotswold breakfast. AE, MC, V.

The best inn in the area, this beautiful, completely refurbished Georgian house behind the Painswick parish church was once a vicarage and is encircled by terraces of formal gardens. Many of your fellow readers have reported that a stay here was the highlight of their Cotswold tour. In accommodation, cuisine, and service, it merits a major detour. The hotel has high standards of cuisine and service in its half-paneled dining room. The rooms are comfortably and attractively furnished, and there's always fresh fruit and bottled water in your room.

Dining: The hotel's chefs are well trained, often from the continent, and they turn out some of the finest cuisine in the area, a medley of English and continental dishes. Reservations are required, and the fixed-price menu, served at lunch and dinner, range from £20.50 ($32.80) to £24.50 ($39.20). The menus change daily, but always emphasize fresh local products. The wine list is expansive and reasonably priced.

Amenities: Concierge, car-rental desk, room service, dry cleaning/laundry, babysitting.

WHERE TO DINE

The Country Elephant. New St. ☎ 01452/813564. Reservations required. Main courses £10.50–£19.50 ($16.80–$31.20); fixed-price lunch £10 ($16); fixed-price dinner £14–£18 ($22.40–$28.80) Tues–Fri, £22 ($35.20) Sat. AE, DC, MC, V. Tues–Sat noon–2pm and 7–10pm. INTERNATIONAL.

Housed in a centrally located building crafted from Cotswold stone, this excellent restaurant serves some of the most imaginative and best food in town. Owned by John Rees, it boasts kitchen walls dating from the 14th century and dining-room walls from the 17th century. Many guests enjoy a predinner drink near the open fireplace of the heavily beamed bar.

Robert Rees, the head chef, trained at Le Gavroche in London and spent 5 subsequent years in Bath at the Royal Crescent Hotel, The Bath Spa Hotel, and The Circus Restaurant. His cuisine is excellent and served in comfortable and relaxed surroundings, including a summer garden. Begin with one of the delightful appetizers—perhaps terrine of sweetened leeks with smoked salmon and Chablis vinaigrette. The kitchen shines when preparing such dishes as Cornish cod lightly flaked with truffles and parsley potatoes with a wasabi dressing, Bresse chicken with a timbale of wild rice, or baked skate wing served with wild mushrooms, bacon, and shallots.

4 Cheltenham

99 miles NW of London; 9 miles NE of Gloucester; 43 miles W of Oxford

Legend has it that the Cheltenham villagers discovered a mineral spring by chance when they noticed pigeons drinking from a spring and observed how healthy they were (the pigeon has been incorporated into the town's crest). King George III arrived in 1788 and launched the town's career as a spa. The duke of Wellington came to ease his liver disorder, and Lord Byron came this way, proposing marriage to Miss Millbanke.

Cheltenham today remains one of England's most fashionable spas, and many visitors come just to see its gardens from spring to autumn. The architecture is mainly Regency, with lots of ironwork, balconies, and verandas. Attractive parks and open spaces of greenery make the town especially inviting. The main street, the Promenade, has been called the most beautiful thoroughfare in Britain. Rather similar are Lansdowne Place and Montpellier Parade (with caryatids separating its stores, Montpellier Walk is one of England's most interesting shopping centers).

ESSENTIALS

GETTING THERE   Twenty-one trains depart daily from London's Paddington Station for the 2-hour-and-15-minute trip. You may have to change trains at Bristol or Swindon. For schedules and information, call ☎ **0345/484950** (in the U.K. only) or 01603/764776. Trains between Cheltenham and Bristol take only an hour, with continuing service to Bath.

National Express offers nine buses daily from London's Victoria Coach Station to Cheltenham. The ride takes about 2½ hours. For schedules and information, call ☎ **0990/808080.**

If you're driving from London, head northwest on the M40 to Oxford, continuing along A40 to Cheltenham.

VISITOR INFORMATION   The **Tourist Information Centre,** 77 Promenade (☎ **01242/522878**), is open September through June, Monday to Saturday from 9:30am to 5:15pm; July and August, Monday to Friday from 9:30am to 6pm, Saturday from 9:30am to 5:15pm, and Sunday from 9:30am to 1:30pm in July only.

SPECIAL EVENTS   The **International Festival of Music** and the **Festival of Literature** take place each year in July and October, respectively, and attract internationally acclaimed performers and orchestras.

WHAT TO SEE & DO

Pittville Pump Room/Gallery of Fashion. East Approach Dr., Pittville Park. ☎ **01242/ 523852.** Pump Room, free; gallery, £1.50 ($2.40) adults, 50p (80¢) children, students, and senior citizens. May–Sept Wed–Mon 10am–4:30pm; Oct–Apr Wed–Mon 11am–4pm. From the town center, take Portland St. and Evesham Rd.

Cheltenham Waters are the only natural, consumable alkaline waters in Great Britain and are still taken at one of the spa's finest Regency buildings. The Pittville Pump Room is open Sundays from the end of May until the end of September for a host of activities, including lunch, afternoon cream teas, live classical music, landau carriage rides around the city, and brass bands playing in Pittville Park—it's real traditional England. The Gallery of Fashion, also located in the pump room, depicts the social history of Cheltenham Spa. Memorabilia include photographs and prints of the U.S. Army when it was stationed at Pittville in the 1940s.

Insider's tip: A prized collection in the gallery is the Hull Grundy Gift, a dazzling display of jewelry from the Regency through the art nouveau periods. You can see tiaras made from glittery paste stones, fine examples of jewelry made from human hair, a brooch made of tiny mosaics, and much more.

Cheltenham Art Gallery & Museum. Clarence St. ☎ **01242/237431.** Free admission. Mon–Sat 10am–5:20pm. Closed bank holidays.

This gallery houses one of the foremost collections of the Arts and Crafts movement, notably the fine furniture of William Morris and his followers. One section is devoted to Edward Wilson, Cheltenham's native son, who died with Captain Scott in the Antarctic in 1912. The gallery is located near Royal Crescent and the Coach Station.

Everyman Theatre. Regent St. ☎ **01242/572573.** Admission £4.50–£21.50 ($7.20–$34.40), depending on the event. Box office Mon–Sat 9:30am–8:30pm on performance days, 9:30am–6pm otherwise. Sun 2 hr. before curtain.

Cheltenham is the cultural center of the Cotswolds, a role solidified by the Everyman Theatre. Designed in the 1890s as an opera house by Frank Matcham, Victorian England's leading theater architect, it retains its ornate cornices, sculpted ceilings, and plush velvets despite extensive renovations to its stage and lighting facilities.

The theater has recently begun to attract some of England's top dramatic companies. Shakespeare, musicals, comedies, and a variety of other genres are performed in the small (658-seat) but charming hall. Last season's works included *The Adventures of Robin Hood, Don Giovanni, Antony and Cleopatra,* and several performances by noted musical groups.

Holst Birthplace Museum. 4 Clarence Rd. ☎ **01242/524846.** Admission £1.50 ($2.40) adults, 50p (80¢) children and seniors. Year-round Tues–Sat 10am–4:20pm.

In 1874, this Regency terrace house saw the birth of the great composer Gustav Theodore Holst, whose works were heavily influenced by English folk music and Hindu literature. He is most famous for "The Planets," which he wrote in 1918. During the first 8 years of his life, he lived here, and visitors can see rooms restored to illustrate the "upstairs-downstairs" lifestyle he and his family enjoyed. The house also includes Holst's original piano, a Regency drawing room, a children's nursery, and a kitchen in working condition.

SHOPPING

The different quarters that make up Cheltenham's shopping district turn shopping into an unusually organized event. Start in the **Montpellier quarter** for a host of individual boutiques and an abundance of craft and specialty shops. Then continue to the nearby **Suffolk quarter** to find most of the town's antique stores.

And an enjoyable short stroll to **the Promenade** will take you by stores featuring attractive women's and men's clothing and shoes, as well as several bookstores. From the Promenade, take Regent Street to **High Street,** which is mostly pedestrian-only, and you'll find several brand-name department stores.

The **weekly market** is in the Henrietta Street car park on Thursday and in Coronation Square on Friday. Weather permitting, markets open around 9am and close toward 4pm.

The Courtyard, on Montpellier Street in the heart of the Montpellier quarter, has become an award-winning shopping mall that offers a fun blend of quality shops specializing in unique fashion, furniture, and gift items. A good mix of restaurants, cafes, and wine bars rounds out the Courtyard. **Hoopers** (☎ **01242/527505**) is a quality department store devoted to designer clothes for men and women. It also has a perfumery, hair and beauty salon, and fully air-conditioned restaurant.

On High Street, you'll find the **Beechwood Shopping Centre.** This mall is touted as Cheltenham's premier shopping center and has restaurants, a car park, and such big-name stores as Debenhams, C&A, and the Disney Store.

Cavendish House, the Promenade (☎ 01242/521300), is a long-established shopping landmark, housing two restaurants, a hair and beauty salon, an immense cosmetic and jewelry hall, and departments devoted to fine fashion, housewares, and furniture.

HITTING THE LINKS

The **Cotswold Hills Golf Club,** Ullenwood, Cheltenham (☎ 01242/515263), is open year-round. The only requirements at this par-71 golf course are a reasonable standard of play, your own clubs, and no jeans or sneakers. Greens fees on weekdays are £24 ($38.40) for 18 holes and £30 ($48) unlimited play; £30 ($48) for 18 holes and £35 ($56) unlimited play on Saturday and Sunday.

The **Tewkesbury Park Golf and Country Club,** Lincoln Green Lane, Tewkesbury, 12 miles north of Cheltenham (☎ 01684/295405), is a par-73 course requiring a reasonable standard of play, a golf bag, and no jeans, sneakers, or club sharing. Clubs are available for rent at £10 ($16). Greens fees for 18 holes are £20 ($32) weekdays and £30 ($48) Saturday and Sunday.

The **Gloucestershire Golf and Country Club,** Matson Lane, Gloucester (☎ 01452/411331 or 01452/525683), is a par-70 course that requires a reasonable standard of play and disallows jeans and sneakers, though tailored shorts are okay. Club rentals are available for £5 to £6 ($8 to $9.60). Eighteen holes costs £19 ($30.40) weekdays, £25 ($40) Saturday and Sunday.

WHERE TO STAY

Central Hotel. 7–9 Portland St., Cheltenham, Gloucestershire GL52 2NZ. ☎ 01242/582172. 15 units, 6 with shower. TV TEL. £40 ($64) double without bathroom, £48 ($76.80) double with shower. AE, DC, MC, V.

Within easy reach of Cheltenham's range of attractions, this white-fronted hotel consists of a pair of stone houses that were originally built in the 1700s and then combined. Today, strictly protected from exterior changes by local building codes, it's a family run hotel, with a street-level public house. Meals are served in the bar for under £10 ($16) each. The rooms are conservatively modern, with everything you need to make tea.

✪ **The Greenway.** Shurdington, near Cheltenham, Gloucestershire GL51 5UG. ☎ 800/543-4135 in the U.S., or 01242/862352. Fax 01242/862780. 19 units. TV TEL. £140–£225 ($224–$360) double. Rates include English breakfast. AE, CB, DC, MC, V. Take A46 less than 4 miles southwest of Cheltenham.

An elegant and beautifully furnished former Elizabethan manor house in a garden setting, this is an ivy-clad Cotswold showpiece. Restored with sensitivity and decorated to a high standard, Greenway rents rooms in both its main house and a converted coach house, all with private bath and shower. Original paintings and antiques abound throughout the hotel. On a chilly day, open fires beckon. Guests are assured of comfort here.

Dining: The dining room is elegantly appointed with an extension added in the Victorian conservatory style. The cooking is superb, using quality produce and good, fresh ingredients that are handled deftly. Lunch is served from 12:30 to 2pm Sunday to Friday, and dinner from 7:30 to 9:30pm Monday to Saturday; only dinner is served on Sunday, at 7:30pm. The cuisine, modern British in style, has continued to improve over the years and is now better than ever. Service is formal, on target, and polite, all at once.

Amenities: Access to nearby health club, car-rental desk, concierge, dry cleaning/laundry.

Hotel de la Bere and Country Club. Southam, Cheltenham, Gloucestershire GL52 3NH. ☎ **01242/237771.** Fax 01242/236016. 57 units. TV TEL. £95–£110 ($152–$176) double. Half board (2-night minimum required) £60 ($96) per person. AE, DC, MC, V. Take B4632 3 miles northeast of town.

Dating from 1500, this Cotswold-stone building near the Cheltenham racecourse has been owned by the de la Bere family for 3 centuries. They converted it into a hotel in 1972 and have made every effort to ensure that it retains its original charm. Five rooms have double four-poster beds, and all have beverage-makers and private bathrooms. All rooms are tastefully decorated and furnished to preserve their individual charm and character. Twenty rooms have recently been refurbished.

Dining: The restaurant, the Elizabethan Room, and the Royalist Room are all paneled in oak, and there is also a Great Hall, complete with minstrel's gallery. The impressive menu uses fresh seasonable ingredients. The hotel restaurant doesn't serve lunch except on Sunday; dinner, however, is offered nightly.

Amenities: Health club, sauna, tennis courts, car-rental desk, concierge, room service, dry cleaning/laundry, baby-sitting, outdoor heated pool.

✪ **Hotel on the Park.** Evesham Rd., Cheltenham, Gloucestershire GL52 2AH. ☎ **01242/518898.** Fax 01242/511526. 12 units. TV TEL. £89.50–£149.50 ($143.20–$239.20) double; from £119.50 ($191.20) suite. Rates include English breakfast. AE, DC, MC, V.

Opened in 1991 in what was formerly the private villa of a local building contractor in the 1830s, this is the most talked-about hotel in town. It is located among similar terraced buildings in the once-prominent village of Pittville Spa, a half mile north of Cheltenham's town center. Owned and operated by Darryl and Lesley-Anne Gregory, who undertook most of the Regency-inspired interior design, it has received several awards. Each bedroom is named after a prominent 19th-century visitor who came here shortly after the villa was built. Comfortable and high-ceilinged, the rooms have stylish accessories and a tasteful assortment of antique and reproduction furniture. A four-poster double is more expensive than one of the junior suites.

Dining: The hotel dining room, called simply the Restaurant, is in the classic Regency style.

Amenities: Access to nearby health club, car-rental desk, room service, dry cleaning/laundry, baby-sitting, courtesy car.

Lawn Hotel. 5 Pittville Lawn, Cheltenham, Gloucestershire GL52 2BE. ☎ or fax **01242/526638.** 9 units, 4 with bathroom. TV. £35–£37 ($56–$59.20) double. Rates include English breakfast. No credit cards. Bus: 1A, 2A, or 3A.

Built in 1830 with a stucco exterior, this elegant landmark Regency house lies just inside the iron gates leading to Pittville Park and the Pump Room. It's one of 300 town houses built in an area landscaped in the early 19th century by Joseph Pitt. Owned by the Armitage family, it offers pleasantly decorated rooms with tea-making equipment and hot and cold running water. Evening meals can be arranged, beginning at £7.50 ($12) per person, as well as afternoon teas. The hotel is convenient to the town center and its Promenade, about a 10-minute walk away.

WHERE TO DINE

81 Bistro & Bar. 81 The Promenade. ☎ **01242/222466.** Bar meals £3–£5 ($4.80–$8); bistro meals £8–£12 ($12.80–$19.20). AE, MC, V. Tues–Sun noon–2pm; Tues–Sat 7–9:30pm. CONTINENTAL/BRITISH.

This bistro features modern British cuisine with a Mediterranean flair along with an extensive selection of wines, all in a less formal setting. Try terrine of duck with foie gras and an apple and walnut dressing, or else confit of duck with butter beans, bacon, and thyme. Such bistro fare is regularly served as a chilled tomato and red pepper soup or else baked fish cakes with an herb hollandaise. Finish off with a rich chocolate mousse with poached pears. The basement cafe-bar is open from 11am to 10pm and is the ideal spot for a cool drink and a quick bite to eat.

♦ **Le Champignon Sauvage.** 24-26 Suffolk Rd. ☎ **01242/573449.** Reservations required. 3-course fixed-price lunch £14.50–£18.50 ($23.20–$29.60); 3-course fixed-price dinner (Mon–Fri) £20 ($32); 3-course fixed-price dinner (Mon–Sat) £33 ($52.80). AE, DC, MC, V. Mon–Fri 12:30–1:30pm; Mon–Sat 7:30–9:15pm. FRENCH/ENGLISH.

This is among the culinary highlights of the Cotswolds. David Everitt-Matthias, a chef of considerable talent, wisely limits the selection of dishes every evening for better quality control. Some evenings he allows his imagination to roam a bit, so dining here is always a surprise, usually a pleasant one. You might begin with leek-and-potato soup drizzled with chive oil and sprinkled with bacon, or the terrine of eggplant with roasted goat's cheese. Main courses might include peppered tuna with a tomato tart and haricot-bean sauce. Matthias was recently named the dessert chef of the year in England, so be sure to try one of the acclaimed sweet treats. Choices include a mango with Thai-spiced cream layered between puff pastry and drizzled with mulled red-wine syrup, and warm carrot cake with caramelized carrot sauce and crystallized carrots.

CHELTENHAM AFTER DARK

The major venue for entertainment is the **Everyman Theatre** (see above), which is the premier sightseeing attraction of Cheltenham. But there's a lot more theater at the **Playhouse,** Bath Road (☎ **01242/522852**), with new local, amateur productions of drama, comedy, dance, and opera being staged at the dizzying pace of every 2 weeks. Tickets are £5 to £8.50 ($8 to $13.60). **Axiom Centre for the Arts,** 57–59 Winchcombe St. (☎ **01242/253183**), is a venue for working artists, musical performance, and traveling exhibitions. The complex houses studio spaces, two galleries featuring works by local artists, a theater specializing in fringe productions, a cafe-bar, and **The Back Bar,** the only local spot for live music, with entertainment Thursday to Saturday and Monday to Tuesday. Bands range from indie to jazz. On Saturday, they break out the turntables with DJs playing an eclectic dance mix. There's usually only a cover charge when bands play.

Dancers flock to **Mondo,** Bath Road (☎ **01242/263456**), which attracts a mixed crowd: Mondays are students-only, but Thursday through Saturday, it's all ages. The cover charge varies from £1 to £3 ($1.60 to $4.80).

You can choose your groove at **Gas,** St. James Square (☎ **01242/527700**); upstairs is generally soul and R&B, whereas downstairs features house and techno Thursday through Saturday nights from 9pm to 2am. The cover charge ranges from £3 to £5 ($4.80 to $8), depending on the night.

A SIDE TRIP TO ROYAL SUDELEY CASTLE

Royal Sudeley Castle. In the village of Winchcombe (6 miles northeast of Cheltenham). ☎ **01242/602949.** Admission £5.50 ($8.80) adults, £4.80 ($7.70) seniors, £3 ($4.80) children, £15 ($24) family ticket. Easter–Oct daily 11am–5pm; grounds open at 10:30am. From Cheltenham, take the regular bus to Winchcombe and get off at Abbey Terrace. Then walk the short distance along the road to the castle. If you're driving, take the B4632 north out of Cheltenham, through Prestbury, and up Cleve Hill to Abbey Terrace, where you can drive right up to the castle.

This 15th-century structure is one of England's finer stately homes. It has a rich history that begins in Saxon times, when the village was the capital of the Mercian kings. Later, Catherine Parr, the sixth wife of Henry VIII, lived and died here. Her tomb is in a chapel on the grounds, which include a host of formal gardens like the Queen's Garden, now planted with old-world roses and dating to the time of Katherine Parr. While exploring the gardens, you're sure to see the waterfowl and flamboyant peacocks that call Sudeley home. For the past 30 years, Lady Ashcombe, an American by birth, has owned the castle and welcomed visitors from the world over. The castle houses many works of art by Constable, Turner, Rubens, and Van Dyck, among others, and has several permanent exhibitions, magnificent furniture and glass, and many artifacts from the castle's past. In the area to the right of the keep, as you enter the castle, workshops are devoted to talented local artisans who continue to use traditional techniques to produce stained glass, textiles, wood and leather articles, and marbled paper.

5 Bibury

86 miles W of London; 30 miles W of Oxford; 26 miles E of Gloucester

On the road from Burford to Cirencester, Bibury is one of the loveliest spots in the Cotswolds. In fact, the utopian romancer of Victoria's day, poet William Morris, called it England's most beautiful village. In the Cotswolds, it is matched only by Painswick for its scenic village beauty and purity. Both villages are still unspoiled by modern invasions.

GETTING THERE
About five trains per day depart from London's Paddington Station for the 1-hour-10-minute trip to Kemble, the nearest station, 13 miles south of Bibury. Some will require an easy change of train in Swindon (the connecting train waits just across the tracks). For schedules and information, call ☎ **0345/484950** (in the U.K. only) or 01603/764776. There are no buses from Kemble to Bibury, but most hotels will arrange transportation if you ask in advance.

Five buses leave London's Victoria Coach Station daily for Cirencester, 7 miles from Bibury. For schedules and information, call ☎ **0990/808080.** There are no connecting buses into Bibury, but local hotels will send a car, and taxis are available.

If you're driving from London, take the M4 to Exit 15, head toward Cirencester, then follow A33 (on some maps this is still designated as B4425) to Bibury.

WHAT TO SEE & DO
On the banks of the tiny Coln River, Bibury is noted for **Arlington Row,** a group of 17th-century gabled cottages protected by the National Trust. These houses were originally built for weavers. They are its biggest and most-photographed attraction, but it's rude to peer into the windows, as many do, because people still live here.

To get a view of something a bit out of the ordinary for the Cotswolds, check out **St. Mary's Parish Church.** As the story goes, the wool merchants who had the power and the money in the area were rebuilding the churches. However, they did not finish the restoration to St. Mary's, and, as a result, much of the original Roman-style architecture has been left intact. The 14th-century decorated-styled windows have even survived the years. This is an often overlooked treasure.

The once-prosperous mill has been silenced and converted into the **Cotswold Country Museum** (☎ **01451/860715**), where visitors are treated to a host of antiquated wagons and machines once used in the area, and a variety of display rooms that illustrate the way people used to handle day-to-day existence. Open mid-March through mid-November, Monday to Saturday from 10:30am to 5pm, and Sunday 2pm to 5pm; mid-November through mid-March, Saturday and Sunday from 10:30am to dusk. Admission is £1.50 ($2.40) for adults, £1.25 ($2) for seniors, and 75p ($1.20) for children.

The Cotswolds feature ✪ **trout fishing** unparalleled in all of England, with the River Test, running through Stockbridge, offering the best, and streams near Bibury and Fairford also providing a challenge. Unfortunately, all are privately owned, so the best way to take advantage of the region's fishing is to stay in a hotel aimed at anglers. Among these, try the **Bibury Court Hotel,** Bibury GL7 5NT (☎ **01285/740337**), the **Swan Hotel,** Bibury GL7 5NW (☎ **01285/740695**), or **Wroxton House Hotel,** Wroxton St. Mary, Wroxton OX15 6PZ (☎ **01295/730777**).

Insider's tip: One of the most delightful **walks** in all the Cotswolds begins at the grounds of the Bibury Court Hotel and winds to the next village of Coln St. Aldwyn, following the riverbank. Tennyson described it well: "Grey twilight poured on dewy pastures, dewy trees, softer than sleep—all things in order stored a haunt of ancient peace."

WHERE TO STAY & DINE

Bibury Court Hotel. Bibury, Gloucestershire GL7 5NT. ☎ **01285/740337.** Fax 01285/740660. 20 units, 17 with bathroom. TV TEL. £87–£95 ($139.20–$152) double; £125 ($200) suite. Rates include continental breakfast. AE, DC, MC, V.

This Jacobean manor house was built by Sir Thomas Sackville in 1633 (parts of it date from Tudor times). Sackville, an illegitimate son of the first Earl of Dorset and a "Knight and gentleman-usher in dailie waiting on the King," James I, launched a family dynasty. His family occupied the house for several generations. Through the female line it passed to the Cresswells, who, eventually, owing to a disputed will and years of litigation, sold the house in the last century to Lord Sherborne. (Charles Dickens is said to have written *Bleak House* with this case in mind.) The house was a residence until it was turned into a hotel in 1968. Over the years, it was reputed to have been visited by Charles II when he attended the Bibury Races, as did the Prince Regent in the reign of George III.

You enter the 8 acres of grounds through a large gateway, and the lawn extends to the Coln River. The structure is built of Cotswold stone, with many gables, huge chimneys, leaded-glass stone-mullioned windows, and a formal graveled entryway. Inside, there are many country-manor furnishings and antiques, as well as a log-burning stone fireplace. Many rooms have four-poster beds, original oak paneling, and antiques.

Dining: Meals are quite special. Dinners are slightly more extravagant than the more reasonably priced bar lunches. After tea and biscuits in the drawing room, walk across the lawn along the river to a little church.

The Swan. Bibury, Gloucestershire GL7 5NW. ☎ **01285/740695.** Fax 01285/740473. 18 units. TV TEL. £150–£220 ($240–$352) double in winter; £140–£250 ($224–$400) double in summer. Rates include English breakfast. AE, MC, V.

Well managed, upscale, and discreet, this hotel and restaurant—the finest in the village originally a riverside cottage in the 1300s, was greatly expanded throughout the centuries, and received its latest enlargement and refurbishment in the early 1990s. Owners Alex and Liz Furtek outfitted parts of the interior in a cozily over-stuffed mode reminiscent of World War II. There's an elegant bar trimmed in oak; rustic but elegant English country pieces; wood-burning fireplaces and murals showing groups of well-wishers during the hotel's most recent renovations. An automatic "pianola" (player piano) provides music in the lobby. The bedrooms are each outfitted with antique furniture and an individualized decor of charm and taste.

Dining: An informal brasserie with outdoor courtyard seating is open daily from 10am to 10pm for coffee, drinks, snacks, and platters of food. There's also a more formal restaurant with crystal chandeliers and heavy damask curtains. Specializing in modern British food, it's open daily only for dinner and Sunday lunch. You may enjoy Bibury trout from a nearby river.

6 Burford

76 miles NW of London; 20 miles W of Oxford

Built of Cotswold stone and serving as a gateway to the area, the unspoiled medieval town of Burford is largely famous for its Norman church (ca. 1116) and its High Street lined with coaching inns. Oliver Cromwell passed this way, as did Charles II and his mistress, Nell Gwynne. Burford was one of the last of the great wool centers, the industry bleating out its last breath as late as Queen Victoria's day. Be sure to photograph the bridge across the Windrush River where Queen Elizabeth I once stood. As the antiques shops along High Street will testify, Burford today is definitely equipped for tourists.

The River Windrush, which toward Burford is flanked by willows through meadows, passes beneath the packhorse bridge and goes around the church and away through more meadows. Strolling along its banks is one of the most delightful experiences in the Cotswolds.

ESSENTIALS

GETTING THERE   Many trains depart daily from London's Paddington Station to Oxford, a 45-minute trip. For schedules and information, call ☎ **0345/484950** (in the U.K. only) or 01603/764776. From Oxford, passengers walk a very short distance to the entrance of the Taylor Institute, from which about three or four buses per day make the 30-minute run to Burford.

A **National Express** bus runs from London's Victoria Coach Station to Burford several times a day, with many stops along the way. It's a 2-hour ride. For schedules and information, call ☎ **0990/808080.**

If you're driving from Oxford, head west on A40 to Burford.

VISITOR INFORMATION   The **Tourist Information Centre** is at the Old Brewery on Sheep Street (☎ **01993/823558**) and is open November to February Monday to Saturday from 10am to 4:30pm; March to October Monday to Saturday from 9:30am to 5:30pm.

SEEING THE SIGHTS

Approaching Burford from the south, you'll experience one of the finest views of any ancient market town in the country. The main street sweeps down to the River Windrush, past an extraordinary collection of houses of various styles and ages. Burford's ancient packhorse bridge is still doing duty at the bottom of the hill. The hills opposite provide a frame of fields and trees and, with luck, panoramic skies.

Although the wool trade has long since vanished, most of Burford remains unchanged in appearance, with its old houses, both great and small, in the High Street and nearby side streets. Nearly all are built of local stone. Many Cotswold towns have a Sheep Street, as does Burford, with many fine stone-built houses covered with roofs of Stonesfield slate. Burford Church (ca. 1175) is almost cathedral-like in proportion.

It was enlarged throughout succeeding centuries until the decline of the wool trade. Little has changed here since about 1500.

Traders and vendors still set up their stalls under the Tolsey on Friday, where from the 12th century the guild has collected tolls from anyone wishing to trade in the town. It still stands at the corner of Sheep Street. On the upper floor is the minor Tolsey Museum, where you can see a medieval seal bearing Burford's insignia, the "rampant cat."

Two miles south of Burford on A361 lies the **Cotswold Wildlife Park** (☎ **01993/823006**). The 120 acres of gardens and forests around this Victorian manor house have been transformed into a jungle of sorts, with a Noah's Ark consortium of animals ranging from voracious ants to rare Asiatic lions. Children can romp around the farmyard and the adventure playground. A narrow-gauge railway runs from April to October, and there are extensive picnic areas plus a cafeteria. Hours are Easter through October daily from 10am to 6:30pm; off-season daily 10am to 5:30pm. Admission is £5.50 ($8.80) for adults, £3.50 ($5.60) for seniors and children 3 to 16, and free for children 2 and under.

And before you leave Burford, we suggest a slight detour to **Swinbrook,** a pretty village by the Windrush River immediately to the east. It's best known as the one-time home of the fabled Mitford sisters. Visit the local parish church to see the grave of writer Nancy Mitford and the impressive tiered monuments to the Fettiplace family.

On High Street in Burford, you'll find several antique shops, including **Manfred Schotten Antiques,** The Crypt, 109 High St. (☎ **01993/822302**). Sporting antiques and collectibles, they also carry library and club furniture. **Jonathan Fyson Antiques,** 50/52 High St. (☎ **01993/823204**), carries English and continental furniture and porcelain, glass, and brass items. On Cheltenham Road, **Gateway Antiques** (☎ **01993/823678**) has a variety of items displayed in large showrooms. English pottery, metalware, and furniture dominate the inventory. Unique arts and crafts items and interesting decorative objects are fun to browse through, even if you don't buy.

WHERE TO STAY

✪ **Bay Tree Hotel.** 12–14 Sheep St., Burford, Oxfordshire OX18 6LW. ☎ **01993/822791.** Fax 01993/823008. 30 units. TV TEL. £115 ($184) double; £160 ($256) suite. Rates include English breakfast. AE, DC, MC, V.

This is the best and most atmospheric of Burford's many interesting old inns. The house was built for Sir Lawrence Tanfield, the unpopular lord chief baron of the Exchequer to Elizabeth I. He definitely was not noted for his hospitality, but time and a major overhaul have erased his unfortunate memory while retaining the splendor of his Cotswold manor house. The house has oak-paneled rooms with stone fireplaces in which burning logs erase the chill. A high-beamed hall has a minstrel's gallery. The guest rooms are tastefully furnished and individually decorated. The 20th-century comforts have been discreetly installed, and the beds are a far cry from the old rope-bottom contraptions of Elizabethan times. Try to get a room overlooking the terraced gardens at the rear of the house.

Dining/Diversions: The hotel has a country-style bar, The Woolsack, offering guests and visitors a choice of light lunches and dinners. The head chef is well known for his tempting menus, with dishes based on local and seasonal produce. The 65-seat oak-beamed restaurant, which overlooks the gardens, retains all of its original charm. The delightful conservatory is now the residents' lounge.

Golden Pheasant Hotel. 91 High St., Burford, Oxfordshire OX18 4QA. ☎ **01993/823223.** Fax 01993/822621. 12 units. TV TEL. £70–£90 ($112–$144) double. Rates include English breakfast. AE, MC, V.

The Golden Pheasant was the 1400s home of a prosperous wool merchant, but it began serving food and drink in the 1730s when it was used both to brew and serve beer. Today it's the second best place to stay in town (it lacks the rich antique furnishings of the best, the Bay Tree Hotel, reviewed above). Like many of its neighbors, the Golden Pheasant is capped with a slate roof and fronted with light gray, hand-chiseled stones. The rooms are comfortable and cozy; one has a four-poster bed.

Inside, within view of dozens of old beams and a blazing fireplace, a candlelit restaurant serves both French and English specialties. The new bar also merits a visit.

✪ **The Lamb Inn.** Sheep St., Burford, Oxfordshire OX18 4LR. ☎ **01993/823155.** Fax 01993/822228. 15 units. TV TEL. £95–£100 ($152–$160) double. Rates include English breakfast. MC, V.

This thoroughly Cotswold house was solidly built in 1430 with thick stones, mullioned and leaded windows, many chimneys and gables, and a slate roof now mossy with age. Vying with the Bay Tree in antique furnishings, it opens onto a stone-paved rear garden, with a rose-lined walk and a shaded lawn. The bedrooms are a mixture of today's comforts, such as good beds and plentiful hot water, and antiques. The public living rooms have heavy oak beams, stone floors, window seats, Oriental rugs, and fine antiques.

Dining: Light lunches and snacks, along with locally brewed ales, are served in the bars and lounges or in the garden in summer. Dinner as well as a traditional Sunday lunch are offered in the beamed dining room with a garden view. If you're dining here in the right season, you can feast on treats of the rivers or forest, such as salmon, trout, and wild boar. See below.

WHERE TO DINE

After you've browsed through the antique shops, head to **Burford House** (☎ 01993/823151) for tea. This old Cotswold favorite serves daily from 11am to 6pm. Freshly baked goods, including flans, scones, cakes, and muffins, are here to tempt.

Lamb Inn Restaurant. Sheep St. ☎ **01993/823155.** Reservations recommended for dinner. 2-course fixed-price menu £19 ($30.40); 3-course fixed-price menu £24 ($38.40); Sun lunch £17.50 ($28); bar lunches from £6 ($9.60). MC, V. Mon–Sat noon–2pm, Sun 12:30–1:30pm; daily 7–9:30pm. ENGLISH/CONTINENTAL.

A meal in this pretty pillared restaurant is the perfect way to cap off a visit to Burford. Good pub lunches dominate the agenda at midday, whereas dinners are more formal, candlelit affairs. The evening menu is beautifully cooked and served. You might begin with a coarse pâté of rabbit and lamb with a walnut-and-honey dressing before moving on to roast rack of lamb with a garlic-and-herb crust or fillet of sea bass on buttered egg noodles with a spring-onion-and-oyster sauce.

The pub here attracts folks from all walks of life. They seem to adore its mellow atmosphere and charm. Guinness, cider, and a carefully chosen collection of ales, including a local brew, Wadworth, are on tap.

7 Bourton-on-the-Water

85 miles NW of London; 36 miles NW of Oxford

You may feel like Gulliver voyaging to Lilliput when you arrive in this scenic Cotswold village. Bourton-on-the-Water lies on the banks of the tiny Windrush River. Its mellow stone houses, its village greens on the banks of the water, and its bridges have earned it the title of the Venice of the Cotswolds. But that label tends to obscure its true charm. Its fans consider Bourton-on-the-Water the quintessential Cotswold village, with a history going back to the Celts and lovely 15th- and 16th-century architecture.

GETTING THERE

Trains go from London's Paddington Station to nearby Moreton-in-Marsh, a trip of 2 hours. For schedules and information, call ☎ 0345/484950 (in the U.K. only) or 01603/764776. From here, take a Pulhams Bus Company coach 6 miles to Bourton on-the-Water. Trains also run from London to Cheltenham and Kingham; while somewhat more distant than Moreton-in-Marsh, both have bus connections to Bourton-on-the-Water.

National Express buses run from Victoria Coach Station in London to both Cheltenham and Stow-on-the-Wold. For schedules and information, call ☎ 0990/808080. Pulhams Bus Company operates about four buses per day from both towns to Bourton-on-the-Water.

If you're driving from Oxford, head west on A40 to the junction with A429 (Fosse Way). Take it northeast to Bourton-on-the-Water.

LILLIPUT, THE BIRDS, VINTAGE CARS & MORE

Within the town are a handful of minor museums, each of which was established from idiosyncratic collections amassed over the years by local residents. They include the **Bourton Model Railway Exhibition and Toy Shop** (☎ 01451/820686) and **Birdland,** described below.

After you've seen them, stop by the quaint little tearoom called **Small Talk,** on High Street (☎ 01451/821596). It's full of dainty lace and fine china and appetizing scones and pastries. Sit at a table overlooking the water and enjoy a pot of tea and some good conversation.

Birdland. Rissington Rd. ☎ 01451/820480. Admission £3.75 ($6) adults, £2.75 ($4.40) seniors, £2 ($3.20) children 4–14; children under 3 free. Apr–Oct daily 10am–6pm; Nov–Mar daily 10am–4pm.

This handsomely designed attraction is set on 8½ acres of field and forests on the banks of Windrush River, about a mile east of Bourton-on-the-Water. It houses about 1,200 birds representing 361 species, many of them on exhibition for the first time. Included is the largest and most varied collection of penguins in any zoo, with glass-walled tanks that allow observers to appreciate their agile underwater movements. There's also an enviable collection of hummingbirds. Birdland has a picnic area and a children's playground in a wooded copse.

Cotswold Motor Museum. The Old Mill. ☎ 01451/821255. Admission £1.75 ($2.80) adults, 80p ($1.30) children. Feb–Nov daily 10am–6pm.

This museum has fun displays of cars, bikes, caravans from the 1920s, toys, and the largest collection of advertising signs in Europe. Visitors can also see village shops from the past. The museum is actually in a historic water mill from the 1700s and is the site where the British TV program *Brum* was filmed.

Cotswold Perfumery. Victoria St. ☎ 01451/820698. Admission £2 ($3.20) adults, £1.75 ($2.80) children and seniors. Apr–Sept Mon–Sat 9:30am–6pm, Sun 10:30am–6pm; Oct–Mar Mon–Sat 9:30am–5pm, Sun 10:30am–5pm. Closed Dec 25–26.

This permanent perfume exhibition details the history of the perfume industry and also focuses on its production. There's an audiovisual show in a "smelly vision" theater, a perfume quiz, a perfume garden full of plants grown exclusively for their fragrance, and a genealogy chart that can be used by visitors to select their own personal perfume. Perfumes are made on the premises and sold in the shop.

The Model Village at the Old New Inn. High St. ☎ **01451/820467.** Admission £2 ($3.20) adults, £1.80 ($2.90) seniors, £1.50 ($2.40) children. Daily 9am–6pm or dusk in summer; daily 10am–4pm in winter.

Beginning in the 1930s, a local hotelier, Mr. Morris, whiled away some of the doldrums of the Great Depression by constructing a scale model (1:9) of Bourton-on-the-Water as a testimony to its architectural charms. This isn't a tiny and cramped display set behind glass—the model is big enough so you can walk through this near-perfect and most realistic model village.

Cotswold Countryside Collection. Fosse Way, Northleach (Cotswold District Council). ☎ **01451/860715.** Admission £1.50 ($2.40) adults, £1.25 ($2) seniors, 75p ($1.20) children, £3.75 ($6) family ticket. Apr–Oct Mon–Sat 10am–5pm, Sun 2–5pm.

This museum of rural life is actually located off the A40 between Burford and Cheltenham. You can see the Lloyd-Baker collection of agricultural history, including wagons, horse-drawn implements, and tools. A Cotswold gallery records the social history of the area. "Below Stairs" is an exhibition of laundry, dairy, and kitchen implements. The museum was once a house of correction, and its history is displayed in the reconstructed cell block and courtroom.

WHERE TO STAY & DINE

Chester House Hotel. Victoria St., Bourton-on-the-Water, Cheltenham, Gloucestershire GL54 2BU. ☎ **01451/820286.** Fax 01451/820471. 23 units. TV TEL. £79–£99 ($126.40–$158.40) double. Rates include continental or English breakfast. AE, CB, DC, MC, V. Closed mid-Dec to early Feb.

This weathered, 300-year-old Cotswold-stone house, built on the banks of the Windrush River, is conveniently located in the center of town. It blends an old building with a row of stables converted into a hotel with comfortable rooms. The hotel also has an intimate bar and a stone-walled restaurant offering reliable English cuisine, including Cotswold lamb.

✪ **Dial House Hotel.** The Chestnuts, High St., Bourton-on-the-Water, Gloucestershire GL54 2AN. ☎ **01451/822244.** Fax 01451/810126. 10 units. TV TEL. £60–£110 ($96–$176) double. Rates include breakfast. MC, V.

Our top choice in the area, this 1698 house is constructed from yellow Cotswold stone, standing right in the heart of the village center. Peter and Lynn Boxhall, your hosts, offer not only a nostalgic retreat but some of the best cuisine in the area (see below).

Set in 1½ acres of manicured gardens, the house overlooks the Windrush River. The Boxhalls have restored all of the rooms, giving each accommodation an individual character, some with four-poster beds. Three bedrooms are no-smoking. Two of the rooms, as charming as those in the main building, are in a converted coach house. Log fires burn on chilly nights, and there are two small dining rooms, one with an inglenook fireplace.

Dining: Under oak beams and on flagstone floors, your candlelit table is the setting for modern British dishes, the best of local game and fish. Try pink salmon fish cakes with a pink champagne sauce or medallions of pork with a pistachio and apricot stuffing. Nonresidents can dine here but should call first for a reservation.

The Old Manse Hotel. Victoria St., Bourton-on-the-Water, Cheltenham, Gloucestershire GL54 2BX. ☎ **01451/820082.** Fax 01451/810381. 15 units. TV TEL. Sun–Thurs £60–£80 ($96–$128) double; £100 ($160) suite. Fri–Sat £72–£96 ($115.20–$153.60) double; £120 ($192) suite. Rates include English breakfast. AE, DC, MC, V.

An architectural gem, this hotel sits in the center of town by the slow-moving river that wanders through the village green. Built of Cotswold stone in 1748, with chimneys, dormers, and small-paned windows, it has been modernized inside. We've

The Great Cotswold Ramble

A walking tour between the villages of Upper and Lower Slaughter, with an optional extension to Bourton-on-the-Water, is one of the most memorable in England. It's a mile each way between the Slaughters, or 2½ miles from Upper Slaughter to Bourton-on-the-Water. This walk could take between 2 and 4 hours.

The architecture of Upper and Lower Slaughter is so unusual that you're likely to remember this easy hike for many years. By striking out on foot, you also avoid at least some of the traffic that taxes the nerves and goodwill of local residents during peak season. En route, you're likely to glimpse the waterfowl that inhabit the rivers, streams, and millponds that crisscross this much-praised region.

A well-worn footpath known as **Warden's Way** meanders beside the edge of the swift-moving River Eye. From its well-marked beginning in Upper Slaughter's central car park, the path passes sheep grazing in meadows, antique houses crafted from honey-colored local stone, stately trees arching over ancient millponds, and footbridges that have endured centuries of foot traffic and rain.

The rushing river powers a historic mill on the northwestern edge of Lower Slaughter. In quiet eddies, you'll see ample numbers of waterfowl and birds, including wild ducks, gray wagtails, mute swans, coots, and Canadian geese.

Most visitors turn around at Lower Slaughter, but Warden's Way continues another 1½ miles to Bourton-on-the-Water by following the Fosse Way, route of an ancient Roman footpath. The path leaves the river's edge and strikes out across cattle pastures in a southerly direction. Most of it from Lower Slaughter to Bourton-on-the-Water is covered by tarmac; it's closed to cars, but ideal for walking or biking. You're legally required to close each of the several gates that stretch across the footpath.

Warden's Way will introduce you to Bourton-on-the-Water through the hamlet's northern edges. The first landmark you'll see will be the tower of St. Lawrence's Anglican Church. From the base of the church, walk south along The Avenue (one of the hamlet's main streets) and end your Cotswold ramble on the Village Green, directly in front of the War Memorial.

You can follow this route in reverse, but parking is more plentiful in Upper Slaughter than in Lower Slaughter.

recently gotten complaints about maintenance, though, so if you stay here, tell us what you think.

Dining: Dining is a treat in Le Jardin du Vin, serving dinner daily from 6:30 to 9:30pm. Typical dishes include such appetizers as homemade venison sausage or sautéed breast of pigeon, followed by Dover sole, stuffed Bibury trout, and roast English lamb. Sometimes roast pheasant is featured.

Old New Inn. High St., Bourton-on-the-Water, Cheltenham, Gloucestershire GL54 2AF. ☎ **01451/820467.** Fax 01451/810236. 17 units, 6 with bathroom. TV. £60 ($96) double without bathroom, £72 ($115.20) double with bathroom. Rates include English breakfast. MC, V.

The Old New Inn is a landmark in the village. On the main street, overlooking the river, it's a good example of Queen Anne design (the miniature model village in its garden was referred to earlier). Hungry or tired travelers are drawn to the old-fashioned comforts and cuisine of this most English inn. The rooms are comfortable, with homelike furnishings and soft beds.

Nonresidents are also welcome here for meals, with lunches at £12 ($19.20) and dinner from £18 ($28.80). You may want to spend an evening in either the redecorated pub-lounge playing darts or chatting with the villagers.

8 Upper & Lower Slaughter

Midway between Bourton-on-the-Water and Stow-on-the-Wold are two of the prettiest villages in the Cotswolds: Upper and Lower Slaughter. Don't be put off by the name—"Slaughter" is actually a corruption of *de Sclotre*, the name of the original Norman landowner. Houses here are constructed of honey-colored Cotswold stone, and a stream meanders right through the street, providing a home for free-wandering ducks, which beg scraps from kindly passersby. Upper Slaughter has a fine example of a 17th-century Cotswold manor house.

The Old Mill, in Lower Slaughter (☎ 01451/820052), is a sturdy 19th-century stone structure built on the River Eye with the sole purpose of grinding out flour. The river still turns the massive water wheel that powers this Victorian flour mill today. Visitors can enjoy an ice-cream parlor and tearoom while visiting the mill.

GETTING THERE

Lower Slaughter and Stow-on-the-Wold are 4 miles apart. From Stow, take A429 (the Main Fosse Way) and follow signs to Cirencester and Bourton-on-the-Water. Turn off the highway when you see signs to Upper and Lower Slaughter. The road will then divide, and you can pick which hamlet you want to head to.

WHERE TO STAY & DINE

✪ **Lords of the Manor Hotel.** Upper Slaughter, near Cheltenham, Gloucestershire GL54 2JD. ☎ **01451/820243.** Fax 01451/820696. 27 units. TV TEL. Summer £180–£210 ($288–$336) standard double, £230–£290 ($368–$464) four-poster room. Winter £130–£165 ($208–$264) standard double, £195–£295 ($312–$472) four-poster room. Rates include English breakfast. AE, DC, MC, V. Take A429 18 miles north of Cheltenham.

A 17th-century house set on several acres of rolling fields, the Lords of the Manor has gardens with a stream featuring brown trout. A quintessentially British hotel of great style and amenities, it's a showplace. It may be modernized, but it has successfully maintained the quiet country-house atmosphere of 300 years ago. Half the rooms are in a converted old barn and granary, and many have lovely views.

Dining: The walls in the lounge bar are hung with family portraits of the original lords of the manor. Another bar overlooks the garden, and chintz and antiques are everywhere. The country atmosphere is carried into the dining room as well, with its antiques and mullioned windows. The well-prepared dishes are all fresh and home cooked.

✪ **Lower Slaughter Manor.** Lower Slaughter, near Cheltenham, Gloucestershire GL54 2HP. ☎ 01451/820456. Fax 01451/822150. 18 units. TV TEL. £150–£215 ($240–$344) double; £275–£335 ($440–$536) suite for 2. Rates include English breakfast. AE, MC, V. Take A429 turnoff at the sign for The Slaughters, and drive ½ mile; manor is on right as you enter the village. No children under 12.

Built in 1658, Lower Slaughter Manor was owned by Sir George Whitmore, high sheriff of Gloucestershire. Today, it's one of the great inns of the Cotswolds, although its charms are matched in every way by Lords of the Manor (see above). It remained in the same family until 1964 when it was sold as a private residence. Standing on its own private grounds, it has beautifully proportioned reception rooms and tastefully furnished rooms, some with four-poster beds.

Dining: The inn was always a solid dining choice, but it's improved its offerings even further under new head chef Alan Dann, who cooks in the modern French style, using the best English produce. Beef and lamb come from specially bred stock in Scotland, the smoked salmon is wild, and the fish is mainly from inshore fishing boats docked at Brixham. The wine list now extends to 500 selections, with emphasis on New York and French vintages.

Amenities: Room service is available from the inn's excellent restaurant. Indoor heated swimming pool, sauna, all-weather tennis court, croquet lawn.

9 Stow-on-the-Wold

9 miles SE of Broadway; 10 miles S of Chipping Campden; 4 miles S of Moreton-in-Marsh; 21 miles S of Stratford-upon-Avon

Stow-on-the-Wold is an unspoiled Cotswold market town, in spite of the busloads of tourists who stop off en route to Broadway and Chipping Campden. In its open market square you can still see the stocks where the townspeople threw rotten eggs at past offenders. The final battle between the Roundheads and the Royalists took place in Stow-on-the-Wold. The town, which is really like a market village today, is a good base for exploring the Cotswolds and Stratford-upon-Avon.

ESSENTIALS

GETTING THERE   Several trains run daily from London's Paddington Station to Moreton-in-Marsh (see below). For schedules and information, call ☎ 0345/484950 (in the U.K. only) or 01603/764776. From Moreton-in-Marsh, Pulhams Bus Company makes the 10-minute ride to Stow-on-the-Wold.

National Express buses also run daily from London's Victoria Coach Station to Moreton-in-Marsh, where you can catch a Pulhams Bus Company coach to Stow-on-the-Wold. For schedules and information, call ☎ 0990/808080. Several Pulhams coaches also run daily to Stow-on-the-Wold from Cheltenham.

If driving from Oxford, take A40 west to the junction with A424, near Burford. Head northwest along A424 to Stow-on-the-Wold.

VISITOR INFORMATION   The **Tourist Information Centre** is at Hollis House, The Square (☎ 01451/831082). It's open April through October Monday to Saturday from 9:30am to 5:30pm, Sunday from 10:30am to 4pm; November through March Monday to Saturday from 9:30am to 4:30pm.

ANTIQUE HEAVEN

Don't be fooled by the village's sleepy, country-bucolic setting: Stow-on-the-Wold has developed over the last 20 years into the antique-buyer's highlight of Britain and has at least 60 merchandisers scattered throughout the village and its environs.

Set within four showrooms inside an 18th-century building on the town's main square, **Anthony Preston Antiques, Ltd.,** The Square (☎ 01451/831586), specializes in English and French furniture, including some very large pieces such as bookcases, and decorative objects that include paperweights, lamps, paintings on silk, and small objects designed to add a glossy accent to carefully contrived interior decors.

Located on Church Street, **Baggot Church Street, Ltd.** (☎ 01451/830370), is the smaller, and perhaps more intricately decorated, of two shops founded and maintained by a well-regarded local antique merchant, Duncan ("Jack") Baggott, a frequent denizen at estate sales of country houses throughout Britain. The shop contains four showrooms loaded with furniture and paintings from the 17th to the 19th century.

More eclectic and wide-ranging is Baggott's second shop, **Woolcomber House,** on Sheep Street (☎ 01451/830662). Among the largest retail outlets in the Cotswolds, it contains about 17 rooms that during the 16th century functioned as a coaching inn, but today are lavishly decorated, each according to a particular era of English decorative history.

Covering about half a block in the heart of town, **Huntington's Antiques Ltd.,** Church Street (☎ **01451/830842**), contains one of the largest stocks of quality antiques in England. Wander at will through 10 ground-floor rooms, then climb to the second floor where a long gallery and a quartet of additional showrooms bulge with refectory tables, unusual cupboards, and all kinds of finds.

After you've shopped till you drop, the best place for tea is a lovely cottage home that goes by the name of **Tea at the Peggums,** on Church Street (☎ **01451/830102**). The place usually sells out well before closing, so get here early. Menu items include a choice of teas and tasty tea breads, scones, and other pastries.

WHERE TO STAY & DINE

Fosse Manor Hotel. Fosse Way, Stow-on-the-Wold, Cheltenham, Gloucestershire GL54 1JX. ☎ **01451/830354.** Fax 01451/832486. 22 units. TV TEL. £94–£114 ($150.40–$182.40) double; £160 ($256) suite. Rates include English breakfast. "Bargain Breaks" (2-night minimum required): £65–£95 ($104–$152) per person, including half board. AE, CB, DC, MC, V. Take A429 1¼ miles south of Stow-on-the-Wold.

Although lacking the charm of the Grapevine, Fosse Manor is at least second best in town, even more inviting than the Stow Lodge. The hotel lies near the site of an ancient Roman road that used to bisect England, its stone walls and neo-Gothic gables almost concealed by strands of ivy. From some of the high stone-sided windows, you can enjoy a view of a landscaped garden with a sunken lily pond, flagstone walks, and an old-fashioned sundial. Inside, the interior is conservatively modern, with homey bedrooms. There's a plushly upholstered bar and a dining room where dinners cost £21 ($33.60).

The Grapevine Hotel. Sheep St., Stow-on-the-Wold, Cheltenham, Gloucestershire GL54 1AU. ☎ **800/528-1234** in the U.S. and Canada, or 01451/830344. Fax 01451/832278. 22 units. TV TEL. £74–£114 ($118.40–$182.40) per person. Rates include breakfast. "Bargain Breaks" (2-night minimum): £69–£119 ($110.40–$190.40) per person, including half board. AE, DC, MC, V.

Facing the village green, The Grapevine mixes urban sophistication with reasonable prices, rural charm, and intimacy. It's the best inn in town, although it doesn't have the charm and grace of Wyck Hill House on the outskirts (see below). It was named after the ancient vine whose tendrils shade and shelter the beautiful conservatory restaurant. Each room has tasteful furnishings, a hair dryer, and a tea- and coffeemaker.

Dining: The reading room, comfortable lounge, and cozy bar with Victorian accessories create a warm ambience for tea, bar snacks, or dinner. Full meals feature English, French, and Italian cuisine and are served from 7 to 9:30pm daily. Bar snacks are served at midday. Dinners are more elaborate, beginning at £24 ($38.40) for a three-course menu, and including seared smoked salmon with herb brioche and a marmalade of caper and onion followed by roasted melon pearls served in a ginger-yogurt topped pastry. The restaurant has a balmy Mediterranean feel.

✪ **The Old Farmhouse Hotel.** Lower Swell, Stow-on-the-Wold, Cheltenham, Gloucestershire GL54 1LF. ☎ **01451/830232.** Fax 01451/870962. 14 units, 12 with private bathroom. TV TEL. £21.50–£24 ($34.40–$38.40) per person double without bathroom, £36–£47.50 ($57.60–$76) per person double with bathroom; £47.50 ($76) per person suite. Rates include English breakfast. MC, V. Take B4068 1¼ miles west of Stow-on-the-Wold.

This small, intimate hotel in the heart of the Cotswolds was converted from a 16th-century farmhouse. It's been completely refurbished and the original fireplaces restored, once again blazing with log fires. The relaxed atmosphere, together with excellent food and wine, has made this a popular stop for visitors, so reserve well in advance. Two accommodations under the eaves share a bath, and all units are different because of the building's farmhouse origin.

Dinner is served daily from 7pm, with last orders taken at 9pm. The table d'hôte menu is changed daily. The hotel has a secluded walled garden.

Stow Lodge Hotel. The Square, Stow-on-the-Wold, Cheltenham, Gloucestershire GL54 1AB. ☎ **01451/830485.** Fax 01451/831671. 21 units. TV TEL. £65–£120 ($104–$192) double. Rates include English breakfast. DC, MC, V.

Stow Lodge dominates the marketplace but is set back far enough to avoid too much noise. Its gardens, honeysuckle growing over the stone walls, diamond-shaped windows, gables, and many chimneys capture the best of country living, even though you're right in the heart of town. The ample, well-furnished, no-smoking rooms have radios, central heating, and beverage-makers.

Dining: Arrange to have your afternoon tea out back by the flower garden. In the lounge, logs burn in a 200-year-old stone fireplace. À la carte dinners, priced from £17 ($27.20), are served daily from 7 to 8:45pm and are likely to feature poached salmon steak, grilled local trout, various steaks, and roast duckling with a choice of sauces.

✪ **Wyck Hill House.** Burford Rd., Stow-on-the-Wold, Cheltenham, Gloucestershire GL54 1HY. ☎ **01451/831936.** Fax 01451/832243. 32 units. TV TEL. £125 ($200) double; £205 ($328) suite. Rates include English breakfast. AE, DC, MC, V. Drive 2½ miles south of Stow-on-the-Wold on A424.

Parts of this otherwise Victorian country house on 100 acres of grounds and gardens date from 1720, when its stone walls were first erected. It was discovered in the course of recent restoration that one wing of the manor house rests on the foundations of a Roman villa. Today, it is the showcase country inn of this area, although not nearly the equal of the premier houses in Upper and Lower Slaughter (see section 8 above). The opulent interior adheres to 18th-century authenticity with room after room leading to paneled libraries and Adam sitting rooms. The well-furnished bedrooms are in the main hotel, in the coach-house annex, or in the orangery.

Dining: Excellent food is served here, with a fixed-price lunch costing £16.95 ($27.10). A set dinner goes for £35 ($56) per meal.

10 Moreton-in-Marsh

83 miles NW of London; 4 miles N of Stow-on-the-Wold; 7 miles S of Chipping Campden; 17 miles S of Stratford-upon-Avon

Near many other villages of interest, Moreton-in-Marsh is an important center for rail passengers headed for the Cotswolds. Don't take the name *Moreton-in-Marsh* too literally, since *Marsh* derives from an old word meaning "border." Look for the 17th-century market hall and the old curfew tower, then walk down the shop-flanked High (the main street), where Roman legions trudged centuries ago along the Fosse Way.

For a fascinating lesson on birds of prey, stop by the **Cotswold Falconry Centre,** Batsford Park (☎ **01386/701043**). These great birds are flown daily by experienced falconers for visitors to see first-hand the remarkable speed and agility of eagles, hawks, owls, and falcons. It's open daily from 10:30am to 5:30pm. Flying displays are daily at 11:30am, 1:30, 3, and 4:30pm. Admission is £3 ($4.80) for adults, £1.50 ($2.40) for children 4 to 16 (free 3 and under).

Touted as a Cotswold farm with a difference, **Sleepy Hollow Farm Park,** 32 Sleepy Hollow Farm Park (☎ **01386/701264**), is a great place for children and adults to explore. This plot of land is the home of many rare and unusual farm animals that coexist with an array of interesting wild animals, including a family of otters, and ever-curious raccoons. Admission is £2.95 ($4.70) adults, £2.20 ($3.50) seniors, and £1.60 ($2.55) children (free 2 and under). It is open daily from 10:30am to 5pm March through October.

GETTING THERE

Trains run from London's Paddington Station to Moreton-in-Marsh, a nearly 2-hour trip. For schedules and information, call ☎ **0345/484950** (in the U.K. only) or 01603/764776. **National Express** buses run from London's Victoria Coach Station to Moreton-in-Marsh daily. For schedules and information, call ☎ **0990/808080.**

If you're driving from Stow-on-the-Wold (see above), take A429 north.

WHERE TO STAY

Manor House Hotel. High St., Moreton-in-Marsh, Gloucestershire GL56 0LJ. ☎ **01608/ 650501.** Fax 01608/651481. 39 units, 1 family suite. TV TEL. £90–£125 ($144–$200) double; £135 ($216) suite. Rates include English breakfast. AE, DC, MC, V.

The town's best hotel, the Manor House comes complete with its own ghost, a priest's hiding hole, a secret passage, and a moot room used centuries ago by local merchants to settle arguments over wool exchanges. On the main street, it's a formal yet gracious house, and its rear portions reveal varying architectural periods of design. Vine-covered walls protect the garden. Inside are many living rooms, one especially intimate with leather chairs and a fireplace-within-a-fireplace, ideal for drinks and swapping "bump-in-the-night" stories. The rooms are tastefully furnished, often with antiques or fine reproductions. Many have fine old desks set in front of window ledges, with a view of the garden and ornamental pond.

Dining/Diversions: The bar, with its garden view through leaded Gothic windows, is a favorite nook. Reliably good evening meals in the two-level dining room are candlelit.

Amenities: The hotel has a heated indoor pool, a spa bath, and a sauna.

Redesdale Arms. High St., Moreton-in-Marsh, Gloucestershire GL56 0AW. ☎ **01608/ 650308.** Fax 01608/651843. 20 units. TV TEL. £42.25 ($67.60) per person double. AE, MC, V.

Although the Manor House is better appointed and more comfortable, this is one of the largest and best-preserved coaching inns in Gloucestershire. Originally established around 1774 as the Unicorn Hotel, it functioned around 1840 as an important link in the Bath-to-Lincoln stagecoach routes, offering food and accommodations to both humans and horses during the arduous journey. Since then, the inn has been considerably upgraded, with modernized and comfortably furnished bedrooms, but much of the old-fashioned charm remains intact.

Dining/Diversions: Guests gravitate to the bar, where drinks are served in front of a 6-foot-high stone fireplace. During nice weather, tables are set up in a sheltered courtyard. The inn is especially well known for its meals and its modern British cuisine, although it offers no serious competition to Marsh Goose or Annie's restaurants (see below).

The White Hart Royal Hotel. High St., Moreton-in-Marsh, Gloucestershire GL56 0BA. ☎ **01608/650731.** Fax 01608/650880. 19 units. TV TEL. £70–£80 ($112–$128) double. Rates include English breakfast. AE, MC, V.

A mellow old Cotswold inn graced by Charles I in 1644, the White Hart provides modern amenities without compromising the personality of yesteryear. It long ago ceased being the premier inn of town but it's still a comfortable place to spend the night. The well-furnished rooms all have hot and cold running water, innerspring mattresses, and a few antiques intermixed with basic 20th-century pieces.

Dining/Diversions: The bar is built of irregular Cotswold stone. You can enjoy drinks in front of the 10-foot open fireplace. Lunches are informal affairs served in the hotel's pub. Dinners are more elaborate sit-down events, with four-course table d'hôte menus featured.

WHERE TO DINE

Annie's. 3 Oxford St. ☎ **01608/651981.** Reservations recommended. Main courses £15–£20 ($24–$32). AE, DC, MC, V. Mon–Sat 7–9:30pm. Closed 3 weeks from late Jan to early Feb. ENGLISH/FRENCH.

In the heart of town, on a side street that merges with the old Roman Fosse Way, lies this stone-sided 3-story house whose walls are 300 to 400 years old. For a decade, David and Anne Ellis have prepared ample portions of English and French country cuisine, garnering enthusiastic responses from weekending Londoners.

The cooking is very straightforward and honest, with dishes standing out for their true flavors and not disguised with heavy sauces. David's tomato-and-rosemary soup is a refreshing beginning, as are the spiced salmon fish cakes with a red-pepper sauce. Appealing main courses are adjusted to make use of the freshest ingredients on the market but might include a duck breast with an orange-and-Noilly-Prat sauce, the chef's homemade pie of the day, or a perfectly done fillet of venison in an even more delectable brandy-and-green-peppercorn sauce. Fresh vegetables, not overcooked, are served with each main dish. Freshly made desserts are also offered.

✪ **Marsh Goose.** High St. ☎ **01608/652111.** Reservations recommended. Lunch main courses £10–£13 ($16–$20.80); 3-course fixed-price lunch £14 ($22.40), on Sun £18.50 ($29.60); 3-course fixed-price dinner £26.50 ($42.40). AE, DC, MC, V. Tues–Sun 12:30–2:30pm; Tues–Sat 7:30–9:30pm. MODERN BRITISH.

The food here is among the best in The Cotswolds. The creative seasonal cuisine showcases the talents of chef Sonya Kidney. Despite its unique allure and country-house elegance, this restaurant is very much an outpost of young and sophisticated Londoners away for a weekend in the country. The unusual cuisine is modern British, with good doses of Caribbean fare thrown in. Examples include panfried scallops served with artichoke hearts, lime dressing, and strips of smoked goose breast; grilled medallions of monkfish on celeriac puree with an orange-and-chive cream sauce; and panfried saddle of rabbit with red-wine risotto, grain mustard, and deep-fried Parma ham. A favorite dessert is the hot dark-chocolate soufflé with white-chocolate sauce. There's an exceptionally cozy bar area with ceiling beams and an open fireplace for before-dinner drinks.

11 Broadway

15 miles SW of Stratford-upon-Avon; 93 miles NW of London; 15 miles NE of Cheltenham

The most overrun and touristy town of the Cotswolds, Broadway is also one of the most beautiful—it's popular for a reason. Many of the prime attractions of the Cotswolds, as well as Shakespeare country, lie within easy reach of Broadway, which is near Evesham at the southern tip of Hereford and Worcester. Overlooking the Vale of Evesham, it's a major stopover for bus tours and is mobbed in summer. Somehow it manages to retain its charm in spite of the annual invasion. Broadway has a wide and beautiful High Street flanked with honey-colored stone buildings, remarkable for their harmony of style and design.

ESSENTIALS

GETTING THERE   Rail connections are possible from London's Paddington Station via Oxford. The nearest railway stations are at Moreton-in-Marsh (7 miles away) or at Evesham (5 miles away). For schedules and information, call ☎ **0345/484950** (in the U.K. only) or 01603/764776. Frequent buses arrive from Evesham, but one has to take a taxi from Moreton.

One bus departs daily from London's Victoria Coach Station to Broadway, a 2½-hour ride. For schedules and information, call ☎ **0990/808080.**

If you're driving from Oxford, head west on A40, then take A434 to Woodstock, Chipping Norton, and Moreton-in-Marsh.

VISITOR INFORMATION   The **Tourist Information Centre** is at 1 Cotswold Ct. (☎ **01386/852937**), open March through December Monday to Saturday from 10am to 1pm and 2 to 5pm.

SEEING THE SIGHTS

The **High Street** is one of the most beautiful in England—perhaps the most beautiful. Many of its most striking facades date from 1620 or a century or two later. The most famous facade is that of the **Lygon Arms,** High Street (☎ **01386/852255**), a venerable old inn. It's been serving wayfarers since 1532, and it stands on its own 3 acres of formal gardens. Even if you're not staying here, you might want to visit for a meal or a drink.

You might also seek out **St. Eadurgha's Church,** a place of Christian worship for more than 1,000 years. It's located just outside Broadway on Snowshill Road, and is open most days, though with no set visiting hours. If it's closed at the time of your visit, a note on the porch door will tell you what house to go to for the key. There are occasional Sunday services here.

Also along the street you can visit the **Broadway Teddy Bear Museum,** 76 High St. (☎ **01386/858323**), a showcase shop for teddy-bear and doll artisans. The site is also the setting for a unique museum displaying hundreds of antique and collectors' teddy bears, toys, and dolls. This 18th-century stone shop offers a historical look at the world of teddy bears, ranging from Steiff to Pooh. Bears from all leading manufacturers are also for sale. Hours are daily from 9am to 6pm from mid-March to mid-November; off-season daily from 10am to 5pm. Admission is £1.50 ($2.40) for adults, £1 ($1.60) for children under 14 and senior citizens.

On the outskirts of Broadway stands the **Broadway Tower Country Park** on Broadway Hill (☎ **01386/852390**), a "folly" created by the fanciful mind of the sixth Earl of Coventry. Today, you can climb this tower on a clear day for a panoramic vista of 12 shires. It's the most sweeping view in the Cotswolds. The tower is open from early April to late October daily from 10am to 6pm. Admission is £2.95 ($4.70) for adults, £1.95 ($3.10) for children. There's also a family ticket costing £7.95 ($12.70). You can also bring the makings for a picnic here and spread it out for your lunch in designated areas.

South of Broadway, a final attraction is **Snowshill Manor,** at Snowshill (☎ **01386/ 852410**), a house that dates mainly from the 17th century. It was once owned by an eccentric, Charles Paget Wade, who collected virtually everything he could between 1900 and 1951. Queen Mary once remarked that Wade himself was the most remarkable artifact among his entire flea market. There's a little bit of everything here: Flemish tapestries, toys, lacquer cabinets, narwhal tusks, mousetraps, and cuckoo clocks—a glorious mess, like a giant attic of the 20th century. The property, now owned by the National Trust, is open October through April, Wednesday through

Monday from 1 to 5pm; May through September, Wednesday through Monday from 1 to 6pm. Admission is £5.50 ($8.80) per person or £13 ($20.80) for a family ticket.

WHERE TO STAY

Broadway Hotel. The Green, Broadway, Hereford and Worcester WR12 7AA. ☎ 01386/852401. Fax 01386/853879. 19 units. TV TEL. £70–£90 ($112–$144) double. Rates include English breakfast. AE, DC, MC, V.

Right on the village green, one of the most colorful places in Broadway, this converted 15th-century house keeps its old-world charm while providing modern comforts. All the pleasantly furnished rooms have beverage-makers and central heating. One room with full private bathroom has a four-poster bed.

Dining/Diversions: The cooking is fine, the service personal, the dining room attractive. The comfortable cocktail bar is well stocked. Locals claim that if you're keeping an eye on costs, the bar is the best lunch place in Broadway. Lunches are served daily from noon to 2pm. Dinner in the main dining room is served daily, featuring English specialties such as fish, duckling, or venison.

✪ **Buckland Manor.** Buckland, near Broadway, Gloucestershire WR12 7LY. ☎ 01386/852626. Fax 01386/853557. 13 units. TV TEL. £198–£325 ($316.80–$520) double. Rates include early morning tea and English breakfast. AE, DC, MC, V. Take B4632 about 2 miles south of Broadway, into Gloucestershire. No children under 12.

The Lygon Arms (see below) reigned supreme in Broadway for so long that people thought it had squatters' rights to the title of top inn in town, both for food and lodging. But along came Buckland Manor on the outskirts, topping The Lygon Arms in every way, especially in cuisine. This imposing slate-roofed manor house is ringed with fences of Cotswold stone, green lawns, sheep, and daffodils. Its jutting chimneys rise a few steps from the Buckland church, with its darkened stone tower. The core of the manor house was erected in the 13th century, with wings added in succeeding centuries, especially the 19th century. The Oak Room, with a four-poster bed and burnished paneling, occupies what used to be a private library. Leaded windows in the room overlook gardens and grazing land with Highland cattle and Jacob sheep. Even the oversize bathrooms each contain at least one antique, as well as carpeting and modern plumbing.

Dining: French-inspired meals are served in the elegant dining room with a baronial fireplace. (You don't have to be a guest to dine here.) Service is daily for breakfast, lunch, and dinner. The chef concocts his imaginative cuisine from first-rate ingredients. He creates happy marriages such as langoustines with shredded root vegetables. You dine in elegance with impeccable service.

Collin House Hotel and Restaurant. Collin Lane, Broadway, Hereford and Worcester WR12 7PB. ☎ 01386/858697. 7 units. £89 ($142.40) standard double, £99 ($158.40) four-poster bed room. Rates include English breakfast. MC, V. From Broadway, follow the signs to Evesham before turning right onto Collin Lane; the hotel is a mile west of Broadway off A44.

On a country lane, this 16th-century Cotswold stone farmhouse has been transformed into a hotel set amid 8 acres of gardens and orchards. The cozy rooms are named for flowers that grow here in profusion. Large structural timbers, tasteful wallpaper, private baths, and mullioned windows make them attractive; Wild Rose, with its sloped ceiling, is the most romantic.

Dining: Traditional English food, flavorfully and freshly prepared, is served by candlelight nightly from 7 to 9pm in a room with stone-rimmed windows and ceiling beams. Lunch is served daily from noon to 2:30pm, either in the bar (inexpensively) or in the more formal dining room.

Dormy House. Willersey Hill, Broadway, Hereford and Worcester WR12 7LF. ☎ **01386/ 852711.** Fax 01386/858636. 49 units. TV TEL. £136 ($217.60) double; £164 ($262.40) four-poster room; £175 ($280) suite. Rates include English breakfast. AE, DC, MC, V. Closed Dec 24–28. Take A44 2 miles southeast of Broadway.

This manor house, high on a hill above the village, boasts views in all directions. Its panoramic position has made it a favorite place whether you're seeking a meal, afternoon tea, or lodgings. Halfway between Broadway and Chipping Campden, it was created from a sheep farm. The owners transformed it, furnishing the 17th-century farmhouse with a few antiques, good soft beds, and full central heating; they also extended these amenities to an old adjoining timbered barn, which they converted into studio rooms with open-beamed ceilings. Bowls of fresh flowers adorn tables and alcoves throughout the hotel. The hotel's Tapestry Restaurant is well recommended; see our review below.

✪ **The Lygon Arms.** High St., Broadway, Hereford and Worcester WR12 7DU. ☎ **01386/852255.** Fax 01386/858611. 65 units. TV TEL. £163–£170 ($260.80–$272) double; from £260 ($416) suite. Value-added tax (VAT) extra. Rates include continental breakfast. AE, CB, DC, MC, V.

Despite the challenge of Buckland Manor, this many-gabled structure with mullioned windows, which looks right out on the road in the center of town, still basks in its reputation as one of the great old English inns. It opens onto a private rear garden, with 3 acres of lawns, trees, and borders of flowers, stone walls with roses, and nooks for tea or sherry. The oldest portions date from 1532 or earlier, and additions have been made many times since then. King Charles I reputedly drank with his friends in one of the oak-lined chambers, and later, his enemy Oliver Cromwell slept here the night before the Battle of Worcester. Today, an earlier century is evoked by the charming cluster of antique-laden public rooms, with cavernous fireplaces, smoke-stained paneling, 18th-century pieces, and polished brass. Many but not all the bedrooms are in the antique style; a new wing offers more of a 20th-century feel. Each room is furnished with a radio, hair dryer, and trouser press.

Dining: You dine in the oak-paneled Great Hall, with a Tudor fireplace, a vaulted ceiling, and a minstrels' gallery.

Amenities: 24-hour room service; laundry service; a country club adjoins the old inn. A health club and many leisure facilities are available here, including a large swimming pool and a sauna.

Olive Branch Guest House. 78–80 High St., Broadway, Hereford and Worcester WR12 7AJ. ☎ and fax **01386/853440.** 8 units, 6 with tub or shower. TV. £45–£56 ($72–$89.60) double with tub or shower. Rates include English breakfast. AE.

In the heart of an expensive village, this is a terrific bargain managed by Mark Riley. The house, dating from the 16th century, retains its old Cotswold architectural features. Behind the house is a large walled English garden and parking area. Guests are given a discount for purchases at the owners' attached antique shop. Tea- and coffeemakers are in each room, and hair dryers and irons are available upon request. Furnishings are basic, but comfortable.

WHERE TO DINE

The best place in Broadway for a cup of tea is **Tisanes,** The Green (☎ **01386/ 852112**). The shop offers perfectly blended teas with a variety of sandwiches and salads.

The Tapestry Restaurant. In Dormy House, off the A44, Willersey Hill, Broadway. ☎ **01386/852711.** Reservations recommended. Lunch main courses (Mon–Fri)

£7.95–£8.75 ($12.70–$14), set price Sun lunch £19.50 ($31.20); dinner main courses £14.80–£20.95 ($23.70–$33.50); fixed-price dinner £27.50–£34 ($44–$54.40). AE, DC, MC, V. Sun–Fri noon–2pm; Mon–Sat 7–9:30pm, Sun 7–9pm. MODERN BRITISH.

Set 2 miles from the center of Broadway, beside the highway leading to Moreton-in-Marsh and Oxford, this is one of the most charming and well-managed restaurants in the region. It's elegant, but not as formal and stuffy as some competitors. The setting is as pastoral as a painting by Constable. You'll dine within a room ringed with Cotswold stone (where there are areas for smokers) or within an adjacent glass-sided conservatory (no smoking here).

Chef Alan Cutler turns out an intelligent and interesting cuisine. You might order an appetizer of seared escalope of Scottish smoked salmon in a caper-and-horseradish butter sauce; a main course of pheasant, grouse, and partridge with a bread-sauce parfait in a rich game sauce; and a dessert of pears poached in mulled wine and glazed with a cinnamon spiced sabayon. The cellar houses a superb collection of wines.

12 Chipping Campden

36 miles NW of Oxford; 12 miles S of Stratford-upon-Avon; 93 miles NW of London

Regardless of how often they visit the Cotswolds, the English are attracted in great numbers to this town, once an important wool center. Off the main road, it's easily accessible to major points of interest, and double decker buses frequently run through here on their way to Oxford or Stratford-upon-Avon.

A Saxon settlement on the northern edge of the Cotswolds above the Vale of Evesham, Campden was recorded in the *Domesday Book*. In medieval times, rich merchants built homes of Cotswold stone along its model High Street, described by historian G. M. Trevelyan as "the most beautiful village street now left in the island." Today the houses have been so well preserved that Chipping Campden remains a gem of the Middle Ages. Its church dates from the 15th century, and its old market hall is the loveliest in the Cotswolds.

ESSENTIALS

GETTING THERE   Trains depart from London's Paddington Station for Moreton-in-Marsh, a 1½- to 2-hour trip. For schedules and information, call ☎ 0345/484950 (in the U.K. only) or 01603/764776. A bus operated by Castleway's travels the 7 miles from Moreton-in-Marsh to Chipping Campden five times a day. Many visitors opt for a taxi from Moreton-in-Marsh to Chipping Campden.

The largest and most important nearby bus depot is Cheltenham, which receives service several times a day from London's Victoria Coach Station. For schedules and information, call ☎ 0990/808080. From Cheltenham, Barry's Coaches are infrequent and uncertain, departing three times per week at most.

If you're driving from Oxford, take A40 west to the junction with A424. Follow it northwest, passing by Stow-on-the-Wold. The route becomes A44 until you reach the junction with B4081, which you take northeast to Chipping Campden.

VISITOR INFORMATION   The summer-only **Tourist Information Centre** is at Noel Court, High Street (☎ 01386/841206). It's open daily from 10am to 5pm.

SEEING THE SIGHTS

In 1907 American horticulturist Maj. Lawrence Johnstone created ✿ **Hidcote Manor Garden,** 4 miles northeast of Chipping Campden and 9 miles south of Stratford-upon-Avon (☎ 01386/438333). Set on 10 acres, this masterpiece is composed of small gardens, or rooms, that are separated by a variety of hedges, old roses, rare shrubs, trees, and herbaceous borders. April through September, the garden is open Monday, Wednesday, Thursday, Saturday and Sunday from 11am to 6pm. October weekend hours are 11am to 6pm. During June and July, the garden is also open on Tuesday from 11am to 7pm. Last admission is at 6pm or 1 hour before sunset. Admission is £5.50 ($8.80) adults, £2.70 ($4.30) children, £13.80 ($22.10) family ticket.

Insider's tip: In summer, Shakespeare is performed on the Theatre Lawn; there is no more memorable experience in the Cotswolds than watching *A Midsummer's Night Dream* performed here on a balmy evening in July.

The poet, artist, and craftsman William Morris (1834–96) called the Cotswold countryside home for most of his life. The worldwide Arts and Crafts movement he led in the late 19th century continues to inspire artists and craftspeople in this area.

At the studio of **D. T. Hart,** The Guild, The Silk Mill, Sheep Street (☎ **01386/ 841100**), silver is expertly smithed by descendants of George Hart, an original member of the Guild of Handicraft, in the original Ashbee workshop. **Robert Welch Studio Shop,** Lower High Street (☎ **01386/840522**), is where Robert Welch has been crafting silverware, stainless steel, and cutlery for more than 40 years. **Ann Smith,** Peacock House (☎ **01386/840879**), creates high-quality, handcrafted 18-carat gold jewelry along with enamel and gem work. **Martin Gotrel,** The Square (☎ **01386/841360**), designs and makes fine contemporary and traditional jewelry.

Campden Needlecraft Centre, High Street (☎ **01386/840583**), is widely known as one of the leading specialist embroidery shops in England with an interesting selection of embroidery and canvas work as well as fabrics and threads. If antiques and antique hunting are your passion, visit **School House Antiques,** High Street (☎ **01386/841474**), or **The Barn Antiques Centre,** Long Marston on the Stratford-upon-Avon Road (☎ **01789/721399**). For new, secondhand, and antiquarian books, look up **Campden Bookshop,** High Street (☎ **01386/840944**), or **Draycott Books,** 1 Sheep St. (☎ **01386/841392**).

WHERE TO STAY & DINE

✪ **Charingworth Manor Hotel.** Charingworth, near Chipping Campden, Gloucestershire GL55 6NS. ☎ **01386/593555.** Fax 01386/593353. 26 units. TV TEL. £140–£260 ($224–$416) double. Rates include English breakfast. AE, DC, MC, V. Take B4035 3¼ miles east of Chipping Campden.

In nearby Charingworth, this elegant country home is even more luxurious than Cotswold House in town. It's the showpiece of the area. A manor has stood on this spot since the time of the *Domesday Book.* The present Tudor-Jacobean house, in honey-colored stone with slate roofs, has 55 acres of grounds. In the 1930s, it was host to such illustrious guests as T. S. Eliot. The old-world charm of the place has been preserved, in spite of modernization; log fires and well-chosen antiques create a delightful country-house ambience. Each room is individually decorated and luxuriously furnished, both in its use of antiques and English fabrics, and offers amenities that include a hair dryer, trouser press, and room safe. Many of the period rooms have four-poster beds. Guests can also wander through a well-manicured garden.

Dining: There's a fixed-price dinner in the elegant restaurant of the hotel, which is situated under low-ceiling beams. Excellent ingredients are deftly handled in the kitchen to create a French and English menu. Game is often featured, and the wine list is carefully chosen.

Amenities: 24-hour room service, laundry service. A modern Leisure Spa consists of a luxurious indoor heated pool built in Romanesque style, a sauna, steam room, solarium, and billiards room, plus there's an all-weather tennis court on the grounds.

⊘ **Cotswold House Hotel.** The Square, Chipping Campden, Gloucestershire GL55 6AN. ☎ **01386/840330.** Fax 01386/840310. 15 units. TV TEL. £120–£150 ($192–$240) double; £160 ($256) four-poster bed. Rates include English breakfast. AE, DC, MC, V.

This is the best place to stay in town. A stately, formal Regency house dating from 1800, right in the heart of the village opposite the old wool market, Cotswold House sits amid 1½ acres of tended, walled garden with shaded seating. Note the fine winding Regency staircase in the reception hall. The bedrooms are furnished with themes ranging from Gothic to French to military.

Dining: The restaurant serves first-class English and French food in a formal, elegant room, or in Forbes Brasserie, open daily from 9:30am to the last orders at 11pm. Light dishes and meals are served here.

Kings Arms Hotel. The Square, Chipping Campden, Gloucestershire GL55 6AW. ☎ **01386/840256.** Fax 01386/841598. 15 units. TV TEL. £60–£70 ($96–$112) double. Rates include English breakfast. AE, MC, V.

Dating from the late 1600s, with many renovations since, this partly Georgian building in the center of town has its own garden, from which come many of the fresh vegetables used in its meals. All the accommodations are well tended, pleasantly furnished, and spotlessly clean. The inn enjoys a good reputation for its cooking. Bar meals are served in the pub, or else you can dine more formally, enjoying a fixed-price dinner or Sunday lunch.

Noel Arms Hotel. High St., Chipping Campden, Gloucestershire GL55 6AT. ☎ **01386/ 840317.** Fax 01386/841136. 26 units. TV TEL. £85–£92 ($136–$147.20) double. Children up to 10 stay free in parents' room. Rates include English breakfast. AE, DC, MC, V.

This old coaching inn has been famous in the Cotswolds since the 14th century. Charles II rested here in 1651 after his defeat at the Battle of Worcester. Tradition is kept alive in the decor, which includes fine antiques, muskets, swords, and shields. Twelve rooms date from the 14th century; the others, comfortably furnished and well appointed, are housed in a modern wing built of Cotswold stone.

Dining/Diversions: There's a private sitting room for residents, but you may prefer the lounge with its 12-foot-wide fireplace. The oak-paneled restaurant offers an extensive menu, with an international wine list. The three-course Sunday lunch is well attended, by both locals and visitors. Typical English dishes are featured, and the hotel's tavern attracts a crowd that enjoys its real ales, malt whiskies, open fires, and Cotswold-stone walls.

13 Shakespeare Country & the Heart of England

After London, Shakespeare Country is the most popular destination in England for North Americans. Many who don't recognize the county name, Warwickshire, know its foremost tourist town, Stratford-upon-Avon, birthplace of Shakespeare and one of the great meccas for writers, readers, and play-goers from around the world.

Shakespeare's hometown is the best center for touring this part of England. You'll want to take in some theater while in Stratford-upon-Avon and branch out for day trips—notably to Warwick Castle in nearby Warwick, to Kenilworth Castle, and to Coventry Cathedral.

And then you have the heart of England at your doorstep. The adventure can begin in nearby Birmingham, England's second largest city. Although abandoned warehouses and bleak factories remain, this industrial city, like the rest of England, is being spruced up. It may even surprise you. From here you can branch out to any number of lovely old market towns and bucolic spots. There's the scenic Malverns, the historic town of Shrewsbury (where Ellis Peters's Brother Cadfael mysteries are set), and Worcester, of Royal Worcester Porcelain fame. And of course, those who are truly passionate about porcelain flock to the fabled Potteries to visit towns like Stoke-on-Trent. Here, factory and outlet shops sell Wedgwood, Portmeirion, and other fine brands of English tableware at a discount.

1 Stratford-upon-Avon

91 miles NW of London; 40 miles NW of Oxford; 8 miles S of Warwick

Crowds of tourists overrun this market town on the Avon River during the summer. In fact, today, Stratford aggressively hustles its Shakespeare connection—everybody seems to be in business to make a buck off the Bard. Will Shakespeare is probably turning over in his grave at the thought of the average tourist buying a Bard T-shirt and a china model of Anne Hathaway's cottage before sampling a Big Mac. The throngs dwindle in winter, however, when you can at least walk on the streets and seek out the places of genuine historic interest.

Aside from the historic sites, the major draw for visitors is the Royal Shakespeare Theatre, where Britain's foremost actors perform during a long season that lasts from early April until late January. Other than the theater, Stratford is rather devoid of any rich cultural life, and you may want to rush back to London after you've seen the literary

Warwickshire

pilgrimage sights and watched a production of *Hamlet*. But Stratford-upon-Avon is also a good center for trips to Warwick Castle, Kenilworth Castle, and Coventry Cathedral (see below).

ESSENTIALS

GETTING THERE   Amazingly, considering the demand, there are no direct trains from London. However, from London's Paddington Station you can take the train to Leamington Spa, where you can change trains for Stratford-upon-Avon. The journey takes about 3 hours and a round-trip ticket costs £20 ($32). For schedules and information, call ☎ **0345/484950** (in the U.K. only) or 01603/764776. The train station at Stratford is on Alcester Road (☎ **01203/555211**). On Sundays from October through May, it is closed, so you'll have to rely on the bus.

Eight **National Express** buses a day leave from London's Victoria Station, with a trip time of 3¼ hours. A single-day round-trip ticket costs £13.50 ($21.60) except Friday when the price is £16 ($25.60). For schedules and information, call ☎ **0990/ 808080.**

If you're driving from London, take M40 toward Oxford and continue to Stratford-upon-Avon on A34.

VISITOR INFORMATION   The **Tourist Information Centre,** Bridgefoot, Stratford-upon-Avon, Warwickshire, CV37 6GW (☎ **01789/293127**), provides any details you might wish to know about the Shakespeare houses and properties and will assist in booking rooms (see "Where to Stay," below). Call and ask for a copy of their free Shakespeare Country Holiday guide. They also operate an American Express currency exchange office. It's open March to October, Monday to Saturday from 9am to 6pm and Sunday from 11am to 5pm; November to February, Monday to Saturday from 9am to 5pm.

To contact **Shakespeare Birthplace Trust,** which administers many of the attractions, call the Shakespeare Centre (☎ **01789/204016**).

THE ROYAL SHAKESPEARE THEATRE

On the banks of the Avon, the ✪ **Royal Shakespeare Theatre,** Waterside, Stratford-upon-Avon CV37 6BB (☎ **01789/295623**), is a major showcase for the Royal Shakespeare Company and seats 1,500 patrons. The theater's season runs from November until September and typically features five Shakespearean plays. The company has some of the finest actors on the British stage.

You'll usually need **reservations for tickets.** There are two successive booking periods, each one opening about 2 months in advance. You can pick these up from a North American or English travel agent. A small number of tickets are always held for sale on the day of a performance, but it may be too late to get a good seat if you wait until you arrive in Stratford. Tickets can be booked through New York agents **Edwards and Edwards** (☎ **800/223-6108** outside New York, or 914/328-2150 in New York), or Keith Prowse (☎ **800/669-8687** or 212/398-1430). Both will add a service charge.

You can also call the **theater box office** directly (☎ **01789/295623**) and charge your tickets. The box office is open Monday to Saturday from 9am to 8pm, although it closes at 6pm on days when there are no performances. Seat prices range from £6.50 to £46 ($10.40 to $73.60). You can make a credit-card reservation and pick up your tickets on the performance day, but you must cancel at least 2 full weeks in advance to get a refund.

Opened in 1986, the **Swan Theatre** is architecturally connected to the back of its older counterpart and shares the same box office, address, and phone number. It seats

Stratford–upon–Avon

Western Rd.
Kendall Av.
St. Gregory's Rd.
Clopton Rd.
Birmingham Rd.
Shakespeare St.
Mulberry St.
Great William St.
Payton St.
Warwick Rd.
Arden St.
Mansell St.
Windsor St.
Guild St.
Henley St.
Union St.
Bus Station
A34
A34
A422
Alcester Rd.
Greenhill St.
Meer St.
Wood St.
Bridge St.
A422
High St.
Ely St.
Sheep St.
Grove Rd.
Rother St.
Chapel St.
Chapel Lane
Waterside
River Avon
Scholars Lane
Albany Rd.
A439
Evesham Pl.
Chestnut Walk
Church St.
Broad St.
West St.
Old Town
Southern Lane
Bull St.
Narrow Lane
Sanctus St.
Trinity St.

Church ‡   Information ⓘ

Anne Hathaway's Cottage ⑩
Hall's Croft ⑧
Harvard House ③
Holy Trinity Church ⑨
Mary Arden's House and the
    Shakespeare Countryside Museum ①

New Place/Nash's House ④
The Other Place ⑦
Royal Shakespeare Theatre ⑤
Shakespeare's Birthplace ❶
Swan Theatre ⑥

3-0-588

430 on three sides of the stage, as in an Elizabethan playhouse, an appropriate design for plays by Shakespeare and his contemporaries. The Swan presents a repertoire of about five plays each season, with tickets ranging from £9 to £30 ($14.40 to $48).

The most recent addition to the Royal Shakespeare complex is **The Other Place,** a small, starkly minimalist theater located on Southern Lane, about 300 yards from its counterparts. It was redesigned in 1996 as an experimental workshop theater without a permanent stage; seats can be radically repositioned (or removed completely) throughout the theater. Examples of recent productions include a "promenade production" of *Julius Caesar,* in which the actors spent the whole play moving freely among a stand-up audience. Tickets are sold at the complex's main box office and generally range from £12 to £18 ($19.20 to $28.80) each, but prices are subject to change.

Within the Swan Theatre is a **painting gallery,** which has a basic collection of portraits of famous actors and scenes from Shakespeare's plays by 18th- and 19th-century artists. It also operates as a base for **guided tours** with lively running commentary through the world-famous theaters. Guided tours are conducted at 1:30 and 5:30pm (excluding Thursday and Saturday, the matinee days), and four times every Sunday afternoon, production schedules permitting. Tours cost £4 ($6.40) for adults and £3 ($4.80) for students, seniors, or children. Call ahead for tour scheduling, which is subject to change.

SEEING THE SIGHTS

Besides the attractions on the periphery of Stratford, there are many Elizabethan and Jacobean buildings in town, many of them administered by the **Shakespeare Birthplace Trust.** One ticket—costing £10 ($16) for adults, £9 ($14.40) for seniors and students, and £5 ($8) for children—lets you visit the five most important sights. You can also buy a family ticket to all five sights (good for two adults and three children) for £18 ($28.80)—a good deal. Pick up the ticket if you're planning to do much sightseeing (obtainable at your first stopover at any one of the Trust properties).

Guided tours of Stratford-upon-Avon leave from near the **Guide Friday Tourism Centre,** Civic Hall, Rother Street (☎ **01789/294466**). In summer, open-top double-decker buses depart every 15 minutes daily from 9:30am to 5:30pm. You can take a 1-hour ride without stops, or you can get off at any or all of the town's five Shakespeare properties. Although the bus stops are clearly marked along the historic route, the most logical starting point is the sidewalk in front of the Pen & Parchment Pub, at the bottom of Bridge Street. Tour tickets are valid all day so you can hop on and off the buses as many times as you want. The tours cost £8 ($12.80) for adults, £6 ($9.60) for seniors or students, and £2.50 ($4) for children under 12.

✪ **Shakespeare's Birthplace.** Henley St. (in the town center near the post office, close to Union St.). ☎ **01789/204016.** Admission £4.50 ($7.20) adults, £2 ($3.20) children; £18 ($28.80) family ticket (2 adults, 3 children) for all 5 Shakespeare-related houses. Mar 20–Oct 19 Mon–Sat 9am–5pm, Sun 9:30am–5pm; off-season Mon–Sat 9:30am–4pm, Sun 10am–4pm. Closed Dec 23–26.

The son of a glover and whittawer (leather worker), the Bard was born on St. George's day, April 23, 1564, and died on the same date 52 years later. Filled with Shakespeare memorabilia, including a portrait and furnishings of the writer's time, the Trust property is a half-timbered structure, dating from the first part of the 16th century. The house was bought by public donors in 1847 and preserved as a national shrine. You can visit the oak-beamed living room, the bedroom where Shakespeare was probably born, a fully equipped kitchen of the period (look for the "babyminder"), and a Shakespeare Museum, illustrating his life and times. Later, you can walk through the garden.

You won't be alone: It's estimated that some 660,000 visitors pass through the house annually.

Built next door to commemorate the 400th anniversary of the Bard's birth, the modern **Shakespeare Centre** serves both as the administrative headquarters of the Birthplace Trust and as a library and study center. An extension houses a visitor center, which acts as a reception area for all those coming to the birthplace.

✪ **Anne Hathaway's Cottage.** Cottage Lane, Shottery. ☎ **01789/292100.** Admission £3.50 ($5.60) adults, £1.50 ($2.40) children; £18 ($28.80) family ticket (2 adults, 3 children) for all 5 Shakespeare-related houses. Mar 20–Oct 19 Mon–Sat 9:30am–5:30pm, Sun 9:30am–5pm; off-season Mon–Sat 9:30am–4:30pm, Sun 10am–4pm. Closed Dec 23–26. Take a bus from Bridge St. or walk via a marked pathway from Evesham Place in Stratford across the meadow to Shottery.

Before she married Shakespeare, Anne Hathaway lived in this thatched, wattle-and-daub cottage in the hamlet of Shottery, 1 mile from Stratford-upon-Avon. It's the most interesting and the most photographed of the Trust properties.

The Hathaways were yeoman farmers, and the cottage provides a rare insight into the life of a family in Shakespearean times. The Bard was only 18 when he married Anne, who was much older. Many of the original furnishings, including the courting settle and utensils, are preserved inside the house, which was occupied by descendants of Shakespeare's wife's family until 1892. After visiting the house, you'll want to linger in the garden and orchard.

New Place/Nash's House. Chapel St. ☎ **01789/204016.** Admission £3 ($4.80) adults, £1.50 ($2.40) children; £18 ($28.80) family ticket (2 adults, 3 children) for all 5 Shakespeare-related houses. Mar 20–Oct 19 Mon–Sat 9:30am–5pm, Sun 10am–5pm; Oct 20–Mar 19 Mon–Sat 10am–4pm, Sun 10:30–4pm. Closed Dec 23–26. Walk west down High St.; Chapel St. is a continuation of High St.

Shakespeare retired to New Place in 1610 (a prosperous man by the standards of his day) and died here 6 years later. Regrettably, the house was torn down, so only the garden remains today. A mulberry tree planted by the Bard was so popular with latter-day visitors to Stratford that the garden's cantankerous owner chopped it down. The mulberry tree that grows here today is said to have been planted from a cutting of the original tree.

You enter the gardens through Nash's House (Thomas Nash married Elizabeth Hall, a granddaughter of the poet). Nash's House has 16th-century period rooms and an exhibition illustrating the history of Stratford. The popular Knott Garden adjoins the site and represents the style of a fashionable Elizabethan garden.

Mary Arden's House and the Shakespeare Countryside Museum. Wilmcote. ☎ **01789/204016.** Admission £4 ($6.40) adults, £2 ($3.20) children; family ticket £11 ($17.60). Mar 20–Oct 19 Mon–Sat 9:30am–5pm, Sun 10am–5pm; off-season Mon–Sat 10am–4pm, Sun 10:30–4pm. Closed Dec 23–26. Take the A3400 (Birmingham) rd. for 3½ miles.

Reputedly this Tudor farmstead, with its old stone dovecote and various outbuildings, was the girlhood home of Shakespeare's mother—or so claimed an 18th-century entrepreneur. There is no definite evidence to prove she lived here, but the house contains country furniture and domestic utensils. In the barns, stable, cowshed, and farmyard, you'll find an extensive collection of farming implements illustrating life and work in the local countryside from Shakespeare's time to the present.

Visitors can also see the neighboring Glebe Farm, whose interior evokes farm life in late Victorian and Edwardian times. Light refreshments are available, and there is a picnic area.

Hall's Croft. Old Town (near Holy Trinity Church). ☎ **01789/292107.** Admission £3 ($4.80) adults, £1.50 ($2.40) children; £18 ($28.80) family ticket (2 adults, 3 children) for all 5 Shakespeare-related houses. Mar 20–Oct 19 Mon–Sat 9:30am–5pm, Sun 10am–5pm; off-season Mon–Sat 10am–4pm, Sun 10:30–4pm. Closed Dec 23–26. To reach Hall's Croft, walk west from High St., which becomes Chapel St. and Church St. At the intersection with Old Town, go left.

It was here that Shakespeare's daughter Susanna probably lived with her husband, Dr. John Hall. Hall's Croft is an outstanding Tudor house with a beautiful walled garden, furnished in the style of a middle-class home of the time. Dr. Hall was widely respected and he built up a large medical practice in the area. Exhibits illustrating the theory and practice of medicine in Dr. Hall's time are on view. Visitors to the house are welcome to use the adjoining Hall's Croft Club, which serves morning coffee, lunch, and afternoon tea.

Holy Trinity Church (Shakespeare's Tomb). Old Town. ☎ **01789/266316.** Church, free; Shakespeare's tomb, donation 60p (95¢) adults, 40p (65¢) students. Mar–Oct Mon–Sat 9am–6pm, Sun 2–5pm; Nov–Feb Mon–Sat 8:30am–4pm, Sun 2–5pm. Walk 4 min. past the Royal Shakespeare Theatre with the river on your left.

In an attractive setting near the Avon River is the parish church where Shakespeare is buried ("and curst be he who moves my bones"). The Parish Register records his baptism in 1564 and burial in 1616 (copies of the original documents are on display). The church is one of the most beautiful parish churches in England.

Shakespeare's tomb lies in the chancel, a privilege bestowed upon him when he became a lay rector in 1605. Alongside his grave are those of his widow, Anne, and other members of his family. You can also see the graves of Suzanna, his daughter, and those of Thomas Nash and Dr. John Hall. Nearby on the north wall is a bust of Shakespeare that was erected approximately 7 years after his death—within the lifetime of his widow and many of his friends.

Harvard House. High St. ☎ **01789/204507.** Admission free. Mar–Oct Tues–Sat 10am–4pm, Sun 10:30am–4pm.

The most ornate home in Stratford, Harvard House is a fine example of an Elizabethan town house. Rebuilt in 1596, it was once the home of Katherine Rogers, mother of John Harvard, founder of Harvard College. In 1909, the house was purchased by a Chicago millionaire, Edward Morris, who presented it as a gift to the famous American university. The rooms are filled with period furniture, and the floors are made of local flagstone. Look for the Bible Chair, used for hiding the Bible during the days of Tudor persecution.

The Royal Shakespeare Theatre Summer House. Avonbank Gardens. ☎ **01789/297671.** Free admission. Apr–Oct daily 10am–6pm; Nov–Mar daily 11am–4pm.

This is a brass-rubbing center, where medieval and Tudor brasses illustrate the knights and ladies, scholars, merchants, and priests of a bygone era. The Stratford collection includes a large assortment of exact replicas of brasses. Entrance is free, but visitors are charged depending on which brass they choose to rub. According to size, the cost ranges from 95p ($1.50) to make a rubbing of a small brass, to a maximum of £19.95 ($31.90) for a rubbing of the largest, a 7-foot behemoth that takes an enthusiast a full day to complete.

SHOPPING

Among the many tacky tourist traps are some quality shops, including the ones described below.

Set within an antique house with ceiling beams, **The Shakespeare Bookshop,** 39 Henley St., across from the Shakespeare Birthplace Centre (☎ **01789/292176**), is the region's premier source for textbooks and academic treatises on the Bard and his works. It specializes in books for every level of expertise on Shakespearean studies, from picture books for junior-high-school students to weighty tomes geared to anyone pursuing a Ph.D. in literature.

The largest shop of its kind in the Midlands, **Arbour Antiques, Ltd.,** Poets Arbour, off Sheep Street (☎ **01789/293493**), sells antique weapons from Britain, Europe, India, and Turkey. If you've always hankered after a full suit of armor, this place can sell you one.

Dianthus, 1 Centre Craft Yard, off Henley Street (☎ **01789/292252**), has a beautiful selection of pottery, and you can watch potters display their technique on their potter's wheels. Prices begin at £3 ($4.80), come in a pleasing assortment of sky and earth tones, and include their oft-duplicated version of a creamware mug.

Everything in the **Pickwick Gallery,** 32 Henley St. (☎ **01789/294861**), is a well-crafted work of art produced by copper or steel engraving plates, or printed by means of a carved wooden block. Hundreds of botanical prints, landscapes, and renderings of artfully arranged ruins, each suitable for framing, can be purchased at prices beginning as low as £1.50 ($2.40) and as much as £150 ($240). Topographical maps of regions of the United Kingdom are also available if you're planning on doing any serious hiking.

At **The National Trust Shop,** 45 Wood St. (☎ **01789/262197**), you'll find textbooks and guidebooks describing esoteric places in the environs of Stratford, descriptions of National Trust properties throughout England, stationery, books, china, pewter, and toiletries.

Once a Tree, Bard's Walk (☎ **01789/297790**), stocks wood-carved objects that range from the functional and utilitarian (kitchen spoons and breadboards) to the whimsical and exotic (carved wooden flowers, chunky jewelry, boxes, bowls, mirror frames, furniture, and mantelpieces).

The **Trading Post,** 1 High St. (☎ **01789/267228**), occupies three floors of an Elizabethan house said to have been occupied by one of Shakespeare's daughters as an adult. It's jam-packed with an assortment of kitschy and nostalgic gift items.

A SIDE TRIP TO RAGLEY HALL

Ragley Hall. Near Alcester (9 miles from Stratford-upon-Avon). ☎ **01789/762090.** Admission to the house, garden, and park £5 ($8) adults, £4.50 ($7.20) seniors, £3.50 ($5.60) children. £4 ($6.40) adults, £3.50 ($5.60) seniors, £3 ($4.80) children for park and gardens only. Easter–Sept Thurs–Sun 11am–5pm (gardens 10am–6pm). You must drive or go by taxi, since there's no good bus service. Ragley Hall is located off A435 or A46 to Evesham, about 1½ miles southwest of the town of Alcester. There is easy access from the main highway network, including the M40 from London.

A magnificent 115-room Palladian country house built in 1680, Ragley Hall is the home of the earl and countess of Yarmouth. The house has been restored and appears much as it did during the early 1700s. Great pains have been taken to duplicate colors and, in some cases, the original wallpaper patterns. The pictures, furniture, and works of art that fill the vast and spacious rooms represent 10 generations of collecting by the Seymour family. Ragley Hall may be a private home, but it has a museumlike quality, and many of its artifacts have great historical importance. The most spectacular attraction is the lavishly painted south staircase hall. Muralist Graham Rust painted a modern trompe l'oeil work depicting the Temptation. A new mural in the tearoom depicts a Victorian kitchen and the characters who inhabit it.

WHERE TO STAY

During the long theater season, you'll need reservations way in advance. The **Tourist Information Centre** (part of the national "Book-a-Bed-Ahead" service) will help find an accommodation for you in the price range you're seeking. The fee for room reservations is 10% of your first night's stay (B&B rate only), which is deductible from your final bill.

VERY EXPENSIVE

✪ **Welcombe Hotel.** Warwick Rd., Stratford-upon-Avon, Warwickshire CV37 0NR. ☎ **01789/295252.** Fax 01789/414666. 68 units. TV TEL. £150–£160 ($240–$256) double; £225–£275 ($360–$440) suite. Rates include English breakfast. AE, DC, MC, V. Take A439 1½ miles northeast of the town center.

For a formal, historic hotel, there is none better in Stratford. The Welcombe is rivaled only by Ettington Park at Alderminster (see below). One of England's great Jacobean country houses, it's a 10-minute ride from the heart of Stratford-upon-Avon. Its keynote feature is an 18-hole golf course. It's surrounded by 157 acres of grounds and has a formal entrance on Warwick Road, a winding driveway leading to the main hall. Guests gather for afternoon tea or drinks on the rear terrace, with its Italian-style garden and steps leading down to flower beds. The public rooms are heroic in size, with high mullioned windows providing views of the park. Regular bedrooms—some seemingly big enough for tennis matches—are luxuriously furnished; however, those in the garden wing, while comfortable, are small.

Dining: The restaurant offers a traditional mix of French and English dishes, although fine cuisine is not the major reason to check in here.

Amenities: 24-hour room service, laundry/dry cleaning, baby-sitting, secretarial services, courtesy car. Sports fans gravitate to the 18-hole, 6,202-yard golf course, tennis courts, and putting green.

EXPENSIVE

Alveston Manor Hotel. Clopton Bridge (off B4066), Stratford-upon-Avon, Warwickshire CV37 7HP. ☎ **800/225-5843** in the U.S. and Canada, or 01789/204581. Fax 01789/414095. 114 units. TV TEL. £120–£145 ($192–$232) double; £185–£225 ($296–$360) suite. AE, DC, MC, V.

This black-and-white timbered manor is perfect for theatergoers; it's just a 2-minute walk from the Avon River. The Welcombe and Ettington Park on the outskirts may have cornered the deluxe trade, but the Alveston, along with the Shakespeare (see below), are the most atmospheric choices within the town itself. The hotel has a wealth of chimneys and gables, and everything from an Elizabethan gazebo to Queen Anne windows. Mentioned in the *Domesday Book*, the building predates the arrival of William the Conqueror. The rooms in the manor house will appeal to those who appreciate old slanted floors, overhead beams, and antique furnishings. Some triples or quads are available in a more modern section, which is connected by a covered walk through the rear garden. The rooms here have built-in pieces and a color-coordinated decor, and 15 are set aside for nonsmokers. The lounges are in the manor; there's a view of the centuries-old tree at the top of the garden—said to have been the background for the first presentation of *A Midsummer Night's Dream*. Logs burn in the Tudor fireplace in the main living room, which has linen-fold paneling.

Dining/Diversions: Meals are served amid oak beams and leaded-glass windows in the softly lit Manor Restaurant. This is not, however, for the serious foodie or an intimate meal (bus tours stop here). The bar, paneled in 16th-century oak, never closes, and is the best place in Stratford for a drink at any time.

Moat House Stratford. Bridgefoot, Stratford-upon-Avon, Warwickshire CV37 6YR. ☎ **01789/279988.** Fax 01789/298589. 249 units. TV TEL. £140 ($224) double; £210 ($336) suite. AE, DC, MC, V.

The Moat House stands on 5 acres of landscaped lawns on the banks of the River Avon near Clopton Bridge. Although lacking the charm of the Alveston Manor or the Shakespeare, this modern hotel offers fine amenities and facilities. It is one of the flagships of the Queen's Moat House, a British hotel chain, and was built in the early 1970s and last renovated in 1995. The hotel hosts many conferences, so don't expect to have the place to yourself. Every bedroom has a high standard of comfort—bathrooms with generous shelf space and large mirrors; tea- and coffeemakers; and hair dryer.

Dining/Diversions: The hotel restaurant features a standard British and continental menu, and the Riverside Restaurant offers a carvery of hot and cold roasts. You can drink in the Tavern Pub and in the Terrace Nightspot, a disco open only on Friday and Saturday. Hotel residents enter the disco free; nonresidents pay a £10 ($16) cover after 10:30pm.

Amenities: 24-hour room service, laundry service, a leisure complex that includes a swimming pool.

Shakespeare. Chapel St., Stratford-upon-Avon, Warwickshire CV37 6ER. ☎ **800/225-5843** in the U.S. and Canada, or 01789/294771. Fax 01789/415411. 67 units. TV TEL. £115 ($184) double; £130 ($208) suite. Children up to 16 stay free in parents' room. AE, DC, MC, V.

Filled with historical associations, the original core of this hotel, which dates from the 1400s, has seen many additions in its long life. Quieter and plusher than the Falcon, it is equaled within the central core of Stratford only by Alveston Manor. Residents relax in the post-and-timber-studded public rooms, within sight of fireplaces and playbills from 19th-century productions of Shakespeare's plays.

The bedrooms are named in honor of noteworthy actors, Shakespeare's plays, or Shakespearean characters. The oldest are capped with hewn timbers, and all have modern comforts. Even the newer accommodations are at least 40 to 50 years old and have rose-and-thistle patterns carved into many of their exposed timbers. The rooms are equipped with tea- and coffeemakers, hair dryers, and trouser presses.

Dining: The hotel restaurant, the David Garrick, serves well-prepared lunches and dinners.

Amenities: 24 hour room service and laundry service.

MODERATE

The Arden Thistle Hotel. 44 Waterside, Stratford-upon-Avon, Warwickshire CV37 6BA. ☎ **01789/294949.** Fax 01789/415874. 62 units. TV TEL. £112 ($179.20) double. AE, DC, MC, V.

Theatergoers flock here, since The Arden is across the street from the main entrance of the Royal Shakespeare and Swan theaters. The Thistle chain completely refurbished the interior after buying the hotel in 1993. Its redbrick main section dates from the Regency period, although over the years a handful of adjacent buildings were included and an uninspired modern extension added. Today, the interior has a well-upholstered lounge and bar; Bards, a dining room with bay windows; a covered garden terrace; and comfortable but narrow bedrooms with trouser presses, hair dryers, and beveragemakers. A fixed-price dinner of pretty run-of-the-mill English and continental fare is served in the restaurant.

Dukes. Payton St., Stratford-upon-Avon, Warwickshire CV37 6UA. ☎ **01789/269300.** Fax 01789/414700. 22 units. TV TEL. £69.50–£115 ($111.20–$184) double. Rates include English breakfast. AE, DC, MC, V. No children under 12.

Located in the center of Stratford north of Guild Street, this little charmer was formed when two Georgian town houses were united and restored. It's a good place to escape the crowds that overrun such hotels as the Falcon. The family operated inn has a large garden and is close to Shakespeare's birthplace. The public areas and bedrooms are attractive, having been restored to an impressive degree of comfort and coziness. The furniture is tasteful, much of it antique. Dukes also serves a good English and continental cuisine.

Falcon. Chapel St., Stratford-upon-Avon, Warwickshire CV37 6HA. ☎ **01789/279953.** Fax 01789/414260. 73 units. TV TEL. £105 ($168) double; £125 ($200) suite. AE, DC, MC, V.

The Falcon blends the very old and the very new. The black-and-white-timbered inn was licensed a quarter of a century after Shakespeare's death. Connected to its rear by a glass passageway is a more sterile bedroom extension added in 1970. In the heart of Stratford, the inn faces the Guild Chapel and the New Place Gardens. You arrive at the rear portion to unload your luggage, just as horse-drawn coaches once dispatched their passengers—except that today you might be jostled by a tour group checking in. The recently upgraded bedrooms in the mellowed part have oak beams, diamond leaded-glass windows, some antique furnishings, and good reproductions. Each room includes an electric trouser press and a beverage-maker, but not enough soundproofing to drown out the BBC on your next-door neighbor's telly.

The comfortable lounges, also recently upgraded, are some of the finest in the Midlands. In the intimate Merlin Lounge is an open copper-hooded fireplace where coal and log fires are kept burning under beams salvaged from old ships (the walls are a good example of wattle and daub, typical of Shakespeare's day). The Oak Bar is a forest of weathered beams, and on either side of the stone fireplace is the paneling removed from the poet's last home, New Place.

Forte Post House. Bridgefoot, Stratford-upon-Avon, Warwickshire CV37 7LT. ☎ **800/225-5843** in the U.S. and Canada, or 01789/266761. Fax 01789/414547. 68 units. MINIBAR TV TEL. £79–£89 ($126.40–$142.40) double, £109–£119 ($174.40–$190.40) suite. AE, DC, MC, V.

An 18th-century Georgian facade with tall, narrow windows fronts this hotel, which looks out over the swans of Avon near Clopton Bridge. The complex is surrounded by gardens on a low, flat area beside a canal, a 5-minute drive south of the Royal Shakespeare Theatre leading toward Oxford. The hotel is on par with The White Swan and Dukes. It is well priced and a decent choice if your expectations are not too demanding. With most of them in a redbrick extension, the bedrooms are comfortably modern and filled with tasteful furnishings. Amenities include a trouser press, hair dryer, and beverage-maker.

The River Bar offers a view of the planting outside. The Swan Nest Restaurant serves à la carte dinners in a room lined with early 19th-century paintings.

Grosvenor House Hotel. 12–14 Warwick Rd., Stratford-upon-Avon, Warwickshire CV37 6YT. ☎ **01789/269213.** Fax 01789/266087. 67 units. TV TEL. £82 ($131.20) double. DC, MC, V.

A pair of Georgian town houses, built in 1832 and 1843, respectively, were joined together to form this hotel, which is one of the second-tier choices of Stratford on equal footing with Dukes or the Arden Thistle. Situated in the center of town, with lawns and gardens to the rear, it is a short stroll from the intersection of Bridge Street and Waterside, allowing easy access to the Avon River, Bancroft Gardens, and the Royal Shakespeare Theatre. All bedrooms have trouser presses and hair dryers, as well as tea- and coffeemakers. The informal bar (open until midnight) and terrace offer relaxation before or after you lunch or dine in the large restaurant, whose floor-to-ceiling windows face the gardens.

The White Swan. Rother St., Stratford-upon-Avon, Warwickshire CV37 6NH. ☎ **800/ 225-5843** in the U.S. and Canada, or 01789/297022. Fax 01789/268773. 39 units. TV TEL. £80 ($128) double; £118.50 ($189.60) suite. Children up to 16 stay free in parents' room. Rates include English breakfast. AE, DC, MC, V.

This cozy, intimate hotel is one of the most atmospheric in Stratford and is, in fact, the oldest building here. In business for more than a century before Shakespeare appeared on the scene, it competes successfully with the Falcon in offering an ancient atmosphere. The gabled medieval front would present the Bard with no surprises, but the modern comforts inside would surely astonish him, even though many of the rooms have been preserved. Paintings dating from 1550 hang on the lounge walls. All the bedrooms are well appointed; the amenities include trouser press and hair dryer. The hostelry has a spacious restaurant where good food is served. The oak-beamed bar is a popular meeting place (see "The Best Places for a Pint," below).

INEXPENSIVE

Sequoia House. 51–53 Shipston Rd., Stratford-upon-Avon, Warwickshire CV37 7LN. ☎ **01789/268852.** Fax 01789/414559. 24 units, 20 with bathroom or shower. TV TEL. £42 ($67.20) double without bathroom, £59–£74 ($94.40–$118.40) double with bathroom. Rates include English breakfast. AE, DC, DISC, MC, V.

This hotel has its own beautiful garden on three-quarters of an acre across the Avon opposite the theater, conveniently located for visiting the major Shakespeare properties of the National Trust. Renovation has vastly improved the house, which was created from two late Victorian buildings. Today it offers rooms with beverage-makers and hot and cold running water. Guests gather in a lounge that has a licensed bar and an open Victorian fireplace. The hotel also has a private parking area.

Stratheden Hotel. 5 Chapel St., Stratford-upon-Avon, Warwickshire CV37 6EP. ☎ and fax **01789/297119.** 9 units. TV TEL. £58–£64 ($92.80–$102.40) double. Rates include English breakfast. MC, V.

A short walk north of the Royal Shakespeare Theatre, the Stratheden Hotel is tucked away in a desirable location. Built in 1673 and today the oldest-remaining brick building in the town center, it has a tiny rear garden and top-floor rooms with slanted, beamed ceilings. Under the ownership of the Wells family for the past quarter century, it has improved again in both decor and comfort with the addition of fresh paint, new curtains, and good beds. You can make a piping hot cup of tea any time of day or night. The glass cupboard in the entry hallway holds family heirlooms and collector's items.

The dining room, with a bay window, has an overscale sideboard that once belonged to the "insanely vain" Marie Corelli (1855–1924), an eccentric novelist, poet, and mystic, and a favorite author of Queen Victoria. You can see an example of her taste: a massive mahogany tester bed in room 4.

Victoria Spa Lodge. Bishopton Lane (1½ miles north of the town center where A3400 intersects A46), Stratford-upon-Avon, Warwickshire CV37 9QY. ☎ **01789/267985.** Fax 01789/204728. 10 units. TV. £48–£60 ($76.80–$96) double; £67.50–£85 ($108–$136) family suite. Rates include English breakfast. MC, V.

Overlooking Stratford Canal, this lodge was originally a spa. Opened in 1837, the year Queen Victoria ascended to the throne, it was the first establishment to be given her name. The queen's eldest daughter, Princess Vicky, stayed here when it was a spa. Once it was the home of the famous cartoonist, Bruce Bairnsfather. Accommodating hosts Paul and Dreen Tozer offer tastefully decorated and comfortable bedrooms with such amenities as hair dryers. A full English breakfast or a vegetarian alternative is served in a cheerful antique-furnished dining room. No smoking.

NEARBY PLACES TO STAY

✪ **Ettington Park Hotel.** Alderminster, near Stratford-upon-Avon, Warwickshire CV37 8BU. ☎ **01789/450123.** Fax 01789/450472. 59 units. TV TEL. £185 ($296) double; £235–£350 ($376–$560) suite. Rates include English breakfast. AE, DC, MC, V. Drive 5 miles south along A3400 just past Alderminster, then take 2nd left (signposted) into Ettington Park.

This Victorian Gothic mansion is one of the most sumptuous retreats in Shakespeare Country, on par with the Welcombe Hotel. It opened as a hotel in 1985, but has a history that spans more than 9 centuries. The land is a legacy of the Shirley family, whose 12th-century burial chapel stands near the hotel. Like a grand private home, the hotel boasts baronial fireplaces, a conservatory, and a charming staff. The Adam ceilings, stone carvings, and ornate staircases have all been beautifully restored. A new wing, assembled with the same stone and neo-Gothic carving of the original house, stretches toward a Renaissance-style arbor entwined with vines. The giant sequoias, ancient yews, and cedars are surrounded by lawns and terraced gardens, whose flowers and ferns cascade toward a rock-lined stream. The bedrooms conjure memories of another era, yet the most modern comforts are concealed behind antique facades. Recent complaints about service aside, this is still one of the finest hotels in Alderminster. Stay clear of the bookcase; the ghost is very temperamental.

Dining: In the dining room, the Shirley family crest is inlaid in hundreds of marquetry depictions in the carved and burnished paneling. The cuisine is a medley of English and French specialties featured in fixed-price dinners.

Amenities: 24-hour room service, laundry, Jacuzzi, indoor swimming pool, sauna, tennis.

Mary Arden Inn. The Green, Wilmcote, Stratford-upon-Avon, Warwickshire CV37 9XJ. ☎ **01789/267030.** Fax 01789/204875. 12 units. TEL TV. £55–£75 ($88–$120) double. Rates include English breakfast. AE, MC, V. Take A3400 3½ miles northwest of Stratford.

Shakespeare's mother, Mary Arden, lived in the tiny village of Wilmcote, some 3½ miles northwest of Stratford. Actually an upgraded village pub-hotel, this place offers not only appealing and well-furnished bedrooms at moderate prices, but also good meals. The inn is relatively unpretentious and offers a welcome respite from the hordes in the center of Stratford. Amenities include beverage-makers, and a four-poster room with a Jacuzzi is available.

Homemade hot and cold bar snacks and meals are served in the popular beamed bar with an open fire and the original well. The bar offers four real ales at lunch and in the evening. Guests can eat outdoors in the large garden with a sun terrace in summer. There is also a restaurant that serves breakfast, lunch, and dinner with an à la carte menu.

WHERE TO DINE

After visiting the birthplace of Shakespeare, pop across the street for tea at **Mistress Quickly,** Henley Street (☎ **01789/295261**). This airy tearoom is tremendously popular, but the very attentive staff more than compensates for the throngs of patrons that grace its doors. Choose from an array of tea blends, cream teas, and various gateaux, pastries, and tea cakes—all freshly baked in their own kitchen.

EXPENSIVE TO MODERATE

The Boathouse. Swan's Nest Lane. ☎ **01789/297733.** Reservations recommended. Main courses £10–£15 ($16–$24); fixed-price lunch £7.50 ($12); fixed-price dinner £19.75 ($31.60). Daily noon–1:50pm; Mon–Sat 5:30–10:30pm. ENGLISH.

The only restaurant set on the Avon, this charming choice is reached from the town center by crossing Clopton Bridge toward Oxford and Banbury. The place is still a working boathouse, and you can rent punts and rowing boats for an intimate view of the Avon. A gondola ferry service transports patrons to the theater if you'd like to dine here before watching one of Shakespeare's plays. The second-floor dining room, opening onto vistas of the river, is decorated with nautical paraphernalia. The cooking is robust and hearty. Try such main courses as sautéed calf's liver with a delicious bubble and squeak (yes, that old horror of boiled potatoes and cabbage), which tastes wonderful here. You might also opt for venison on a bed of leeks or a tempura of codfish served with a sun-dried tomato pesto sauce.

The Box Tree Restaurant. In the Royal Shakespeare Theatre, Waterside. ☎ 01789/293226. Reservations required. Matinee lunch £16.50 ($26.40); dinner £25.50–£26.50 ($40.80–$42.40). AE, MC, V. Thurs–Sat noon–2:30pm; Mon–Sat 5:45pm–midnight. FRENCH/ITALIAN/ENGLISH.

This restaurant enjoys the best location in town—right in the theater itself, with glass walls providing an unobstructed view of swans on the Avon. You can have an intermission snack feast of smoked salmon and champagne, or dine by flickering candlelight after the performance. Many dishes, such as apple-and-parsnip soup, are definitely old English; others reflect a continental touch, such as fried polenta with fillets of pigeon and bacon. For your main course, you might select Dover sole, pheasant supreme, or roast loin of pork. Homemade crème brûlée is an old-time favorite at The Box Tree. There's a special phone for reservations in the theater lobby.

The Greek Connection. 1 Shakespeare St. ☎ 01789/292214. Reservations recommended. Main courses £8.25–£15.95 ($13.20–$25.50); 3-course early evening fixed-price dinner £9.75 ($15.60) from 5:30–7pm only. DC, MC, V. Daily noon–2:30pm in summer; daily 5:30pm–late year-round. GREEK/INTERNATIONAL.

Situated in the heart of Stratford, within a 3-minute walk of Shakespeare's birthplace, the Greek Connection occupies what was formerly a Methodist chapel built in 1854 (it also functioned for a brief period as an automobile museum). A warm welcome awaits you here, along with authentic Greek cuisine, live Greek music, and dancing nightly. Chefs Spiros and George serve a variety of Greek and international dishes (some vegetarian). We are especially fond of their moussaka.

INEXPENSIVE

Hussain's. 6A Chapel St. ☎ 01789/267506. Reservations recommended. Main courses £6.75–£11.95 ($10.80–$19.10). AE, DC, MC, V. Daily noon–2:30pm and 5pm–midnight. INDIAN.

This restaurant has many admirers—it's one of the brighter spots on the bleak culinary landscape hereabouts. The owner has chosen a well-trained, alert staff, which welcomes guests, advising them about special dishes. You can select from an array of northern Indian dishes, many from the tandoor, plus various curries with lamb or prawn. There is a three-course lunch from 12:30 to 2:30pm for £6.95 ($11.10). Fixed-price pre- and post-theater dinners are also available. Hussain's is across from the Shakespeare Hotel and historic New Place.

The Opposition. 13 Sheep St. ☎ 01789/269980. Reservations recommended. Main courses £6–£15 ($9.60–$24). MC, V. Daily noon–2pm and 5:30–11pm. INTERNATIONAL.

Located in the heart of Stratford, within a 16th-century building whose twin dining rooms are both sheathed with exposed timbers and old bricks, this refreshingly unpretentious restaurant serves up good bistro cooking at reasonable prices. Morning coffee, tea cakes, and croissants are sold Monday to Saturday from 11am to noon, but most people appreciate the place for a real sit-down meal. Menu choices include chicken cooked with spinach, stuffed with mango and curry, or prepared Cajun-style; salmon either grilled or poached and served with hollandaise; and grilled sirloin or fillet of beef.

Russons. 8 Church St. ☎ **01789/268822.** Reservations required. Main courses £8.95–£12.95 ($14.30–$20.70). AE, MC, V. Tues–Sat 11:30am–2pm and 5:30–10pm. INTERNATIONAL.

Since the theater is a short stroll away, this is a great place for a preshow meal. The restaurant is housed in a 400-year-old building and the two simply furnished dining rooms, one with a hardwood floor, the other with flagstones, both feature inglenook fireplaces. The menu changes regularly to reflect the availability of seasonal ingredients; and fresh seafood is their specialty. Daily specials are posted on a blackboard, and include rack of lamb, guinea fowl, and numerous vegetarian dishes. Finish with one of their simple but delicious homemade desserts.

THE BEST PLACES FOR A PINT

✪ The Black Swan ("The Dirty Duck"). Waterside. ☎ **01789/297312.** Reservations required for dining. Main courses £7–£15 ($11.20–$24); bar snacks £1.50–£4 ($2.40–$6.40). MC, V (in the Grill Room only). Pub, Mon–Sat 11am–11pm, Sun noon–3pm and 7–10:30pm. Grill Room, Tues–Sun noon–2pm, Mon–Sat 6–11:30pm. ENGLISH.

Affectionately known as The Dirty Duck, this has been a popular hangout for Stratford players since the 18th century. The wall is lined with autographed photos of its many famous patrons. The front lounge and bar crackles with intense conversation. In the spring and fall, an open fire blazes. Typical English grills, among other dishes, are featured in the Dirty Duck Grill Room, although no one ever accused it of serving the best food in Stratford. You'll have a choice of a dozen appetizers, most of which would make a meal in themselves. In fair weather you can have drinks in the front garden and watch the swans glide by on the Avon.

The Garrick Inn. 25 High St. ☎ **01789/292186.** Main courses £5–£9 ($8–$14.40). MC, V. Meals daily noon–8:30pm. Pub Mon–Sat 11am–11pm, Sun noon–10:30pm. ENGLISH.

Near Harvard House, this black-and-white timbered Elizabethan pub, dating from 1595, has an unpretentious charm. The front bar is decorated with tapestry-covered settles, an old oak refectory table, and an open fireplace that attracts the locals. The back bar has a circular fireplace with a copper hood and mementos of the triumphs of the English stage. The specialty is homemade pies such as steak and kidney or chicken and mushroom.

The White Swan. In The White Swan hotel, Rother St. ☎ **01789/297022.** Dinner reservations recommended. Bar snacks £2.25–£6 ($3.60–$9.60); 3-course fixed-price dinner £19.95 ($31.90). AE, DC, MC, V. Morning coffee daily 10am–noon; self-service bar snacks daily 12:30–2pm; afternoon tea daily 2–5:30pm; dinner Mon–Thurs 6–9pm, Fri–Sat 6–9:30pm, Sun 7–9pm. ENGLISH.

In the town's oldest building you'll find this atmospheric pub, with cushioned leather armchairs, oak paneling, and fireplaces. You're likely to meet amiable fellow drinkers, who revel in a setting once enjoyed by Will Shakespeare himself when it was known as the Kings Head. At lunch you can partake of the hot dishes of the day, along with fresh salads and sandwiches.

2 Warwick: England's Finest Medieval Castle

92 miles NW of London; 8 miles NE of Stratford-upon-Avon

Most visitors come to this town just to see Warwick Castle, the finest medieval castle in England. Some combine it with a visit to the ruins of Kenilworth Castle (see below), but the historic center of ancient Warwick has a lot more to offer.

Warwick cites Ethelfleda, daughter of Alfred the Great, as its founder. But most of its history is associated with the earls of Warwick, a title created by the son of William the Conqueror in 1088. The story of those earls—the Beaumonts, the Beauchamps (such figures as "Kingmaker" Richard Neville)—makes for an exciting episode in English history.

A devastating fire swept through the heart of Warwick in 1694, but a number of Elizabethan and medieval buildings still survive, along with some fine Georgian structures from a later date.

ESSENTIALS

GETTING THERE   Trains run frequently between Stratford-upon-Avon and Warwick. Call ☎ **0345/484950** (in the U.K. only) or 01603/764776 for schedules and information.

One Midland Red bus per hour (no. 18 or no. X16) departs Stratford-upon-Avon during the day. The trip takes 15 to 20 minutes. Call the tourist office (☎ **01789/ 293127**) for schedules.

Take A46 if you're driving from Stratford-upon-Avon.

VISITOR INFORMATION   The **Tourist Information Centre** is at The Court House, Jury Street (☎ **01926/492212**), and is open daily from 9:30am to 4:30pm; closed December 24 to 26 and January 1.

SEEING THE SIGHTS

✪ **Warwick Castle.** ☎ **01926/406600.** Admission £8.95 ($14.30) adults, £5.40 ($8.65) children 4–16, £6.40 ($10.25) seniors and students; free for children 4 and under. Apr–Oct daily 10am–6pm; Nov–Mar daily 10am–5pm. Closed Christmas Day.

Perched on a rocky cliff above the Avon River in the town center, a stately late 17th-century-style mansion is surrounded by a magnificent 14th-century fortress, the finest medieval castle in England. Even 3 hours may not be enough time to see everything. Surrounded by gardens, lawns, and woodland, where peacocks roam freely, and skirted by the Avon, Warwick Castle was described by Sir Walter Scott in 1828 as "that fairest monument of ancient and chivalrous splendor which yet remains uninjured by time."

The first significant fortifications were built here in 914 by Ethelfleda, daughter of Alfred the Great. William the Conqueror ordered the construction of a motte-and-bailey castle in 1068, 2 years after the Norman Conquest. The mound is all that remains today of the Norman castle, which was sacked by Simon de Montfort in the Barons' War of 1264.

The Beauchamp family, the most illustrious medieval earls of Warwick, are responsible for the appearance of the castle today, and much of the external structure remains unchanged from the mid–14th century. When the castle was granted to Sir Fulke Greville by James I in 1604, he spent £20,000 (an enormous sum in those days) converting the existing castle buildings into a luxurious mansion. The Grevilles have held the earl of Warwick title since 1759, when it passed from the Rich family.

The staterooms and Great Hall house fine collections of paintings, furniture, arms, and armor. The armory, dungeon, torture chamber, ghost tower, clock tower, and Guy's tower create a vivid picture of the castle's turbulent past and its important role in the history of England.

The private apartments of Lord Brooke and his family, who in recent years sold the castle to Tussaud's Group, are open to visitors. They house a display of a carefully reconstructed Royal Weekend House Party of 1898. The major rooms contain wax portraits of important figures of the time, including a young Winston Churchill. In the Kenilworth bedroom, the likeness of the Prince of Wales, who later became King Edward VII, reads a letter. The duchess of Marlborough prepares for her bath in the red bedroom. Among the most lifelike of the figures is a little uniformed maid bending over to test the temperature of the water running into a bathtub.

You can also see the Victorian rose garden, a re-creation of an original design from 1868 by Robert Marnock. Near the rose garden is a Victorian alpine rockery and water garden.

St. Mary's Church. Church St. ☎ **01926/400771.** Free admission; donations accepted. Apr–Sept daily 10am–5pm; Oct–Mar daily 10am–6pm. All buses to Warwick stop at Old Sq.

Destroyed in part by the fire of 1694, this church, with its rebuilt battlemented tower and nave, is among the finest examples of late 17th- and early 18th-century architecture. The Beauchamp Chapel, spared from the flames, encases the Purbeck marble tomb of Richard Beauchamp, a well-known earl of Warwick who died in 1439 and is commemorated by a gilded bronze effigy. Even more powerful in his day than King Henry V, Beauchamp has a tomb that's one of the finest remaining examples of Perpendicular-Gothic style from the mid–15th century. The tomb of Robert Dudley, earl of Leicester, a favorite of Elizabeth I, is against the north wall. The Perpendicular-Gothic choir dates from the 14th century, and the Norman crypt and the chapter house are from the 11th century.

Lord Leycester Hospital. High St. ☎ 01926/491422. Admission £2.50 ($4) adults, £1.75 ($2.80) students and seniors, £1.25 ($2) children. Easter–Oct Tues–Sun 10am–5pm; Nov–Easter Tues–Sun 10am–4pm.

The great fire also spared this group of half-timbered almshouses at the West Gate. The buildings were erected around 1400, and the hospital was founded in 1571 by Robert Dudley, earl of Leicester, as a home for old soldiers. It's still used by ex-service personnel and their spouses. On top of the West Gate is the attractive little chapel of St. James, dating from the 12th century but renovated many times since. Closed to the public since 1903, the gardens in back of the hospital were recently restored. Nathaniel Hawthorne wrote of his visits to the gardens in 1855 and 1857. Based on his observations, the gardens were restored as he wrote of them. The queen herself along with Prince Philip arrived in 1996 for a well-publicized visit.

Warwick Doll Museum. Oken's House, Castle St. (off Jury St. in the town center). ☎ 01926/495546. Admission £1 ($1.60) adults, 70p ($1.10) children. Easter–Sept Mon–Sat 10am–5pm, Sun 1–5pm; Oct–Easter Sat 10am–5pm.

One of the most charming Elizabethan buildings in Warwick houses this doll museum near St. Mary's Church. Founded in 1955, its seven rooms display an extensive collection of dolls in wood, wax, porcelain, and fabric.

Warwickshire Museum. Market Hall, The Market Place. ☎ 01926/412500. Free admission. Mon–Sat 10am–5:30pm, Sun (May–Sept) 2–5pm. From Jury St. in the town center, take a right onto Swan St., which leads to the museum.

This museum was established in 1836 to house a collection of geological remains, fossils, and an exhibit of amphibians from the Triassic period. There are also displays illustrating the history, archaeology, and natural history of the county, including the famous Sheldon tapestry map.

St. John's House Museum. St. John's, at the crossroads of the main Warwick-Leamington rd. (A425/A429) and the Coventry rd. (A429). ☎ 01926/412021. Free admission. Tues–Sat (and bank holidays) 10am–12:30pm and 1:30–5:30pm.

At Coten End, not far from the castle gates, this early 17th-century house has exhibits on Victorian domestic life. A schoolroom is furnished with original 19th-century furniture and equipment. During the school term, Warwickshire children dress in period costumes and learn Victorian-style lessons. Groups of children also use the Victorian parlor and the kitchen. Since it's impossible to display more than a small number of items at a time, a study room is available where you can see objects from the reserve collections. The costume collection is a particularly fine one, and visitors can study the drawings and photos that make up the costume catalog. These facilities are available by appointment only. Upstairs is a military museum, tracing the history of the Royal Warwickshire Regiment from 1674 to the present.

WHERE TO STAY

Many people prefer to stay in Warwick and commute to Stratford-upon-Avon, though the accommodations here are not as special as those at Stratford.

Hilton National Warwick/Stratford. Warwick Bypass (A429 Stratford Rd.), Warwick, Warwickshire CV34 6RE. ☎ **800/445-8667** in the U.S. and Canada, or 01926/499555. Fax 01926/410020. 181 units. TV TEL. £115 ($184) double. AE, DC, MC, V. Take A429 2 miles south of Warwick (7 miles north of Stratford-upon-Avon). Junction 15 off M40 from London.

Although it's outside of town, the Hilton is the best choice in the area. Lying at the junction of a network of highways, it's popular with business travelers and hosts many conferences for local companies. But tourists also find that its comfort and easy-to-find location make it a good base for touring Warwick and the surrounding regions. It's a low-rise modern design of earth-colored brick and sports a series of interconnected bars, lounges, and public areas, a heated indoor swimming pool, fitness room, and solarium. Room furnishings are bland but comfortable. The hotel's Sonnetts Restaurant offers a three-course carvery lunch and dinner, and there is 24-hour room service.

Lord Leycester Hotel (Calotels). 17 Jury St., Warwick, Warwickshire CV34 4EJ. ☎ **01926/491481**. Fax 01926/491561. 51 units. TV TEL. £49.50 ($79.20) double. Rates include English breakfast. AE, DC, MC, V.

This affordable choice lies within walking distance of the castle and the other historic buildings of Warwick. In 1726, this manor house belonged to Lord Archer of Umberslade; in 1926, it was finally turned into this modest hotel. Each comfortable bedroom is equipped with a trouser press and beverage-maker. A small English menu is offered in the dining room, and snacks are available 24 hours a day in Alexander's Bar. There's a large parking lot at the rear of the hotel.

Tudor House Inn & Restaurant. 90–92 West St. (opposite the main Warwick Castle car park, ½ mile south of town on A429), Warwick, Warwickshire CV34 6AW. ☎ **01926/495447**. Fax 01926/492948. 11 units, 8 with bathroom or shower. TV TEL. £65–£70 ($104–$112) double with bathroom. Rates include English breakfast. AE, MC, V.

At the edge of town, on the main road from Stratford-upon-Avon to Warwick Castle, is a black-and-white-timbered inn built in 1472. It's one of the few buildings to escape the fire that destroyed High Street in 1694. Off the central hall are two large rooms, each of which could be the setting for an Elizabethan play. All the simply furnished bedrooms have washbasins, and two contain doors only 4 feet high. In the corner of the lounge is an open turning staircase. Bar snacks are available, and the restaurant offers a standard English and continental menu.

WHERE TO DINE

When you're ready to take a break from sightseeing, it's hard to beat the ancient ambiance of tea at **Brethren's Kitchen,** Lord Leycester Hospital (☎01926/491580). This tearoom is part of a 16th-century hospital the earl established in the year 1571. It has cool stone floors and wonderful exposed oak beams. Indian, Chinese, and herbal teas are all available, as well as scones with fresh cream, sponge cake, and fruit cake.

Open Tuesday before Good Friday to the end of October. Closed Monday, but open on bank holidays.

Fanshaw's Restaurant. 22 Market Place. ☎ **01926/410590.** Reservations recommended. Main courses £8–£16.50 ($12.80–$26.40). Set menus £13–£16 ($20.80–$25.60). AE, MC, V. Mon–Sat 6–10pm. BRITISH/FRENCH.

In the heart of Warwick, at the edge of the city's commercial center, this restaurant occupies a late Victorian building whose somber brick facade is enlivened by flowered window boxes. Inside, there are only 32 seats within a well-maintained, rather flouncy dining room accented in pink and white, filled with fresh flowers, and lined with mirrors to give the illusion that it's actually bigger than it is. A well-trained staff serves food from a menu that changes every 2 months, and that usually includes sirloin steak; fillet of beef Wellington-style, with a red wine and shallot sauce; breast of pheasant with a shiitake and oyster mushroom brandy sauce; and sautéed lamb kidneys with Dijon sauce in a puff pastry "pillow." Especially elegant, usually offered during game season, is a brace of quail with a hazelnut and apricot stuffing.

Findon's Restaurant. 7 Old Sq. ☎ **01926/411755.** Reservations recommended. Set lunches £6.95–£22.95 ($11.10–$36.70); set dinners £15.95–£22.95 ($25.50–$36.70). AE, DC, MC, V. Sun and Tues–Fri noon–2pm and Tues–Sat 7–9:30pm. BRITISH.

The building is authentically Georgian, constructed in 1700. You'll dine surrounded by original stone floors and original cupboards, within a setting for only 43 diners to dine in snug comfort. Michael Findon, owner and sometime chef, works hard at orchestrating a blend of traditional and modern British cuisine. The set menus include such dishes as chicken livers with Calvados and sliced apples, and baked goat's cheese with a mushroom crust, red onion relish, and an herb salad. À la carte meals might include medallions of venison with a mousse of peas and a port sauce; "chump" of lamb with green lentils and garlic with a mint and basil fumet; flaked smoked haddock with savoy cabbage and an English mustard sauce; and a filet of beef with a green tapenade and truffle jus. Consider a lunchtime visit to this place, when a two-course "plat du jour" includes a soup of the day followed by such platters as venison sausages with a mustard sauce and fresh vegetables (or a suitable vegetarian substitute), all for only £6.95 ($11.10), a great deal considering that's about what you'd pay for a mediocre lunch in a local pub.

3 Kenilworth Castle

102 miles NW of London; 5 miles N of Warwick; 13 miles N of Stratford-upon-Avon

The big attraction in the village of Kenilworth, an otherwise dull English market town, is Kenilworth Castle—and it's reason enough to stop here.

ESSENTIALS

GETTING THERE　InterCity train lines make frequent and fast connections from London's Paddington and Euston stations to either Coventry or Stratford-upon-Avon. For schedules and information, call ☎ **0345/484950** (in the U.K. only) or 01603/764776. Midland Red Line buses make regular connections from both towns to Kenilworth.

If you're driving from Warwick, take A46 toward Coventry.

VISITOR INFORMATION　The **Tourist Information Centre** is in the village at the Kenilworth Library, 11 Smalley Place (☎ **01926/852595**). It's open Monday, Tuesday, Thursday, and Friday from 9:30am to 7pm, and Saturday from 9:30am to 4pm.

THE MAGNIFICENT RUINS OF KENILWORTH CASTLE

✪ **Kenilworth Castle.** Admission £3.10 ($4.95) adults, £2.75 ($4.40) seniors, £1.60 ($2.55) children 5–16; free for children under 5. ☎ **01926/852078.** Good Friday to Sept daily 10am–6pm; other months daily 10am–4pm. Closed Jan 1 and Dec 24–26.

The castle was built by Geoffrey de Clinton, a lieutenant of Henry I. At one time, its walls enclosed an area of 7 acres, but it is now in magnificent ruins. Caesar's Tower, with its 16-foot-thick walls, is all that remains of the original structure.

Edward II was forced to abdicate at Kenilworth in 1327 before being carried off to Berkeley Castle in Gloucestershire, where he was undoubtedly murdered. In 1563, Elizabeth I gave the castle to her favorite, Robert Dudley, earl of Leicester. He built the gatehouse, which the queen visited on several occasions. After the civil war, the Roundheads were responsible for breaching the outer walls and towers and blowing up the north wall of the keep. This was the only damage inflicted following the earl of Monmouth's plea that it be "Slighted with as little spoil to the dwellinghouse as might be."

The castle is the subject of Sir Walter Scott's romance, *Kenilworth*. In 1957, Lord Kenilworth presented the decaying castle to England, and limited restoration has since been carried out.

WHERE TO STAY

Clarendon House Hotel. 6-8 Old High St., Kenilworth, Warwickshire CV8 1LZ. ☎ **01926/ 857668.** Fax 01926/850669. 31 units. TV TEL. £75 ($120) double. Rates include English breakfast. MC, V.

A family run hotel and restaurant, the Clarendon House is in the old part of Kenilworth. The oak tree around which the original alehouse was built in 1430 is still supporting the roof of the building today. The bedrooms are tastefully decorated.

Before the evening meal, guests gather in the timbered and oak-paneled Royalist Retreat Bar and lounges. The hotel's Cromwell's Bistro restaurant is housed in what was once the inn's stable. The oddly timbered room is decorated with antique maps and armor, constant reminders that a Cromwellian garrison once stayed at the inn during a siege of Kenilworth Castle. In season, you can dine on such specialties as jugged hare or pheasant *georgienne* (marinated in Madeira wine with oranges, grapes, and walnuts).

WHERE TO DINE

Restaurant Bosquet. 97A Warwick Rd. ☎ **01926/852463.** Reservations required. Main courses £14–£16 ($22.40–$25.60); 3-course lunch or dinner £23 ($36.80). AE, MC, V. Tues–Sat noon–2pm and 7–9pm. Closed 1 week for Christmas and the last 3 weeks in Aug. FRENCH.

This narrow, stone-fronted town house from the late Victorian age is a culinary oasis. It's owned and operated by French-born Bernard Lignier, who does the cooking, and his English wife, Jane, who supervises the dining room. The à la carte menu changes every 2 months and might include such offerings as terrine of wild duck with foie gras and truffles, saddle of venison with mandarin oranges and juniper berries, saddle of lamb coated with truffles, and a dessert specialty known as an *assiette* of chocolates.

4 Coventry

100 miles NW of London; 20 miles NE of Stratford-upon-Avon; 18 miles SE of Birmingham; 52 miles SW of Nottingham

Coventry has long been noted in legend as the ancient market town through which Lady Godiva took her famous ride in the buff (giving rise to the term Peeping Tom).

The veracity of the Lady Godiva story is hard to pin down. It's been suggested that she never appeared nude in town, but was the victim of scandalmongers. Coventry today is a Midlands industrial city. The city was partially destroyed by German bombers during World War II, but the restoration is miraculous.

ESSENTIALS

GETTING THERE Trains run every half hour from London's Euston Station to Coverntry (trip time: 1 hour, 15 minutes). For schedules and information, call ☎ **0345/484950** in the U.K., or 01603/764776.

From London's Victoria Coach Station, buses depart every hour throughout the day for the 2-hour trip. From Stratford, bus no. X-16 runs from the town's bus station every hour for Coventry's bus station at Pool Meadow, Fairfax Street. This bus takes 60 to 90 minutes, and stops at Kenilworth and Warwick en route. For schedules and information, call ☎ **0990/808080.**

VISITOR INFORMATION The **Coventry Tourist Office,** Bayley Lane (☎ **01203/832303**), is open Easter to mid-October, Monday to Friday from 9:30am to 5pm, and Saturday from 10am to 4:30pm; mid-October to Easter, Monday to Friday from 9:30am to 4:30pm, and Saturday and Sunday from 10am to 4:30pm.

TOURING COVENTRY CATHEDRAL

✪ **Coventry Cathedral.** Priory Row. ☎ **01203/227597.** Suggested donation of £2 ($3.20) to cathedral. Admission to tower £1 ($1.60) adults, 50p (80¢) children; to visitor center £1.25 ($2) adults, 75p ($1.20) children ages 6–16, free for children under 6. Cathedral Easter–Sept daily 9:30am–6pm; Oct–Easter daily 9:30am–5:30pm. Visitor center Easter–Oct Mon–Sat 10am–4pm.

Consecrated in 1962, Sir Basil Spence's controversial Coventry Cathedral is the city's main attraction. The cathedral is on the same site as the 14th-century Perpendicular building, and you can visit the original tower. Many locals maintain that the structure is more likely to be appreciated by the foreign visitor, since Brits are more attached to traditional cathedral design. Some visitors consider the restored site one of the most poignant and religiously evocative modern churches in the world.

Outside is Sir Jacob Epstein's bronze masterpiece, *St. Michael Slaying the Devil.* Inside, the outstanding feature is the 70-foot-high altar tapestry by Graham Sutherland, said to be the largest in the world. The floor-to-ceiling abstract stained-glass windows are the work of the Royal College of Art. The West Screen (an entire wall of stained glass installed during the 1950s) depicts rows of stylized saints and prophets with angels flying around among them.

In the undercroft of the cathedral is a visitor center, where a 20-minute documentary film is shown more or less continually. Also within the visitor center is the Walkway of Holograms, whose otherwise plain walls are accented with three-dimensional images of the stations of the cross created with reflective light. One of the most evocative objects here is a charred cross wired together by local workmen from burning timbers that crashed to the cathedral's floor during the Nazi bombing. An audiovisual exhibit on the city and church includes the fact that 450 aircraft dropped 40,000 firebombs on the city in 1 day.

5 Birmingham

120 miles NW of London; 25 miles N of Stratford-upon-Avon

England's second-largest city may fairly lay claim to the title "Birthplace of the Industrial Revolution." It was here that James Watt first used the steam engine with success

Birmingham Museum and Art Gallery (6)
Central Library (5)
Council House (6)
Gas Street Basin (2)
Hall of Memory (3)

International Convention Centre (1)
Museum of Science and Industry (4)
St. Chad's Cathedral (7)
St. Martin's-In-The-Bull-Ring (9)
St. Philip's Cathedral (8)

to mine the Black Country. Watt and other famous 18th-century members of the Lunar Society regularly met under a full moon in the nearby Soho mansion of manufacturer Matthew Boulton. Together Watt, Boulton, and other "lunatics," as Joseph Priestly, Charles Darwin, and Josiah Wedgwood cheerfully called themselves, launched the revolution that thrust England and the world into the modern era.

Today, this brawny, unpretentious metropolis still bears some of the scars of industrial excess and the devastation of the Nazi Luftwaffe bombing during World War II. But there's been an energetic building boom in recent years, and Brummies have nurtured the city's modern rebirth by fashioning Birmingham into a convention city that hosts 80% of all trade exhibitions in the United Kingdom.

Birmingham has worked diligently in recent decades to overcome the blight of overindustrialization and poor urban planning. New areas of green space and the city's cultivation of a first-rate symphony and ballet company, as well as art galleries and museums, have all made Birmingham more appealing.

Although not an obvious tourist highlight, Birmingham serves as a gateway to England's north. With more than one million inhabitants, Birmingham serves up a vibrant nightlife and restaurant scene. Its three universities, 6,000 acres of parks and nearby pastoral sanctuaries, and restored canal walkways also offer welcome quiet places.

ESSENTIALS

GETTING THERE   By Plane   Three major international carriers fly transatlantic flights directly to **Birmingham International Airport (BHX)** from four North

American gateways. **British Airways** (☎ 800/AIRWAYS in the U.S. and Canada, or 0345/222111) has daily direct flights from Toronto and New York's JFK airport. **American Airlines** (☎ 800/882-8880) flies nonstop 7 days a week from Chicago's O'Hare Airport and Birmingham. **Continental Airlines** (☎ 800/525-0280) flies a 183-passenger 757 every evening from Newark, New Jersey, to Birmingham, departing at 8pm. Flight time is 6 hours, 45 minutes.

Details on Birmingham flights and schedules are available through the airport (☎ 0121/7675511), brochure hot line (☎ 0121/7677000), or the Web site **www.bhx.co.uk**.

Direct air service between Birmingham and London is almost nonexistent. Many air carriers, however, maintain a virtual air shuttle service between London airports and nearby Manchester, which is a 1½-hour trip to Birmingham via ground transport. For example, British Airways (BA) operates 28 daily flights from London's Heathrow to Manchester, 17 daily flights from London's Gatwick, and 6 daily flights from Stansted to Manchester. BA runs even more return flights daily from Manchester to London.

Birmingham's airport lies about 8 miles southeast of the Birmingham City Centre and is easily accessible by public transportation. **AirRail Link** offers a free shuttle bus service every 10 minutes from the airport to the Birmingham International Rail Station and National Exhibition Centre (NEC). **InterCity** train services operate a shuttle from the airport to New Street Station in the City Centre, just a 10-minute trip.

By Train   InterCity offers half-hourly train service (Monday through Friday) between London's Euston Station and Birmingham, a 90-minute rail trip. Regular train service is also available from London's Euston Station. Trains depart every 2 hours for Birmingham. Birmingham's New Street Station in City Centre and the airport's International Station link the city to the national rail network.

Trains leave Manchester's Piccadilly Station nearly every hour for Birmingham. The trip takes 90 minutes.

Call ☎ 0345/484950 (in the U.K. only) or 01603/764776 for train schedules and current fares.

By Bus   National Express (☎ 0990/808080) and **Flightlink** (☎ 0990/757747) provide regular bus service between Birmingham and London, Manchester, and regional towns.

By Car   From London drive north on M5 to A38, which leads directly to the Bristol Street/Suffolk Street Queensway and the City Centre. The drive takes about 2 to 2½ hours, depending on traffic conditions. Parking is available at various city locations. Contact **National Car Parks** (☎ 0121/7677861) for parking lot locations.

VISITOR INFORMATION   The **Birmingham Convention & Visitor Bureau** (BCVB), 2 City Arcade, near New Street in the City Centre (☎ 0121/6432514), is open Monday through Saturday from 9:30am to 5:30pm and Sunday from 10am to 4pm. The BCVB assists travelers in arranging accommodations, obtaining theater or concert tickets, and planning travel itineraries. The BCVB also operates offices at the National Exhibition Centre, International Exhibition Centre, and at 130 Colmore Rd., Victoria Square.

GETTING AROUND   Birmingham's City Centre hosts a number of attractions within easy walking distance. **Centro** (☎ 0121/2002700) provides information on all local bus and rail service within Birmingham and the West Midlands area. A **Day Saver Pass** costs £2.40 ($3.85) and is an economical way to use the Centro bus and local train system. A weekly **Centro Card** costs £13 ($20.80). Exact change is required on one-way local bus and train trips.

Centro (☎ 0121/2002700) links Birmingham and surrounding Midland towns with regular bus service. Taxis queue at various spots in City Centre, rail stations, and the National Exhibition Centre. Travelers can also ring up radio cab operators such as BB's (☎ 0121/6933333) and Beaufort Cars (☎ 0121/7844444).

EXPLORING BIRMINGHAM

Stephenson Place, at the intersection of New and Corporation streets, is a good starting point for sampling the attractions of City Centre. A 5-minute stroll along New Street leads to Victoria Square, where **Council House,** Colmore Row (☎ 0121/3032040), the city's most impressive Victorian building, anchors the piazza. Built in 1879, it is still the meeting place for the Birmingham City Council and an impressive example of the Italian Renaissance style.

Along Broad Street is the **Gas Street Basin** (☎ 0121/2369811). Operated by Second City Canal Cruises, it forms the hub of the 2,000-mile canal network that runs in all directions from Birmingham to Liverpool, London, Nottingham, and Gloucester. From the Basin, you can take a cruise along the canals, or just walk by the towpaths.

Just a 10-minute walk from City Centre is the **Jewelry Quarter** at 77–79 Vyse St. (☎ 0121/5543598). This complex includes more than 100 jewelry shops. The skill of the jeweler's craft can be viewed at the Discovery Centre's restored Smith and Pepper factory displays or by visiting shop workbenches that still produce most of the jewelry made in Britain. A unique time capsule of the ancient craft of jewelry making and working with precious metals, the quarter offers bargain-hunters the opportunity to arrange repairs, design a custom piece, or just browse. Admission to the Discovery Centre is £2 ($3.20), seniors £1.50 ($2.40). It is open Monday through Friday from 10am to 4pm and Saturday from 11am to 5pm.

Birmingham Museum and Art Gallery. Chamberlain Sq. ☎ 0121/3032834. Free admission. Special exhibition charge. Mon–Sat 10am–5pm, Sun 12:30–5pm.

Known chiefly for its collection of pre-Raphaelite paintings (including works by Ford Maddox Brown, Dante Gabriel Rossetti, Edward Burne-Jones, and Holman Hunt), the gallery also houses exceptional paintings by English watercolor masters from the 18th century. The BMAG is instantly recognized by its "Big Brum" clock tower.

Barber Institute of Fine Arts. University of Birmingham (just off Edgbaston Rd., near the University's East Gate, 2½ miles south of City Centre). ☎ 0121/4147333. Free admission. Mon–Sat 10am–5pm, Sun 2–5pm. Bus: 61, 62, or 63 from City Centre.

Don't be put off by the stark, stone-and-brick building that houses the Barber Institute collection. Some critics consider it the finest small art museum in England and the equal of any museum outside London. The choice selection of paintings includes works by Bellini, Botticelli, Brueghel, Canaletto, Delacroix, Gainsborough, Gauguin, Guardi, Murillo, Renoir, Rubens, Turner, van Gogh, and Whistler.

The Black Country Museum. Tipton Rd., Dudley (3 miles north of the Junction 2 exit on the M5). ☎ 0121/5579643. Admission £6.95 ($11.10) adults, £5.95 ($9.50) seniors, £4.50 ($7.20) children. Family ticket £19.50 ($31.20). Mar–Oct daily 10am–5pm, Nov–Feb Wed–Sun 10am–4pm.

Much of the area immediately surrounding Birmingham is called the Black Country (after the black smoke that billowed over the city and its environs during the iron-working era). That period is best preserved at the Black Country Museum in Dusley, a town about 10 miles northwest of Birmingham. The museum occupies a sprawling landscape in the South Staffordshire coal fields, an early forge of the Industrial Revolution, and it re-creates what it was like to work and live in the Black Country of the

1850s. An electric tramway takes visitors to a thick underground coal seam, and trolleys move through a reconstructed industrial village with a schoolhouse, anchor forge, rolling mill, working replica of a 1712 steam engine, and trade shops.

WHERE TO STAY
EXPENSIVE

Hyatt Regency. 2 Bridge St., Birmingham B1 2JZ. ☎ **800/400-3319** in the U.S. and Canada, or 0121/6431234. Fax 0121/6162323. 331 units. MINIBAR TV TEL. Mon–Fri £120–£180 ($192–$288) double, Sat–Sun £89 ($142.40) double; from £280–£700 ($448–$1,120) suite. Rates include continental breakfast. AE, CB, DC, DISC, MC, V.

The town's premier choice, this sheer, 24-story, glass-skinned hotel, linked by footbridge to the Convention Centre, affords one of the best views of Birmingham from its upper floors. In the heart of Birmingham, it opens onto a canal-side setting with a dramatic glazed atrium that's the epitome of elegance and style. Rooms are tastefully appointed with modern furnishings, marble-floored baths, and an open design. The best accommodations are in the Regency Club, with its own lounge on the 22nd floor.

Dining: Even if you're not a guest, consider a meal at Number 282, nicknamed "The Brasserie on Broad Street." Its menu incorporates the day's news headlines, and reflects the very freshest of market ingredients. Here, the fish-and-chips is made with deep-fried monkfish. For a change, the chips are made with sweet potatoes.

Amenities: Secretarial services, health club, conference rooms.

New Hall Country House Hotel. Walmley Rd., Royal Sutton, Coldfield, W. Midlands B76 1QX. ☎ **0121/3782442.** Fax 0121/3784637. 68 units. MINIBAR TV TEL. £148–£225 ($236.80–$360) double; £190–£345 ($304–$552) suite. AE, DC, MC, V.

Set amid 26 acres of private gardens, only 7 miles northeast of the city, this place claims to be the oldest moated manor house in England, complete with inviting formal gardens. Guest rooms feature marble-tile baths and English country furnishings. The most luxurious and desirable accommodations are in the antique part of the house, which opens onto a view of the moat. However, even the more modern wing, built around a courtyard, has traditional English styling and grace.

Dining: The formal restaurant is an elegant oak-paneled, no-smoking room with an award-winning menu of classic English offerings.

Amenities: Meeting rooms, a tennis court, a 9-hole par-3 golf course, and a croquet lawn.

MODERATE

The Apollo Hotel. Hagley Rd., Edgbaston, Birmingham B16 9RA. ☎ **800/847-4358** in the U.S., or 0121/4550271. Fax 0121/4562394. 132 units. TEL. £85–£105 ($136–$168) double; from £150 ($240) suite. AE, DC, MC, V. Take Exit 3 from the M5, or Exit 6 from the M6.

A 5-minute drive from City Centre, this hotel offers comfortable modern rooms, two restaurants, and a location convenient to the convention centers or the countryside. Rooms are often a bit cramped, but are filled with such amenities as trouser presses, hair dryers, and beverage-makers. Double-glazed windows cut down noise. The suites are a good value here, as they incorporate a minibar, private kitchen, and their own dining and lounge facilities. Restaurant Burgundy provides French cuisine in an elegant setting, whereas the Rib Room offers rich country English fare.

✪ **Jonathans.** 13-24 Wolverhampton Rd., Oldbury (at the crossroads of A456 and A4123, just off Exit J2 or 3 on the M5), Birmingham B68 0LH. ☎ **0121/4293757.** Fax 0121/4343107. 55 units. MINIBAR TV. £85–£125 ($136–$200) double; from £125 ($200) suite. Rates include English breakfast. AE, DC, MC, V.

Filled with Victorian antiques, this charming choice features two highly rated restaurants, a tavern, and plenty of business amenities, all set within a classic 19th-century country-house hotel 5 miles from New Street Station in City Centre. Jonathans derives its name from its two owners, each of whom is named Jonathan (one cooks and the other attends to guests). Visitors enjoy a sojourn back to the 1880s, right down to the mock Victorian street and secret boardroom tucked behind a book-lined dining room wall.

INEXPENSIVE

Ashdale House Hotel. 39 Broad Rd., Acock's Green B27 7UX. ☎ **0121/7063598.** Fax 0121/7063598. 9 units, 6 with bathroom. TV. £32 ($51.20) double without bathroom, £38 ($60.80) double with bathroom. Rates include English breakfast. AE, DC, MC, V.

A spacious Victorian terrace house, this is one of Birmingham's best B&Bs. Your hosts, David and John, invite you to use their library with television. The rooms are cozy, comfortable, and well maintained. Organic produce is offered at breakfast along with some vegetarian choices. Naturally in such an ecofriendly environment, smoking isn't allowed. It's a very inviting and homelike place for an affordable stay in Birmingham.

Awentsbury Hotel. 21 Serpentine Rd., Selly Park B29 7HU. ☎ and fax **0121/4721258.** 16 units, 11 with shower. TV TEL. £42 ($67.20) double without shower, £46–£50 ($73.60–$80) double with shower. Rates include English breakfast. AE, DC, MC, V. Take the A38 from City Centre for about 2 miles, turn left at Bournebrook Rd., then take the first right onto Serpentine Rd.

University and Pebble Mill Studio visitors will find this lodging convenient and comfortable. The place is kept spick-and-span, and the rooms, while not stylish, are acceptable in every other way, with beverage-makers. One room is large enough for families. No smoking is allowed in the dining room, where a large English breakfast is served.

Lyndhurst Hotel. 135 Kingsbury Rd., Erdington B24 8QT. ☎ and fax **0121/3735695.** 14 units. TV. £42.50–£56 ($68–$89.60) double. Rates include English breakfast. AE, DC, MC, V. From junction 6 of the M6 motorway, follow A5127; take the right signposted Minworth onto Kingsbury Rd. The hotel is on the right.

Nine miles from the airport, this stone-exterior Victorian hotel in the northern suburbs is convenient to the Convention and City Centres and Aston University. The rooms are well maintained and well equipped, with everything from a hostess tray to a hair dryer. Although the house is Victorian, furnishings are contemporary. Those who have trouble with steep steps may prefer the ground-floor rooms. A bar and homelike dining room serve guests, as does a separate TV lounge. The garden-view restaurant serves standard but very affordable dishes in a relaxed environment.

WHERE TO DINE

A growing phenomenon, which we can only call the **Birmingham Balti Experience,** may interest those who love spicy food. *Balti* literally means bucket, but it refers to a Kashmiri style of cooking over a fast, hot flame. With the city's large Kashmiri population, there are now many *baltihouses* in Birmingham. Most of these restaurants are bare-bones, BYOB affairs. Two of the better ones are **Celebrity Balti,** 44 Broad St. (☎ **0121/6326074**), close to the Convention Centre, which is open daily from 6pm to 1:30am; and **Selecta Balti,** 884 Lode Lane in Solihull (☎ **0121/7437883**), open daily 6pm to midnight.

Chung Ying. 16 Wrottesley St., City Centre. ☎ **0121/6225669.** Main courses £5.50–£15 ($8.80–$24). AE, DC, MC, V. Mon–Sat noon–11:30pm, Sun noon–10:30pm. CHINESE.

There are more than 300 flavorful items on this predominantly Cantonese menu (40 dim sum items alone). Samples include pan-cooked Shanghai dumplings, stuffed crispy duck packed with crabmeat, steamed eel in bean sauce, and a variety of tasty casseroles. If you want to go really authentic and sample some of the dishes the local Chinese community likes, try fried frogs' legs with bitter melon, steamed pork pie with dried or fresh squid, or fish cakes.

The **Chung Ying Garden,** another restaurant owned by the same proprietor, is at 17 Thorpe St. (☎ **0121/6666622**).

Left Bank. 79 Broad St., City Centre. ☎ **0121/6434464.** Main courses £12–£19 ($19.20–$30.40). AE, DC, MC, V. Mon–Fri noon–2pm, Mon–Sat 7–10:30pm. BRITISH.

This winning restaurant, in a former bank's premises near the International Convention Centre, occupies the ground floor of a grand Victorian building. It's one of the few places in Birmingham where you can almost be guaranteed a good meal. The bistro has a high, coffered ceiling, with gilt, oil paintings, and seating in wicker chairs. The menu from the talented chef, William Marmion, is eclectic. Some of the more delectable items include rump of lamb cooked with beans, a confit of duck with chile salsa and wild rice, a mille-feuille of salmon and spinach in an herb-flavored sauce, and charcoal-grilled chicken with couscous risotto and a tomato salsa.

Maharaja. 23 Hurst St., near the Hippodrome. ☎ **0121/6222641.** Main courses £6–£7.75 ($9.60–$12.40). AE, DC, MC, V. Mon–Sat noon–2pm and 6–11pm. INDIAN.

Set a few doors down from the Birmingham Hippodrome, this rather good restaurant specializes in Mughlai and North Indian dishes. Dining is on two floors, with light oak paneling and framed fragments of Indian printed cloth on the walls. The menu features such dishes as *lamb dhansak* (cubes of lamb in thick lentil sauce), *chicken patalia* (chicken cooked in spices, herbs, and fruit), and prawn madras. The kitchen's balanced use of spices, herbs, and other flavorings lends most dishes an aromatic but delicate taste.

Shimla Pinks. 215 Broad St., City Centre. ☎ **0121/6330366.** Main courses £13–£20 ($20.80–$32). AE, DC, MC, V. Mon–Fri noon–2pm; daily 6–11pm. INDIAN.

A carefully selected menu featuring mostly Indian and Sri Lankan dishes is served by a very courteous staff in this relaxed, elegant restaurant. Try the achari chicken from Uttar Pradesh, or sample the Karachi dishes from the north. Special buffets complement the main menu on Sunday and Monday nights. Parking is available on Tennent Street behind the restaurant.

Another Shimla Pinks is located at 44 Station Road, Solihull (☎ **0121/7040344**).

BIRMINGHAM AFTER DARK
THE PERFORMING ARTS

Connected to the Convention Centre, **Symphony Hall,** at Broad Street (☎ **0121/2123333**), has been hailed as an acoustical gem since its completion in 1990. Home to the **City of Birmingham Symphony Orchestra,** it also hosts special classical music events.

The **National Indoor Arena,** King Edward's Road (☎ **0121/2002202**), seats 13,000 and is a favorite site for jazz, pop, and rock concerts; sporting events; and conventions.

The **Birmingham Repertory Theatre** on Broad Street at Centenary Square (☎ **0121/2364455**), houses one of the top companies in England. Some of the world's greatest actors have performed with the repertory company over the years, including Lord Olivier, Albert Finney, Paul Scoffield, Dame Edith Evans, and Kenneth Branagh. The widely known "Rep" comprises the **Main House,** which seats 900 theatergoers, and the **Studio Theatre,** a more intimate 140-seat venue that often stages new and innovative works. The box office is open from 9:30am to 8pm Monday through Saturday. Tickets cost £8 to £15 ($12.80 to $24).

Midlands Arts Centre (MAC) in Cannon Hill Park (☎ **0121/4403838**) is close to the Edgbaston Cricket Ground and reached by car or bus (routes 1, 35, 45, 47, 61, 62, 63). The MAC houses three performance areas and stages a lively range of drama, dance, and musical performances, as well as films. The box office is open daily from 9am to 8:45pm.

The **Alexandra Theatre,** Station Street (☎ **0121/6431231**), hosts national touring companies, including productions from London's West End. Tickets for all theaters are available through Birmingham visitor offices. The theater serves as a temporary home to many of England's touring companies. Contact the box office for show details.

The **Birmingham Hippodrome,** Hurst Street (☎ **0121/6227486**), is home to the **Birmingham Royal Ballet** and visiting companies from around the world. It hosts a variety of events from the Welsh National Opera and musicals to dance. The box office is open Monday through Saturday from 10am to 10pm.

CLUBS & PUBS

Bobby Brown's The Club, 48 Gas St., along the City Centre canal (☎ **0121/6432573**), is a converted warehouse with several small bars and a disco. **Ronnie Scott's,** 258 Broad St. (☎ **0121/6434525**), lets guests unwind with live jazz in a casual setting. **Liberty's,** 184 Hagley Rd. (☎ **0121/4544444**), is a large, fashionable club featuring French cuisine in the Piano Bar restaurant, champagne, cocktails, and other smaller bars.

The **Old Varsity Tavern Public House,** 56 Bristol Rd. (☎ **0121/4723186**), is ranked as the third largest pub in England and is popular with university students. Says one local fan and reviewer: It's "good for dodgy music," but another laments that while it is "generally a good pub, there are vast numbers of wasted students." The **City Tavern Public House,** Bishopsgate Street (☎ **0121/6434394**), dates from 1901 and is a popular, 3-story pub with live music.

6 Evesham

99 miles NW of London; 30 miles S of Birmingham; 32 miles SW of Coventry

Evesham sits in the center of the Vale of Evesham, along the banks of the Avon River, and has the traditional atmosphere of a bustling and ancient market town. Rich with gardens and riverside parks, Evesham also has several interesting buildings, including a 16th-century bell tower—the only surviving evidence of the Benedictine abbey that once stood here, commemorating the vision of the Virgin Mary that the swineherd saw around the year 700. The town is located in the middle of a host of small farms and orchards. In the springtime, the blossom trail, which begins in the town, bursts into delightful color and flows over the gently rolling hills, making for a memorable walk.

ESSENTIALS

GETTING THERE   Seven days a week, trains run every 2 hours from London's Paddington Station to Evesham. For schedules and information, call ☎ **0345/484950** (in the U.K. only) or 01603/764776.

A **National Express** bus departs Victoria Coach Station in London every day at 5:30pm for Evesham. For schedules and information, call ☎ **0990/808080.**

From London by car, take the M40 toward Oxford, where you'll exit onto A44. Follow it straight into Evesham. Give yourself about 3 hours for this drive.

VISITOR INFORMATION   The **Evesham Tourist Information Centre,** Almonry Museum, Abbey Gate (☎ **01386/446944**), is open year-round Monday to Saturday from 10am to 5pm and Sunday from 2pm to 5pm.

SEEING THE SIGHTS

Other sites include the **Abbey Park,** with its Victorian bandstand (music on Sunday afternoons from June to September), and the **Bell Tower**—all that is left of the once great abbey that was destroyed when Henry VII closed England's monasteries in 1540.

Almonry Heritage Centre. Abbey Gate. ☎ **01386/446944.** Admission £2 ($3.20) adults, £1 ($1.60) children 16 and over, students, and seniors; free for children under 16. Mon–Sat 10am–5pm, Sun 2–5pm.

This ancient house, built in the 14th century, is a superb example of early English architecture. Once the home of the Abbey's Almoner, the monk responsible for looking after the poor and the sick of the town, it now houses a unique collection of artifacts from the town and the Vale, as well as exhibitions on the history of the great abbey and the defeat of Simon de Montfort at the Battle of Evesham in 1265.

WHERE TO STAY & DINE

Bretforton Manor. Bretforton (3½ miles east of Evesham on B4035), Evesham, Hereford and Worcester WR11 5JH. ☎ and fax **01386/833111.** 3 units. TV. £95 ($152) double. Rates include breakfast. AE.

Its owners, Brian and Janet Crittenden, are as informative as they are hospitable, and are successful at showcasing the historical highlights of their stately Elizabethan home. The house has a black slate roof and a facade of blue-tinged Cotswold stone. Completed around 1550, it was constructed from the vestiges of ecclesiastical buildings dating from the 12th and 13th centuries. Today, the atmosphere is charming, relaxed, and exclusive. Bedrooms are outfitted with a scattering of mostly 19th-century heirlooms and cozy touches like decanters of sherry, positioned atop a communal refrigerator where guests can store their munchies. Other than breakfast, no meals are served, although the village pub, a historic affair with flagstone floors, is a 5-minute walk from the hotel. There's a pond, stream, and meadow with grazing sheep scattered across the property's 7 acres. Still standing on the grounds is a wood contraption that functioned during the 1700s as the village stocks, where wrongdoers were incarcerated for public display. Today, they're purely decorative reminders of naughtiness past.

The Evesham Hotel. Cooper's Lane, off Waterside, Evesham, Worcester WR11 6DA. ☎ **01386/765566.** Fax 01386/765443. 41 units. TV TEL. £78–£90 ($124.80–$144) double; £125 ($200) suite. AE, DC, MC, V.

The family that runs the place, the Jenkinsons, may be savvy business folk, but they bring lots of tongue-in-cheek humor to their hotel (rubber ducks in the bath, teddy bears attached to room keys, radios and magazines within each of the public toilets, and cartoons that gently satirize themselves and vacations in general). Most guests find it enchanting.

The setting is authentically historic. Built in 1540 as a farmhouse, it was "modernized" in 1810 into the solidly elegant Georgian appearance it maintains today. Half a dozen mulberry trees are believed to have been planted by monks around 1500, and a stately cedar of Lebanon, the hotel's horticultural pride, dates from 1809. Bedrooms are loaded with thoughtful and sometimes quirky touches (playing cards are provided). Most have traditional bedspreads and upholsteries, and many have either the original beams, or carefully maintained antique paneling.

Dining: The Cedar has a large bay window overlooking the garden, and gracious service that many guests will remember long after their meal. There are special high teas (actually, early suppers) for the children of guests every day from 5:30 to 6:30pm. These are whimsical Christopher Robin and Winnie-the-Pooh–type affairs. The dinner menu, served from 7 to 9:30pm, might start with a lentil-and-goat-cheese salad then move on to veal steak bordelaise or lamb cutlets flavored with walnut crumbs and served with a creamy peppercorn sauce. Desserts include ice cream scented with rose petals and served with chocolate sauce (they call it "Turkish delight"), and an award-winning version of Banoffi pie, made with toffee, bananas, and coffee ice cream.

The Mill at Harvington. Anchor Lane, Harvington (4 miles north of Evesham, via A4188 and A435), Evesham, Hereford, and Worcester WR11 5NR. ☎ and fax **01386/870688.** 21 units. TV TEL. £82–£112 ($131.20–$179.20) double. Rates include breakfast. AE, DC, MC, V.

This is the most stately looking hotel in Evesham, with a redbrick Georgian-inspired setting that abuts the verdant bank of the River Avon. Beginning around 1750, it functioned as a bakery, and today, the property retains many of its original features, such as the old bakery's ovens (with ornate iron doors), but is now surrounded with bucolic gardens and a stream with nesting swans and herons. Rooms are conservatively furnished with solidly comfortable, albeit somewhat unimaginative, furniture. The real appeal of the place lies in the walks and strolls you'll take around its impressive exterior rather than the time you'll spend inside.

Dining: The restaurant serves an imaginative and well-prepared menu. Lunches are less elaborate than dinners, but everything served here has an international panache hard to find at most nearby establishments. At dinner, you might order a tartlet of "arbroath smokies" (young haddock), green and white tagliatelle with ham and sherry, or half of a roasted Gressingham duck served with orange-and-ginger sauce.

Riverside Restaurant and Hotel. The Parks, Offenham Rd. (2 miles west of Hereford beside B4510), Hereford and Worcester WR11 5JP. ☎ **01386/446200.** Fax 01386/40021. 7 units. TV TEL. £80 ($128) double. Rates include breakfast. MC, V. Closed Tues–Fri during a 3-week period in Jan; closed Sun night and all day Mon.

Stately and sprawling, this white-sided Edwardian home set within 3 acres of gardens boasts prominent rows of bay windows overlooking the Avon River and its verdant banks. It's intimate, charming, and very English. Public rooms contain lavish draperies with ribbons and swags, and a 19th-century ambience. Rooms are cozy, sunny, individually decorated, and meticulously maintained.

Dining: Within the pleasant, if conservative-looking dining room, imaginative, well-prepared meals are served for lunch and dinner. There are garden and Avon River views from the big bay windows, and the service is sensitive and well timed. Your choices include a carefully dressed, whole Cornish crab served with creamy mayonnaise, deviled soft herring roe on granary toast, and English lamb kidneys with a mushroom and Madeira sauce.

7 Worcester

124 miles NW of London; 26 miles SW of Birmingham; 61 miles N of Bristol

Awash with some of the most magnificent and lush river scenery in all of Europe, the River Wye Valley contains some of the most charming small villages in west-central England. Where wool used to be the main industry in this area, most of the locals today make their living by fruit growing, dairy farming, and, to an increasing degree, tourism.

Worcestershire has become a household name around the world, thanks to the famous sauce that is used to accent a myriad of dishes and to perk up any respectable Bloody Mary. One of the quaintest of the Midland counties, it covers portions of the rich valleys of the Severn and Avon rivers. Between the two cathedral cities of Hereford and Worcester, the ridge of the Malverns rises from the Severn Plain.

The River Severn flows through the heart of Worcester, a world-famous porcelain center. In medieval times, the river—just a short distance away from the bustling High Street—served as the hub of the city's commercial life. Today, it plays host to more leisurely activities like boat trips, fishing, and rowing. The river's bridge also affords the city's best views of 900-year-old Worcester Cathedral, with its 200-foot-high tower.

ESSENTIALS

GETTING THERE   Regular trains depart London's Paddington Station for Worcester, arriving about 2¼ hours later. For schedules and information, call ☎ **0345/484950** (in the U.K. only) or 01603/764776.

National Express buses leave throughout the day from London's Victoria Coach Station. For schedules and information, call ☎ **0990/808080.**

Driving from London, take the M5 to Junction 7 toward Worcester. Give yourself about 3 hours. From Hereford, it's a short drive to Worcester. Just take A449 26 miles west.

VISITOR INFORMATION   The **Worcester Tourist Information Centre,** in the Queen Anne's Guildhall on High Street (☎ **01905/726311**), keeps hours of 10:30am to 5:30pm Monday to Saturday from mid-March to the end of October, and 10:30am to 4pm Monday to Saturday from November to mid-March.

SPECIAL EVENTS   The **Three Choirs Festival** was founded in 1715 by the cathedrals choir of Worcester, Gloucester, and Hereford. The cathedrals rotate every year as hosts, with the other two choirs as guests. In 1999, Worcester will serve as host from August 21 to 27, with a program that will feature the works of Elgar, among others. Ticket prices range from £4 ($6.40) to £29 ($46.40).

WHAT TO SEE & DO

Bickerline River Trips, on the south quay near the cathedral (☎ **01531/670679**), lets you see Worcester from the river aboard the 88-passenger *Marianne*. These 45-minute trips set sail every day on the hour from 11am to 5pm and until 6pm on Saturday and Sunday. Light refreshments are served and party bookings are available.

If you're interested in shopping, you might want to take a stroll down the architecturally important **Friar Street,** taking in the eclectic collection of individual timber-framed and brick shops. **G. R. Pratley & Sons,** Shambles ☎ **01905/22678** or 01905/28642), offers a smorgasbord of glass, china, and earthenware; it's an agent for Royal Worcester, Royal Doulton, Wedgwood, Spode, Duchess Fine Bone China, and Wood & Sons Ltd. You can also find finely woven Oriental rugs and carpets and top-quality furniture here.

Bygones of Worcester, 55 Sidbury and Cathedral Square (☎ **01905/23132** or 01905/25388), is actually two shops packed with an intriguing collection of antiques and odds and ends. Wander through this store to find furnishings for your home that range from the bizarre to the decorative and fanciful—all from cottages and castles in England.

Worcester Cathedral. College Yard at High St. ☎ **01905/611002.** Admission free, but adults asked for a £2 ($3.20) donation. Daily 7:30am–6pm.

Historically speaking, the most significant part of Worcester Cathedral is its crypt, a classic example of Norman architecture that dates from 1084. Still in use today, it contains the tombs of King John, whose claim to fame is the Magna Carta, and Prince

Arthur, the elder brother of Henry VII. Both tombs can be found near the high altar. The 12th-century chapter house is one of the finest in England and, along with the cloisters, evokes the cathedral's rich monastic past. The cathedral is also known for a distinguished history of fine choral music, and, rotating with the cathedrals of Gloucester and Hereford, hosts the oldest choral festival in Europe, the **Three Choirs Festival.**

Royal Worcester Porcelain Factory. Severn St. ☎ **01905/23221.** Factory tours available Mon–Fri beginning at 10:25am; cost is £4.95 ($7.90) adults, £4.50 ($7.20) seniors, £3.25 ($5.20) children over 11. Call ahead to reserve (for a same-day tour, phone before 10am). Museum admission £1.75 ($2.80) adults, £1 ($1.60) seniors and children. Museum open Mon–Sat 9am–5:30pm.

This factory has been achieving its goal of creating "ware of a form so precise as to be easily distinguished from other English porcelain" ever since its founding in 1751. It produces a unique range of fine china and porcelain that remains unsurpassed throughout the world. Behind-the-scenes tours last about 45 minutes and do not accept children under 11, very elderly visitors, or persons with disabilities, because of safety regulations.

The **Retail and Seconds Shops** at the factory are open to all, and offer a unique chance to buy the beauty of Royal Worcester at bargain prices. Many of the pieces are marked as seconds, but most of the time you won't be able to tell why. The **Dyson Perrins Museum** is also located at the factory and houses the world's largest collection of Worcester Porcelain.

The **Commandery,** Sidbury (☎ **01905/355071**), originally the 11th-century Hospital of St. Wulstan, was transformed over the years into a sprawling 15th-century, medieval timber-framed building that served as the country home of the Wylde family. This was the headquarters of King Charles II during the Battle of Worcester in 1651, the last battle in the English civil war. The Great Hall has a hammer-beam roof and a minstrels' gallery. England's premier **Civil War Centre** is now situated here. This exciting, interactive, and hands-on museum marvelously incorporates life-size figures, sound systems, and videos to take you through the bloody and turbulent years of England's civil war. You can even try on helmets, handle weapons, and pick up cannon balls. The Commandery also has canal-side tearooms, a picnic area, and a Garden of Fragrance. The house is open from 10am to 5pm Monday to Saturday and 1:30pm to 5:30pm on Sunday. Admission is £3.50 ($5.60) for adults, £2.35 ($3.75) for children and seniors, and £9.30 ($14.90) for a family ticket. The Commandery is a 3-minute walk from Worcester Cathedral.

Queen Anne's Guildhall. High St. ☎ **01905/723471.** Admission free. Mon–Sat 9am–5pm.

The guildhall was built between 1721 and 1723. Here you'll find statues dutifully erected by the Royalists honoring Charles I and Charles II, as well as one of the most beautifully decorated Queen Anne rooms in England. The tourist office is located here.

Sir Edward Elgar's Birthplace Museum. Crown East Lane, Lower Broadheath. ☎ **01905/333224.** Admission £3 ($4.80) adults, £2 ($3.20) seniors, 50p (80¢) children. Summer Thurs–Tues 10:30am–6pm; winter Thurs–Tues 1.30–4:30pm Closed mid Jan to mid-Feb. Drive out of Worcester on the A44 toward Leominster. After 2 miles, turn off to the right at the sign. The house is in the village, ½ mile down a side road.

This charming and inviting redbrick country cottage, stable, and coach house is set on well-tended grounds. Elgar, perhaps England's greatest composer, was born in this early 19th-century house on June 2, 1857. Today, the cottage houses a unique collection of manuscripts and musical scores, photographs, and other personal memorabilia.

WHERE TO STAY

Diglis House Hotel. Severn St., Worcester WR1 2NF. ☎ **01905/353518.** Fax 01905/767772. 25 units. TV TEL. Mon–Fri £77.75–£130 ($124.40–$208) double, Sat–Sun £60–£130 ($96–$208) double; £172 ($275.20) suite. Rates include breakfast. AE, MC, V.

Set within gardens at the edge of the Severn River, this brick-sided mansion was built in the 1700s as a guest house for visitors to the nearby cathedral. Later, it was the family home of noted landscape architect Benjamin Williams Leader, whose paintings of bucolic England have graced the cover of Christmas cards for many generations of English letter-writers. The building's interior was upgraded to country-house hotel standards, and includes chintz curtains, mahogany furniture, and a polite but sometimes not terribly alert staff. There's a restaurant (The Conservatory) on the premises, set within a glass-sided greenhouse-style wing of the stately building.

✪ **The Elms Hotel.** On the A443 (2 miles west of Abberley, near Worcester), Hereford and Worcester WR6 6AT. ☎ **01299/896666.** Fax 01299/896804. 16 units. TV TEL. £110–£135 ($176–$216) double. Rates include breakfast. AE, DC, MC, V. Take the A443 for 6 miles west of Worcester, following the signs to Tenbury Wells.

One of the most stately and impressive hotels in the region was built in 1710 by Gilbert White, a disciple of Sir Christopher Wren. It is chic, fun, sophisticated, and international, and lies on the outskirts of Worcester. Sheathed in cream-colored stucco, and surrounded by 10 acres of field, park, and forest, it's outfitted with what some visitors consider a fantasy version of the best of England, complete with acres of formal draperies, mahogany or walnut 18th- and 19th-century antiques, an intriguing collection of clocks and oil paintings, and log-burning fireplaces.

There's a restaurant on the premises that's open daily for lunch and dinner.

Fownes Hotel. City Walls Rd., Worcester WR1 2AP. ☎ **01905/613151.** Fax 01905/23742. 61 units. TV TEL. £95 ($152) double; £120 ($192) suite. AE, DC, MC, V.

A 5-minute walk west of Worcester's cathedral, this hotel occupies the industrial-age, brown-brick premises of the Fownes Glove Factory (ca. 1892). A civic monument, and source of income for many local residents until glove-wearing went out of fashion, it was converted in the 1980s into Worcester's most interesting large hotel. Public rooms are attractively outfitted with spot lighting, tile or carpeted floors, pastel colors, and English-style chintz, and are unified by a decorating theme that includes gilt-edged photographs of what each area of the hotel looked like during its glove-making heyday. Bedrooms are cozy and furnished in a conservative English style that includes botanical prints, mahogany furnishings, and, best of all, the wide or tall many-paned windows of the factory's original construction. There's a cocktail bar on the premises, and a dining room, The King's Restaurant.

The Giffard Hotel. High St., Worcester WR1 2QR. ☎ **01905/726262.** Fax 01905/723458. 103 units. TV TEL. £69 ($110.40) double; £89 ($142.40) suite. AE, DC, MC, V. Parking £3 ($4.80).

Although this hotel is located directly across from the city's cathedral, absolutely no effort was made to blend the bland modern architecture of this 1967, six-story hotel into the historic area surrounding it. A member of the Forte chain since its inception, it offers clean, conservatively modern, earth-toned rooms that are favored by tour groups and business conventions. There's a cocktail bar on the premises, and a restaurant. Room service is available 24 hours a day.

WHERE TO DINE

Across from the cathedral, **The Pub at Ye Old Talbot Hotel,** Friar Street (☎ 01905/ 23573), contains lots of Victorian nostalgia and old-fashioned wood paneling that's been darkened by generations of cigarette smoke and spilled beer. It offers predictable pub grub that's a bit better than expected, especially when it's accompanied with a pint of the house's half dozen ales on tap.

One of Worcester's most whimsical pubs is the **Little Sauce Factory,** London Road (☎ 01905/350159). The entire place is a takeoff on Worcester's famous sauce, with posters advertising food flavorings, all the accessories of an old-fashioned kitchen, and an enormous ceiling map of Britain in ceramic tiles.

Il Pescatore. 34 Sidbury. ☎ **01905/21444.** Reservations recommended. Set lunches £4.90 ($7.85); main courses £8–£16 ($12.80–$25.60). MC, V. Tues–Sat noon–2pm; Mon–Sat 6:45–10pm. Closed 2 weeks in late July. TUSCAN.

Set within 200 yards of the cathedral in a half-timbered, 16th-century Elizabethan building, this restaurant has an ambience that's a lot more international and suave than the very English exterior suggests. It's the domain of Giuliano Ponzi, a former resident of L'Aquila, north of Rome. An excellent chef, his menu includes *finocchiona* (Tuscan-style, fennel-flavored sausages) served with cannellini beans; daily homemade pastas, such as crabmeat-stuffed ravioli or smoked salmon and basil tagliatelle; and a succulent sea bass garnished with Martini-and-beurre-blanc sauce. For dessert, the tiramisu served in a chocolate cup is an enduring favorite.

8 The Malverns

127 miles NW of London; 34 miles SW of Birmingham

Once part of the ancient and formidable kingdom of Mercia, the beautiful and historic Malvern Hills lie just west of Worcester, rising suddenly and drastically from the Severn Valley and stretching for 9 miles. This tranquil area is rich in natural beauty. The towns are especially famous for their healing waters, refreshing air, and inspiring vistas.

Six townships cling to the Malvern Hills, making this an outstanding place to strike out for easy day hikes while you're staying in Worcester or Hereford. You can wander through Great Malvern, Malvern Link, West Malvern, Welldon, Malvern Wells, Little Malvern, and several other hamlets in a day's stroll. Great Malvern is resplendent with Victorian grandeur, much of which was gained from its importance as a 19th-century spa resort. The town boasts the largest priory church in the area, dating from the 15th century and boasting some fine stained-glass windows, as well as a great Gothic tower. The monks' stalls have superb misericords and medieval titles. The greatest and most beloved singer of the 19th century, the wildly talented "Swedish Nightingale" Jenny Lind, as well as that century's greatest English composer, Sir Edward Elgar, both called this area home.

The Malvern hills provide a breathtaking backdrop for hiking and biking. You can take in immense views, eastward to the Cotswolds and westward to the Wye Valley and the Welsh mountains, while exploring the most beautiful countryside in England. The Malvern Tourist Information Centre (see below) can provide you with detailed maps and route descriptions.

St. Wulstan's Church, 2 miles out of Great Malvern on the Ledbury Road, is where the composer Sir Edward Elgar is buried with his wife and daughter. You'll find a bronze bust of the composer in Priory Park, and he lived at Craeglea on the Malvern

Wells Road and at Forli in Alexandra Road, where he composed the *Enigma Variations, Sea Pictures,* and the *Dreams of Gerontius.*

ESSENTIALS

GETTING THERE   From London, trains leave regularly from Paddington Station for this 2-hour trip. For schedules and information, call ☎ **0345/484950** (in the U.K. only) or 01603/764776.

One **National Express** bus departs daily from Victoria Coach Station in London, arriving in Great Malvern 2½ hours later. Call ☎ **0990/808080** for more information.

If you're driving from London, take M5 to A4104 west, then A449 north toward Great Malvern. Depending on traffic, the drive takes about 2 hours.

VISITOR INFORMATION   The **Malverns Tourist Information Centre,** 21 Church St., Malvern, Worcestershire WR14 2AA (☎ **01684/892289**), is open from 10am to 5pm daily year-round.

WHERE TO STAY

The Cotford Hotel. Graham Rd., Malvern, Worcestershire WR14 2JW. ☎ **01684/574642.** 16 units. TV TEL. £65–£75 ($104–$120) double. Rates include breakfast. AE, MC, V.

A 5-minute walk east of Malvern's town center, on an acre of lawns and rock gardens, this towering and stately home was built in 1851 as the local bishop's residence. Constructed of beige-brown Cotswold stone, and accented with lavish gingerbread, it retains a vaguely ecclesiastical air despite the modern-day overlays of comfy armchairs, simple contemporary draperies, and patterned carpeting. Views extend over the garden through elaborate windows carved from wood to resemble Gothic tracery. The main appeal of the place derives from its monumental historic premises, the warm welcome, and such Victorian touches as the tile-floored wide entrance hallway; not from the simple modern furnishings it contains today. Evening meals can be prepared, but are usually restricted to residents and their guests.

✪ **Cottage in the Wood.** Holywell Rd., Malvern Hills, Great Malvern, Hereford and Worcester WR14 4LG. ☎ **01684/575859.** Fax 01684/560662. 20 units. TV TEL. £89.50–£139 ($143.20–$222.40) double. AE, MC, V. After leaving Great Malvern on A449, turn right just before the gas station. The inn is on the right.

There is indeed a cottage in the woods associated with this hotel (it contains four cozy bedrooms and dates from the 17th century). But most of the inn occupies a nearby Georgian house from the late 1700s. Originally built for the semiretired mother of the lord of a neighboring estate, it's referred to as "The Dower House" and is appropriately outfitted throughout in an attractive Laura Ashley style. The bedrooms are quite small, but this place is so charming and offers such panoramic views that most visitors don't mind. Your hosts are John and Sue Pattin, whose skill is especially visible within their restaurant (see below).

The Foley Arms. 14 Worcester Rd., Malvern, Hereford and Worcester WR14 4QS. ☎ **01684/573397.** Fax 01684/569665. 28 units. TV TEL. £82–£88 ($131.20–$140.80) double. Rates include breakfast. AE, DC, MC, V.

Home to one of the town's most bustling pubs, the Foley Arms is the oldest hotel in Malvern, with a Georgian pedigree from 1810 when it welcomed the affluent and exhausted for curative sessions at the nearby spa. Close to the town center, it rises from a very steep hillside, which makes it inconvenient for mobility-impaired guests, but also gives it glorious views over the Severn River to the edge of the Cotswolds from many of its bedroom windows. Accommodations contain old, usually antique, furniture and heavy draperies; they have all the modern conveniences but still seem old-fashioned. The in-house restaurant has a bay window with views over the valley, thoughtful service, and good-value set meals

WHERE TO DINE

The Cottage in the Wood. Holywell Rd., Malvern Wells. ☎ **01684/575859.** Reservations recommended. Light set lunch (Mon–Sat) £11.95 ($19.10); set-price Sun lunch £14.55 ($23.30). Main courses £12.50–£16.50 ($20–$26.40). AE, MC, V. Daily 12:30–2pm and 7–9pm. MODERN BRITISH.

The setting is an 18th-century Georgian-style dower's house, set on a steeply sloping, wooded plot of land with panoramic views over the Herefordshire countryside. The setting manages to be elegant, cozy, and nurturing at the same time, thanks to the hard work and charm of resident owners John and Sue Pattin. They offer modern adaptations of traditional British favorites, including slices of fillet steak with deep-fried parsnips and celeriac on a bed of cream-based spring-onion sauce, and roasted breast of pigeon with savoy cabbage and bacon in a port sauce. English cheeses or such desserts as a Drambuie pot are particularly appealing.

✪ Restaurant Croque-en-Bouche. 221 Wells Rd., Malvern Wells. ☎ **01684/565612.** Set menus £25–£27 ($40–$43.20) Thurs; £33.50–£36 ($53.60–$57.60) Fri–Sat. MC, V. Thurs–Sat 7–9pm. MODERN INTERNATIONAL.

Within a dark and woodsy neo-Victorian setting, the Joneses offer only as many tables as can be personally served by Robin (who waits alone on tables) and Marion (who cooks everything herself, often incorporating salads and vegetables from their garden). Menu items are heavily influenced by the traditions of Italy and Japan, and are likely to include vegetable tempura; vegetarian parcels wrapped in phyllo pastry; a frequently changing list of soups, including fish chowder served with *rouille* and garlicky croutons; roasted leg of Welsh lamb served with braised garlic, Pinot Noir, and glazed shallots; or perhaps Cornish codfish spiced with ginger and coriander on a bed of lentils and exotic greens. For such a small and intimate restaurant, the wine list, containing an estimated 1,500 vintages, is amazingly varied.

9 Ledbury

119 miles NW of London; 14 miles W of Hereford; 16 miles SW of Worcester

A thriving market town since 1120, Ledbury has a wealth of historic black-and-white, half-timbered buildings set against a rustic backdrop, especially in springtime when bluebells and wild daffodils abound and the scent of apple blossoms fills the air. Famous 19th-century poet Elizabeth Barrett Browning spent her childhood in nearby Wellington at Hope End (now a hotel), and the renowned poet laureate John Mansfield was born and reared in Ledbury.

ESSENTIALS

GETTING THERE   Six trains depart London's Paddington Station for Ledbury daily (a 2½-hour ride). For schedules and information, call ☎ **0345/484950** (in the U.K. only) or 01603/764776.

Two **National Express** buses leave daily from London's Victoria Coach Station for the 3-plus-hour trip to Ledbury. For schedules and information, call ☎ **0990/808080.**

If you're driving from London, take the M50 south toward Wales. Then take exit NW on A417 toward Ledbury.

VISITOR INFORMATION   The **Ledbury Tourist Information Centre** is located at 3 The Homend (☎ 01531/636147), and is open from 10am to 5pm daily year-round; closed Sunday in winter.

SEEING THE SIGHTS

Within easy walking distance of the Tourist Information Centre is the delightfully cobbled **Church Lane,** which is so well preserved it's often used as a movie set. *Little Lord Fauntleroy* and *By the Sword Divided* are two films in which you'll be able to spy Church Lane.

The **Painted Room** (☎ 01531/632306), located in the Old Council Offices in Church Lane, features a series of 16th-century frescoes found during a 1991 renovation to the building. It's open daily from 11am to 2pm if a staff member is available, or a tour can be arranged by phoning ahead. Tours cost £1 ($1.60) per person.

Almost every street in town is worth exploring for its unique craft galleries and antique shops. It's a wonderful place for finding quality craft work. Just one example is **Homend Pottery,** 205 The Homend (☎ 01531/634571), a gallery and showroom featuring beautiful hand-thrown wares made right on the premises.

Eastnor Castle. 2½ miles east of Ledbury on A438. ☎ 01531/633160. Admission £4 ($6.40) adults, £2 ($3.20) children. Easter–June and Sept Sun and bank holiday Mondays 11am–5pm; July–Aug Sun–Fri 11am–5pm. Closed Oct–Easter.

The castle transports you back to a more romantic time. Built in 1812 by a local aristocrat, Eastnor has undergone a virtual renaissance thanks to the hard work, dedication, and youthful vitality of the Hervey-Bathursts, descendants of the castle's original owner. The many rooms are spectacularly appointed and overflow with early Italian fine art, 17th-century Venetian furniture and Flemish tapestries, plus medieval armor and paintings by Van Dyck, Reynolds, Romney, and Watts. Lunches and teas are also available.

Hellen's Much Marcle. 4 miles southwest of Ledbury in Much Marcle. ☎ 01531/660668. Admission £3 ($4.80) adults, £1 ($1.60) children. Guided tours on the hour 2–5pm daily from Good Friday to beginning of Oct.

Begun in 1292, Much Marcle was the boyhood home of one of the original Knights of the Garter, a knighthood that is only bestowed upon those men who have accomplished something extraordinarily courageous or exceptional for Great Britain. This ancient manor, brimming with a haunting atmosphere, still houses the great fireplace by which Queen Isabella of England waited for the Great Seal and abdication of King Edward II in 1326 as well as the bedroom prepared for Bloody Mary, Queen of England, in 1554.

Westons Cider Mill. The Bounds, Much Marcle. ☎ 01531/660233. Tours £3 ($4.80) adults, £2 ($3.20) children. Mill open year-round Mon–Fri 9:30am–4:30pm, Sat 10am–1pm. Tours Mon, Wed, and Fri at 2:30pm.

Situated in the middle of apple and pear orchards, this cider mill was established in 1880. Although the tour is long (2½ hours), it's a real treat, including a tasting of ciders and perries (fermented pear juices) in the Visitors Centre and Shop. Tours need to be booked in advance. If your time is limited, skip the tour, but drop into the shop for a free cider tasting. A new restaurant, Scrumpy's House, opened in January 1998, serving sandwiches and salads for lunch Monday to Saturday; dinner, consisting of traditional British fare, is served evenings Thursday to Saturday.

WHERE TO STAY & DINE

The Feathers Hotel. High St., Ledbury, Hereford, and Worcester HR8 1DS. ☎ 01531/635266. Fax 01531/632001. 24 units. TV TEL. £80–£120 ($128–$192) double. Rates include breakfast. AE, DC, MC, V.

This is one of the most prominent buildings on Ledbury's High Street, an Elizabethan fantasy of blackened timbers and meticulously maintained stucco. It's the most evocative and charming choice in town. Rooms combine rugged-looking half-timbering with patterned chintz fabrics and upholsteries. Each has an electric kettle and tea, plus the requisite squeaking floors, and is accessible only by somewhat irregular and very old-fashioned staircases. However rustic, the hotel recently completed renovations that added a conference center, a swimming pool, and a gym, complete with a steam room.

At the more appealing of the hotel's two restaurants, Fuggles, you'll find dishes that range from the informal (burgers and hearty soups) to the more elaborate (spinach-and-ricotta tart). The other dining area, Quills, is only open for dinner on Friday and Saturday nights, and is rather staid and stiff.

10 Hereford

133 miles NW of London; 51 miles SW of Birmingham

Situated on the Wye River, the city of Hereford is one of the most colorful towns in England. It was the birthplace of both David Garrick—the actor, producer, and dramatist who breathed life back into London theater in the mid-18th century—and Nell Gwynne, an actress who was the mistress of Charles II. Dating from 1080, the red sandstone Hereford Cathedral contains an eclectic mix of architectural styles from Norman to Perpendicular.

Surrounded by pristine countryside, including orchards and lush pasturelands, Hereford is home to the world-famous, white-faced Hereford cattle and some of the finest cider around, best sampled in one of the city's traditional and atmospheric pubs.

ESSENTIALS

GETTING THERE   By train from London's Paddington Station, Hereford is a 3-hour trip. For schedules and information, call ☎ **0345/484950** (in the U.K. only) or 01603/764776.

To make the 4-hour-plus trip by bus from London, you'll need to catch a **National Express** bus from Victoria Coach Station. For schedules and information, call ☎ **0990/808080.**

The trip to Hereford makes a scenic 3-hour drive from London. Take M5 to either Ledbury or Romp-on-Wye, then turn onto A49 toward Hereford.

VISITOR INFORMATION   Hereford's **Tourist Information Centre** (☎ **01432/268430**) is located at 1 King St., and is open daily from 9am to 5pm in summer, and Monday through Saturday from 9am to 5pm off-season.

WHAT TO SEE & DO

There's interesting shopping within a labyrinth of historic and characterful buildings known collectively as **High Town.** Limited only to pedestrians, it's enhanced with street performers and visiting entertainers. Principal shopping streets include Widemarsh Street, Commercial Road, St. Owen's Street, and perhaps the most charming and artfully old-fashioned of them all, Church Street.

Also near the town center is **Hereford Market,** which evokes West Country street fairs of old with its cornucopia of collectibles and junk displayed in an open-air setting. It's conducted throughout the year, every Wednesday and Saturday morning from 8am to 1pm. The area literally pulsates with life as vendors sell items ranging from sweatshirts and saucepans to paintings and pet food.

Andrew Lamputt, The Silver Shop, 28 St. Owen St. (☎ **01432/274961**), is the place to pick up the perfect silver gift. It boasts an extensive array of quality silverware and fine gold jewelry, and maintains a stable of skilled craftspeople who restore old pieces.

Hereford Cathedral. Hereford city center. ☎ **01432/59880.** Cathedral open year-round, with free admission. Guided tours £1.50 ($2.40) per person. Mappa Mundi and Chained Library exhibition also open Mon–Sat 10am–4:15pm, Sun noon–3:15pm. Admission for exhibitions £4 ($6.40) adults, £3 ($4.80) children and seniors, free for children under 5; family ticket (2 adults and 3 children) £10 ($16).

This is one of the oldest cathedrals in England (its cornerstone was laid in 1080). The cathedral is primarily Norman, and includes a 13th-century Lady Chapel erected in 1220, as well as a majestic "Father" Willis organ, one of the finest in the world. Exhibited together in the new library building at the west end of the Hereford Cathedral are two of Hereford's unique and priceless historical treasures: the Mappa Mundi of 1290, which portrays the world oriented around Jerusalem, and a 1,600-volume library of chained books, with some volumes dating from the 8th century. The cathedral also contains the Diocesan Treasury and the St. Thomas Becket Reliquary.

The Cider Museum and King Offa Cider Brandy Distillery. Pomona Place, Whitecross Rd. (a 5-minute walk from the city center and ¼ mile from the city ring rd. on the A438 to Brecon). ☎ **01432/354207.** Admission £2.20 ($3.50) adults, £1.70 ($2.70) children. Family ticket £6.10 ($9.75). Museum Apr–Oct daily 10am–5:30pm; Nov–Mar Tues–Sun 11am–3pm.

This museum tells the story of traditional cider making from its heyday in the 17th century right through to modern factory methods. The King Offa Distillery has been granted the first new license to distill cider in the United Kingdom in more than 250 years, and visitors can see it being produced from beautiful copper stills brought from Normandy. The museum shop sells cider, cider brandy, cider brandy liqueur, and Royal Cider, the real wine of old England, as well as a good selection of gifts and souvenirs.

The Old House. High Town. ☎ **01432/364598.** Admission £1 ($1.60) adults, 40p (65¢) children. Combination tickets available to see The Churchill Gardens Museum and Hatton Gallery as well. Summer Tues–Sun 10am–5:30pm; winter Tues–Sat 10am–1pm and 2–5:30pm.

This is a completely restored Jacobean-period museum with 17th-century furnishings on three floors. The painstakingly restored half-timbered building was constructed in 1621 and includes a kitchen, hall, and rooms with four-poster beds.

The Churchill Gardens Museum and Hatton Gallery. Venns Lane, at the top of Aylestone Hill, on the outskirts of town (off the main Worcester rd./A465, a 10-minute walk from the city center). ☎ **01432/267409.** Combination tickets available to see The Old House as well. Admission £1 ($1.60) adults, 60p (95¢) children and seniors over 60. Summer Tues–Sun 2–5pm; winter Tues–Sat 2–5pm.

Located in a large park, the museum boasts collections of fine furniture, costumes, and paintings from the 18th and 19th centuries. The Hatton Gallery is devoted to the work of a local artist, Brian Hatton, who was killed in World War I.

WHERE TO STAY

Castle Pool Hotel. Castle St., Hereford HR1 2NR. ☎ and fax **01432/356321.** 27 units. TV TEL. £58–£70 ($92.80–$112) double. Rates include breakfast. AE, DC, MC, V.

Built in the 19th century as a rectory for the bishop who administered the nearby cathedral, this place is sometimes called "the bishop's palace." Despite that, don't expect anything opulent: The Castle Pool is simply a clean, comfortable, and competent choice at an affordable price. That said, it's still one of the three finest hotels in Hereford, with rooms outfitted with straightforward contemporary furnishings and

matching fabrics. A limited number retain the deep-cove moldings and ornate plasterwork of the building's original grandeur, with rates that vary depending on their
size. There's a somewhat formal cocktail lounge on the premises, and a restaurant that's
recommended below.

The Green Dragon. Broad St., Hereford HR4 9BG. ☎ **01432/272506.** Fax 01432/352139.
83 units. TV TEL. £80 ($128) double. AE, DC, MC, V.

The Green Dragon is the oldest, most historic hotel in Hereford, and quite possibly
the best. In 1857, this attractive inn, situated near the cathedral, had already been in
business for 300 years when the then-owners decided to replace its front with the
stately neoclassical facade you see today. Rooms are scattered over three upper floors,
and have all the high ceilings, thick walls, and squeaky floors you'd expect from an old
treasure like this. Each has reasonably modern furnishings and a tea maker. There's a
cocktail bar on the premises, as well as a rowdier (and more fun) pub, and a restaurant, The Shires, that's recommended below.

Three Counties Hotel. Belmont Rd. (Hwy. A465), Hereford HR2 7XB. ☎ **01432/299955.**
Fax 01432/275114. 60 units. TV TEL. £50–£65 ($80–$104) double. AE, DC, MC, V.

Set a mile south of Hereford's center on the opposite bank of the River Wye, this
Polish-owned hotel has a distinctive hip-roofed, barnlike design that's more common
in central Europe than England. You can't miss its prominent tawny-colored tile roof
from a distance. The hotel caters to business travelers and bus tours. Rooms are monochromatic and modern, nothing fussy. Cozier, woodsier, and more British-looking are
the ground-level cocktail lounges and in-house restaurant.

WHERE TO DINE

The Restaurant at the Castle Pool Hotel. Castle St. ☎ **01432/356321.** Reservations
recommended. Set lunch £8.90 ($14.25); set dinner £15 ($24); main courses £7.95–£12.50
($12.70–$20). AE, DC, MC, V. Daily noon–2pm; Sun–Thurs 7:30–9:30pm, Fri–Sat
7:30–10:30pm. ENGLISH/INTERNATIONAL.

This restaurant is rivaled only by the dining room at the Green Dragon Hotel, with
which it is frequently compared. Set within the severely dignified walls of a 19th-
century bishop's residence, it's decorated in vibrant shades of peach and maroon, and
overlooks a well-planned garden from a modern extension to the original house.
Lunches are straightforward, inexpensive, mostly British affairs (steak and kidney pies
and fisherman's platters). Dinners are more experimental, with selections like chicken
San Remo, spinach Verona, or Polynesian pork satay. The food is well prepared and
more imaginative than what you'll get at almost any other place around.

Shires Restaurant. In The Green Dragon Hotel, Broad St. ☎ **01432/272506.** Main lunch
courses £6.50 ($10.40); main dinner courses £12.95–£16.95 ($20.70–$27.10). AE, DC, MC,
V. Daily 12:30–2pm and 6:45–9:15pm. ENGLISH/FRENCH.

Set within the street level of the town's most historic and prestigious hotel, this restaurant is sheathed with very old paneling, some of it from the 17th century, carved from
Herefordshire oak. Everyone in town considers it the stateliest restaurant around, suitable for formal family celebrations. Main courses at lunchtime are selected from an all-
English carvery table, where a uniformed attendant will carve from roasted joints of
beef, turkey, or ham, garnished with all the traditional fixings. Dinners are more
French in their flavor, and are conducted with as much fanfare as anything else. Menu
items include a pâté of duck meat and wild mushrooms served with a juniper chutney;
fillet of beef with red-wine-and-mushroom sauce; and fillet of salmon with white-wine
sauce and sorrel.

A FAVORITE LOCAL PUB

One of the most consistently popular pubs is the **Orange Tree,** 16 King St. (☎ 01432/267698), attracting beer lovers and tipplers from across the county. There's nothing particularly unusual about this woodsy pub (it's mostly a place to soak up local color), but its beers on tap include Buddington's and a changing roster of ales and lagers sent on spec from local breweries, sometimes as part of local sales promotions.

11 Ludlow

162 miles NW of London; 29 miles S of Shrewsbury

An outpost on the Welsh border during Norman times, this mellow town on the tranquil Teme River is often referred to as "the perfect historic town." Indeed, a tremendous amount of history whispers through its quiet lanes and courts, all lined with Georgian and Jacobean timbered buildings. The two little princes who died in the Tower of London lived here, and it was once the refuge of Henry VIII's first wife, Catherine of Aragon. You can still visit the church where the unhappy queen prayed. The town's most colorful street is the "Broad," which rises from the old Ludford Bridge to Broadgate, the last remains of a wall erected in the Middle Ages. Be sure to visit the Butter Cross and Reader's House, in particular, as well as A. E. Housman's grave in the town cemetery.

ESSENTIALS

GETTING THERE   Trains run hourly from Paddington Station in London to Ludlow, with a transfer at Newport. It's approximately a 3-hour journey. For schedules and information, call ☎ **0345/484950** (in the U.K. only) or 01603/764776.

National Express buses depart London's Victoria Coach Station for Shrewsbury, where you must change to the local line to reach Ludlow. It's a slow, approximately 5½-hour journey, but for those who are still interested, call ☎ **0990/808080** for the current schedule.

By car, it's a much shorter, 3-hour drive. Follow the M25 out of London to the M40 at Oxford. Take the M40 to Bromsgrove. Once at Bromsgrove, follow the M42 until Kidderminster. From here, take A456 to Ludlow.

VISITOR INFORMATION   The **Ludlow Tourist Information Centre,** Castle Street (☎ 01584/875053), is open November to March, Monday to Saturday from 10am to 5pm; from April to October, it is also open on Sunday from 10:30am to 5pm.

SPECIAL EVENTS   The ✪ **Ludlow Festival,** held annually in late June and early July, is one of England's major arts festivals. The centerpiece is an open-air Shakespeare performance within the Inner Bailey of Ludlow Castle. Orchestral concerts, historical lectures, readings, exhibitions, and workshops round out the festival. From March onward, a schedule can be obtained from the box office. Write to The Ludlow Festival box office, Castle Square, Ludlow, Shropshire SY8 1AY, enclosing a self-addressed stamped envelope, or call ☎ **01584/872150.** The box office is open daily beginning in early May.

EXPLORING THE TOWN

Whitcliffe Common was the common land of Ludlow during the Middle Ages. From here, you can enjoy panoramic views of Ludlow as you stroll. Leave town by one of two bridges across the River Teme and follow any of a number of paths through the Common.

A colorful Sunday **flea market** is held on Castle Square on alternate Sundays throughout the year from 9am to approximately 4pm.

In addition, the town is filled with traditional family businesses; of particular interest are the many antique, book, arts-and-crafts, and gift shops. **The Marches Pottery,** 45 Mill St. (☎ 01584/878413), produces a wide selection of hand-thrown tableware and individual pieces decorated with subtle Chinese glazes, including a host of terra-cotta flowerpots.

Lower Hundred Craft Workshop, off A49, 7 miles south of Ludlow (☎ 01584/ 711240), nestled in peaceful country settings, offers a full range of candles, fabric boxes, and pottery. Tea, coffee, and homemade cakes are also available.

Ludlow Castle. Ludlow Town Centre. ☎ 01584/873355. Admission £2.50 ($4) adults, £2 ($3.20) seniors, £1.50 ($2.40) children, £7.50 ($12) family. Jan Sat–Sun only, 10am–4pm; Feb–Apr and Oct–Dec daily 10am to 4pm; May–Sept daily 10am–5pm.

This Norman castle was built around 1094 as a frontier outpost to keep out the as yet unconquered Welsh. The original castle, or the inner bailey, was encircled in the early 14th century by a very large outer bailey and transformed into a medieval palace by Roger Mortimer, the most powerful man in England at the time. After the War of the Roses, the castle was turned into a royal residence, and Edward IV sent the Prince of Wales and his brother (the "Princes in the Tower") to live here in 1472. It was also the seat of government for Wales and the Border Counties. Catherine of Aragon and Mary Tudor and her court also spent time in this 900-year-old home. Norman, Medieval, and Tudor architectural styles can be found throughout the castle. Many of the original buildings still stand, including the Chapel of St. Mary Magdalene, with one of England's last remaining circular naves. Excellent views of the castle can be spied from the banks of the River Teme.

Ludlow Museum. The Assembly Rooms, Castle Sq. ☎ 01584/875384. Admission £1 ($1.60) adults, 50p (80¢) children and seniors. Apr–Oct daily 10:30am–1pm and 2–5pm. Guided tours available.

This museum tells the story of Ludlow town: the construction of its castle 900 years ago, the prosperity gained from wool and agriculture during the Middle Ages, and its rise in political importance. The museum also houses natural-history displays; and the Norton Gallery contains "Reading the Rocks," an exhibit that celebrates Ludlow's unique contribution to international geology. There are several hands-on, interactive displays, including a video microscope that lets you examine geological specimens. Visitors can also try on helmets used in England's civil war. It's a great place for kids.

WHERE TO STAY

Dinham Hall Hotel. Dinham by the Castle, Ludlow, Shropshire SY8 1EJ. ☎ 01584/ 876464. Fax 01584/876019. 14 units. TV TEL. £95–£125 ($152–$200) double. Rates include breakfast. AE, DC, MC, V.

Not to be confused with a less desirable competitor, Ludlow's Dinham Weir Hotel, the Dinham Hall Hotel rises in severe gray-stoned dignity, immediately across the road from Ludlow Castle. Built in 1792, it was constructed by the earl of Mortimer, and served through the 1960s and 1970s as a dormitory for the nearby public boys' school. Many of the comfortable but very simple bedrooms bear the names of that school's former headmasters. Especially popular with participants of Ludlow's annual Shakespeare festival, it offers a kind of Georgian-era, stately ambience, as opposed to the Elizabethan ambience of its major competitor, the Feathers. On the premises is a worthwhile restaurant that offers relatively formal, well-prepared lunches and dinners every day of the year.

The Feathers at Ludlow. Bull Ring, Ludlow, Shropshire SY8 1AA. ☎ **01584/875261.** Fax 01584/876030. 39 units. TV. £80 ($128) double; £108 ($172.80) suite. AE, DC, MC, V.

The New York Times hailed this as "the most handsome inn in the world," and after a glance at its lavishly ornate half-timbered facade, you might agree. Originally built as a private home in 1603 and enlarged many times since, it boasts a winning combination of formal, high-style plasterwork ceilings as well as rustic, Elizabethan-style half-timbering and exposed stone, especially in the pub (the Comus) and restaurant (the Housman). Only the suite and a few of the rooms have exposed Tudor-style beams; the others are traditional and conservative, but without the medieval vestiges of the building's exterior. Nevertheless, each is comfortable, cozy, and well maintained. Some rooms have massive headboards skillfully fashioned from antique overmantels or mirror frames. The hotel's antique conference rooms and its "Olde-Englandy" pub are favorite meeting places for local civic groups.

WHERE TO DINE

Les Marches. In the Overton Grange Hotel, Overton, near Ludlow. ☎ **01584/873500.** Reservations recommended. Lunch main courses £7–£15 ($11.20–$24); set dinner menus £20 ($32). MC, V. Daily noon–2:30pm and 7–9:45pm. MODERN BRITISH/FRENCH.

This is a well-recommended and rather stylish restaurant with an ambitious menu that usually succeeds with flair. The richly oak-paneled dining room, with touches of restful green, evokes the grand age of private dinner parties. Menu items are prepared by Claude Bosi or his assistants, and make straightforward but intelligent use of fresh ingredients. Examples include grilled rib eye of Scottish beef with celeriac tart and tomato confit, roasted red-snapper filet with pot-roasted vegetables and fondant potatoes, and roast wild duck with Gavroche potato and roast onions. The wine list boasts over 250 selections.

✪ **The Merchant House.** Lower Corve St. ☎ **01584/875438.** Reservations required. Set menu £27.50 ($44). AE, MC, V. Fri–Sat noon–2:30pm; Tues–Sat 7–9:30pm. MODERN BRITISH.

The Merchant House is the best restaurant in town. In virtually any other city in the world, much attention and fuss would be made over the half-timbered facade of this late 16th-century building (the former home of a wool merchant), but in Ludlow, it blends right in. Within a half-timbered room where you could imagine Will Shakespeare concocting some of his sonnets, you'll enjoy a view over the River Corve. The only drawbacks are a comparatively small dining room (with seating for only 24) and limited hours.

The creative forces here are Shaun (who prepares the food) and Anja (the Finnish-born manager) Hill, whose cuisine is based on a deep respect for fresh local ingredients. Enjoy roasted venison with celeriac and gnocchi stuffed with fresh goat cheese, a medley of calf's kidneys and sweetbreads in a caper-and-chive sauce, or an artfully arranged chunk of brill surrounded with perfectly prepared vegetables and drizzled with a watercress-and-vermouth sauce. One of the best desserts is a chocolate-flavored *pativier* that elevates an old-fashioned almond tart to chocoholic heaven.

A FAVORITE LOCAL PUB

The town's most atmospheric and evocative pub, **The Church Inn,** Church Street, Buttercross (☎ **01584/872174**), is everybody's favorite source for beer, gossip, and good cheer. Beer, mead, and wine have flowed here since at least 1446 and according to some historians, even earlier. Meals are served daily from noon to 2pm, and Monday to Saturday from 6:30 to 9pm. Whether you eat informally in the bar or head for the more formal restaurant, the food and prices are exactly the same. Main courses range from £5 to £8.50 ($8 to $13.60). Cuisine is straightforward, British, and rib-sticking, with traditional pub grub like steak and kidney pie, fried prawns, and omelettes. The bar is open Monday to Saturday from 11am to 11pm, and Sunday from noon to 2:30pm and 7 to 10:30pm.

12 Shrewsbury

164 miles NW of London; 39 miles SW of Stoke-on-Trent; 48 miles NW of Birmingham

The finest Tudor town in England, Shrewsbury is noted for its black-and-white buildings of timber and plaster, including Abbot's House (dating from 1450), and the tall gabled Ireland's Mansion (ca. 1575) on High Street. These houses were built by the powerful and prosperous wool traders, or drapers. Charles Dickens wrote of his stay in Shrewsbury's Lion Hotel, "I am lodged in the strangest little rooms, the ceilings of which I can touch with my hands. From the windows I can look all downhill and slantwise at the crookedest black-and-white houses, all of many shapes except straight shapes." The town also has a number of Georgian and Regency mansions, some old bridges, and handsome churches, including the Abbey Church of Saint Peter, and St. Mary's Church.

ESSENTIALS

GETTING THERE Shrewsbury-bound trains depart London's Euston Station daily every half hour. There's a change of trains in Birmingham before you arrive in Shrewsbury 3 hours later. For schedules and information, call ☎ **0345/484950** (in the U.K. only) or 01603/764776.

Three **National Express** buses depart daily from London's Victoria Coach Station for the 5-hour trip. For schedules and information, call ☎ **0990/808080.**

By car from London, the drive is 2½ hours; take the M1 to the M6 to the M54 to reach A5, which will take you directly to Shrewsbury.

VISITOR INFORMATION From May 26 to September 30, the **Shrewsbury Tourist Information Centre,** The Square (☎ **01743/350761**), is open from 10am to 6pm Monday to Saturday, and 10am to 4pm Sunday. From October to late May, its hours are 10am to 5pm Monday to Saturday, and 10am to 4pm Sunday. It is closed during the month of April and all bank holidays.

SEEING THE SIGHTS

Many tales and stories are locked within Shrewsbury's winding narrow streets and black-and-white buildings. The best way to learn this local lore is to take one of the many walking or coach tours hosted by official Shrewsbury guides. Special themed walking tours such as Ghosts, Brother Cadfael, and the Civil War are also available. A typical tour starts in the town center and lasts 1½ hours. Tickets can be purchased from the Tourist Information Centre (see above).

Shrewsbury Castle. Castle St. ☎ **01743/358516.** £3 ($4.80) adults, £1.50 ($2.40) students and seniors, £1 ($1.60) children 5–15 (free 4 and under). Tues–Sat 10am–4:30pm; also Sun 10am–4pm Easter–Sept.

Built in 1083 by a Norman earl, Roger de Montgomery, this castle was designed as a powerful fortress to secure the border with Wales. The Great Hall and walls were constructed during the reign of Edward I, but 200 years ago, Thomas Telford extensively remodeled the castle. Today, it houses the Shropshire Regimental Museum, which includes the collections of the King's Shropshire Light Infantry, the Shropshire

Yeomanry, and the Shropshire Royal Horse Artillery. These collections represent more than 300 years of regimental service, and include a lock of Napoléon's hair and an American flag captured during the seizure and burning of the White House during the War of 1812.

Rowley's House Museum. Barker St. ☎ **01743/361196.** Admission £3 ($4.80) adults, £1.50 ($2.40) students and seniors, £1 ($1.60) children. Tues–Sat 10am–5pm, plus Sun 10am–4pm Easter–Sept.

This museum is housed in a fine 16th-century timber-frame warehouse and an adjoining 17th-century brick-and-stone mansion dating from 1618. The museum includes displays on art, local history, Roman and prehistoric archaeology, geology, costumes, and natural history. The great treasures include the Hadrianic forum inscription and silver mirror, both from the nearby Roman city of Viroconium (Wroxeter).

Clive House Museum. College Hill. ☎ **01743/354811.** Admission £3 ($4.80) adults, £1.50 ($2.40) students and seniors, £1 ($1.60) children. Tues–Sat 10am–4pm, plus Sun 10am–4pm Easter–Sept.

This Georgian town house, home to Clive of India when he served as mayor and member of parliament for Shrewsbury in the 1760s, contains period rooms and local pottery and porcelain, early watercolors, and textiles, plus displays on the natural historians of 19th-century Shrewsbury such as Charles Darwin. There is also a secluded walled garden.

Attingham Park. Shrewsbury. ☎ **01743/709203.** House admission £4 ($6.40) adults, £2 ($3.20) children, £10 ($16) families. Park and grounds £1.50 ($2.40) adults, 75p ($1.20) children. House, tearoom, and shop Mar 28–Nov 1 Sat–Wed 1:30–5pm (the tearoom opens an hour earlier for lunch); park and grounds open winter daily 8am–5pm, until 9pm in summer.

This elegant classical house set on 250 acres of woodlands and landscaped deer park is graced with superbly decorated state rooms, including a red dining room and blue drawing room. Treasures of the house include Regency silver used at 19th-century ambassadorial receptions and elegant Italian furniture. A tearoom and gift shop on the grounds make a pleasant stop before or after you've toured the house.

Shrewsbury Abbey. Abbey Foregate. ☎ **01743/232723.** Admission free, but donations requested for the Abbey Fund. Easter–Oct daily 9:30am–5:30pm, Nov–Easter daily 10:30am–3pm.

Founded in 1083, Shrewsbury Abbey became one of the most powerful Benedictine monasteries in England. It's the setting of the Brother Cadfael tales, a series of mysteries written by Ellis Peters that have recently been adapted for television. The church remains in use to this day, and visitors can see displays devoted to the abbey's history as well as the remains of the 14th-century shrine of St. Winefride.

The Shrewsbury Quest. Abbey Foregate. ☎ **01743/243324** or 01743/355990. Admission £3.95 ($6.30) adults, £3.35 ($5.35) seniors and students, £2.95 ($4.70) children under 12. Family ticket £12.60 ($20.15). Apr–Oct daily 10am–5pm; Nov–Mar daily 10am–4pm. Closed Dec 25 and Jan 1.

On the site of the 5-century-old Benedictine Abbey of St. Peter and St. Paul, the world of the medieval monastery comes to life, with busy tradespeople, a great store, sweet sounds of dulcimer, harp, and lute, vespers bells, plus monastic gardens planted with a collection of herbs dating from the 12th century. Visitors can participate in different activities, including making a decorated manuscript in the Scriptorium, solving mysteries like Ellis Peters's Brother Cadfael, and playing ancient games of skill in the Cloisters.

SHOPPING

The narrow, cobbled streets of Shrewsbury host wonderful, small shops in Tudor-fronted buildings, selling everything from secondhand books and art-deco bric-a-brac to geological specimens, musical instruments, and antiques.

St. Julian's Craft Centre, Wyle Cop (☎ 01743/353516), housed in a 12th-century tower, has been the place to purchase high-quality, locally made crafts for over 15 years. Shoppers can see artisans at work in the center of the tower, or browse Saturday craft fairs and art exhibitions, which change every 2 weeks.

The staff at **Mansers Antiques,** 53/54 Wyle Cop (☎ 01743/351120), is always ready to dispense free advice, and offers one of the largest comprehensive stocks of antiques in the United Kingdom. Items for sale include furniture of all periods, silver and plate, china and glass, clocks and metal goods, jewelry, linen, paintings, and Oriental items. There's a restoration department, and the shop will ship purchases.

Carnival Crafts, 26/27 The Parade Shops, St. Mary's Place (☎ 01743/366713), boasts a fun and beautiful assortment of unusual handcrafted gifts from Britain and around the world. Crafts available include African and Balinese carvings, Italian music boxes and ceramics, and unique glass from Britain, Gozo, and Gibraltar.

For secondhand and antiquarian books, head to **Quarry Books** at 24 Clarmemont Hill (☎ 01743/361404); for prints, the **Victorian Gallery** at 40 St. John's Hill (☎ 01743/356351), is the place to go.

WHERE TO STAY

✪ **Albright Hussey Hotel.** Ellesmere Rd., Shrewsbury, Shropshire SY4 3AF. ☎ 01939/290571. Fax 01939/291143. 14 units. TV TEL. £141–£178 ($225.60–$284.80) double. Rates include breakfast and dinner. AE, DC, MC, V. 2½ miles southeast of Shrewsbury along A528.

Its unusual name derives from the feudal family (the Husseys) who occupied it between 1292 and the 1600s. Today, it's one of the best examples of an elaborate Tudor timber frame building in Shrewsbury. The brick-and-stone wing was added around 1560. The interior contains all the old-world charm and eccentricities you could hope for, including oak panels, fireplaces large enough to roast an ox, and a moated garden with several pairs of fiercely territorial black swans. Furnishings tend to date from the early 19th century, and contrast well with the dozens of beams that have been artfully exposed in the ceilings and walls of bedrooms and public areas.

Dining: The owners are Tuscany-born Franco Subbiani and his German/Czech wife, Vera. Together, they produce fine cuisine derived from Italy, France, and England that changes frequently. Dishes might include ravioli with wild mushrooms in a saffron cream sauce, or shredded duck with orange sauce presented in a potato galette on a bed of exotic greens.

The Lion. Wyle Cop, Shrewsbury, Shropshire SY1 1UY. ☎ 01743/353107. Fax 01743/352744. 59 units. TV TEL. £70 ($112) double; £90 ($144) suite. Discounts of £10 ($16) per room Fri–Sun. AE, DC, MC, V.

Housed on the site of a 17th century coaching inn that claims to have origins in the 14th century, this is easily the most evocative hotel in Shrewsbury. The roster of former guests includes Paganini, Jenny Lind, Benjamin Disraeli, and Charles Dickens. Since then, the rooms have been enlarged, and the setting has been lavishly gentrified with lots of patterned chintz and modern amenities. Only the suite contains artfully gnarled oaken beams—other rooms are comfortable but chain-motel modern.

Dining: The pub has all the old England touches you could hope for. A restaurant, The Shires, is open daily from noon to 2pm, and 7 to 9:30pm. There, amid a not particularly antique looking decor, you can order elaborate, if not innovative, dishes such as duck breast with Grand Marnier and oranges.

Prince Rupert Hotel. Butcher Row, Shrewsbury, Shropshire SY1 1UQ. ☎ **01743/499955.** Fax 01743/357306. 65 units. Mon–Thurs £70–£80 ($112–$128) double, Fri–Sun £60 ($96) double; suites £80–£115 ($128–$184) all week long. Rates include breakfast. AE, DC, MC, V.

Its half-timbered Elizabethan core is one of the most historic structures in this very historic town. In the 17th century, it was the home of the Bohemian-born Prince Rupert, nephew to Charles I, who commanded Royalist forces here during the English civil war. In the 1980s, a modern wing, not inconsistent with the architecture of the original design, was added, transforming the site into a large, somewhat conventional chain hotel. Only about half a dozen of the accommodations contain exposed beams from the building's early origins; the others are conservatively modern and somewhat bland. In 1996, the hotel was taken over by independent managers, sophisticated hoteliers in their own right, who upgraded the standards, especially the restaurant. Today, a well-executed cuisine that's roughly 80% British and 20% international is served daily at lunch and dinner. The latest restaurant, Chambers, which opened in 1997, serves both English and continental fare.

WHERE TO DINE

Country Friends. Dorrington (6 miles south of Shrewsbury via A49), Shropshire S45 7JD. ☎ **01743/718707.** Light luncheon platters £5–£9 ($8–$14.40); set menus £27 ($43.20). MC, V. Tues–Sat noon–2pm and 7–9pm. MODERN BRITISH.

Originally built in 1673 as a private home, this pleasant restaurant today boasts a much-restored Tudor facade amid attractive gardens. Inside, a hardworking kitchen concocts modern reinventions of such old-fashioned dishes as lamb noisettes roasted in mustard crust with mint hollandaise and venison with a black-currant sauce. Some aspects of the menu change almost every week, but it usually includes roasted guinea fowl with grapes or roasted duck with bacon on a bed of lentils—both excellent choices. They also feature three bedrooms at a rate of £102 ($163.20) double occupancy, including dinner.

The Peach Tree. 21 Abbey Foregate. ☎ **01743/355055.** Reservations recommended. Main courses £7.95–£13.50 ($12.70–$21.60). AE, MC, V. Tues–Sun 12:30–2pm; Tues–Sat 7–9:30pm. BRITISH/EUROPEAN.

Its name derives from the hundreds of ripe peaches, peach trees, and peach boughs that someone laboriously stenciled onto the walls. The setting dates from the 15th century, when this was a weaver's cottage adjacent to the abbey. The food is based on solid, time-tested recipes made with fresh ingredients and loads of European savoir-faire. It's some of the best in town. Main courses include roasted breast of duck with traditional blackberry-and-red-wine sauce; and such vegetarian main courses as a cashew-and-hazelnut loaf served with an apricot-and-ginger sauce. The dessert that keeps everyone coming back for more is homemade meringue with ice cream, traditional butterscotch sauce, and shreddings of roasted coconut. Although the upstairs restaurant is more fancy, you can have any of the platters informally in the street-level bar if you're alone or in a hurry.

SHREWSBURY AFTER DARK

Quench your thirst or have a bite to eat at the **Lion & Pheasant Hotel** bar, 49–50 Wyle Cop (☎ **01743/236288**), where in colder months, an inviting firelight ambience presides. Or check out the **Boat House Pub,** New Street (☎ **01743/362965**), located beside a beautiful old park on the River Severn. In summer, they open up the terrace overlooking the river, and it becomes a popular date place. Couples enjoy a healthy selection of beers and ales, along with a tasty pub grub that ranges from soup and sandwiches to pies.

The **Buttermarket Nightclub** (☎ 01743/241455), set in the old butter market on Howard Street, caters to the over-25 crowd. It has two theme nights: Saturday (disco) and Thursday (world music).

Other clubs include the **Park Lane Nightclub,** Ravens Meadows (☎ 01743/358786). **The Music Hall,** The Square (☎ 01743/244255), hosts musicals, plays, and concerts year-round. Tickets range from £10 to £20 ($16 to $32).

13 Ironbridge

135 miles NW of London; 36 miles NW of Birmingham; 18 miles SE of Shrewsbury

Ironbridge, located in the Ironbridge Gorge, is famous for kicking off an early stage of the Industrial Revolution. Indeed, this stretch of the Severn River valley has been an important industrial area since the Middle Ages because of its iron and limestone deposits. But the event that clinched this area's importance came in 1709, when the Quaker ironmaster, Abraham Darby I, discovered a method for smelting iron by using coke as a fuel, instead of charcoal. This paved the way for the first iron rails, boats, wheels, aqueducts, and bridge, cast in Coalbrookdale in 1779. So momentous was this accomplishment that the area, originally called Coalbrookdale, was renamed Ironbridge. The area literally buzzed with the new transportation and engineering innovations that soon followed.

Today, you'll find an intriguing complex of museums that documents and brings to life the rich history of Ironbridge Gorge. The gift shops and other stores in town have plenty of unusual souvenirs to help you remember your visit.

ESSENTIALS

GETTING THERE   Seven days a week, trains leave London's Euston Station hourly for Telford Central Station in Telford. From here, take a bus or taxi into Ironbridge. The entire journey takes about 3 hours. For schedules and information, call ☎ 0345/484950 (in the U.K. only) or 01603/764776.

Three buses depart daily from London's Victoria Coach Station, arriving in Telford about 5 hours later. Call ☎ 0990/808080 for more information. Local buses that leave Telford for the 20-minute ride to Ironbridge include nos. 6, 8, 9, and 99.

If you're driving a car from London, take the M1 to the M6 to the M54, which leads directly to Ironbridge.

VISITOR INFORMATION   The **Ironbridge Gorge Tourist Information Centre,** 4 The Wharfage (☎ 01952/432166), is open Monday through Friday from 9am to 5pm and Saturday and Sunday from 10am to 5pm.

EXPLORING THE AREA

The Ironbridge Valley plays host to seven main museums and several smaller ones, collectively called the **Ironbridge Gorge Museums,** Ironbridge, Telford (☎ 01952/43352 on weekdays and 01952/432166 on Saturday and Sunday). These include the **Coalbrookdale Museum,** with its Darby Furnace of iron and sound-and-light display, as well as restored 19th-century homes of the Quaker ironmasters; the **Iron Bridge,** with its original tollhouse; the **Jackfield Tile Museum,** where you can see demonstrations of tile-pressing, decorating, and firing; the **Blists Hill Open Air Museum,** with its re-creation of a 19th-century town; and the **Coalport China Museum.** A passport ticket to all museums in Ironbridge Gorge is £9.30 ($15.20) for adults, £8.50 ($13.60) for seniors, £5.50 ($8.80) for students and children, and £29 ($46.40) for a family of two adults and up to five children. The sites are open September to June daily from 10am to 5pm and July and August daily from 10am to 6pm. The Iron Bridge Tollhouse and Rosehill House are closed from November to March.

There's also some good shopping. You can buy Coalport china at the **Coalport China Museum** and decorative tiles at the **Jackfield Tile Museum.** Another place worth visiting is just beyond the Jackfield Museum. **Maws Craft Workshops** (☎ **01952/883967**) is the site of 25 workshops situated in an old Victorian tile works beside the River Severn. Here you can browse for porcelain dolls, glass sculptures, dollhouses, original and Celtic art, pictures with frames made while you wait, pottery, jewelry, woodcraft, stained glass, hats, and children's clothes. There's also a tearoom on site that's open for lunch and afternoon tea.

WHERE TO STAY

Bridge House. Buildwas, Telford, Shropshire TF8 7BN. ☎ **01952/432105.** 4 units. £52 ($83.20) double. Rates include breakfast. AE, MC, V. Closed for 2 weeks at Christmas.

Set 1½ miles west of Ironbridge, on the outskirts of the hamlet of Buildwas, this ivy-draped, half-timbered building originated in 1620 as a coaching inn. Resident proprietor Janet Hedges will tell you unusual stories about the house, such as the 365 nails (one for every day of the year) that hold together the planks of the front door, or the fact that the building's front porch was removed from the nearby abbey. Rooms are cozy, genteel, and comfortable, sometimes with touches of Edwardian drama (lavishly draped beds, in some cases). Others have exposed beams, and all have creaking floors and uneven walls that testify to the age of the building.

The Valley House. Ironbridge, Telford, Shropshire, 01952. ☎ **01952/432247.** Fax 01952/432308. 35 units. TV TEL. £95 ($152) double. Rates include breakfast. AE, DC, MC, V.

Originally built as a private home around 1750, this riverside inn was enlarged over the years into the sprawling, light-brown brick design you see today. The high-ceilinged interior contains hints of its original grandeur, including a worthwhile restaurant, the Chez Maw (see below). Fifteen of the hotel's rooms lie within the original stable, and are accessible via a glass-roofed courtyard. Although rooms in the main house usually have more panoramic views, many visitors prefer the coziness of the former stables. All rooms are clean and modernized and have coffee makers.

WHERE TO DINE

Restaurant Chez Maw. In The Valley House Hotel. ☎ **01952/432247.** Reservations recommended. Main courses £9–£20 ($14.40–$32); fixed-price menu £19.50 ($31.20). AE, DC, MC, V. Daily noon–2pm and 7–9:30pm. BRITISH.

The name refers to Arthur Maw, long-ago owner of the house, and founder of a nearby factory that produced decorative tiles during the 19th century. Prized examples of his ceramic creations line the reception area and the monumental staircase. Outfitted with crisp napery, Windsor-style chairs, formal draperies, and a high ceiling, the restaurant serves such updated British food as tortellini laced with cream, herbs, and slices of Parma ham; platters of smoked tuna and marinated salmon; and fillets of pork and beef drizzled with sauce made from Shropshire blue cheese.

A FAVORITE LOCAL PUB

A rebuilt Victorian pub complete with a chicken coop in the backyard? Yes, it's the **New Inn,** located within the Blists Hill Museum complex (☎ **01952/586063**). It has atmosphere galore, with its gas lamps, sawdust floors, and knowledgeable and friendly staff sporting vintage Victorian garb. You'll find a goodly selection of ales, hearty, rib-sticking home-cooked meals, and plenty of pub games.

14 Stoke-on-Trent: The Potteries

162 miles NW of London; 46 miles N of Birmingham; 59 miles NW of Leicester; 41 miles S of Manchester

Situated halfway between the Irish and the North seas, Staffordshire is a county of peaceful countryside, rugged moorlands, and Cheshire plains. While there are several charming country inns here, pottery is Staffordshire's real claim to fame. Although it's been created in the area since 2000 B.C., it wasn't until the Romans rolled through in A.D. 46 that the first pottery kiln was set up at Trent Vale. Now it's **Stoke-on-Trent,** a loose confederation of six towns (Tunstall, Burslem, Stoke, Fenton, Longton, and Hanley, the most important town) covering a 7-mile area, that's the real center of the pottery trade. During the Industrial Revolution, the area known collectively as Stoke-on-Trent became the world's leading producer of pottery, and today it's become a tourist attraction.

ESSENTIALS

GETTING THERE   It's a direct train ride of 2 hours to Stoke-on-Trent from London's Euston Station. Trains make hourly departures daily. For schedules and information, call ☎ **0345/484950** (in the U.K. only) or 01603/764776.

Six **National Express** buses leave London's Victoria Coach Station daily for the 4- to 5-hour trip to Stoke. For schedules and information, call ☎ **0990/808080.**

By car from London, drive along the M1 to the M6 to A500 at Junction 15. It will take you 2 to 3 hours by car.

VISITOR INFORMATION   The **Stoke-on-Trent Tourist Information Centre,** Quadrant Road, Hanley, Stoke-on-Trent (☎ **01782/236000**), is open Monday through Saturday from 9:15am to 5:15pm. Here you can pick up a China Experience visitor map, which notes most potteries, shops, and museums in the area.

HISTORY FIRST: TWO WORTHWHILE MUSEUMS

The Potteries Museum and Art Gallery. Bethesda St., Hanley. ☎ **01782/232323.** Admission free. Mon–Sat 10am–5pm, Sun 2–5pm.

Start here for an overview of Stoke-on-Trent history. It houses departments of fine arts, decorative arts, natural history, archaeology, and social history. It also has one of the largest and finest collections of ceramics in the world. It's a great place for training your eyes before exploring the factories and shops of Stoke-on-Trent.

The Gladstone Pottery Museum. Uttoxeter Rd. at Longton. ☎ **01782/319232.** Admission £3.75 ($6) adults, £2.75 ($4.40) seniors and students, £2.25 ($3.60) children. Daily 10am–5pm; last admission at 4pm.

This is the only Victorian pottery factory that has been restored as a museum, with craftspeople providing daily demonstrations in original workshops. Various galleries depict the rise of the Staffordshire pottery industry, tile history, and so on (check out the toilets of all shapes, sizes, colors, and decoration!). Great hands-on opportunities for plate painting, pot throwing, and ornamental flower making.

TOURING & SHOPPING THE POTTERIES

With more than 40 factories in Stoke-on-Trent, you'll need to get in shape for this adventure. All have gift shops and seconds shops on site—in fact, some have several shops, selling everything from fine china dinner services to hand-painted tiles.

Seconds are always a great bargain. They're still high-quality pieces with imperfections that only the professional eye can detect. But don't expect bargains on top-of-the-line pieces. Shops discount their best wares once in a while, but most of the time, prices for first-quality items are the same here as they are in London, elsewhere in England, or in America.

During the big January sales in London, many department stores, including Harrods, truck in seconds from the factories in Stoke, so if you're in London then, you don't have to visit here to bring home a bargain.

Each of the factories we discuss below offers shipping and can help you with your value-added tax (VAT) refund. Expect your purchases to be delivered within 1 to 3 months.

Wedgwood Visitor Centre. Barlaston. ☎ **01782/204218.** Tours £7.25 ($11.60) adults, seniors, students, and children 15 and older. Admission to everything else £3.25 ($5.20) adults; £1.60 ($2.55) seniors, students, and children; £7.95 ($12.70) family ticket (up to 2 adults and 3 children). Factory tours Mon–Thurs at 10am and 2pm; they last 2 hours and must be booked in advance. Centre open Mon–Fri 9am–5pm, Sat 10am–5pm, Sun 10am–4pm. It's easiest to get here by taxi from the Stoke-on-Trent train station, a 6-mile trip that will cost around £6.50 ($10.40). If you're driving from London, head north along the M1 until you reach the M6. Continue north to Junction 14, which becomes the A34. Follow the A34 to Barlaston and follow the signs to Wedgewood.

The visitor center includes a demonstration hall where you can watch clay pots being formed on the potter's wheel, and witness how plates are turned and fired, then painted. Highly skilled potters and decorators are happy to answer your questions. An art gallery and a gift shop showcase samples of factory-made items that also can be purchased. (Note that the prices at this shop are the same as those found elsewhere.) Tours must be booked in advance.

Also located at the Wedgwood Centre, the **Wedgwood Museum** covers 3 centuries of design and features living displays including Josiah Wedgwood's Etruria factory and his Victorian showroom. Other room settings can also be seen at the museum. The Josiah Wedgwood Restaurant is the perfect place to relax with a cup of coffee or a full meal.

Wedgwood seconds, which are available at reduced prices, are not sold at the center but are available at the **Wedgwood Group Factory Shop,** King Street, Fenton (☎ **01782/316161**).

Royal Doulton Pottery Factory. Nile St. Burslem, near Stoke-on-Trent. ☎ **01782/ 292434.** Admission for both tour and Visitor Centre £5.75 ($9.20) adults; £4.75 ($7.60) children ages 10–16, students, and seniors; £17 ($27.20) family tickets. Admission to just Visitor Centre £3 ($4.80) adults; £1 ($1.60) children ages 5–9; £2 ($3.20) children ages 10–16, students, and seniors; £7 ($11.20) family tickets. Tours offered Mon–Thurs 10:30am–1:15pm, Fri 10:30am–1:30pm; they must be booked in advance. Visitor Centre open Mon–Sat 9:30am–5pm, Sun 10am–4pm; shop open Mon–Sat 9am–5:30pm, Sun 10am–4pm. A taxi from the Stoke-on-Trent train station will cost about £3.50 ($5.60). If you're driving from London, follow the M1 north until you reach M6. Take it to Junction 15, which becomes the A500. Follow the brown signs to the factory.

Wear some comfortable shoes if you take the tour here—you'll walk nearly a mile and tackle upwards of 250 steps, but you will see exactly how plates, cups, and figures are made from start to finish. Live demonstrations of how figures are assembled from a mold and decorated are given at the **Visitor Centre,** which also has the world's largest collection of Royal Doulton figures. Next door to the Visitor Centre is the **Minton Fine Art Studio,** where plates and pill boxes are hand-painted and richly decorated with gold before your eyes.

The Gallery Restaurant serves cakes and coffee, light lunches, and afternoon tea. Of course, everything is served on the finest bone china. The gift shop is stocked with a full range of Royal Doulton figures and tableware, featuring a selection of bargains.

John Beswick Studios of Royal Doulton. Gold St., Longton, near Stoke-on-Trent. ☎ **01782/291237.** Factory tours Mon–Thurs at 10:15am and 2pm, Fri at 10:15am and 1:30pm. Tours need to be booked in advance by calling 01782/291770; tour price is £2.50 ($4) adults, £2.25 ($3.60) seniors and children 10 and older; free for children under 10. Shop hours Mon–Fri 9am–4:30pm. The easiest way to get here from the Stoke-on-Trent train station is by taxi, which will run you about £5 ($8). If you're driving from London, follow the M1 north until you reach the M6. Take it to Junction 14, which becomes the A34. Follow the signs.

The staff here has been building a reputation for fine ceramic sculpture since 1896. Most renowned for its authentic studies of horses, birds, and animals, the studio also creates the famed Character and Toby Jugs of Royal Doulton. You may be lucky enough to see Peter Rabbit and other Beatrix Potter figures in the making during a visit. The 1½-hour tour ends in the factory shop.

Spode. Church St., Stoke-on-Trent. ☎ **01782/744011.** Tours Mon–Thurs at 10am and 1:30pm, Fri at 10am. Tours must be booked in advance. Regular factory tour £4 ($6.40) adults; £2.50 ($4) children 12 years and older, students, and seniors. Connoisseur factory tour £6.50 ($10.40) adults; £4.50 ($7.20) children 12 years and older, students, and seniors. Spode Visitor Centre and accompanying sights open Mon–Sat 9am–5pm, Sun 10am–4pm. Admission for Visitor Centre and Museum £2.50 ($4) adults; £1.50 ($2.40) children 5 years and older, students, and seniors; free for children under 5. Spode is a 10-minute walk from the Stoke-on-Trent train station. Head out on Station Rd., making a left on Coveland St. just past the canal. You will be directly behind the building. If you're driving from London, follow the M1 north until you reach M6. Take it north to Junction 15, which becomes the A500. Follow the signs.

The oldest English pottery company still operating on the same site since 1770 and the birthplace of fine bone china, Spode offers regular factory tours lasting approximately 1½ hours and connoisseur tours lasting 2½ hours. In the **Craft Centre,** visitors can also see demonstrations of engraving, lithography, hand painting, printing, and clay casting. An unrivaled collection of Spode's ceramic masterpieces is on display in the **Spode Museum.** The Blue Italian Restaurant cooks up refreshments and lunch—all served on Spode's classic blue tableware, Blue Italian. The Factory Shop sells seconds at reduced prices.

Moorcroft Pottery. West Moorcroft, Sandbach Rd., Burslem, Stoke-on-Trent. ☎ **01782/ 207943.** Factory tours Mon, Wed, and Thurs at 11am and 2pm; Fri at 11am. Tours must be booked in advance; cost is £2.50 ($4) adults, £1.50 ($2.40) seniors and children under 16. Museum and shop open Mon–Fri 10am–5pm, Sat 9:30am–4:30pm. A taxi from the Stoke-on-Trent train station will run about £5 ($8). If you're driving from London, follow the M1 north to the M6. Take it north to Junction 15, which becomes the A500. Follow the signs.

Moorcroft is a welcome change from the world-famous names you've just seen. It was founded in 1898 by William Moorcroft, who produced his own special brand of pottery and was his own exclusive designer until his death in 1945. Decoration is part of the first firing here, giving it a higher quality of color and brilliance than, say, Spode. Today, the design is in the hands of William's son, John, who carries on the personal traditions of the family firm, creating floral designs in bright, clear colors (think of it as the art nouveau of the pottery world). There is much to admire and buy in the factory seconds shop. There is always someone around to explain the various processes and to show you around the museum, with its collections of early Moorcroft.

WHERE TO STAY

George Hotel. Swan Sq., Burslem, Stoke-on-Trent ST6 2AE. ☎ **01782/577544.** Fax 01782/837496. 39 units. TV TEL. £80 ($128) double. AE, DC, MC, V.

This is one of the most upscale, formal, and dignified hotels in town, the kind of place where the mayor might invite some cronies or a businessperson might bring an important client. Built in 1929 of red brick, it rises three floors from the hamlet of Burslem, one of the six villages comprising the Stoke-on-Trent district. Public areas are outfitted with high ceilings, solid, traditional furniture, and large 19th-century oil paintings of the town and region. Rooms are dignified, conservative, and comfortable, and each contains tea-making facilities. The restaurant serves solid and reliable fare.

Haydon House Hotel. 1-9 Haydon St., Basford, Stoke-on-Trent, Staffordshire ST4 6JD. ☎ **01782/711311.** Fax 01782/717470. 30 units. TV TEL. Mon–Thurs £62.50 ($100) double; £120 ($192) suite. Fri–Sun £50 ($80) double; £100 ($160) suite. AE, DC, MC, V.

This imposing, dark-brick, late Victorian house has long been the home of the Machin family, which also acquired a pair of smaller but roughly equivalent houses across the road. They've added a collection of built-in mahogany furniture to the bedrooms, and reconfigured their home and their lives to welcome overnight guests. Today, you'll find many of the original Victorian fittings (paneling, elaborate cove moldings, bay windows, a dignified staircase), an unusual collection of clocks, and many of the modern amenities to make your stay comfortable. A restaurant on the premises serves lunch and dinner, and suites each have efficiently arranged kitchenettes.

Stoke-on-Trent Moat House. Etruria Hall, Festival Way, Etruria, Stoke-on-Trent, Staffordshire ST1 5BQ. ☎ **01782/609988.** Fax 01782/284500. 143 units. TV TEL. £122 ($195.20) double; £155 ($248) suite. AE, DC, MC, V.

Originally built in the 18th century as the home of Josiah Wedgwood, father of the ceramics company that bears his name today, this redbrick house functioned for many years as an administrative office for British Steel. By the time the Queen's Moat House chain bought it in the late 1980s, many of the architectural nuances had been removed, except for the sweeping staircase and a few remnants. The new owners subsequently began the laborious process of enlarging and restoring the premises. The result is a 4-story annex wing—joined to the historic core by a glass-sided corridor—in which the bulk of the accommodations lie. Its redbrick walls more or less match those of the original premises. The result is a modern, chain-style hotel. In spite of this, the place retains a sense of history, which its hardworking staff strives to maintain.

Amenities: On site are two bars and a restaurant, the Viva Brasserie, open daily for lunch and dinner. There's also a heated swimming pool, a health club/gymnasium, and a business center.

WHERE TO DINE

Reagan's. 325 Hartshill Rd., Hartshill. ☎ **01782/634925.** Main courses £5.60–£10.25 ($8.95–$16.40). AE, DC, MC, V. Daily noon–midnight. INTERNATIONAL.

This is one of the most whimsical and fun restaurants in the district. You'll find it 2 miles outside of Stoke, beside the road leading to Newcastle, within a stone-sided cottage built 200 years ago. Peter Harber is the place's creative force. There's a bar (either the Hollywood Bar or the Ivy League Bar, depending on whom you ask) on the ground floor, and a restaurant upstairs. Both are outfitted with American memorabilia that includes framed letters of recognition from the restaurant's namesake (former U.S. president Ronald Reagan). The menu? Stiff drinks, plus eight kinds of burgers, fillet and/or sirloin steaks, half a dozen pastas and pizzas, salads, and daily specials of fish, vegetarian dishes, pork, or lamb, each competently prepared with fresh ingredients.

15 Stafford

142 miles NW of London, 26 miles N of Birmingham, 17 miles S of Stoke-on-Trent

The county town of Staffordshire was the birthplace of Izaak Walton, the British writer and celebrated fisherman. Long famous as a boot-making center, it contains many historic buildings, notably St. Chad's, the town's oldest church; St. Mary's, with its unusual octagonal tower; and the Ancient High House, the largest timber-frame town house in England.

ESSENTIALS

GETTING THERE   To get here from London, take a train from Euston Station for the approximately 2-hour trip. For schedules and information, call ☎ **0345/484950** (in the U.K. only) or 01603/764776.

National Express buses depart London's Victoria Coach Station, arriving about 5 hours later. For schedules and information, call ☎ **0990/808080.**

For the 3-hour car trip, take the M40 to the M6, which leads directly to Stafford.

VISITOR INFORMATION   Visitor information is available from the **Stafford Tourist Information Centre,** located in the Ancient High House, Greengate Street (☎ **01785/240204**). It is open Monday to Friday from 9am to 5pm and Saturday from 10am to 3pm (November to March) and Saturday from 10am to 4pm (April to October).

EXPLORING THE TOWN

Stafford's **shopping** opportunities run the gamut from dusty antiquarian bookshops to upscale, one-of-a-kind galleries. The **Schott Zwiesel Factory Shop,** Drummond Road, Astonfields Industrial Estate (☎ **01785/223166**), is Europe's largest manufacturer of blown crystal glassware. It combines advanced glass technology with the finest quality and design. You can find plain or fine-cut crystal stemware, giftware, and blown decorative crystal.

The Shire Hall Gallery, Market Square (☎ **01785/278345**), housed in the richly restored historic courthouse built in 1798, is an important visual-arts complex that offers a lively program of exhibitions and a craft shop that stocks a wide range of contemporary ceramics, textiles, jewelry, and glass objects. All are chosen for their quality and displayed in original surroundings.

Ancient High House. Greengate St. ☎ **01785/240204.** Admission £1.60 ($2.55) adults; £1 ($1.60) students, children, and seniors; £4 ($6.40) family ticket for 2 adults, 2 children. Year-round Mon–Fri 9am–5pm; Sat 10am–4pm Apr–Oct, 10am–3pm Nov–Mar.

The Ancient High House was built in 1595 and served as living quarters for King Charles I and his nephew Prince Rupert at the start of England's civil war in 1642. The next year, the house was turned into a prison for Royalist officers by the Parliamentarians. Many of the rooms throughout the house have been restored, and each corresponds with an important period in the house's history.

Stafford Castle. Newport Rd. ☎ **01785/257698.** Admission £1.75 ($2.80) adults; £1.10 ($1.75) students, children, and seniors; £4 ($6.40) family ticket for 2 adults, 2 children. May–Sept Tues–Sun 10am–5pm; Oct–Apr Tues–Sun 10am–4pm.

Built on an easily defensible promontory, Stafford Castle began as a timber fortress in A.D. 1100, a scant 40 years after the Norman invasion. Its long history peaked in 1444 when its owner, Humphrey Stafford, became the duke of Buckinghamshire. In the 17th century, during the English civil war, the castle was defended by Lady Isabel but was eventually abandoned and almost entirely destroyed. In 1813, the ruins of the castle were reconstructed in the Gothic Revival style but nonetheless fell into disarray by the middle of this century. The Visitor Centre has the floor plan of a Norman guardhouse from the 12th century, and, along with its collection of artifacts from on-site excavations, is designed to bring to life the tumultuous history of Stafford Castle. Many programs, events, and reenactments are scheduled throughout the year (during winter, torchlight tours of the castle can be arranged for organized groups). The castle also has a 16-bed herb garden and a host of arms and armor that visitors can try on.

Izaak Walton Cottage. Worston Lane. ☎ 01785/760278 Apr–Oct, or 01785/240204 Nov–Mar. Admission £1.60 ($2.55) adults; £1 ($1.60) children, students, and seniors; £4 ($6.40) family ticket for 2 adults, 2 children. Apr–Oct Tues–Sun 11am–4:30pm.

In 1654, after publishing *The Compleat Angler,* Izaak Walton bought a 16th-century, typical mid-Staffordshire cottage that's now open to visitors. To this day, Walton's work is recognized as one of the greatest books on fishing ever written. After a difficult history that's included two fires in the 20th century alone, the cottage has been rethatched and restored to its original condition. A cottage garden and an angling museum can be found on the grounds, too.

WHERE TO STAY

The Garth. Wolverhampton Rd., Moss Pitt, near Stafford ST17 9JR. ☎ **01785/256124.** Fax 01785/255152. 60 units. TV TEL. Mon–Thurs £77 ($123.20) double; Fri–Sun £47 ($75.20) double. Rates include breakfast. AE, DC, MC, V.

This Edwardian-era house enjoys a garden setting in the suburb of Moss Pitt, 2 miles southeast of the center of Stafford. It's been altered and enlarged extensively since the 1950s (the interior was renovated more successfully than the exterior). Additional refurbishments continued in 1992 and 1996. Today, the only authentic vestige of the building's original turn-of-the-century architecture lies within the richly paneled cocktail lounge. The rest of the hotel is attractively traditional, with well-trained service, but with fewer lush reminders of England's Age of Empire than you might have hoped for. Each of the rooms has everything you need to make tea, and stylish draperies worthy of a stately home. There's a restaurant and bar on the premises.

Tillington Hall. Eccleshall Rd., Stafford ST16 1JJ. ☎ **01785/253531.** Fax 01785/259223. 90 units. TV TEL. Mon–Thurs £100 ($160) double; Fri–Sun £83 ($132.80) double. AE, MC, V.

This, along with the Garth, is one of the two best hotels in Stafford, and Tillington Hall lies closer to the town center. Its historic core is a late 19th-century manor house whose severely dignified design was enlarged in the 1980s with a new, brick-built, 3-story wing that contains most of the accommodations. These are comfortable, contemporary rooms like those you'd find in any British chain hotel. It offers an indoor swimming pool, gym, and sauna, as well as a nearby tennis court. Favored by business travelers, the hotel contains its own cocktail lounge and restaurant serving English and international cuisine.

WHERE TO DINE

Spaggos. 13 Bailey St., Woodlings Yard. ☎ **01785/246265.** Reservations recommended. Main courses £6.50–£10.50 ($10.40–$16.80). AE, DC, MC, V. Mon–Sat noon–2pm and 7–10:30pm. ITALIAN.

This place just opened in 1997, in a spot previously occupied by another fine Italian restaurant. Despite the changes since the new owner, Andrew Dean, took over, it's still the best choice in town, providing Mediterranean flair from a white-sided Victorian cottage adjacent to downtown Stafford's only cinema. The menu is a welcome relief from British staples. Pastas include succulent spaghetti marinara, Bolognese, or carbonara. There's also a very popular swordfish with olive oil, coriander, and lime juice. Medallions of beef with balsamic vinegar is a fine choice, as are paupiettes of veal with tomato and red pepper salsa.

PUBS

The Stafford Arms, 43 Railway St. (☎ 01785/253313), tends to be a very happening place, drawing patrons from all walks of life. It always has a fun, friendly feel. The staff is outgoing, serving a fine array of ales, ever-changing microbrewery specials, and good inexpensive grub.

The Malt & Hops, 135 Lichfield Rd. (☎ 01785/258555), is more laid-back than the Stafford Arms, though it attracts an energetic young crowd on weekend nights. It, too, has a wise choice of ales and good food.

16 Lichfield

128 miles NW of London, 16 miles N of Birmingham, 30 miles SE of Stoke-on-Trent

Set near the heartland of the English Midlands, Lichfield, which dates from the 8th century, has escaped excessive industrialization. Visitors can reflect on earlier times while strolling down the medieval streets, complete with a mix of Georgian, Tudor, and Victorian architectural styles. Fans of Samuel Johnson take pilgrimages to this historic city to see where the author of the first important English dictionary was born in 1709. The city is noted for its cathedral, whose three spires are known as "Ladies of the Vale." The half-timbered houses in the vicar's close and the 17th-century bishop's palace have survived a tremendous number of sieges down through the years.

ESSENTIALS

GETTING THERE   A few direct trains leave daily out of London's Euston Station in the early morning and evening. The trip takes about 2½ hours. For schedules and information, call ☎ 0345/484950 (in the U.K. only) or 01603/764776.

To travel here by bus, take the **National Express** from London's Victoria Coach Station to Birmingham, then change to local bus no. 912 to reach Lichfield. Plan on about 4 hours for the bus trip, depending on your connection in Birmingham. (The Birmingham-Lichfield leg takes approximately an hour.) For schedules and information, call ☎ 0990/808080.

If you plan on making the 3-hour drive from London yourself, take the M1 to the M42 to A38.

VISITOR INFORMATION   The **Lichfield Tourist Information Centre,** Donegal House, Bore Street, Lichfield (☎ 01543/252109), provides visitor information Monday through Saturday between 9am and 5pm from September to May; and Monday through Saturday from 9am to 6pm and Sunday 1 to 5pm during the summer months.

SPECIAL EVENTS   In summer, Lichfield District is home to many small but fun events. June brings a jazz and blues festival, a real ale festival with more than 50 different brews to sample, and a folk festival. The Lichfield Festival plus Fringe occurs in July and is a music, arts, and drama extravaganza. Contact the Tourist Information Centre for exact dates.

SEEING THE SIGHTS

The Samuel Johnson Birthplace Museum. Breadmarket St. ☎ 01543/264972. Admission £1.20 ($1.90) adults, 70p ($1.10) children and seniors, £3.20 ($5.10) family ticket (up to

2 adults, 4 children). Feb–Oct Mon–Sun 10:30am–4:30pm, Nov–Jan Mon–Sat 10:30am–4:30pm. Last admission at 4:15pm.

Dedicated to one of England's most gifted writers, this museum occupies the restored house where Dr. Johnson was born in 1709. Johnson wrote poetry, essays, biographies, and, of course, the first important English dictionary. The museum contains tableaux rooms revealing how the house looked in the early 18th century, four floors of exhibits illustrating Johnson's life and work, a bookshop, a reading room, and displays of Johnson's manuscripts and other personal effects.

Heritage Centre & Treasury. In St. Mary's Centre, Breadmarket St. in Market Square. ☎ 01543/256611. Across the street from Dr. Johnson's Birthplace Museum stands the Heritage Centre & Treasury. Admission £1.30 ($2.10) adults; 80p ($1.30) children, seniors, and students; £3.30 ($5.30) family ticket. Viewing platform admission £1 ($1.60) adults, 80p ($1.30) children over 10, students, and seniors. Daily 10am–5pm (last admission at 4:15pm).

The former parish church, which still maintains the Dyott Chapel for worship, has been transformed into a treasury and exhibition room with a coffee shop and a gift shop. And the best panoramic views of the town can be seen from the 40-meter (44-yd.) viewing platforms in the spire of St. Mary's Centre.

Guildhall. Bore St. ☎ 01543/250011. Admission 30p (50¢) adults, 20p (30¢) seniors and children. Dungeons open June to mid-Sept on Sat 10am–4pm.

Just behind the Heritage Centre is the Victorian Gothic Guildhall. Rebuilt in 1846, this former meeting place of the city council is actually constructed over the medieval city dungeons where it is reported that a man was imprisoned for 12 years for counterfeiting a sixpence. Many of its prisoners were burned at the stake in Market Square.

Lichfield Cathedral. The Old Registry, The Close. ☎ 01543/306240. Free admission. Cathedral daily 7:45am–5:30pm; Visitors Study Centre June–Sept daily 7:45am–5:30pm.

The west front end of Lichfield Cathedral was built around 1280. The entire cathedral received heavy damage during the civil war but was restored in the 1660s and later in the 1800s. Thanks to the careful restoration, its three spires, known as the "Ladies of the Vale," can still be seen from miles around, with its tallest spire rising more than 250 feet. The cathedral's many treasures include the illuminated manuscript known as "the Lichfield Gospels"; Sir Francis Chantrey's famous sculpture *The Sleeping Children;* 16th-century Flemish glass in the Lady Chapel; and a High Victorian pulpit and chancel screen by Gilbert Scott and Francis Skidmore.

WHERE TO STAY

Little Barrow Hotel. Beacon St., Lichfield, Staffordshire WS13 7AR. ☎ 01543/414500. Fax 01543/415734. 25 units. TV TEL. £60 ($96) double. Family room £60–£70 ($96–$112). AE, MC, V.

This place was enlarged and improved so frequently during its lifetime that the exterior today includes everything from half-timbering to relatively modern stucco. This is the largest hotel in Lichfield, and its interior seems like a personalized version of a modern, upscale chain hotel run by a well-trained staff. Bedrooms are warm, clean, and cozy, each with an electric kettle and tea. There's a cocktail lounge and a restaurant.

The Swan Hotel. Bird St., Lichfield, Staffordshire WS13 6PT. ☎ 01543/414777. Fax 01543/411277. 19 units. TV TEL. Mon–Thurs £64.50 ($103.20) double; Fri–Sun £52.50 ($84) double. AE, DC, MC, V.

This place has thrived since the 1700s, partly because of its location near the cathedral and its rustic warmth. The heart and soul of the place is its old-fashioned pub, where ceiling beams and evocatively battered oaken panels frame a busy scene where half a dozen ales and lagers are available on tap, and simple platters of conventional but filling food are served every day at lunch. Eleven of the bedrooms lie within the main building, and in most cases come with all the dark woodwork, ceiling beams, and old-fashioned charm you'd expect. Another eight rooms, in a 1970s-era annex, are comfortable but have a chain-hotel appearance. The staff is helpful and cheery.

WHERE TO DINE

Champs-Élysées. Minster House, Pool Walk. ☎ **01543/253788.** Reservations recommended. Fixed-price lunch £8.95 ($14.30); fixed-price dinner £12.95 ($20.70). Main courses £14.75–£19.45 ($23.60–$31.10). AE, MC, V. Daily 12:30–2pm; Mon-Sat 7:30–9:30pm. FRENCH.

Firmly committed to preparing fine French food, this restaurant occupies two floors of a house built around 1760. The setting offers a collection of photographs of Paris in the late 19th century, and the service is provided by a crew that's familiar with the language and customs that prevail on the opposite side of *La Manche*. Menu items include chicken stuffed with crabmeat, served on a bed of lobster bisque; king prawns in a brandy cream and garlic sauce; and a mousse of smoked fish.

Oakleigh House. 25 Chad's Rd. ☎ **01543/262688.** Reservations recommended. Main courses £7.50–£18 ($12–$28.80); set dinner menus £14.75 ($23.60). MC, V. Daily noon–2pm and 7–9:15pm. INTERNATIONAL.

This place provides warmth, whimsy, and well-prepared food that's less expensive than you might think, considering its quality and finesse. Menu items change according to the seasonality of the ingredients and the inspiration of the chef, but might include panfried noisettes of lamb with apricots and roasted almonds, served with a reduction of red currants and port; and the chef's signature version of salmon inlaid with scallops and watercress mousse and set on a fish glaze. Vegetarian choices are always available. Everyone's favorite dessert is an old-fashioned version of English spotted dick with *sauce anglaise*. Look forward to a drink in the bar before your meal, beneath the house's most unusual ceiling, where co-owner Andrew Usher mixes drinks and carries on conversations.

PUBS

The King's Head, Bird Street (☎ **01543/256822**), saw quite a bit of action during the English civil war and has no problem still attracting a noisy, animated, and frenetic crowd. In a 15th-century coaching inn decorated with military memorabilia, the town's under-25 crowd enjoys live music, reasonable ales, good food, and a disco on Friday, Saturday, and Sunday.

    The Shoulder of Mouton, London Road (☎ **01543/263279**), has been recently renovated and has a more relaxed atmosphere and an older crowd than the King's Head. This is a friendly place filled with lots of big comfy chairs just perfect for listening to its Monday-evening live jazz sessions. Traditional pub-style food and drink are available.

    One of the town's most cheerful and comfortably old-fashioned pubs is in the **Swan Hotel,** Bird Street (☎ **01543/414777**). Its interior hasn't changed much since the days of Charles Dickens. Ales on tap (management refers to them as "cask ales") and lagers are served along with pub-style lunches, really simple platters of British staples. *Dance alert:* Disco isn't dead, at least not in Lichfield. Every Friday and Saturday night, from 8pm till the 11pm closing, the site is transformed into a disco. The only cover charge you'll pay is the purchase of a pint.

    Where to wander next? Try the **Pig & Truffle Bar & Bistro,** Tamworth Street (☎ **01543/262312**), where diners and drinkers alike congregate in a wood-paneled, stone-trimmed setting for burgers, stuffed jacket potatoes, and baguettes. Lunches are served daily from noon to 2:30pm, dinner only Monday to Thursday from 6 to 9pm.

17 Tutbury

132 miles NW of London, 33 miles N of Birmingham, 27 miles SE of Stoke-on-Trent

Once a stronghold of the Anglo-Saxon kings of Mercia, and mentioned in the *Domesday Book,* Tutbury is a small town on the Dove River that lies 4 miles north of Burton-upon-Trent. Over the centuries, this town has borne more than its fair share of violent history. It has been scarred by the armies of Parliamentarians, Royalists, Welsh mercenaries, and marauding Danes. Some of the most famous figures in English history have placed their mark on Tutbury, too, including Ethelred I, John of Gaunt, King John, Henry II and his Queen Eleanor, Henry IV and Henry V, Mary Queen of Scots, James I, Charles I, and even Queen Elizabeth II. It also has a fine Norman church and the ruins of Tutbury Castle.

ESSENTIALS

GETTING THERE   There are no direct trains from London to Tutbury. All the London trains arrive in the nearby town of Burton-upon-Trent. And you'll need to take a 15-minute bus ride to complete the trip to Tutbury. Trains depart from two London stations daily. If you leave from Euston Station, you'll have to change in Birmingham. From St. Pancras Station, the change is in Derby. Either way, the train trip takes about 3 hours. For schedules and information, call ☎ **0345/484950** (in the U.K. only) or 01603/764776.

National Express buses depart daily from London's Victoria Coach Station for nearby Burton-upon-Trent. The ride takes about 5 hours. For schedules and information, call ☎ **0990/808080.** Once in Burton-upon-Trent, local buses no. 401 and no. 83 will take you to Tutbury. Again, this is about a 15-minute ride.

You can drive from London to Tutbury in approximately 3 hours by taking the M1 to A50.

VISITOR INFORMATION   For visitor information on Tutbury, contact the **Burton-upon-Trent Tourist Information Centre,** New Street, Burton-upon-Trent (☎ **01283/516609**). It is open year-round Monday through Friday from 10am to 5:30pm and Saturday from 10am to 4pm.

WHAT TO SEE & DO

Tutbury is an important center for glassblowing and a virtual treasure trove of crystal glassware. Both **Tutbury Crystal,** Burton Street (☎ **01283/813281**), and **Georgian Crystal,** Silk Mill Lane (☎ **01283/814534**), specialize in full lead-crystal manufacturing and have factory shops. There is also any number of crystal shops in town that complement the factory shops by offering their own unique items. For a shop specializing in hand-cut crystal, visit **The Crystal Studio,** 22 High St. (☎ **01283/520917**).

Tutbury Castle. ☎ **01283/812123.** Admission £2 ($3.20) adults; £1 ($1.60) students, children, and seniors. Good Friday to Sept Mon–Wed 10am–5:30pm, Sat noon–6pm, Sun 10am–6pm.

Built in a motte-and-bailey style, Tutbury Castle has a chapel that dates from the 12th century, even if most of its remaining structures are from the 15th century. Mary Queen of Scots was imprisoned here from 1569 to 1585, before she left for Fotheringhay and eventual execution.

Priory Church of Saint Mary the Virgin. ☎ **01283/813127.** Admission free. Not open regularly, but appointments to see the church can be made in advance by contacting the vicar.

Originally built in 1089, the church was almost completely destroyed during the Reformation. Only the west door remained intact. This famous west front is 14 feet high and 9 feet wide and is set in a series of six receding arches and a square table. The size of this church attests to the fact that it was truly important during Norman times. It has a noteworthy Norman nave and unique quatrefoil pillars. Note the lectern that was carved from one piece of bog oak that is at least 6,000 years old.

WHERE TO STAY & DINE

✪ **Ye Olde Dog & Partridge.** High St., Tutbury (near Burton-upon-Trent), Staffordshire DE13 9LS. ☎ **01283/813030.** Fax 01283/813178. 17 units. MINIBAR TV TEL. Mon–Thurs £75–£90 ($120–$144), Fri–Sun £60–£90 ($96–$144) double. Rates include breakfast. AE, MC, V.

Set within a pair of side-by-side 15th-century buildings on Tutbury's main street, this is one of the most evocative and historic inns in the west of England. It's been wining and dining guests since the outbreak of the Wars of the Roses, and became a coaching inn servicing the busy traffic between Liverpool and London in the 18th and 19th centuries. Rooms have been upgraded to contemporary standards of elegance, with wall-to-wall carpets, and, in many cases, deep cove moldings. Only three of them (nos. 31, 32, and 33; all within the hotel's Tudor-era main core), are accented with the building's original heavy beams. The remainder are within the Georgian-style house next door, and have a pleasant mixture of 19th-century styles, always with dignified copies of 18th-century antiques and patterned draperies. Notice the wonderful sinuous staircase that winds upward from the ground floor of the hotel's annex.

Dining/Diversions: There's a pub and a slightly more formal cocktail lounge, and a carvery-style restaurant where, amid polished brass and copper and the music of a resident pianist, you can enjoy the English country life along with as many as 150 other diners. Menu items include platters of venison sausage, roast beef, ham, and turkey; lamb with wine or mint sauce; roasted pheasant in season; and Dover sole with lemon-butter sauce.

14 Cambridge & East Anglia

The four essentially bucolic counties of East Anglia (Essex, Suffolk, Norfolk, and Cambridgeshire) were an ancient Anglo-Saxon kingdom dominated by the Danes. In part, it's a land of heaths, fens, marshes, and inland lagoons known as "broads." Many old villages and market towns abound, and bird watchers, anglers, walkers, and cyclists are all drawn to the area.

Suffolk and Essex are Constable Country, and boast some of England's finest landscapes. (The little village of Thaxted makes a good base for exploring Essex. Either Long Melford or Lavenham are the most idyllic centers for exploring Suffolk.)

Many visitors drive through Essex on the way to Cambridge. Even though it's close to London and is itself industrialized in places, this land of rolling fields has rural areas and villages, many on the seaside. Essex stretches east to the English Channel, where its major city, Colchester, is known for oysters and roses. Fifty miles from London, Colchester was the first Roman city in Britain and is the oldest recorded town in the kingdom.

Since Colchester is not on the route of most visitors, we have focused instead on tiny villages in the western part of Essex, such as Thaxted, which is just south of Cambridge, and easily explored on your way there from London.

The easternmost county of England, Suffolk is a refuge for artists, just as it was in the day of its famous native sons, Constable and Gainsborough, who preserved its landscapes on canvas. Although a fast train can whisk visitors from London to East Suffolk in approximately 1½ hours, its fishing villages, historic homes, and national monuments remain off the beaten track for most tourists. To capture the true charm of Suffolk, you must explore its little market towns and villages. Beginning at the Essex border, we'll head toward the North Sea, highlighting the most scenic villages as we move eastward across the shire.

Seat of the dukes of Norfolk, Norwich is less popular, but those who do venture toward the North Sea will be rewarded with some of England's most beautiful scenery. An occasional dike or windmill makes you think you're in the Netherlands. From here you can branch out and visit the "Broads."

The resort town of Wroxham, capital of the Broads, is easily reached from Norwich, only 8 miles to the northeast. Motorboats regularly take parties on short trips from Wroxham. Some of the best

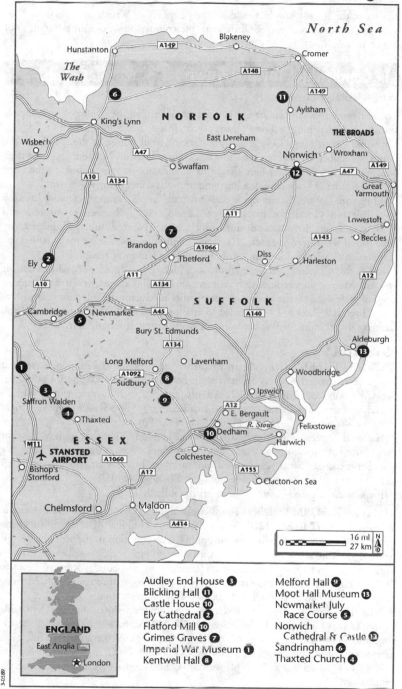

East Anglia

North Sea

Blakeney

Hunstanton

The Wash

A149

Cromer

A148

6

A149

11

Aylsham

King's Lynn

N O R F O L K

Wisbech

East Dereham

THE BROADS

Norwich

Wroxham

A47

Swaffam

12

A47

A149

A10

A134

Great Yarmouth

Lowestoft

A11

A143

Beccles

Ely

2

Brandon

7

Diss

Harleston

A10

A1066

Thetford

A12

A11

A134

Cambridge

S U F F O L K

A45

Newmarket

5

A140

Aldeburgh

Bury St. Edmunds

13

A134

Long Melford

Lavenham

Woodbridge

A1092

8

Sudbury

9

Ipswich

1

A12

Felixstowe

3

E. Bergault

R. Stour

Saffron Walden

10

Dedham

Harwich

4

Thaxted

Colchester

M11

E S S E X

STANSTED AIRPORT

A1060

A135

Bishop's Stortford

A12

Clacton-on Sea

Chelmsford

Maldon

A414

0   16 ml
     27 km

N

ENGLAND

East Anglia

★ London

Audley End House **3**
Blickling Hall **11**
Castle House **10**
Ely Cathedral **2**
Flatford Mill **10**
Grimes Graves **7**
Imperial War Museum **1**
Kentwell Hall **8**

Melford Hall **9**
Moot Hall Museum **13**
Newmarket July Race Course **5**
Norwich Cathedral & Castle **12**
Sandringham **6**
Thaxted Church **4**

3-0589

scenery of the Broads is to be found on the periphery of Wroxham. Also from Norwich you can make a trip to Sandringham, the country home of four generations of British monarchs.

1 Cambridge: Town & Gown

55 miles N of London; 80 miles NE of Oxford

The university town of Cambridge is a collage of images: the Bridge of Sighs; spires and turrets; drooping willows; dusty secondhand bookshops; carol-singing on Christmas Eve in King's College Chapel; dancing until sunrise at the May balls; the sound of Elizabethan madrigals; narrow lanes where Darwin, Newton, and Cromwell once walked; the "Backs," where the lawns of the colleges sweep down to the Cam River; the tattered black robe of a hurrying upperclassman flying in the wind.

Along with Oxford, Cambridge is one of Britain's ancient seats of learning. In many ways their stories are similar, particularly the age-old conflict between town and gown. As far as the locals are concerned, alumni such as Isaac Newton, John Milton, and Virginia Woolf aren't from yesterday. Cambridge continues to graduate many famed scientists such as Stephen Hawking, author of *A Brief History of Time.*

In the '90s Cambridge became known as a high-tech outpost, or "a silicon fen," if you will. More and more high-tech ventures are installing themselves here to produce new software—thousands of start-up companies producing $3 billion a year in revenues. Even Bill Gates in 1997 decided to finance an $80 million research center here, claiming that Cambridge was becoming "a world center of advanced technology."

ESSENTIALS

GETTING THERE Trains depart frequently from London's Liverpool Street and King's Cross stations, arriving an hour later. For inquiries, call ☎ **0345/484950** (in the U.K. only) or 01603/764777. An off-peak, same-day round-trip is £13.20 ($21.10). A peak-time, same-day round-trip is £15.60 ($24.95). An off-peak, longer stay round-trip (up to 5-day period) is £17.80 ($28.50).

National Express buses run hourly between London's Victoria Coach Station for the 2-hour trip to Drummer Street Station in Cambridge. A one-way or same-day round-trip costs £7.50 ($12). If you'd like to return in a day or two the cost is £9 ($14.40). For schedules and information, call ☎ **0990/808080.**

If you're driving from London, head north on the M11.

VISITOR INFORMATION The **Cambridge Tourist Information Centre,** Wheeler Street (☎ **01223/322640**), is in back of the Guildhall. The center has a wide range of information, including data on public transportation in the area and on different sightseeing attractions. It's open April through June and September, Monday to Friday from 9am to 6pm, Saturday from 9am to 5pm, and Sunday from 10:30am to 3:30pm; July and August, daily from 9am to 7pm; October through March, Monday to Friday from 9am to 5:30pm and Saturday from 9am to 5pm.

A tourist reception center for Cambridge and Cambridgeshire is operated by **Guide Friday Ltd.** at Cambridge Railway Station (☎ **01223/362444**). The center, on the concourse of the railway station, sells brochures and maps. Also available is a full range of tourist services, including accommodations booking. Open in summer daily from 9:30am to 6pm (closes at 3pm off-season). Guided tours of Cambridge leave the center daily.

GETTING AROUND The center of Cambridge is made for pedestrians, so leave your car at one of the many car parks (they get more expensive as you approach the city center) and stroll to some of the colleges spread throughout the city. Follow the

Cambridge

0 — .4 km / .25 mi N

To Ely →

Victoria Rd.

Chesterton Rd.

River Cam

JESUS GREEN

To Bedford ←

Castle St.

Chesterton Lane

Northampton St.

Magdalen St.

Park Parade

Portugal Pl.

Park St.

MIDSUMMER COMMON

BUTTS GREEN

Victoria Ave.

To → Newmarket

Fitzroy St.

Round Church St.

St. John's St.

Jesus Lane

Malcolm St.

King St.

Green St.

CHRISTS PIECES

New Sq.

Eden St.

City Rd.

Sidney St.

Hobson St.

"The Backs"

River Cam

Queen's Rd.

Trinity St.

Market Hill

Petty Curry

St. Andrews St.

Emmanuel Rd.

Clarendon St.

Benet St.

Corn Exchange St.

Emmanuel St.

Drummer St.

Parker St.

Downing St.

Downing Pl.

Park Terrace

Parkside

PARKERS PIECE

Gonville Pl.

East Rd.

Mill Rd.

West Rd.

Pembroke St.

Kings Parade

Silver St.

Mill Lane

Little St. Mary's Lane

Trumpington St.

Regent St.

Sidgwick Ave.

THE FEN

SHEEPS GREEN

BOTANIC GARDENS

Tennis Court Rd.

Hills Rd.

Harvey Rd.

Cresham Rd.

Newnham Rd.

The Fen

Causeway

Lensfield Rd.

To London ↓

To Colchester ↓

Information ⓘ

The Bridge of Sighs ⑩
British Rail Station ㉙
Bus Station ⑬
Christ's College ⑫
Clare College ⑲
Corpus Christi College ㉔
Downing College ㉘
Emmanuel College ⑮
Fitzwilliam Museum ㉗
Folk Museum ③
General Post Office ⑯

Gonville & Caius College ⑪
Great St. Mary ⑭
Jesus College ⑥
King's College ⑱
Magdalene College ④
Newnham College ㉓
Pembroke College ㉕
Peterhouse College ㉖
Punts ⑤
Queen's College ㉑

St. Catharine's College ⑳
St. John's College ⑧
Selwyn College ㉒
Sidney Sussex College ⑦
Swimming Pool ①
Tourist Information Office ⑰
Trinity College ⑨
Westminster College ②

3-0430

531

courtyards through to the "Backs" (the college lawns) and walk through to Trinity (where Prince Charles studied) and St. John's Colleges, including the Bridge of Sighs.

Next to walking, the most popular way of getting around is bicycling. **Geoff's Bike Hire,** 65 Devonshire Rd. (☎ 01223/365629), has bicycles for rent for £4 ($6.40) for 3 hours, £6 ($9.60) per day, or £15 ($24) per week. A deposit of £25 ($40) is required. Open daily in summer from 9am to 6pm; off-season Monday to Saturday from 9am to 5:30pm. Geoff's also operates tours by bike (see below).

Stagecoach Cambus, 100 Cowley Rd. (☎ 01223/423554), services the Cambridge area with a network of buses, with fares ranging in price from 50p (80¢) to £1.60 ($2.55). The local tourist office has bus schedules.

SPECIAL EVENTS   Cambridge has an artistic bent that comes to a head from June 25 to July 25 during **Camfest** (☎ 01223/359547), a visual and performing arts festival. Event tickets are generally between £3.50 and £7 ($5.60 and $11.20).

ORGANIZED TOURS

A good person to know if you're in the Cambridge area is Mrs. Isobel Bryant, who operates **Heritage Tours** from her 200-year-old home, Manor Cottage, Swaffham Prior CB5 0JZ (☎ 01638/741440). An expert on the region, she will arrange small tours starting from your hotel or Cambridge railway station to Lavenham, with its thatched and timbered houses, to the fine medieval churches of the Suffolk villages, to Ely Cathedral, or to one of the nearby grand mansions with their many treasures. The charge of £100 ($160) is for the day for up to three people, or £110 ($176) for four passengers and all travel expenses, including the service of the driver-guide. Lunch in a village pub and admission fees add £3 to £6 ($4.80 to $9.60) per person.

Mrs. Bryant also offers walking tours around the Cambridge colleges; they cost £35 ($56) for a family-size party and last about 2 hours. A day tour takes in Cambridge, then a country tour, pub lunch, and visits of interest in the area. The total cost of £100 ($160) covers all travel and driver-guide for up to four persons.

For an informative spin on Cambridge, join in on one of the **Guided Walking Tours** given by a Cambridge Blue Badge Guide (☎ 01223/322640). Two-hour walking tours leave the Tourist Information Centre (see above) and wind through the streets of historic Cambridge, visiting at least one of the colleges and the famous "Backs." From mid-June through August, drama tours are conducted during which participants may see various costumed characters walk in and out of the tour. Henry VIII, Queen Elizabeth I, Isaac Newton, and others help to breathe life into the history of Cambridge during the drama tours. Regular tours are given April through mid-June, daily at 11:30am and 1:30pm; mid-June through September, daily at 10:30am, 11:30am, 1:30pm, and 2:30pm; October through March, daily at 1:30pm and Saturday at 11:30am. Drama tours are offered mid-June through August, daily at 6:30pm. Admission for regular tours is £5.75 ($9.20) per person and for drama tours is £3.90 ($6.25) per person.

In addition to its visitor information services (see "Essentials," above), **Guide Friday Ltd.,** on the concourse of Cambridge Railway Station (☎ 01223/362444), has daily guided tours of Cambridge via open-top, double-decker buses. In summer, they depart every 30 minutes from 9:45am to 2:45pm. Departures are curtailed off-season depending on demand. The tour can be a 1-hour ride, or you can get off at any of the many stops and rejoin the tour whenever you wish. Tickets are valid all day. The fare is £7.50 ($12) for adults, £6.50 ($10.40) for senior citizens and students, £2 ($3.20) for children 5 to 12, and free for kids 4 and under. Office hours are daily 9:30am to 3pm.

Geoff's Bike Hire, 65 Devonshire Rd. (☎ **01223/365629**), has guided bicycle tours on Tuesday, Wednesday, Thursday, and Saturday at 2:30pm. A 10:30am tour on Saturday is also offered. These cost £7.50 ($12) including bike rental. Or you can just rent a bike, which is £6 ($9.60).

EXPLORING THE UNIVERSITY

Oxford University predates Cambridge, but by the early 13th century, scholars began coming here, too. Eventually, Cambridge won partial recognition from Henry III, rising or falling with the approval of subsequent English monarchs. Cambridge consists of 31 colleges for both men and women. Colleges are closed for exams from mid-April until the end of June.

A word of warning: Unfortunately, because of the disturbances caused by the influx of tourists, Cambridge has had to limit visitors, or even exclude them altogether, from various parts of the university. In some cases, a small entry fee will be charged. Small groups of up to six people are generally admitted with no problem, and you can inquire with the local tourist office about visiting hours (see above). All colleges are closed during exams and graduation, on Easter and all bank holidays, and at other times without notice.

The following is only a sample of some of the more interesting colleges.

✪ **KING'S COLLEGE**   The adolescent Henry VI founded King's College on King's Parade (☎ **01223/331212**) in 1441. Most of its buildings today are from the 19th century, but its crowning glory, the Perpendicular **King's College Chapel,** dates from the Middle Ages and is one of England's architectural gems. Henry James called the chapel "the most beautiful in England." Its most characteristic features are the magnificent fan vaulting, all of stone, and the great windows, most of which were fashioned by Flemish artisans between 1517 and 1531. The stained glass portrays biblical scenes, in hues of red, blue, and amber. The chapel also houses Rubens's *The Adoration of the Magi.* The rood screen is from the early 16th century.

The chapel is open during vacation time, Monday to Saturday from 9:30am to 4:30pm, and on Sunday from 10am to 4:30pm. During the term, the public is welcome to attend choral services Tuesday to Saturday at 5:30pm and on Sunday at 10:30am and 3:30pm. During the term, the chapel is open to visitors Monday to Saturday from 9:30am to 3:15pm and on Sunday from 1:15 to 2:15pm and 5 to 5:30pm; it is closed December 23 to January 1. It may be closed at other times for recording sessions, broadcasts, and concerts.

There is an exhibition in the seven northern side chapels showing why and how the chapel was built. Admission to the college and chapel, including the exhibition, is £3 ($4.80) for adults, £2 ($3.20) for students and children 12 to 17, and free for children under 12.

PETERHOUSE   This college, on Trumpington Street (☎ **01223/338200**), is the oldest Cambridge college, founded in 1284 by Hugh de Balsham, the bishop of Ely. Of the original buildings, only the hall remains, but this was restored in the 19th century and now boasts stained-glass windows by William Morris. Old Court, constructed in the 15th century, was renovated in 1754; the chapel dates from 1632. Ask permission to enter at the porter's lodge.

TRINITY COLLEGE   On Trinity Street, Trinity College (not to be confused with Trinity Hall) is the largest college in Cambridge. It was founded in 1546 by Henry VIII, who consolidated a number of smaller colleges that had existed on the site. The courtyard is the most spacious in Cambridge, built when Thomas Nevile was master.

Punting on the Cam

Punting on the River Cam in a wood-built, flat-bottomed boat (which looks somewhat like a Venetian gondola) is a traditional pursuit of students and visitors to Cambridge. Downstream, you pass along the ivy-covered "Backs" of the colleges, their lush gardens sweeping down to the Cam.

People sprawled along the banks of the Cam on a summer day wait to judge and tease you as you maneuver your punt with a pole about 15 feet long. The river's floor is muddy, and many a student has lost his pole in the riverbed shaded by the willows. If your pole gets stuck, it's better to leave it sticking in the mud instead of risking a plunge into the river.

About 2 miles upriver lies Grantchester, immortalized by Rupert Brooke. Literary types flock to Grantchester, which can be reached by punting or by taking the path following the River Granta for less than an hour to Grantchester Meadows (the town lies about a mile from the meadows). When the town clock stopped for repairs in 1985, its hands were left frozen "for all time" at 10 minutes to 3, in honor of Brooke's famed sonnet "The Soldier."

After so much activity, you're bound to get hungry or thirsty, so head to **The Green Man,** 59 High St. (☎ **01223/841178**), a 400-year-old inn named in honor of Robin Hood, where a crackling fire warms you in cold weather and summer features a back beer garden, leading off toward the river, where your punt is waiting to take you back to Cambridge.

Scudamore's Boatyards, Granta Place (☎ **01223/575431**), by the Anchor Pub, has been in business since 1910. Punts and rowboats rent for £10 ($16) per hour. A £40 ($64) cash or credit-card deposit is required. There is a maximum of six persons per punt. They are open from March to late September or October daily from 9am until dusk, depending on the weather and number of clients. You may prefer a chauffeur, in which case there is a minimum cost of £20 ($32) for two people and £5 ($8) per person after that.

The **Cambridge Punt Company,** working out of The Anchor Pub, Silver Street (☎ **01223/327280**), is well recommended for its 45-minute punt tours. A guide (usually a Cambridge student) appropriately dressed in a straw boater hat will both punt and give running commentary to groups of between one and six persons. Tours cost a minimum of £20 ($32) for two and £5 ($8) per each extra adult, and £2.50 ($4) for children 5 to 12. Kids 4 and under ride free. The Anchor Pub's service staff can call a guide over to your table. If you want to row yourself along the Cam, "unchauffeured" boats rent for £10 ($16) per hour. The company is open daily from 9am to dusk, although everyone packs up and goes home if it rains or if the winds get too high.

Sir Christopher Wren designed the library. For entry to the college, apply at the porter's lodge, or call ☎ **01223/338400** for information. There is a charge of £1.50 ($2.40) from March to May 4 and June 21 to November 2.

EMMANUEL COLLEGE　On St. Andrew's Street, Emmanuel (☎ **01223/ 334274**) was founded in 1584 by Sir Walter Mildmay, a chancellor of the exchequer to Elizabeth I. Harvard grads, take note: John Harvard, patron of Harvard University, studied here. You can take a nice stroll around its attractive gardens and visit the chapel designed by Sir Christopher Wren and consecrated in 1677. Both the chapel and college are open daily from 9am to 6pm.

QUEENS' COLLEGE   On Queens' Lane, Queens' College (☎ 01223/335511) is the loveliest of Cambridge's colleges. Dating from 1448, it was founded by two English queens, one the wife of Henry VI, the other the wife of Edward IV. Its second cloister is the most interesting, flanked by the early 16th-century half-timbered President's Lodge. Admission is £1 ($1.60); free for children under 12 accompanied by parents. A short printed guide is issued. Individual visitors are normally admitted daily from 1:45 to 4:30pm, but during March through October the college is also open to visitors daily from 10:15am to 12:45pm. Entry and exit is by the old porter's lodge in Queens' Lane only. The old hall and chapel are usually open to the public when not in use.

Insider's tip: The Grove fronts the west bank of the River Cam on the north side of the bridge. It's a riot of blossoms in spring. The walk along the riverbank reveals the best view of King's College but ends at a small branch channel in the river. Beyond the lawn on the other side of the river, the high stone wall dividing the two colleges is the last remaining fragment of a Carmelite monastery dissolved in 1538.

ST. JOHN'S COLLEGE   On St. John's Street, this college (☎ 01223/338600) was founded in 1511 by Lady Margaret Beaufort, mother of Henry VII. A few years earlier she had founded Christ's College. Before her intervention, an old hospital had stood on the site of St. John's. The impressive gateway bears the Tudor coat of arms, and Second Court is a fine example of late Tudor brickwork. But its best-known feature is the Bridge of Sighs crossing the Cam, built in the 19th century and patterned after the bridge in Venice. It connects the older part of the college with New Court, a Gothic Revival on the opposite bank from which there is an outstanding view of the famous Backs. The **Bridge of Sighs** is closed to visitors but can be seen from the neighboring Kitchen Bridge. Wordsworth was an alumnus of St. John's College. The college is open from March to October daily from 9:30am to 5pm. Admission is £1.75 ($2.80) for adults and £1 ($1.60) for children. Visitors are welcome to attend choral services in the chapel.

CAMBRIDGE'S OTHER ATTRACTIONS

✪ The Fitzwilliam Museum. Trumpington St., near Peterhouse. ☎ 01223/332900. Free admission. Tues–Sat 10am–5pm, Sun 2:15–5pm. Guided tours Sun 2:30pm. Closed Jan 1, Good Friday, May Day, and Dec 24–31.

One of the finest museums in Britain is worth the trip here. Although it features temporary exhibitions, its permanent collections are noted for their antiquities from ancient Egypt, Greece, and Rome. The Applied Arts section features English and European pottery and glass, along with furniture, clocks, fans, and armor, Chinese jades and ceramics from Japan and Korea, plus rugs and samplers. The museum is also noted for its rare-coin collection. Many rare printed books and illuminated manuscripts, both literary and musical, are also on display.

But the best for last: The paintings include masterpieces by Simone Martini, Domenico Veneziano, Titian, Veronese, Rubens, Van Dyck, Canaletto, Hogarth, Gainsborough, Constable, Monet, Degas, Renoir, Cézanne, and Picasso. There is also a fine collection of other 20th-century art, miniatures, drawings, watercolors, and prints.

Insider's tip: Occasional musical events, including evening concerts, are held in Gallery III. For more details, call ☎ 01223/332900. Some of the best lectures in England are staged here throughout the year. Call the number above for more details.

Great St. Mary's. King's Parade. ☎ 01223/350914. Admission to tower £1.50 ($2.40) adults, 50p (80¢) children. Tower Mon–Sat 10am–4:30pm, Sun 12:30–4:30pm; church daily 9am 6pm.

Cambridge's central church was built on the site of an 11th-century church, but the present building dates largely from 1478. It was closely associated with events of the Reformation. The cloth that covered the hearse of King Henry VII is on display in the church. There is a fine view of Cambridge from the top of the tower. Great St. Mary's is the university church.

SHOPPING

Forage around the shops lining St. John's Street, Trinity Street, King's Parade, and Trumpington Street.

Check out **English Teddy Bear Company,** 1 King's Parade (☎ 01223/300908), which sells teddy bears handmade in cottages all over the United Kingdom—a real British souvenir.

Primavera, 10 King's Parade (☎ 01223/357708), is a showplace of British crafts, featuring pottery, glass, ceramics, jewelry, ironwork, and fabric crafts ranging from ties to wall hangings. Be sure to explore their basement exhibition of paintings and craft items.

Music buffs will want to visit the **Cambridge Music Shop,** 1-A All Saints Passage (☎ 01223/351786), which carries stringed instruments, musical scores, music books, and accessories.

For a bit of energy to fuel your shopping frenzy, stop by **Fitzbillies,** 52 Trumptin St. (☎ 01223/352500), a bakery since 1922, and try the house specialty: a devilishly delectable sticky Chelsea bun. They also make cakes, pastries, bread, and pack picnic baskets with a hearty assortment of goodies. Their upstairs restaurant is open for breakfast, lunch, and dinner, Wednesday through Saturday.

Another well-defined shopping district is comprised of Bridge Street, Sidney Street, St. Andrew's Street, and Regent Street. Particularly worth noting in this area is **James Pringle Weavers,** 11 Bridge St. (☎ 01223/361534), a Scottish haven. You'll find a mind-boggling array of Scottish tartans, kilts, tweeds, fine knitwear, Scottish food, and, of course, postcards.

For unique British-designed jewelry, stop in **Workshop,** 3 Bridge St. (☎ 01223/354326). You can also get pieces made to order and shop for studio glass as well as handmade leather goods.

A posh area of extremely chic, small, and exclusive shops runs between Market Square and Trinity Street and is called **Rose Crescent.** Here you can buy leather goods, smart women's clothing, fine hats, as well as jewelry and a host of very expensive gift items.

Cambridge's pedestrian shopping district runs between Market Square and St. Andrew's Street and is known as the **Lion Yard. Culpepper the Herbalists,** 25 Lion Yard (☎ 01223/367370), carries a complete herbal line that includes everything from extracts of plants to jellies, honeys, teas, cosmetics, bath products, pillows, and potpourri.

If you're a book lover, Cambridge's bookstores will truly delight you. **Heffers of Cambridge** is a huge book, stationery, and music store with six branches, all of which can be contacted through their central phone number (☎ 01223/568568). The main store, at 20 Trinity St., carries academic books; the children's book shop is at 30 Trinity St.; the stationery store can be found at 19 Sydney St.; Heffers's paperback and video shop is at 31 St. Andrews St.; their art and graphics shop has an address of 15-21 King St.; and the music store at 19 Trinity St. features classical and popular cassettes, CDs, and choral college music. Heffers also has a shop in the mall at Grafton Centre that carries new fiction and nonfiction titles.

Also owned by Heffers, **Deighton, Bell & Co.,** 13 Trinity St. (☎ **01223/568568**), sells art and architectural books downstairs and antiquarian as well as secondhand books upstairs. **G. David,** 16 St. Edward's Passage (☎ **01223/354619**), hawks secondhand books, publishers' overruns at reduced prices, and antiquarian books. **Dillons,** 22 Sydney St. (☎ **01223/351688**), deals exclusively in new books on a variety of subjects. The **Haunted Bookshop,** 9 St. Edward's Passage (☎ **01223/312913**), specializes in out-of-print children's books and first editions. **W. H. Smith,** 14-15 Market St. (☎ **01223/311313**), peddles magazines, newspapers, stationery, books, and videos.

WHERE TO STAY
VERY EXPENSIVE

Cambridge Garden House Moat House. Granta Place, Mill Lane, Cambridge, Cambridgeshire CB2 1RT. ☎ **01223/259988.** Fax 01223/316605. 118 units. MINIBAR TV TEL. £150–£185 ($240–$296) double; £295 ($472) suite. AE, DC, MC, V.

This modern hotel, the best in Cambridge, is situated between the riverbank and a cobblestone street in the oldest part of town, a short stroll from the principal colleges. Because of its riverside location, we prefer it over its nearest competitor, the University Arms, which is in the center of town. It offers ample parking. You can rent punts at a boatyard next door. Visitors can relax on comfortable sofas and chairs in the bars and lounge. The standardized bedrooms are equipped with soundproof windows, beverage-makers, and hair dryers. Most rooms have balconies and river views.

Dining/Diversions: Overlooking the river and gardens, the hotel's Le Jardin Restaurant offers fixed-price and à la carte menus, including vegetarian meals, at lunch and dinner. The Riverside Lounge provides light meals, accompanied in the evening by piano music. The hotel has a series of outdoor terraces where drinks and afternoon tea are served in nice weather.

Amenities: Fitness center with pool, gym, and aerobics; 24-hour room service; laundry/dry cleaning; valet parking; business center.

EXPENSIVE

University Arms Hotel. Regent St., Cambridge, Cambridgeshire CB2 1AD. ☎ **01223/351241.** Fax 01223/315256. 116 units. TV TEL. £130–£145 ($208–$232) double; £280 ($448) suite. Rates include English breakfast. AE, MC, V. Bus: 1.

Built in 1834, this hotel maintains much of its antique charm and many of its original architectural features despite discreet modernization over the years. This is the only real rival in town to the Garden House, although it lacks the river location and time-worn Edwardian elegance of the former. Near the city center and the university, it offers tastefully decorated bedrooms with central heating, electric-razor outlets, trouser presses, and hair dryers. Suite residents will also find fresh flowers, fruits, and chocolates in their rooms. The porter can arrange a guided tour of the city.

Dining: The Octagon Lounge, with its stained-glass domed ceiling and open log fire, is a popular place to meet for tea. There's also a spacious oak-paneled restaurant.

Amenities: Concierge, room service, dry cleaning/laundry, baby-sitting, valet parking.

MODERATE

Arundel Hotel. 53 Chesterton Rd., Cambridge, Cambridgeshire CB4 3AN. ☎ **01223/367701.** Fax 01223/67721. 105 units. TV TEL. £60–£90 ($96–$144) double. Rates include continental breakfast. AE, DC, MC, V. Bus: 3 or 5.

The Arundel has a great location. Until recently, it consisted of six identical Victorian row houses, connected many years ago. In 1994, after two additional row houses were purchased from the university, the hotel was enlarged, upgraded, and expanded into the well-maintained place you'll see today. Rooms overlooking the River Cam and Jesus Green cost more than those facing the other way; and because there's no elevator, rooms on lower floors go for more than those upstairs. Regardless of their location, all accommodations are clean, simple, and comfortable. A coin-operated launderette is on the premises. There's a bar and restaurant (see "Where to Dine," below) and a garden with outdoor tables for drinks in warm weather; the Arundel offers the best dining of any hotel in town.

Cambridgeshire Moat House. Huntingdon Rd., Bar Hill, Cambridge, Cambridgeshire CB3 8EU. ☎ **01954/249988.** Fax 01954/780010. 100 units. TV TEL. £105 ($168) double. Children 12 and under stay free in parents' room. AE, DC, MC, V. Take A14 5½ miles northwest of the town center.

This place, a more affordable member of the same chain that manages the Cambridge Garden House Moat House (reviewed above), offers the best sports facilities in the Cambridge area. Built around 1977, it has conservatively modern public areas, comfortable bedrooms with nice views, a heated indoor swimming pool, a sauna, two outdoor tennis courts, putting green, and an 18-hole championship golf course where greens fees range from £12.50 to £22 ($20 to $35.20). The bedrooms, each comfortably furnished, are equipped with hair dryers, trouser presses, and beverage-makers. There's a restaurant in the hotel, although the food is just standard stuff. Meals are also served daily in the bar.

Gonville Hotel. Gonville Place, Cambridge, Cambridgeshire CB1 1LY. ☎ **800/528-1234** in the U.S. and Canada, or 01223/366611. Fax 01223/315470. 62 units. TV TEL. £101 ($161.60) double. Rates include English breakfast. AE, CB, DC, MC, V.

Only a 5-minute walk from the center of town, this comfortable hotel and its grounds are opposite Parker's Piece. The Gonville has been much improved in recent years, and is now better than ever. It's not unlike a country house, with shade trees and a formal car entry. It attracts businesspeople as well as tourists. The recently refurbished rooms are comfortable and furnished in a modern style. There is central heating throughout and air-conditioning in the restaurant.

Post House Hotel. Lakeview, Bridge Rd., Lakeview Bridge, Impington, Cambridge, Cambridgeshire CB4 4PH. ☎ **800/225-5843** in the U.S. and Canada, or 01223/237000. Fax 01223/233426. 118 units. TV TEL. Sun–Thurs £89–£129 ($142.40–$206.40) double; Fri–Sat £59–£99 ($94.40–$158.40) double. AE, DC, MC, V. Bus: 104. Drive 2 miles north of Cambridge on B1049 (Histon Rd.) to the A45 intersection.

Located a short walk from a small artificial lake, which the bedrooms overlook, this modern 2-story hotel was vaguely influenced by the designs of nearby country houses. Like the Moat House, it emphasizes leisure facilities (though it doesn't offer golf), and of the two, it has better bedrooms. There's a grassy courtyard partially enclosed by the hotel's wings. Peak-ceilinged public rooms are furnished with scattered clusters of sofas and chairs. The bedrooms have large windows with pleasant views. Facilities include a heated indoor swimming pool, a Jacuzzi, a sauna, and a lobby bar. The restaurant has mahogany paneling and reproductions of paintings created by Sir Winston Churchill. The hotel has recently enlarged its health-and-fitness room.

Regent Hotel. 41 Regent St., Cambridge, Cambridgeshire CB2 1AB. ☎ **01223/351470.** Fax 01223/566562. 26 units. TV TEL. £79.50 ($127.20) double. Rates include English breakfast. AE, DC, MC, V.

This is one of the nicest of the reasonably priced small hotels in Cambridge. Right in the city center, overlooking Parker's Piece, the house was built in the 1840s as the original site of Newham College. It became a hotel when the college outgrew its quarters. The attractive, comfortable bedrooms have radios, hair dryers, and trouser presses. There's a cocktail bar on the street level, and the coffee bar serves breakfast, late snacks, and afternoon tea.

INEXPENSIVE

Parkside Guest House. 25 Parkside, Cambridge, Cambridgeshire CB1 1JE. ☎ 01223/ 311212. Fax 01223/356926. 11 units, 5 with shower. TV TEL. £51 ($81.60) double without shower, £54 ($86.40) double with shower. Rates include English breakfast. No credit cards. Bus: no. 78 or 79.

Originally built in the 1850s as a residence for lecturers at Peterhouse College, this house was transformed during World War II into the headquarters for the Peterhouse Jewish Association, and sheltered Jewish academics from other parts of Europe. Later, the organist from St. John's College lived here and, after a brief period when it was owned by another college (Robinson College) within Cambridge University, it was sold to Mr. John Sutcliffe and Mrs. Shirley Heaton, who operate it today as a hotel. Located very close to the town center, it's one of the city's better B&Bs. The rooms are a good safe haven if not overly charming. There's a tiny laundry, a bar and lounge, a small walled garden, a collection of reference books about the city and university, and a variety of breakfast cereals for those who wish to supplement the bacon and eggs. With advance notice, an evening meal can be arranged.

Regency Guest House. 7 Regent Terrace, Cambridge, Cambridgeshire CB2 1AA. ☎ 01223/329626. Fax 01223/301567. 8 units, 3 with bathroom. TV. £48–£50 ($76.80–$80) double without bathroom, £58–£60 ($92.80–$96) double with bathroom. Rates include continental breakfast. No credit cards. Bus: no. 5.

In a desirable location near the town center, overlooking the verdant city park known as Parker's Piece, this hotel was built around 1850. Set behind a stone facade, and similar in design to many of its neighbors, it offers bedrooms with tea makers and 1950s-style retro furniture. The rooms are painted about every 6 months and have a bright, fresh look. Breakfast includes ample portions of continental-inspired selections, although cooked English breakfasts can be arranged for a supplement of £3 ($4.80).

WHERE TO DINE

Drop down into the cozy **Rainbow Vegetarian Bistro,** King's Parade, across from King's College (☎ 01223/321551), for coffee, a slice of fresh-baked cake, or a meal from their selection of whole-food and vegetarian offerings. A main course lunch or dinner goes for only £5.45 ($8.70); if you're around for breakfast, an egg with vegetarian sausage is just £3.75 ($6). Open daily from 9am to 9pm. The café lies at the end of a lily lined path.

VERY EXPENSIVE

✪ **Midsummer House.** Midsummer Common. ☎ 01223/69299. Reservations required. 3-course lunch £23 ($36.80); Sun lunch £24.95 ($39.90); 3-course fixed-price dinner £39.50 ($63.20); 6-course fixed-price dinner £50 ($80). AE, MC, V. Tues–Fri and Sun 12:30–1:45pm; Tues–Sat 7:30–9:30pm. CONTINENTAL

Located in an Edwardian-era cottage near the River Cam, the Midsummer House is a real find. We prefer to dine in the elegant conservatory, but you can also find a smartly laid table upstairs. The fixed-price menus are wisely limited, and quality control and high standards are much in evidence here. Anton Escalera, of Spanish and Dutch origins, is the master chef, and he is known for creating such specialties as roast suckling pig with lemon-scented juices, poached langoustine and crab ravioli in a saffron cream sauce, or meltingly tender oxtail served with Yorkshire pudding and sautéed onions. His passion for food is clearly evident and he pays attention to small details, even offering a choice of butters: paprika, herb, garlic, anchovy, or unsalted.

MODERATE

Arundel House Restaurant. 53 Chesterton Rd. ☎ **01223/367701.** Reservations recommended. Main courses £9–£13 ($14.40–$20.80); 2-course fixed-price lunch £9.75 ($15.60); 3-course fixed-price lunch £10.95 ($17.50); Sun lunch £11.95 ($19.10); 2-course fixed-price dinner £13.50 ($21.60); 3-course dinner £15.95 ($25.50). AE, DC, MC, V. Daily 12:15–1:45pm and 6:30–9:30pm. Bus: 3 or 5. FRENCH/BRITISH/VEGETARIAN.

One of the best and most acclaimed restaurants in Cambridge is in a hotel overlooking the River Cam and Jesus Green, a short walk from the city center. Winner of many awards, it's noted not only for its excellence and use of fresh produce, but also for its good value. The decor is warmly inviting with Sanderson curtains, Louis XV upholstered chairs, and spacious tables. The menu changes frequently, and you dine both à la carte or from the set menu. There is also a children's menu where the maximum price is £2.25 ($3.60). Perhaps you'll begin with a homemade golden-pea-and-ham soup or a white-rum-and-passion-fruit cocktail. Fish choices might include plaice or salmon; or try the country venison pie, marinated venison and seasonal root vegetables in a short-crust pastry.

Browns. 23 Trumpington St. (5 minutes from King's College and opposite the Fitzwilliam Museum). ☎ **01223/461655.** Main courses £7.45–£14.95 ($11.90–$23.90). AE, MC, V. Mon–Sat 11am–11:30pm, Sun noon–11:30pm. Bus: 2. ENGLISH/CONTINENTAL.

With a neoclassical colonnade in front, Browns has all the grandeur of the Edwardian era, but inside, it's the most lighthearted restaurant in the city, with wicker chairs, high ceilings, pre–World War I woodwork, and a long bar covered with bottles of wine. The extensive bill of continually varied fare includes pasta, scores of fresh salads, several selections of meat and fish (from charcoal-grilled leg of lamb with rosemary to fresh fish in season), hot sandwiches, and the chef's daily specials posted on a blackboard. If you drop by in the afternoon, you can also order thick milk shakes or natural fruit juices. In fair weather, there's outdoor seating.

✪ **Twenty Two.** 22 Chesterton Rd. ☎ **01223/351880.** Reservations required. Fixed-price menu £22.50–£28.50 ($36–$45.60). AE, MC, V. Tues–Sat 7:30–10pm. ENGLISH/CONTINENTAL.

Who would expect to find one of the best restaurants in Cambridge in this quiet residential and hotel district near Jesus Green? This is a secret jealously guarded by the locals, a homelike but elegant Victorian dining room that offers an ever-changing fixed-price menu based on fresh market produce. Owners David Carter and Louise Crompton use time-tested recipes along with their own inspirations, offering creations such as warm squid salad with ginger dressing or roast chump of lamb with braised white cabbage.

INEXPENSIVE

Charlie Chan. 14 Regent St. ☎ **01223/61763.** Reservations recommended. Main courses £5.80–£9.95 ($9.30–$15.90); fixed-price menus £13.50–£28 ($21.60–$44.80). AE, MC, V. Daily noon–2pm and 6–11pm. CHINESE.

Most people agree that this is the finest Chinese restaurant in Cambridge. We've always found Charlie Chan reliable and capable, which is remarkable given its huge menu. Downstairs is a long corridor-like restaurant, with pristine decor and tile floors. The ambience is lusher in the Blue Lagoon upstairs. Most of the dishes here are inspired by the traditional cuisine of Beijing. The specialties we've most enjoyed include an aromatic and crispy duck, lemon chicken, and prawn with garlic and ginger.

CAMBRIDGE AFTER DARK

You can take in a production where Emma Thompson and other well-known thespians got their start at **The Amateur Dramatic Club,** Park Street near Jesus Lane (☎ 01223/359547; box office 01223/504444). It presents two student productions nightly, Tuesday through Saturday, with the main show tending toward classic and modern drama or opera, and the late show being of a comic or experimental nature. The theater is open 40 weeks a year, closing in August and September, and tickets run from £2.50 ($4) to £5.50 ($8.80).

Then there's the most popular Cantebridgian activity: the pub crawl. There are too many pubs in the city to list them all here, but you might as well start at Cambridge's oldest pub, the **Pickerel,** on Bridge Street (☎ 01223/355068), which dates from 1432. English pubs don't get more traditional than this. If the ceiling beams or floorboards groan occasionally—well, they've certainly earned the right over the years. Real ales on tap include Bulmer's Traditional Cider, Old Speckled Hen, or Theakston's 6X, Old Peculiar, and Best Bitter. **The Maypole,** Portugal Place at Park Street (☎ 01223/352999), is the local hangout for actors when they're not in the nearby ADC Theatre. It's known for cocktails instead of ales, but you can get a Tetley's 6X or Castle Eden anyway.

The Eagle, Benet Street off King's Parade (☎ 01223/505020), will be forever famous as the place where Nobel Laureates Watson and Crick first announced their discovery of the DNA double helix. Real ales include Icebreaker and local brewery Greene King's Abbott, so make your order and raise a pint to the wonders of modern science.

To meet up with current Cambridge students, join the locals at the **Anchor,** Silver Street (☎ 01223/353554), or **Tap and Spicl (The Mill),** Mill Lane, off Silver Street Bridge (☎ 01223/357026), for a pint of Greene King's IPA or Abbott. The crowd at the Anchor spills out onto the bridge in fair weather, whereas the Tap and Spiel's clientele lay claim to the entire riverside park.

There's also musical entertainment to be had, and you can find out who's playing by checking out flyers posted around town, or reading the *Varsity.* **The Corn Exchange,** Wheeler Street and Corn Exchange (☎ 01223/357851), hosts everything from classical concerts to bigger-name rock shows. The **Fresher & Firkin,** 16 Chesterton Rd. (☎ 01223/324325), a pub located in a former movie theater, has live music or DJs on Friday and Saturday, with no cover charge.

Entertainment in some form can be found nightly at **The Junction,** Clifton Road, near the train station (☎ 01223/511511), where an eclectic mix of acts take to the stage weeknights to perform all genres of music, comedy, and theater, and DJs take over on the weekend. Cover charges vary from £7.50 to £10 ($12 to $16), depending on the event.

5th Avenue, Lion Yard (☎ 01223/364222), a second-story club, has a huge dance floor and plays everything from house to the latest pop hits, Monday through Saturday from 9pm until 2am. Sometimes they even DJ the old-fashioned way, by taking requests. The cover charge ranges from £3 to £5 ($4.80 to $8), depending on what night you're here.

SIDE TRIPS FROM CAMBRIDGE
A GLIMPSE OF WARTIME BRITAIN

✪ **Imperial War Museum.** Duxford Airfield, on A505, at Junction 10 of M11. ☎ **01223/835000.** Admission £7 ($11.20) adults, £4.70 ($7.50) seniors, £3.50 ($5.60) children and students, £20 ($32) family ticket. Mid–Mar to Oct daily 10am–6pm; Nov to mid–Mar daily 10am–4pm. Closed Dec 24–26. Bus: Cambus no. 103 from Drummer St. Station in Cambridge. By car, take M11 to Junction 10, 8 miles south of Cambridge.

In this former Battle of Britain station and U.S. Eighth Air Force base in World War II, you'll find a huge collection of historic civil and military aircraft from both world wars, including the only B-29 Superfortress in Europe. Other exhibits include midget submarines, tanks, and a variety of field artillery pieces, as well as a historical display on the U.S. Eighth Air Force.

In summer 1997, Elizabeth I opened the American Air Museum here as part of the larger complex. It houses Europe's finest collection of historic American combat aircraft and is the largest precast concrete structure in Europe. Aircraft on show range from a World War I biplane to the giant B-52 jet bomber. A number are dramatically suspended from the ceiling as if in flight.

THAXTED

The nearby village of Thaxted is famous for its well-preserved Elizabethan houses and for hosting the famous **Morris Ring,** the first weekend after Spring Bank Holiday, a processional street dance that attracts more than 300 dancers and culminates with a haunting horn dance as dusk falls.

Thaxted is 5 miles south of Saffron Walden. To get here from Saffron Walden, drive along B184 (the Thaxted Road), following signs to Thaxted and Great Dunmow. A bus follows this route Monday to Saturday five to six times a day.

Thaxted has the most beautiful small church in England, the ✪ **Church of St. John the Baptist, Our Lady and St. Lawrence** (☎ **01371/830221**), whose graceful spire can be seen for miles around. Its belfry has special chimes that call parishioners to church services. Dating from 1340, the church is a nearly perfect example of religious architecture.

Other sights include the **Thaxted Guildhall** (no phone), located next to the church and the site of a medieval market place. It is a fine example of a medieval Guildhall, few of which now remain. It was built between 1393 and 1420, possibly by the Cutlers Guild. Open April through September, Sunday and Monday, except bank holidays, from 2 to 6pm.

Where to Stay Near Thaxted

Whitehall. Church End, Broxted, Essex CM6 2BZ. ☎ **01279/850603.** Fax 01279/850385. 25 units. TV TEL. £120–£150 ($192–$240) double. Rates include English breakfast. AE, DC, MC, V. Take B1052 about 4 miles southwest of Thaxted. If you're driving from Stansted Airport, follow the signs to Broxted for the 7-minute drive.

This hotel lies adjacent to the village church of Broxted, with a garden behind it and lots of open land nearby. It's also very convenient for passengers using Stansted Airport outside London. In the 18th century, this property was attached to almost 28,000 acres of prime farmland. By the 1900s, Daisy, the countess of Warwick, then its mistress, entertained King Edward VII within these baronial walls. One of the renowned hostesses of the Edwardian era, the countess was also the mistress of Victoria's son. In an elegant simplicity, today's guests are still entertained more or less royally. Some bedrooms are uniquely furnished in 18th-century style; all have thoughtful extras and views of the 300-year-old yew trees in the ancient walled garden. Half of the rooms lie within a modern wing that was added in 1985. The new-wing rooms are conservatively traditional, with country-house accessories.

Dining: A medieval brew house with a soaring ceiling is the dining venue for specialties prepared with fresh ingredients, subtle flavors, and imaginative presentation. The specialty fixed-price menu costs £37.50 ($60) for a six-course "menu surprise."

2 Ely

70 miles NE of London; 16 miles N of Cambridge

Ely Cathedral is the top attraction in the fen country, outside of Cambridge. After you've seen the cathedral, you can safely be on your way, as Ely is simply a sleepy market town that can't compete with the life and bustle found at Cambridge.

ESSENTIALS

GETTING THERE Ely is a major railway junction served by express trains to Cambridge. Service is frequent from London's Liverpool Street Station. For schedules and information, call ☎ **0345/484950** (in the U.K. only) or 01603/764777.

Campus buses run frequently between Cambridge and Ely. Call ☎ **01223/423554** for schedules and information.

If you're driving from Cambridge, take A10 north.

VISITOR INFORMATION The **Tourist Information Centre** is at Oliver Cromwell's House, 29 St. Mary's St. (☎ **01353/662062**); open April through September daily from 10am to 5pm; October through March, Monday to Saturday from 10am to 4:30pm.

SEEING THE SIGHTS

✪ **Ely Cathedral.** ☎ **01353/667735.** Admission £3.50 ($5.60) adults; £3 ($4.80) seniors, students, and children ages 12–16; free for children under 12. Apr–Oct daily 7am–7pm; Nov–Mar Mon–Sat 7:30am–6pm, Sun 7:30am–5pm

The near-legendary founder of this cathedral was Etheldreda, the wife of a Northumbrian king who established a monastery on the spot in 673. The present structure dates from 1081. Visible for miles around, the landmark octagonal lantern is the crowning glory of the cathedral. Erected in 1322 following the collapse of the old tower, it represents a remarkable engineering achievement. Four hundred tons of lead and wood hang in space, held there by timbers reaching to the eight pillars.

You enter the cathedral through the Galilee West Door, a good example of the early English style of architecture. The lantern tower and the Octagon are the most notable features inside, but visit the lady chapel too. Although its decor has deteriorated over the centuries, it's still a handsome example of the Perpendicular style, having been completed in the mid–14th century. The entry fee goes to help preserve the cathedral. Monday to Saturday, guided tours gather at 11:15am and 2:15pm; in the summer, tours occur throughout the day.

There's also a Brass Rubbing Centre, where a large selection of replica brass is available for you to rub. These can produce remarkable results for wall hangings or special gifts. The center is open year-round in the North Aisle, outside the Cathedral Shop

Ely Museum. The Old Gaol, Market St. ☎ **01353/666655.** Admission £1.80 ($2.90) adults; £1.25 ($2) children, students, and seniors; free for children 6 and under. Tues–Sun and Mon bank holidays 10:30am–4:30pm.

A gallery presents a chronological history of Ely and the Isle from the Ice Age to the present day. Displays include archaeology, social history, rural life, local industry, and military, as well as a tableaux of the debtor's cell and condemned cell, which are also on view.

Oliver Cromwell's House. 29 St. Mary's St. (next to St. Mary's Church). ☎ 01353/ 662062. Admission £2.50 ($4) adults; £2 ($3.20) children, seniors, and students; £5.25 ($8.40) family ticket. Apr–Sept daily 10am–5pm; off-season Mon–Sat 10am–4:30pm.

This recently restored house was owned by the Puritan Oliver Cromwell, a name hardly beloved by the royals, even today. He rose to fame as a military and political leader during the English civil wars of 1642 to 1649. These wars led to the execution of Charles I and the replacement of the monarchy by the Commonwealth. In 1653 Cromwell was declared lord protector, and this local farmer became the most powerful man in the land until his death in 1658. Exhibitions, displays, and period rooms offer insight into Cromwell's character and 17th-century domestic life. The tourist center is also located here.

Grimes Graves. On the B1107, 2¾ miles northeast of Brandon, Norfolkshire. ☎ 01842/ 810656. Admission £1.60 ($2.55) adults, £1.20 ($1.90) students and seniors, 80p ($1.30) children 5–15; free for children 4 and under. Apr–Oct daily 10am–1pm and 2–6pm; Nov–Mar Wed–Sun 10am–1pm and 2–4pm. Take the A134 for 7 miles northwest of Thetford, then transfer to B1107.

This is the largest and best-preserved group of Neolithic flint mines in Britain; it produced the cutting edges of spears, arrows, and knives for prehistoric tribes throughout the region. Because of its isolated location within sparsely populated, fir-wooded countryside, it's easy to imagine yourself transported back through the millennia.

A guardian will meet you near the well-signposted parking lot. After determining that you are not physically impaired, he or she will open one or several of the mine shafts, each of which requires a descent down an almost-vertical 30-foot ladder (a visit here is not recommended for very young children, elderly travelers, or those with disabilities). Since the tunnel and shaft have been restored and reinforced, it's now possible to see where work took place during Neolithic times. Although it's not essential, many archaeologists, professional and amateur, bring their own flashlights with them. The mines, incidentally, are situated close to the military bases that housed thousands of American air force personnel during World War II.

WHERE TO STAY

Lamb Hotel. 2 Lynn Rd., Ely, Cambridgeshire CB7 4EJ. ☎ 01353/663574. Fax 01353/ 662023. 32 units. TV TEL. £84 ($134.40) double. Rates include English breakfast. AE, DC, MC, V. Bus: 109.

Right in the center of town, this hotel is a former 14th-century coaching inn whose ground-floor areas, including the lounge and bars, were completely refurbished in 1996. In the shadow of the cathedral, this hotel offers renovated bedrooms with beverage-makers. In the 1400s, this place was known as the "Holy Lambe," a stopping-off spot for wayfarers, often pilgrims, passing through East Anglia. Rather standard English meals are served.

WHERE TO DINE

Around the corner from St. Mary's Church is **Steeplegate,** 16–18 High St. (☎ 01353/664731), a tearoom and craft shop with wooden tables and ancient windows. There are tea selections plus light lunch items, scones, and creamy gateaux. After tea, venture downstairs to the craft shop and have a look at the variety of handmade pottery, glass, and baskets.

An unusual choice is **The Almonry Restaurant & Tea Rooms** in The College, Ely Cathedral (☎ 01353/666360). Housed in the medieval college buildings on the north side of the Cathedral, this is a comfortable tearoom with table service in a beautiful 12th-century undercroft licensed to sell drinks. You can take your tea out to a garden seat in good weather. It is open for late morning coffee, lunches, and afternoon teas. Meals start at £5 ($8).

The Old Fire Engine House. 25 St. Mary's St. (opposite St. Mary's Church). ☎ **01353/ 662582.** Reservations required. Main courses £12–£14.50 ($19.20–$23.20). MC, V. Daily 12:30–2pm; Mon–Sat 7:30–9pm (last entry). Bus: 109. ENGLISH.

It's worth making a special trip to this converted fire station in a walled garden, within a building complex that includes an art gallery. Soups are served in huge bowls, accompanied by coarse-grained crusty bread. Main dishes include duck with orange sauce, jugged hare, baked stuffed pike, and pigeon with bacon and black olives. In summer you can dine outside in the garden and even order a cream tea.

3 Newmarket

62 miles NE of London; 13 miles NE of Cambridge

This old Suffolk town has been famous as a horse-racing center since the time of James I. Visitors can see Nell Gwynne's House, but mainly they come to visit Britain's first and only equestrian museum.

GETTING THERE

Trains depart from London's Liverpool Street Station every 45 to 60 minutes for Cambridge (see above). In Cambridge, passengers change trains and head in the direction of Mildenhall. Three stops later, they arrive at Newmarket.

About eight **National Express** buses depart from London's Victoria Coach Station for Norwich every day, stopping at Stratford, Stansted, and (finally) Newmarket along the way. For schedules and information, call ☎ **0990/808080.**

If you're driving from Cambridge, head east on A133.

OFF TO THE RACES

Britain's most prestigious racecourse lies at Newmarket, a small country town whose main draw for tourists is the series of warm-weather horse races whose origins date from the days of James I and Charles II. Charles II was so enthusiastic about racing that he frequently ordered most of his Restoration-era court up from London to attend the races.

The headquarters of British racing, and the venue where precedents and policies are hammered out before being applied to the more formal venue of Ascot, Newmarket is the only racecourse in Britain with two separate racetracks.

The more bucolic of these is the **July Race Course,** where races are held during the heat and glare of June, July, and August. It's the site of the prestigious July Cup. Smaller than the other course, the Rowley Mile, it's known for its rows of beech trees that shade the saddling boxes and promenade grounds, as well as the thatched roofs that add an old English charm to the ornamental entranceways and some of the showcase buildings used by investors, owners, and fans. The grandstands, however, have conventional roofs shielding fans from the sun and the rain.

The more industrial-looking racetrack is the **Rowley Mile,** used during the racing season's cooler months (mid-April to late May and early September to November 2). Dress codes are less strictly observed here and at the July Race Course, where men wear jackets and ties, but the venue at Rowley Mile attracts a bigger and brasher crowd. At the Rowley Mile, prestigious races such as the Guineas Races, the Cesarewitch Handicap, and the Champion Stakes are run.

The two courses lie within a half mile of each other, and share the same administration. For more information, contact **The Clerk of the Course,** Westfield House, The Links, Newmarket, Suffolk CB8 0TG (☎ 01638/663482).

National Horseracing Museum. 99 High St. ☎ **01638/667333.** Admission £3.50 ($5.60) adults, £1.50 ($2.40) children, £2.50 ($4) seniors. Tues–Sat 10am–5pm, Sun noon–4pm (plus Mon bank holidays). Closed Nov–Mar 2.

Visitors can see the history of horse racing over 300 years in this museum housed in the old subscription rooms, early 19th-century rooms used for betting. There are fine paintings of famous horses, paintings on loan from Queen Elizabeth II, and copies of old parliamentary acts governing races. A continuous 53-minute audiovisual presentation shows races and racehorses.

To make history come alive for visitors, they also offer equine tours of this historic town. Guides take you to watch morning gallops on the heath where you'll see bronzes of horses from the past and other points of interest. An optional tour of a famous training establishment is offered, plus a visit to the Jockey Club rooms, known for their fine collection of paintings. Reservations are necessary. Tours depart every day when the museum is open except Sundays and in October. Departures are on Tuesday, Thursday, Saturday, and race days at 9:25am, costing £20 ($32) for adults, £16 ($25.60) for seniors, students, and children.

The National Stud. July Race Course. ☎ **01638/666789.** Admission £3.80 ($6.10) adults, £2.80 ($4.50) children and seniors. Mar–Aug and Sept–Oct race day only. Guided tours Mon–Fri 11:15am and 2:30pm, Sat 11:15am, Sun 2:30pm. Closed Nov–Feb.

Next to Newmarket's July Race Course, 2 miles southwest of the town, this place is home to some of the world's finest horses, and a renowned breeding stud operation. A tour lasting about 75 minutes lets you see many mares and foals, plus top-class stallions. Reservations for tours must be made at the National Stud office or by phoning the number given above.

WHERE TO STAY & DINE

Heath Court Hotel. Moulton Rd., Newmarket, Suffolk CB8 8DY. ☎ **01638/667171.** Fax 01638/666533. 43 units. TV TEL. Mon–Thurs £88–£105.95 ($140.80–$169.50) double, Fri–Sun £78–£95 ($124.80–$152) double. All week £105 ($168) family room for 3; £140 ($224) suite. Extra bed £25 ($40). Rates include English breakfast. AE, DC, MC, V.

A member of Queen's Moat House hotel chain, this brick-fronted hotel is near The Gallops, the exercise area for the stables at the Newmarket Heath racetrack, about a 5-minute walk from the center of town. Built in the mid-1970s, it's a favorite of the English horse-racing world and is fully booked during the racing season. It is decorated in an appropriate country-elegant style in its public rooms, including oil portraits of horses and souvenirs of the racing life in its bar and restaurant. The bedrooms are well appointed, conservatively modern, and comfortable.

Bertie's Brasserie is an informal restaurant serving an English and continental menu, ranging from pink-roasted knuckle of lamb to paella, including Newmarket bangers and mash.

Swynford Paddocks. Six Mile Bottom, Cambridgeshire CB8 0UE. ☎ **01638/570234.** Fax 01638/570283. 15 units. TV TEL. £127–£148 ($203.20–$236.80) double. Rates include English breakfast. AE, DC, MC, V. Take A1304 6 miles southwest of Newmarket.

This well-appointed country house, one of the finest in the area, is situated on a 60-acre stud farm surrounded by beautiful grounds. It was once a retreat of Lord Byron, who wrote many of his works at the foot of a now-felled beech. The house then became the home of Lord and Lady Halifax until 1976 when it was converted into a luxury hotel. Many guests use it as a base for exploring not only Newmarket but Cambridge as well. Each of the bedrooms, opening onto scenic views, is individually decorated with a special character. Rooms are spacious and contain many amenities such as beverage-makers, trouser presses, and hair dryers. For extraspecial occasions, there's a suite of rooms or two sumptuous four-posters. The rates are expensive, but you get a lot of quality here. The restaurant serves a first-rate English, French, and Irish cuisine.

4 Bury St. Edmunds

79 miles NE of London; 27 miles E of Cambridge; 12 miles N of Lavenham

Bury St. Edmunds is "a handsome little town, of thriving and cleanly appearance." That's how Charles Dickens described it in *Pickwick Papers* and it holds true today. This historical town, founded around the powerful Benedictine Abbey in 1020, derives its name from St. Edmund, King of the East Angles in the mid–9th century. It was in the Abbey Church that the barons of England united and forced King John to sign the Magna Carta in 1214. Even though it's sometimes hard to tell, Bury is filled with many original medieval buildings. (Many buildings were given face-lifts in the 17th and 18th centuries; it's only when you step inside that their medieval roots become clear.) During the 18th century, this market town was quite prosperous and had a thriving cloth-making industry. The large number of fine Georgian buildings bear testament to the wealth of the day.

Upon the Vikings' arrival to the area, they dubbed it "The Summer Country." And, indeed, the summer, when the town bursts into bloom, is the best time to visit. Most of the historic sites and gardens open for the season on Easter.

ESSENTIALS

GETTING THERE   Trains leave regularly from either Liverpool Street Station or King's Cross Station in London; however, none are direct. Leaving from Liverpool Street, you will change at Ipswich. And from King's Cross Station, you'll have to switch trains at Cambridge. The trip takes approximately 1½ hours. For schedules and information, call ☎ 0345/484950 (in the U.K. only) or 01603/764776.

National Express runs several direct buses every day from London's Victoria Coach Station, which reach Bury in 2 hours. For schedules and information, call ☎ 0990/808080.

By car, take M11 north out of London. As you near Cambridge, get on A45 and continue on to Bury. The drive takes about 1½ hours.

It's also possible to get here by train or bus from Cambridge. Regular trains leave from the Cambridge Rail Station and arrive about 45 minutes later in Bury St. Edmunds. **Cambus Bus Company** runs three or four buses a day to Bury from the Drummer Street Bus Station in Cambridge, a 1-hour ride. Call ☎ 01223/423554 for information and schedules. By car, simply take A45 directly from Cambridge. It's a 45-minute drive.

VISITOR INFORMATION   The **Bury St. Edmunds Tourist Information Centre,** 6 Angel Hill (☎ 01284/764667), is open November through Easter, Monday to Friday from 10am to 4pm and Saturday from 10am to 1pm; Easter through October, Monday to Saturday from 9:30am to 5:30pm and Sunday from 10am to 3pm.

SPECIAL EVENTS   The **Bury St. Edmunds Festival** (☎ 01284/757099) is held annually in May. The 17-day festival includes performances from leading ensembles and soloists ranging from classical to contemporary. Exhibitions, talks, walks, films, plays, and a fireworks display are integral parts of this internationally renowned festival.

EXPLORING THE TOWN

For a bit of easy and always interesting sightseeing, take one of the hour-long **guided walks** around Bury St. Edmunds. Choices include a Blue Badge Guided Tour and theme tours with Bury's historical monk, Brother Jocelin, or gravedigger William Hunter. Tours leave from the Tourist Information Centre (see above) where tickets can also be purchased.

The normally quiet town center becomes a hub of hustle and bustle on Wednesday and Saturday mornings when the **market** arrives. Weather permitting, hours are approximately 9am to 4pm. You'll find a pleasing mix of family run businesses and High Street names for shopping in and around the town and its pedestrian zones.

The Bury St. Edmunds Art Gallery, Market Cross, Cornhill (☎ **01284/762081**), hosts eight fine art and craft exhibitions each year and serves as a venue for local crafts-people and artists. A craft shop located in the gallery sells ceramics, prints, books, glassware, and jewelry. **The Parsley Pot,** 17 Abbeygate St. (☎ **01284/760289**), sells an assortment of gift items, including china and porcelain.

Several parks are located just outside of town. Seven miles north of Bury is the 125-acre **West Stow Country Park** with heathland, woodland, and a large lake bordered by the River Lark. This diverse area is perfect for the proverbial "walk in the park" with a rustic twist. **The West Stow Anglo-Saxon Village** (☎ **01284/728719**) is part of West Stow Country Park. This reconstructed village is built on the excavated site of an ancient Anglo-Saxon village, and period reenactments take place throughout the year. The park is open October to March daily from 8am to 5pm and April to September daily from 8am to 8pm. Admission is free. The village is open year-round from 10am to 5pm. Admission is £3 ($4.80) for adults and £2 ($3.20) for children.

Nowton Park (☎ **01284/756127**) is 1½ miles outside of Bury on 200 acres of Suffolk countryside. Landscaped a century ago, the park is typically Victorian and has many country-estate features. In the springtime, walk the avenue of lime trees with its masses of bright yellow daffodils. Marked walking paths snake through the park. Depending on the path, walks take between 20 and 75 minutes. It's open daily from 8:30am to dusk; free admission.

The Abbey. Samson's Tower. ☎ **01284/763110** for Visitor Centre. Free admission. Visitor Centre Easter through Oct daily 10am–5pm. Abbey Gardens and ruins year-round Mon–Sat 7:30am to half hour before dusk, Sun 9am to half hour before dusk.

The **Visitor Centre** is a good starting point for a visit to the entire Abbey precinct. (The Abbey itself is in ruins today and sits in the middle of the Abbey Gardens.) The Visitor Centre is housed in the west front of the Abbey of St. Edmunds's remains and uses a clever series of displays to give the visitor an idea of what life was like in this powerful abbey from its beginnings in 1020 to its dissolution in 1539.

Moving on to the formal **Abbey Gardens** with its flower beds and well-kept lawns, you'll see the ruins of the abbey. When the long shadows cast themselves across the weathered ruins, the landscape becomes surreal and looks much like a Dalí master-piece. In reality, the abandoned abbey was used as a quarry for the townspeople down through the ages, and that is the reason for the extremely worn condition and melted character of the ruins. A rather interesting tour of the Abbey Gardens is led by medieval monk Brother Jocelin, bookable through the Tourist Information Centre at ☎ **01284/764667.**

Moyse's Hall Museum. Cornhill. ☎ **01284/757488.** Admission £1.50 ($2.40) adults, .95p ($1.50) seniors, children. Free. 4–5pm. Mon–Sat 10am–5pm, Sun 2–5pm.

Located in one of England's last surviving Norman stone houses, this museum has nationally important archaeological collections and local artifacts.

Manor House Museum. Honey Hill. ☎ **01284/757072.** Admission £2.70 ($4.30) adults, £1.75 ($2.80) seniors and children, £7.50 ($12) family ticket. Tues–Sun 10am–5pm.

Housed in a restored Georgian mansion, this museum uses touch-screen computers to help interpret its displays of fine and decorative art.

The Cathedral Church of St. James. Angel Hill. ☎ **01284/754933.** Free admission. Daily 8:30am–dusk.

Dating from the 16th century, this church has a magnificent font, beautiful stained-glass windows, and a display of 1,000 embroidered kneelers.

St. Mary's Church. Crown St. ☎ **01284/706668.** Call the church to arrange a tour. Free admission.

St. Mary's was built on the site of a Norman church in 1427. Note its impressive roof and nave. It is also where Henry VIII's sister, Mary Rose, is buried.

Ickworth House. 3 miles south of Bury at Horringer. ☎ **01284/735270.** Admission £5.20 ($8.30) adults, £2.20 ($3.50) children, £9.50 ($15.20) family ticket. Mar–Nov Tues–Wed and Thurs–Sun 1–5pm.

This National Trust property was built in 1795 and contains an impressive rotunda, state rooms, and art collections of silver and paintings. An Italian garden surrounds the house, and all is set in a peaceful, landscaped park.

WHERE TO STAY

Angel Hotel. Angel Hill, Bury St. Edmunds, Suffolk IP33 1LT. ☎ **01284/753926.** Fax 01284/750092. 43 units. TV TEL. £76–£130 ($121.60–$208) double; £150 ($240) suite AE, DC, MC, V.

Originally a coaching inn dating from 1452, the hotel received an exterior face-lift during the Georgian era, and its front facade is now completely covered with lush ivy. The location is ideal for sightseeing and shopping, as both are only a short walk from the hotel. Look out the window of any of the front-facing rooms or walk out the front door, and you'll see the romantic Abbey Gardens. Each of the rooms is individually decorated with freestanding furnishings and some even have four-poster beds. Room 36 is one of the more popular rooms with its four-poster bed, bold peach-colored walls (a shade you can almost taste), and chintz curtains and armchairs. You'll find tea makers in all the rooms.

The hotel runs two restaurants: The Vault, located in the cellar, serves an informal lunch and dinner, and the more formal Regency serves breakfast, dinner, and lunch on Sunday.

Butterfly Hotel. Symonds Rd., Bury St. Edmunds, Suffolk IP32 7BW. ☎ **01284/760884.** Fax 01284/755476. 69 units. TV TEL. Mon–Fri £59.50 ($95.20) double, Sat–Sun £49.50 ($79.20) double; £80 ($128) suite. AE, DC, MC, V.

This standard, rather ordinary hotel, built relatively recently, is located 10 minutes from Bury on the A14 motorway. The grassy grounds are landscaped, and there is a sunny patio for dining alfresco. All the rooms are decorated in the same style (bland) with landscape pictures and an armchair or two, along with an accompanying desk. Because of the proximity to the motorway, the windows are double-paned to reduce traffic noise and to help guests get a better night's rest. Tea-making equipment is provided in every room, and The Walt, the hotel's restaurant, serves three standard meals a day.

Ravenwood Hall. Rougham, Bury St. Edmunds, Suffolk IP30 9JA. ☎ **01359/270345.** Fax 01359/270788. 14 units. TV TEL. £79–£109 ($126.40–$174.40) double. Rates include breakfast. AE, DC, MC, V.

Located 3 miles outside of town, this Tudor hall dates from the 1500s and is set in a very peaceful 7-acre park with well-manicured lawns, gardens, and forest. There are also tennis courts and an outdoor swimming pool (not heated). This rustic country place is filled with oak beams and has a magnificent fireplace that is the focal point of the restaurant, where diners enjoy an à la carte menu. The individually decorated rooms are comfortable, full of atmosphere, and have tea- and coffeemakers. If you're a fancier of fine beds, check out the oak room with its four-poster bed and the bridal suite with its brass bed. There is also an informal, somewhat cozy bar that offers snacks and drinks.

WHERE TO DINE

Maison Bleve at Mortimer's. 31 Churchgate St. ☎ **01284/760623.** Reservations recommended. Main courses £10–£20 ($16–$32). AE, MC, V. Mon–Fri noon–2pm; Sat 6:30–9pm. SEAFOOD.

This restaurant has quickly become the town's best, although a change in management may bring some changes here during the lifetime of this edition. The open and airy dining room has a nautical theme, in keeping with the fresh seafood that's served here. The same menu is available for both lunch and dinner and changes regularly with the season. Favorites include halibut Florentine, Dover sole charcoal-grilled over an open flame, and skate with a light black-butter sauce and capers. All main courses are presented with new potatoes.

BURY ST. EDMUNDS AFTER DARK

Throughout the centuries, Bury has enjoyed a well-deserved reputation as a small center of arts and entertainment. **The Theatre Royal,** Westgate Street (☎ **01284/769505**), is the oldest purpose-built theater in England. Its Georgian building has been lovingly and richly restored to its original grandeur. Programs include opera, dance, music, and drama from the best touring companies. Tickets are £3 to £15 ($4.80 to $24) and can be purchased at the box office (☎ **01284/769505**).

Stop by the 17th-century pub **Dog and Partridge,** 29 Crown St. (☎ **01284/764792**), and see where the bar scenes from the BBC hit series *Lovejoy* were filmed while you sample one of the region's Greene King Ales. Also try wiggling your way into the **Nutshell,** corner of The Traverse and Abbeygate Street (☎ **01284/764867**). This pub has been notoriously dubbed the smallest pub in all of England and is a favorite tourist stop. **The Masons Arms,** 14 Whiting St. (☎ **01284/753955**), features more of a family atmosphere and welcomes children. Home-cooked food is served along with a standard selection of ales. There's a patio garden in use in summer.

A SIDE TRIP TO SUDBURY

Twenty miles south of Bury St. Edmunds along A134 is Sudbury, a town that has prospered through the ages thanks to its sheep (the wool industry) and prime location along the banks of the River Stour. A handful of medieval half-timbered buildings and Georgian homes attest to the town's ripe old age. Its most famous native son is Thomas Gainsborough, who was born in 1727 and went on to become one of England's most well-liked painters.

His birthplace, **Gainsborough's House,** 46 Gainsborough St. (☎ **01787/372958**), is a museum and arts center that has many of his works of art on display.

Visitors will notice that several different architectural styles make up the house, and there is a walled garden in back worth seeing. It's open mid-April to October, Tuesday through Saturday from 10am to 5pm and Sunday from 2 to 4pm; November to mid-April, Tuesday through Saturday from 10am to 4pm and Sunday from 2 to 4pm. Admission is £2.50 ($4) during the year, but it is free during the month of December.

WHERE TO STAY

The Mill Hotel. Walnuttree Lane, Sudbury CO10 6BD. ☎ **01787/375544.** Fax 01787/373027. 56 units. TV TEL. £59–£70 ($94.40–$112) double. AE, DC, MC, V.

As can be gathered from its name, this hotel is located in the shell of an old mill. In fact, the River Stour, which runs under the hotel, still turns the mill's 16-foot water wheel, now encased in glass and on display in the hotel's restaurant and bar. Rooms vary in size; some have heavy oak beams and massive columns, but all are outfitted with comfortable furnishings. You may even be able to watch the local cows pass some time by the water's edge, as many of the rooms have a river or millpond view. The restaurant and bar areas are welcoming with their polished hardwood floors, stylish Oriental carpets, and antiques.

WHERE TO DINE

Brasserie 47. 47 Gainsborough St. ☎ **01787/374298.** Reservations recommended for dinner. Lunch £12–£14 ($19.20–$22.40); main courses £6.95–£11.95 ($11.10–$19.10). AE, DC, MC, V. Tues–Sat 10am–2pm and 6–10pm. Closed 5 days during Christmas. INTERNATIONAL.

Right next door to the Gainsborough House, this friendly brasserie, full of pine furnishings and lots of earthy terra-cotta and navy accents, is ideal for lunch or dinner. In fact, the same menu is used for both, along with a host of specials that change daily. Popular main dishes include the duck and bacon salad with red-wine sauce and tarragon dressing, lamb steak in rosemary sauce served with couscous and a leafy salad, and grilled salmon with lemon butter and new potatoes. Homemade ice creams and exotic sorbets like orange caramel and toasted poppy seed open the dessert selection. But the hot syrup sponge cake with vanilla custard sauce is hands-down the most deservedly popular dessert.

5 Lavenham

66 miles NE of London; 35 miles SE of Cambridge

Once a great wool center, Lavenham is the classic Suffolk village, beautifully preserved today. It features a number of half-timbered Tudor houses washed in the characteristic Suffolk pink. The town's wool-trading profits are apparent in its guildhall, on the triangular main "square." Inside are exhibits on Lavenham's textile industry, showing how yarn was spun, then "dyed in the wool" with woad (the plant used by the ancient Picts to dye themselves blue), and following on to the weaving process. There is also a display showing how half-timbered houses were constructed.

The Church of St. Peter and St. Paul, at the edge of Lavenham, has interesting carvings on the misericords and the chancel screen, as well as ornate tombs. This is one of the "wool churches" of the area, built by pious merchants in the Perpendicular style with a landmark tower.

ESSENTIALS

GETTING THERE Trains depart London's North Street Station at least once an hour, sometimes more often, for Colchester, where they connect quickly to the town of Sudbury. For schedules and information, call ☎ **0345/484950** (in the U.K. only) or 01603/764776. From Sudbury, Beeston's Coaches, Ltd., has about nine daily buses making the short run to Lavenham. The trip from London takes between 2 and 2½ hours.

National Express buses depart from London's Victoria Coach Station, carrying passengers to the town of Bury St. Edmunds, some 9 miles from Lavenham. For schedules and information, call ☎ **0990/808080.** From Bury St. Edmunds, you can take another bus onto Lavenham. The trip takes about 2½ hours.

If you're driving from Bury St. Edmunds, continue south on A134 toward Long Melford, but cut southeast to Lavenham at the junction with A1141.

VISITOR INFORMATION The **Tourist Information Centre** is on Lady Street (☎ 01787/248207) and is open daily April through October from 10am to 4:45pm.

SHOPPING & TEATIME

Shoppers from all over East Anglia flock to **Timbers,** 13 High St. (☎ 01787/ 247218), a center housing 24 dealers specializing in antiques and collectibles, including books, toys, military artifacts, glass, porcelain, and much more. It's open Thursday through Tuesday.

After strolling the medieval streets of Lavenham, stop by **Tickle Manor Tea Rooms,** High Street (☎ 01787/248438). This 2-story timber frame home was built by the son of a priest in 1530 and provides an ample dose of history for patrons to absorb while sipping any one of a selection of teas that are served with English breakfast, sandwiches, or a piece of cake.

WHERE TO STAY

The Great House (see "Where to Dine," below) also rents rooms.

✪ **The Swan.** High St., Lavenham, Sudbury, Suffolk CO10 9QA. ☎ **800/225-5843** in the U.S. and Canada, or 01787/247477. Fax 01787/248286. 50 units. MINIBAR TV TEL. £117.90 ($188.65) double; £136–£172 ($217.60–$275.20) suite. AE, DC, MC, V.

This lavishly timbered inn, the best accommodation in Suffolk, is one of the oldest and best-preserved buildings in a relatively unspoiled village. It's been so successful that it's expanded into an adjoining ancient wool hall, which provides a high-ceilinged and timbered guest house and raftered, second-story bedrooms opening onto a tiny cloistered garden. The bedrooms vary in size, according to the eccentricities of the architecture. Most have beamed ceilings and a mixture of traditional pieces that blend well with the old. The more expensive rooms feature four-poster beds. There are nearly enough lounges for guests to try a different one every night of the week.

Dining/Diversions: The Garden Bar opens onto yet another garden, with old stone walls and flower beds. Londoners often visit on weekends for dinner and chamber-music concerts, which are performed in October, December, and March. Meals in the 2-story-high dining room, where you sit on leather-and-oak chairs with brass studs, have their own drama. Even if you're not spending the night, you can sample the three-course lunch or an evening table d'hôte dinner. During World War II, Allied pilots made the Swan their second home and carved their signatures into the bar, in a longish room with a timbered ceiling and a fine weapons collection.

WHERE TO DINE

✪ **The Great House.** Market Place. ☎ 01787/247431. Fax 01787/248007. Reservations recommended. Snacks 60p–£8.95 (95¢–$14.30); fixed-price meals £10.95–£12.95 ($17.50–$20.70) at lunch and £18.95 ($30.30) at dinner (Tues–Fri). AE, MC, V. Tues–Sun noon–2:30pm; Tues–Sat 7–9:30pm. FRENCH.

With its Georgian facade and location near the marketplace, The Great House is the town's finest place to dine, a quintessentially French hotel in a beautiful English town. The interior is also attractively decorated, with Laura Ashley prints, an inglenook, and old oak beams. Assisted by his wife, Martine, owner Régis Crépy does double duty as the *chef de cuisine*. He is an inventive, quixotic cook, as reflected by such dishes as breast of duck in green-olive sauce, sauté of sweetbreads with a wild mushroom sauce, and medallions of lamb fillet in lime sauce.

The house also rents four elegantly decorated suites for £52 to £81 ($83.20 to $129.60) double, including English breakfast and dinner. The units have TVs, phones, and private bathrooms or showers.

6 Two Stately Homes in Long Melford

61 miles NE of London; 34 miles SE of Cambridge

Long Melford has been famous since the days of the early cloth makers. Like Lavenham, it attained prestige and importance during the Middle Ages. Of the old buildings remaining, the village church is often called "one of the glories of the shire." Along its 3-mile-long High Street—said to boast the highest concentration of antique shops in Europe—are many private homes erected by wealthy wool merchants of yore. Of special interest are Long Melford's two stately homes, Melford Hall and Kentwell Hall.

ESSENTIALS

GETTING THERE   Trains run from London's Liverpool Street Station toward Ipswich and on to Marks Tey. Call ☎ **0345/484950** (in the U.K. only) or 01603/764776 for information and schedules. Here you can take a shuttle train going back and forth between that junction and Sudbury. From the town of Sudbury, it's a 3-mile taxi ride to Long Melford.

From Cambridge, take a Cambus Bus Company coach to Bury St. Edmunds, then change for the final ride into Long Melford. These buses run about once an hour throughout the day and early evening.

If driving from Newmarket, continue east on A45 to Bury St. Edmunds, but cut south on A134 (toward Sudbury) to Long Melford.

VISITOR INFORMATION   There is a **Tourist Information** office in the Town Hall, Sudbury (☎ **01787/881320**), that's open Monday through Saturday from 10am to 4:45pm.

BEATRIX POTTER'S ANCESTRAL HOME & A TUDOR MANSION

Melford Hall. On the east side of A134, Long Melford. ☎ **01787/880286.** Admission £4 ($6.40) adults, £2 ($3.20) children. May–Sept Wed–Sun and bank holiday Mon 2–5:30pm; Apr and Oct Sat–Sun and bank holiday Mon 2–5:30pm.

This is the ancestral home of Beatrix Potter, who often visited. Jemima PuddleDuck still occupies a chair in one of the bedrooms upstairs, and some of her other figures are on display. The house, built between 1554 and 1578, has paintings, fine furniture, and Chinese porcelain. The gardens alone make a visit here worthwhile.

Kentwell Hall. On the A134 between Sudbury and Bury St. Edmunds. ☎ **01787/310207.** Admission £5.20 ($8.30) adults, £4.40 ($7.05) seniors, £3.20 ($5.10) children. July–Sept daily noon–5pm; Mar–June and Oct Sun only, noon–5pm. The entrance is north of the green in Long Melford on the west side of A134, about half a mile north of Melford Hall.

At the end of an avenue of linden trees, the redbrick Tudor mansion called Kentwell Hall, surrounded by a broad moat, has been restored by its owners, Mr. and Mrs. Patrick Phillips. A 15th-century moat house, interconnecting gardens, a brick-paved maze, and a costume display are of interest. There are also rare-breed farm animals here. Two gatehouses are constructed in 16th-century style. The hall hosts regular recreations of Tudor domestic life, including the well-known annual events for the weeks of June 16 to July 7 when admission prices tend to escalate slightly.

WHERE TO STAY

✪ **Bull Hotel.** Hall St., Long Melford, Sudbury, Suffolk CO10 9JG. ☎ **01787/378494.** Fax 01787/880307. 25 units. TV TEL. £85 ($136) double; £105–£120 ($168–$192) suite. Leisure breaks (2-night minimum) Mon–Thurs £79.50 ($127.20) per person double, Fri–Sun £72 ($115.20) per person double, including half board. AE, CB, DC, MC, V.

Here is an opportunity to experience life in one of the great old inns of East Anglia. Built by a wool merchant in 1540, this is Long Melford's finest hotel and its best-preserved building, with lots of improvements and modernizations added over the years. The rooms here, a mix of the old and the new, are better than those of its closest competitor, the Black Lion. A medieval weavers' gallery and an open hearth with Elizabethan brickwork have been incorporated into the hotel's design.

Dining: The Cordell Restaurant is the outstanding part of the Bull, with its high-beamed ceilings, trestle tables, and handmade chairs, as well as a 10-foot fireplace. The English and continental cuisines are worth a stop even if you're not staying here. Menu choices are likely to include poached fillet of plaice with white-wine-and-mushroom sauce.

The Countrymen. The Green, Long Melford, Suffolk CO10 9DN. ☎ **01787/312356.** Fax 01787/374557. 9 units. TV TEL. £70–£80 ($112–$128) double; £95 ($152) suite. Rates include English breakfast. AE, MC, V.

There has been some type of inn on this spot since the 1100s. Fourteenth-century documents mention it as the spot where drinks were dispensed to revolutionaries during one of the peasants' revolts. The present building dates from the early 1800s; it has been richly restored by its present owners. Although the Bull (see above) remains the most atmospheric choice here, the Countrymen overlooks one of the loveliest village greens in Suffolk. Each of the individually decorated bedrooms features tea- and coffeemakers.

An added bonus is the hotel's well-patronized Countrymen bistro, which offers lighter meals and a well-chosen wine list. Fixed-price meals are served at both lunch and dinner. Bar lunches are a simpler, cheaper option. Their special is pastas made fresh daily by chefs/owners Stephen and Janet Errington.

WHERE TO DINE

Chimneys. Hall St. ☎ **01787/379806.** Reservations recommended. Fixed-price lunch £18.50 ($29.60); fixed-price dinner £20.50–£29.50 ($32.80–$47.20). MC, V. Daily noon–2pm; Mon–Sat 7–9pm. BRITISH/CONTINENTAL.

This is the most venerable restaurant in town, with a more refined cuisine than that served at Scutchers Bistro (see below). The building here was erected in the 16th century and retains its original dark-stained oaken beams and mellow brick walls in the dining room. A walled garden is in back. The fixed-price menus offer a wide choice of foods, influenced by the best modern British cuisine trends. Begin, perhaps, with warm salad of pigeon breast with a red currant jus or else baked phyllo parcels of prawns and feta cheese. Main courses are equally delectable, especially slow-cooked lamb shanks with rosemary and creamed potatoes or monkfish and spinach wrapped in crisp pastry and served with a lobster sauce. Few desserts equal the hot apple and blackberry pie with a fresh egg custard.

Scutchers Bistro. Westgate St. ☎ **01787/310200.** Reservations recommended. Main courses £7.95–£15 ($12.70–$24). AE, MC, V. Tues–Sat noon–2pm and 7–9:30pm. BRITISH.

This upscale bistro has earned favorable recommendations from many locals throughout Suffolk. The building was erected in stages between the 1600s and the 1800s and was named after the workers (scutchers) who, in olden days, rendered flax into linen. As The Scutchers Arms, it was a favorite pub—until the new owners painted its facade bright yellow and covered its heavily beamed interior with vivid Mediterranean colors. Menu choices change daily. Your meal might include sautéed tiger prawns with mushrooms, bacon, and garlic; steamed scallops with asparagus and lemon-flavored hollandaise; warm smoked salmon with green beans and marinated artichokes; and a very English version of steamed fruit pudding with custard.

7 Dedham

63 miles NE of London; 8 miles NE of Colchester

Remember Constable's *Vale of Dedham?* The Vale of Dedham lies between the towns of Colchester and Ipswich in a wide valley through which runs the River Stour, the boundary between Essex and Suffolk. It's not only the link with Constable that has made this vale so popular. It is one of the most beautiful, unspoiled areas left in southeast England. In this little Essex village on the Stour River you're in the heart of Constable Country. Flatford Mill is only a mile farther down the river. The village, with its Tudor, Georgian, and Regency houses, is set in the midst of the water meadows of the Stour. Constable painted its church and tower. Dedham is right on the Essex-Suffolk border and makes a good center for exploring both North Essex and the Suffolk border country.

GETTING THERE

Trains depart every 20 minutes from London's Liverpool Street Station for the 50-minute ride to Colchester. For schedules and information, call ☎ **0345/ 484950** (in the U.K. only) or 01603/764777. From Colchester, it's possible to take a taxi from the railway station to the bus station, then board a bus run by the Eastern National Bus Company for the 5-mile trip to Dedham. (Buses leave about once an hour.) Most people take a taxi from Colchester directly to Dedham.

National Express buses depart from London's Victoria Coach Station for Colchester, where you have the choice of taking either another bus or a taxi to Dedham. For schedules and information, call ☎ **0990/808080.**

If you're driving from the London ring road, branch northeast on A12 to Colchester, turning off at East Bergholt onto a small secondary road leading east to Dedham.

VISITING THE PAINTERS' HOMES

Less than a mile from the village center is **The Sir Alfred Munnings Art Museum,** East Lane (☎ **01206/322127**), home of Sir Alfred Munnings, president of the Royal Academy from 1944 to 1949 and painter extraordinaire of racehorses and other animals. The house and studio, which have sketches and other works, are open from early May to early October, on Sunday, Wednesday, and bank holidays (plus Thursday and Saturday during August) from 2 to 5pm. Admission is £3 ($4.80) for adults, 50p (80¢) for children.

The English landscape painter John Constable (1776–1837) was born at East Bergholt, directly north of Dedham. Near the village is **Flatford Mill,** East Bergholt (☎ 01206/298283), subject of one of his most renowned works. The mill, in a scenic setting, was given to the National Trust in 1943, and has since been leased to the Field Studies Council for use as a residential center. The center offers more than 170 short courses each year in all aspects of art and the environment. Fees are £105 ($168) for a weekend (Saturday and Sunday) and £250 to £350 ($400 to $560) for a full week. The fee includes accommodation, meals, and tuition. Write to Director of Studies, Field Studies Council, Flatford Mill Field Centre, East Bergholt, Colchester, Essex CO7 6UL.

WHERE TO STAY
Dedham Hall/Fountain House Restaurant. Brook St., Dedham CO7 6AD. ☎ **01206/ 323027.** Fax 01206/323293. 16 units. TV. £60 ($96) double. Rates include English breakfast. MC, V.

A 3-minute walk east of the center of town, this well-managed hotel has flourished since its adoption by Jim and Wendy Sarton in 1991. Set on 5 acres of grazing land whose centerpiece is a pond favored by geese and wild swans, it consists of a 400-year-old brick-sided cottage linked to a 200-year-old home of stately proportions. The older section is reserved for the breakfast room, a bar, and a sitting room for residents of the six second-floor bedrooms. Accommodations are cozy and comfortable, with tea makers. A cluster of three converted barns provide accommodations for many artists who congregate here several times throughout the year for painting seminars and art workshops.

Dining: Beneath beamed ceilings, near a crackling fire, you can enjoy a fixed-price lunch at the Fountain House Restaurant on Sunday for £18.50 ($29.60) or fixed-price dinners daily for £19.95 ($31.90). There's a wide selection of dishes with all-fresh ingredients and an abundance of natural flavors.

✪ **Maison Talbooth.** Stratford Rd., Dedham, Colchester, Essex CO7 6HN. ☎ **01206/ 322367.** Fax 01206/322752. 15 units. MINIBAR TV TEL. £120–£185 ($192–$296) double. Rates include continental breakfast. AE, DC, MC, V. Take Stratford Rd. half a mile west of the town center.

This small and exclusive hotel is located in a handsomely restored Victorian country house on a bluff overlooking the river valley, with views that stretch away to the medieval Church of Stratford St. Mary. Accommodations here consist of spacious suites distinctively furnished by one of England's best-known decorators. High-fashion colors abound, antiques are mixed discreetly with reproductions, and the original architectural beauty has been preserved. A superluxury suite has a sunken bath and a draped bed, and each suite has its own theme. Fresh flowers, fruit, and a private bar are standard amenities in the suites. The restaurant, Le Talbooth, is award-winning (see below).

WHERE TO DINE
✪ **Le Talbooth.** Gun Hill. ☎ **01206/323150.** Reservations required. Main courses £14.95–£22.50 ($23.90–$36); fixed-price lunch £18.50 ($29.60) for 2 courses and £19–£22 ($30.40–$35.20) for 3 courses. AE, DC, MC, V. Daily noon–2pm and 7–9:30pm. ENGLISH/FRENCH.

A hand-hewn, half-timbered weaver's house is the setting for this restaurant standing amid beautiful gardens on the banks of the River Stour. Le Talbooth was featured in Constable's *Vale of Dedham.* You descend a sloping driveway leading past flowering terraces. A well-mannered staff will usher you to a low-ceilinged bar for an aperitif.

If you're tall, beware of low ceiling beams, which add an atmospheric touch from another era.

Owner Gerald Milsom has brought a high standard of cooking to this rustically elegant place, where a well-chosen wine list complements the good food. An à la carte menu changes six times a year, and special dishes are altered daily, reflecting the best produce available at the market. You'll get off to a fine start with half a dozen native oysters from nearby Colchester. The velvety smooth parfait of foie gras and duck livers is hard to resist. Each night a different roast is featured, ranging from honey-coated ham to leg of lamb. Your main course, inevitably a delight, might be breast of pheasant with braised cabbage (filled with its own mousseline on a juniper-scented jus).

8 Woodbridge & Aldeburgh

Woodbridge: 81 miles NE of London; 47 miles S of Norwich
Aldeburgh: 97 miles NE of London; 41 miles SE of Norwich

On the Deben River, the market town of Woodbridge is a yachting center. Its best-known, most famous resident was Edward FitzGerald, Victorian poet and translator of the "Rubaiyat of Omar Khayyam." Woodbridge is a good base for exploring the East Suffolk coastline, particularly the small resort of Aldeburgh, noted for its moot hall.

On the North Sea, 15 miles from Woodbridge, Aldeburgh is an exclusive resort, and it attracts many Dutch visitors, who make the sea-crossing via Harwich and Felixstowe, both major entry ports for traffic from the Continent. Aldeburgh dates from Roman times, and has long been known as a small port for North Sea fisheries. The Aldeburgh Festival, held every June, is the most important arts festival in East Anglia, and one of the best attended in England.

ESSENTIALS

GETTING THERE   Woodbridge is on the rail line to Lowestoft from either Victoria Station or Liverpool Street Station in London. Get off two stops after Ipswich. For schedules and information, call ☎ 0345/484950 (in the U.K. only) or 01603/764776. The nearest rail station to Aldeburgh is on the same line, at Saxmundham, six stops after Ipswich. From Saxmundham, you can take a taxi or one of six buses that run the 6 miles to Aldeburgh during the day.

One **National Express** bus a day passes through Aldeburgh and Woodbridge on the way from London's Victoria Coach Station to Great Yarmouth. It stops at every country town and narrow lane along the way, so the trip to Aldeburgh takes a woeful 4½ hours. For schedules and information, call ☎ 0990/808080. Many visitors reach both towns by Eastern County Bus Company's service from Ipswich. That company's no. 80/81 buses run frequently between Woodbridge and Aldeburgh.

If you're driving from London's ring road, take A12 northeast to Ipswich, then continue northeast on A12 to Woodbridge. To get to Aldeburgh, stay on A12 until you reach the junction with A1094, then head east to the North Sea.

VISITOR INFORMATION   The **Tourist Information Centre** is at the Cinema, 51 High St., Aldeburgh (☎ 01728/453637), and is open Easter through October, Monday to Friday from 9am to 4:30pm and on Saturday and Sunday from 10am to 4:30pm.

SPECIAL EVENTS   Aldeburgh was the home of Benjamin Britten (1913–76), renowned composer of the operas *Peter Grimes* and *Billy Budd,* as well as many orchestral works. Many of his compositions were first performed at the ❍ **Aldeburgh**

Festival, which he founded in 1946. The festival takes place in June, featuring internationally known performers. There are other concerts and events throughout the year. Write or call the tourist office for details. The Snape Maltings Concert Hall nearby is one of the more successful among the smaller British concert halls; it also houses the Britten-Pears School of Advanced Musical Studies, established in 1973.

WHAT TO SEE & DO IN ALDEBURGH

There are two local golf courses, one at Aldeburgh and another at Thorpeness, 2 miles away. A yacht club is situated on the River Alde, 9 miles from the river's mouth. There are also two bird sanctuaries nearby, Minsmere and Havergate Island. Managed by the Royal Society for the Protection of Birds, they are famous for their waterfowl.

Insider's tip: Seek out **Crag Path,** running along Aldeburgh's wild shore. It is unusually attractive, with its two lookout towers built early in the 19th century to keep watch for vessels putting down or needing pilots.

Constructed on a shelf of land at the sea level, the High Street runs parallel to the often turbulent waterfront. A cliff face rises some 55 feet above the main street. A major attraction is the 16th-century **Moot Hall Museum,** Market Cross Place, Aldeburgh (☎ **01728/453295**). The hall dates from the time of Henry VIII, but its tall twin chimneys are later additions. The timber-frame structure displays old maps, prints, and Anglo-Saxon burial urns, as well as other items of historical interest. It is open July and August daily from 10:30am to 12:30pm and 2:30 to 5pm. It is also open Easter to June and in September daily from 2:30 to 5pm. Admission is 50p (80¢) for adults and free for children.

Aldeburgh is also the site of the nation's northernmost martello tower, erected to protect the coast from a feared invasion by Napoléon.

WHERE TO STAY & DINE
NEAR WOODBRIDGE

✪ **Seckford Hall.** On A12 (1½ miles from the Woodbridge rail station), Woodbridge, Suffolk IP13 6NU. ☎ **01394/385678.** Fax 01394/380610. 32 units. TV TEL. £110–£135 ($176–$216) double; £125–£150 ($200–$240) suite. Rates include English breakfast. AE, DC, MC, V.

This ivy-covered estate's pure Tudor, crow-stepped gables, mullioned windows, and ornate chimneys capture the spirit of the days of Henry VIII and his strong-willed daughter Elizabeth (the latter may have held court here). Today it provides some of the finest accommodations in Suffolk, rivaling those at The Swan in Lavenham (see above). You enter through a heavy, studded Tudor door into a flagstone hallway with antiques. The butler will show you to your bedroom. Many rooms have four-poster beds, one of them a monumental 1587 specimen.

If you arrive before sundown, you may want to stroll through the 34-acre gardens, which include a rose garden, herbaceous borders, and greenhouses. At the bottom of the garden is an ornamental lake, complete with weeping willows and paddling ducks.

Dining: At 4pm you can enjoy a complete tea in the Great Hall. Sip your brew slowly as you enjoy the atmosphere of heavy beams and a stone fireplace. Your chair may be Queen Anne, your table Elizabethan. Dinner will be announced by the butler. Good English meals are served in a setting of linen-fold paneling and Chippendale and Hepplewhite chairs. After-dinner coffee and brandy are featured in the Tudor Bar. (Call ahead for reservations if you're not staying here.)

Amenities: Heated indoor swimming pool.

IN ALDEBURGH

Brudenell Hotel. The Parade, Aldeburgh, Suffolk IP15 5BU. ☎ **01728/452071.** Fax 01728/454082. 47 units. TV TEL. £85–£105 ($136–$168) double. AE, DC, MC, V.

Located on the waterfront, this hotel was built at the beginning of the 20th century and has been remodeled and redecorated to achieve a pleasant interior. Many of the bedrooms face the sea, and each has a radio, tea- and coffeemakers, central heating, and comfortable beds. The dining room, with an all-glass wall overlooking the coast, is an ideal spot for lunch; dinner is also served.

Wentworth Hotel. Wentworth Rd., Aldeburgh, Suffolk IP15 5BD. ☎ **01728/452312.** Fax 01728/454343. 38 units, 35 with bathroom. TV TEL. £144 ($230.40) double with bathroom. Rates include English breakfast and dinner. AE, DC, MC, V. Closed Dec 27–Jan 9.

A traditional country-house hotel with tall chimneys and gables, the Wentworth over-looks the sea. Built in the early 19th century as a private residence, it was converted into a hotel around 1900. The Pritt family has welcomed the world here since 1920, including Sir Benjamin Britten and the novelist E. M. Forster. In summer, tables are placed outside so guests can enjoy the sun, but in winter the open fires in the lounges, even the cozy bar, are a welcome sight. Many guest rooms, seven of which are reserved for nonsmokers, have panoramic views. There's a 19th-century building across the road from the main house that's a comfortable, seven-room annex. The standards here match those of the main house, though a few singles do not have bathrooms.

Dining: Many come here just to enjoy the good food and wine. Bar lunches range from £7 ($11.20), with a table d'hôte dinner costing £14.50 ($23.20) Sunday to Friday, rising to £16.50 ($26.40) on Saturday.

9 Norwich

109 miles NE of London; 20 miles W of the North Sea

Norwich still holds to its claim as the capital of East Anglia. Despite its partial indus-trialization, it's a charming and historic city. In addition to its cathedral, it has more than 30 medieval parish churches built of flint. It's also the most important shopping center in East Anglia and has a lot to offer in the way of entertainment and interesting hotels, many of them in its narrow streets and alleyways. There also is a big open-air market, busy every weekday, where fruit, flowers, vegetables, and other goods are sold from stalls with colored canvas roofs.

ESSENTIALS

GETTING THERE   There is hourly train service from London's Liverpool Street Station. The trip takes nearly 2 hours. For schedules and information, call ☎ **0345/ 484950** (in the U.K. only) or 01603/764776.

National Express buses depart London's Victoria Coach Station once each hour for the 3-hour ride. For schedules and information, call ☎ **0990/808080.**

If you're driving from London's ring road, head north toward Cambridge on the M11. Turn northeast at the junction with A11, which will take you all the way to Nor-wich.

GETTING AROUND   Norwich and its surrounding countryside is best seen from the seat of a bicycle. **East Anglia Cycles,** 72-A Gloucester St. (☎ **01603/632467**), has the best selection. Bicycles are rented by the day or the week. Hours are Monday to Saturday from 9am to 6pm, and rates are £5 ($8) per day. There's a 20% discount for rentals over 7 days as well as a discount for card-carrying students.

WHAT TO SEE & DO

Norwich Cathedral. 62 The Close. ☎ **01603/764385.** Free admission, but £2 ($3.20) donation suggested. Oct–May daily 7:30am–6pm; June–Sept daily 7:30am–7pm.

Dating from 1096 and principally of Norman design, Norwich Cathedral is noted primarily for its long nave with lofty columns. Built in the late Perpendicular style, the spire rises 315 feet; together with the keep of the castle, it forms a significant landmark on the Norwich skyline. More than 300 bosses (knoblike ornamental projections) on the ceiling depict biblical scenes. The impressive choir stalls with handsome misericords date from the 15th century. Edith Cavell, an English nurse executed by the Germans during World War I, is buried on the cathedral's Life's Green. The quadrangular cloisters, which date from the 13th century, are the largest monastic cloisters in England.

The cathedral visitor center includes a refreshment area and exhibition and film room with tape/slide shows about the cathedral. Inquire at the information desk about guided tours from June through September. A short walk from the cathedral will take you to Tombland, one of the most interesting old squares in Norwich.

Norwich Castle Museum. Castle Meadow. ☎ **01603/223624.** Admission Oct–June £2.30 ($3.70) adults, £1 ($1.60) children; July–Sept £3.10 ($4.95) adults, £1.40 ($2.25) children. Museum Mon–Sat 10am–5pm, Sun 2–5pm.

Formerly the county jail, the castle sits in the center of Norwich on a partly artificial mound. Its huge 12th-century Norman keep and the later prison buildings are used as a civic museum and headquarters of the countywide Norfolk Museums Service. There are guided tours of the battlements and dungeons throughout the day.

The museum's art exhibits include an impressive collection of paintings by artists of the Norwich School, the most distinguished of whom were John Crome (b. 1768) and John Sell Cotman (b. 1782). The castle museum also has the best collection of British ceramic teapots in the world and unrivaled collections of Lowestoft porcelain and Norwich silver. Rare prehistoric gold jewelry and other archaeological finds help to illustrate Norfolk's wealth and importance and the life of its people.

✪ Sainsbury Centre for Visual Arts. University of East Anglia, Earlham Rd. ☎ **01603/ 456060.** Admission £2 ($3.20) adults, £1 ($1.60) children and students. Tues–Sun 11am–5pm. Bus: 3, 4, 12, 27, or 76 from Castle Meadow.

The center was the gift in 1973 of Sir Robert and Lady Sainsbury, who contributed their private collection to the University of East Anglia, 3 miles west of Norwich on Earlham Road. Together with their son David, they gave an endowment to provide a building to house the collection. Designed by Foster Associates, the center was opened in 1978 and has since won many national and international awards. Features of the structure are its flexibility, allowing solid and glass areas to be interchanged, and the superb quality of light, which permits optimum viewing of works of art. Special exhibitions are often presented in the 1991 Crescent Wing extension. The Sainsbury Collection is one of the foremost in the country, including modern, ancient, classical, and ethnographic art. Its most prominent works are those by Francis Bacon, Alberto Giacometti, and Henry Moore.

The Mustard Shop Museum. 3 Bridewell Alley. ☎ **01603/627889.** Free admission. Mon–Sat 9:30am–5pm. Closed bank holidays.

The Victorian-style Mustard Shop displays a wealth of mahogany and shining brass. The standard of service and pace of life reflect the personality and courtesy of a bygone age. The Mustard Museum features exhibits on the history of the Colman Company and the making of mustard, including its properties and origins. There are old advertisements, as well as packages and "tins." You can browse in the shop, selecting whichever mustards you prefer, including the really hot English type. The shop also sells aprons, tea towels, pottery mustard pots, and mugs.

Second Air Division Memorial Library. 71 Ber St. ☎ **01603/215206.** Free admission. Mon–Fri 10am–5pm, Sat 9am–5pm.

A memorial room honoring the Second Air Division of the Eighth U.S. Army Air Force is part of the central library. The library staff will assist veterans who wish to visit their old air bases in East Anglia. At the library, you can find pertinent books, audiovisual materials, and records of the various bomber groups.

Blickling Hall. Blickling, near Aylsham. ☎ **01263/733084.** House and gardens, Tues–Sat £6 ($9.60) adults, £3 ($4.80) children. Gardens only, Tues–Sat £3.50 ($5.60) adults, £1.75 ($2.80) children. Apr–Oct Wed–Sun, bank holiday Mon, and Tues during Aug 1–4:30pm. (Garden, shop, restaurant, and Plant Centre open Thurs–Sun and bank holiday Mon 10:30am–5:30pm). Blickling Hall lies 14 miles north of the city of Norwich, 1½ miles west of Aylsham on B1354; take A140 toward Cromer and follow the signs. Telephone before visiting to confirm opening arrangements.

Massive yew hedges bordering a long drive frame your first view of Blickling Hall, a great Jacobean house built in the early 17th century, one of the finest examples of such architecture in the country. The long gallery has an elaborate 17th-century ceiling, and the Peter the Great Room, decorated later, has a fine tapestry on the wall. The house is set in ornamental parkland with a formal garden and an orangery.

EXPLORING THE BROADS

Wroxham, 7 miles northeast of Norwich, is the best center for exploring the Broads, mostly shallow lagoons connected by streams. These are fun to explore by boat, of course, but some folks prefer to ride their bikes along the Broads.

To get to Wroxham from Norwich, take bus 51. The 30-minute ride costs £2 ($3.20) for a return ticket. Information about touring the Broads is provided by the **Hoveton Tourist Office,** Station Road (☎ **01603/782281**), open Easter through October daily from 9am to 1pm and 2 to 5pm. At this office you can get a list of boat-rental facilities.

If you don't want to handle your own boat, you can take an organized tour. The best ones are offered by **Broads Tours,** near the Wroxham bridge (☎ **01603/782207**). Their cruises last 1¼ to 3½ hours. In summer, most departures are at either 11:30am or 2:30pm. The cost ranges from £4.40 to £6.75 ($7.05 to $10.80) for adults, and £3.40 to £5 ($5.45 to $8) for children.

SHOPPING

For the best in antiques, books, crafts, and pleasant scenery, shoppers can search out the historic lanes and alleys of the town center.

The **Norwich Antiques Centre,** 14 Tombland (☎ **01603/619129**), is a three-floor house opposite the cathedral where 60-plus dealers set up shop. The selection is wide and varied and includes everything from small collectibles to antique furniture. There's also a small coffee shop in the house.

Right next to the Antiques Centre, **James and Ann Tillett,** 12-13 Tombland (☎ **01603/624914**), have a marvelous shop specializing in antique silver, barometers, and new as well as antique jewelry.

St. Michael-at-Plea, Bank Plain (☎ **01603/618989**), calls a 13th-century church home. The church's stained-glass windows were stolen by Henry VIII. Here, 30 dealers sell toys, books, linens, ceramics, and furniture, among other things. Browsers can get snacks, sandwiches, and coffee at the small on-site restaurant.

For book fanciers, **Peter Crowe,** 75 Upper St. Giles St. (☎ **01603/624800**), specializes in 17th- and 18th-century scholarly books, well-bound and illustrated 19th-century books, general secondhand books, and modern first editions.

The **Black Horse Bookshop,** 8–10 Wensum St. (☎ **01603/626871**), rates itself the best general bookstore in the city, but its specialty is fine art tomes. This store is also the official agency for British government publications.

If you're into dolls, don't miss the **Elm Hill Craft Shop,** 2 Elm Hill (☎ **01603/ 621076**), with its custom-made dollhouses and furnishings, plus traditional children's toys, books, and children's jewelry.

WHERE TO STAY
EXPENSIVE

Sprowston Manor Hotel. Sprowston Park, Wroxham Rd., Norwich, Norfolk NR7 8RP. ☎ **01603/410871.** Fax 01603/423911. 91 units. MINIBAR TV TEL. £110 ($176) double; £149 ($238.40) suite. Children under 16 stay free in parents' room. Rates include English breakfast. AE, DC, MC, V.

Norfolk's premier hotel had a long and illustrious history as a private home before it became a hotel in the 1970s. Built in 1559 by a Protestant family prominent in the civil war of the 1640s, it was eventually sold to the lord mayor of Norwich in the late 1800s. It wasn't until 1991, however, that a comprehensive redevelopment added 87 new bedrooms and leisure and conference facilities.

The hotel lies at the end of an oak-lined driveway in 10 acres of parkland surrounded by the 18-hole Sprowston Park Golf Course. Elegance and informality are its hallmarks. Opening onto views, the bedrooms are spacious, quiet, and filled with stylish furniture.

Dining: Some of Norfolk's best cuisine is served here, either in The Manor Restaurant, restored with ancient mahogany reed columns, oil paintings, and crystal chandeliers, or else in The Orangery, draped with Gothic arched windows, a wall fountain, and ferns.

Amenities: There's an indoor swimming pool, spa bath, sauna, steam room, beauty salon, gym and solarium, even a guest laundry room. The **La Fontana Health & Beauty Spa** (☎ 01603/788788) is also located at the Sprowston Hotel and is resplendent with palms and stone balustrades. At the spa, you can balance your mind and your body with a wide range of therapeutic spa treatments. La Fontana also offers a variety of packages.

MODERATE

Hotel Nelson. 121 Prince of Wales Rd., Norwich, NR1 1DX. ☎ **01603/760260.** Fax 01603/620008. 132 units. TV TEL. £85 ($136) double; £95 ($152) suite. AE, DC, MC, V.

Located by the water near Thorpe Station and Foundry Bridge, this 4-story hotel has the best modern amenities and facilities in town, although it lacks the character and atmosphere of Maid's Head (see below). Each of the bedrooms provides a view of either the river or a pleasant courtyard.

The Quarterdeck restaurant offers fast, cheerful service and a choice of dishes such as Cromer fish pie or beef-and-beer casserole with mushrooms and noodles. It's open daily for coffee and drinks, lunch, and informal dinners. There's also the more formal Trafalgar dining room. Facilities include a swimming pool, sauna, and gym.

Maid's Head Hotel. Palace St., Tombland, Norwich, Norfolk NR3 1LB. ☎ **01603/209955.** Fax 01603/209955. 89 units. TV TEL. £99 ($158.40) double; £139–£145 ($222.40–$232) suite. AE, DC, MC, V.

The Royal Residence of Sandringham

Some 110 miles northeast of London, 7,000-acre Sandringham has been the country home of four generations of British monarchs, ever since Queen Victoria's son, the Prince of Wales (later King Edward VII), purchased it in 1861. He and his Danish wife, Princess Alexandra, rebuilt the house, which in time became a popular meeting place for British society. The redbrick and stone Victorian-Tudor mansion consists of more than 200 rooms, some of which are open to the public, including two drawing rooms, the ballroom, and a dining room. The atmosphere of a well-loved family home is a contrast to the formal splendor of Buckingham Palace. Guests can also view a loft salon with a minstrel's gallery used as a sitting room by the royal family and full of photographs and mementos.

A **Land Train** designed and built on the estate makes it easy for visitors to reach Sandringham House, which sits at the heart of 60 acres of beautiful grounds. The train's covered carriages have room for wheelchairs.

The **Sandringham Museum** holds a wealth of rare items relating to the history of the royal family's time here, and displays tell the story of the monarchs who have owned the estate since 1862. Visitors can see the big-game trophies in settings that include a safari trail.

Sandringham is some 50 miles west of Norwich and 8 miles northeast of King's Lynn (off A149). King's Lynn is the end of the main train route from London's Liverpool Street Station that goes via Cambridge and Ely. Trains from London arrive at King's Lynn every 2 hours, a trip of 2½ hours. From Cambridge, the train ride takes only 1 hour. Buses from both Cambridge and Norwich run to King's Lynn, where you can catch bus no. 411 to take you the rest of the way to Sandringham.

The grounds and museum of Sandringham (☎ **01553/772675**) are open Easter to July 20 and August 17 to October 2 daily from 11am to 4:45pm. Admission to the house, grounds, and museum is £4.50 ($7.20) for adults, £3.50 ($5.60) for senior citizens, £2.50 ($4) for children. Admission to the grounds and museum is £3 ($4.80) for adults, £2.50 ($4) for senior citizens, and £2 ($3.20) for children.

In business since 1272, the Maid's Head claims to be the oldest continuously operated hotel in the United Kingdom. Located next to Norwich Cathedral in the oldest part of the city, it has Elizabethan and Georgian architectural styles. The Georgian section has a prim white entry and small-paned windows. The bedrooms are supplied with bowls of fresh fruit and newspapers. Traditional services such as shoe cleaning, breakfast in bed, and afternoon cream teas are offered. The four-poster Queen Elizabeth I Suite (where the Tudor monarch allegedly once slept) is much sought after.

Breakfast and lunch are served in an indoor/outdoor restaurant called the Courtyard Carvery. Here, lunch, tea, coffee, and sandwiches are served every day to nonresidents from 9am to 5:30pm. Dinner is more elaborate—it is usually served amid the Georgian-era paneling of the Minstrel Room.

INEXPENSIVE

Forte Post House Hotel. Ipswich Rd., Norwich, Norfolk NR4 6EP. ☎ **01603/456431.** Fax 01603/506400. 116 units. MINIBAR TV TEL. Sun–Thurs £69 ($110.40) double, Fri–Sat £59 ($94.40) double. AE, DC, MC, V. Take A140 (Ipswich Rd.) 2 miles from city center and 1 mile from A11 (London Rd.)

Situated on a sloping hillside about 2 miles from the city center, this redbrick building offers comfortably contemporary accommodations for business travelers and tourists. Although uninspired, it's a good, clean, and safe haven. Many of the bedrooms feature sitting areas with sofas and armchairs and soothingly monochromatic color schemes. On the premises is Trader's Restaurant and Bar as well as an activity center with an indoor pool, gym, and sauna.

Jarvis Lansdowne Hotel. 116 Thorpe Rd., Norwich, Norfolk NR1 1RU. ☎ **01603/ 620302.** Fax 01603/761706. 45 units. TV TEL. Mon–Thurs £60 ($96) double, Fri–Sun £70 ($112) double. Weekend rates include English breakfast. AE, DC, MC, V. Take Thorpe Rd. a half mile east of city center.

This hotel was originally constructed in the 18th century as a residence for the local lord mayor. The refurbished bedrooms are situated in the main building, as well as in two semidetached cottages. The cottages have bay windows and wooden beams, as well as a private garden.

The reception area's chandeliers light the way up the elegant staircase to the restaurant, where fixed-price lunches and dinners for £13.95 ($22.30) are served. Meals get off to a promising start with appetizers such as a perfectly prepared terrine of peppers and tomato with baby fennels. Main dish temptations include the likes of roast turbot with vermicelli and a green bean salad. A special delight is the breast, foie gras, and leg of a duck with the perfect accompaniments of buttered lentils and a red wine sauce.

WHERE TO DINE

✪ **Adlard's.** 79 Upper St. Giles St. ☎ **01603/633522.** Reservations required. Lunch main course £11.50 ($18.40); 3-course dinner £33 ($52.80), 4-course dinner £35 ($56). MC, V. Tues–Sat 12:30–1:45pm; Mon–Sat 7:30–10:30pm. MODERN BRITISH.

Chef/proprietor David Adlard and his head chef Aiden Byrne are clearly the culinary stars of Norwich. This stylish dining room has a clean crisp decor of green and white, with candlelit tables and a collection of paintings. David sees to it that service is correct in every way but also relaxed enough to make diners comfortable. The chef specializes in modern British cookery, bringing his own interpretation to every dish. These might include terrine of crab and avocado with caviar, steamed squab with Merlot sauce, or seared turbot with saffron sauce, fennel, and roast salsify.

Brasted's. 8–10 St. Andrews Hill. ☎ **01603/625949.** Reservations required. Main courses £11.95–£21.50 ($19.10–$34.40). MC, V. Mon–Fri noon–2pm; Mon–Sat 7–10pm. ENGLISH/ FRENCH.

Within an easy stroll of both the cathedral and the castle, Brasted's is housed in a lovely home with a rather flamboyant interior. Come here to sample the savory cooking of Adrian Coarke, the chef who replaced the restaurant's namesake but who possesses an equal mastery of cooking techniques and innovations. He has a special skill with soufflés. Other dishes, including roast Norfolk pheasant, vegetarian dishes, and desserts, seem equally well prepared.

Greens Seafood Restaurant. 82 Upper St. Giles St. ☎ **01603/623733.** Reservations recommended. Main courses £9–£16 ($14.40–$25.60); set-price lunches £13–£16 ($20.80– $25.60). MC, V. Tues–Fri noon–2:15pm; Tues–Sat 7–10:30pm. Closed Christmas, Boxing Day, and New Year's Day. SEAFOOD.

Owner-chef Dennis Crompton's restaurant is painted green inside in honor of its name. Surrounded by sepia-toned engravings of the seafaring life, you'll enjoy the best and freshest fish in the region. Menu choices include both intricate and complicated preparations of fresh seafood influenced by classic European traditions, as well as a wide selection of less complicated grilled fish served with a variety of sauces. There's also a "classic menu" including the likes of ravioli stuffed with a puree of scallops and served with bean sprouts, oyster mushrooms, and a coriander-ginger sauce. A live pianist provides music for about half of each dinner hour

Marco's. 17 Pottergate. ☎ **01603/624044.** Reservations required. Main courses £15.50–£17.80 ($24.80–$28.50); fixed-price lunch £14.70 ($23.50). AE, DC, MC, V. Tues–Sat noon–2pm and 7–10pm. NORTHERN ITALIAN.

Norwich's premier Italian restaurant is located in a Regency house, a 2-minute walk from Market Place. It's not the kind of place where Chianti bottles hang from the ceiling and troubadours serenade you. Instead, you'll find one of the smallest dining rooms in town, its six tables decorated with elegant cove moldings, the building's original marble fireplace, and soothing tones of buttermilk, gold, and black. Although smoking is not allowed in the dining room, you can have before- or after-dinner puffs and drinks in a comfortable bar/lounge decorated in the Chinese style (in honor of another Italian, Marco Polo). Try such tasty dishes as baked saddle of lamb with a red-currant, mint, and orange sauce, or perhaps chicken breast with slices of Parma ham served with a marsala sauce.

NORWICH AFTER DARK

From fine art to pop art, there's quite a lot happening around Norwich at night. Information on almost all of it can be found at **The Ticket Shop,** Guildhall (☎ **01603/764764**), where you can also pick up tickets to just about any event.

The **Theatre Royal,** Theatre Street (box office ☎ **01603/630000**), hosts touring companies performing drama, opera, ballet, and modern dance. The Royal Shakespeare Company and London's Royal National troupe are among the regular visitors. Ticket prices run £10 to £25 ($16 to $40), with senior and student discounts usually available for Wednesday, Thursday, and Saturday matinees. The box office is open Monday through Saturday from 9:30am until 8pm on performance days, and closes at 6pm on nonperformance days.

Hosting productions of classic drama on most evenings, the **Norwich Playhouse,** Gun Wharf, 42-58 St. George's St. (☎ **01603/766466**), offers tickets ranging from £3.50 to £12.50 ($5.60 to $20). The box office is open daily from 10am until 8pm.

An Elizabethan-style theater, the **Maddermarket Theatre,** 1 St. John's Alley (☎ **01603/620917**), is home to the amateur Norwich Players' productions of classical and contemporary drama. Tickets, ranging from £3.50 to £7.50 ($5.60 to $12), and schedules are available at the box office, Monday through Saturday from 10am to 5pm. On nonperforming Saturdays it closes at 1pm.

The city's **Theatre in the Parks** (☎ **01603/212137**) includes about 40 outdoor performances every summer in various venues.

Located in a converted medieval church, **Norwich Puppet Theatre,** St. James, Whitefriars (☎ **01603/629921**), offers original puppet shows most afternoons and some mornings in an octagonal studio that holds about 50 people. Tickets are £5 ($8) for adults, £3.75 ($6) for children, and are available at the box office Monday through Saturday from 9:30am to 5pm.

The most versatile entertainment complex in town, the **Norwich Arts Centre,** Reeves Yard, St. Benedict's Street (☎ **01603/660352**), hosts performances of ballet, comedy, poetry, and an emphasis on ethnic music. Tickets are £3 to £10 ($4.80 to $16), and the box office is open Monday through Friday from 10am to 5pm, and Saturday from 11am to 1pm.

Before or after your cultural event, check out the local culture at **Adam and Eve,** 17 Bishopgate (☎ **01603/667423**), the oldest pub in Norwich, founded in 1249, which serves a well-kept John Smith's or Old Peculiar. A traditional bare-wood pub, the **Finnesko & Firkin,** 10 Dereham Rd. (☎ **01603/666821**), serves five real ales brewed on the premises, and **The Gardener's Arms,** 2–4 Timberhill (☎ **01603/ 621447**), pours Boddington's and London Pride to a lively crowd of locals and students. A good place to wait for the next film, **Take 5,** St. Andrew's Street (☎ **01603/763099**), a cafe-bar located next door to Cinema City, is the hangout for the local arts crowd.

The East Midlands 15

This region is a mix of dreary industrial sections and incredible scenery, particularly in the Peak District National Park, centered in Derbyshire. Byron said that the landscapes in the Peak District rivaled those of Switzerland and Greece. In the East Midlands you'll also find the tulip land of Lincolnshire, the 18th-century spa of Buxton in Derbyshire, and the remains of Robin Hood's Sherwood Forest in Nottinghamshire. George Washington looked to Sulgrave Manor in Northamptonshire as his ancestral home. If you have Pilgrims in your past, you can trace your roots to the East Midlands.

Except for Sulgrave Manor and Althorp House, where Princess Di spent her girlhood, Northamptonshire is not on the tourist circuit. If you do decide to stop here, the best place to base yourself is Northampton, the capital.

In Leicestershire, you can use the industrialized county town of Leicester as a base to explore many notable sights in the countryside, including Belvoir Castle, setting for Spielberg's *Young Sherlock Holmes*, and Bosworth Battlefield, site of one of England's most important battles.

Derbyshire is noted primarily for the Peak District National Park, but it also has a number of historic homes—notably Chatsworth, the home of the 11th duke of Devonshire. The best places to base yourself here are Buxton, Bakewell, and Ashbourne.

In Nottinghamshire, the city of Nottingham is a good center for exploring what's left of Sherwood Forest, the legendary stomping grounds of Robin Hood.

If you're headed for Lincolnshire, the highlight is the cathedral city of Lincoln itself, with stopovers at the old seaport of Boston, which lent its name to the famous American city.

1 Northamptonshire

In the heart of the Midlands, Northamptonshire has been inhabited since Paleolithic times. Traces have been found here of Beaker and other Bronze Age people, and remains of a number of Iron Age hill-forts can still be seen. Two Roman roads—now Watling and Ermine streets—ran through the county, and relics of Roman settlements have been discovered at Towcester, Whilton, Irchester, and Castor. West Saxons and Anglicans invaded in the 7th century. In 655, the first abbey was established at Medehamstede, now Peterborough. In the

Middle Ages, castles and manor houses dotted a country rich in cattle, sheep farms, and the production of leather work.

American visitors mostly come here today to see Sulgrave Manor, George Washington's ancestral home.

NORTHAMPTON

69 miles NW of London; 41 miles NE of Oxford

Fortified after 1066 by Simon de Senlis (St. Liz), the administrative and political center of Northamptonshire was a favorite meeting place of Norman and Plantagenet kings.

The barons trying to force policy changes that finally resulted in the Magna Carta besieged King John here. During the War of the Roses, Henry VI (before he achieved that title) was defeated and taken prisoner, and during the civil war, Northampton stuck with Parliament and Cromwell. On the River Nene, it has long been an important center for the production of boots and shoes, as well as other leather work, pursuits that are traced through the centuries in two of the city's museums.

From reports of the time, Northampton before 1675 was a fascinating town architecturally, but a fire destroyed the medieval city. Defoe once called it "the handsomest and best town in this part of England." That is no longer true. Nothing of the castle (ca. 1100) where Thomas à Becket stood trial in 1164 is left standing. The town you see today was created essentially after the railway came in the mid–19th century. If ancient architecture is your interest, you'll find Lincoln more interesting.

ESSENTIALS

GETTING THERE   Trains depart from London's Euston Station every hour and 5 minutes throughout the day for the 1-hour trip to Northampton. For information in Northampton and the rest of the Midlands, call the ☎ 0345/484950 (in the U.K. only) or 0163/764776.

Between three and five motor coaches depart every day from London's Victoria Coach Station, requiring about 2 hours for the ride to Northampton, with many annoying stops in between. For schedules and information, call ☎ 0990/808080.

If you're driving from London, follow the M1 due north to junction 15, then follow the signs into Northampton. Depending on traffic, the trek takes about an hour.

VISITOR INFORMATION   The **Northampton Visitor Center** is at Mr. Grant's House, St. Giles Sq. (☎ 01604/622677). It's open Monday to Friday from 9:30am to 5pm, Saturday from 9:30am to 4pm, and Sunday from early June to late August from noon to 4pm.

SEEING THE SIGHTS

The **Church of the Holy Sepulchre,** on Sheep Street, is one of five Norman round churches in England. It was founded by Simon de Senlis, famous veteran of the First Crusade. You can see its circular ambulatory and round nave. Victorian Gothic architecture swept Northampton after the coming of the railway, and the style is best exemplified by the **Guidehall,** on St. Giles Square. It was built by Edward Godwin in the 1860s, an architect then only in his 20s.

Central Museum & Art Gallery. Guildhall Rd. ☎ 01604/639415. Free admission. Mon–Sat 10am–5pm, Sun 2–5pm.

One of Britain's most unusual provincial museums and Northampton's key attraction celebrates Northampton's rich cultural and industrial traditions. Proud of the city's status as the boot- and shoe-making capital of Britain, it devotes much of its gallery space to exhibitions of the largest collection of antique shoes in the world, spanning

The East Midlands

Althorp House **8**
Ashby Castle **4**
Belvoir Castle **6**
Bosworth Battlefield **5**
Chatsworth **1**
Hardwick Hall **2**
Melbourne Hall **3**
Stapleford Park **7**
Stoke Bruerne **9**
Sulgrave Manor **10**

Buxton
Sheffield
Bawtry
A1
M1
A6075
Bakewell **1**
6
Matlock
Edwinstowe
2
614
Ashbourne
Lincoln
52
Southwell
Derby
612
Newark
Eastwood
15
Nottingham
E15
515
Melbourne
6
Ashby-
de-la-Zouch
3
60
Grantham
Boston
5
4
453
Melton Mowbray
7
607
Stapleford
15
17
Leicester
Nuneaton
Oakham
Stamford
M1
M6
43
Peterborough
508
1
8
Huntingdon
Northampton
45
10
Towcester
9
428
M40
Cambridge
422
E15
14
34
Milton
Keynes
5
M11
Oxford
Luton
A1

0   15 mi
24 km   N

E30
Reading
E30
London
M3

centuries of footwear, with emphasis on the Victorian era. Also on display are artworks from Italy spanning the 15th to the 18th centuries, a wide spectrum from the history of British art, and objects uncovered from nearby archaeological sites dating from the Stone Age.

WHERE TO STAY IN & AROUND NORTHAMPTON

Crossroads Hotel. High St., Weedon, Northamptonshire NN7 4PX. ☎ **01327/340354.** Fax 01327/340849. 47 units. TV TEL. £44.25 ($70.80) double. AE, DC, MC, V. Take the A45 8 miles west of Northampton.

This hotel was acquired in the early 1990s by a competent but unpretentious nation-wide chain, which enlarged and renovated it into a simple and rather standard format suited to business travelers. Hints of the building's original antique core are visible in the stone facade, which originally sheltered a tollbooth that long ago taxed travelers between Northampton and nearby Daventry. Bedrooms contain tea-makers and hair dryers. Set on Weedon's main street, the hotel contains a straightforward restaurant serving English fare.

Northampton Moat House Inn. Silver St., Northampton, Northamptonshire NN1 2TA. ☎ **01604/739988.** Fax 01604/230614. 140 units. TV TEL. £110 ($176) double; £130 ($208) suite. AE, DC, MC, V.

The Moat House is often booked by conventioneers and business travelers who appreciate its comfort and its location near the heart of town. Built in the mid-1970s in an efficient, no-nonsense format of concrete and glass, it lies close to the western edge of the Inner Ring Road. The restaurant and bar have exposed stone, flickering candles, and varnished wood trim. The comfortable bedrooms are what you'd expect from an upscale chain hotel. Overall, it's a fine if not particularly historic choice for an overnight stay.

Swallow Hotel. Eagle Dr., Northampton, Northamptonshire NN4 7HW. ☎ **01604/ 768700.** Fax 01604/769011. 124 units. MINIBAR TV TEL. Mon–Thurs £115 ($184) double, Fri–Sun £80 ($128) double; £145 ($232) suite. Rates include English breakfast. AE, DC, MC, V.

Unlike the Moat House, this 1980s-vintage hotel, 3 miles east of Northampton's center, has a country setting, easy access to a golf course, and an on-site health club with swimming pool, sauna, steam bath, and exercise equipment. It also contains two restaurants—an Italian trattoria and a more formal French and English restaurant—that, for lack of anything better near the town center, are popular local choices. Bedrooms are not excessively large, but comfortably outfitted with monochromatic modern furnishings. They're better maintained than any other lodgings in town. The Swallow is friendly and competently run.

WHERE TO DINE

The restaurant situation in Northampton's center is pretty dismal. Many visitors prefer to dine at the Swallow Hotel (see above) or head out of town to The Pavilion.

The Pavilion. 160 Kettering Rd. ☎ **01604/621292.** Reservations recommended. Set lunch £6.75 ($10.80); set dinner £14.95 ($23.90). Main courses £6–£12 ($9.60–$19.20). AE, DC, MC, V. Daily 10am–9:30pm. BRITISH/CONTINENTAL.

Up three flights of stairs, this long and narrow dining room overlooks tennis courts, bowling greens, and the rusted hulk of Victorian bleachers surrounding a racecourse that hasn't seen any action since 1870. Scholars of the Industrial Revolution consider the intricate but rusted ironwork comparable to the elaborate structure of Paris's Eiffel Tower, and something of a sightseeing attraction in its own right.

Rich and copious fare is this restaurant's trademark, including salmon *Coullibiac* (prepared with mushrooms, prawns, and lobster sauce, all presented in puff pastry). Rack of New Zealand lamb is served with red currants and mint sauce. "Pavilion smokies" are smoked haddock poached in white wine, herbs, and cream, and topped with English cheddar.

SULGRAVE MANOR:
GEORGE WASHINGTON'S ANCESTRAL HOME

Sulgrave Manor. Manor Rd. ☎ **01295/760205.** Admission £3.75 ($6) adults, £2 ($3.20) children ages 5–16; free for children under 5. Apr–Oct Mon–Tues and Thurs–Fri 2–5:30pm, Sat–Sun 10:30am–1pm and 2–5:30pm; Nov–Dec Sat–Sun 10:30am–1pm and 2–4:30pm. Closed Jan–Feb except for schools and prebooked groups. From Northampton, drive 18 miles southwest on A43, then B4525 to Sulgrave. From Stratford-upon-Avon, take A422 via Banbury (whose famous cross entered nursery-rhyme fame) and continue to Brackley; 6 miles from Brackley, leave A422 and join B4525, which goes to the tiny village of Sulgrave. Signs will lead you to Sulgrave Manor.

American visitors will be especially interested in this small mid–16th-century Tudor manor, the ancestral home of George Washington. As part of a plan to dissolve the monasteries, Henry VIII sold the priory-owned manor in 1539 to Lawrence Washington, who had been mayor of Northampton. The Washington family occupied Sulgrave for more than a century, but in 1656, Col. John Washington left for the New World. Born in Virginia, George Washington was a direct descendant of Lawrence (seven generations removed).

A group of English people bought the manor in 1914 in honor of the friendship between Britain and the United States. Beginning with a large donation in 1927, the Colonial Dames have been largely responsible for raising the money for a major restoration to return it as much as possible to its original state. Appropriate furnishings and portraits, including a Gilbert Stuart original of the first president, have been donated on both sides of the Atlantic. The Washington family coat of arms on the main doorway—two bars and a trio of mullets—is believed to have been the inspiration for the Stars and Stripes.

ALTHORP HOUSE: THE GIRLHOOD HOME
& FINAL RESTING PLACE OF PRINCESS DIANA

Althorp House. 6 miles northwest of Northampton on A428 in Althorp, near Harlestone. ☎ **01604/592020.** www.althorp-house.co.uk. Admission £10.50 ($16.80) adults, £7.75 ($12.40) seniors, £5.50 ($8.80) children under 14. Open only July 1–Aug 30.

Originally built in 1508 by Sir John Spencer, Althorp House has brought a sometimes unwelcome dose of fame to the surrounding rural area because it was the girlhood home of Princess Diana. It was brought back to life and a degree of glamour by Raine Spencer, Diana's stepmother. At least part of the beauty and historical authenticity of this frequently renovated site is the result of her efforts.

Since the death of Lord Spencer, Diana's father, the house has been under the jurisdiction of Charles Spencer, Diana's older brother, who emigrated to South Africa partly because of the glare from the British monarchy's fall from grace. The house collection includes paintings by Van Dyck, Reynolds, Gainsborough, and Rubens, as well as an assortment of rare French and English furniture, and porcelain by Sèvres, Bow, and Chelsea.

To visit, *you must book ahead.* Following the tragic death of Princess Diana in August 1997, a ticket to Althorp House became extremely difficult to obtain. More than 200, 24-hour telephone lines handle orders for tickets. Althorp is open to the public only from July 1, Diana's birthday, to August 30, the day before the anniversary of her death.

Diana was buried on an island in an artificial lake on the property. Visitors do not have access to the island, but have a clear view of it across the lake. A museum celebrating Diana's life, complete with schoolgirl letters, her wedding dress, and some of her high fashion outfits, also opened here in the summer of 1998.

STOKE BRUERNE: HEART OF THE CANAL NETWORKS

Stoke Bruerne is the center of the East Midland canal networks, the water-going equivalent of a modern motorway junction. The canal reached Stock Bruerne in 1800, and it has played a central role in the canal system ever since. Today, you can visit the Canal Museum and take a cruise on the waterways.

Stoke Bruerne is 9 miles southwest of Northampton near Towcester, just south of the Blisworth Tunnel (take the A508 from the M1 junction 15 or the A5).

SEEING THE SIGHTS

A ride along the canal complements a visit to the Canal Museum. The most convenient operator is **Indian Chief Cruises** (☎ 01604/862428), at the pub of The Boat Inn (see "Where to Dine," below). Two competitors are **Linda Cruises** (☎ 01604/862107), from a base adjacent to the museum, and **Blisworth Tunnel Boats** (☎ 01604/858868), which operates from the village of Blisworth, 3 miles to the north.

Any of the three can arrange daylong rentals of 30-foot "narrows" boats—long, shallow-bottomed motorboats suitable for up to 12 occupants. The companies offer the same loosely scheduled services, hauling groups of passengers up and down the canal for rides that last between 25 minutes and 6 hours depending on the cruise selected. There are no timetables, and the prices vary depending on the company and on the length of the cruise. Indian Chief Cruises charges £1.50 ($2.40) for adults and £1 ($1.60) for children for a 25-minute cruise and as much as £10 ($16) for adults and £6 ($9.60) for children for a 6-hour cruise with a pub stop for a meal. Linda Cruises charges from £1.50 to £9.50 ($2.40 to $15.20) for adults and £1.25 to £6.50 ($2 to $10.40) for children for cruises lasting from a half hour to 6 hours. Blisworth Tunnel Boats rents boats that hold 8 to 12 people for £80 to £95 ($128 to $152) for the day. Rentals require a refundable deposit of £25 ($40), and are always accompanied with instruction on how to operate and navigate them. Be warned that the operations are extremely fluid, and depend a lot on the season and the weather.

Canal Museum. Rte. A508, Stoke Bruerne. ☎ **01604/862229.** Admission £3 ($4.80) adults, £2 ($3.20) children under 16 and seniors. Apr–Oct daily 10am–6pm; off-season Tues–Sun 10am–4pm.

Set within a restored corn mill beside the banks of the Grant Union Canal, this organization celebrates 200 years of traditions that developed around the inland canals and waterways of the Midlands. Its exhibits include videos, a collection of horse-drawn barges and motorized vessels from the earliest years of the Industrial Revolution, memorabilia, tools and artifacts, period costumes, and a well-attended museum shop containing posters, postcards, books, and more.

WHERE TO DINE

The Boat Inn. Stoke Bruerne. ☎ **01604/862428.** Reservations recommended for upstairs restaurant, not accepted in street-level bars and bistros. Restaurant, fixed-price menus £12.95 ($20.70). Bistro and pubs, main courses £4–£9 ($6.40–$14.40), tea with pastries or sandwiches £4 ($6.40). AE, DC, MC, V accepted in restaurant only, no credit cards in bars or bistro. Restaurant Tues–Sun noon–2pm and daily 7:30–9:15pm. Street-level bars daily 9am–11pm. BRITISH/FRENCH.

This is the largest and most popular restaurant in Stoke Bruerne, a canal-side complex that manages to incorporate four bars, cocktail lounges, and dining rooms into an interconnected row of 17th-century cottages. Most of the original character resides in the street-level bars, which boast a thatched roof, limestone walls, stone floors, and open fireplaces. You can order platters of simple food along with your beer (which includes lagers and eight kinds of bitter).

More formal meals, with more elaborate service, are offered upstairs in the restaurant, a barn-style extension with lots of exposed wood and a view over the canal. Menu items change with the season but include venison with red-wine sauce, guinea fowl, lobster Thermidor, salmon, trout, and chicken.

✪ **Bruerne's Lock Restaurant.** 5 The Canalside. ☎ **01604/863654.** Reservations recommended. Set-price lunch £17.50 ($28); dinner main courses £15–£18 ($24–$28.80). AE, MC, V. Tues–Fri and Sun 12:30–2pm and Tues–Sat 7:30–9:30pm. CONTINENTAL/MODERN ENGLISH.

This is the most sophisticated and, at least in terms of cuisine, elegant restaurant in Northamptonshire, a destination sought out by gastronomes as far away as Birmingham and Manchester. Its present allure dates from 1989, when a trio of Franco-British entrepreneurs took over a thick-walled Georgian building whose foundations were built in the 17th century. Past functions of the building, which is situated near the uppermost of the town's seven canal locks, have included roles as a post office, a surgeon's office, and a nursery.

Within a warm and formal setting that contains antique photographs of canal life in the early 20th century, you can enjoy the most creative and imaginative cuisine in the region. Examples might include braised mushrooms in a cheese galette with an artichoke salad; cold sliced breast of duck flavored with the smoke from burning tea leaves, served with a duck-liver mousse; fillet of beef layered with horseradish mousse and a grainy mustard sauce. Desserts are equally imaginative and include an astonishing version of sweet fettuccine noodles laced with honey, rum, and sweet cream.

2 Leicester

107 miles NW of London; 43 miles NE of Birmingham; 24 miles NE of Coventry; 26 miles S of Nottingham

Hang on to your hats, because this county town is definitely no Sleepy Hollow. Leicester, pronounced "*Les*-ter," one of the 10 largest cities in England, overflows with hustle and bustle and is by far the most cosmopolitan city in the East Midlands. This city of firsts—Beethoven's music was first performed here, the BBC's first local radio station was BBC Radio Leicester—thrives on the spirit of discovery and adventure. More recently, it gave birth to genetic fingerprinting.

Although it has some historic attractions, think of Leicester as a base for exploring the surrounding countryside. Its real lure with locals and tourists alike is its shopping, art scene, and nightlife.

ESSENTIALS
GETTING THERE Trains depart from London's St. Pancras Station every 30 minutes throughout the day for Leicester, a trip of about 90 minutes. The fare costs £26 ($41.60) each way Saturday through Thursday and £32 ($51.20) on Friday. For schedules and information, call ☎ **0345/484950** (in the U.K. only) or 01603/764776.

About 10 buses a day leave London's Victoria Coach Station for Leicester. They call at several secondary stops en route, thus taking 2 hours and 45 minutes each way. The round-trip fare is £15.75 ($25.20) Saturday to Thursday and £19 ($30.40) on Friday, a considerable savings over the price of the train if you don't mind the relative inconvenience. For schedules and information, call ☎ **0990/808080.**

If you're driving from London, follow the M1 north to junction 21 toward Leicester. The drive takes 2 hours.

VISITOR INFORMATION   The main tourist information office is at 7-9 Every St., Town Hall Square (☎ **0116/2650555**). It's open Monday to Wednesday and Friday from 9am to 5:30pm, Thursday from 10am to 5:30pm, and Saturday from 9am to 5pm. They'll supply a useful map. Blue Badge guided walks are offered at ☎ **0116/2862252.**

SPECIAL EVENTS   The **Leicester Early Music Festival** (☎ **0116/2707820**) takes place in May and June. Tickets for the whole series cost £20 to £25 ($32 to $40). Also in June, the **Leicester International Music Festival** (☎ **0116/2517759**) attracts some of the biggest names in classical music. Ticket prices vary, but average about £6 to £7 ($9.60 to $11.20).

EXPLORING THE TOWN

Leicester is worth a look if you have an afternoon to spare. In addition to the sights mentioned below, the town has a boating lake, riverside walks, and ornamental gardens.

An exciting wave of new shops has opened in Leicester. In addition to Victorian-style **Shires Shopping Centre,** with its designer and collectible stores, wide walkways, fountains, and sunny skylights, there's **St. Martins Square** in the city center, which has given new life to old restored buildings, with new retailers, cafes, and tea shops. A wealth of specialty shops out a quarter mile on either side of the railway station, and several antique stores line Oxford Street and Western Boulevard.

Venture out from the center of town to Belgrave Road and you'll discover the **"Golden Mile."** This neighborhood is home to the largest sari shop outside of India, and the store windows along Belgrave Road overflow with fine Indian silks, organzas, and cottons. Sari shops also generally carry a variety of accessories including bags, jewelry, shoes, and shawls. **Alankar,** 95–101 Belgrave Rd. (☎ **0116/2612594**), creates a traditional Indian atmosphere for shoppers with Moghul-style decor and provides free refreshments. They receive new shipments of saris from India every 8 weeks. **Benzer,** 153 Belgrave Rd. (☎ **0116/2611411**), carries tussah silk saris, *salwar kameez* (trouser suits) in cotton and silks, and men's traditional wedding outfits.

Jewry Wall and Archeology Museum. St. Nicholas Circle (about ¼ mile from the town center, adjacent to the Holiday Inn). ☎ **0116/2473021.** Free admission. Mon–Sat 10am–5:30pm, Sun 2–5:30pm.

Set near the excavation of an ancient Roman bath, this museum has nothing at all to do with Jewish history. Its name derives from a corruption of the Norman French "Jurad," which referred to the governing magistrates of an early medieval town, who used to gather in the shadow of this wall for their municipal decisions. More than 40 feet high, the wall is higher than Hadrian's Wall, the Baths at Cirencester, or any other piece of ancient Roman architecture in Britain. Exhibits within the museum include a pair of ancient Roman mosaics, the Peacock Pavement and the Blackfriars Mosaic, which are the finest of their kind in the British Midlands. Each was laboriously sliced from the masonry of ancient villas within the district and set into new masonry beds here.

Leicester Abbey. Abbey Park, Abbey Park Rd. ☎ **0116/2510641.** Free admission. Daily dawn to dusk.

Set within a verdant public park that's favored by joggers and picnickers, about three quarters of a mile north of Leicester's historic core, these evocative, poetically shattered remains are all that's left of the richest Augustinian monastery in England, built in 1132. In 1530, Cardinal Wolsey came here to die, demoralized and broken after his political and religious conflicts with Henry VIII. The abbey was torn down during the Reformation and stones were used in the construction of Cavendish House next door.

Leicester Guildhall. Guildhall Lane. ☎ **0116/2532569.** Free admission. Mon–Sat 10am–5:30pm, Sun 2–5:30pm.

Built in stages between the 14th and 16th centuries, the city's most prominent public building was Leicester's first town hall and contains one of the oldest libraries in Britain. Plaques commemorate its role as a die-hard last bastion of the Parliamentarians during the civil war. On its ground floor, you'll see a 19th-century police station with a pair of original prison cells, whose mournful effigies afford a powerful testimony to the horrors of the Victorian penal system. Shakespeare's troupe is said to have appeared here.

Leicestershire Museum and Art Gallery. 96 New Walk. ☎ **0116/2554100.** Free admission but donations accepted. Mon–Sat 10am–5:30pm, Sun 2–5:30pm.

This multipurpose museum has two distinctly separate features. The street level contains exhibits of archaeology and natural history: a dinosaur bone found in a field near Leicester; a collection of Egyptian mummies and artifacts brought back to the Midlands by Thomas Cook, the 19th-century travel mogul; and geological exhibits. One floor above street level is a collection of paintings by British and European artists (including some by Gainsborough) from the 18th through 20th centuries. The collection of early 20th-century canvasses by German expressionists is one of the largest in Europe.

St. Martin's Cathedral. 1 St. Martin's E. ☎ **0116/2625294.** Free admission. Daily 7:30am–5pm.

It may not have the soaring grandeur of the cathedrals of York or Lincoln, but this is the most venerated and historic church in Leicester. In 1086, it was one of the region's parish churches, and it was enlarged during the 1300s and the 1500s. In 1927, it was designated as the cathedral of Leicester, a nomenclature that adds considerably to its pomp and circumstance. The oak vaulting beneath the building's north porch is one of the most unusual treatments of its kind in England. For walking tours contact, Mr. A. Joyce at the tourist office.

WHERE TO STAY

Jarvis Grand Hotel. 73 Granby St., Leicester, Leicestershire LE1 6ES. ☎ **0116/2555599.** Fax 0116/2544736. 92 units. TV TEL. Mon–Thurs £109 ($174.40) double; £165 ($264) suite. Fri–Sun £69 ($110.40) double; £115 ($184) suite. Weekend rates include English breakfast. AE, DC, MC, V.

Jarvis Grand is the finest choice in the city itself. When it was built in 1898, no expense was spared. The original oak and mahogany paneling has been retained, even though the building was enlarged in the 1970s, later taken over by the nationwide Jarvis chain, and completely renovated between 1995 and 1996. Bedrooms are more streamlined and contemporary than the semiantique public areas suggest.

Dining/Diversions: On the premises are the Sports Bar, the slightly more formal Club Bar, a bistro and cafe, and the Club Restaurant, an antique-looking carvery-style restaurant touting fixed-priced lunches and dinners.

Two Great Country-House Hotels

Outside Melton Mowbray are two of the great country houses of England, and the finest places to stay or dine in Leicestershire itself.

○ **Stapleford Park,** 5 miles east of Melton Mowbray on Highway B676 (Stapleford Road; ☎ 01572/787522; fax 01572/787651), has it all. Capability Brown himself laid out the 500 acres of parkland surrounding the 19th-century mansion, with parts dating from the 16th century. In the 17th century, it functioned as the seat of the earls of Harlborough. It was magnificently renovated by the estate's former owner, the late Bob Payton, founder of the Chicago Pizza Factory chain. The present decor was selected by another pair of former owners, David Hicks and Nina Campbell, who defined the place as a "sporting estate," partly because the site has a school of falconry, colonies of trained hawks and owls, a stable with half a dozen horses, and a group of hunt masters who take guests out on game shoots. The present owner, Peter DeSavary, purchased the property in 1996. The lush bedrooms are outfitted with modern comforts, 18th-century antiques, and have 24-hour room service. Rates for the 52 units, which have televisions and telephones, are £165 to £250 ($264 to $400) for a double and £375 to £495 ($600 to $792) for a suite. Major credit cards are accepted.

With sophisticated and elegant Mediterranean and continental cuisine, the dining room here is opulent and highly acclaimed. The offerings aren't quite on the level of Hambleton Hall, but you'll dine in a lavishly outfitted dining room that's as spectacular as 400 years of British tradition and gobs of recent money can provide. Even the yellow-painted wall carvings are historically important, carved by Grinling Gibbons, who was to wood carvings what Thomas Chippendale was to furniture. Menu items include charcoal-grilled king-prawn gazpacho as an appetizer, or else a peppered duck-breast salad. Technically precise main courses may feature sautéed wild mallard or a perfectly spiced crab cake with sautéed

---

Rothley Court Hotel. Westfield Lane, Rothley, Leicester, Leicestershire LE7 7LG. ☎ 0116/2374141. Fax 0116/2374483. 32 units. TV TEL. £90 ($144) double; £100 ($160) suite. AE, DC, MC, V. Head 6 miles north of Leicester on the B5328 rd., just off the A6 between Leicester and Loughborough.

This hotel stands on the edge of Charnwood Forest, a royal hunting ground for centuries. In 1231, Henry III granted the manor and "soke" (right to hold court under feudal law) to the Knights Templar. The chapel erected next to the existing abbey around 1240 is second only to the Temple in London as the best preserved Templar chapel in Britain.

Standing on 6 acres of grounds, the hotel is surrounded by open farmland. Stone fireplaces, oak paneling, and stained-glass windows evoke its rich historical associations. Bedrooms have been handsomely restored and are comfortable, with modern conveniences. Accommodations come in different sizes (some are quite spacious), and many are furnished with antiques. The less desirable rooms with standard furnishings are in a modern annex.

The hotel serves some of the finest cuisine in the area (see below).

WHERE TO DINE

Rothley Court Hotel Restaurant. Westfield Lane, Rothley. ☎ 0116/2374141. Reservations recommended. Set-price lunch £12.95–£13.95 ($20.70–$22.30), set-price dinner scallops. On occasion, roasted venison cutlet with Savoy cabbage and lentils is served. The dining room is open daily from noon to 2:30pm and from 7:30 to 9:30pm. Reservations are required.

○ **Hambleton Hall,** on A606, 3 miles east of Oldham and 26 miles northeast of Leicester, in the small village of Hambleton, near Oakham, Leicestershire (☎ **01572/756991;** fax 01572/724721), is another great country house, with a fabulous restaurant.

Originally built in 1881 as a hunting lodge by a Victorian industrialist named Walter Marshall, it sits on 12 acres of landscaped park at the edge of an artificial lake, Rutland Water. Everything about the place evokes a Victorian/Edwardian country house, including the many flower arrangements and comfortable but severely dignified furniture. Bedrooms have the chintz curtains and scatterings of Victorian antiques you'd expect. Terraced gardens run down to the edge of the lake. Rates for the 15 rooms, which have televisions and telephones, are £140 to £295 ($224 to $472) for a double, including breakfast. Major credit cards are accepted.

Hambleton Hall is widely known for its prestigious formal dining room, which is open to the public. You dine here amid walls upholstered in russet-colored silk and order from a menu that changes according to the practiced but imaginative whims of chef Aaron Patterson, who takes full advantage of the game available from the surrounding countryside and even grows some of the produce in the hotel's walled garden. Menu items include roasted scallops with a sauce *vierge;* fillet of Angus beef with caramelized shallots and a red-wine sauce; whole boneless quail with a ravioli Florentine and *Pineau des Charontes* sauce. It's open daily from noon to 1:30pm and from 7 to 9:30pm. Reservations are recommended.

£16.95–£19.95 ($27.10–$31.90); main courses £12.95–£19.95 ($20.70–$31.90). AE, DC, MC, V. Daily 7–9:30am, noon–2:30pm, and 7–9:30pm. ENGLISH.

Part of the fun of dining at this hotel involves a pre- or postmeal visit to one of Britain's best-preserved strongholds of the Knights Templar, a 13th-century semi-fanatical sect that played an important role in the Crusades. Within the venerable walls of a historic manor house surrounded with parks and farmland, you can enjoy a sophisticated blend of modern and traditional English cuisine—say, a medley of monkfish and crayfish with lime juice, coriander, and artichoke hearts; braised shank of lamb with rosemary glaze and Provençale vegetables; or seared filet of Scottish salmon with nut-brown butter sauce. Not all these dishes reach gastronomic heights, but this is as good as it gets in the Leicester area.

Welford Place. 9 Welford Place. ☎ **0116/2470758.** English breakfast £6.25 ($10); main courses £7.50–£15.25 ($12–$24.40); set menus £12–£15 ($19.20–$24). AE, DC, MC, V. Bar daily 8am–11pm; restaurant daily noon–11pm. BRITISH/ITALIAN.

This place serves everything from midmorning coffee to a steaming pot of midafternoon tea, as well as drinks and full meals. Menu items include bowls of ratatouille with garlic bread; a prawn and curried-mayonnaise sandwich; polenta with spinach and mozzarella in a mushroom-garlic sauce; and panfried Greshingham duck with pears. All of it is dispensed with good cheer and an utter lack of pretension by members of the hardworking Hope family. The dignified building within Leicester's center was originally constructed in 1877 as a private men's club, and the interior retains its original shoulder-height oaken paneling and Victorian motifs.

LEICESTER AFTER DARK

The **Haymarket Theatre,** Belgrave Gate (☎ **0116/2539797**), one of the nation's leading provincial theaters, has been the launching point for many successful West End productions, including *Hot Stuff, Me and My Girl,* and *Mark & Mabel.* Popular musicals like these are the house specialty, but don't be surprised to see anything from contemporary drama to visiting dance companies gracing the stage.

The **Phoenix Arts Centre,** Newarke Street (☎ **0116/2554854**), hosts dance, music, and theatrical productions from around the world, but local dancers, musicians, and actors also entertain from its stage, and there's even an occasional film screening.

On weekends, the area around the **Clock Tower** in the center of town is alive with bustling crowds headed out to the clubs and bars on Church Gate, Silver Street, and High Street. **Krystals,** 97 Church Gate (☎ **0116/2625720**), offers varied entertainment acts from around the world to crowds that flock in from all over the Midlands. Call ahead, since cover charges depend on the act.

The **Mud Club,** 28 Newarke St. (no phone), and **Gold's,** St. Peters Lane (☎ **0116/2531365**), offer a full range of contemporary dance beats in intimate and atmospheric surroundings.

As you might expect of a university town, Leicester has a variety of pubs, but the two most favored by locals are the **Pump and Tap,** Duns Lane (☎ **0116/2540324**), and **The Magazine,** Newarke Street (☎ **0116/2540523**). Stop by either to sample ales by Leicestershire's three home brewers: Everards, Ruddles, and Hoskins.

HISTORIC SIGHTS NEAR LEICESTER

Bosworth Battlefield Visitor Centre and Country Park. 18 miles southwest of Leicester between the M1 and the M6 (near the town of Nuneaton). ☎ **01455/290429.** Admission £2.80 ($4.50) adults, £1.80 ($2.90) children under 16 and seniors; family ticket £7.40 ($11.85). Battlefield can be visited anytime during daylight hours year-round. Visitor center Apr–June and Sept–Oct Mon–Fri 1–5pm, Sat–Sun 11am–6pm; July–Aug Mon–Fri 11am–5pm, Sat–Sun 11am–6pm.

This site commemorates the 1485 battle that ended one of England's most important conflicts. The Battle of Bosworth ended the War of the Roses between the houses of York and Lancaster. When the fighting subsided, King Richard III, last of the Yorkists, lay dead, and Henry Tudor, a Welsh nobleman who had been banished to France to thwart his royal ambition, was proclaimed the victor. Henry thus became King Henry VII, and the Tudor dynasty was born.

Today, the appropriate standards fly where the opponents had their positions. You can see the whole scene by taking a 1¾-mile walk along the marked battle trails. In the center are exhibitions, models, book and gift shops, a cafeteria, and a theater where an audiovisual introduction with an excerpt from the Lord Laurence Olivier film version of Shakespeare's *Richard III* is presented.

Ashby Castle. Ashby-de-la-Zouch (18 miles northwest of Leicester). ☎ **01530/413343.** Admission £1.60 ($2.55) adults, £1.20 ($1.90) seniors, 80p ($1.30) children under 16. Apr–Oct daily 10am–6pm; off-season Wed–Sun 10am–4pm.

If you've read Sir Walter Scott's *Ivanhoe,* you will remember Ashby-de-la-Zouch, a town that retains a pleasant country atmosphere. The main attraction here is the ruined Norman manor house, Ashby Castle, where Mary Queen of Scots was imprisoned. The building was already an antique in 1464 when its thick walls were converted into a fortress.

Melbourne Hall. 8 miles south of Derby on A447, on Church Square. ☎ **01332/862502.** Admission to house and garden £4.50 ($7.20) adults, £3.50 ($5.60) students and seniors, £2.50 ($4) children 5–15; free for children 4 and under. House only, £2.50 ($4) adults, £2 ($3.20) students and seniors, £1 ($1.60) children 5–15. Gardens only, £3 ($4.80) adults, £2 ($3.20) students, children 5–15, and seniors. House open Aug only, daily 2–5pm (closed the first 3 Mondays). Gardens Apr–Sept Wed, Sat–Sun, and bank holidays 2–6pm.

Originally built by the bishops of Carlisle in 1133, Melbourne Hall stands in one of the most famous formal **gardens** in Britain. The ecclesiastical structure was restored in the 1600s by one of the cabinet ministers of Charles I and enlarged by Queen Anne's vice chamberlain. It was the home of Lord Melbourne, who was prime minister when Victoria ascended to the throne. Lady Palmerston later inherited the house, which contains an important collection of pictures, antique furniture, and works of art. A special feature is the beautifully restored wrought-iron pergola by Robert Bakewell, noted 18th-century iron smith.

Belvoir Castle. 7 miles southwest of Grantham, between the A607 to Melton Mowbray and the A52 to Nottingham. ☎ **01476/870262.** Admission £5 ($8) adults, £4 ($6.40) seniors, £3 ($4.80) children under 16; £14 ($22.40) family ticket (2 adults, 2 children). Apr–Sept Tues–Thurs and Sat–Sun 11am–5pm.

On the northern border of Leicestershire overlooking the Vale of Belvoir (pronounced *Beaver*), Belvoir Castle has been the seat of the dukes of Rutland since the time of Henry VII. Rebuilt by Wyatt in 1816, the castle contains paintings by Holbein, Reynolds, and Gainsborough, as well as tapestries in its magnificent state rooms. The castle was the location of the movies *Little Lord Fauntleroy* and Steven Spielberg's *Young Sherlock Holmes*. In summer, it's the site of medieval jousting tournaments.

3 Derbyshire & Peak District National Park

The most magnificent scenery in the Midlands is found in Derbyshire, between Nottinghamshire and Staffordshire. Some travelers avoid this part of the country because it's ringed by the industrial sprawl of Manchester, Leeds, Sheffield, and Derby. But missing this area is a pity, for Derbyshire has actually been less defaced by industry than its neighbors.

The north of the county, containing the Peak District National Park, contains waterfalls, hills, moors, green valleys, and dales. In the south, the land is more level and the look becomes, in places, one of pastoral meadows. Dovedale, Chee Dale, and Millers Dale are worth a detour.

EXPLORING PEAK DISTRICT NATIONAL PARK

✪ **Peak District National Park** covers some 542 square miles, most of it in Derbyshire, with some spilling over into South Yorkshire and Staffordshire. It stretches from Holmfirth in the north to Ashbourne in the south, and from Sheffield in the east to Macclesfield in the west. The best central place to stay overnight is Buxton (see below).

The peak in the name is a bit misleading, since there is no actual "peak"—the highest point is just 2,100 feet. The park has some 4,000 walking trails that cover some of the most beautiful hill country in England.

The southern portion of the park, called **White Peak,** is filled with limestone hills, tiny villages, old stone walls, and hidden valleys. August and September are the best and most beautiful times to hike these rolling hills.

In the north, called **Dark Peak,** the scenery changes to rugged moors and deep gullies. This area is best visited in the spring when the purple heather, so beloved by Emily Brontë, comes into bloom.

Many come to the park not for its natural beauty but for the **"well dressings."** A unique park tradition, this festival with pagan origins is best viewed in the villages of Eyam, Youlgrave, Monyash, and Worksworth, which lie within the park's parameters. Local tourist offices will supply details. The dressings began as pagan offerings to local "water spirits," but later became part of Christian ceremonies. Dressings of the wells take place from early May to August of every year. Designs are pricked on large boards covered in clay. The board is then decorated with grasses, lichens, bark, seeds, and flowers and placed by the spring or well and blessed.

If you're planning an extensive visit to the park, write for details to the **Peak Park Joint Planning Board,** National Park Office, Aldern House, Bakewell, Derbyshire DE45 1AE. A list of publications will be sent to you, and you can order according to your wishes.

GETTING TO THE PARK   You can reach Buxton (see below) by train from Manchester. It's also possible to travel by bus, the Transpeak, taking 3½ hours from Manchester to Nottingham, with stops at such major centers as Buxton, Bakewell, Matlock, and Matlock Bath. If you're planning to use public transportation, consider purchasing a **Derbyshire Warfarer,** sold at various rail and bus stations; for £6.95 ($11.10) for adults or £3.50 ($5.60) for children, you can ride all the bus and rail lines within the peak district for a day.

If you're driving, the main route is A515 north from Birmingham, with Buxton as the gateway. From Manchester, route 6 heads southeast to Buxton.

GETTING AROUND THE PARK   Many visitors prefer to walk from one village to another. If you're not so hearty, you can take local buses, which connect various villages. Instead of the usual Sunday slowdown in bus service, more buses run on that day than during weekdays because of the increased demand, especially in summer. Call ☎ **01298/23098** daily between the hours of 7am to 8pm for bus information.

Another popular way to explore the park is by bicycle. Park authorities operate six **Cycle Hire Centres,** renting bikes for £8 ($12.80) a day for adults and £5.50 ($8.80) for children 15 and under, with a £20 ($32) deposit, helmet included. Centers are at Mapleton Lane in Ashbourne (☎ **01335/343156**); near the Fairholmes Information Centre at Derwent (☎ **01433/651261**); near New Mills on Station Road in the Sett Valley at Hayfield (☎ **01663/746222**); near Matlock on the High Peak Trail at Middleton Top (☎ **01629/823204**); at the junction of Tissington and High Peak Trails at Parsley Hay (☎ **01298/84493**); and between Ashbourne and Leek on the A523 near the southern tip of the Manifold Truck at Waterhouses (☎ **01538/308609**).

BUXTON: A LOVELY BASE FOR EXPLORING THE PARK

172 miles NW of London; 38 miles NW of Derby; 25 miles SE of Manchester

One of the loveliest towns in Britain, Buxton rivaled the spa at Bath in the 18th century. Its waters were known to the Romans, whose settlement here was called *Aquae Arnemetiae.* The thermal waters were pretty much forgotten from Roman times until the reign of Queen Elizabeth I, when the baths were reactivated. Mary Queen of Scots was brought here to take the waters by her caretaker, the earl of Shrewsbury.

Buxton today is mostly the result of the 18th-century development carried out under the direction of the duke of Devonshire. Its spa days have come and gone, but it's still the best center for exploring the peak district. The climate is amazingly mild, considering that at 1,000 feet altitude, Buxton is the second highest town in England.

ESSENTIALS

GETTING THERE   Trains depart from Manchester (see chapter 16) at least every hour during the day. It's a 30-minute trip.

About half a dozen buses also run between Manchester and Sheffield, stopping in Buxton en route, after a 40-minute ride.

VISITOR INFORMATION   The **Tourist Office** is at The Crescent (☎ 01298/ 25106) and is open between March and October daily from 9:30am to 5pm; off-season daily from 10am to 4pm. It arranges a limited roster of 2-hour guided walking tours of the town between June and September on Monday at 10:30am. Although they're free, a gratuity to the guide is appreciated. More practical are the self-guided tours that meander through the historic streets of the town, beginning and ending at the tourist office. Most visitors require between 75 and 90 minutes for the circuit. The tourist office also sells pamphlets outlining the town's most remarkable sites for 30p (50¢) a copy.

SPECIAL EVENTS   The town hosts a well-known **opera festival** during a 2½-week period in July, followed by a 2½-week **Gilbert and Sullivan festival** that draws people from around the world. The tourist office will supply details.

SEEING THE SIGHTS

Water from nine thermal wells is no longer available for spa treatment except in the hydrotherapy pool at the Devonshire Royal Hospital, behind The Crescent. It is also used in the swimming pool at the 23-acre **Pavilion Gardens** (which are open at all times; admission is free). You can purchase a drink of spa waters at the tourist information center or help yourself at the public fountain across the street.

Another sight, **Poole's Cavern,** Buxton Country Park, Green Lane (☎ 01298/ 26978), is a cave that was inhabited by Stone Age people, who may have been the first to marvel at the natural vaulted roof bedecked with stalactites. Explorers can walk through the spacious galleries, viewing the incredible horizontal cave, which is electrically lighted. It is open daily from March through October from 10am to 5pm. Admission is £4.20 ($6.70) for adults, £2.20 ($3.50) for children 5 to 15, and free for kids 4 and under.

Set about 1¼ miles south of Buxton's town center is one of the oddest pieces of public architecture in the Midlands, **Solomon's Temple,** whose circular design might remind you of a straight castellated Tower of Pisa as interpreted by the neo-Gothic designers of Victorian England. It was conceived as a folly in 1895, and donated to the city by a prominent building contractor, Solomon Mycock. It sits atop a tumulus (burial mound) from Neolithic time. Climb a small spiral staircase inside the temple for impressive views over Buxton and the surrounding countryside. It's open all the time, day and night, and admission is free.

WHERE TO STAY

Lee Wood Hotel. The Park, 13 Manchester Rd. (Hwy. A5004), Buxton, Derbyshire SK17 6TQ. ☎ 800/528-1234 in the U.S. and Canada, or 01298/23002. Fax 01298/23228. 38 units. TV TEL. £88–£100 ($140.80–$160) double. Rates include English breakfast. AE, MC, V.

Within a 15-minute walk north of the town center and overlooking Buxton's most popular cricket ground, this hotel was built adjacent to a forest during the Victorian age of Derbyshire limestone. It's the most sophisticated hotel in town. Renovated during the 1990s, it has comfortable but rather plain bedrooms.

Dining: A glassed-in restaurant, The Conservatory, isn't as cozy and charming as The Columbine restaurant (see below), but its food is almost as good, with more of an emphasis on recipes considered exotic by the locals. Set-price menus range from

£16 to £26.50 ($25.60 to $42.40) in the conservatory, and are likely to include breast of duck with honey, garlic, and port-wine sauce; venison with dark-chocolate sauce; and noisettes of lamb with rosemary sauce. Less ambitious platters and snacks are served in The Beer Keller, a popular pub.

WHERE TO DINE

The Columbine. 7 Hallbank. ☎ **01298/78752.** Reservations recommended. Main courses £8–£12 ($12.80–$19.20). AE, MC, V. Thurs and Sat noon–2pm; Mon and Wed–Sat 7–10pm. CONTINENTAL/MODERN ENGLISH.

Here is Buxton's most charming restaurant, serving the town's best food. It's reasonably priced but still rivals some of the more formal and expensive country-house hotels outside the center of town. Set behind a facade of gray Derbyshire stone, it was built during the Victorian age as a private home and retains some of its oldest vestiges within an atmospheric cellar. The place is especially popular during the town's annual music festivals; it sometimes prepares pre- and post-theater suppers. Menu items are straightforward and unpretentious, but fresh and flavorful, served in a bistro-style setting. Dishes might include roasted goat cheese on a bed of leaves with a nut-oil dressing; breast of duckling with fresh mango, apples, and cream; and fillet of salmon with a wild-mushroom-and-chive sauce.

THE HISTORIC MARKET TOWN OF ASHBOURNE

146 miles NW of London; 48 miles SE of Manchester; 33 miles NW of Nottingham

Another center for exploring the Peak District, this historic market town has a 13th-century church, a 16th-century grammar school, ancient almshouses, a population that doesn't exceed 5,000, and no fewer than 13 pubs, more than virtually any town its size in the district. The River Dove, which runs nearby, is known for outstanding trout fishing.

ESSENTIALS

GETTING THERE   There's no train service to Ashbourne, as the rail lines that used to run into the village have been reconfigured into a walking trail.

The bus connecting Manchester with Derby stops in Ashbourne en route. It runs five times a day, and takes about 1¼ hours.

From Nottingham, you can take the train to Derby, then transfer to the Trent Bus no. 107. The bus takes about an hour and runs hourly from Monday to Saturday.

If you're driving from London, take the N1 motorway north, getting off at Junction 24. Continue east along A50 for the next 10 miles, turning onto A515 north into Ashbourne. From Manchester, take the A6 south as far as Buxton, continuing south along A515 into Ashbourne.

VISITOR INFORMATION   The town's **Information Centre** is at 13 Market Place (☎ **01335/343666**) and is open from early March through June and September and October, Monday to Saturday from 9:30am to 5pm; July and August daily from 9:30am to 5pm; off-season Monday to Saturday from 10am to 4pm.

WHERE TO STAY & DINE

For the best pot of tea around, try **The Old Post Office Tea Room,** Alstonefield, near Ashbourne (☎ **01335/310201**). Ernie and Jean Allen, owners and tea aficionados, offer a set tea menu. They also prepare an assortment of homemade goodies such as baked quiche, soup, and cold roasted meats—all perfect for a light lunch.

Callow Hall. Mappleton Rd., Ashbourne, Derbyshire DE6 2AA. ☎ **01335/343403.** Fax 01335/343624. 16 units. TV TEL. £115–£140 ($184–$224) double; £170 ($272) suite. Rates include breakfast. AE, DC, MC, V.

This is by far the most historic, appealing, and comfortable hotel in town, and it also sports Ashbourne's most prestigious restaurant. Originally built in 1848 as a private home, it was transformed into a well-managed hotel in the early 1980s. Most of the 30 acres of land have been leased to neighboring farmers. Set about a half mile northwest of Ashbourne, the Gothic-looking, stone-sided house has been skillfully reincarnated to receive paying guests. Bedrooms are old-fashioned, with hints of the Victorian and Edwardian ages.

Dining: Rather pricey meals are served in a trio of dining rooms with flocked wallpaper and views over the garden. Menu items include escalope of veal with Dijon mustard, mustard seeds, and asparagus tips; and a breast of chicken stuffed with smoked salmon, morels, and cream sauce.

Izaak Walton Hotel. Dovedale, near Ashbourne, Derbyshire DF6 2AY. ☎ 01335/350555. Fax 01335/350-359. 31 units. TV TEL. £67 ($107.20) per person double. Rates include half board. AE, DC, MC, V. From Ashbourne, drive north along the A515, following signs to Buxton. Two miles later, turn left and follow signs to Thorpe and Dovedale. The hotel is on the outskirts of Dovedale.

Set adjacent to the River Dove, a stream noted for its springtime trout fishing, this hotel was named after Izaak Walton, the 18th-century sportsman. The hotel occupies the site of a cottage set on the premises of what used to be Half Head Farm, where Walton was born and where in 1653 he wrote *The Compleat Angler,* one of the English language's definitive texts on fly-fishing. Set amid fields of grazing sheep in an isolated position about a mile west of Thorpe, it was built in the 17th century as a farmhouse. Today, it's an ivy-covered, overgrown cottage with stone walls and rustic grandeur. Bedrooms lie within both an original and a more recent wing, and each contains tea-making facilities and an iron. All were last renovated in 1995.

Dining: Even if you're not a resident of the hotel, you'll be welcomed for bar snacks in the cozy lounge or for full-fledged dinners in the dining room.

BAKEWELL
160 miles NW of London; 26 miles N of Derby; 37 miles SE of Manchester; 33 miles NW of Nottingham

Lying 12 miles southeast of Buxton, Bakewell is yet another possible base for exploring the southern Peak District, especially the beautiful valleys of Ashwood Dale, Monsal Dale, and Wyedale. On the River Wey, Bakewell is just a market town, but its old houses constructed from gray-brown stone and its narrow streets give it a picturepostcard look. Its most spectacular feature is a medieval bridge across the river with five graceful arches.

Still served in local tearooms is the famous Bakewell Tart, which was supposedly created by accident. A local chef spilled a rich cake mixture over some jam tarts, and tearoom history was made.

The best time to be here is on Monday, **market day,** when local farmers come in to sell their produce. Entrepreneurs from throughout the Midlands also set up flea market stands in the town's main square, The Market Place. Sales are conducted from 8:30am until 5:30pm in winter, and until 7:30pm in summer.

ESSENTIALS
GETTING THERE To reach Bakewell from Derby, take the A6 north to Matlock, passing by the town and continuing on the A6 north toward Rowsley. Just past Rowsley, you'll come to a bridge. Follow the signpost across the bridge into Bakewell.

From London, take the M1 motorway north to Junction 28. Then follow A38 for 3 miles, connecting with the A615 signposted to Matlock. Once you're at Matlock, follow the A6 into Bakewell.

VISITOR INFORMATION   The **Bakewell Information Centre** (☎ 01629/
813227) is at the Old Market Hall, Bridge Street. It's open Easter to October from
9:30am to 5:30pm Monday through Friday and 9:30am to 6pm weekends and bank
holidays; November to Easter 9:30am to 5pm Friday through Wednesday, and 9am to
1pm Thursday.

WHERE TO STAY & DINE IN THE AREA

For a look at a working 19th-century flour mill, stop in at **Caudwell's Mill,** Bakewell
Road (☎ 01629/733185). Here you can have afternoon tea with freshly baked cakes,
breads, and pastries made right here at the mill, and then stroll through a variety of
shops, including a handcrafted-furniture store, glassblowing studio, jewelry shop, and
art gallery.

✪ **Cavendish Hotel.** Baslow, Bakewell, Derbyshire DE4 1SP. ☎ 01246/582311. Fax
01246/582312. 24 units. MINIBAR TV TEL. £99–£114 ($158.40–$182.40) double; £135
($216) suite. AE, DC, MC, V.

Four miles east of Bakewell, the Cavendish is one of the most stately country hotels of
England. The stone-sided building was constructed in the 1780s as the Peacock Inn,
and because of its location on the duke of Devonshire's private estate, has remained
closely associated with that family.

The duke and duchess took personal charge of the hotel and its lavish restoration
in 1975, furnishing the public areas and the more expensive bedrooms with antiques
from nearby Chatsworth, a 15-minute walk to the south. The hotel is lavish, aristocratic, and charming.

Dining: On the premises is a woodsy-looking pub, the informal Garden Restaurant, and another rather formal and elegant restaurant.

Riber Hall. Riber, Matlock, Derbyshire DE4 5JU. ☎ 01629/582795. Fax 01629/580475. 14
units. MINIBAR TV TEL. £115–£157 ($184–$251.20) double. Rates include continental breakfast. AE, DC, MC, V.

Directly south of Bakewell along Route 6, this symmetrically gabled structure was
built from gray-toned Derbyshire stone around 1450, enlarged and discreetly altered
by the Jacobeans, and intricately restored to what you'll see today by the present
owners. Public areas are as richly historic and atmospheric as anything in the district.
Bedrooms occupy the premises of a converted stable and are charmingly furnished,
each with a four-poster bed and a roster of tasteful chintzes and antiques.

Dining: Many residents of the shire consider the hotel restaurant their favorite local
haunt. It features elaborate table settings, well-informed cuisine, and is rather formal.
Menu items include fillet of beef wrapped in bacon and herbs, topped with baked goat
cheese with Provençale sauce; lamb served on spinach, tomatoes, and mushroom with
garlic and white-wine sauce; and succulent desserts.

Rutland Arms Hotel. The Square, Bakewell, Derbyshire DE45 1BT. ☎ 01629/812812. Fax
01629/812309. 37 units. TV TEL. £80–£90 ($128–$144) double; £105 ($168) suite. Rates
include breakfast. AE, DC, MC, V.

A dignified early Georgian building set behind a gray stone facade originally built in
1804, this is a landmark in the town, and a good base for visiting nearby Haddon Hall
and Chatsworth House. Jane Austen rewrote part of *Pride and Prejudice* while staying
here. Its original owner operated a prosperous livery stable; some of the bedrooms are
in the old stable block in back. Last renovated in 1995, the hotel offers cozy, well-
maintained bedrooms.

Dining: Today, the restaurant offers more sophisticated and flavorful dishes than
when Ms. Austen was in residence. Lunch and dinner might include roasted Barbary

duck with pear-and-port-wine sauce; grilled fillet of sole with herb butter and lemon sauce; and medallions of pork with glazed apples and a cider-flavored cream sauce.

HISTORIC HOMES NEAR BAKEWELL

The tourist office in Bakewell (see above) will provide you with a map outlining the best routes to take to reach each of the attractions below.

✪ **Chatsworth.** 4 miles east of Bakewell, beside the A623 (10 miles north of Matlock). ☎ **01246/582204.** Admission £6.20 ($9.90) adults, £3 ($4.80) children 5–15; free for children 4 and under. Mar 18–Nov 1 daily 11am–4:30pm.

Here stands one of the great country houses of England, the home of the 11th duke of Devonshire and his duchess, the former Deborah Mitford. With its lavishly decorated interior and a wealth of art treasures, it has 175 rooms, the most spectacular of which are open to the public.

Dating from 1686, the present building stands on a spot where the eccentric Bess of Hardwick built the house in which Mary Queen of Scots was held prisoner upon orders of Queen Elizabeth I. Capability Brown (who seems to have been everywhere) worked on the landscaping of the present house. But it was Joseph Paxton, the gardener to the sixth duke, who turned the garden into one of the most celebrated in Europe. Queen Victoria and Prince Albert were lavishly entertained here in 1843. The house contains a great library and such paintings as the *Adoration of the Magi* by Veronese and *King Uzziah* by Rembrandt. On the grounds you can see spectacular fountains, and there is a playground for children in the farmyard.

Hardwick Hall. Doe Lea, 9½ miles southeast of Chesterfield. ☎ **01246/850430.** Admission £6 ($9.60) adults, £3.10 ($4.95) children. House Apr–Oct Wed–Thurs, Sat–Sun, and bank holiday Mondays 12:30–5pm. Grounds open daily year-round. Take junction 29 from the M1 motorway.

Hardwick Hall was built in 1597 for Bess of Hardwick, a woman who acquired an estate from each of her four husbands. It is particularly noted for its "more glass than wall" architecture. The high great chamber and long gallery crown an unparalleled series of late 16th-century interiors, including an important collection of tapestries, needlework, and furniture. The house is surrounded by a 300-acre country park, featuring walled gardens, orchards, and an herb garden.

MORE ATTRACTIONS AROUND THE REGION

National Tramway Museum. At Crich, near Matlock. ☎ **01773/852565.** Admission £5.90 ($9.45) adults, £5.10 ($8.15) seniors, £3 ($4.80) children 5–15; £16.20 ($25.90) family ticket (2 adults, 3 children). April and June–Aug daily 10am–5:30pm; May and Sept–Oct Sat–Thurs 10am–5:30pm.

The National Tramway Museum is a paradise of vintage trams—electric, steam, and horse-drawn—from England and overseas, including New York. Your admission ticket allows you unlimited rides on the trams, which make the 2-mile round-trip to Glory Mine with scenic views over the Derwent Valley via Wakeridge, where a stop is made to visit the Peak District Mines Historical Society display of lead mining. It also includes admission to various tramway exhibitions.

Peak District Mining Museum. At the Pavilion, Matlock Bath. ☎ **01629/583834.** Admission £2 ($3.20) adults, £1.50 ($2.40) children. Apr–Sept daily 10am–5pm; off-season daily 11am–4pm.

This museum traces 2,000 years of Derbyshire lead mining. Its centerpiece is a giant water-pressure engine that used to pump water from a lead mine 360 feet underground in the early 19th century. You can crawl through a simulated mine level and climbing shaft.

The Royal Crown Derby Factory. 194 Osmaston Rd., Derby. ☎ **01332/7128000.** Tours £5.50 ($8.80) per person; free admission to museum. Tours Mon–Thurs 10:30am and 1:45pm and Fri 10:30am–1:15pm; museum Mon–Sat 9:30am–5pm and Sun 10am–4pm.

This is the only pottery factory allowed to use both the words *royal* and *crown* in its name, a double honor granted by George III and Queen Victoria. At the end of a 90-minute tour, you can treat yourself to a bargain in the gift shop and visit the Royal Crown Derby Museum.

4 Nottinghamshire: Robin Hood Country

"Notts," as Nottinghamshire is known, lies in the heart of the East Midlands. Its towns are rich in folklore or have bustling markets. Many famous people have come from Nottingham, notably those 13th century outlaws from Sherwood Forest, Robin Hood and his Merry Men. It also was home to the romantic poet Lord Byron; you can visit his ancestral home at Newstead Abbey. D. H. Lawrence, author of *Sons and Lovers* and *Lady Chatterley's Lover,* was born in a tiny miner's cottage in Eastwood, which he later immortalized in his writings.

NOTTINGHAM

121 miles N of London; 72 miles SE of Manchester

Although it's an industrial center, Nottingham is still a good base for exploring Sherwood Forest and the rest of the shire. Nottingham is known to literary buffs for its association with author D. H. Lawrence and its medieval sheriff, who played an important role in the Robin Hood story.

It was an important pre-Norman settlement guarding the River Trent, the gateway to the north of England. Followers of William the Conqueror arrived in 1068 to erect a fort here. In a later reincarnation, the fort saw supporters of Prince John surrender to Richard the Lionheart in 1194. Many other exploits occurred here—notably Edward III's capture of Roger Mortimer and Queen Isabella, the assassins of Edward II. From Nottingham, Richard III marched out with his men to face defeat and his own death at Bosworth Field in 1485.

With the arrival of the spinning jenny in 1768, Nottingham was launched into the forefront of the Industrial Revolution. It's still a center of industry and home base to many well-known British firms, turning out such products as John Player cigarettes, Boots pharmaceuticals, and Raleigh cycles.

Nottingham doesn't have many attractions, but it's a young and vital city, very student-oriented. Its Hockley neighborhood is as hip as anything this side of Manchester or London. A look at one of the alternative newspapers or magazines freely distributed around town can connect you with the city's constantly changing nightlife scene.

ESSENTIALS

GETTING THERE   The best rail connection is via Lincoln, from which 28 trains arrive Monday through Saturday, and about eight trains on Sunday. The trip takes about 45 minutes. Trains also leave from London's St. Pancras Station; the trip takes about 2½ hours. For schedules and information, call ☎ **0345/484950** (in the U.K. only) or 01603/764776.

Buses from London arrive at the rate of about seven per day. For schedules and information, call ☎ **0990/808080.**

If you're driving from London, the M1 motorway runs to a few miles west of Nottingham. Feeder roads, including the A453, are well marked the short distance into town. The drive takes about 3 to 3½ hours.

The Search for Pilgrim Roots

Many North Americans who trace their ancestry to the Pilgrims come to this part of England to see where it all started.

The Separatist Movement had its origin in a small area north of Nottingham and south of York called Bassetlaw. Hamlets that were the strongholds of the Separatist membership are clustered into a relatively small area interconnected to Nottingham via the A60 and the A614 highways, between 30 and 35 miles north of Nottingham's center. In the order you'll reach them from Nottingham, they include Babworth, Blyth, Scrooby, and Austerfield Bawtry (you'll see it on maps simply as Bawtry).

Pilgrim patriarchs associated with these villages include William Brewster (usually identified with Scrooby) and William Bradford, who was born in a manor house still standing in Austerfield Bawtry. During the Industrial Revolution, Babworth was inhabited mostly by owners and employees of the region's many coal mines.

Blyth is the most beautiful of the villages. It's no surprise that it looks like a New England town, with a green surrounded by well-kept old houses. The parish church was developed from the 11th-century nave of a Benedictine priory church. On the green is a 12th-century stone building which was once the Hospital of St. John.

Scrooby is a tiny village of some 160 inhabitants where the Pilgrim leader William Brewster was born in 1566. His father was bailiff of the manor and master of the postes, so the infant Brewster first saw the light of day in the manor house. The original house dated from the 12th century, and the present manor farm, built on the site in the 18th century, has little except its historical association to offer. Brewster Cottage, with its pinfold where stray animals were impounded, lies beside the village church of St. Wilfred, but it's uncertain whether Brewster ever lived in it.

The village also contains Monks Mill on the River Ryton, now almost a backwater but once a navigable stream down which Brewster and his companions may have escaped to Leyden in Holland and on to their eventual freedom.

A turnpike ran through Scrooby in the 18th century, and there are many stories of highwaymen, robberies, and murders. The remains of one John Spencer dangled here for more than 60 years as a reminder of the penalties of wrongdoing. He had attempted to dispose of the bodies of the keeper of the Scrooby tollbar and his mother in the river.

The tourist office at Nottingham can offer advice on exploring these villages.

VISITOR INFORMATION Information is available at the **City Information Centre,** 1–4 Smithy Row (☎ **0115/9155330**). It's open Easter to the first week in October, Monday through Friday from 8:30am to 5pm, Saturday from 9am to 5pm, and Sunday from 10am to 4pm; the rest of the year, it's open Monday to Friday from 8:30am to 5pm and Saturday from 9am to 5pm.

SPECIAL EVENTS Culturally, Nottingham is on the maps with its **Nottingham Festival,** a premier musical and artistic festival lasting throughout the summer. The tourist office will provide you with complete details.

EXPLORING THE AREA

Put on your most comfortable shoes and prepare to tackle the more than 800 shops in and around town—Nottingham boasts some of England's best shopping. Start in the city center, with its maze of pedestrian streets, and work your way out toward the two grand indoor shopping malls, the Victoria and the Broad Marsh, located to the north and to the south of the center of town. Then head over to Derby Road for your fill of antiques.

Fine Nottingham lace can be found in the **Lace Centre**, Castle Road, across the street from Nottingham Castle (☎ **0115/9413539**), or in the shops around the area known as the **Lace Market** along High Pavement.

Then, to catch up on the hippest and latest in fashion and furnishing trends, explore the many boutiques in the Hockley area, the Exchange Arcade, and the Flying Horse Mall, all in the city center.

Of course, in a shopping mecca like Nottingham, unique art items abound. **International Fine Arts,** No. 5, The Poultry (☎ **0115/9412580**), is a prestigious art gallery, selling original oil paintings, watercolors, limited editions, and collections by David Shepherd, Sir William Russell Flint, Gordon King, and L. S. Lowry. **Patchings Farm Art Centre,** Oxton Road, near Calverton (☎ **0115/9653479**), is a 60-acre art haven. Restored farm buildings house three galleries, working art and pottery studios, a gift shop, and art and framing shops.

And long known as Britain's first real craft center, **Longdale Craft Centre,** Longdale Lane, Ravenshead (☎ **01623/794858**), is a labyrinth of re-created Victorian streets where professional craftspeople work on a whole range of craft items, including jewelry, pottery, and prints.

Nottingham Castle Museum. Castle Rd. ☎ **0115/9153700.** Admission Sat–Sun £1 ($1.60) adults, 50p (80¢) children; free Mon–Fri. Mar–Oct daily 10am–5pm; Nov–Feb Mon–Thurs and Sat–Sun 10:30am–5pm, Fri 1–5pm.

Overlooking the city, Nottingham Castle was built in 1679 by the duke of Newcastle on the site of an old Norman fortress. After restoration in 1878, it was opened as a provincial museum surrounded by a charmingly laid-out garden. Of particular interest is the History of Nottingham Gallery, re-creating the legends associated with the city, plus a rare collection of ceramics and a unique exhibition of medieval alabaster carvings, which were executed between 1350 and 1530. These delicately detailed scenes illustrate the life of Christ, the Virgin Mother, and various saints. Paintings cover several periods but are strong on 16th-century Italian, 17th-century French and Dutch, and the richest English paintings of the past 2 centuries.

The only element from the original Norman castle to survive is a subterranean passage called Mortimer's Hole. The passage leads to **Ye Olde Trip to Jerusalem,** 1 Brewhouse Yard at Castle Rd. (☎ **0115/9473171**), dating from 1189 and said to be the oldest inn in England. King Edward III is said to have led a band of noblemen through these secret passages, surprising Roger Mortimer and his queen, killing Mortimer and putting his lady in prison. A statue of Robin Hood stands at the base of the castle.

Brewhouse Yard Museum. Brewhouse Yard, Castle Rock. ☎ **0115/9153640.** Admission Sat–Sun £1 ($1.60) adults, 50p (80¢) children; free Mon–Fri. Daily 10am–4pm. Closed Christmas Day, Boxing Day, and New Year's Day.

This museum consists of five 17th-century cottages at the foot of Castle Rock, presenting a panorama of Nottingham life in a series of furnished rooms and shops. Some of them, open from cellar to attic, display much local history, and visitors are encouraged to handle the exhibits. The most interesting features are in a series of cellars cut into the rock of the castle instead of below the houses, plus an exhibition of a Nottingham shopping street from around 1919 to 1939. This is not a typical folk museum, but attempts to be as lively as possible, involving both visitors and the Nottingham community in expanding displays and altering exhibitions on a bimonthly basis.

Museum of Costume & Textiles. 51 Castle Gate. ☎ **0115/9153500.** Free admission. Daily 10am–5pm.

This is one of the half dozen or so best collections of period costumes in Britain, with exhibitions ranging from the 17th century to the Carnaby Street era of the 1960s. Many garments date from the 1700s, and include exhibitions of "fallals and fripperies" (gewgaws and accessories as designated by the disapproving Puritans), as well as lace, weavings, and embroideries, each of them a celebration of the textile industry that dominated part of Nottingham's economy for many generations. Look for the Eyre Map Tapestries, woven in 1632 and depicting the geography of the region.

Historic Homes Near Nottingham

Newstead Abbey. On A60 (Mansfield Rd.), 12 miles north of Nottingham center in Linby. ☎ **01623/793557.** Admission to house and grounds £4 ($6.40) adults, £2 ($3.20) students and seniors, £1 ($1.60) children. Gardens only £2 ($3.20) adults, £1.50 ($2.40) children. House Apr–Oct daily noon–6pm; gardens open year-round daily 9:30am–dusk.

Lord Byron once made his home at Newstead Abbey, one of eight museums administered by the city of Nottingham. Some of the original Augustinian priory, purchased by Sir John Byron in 1540, still survives. In the 19th century, the mansion was given a neo-Gothic restoration. Mementos, including first editions and manuscripts, are displayed inside. You can explore the parkland of some 300 acres, with waterfalls, rose gardens, a Monk's Stew Pond, and a Japanese water garden.

Wollaton Hall. In Wollaton Park, 3 miles from Nottingham center. ☎ **0115/9153900.** Admission on Sat–Sun and bank holiday Mondays £1.50 ($2.40) adults, 80p ($1.30) children. Free other days. Apr-Sept Mon–Sat 10am–5pm, Sun 1–5pm; off-season Mon–Sat 10am–4:30pm, Sun 1:30-4:30pm. Drive southwest along the A609 (Ilkeston Rd.), which will become Wollaton Rd.

This well-preserved Elizabethan mansion, finished in 1588, is the most ornate in England. Today it houses a natural-history museum with lots of insects, invertebrates, British mammals, birds, reptiles, amphibians, and fish. The hall is surrounded by a deer park and garden. See the camellia house with the world's earliest cast-iron front dating from 1823. The bird dioramas here are among the best in Britain.

WHERE TO STAY

Nottingham Moat House. 296 Mansfield Rd., Nottingham, Nottinghamshire NG5 2BT. ☎ **0115/9359988.** Fax 0115/9691506. 175 units. TV TEL. £115 ($184) double; £130 ($208) suite. AE, MC, V.

If you're driving, you'll appreciate this chain hotel's easy access from the A60 highway, and its location less than a mile north of the city center. It was built in 1968 as a modern alternative to the town's B&Bs. The rooms are standard but are well maintained; half are designated for nonsmokers. Business travelers might be comfortable entertaining clients in the Churchill Restaurant.

If this hotel is full, a desk employee will be glad to refer you to the hotel's sibling, the **Royal Moat House Nottingham,** Wollaton Street (☎ **0115/9369988;** fax 0115/947-5667), where 218 units await. Doubles here cost £130 ($208), suites £130 to £180 ($208 to $288). Although bedrooms are a bit more modern, and although it contains four different restaurants and bars, many travelers prefer to save a few pounds by staying at the Nottingham Moat House.

Strathdon Thistle Hotel. 44 Derby Rd., Nottingham, Nottinghamshire NG1 5FT. ☎ **0115/9418501.** Fax 0115/948-3725. 68 units. TV TEL. Mon–Thurs £109 ($174.40) double, Fri–Sun £69 ($110.40) double. AE, DC, MC, V.

This is a solid and unpretentious member of a nationwide chain. Built in the 1970s of gray-colored brick in the heart of town, it has seven floors, neutral public areas, and two bars. Bedrooms are nondescript but well designed, with satellite TVs and 24-hour room service.

We much prefer the informal Boston Bean Bar, a combination saloon and diner watering hole, to the sedate cocktail lounge. More elaborate meals are served in Bobbins, a well-run but somewhat lackluster restaurant.

WHERE TO DINE

When it's teatime, head for the **Lace Hall,** High Pavement (☎ **0115/9484221**), where you can sit in an ancient chapel and admire the softly colored sunlight filter through the stained-glass windows.

Sonny's. 3 Carlton St. ☎ **0115/9473041.** Reservations required. Main courses £8.95–£23.95 ($14.30–$38.30). AE, DC, MC, V. Daily 11am–3:30pm; Sun–Thurs 7–10:30pm, Fri–Sat 7–11pm. MODERN PACIFIC RIM/BRITISH/FRENCH.

This choice, in the fashionable neighborhood of Hockley, seems almost like a hip London restaurant of the moment. Dishes include charcoal-grilled peppered duck with mango and sesame-seed oil; Yucatan-style spiced charcoal-grilled chicken with black-bean salsa; and roast shallot-and-leek tart served with a gruyère crust. Desserts such as sticky toffee pudding and lemongrass-and-coconut parfait are deliberately conceived to raise eyebrows; many are delicious.

SHERWOOD FOREST

Second only to Germany's Schwarzwald in European lore and legend, ☻ **Sherwood Forest** comprises 450 acres of oak and silver birch trees owned and strictly protected by a local entity, the Thoresby Estate, and maintained by the county of Nottinghamshire. Actually, very little of this area was forest even when it provided cover for Robin Hood, Friar Tuck, and Little John.

Robin Hood, the folk hero of tale and ballad, fired the imagination of a hardworking, impoverished English people, who particularly liked his adopted slogan: "Take from the rich and give to the poor."

Celebrating their freedom in verdant Sherwood Forest, Robin Hood's eternally youthful band rejoiced in "hearing the twang of the bow of yew and in watching the gray goose shaft as it cleaves the glistening willow wand or brings down the king's proud buck." Life was one long picnic beneath the splendid oaks of a primeval forest, with plenty of ale and flavorful venison poached from the forests of an oppressive king. The clever guerrilla rebellion Robin Hood waged against authority (represented by the haughty, despotic, and overfed sheriff of Nottingham) was full of heroic exploits and a desire to win justice for the victims of oppression.

Now, as then, the forest consists of woodland glades, farm fields, villages, and hamlets. But the surroundings are so built up that Robin Hood wouldn't recognize them today.

Sherwood Forest Visitor Centre (☎ **01623/823202**) is in Sherwood Forest Country Park at Edwinstowe, some 18 miles north of Nottingham city off the A614, or 8 miles east of Mansfield on B6034. It stands near the Major Oak, popularly known as Robin Hood's tree, although analysis of its bark reveals that it wasn't around in the 13th century. Many marked walks and footpaths lead from the visitor center through the woodland. There's an exhibition of life-size models of Robin and the other well-known outlaws, as well as a shop with books, gifts, and souvenirs. The center will provide as much information as is known about the Merry Men and Maid Marian, whom Robin Hood is believed to have married at Edwinstowe Church near the visitor center. Little John's grave can be seen at Hathersage (36 miles away), Will Scarlet's at Blidworth (9½ miles away).

The center also contains a visitor information facility and the **Forest Table,** which offers cafeteria service and meals with an emphasis on traditional English country recipes.

Opening times for the country park are dawn to dusk, and for the visitor center, April to October daily from 10:30am to 5pm and November to March from 10:30am to 4:30pm. Entrance to the center is free, and "Robin Hood's Sherwood" exhibition is also free. There is a charge of 50p (80¢) for adults, 25p (40¢) for children and senior citizens. A year-round program of events is presented, mainly on weekends and during national and school holiday periods. Parking costs £1.50 ($2.40) per car per day from April to October.

An odd and somewhat archaic holdover from medieval times are **The Dukeries,** large country estates that contain privately owned remnants of whatever trees and vales remain of Sherwood Forest. Most lie on the edge of heavily industrialized towns, and may or may not have privately owned houses of historic merit. Very few can actually be visited without special invitations from their owners. On the other hand, **Clumber Park,** a 3,800-acre tract of park and woodland maintained by National Trust authorities, is favored by local families for picnics and strolls. It contains an 80-acre lake at its center, a monumental promenade flanked with venerable lime (linden) trees, and the Gothic-Revival **Clumber Chapel.** Built between 1886 and 1889 as a site of worship for the private use of the seventh duke of Newcastle, it's open from early March until mid-January, daily from 10am to 4pm.

The park itself is open year-round during daylight hours, although its allure and the services it provides are at their lowest ebb during November and December. The gift shop and tearoom are open January through March daily from 10:30am to 4pm, and from April to late October daily from 10:30am to 6pm. Admission to the park, including the chapel, ranges from £3 to £14 ($4.80 to $22.40), depending on the size of your vehicle.

If you're specifically interested in the botany and plant life, head for the park's **Conservation Centre,** a walled garden with extensive greenhouses. It's open from April 1 to September 24 on Saturday, Sunday, and bank-holiday Mondays from 1 to 5pm. For information about the park and its features, contact the **Clumber Park Estate Office,** Worksop, Nottingham SKO 3AZ (☎ **01909/476592**).

SOUTHWELL

135 miles NW of London; 24 miles SW of Lincoln; 14 miles NE of Nottingham

If you don't want to stay in Nottingham, the ancient market town of Southwell, England's smallest cathedral town, about a half-hour drive from Lord Byron's Newstead Abbey, is a good center for exploring Robin Hood country. From Nottingham's center, drive northeast along the B686 (the Southwell Road), then transfer onto the A612 for the remaining distance into Southwell. It's a 17-mile drive.

ONE OF ENGLAND'S MOST BEAUTIFUL CHURCHES

✪ **Southwell Minster.** Admission free but a donation is suggested. Daily 8am–dusk.

The old twin-spired cathedral is an unexpected gem in this part of England. James I found that it held up with "any other kirk in Christendom." The Minster is the only cathedral in England to boast three Norman towers. The west front is pierced by a

Perpendicular, seven-light window. Interior architectural highlights include a screen built in the mid-1300s and depicting 286 images of gods, men, and devils. Look also for a stunning early English choir and chapter house from 1288, the first single-span, stone-vaulted chapter house in the Christian world. The chapter house is noted for its "Leaves of Southwell," stone foliage so realistic you can distinguish oak from hawthorn, buttercup from ivy.

WHERE TO STAY

Saracen's Head. Market Place, Southwell, Nottinghamshire NG25 0HE. ☎ **01636/ 812701.** Fax 01636/815408. 27 units. TV TEL. £85 ($136) double. AE, DC, MC, V.

Other than Southwell Minster, this is the town's most famous and historic building. Built during the Elizabethan age, it retains its original Tudor-style, black-and-white, half-timbered facade. Both Charles I and James I dined here, and Charles I was imprisoned here before the Scots handed him over to the Parliamentarians. After he was beheaded, the name of the inn was changed from the King's Arms to the Saracen's Head. Commanding the junction of the main ancient thoroughfares leading into the town, the old inn frequently entertained Byron. Today, you'll find cozy bedrooms strewn with nostalgic reminders of old England, a pair of cozy bars with exposed beams and paneling, and a restaurant serving well-prepared traditional table d'hôte meals.

WHERE TO DINE

Vineyard Cafe & Bistro, 12 King St. ☎ **01636/816573.** Reservations recommended. Main courses £9.50–£15 ($15.20–$24); fixed-price lunch £12.95 ($20.70). Tues–Sat noon–2:30pm and 7–9:30pm. BRITISH.

If you don't dine at the Saracen's Head (see above), this is the other fine choice in town, an inviting little bistro on the town's main street. The atmosphere is appropriately rustic, with wooden plank floors and low ceilings with beams. The chef and owner, Tim Hooton, believes in market-fresh ingredients and he adjusts the menu based on what's good in any season. The cooking is full of flavor and uses the best of British produce when available, and it's accompanied by a wine list with lots of moderately priced selections. No smoking.

A SIDE TRIP TO NEWARK CASTLE

While based at Southwell, you can easily visit the ancient riverside market town of **Newark-on-Trent,** 7 miles to the east on the A612 and the A617, which is on the Roman Fosse Way.

King John died in **Newark Castle** in 1216. Constructed between the 12th and 15th centuries, the castle survived three sieges by Cromwell's troops, finally falling in 1646. Now in ruins, all that remains are a series of two watch towers, a gate, and a stretch of wall.

Although the ruins are unsafe to walk on or about, Newark has transformed a nearby building that was conceived in the 1880s as a public library into **The Gilstrap Center,** Castlegate (☎ 01636/611908), an exhibition center and tourist information office. It commemorates the castle's role in English history. The main allure is an exhibit, The Newark Castle Story and Crossroads, and three videos are available for viewing. The center is open from April through October daily from 10am to 5:45pm. Off-season hours are daily from 10am to 4:45pm. Admission is free.

The castle gardens are never locked and are open day and night. Technically, however, open hours are daily from 9am to dusk. Admission is free.

The **Parish Church of Mary Magdalen,** Church Street (☎ 01636/706473), the town's delicately detailed parish church, is among the finest such structures in the country. Its 252-foot spire overshadows the Market Place. In the interior, seek out its vast transept windows. A stunning wall painting, *Dance of Death,* in the south chantry chapel, dates from around 1520 (exact year of its origin unknown). Open from October to Easter, Monday to Saturday from 8:30am to noon and 2 to 4pm, and Easter Sunday to the end of September daily 8:30am to noon and 2 to 4:30pm. Admission is free, but there is a donation box.

The **Millgate Museum of Social and Folk Life,** 48 Millgate (☎ 01636/679403), is housed in a 19th-century oil-seed mill. Today it contains portrayals of social and industrial life in the area from around 1750 until the dawn of World War II. Agricultural, malting, and printing artifacts are displayed, and a series of rooms depict domestic life in bygone times. The museum is open Monday to Friday from 10am to 5pm and Saturday and Sunday, and bank holidays, from 1 to 5pm. Admission is free.

EASTWOOD: A STOP FOR D. H. LAWRENCE FANS
100 miles N of London; 7½ miles NW of Nottingham

D. H. Lawrence was born in the Nottinghamshire village of Eastwood on September 11, 1885, son of a coal miner who labored in the nearby mines at Brimsley.

The site is commemorated with the **D. H. Lawrence Birthplace Museum,** 8A Victoria St, (☎ 01773/763312). The memorabilia and furnishings authentically replicate what you might have found in a miner's home in 1885, with an audiovisual presentation that pays tribute to the conditions of the working class during Victorian times. Admission is £1.75 ($2.80) for adults, £1 ($1.60) for children 5 to 15 and senior citizens, and free for kids 4 and under. The museum is open from April to October daily from 10am to 5pm; from November to March daily from 10am to 4pm.

If your interest in Lawrence is still piqued, you might want to stop into **Eastwood's Public Library,** Nottingham Road (☎ 01773/712209), which devotes a room to folios, manuscripts, and memorabilia associated with the town's famous and iconoclastic writer. It's open Monday, Tuesday, and Thursday from 9:30am to 7pm, Friday from 9:30am to 6pm, and Saturday from 9:30am to 1pm. Admission is free.

Either the museum or the public library can provide a free pamphlet for the town's self-guided "Blue Line Tour." A badly scuffed but still visible blue line will lead you along the village's sites that played a role in Lawrence's life. The museum staff will describe for you a sojourn to the nearby coal mines at Brimsley, where Lawrence's father labored, and an excursion to Cossall, a nearby hamlet that was the home of Lawrence's fiancée and provided the setting for scenes in his novel *The Rainbow.*

To reach Eastwood from Nottingham, go to Victoria Station and board either Bus 231 or R11. Or you can drive for 7½ miles northwest along the A610.

5 Lincoln
140 miles N of London; 94 miles NW of Cambridge; 82 miles SE of York

The ancient city of Lincoln was the site of a Bronze Age settlement, and later, in the 3rd century, was one of the four provincial capitals of Roman Britain. In the Middle Ages it was the center of Lindsey, a famous Anglo-Saxon kingdom. After the Norman conquest, it grew increasingly important and was known throughout the land for its cathedral and castle. Its merchants grew rich by shipping wool directly to Flanders.

Much of the past remains in Lincoln today to delight visitors who wander past half-timbered Tudor houses, the Norman castle, and the towering Lincoln Cathedral. Medieval streets climbing the hillsides and cobblestones re-create the past. Lincoln, unlike other East Midlands towns such as Nottingham and Leicester, maintains somewhat of a country-town atmosphere. But it also extends welcoming arms to tourists, the mainstay of its economy.

Lincoln

Castle ③
Central Station ⑯
City Hall ⑧
Civic Center ⑭
Greyfriars City and
    County Museum ⑩
Lincoln Cathedral ⑤
Museum of Lincolnshire Life ①
Newport Arch ②
Post Office ⑫
Royal Theatre ⑨
St. Benedict's Church ⑬
St. Mary's Church ⑮
St. Michael's Church ⑥
St. Swithin's Church ⑪
Visitor Information Centre ④
Usher Art Gallery ⑦

ESSENTIALS

GETTING THERE   Trains arrive every hour during the day from London's King's Cross Station, a 2-hour trip usually requiring a change of trains at Newark. Trains also arrive from Cambridge, again requiring a change at Newark. For schedules and information, call ☎ **0345/484950** (in the U.K. only) or 01603/764776.

National Express buses from London's Victoria Coach Station service Lincoln, a 3-hour ride. For schedules and information, call ☎ **0990/808080.** Once in Lincoln, local and regional buses service the county from the City Bus Station, off St. Mary's Street opposite the train station.

If you're driving from London, take the M1 north to the junction with A57, then head east to Lincoln.

VISITOR INFORMATION   The **Tourist Information Centre** is at 9 Castle Hill (☎ **01522/529828**) and is open Monday to Thursday from 9:30am to 5:30pm, Friday from 9am to 5pm, and Saturday and Sunday from 10am to 5pm.

EXPLORING THE CITY

The best lanes for strolling are those tumbling down the appropriately named Steep Hill to the Witham River.

The cathedral is a good starting point for your shopping tour of Lincoln, as the streets leading down the hill (you won't be working against gravity this way) are lined with a mélange of interesting stores. Wander in and out of these historic lanes, down Steep Hill, along Bailgate, around the Stonebow gateway and Guildhall, and then down High Street. Following this route, you'll find all sorts of clothing, books, antiques, arts and crafts, and gift items.

While walking down Steep Hill, stop in the **Harding House Gallery,** 53 Steep Hill (☎ 01522/523537), to see some of the best local crafts: ceramics, teddy bears, textiles, wood, metal sculptures, and jewelry. You can peek down St. Paul's Lane, just off Bailgate, to investigate **Cobb Hall Centre,** St. Paul's Lane (☎ **01522/527317**), a small cluster of specialty shops selling outdoor gear, candies and gift items, German figures, and antiques.

✪ **Lincoln Cathedral.** ☎ **01522/544544.** Suggested donation £3 ($4.80) adults, £1 ($1.60) seniors, students, and children. June–Aug Mon–Sat 7:15am–8pm, Sun 7:15am–6pm; Sept–May Mon–Sat 7:15am–6pm, Sun 7:15am–5pm.

No other English cathedral dominates its surroundings as does Lincoln's. Visible from up to 30 miles away, the central tower is 271 feet high, which makes it the second tallest in England. The central tower once carried a huge spire, which, before heavy gale damage in 1549, made it the tallest in the world at 525 feet.

Construction on the original Norman cathedral was begun in 1072, and it was consecrated 20 years later. It sustained a major fire and, in 1185, an earthquake. Only the central portion of the West Front and lower halves of the western towers survive from this period.

The present cathedral is Gothic in style, particularly the early English and decorated periods. The nave is 13th century, but the black font of Tournai marble originates from the 12th century. In the Great North Transept is a rose medallion window known as the Dean's Eye. Opposite it, in the Great South Transept, is its cousin, the Bishop's Eye. East of the high altar is the Angel Choir, consecrated in 1280, and so called after the sculpted angels high on the walls. The exquisite wood carving in St. Hugh's Choir dates from the 14th century. Lincoln's roof bosses, dating from the 13th and 14th centuries, are handsome, and a mirror trolley assists visitors in their appreciation of these features, which are some 70 feet above the floor. Oak bosses are in the cloister.

In the Seamen's Chapel (Great North Transept) is a window commemorating Lincolnshire-born Capt. John Smith, one of the pioneers of early settlement in America and the first governor of Virginia. The library and north walk of the cloister were built in 1674 to designs by Sir Christopher Wren. In the Treasury is fine silver plate from the churches of the diocese.

Museum of Lincolnshire Life. Burton Rd. ☎ **01522/528448.** Admission £2 ($3.20) adults, 60p (95¢) children. Mon–Sat 10am–5:30pm, Sun 2–5:30pm. Closed Good Friday, Dec 24–27, and New Year's Day.

This is the largest museum of social history in the Midlands. Housed in what was originally built as an army barracks in 1857, it's a short walk north of the city center. Displays here range from a Victorian schoolroom to a collection of locally built steam engines.

WHERE TO STAY

Castle Hotel. Westgate, Lincoln, Lincolnshire LN1 3AS. ☎ **01522/538801.** Fax 01522/575457. 20 units. TV TEL. £75 ($120) double. Rates include English breakfast and newspaper MC, V.

This redbrick, 3-story, traditional English hotel sited in old Lincoln has been carefully converted from what was the North District National School, dating from 1858. It boasts splendid views of the castle and cathedral, which is just a 3-minute walk away. The bedrooms have been individually decorated and are named after British castles. Good English-style cooking can be enjoyed by candlelight amid tapestry screens in the oak-paneled Knights restaurant.

Disney Place Hotel. Eastgate, Lincoln, Lincolnshire LN2 4AA. ☎ **01522/538881.** Fax 01522/511321. 17 units. TV TEL. £75–£95 ($120–$152) double. Rates include English breakfast. AE, DC, MC, V. Bus: 1A or 8.

This family-owned hotel is close to the cathedral, the minster yard, the castle, and the Bailgate shops. It was built in 1735 and later enlarged. The southern boundary of the house gardens is formed by the wall of the cathedral close and towers, which were constructed in 1285. Not as luxurious as the White Hart Hotel or comfortable as Forte Poste House (see below), it is nevertheless one of the best bets in Lincoln. Each room is uniquely decorated and includes a radio and beverage-maker. Some units have four-poster beds and Jacuzzi baths.

Forte Poste House Hotel. Eastgate, Lincoln, Lincolnshire LN2 1PN. ☎ **800/225-5843** in the U.S. and Canada, or 01522/520341. Fax 01522/510780. 70 units. TV TEL. Sun–Thurs £69 ($110.40) double, Fri–Sat £59 ($94.40) double. AE, DC, MC, V. Bus: 1A or 8.

When workmen were digging the foundations here in the mid-1960s, they discovered the remnants of the north tower of the East Gate of the Roman city wall, a preserved part of which is included in the rear garden. The hotel faces Lincoln Cathedral and is attached to a Victorian mansion (now the Eastgate Bar). All the recently refurbished bedrooms have radios and beverage-makers. Breakfast, lunch, and dinner are served in the Trader's Bar and Restaurant, which serves fine but unremarkable food.

✪ **Hillcrest Hotel.** 15 Lindum Terrace, Lincoln, Lincolnshire LN2 5RT. ☎ and fax **01522/510182.** 17 units. TV TEL. Mon–Thurs £69 ($110.40) double, Fri–Sun £64 ($102.40) double. Rates include English breakfast. AE, MC, V. From Wragby Rd., connect with Upper Lindum St.; continue to the bottom of this st., make a left onto Lindum Terrace, and the hotel is 200 yd. along on the right.

This fine redbrick house was built in 1871 as the private home of a local vicar, and although it has been converted into a comfortable, small, licensed hotel, it retains many of its original features. The Hillcrest offers a cozy atmosphere and tries to accommodate personal requests. It's on a quiet, tree-lined road overlooking 26 acres of parkland, in the old high town and within easy walking distance of Lincoln Cathedral and the Roman remains. All bedrooms are well furnished and kept in shape. The Terrace Restaurant offers a wide variety of English dishes with a European flavor cooked to order, with special menus for vegetarians and children.

✪ **White Hart Hotel.** Bailgate, Lincoln, Lincolnshire LN1 3AR. ☎ **01522/526222.** Fax 01522/531798. 60 units. TV TEL. £90–£115 ($144–$184) double; £125–£160 ($200–$256) suite. AE, DC, MC, V. Bus: 1A.

The White Hart is named after the emblem of Richard II, who visited this region shortly before this hotel was constructed and probably stayed at an inn on the site. A letter written in 1460 by a London woman who paid sixpence for her room complains that her bed was lumpy.

The inn's facade dates from the 1700s, when it was a luxurious private home. Its life as a modern hotel began in 1913 when the live-in owners started accepting paying guests (only if they came with ironclad references). The hotel also hosted several meetings between Churchill and Eisenhower in the darkest days of World War II. Other guests have included David Lloyd George, Edward VIII, and Margaret Thatcher.

The inn is still going strong today and is still the best choice in town. The lumpy beds are long gone, although the inn does have a superb collection of antiques. Enter through a revolving mahogany door into a large and finely proportioned lounge filled with fine antiques, rare and unusual clocks, and display cabinets of rare silver, glass, and porcelain. Each of the accommodations, many of which were restored in 1995, has some antique furniture, a well-accessorized bathroom, and views of the old city. You'll have to negotiate a labyrinth of narrow halls and stairways to reach your room. The Georgian-style main dining room has elegant furnishings and well-prepared lunches and dinners.

WHERE TO DINE

Jews House Restaurant. The Jews House, 15 The Strait. ☎ **01522/524851.** Reservations required. Main courses £9.95–£16 ($15.90–$25.60); fixed-price lunch £13.95 ($22.30), fixed-price dinner £26 ($41.60). AE, DC, MC, V. Tues–Fri noon–2pm; Tues–Sat 7–9pm. Bus: 1A or 8. CONTINENTAL.

Originally constructed around 1150, this stone fronted building is said by local historians to be the oldest occupied house in Europe. Today it offers the finest food in Lincoln. The dining room has a low-beamed ceiling, a cast-iron fireplace, and medieval features. Two of the massive ceiling beams are known to date from the construction of the original house. Seating only about 28 diners, the restaurant is run by chef-proprietor Richard Gibbs and his wife, Sally. Their menu features stylish dishes that change weekly according to market ingredients and the inspiration of the chef—perhaps grilled goat cheese served on a bed of fresh spinach with croutons and bacon, or roast rack of lamb with a pesto crust. All these dishes are savory and prepared in an up-to-date, modern style without heavy saucing. No smoking in the main restaurant.

Wig & Mitre. 29 Steep Hill. ☎ **01522/523705.** Reservations recommended. Main courses £5.50–£16.50 ($8.80–$26.40); sandwiches £4.75–£5.50 ($7.60–$8.80). AE, DC, MC, V. Daily 8am–11pm. Bus: 1A or 8. INTERNATIONAL.

This is not only the best pub in old Lincoln, but it serves fine food, too. Sitting on the aptly named Steep Hill near the cathedral, and loaded with an Old English atmosphere, it operates somewhat like a cafe-brasserie. The main restaurant, behind the bar on the second floor, has oak timbers, Victorian armchairs, and settees. The 14th-century pub, which has been substantially restored over the years, opens to a summer beer garden. If the restaurant is full, all dishes can be served in the bar downstairs. Starters are always intriguing, ranging from a smoked mackerel mousse to a warm salad of goat cheese with grapes and hazelnuts. The menu is never staid and old-fashioned, but is constantly kept up-to-date, like in a trendy London wine bar.

FAVORITE LOCAL PUBS

Drop by the **Adam & Eve Tavern,** Lindum Hill (☎ **01522/537108**), the oldest pub in Lincoln, dating from 1701, where you can knock back a Magnet, Old Speckled Hen, or Theakston's Best Bitter in a homey, cottage atmosphere complete with gas fires and a large front garden for warm-weather drinking and browsing.

The **Jolly Brewer,** 27 Broadgate (☎ **01522/528583**), dates from 1850, and it's a basic wooden-floorboards place where you'll be welcomed into a mixed straight and gay crowd. If you're hungry, there's pub grub at lunchtime only, and draft ales include Spitfire no. 3 and Bass, as well as rotating guests.

If you're looking for a drink and maybe a band in a unique atmosphere, visit **Cornhill Vaults,** Cornhill Exchange, opposite the Central Market (☎ **01522/535113**), a Roman wine cellar converted into a subterranean pub and club full of nooks and crannies scattered with brewery relics. Weekends often feature hard-rock bands, and the place gets packed and smoky.

A SIDE TRIP TO BOSTON

122 miles N of London; 35 miles SE of Lincoln; 55 miles E of Nottingham

New Englanders like to visit this old seaport, which gave its name to the more famous Massachusetts city. But it's ironic that the Pilgrims chose to name their seaport after this English town, for they suffered a great deal here.

In 1607, about a dozen years before their eventual transit to the New World on the *Mayflower*, some Pilgrims arranged for a ship to carry them to new lives in Holland via The Wash and the sea lanes of the North Sea. The captain of the ship betrayed them and absconded with their money; as a result, the group was imprisoned in Boston's guildhall for a month for attempting to emigrate from England without the king's permission. The cells they occupied can still be visited within Boston's guildhall. Also at Scotia Creek, on a riverbank near town, is a memorial to those early Pilgrims.

GETTING THERE

From Lincoln, there are about half a dozen trains a day, each of which require a transfer in the town of Sleaford. The trip takes about an hour. From London, about 10 trains a day depart from King's Cross Station for the 2½-hour trip. For schedules and information, call ☎ **0345/484950** (in the U.K. only) or 01603/764776.

There's no bus service from Lincoln, and perhaps one or two buses a day depart from London's Victoria Coach Station to Boston. For schedules and information, call ☎ **0990/808080.**

If you're driving from Lincoln, take A17 southeast for 35 miles; the trip takes about 45 minutes. From London, take the A1 motorway north to Peterborough, then follow the signs to Boston. It's about a 3½-hour drive.

SEEING THE SIGHTS

The center of Boston is closed to cars, so you will have to walk to visit attractions such as the **Boston Stump,** the lantern tower of the Church of St. Botolph with a view for miles around of the all-encircling fens. As it stands, the tower was finished in 1460. In the 1930s, the people of Boston, Massachusetts, paid for the restoration of the tower, known officially as St. Botolph's Tower. The stairs aren't in good shape, so we don't recommend that you climb the tower. The city officials were going to add a spire, making it the tallest in England, but because of the wind and the weight, they feared the tower would collapse. Therefore, it became known as "the Boston Stump." An elderly gentleman at the tower assured us it was the tallest in England—that is, 272½ feet tall.

The **Boston Guildhall Museum,** South Street (☎ **01205/365954**), is a 15th-century guildhall that contains the courtrooms where the Pilgrims were tried and the cells where they were imprisoned. It is open year-round, Monday to Saturday from 10am to 5pm. From April through September, it is also open on Sunday from 1:30 to 5pm. The admission of £1.20 ($1.90) for adults or 80p ($1.30) for senior citizens includes a 45-minute audio guided tour. Thursday is free. Children accompanied by adults are admitted free.

Next door to the guildhall, the 1700s **Fydell House** (☎ **01205/351520**) is an adult education center but has a room set aside to welcome visitors not only from Boston, Massachusetts, but also from the rest of the United States. It is open Monday to Friday from 9:30am to 12:30pm and 1:30 to 4:30pm. Admission is free.

WHERE TO STAY & DINE

Comfort Friendly Inn. Bicker Bar (8 miles southwest of Boston at the junction of A17 and A52), Lincolnshire PE20 3AM. ☎ **01205/820118.** Fax 01205/820228. 54 units. TV TEL. £39.75 ($63.60) double. AE, DC, MC, V.

This 2-story redbrick hotel, built in 1993, is the largest hotel in the area. It's run better and its amenities are more up-to-date than any of the hotels in Boston's center, although its location southwest of the city is somewhat inconvenient. The comfortable and well-upholstered bedrooms are favored by business travelers, who also appreciate the hotel's many conference facilities and small gym. On the premises is a well-managed restaurant where set menus are reasonably priced and a cocktail bar where simple platters of pub-style food, such as stuffed baked potatoes, are offered daily.

New England Hotel. 49 Wide Bargate, Boston, Lincolnshire PE21 6SH. ☎ **01205/365255.** Fax 01205/310597. 25 units. TV TEL. £75 ($120) double. AE, DC, MC, V.

Originally built a century ago as a coaching inn near the Market Square (which at the time was on the outskirts of the city), this is the most appealing hotel in the town center. Its bedrooms were renovated in 1994 and 1995 into a bland contemporary format that is nonetheless very comfortable. Each contains the hardware you'll need to brew a cup of tea.

Magellan's is one of the best restaurants in town, offering an array of pastas, Cajun chicken, Middle Eastern kabobs, king-prawn sizzlers, and many stir-fried dishes inspired by China and Southeast Asia. There's also a cocktail lounge and a lobby bar, which is a bit grander than a pub.

16 The Northwest

The great industrial shadow of the 19th century cast such a darkness over England's northwest that the area has been relatively neglected by visitors. Most Americans rush through, heading for the Lake District and Scotland. But in spite of its industry and bleak commercial area, the northwest still has a lot to offer, including some beautiful countryside that remains unspoiled.

We will concentrate, however, on only three of its more important cities—Manchester, Liverpool, and Chester—plus a side trip to Blackpool, a huge Coney Island–style resort. You may want to visit it not so much for its beaches but for its kitschy, old-world appeal.

1 Manchester: Gateway to the North

202 miles NW of London; 86 miles N of Birmingham; 35 miles E of Liverpool

The second-largest city in England, Manchester is becoming increasingly important, as major airlines now fly here from North America, making the city a gateway to northern England. In recent years, Manchester has made great strides to shake its image as an industrial wasteland. Although chimneys still spike the skyline, they no longer make the metropolitan sky an ash-filled canopy. Abandoned warehouses are being renovated to provide sleek new loft apartments for yuppies. Rustic factory equipment turns up in museums rather than piling up in salvage yards. Even the old Victorian architecture has been given a facelift. The overall effect is a gritty kind of charm.

Manchester's roots date from A.D. 79, when the Romans settled here. It remained under Roman occupation until A.D. 410 when the empire began its storied fall. The west gate has since been reconstructed upon its original site. Little is known of Manchester's Middle Ages.

But then in the mid–17th century, the city began to capitalize on the wealth of opportunity that the burgeoning textile industry offered. Manchester eventually became the Dickensian paradigm of the industrial complex and the plight of cities. The railways were equally responsible for catapulting the city to the forefront of the industrial movement. England found Manchester both a convenient terminus and refinement center through which raw goods became viable exports. It is apt indeed that the Museum of Science and Technology resides here.

The Northwest

ENGLAND

The Northwest

★ London

Keswick

Ullswater

LAKE DISTRICT
NATIONAL PARK

A591

Grasmere ○ Rydal

○ Ambleside

A6 M6

Hawkshead ○

Coniston ○

○ Windermere

A595

A5074

A5084 A592 ○ Bowness

T
H
E

P
E
N
N
I
N
E
S

○ Kirby Lonsdale

A6068

Barrow-in-Furness ○

*Morecambe
Bay*

YORKSHIRE DALES
NATIONAL PARK

A6

Morecambe ○

Heysham ○

M6

○ Lancaster A65

Fleetwood ○

A6

M6

L A N C A S H I R E

○ Keighley

Irish Sea

M55

Blackpool ●

Preston ○

M65

○ Burnley

Blackburn

Huddersfield ○

Halifax ○

Southport ○

A59

M6

Rochdale ○

A565

A6

Bolton ○

Bury ○

○ Wigan

Oldham ○

Liverpool Bay

A580

M62

A628

Birkenhead ○

● Liverpool

M62

Warrington ○

Manchester ●

M53

R. Hersey

○ Stockport

A55

Chester ●

A54

Northwich ○

A34

Macclesfield ○

M6

A34

A53

0 ———— 85 km
      50 mi

N

↓ Stoke-on-Trent

3-0590

601

Many of the factory laborers were immigrants who flocked to the city for the promise of work. The atrocity of their conditions is well documented. But these immigrants had a profound effect on the city's culture. Today, nearly 20,000 descendants of Chinese immigrants give Manchester England's highest Chinese population outside London. The Chinese residents have amalgamated their surroundings to fit their heritage. Falkner Street, particularly the monumental Imperial Chinese Archway, is brought to life by the murals, gardens, and vibrant decor that pay homage to the once-displaced working force.

The stars of Manchester today are Oasis, best known in America for their album (*What's the Story*) *Morning Glory*. These rock stars haven't exactly done for Manchester what the Beatles did to put Liverpool on the map, but they're on their way. Of course, these self-styled "hard-drinking, groupie-shagging, drug-snorting geezers" make the Beatles seem like choir boys. As Manchester is increasingly cited for its hipness, Oasis, whose *Definitely Maybe* was the fastest-selling debut album in British history, helped make it so.

ESSENTIALS

GETTING THERE   By Plane   More and more North Americans are flying directly to Manchester to begin their explorations of the United Kingdom. **British Airways** (BA) (☎ **800/247-9297** in the U.S. and Canada, or 0345/222111 in the U.K.) has daily flights departing New York's JFK airport for Manchester at 5:30pm on Wednesday, Thursday, and Saturday; 6:30pm on Monday, Tuesday, and Friday, arriving after 7 hours in the air. You can also fly from BA's many North American gateways nonstop to London, and from here, take the almost shuttlelike service from either Gatwick or Heathrow airports to Manchester, a 50-minute flight.

American Airlines (☎ **800/433-7300** in the U.S. and Canada) offers a daily nonstop flight to Manchester from Chicago's O'Hare Airport that departs at 6:10pm, arriving the following morning. American also flies from London's Heathrow back to Chicago.

Manchester is also served by dozens of flights from the Continent. For example, **Lufthansa** (☎ **800/645-3880**) has frequent nonstop flights each week between Frankfurt and Manchester, depending on the season. Flight time is 1 hour and 45 minutes.

For airport information, call ☎ **0161/4993322.**

Manchester's airport, 15 miles south of the town center, is served by both public transportation and a motorway network. The **Airport Link,** a modern aboveground train, connects the airport terminal to the Piccadilly Railway Station downtown in Manchester. Trains leave every 15 minutes from 5:15 to 10:10pm, sometimes through the night. The ride takes 25 minutes. Direct rail lines link the airport to surrounding northern destinations such as Edinburgh, Liverpool, and Windermere.

Buses no. 44 and 105 run between the airport and Piccadilly Gardens Bus Station every 15 minutes (hourly during the evenings and on Sunday). The bus ride takes 55 minutes.

By Train, Bus & Car   Trains from London's Euston Station travel directly to Manchester ☎ **0345/484950** (in the U.K. only) or 01603/764776. The trip takes 2½ hours.

National Express (☎ **0990/808080,** only accessible in the U.K.) buses serve the Manchester region from London's Victoria Coach Station.

If you're driving from London to Manchester, go north on the M1 and the M6. At junction 21A, go east on the M62, which becomes the M602 as you enter Manchester.

Manchester

BBC's New Broadcasting House **11**
Bridgewater Hall **9**
Cathedral **2**
City Art Gallery **4**
Granada TV Studio **7**
The Green Room **10**
The Jewish Museum **1**
Manchester Museum **12**

Manchester Town Hall **5**
Museum of Science
 and Technology **8**
The Pumphouse People's
 History Museum **6**
The Royal Exchange **3**
Whitworth Art Gallery **13**

The trip from London to Manchester usually takes from 3 to 3½ hours, but it could be longer because of traffic and construction.

VISITOR INFORMATION The **Manchester Visitor Centre,** Town Hall Extension, Lloyd Street (☎ **0161/2343157**) is open Monday to Saturday from 10am to 5:30pm and Sunday from 11am to 4pm. To reach it, take the Metrolink tram to St. Peter's Square. Especially useful are a series of four free pamphlets with information on accommodations, dining, city attractions, and cultural/entertainment options.

GETTING AROUND It's not a good idea to try to hoof it in Manchester. It's better to take the bus and Metrolink. Timetables, bus routes, fare information, and a copy of a helpful leaflet, the *Passenger's Guide,* are available from **The Kiosk,** a general information booth within the Piccadilly Gardens Bus Station, Market Street (☎ **0161/627 2828**), open Monday through Saturday from 7am to 6:30pm and Sunday from 10am to 2pm and 3 to 6pm.

Buses begin running within Manchester at 6am and operate in full force until 11pm, then continue with limited routes until 3am. Tickets are sold at a kiosk at Piccadilly Gardens Bus Station.

A day pass, the **Wayfarer** (☎ **0161/2287811**) costs £5.60 ($8.95) for adults and £3 ($4.80) for children 5 to 15 and is valid for a complete day of public bus travel.

Another source of bus information is **Stagecoach** (☎ **0161/2733377**).

Metrolink (☎ **0161/2052000**) streetcars connect the bus stations and provide a useful north–south conduit. Self-service ticket machines dispense zone-based fares. The streetcars operate Monday to Thursday from 6am to midnight (Friday and Saturday 6am to 1am), and on Sunday from 7am to 11pm. They are wheelchair accessible.

SEEING THE SIGHTS

✪ **City Art Gallery.** Mosley St. ☎ **0161/2365244.** Free admission. Mon 11am–5:30pm, Tues–Sat 10am–5:30pm, Sun 2–5:30pm. Metrolink tram to Albert Sq.

These stately neoclassical premises, built between 1827 and 1834, contain many paintings accumulated by the city's wealthy industrialists during the heyday of their prosperity. The museum boasts one of the best collections of pre-Raphaelite paintings in Britain, with at least 30 by one of the genre's leaders, Ford Madox Brown. The entrance hall is lined with plaster castings made directly from the Elgin Marbles, exact duplicates of the originals in London (made using a process that would never be allowed today!). Other artworks include an eclectic collection of British and European art dating from the 1300s to the present, including some works by Gainsborough, Turner, and such postwar artists as Derek Jarman. The gallery's summer 1998 £20 million expansion program only promises to enrich the experience.

If you're here between May and September, consider a visit to **Heaton Hall,** the museum's annex, 4 miles to the east. It's the centerpiece of 650 acres of rolling parkland, and accessible via the Metrolink tram (get off at Heaton Park). Built of York stone in 1772, and filled with furniture and decorative art of the 18th and 19th centuries, it is open only between May and September. Contact the City Art Gallery for opening hours; admission is free.

Manchester Town Hall. St. Peter's Ct. ☎ **0161/2343157.** Free admission. Mon–Fri 10am–5:30pm, Sun 11am–4pm. Closed Dec 25–26 and New Year's Day. Guided tours 2nd and 4th Wed at 2pm.

Alfred Waterhouse designed this neo-Gothic structure that first opened in 1877, and extensions were added just before World War II. The tower rises nearly 300 feet above the town. The Great Hall and its signature hammer-beam roof houses 12 pre-Raphaelite murals by Ford Madox Brown, commissioned between 1852 and 1856. The paintings chronicle the town's storied past from 1st century Roman occupation to the Industrial Revolution of the 19th century.

Manchester Cathedral. Victoria St. Daily 8am–5pm.

Originally just a medieval parish in 1421, Manchester achieved cathedral status in 1847 with the creation of the new diocese. The cathedral's nave, the widest of its kind in Britain, is formed by six bays, as is the choir. The choir stall features unique 16th-century misericord seats—caricatures of medieval life. The choir screen is a wood carving from the same era. Carel Weight provides her 20th-century canvas rendition of the beatitudes and there's also a sculpture by typographer Eric Gill.

The Jewish Museum. Cheetham Hill Rd. ☎ **0161/8349879.** Admission £2.75 ($4.40) adults, £1.95 ($3.10) children, students, and seniors, £6.50 ($10.40) family. Mon–Thurs 10:30am–4pm, Sun 10:30am–5pm. Bus: 21, 59, 60.

The premises here were originally built in the Moorish revival style in 1874 as a Sephardic synagogue. It's one of only two such museums in Britain (the other is in London). It traces the culture and history of Manchester's Jewish community, estimated today at around 40,000. Part of the emphasis is on the experiences of immigrants, many from Eastern Europe, whose recorded voices describe the experience of life in Manchester's Jewish quarter in the years before World War II.

The Pumphouse People's History Museum. Left Bank, Bridge St. ☎ **0161/8396061.** Admission £1 ($1.60) adults Sat–Thurs, free Fri; free for students, seniors, and children. Tues–Sun 11am–4:30pm. Tram: Metrolink to St. Peter's Sq.

Few other museums in Europe catalog and commemorate the social history of the working class as carefully and with as much objectivity as this one. The museum began to take shape in 1990 when this was designated as the archive of Britain's communist party. Despite the fact that every exhibit is carefully couched in apolitical terms, it remains the most controversial museum in the Midlands. Of special note are exhibitions that relate the 1819 Peterloo Massacre of trade union activists by government forces, and the ongoing struggles of the coal miners of Yorkshire in their fight for higher wages and better working conditions.

Manchester Museum. University of Manchester, Oxford Rd., near Booth St. ☎ **0161/2752634.** Free admission. Mon–Sat 10am–5pm. Metrolink tram to St. Peter's Sq., then bus no. 41, 42, or 45.

This venerable museum showcases an eclectic and sometimes eccentric collection of the spoils brought back by local industrialists from their adventurous forays outside of England; there are archaeological finds from all over the world, including England's largest collection of ancient Egyptian mummies outside the British Museum in London.

EXPLORING CASTLEFIELD

Manchester had its origins in Castlefield, the city's historic core that local authorities have recently designated an "urban heritage park." It comprises the densely populated neighborhood that housed as many as 2,000 civilians beginning in A.D. 79, when Manchester was *Mancestra,* a fortified Roman camp strategically positioned between other Roman outposts, Chester and Carlisle. The roots of modern-day Manchester grew from here, providing the basic goods and services that supplied the soldiers in the nearby fort. After the Romans abandoned their fortress in A.D. 411, the settlement stood alone throughout the Dark Ages

Castlefield's next major development was the **Bridgewater Canal,** which transferred coal from Worsley. Many other goods passed through this center because of the ease of transportation. Warehouses arose around the wharves, their names suggesting their wares (for example, Potato Wharf). Later, Liverpool Road housed the world's first passenger railway station, today home to the Museum of Science and Technology.

Although the city atrophied for decades after its reign as industrial capital of the world, an interest in urban renewal emerged in the 1970s. Many of the grand canals and warehouses have been restored, and Castlefield is once again a thriving, vibrant area full of attractions.

Granada TV Studio. Water St. (tour entrance across the st. from the Victoria & Albert Hotel), Castlefield. ☎ **0161/8329090.** Tour and exhibits £15 ($24) adults, £10 ($16) children 5–12 and seniors, free for kids 4 and under. May–Sept tours Tues–Sun 9:45am–4:30pm; Oct–Apr tours Wed–Sun 9:45am–7pm.

This facility produces many of the most popular and most widely distributed TV series in Britain. A private corporation, Grenada is Britain's second largest producer of television programs, behind only the BBC. Many of its made-for-TV movies and series (*A Tale of Two Cities, Adventures of Sherlock Holmes,* and *Children's Ward*) have been public television staples in the United States.

Granada opens the backstage area of its studios to the public every day except when areas are restricted for filming. The studio is one of the most popular attractions in the Midlands. Although tours last only 45 minutes, there are so many exhibitions and displays on view that many participants extend their visits to fill several hours touring through the memorabilia of TV shows that are household words throughout the United Kingdom. Advance tour reservations are a good idea, if only to learn about last-minute changes to the activities and opening hours.

Museum of Science and Industry. Liverpool Rd. (a mile north of Manchester's center), Castlefield. ☎ **0161/8321830.** Admission £5 ($8) adults, £3 ($4.80) children. Daily 10am–5pm. Closed Dec 24–26. Parking £1.50 ($2.40). Bus: 33.

Set within five separate and antique buildings, the premises were built in 1830 as the first railway station in the world. Its many exhibits celebrate the Industrial Revolution and its myriad inventions and developments, such as printing, the railway industry, electricity, textile manufacturing, and industrial machinery, plus the history of flight and aerospace exploration.

Whitworth Art Gallery. At the University of Manchester, on Oxford Rd., near the corner of Denmark Rd. ☎ **0161/2757450.** Free admission. Mon–Sat 10am–5pm, Sun 2–5pm. Metrolink to St. Peter's Sq., then bus no. 41, 42, or 45.

Whitworth was originally established in 1889 with a bequest to the city from a wealthy industrialist. The gallery was opened to the public in 1908. Behind the magnificent redbrick facade lies a light and spacious interior. The gallery is one of the richest research sources in England for antique patterns of wallpaper and textiles and the weaving techniques that produced them. There's a superb collection of 18th- and 19th-century watercolors on display, including many by Turner.

SHOPPING

Not only does Manchester offer a vast number and variety of boutiques, shops, galleries, and craft centers, but it's one of the best hunting grounds for bargains in all of England.

Most of the larger shopping areas in the city are pedestrian-only. These include **King Street** and **St. Ann's Square,** full of exclusive boutiques and designer stores; **Market Street,** with its many major chain and department stores; **Arndale Centre,**

Manchester's largest covered shopping center; and the recently revitalized **Piccadilly** and **Oldham streets,** for fashion, music, and plenty of bargains. **Deansgate Street** is not pedestrian-only but does have a lot of adventure-sports shops.

ANTIQUES & FINE ART   Those of you who like to search through dusty stacks of stuff searching for treasures will find Manchester and the greater Manchester area prime hunting grounds.

For "recent antiques" and hip collectibles, go to **Design Goes Pop,** Basement Cafe Pop, 34–36 Oldham St. (☎ **0161/2379688**). They have original decorations and finds from the 1950s through the 1970s. **The Ginnel Antique Centre,** 18–22 Lloyd St. (☎ **0161/8339037**), has a massive selection of books, collectibles, art-deco and art-nouveau pottery, glass, and furniture. Check out **The Antiques Gallery,** Royal Exchange Shopping Centre, St. Ann's Square (☎ **0161/8288213**), for a stash of all kinds of wares down through the ages.

More pricey antiques can be found along Bury New Road in Prestwich village, just outside of Manchester.

ART GALLERIES   If you're into contemporary art, stop by the artist-run **Castle-field Gallery,** Liverpool Road (☎ **0161/8328034**). **The Gallery Manchester's Art House,** 131 Portland St. (☎ **0161/2373551**), focuses on artists whose work can be classified as being from the Northern School.

ARTS & CRAFTS   You can really rack up a lot of one-of-a-kind items while exploring the many shops devoted to craftspeople and their art. For ceramics, glass, textiles, jewelry, toys, dollhouses, and the like, visit the exquisite Victorian building that houses Manchester Craft Centre, 17 Oak St. (☎ 0161/8324274); The Alexandra Craft Centre, Upper Mill, Oldham (☎ 01457/876675); and St. George's Craft Centre, St. George's Road, Bolton (☎ 01204/398071).

FASHION   Most of the fashion stores are centered around St. Ann's Square and King Street.

Men's and women's avant-garde clothing can be found at **Flannels,** Police Street (☎ **0161/8349442**). Classic and unisex clothing is sold at **Racing Green,** 33 King St. (☎ **0161/8352022**). British designers reign supreme at **De La Mode,** 24 Deansgate (☎ **0161/2375991**).

MARKETS   Here in the north, markets are a tradition and offer you a chance to jump in and barter with the locals. Tourists tend to steer clear of them, so this is a great chance for a really authentic experience.

Although markets tend to sell everyday items and foodstuff, some stalls are devoted to flea-market goods and "antiques." Market days vary throughout the city, but you're bound to find at least one in full swing each day of the work week.

The major ones include Arndale Market and Market Hall in Manchester Arndale Centre; Grey Mare Lane Market and Beswick District Shopping Centre in Beswick; Moss Side Market and Moss Lane East in Moss Side. For information on Manchester's markets, call ☎ 0161/2341282.

MILL SHOPS   Manchester is an industrial stronghold with lots of textile mills. Most mills used to have a store, or mill shop, on site where customers could come to buy mill goods. Today, more and more of the mills are setting up shop in towns across the country.

Bury New Road in Cheetham Hill, near Boddington's Brewery, has a great selection of factory shops, discount stores, warehouses, cash-and-carry outlets, and street stalls on Sunday mornings. Some of the stores along this road do not sell to the general public and others require a minimum purchase.

The **Jaeger Factory Shop,** Thomas Burnley, Gomersal, Cleakheaton (☎ 01274/852303), has developed an extensive chain of outlet stores all over England. Jaeger will provide you with a complete list of stores and addresses. Stock includes overruns, damages, and imperfectly colored men's and women's clothing. This is the place to find the best price in the world on cashmere sweaters and factory knit seconds. A good line of Van Heusen shirts is also available.

A. Sanderson & Sons, 2 Pollard St., Ancoats (☎ 0161/2728501), is one of England's most famous brands. The shop is right outside the heart of downtown and easy to get to. It's clean, modern, and fun to shop for fabrics by the yard, gift items made of Sanderson fabrics, as well as bed linen, carpet, and draperies.

MUSIC   Audiophiles take note: There's more than live Britpop to be found in Manchester. The largest secondhand album and CD shop in all of England is the city's **Vinyl Exchange Used Record & CD Shop,** 18 Oldham St. (☎ 0161/2281122), with recordings from all musical genres split between vinyl on the first floor, and CDs upstairs. With more than 25,000 selections in stock, it's worth setting aside some browsing time. You may just walk out with that single you've been trying to track down for the past few years.

Also check out the secondhand music stalls found near Piccadilly Station along Church Street.

For newer music, go to the **Virgin Megastore,** 52–56 Market St. (☎ 0161/8331111).

WHERE TO STAY
EXPENSIVE TO MODERATE

Etrop Grange Hotel. Thorley Lane, Manchester Airport M90 4EG. ☎ 0161/4990500. Fax 0161/499-0790. 66 units. TV TEL. Mon–Thurs £135–£160 ($216–$256) double; £170 ($272) suite. Fri–Sun £90–£125 ($144–$200) double; £135 ($216) suite. AE, DC, MC, V.

Of the many hotels near Manchester Airport, this is the most historic; it carefully cultivates its image as an antique manor house. Originally built of red brick in 1760, with a modern wing added in the late 1980s in the same architectural style as the original bedrooms, it lies only a couple of minutes drive east of the airport. Don't expect lush meadows and views of fen and forest: The setting, like those of every other hotel at the airport, is one of sprawling parking lots and industrial-looking warehouses. But inside you'll find open fireplaces, ornate chandeliers, Edwardian windows, and many of the architectural features of the building's original construction. Bedrooms are often small but comfortably appointed, and many antique beds are used. There's a bar, plus an informal restaurant with well-prepared food.

Forte Posthouse. Manchester Airport, Ringway Rd. (off Junction 5 of M56 beside Terminal One), Wythenshawe, Manchester M90 3NS. ☎ 0161/4375811. Fax 0161/4362340. 285 units. MINIBAR TV TEL. Mon–Thurs £89–£99 ($142.40–$158.40) double, Fri–Sun £79 ($126.40) double. AE, DC, MC, V.

Among the first of Manchester's many airport hotels, this sprawling, 4-story structure was built in 1961. It was refurbished in 1996 and is now quite modern. All bedrooms feature tea- and coffeemakers; TVs that can provide wake-up calls, guest information, room-service menus, and bill viewing; hair dryers; and hospitality trays.

Dining/Diversions: You can dine at Gazingi's Brasserie with its modern style and innovative cuisine, or have a light meal in Gazingi's bar and lounge while eavesdropping on the multilingual conversations going on around you.

Amenities: Health-and-fitness club with indoor swimming pool, gym, and sauna; courtesy bus to and from the airport; 23-hour room service.

Four Seasons Hotel. Hale Rd., Hale Barns, near Altrincham (2 miles from the airport, near Exit 6 of M56), Manchester WA15 8XW. ☎ **0161/9040301.** Fax 0161/980-1787. 94 units. TV TEL. Mon–Thurs £110 ($176) double; £120–£170 ($192–$272) suite. Fri–Sun £69.50 ($111.20) double; £85.50–£145 ($136.80–$232) suite. AE, DC, MC, V.

Of the many airport accommodations, this one most closely emulates an American-style courtyard hotel, with a verdant oasis surrounded by a 2-story block of motel-style bedrooms. Although the enclosed garden is very attractive, there's no pool or health club facility, and rooms are done in the modern chain-hotel style you'd expect. Stiff drinks and filling meals are served in two in-house bars and two restaurants.

Hilton International. Outwood Lane (near Junction 5 of the M56), Manchester Airport, Manchester M90 4WP. ☎ **800/445-8667** in the U.S. and Canada, or 0161/436-4404. Fax 0161/436-1521. 223 units. A/C MINIBAR TV TEL. Mon–Thurs £140–£250 ($224–$400) double, Fri–Sun £75–£95 ($120–$152) double. AE, DC, MC, V.

This is the best of the many modern hotels that flank Manchester's airport. Built during the mid-1980s, it features conservative but modern bedrooms with sound-proofed windows. The 60 more expensive "Plaza Club" rooms feature a wider assortment of perks and amenities than the less expensive accommodations.

Dining/Diversions: Meals are served in both a cheerful and unpretentious coffee shop and a more formal restaurant, The Portico, where food always seems to be most felicitously preceded with a round of drinks in the Lounge Bar.

Amenities: Room service, shuttle service to and from the airport. There's a health club with its own swimming pool, a garden, and a business center.

Holiday Inn Crowne Plaza Midland Hotel. Peter St., Manchester M60 2DS. ☎ **0800/897121** or 0161/2363333. Fax 0161/9324100. 303 units. MINIBAR TV TEL. Mon–Thurs £150 ($240) double, Fri–Sun £99 ($158.40) double; daily £220–£450 ($352–$720) suite. Breakfast £11.50 ($18.40) Mon–Thurs for doubles, and for occupants of suites all week. Fri–Sun double rates include breakfast. AE, DC, MC, V. Tram: Metrolink to Piccadilly.

This is one of the leading hotels in Manchester, a 6-story, redbrick structure originally built in 1903 as the city's railway station hotel. Holiday Inn acquired it in 1985 and radically renovated and upgraded it as one of its top-of-the-line offerings, a Crowne Plaza Hotel. Although comfortable, bedrooms are rather anonymous looking, with none of the Edwardian flair retained in some of the public areas, which have high ceilings, skylights, arches, and majestic columns of their original construction.

Dining: The most formal dining room is the French Restaurant. The more casual and least expensive choice is the Wyvern Bar and Grill, offering international dishes from Mexico to Asia to Italy. Somewhere in the middle is a staid but solid carvery, Trafford Room, which serves British roasts.

✪ **Victoria & Albert Hotel.** Water St., Castlefield, Manchester M3 4JQ. ☎ **0161/8321188.** Fax 0161/834-2484. 160 units. MINIBAR TV TEL. Mon–Thurs £149–£185 ($238.40–$296.00) double, Fri–Sun £99–£125 ($158.40–$200) double; daily £250–£450 ($400–$720) suite. Rates include breakfast Fri–Sun only. AE, DC, MC, V.

One of the most unusual hotels in Britain occupies a renovated brick-sided pair of warehouses, originally conceived in 1843 to store bales of cotton being barged along the nearby Irwell River and the Manchester Ship Canal to looms and mills throughout the Midlands. About a decade ago, Granada TV transformed the then-decrepit buildings into lodgings for their out-of-town guests, and a showcase for many of their creative ideas.

Bedrooms here are dripping with the authenticity and charm of the Victorian age. Each has exposed brick walls, massive ceiling beams, an individualized shape and themed decor, and in many cases, the ornate cast-iron columns of its earlier warehouse manifestation. Each room carries the name of a Granada TV show or series, all instantly recognizable to millions of Brits.

Dining/Diversions: The Sherlock Holmes is one of the most clever restaurants in the Midlands (see "Where to Dine," below). There's also a bar named after Dr. Holmes's sidekick, Dr. Watson, and a French-style bistro, the Maigret.

INEXPENSIVE
Kempton House Hotel. 400 Wilbraham Rd., Chorlton-Cum-Hardy M21 0UH. ☎ and fax **0161/881-8766.** 13 units, 6 with bathroom. TV. £29 ($46.40) double without bathroom, £39 ($62.40) double with bathroom. Rates include English breakfast. MC, V.

A large Victorian house located 2½ miles south of the city center, this hotel provides basic, centrally located accommodations at a reasonable rate. Rooms include tea- and coffeemakers, and the hotel features a small bar and lounge. Several buses run by the hotel on a regular basis.

New Central Hotel. 144-146 Heywood St., Cheetham, M8 0PD. Tel and fax **0161/205-2169.** 10 units, 7 with shower. TV. £33 ($52.80) double without shower, £35 ($56) double with shower. Rates include English breakfast. MC, V.

Located just off the A665 Cheerham Hill Road, 1½ miles from Victoria Station, this hotel offers simple but comfortable accommodations, each with a tea- and coffeemaker. There is a lounge and a bright, pleasant dining room where you can arrange dinner service upon request. Be sure and specify your needs when booking a room, since three rooms share all facilities, and none has private toilet facilities.

WHERE TO DINE
EXPENSIVE
✪ **Market Restaurant.** 19 Edge St. or 104 High St. ☎ **0161/8343743.** Reservations recommended. Main courses £9.95–£14.95 ($15.90–$23.90). AE, DC, MC, V. Wed–Fri 6–9:30pm, Sat 7–9:30pm. Tram: Metrolink to Piccadilly or Victoria Station (best to take a taxi). BRITISH.

The Market offers genuine nostalgia and unpretentious cheerfulness. Set in a 19th-century industrial building, it's outfitted with pieces made between 1930 and 1955. The seasonally changing repertoire is based on sophisticated but earthy interpretations of cuisine from throughout Britain and, to a lesser extent, some of its former colonies. Examples include a marinated fillet of lamb wrapped in vine leaves and phyllo pastry; and breast of Barbary duck with Szechuan pepper-and-plum sauce. About a third of the dishes are vegetarian, and might include crispy risotto with a chestnut-and-mushroom sauce. Desserts are nothing short of splendid, raising syllabubs, puddings, and trifles to levels of bliss rarely experienced by diners of yesteryear. The rhubarb crumble ice cream served with a compote of rhubarb is as delicious as it is British.

Moss Nook. Ringway Rd., Moss Nook, ¾ mile from the Manchester Airport. ☎ **0161/4374778.** Reservations recommended. 5-course set lunch £16.95 ($27.10), 7-course set dinner £29.95 ($47.90); main courses £17.95–£19.50 ($28.70–$31.20). AE, MC, V. Tues–Fri noon–1:30pm (last order); Tues–Sat 7–9:30pm (last order). CONTINENTAL.

This restaurant, named after the village of Moss Nook where it is located, is a favorite local choice for an upscale dinner. The setting, complete with red suede wallpaper, hefty cutlery, and elaborate table settings, is rather formal and heavy. The service is not only professional but warm and friendly, too. Menu choices include everything from the standard to the exotically imaginative—breast of duckling can be served in an orange sauce, or with red-currant-and-elderflower dressing. Especially good is a soufflé of Swiss cheese with chives and red-pepper sauce or halibut with scallops prepared in a parsley sauce.

✪ **Sherlock Holmes Restaurant.** In the Victoria & Albert Hotel, Water St. ☎ **0161/ 8321188.** Reservations recommended. 3-course fixed-price dinner £35 ($56). AE, DC, MC, V. Mon–Sat 7–9:30pm. BRITISH.

This is the most hip and interesting restaurant in Manchester. The setting—a converted cotton warehouse from 1843—combines soaring brick walls, heavy ceiling beams, dozens of verdant plants, cast-iron columns, and views of the Irwell River with a lively association with Granada, Britain's second-largest TV studio.

Your meal might include what the menu describes as "snobby queen scallops and expensive wild-mushroom stew with layered potatoes," "mega-trendy terrine of salmon and herbs with lobster-flavored mayonnaise and a prawn and olive-oil dressing in the style of Paris House," and "Hay and Lavender-baked rump of English lamb resting nicely on straw potatoes with a polite ratatouille stew." Whether you come here to ogle, dine, or both, you'll have lots of company. Anyone from a hopeful job applicant to a media wanna-be from London might be at the next table.

The adjacent bar, Dr. Watson's, is warmly comfortable—a re-creation of the fussy but masculine parlor you might have found within the sleuth's apocryphal Victorian town house on London's Baker Street.

MODERATE

Yang Sing. 34 Princess St. ☎ **0161/2362200.** Reservations required. Main courses £6– £13 ($9.60–$20.80). AE, MC, V. Daily noon–11:30pm. Metrolink tram to Piccadilly. CANTONESE.

Manchester has a large population of immigrants from China, Hong Kong, and India. Many of them consider Yang Sing their favorite restaurant, as proven by the cacophony of languages spoken within its scarlet-colored basement dining room. It's loud but efficient, with a fast turnover of tables. Dim sum, those delicate dumplings, are served in a blissful array of choices from a pair of oversized carts in the dining room's center. Menu items cover the gamut of the Cantonese repertoire.

In 1996, Yang Sing began offering a street-level "steamboat restaurant," where containers of bubbling broth are brought to your table accompanied with an assortment of raw chicken, fish, chopped vegetables, and beef. Use your chopsticks to dunk the tidbits into the hot broth (think of it as a Chinese version of a Swiss fondue). Despite this street-level newcomer, the basement-level room remains more popular. The restaurant was destroyed by fire in 1997, but should have risen like the phoenix from the ashes by the time of your visit.

MANCHESTER AFTER DARK
THE CLUB & MUSIC SCENE

Above all else, Manchester is known for its recent contributions to pop music. From The Smiths and New Order to Oasis and the Stone Roses, the "Manchester sound" has been known throughout the world for over a decade. Yet surprisingly enough, live music went by the wayside in the early 1990s, and clubs were in short supply until they started making a steady comeback in the last couple of years.

The city's most famous landmark, **The Hacienda,** sadly has closed. It used to book some of the top music groups in England, and fans still come here looking for the site. Hooking up with the same booking agents, the **Boardwalk,** Little Peter Street (☎ **0161/2283555**), has gained popularity by hosting "Stone Love II," an extension of the former Hacienda's showcase.

Other nights of the week, head to **The Roadhouse,** Newton Street (☎ **0161/ 2281789**), the hottest small venue in Manchester, which hosts bands up to 7 nights a week. Monday through Saturday check out **Band on the Wall,** 25 Swan St., at Oak

Street (☎ 0161/8326625), where live rock, blues, jazz, and reggae can be heard. For edgier music, check the stage at **Star & Garter,** Barefield Street (☎ 0161/2736726), on Wednesday through Friday, when harder rock and hard-core acts will get in your face.

Dance clubs have taken over the town in the '90s. Just stroll through the Castlefield district on a weekend night and check out all the bars featuring a DJ. Clubs are everywhere.

On York Street near Oxford Road, **The Holy City Zoo** (☎ 0161/2737467) offers up everything from garage to house on Thursday through Saturday nights.

Located in the old 3-story headquarters of Factory Records, Paradise Factory, 112-116 Princess St. (☎ 0161/2735422), offers up techno and disco to a mainly gay crowd.

A Pub Crawl

Peveril of the Peak, Great Bridgewater Street (☎ 0161/2366364), is easy enough to find—just look for a 380-year-old triangular building covered in tile from top to bottom. No one seems to know why it was designed or built that way, but you can step inside and enjoy a pint of Wilson's Original, Theakston's Best Bitter, Yorkshire Terrier, or Webster's Best Bitter while you puzzle over it.

Manto, 46 Canal St., behind Chorlton Street Coach Station (☎ 0161/2362667), is more than a gay pub; it's a major scene, and serves as a sort of clearinghouse of information on the hottest happenings in the gay community. Read the flyers posted around the interior and strike up a conversation with an employee or regular to find out what's what if you're out and about.

A late-Victorian drinking house renowned for its environment as well as its ales, the **Marble Arch,** 73 Rochdale Rd., Ancoats, at the corner of Gould Street (☎ 0161/8325914), just east of Victoria Station, has high barrel-vaulted ceilings, extensive marble and tile surfaces, a mosaic barroom floor, carved wooden mantelpiece, and glazed brick walls. It's a great place to linger over a pint of Hopwood Bitter, Oak Wobbly Bob, or Titanic Captain Smith. If you get hungry, they offer breakfast or chili all day long. If you like slapstick, the Laurel and Hardy Preservation Society shows old movies here on the 3rd Wednesday of the month. Recent improvements include the opening of their own microbrewery featuring four of their homemade suds.

The Performing Arts

Everyone knows about the rock scene in Manchester, but the fine arts are thriving as well. For information on what's happening when you visit, contact **Arts About Manchester,** 23 New Mount St. (☎ 0161/9534035).

For drama with an unobstructed view, go to the nation's largest theater-in-the-round, **The Royal Exchange,** St. Ann's Square (☎ 0161/8339833), which is housed in a futuristic glass-and-steel structure built within the Great Hall of Manchester's former Cotton Exchange, and offers 48 weeks of in-house dramaturgy every year.

Home of the renowned **Halle Orchestra, The Bridgewater Hall,** Lower Mosley Street (☎ 0161/950000), is a state-of-the-art, 2,400-seat concert hall. In addition to the orchestra's season, it also presents other classical performances as well as some pop and comedy, too.

The University of Manchester's Department of Music, Dunmark Road (☎ 0161/2754982), is home to one of the nation's most distinctive classical string quartets, the **Lindsay String Quartet,** which performs a series of eight evening concerts in the department's auditorium during the year. For a real bargain, check on its luncheon recital series, which is free.

The BBC's **New Broadcasting House,** Oxford Road (☎ **0161/2444001**), has free tickets to musical performances that are taped in its Studio Seven for broadcast on BBC Radio 3. Renowned ensembles perform chamber music on Tuesday and/or Friday evenings, and there's a brass festival held annually in February.

The internationally acclaimed **BBC Philharmonic** performs Saturday-evening concerts 12 times a year at Bridgewater Hall (box office ☎ **0161/9079000**).

Presenting new theater, dance, and live art at the local, national, and international levels, **The Green Room,** Whitworth West Street (☎ **0161/9505777,** or 0161/9505900 for the box office), a theater-cafe bar, hosts performances mainly during its two seasons, spring (February through May) and autumn (September through December).

2 Liverpool

219 miles NW of London; 103 miles NW of Birmingham; 35 miles W of Manchester

Liverpool, with its famous waterfront on the River Mersey, is a great shipping port and industrial center. King John launched it on its road to glory when he granted it a charter in 1207. Before that, it had been a tiny 12th-century fishing village, but it quickly became a port for shipping men and materials to Ireland. In the 18th century, it grew to prominence as a result of the sugar, spice, and tobacco trade with the Americans. By the time Victoria came to the throne, Liverpool had become Britain's biggest commercial seaport.

Recent refurbishing of the Albert Dock, the establishment of a Maritime Museum, and the conversion of warehouses into little stores similar to those in Ghirardelli Square in San Francisco have made this an up-and-coming area once again, with many attractions for visitors. Liverpudlians are proud of their city, with its new hotels, two cathedrals, shopping and entertainment complexes, and parks. And of course, whether they're fans of the Fab Four or not, most visitors to Liverpool want to see where Beatlemania began.

ESSENTIALS

GETTING THERE   Liverpool has its own airport, **Speke** (☎ **0151/4868877**), which has frequent daily flights from many parts of the United Kingdom, including London, the Isle of Man, and Ireland.

Frequent express trains depart London's Euston Station for Liverpool, a 2¾-hour trip. For schedules and information, call ☎ **0345/484950** (in the U.K. only) or 01603/764776. There is also frequent service from Manchester, a 1-hour ride away.

National Express buses depart London's Victoria Coach Station every 3 hours for the 4¼-hour trip to Liverpool. Buses also arrive every hour from Manchester, a 1-hour ride away. For schedules and information, call ☎ **0990/808080.**

If you're driving from London, head north on the M1, then northwest on the M6 to the junction with M62, which heads west to Liverpool.

VISITOR INFORMATION   The **Tourist Information Centre** is at the Atlantic Pavilion, Albert Dock (☎ **0151/7088854**), and is open daily from 10am to 5:30pm. There is also a Tourist Information Centre in the City Centre: **Merseyside Welcome Centre,** Clayton Square (☎ **0151/7088858**). It's open Monday and Wednesday through Saturday from 9:30am to 5:30pm, and Tuesday from 10am to 5:30pm.

SPECIAL EVENTS   At the end of August and running into the first couple of days of September, the annual **International Beatles Week** attracts about 100,000 fans to Liverpool for a 7-day celebration highlighted by concerts from bands from Argentina to Sweden (with names like Lenny Pane, Wings Over Liverpool, and The Beats). You can hear the news today at the Sgt. Pepper concert, and take in many other Beatles tributes, auctions, and tours. **Cavern City Tours,** a local company, offers hotel and festival packages that include accommodations and tickets to tours and events, starting around £75 ($120) for two nights. For information, contact Cavern City Tours at ☎ 0151/7088838 or the Tourist Information Centre in Liverpool at ☎ 0151/7088854.

SEEING THE SIGHTS

Later in this section, we've outlined a detailed walking tour of Beatles sights that you can take on your own. If you'd like a bus tour, **Cavern City Tours** (☎ 0151/2369091) presents a daily 2-hour Magical Mystery Tour, departing from Albert Dock at 2:20pm and from Clayton Square at 2:30pm. This bus tour covers the most famous attractions associated with the Beatles. Tickets cost £8.95 ($14.30) and are sold at the Tourist Information Centre at the Atlantic Pavilion on Albert Dock or at the Merseyside Welcome Center on Clayton Square. For more information about tickets, call either ☎ 0151/7088838 or 0151/2369091.

In the Britannia Pavilion at Albert Dock, you can visit **"The Beatles Story"** (☎ 0151/7091963), a museum housing memorabilia of the famous group, including a yellow submarine with live fish swimming past the portholes. It's open daily from 10am to 6pm. Admission is £5.95 ($9.50) for adults and £4.25 ($6.80) for children and students, and a family ticket is £14.50 ($23.20).

Although we'll explore the former footsteps of the Beatles in more detail in the walking tour, we know that everyone's curious about **Penny Lane** and **Strawberry Field.** Actually, the Beatles song about Penny Lane ("There are places I'll remember") didn't refer to the small lane itself, but to the area at the top of the lane called Smithdown Place. Today, this is a bustling thoroughfare for taxis and buses—hardly a place for nostalgic memories.

John Lennon lived nearby and attended school in the area. When he studied at Art College, he passed here almost every day, these bus journeys inspiring the original lyrics. To reach Penny Lane and the area referred to, head north of Sefton Park. From the park, Green Bank Lane leads into Penny Lane itself, and at the junction of Allerton Road and Smithdown Road stands the Penny Lane Tramsheds. This is John Lennon country—or what's left of it.

Only the most diehard fans will want to make the journey to **Strawberry Field** along Beaconsfield Road which is reached by taking Menlove Avenue east of the center. Today, you can stand at the iron gates and look in at a children's home run today by the Salvation Army. As a child John played on the grounds and in 1970, he donated a large sum of money to the home. A garden party held every summer here was attended by John. His son, Sean, and Yoko Ono made two visits here in 1984. The first was a media circus, but the second was conducted in secrecy. Yoko spent many hours talking to the children and bringing them gifts, along with $80,000 to help run their home.

Since these sights are hard to reach by public transport and lie outside the center, you may want to take one of the Cavern City Tours (see above) which feature both Strawberry Field and Penny Lane.

A fun thing to do is to take the famous **Mersey Ferry** that travels from the Pier Head to both Woodside and Seacombe. Service operates daily from early morning to early evening throughout the year. Special cruises run throughout the summer including trips along the Manchester Ship Canal. For more information, contact **Mersey Ferries,** Victoria Place, Seacombe, Wallasey (☎ **0151/6301030**).

Liverpool

Albert Dock. Albert Dock Co. Ltd. ☎ **0151/7088838.** Free admission. Shops daily 10am–6pm. Bars and restaurants daily 10am–11pm. Smart Bus from city center.

Built of brick, stone, and cast iron, this showpiece development on Liverpool's waterfront opened in 1846, saw a long period of decline, and has now been extensively renovated and refurbished. The dockland warehouses now house shops, restaurants, cafes, an English pub, and a cellar wine bar. One pavilion encompasses the main building of the Merseyside Maritime Museum (see below) and another is the home of the Tate Gallery Liverpool, the National Collection of modern art in the north of England (see below). Parking is available.

✪ **Tate Gallery Liverpool.** Albert Dock. ☎ **0151/7093223.** Free admission except special exhibitions, £2.50 ($4) adults, £1 ($1.60) children. Tues–Sun 10am–6pm. Bus: "Albert Dock Shuttle" from city center.

This museum displays much of the National Collection of 20th-century art, complemented by changing art exhibitions of international standing. Three- and four-month special exhibitions are frequently mounted here, perhaps the prints of Joan Miró or the sculptures of the iconoclastic British sculptress Rachel Whiteread. The tourist office has full details of all special exhibitions, or you can call the museum directly.

✪ **Merseyside Maritime Museum and the Museum of Liverpool Life.** Albert Dock. ☎ **0151/4784499.** Admission £3 ($4.80) adults, £1.50 ($2.40) children, students, and seniors; family ticket £7.50 ($12). Daily 10am–5pm. Bus: "Albert Dock Shuttle" from city center.

Set in the historic heart of Liverpool's waterfront, this museum provides a unique blend of floating exhibits, craft demonstrations, working displays, and special events. In addition to restored waterfront buildings, exhibitions present the story of mass emigration through Liverpool in the last century, shipbuilding on Merseyside, the Battle of the Atlantic Gallery, and Transatlantic Slavery. There is wheelchair access.

The Conservation Centre. Whitechapel, Liverpool. ☎ **0151/4784999.** Admission £1.50 ($2.40) adults, £1 ($1.60) children, students, and seniors; family ticket £7.50 ($12). Mon–Sat 10am–5pm, Sun noon–5pm. Closed Dec 23–26 and Jan 1.

The Conservation Centre, in the heart of Liverpool, is the first of its kind in Europe. The Caught in Time exhibition uncovers the secret world of museum conservation and reveals how the 1.2 million artifacts in national museums and galleries on Merseyside collections are kept from the ravages of time. Using state-of-the-art hand-held audio guides, video linkups, demonstrations, behind-the-scenes tours, and interactive displays, visitors can see how everything from fine art and a Beatles gold disc to a mummified crocodile are saved from decay by expert conservators using the most up-to-date techniques.

✪ **Walker Art Gallery.** William Brown St. ☎ **0151/4784199.** Admission £3 ($4.80) adults, £1.50 ($2.40) seniors, students, and children under 16; family ticket £7.50 ($12). Mon–Sat 10am–5pm, Sun noon–5pm. Closed Dec 23–26 and Jan 1.

One of Europe's finest art galleries offers an outstanding collection of European art from 1300 to the present day. The gallery is especially rich in European old masters, Victorian and pre-Raphaelite works, and contemporary British art. It also has an award-winning sculpture gallery, featuring works from the 18th and 19th centuries. Seek out, in particular, Simone Martini's *Jesus Discovered in the Temple* and Salvator Rosa's *Landscape with Hermit*. Rembrandt is on show, as is an enticing *Nymph of the Fountain* by Cranach. The work of British artists is strongest here, ranging from *Horse Frightened by a Lion* by Stubbs to *Snowdon from Llan Nantlle* by Richard Wilson.

Among the pre-Raphaelites is Ford Madox Brown's *Coat of Many Colours* and narrative paintings such as *When Did You Last See Your Father?* by W. R. Yeames. French impressionists include the works of Monet, Seurat, and Degas, among others. Modern British paintings include works by Lucian Freud and Stanley Spencer. The admission charged is good for 1 year's admission into any and all of the eight museums and galleries on Merseyside.

✪ **Liverpool Museum.** William Brown St. ☎ **0151/2070001.** Free admission. Mon–Sat 10am–5pm, Sun noon–5pm.

One of Britain's finest museums features collections from all over the world—from the earliest beginnings with giant dinosaurs through centuries of great art and inventions. At the Natural History Centre you can use microscopes and video cameras to learn about the natural world. Living displays from the vivarium and aquarium form a large part of the collections, and a planetarium features daily programs covering modern space exploration—an armchair tour toward the beginning of the universe and the far-flung reaches of the cosmos. There is a small charge for the planetarium and temporary exhibitions.

✪ **Cathedral Church of Christ.** St. James Mt. ☎ **0151/7096271.** Admission to cathedral free; tower and embroidery gallery £2 ($3.20) adults, £1 ($1.60) children. Daily 8am–6pm.

The great new Anglican edifice overlooking the River Mersey was begun in 1904 and was largely completed 74 years later; it was the last Gothic-style cathedral to be built worldwide. Dedicated in the presence of Queen Elizabeth II in 1978, it is the largest church in England and the fifth largest in the world. Its vaulting under the tower is 175 feet high, the highest in the world, and its length, 619 feet, makes it one of the longest cathedrals in the world. The organ has nearly 10,000 pipes, the most found in any church. The tower houses the highest (219 ft.) and the heaviest (31 tons) bells in the world, and the Gothic arches are the highest ever built. From the tower, you can see to North Wales.

A Visitor Centre and Refectory features an aerial sculpture of 12 huge sails, with a ship's bell, clock, and light that changes color on an hourly basis. You can enjoy full meals in the charming refectory.

✪ **Roman Catholic Metropolitan Cathedral of Christ the King.** Mt. Pleasant. ☎ **0151/7099222.** Free admission. Daily 8am–6pm (closes 5pm Sun in winter).

Half a mile away from the Anglican cathedral stands the Roman Catholic cathedral—the two are joined by a road called Hope Street. The construction of the cathedral, designed by Sir Edwin Lutyens, was started in 1930, but when World War II interrupted in 1939, not even the granite and brick vaulting of the crypt was complete. At the end of the war it was estimated that the cost of completing the structure as Lutyens had designed it would be some £27 million. Architects throughout the world were invited to compete to design a more realistic project to cost about £1 million and to be completed in 5 years. Sir Frederick Gibberd won the competition and was commissioned to oversee the construction of the circular cathedral in concrete and glass, pitched like a tent at one end of the piazza that covered all the original site, crypt included.

Construction was completed between 1962 and 1967, and today the cathedral provides seating for more than 2,000, all within 50 feet of the central altar. Above the altar rises a multicolored glass lantern weighing 2,000 tons and rising to a height of 290 feet. Called a space-age cathedral, it has a bookshop, a tearoom, and tour guides.

WALKING TOUR
In the Footsteps of the Fab Four

Wherever you turn in Liverpool today, somebody is hawking a Beatles tour. But if you'd like to set your own pace, put on a pair of walking shoes and head out on your own trail with a little help from your friends (meaning us).

At The Cavern (see below), now touted as "The Most Famous Club in the World," you can pick up a Cavern City Tour map to find locations in the city center. More in-depth exploration will require the *Liverpool A to Zed* map, which is available at most newsstands.

Start: Town Hall

Finish: St. Silas School

Time: 2½ leisurely hours

Best Time: Daily 9:30am to 4:30pm to avoid rush hour traffic.

Start your tour at:

1. **Town Hall,** Water Street, where the city of Liverpool held a civic reception for The Beatles on July 10, 1964, while they were in town for the northern premiere of their first feature film, *A Hard Day's Night.* Nearly a quarter of a million fans turned out, lining the way from Liverpool Airport into the city center, and there was an explosion of cheering when John, Paul, George, and Ringo finally appeared on the Town Hall's balcony.

    Near the intersection of Water and Castle streets, John first wooed girlfriend Thelma Pickles (yes, Pickles) in 1958 on the steps of:

2. **Victoria Monument.** A fellow art school student also abandoned by her father, she is best remembered for helping John come to terms with his mother's tragic death. Thelma was hit by a car and killed while walking on July 15, 1958.

    Walk up Castle Street (which starts at Water Street), turn left onto Cook Street, and take a right on North John Street. Almost immediately, you'll turn left onto Mathew Street, site of the legendary:

3. **Cavern,** 10 Mathew St., where The Beatles played 292 gigs between 1961 and 1963. The first show was on March 21, 1961, for which they were paid the rather less-than-princely sum of £5 ($8). Manager Brian Epstein first saw them here on November 9, 1961. By December 10, he had signed a contract with the band.

    Through much of its heyday, The Cavern was without a drinking license, so The Beatles and other bands would cross Mathew Street and enter:

4. **The Grapes** pub for a quick drink. Occasionally, after being barred from The Grapes for rowdy or drunken behavior, the boys would find it necessary to venture up the street and hang a right onto Rainford Gardens, where:

5. **The White Star** stood ready to haul out the pints.

    Heading back to Mathew Street, continue away from The Cavern, and you'll dead-end on Stanley Street. Hang a right, and just around the corner stands:

6. **Hessy's Music Shop,** where Aunt Mimi bought John his first guitar for £17 ($27.20) in 1957.

    Continue up Stanley Street and you'll come to Whitechapel. Take a right to find:

7. **12-13 Whitechapel St.,** situated on your left. Now an appliance store called Rumbelows, this was the home of **NEMS** (Northern End Music Stores), Brian Epstein's family owned record shop, where repeated requests for The Beatles

1. Town Hall
2. Victoria Monument
3. The Cavern
4. The Grapes
5. The White Star
6. Hessy's Music Store
7. 12–13 Whitechapel Street
8. Rushworths
9. Reece's Cafeteria
11. Lewis's Department Store
10. The Adelphi Hotel
12. The Jacaranda
15. Blue Angel
17. 64 Mount Pleasant
14. Oxford Street Maternity Hospital
16. Ye Cracke
17. Liverpool Institute
18. Liverpool Art College
19. 3 Gambier Terrace
20. 22 Huskisson Street
21. Rosebury Street

record (actually a single by fellow Hamburg nightclub performer Tony Sheridan, on which The Beatles appeared as "The Beat Brothers") made him curious enough to head to The Cavern and catch a show.

Backtrack now, walking past the intersection with Stanley Street again. Also located on the east side of Whitechapel, you'll find Hessy's competitor:

8. Rushworths, the shop that upgraded John and George to Gibson acoustic guitars in 1962—their prize for being named Liverpool's best band in a *Mersey Beat* poll.

Now turn around, backtrack a bit on Whitechapel, and make a left onto Church Street. After about 3 blocks, you'll come to:

9. Reece's Cafeteria, site of John and Cynthia's wedding reception on August 23, 1962. Brian Epstein escorted them to lunch here after their ceremony, with witnesses George and Paul in tow. Brian not only picked up the bill, but also announced that he was giving them his comfortable apartment at 36 Falkner St. as a wedding present (his real motive was actually to protect John's sexy single image by hiding away the pregnant Cynthia).

Backtrack along Elliot Street, and turn right on Great Charlotte Street. Keep going and turn left on Ranelagh Street. To your right will be:

10. Lewis's Department Store. Upon returning to home life after the excitement of Hamburg, Paul was instructed by his father to quit moping around the house, so he found short-lived employment here as a delivery-van assistant during the 1960 Christmas season. The doorway of this store is also where John and Cynthia met to start many an evening on the town when they were dating.

Just across Renshaw Street, between Copperas Hill and Brownlow Hill, sits the:

11. Adelphi Hotel, Ranelagh Place, where John's father, Freddie Lennon, worked in his youth. This is also where John the art student, dressed as a vicar, persuaded the staff to lend him a mop and bucket. He proceeded to mop the pedestrian crosswalk out front while singing at the top of his lungs. Later, in the mid-1960s, the hotel housed not only The Beatles, but other pop luminaries, including Bob Dylan, when they passed through town.

Head to the intersection of Renshaw Street and Brownlow Hill. Take Brownlow for 1 block, then veer off to your right onto Mount Pleasant. After two and a half blocks, you'll come to:

12. 64 Mount Pleasant, the site of the former Register Office where John and Cynthia were married on August 23, 1962, with Brian, George, and Paul in attendance.

Continue along Mount Pleasant until it becomes Oxford Street. Just past the intersection of Hope Street is the:

13. Oxford Street Maternity Hospital, Cambridge Street, where John was born during a 7am air raid on October 9, 1940.

Now start heading down Hope Street. After several blocks, you'll come to Rice Street, where you can take a much-deserved break and have a pint at:

14. Ye Cracke. Located close to the Liverpool Art College, this was a hangout frequented by John Lennon and Stuart Sutcliffe in their art-school days. It was here that John brought future first wife Cynthia, plying her with alcohol until she agreed to return with him to Stuart's flat at 3 Gambier Terrace, Hope Street, where he seduced her for the first time. (*Note:* Regulars here are sick of talking to tourists about John's drinking days in the pub. Just absorb the atmosphere and move on.)

Backtrack to Hope Street, where you'll turn right. The next intersection on your right is with Mount Street. Sitting at the corner, on Mount Street, is the:

15. Liverpool Institute, the high school of both George and Paul.

Adjacent to it on Hope Street is the old:

16. Liverpool Art College, now John Moores University, where John Lennon enrolled in 1958 majoring in lettering. It was here that John met Cynthia, Stuart, and Bill Harry, his art-school friend. Owing to the proximity of their schools, Paul and George often took their guitars to school and met John at the art college, holding impromptu jam sessions in the canteen or in Room 21.

Keep heading down Hope Street; it will change names here and become Gambier Terrace. Stuart's former apartment is at:

17. 3 Gambier Terrace, on the left. This is the Liverpool apartment shared by John and Stuart in early 1960. An unknown John appears sprawled on the floor of this apartment in a photo accompanying a derogatory article about beatniks in a July 1960 article from *The People*. This is where John first seduced Cynthia and used to sleep in a satin-lined coffin because he claimed it was comfortable.

Continue south on Gambier Terrace, and turn left on Huskisson Street, where, situated on your right, you'll find a large, 4 story Victorian house at:

18. 22 Huskisson St., the childhood home of John's mother, Julia, Aunt Mimi, and his other three aunts.

Backtrack to Gambier Terrace, turn left, take a left on Upper Parliament Street, then go right on Princess Road. To your left you'll find:

19. Rosebury Street. A block party held here, to celebrate the 750th anniversary of Liverpool receiving its first royal charter from King John, is touted as "The Quarry Men's" first professional gig, on June 22, 1957, on the back of a coal lorry. A picture from this gig of John Lennon playing and singing in a checkered shirt is famous today as the first photo of the future superstar at work. The gig was so successful that The Quarry Men had to wait inside a friend's home for a police escort, as some local toughs, noticing the amount of female attention they were receiving, threatened them with bodily harm.

Now backtrack to Gambier Terrace and head back up. Make a left on Upper Duke Street, continuing for a few blocks until you reach Berry Street. Turn right onto Berry. Walk up well past Knight Street and on your left will be a club called:

20. The Blue Angel, at 108 Seel St. In May 1960 (when it was called "Wyvern Social Club"), the band auditioned here as the Silver Beatles for British promoter Larry Parnes (the United Kingdom's answer to Col. Tom Parker). The band was chosen to accompany Parnes's crooner, Johnny Gentle, on a nine-stop tour of Scotland—their first professional gig as The Beatles. In August that year, desperately needing a drummer to accept their infamous Hamburg gig, they auditioned Pete Best on this stage. It actually opened as the Blue Angel on March 22, 1961, and was later the site of the first meeting between Ringo and Brian.

Keep going on Seel Street for a couple of blocks until you reach the intersection of Seel and Slater. Here you'll find:

21. The Jacaranda, 23 Slater St., Allan Williams's wine cellar, which has been converted into a music club with a dance floor. Although he claimed to have never liked their music, Williams acted as the quartet's first manager and occasionally booked them here in 1960. It is from this location that Williams drove them to the ferry on their way to Hamburg in August 1960. Murals still visible on the walls were supposedly painted by John and Stuart when the club was preparing to open.

SHOPPING

Pedestrian shopping areas with boutiques, specialty shops, and department stores include Church Street, Lord Street, Bold Street, Whitechapel, and Paradise Street. Right on the river, Albert Dock also houses a collection of small shops.

For shopping centers, go to **Cavern Walks** on Mathew Street, the heart of Beatleland (☎ **0151/2369082**), or **Quiggins Centre,** 12-16 School Lane (☎ **0151/7092462**).

If you want to buy that special piece of Beatles memorabilia, wander through the **Beatles Shop,** 31 Mathew St. (☎ **0151/2368066**), or the **Heritage Shop,** 1 The Colonnades, Albert Dock (☎ **0151/7097474**).

For a huge selection of British crafts, visit **Bluecoat Chambers,** School Lane (☎ **0151/7094014**), with its gallery of metal, ceramics, glass, jewelry, and wood pieces by some 350 British craftspeople.

Frank Gzeen's, 10 Britannia Pavilion, Albert Dock (☎ **0151/7093330**), is where you'll find prints by this famous local artist who has been capturing the Liverpool scene on canvas since the 1960s. His work includes city secular buildings, churches, and street life.

Two of Liverpool's best bookshops include **Waterstone's,** 52 Bold St. (☎ **0151/7090866**), and **Gallery Shop,** Tate Gallery, Albert Dock (☎ **0151/709131**). Since the Gallery Shop is located in Tate Gallery, it also carries gallery-related merchandise.

A couple of other specialty shops that warrant a visit include **Sewill Marine,** Cornhill House, 24 Cornhill St. (☎ **0151/7087744**), which has been making nautical instruments longer than anyone in the known world; and **Thornton's,** 6 Whitechapel (☎ **0151/7086849**), where you can choose from a dizzying selection of continental and traditional English chocolates, toffees, and mints.

WHERE TO STAY
EXPENSIVE

Atlantic Tower Thistle. 30 Chapel St., Liverpool, Merseyside L3 9RE. ☎ **800/847-4358** in the U.S., or 0151/2274444. Fax 0151/236-3973. 226 units. A/C TV TEL. £108 ($172.80) double; £190 ($304) suite. Weekends £80 ($128) double including breakfast. AE, DC, MC, V.

Showcased in an austere high-rise evoking the bow of a great luxury liner, the Atlantic Tower is one of the two or three top hotels in the city. It caters largely to business travelers. You check in to a spacious lobby and are shown to one of the well-furnished but pretty standard bedrooms. Many bedrooms, although quite small, provide views of the River Mersey, and you can request a minibar.

Dining: You can dine in the Stateroom Restaurant, enjoying drinks in a bar that resembles a Pullman coach.

Liverpool Moat House. Paradise St., Liverpool, Merseyside O1 8JD. ☎ **0151/4719988.** Fax 0151/709-2706. 255 units. A/C TV TEL. Mon–Thurs £125 ($200) double, Fri–Sun £82 ($131.20) double; daily £150 ($240) suite. Weekend rates include English breakfast. AE, DC, MC, V.

This hotel might have zoomed past the Britannia Adelphi and the Atlantic Tower in the race for the title of Liverpool's best hotel, but that doesn't mean it's a world-class hotel like you'll find in Manchester or even Chester. Located in the center of the city, it is nonetheless one of the most comfortable, efficient hotels in Merseyside. The spacious bedrooms are spread across eight floors, three of which are designated for non-smokers. Typically favored by businesspeople, the hotel is also a perfectly nice choice for sightseers.

Dining: The coffee shop stays open until 10:30pm for late arrivals. It also offers the Garden Restaurant serving British and French dishes.

Amenities: Solarium, gym, indoor swimming pool, and garden.

MODERATE

Britannia Adelphi Hotel. Ranelagh Place, Liverpool, Merseyside L3 5UL. ☎ **0151/ 7097200.** Fax 0151/708-0743. 419 units. TV TEL. Mon–Thurs £87 ($139.20) double; £120 ($192) suite. Children under 13 stay free in parents' room. AE, DC, MC, V. Parking £5–£10 ($8–$16).

This grand hotel, built in 1914, is known for its fine Edwardian rooms and good cuisine. Past the elegant entrance, you enter an overblown world of marble corridors, molded ceilings, and dark polished wood. These traditional features are complemented by modern amenities, since the hotel has been completely refurbished. Many still view this as the best address in town; others disagree. We rank it number three, after the Liverpool Moat House and Atlantic Tower Thistle (see above); given the price difference, it's a better buy. Each bedroom is well furnished and attractively appointed, although some accommodations appear faded. Facilities include three restaurants, four bars, a disco/wine bar, hair and beauty salons, and a health club with swimming pool, gym, solarium, and Jacuzzi. There is garage space for 100 cars.

✪ **Trials.** 56-62 Castle St., Liverpool, Merseyside L2 7LQ ☎ **0151/2271021.** Fax 0151/ 236-0110. 20 suites. MINIBAR TV TEL. £95–£140 ($152–$224) suite. AE, MC, V. Parking £6.50 ($10.40).

Although it's small, this rather luxurious hotel has charm and character. It was created in 1986 from a centrally located Victorian structure that had once been a bank. Now beautifully converted, it's often the choice of discriminating visitors. The plush accommodations are all split-level suites with Jacuzzis, trouser presses, and hair dryers. Trials Restaurant offers breakfast only, whereas the Trials Bar serves lunch. The hotel has 24-hour room service.

INEXPENSIVE

Feathers Hotel. 119-125 Mt. Pleasant, Liverpool, Merseyside L3 5TF. ☎ **0151/7099655.** Fax 0151/7093838. 78 units, 60 with bathroom. TV TEL. £54.95 ($87.90) double without bathroom, £69.95 ($111.90) double with bathroom. Rates include English breakfast. AE, DC, MC, V. Bus: 80 (the airport bus).

This brick-fronted hotel is composed of four separate Georgian-style town houses. It sits in the heart of the city, adjacent to the modern Metropolitan Cathedral. The hotel contains a cocktail lounge (Zach's) serving bar snacks, as well as the Peacock Restaurant. The bedrooms are comfortable, with simple traditional furniture, but don't expect much charm.

WHERE TO DINE

For such a world-famous city, Liverpool has yet to have a world-class restaurant. Here are the best nonhotel restaurants it has to offer.

La Grande Bouffe, 48A Castle St. (☎ **0151/2363375**), is a basement restaurant offering mostly self-service lunches weekdays from noon to 3pm. The steamed monkfish *à la niçoise* places you on the French Riviera, but homemade black pudding returns you squarely to the northwest of England. Dinners are also served Thursday to Saturday from 6 to 10:30pm.

Armadillo. 20 Mathew St. ☎ **0151/2364123.** Reservations required. Main courses £9.95–£14.95 ($15.90–$23.90). AE, MC, V. Tues–Fri noon–3pm and 5 6:30pm; Tues–Sat 7:30–10:30pm. MODERN BRITISH.

With a conservative modern decor and big windows, this restaurant seems to be near the top of everybody's list of favorites in Liverpool. It's housed in the solid stone walls of a converted Victorian warehouse across the street from the site of the famous Cavern, where the Beatles got their start. The menu includes such dishes as seafood gazpacho, sirloin with garlic sauce, panfried Dover sole with peppercorn and pomegranate, or roast pheasant with chorizo sausages and lamb kidneys. The cooking has some artful touches, and ingredients are above average.

✪ **Becher's Brook.** 29A Hope St. ☎ **0151/7070005.** Reservations recommended. Main courses £10.50–£16 ($16.80–$25.60); fixed-price lunch £16 ($25.60). AE, DC, MC, V. Mon–Fri noon–2:30pm; Mon–Sat 5–10pm. Bus 14 or 79. INTERNATIONAL.

Close to both cathedrals, this new restaurant has received a lot of attention locally. A challenge to the oldtime favorites, its run by David Cooke and Gerard Mogan, who operate from a restored Georgian townhouse with a bar in the cellar. A rustic look prevails, with bare wood-planked floors and brick walls decorated with clusters of fresh herbs. Flavors are carefully thought out here, and main dishes are full of good taste and freshness. The appetizers are especially satisfying, notably lobster salad. Then it's on to such main courses as tender braised lamb shank with roast parsnips and green beans or else a peppery rabbit prepared to perfection. Most wines are reasonably priced.

Far East. 27-35 Berry St. ☎ **0151/7093141.** Reservations required. Main courses £7–£20 ($11.20–$32); fixed-price meals £7–£14 ($11.20–$22.40) at lunch, £14.50–£20 ($23.20–$32) at dinner. AE, DC, MC, V. Sun–Thurs noon–11:30pm; Fri–Sat noon–1am. CANTONESE/ BEIJING.

Liverpool is famous for its Chinese restaurants—not surprising since the city has one of the largest Chinese populations in Europe and its own Chinatown. Far East is a great Chinese restaurant. You might enjoy a dim sum lunch, later returning in the evening for more haute Chinese fare. You face a vast array of Cantonese specialties, including our favorite chile-flavored large prawns. The chefs also do marvelous things with duck.

Jenny's Seafood Restaurant. Old Ropery, Fenwich St. ☎ **0151/2360332.** Reservations required. Main courses £8–£34 ($12.80–$54.40); fixed-price lunch or dinner £18.50 ($29.60). AE, MC, V. Mon–Fri noon–2:15pm; Tues–Sat 7–10pm. Closed Aug 15–31 and 2 weeks at Christmas. SEAFOOD.

This restaurant has been a Liverpool staple for as long as anyone can remember. You'll find Jenny's near the harbor, in a big white Victorian building on a cul-de-sac at the lower end of Fenwich Street. Small, cozy, and select, it serves the city's best fresh seafood, which might include grilled Dover sole in Newburgh sauce or in white wine, prawn, and mushroom sauce; at least three different preparations of sea bass, including one baked in a salt crust; and monkfish, flounder, prawns, and North Atlantic lobsters. Sure, the cooking is old-fashioned, but Liverpudlians wouldn't change a thing.

LIVERPOOL AFTER DARK

Liverpool's nightlife is nothing if not diverse. There are several publications and places that will help you get a handle on the entertainment options around town. The evening *Liverpool Echo* is a good source of daily information about larger and fine-arts events; the youth-oriented *L: Scene* magazine will provide you with a thorough calendar of club dates and gigs for £1 ($1.60); and the free *City X Blag*, available in most clubs and pubs, will do the same. Available free in gay clubs and pubs, *Pulse* lists gay activities and events throughout the region.

The **Student Entertainment Office** (☎ **0151/7944143**) at the University of Liverpool can tell you about the range of activities sponsored by the school, or you can stop by the student union on Mount Pleasant and check out the bulletin board. Two other good places for finding out about the underground scene are **The Palace,** Slater Street (☎ 0151/7088515), and **Quiggins Centre,** School Lane (☎ 0151/7092462). Each is overflowing with flyers advertising local events.

Open year-round, the **Liverpool Empire,** Lime Street (☎ 0151/7091555), hosts visiting stage productions ranging from dramas and comedies to ballets and tributes. The box office is open Monday through Saturday from 10am until 8pm on show days, and closes at 6pm when there's no show.

The **Philharmonic Hall,** Hope Street (☎ 0151/2102895), is home to **The Royal Philharmonic Orchestra,** one of the best orchestras outside of London, which performs twice weekly. When the orchestra is not on, there are often concerts by touring musicians, and films are sometimes shown as well.

Open Wednesday through Saturday nights, **Lomax,** 34 Cumberland St. (☎ 0151/2366458), is a good place to catch local and touring indie bands.

Krazy House, Wood Street (☎ 0151/7085016), hosts live music 2 to 3 nights a week on a small and a larger stage. Within its split-level layout, you can catch everything from unknown locals to popular touring bands.

The best of both worlds, **The Buzz,** Skelhorne Street (☎ 0151/7072122), hosts uplifting house piano on Friday, but its reputation as a dance club is unparalleled.

House music keeps the dance floor rocking all week at **Mello Mello,** 40–42 Slater St. (☎ 0151/7070898), where there's no cover charge.

At the **Zanzibar Club,** 43 Seel St. (☎ 0151/7070633), DJs spin salsa and other Latin sounds Monday through Saturday nights, and if you like your dancing exotic, the first Friday of each month has a Brazilian Carnival theme, with samba music, costumed dancers, stilt walkers, and a rowdy, party atmosphere.

Cream/Nation, Parr Street, north of Slater Street (☎ 0151/7091693), is where the Nation, a huge warehouse club, hosts one of England's top-rated dance clubs, Cream, every Saturday night. The last Friday of every month, Cream pulls an all-nighter and attracts club-goers from all over England. Admission to Cream is a pricey £7 to £10 ($11.20 to $16).

A mixed/gay nightclub, **Garlands,** 8–10 Eberle St., off Dale Street (☎ 0151/2363307), sometimes hosts bizarre special events, but you can always count on dancing Thursday through Saturday, when the cover charge will range from £7 to £10 ($11.20 to $16).

A cafe by day, **Baa Bar,** 43–45 Fleet St. (☎ 0151/7070610), still serves tapas at night, but free dancing to a DJ brings in a lot of the evening's business.

A pub with a Fab Four spin, **Ye Cracke,** Rice Street (☎ 0151/7094171), was a favorite watering hole of John Lennon in pre- and early Beatles days (but expect regulars to suggest you quit living in the past if you ask about it). Better just soak up the little-changed atmosphere over a pint of Oak Wobbly Bob, Cains, or Pedigree.

A hangout for gay groups and clubs, **Time Out,** 30 Highland Rd. (☎ 0151/2366768), is a continental pub that offers all the latest information on happenings in the local gay scene. A friendly place, it's mainly for men.

3 The Walled City of Chester

207 miles NW of London; 19 miles S of Liverpool; 91 miles NW of Birmingham

A Roman legion founded Chester on the Dee River in the 1st century A.D. It reached its pinnacle as a bustling port in the 13th and 14th centuries but declined following the gradual silting up of the river. While other walls of medieval cities of England were either torn down or badly fragmented, Chester still has 2 miles of fortified city walls intact. The main entrance into Chester is Eastgate, which dates only from the 18th century. Within the walls are half-timbered houses and shops, although not all of them date from Tudor days. Chester is unusual in that some of its builders used black-and-white timbered facades even during the Georgian and Victorian eras.

Chester today has aged gracefully and is a lovely old place to visit, if you don't mind the summer crowds who overrun the place. It has far more charm and intimacy than either Liverpool or Manchester, and is one of the most interesting medieval cities in England.

ESSENTIALS

GETTING THERE   About 21 trains depart London's Euston Station every hour daily for the 3-hour trip to Chester. Trains also run every hour between Liverpool and Chester, a 45-minute ride. For schedules and information, call ☎ **0345/484950** (in the U.K. only) or 01603/764776.

One **National Express** bus runs every hour between Birmingham and Chester; the trip takes 2 hours. The same bus line also offers service between Liverpool and Chester. It's also possible to catch a National Express coach from London's Victoria Coach Station to Chester. For schedules and information, call ☎ **0990/808080.**

If you're driving from London, head north on the M1, then take the M6 at the junction near Coventry. Continue northwest to the junction with A54, which leads west to Chester.

VISITOR INFORMATION   The **Tourist Information Centre** is at the Town Hall, Northgate Street (☎ **01244/402111**). It offers a hotel-reservation service as well as information. Arrangements can also be made for coach tours or walking tours of Chester (including a ghost-hunter tour). It's open May through October, Monday to Saturday from 9am to 7:30pm and Sunday from 11am to 4pm; off-season, Monday to Saturday from 9am to 5pm (except on Wednesdays when they close at 4:45pm), Sunday from 10am to 4pm.

SPECIAL EVENTS   The last 2 weeks of July are an active time in Chester, as the **Chester Summer Music Festival** (☎ **01244/320700** or 01244/341200, Monday through Saturday from 9:30am to 5:30pm) hosts orchestras and other classical performers from around Britain in lunch concerts, with tickets averaging £5 ($8); small indoor evening concerts, where tickets cost between £8 and £20 ($12.80 and $32); and large outdoor shows, with tickets ranging from £14 to £20 ($22.40 to $32). For additional information about the music festival, you can also write to the Chester Summer Music Festival Office, Gateway Theatre, Hamilton Place, Chester CH1 2BH.

Occurring simultaneously, the **Chester Fringe Festival** (☎ **01244/340392**) focuses on other musical genres, offering Latin, rock, Cajun, folk, and jazz concerts. Ticket prices vary widely, depending on the performer.

SEEING THE SIGHTS

In a big Victorian building opposite the Roman amphitheater, the largest uncovered amphitheater in Britain, the **Chester Visitor Centre,** Vicars Lane (☎ **01244/ 319019**), offers a number of services to visitors. A visit to a life-size Victorian street, complete with sounds and smells, helps your appreciation of Chester. The center has a gift shop and a licensed restaurant serving meals and snacks. Admission is free, and the center is open daily from 9am to 6pm. Guided walking tours of the city depart daily at 10:30am in the winter and at 10:30am and 2pm in the summer.

To the accompaniment of a hand bell, the **town crier** appears at the City Cross—the junction of Watergate, Northgate, and Bridge streets—from April to September at

Chester

0 | .2 km
.12 ml

N

City Walls

Canal St.

George St.

King St.

Abbey St.

St. Martin's Way

Hunter St.

Northgate St.

Princess St.

Bedward Row

City Walls Rd.

Stanley St.

St. Werburgh St.

Lee Lane

Hamilton Pl.

Eastgate St.

Foregate St.

Frodsham St.

St. John St.

Watergate St.

Commonhall St.

Bridge St.

Newgate St.

Nicholas St.

Weaver St.

White Friars

Grey Friars

Black Friars

Grosvenor St.

Lower Bridge St.

Pepper St.

Nuns Rd.

Castle St.

Duke St.

The Groves

City Walls

The Roodee

Castle Square

Grosvenor Rd.

Castle Dr.

River Dee

HandBridge

City Walls

Church ✝ Information ⓘ

Agricola's Tower ⑳
Bishop Lloyd's
  House ⑦
Bridgegate ⑱
Chester Castle ⑲
Chester Cathedral ✝
Chester
  Heritage Center ⑭

Chester Visitor Center ⑰
The City Cross ⑩
Eastgate ⑪
Flag Tower ㉑
God's
  Providence House ⑨
Guildhall ⑤
The Leche House ⑧

Newgate ⑮
Roman Bath ⑬
Roman Ampitheater ⑯
The Rows ⑫
St. Nicholas's Chapel
St. Peter's Church ④
Town Hall ①
Watergate ⑥

3-0599

627

noon and 3pm Tuesday to Saturday to shout news about sales, exhibitions, and attractions in the city.

In the center of town, you'll see the much-photographed **Eastgate clock.** Climb the nearby stairs and walk along the top of the **city wall** for a view down on Chester. Passing through centuries of English history, you'll go by a cricket field, see the River Dee, formerly a major trade artery, and get a look at many 18th-century buildings. The wall also goes past some Roman ruins, and it's possible to leave the walkway to explore them. The walk is charming and free.

Eastgate Street is now a pedestrian way, and musicians often perform for your pleasure beside St. Peter's Church and the Town Cross.

The Rows are double-decker layers of shops, one tier on the street level, the others stacked on top and connected by a footway. The upper tier is like a continuous galleried balcony—walking in the rain is never a problem here.

Chester Cathedral. St. Werburgh St. ☎ **01244/324756.** £2 ($3.20) donation suggested. Daily 7:30am–6:30pm.

The present building, founded in 1092 as a Benedictine abbey, was made an Anglican cathedral church in 1541. Many architectural restorations were carried out in the 19th century, but older parts have been preserved. Notable features include the fine range of monastic buildings, particularly the cloisters and refectory, the chapter house, and the superb medieval wood carving in the choir (especially for misericords). Also worth seeing are the long south transept with its various chapels, the consistory court, and the medieval roof bosses in the lady chapel.

✪ **Chester Zoo.** Off A41, Upton-by-Chester, 2 miles north of the town center. ☎ **01244/380216.** Admission £8.50 ($13.60) adults, £6.50 ($10.40) seniors, £6 ($9.60) children 3–15. Family ticket £30 ($48). Monorail £1 ($1.60) adults, 50p (80¢) children, £26 ($41.60) family ticket. Free for kids under 3. Daily 10am–3:30 or 5:30pm, depending on season (last admission). Closed Dec 25. From Chester's center, head north along Liverpool Rd.

The Chester Zoo is the largest repository of animals in the north of England. It is also the site of some of the most carefully manicured gardens in the region—110 acres that feature unusual shrubs, rare trees, and warm-weather displays of carpet bedding with as many as 160,000 plants timed to bloom simultaneously.

Many rare and endangered animal species breed freely here; the zoo is particularly renowned for the most successful colonies of chimpanzees and orangutans in Europe. The water bus, a popular observation aid that operates exclusively in summer, allows you to observe hundreds of water birds that make their home on the park's lake. There's also a monorail, which stops at the extreme eastern and western ends of the zoo, making visits less tiring. Youngsters love the Monkey's Island exhibit.

SHOPPING

There are three main shopping areas.

The **Grosvenor Precinct** is filled with classy, expensive shops and boutiques that sell a lot of trendy fashion and art items. This area is bordered on three sides by Eastgate Street, Bridge Street, and Pepper Street.

For stores with more character and lower prices, explore **the Rows,** a network of double-layered streets and sidewalks with an assortment of shops. The Rows runs along Bridge Street, Watergate Street, Eastgate Street, and Northgate Street. Shopping upstairs is much more adventurous than down on the street. Thriving stores operate in this traffic-free paradise: tobacco shops, restaurants, department stores, china shops, jewelers, and antique dealers. For the best look, take a walk on arcaded Watergate Street.

Another shopping area to check out is **Cheshire Oaks,** a huge retail village of 60 shops, mainly clothing, perfume, and shoe outlet stores. Cheshire Oaks is located about 8 miles north of Chester on M53.

Another town worth exploring in the environs is **Boughton;** every transatlantic dealer seems to go here. Along A41, a mile from the heart of town, Boughton is filled with antique shops along Christleton Road. It doesn't have the charm of Chester, but shopping values are often better here than in the more historic city. Some outlets have as many as a dozen showrooms, even though they often are hidden behind rather dreary facades.

Chester has a large concentration of antique and craft shops. Some of the better ones include **Lowe & Sons,** 11 Bridge St. Row (☎ 01244/325850), with their antique silver and estate jewelry; **The Antique Shop,** 40 Watergate St. (☎ 01244/316286), specializing in brass, copper, and pewter items; **Adam's Antiques,** 65 Watergate Row (☎ 01244/319421), focusing on 18th- and 19th-century antiques; and **Melodies Galleries,** 32 City Rd. (☎ 01244/328968), a cluster of eight antique dealers in a 3-story 18th-century grain-storage building. **Three Kings Studios,** 90-92 Lower Bridge St. (☎ 01244/317717), is a gallery for local artisans and craftspeople that sells pottery, prints, embroidery, and wood items.

Weekly antique shows and auctions are held on Thursday at the Guildhall in Chester. Call the **Tourist Information Board** in Chester at ☎ 01244/402111.

One of the better shops for jewelry is **Boodle and Dunthorne,** 52 Eastgate St. (☎ 01244/326666). Since the days of George III, **Brown's of Chester,** Eastgate Street (☎ 01244/350001), has carried women's fashions and perfumes.

For a good selection of cheeses, chutneys, olives, pastas, and English fruit wines, seek out **The Cheese Shop,** 116 Northgate St. (☎ 01244/346240). Another specialty food store is **Owen Owen,** Bridge Street (☎ 01244/321555), where you can get spices and preserves, a variety of coffee and teas, chocolates, and even prepared picnic baskets.

WHERE TO STAY
VERY EXPENSIVE

✪ **Chester Grosvenor Hotel.** Eastgate, Chester, Cheshire CH1 1LT. ☎ **01244/324024.** Fax 01244/313246. 85 units. A/C MINIBAR TV TEL. £155–£190 ($248–$304) double; £325–£425 ($520–$680) suite. Children under 15 stay free in parents' room. AE, DC, MC, V.

This fine, half-timbered, 5-story building in the heart of Chester is one of the most luxurious hotels in northern England. Its reputation is well deserved. It is owned and named after the family of the dukes of Westminster, and its origin can be traced from the reign of Queen Elizabeth I. Started as a Tudor inn, it became a political headquarters in Hanoverian days, was later transformed into a glittering mecca for the Regency and Victorian set, and continued to be a social center during the Edwardian era. It's hosted its share of royalty, including Prince Albert, Princess Diana, and Prince Rainier.

The high-ceilinged, marble-floored foyer of the hotel, with its 200-year-old chandelier, carved wooden staircase, and antiques, sets the tone. The large, well-furnished bedrooms have radios and hair dryers.

Dining: This grand hotel has the finest dining rooms in the county. See "Where to Dine," below, for details about its formal restaurant, Arkle, and the more informal La Brasserie.

Amenities: 24-hour room service, laundry, sauna, gym, solarium, business center.

✪ **Crabwall Manor.** Parkgate Rd., Mollington, Chester, Cheshire CH1 6NE. ☎ **800/525-4800** in the U.S. and Canada, or 01244/851666. Fax 01244/851400. 48 units. TV TEL.

£150 ($240) double; from £170 ($272) suite. AE, DC, MC, V. Bus: 22 or 23. Take A540 2¼ miles northwest of Chester.

Chester's premier country-house hotel, the imposing crenellated Crabwall Manor traces its origins from the 16th century, although most of the present building dates from the early 1800s. It has a more peaceful location than the Chester Grosvenor, although it lacks the facilities and the top-notch service of its more highly rated competitor. Standing amid 11 acres of private grounds and gardens, the capably managed hotel rents well-furnished bedrooms. Most rooms are quite large and show a certain flair in their decoration, and the bathrooms are first class, with bidets and separate showers for the most part.

Dining: The finest of contemporary English and French dishes are offered in a conservatory restaurant overlooking the gardens. Nonresidents are also welcome to enjoy the harmonious flavors, the subtle sauces, and the well-chosen menu.

Amenities: 24-hour room service.

MODERATE

Blossoms Hotel. St. John's St., Chester, Cheshire CH1 1HL. ☎ **800/225-5843** in the U.S. and Canada, or 01244/323186. Fax 01244/346433. 64 units. TV TEL. £90 ($144) double; £100 ($160) minisuite; £130 ($208) full suite. AE, DC, MC, V.

Blossoms Hotel has been in business since the mid–17th century, although the present structure was rebuilt late in Victoria's day. An old open staircase in the reception room helps set the tone here, but otherwise the public rooms are uninspired. Each of the traditionally furnished bedrooms is equipped with central heating and a coffeemaker. Maintenance could be a bit better. Lunch and dinner are served in the Brooks Restaurant, and there's also the Malt Shop bar.

Mollington Banastre. Parkgate Rd., Chester, Cheshire CH1 6NN. ☎ **800/528-1234** in the U.S. and Canada, or 01244/851471. Fax 01244/851165. 65 units. TV TEL. £105 ($168) double; £135 ($216) family unit (2 adults and up to 4 children), £145 ($232) suite for 2. Children 15 and under stay free in parents' room. AE, DC, MC, V. Take A540 2 miles northwest of the center of Chester. Or take Junction 16 of the M56 and continue for 1½ miles.

This Victorian mansion, surrounded by gardens, has been successfully converted into one of the leading country-house hotels in Cheshire, now affiliated with the Best Western reservation system. A gabled house, it offers a health club complex, along with two dining rooms and well-furnished bedrooms. It's not the most opulent choice in town, but it's a great value for the money, especially with all its facilities, including a sauna, solarium, indoor swimming pool, and a gym. There's also a beauty salon and a coffee shop.

Rowton Hall Hotel. Whitchurch Rd., Rowton, Chester, Cheshire CH3 6AD. ☎ **01244/335262.** Fax 01244/335464. 42 units. TV TEL. £99–£140 ($158.40–$224) double. Rates include English or continental breakfast. AE, DC, MC, V. Take A41 2 miles from the center of Chester.

This stately home stands on the site of the Battle of Rowton Moor, which was fought in 1643 between the Roundheads and the Cavaliers. Built in 1779 with a wing added later, the house has an 8-acre garden, with a formal driveway entrance. Rowton Hall has comfortable traditional and contemporary furnishings. The better and more stylish rooms, with chintzy fabrics, are in the old house. Make sure you get a room there; an adjoining wing contains more sterile and uninspired units, which some readers have complained about.

Good English meals are served in an oak-paneled dining room with a Tudor fireplace. Fresh vegetables and herbs are supplied by the hall's kitchen garden.

Overlooking the garden, the conservatory-style Hamilton Lounge is an ideal venue for coffee, afternoon tea, or drinks. Special features include the hotel's swimming pool and its gym, which offers massages, aerobics classes, and a personal trainer.

WHERE TO DINE

✪ **Arkle Restaurant.** In the Chester Grosvenor Hotel, Eastgate. ☎ **01244/324024.** Reservations required. Fixed-price meals £38–£45 ($60.80–$72); fixed-price menu gourmand £40 ($64). AE, DC, MC, V. Tues–Sun noon–2:30pm; Mon–Sat 7–9:30pm. BRITISH/CONTINENTAL.

Arkle is the premier restaurant in this part of England. The 45-seat formal, gourmet restaurant has a superb *chef de cuisine* and a talented 40-strong team that uses the freshest ingredients to create modern British and continental dishes prepared with subtle touches and a certain lightness. Main course might include roasted Bresse pigeon with Savoy cabbage and thyme-scented juices; fillet of beef on a bed of flaked oxtail topped with foie gras and roasted bay vegetables; or locally caught poached turbot with panfried foie gras and truffle juices. Desserts are equally luscious and tempting. Arkle has an award-winning cheese selection and a choice of at least six unique breads daily.

Garden House Restaurant. 1 Rufus Ct., Northgate St. ☎ **01244/320004.** Reservations recommended. Main courses £11.25–£18 ($18–$28.80); set menus £12–£15 ($19.20–$24). AE, DC, MC, V. Mon–Sat noon–2pm and 6:30–9:30pm. INTERNATIONAL.

Both the renovation of this restaurant and the food it serves have won several civic awards. It's located within a complex of Georgian buildings originally designed as an archbishop's palace and later occupied by the city's hangman. You can enjoy a cocktail on either of two levels that are connected with a sweeping Georgian staircase lined with oil portraits and silver candelabrum. (Upstairs offers a setting overlooking the park and city wall, more elegant than the downstairs bar and lounge.) During nice weather, additional tables are set in the large outdoor garden.

Flavors are delicate but distinct. Begin perhaps with a homemade chicken liver pâté or else one of the chef's tasty soups of the day. For a main course, you might opt for our favorite, a medley of market-fresh fish, or panfried loin of pork layered with an apricot and apple puree.

La Brasserie. In the Chester Grosvenor Hotel, Eastgate St. ☎ **01244/324024.** Main courses £8–£25 ($12.80–$40). AE, DC, MC, V. Mon–Sat noon–10:30pm, Sun noon–10pm. ENGLISH/FRENCH.

This is perhaps the best all-around dining choice in Chester for convenience, price, and quality. In a delightful art-nouveau setting, the Brasserie offers an extensive à la carte menu to suit most tastes and pocketbooks. You get robust flavors and hearty ingredients. Main dishes might include Grosvenor beef and Guinness sausage with mashed potatoes and onion gravy; grilled whole lemon sole with tartar sauce; shank of lamb with sage, onions, and black-pudding potatoes; and other hearty brasserie food.

CHESTER AFTER DARK

If you want to relax in a pub, grab a pint of Marston's at the **Olde Custom House,** Watergate Street (☎ **01244/324435**), a 17th-century customhouse with many original features still intact. The **Pied Bull,** Northgate Street (☎ **01244/325829**), is an 18th-century coaching inn where you can still eat, drink, or rent a room. Real ales on tap include Flowers, and Greenall's Bitter and Traditional. At **Ye Olde King's Head,** Lower Bridge Street (☎ **01244/324855**), ales are not the only spirits you might encounter. This B&B pub, built in 1622, is said to be haunted by three ghosts: a crying woman and baby in room no. 6, and the ghostly initials "ST" that appear in steam on the bathroom mirror of room no. 4. If you prefer your spirits in a glass, stick to the pub, where you can sip on a Boddington's Bitter, or Greenall's Original or Local.

Live Irish music and atmosphere can be sampled at **Scruffy Murphy's,** 59 Northgate St. (☎ **01244/321750**), where you can hear traditional music on Wednesday and Friday nights for the price of a pint of Guinness. **Alexandre's,** Rufus Court off Northgate Street (☎ **01244/340005**), offers more varied entertainment.

For dancing, head to **Raphael's,** Love Street off Foregate (☎ **01244/340754**), or **Connections,** 39 Watergate St. (☎ **01244/320619**), Chester's only gay club, on weekends.

4 Blackpool: Playground of the Midlands

246 miles NW of London; 88 miles W of Leeds; 56 miles N of Liverpool; 51 miles NW of Manchester

This once-antiquated Midlands resort is struggling to make a comeback by marketing itself to a new generation of vacationers. The result may remind you of Atlantic City or even Las Vegas (with a weird Victorian twist). The city has a midwinter population of 125,000 that swells to three or four times that many in midsummer.

The country's largest resort makes its living from conferences, tour groups, families, and couples looking for an affordable getaway. Its 7 miles of beaches, 6 miles of colored lights, and dozens of Disney-like attractions and rides make Blackpool one of the most entertaining (and least apologetic) pieces of razzle-dazzle in England.

Disadvantages include unpredictable weather that brews over the nearby Irish Channel; a sandy, flat-as-a-pancake landscape that's less than inspiring; and a (sometimes undeserved) reputation for dowdiness. But some people love the brisk sea air, the architectural remnants of Britain's greatest Imperial Age, the utter lack of pretentiousness, and the poignant nostalgia that clings to the edges of places like Coney Island, where people look back fondly on the carefree fun they had in a simpler time.

ESSENTIALS

GETTING THERE   Two trains from Manchester pull in every hour (trip time: 1½ hours), and there's one every hour from Liverpool (trip time: 2 hours). For schedules and information, call ☎ **0345/484950** (in the U.K. only) or 01603/764776.

National Express buses arrive from Chester at the rate of three per day (trip time: 4 hours), Liverpool at the rate of six per day (trip time: 3½ hours), Manchester, five per day (trip time: 2 hours), and London, six per day (trip time: 6½ hours). For schedules and information, call ☎ **0990/808080.**

If you're driving from Manchester, take M61 north to M6 then M55 toward Blackpool. The trip takes about 1 hour.

VISITOR INFORMATION   The helpful **Tourist Office** staff is at 1 Clifton St. (☎ **01253/621623**). The office is open Monday through Thursday and Saturday from 9am to 5pm, Friday from 9:30am to 5pm, and Sunday from 10am to 3:45pm.

WHERE TO PLAY

Blackpool is famous for the **Illuminations,** an extravaganza of electric lights affixed to just about any stationary object along the Promenade. It features hundreds of illuminated figures, including Diamonds Are Forever, Santa's Workshop, Lamp Lighters, and Kitchen Lites. The tradition began in 1879 with just eight electric lights and has grown with time and technology to include 6 miles of fiber optics, low-voltage neon tubes, and traditional lamps. The illuminations burn bright into the night from the end of August to the end of November. Take a tram ride down the Promenade for a great view of these tacky but festive lights.

Without a doubt, the most famous landmark in this town is the **Tower** along the Central Promenade (☎ **01253/22242**). In 1891, during the reign of Queen Victoria, a madcap idea started floating around to construct a 518-foot tower that resembled Paris's Eiffel Tower at half the size. The idea was first formerly presented to the town leaders of Brighton, who laughed at the idea, thinking it was a joke. But the forward-thinking leaders of Blackpool, when presented the plan, immediately saw the advantages of having such an attraction, and quickly approved the tower's construction. You be the judge.

Lighted by more than 10,000 bulbs, this landmark has become a tower of fun. It is truly an indoor entertainment complex both day and night and features the Tower Ballroom (one of the great Victorian ballrooms of Britain), the Tower Circus, the Hornpipe Galley, and Jungle Jim's Indoor Adventure Park and Dawn of Time dinosaur ride for kids, as well as the Tower Aquarium. An elevator takes visitors to the top of the Tower for a 60-mile view. The Tower is open from Good Friday through October daily from 10am to 11pm. The circus has two shows daily (with the exception of Friday evening) at 2:30pm and 7:30pm. Tower admission is £5 ($8).

WHERE TO STAY

De Vere Blackpool. E. Park Dr., Blackpool, Lancashire FY3 8LL. ☎ **01253/838866.** Fax 01253/798800. 168 units. TV TEL. £55–£220 ($88–$352) double; from £160 ($256) suite. AE, DC, MC, V.

This hotel symbolizes the renewal of Blackpool. It was erected on 236 flat and sandy acres in 1992, adjacent to the town's zoo and Stanley Park. Designed in a postmodern style that some visitors liken to a mansard-roofed French château, it evokes Las Vegas with a Midlands accent, partly because of the cheerful razzle-dazzle its hardworking staff throw into their jobs, and partly because of the many diversions on hand right here. These include an 18-hole golf course, pool tables, squash courts, a health spa and exercise room, and a large indoor swimming pool. There are also three bars and three restaurants, the most upscale of which is The Grill. Bedrooms are traditional but modern, done with light woods, and despite their relative youth, were renovated early in 1997.

The Imperial Hotel. N. Promenade, Blackpool, Lancashire FY1 2HB. ☎ **01253/623971.** Fax 01253/751784. 183 units. £144 ($230.40) double; £249 ($398.40) suite. AE, DC, MC, V.

Operated by the Forte chain, and noted as a stylish venue for group conferences, this hotel was built by the Victorians as a massive redbrick pile. It's still a major landmark in town. Recent renovations added vestiges of 19th-century country-house stateliness to the public areas and some of the bedrooms, and a scattering of artwork related to such genteel pleasures as "the hunt." There's also the occasional touch of color that relieves an otherwise heavy use of beige and neutral tones. Everything is pretty anonymous and standard. There are two bars and a restaurant, plus 24-hour room service.

The Savoy Hotel. Queens Promenade, Blackpool FY2 9SJ. ☎ **01253/352561.** Fax 01253/500735. 131 units. TV TEL. £55–£120 ($88–$192) double; £110–£185 ($176–$296) suite. AE, DC, MC, V.

The roots of this hotel stretch back to the late 19th century, when its redbrick tower and bay windows beckoned vacationers to its seaside location near the North Pier. Since then, ongoing refurbishment has kept the place well carpeted, well painted, and well upholstered. Bedrooms are conservatively up to date and restful. On the premises is an attractive restaurant, Gilbert's Bistro, whose paneled interior attracts its own rather active bar trade.

WHERE TO DINE

September Brasserie. 15–17 Queen St. ☎ **01253/623282.** Reservations recommended. Main courses £12–£14 ($19.20–$22.40); set-price dinner £17.50 ($28). AE, DC, MC, V. Tues–Sat noon–2pm and 7–9:30pm. MODERN BRITISH/INTERNATIONAL.

Set within a 3-story building that originally functioned as a Victorian-era haber-dashery, this noteworthy restaurant developed from the core of a hairdressing salon that still flourishes on the street level today. Both elements of the place are the domain of the Golowicz family, which maintains (with a smile) that the staff that works inside are probably the best-coifed restaurant employees in the west of England. The restaurant prides itself on its sophisticated, modern, British cuisine (a step up from the pub grub and fish-and-chip parlors that proliferate in the surrounding neighborhood). Menu items include a tartare of tuna with sushi rice, and a saddle of rabbit with Parma-style ham, sun-dried tomatoes, and ricotta.

The Lake District 17

The Lake District, one of the most beautiful parts of Great Britain, is actually quite small, measuring about 35 miles wide. Most of the district is in Cumbria, although it begins in the northern part of Lancashire.

Bordering Scotland, the far-northwestern part of the shire is generally divided geographically into three segments: the Pennines, dominating the eastern sector (loftiest point at Cross Fell, nearly 3,000 feet high); the Valley of Eden; and the lakes and secluded valleys of the west, which are by far the most interesting.

So beautifully described by the romantic poets, the area enjoys many literary associations with William Wordsworth, Samuel Taylor Coleridge, Charlotte Brontë, Charles Lamb, Percy Bysshe Shelley, John Keats, Alfred Lord Tennyson, and Matthew Arnold. In Queen Victoria's day, the Lake District was one of England's most popular summer retreats.

The largest town is Carlisle, up by the Scotland border, which is a possible base for exploring Hadrian's Wall (see chapter 18)—but for now, we will concentrate on the district's lovely lakeside villages. **Windermere** is the best base for exploring the Lake District.

WALKS & RAMBLES

Driving in the wilds of this scenic shire is fine for a start, but the best way to take in its beauty is by walking—an art best practiced here with a crooked stick. There is a great deal of rain and heavy mist, and sunny days are few. (Pack some good waterproof hiking boots and a lightweight rain jacket—even if you set out on a nice morning, you need to be prepared for changing conditions.) When the mist starts to fall, do as the locals do and head for the nearest inn or pub, where you can drop in and warm yourself beside an open fireplace. You'll be carried back to the good old days, since many places in Cumbria have valiantly resisted change.

If you want to make hiking in the Lake District a focus of your entire vacation, you might prefer an organized outing. **Countrywide Holidays,** Grove House, Wilmslow Road, Didsbury, Manchester M20 2HU (☎ **0161/448-7112**), has offered walking and special-interest vacations for more than 100 years. Safe and sociable guided walks are led by experienced guides for all ages and abilities. It's ideal for independent walkers, with boot drying rooms provided. They have four comfortable, informal, and welcoming guest houses set in beautiful Lakeland locations.

Lakeland Natural Walking Holidays, Low Slack, Queens Road, Kendal LA9 4PH (☎ **01539/733011**), explores the Lakeland Fells on its 2-, 5-, and 7-day vacations, all led by qualified, informative guides. Then, you can relax and delight in one of the vegetarian guest houses in Kendal where you'll find comfort, plentiful food, and wine.

1 Kendal

270 miles NW of London; 64 miles NW of Bradford; 72 miles NW of Leeds; 9 miles SE of Windermere

The River Kent winds its way through a rich valley of limestone hills and cliffs, known as "fells," and down through the "Auld Grey Town" of Kendal, whose moniker refers to the large number of gray stone houses found in and about the town. Many visitors to the Lake District simply pass through Kendal on their way to more attractive destinations—the town is a gateway rather than a true stopping place. It's never depended entirely on the tourist dollar. This fact should not deter you, however, from taking a bit of time to discover some of this market town's more intriguing areas.

Kendal contains the ruins of a castle where Catherine Parr, the last wife of Henry VIII, was allegedly born. Recent speculation about her actual birthplace has led to a clouding of the historic record. Even if she wasn't born here, it is still said that she most likely lived at the castle at some time in her life. Among other historic sites, Kendal has a 13th-century parish church that merits a visit.

Today, Kendal is famous for its mint cake and its surrounding limestone fells, which offer excellent vistas of the area and make for great hikes.

ESSENTIALS

GETTING THERE   Trains from London's Euston Station do not go directly to Kendal; seven daily trains arrive in Oxenholme, about 1½ miles away. From here, you'll be able to hop a cab or take one of the local trains that leave approximately every hour to Kendal proper (total trip time: 3½ hours). For train schedules and information, call ☎ **0345/484950** (in the U.K. only) or 01603/764776.

To Kendal from London by bus, take one of the three daily National Express buses (trip time: 7 hours). For schedules and information, call **National Express** at ☎ **0990/808080.**

If you're driving, follow the M1 out of London, then the M6 to Kendal (trip time: 5 hours).

VISITOR INFORMATION   The **Tourist Information Centre,** Town Hall, Highgate (☎ **01539/725758**), is open November to Easter, Monday to Saturday from 9am to 5pm; Easter through October, Monday to Saturday from 9am to 5pm, and Sunday from 10am to 4pm.

SEEING THE SIGHTS

Kendal Museum. Station Rd. ☎ **01539/721374.** Admission £2.80 ($4.50) adults, £2.50 ($4) seniors, £1.25 ($2) children. Mid-Feb to Mar daily 10:30am–4pm; Apr–Oct daily 10:30am–5pm. Closed Nov to mid-Feb.

One of England's oldest museums takes visitors on a journey of discovery from Roman times to the present. A natural-history section includes a nature trail from mountaintop to lakeside, on which visitors are brought face to face with many of the inhabitants of the area. The World Wildlife Gallery displays a vast collection of exotic animals. One of the exhibitions introduces visitors to the fell-tops' best-known visitor,

The Lake District

Alfred Wainwright, who walked, talked, and wrote with a passion and flair about the region. Wainwright worked diligently until his death in 1991.

Museum of Lakeland Life and Industry. Kirkland. ☎ **01539/722464.** Admission £2.80 ($4.50) adults, £2.50 ($4) seniors, £1.25 ($2) children. Mid-Feb to Mar daily 10:30am–4pm; Apr to late Dec daily 10:30am–5pm. Closed late Dec to mid-Feb.

From the re-creation of a Victorian Kendal street, complete with pharmacy and market, the visitor can discover the lost craft and trades of the region and the ways of life that accompanied them.

Abbot Hall Art Gallery. Kirkland. ☎ **01539/722464.** Admission £2.80 ($4.50) adults, £2.50 ($4) seniors, £1.50 ($2.40) children. Mid-Feb to Mar daily 10:30am–4pm; Apr to late Dec daily 10:30am–5pm.

The Georgian elegance of Kendal's Abbot Hall Art Gallery has created an ideal setting for its display of fine art. Paintings by the town's famous son, 18th-century portrait painter George Romney, fill the walls of rooms furnished by Gillows of Lancaster. A major display of work by 20th-century British artists such as Graham Sutherland, John Piper, and Ben Nicholson are on permanent display. Visitors can see the region through the eyes of the many painters who have been inspired by the landscapes in another of the gallery's permanent exhibitions housed in The Peter Scott Gallery.

Sizergh Castle. 3½ miles south of Kendal (northwest of interchange A590/591). ☎ 015395/60070. Admission £3.80 ($6.10) adults, £1.90 ($3.05) children, £10 ($16) family ticket (2 adults and 2 children). Apr–Oct Sun–Thurs 1:30–5:30pm (last admission 5pm).

The castle has a pele tower that dates from the 14th century. Inside, visitors can see a collection of Elizabethan carvings and paneling, fine furniture, and portraits. The complete garden, largely from the 18th century, incorporates a rock garden and a famous planting of hardy ferns and dwarf conifers. The castle is surrounded by a show of fiery colors in autumn.

Levens Hall. Levens Park, Levens (4 miles south of Kendal). ☎ 015395/60321. Admission £5.20 ($8.30) for house and gardens; £3.80 ($6.10) for gardens only. Apr–Sept Sun–Thurs 11am–5pm.

This Elizabethan mansion was constructed in the 1500s by James Bellingham. Today the house is filled with Jacobean furniture and a working model of steam collection. The estate also has a **topiary garden** dating from 1692, with a host of yews and box hedges clipped into a variety of intriguing shapes.

WHERE TO STAY

Garden House Hotel. Fowling Lane, Kendal, Cumbria LA9 6PH. ☎ 01539/731131. Fax 01539/740064. 10 units. TV TEL. £75 ($120) double. £6 ($9.60) extra bed or cot for child. Rates include English breakfast. AE, DC, MC, V.

Built in 1812, this Georgian country house was once a convent for local nuns, and has been a hotel for the past 30 years or so. It's nestled in 2 acres of walled garden and green pastureland, and is perfectly serene. The guest rooms are medium in size, some have fireplaces and four-poster beds, and all are decorated in pastels with lots of lace, soft fabrics, and contemporary furnishings. The public areas include a somewhat formal sitting room, an informal lounge bar with lots of seating, an elegant breakfast room with a dark mahogany fireplace, and a restaurant conservatory. The restaurant serves four- and five-course dinners, or guests can take an easy 5-minute walk into the center of Kendal for an interesting choice of restaurants.

Lane Head House. Helsington, Kendal LA9 5RJ. ☎ 01539/731283. Fax 01539/721023. 8 units. TV TEL. £60 ($96) double; £70 ($112) suite. Rates include English breakfast. V.

This 17th-century manor house was built on an elevated plot of land alongside the ruins of a pele tower, a fortress used during battles between the English and Scots centuries ago. The average-sized guest rooms have their original oak beams from the 1600s and are appointed with period-style reproductions. All rooms have romantic arch windows with views of the landscaped gardens, including an Elizabethan knot garden and maze and an orchard of apple, pear, and plum trees, with glimpses of the River Kent and pastureland beyond. If prearranged, a three-course dinner can be served.

WHERE TO DINE

Déjà Vu. 124 Stricklandgate. ☎ 01539/724843. Reservations recommended. Main courses £8.95–£11.95 ($14.30–$19.10). MC, V. Daily 7–10:30pm. FRENCH.

The interior of this small and cozy French cabaret was inspired by one of van Gogh's landscape paintings. People come for good food and a fun time. A wide range of appetizers evoke a taste of Paris, featuring scallop and asparagus salad, fresh mussels cooked in white wine and shallots, or frogs legs sautéed in garlic butter and parsley. Follow with such main dishes as pork tenderloin flavored with cumin, apple brandy, and cream. Chicken breast is prepared chasseur style (mushrooms, shallots, white wine, tarragon, and tomato). Veal escalope is especially pleasing, flavored with walnuts and served with a blue cheese sauce. Desserts feature many classic French favorites, including our pick, the delicate pear cake.

Moon. 129 Highgate. ☎ **01539/729254.** Main courses £8.45–£10.75 ($13.50–$17.20). MC, V. Tues–Fri and Sun 6:30–10pm; Sat 6–10pm. INTERNATIONAL.

This bistro cooks up the best food in Kendal. Set in a building that's more than 250 years old and was once a grocery store, the dining room offers patrons a close, friendly, and informal environment. The food is interesting without being gimmicky. The owners take pride in offering market-fresh ingredients when available. Main courses include fillet steak in Roquefort cheese sauce wrapped in phyllo pastry and served with mushroom coulis; monkfish prepared in Thai tomato, lime, and coriander sauce; and, for vegetarians, creamed parsnip, lentil, and tomato tortillas with Parmesan sauce.

2 Windermere & Bowness

274 miles NW of London; 10 miles NW of Kendal; 55 miles N of Liverpool

The largest lake in England is Windermere, whose eastern shore washes up on the town of Bowness (or Bowness-on-Windermere), with the town of Windermere 1½ miles away. From either town, you can climb **Orrest Head** in less than an hour for a panoramic view of the Lakeland. From that vantage point, you can even view **Scafell Pike,** rising to a height of 3,210 feet—it's the tallest peak in all of England.

ESSENTIALS

GETTING THERE   Trains to Windermere meet the main line at Oxenholme for connections to both Scotland and London. Information about rail services in the area can be obtained by calling the railway information line at ☎ **0345/484950** (in the U.K. only) or 01603/764776. Frequent connections are possible throughout the day. To get to Bowness and its ferry pier from Windermere, turn left from the rail terminal and cross the center of Windermere until you reach New Road, which eventually changes its name to Lake Road before it approaches the outskirts of Bowness. It's about a 20-minute walk downhill. The CMS Lakeland Experience bus also runs from the Windermere Station to Bowness every 20 minutes.

The **National Express** bus link, originating at London's Victoria Coach Station, serves Windermere, with good connections also to Preston, Manchester, and Birmingham. For schedules and information, call ☎ **0990/808080.** Local buses operated mainly by **Cumberland Motor Services (CMS)** (☎ **01946/63222**) go to Kendal, Ambleside, Grasmere, and Keswick. Call for information on various routings within the Lake District.

If you're driving from London, head north on the M1 and M6 past Liverpool until you reach the A685 junction heading west to Kendal. From Kendal, A591 continues west to Windermere.

VISITOR INFORMATION   The **Tourist Information Centre** at Windermere is on Victoria Street (☎ **015394/46499**). From November to February, it's open daily from 9am to 5pm; from March through June, 9am to 6pm, and until 7:30pm in July and August. The **Tourist Information Centre** at The Glebe in Bowness (☎ **015394/ 42895**) is open April through October daily from 9:30am to 5:30pm.

EXPLORING THE AREA

There is regular **steamer service** around Windermere, the largest of the lakes, about 10½ miles long. It's also possible to take a steamer on Coniston Water, a small lake that Wordsworth called "a broken spoke sticking in the rim." Coniston Water is a smaller and less heavily traveled lake than Windermere.

There are launch and steamer cruises from Bowness daily throughout the year operated by **Windermere Lake Cruises Ltd. (☎ 015394/43360)**. Service is available from Bowness to Ambleside and to Lakeside at rates ranging from £5.50 to £9 ($8.80 to $14.40) for adults and £2.75 to £4.50 ($4.40 to $7.20) for children. There is a 45-minute Island Cruise for £4.30 ($6.90) for adults and £2.15 ($3.45) for children.

At Lakeside you can ride a steam train to Haverthwaite. A combination boat/train ticket is £8.15 ($13.05) for adults and £4.15 ($6.65) for children. An attraction at Lakeside, near Newby Bridge, is the **Aquatarium (☎ 015395/30153)**, with an exhibit of fish and wildlife. Combination boat/admission tickets are £12.50 ($20) for adults, £7.10 ($11.35) for children, and £36.75 ($58.80) for a family ticket from Ambleside; and £9.15 ($14.65) for adults, £5.30 ($8.50) for children.

Directly south of Windermere, **Bowness** is an attractive old lakeside town with lots of interesting architecture, much of it dating from Queen Victoria's day. This has been an important center for boating and fishing for a long time, and you can rent boats of all descriptions to explore the lake.

Windermere Steamboat Museum. Rayrigg Rd. ☎ 015394/45565. Admission £3 ($4.80) adults, £2.50 ($4) children. Daily 10am–5pm. Closed Nov–Mar 23.

This museum houses the finest collection of steamboats in the world. Important examples of these elegant Victorian and Edwardian vessels have been preserved in working order. The steamboats are exhibited in a unique wet dock where they are moored in their natural lakeside setting. The fine display of touring and racing motorboats in the dry dock links the heyday of steam with some of the most famous names of powerboat racing and record-breaking attempts on Windermere, including Sir Henry Segrave's world water-speed record set in 1930.

All the boats have intriguing stories, including the veteran SL *Dolly,* built around 1850 and probably the oldest mechanically driven boat in the world. The vessel was raised from the lake bed of Ullswater in 1962 and, following restoration, ran for 10 years with its original boiler. The *Dolly* is still steamed on special occasions.

The SL *Osprey* (1902) is steamed most days and visitors can make a 50-minute trip on the lake, at a cost of £4.75 ($7.60) for adults and £3.50 ($5.60) for children, with the crew serving tea or coffee made using the Windermere steam kettle.

The World of Beatrix Potter. The Old Laundry, Bowness-on-Windermere. ☎ 015394/88444. Admission £2.99 ($4.80) adults, £1.99 ($3.20) children. Easter–Sept daily 10am–5:30pm; rest of year daily 10am–5pm. Take A591 to Lake Rd. and follow the signs.

This exhibit uses the latest technology to tell the story of Beatrix Potter's fascinating life. A video wall and special film describe how her tales came to be written and how she became a pioneering Lakeland farmer and conservationist. There is also a shop with a wealth of top-quality Beatrix Potter merchandise, from Wedgwood ceramics to soft toys. It's mobbed on summer weekends; try to come at any other time.

WHERE TO STAY
VERY EXPENSIVE

Holbeck Ghyll. Holbeck Lane (on the A591 3½ miles northwest of town center), Windermere, Cumbria LA23 1LU. ☎ 015394/32375. Fax 015394/34743. 14 units. TV TEL. £79–£110 ($126.40–$176) per person double; £130 ($208) per person double with breakfast and dinner. Children under 17 stay for half price when sharing parents' room. AE, DC, MC, V.

This country-house hotel was once a 19th-century hunting lodge owned by Lord Lonsdale, one of the richest men in Britain. It still has a wealth of oak paneling and stained glass. Overlooking Lake Windermere, this hotel has a high price tag, but offers a lot for the money. An inglenook fireplace welcomes visitors. Bedrooms are well maintained and have an unpretentious decor.

Dining: The hotel's primary dining room is one of the finest restaurants in the Lake District. The menu changes every day and is never repeated. Appetizers are likely to include tender chicken liver and foie gras parfait with dried fruit compote. That might be followed by a braised shank of Cumbria lamb served with mashed potatoes and savoy cabbage. A second restaurant now offers lunch.

Amenities: The property includes woods with walking paths, streams, ponds, an all-weather tennis court, and a health spa.

Langdale Chase Hotel. On the A591 (2 miles north of town, toward Ambleside), Windermere, Cumbria LA23 1LW. ☎ **015394/32201.** Fax 015394/32604. 29 units. TV TEL. £75–£100 ($120–$160) per person double. Rates include breakfast and dinner. AE, DC, MC, V. Bus: 55.

A grand old lakeside house, this hotel resembles a villa on Italy's Lake Como. It has better rooms than Miller Howe (see below), although the food is not as good. The bedrooms have excellent furniture, and many were recently refurbished. The interior of the Victorian stone château, with its many gables, balconies, large mullioned windows, and terraces, is a treasure trove of antiques. The main lounge hall looks like a setting for one of those English drawing-room comedies. On the walls are distinctive paintings, mostly Italian primitives, although one is alleged to be a Van Dyck.

Dining: The dining room ranks among the finest in the Lake District, with tables offering a view of the lake. The cuisine is highly personal, mostly updated English fare, supported by a fine wine list.

Amenities: There's waterskiing, rowing, swimming in the lake, tennis, croquet, and fishing.

Lindeth Fell Hotel. Lyth Valley Rd. (on the A5074 a mile south of Bowness), Bowness-on-Windermere, Cumbria LA23 3JP. ☎ **015394/43286.** Fax 015394/47455. 14 units. TV TEL. £125–£150 ($200–$240) double. Rates include breakfast and dinner. MC, V. Closed Jan–Feb 14.

High above the town is this traditional large Lakeland house, built of stone and brick in 1907. Many of its rooms overlook the handsome gardens and the lake. The owners, the Kennedys, run the place more like a country house than a hotel, achieving an atmosphere of comfort in pleasingly furnished surroundings. All the cozy bedrooms have beverage-makers.

Dining: The cooking is supervised by Diana Kennedy and a resident chef, with local produce used whenever possible to prepare a variety of Lakeland and traditional English dishes, including noisettes of border lamb with mint and onion puree, and poached Scottish salmon with chive and lemon-butter sauce.

Amenities: The Kennedys offer tennis, croquet, and putting on the lawn, as well as a private tarn for fishing.

✪ **The Linthwaite House Hotel.** Crook Rd., Bowness-on-Windermere, Cumbria LA23 3JA. ☎ 015394/88600. Fax 015934/88601. 18 units. TV TEL. £120–£190 ($192–$304) double. Rates include English breakfast. AE, MC, V.

This hotel, built in 1900 and surrounded by woodlands and gardens, has a panoramic view of Lake Windermere, Bell Isle, and the distant mountains. The bedrooms are

Lake District National Park

Despite the reverence with which the English treat the Lake District, it required an act of Parliament in 1951 to protect its natural beauty. Sprawling over 885 square miles of hills, eroded mountains, forests, and lakes, the **Lake District National Park** is the largest and one of the most popular national parks in the United Kingdom, with 14 million visitors a year. Its scenery and literary references (Wordsworth, Beatrix Potter, John Ruskin, and Samuel Taylor Coleridge were among its most ardent fans) add an academic gloss to one of the most idealized regions of Britain. Lured by descriptions from the romantic lake poets, visitors arrive to take in the mountains, wildlife, flora, fauna, and secluded waterfalls. Much of the area is privately owned, but landowners work with national park officers to preserve the landscape and its 1,800 miles of footpaths.

Alas, the park's popularity is now one of its major drawbacks. Hordes of weekend tourists descend, especially in summertime and on bank-holiday weekends. During mild weather in midsummer, Windermere, Keswick, and Ambleside are likely to be among the most crowded towns of their size in England. But despite the crowds, great efforts are made to maintain the trails that radiate in a network throughout the district. Rigid building codes manage to accommodate the scores of tourist-industry facilities, while preserving the purity of a landscape that includes more than 100 lakes and countless numbers of grazing sheep.

Before setting out to explore the lake, stop in at the **National Park Visitor Centre** (☎ 015394/146601), located on the lakeshore at Brockhole, on the A591 between Windermere and Ambleside. It can be reached by bus or by one of the lake launches from Windermere. Here you can pick up useful information and explore 30 acres of landscaped gardens and parklands; lake cruises, exhibitions, and film shows are also offered. Lunches and teas are served in Gaddums

beautifully decorated and offer many amenities, including bathrobes, satellite TVs, tea- and coffeemakers, and hair dryers.

Dining: Since chef Ian Bravery has numerous requests for his secrets, the hotel has decided to produce its own cookbook containing some of the most sought-after recipes, such as sticky toffee pudding, bread-and-butter pudding, gin-and-tonic sorbet, and Lakeland lamb rosemary and thyme jus.

Amenities: The rates include complimentary use of the nearby leisure spa, which has a pool, sauna, steam room/plunge pool, spa bath, and gym.

✪ **Miller Howe Hotel.** Rayrigg Rd. (on A592 between Windermere and Bowness), Windermere, Cumbria LA23 1EY. ☎ **015394/45664.** Fax 015394/45664. 12 units. TV TEL. £70–£125 ($112–$200) per person per night. Rates include English breakfast and 4-course dinner. AE, DC, MC, V. Closed mid-Dec to mid-Mar.

International guests come to this inn, which bears the unique imprint of its creator, former actor John Tovey, who treats his guests as if they had been invited to a house party. His country estate overlooks Lake Windermere (with views of the Langdale Pikes), and offers stylish accommodations and exquisite cuisine. The house was built in 1916 in the Edwardian style, sitting on 4½ acres of statue-dotted garden and parkland. The large, graciously furnished rooms have names (not numbers), and each is supplied with binoculars to help guests fully enjoy the view. There are even copies of *Punch* from the 1890s. Antiques are scattered lavishly throughout the house.

tearooms with terrace seating. Normally there is free admission, except for special events staged here. Parking costs £2.75 ($4.40) for 2 hours or £3.50 ($5.60) for the day.

When setting out anywhere in the Lake District, it's wise to take adequate clothing and equipment, including food and drink. Weather conditions can change rapidly in this area, and in the high fells it can be substantially different from that found at lower levels. A **weather** line (☎ **017687/75757**) provides the latest conditions.

Tourist information offices within the park are richly stocked with maps and suggestions for several dozen bracing rambles—perhaps a 4-mile loop around the town of Windermere; a long (7-mile) or short (3½-mile) hike between Ambleside and Grasmere; or a boat ride from Windermere to the southern edge of the town's lake, followed by a trek northward along the lake's scenic western shore.

Regardless of the itinerary you select, you'll spot frequent green-and-white signs, or their older equivalents in varnished pine with Adirondack-style routed letters, announcing FOOTPATH TO. . . .

Be aware before you go that the Lake District receives more rainfall than any other district of England, and that sturdy walking shoes and rain gear are essential. Hiking after dark is not recommended under any circumstances.

Any tourist information office within the park can provide leaflets describing treks through the park. The **Windermere Tourist Information Centre,** Victoria Street, Windermere, Cumbria LA23 1AD (☎ **015394/46499**), is especially helpful.

See also section 5 of this chapter, "Coniston & Hawkshead," for additional details about boating in the national park.

Dining: Dinner at Miller Howe is worth the drive up from London. Susan Elliott, the head chef, has introduced lighter dishes; she uses hot and cold vinaigrettes rather than rich cream sauces, cutting out many of the garnishes and getting back to basics. Even if you can't stay overnight, at least consider a meal here, for which you must make a reservation.

Quarry Garth Country House. Troutbeck Bridge (2 miles northwest of town on A591), Windermere, Cumbria LA23 1LF. ☎ **015394/88282.** Fax 015394/46584. 11 units, one 4-room lodge. TV TEL. £65–£79 ($104–$126.40) per person double; lodge £1,000 ($1,600) per week in summer, £75 ($120) per person per night in winter. Rates include breakfast and dinner. DC, MC, V.

A hotel of character, this country house is the home of Huw and Lynne Phillips, who run the place with efficiency and precision. It is far less pretentious than the choices previously mentioned. Set on 8 well-maintained acres, the hotel has leaded, mullioned windows and a terrace. With its gardens, woods, and banks of wildflowers, it offers peace and tranquillity. The bedrooms are attractively furnished in traditional English styling; the bathrooms have big, fluffy towels. Amenities include hair dryers, radios, and coffeemakers.

Dining: The menu features dishes such as gently poached Lakeland trout fillets topped with a julienne of zucchini and surrounded by a dill-infused caper cream sauce. Fresh local produce is used whenever possible. Nonresidents who'd like to have dinner here can call to reserve a table d'hote dinner.

MODERATE

Cedar Manor. Ambleside Rd. (A591), Windermere, Cumbria LA23 1AX. ☎ **015394/ 43192.** Fax 015394/45970. 12 units. TV TEL. £78–£106 ($124.80–$169.60) double. Half board £47–£58 ($75.20–$92.80) per person. Rates include breakfast. MC, V.

One of the most desirable country-house hotels in the area is Cedar Manor. Originally built in 1860, with gables and chimneys, it was the summer getaway home for a wealthy industrialist from Manchester. But since those times, it has been converted into a small hotel of exceptional merit, with well-furnished bedrooms. The hotel takes its name from a cedar tree, perhaps from India, which has grown in the garden for some 2 centuries.

Meals are good and wholesome. Typical dishes include roast leg of lamb, fresh Scottish salmon steak, and roast leg of pork.

Lindeth Howe. Longtail Hill, Storrs Park, Bowness-on-Windermere, Cumbria LA23 3JF. ☎ **015394/45759.** Fax 015394/46368. 15 units. TV. £66–£106 ($105.60–$169.60) double. Rates include English breakfast. MC, V. Take B5284 south of Bowness.

This is a country house in a scenic position above Lake Windermere, with 6 acres of grounds. Part stone and part red brick, with a roof of green Westmoreland slate, the house was built for a wealthy mill owner in 1879, but its most famous owner was Beatrix Potter, who installed her mother here while she lived across the lake at Sawrey. The present owners, Eileen and Clive Baxter, have furnished it in fine style. Most of the bedrooms open onto lake views and are comfortably furnished, with in-house movies, beverage-makers, and central heating. Four rooms have handsome four-poster beds and some rooms have spa baths.

The dining room has two deep bay windows overlooking the lake. The lounge features a brick fireplace with a solid oak mantel. The hotel has a sauna and solarium and access to the Leisure Club opposite the beautiful grounds which includes a swimming pool, steam room, and Jacuzzi.

INEXPENSIVE

Beaumont Hotel. Holly Rd., Windermere, Cumbria LA23 2AF. ☎ and fax **015394/47075.** 10 units. TV. £46–£76 ($73.60–$121.60) double. Rates include English breakfast. AE, MC, V.

This stone-sided Lakeland villa, originally built in the 1850s, is on a quiet residential street about a minute's walk from Windermere's commercial center. In 1992, owners Kathy and Malcolm Cox massively upgraded what had been a rather dowdy interior. Each of the bedrooms is named after one of the characters in the Beatrix Potter sagas (our favorite is Jemima PuddleDuck) and contains either some kind of elaborate canopy or a four-poster bed. Each also has a tea-maker. No meals are served other than breakfast, so the owners keep local restaurant menus on hand for their guests to consult.

Fir Trees. Lake Rd., Windermere, Cumbria LA23 2EQ. ☎ and fax **015394/42272.** 7 units. TV. £44–£56 ($70.40–$89.60) double. Rates include English breakfast. AE, MC, V.

This is one of the finest guest houses in Windermere. It's very well run, essentially providing hotel-like standards at B&B prices. Opposite St. John's Church, halfway between the villages of Bowness and Windermere, Fir Trees is a Victorian house furnished with antiques. Proprietors Allene and Ira Fishman offer a warm welcome and rent well-furnished and beautifully maintained bedrooms, each with a beverage-maker and other thoughtful amenities. Some units are large enough for families. The Fishmans know the Lake District extremely well and provide their guests with detailed information on restaurants, country pubs, or where to go and what to see. No smoking.

Rockside Guest House. Ambleside Rd., Windermere, Cumbria LA23 1AQ. ☎ 015394/ **45343.** Fax 015394/45533. 15 units, 10 with shower. TV TEL. £36 ($57.60) double without shower, £39–£49 ($62.40–$78.40) double with shower. Rates include English breakfast. MC, V.

This guest house near the train station is run by Neville and Mavis Fowles, who came to this area to achieve their ambition of living in "the most beautiful corner of England." They have since made Rockside one of the best B&Bs in the area. Standard rooms have hot and cold running water basins; "top choice" rooms contain private showers and toilets, beverage-makers, and hair dryers. The breakfast menu gives you a wide choice. At the rear of the house is a parking area for 12 cars, but Rockside is only a 2-minute walk from the bus, train, or village of Windermere. The Fowles, who like to make sure their guests see what the area has to offer, can also organize a half- or full-day minibus tour of the Lake District.

WHERE TO DINE

✪ **Roger's.** 4 High St., Windermere. ☎ 015394/44954. Reservations required. Main courses £6.50–£12.50 ($10.40–$20); fixed-price dinner £16.50 ($26.40). AE, DC, MC, V. Mon–Sat 7–9:30pm. ENGLISH/INTERNATIONAL.

Cumbria's stellar French dining room, Roger's carries the name of its skilled chef de cuisine, Roger Pergl-Wilson. For almost a decade, he has been going strong at this location (a part of England where restaurants seem to have a high mortality rate). That means he's doing something right. You can judge for yourself.

A table d'hôte dinner is a superb value, but you're most likely to be tempted to order à la carte. Homegrown ingredients go into the cooking whenever possible. Deer from the field, salmon from the rivers, char from Lake Windermere, and local pheasant and duck—everything seems fresh and deftly handled here. Care also goes into the presentation, and the service is polite and efficient without being overly formal.

FAVORITE LOCAL PUBS

Drive a short distance south of Windermere to Cartmel Fell, situated between A592 and A5074, and you'll find a pub-lover's dream. The **Mason Arms,** Strawberry Bank (☎ 01539/568486), is a Jacobean pub with its original oak paneling and flagstone floors. There's sturdy, comfortable wooden furniture spread through a series of five rooms in which you can wander or settle. The outside garden, attractive in its own right, offers a dramatic view of the Winster Valley beyond. The pub offers so many beers that they have a 24-page catalog to help you order. There's also Knickerbocker-breaker, a hard cider from local apples, plus a creative, reasonable menu that includes several tasty vegetarian options.

Or sample the offerings at the **Watermill** (☎ 01539/821309), just east of Windermere off A591 in Ings. Choose a padded or wooden chair, pew, or stool, then look over the selection of ales and more than 50 whiskies. There's good traditional pub grub here as well.

Southeast of the village, off A5074 in Crosthwaithe, the **Punch Bowl** (☎ 015395/ 68237) is a 16th-century pub; the central room features a high-beamed ceiling with upper minstrel galleries on two sides. Outdoors, a stepped terrace on the hillside offers a tranquil retreat. Theakstons Best, Jennings Cumberland, or Cocker Hoop are available on tap.

A popular 17th-century pub, **The Queens Head,** on A592 north of Windermere (☎ 015394/32174), uses a gigantic Elizabethan four-poster bed as its serving counter, and has an eclectic mix of antiques strewn in with basic bar furnishings. There are half a dozen rooms in which you can settle with a pint of Mitchells Lancaster Bomber, Tetleys, or Buddington's.

Established in 1612, the **Hole in t' Wall**, Lowside (☎ **01539/443488**), is the oldest pub in Bowness, a real treasure for its character and friendliness. The barroom is decorated with a hodgepodge of antiquated farming tools, and there's a large slate fireplace lending warmth on winter days plus a good selection of real ales on tap. The menu is determined daily and there's real ingenuity illustrated in an eclectic mix of vegetarian, seafood, and local game dishes. There's a small flagstoned terrace in the front for lingering on warmer days and evenings.

3 Ambleside & Rydal

278 miles NW of London; 14 miles NW of Kendal; 4 miles N of Windermere

An idyllic retreat, Ambleside is just a small village, but it's one of the major places to stay in the Lake District, attracting pony trekkers, hikers, and rock climbers. It's wonderful in warm weather, and even through late autumn, when it's fashionable to sport a mackintosh. Ambleside is perched at the north end of Lake Windermere.

Between Ambleside and Wordsworth's former retreat at Grasmere is Rydal, a small village on one of the smallest lakes, Rydal Water. The village is noted for its sheep-dog trials at the end of summer. It's 1½ miles north of Ambleside on A591.

ESSENTIALS
GETTING THERE   Take a train to Windermere (see above), then continue the rest of the way by bus.

Cumberland Motor Services (☎ **01946/63222**) has hourly bus service from Grasmere and Keswick (see below) and from Windermere. All these buses into Ambleside are labeled either no. 555 or no. 557.

If you're driving from Windermere, continue northwest on A591.

VISITOR INFORMATION   The **Tourist Information Centre** is at Old Courthouse, Church Street, in Ambleside (☎ **015394/32582**), and is open April through October daily from 9am to 5pm, and from November through March from Tuesday to Saturday with reduced hours.

EXPLORING THE AREA
Lakeland Safari Tours, 23 Fisherbeck Park, Ambleside (☎ **015394/33904**), help you discover the Lakeland's hidden beauty, heritage, and traditions. The owner, a qualified Blue Badge Guide, provides an exciting selection of full-day and half-day safaris in his luxury six-seat vehicle. A half-day safari is £17 ($27.20) per person; a day-long trek is £27 ($43.20) per person.

✪ **Rydal Mount.** Off the A591, 1½ miles north of Ambleside. ☎ **015394/33002.** Admission £3 ($4.80) adults, £2.50 ($4) seniors and students, £1 ($1.60) children ages 5–16; free for kids 4 and under. Entrance to the garden is £1.50 ($2.40). Mar–Oct daily 9:30am–5pm; Nov–Feb Wed–Mon 10am–4pm.

This was the home of William Wordsworth from 1813 until his death in 1850. Part of the house was built as a farmer's lake cottage around 1575. A descendant of Wordsworth now owns the property, which displays numerous portraits, furniture, and family possessions, as well as mementos and the poet's books. The 4½-acre garden, landscaped by Wordsworth, is filled with rare trees, shrubs, and other features of interest.

WHERE TO STAY & DINE
EXPENSIVE
Kirkstone Foot. Kirkstone Pass Rd., Ambleside, Cumbria LA22 9EH. ☎ **015394/32232.** Fax 015394/32805. 30 units. TV. Apr–Oct £116–£138 ($185.60–$220.80) double; Nov–Mar

£104–£120 ($166.40–$192) double. Rates include English breakfast. MC, V. Closed 1st 2 weeks in Dec. Take Rydal Rd. north, turning right onto Kirkstone Pass Rd.

This country house is one of the finest places to stay in the area. There's the main 17th-century manor house plus several self-catering apartments in the surrounding parklike grounds. The original building is encircled by a well-tended lawn, whereas the interior is cozily furnished with overstuffed chairs and English paneling. The comfortable accommodations—15 in the main house and 15 in the less desirable outlying units—are tastefully decorated. The rooms that face the front are the most sought after.

Dining: The restaurant offers home-cooked English meals. Fresh produce is used whenever possible. A five-course dinner costs 21.95 ($35.10) April to October and 20.95 ($33.50) November to March for nonresidents.

Amenities: Dry cleaning/laundry, baby-sitting, room service.

Nanny Brow Hotel. Clappersgate (on A593 about a mile west of Ambleside), Ambleside, Cumbria LA22 9NF. ☎ 015394/32036. Fax 015394/32450. 17 units. MINIBAR TV TEL. £131 ($209.60) double; £220 ($352) suite for 2. Rates include English breakfast and dinner. AE, DC, MC, V.

Situated on a hill, this former private home, built in 1904, has been turned into one of the most successful hotels in the area, a worthy competitor of Rothay Manor (see below). The Tudor-style gabled house is reached via a steep tree-lined drive. Once you arrive, you find a country-house setting containing a lovely sitting room with intricate cove moldings and a log fire. The rooms are in both the main house and a garden wing (the latter offers the best accommodations). Some of the suites have half-tester beds.

Dining: The food is well prepared, using fresh ingredients.

Amenities: Solarium and whirlpool bath, plus free access to the pool, sauna, and gym at the nearby local time-share complex.

✪ Rothay Manor. Rothay Bridge, Ambleside, Cumbria LA22 0EH. ☎ 015394/33605. Fax 015394/33607. 18 units. TV TEL. £106–£118 ($169.60–$188.80) double; £150–£166 ($240–$265.60) suite. Rates include English breakfast. AE, DC, MC, V. Take A593 ½ mile south of Ambleside.

At this spot, which is reminiscent of a French country inn, the stars are the cuisine, the well-chosen French wines, and comfortable, centrally heated bedrooms and suites. It's our top choice in an area where the competition is stiff in the country-house race. Each of the bedrooms is individually decorated (two are wheelchair accessible). Most have shuttered French doors opening onto a sun balcony and a mountain view. Throughout the estate you'll find an eclectic combination of antiques (some Georgian blended harmoniously with Victorian), flowers, and enticing armchairs.

Dining: The manor is also a restaurant open to nonresidents, serving the finest cuisine in Ambleside. The spacious dining room is decked with antique tables and chairs. The flawless appointments include fine crystal, silver, and china. A traditional Sunday lunch always features a whole sirloin of roast beef with Yorkshire pudding. Dinners are more ambitious. The chef is likely to prepare everything from a savory loin of pork roasted with rosemary and onion to salmon gently poached in a white-wine court bouillon, its essential goodness enhanced by a fresh dill sauce.

Waterdge Hotel. Borrans Rd. (on A591, a mile south of Ambleside), Waterhead, Ambleside, Cumbria LA22 0EP. ☎ 015394/32332. Fax 015394/31878. 22 units. TV TEL. £110–£186 ($176–$297.60) double. Rates include breakfast and dinner. AE, MC, V. Closed mid-Dec to mid-Jan.

The center of this hotel was formed long ago from two 17th-century fishing cottages. Wateredge was, in fact, listed as a lodging house as early as 1873, and further additions were made in the early 1900s. Situated in a beautiful garden overlooking Lake Windermere, the hotel also serves some of the best food in the area. Public rooms have many little nooks for reading and conversation, and there is a cozy bar. However, on sunny days guests prefer to relax in one of the chairs on the lawn. The rooms vary in size and appointments; some are spacious, others much smaller.

Dining: A six-course, well-balanced, fixed-price dinner is offered to nonresidents nightly if hotel guests don't take all the tables. Fresh produce is used, and the quality of cooking is high—self-styled as a "traditional farmhouse cuisine." In winter, a log fire will greet you.

Amenities: Access to nearby health club and tennis courts; car-rental desk, room service, concierge, dry cleaning/laundry, baby-sitting.

MODERATE TO INEXPENSIVE

Glen Rothay Hotel. On A591, Rydal, Ambleside, Cumbria LA22 9LR. ☎ **015394/34500.** Fax 015394/31079. 13 units. TV TEL. £50–£70 ($80–$112) double; from £116 ($185.60) suite for 2. Rates include English breakfast. AE, DC, MC, V. On A591 1½ miles northwest of Ambleside.

Built in the 17th century as a wayfarer's inn, this hotel adjoins Dora's Field, immortalized by Wordsworth. Set back from the highway, it has a stucco-and-flagstone facade. Inside, the place has been modernized, but original details remain, including beamed ceilings and paneling. There is a popular street-level pub, plus a more formal cocktail lounge with a fireplace and comfortable armchairs, as well as a dining room serving solid English food. The comfortable bedrooms upstairs have central heating and coffeemakers, and a few offer four-poster beds.

Queens Hotel. Market Place, Ambleside, Cumbria LA22 9BU. ☎ **015394/32206.** Fax 015394/32721. 26 units. TV TEL. Mon–Thurs £42–£50 ($67.20–$80) double, Fri–Sun £54 ($86.40) double. AE, DC, MC, V.

In the heart of this area is the Queens, an old-fashioned family run hotel where guests are housed and fed well. It began as a private home in the Victorian era, and it was later transformed into a hotel, with some restoration completed in 1992. It's centrally heated in winter.

Since the hotel has two fully licensed bars and restaurants, you may want to dine here. The food is good and hearty. Locals and tourists alike gravitate to the hotel bar. Bar meals are served throughout the day.

Riverside Hotel. Near Rothay Bridge, Under Loughrigg, Ambleside, Cumbria LA22 9LJ. ☎ **015394/32395.** Fax 015394/32395. 4 units. TV TEL. £60 ($96) double; £65 ($104) suite. Rates include breakfast. V. Closed Nov–Feb. From Windermere on the A591, take the left fork at Waterhead toward Coniston. Follow Coniston Rd. for about a mile until you come to the junction at Rothay Bridge. Turn left across the bridge and then immediately make a sharp right along the small lane signposted UNDER LOUGHRIGG.

Secluded on a quiet lane, this small country hotel was formed by combining three adjoining riverside houses dating from the 1820s. It has the solid slate-block walls and slate roof common to Cumbria and, despite its peaceful location, lies a few minutes' walk from the center of Ambleside. Each of the painstakingly decorated rooms has a hair dryer and central heating; two feature four-poster beds and the suite has a Jacuzzi. Guests have access to a nearby health club.

Riverside Lodge Country House. Near Rothay Bridge, Ambleside, Cumbria LA22 0EH. ☎ **015394/34208.** 5 units. TV. £25–£31 ($40–$49.60) per person per night. Rates include English breakfast. MC, V. From Ambleside, take A593, which crosses Rothay Bridge.

This early Georgian house is set on a riverbank, a short walk from the town center, near the foot of Loughrigg Fell, on 3 acres of grounds. The property is run by Alan and Gillian Rhone. Bonnie Prince Charlie rested here in 1745. The lodge has some beamed ceilings and offers well-furnished bedrooms, some with river views. The breakfast room overlooks the river, and there's an intimate lounge with an open fire.

WHERE TO SHARE A PINT

The friendliest pub in Ambleside is the **Golden Rule,** Smithy Brow (☎ 01539/ 433363), named for the brass yardstick mounted over the bar. There's a country hunt theme in the barroom, which features comfortable leather furniture and cast-iron tables. You can step into one side room and throw darts, or go into the other for a quiet, contemplative pint. Behind the bar, a small but colorful garden provides a serene setting in warm weather. There's inexpensive pub grub if you get hungry.

Located 3 miles west of town, off the A593 in Little Langdale, **Three Shires** (☎ 015394/37215), a stone-built pub with a stripped timber-and-flagstone interior, offers stunning views of the valley and wooded hills. You can get good pub grub here, as well as a pint of Black Sheep Bitter, Ruddles County, or Websters Yorkshire. Malt whiskies are well represented, too.

4 Grasmere

282 miles NW of London; 18 miles NW of Kendal; 43 miles S of Carlisle

On a lake of the same name, Grasmere was the home of Wordsworth from 1799 to 1808. He called this area "the loveliest spot that man hath ever known."

ESSENTIALS

GETTING THERE   Take a train to Windermere (see above) and continue the rest of the way by bus.

Cumberland Motor Services (☎ 01946/63222) runs hourly bus service to Grasmere from Keswick (see below) and Windermere (see above). Buses running in either direction are marked no. 555 or no. 557.

If you're driving from Windermere (see above), continue northwest along A591.

VISITOR INFORMATION   The summer-only **Tourist Information Centre** is on Red Bank Road (☎ 015394/35245), and is open April through October daily from 9:30am to 5:30pm.

A LITERARY LANDMARK

Afternoon tea is served in the **Dove Cottage Tearoom and Restaurant** (☎ 015394/ 35268). A good selection of open sandwiches, scones, cake, and tea breads is offered along with Darjeeling, Assam, Earl Grey, and herbal teas. The tearoom is open from 10am to 5pm Sunday to Thursday, 6:30 to 9pm Friday and Saturday.

✪ **Dove Cottage/The Wordsworth Museum.** On A591, south of the village of Grasmere on the road to Kendal. ☎ 015394/35544. Admission to both Dove Cottage and the adjoining museum £4.25 ($6.80) adults; family ticket £6.15 ($9.85) Daily 9:30am–5:30pm. Closed Dec 24–26 and Jan 6–Feb 2.

Wordsworth lived with his writer-and-diarist sister, Dorothy, at Dove Cottage, which is now part of the Wordsworth Museum and administered by the Wordsworth Trust. Wordsworth, the poet laureate, died in spring 1850 and was buried in the graveyard of the village church at Grasmere. Another tenant of Dove Cottage was Thomas De Quincey (*Confessions of an English Opium Eater*). The Wordsworth Museum houses manuscripts, paintings, and memorabilia. There are also various special exhibitions throughout the year that explore the art and literature of English romanticism.

WHERE TO STAY & DINE
VERY EXPENSIVE

✪ **Michael's Nook.** ¼ mile east of A591, Grasmere, Cumbria LA22 9RP. ☎ **800/544-9941** in the U.S., or 015394/35496. Fax 015394/35645. 16 units. TV TEL. £192–£296 ($307.20–$473.60) double; £410 ($656) suite. Rates include English breakfast and 5-course dinner. AE, DC, MC, V.

This country-house hotel, once a private residence, is situated on its own secluded 3-acre garden and provides the finest and most tranquil stopover in Grasmere. The name honors a hill shepherd, Michael, subject of a Wordsworth poem. A Lakeland home of stone, it is adorned with fine mahogany woodwork and paneling, especially its elegant staircase. Throughout the house, which is owned by Grasmere antique dealer Reg Gifford and his wife, Elizabeth, are many fine antiques, enhanced by the glow of log fires or vases of flowers. Amenities include hair dryers and sandalwood sachets in drawers; one room has a four-poster bed. During some peak weekends, a minimum 3-night stay is requested, but shorter bookings are accommodated whenever possible.

Dining: Only about 20 people can be served in the intimate dining room, which accepts reservations from nonresidents for both lunch and dinner. Additional seating is available in the Oak Room. Meals are carefully prepared, with menus changing daily. Michael's Nook is now recognized by the British AA as being the best hotel restaurant in the north of England, and it's been awarded four rosettes (out of a possible five) for its cuisine. Room service is available.

White Moss House. On A591 (1½ miles south of town), Rydal Water, Grasmere, Cumbria LA22 9SE. ☎ **015394/35295.** Fax 015394/35516. 7 units. TV TEL. £120–£190 ($192–$304) double. Rates include breakfast and dinner. MC, V. Closed Dec–Jan.

This 1730 Lakeland cottage, once owned by Wordsworth, overlooks the lake and the fells. You'll be welcomed here by Peter and Susan Dixon, who will pamper you with morning tea in bed, turn down your bedcovers at night, and cater to your culinary preferences. The rooms are comfortably furnished and well heated in nippy weather. All units have trouser presses, hair dryers, and such amenities as herbal bath salts. There's also Brockstone, their cottage annex, a 5-minute drive along the road, where two, three, or four guests can be accommodated in utter peace.

Dining: Dinner is a leisurely affair in a little cottage-style room. You're served five courses, which might include roast of lamb with an orange-and-red-currant sauce or quail with a chicken and brown-rice stuffing. For dessert, hope that Mrs. Beeton's chocolate pudding is featured. You must reserve a table early. Room service is available.

Amenities: Access to nearby health club and tennis courts; car-rental desk, dry cleaning/laundry, baby-sitting.

Wordsworth Hotel. Stock Lane, Grasmere, Cumbria LA22 9SW. ☎ **015394/35592.** Fax 015394/35765. 39 units. TV TEL. £140–£172 ($224–$275.20) double; from £220 ($352) suite. Rates include English breakfast. AE, DC, MC, V. Turn left on A591 at the Grasmere Village sign and follow the road over the bridge past the church, and around an S-bend; the Wordsworth is on the right.

This choice in the heart of the village is situated in a 3-acre garden next to the churchyard where Wordsworth is buried. An old stone Lakeland house that once was the hunting lodge of the earl of Cadogan, the Wordsworth has been completely refurbished to provide luxuriously appointed bedrooms with views of the fells, as well as modern baths, hair dryers, and trouser presses. Three rooms have four-poster beds. The original master bedroom contains a Victorian bathroom with a brass towel rail and polished pipes and taps. Rooms vary widely in size and configurations.

Dining/Diversions: There are several lounges, with comfortable armchairs. A buffet lunch is served in the cocktail lounge, including the chef's hot dish of the day. The cuisine is modern English, and local produce, deftly handled by the kitchen staff, is used whenever possible.

Amenities: 24-hour room service, laundry service, large swimming pool, sauna, and minigym.

EXPENSIVE TO MODERATE

Red Lion Hotel. Red Lion Sq., Grasmere, Cumbria LA22 9SS. ☎ 015934/35456. Fax 015394/35579. 34 units. TV TEL. £39.50–£51 ($63.20–$81.60) per person per night. Rates include English breakfast. AE, DC, MC, V.

This 200-year-old coaching inn is only a short stroll from Wordsworth's Dove Cottage, and it's assumed that the poet often stopped here for a meal, drink, or to warm himself by the fire. Recently refurbished, the hotel offers comfortably furnished bedrooms, half with spa baths. A fitness room includes Nautilus weights, sauna, steam room, Jacuzzi, and solarium. Enjoy a drink or lunch in the airy surroundings of the Easdale Bar, or try the Lamb Inn and Buttery for a more traditional pub atmosphere. In the dining room, The Courtyard Restaurant, you'll be served some of the finest fare in the district.

Swan Hotel. On A591 (on the road to Keswick, ½ mile outside Grasmere), Grasmere, Cumbria LA22 9RF. ☎ 800/225-5843 in the U.S. and Canada, or 015394/35551. Fax 015394/35741. 36 units. TV TEL. £120–£140 ($192–$224) double. Apr–Aug leisure-break packages available Fri–Sun, £79 ($126.40) per person with half board. AE, DC, MC, V.

This is one of the best moderately priced choices. Many bedrooms are in a modern wing, added in 1975, that fits gracefully onto the building's older core (only the shell of the original 1650 building remains). Sir Walter Scott used to slip in for a secret drink early in the morning, and Wordsworth mentioned the place in "The Waggoner." In fact, the poet's wooden chair is in one of the rooms.

INEXPENSIVE

Riversdale. Grasmere, Cumbria LA22 9RQ. ☎ 015394/35619. 3 units. TV. £46–£60 ($73.60–$96) double. Rates include English breakfast. No credit cards. Drive 10 miles north of Windermere along A591 (signposted to Kenwick), then turn left by the Swan Hotel. In 400 yd., you'll find the inn on the left side of the rd. facing the river.

This lovely old house, built in 1830 of traditional Lakeland stone, is quietly situated on the outskirts of the village of Grasmere along the banks of the River Rothay. The bedrooms are tastefully decorated and offer every comfort, including hair dryers, toiletries, tea- and coffeemakers, and hospitality trays, as well as views of the surrounding fells. Mrs. Joyce Edwards and her sister Jean Newnes are gracious, witty, and full of fun. They are a wealth of information on day trips, whether by car or hiking. Their breakfasts, which are a delight, are served in a dining room overlooking Silver How and the fells beyond Easdale Tarn. No smoking.

5 Coniston & Hawkshead

263 miles NW of London; 52 miles S of Carlisle; 19 miles NW of Kendal

At Coniston, you can visit the village famously associated with John Ruskin. It's also a good place for hiking and rock climbing. The Coniston "Old Man" towers in the background, at 2,633 feet, give mountain climbers one of the finest views of the Lake District.

Just 4 miles east of Coniston, discover for yourself the village of Hawkshead, with its 15th-century grammar school where Wordsworth studied for 8 years (he carved his name on a desk that is still there). Nearby, in the vicinity of Esthwaite Water, is the 17th-century Hill Top Farm, former home of author Beatrix Potter.

ESSENTIALS
GETTING THERE   Take a train to Windermere (see above) and proceed the rest of the way by bus.

Cumberland Motor Services (☎ 01946/63222) runs three buses from Windermere to Hawkshead and Coniston from Monday to Saturday, two on Sunday. Take either bus no. 505 or no. 515 from Windermere.

By car from Windermere, proceed north on A591 to Ambleside, cutting southwest on B5285 to Hawkshead.

Windermere Lake Cruises Ltd. (☎ 015394/43360) operates a ferry service in summer from Bowness, directly south of Windermere, to Hawkshead. It reduces driving time considerably (see "Windermere & Bowness," above).

VISITOR INFORMATION   The **Tourist Information Centre** (☎ 015394/36525) is at Hawkshead in the Main Car Park and is open March 23 through October daily from 9:30am to 5:30pm.

EXPLORING THE AREA
Of the many places to go boating in the Lake District, Coniston Water in the Lake District National Park may be the best. Coniston Water lies in a tranquil wooded valley between Grisedale Forest and the high fells of Coniston Old Man and Wetherlam. The **Coniston Boating Centre,** Lake Road, Coniston LA21 (☎ 015394/41366), occupies a sheltered bay at the northern end of the lake. The center provides launching facilities, boat storage, and parking. You can rent rowing boats that carry from two to six people, sailing dinghies carrying up to six passengers, or Canadian canoes that transport two. There is a picnic area and access to the lakeshore. From the gravel beach you may be able to spot the varied water birds and plants that make Coniston Water a valuable but fragile habitat for wildlife.

You can also cruise the lake in an original Victorian steam-powered yacht, the *Gondola.* Launched in 1859 and in regular service until 1937, this unique boat was rescued and completely restored by the National Trust. Since 1980 it has become a familiar sight on Coniston, and sailings to Park-a-Moor and Brantwood run throughout the summer. Service is subject to weather conditions, of course. For more information, call ☎ 015394/41288.

Coniston Launch is a traditional timber boat that calls at Coniston, Monk Coniston, Torver, and Brantwood. (Discounts are offered in combination with admission to Brantwood house; see below.) This exceptional boating outfitter offers special cruises in summer (a "Swallows and Amazons" tour was inspired by Arthur Ransome's classic story). For more information, call or fax ☎ 015394/36216.

Summitreks operates from the lakeside at Coniston Boating Centre, offering qualified instruction in canoeing and windsurfing. A wide range of equipment can be rented from the nearby office at Lake Road (☎ 015394/41212).

In Hawkshead, the **Beatrix Potter Gallery** (☎ 015394/36355) has an annually changing exhibition of Beatrix Potter's original illustrations from her children's storybooks. The building was once the office of her husband, the solicitor William Heelis, and the interior remains largely unaltered since his day. To get here, take bus 505 from Ambleside-Coniston to the square in Hawkshead.

Brantwood. Coniston. ☎ **015394/41396.** Admission £3.90 ($6.25) adults, £2.10 ($3.35) students, £1 ($1.60) children 5–16. Nature walk £1.75 ($2.80) adults, £1 ($1.60) children.

Mid-Mar to mid-Nov daily 11am–5:30pm; mid-Nov to mid-Mar Wed–Sun 11am–4pm. Closed Christmas Day and Boxing Day.

John Ruskin, poet, artist, and critic, was one of the great figures of the Victorian age and a prophet of social reform, inspiring such diverse men as Proust, Frank Lloyd Wright, and Gandhi. He moved to his home, Brantwood, on the east side of Coniston Water, in 1872 and lived here until his death in 1900. The house today is open for visitors to see his memorabilia, including some 200 pictures by him.

Part of the 250-acre estate is open as a nature trail. The Brantwood stables, designed by Ruskin, have been converted into a tearoom and restaurant, the Jumping Jenny. Also in the stable building is the Coach House Craft Gallery, which follows the Ruskin tradition of encouraging contemporary craft work of the finest quality.

Literary fans may want to pay a pilgrimage to the graveyard of the village church, where Ruskin was buried; his family turned down the invitation to have him interred at Westminster Abbey.

John Ruskin Museum. Yewdale Rd., Coniston. ☎ 015394/11164. Admission £2 ($3.20) adults, £1 ($1.60) children. Easter–Oct daily 10am–1pm and 2–4pm. Closed Nov–Easter.

At this institute, in the center of the village, you can see Ruskin's personal possessions and mementos, pictures by him and his friends, letters, and his collection of mineral rocks.

WHERE TO STAY

Coniston Sun Hotel. Brow Hill (off the A593), Coniston, Cumbria LA21 8HQ. ☎ 015394/41248. Fax 015395/41219. 11 units. TV TEL. £60–£70 ($96–$112) double. Rates include English breakfast. MC, V.

This is the most popular, traditional, and attractive pub, restaurant, and hotel in Coniston. It's a country-house hotel of much character, dating from 1902, although the inn attached to it is from the 16th century. Situated on beautiful grounds above the village, 150 yards from the town center, it lies at the foot of the Coniston "Old Man." Donald Campbell established his headquarters here during his attempt to break the world water-speed record. Each bedroom is decorated with style and flair, and two of them have four-posters.

Fresh local produce is used whenever possible in the candlelit restaurant. Log fires take the chill off a winter evening, and guests relax informally in the library-like lounge. Many outdoor activities can be arranged, including water sports, pony rides, and mountain biking.

Highfield House. Hawkshead Hill (¾ mile east of Hawkshead, on the road to Coniston), Hawkshead, Ambleside, Cumbria LA22 OPN. ☎ 015394/36344. Fax 015394/36793. 11 units. TV. £76–£86 ($121.60–$137.60) double. Rates include English breakfast. MC, V.

This solidly built stone-sided house sits on the side of a hill and on clear days enjoys sweeping views over the Lake District. Constructed around 1870, it is surrounded by 2½ acres of its own land. Operated by members of the Bennett family, it has cozy bedrooms, either with pastel colors or wallpaper inspired by the turn-of-the-century designs of William Morris. Rooms were recently refurbished.

A four-course dinner with such dishes as pink fillet baked with poppy seeds, or grilled salmon with dill and cucumber sauce is always available, but advance notice is recommended.

WHERE TO DINE

Grizedale Lodge. Grizedale, Hawkshead. ☎ 015394/36532. Reservations required. Bar lunches £3.50–£9.50 ($5.60–$15.20); fixed-price dinner £23.50 ($37.60). AE, MC, V. Daily

12:30–1:30pm and 7–8pm. Closed Jan 2–Feb 7. From Hawkshead take Newby Bridge Rd. for about 500 yd., then turn right (signposted GRIZEDALE & FOREST PARK CENTER) and follow this road for 2 miles. ENGLISH/FRENCH.

The best place for food in the area is this country *restaurant avec chambres,* which was built in 1902 as a hunting lodge for the chairman of the Cunard Line. Many people come here just to dine because the cuisine is top-notch. During the day, guests order bar lunches, but at night they can enjoy a memorable five-course meal in a tranquil setting. Service is personable.

Mr. and Mrs. Dawson offer nine handsomely furnished bedrooms for guests, each with a private bathroom and TV. For half board, charges are from £49.50 to £59.50 ($79.20 to $95.20) per person.

WHERE TO ENJOY A PINT

A display case of fishing lures is the first tip-off, then there's the pond itself—yes, it's true, you can fish while you drink at the **Drunken Duck,** Barnsgate (☎ **01539/ 436347**). Or you can just sit on the front porch and gaze at Lake Windermere in the distance. Inside, you can choose from an assortment of cushioned settles, old pews, and tub or ladder-back chairs, then order a wild-boar steak or minted lamb casserole to go with a pint of Mitchells Lancaster Bomber, Yates Bitter, or Yates Drunken Duck Bitter, brewed especially for the pub. If you want stronger spirits, there are more than 60 malt whiskies to choose from.

Overlooking the central square of the village, the **Kings Arms** (☎ **01539/436372**) offers a pleasant front terrace or lots of plush leather-covered seating inside the cozy barroom. Traditional pub grub is supplemented with a few pasta dishes, and ales include Greenall's Original, Tetleys, and Theakstons XB. Malt whiskies are well represented also.

6 Keswick

22 miles NW of Windermere; 294 miles NW of London; 31 miles NW of Kendal

Keswick opens onto Derwentwater, one of the loveliest lakes in the region, and the town makes a good base for exploring the northern half of Lake District National Park. Keswick has two landscaped parks, and above the small town is a historic stone circle thought to be some 4,000 years old.

St. Kentigern's Church dates from A.D. 553, and a weekly market held in the center of Keswick can be traced from a charter granted in the 13th century. It's a short walk to Friar's Crag, the classic viewing point on Derwentwater. The walk will also take you past boat landings with launches that operate regular tours around the lake.

Around Derwentwater there are many places with literary associations that evoke memories of Wordsworth, Robert Southey, Coleridge, and Hugh Walpole. Several of Beatrix Potter's stories were based at Keswick. The town also has a professional repertory theater that schedules performances in the summer. There's a swimming pool complex, plus an 18-hole golf course at the foot of the mountains 4 miles away.

ESSENTIALS

GETTING THERE   Take a train to Windermere (see above) and proceed the rest of the way by bus.

Cumberland Motor Services (☎ **01946/63222**) has a regular bus service from Windermere and Grasmere (bus no. 555).

From Windermere, drive northwest on A591.

VISITOR INFORMATION   The **Tourist Information Centre,** at Moot Hall, Market Square (☎ **017687/72645**), is open daily April to June from 9:30am to 5:30pm, in July and August daily from 9:30am to 7pm, and from September through March daily from 10am to 4pm. It's closed Christmas and New Year's days.

SEEING THE SIGHTS

Internationally known for its unique handmade teapots, **The Teapottery,** off Heads Road (☎ **017687/73983**), now has a branch in Keswick open to visitors who can watch the craftspeople at work. You can experience the history of tea and see the whole range of wild and wonderful teapots in this shop. To get here, go to Keswick's central car park, off Heads Road. It's by the entrance to the car park.

Mirehouse. On the A591, 3½ miles north of Keswick. ☎ **017687/72287.** Admission to house and gardens plus a lakeside walk £3.50 ($5.60) adults, £1.75 ($2.80) children and seniors; family ticket (2 adults plus 4 kids ages 5–16) £9.50 ($15.20). House or gardens alone £1.50 ($2.40) adults, 80p ($1.30) children. House open Aug only, Sun, Wed, and Fri 2–4:30pm. Tearoom and grounds Apr–Oct daily 10am–5:30pm.

A tranquil Cumbrian family home that has not been sold since 1688, Mirehouse has unusually wide-ranging literary and artistic connections. The piano is played on afternoons when guests stop by to visit. The park around it stretches to Bassenthwaite Lake, and has extensive gardens, plus woodland adventure playgrounds. It is in easy reach of the ancient lakeside church and the Old Sawmill Tearoom, which is known for its generous Cumbrian cooking.

WHERE TO STAY

Brundholme Country House. Brundholme Rd., Keswick, Cumbria CA12 4NL. ☎ and fax **017687/74495.** 7 units. TV TEL. £60 ($96) double; £300–£600 ($480–$960) per week for apt. Rates include English breakfast. No credit cards. At the A66 Keswick roundabout, turn left toward Brundholme.

Coleridge wrote that this Regency villa above the River Greta was "in a delicious situation," referring to the views over Keswick to the enveloping hills. Wordsworth was also known to visit here. It was restored and opened as a choice hotel in 1988. Owner Ian Charlton has recently reconfigured the house. His well-chosen staff is one of the most helpful in the area. There are now three well-furnished bedrooms, plus several apartments that are fully furnished with dishes, kitchen equipment, sheets, and towels. The hotel also has a garden.

Grange Country House. Manor Brow, Ambleside Rd. (on the southeast side of Keswick, overlooking the town, just off A591), Keswick, Cumbria CA12 4BA. ☎ **017687/72500.** 10 units. TV TEL. £67–£77 ($107.20–$123.20) double. Rates include English breakfast. MC, V. Closed Nov to mid-Mar.

A tranquil retreat, this charming hotel and its gardens are situated on a hilltop. Dating from the 1840s, it is furnished in part with antiques. Guests enjoy the crackling log fires in chilly weather. Many of the attractively furnished, well-kept rooms open onto scenic views of the Lakeland hills. The hotel, run by Jane and Duncan Miller, also offers first-rate cuisine from a varied dinner menu.

Skiddaw Hotel. Market Sq., Keswick, Cumbria CA12 5BN. ☎ **017687/72071.** Fax 017687/74850. 40 units. TV TEL. £62–£70 ($99.20–$112) double. Rates include English breakfast. AE, MC, V.

This hotel has an impressive facade and entrance marquee built right onto the sidewalk in the heart of Keswick at the market square. The owners have refurbished the interior, retaining the best features. Bedrooms are compact and eye catching, have beverage-makers, and are gradually being refurbished. Guests may use the pool and spa at Armathwaite Hall and golf at Keswick Golf Club during the week.

Folks gather in the lounge or the popular cocktail bar, with its art nouveau ambience. The meals at Gillespies feature well-prepared English and continental cuisine, available à la carte all day. In addition, a chef's special, such as Cumbria hot pot, is offered at lunch, and afternoon teas are served in the restaurant and in the lounge bar. There is a wide selection of wines.

A NEARBY PLACE TO DINE
The Yew Tree Restaurant. Seatoller. ☎ **017687/77634.** Reservations recommended. Main courses £3.85–£12 ($6.15–$19.20). Daily noon–9:30pm. Closed Jan and Mon from Nov–Mar. Take the B5289 8 miles south of Keswick. BRITISH.

This restaurant in the Borrowdale region lies in the hamlet of Seatoller. Named after the 500-year-old yew that broods timelessly near the front entrance, this restaurant occupies an interconnected pair of stone-sided cottages that were built in 1628 as the home of two German-born miners. If you've been out hiking, fortify yourself with simple but nourishing dishes that include soup, Cumberland sausages with salads, and lamb cobbler. Evening meals tend to be more elaborate, and include local trout with almonds. The interior of the place, loaded with oaken beams and memorabilia, is about as evocative as it gets.

SIDE TRIPS FROM KESWICK
BORROWDALE
One of the most scenic parts of the Lake District, Borrowdale stretches south of Derwentwater to Seathwaite in the heart of the county. The valley is walled in by fell sides, and it's an excellent center for exploring, walking, and climbing. Many use it as a center for exploring **Scafell,** England's highest mountain, at 3,210 feet.

This resort is in the Borrowdale Valley, the southernmost settlement of which is Seatoller. The village of Seatoller, at 1,176 feet, is the terminus for buses to and from Keswick. It's also the center for a **Lake District National Park Information Centre** at Dalehead Base, Seatoller Barn (☎ **01768/777294**).

After leaving Seatoller, B5289 takes you west through the Honister Pass and Buttermere Fell, one of the most dramatic drives in the Lake District. The road is lined with towering boulders. The lake village of Buttermere also merits a stopover.

Where to Stay & Dine
Borrowdale Gates Hotel. Grange-in-Borrowdale, Keswick CA12 5UQ. ☎ **01768/777204.** Fax 01768/777254. 28 units. TV. £112–£165 ($179.20–$264) double. Rates include English breakfast and dinner. AE, MC, V. From Keswick, take B592 4 miles south to Grange, go over the bridge and the inn sits on the right, just beyond the curve in the road.

The proprietors of this hotel, Terry and Christine Parkinson, have welcomed John Major here for afternoon tea. It was quite the affair around these parts. Their 1860 Victorian country house, built of Lakeland stone, has just received a new addition of nine rooms that faithfully matches the Victorian style. All the rooms range in size from medium to large and are decorated with rich Victorian colors and period reproductions. The public areas, with their antiques and open-log stone fireplaces, sprawl along the ground floor and include a bar, restaurant and dining area, and four sitting lounges. They are all airy and bright with views of the surrounding gardens which roll into the outlying countryside.

Dining: The kitchen is the domain of chef Michael Heathcote, whose passion for good food accounts for the excellence of the cuisine, which relies on the fresh local produce. You can dine here every night and always have a different menu to choose from. Try such delights as a duckling and vegetable spring roll followed by a panache of seafood with a fish mousseline. The kitchen leans heavily on British favorites, but also has a continental flair.

Amenities: Dry cleaning/laundry; access to health club 4 miles away.

Borrowdale Hotel. Borrowdale Rd. (B5289), Borrowdale, Keswick, Cumbria CA12 5UY. ☎ **017687/77224.** Fax 017687/77338. 34 units. TV TEL. £55–£79 ($88–$126.40) per person double. Rates include English breakfast and dinner. MC, V. On B5289 3½ miles south of Keswick.

When the weather is damp, log fires welcome guests in this Lakeland stone building, which was originally a coaching inn (ca. 1866). The rooms are comfortable and many have fine views. All have intercom units and hair dryers. Some traditional four-poster beds are available.

Dining: The restaurant fusses over the presentation of its dishes. From Monday to Saturday, lunches are served in the bar, and feature a choice of at least 20 main courses that range from soup and sandwiches to chicken Kiev. Sunday lunch is a more formal, fixed-price affair. At dinner, the restaurant serves six-course set menus with a choice of at least six different dishes. Cuisine from all parts of the globe is offered, and the menu changes daily. If you would like to have the daily roast, the chef will carve it at your table from a silver cart.

Amenities: Free access to a health club and golf course.

Stakis Lodore Swiss Hotel. Borrowdale Rd. (B5289), Borrowdale, Keswick, Cumbria CA12 5UX. ☎ **017687/77285.** Fax 017687/77343. 75 units. MINIBAR TV TEL. £128–£148 ($204.80–$236.80) double; £175–£340 ($280–$544) suite. Winter discounts available. AE, DC, MC, V. Indoor parking £4 ($6.40); outdoors, free. On B5289 3½ miles south of Keswick.

The Stakis hotel chain runs this hotel, which overlooks Derwentwater from fields where cows graze. With its spike-capped mansard tower, symmetrical gables, and balcony-embellished stone facade, it seems straight out of the Swiss Alps. (Ironically, the Swiss owners who built this place in the 19th century were named England. Their tradition of good rooms, food, and service continues today.) The interior has been completely modernized, and each of the well-furnished bedrooms has a hair dryer and coffeemaker.

Dining: The food here is exceptional for the area, with fixed-price meals available to nonresidents. Dishes include roast topside of English beef with Yorkshire pudding, Morecambe Bay shrimp, and plaice sautéed in butter. Call for a reservation, especially at dinner.

Amenities: 24-hour room service, indoor swimming pool and garden, laundry service.

BASSENTHWAITE

In the Lake District National Park, 6 miles north of Keswick, Bassenthwaite is one of the most beautiful of Lakeland villages, and makes the best center for exploring the woodlands of Thornthwaite Forest and Bassenthwaite Lake nearby. Bassenthwaite Lake is the northernmost and only true "lake" in the Lake District, and it's visited yearly by many species of migratory birds from the north of Europe.

Where to Stay

✪ **Armathwaite Hall Hotel.** Bassenthwaite Lake (on B5291, 7 miles northwest of Keswick, 1½ miles west of Bassenthwaite), Keswick, Cumbria CA12 4RE. ☎ **017687/76551.** Fax 017687/76220. 42 units. TV TEL. £110–£180 ($176–$288) double; £198 ($316.80) suite. Rates include English breakfast. AE, DC, MC, V.

Rich in history, this hotel was originally built in the 1300s as a house for Benedictine nuns. During the Middle Ages, it was plundered frequently, leaving the sisters wretchedly poor. By the 17th century, a series of wealthy landowners had completed the severe Gothic design of its stately facade, and an architecturally compatible series of wings were added in 1844. It was converted into a hotel during the 1930s. Sir Hugh Walpole, who once stayed here, found it "a house of perfect and irresistible charm." Ringed with almost 400 acres of woodland (some bordering the lake), the place offers a magnificent entrance hall filled with hunting trophies and sheathed with expensive paneling; the bedrooms are also handsomely furnished. A Victorian billiard room is lined with old engravings.

There's a small but diverting attraction on its premises: a minizoo featuring unusual breeds of both barnyard and wild animals. The collection includes potbellied pigs, llamas, goats, rabbits, and owls. They also have a reptile house, bird of prey center, animated display, tearoom, and wet-weather facilities. Only a 5-minute walk from the hotel, Trotters & Friends is open daily from 10am to 5pm. Adults pay £2.85 ($4.55); children age 3 to 14, £1.95 ($3.10). Kids 3 and under enter free.

Dining: A first-class restaurant offers a view of the lake.

Amenities: An indoor swimming pool is ringed with stone walls and sheltered from the rain by a roof of wooden trusses. The hotel also provides the finest equestrian center in the area.

The Castle Inn Hotel. Bassenthwaite (6 miles north of Keswick on A591), Cumbria CA12 4RG. ☎ and fax **017687/76401.** 48 units. TV TEL. £115 ($184) double; £150 ($240) suite. Rates include English breakfast. AE, DC, MC, V. From Keswick, take the A591 6 miles north of town; the inn is on the left.

Don't expect a castle. Although this place plays up its historical importance, you'll find there is an "old" core (no one on the staff is sure of how old), with many newer additions that don't exactly gracefully merge into a unified whole. The result is a hotel that's neither whimsically antique nor strikingly modern—but nor is it dowdy. There are two bars on the premises, and of the two restaurants, the De Quincey is the more upscale. The premises contain both a solarium and a gymnasium/health club.

Overwater Hall. Overwater, Ireby, near Keswick CA5 1HH. ☎ **01768/776566.** 12 units. TV TEL. £84 ($134.40) double. Rates include English breakfast. MC, V.

Built in the late 18th century, this Georgian mansion had battlements added to it by the Victorians, and is reminiscent of a castle and comes complete with a tragic ghost story. When the house was still new, its owner became involved with an alluring Jamaican mistress who became too much of an embarrassment to him. So in a fit of desperation, he threw her to the depths of the nearby lake, cutting off her hands so she could not climb back into the boat. According to all reports, her handless spirit wanders the guest rooms during the night in a harmless manner.

Despite its sad past, this B&B is anything but somber. All the bedrooms, though standard in size, are extremely ritzy (which may be why Overwater's phantom has chosen to stay), having been furnished with top-quality antiques. Some even have oak-paneled four-poster beds. Guests can enjoy the regal surroundings of the public rooms with their intricate and rich cove molding and formal Victorian antiques. The drawing room is a great place for afternoon tea, and the piano bar actually has a baby grand piano. The restaurant's elegant dining room serves breakfast and a five-course dinner. Overwater Hall also offers guests the use of their own putting green and abundant fishing for pike on Overwater Tarn.

The Pheasant Inn. Bassenthwaite Lake, Cockermouth, Cumbria CA13 9YE. ☎ **017687/ 76234.** Fax 017687/76002. 20 units. TV. £80–£108 ($128–$172.80) double. MC, V.

Set amid conifers near the northwestern tip of Bassenthwaite Lake, this place originated in the 17th century as a coaching inn; a series of extensions were later added.

Everything about it evokes old-fashioned English coziness. Coal- and log-burning fireplaces warm a moderately eccentric bar area, a mishmash of antique and merely old-fashioned furniture, and bedrooms whose smallish windows overlook 60 acres of forest and parkland associated with the hotel. Three of the rooms are in a separate bungalow. The restaurant is open for breakfast and dinner only during the week and for lunch on Sunday, serving traditional English fare.

Where to Dine

The Sun. Bassenthwaite Village. ☎ **017687/76439.** Reservations not accepted. Main courses £5.50–£9.50 ($8.80–$15.20). No credit cards. Daily noon–2pm; Mon–Sat 6–11pm. BRITISH.

Originally built in the 16th century as a farmhouse, and now Bassenthwaite Village's only pub, this place has oaken beams, squeaking floors, and as much old-world charm as you can digest at a single sitting. It offers the products from a nearby brewery (Jennings), selling ample amounts of such brand names as Jennings Bitter and Jennings Old Smoothie. Menu items are as traditional as the architecture itself: ham or beef-steaks, squid, sausages, salads, ploughman's lunches, and steaming bowls of Lancashire hot pot. Everybody's favorite dessert is sticky toffee pudding. Lunch in winter often is not available; call ahead before you visit.

7 Ullswater

296 miles NW of London; 26 miles SE of Keswick

Set in a region that is home to contrasting vistas of gently rolling fields and dramatic mountain rises, Ullswater is a favorite with those who enjoy spectacular natural beauty. Ullswater itself is a 9-mile expanse of water, stretching from Pooley Bridge to Patterdale and is the second-largest lake in the district. It is a magnet for outdoor types of all levels of ability, offering activities that range from walks and hikes around the shore to rock climbing, mountain biking, canoeing, sailing, and even windsurfing.

This part of the Lakeland, where the majesty of nature tends to entrance and envelope, has always held a special attraction for artists and writers. The area gained most of its fame from writings by the likes of Wordsworth during the early 19th century. It was on the shores of Ullswater that Wordsworth saw his "host of golden daffodils." Aira Force waterfall, near the National Trust's Gowbarrow, inspired both Wordsworth and Coleridge by its beauty. While using this area as a base for outdoor activities, you can also easily explore the many places of prehistoric and historic significance, from the times of the ancient Celts right through to modern day. Two noteworthy sites include Long Meg and her "daughters," an ancient stone circle near Penrith, and Hadrian's Wall, marking the northern extent of the Roman empire, east of Carlisle (see chapter 18).

In Ullswater, two 19th-century **steamers** provide the best way to see the area's panoramic mountain scenery around the lake. In season, there are three scheduled services daily between Glenridding, Howtown, and Pooley Bridge as well as five shorter 1-hour cruises. Passengers may choose to walk back along the lakeside path or break for lunch at either end of the lake. The steamers run from the end of March to the beginning of November and cost £1.95 to £5.30 ($3.10 to $8.50) per person. For more information, call ☎ **01539/721626.** Glenridding is on A592 at the southern end of Ullswater. Pooley Bridge is 5 miles from the M6 junction 40 Penrith.

ESSENTIALS

GETTING THERE   About three trains from London's Euston Station arrive daily in Penrith, this region's main rail junction. Usually a change of trains isn't necessary.

For schedules and information, call ☎ **0345/484950** (in the U.K. only) or 01603/764776. Once in Penrith, passengers usually take a taxi to Ullswater.

Two buses operated by **Cumberland Motor Services** (☎ **01946/63222**) stop at the Penrith Rail Station on their way between Carlisle and Bowness-on-Windermere from June 24 to September 29. Passengers must take a taxi from Penrith to Ullswater.

If you're driving from Penrith, go southeast on B5320.

VISITOR INFORMATION   The summer-only **Tourist Information Centre** for the lake is at The Square, Pooley Bridge (☎ or fax **017684/86530**); it's open daily April through November from 10am to 5pm.

WHERE TO STAY & DINE

Gowbarrow Lodge. Watermillock, Ullswater, Cumbria CA11 0JP. ☎ **01768/486286.** 8 units. TV. £50 ($80) double. Rates include English breakfast. MC, V.

Named for the large limestone fell running behind the hotel, Gowbarrow Lodge was a filling station 3 years ago—and you never could tell it today from looking at its stone facade. The lodge affords fantastic views of the green fields, large lake, and distant fells across the road. This view was part of the reason the Whitehead family decided to convert their filling station, which people often described as being "the best filling station around simply because of its view." The bedrooms upstairs are of a medium size, decorated with contemporary, functional furnishings. Downstairs, the public rooms, including a small restaurant, lounge, and bar, are full of dark, polished wood with local maps and photographs adorning the walls. The restaurant serves good home-cooked meals.

Land Ends Country Lodge. Watermillock, Penrith, Cumbria CA11 0NB. ☎ **01768/486454.** Fax 01768/486959. 9 units. TV. £50–£52 ($80–$85.80) double. Rates include English breakfast. No credit cards.

This rustic, 2-story converted farmhouse sits rather majestically in the middle of 7 acres of well-tended gardens and lush forest. The years have worn a welcoming charm into the facade of this B&B with its eclectic collection of modern and antique furnishings. The average-sized but pleasantly appointed guest rooms look out onto the countryside and two large ponds, where guests can get in a little trout fishing. The B&B also provides a lounge/sitting room that has an honor bar for guests to use and congregate around.

✪ Sharrow Bay Country House Hotel. Howtown Rd., Lake Ullswater, near Penrith, Cumbria CA10 2LZ. ☎ **01768/486301.** Fax 017684/86349. 28 units. TV TEL. £290–£350 ($464–$560) double; £330–£350 ($528–$560) suite for 2. Rates include half board. No credit cards. Howtown Rd. 2 miles south of Pooley Bridge.

This was Britain's first country-house hotel and the oldest British Relais & Châteaux. It's an unusual Victorian house with a low angled roof and wide eaves. It had been a private home until purchased by Francis Coulson in 1948. Realizing its potential, Coulson restored the structure, sleeping on the floor while work was in progress. Three years later he was joined by Brian Sack, and together they turned Sharrow into one of England's finest places to dine. Today the hotel offers 28 antique-filled bedrooms, 17 of them in the gatehouse and cottages. Individually decorated, each is named after one or another of the glamorous (and often famous) women who have swept in and out of the lives of the articulate owners. Some of the rooms offer views of the lakes, trees, or Martindale Fells.

Dining: The 6-course, fixed-price menu offers a formidable list of choices, all of them made with ultrafresh ingredients and superb vegetables, many of them home-grown. Choices might include honey-glazed roast breast of Lunesdale duckling with a confit of onions, ginger, and coriander in a pastry parcel, orange segments, and a spicy sauce, and, in season, a wide array of game dishes.

Amenities: Room service, laundry/dry cleaning.

8 Penrith

290 miles NW of London; 31 miles NE of Kendal

This one-time capital of Cumbria, in the old Kingdom of Scotland and Strathclyde, takes its name, some say, from the Celts who called it "Ford by the Hill." The namesake hill is marked today by a red-sandstone beacon and tower. Because of Penrith's central location right above the northern Lake District and beside the Pennines, this thriving market center was important to Scotland and England from its very beginning, eventually prompting England to take it over in 1070.

The characteristically red-sandstone town has been home to many famous and legendary figures through the ages, including Richard, duke of Gloucester; William Cookson, the grandfather of William and Dorothy Wordsworth; and, it is said, the giant Ewan Caesarius, a slayer of monsters, men, and beasts. Caesarius's grave allegedly rests in St. Andrew's Churchyard. Today, Penrith still remains best known as a lively market town.

ESSENTIALS

GETTING THERE   Trains from London's Euston Station arrive in Penrith four times a day. The trip takes 4 hours. For train schedules and information, call ☎ **0345/484950** (in the U.K. only) or 01603/764776.

To take a bus from London to Penrith, hop on one of the two daily National Express buses to Carlisle and then take a Stage Coach Cumberland bus to Penrith, a total journey of 8 hours. The Stage Coach Cumberland buses leave every hour. For schedules and information, call **National Express** at ☎ **0990/808080** and **Stage Coach Cumberland** at ☎ **01946/63222**.

To drive, take the M1 out of London, getting on the M6 to Penrith. The trip should take no more than 6 hours.

VISITOR INFORMATION   The **Tourist Information Centre,** Robinson's School, Middlegate, Penrith (☎ **01768/867466**), is open November to Easter, Monday to Saturday from 9:30am to 5pm; Easter through May and the month of October, Monday to Saturday from 9:30am to 5pm and Sunday from 1 to 5pm; June through September, Monday to Saturday from 9:30am to 6pm and Sunday from 1 to 6pm.

EXPLORING THE AREA

It's a small town of 12,500 people, but there are lots of shops to explore. Major shopping areas include the covered **Devonshire Arcade** with its name-brand stores and boutiques, the pedestrian-only **Angel Lane** and **Little Dockray,** with an abundance of family run specialty shops, as well as **Angel Square** just south of Angel Lane.

For handmade earthenware and stoneware from the only remaining steam-powered pottery in Britain, stop by **Wetheriggs Country Pottery,** Clifton Dykes, 2 miles south of Penrith on the A6 (☎ **01768/892733**).

In the 130-year-old **Briggs & Shoe Mines,** Southend Road (☎ **01768/899001**), you'll have a shoe-shopping extravaganza. It is the largest independent shoe shop in the Lakelands, carrying famous names and offering great bargains, including sportswear, walking boots, clothing, and accessories.

The **Eden Valley Woollen Mill,** Armathwaite, along the M6 heading toward Carlisle (☎ 016974/72457), is where Steve Wilson and his small and talented team design and weave using restored looms dating from the early 1900s. Their wares include jackets and skirts in traditional and modern tweeds, rugs, throws, ruanas, hats, ties, and scarves. The showroom also carries individual knitwear and yarns.

Penrith Museum. Robinson's School, Middlegate. ☎ **01768/212228.** Free admission. June–Sept Mon–Sat 9:30am–6pm, Sun 1–6pm; Oct–May Mon–Sat 10am–5pm.

For perspective on Penrith and the surrounding area, a visit here isn't a bad idea. Originally constructed in the 1500s, the museum building was turned into a poor-girls school in 1670. Today, the museum offers a survey of the archaeology and geology of Penrith and the Eden Valley, which was a desert millions of years ago.

Penrith Castle. Just across from the train station along Ullswater Rd. No phone. Free admission. Park and ruins June–Sept daily 7:30am–9pm; Oct–May daily 7:30am–4:30pm.

This park contains the massive ruins of the castle, whose construction began in 1399, ordered by William Strickland, the bishop of Canterbury. For the next 70 years, the castle continued to grow in size and strength until it finally became the royal castle and oftentimes residence for Richard, duke of Gloucester.

Acorn Bank Garden. Temple Sowerby, 6 miles east of Penrith on A6. ☎ **017683/61893.** Admission £2.10 ($3.35) adults, £1 ($1.60) children; family ticket (2 adults, 2 children) £5.50 ($8.80). Daily 10am–5:30pm (last admission at 5pm). Closed mid-Oct to Good Friday.

For a stroll in an English garden, see the Acorn Bank Garden with its varied landscape of blooming bulbs, plants, and walled spaces. Its claim to fame is its extensive herb garden, said to be the best in all of northern England. The Acorn Bank Garden is part of an estate dating from 1228 and is now owned by the National Trust. Buildings on the estate include a partially restored water mill, parts of which also date from the 13th century, and a red-sandstone primarily Tudor house, which is presently not open to the public.

WHERE TO STAY

Clifton Hill. Clifton, Penrith, Cumbria CA10 2EJ. ☎ **01768/862717.** Fax 01768/867182. 62 units. TV. £50 ($80) double. Rates include English breakfast. No credit cards.

This hotel/motel combo sits on 4½ acres, part of which has been turned into a large garden area in the front to welcome guests as they get off their tour buses. Many of these tours are organized by the owners themselves to fill the hotel. The main building was constructed in 1912 by Lord Longsdale, one of the founders of the British Automobile Association. Later, to accommodate the larger crowds, a motel section was added onto the main building. Rooms vary in size—larger ones in the main building and smaller ones in the motel section—but the furnishings are all similar and blend modern with old-world styles. Guests can take tea on the veranda and eat breakfast in the hotel's lounge bar.

George. Devonshire St., Penrith, Cumbria CA11 7SU. ☎ **01768/862696.** Fax 01768/868223. 31 units. TV. £56–£70 ($89.60–$112) double. Rates include English breakfast. MC, V.

This 300-year-old coaching inn, built right in the heart of town, welcomed Bonnie Prince Charlie in 1745. The front of the George looks out on a street of small specialty shops, and the average-size guest rooms are spread among three floors, individually decorated with light colors and up-to-date furnishings. Full of oak beams and paneling, the lounge, two bars, and restaurant with dining room provide everything guests will need during their stay.

North Lakes Hotel. Ullswater Rd., Penrith, Cumbria CA11 8QT. ☎ **01768/868111.** Fax 01768/868291. 95 units. TV TEL. £130–£146 ($208–$233.60) double; £162 ($259.20) suite. Rates include English breakfast. AE, DC, MC, V.

The exterior may lack character, but you'll find compensation inside. A member of the Shire Inns chain, this hotel is designed to meet the needs of businesspeople during the week and vacationers on weekends. Rooms are bright and spacious, decorated with classic wood furniture, large couches, and soft pastel accents. Guests enjoy an inviting lobby sitting area with a grand, barn-style, open ceiling with rustic beams, a huge stone fireplace, and hardwood floors.

Dining: There's an intimate bar and a comfortable restaurant specializing in English and French dishes.

Amenities: The hotel's leisure club has a large indoor pool, whirlpool, sauna, solarium, two squash courts, and a gym.

WHERE TO DINE

Passepartout. 51 Castlegate. ☎ **01768/865852.** Main courses £8–£15 ($12.80–$24). MC, V. Tues–Sat 7–11pm. FRENCH/ENGLISH.

Housed in a 400-year-old building, this cozy, candlelit dining room is set among painted stone walls. The chef has designed an imaginative menu around fresh local items, and dishes may include Scottish venison marinated in red wine and herbs. Desserts range from homemade butterscotch ice cream to a hot cherry meringue with chocolate. In warmer months, folks relax with drinks in a Spanish-style open courtyard in back of the dining room.

18 Yorkshire & Northumbria

Yorkshire, known to readers of *Wuthering Heights* and *All Creatures Great and Small*, embraces both the moors of North Yorkshire and the dales.

Across this vast region came the Romans, the Anglo-Saxons, the Vikings, the monks of the Middle Ages, kings of England, lords of the manor, craftspeople, hill farmers, and wool growers, all leaving their own mark. You can still see Roman roads and pavements, great abbeys and castles, stately homes, open-air museums, and craft centers, along with parish churches, old villages, and cathedrals.

Some cities and towns still carry the taint of the Industrial Revolution, but there's also wild and remote beauty to be found—limestone crags, caverns along the Pennines, mountainous uplands, rolling hills, chalk land wolds, heather-covered moorlands, broad vales, and tumbling streams. Yorkshire offers not only beautiful inland scenery, but also 100 miles of shoreline, with rocky headlands, cliffs, and sandy bays, rock pools, sheltered coves, fishing villages, bird sanctuaries, former smugglers' dens, and yachting havens. And in summer, the moors in North York Moors National Park bloom with purple heather. You can hike along the 110-mile Cleveland Way National Trail, encircling the park.

Yorkshire's most visited city is the walled city of York. York Minster, part of the cathedral circuit, is noted for its 100 stained-glass windows. In West Yorkshire is the literary shrine of Haworth, the home of the Brontës.

On the way north to Hadrian's Wall, we suggest you spend the night in the ancient cathedral city of Durham. This great medieval city is among the most dramatically sited and most interesting in the north.

Northumbria is made up of the counties of Northumberland, Cleveland, and Durham. The Saxons, who came to northern England centuries ago, carved out this kingdom, which at the time stretched from the Firth of Forth in Scotland to the banks of the Humber in Yorkshire. Vast tracts of that ancient kingdom remain natural and unspoiled. Again, this slice of England has more than its share of industrial towns, but you should explore the wild hills and open spaces and cross the dales of the eastern Pennines.

The whole area evokes ancient battles and bloody border raids. Space constraints don't permit us to cover this area in great detail, as

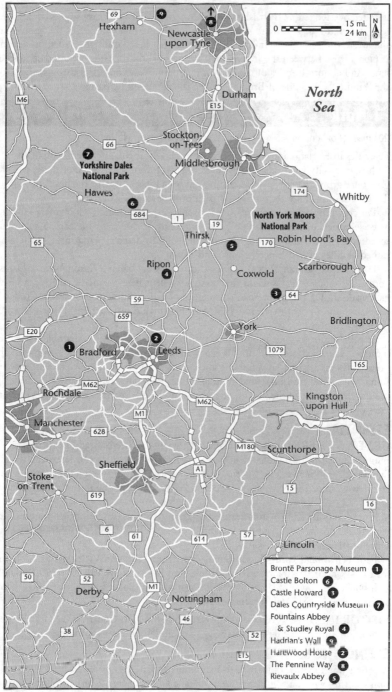

The Northeast: Yorkshire & Northumbria

0 ___ 15 mi.
  ___ 24 km

N

Hexham

Newcastle
upon Tyne

Durham

North
Sea

Stockton-
on-Tees

Middlesbrough

Yorkshire Dales
National Park

Hawes

Whitby

North York Moors
National Park

Thirsk

Robin Hood's Bay

Ripon

Coxwold

Scarborough

York

Bridlington

Bradford

Leeds

Rochdale

Kingston
upon Hull

Manchester

Sheffield

Scunthorpe

Stoke-
on-Trent

Lincoln

Derby

Nottingham

Brontë Parsonage Museum **1**
Castle Bolton **6**
Castle Howard **3**
Dales Countryside Museum **7**
Fountains Abbey
  & Studley Royal **4**
Hadrian's Wall **9**
Harewood House **2**
The Pennine Way **8**
Rievaulx Abbey **5**

Road numbers: M6, 66, 69, E15, 174, 65, 684, 1, 19, 170, 59, 64, 659, E20, 1079, 165, M62, M1, 628, A1, 619, 15, 16, 6, 61, 614, 57, 50, 52, 46, 38, 52, E15 it's often overlooked by the rushed North American visitor. But we suggest that you at least venture to see Hadrian's Wall, a Roman structure that was one of the wonders of the Western world. The finest stretch of the wall lies within the Northumberland National Park, between the stony North Tyne River and the county boundary at Gilsland. And about 40 miles of the 150-mile Pennine Way meanders through the park; the Pennine Way is one of Britain's most challenging hiking paths.

1 York

203 miles N of London; 26 miles NE of Leeds; 88 miles N of Nottingham

Few cities in England are as rich in history as York. It is still encircled by its 13th- and 14th-century city walls, about 2½ miles long, with four gates. One of these, Micklegate, once grimly greeted visitors coming up from the south with the heads of traitors. To this day, you can walk on the footpath of the medieval walls.

The crowning achievement of York is its minster, or cathedral, which makes the city an ecclesiastical center equaled only by Canterbury. It can easily be seen on a drive up to Edinburgh. Or, after visiting Cambridge, you can make a swing through the great cathedral cities of Ely, Lincoln, York, and Ripon.

There was a Roman York (Hadrian came this way), then a Saxon York, a Danish York, a Norman York (William the Conqueror slept here), a medieval York, a Georgian York, and a Victorian York (the center of a flourishing rail business). Today, a large amount of 18th-century York remains, including Richard Boyle's restored Assembly Rooms.

At some point in your exploration, you may want to visit the Shambles; once the meat-butchering center of York, it dates from before the Norman Conquest. The messy business is gone now, but the ancient street survives, filled today with jewelry stores, cafes, and buildings that huddle so closely together that you can practically stand in the middle of the pavement, arms outstretched, and touch the houses on both sides of the street.

ESSENTIALS

GETTING THERE   British Midland flights arrive at Leeds/Bradford Airport, a 50-minute flight from London's Heathrow Airport. For schedules and fares, call the airline at ☎ **0345/554-554** (in the U.K. only) or 1332/854-854 from outside the country. Connecting buses at the airport take you east and the rest of the distance to York.

From London's King's Cross Station, York-bound trains leave every 10 minutes. The trip takes 2 hours. For schedules and information, call ☎ **0345/484950** (in the U.K. only) or 01603/764776.

Four **National Express** buses depart daily from London's Victoria Coach Station for the 4½-hour trip to York. For schedules and information, call ☎ **0990/808080.**

If you're driving from London, head north on M1, cutting northeast below Leeds at the junction with A64, heading east to York.

VISITOR INFORMATION   The **Tourist Information Centre** at De Grey Rooms, Exhibition Square (☎ **01904/621756**), is open daily from 9am to 5pm.

SEEING THE SIGHTS

The best way to see York is to go to Exhibition Square (opposite the Tourist Information Centre), where a volunteer guide will take you on a **free 2-hour walking tour** of the city. You'll learn about history and lore through numerous intriguing stories. Tours are given April through October, daily at 10:15am and 2:15pm, plus 7pm from June

Bailey Hall **8**
Clifford's Tower **13**
Guildhall **3**
Jorvik Viking Centre **11**
King's Arms **12**

Mansion House **4**
Merchant
  Adventurer's Hall **10**
Micklegate **15**
National Railway
  Museum **1**

St. William's College **7**
The Shambles **9**
Treasurer's House **5**
York Castle Museum **14**
York Minster **6**
Yorkshire Museum **2**

to August; from November to March, a daily tour is given at 10:15am. Groups can book by prior arrangement by contacting the **Association of Volunteer Guides,** De Grey Rooms, Exhibition Square, York YO1 2I IB (**☎ 01904/640780**).

✪ York Minster. At the converging point of Deangate, Duncombe Place, Minster Yard, and Petergate. **☎ 01904/639347.** Admission to Chapter House 70p ($1.10) adults, 30p (50¢) children; crypt 60p (95¢) adults, 30p (50¢) children; foundations and treasury £1.80 ($2.90) adults, 70p ($1.10) children; tower £2 ($3.20) adults, £1 ($1.60) children. Chapter House, foundations, treasury, and tower Mon–Sat 10am–6pm, Sun 2–6pm (closing time in winter 4:30pm). Crypt Mon–Fri 10am–4:30pm, Sat 10am–3:30pm, Sun 1–3 30pm. Call ahead to verify times, as they are subject to change.

One of the great cathedrals of the world, York Minster traces its origins from the early 7th century; the present building, however, dates from the 13th century. Like the cathedral at Lincoln, York Minster is characterized by three towers built in the 15th century. The central tower is lantern-shaped in the Perpendicular style, and from the top of the tower on a clear day there are panoramic views of York and the Vale of York. The climb up a stone spiral staircase is steep and not recommended for very elderly or very young visitors, or anyone with a heart condition or breathing difficulties.

The outstanding characteristic of the cathedral is its **stained glass** from the Middle Ages—in glorious Angelico blues, ruby reds, forest greens, and honey-colored ambers. See especially the Great East Window, the work of a 15th-century Coventry-based glass painter. In the north transept is an architectural gem of the mid–13th century: the Five Sisters Window, with its five lancets in grisaille glass. The late–15th-century choir screen has an impressive lineup of historical figures—everybody from William the Conqueror to the overthrown Henry VI.

At a reception desk near the entrance to the minster, groups can arrange a guide, if one is available. Conducted tours are free but donations toward the upkeep of the cathedral are requested.

Insider's tip: Check out **St. William's Restaurant** at the front of St. William's Cottage (☎ **01904/634830**), close to the east end of the minster. This splendid timbered building provides a setting daily for coffee, an affordable lunch, or tea. Here you can get tasty quiches, homemade soups, and luscious desserts. Not only that, if you can arrange for a party of 35 or more, you can have a medieval banquet staged on your behalf, complete with minstrels, jesters, and jugglers. One way to do this is to post a notice at your hotel and get people to sign up and invite their newly made acquaintances. In one day our party swelled to nearly 50 and we were regally fed and entertained. For more information, call ☎ **01904/634830.**

Treasurer's House. Minster Yard. ☎ **01904/624247.** Admission £3.50 ($5.60) adults, £1.75 ($2.80) children, £8 ($12.80) family ticket. Sat–Thurs 10:30am–5pm (last entry 4:30pm). Closed Nov–Mar.

The Treasurer's House lies on a site where a continuous succession of buildings has stood since Roman times. The main part of the house, built in 1620, was refurbished by Yorkshire industrialist Frank Green at the turn of the century; he used this elegant town house to display his collection of 17th- and 18th-century furniture, glass, and china. An audiovisual program and exhibit explain the work of the medieval treasures and the subsequent fascinating history of the house. It has an attractive small garden in the shadow of York Minster.

✪ **York Castle Museum.** Eye of York off Tower St. ☎ **01904/653611.** Admission £4.50 ($7.20) adults, £3.15 ($5.05) children. Easter–Nov Mon–Sat 9:30am–5:30pm, Sun 10am–4pm; off-season Mon–Sat 9:30am–4pm, Sun 10am–4pm.

On the site of York's Castle, this is one of the finest folk museums in the country. Its unique feature is a re-creation of a Victorian cobbled street, Kirkgate, named for the museum's founder, Dr. John Kirk. He acquired his large collection while visiting his patients in rural Yorkshire at the beginning of this century. The period rooms range from a neoclassical Georgian dining room to an overstuffed and heavily adorned Victorian parlor to the 1953 sitting room with a brand-new television set purchased to watch the coronation of Elizabeth II. In the Debtors' Prison, former prison cells display craft workshops. There is also a superb collection of arms and armor. In the Costume Gallery, displays are changed regularly to reflect the collection's variety. Half Moon Court is an Edwardian street, with a gypsy caravan and a pub (sorry, the bar's closed!). During the summer, you can visit a water mill on the bank of the River Foss. Allow at least 2 hours for your museum visit.

✪ **National Railway Museum.** Leeman York Rd. ☎ **01904/621261.** Admission £4.95 ($7.90) adults, £3.15 ($5.05) children. Daily 10am–6pm. Closed Dec 24–26.

0   20 m
     65 ft   z

Chapterhouse

Five Sisters
Window ❷

North
Transept

West
End ❶   Nave   Central
Tower ❸   Choir ❹   Presbytery ❺   Lady
Chapel   East
End ❼

❻

St. William's Window ❻

South
Transept

❾ ❽

Choir Screen ❸	Great East Window ❼
Entrances to crypt ❹	Great West Window ❶
Entrance to The Foundations ❾	High Altar ❺
"Five Sisters" Window ❷	Rose Window ❽
	St. William's Window ❻

3-0600

This was the first national museum to be built outside London, and it has attracted millions of train buffs. Adapted from an original steam-locomotive depot, the museum gives visitors a chance to see how Queen Victoria traveled in luxury and to look under and inside steam locomotives. In addition, there's a collection of railway memorabilia, including an early 19th-century clock and penny machine for purchasing tickets on the railway platform. More than 40 locomotives are on display. One, the *Agenoria*, dates from 1829 and is a contemporary of Stephenson's well known *Rocket*. Of several royal coaches, the most interesting is Queen Victoria's Royal Saloon; it's like a small hotel, with polished wood, silk, brocade, and silver accessories.

Jorvik Viking Centre. Coppergate ☎ 01904/643211. Admission £5 ($8) adults, £4 ($6.40) children, £4.60 ($7.35) seniors and students. Family ticket £16.50 ($26.40). Apr–Oct daily 9am–5:30pm; Nov–Mar daily 9am–3:30pm.

This Viking city, discovered many feet below present ground level, was reconstructed as it stood in 948. In a "time car," you travel back through the ages to 1067, when Normans sacked the city, and then you ride slowly through the street market peopled

Is York Haunted?

After London, York has been the site of more beheadings, medieval tortures, and human anguish than any other city in Britain. Psychics and mystics insist that dozens of lost souls wander among the city's historic core reliving the traumatic moments of their earthly lives. Ghost walks are held every evening in York, allegedly England's most haunted city.

Several outfits conduct these tours, but the most charming one, **"The Original Ghost Walk of York,"** leaves at 8pm every night from The Kings Arms Pub, located at the Ouse Bridge. The 1½-hour tour costs £3 ($4.80) per person. Be prepared for lively commentary and more ghoulishness than you might have expected. Advance reservations aren't necessary: Just show up at The Kings Arms in time for a pint before the tour departs (the fun of this tour tends to be enhanced after a tipple or two).

by faithfully modeled Vikings. You also go through a house where a family lived and down to the river to see the ship chandlers at work and a Norwegian cargo ship unloading. At the end of the ride, you pass through the Finds Hut, where thousands of artifacts are displayed. The time car departs at regular intervals.

SHOPPING

Several of the main areas to explore include **Gillygate** for antique dealers, **St. Mary's Square** and its **Coppergate** pedestrian mall for name brands and chain stores, and **Newgate Marketplace** for local vendors selling a variety of wares Monday through Saturday.

Ellerker's of York, 25 Walmgate (☎ 01904/654417), has been selling various and sundry articles of English country life for more than 200 years. They have Jeffries saddles and bridles, shoes and riding boots, shooting and lounge tweeds (both Scottish and Irish), and Australian stockman's clothing by Drizabone.

Several specialty shops that have ideal gift items include **Maxwell and Kennedy,** 79 Low Petergate (☎ 01904/610034), a candy store specializing in both Belgian chocolate and Cambridge Wells dark, milk, and white chocolate; **Mulberry Hall,** 17 Stonegate (☎ 01904/620736), housed in a medieval house from 1436, with 16 showrooms on three floors devoted to the best in British and European porcelain, fine china, crystal, and some antiques; and **Wooden Horse,** 9 Goodramgate (☎ 01904/626012), featuring an eclectic mixture of ethnic items such as shirts, tops, jewelry, cushions, rugs, and throws from Africa, India, China, and Mexico.

WHERE TO STAY
EXPENSIVE

✪ **Dean Court Hotel.** Duncombe Place, York, N. Yorkshire YO1 2EF. ☎ **800/528-1234** in the U.S., or 01904/625082. Fax 01904/620305. 41 units, some with shower only. TV TEL. £105–£155 ($168–$248) double. Children under 17 stay free in parents' room. Rates include English breakfast. AE, DC, MC, V.

This 1850 building lies right beneath the towers of the minster. It was originally constructed to provide housing for the clergy of York Minster and then converted to a hotel after World War I. All the well-furnished rooms have bathtubs or showers (ask for your preference). It may not be the most atmospheric choice in York, but recent refurbishments have vastly improved the accommodations. The rooms are simple yet comfortable, as are the public rooms, which are decorated in more traditional styles.

Dining: Snacks are served in a coffee lounge from 10am to 6pm. The restaurant serves both traditional English and international dishes at lunch and dinner.

Amenities: Concierge, room service, dry cleaning/laundry, baby-sitting, courtesy car; access to nearby health club.

♻ Middlethorpe Hall Hotel. Bishopthorpe Rd. (on the A64, 1½ miles south of town), York, N. Yorkshire YO2 1QB. ☎ **800/260-8338** in the U.S., or 01904/641241. Fax 01904/620176. 30 units. TV TEL. £140–£215 ($224–$344) double; £175–£230 ($280–$368) suite. AE, MC, V.

Set on a 26-acre park, this hotel is on the outskirts of York, near the racecourse and away from the traffic. It's clearly York's leading hotel. Built in 1699, the stately, red-brick William-and-Mary country house was purchased by Historic House Hotels and beautifully restored, both inside and out. Fresh flowers are displayed profusely and lots of antiques create the ambience of a classic manor house. The rooms are located in the main house and restored outbuildings. Chintz-covered chairs and Edwardian-style baths are the order of the day. Accommodations in the wing have less drama and flair, although you can enjoy greater privacy here. Guests find in their room such niceties as homemade cookies and bottles of mineral water, as well as bathrobes.

Dining: Distinguished meals are served in two restaurants, one oak-paneled and one a grill room. A choice of either international or English traditional meals is offered.

Amenities: Concierge, car-rental desk, dry cleaning/laundry.

Viking Moat House. North St., York, N. Yorkshire YO1 1JF. ☎ **01904/459988.** Fax 01904/641793. 201 units. TV TEL. £120–£130 ($192–$208) double; £140 ($224) suite. AE, DC, MC, V. Parking £5 ($8).

Within the ancient city walls, this modern hotel overlooks the River Ouse and is the leading hotel within the center of York. Built in the 1970s, the hotel is today the largest in town and is conveniently located for sightseeing. The well-furnished and modern bedrooms, many with views looking toward the minster, have trouser presses, hair dryers, and beverage-makers.

Dining/Diversions: The hotel's two restaurants offer a variety of dining. In both restaurants, the Regatta and the Waterfront, fixed-price lunches and dinners are offered daily. Each one has a bar and offers a welcoming atmosphere.

Amenities: 24-hour room service, Jacuzzi, sauna, solarium, gym, dry cleaning/laundry, baby-sitting.

MODERATE

Hudson's Hotel. 60 Bootham, York, N. Yorkshire YO3 7BZ. ☎ **01904/621267.** Fax 01904/654719. 34 units. TV TEL. £80–£95 ($128–$152) double; £90–£95 ($144–$152) triple. Rates include English breakfast. AE, DC, MC, V.

Just a short walk from the minster, this hotel offers personal service. The owner converted two Victorian houses into the main hotel building in 1981 and later added an extension in the Victorian style. All accommodations are comfortably furnished and have tea- and coffeemakers. Hudson's has its own large parking lot. Both bar food and an English/French menu are offered.

The Judges Lodging. 9 Lendal, York, N. Yorkshire YO1 2AQ. ☎ **01904/638733.** Fax 01904/679947. 14 units. TV TEL. £75–£135 ($120–$216) double. Rates include English breakfast. AE, DC, MC, V.

The earliest historical fact about this charming house is that it was the home of a certain Dr. Wintringham in 1710. It is listed as having been a judges' lodging at the beginning of the 19th century. To get to your room, you'll climb a circular wooden staircase, the only one of its type in the United Kingdom. Some bedrooms have four-poster beds. If you want to spoil yourself, book the large Prince Albert room, a twin-bedded room with three large windows overlooking the minster (Prince Albert actually slept in the room once). Each room has a different decor and is named accordingly.

There are two dining rooms; in each, candles flicker and the carefully trained staff attends to your every need. All meat, fish, and vegetables are fresh. Down in the old cellars, they found bits of Roman pottery, antique pieces of glass, and other relics of the house's varied past—you'll find a cocktail bar, open to the public. A private bar that serves simple meals is also open to guests only.

Mount Royale Hotel. 119 The Mount, York, N. Yorkshire YO2 2DA. ☎ **01904/628856.** Fax 01904/611171. 23 units. TV TEL. £72–£85 ($115.20–$136) double; £95 ($152) suite. Rates include English breakfast. AE, DC, MC, V.

A short walk west of York's city walls, in a neighborhood known as The Mount, this hotel is the personal statement of two generations of the Oxtaby family. They work hard to create a friendly, homelike atmosphere. The main house was built as a private home in 1833, although several years ago the owners merged a neighboring house of the same era into the original core. Accommodations and public rooms are furnished with both antiques and modern pieces. Some bedrooms have private terraces leading into the garden. Room service, laundry, and a swimming pool are available.

The restaurant features roasts with interesting accompaniments. There's also an extensive fixed-price menu. Reservations are recommended. The dining room opens onto an attractive garden.

INEXPENSIVE

Beechwood Close Hotel. 19 Shipton Rd. (on the A19 north of the city), Clifton, York, N. Yorkshire YO3 6RE. ☎ **01904/658378.** Fax 01904/647124. 14 units. TV TEL. £70 ($112) double. Rates include English breakfast. AE, DC, MC, V.

Beechwood is a large house surrounded by trees, a garden with a putting green, and a parking area. Mr. and Mrs. Blythe run the small hotel, which offers comfortable bedrooms with central heating and beverage-makers. Good dinners or bar meals are served in the dining room overlooking the garden. The hotel is a 15-minute walk to the minster, either by road or along the river.

Cottage Hotel. 3 Clifton Green, York, N. Yorkshire YO3 6LH. ☎ **01904/643711.** Fax 01904/611230. 22 units. TV TEL. £50–£70 ($80–$112) double. Rates include English breakfast. AE, DC, MC, V.

About a 10-minute walk north of York Minster, this hotel comprises two refurbished and extended Victorian houses overlooking the village green of Clifton. The hotel offers cozy bedrooms with simple furnishings and hot-beverage makers. Some 400-year-old timbers rescued from the demolition of a medieval building in one of the city's historic streets (Micklegate) grace the restaurant and bar, which does a thriving business in its own right. The hotel provides secured parking for its guests.

Grasmead House Hotel. 1 Scarcroft Hill, York Y02 1DF. ☎ and fax **01904/629996.** 6 units. TV. £60–£65 ($96–$104) double. Rates include English breakfast. AE, MC, V.

This house was built in 1896 on a narrow strip of land between an ancient drovers' road leading to the walled center of York and a residential street. It was converted to a small hotel in 1951 and has been thriving ever since. A 15-minute walk south of the town center, this lovely B&B features antique four-poster beds in each of its six rooms, with the oldest bed dating from 1740. It's perfect for a romantic getaway, but families are welcome as well; two rooms are larger suites with an extra single bed. For proprietors Stan and Sue Long, the hotel is their home and their guests are extended family, so just ask for anything from advice to aspirin. Each room, individually decorated with antiques and in a Victorian style, has its own bathroom, heating, alarm clock, and beverage-makers. There's also a sitting room, complete with a licensed bar for guests, and a full English breakfast is served every morning in the Tea Room dining room.

Heworth Court. 76 Heworth Green, York, N. Yorkshire YO3 7TQ. ☎ **01904/425156.** Fax 01904/415290. 27 units. TV TEL. £50–£76 ($80–$121.60) double. Rates include English breakfast. AE, DC, MC, V. Take the A1036 to the east side of the city.

Just a 10- to 15-minute walk east of the city center is this 3-story redbrick Victorian structure (many of its bedrooms are located in a modern extension added during the 1980s). The rooms are agreeably furnished and some open onto the courtyard. The hotel also offers really fine food.

WHERE TO DINE

Oscar's Wine Bar & Bistro, 8A Little Stonegate (☎ **01904/652002**), offers heaping plates of meats and salads, attracting a young crowd (often because of the inexpensive beer). There's a courtyard and a large menu. A DJ spins dance music on Friday and Saturday. Open daily from 11am to 11pm.

The best place for afternoon tea is **Betty's Café & Tea Rooms,** 6–8 St. Helen's Sq. (☎ **01904/659142**). We also recommend **St. William's College Restaurant,** 3 College St. (☎ **01904/634830**), and **Theatre Royal Café Bar,** St. Leonard's Place (☎ **01904/632596**).

The Ivy/The Seafood Bar/The Brasserie. In the Grange Hotel, 1 Clifton (off Bootham Rd.), York, N. Yorkshire YO3 6AA. ☎ **01904/644744.** Fax 01904/612453. Reservations recommended in The Ivy and The Seafood Bar; not necessary in The Brasserie. Fixed-price 3-course menu in The Ivy £25 ($40); fixed-price 2-course menu in The Seafood Bar £7.95–£10.95 ($12.70–$17.50); main courses in The Brasserie £7.50–£9.50 ($12–$15.20). AE, DC, MC, V. The Ivy Sun–Fri noon–2pm, daily 7–10pm; Seafood Bar daily 6:30–10pm; The Brasserie Mon–Sat noon–2:30pm and 6–10:30pm, Sun 7–10pm. FRENCH/ENGLISH.

A 10-minute walk west of York Minster, this dining complex is one of the most appealing in town. It's housed within an ivy-covered Regency town house that's also a 30-room hotel.

The least formal venue is The Brasserie, a paneled, candlelit hideaway in the cellar. The hearty menu items include steaks, grilled fish, and ale. It's the most crowded of the three restaurants within the complex.

On the building's street level, The Ivy restaurant and The Seafood Bar are set adjacent to one another. Cuisine in The Ivy is more upscale than that in the cellar, and includes dishes such as sautéed fillet of John Dory with smoked bacon, oyster mushrooms, leeks, and hazelnut oil.

A few steps away, The Seafood Bar has a great trompe l'oeil panoramic mural of York's Racecourse, complete with views of the city's skyline. The menu here is mostly seafood prepared many ways. Examples include roasted filet of sea bass with creamed celeriac, red wine, and truffles.

Kites. 13 Grape Lane. ☎ **01904/641750.** Reservations required. Main courses £8.25–£14.95 ($13.20–$23.90). AE, DC, DISC, MC, V. Mon–Tues and Thurs–Sun noon–2pm and 6:30–10:30pm. INTERNATIONAL.

About a 5-minute walk from the minster, this restaurant is in the heart of York, on a small street near Stonegate (walk up a narrow staircase to the second floor). This is a simple York bistro where the food is good and the atmosphere and service are unpretentious. Kites's many fans are attracted to its eclectic brand of cooking. One recipe might have been a dish served in the Middle Ages in England (perhaps with adaptations), the next might come from Thailand. Kites might feature trout, game, tuna, or pork depending on what the hunters and gatherers return with. Fondues, fresh salads, and vegetarian meals are also available.

✪ **Melton's Restaurant.** 7 Scarcroft Rd. ☎ 01904/634341. Reservations required. Main courses £9.50–£14.95 ($15.20–$23.90); fixed-price menu (Mon–Sat) £19.50 ($31.20). MC, V. Tues–Sun noon–2pm; Mon–Sat 5:30–10pm. Closed Aug 25–Sept 2 and Dec 24–Jan 11. CONTINENTAL/ENGLISH.

Some local food critics claim that Michael and Lucy Hjort serve the finest food in York, and we agree. Their small and unpretentious restaurant is approximately 1 mile from the heart of the city. Mr. Hjort trained with the famous Roux brothers of Le Gavroche in London, but he doesn't charge their astronomical prices. His cuisine reflects his own imprint.

In what has always been known as a sleepy culinary backwater, the Hjorts have created some local excitement at this family friendly place. Their menu changes frequently, but might include poached salt pork with apples and horseradish sauce, rack of lamb with herbs, or sea bass with baked fennel in the style of the French Riviera. Vegetarian meals are also available, and families with children are welcome.

19 Grape Lane. 19 Grape Lane. ☎ 01904/636366. Reservations recommended for dinner. Main courses £8.95–£13.50 ($14.30–$21.60). MC, V. Tues–Sat noon–10pm; Sun–Mon noon–4pm. Closed 1st 2 weeks in Feb and last 2 weeks in Sept. ENGLISH.

In the heart of York, this restaurant occupies two floors of a timbered building with a wealth of its original features. With such a name, you expect a very British restaurant and you get that, but with a very contemporary touch. You might begin with crispy duck, bacon, and mushroom salad. The menus are wisely limited to about 10 main courses, so that every dish will be fresh. The cooking is without needless adornment. The wine list is ever-growing, and service is thoughtful and considerate. The location is on a cobbled lane off Petergate.

A YORK PUB CRAWL

One of the city's oldest inns, **The Black Swan,** Peaseholme Green (☎ 01904/686911), is a fine, timbered, frame house that was once the home of the lord mayor of York in 1417; the mother of Gen. James Wolfe of Québec also lived here. You can enjoy pub meals in front of a log fire in a brick inglenook. There are sandwiches, homemade soups, and Yorkshire puddings filled with beef stew. This is one of York's "musical pubs," featuring live jazz on Monday and folk on Tuesday, with a small cover charge.

Situated at the base of the Ouse Bridge, a few steps from the edge of the river, the 16th-century **Kings Arms Public House,** King's Staith (☎ 01904/659435), is boisterous and fun. A historic monument in its own right, it's filled with charm and character and has the ceiling beams, paneling, and weathered brickwork you'd expect. In summer, rows of outdoor tables are placed beside the river. Your hosts serve a full range of draft and bottled beers, the most popular of which (Samuel Smith's) is still brewed in Tadcaster, only 10 miles away. The ghost walk we recommend leaves here every night at 8pm (see box above).

On a pedestrian street in Old York, **Ye Olde Starre Inne,** 40 Stonegate (☎ 01904/623063), dates from 1644 and is York's oldest licensed pub. Some inn (of one kind or another) might have stood on this spot since 900. In a pub said to be haunted by an old woman, a little girl, and a cat, you enter into an atmosphere of cast-iron tables, an open fireplace, oak Victorian settles, and time-blackened beams. Recently, the owners have added a year-round glassed-in garden. In all types of weather, guests can enjoy the plants and the view of the minster from their tables here.

2 Leeds

204 miles NW of London; 75 miles NE of Liverpool; 43 miles NE of Manchester; 74 miles N of Nottingham

The foundations for a permanent community were laid nearly 2,000 years ago when the Romans set up a small camp here called Cambodunum, but the next step toward modern Leeds didn't come until the 7th century, when the Northumbrian King Edwin established a residence. Kirkstall Abbey was founded in 1152, and in 1207 Leeds finally obtained its charter and laid out the grid pattern still evident in the streets today.

During the medieval era, Leeds took the Golden Fleece as its coat of arms, representative of its growth and importance as a wool town. In time it became the greatest center of cloth trade in the region. Industrial advancements have played a great role in the development of the city, with the introduction of steam power leading to the development of the coal fields to the south. Other innovations allowed the continued growth of its textile industry, as well as the rapid development of such upstart industries as printing, tailoring, and engineering. The Victorian era marked the city's glory days.

After languishing for years and being dismissed for its industrial blight, the city is moving progressively forward again today. It's experiencing some economic growth, and many of the great Victorian buildings have been renovated in its bustling central core: The Corn Exchange, The Grand Theatre, and the Victoria Quarter. Add to this the recently passed "24-Hour City Initiative," making it the only U.K. location to not only allow but encourage around-the-clock work and entertainment options, and you've got an up-and-coming city with a lot of new energy.

ESSENTIALS

GETTING THERE   **Leeds-Bradford International Airport** (☎ 0113/2509696), has daily flights to and from London and Manchester, with air transport taking less than an hour. There is also a 24-hour direct rail link between Manchester airport and Leeds.

Trains from London's King's Cross Station arrive hourly during the day, with the trip taking about 2 hours. For schedules and information, call ☎ 0345/484950 (in the U.K. only) or 01603/764776.

Leeds is also serviced daily by **National Express** buses from London. For schedules and information, call ☎ 0990/808080.

Leeds lies at the crossroads of the North/South M1 and East/West M62 routes, making it easily accessible by car from anywhere in England or Scotland.

VISITOR INFORMATION   The **Gateway Yorkshire Regional Travel & Tourist Information Centre,** The Arcade, City Station (☎ 0113/2425242), is open Monday through Saturday from 9am to 6pm and Sunday from 10am to 4pm. Leeds has a Web site (**www.leeds.gov.uk/**) with information on transportation, lodging, dining, shopping, and entertainment in the city; and **Leeds On Line** (☎ 0891/137400) is a 24-hour telephone information line accessed in the United Kingdom only.

Information on local bus and train routes and times is available by calling **Metroline** at ☎ 0113/2457676.

SPECIAL EVENTS   In July, more than 40,000 opera lovers turn out at Temple Newsam, Temple Newsam Road, off Selby Road (☎ 0113/2425242), for the single performance of **Opera in the Park,** the largest free outdoor opera concert in the United Kingdom. The gargantuan **Party in the Park** (☎ 0113/24/8222), also held at Temple Newsam, is one of the largest free pop and rock concerts in the United Kingdom. It's usually held the day following Opera in the Park, and features some of the hottest acts in rock music.

Film buffs turn out in droves for the annual **Leeds International Film Festival** (☎ 0113/2478308). Screened in October at cinemas throughout Leeds, it's the only theme-based film festival in the United Kingdom. It regularly features British as well as world-premiere films, and hosts film-related lectures, seminars, and workshops.

EXPLORING LEEDS

Despite its longtime reputation as a grimy northern industrial city, Leeds will surprise you with the beauty and diversity of its **City Centre,** where £400 million ($640 million) has been invested in both new construction and renovation of warehouses and landmark Victorian structures into homes, lodging, shops, and restaurants along The Waterfront and in the central shopping district.

✪ **Leeds City Art Gallery.** The Headrow. ☎ 0113/2478248. Free admission. Mon–Tues and Thurs–Sat 10am–5pm, Wed 10am–8pm, Sun 1–5pm.

Spread over three floors, this gallery, founded in 1888, houses England's best collection of 20th-century art outside of London, including impressive collections of French postimpressionist paintings, contemporary British sculpture, prints, watercolors, and drawings. Throughout the year it also hosts visiting exhibits, enhanced by workshops, talks, and other related events.

Located within the gallery, the **Craft Centre and Design Gallery** (☎ 0113/2478241), showcases contemporary ceramics, jewelry, prints, textiles, and applied arts from around the world, as well as hosts openings and exhibits by local and regional artists working within these mediums.

Leeds City Museum. The Headrow. ☎ 0113/2637861. Free admission. Tues–Sat 10am–5pm. Closed Tues following bank holidays.

One of the top 10 natural-history collections in England, the gallery's rotating exhibitions include everything from Bengal tigers and dinosaurs to Egyptian mummies and Roman coins and medals—and no wonder, since their collection, largely provided by the Leeds Philosophical and Literary Society in the 19th century, includes nearly a million artifacts, with perhaps 10,000 on display at any given time.

The Henry Moore Institute. 74 The Headrow. ☎ 0113/2343158. Mon–Tues and Thurs–Sun 10am–5:30pm, Wed 10am–9pm.

Located next door to the City Art Gallery, this is the largest sculpture gallery in Europe, as well as the first devoted to the display, study, and research of sculpture from all periods and cultures. The institute is named after the greatest British sculptor of the 20th century, Henry Moore (1898–1986), who was a Yorkshireman. This center shows the range of his accomplishments, from his early *Reclining Figure* (1929) to his most powerful postwar statements like *Meat Porters.* The works of many of Moore's contemporaries are also displayed. Lectures throughout the year supplement the institute's exhibitions.

Royal Armouries Museum. Armouries Dr. ☎ 0113/2201999. Admission £7.95 ($12.70) adults, £6.95 ($11.10) seniors and students, £4.95 ($7.90) children, £23.95 ($38.30) family ticket. Mar 4–Nov 8 daily 10:30am–5:30pm; off-season Mon–Fri 10:30am–4:30pm, Sat–Sun 10:30am–5:30pm.

A notable new construction along The Waterfront, this £42 million ($67.2 million) facility is the home of London Tower's Royal Armouries, England's oldest museum, dating from the working arsenal of the medieval kings. It is designed to exhibit the many pieces that have been in perpetual storage because of inadequate facilities in

London. The museum illustrates the development and use of arms and armor for war, sport, hunting, self-defense, and fashion.

Temple Newsam House. Temple Newsam Rd. (off Selby Rd.; 4 miles from Leeds City Centre off the A63). ☎ **0113/2647321.** Admission £2 ($3.20) adults, 50p (80¢) for children accompanied by adult. Tues–Sun 10am–4pm.

This was the birthplace in 1545 of the ill-fated Lord Darnley, husband of Mary Queen of Scots. Construction of this Tudor-Jacobean mansion was begun in 1521 by Thomas, Lord Darcy, and substantial remodeling occurred in both the 17th and late 18th centuries. It stands as an odd but beautiful tribute to several eras of architecture. Today, it houses a splendid collection of silver and Chippendale furniture. The surrounding 1,200 acres of parkland includes the popular Home Farm, a breeding ground for rare farm animals, and the annual venue for Opera in the Park.

Tetley's Brewery Wharf. The Waterfront. ☎ **0113/2420666.** Admission £4.95 ($7.90). Apr–Oct Tues–Sun 10:30am–3:30pm; off-season Wed–Sun 10:30am–3:30pm.

Joshua Tetley & Sons have been brewing beer in Leeds since 1822, and produce Yorkshire's favorite ales. Opened in 1994, this £6 million ($9.6 million) visitor center gives you ample opportunity to sample their products while leading you through a series of settings designed to showcase the history of the English pub. Included are a medieval pub, Jacobean tavern, Georgian drinking club, Victorian Music Hall, and a "Pub of the Future," run by robots serving somewhat disturbing fluorescent brews. You can also tour the working brewery and see the famous Shire Horses.

WHERE TO STAY

If you'd like advice on local lodging, or if you'd just like to tell someone your price range and requirements and let them book you a room, contact the **Gateway Yorkshire Accommodation Booking Line** (☎ **0800/808050** or 0113/242-5242). For a £1.25 ($2) handling fee and a refundable deposit of 10% of your first night's stay, they'll find you a bed for the night.

Aragon Hotel. 250 Stainbeck Lane, Leeds LS7 2PS. ☎ **0113/2759306.** Fax 0113/275-7166. 13 units. TV TEL. £47.80–£49.50 ($76.50–$79.20) double. Rates include English breakfast. AE, DC, MC, V. From Leeds, follow A61 Harrogate signs out of the city. This becomes Scott Hall Rd. (A61). Take the 2nd roundabout, turning left onto Stainbeck Lane, and follow it down one hill and up another. The hotel is on the right. It is also conveniently located about 200 yd. from a bus stop with routes to Leeds and the surrounding area.

Located only 2 miles from City Centre, this small family-run hotel is set well back from the road in an acre of gardens. The surrounding properties stretch out in open fields and woods. Accommodations, while not luxurious, are neat and comfortable, and each room includes tea- and coffee-making facilities. There's a pleasant residents' lounge, featuring a large marble fireplace, as well as a full bar, both of which look out over the gardens. When you get hungry, lunch and dinner are available in the 22-seat dining room.

✪ **42 The Calls.** 42 The Calls, Leeds LS2 7EW. ☎ **0113/2440099.** Fax 0113/2344100. 41 units. MINIBAR TV TEL. £135–£155 ($216–$248) double; from £185 ($296) suite. AE, DC, MC, V.

Overlooking the River Aire in the heart of Leeds, this is a small but deluxe hotel. It's the most tranquil and elegant choice in Leeds, created from an 18th-century grain mill in a once dilapidated waterfront area that's all high-tech and high-comfort now. Each room is individually designed with its own fabrics and color scheme, ranging from more traditional rooms to the Black Room, with a huge black bed and black-striped walls, or Room 303, with an original winch hanging from the ceiling—a nod to the building's origins. Business travelers will appreciate the three phones in every room, the full-size work desk, an individual fax machine on request, and dictation by arrangement. Each room includes a CD player, satellite TV, a coffeemaker, a hair dryer, and trouser press. Baths feature deluxe toiletries and plush towels and bathrobes. There's a comfortable small bar tucked away in a corner of the lobby, and a nice selection of CDs and videos are available from the lobby.

You can order breakfast in, and have it passed into your room without disturbance via an ingenious "two-way pass" system, or you can enjoy excellent meals at the neighboring Brasserie 44 or Pool Court at 42.

Amenities: Access to nearby health club, car-rental desk, concierge, room service, dry cleaning/laundry, baby-sitting, secretarial services, courtesy car.

Haley's Hotel & Restaurant. Shire Oak Rd. (2 miles from Leeds City Centre and 7 miles from Leeds/Bradford International Airport), Headingley, Leeds LS6 2DE. ☎ **0113/2784446.** Fax 0113/2753342. 29 units. TV TEL. £120–£140 ($192–$224) double; from £210 ($336) suite. Rates include English or continental breakfast. AE, DC, MC, V.

Located in a quiet, tree-lined cul-de-sac just off the main Otley-Leeds road (A660), this town-house hotel, set up in a Victorian mansion, makes it easy to forget you're in the suburbs of a major metropolitan area. The hotel's rooms are comfortably laid out and opt for tasteful individuality, each with its own fabrics and period-specific, polished, natural wood antiques. Features include a work desk with telephone, trouser press, iron and ironing board, hair dryer, and tea- and coffeemakers. The staff is diligent, accommodating guests with such options as a late supper or shoe-cleaning service.

Dining: Haley's Restaurant offers modern British table d'hôte and à la carte options—so enticing that it's earned two AA rosettes for cuisine. In fact, it's so popular you'd better make your dinner reservations when you book a room. See below for a review.

Amenities: Concierge, room service, dry cleaning/laundry.

✪ **Oulton Hall.** Rothwell Lane (5½ miles from Leeds by A61 and A639), Oulton, Leeds LS26 8HN. ☎ **0113/2821000.** Fax 0113/2828066. 159 units. MINIBAR TV TEL. £100–£150 ($160–$240) double; £205–£245 ($328–$392) suite. Rates include English breakfast. AE, DC, MC, V.

A painstakingly restored 1850s Italianate mansion, this hotel has an atmosphere of pure elegance, from the black-and-white tiled front entrance and the damask-hung walls of the public rooms with their great crystal chandeliers, to the library with its mahogany wall paneling and window seat. You can enjoy butler service in the drawing room, a drink in the plush red-leather interior of the Calverley Bar, or stroll through formal gardens re-created to the original 19th-century plans. Most of the well-furnished bedrooms are in the modern wing; the grand suites are in the original house. Most of the rooms are no-smoking, and two are equipped for persons with disabilities.

Dining: In the Brontë Restaurant, which was awarded an AA rosette for its cuisine, the service is impeccable and the wine list will please any palate.

Amenities: Championship 9- and 18-hole golf courses and driving range, croquet lawn, squash courts, full gym, indoor heated pool, Jacuzzi, sauna, steam room, aerobics classes, and beauty therapy.

WHERE TO DINE

Haley's Restaurant. In Haley's Hotel, Shire Oak Rd., Headingley. ☎ **0113/2784446.** Reservations required well in advance. Main courses £18–£22 ($28.80–$35.20); fixed-price Sun lunch £14.95 ($23.90) for 3 courses. AE, DC, MC, V. Mon–Sat 7:15–9:30pm, Sun 12:15–1:45pm. BRITISH.

This hotel restaurant, in a beautifully restored Victorian mansion, is so popular among locals that even the guests have to reserve long in advance. The understated browns and creams of the restaurant's decor contribute to a relaxed atmosphere.

Chef John Vennell changes his à la carte dinner menu monthly to use the freshest, best market ingredients, offering appetizers such as a terrine of mixed game and pistachios, main courses like home-cured duck breast with sweet-potato relish, and desserts such as lemon mousse with stewed black cherries or an iced Grand Marnier soufflé. The wine cellar has interesting offerings from around the world.

Leodis Brasserie. Victoria Mill, Sovereign St. ☎ **0113/2421010.** Reservations recommended. Main courses £7.90–£15.90 ($12.65–$25.45); fixed-price lunch £12.95 ($20.70). AE, DC, MC, V. Mon–Fri noon–2pm and 6–11pm, Sat 6–11pm. BRITISH.

Another fine choice in the revitalized canal district, Leodis is housed in an artfully renovated old mill. You dine in a comfortable dining space created from the mill's original cast-iron columns and new glass screens.

The menu here changes weekly. At lunch, there are four three-course set meals to choose from, plus several à la carte options. Dishes are often quite simple, yet incredibly well prepared. Starters might include fish cakes in tomato-lime salsa or sautéed chicken livers, followed by a main course of roast cod with warm Italian dressing or a perfectly braised lamb shank, finished with caramelized burnt orange crème or a chocolate marquise. There's a full bar and a lengthy wine list as well.

⭐ **Pool Court at 42.** 42–44 The Calls. ☎ **0113/2444242.** Reservations recommended. Fixed-price 2-course lunch £12.50 ($20), £17 ($27.20) for 3 courses; Fixed-price 2-course dinner £24.50 ($39.20), £29.50 ($47.20) for 3 courses. AE, DC, MC, V. Mon–Fri noon–2pm; Mon–Thurs 7–10pm, Fri–Sat 7–10:30pm. CONTINENTAL.

This small, elegant restaurant with its popular riverside terrace is built into the lodging at 42 The Calls, but functions independently and has a private street entrance. It's an intimate space, seating only 38 diners, and the modern decor is stylish and refined. It's a comfortable spot, with great attention to detail and delectable food.

The menu is entirely a set-price affair, though you'll have a few choices for each course. Chef Jeff Baker scours the markets to see what's freshest and most abundant, then updates his menu often, with creations such as creamed eggs with Beluga caviar or risotto and wild mushrooms with truffles. You can finish with one of the *assiettes*, a combination of three desserts, usually with a central theme, such as assiette of chocolate. There are some unusual selections on the wine list as well.

Rascasse. Canal Wharf, Water Lane. ☎ **0113/2446611.** Reservations recommended. Fixed-price 2-course lunch £13.50 ($21.60), £17 ($27.20) for 3 courses; main courses £13–£16.50 ($20.80–$26.40). AE, DC, MC, V. Mon–Fri noon–2pm; Mon–Thurs 7–10pm; Fri–Sat 7–10:30pm. CONTINENTAL.

When you step into this airy, light restaurant, you might forget that you're setting foot in an early 19th-century extension of a granary. Located in the revitalized canal district, owner/chef Simon Gueller's restaurant has taken what's best about its surroundings—a large, solid room and waterfront location—and reworked them into a stylish modern restaurant.

The same can be said of his menu, a seasonal offering of classic dishes and ingredients. He reinterprets golden oldie recipes with flavor and flair. Examples include starters like sea scallops with fillet of lamb and truffles, or deep-fried goat's cheese with an apple-and-walnut salad. Main courses include roast squab with a galette of foie gras and jus of thyme, or sea bass in olive crust served over market vegetables. A lusciously tempting dessert is hot chocolate pudding with a melting fondant core and coconut-flecked ice cream. There's an extensive wine list.

LEEDS AFTER DARK

Thanks to a recently passed city initiative aimed at relaxing licensing restrictions and increasing late-night entertainment options, it's safe to say that Leeds now rocks around the clock. It was already humming with classical concerts, opera, jazz, dance, theater, cinema, rock and dance clubs, cafes, and pubs.

THE CLUB & MUSIC SCENE   Leeds has a thriving rock scene, with recent bands like Sisters of Mercy and The Mission rising out of the music scene at The Warehouse. Today's up-and-coming music scene is, not surprisingly, very influenced by the Manchester scene, but innovative bands like Black Star Liner, Bedlam A Go Go, and Embrace show that Leeds still has a musical voice all its own.

The **Cockpit,** Bridge House, Swinegate (☎ 0113/2443446), can host about 600 fans, who turn out to hear the latest indie bands in a converted railway arch setting.

For real intimacy, you can't beat the **Duchess of York,** Vicar Lane (☎ 0113/ 2453929), the city's most famous music pub, unrivaled in its nightly schedule of up-and-coming bands.

When you'd rather groove to the beat than watch the guitarist, you can head to a vast array of dance clubs around town. Leeds' dance-music scene is absolutely thriving, as is evident by the presence of internationally acclaimed DJs **Trannies With Attitude,** who set up at **The Warehouse,** Somers Street (☎ 0113/2461033), on

Saturday, with admission for £10 ($16). **The Pleasure Rooms,** 9 Lower Merrion St. (☎ 0113/2450923), is also incredibly popular, offering three separate rooms of music. Cover charge is £5 to £7 ($8 to $11.20) on Friday, depending on which room you want to visit, and Saturday's hefty £12 ($19.20) cover lets you roam through the entire complex.

You'll find the jazz you're looking for at **Arts Café,** 42 Call Lane (☎ 0113/2438243), a European-style cafe bar that offers tapas, bottled beers, and coffees to accompany its live jazz on Tuesday. **Think Tank,** The Basement, 107 Kirkgate (☎ 0113/2428522), has a "cantina" atmosphere with fiery Mexican food and jazz to match on Thursday nights. **The Underground,** Cookridge Street, at the back of the Town & Country Club (☎ 0113/2302113), offers lunch and evening jazz, featuring Thursday-night salsa and other Latin music.

There's also a substantial gay scene. Step into **Primos 2,** New York Street (☎ 0113/2343863), Leeds's most prominent gay club, where you can shake it every night of the week (until 6am on weekends). **The New Penny,** Call Lane, next to The Bridge Inn (no phone), is the best known mixed/gay club. This is a festive place, in spite of the grim exterior and blacked-out windows. It gets downright hopping during its regularly scheduled cabarets.

PUBS   Stop by **Whitelocks,** Turks Head Yard (☎ 0113/2453950), in the alley of Briggate, opposite Debenhams and Littlewoods. There's a copper-topped bar with a handmade ceramic-tile front, a marble sandwich bar, old advertising mirrors, and stained-glass windows. Locals keep the conversation flowing in a thick, northern accent. If you get hungry, there's cheap traditional pub grub. Tap selections are varied and quite good, including McEwans 80, Youngers IPA, Scotch, No. 3, and Theakston's Bitter.

Hearkening back to Leeds' glory days, **Victoria,** Great George Street (☎ 0113/2451386), is every bit as Victorian as its name suggests, with ornate globe lamps, etched mirrors, and a well-adorned bar. Politicians and lawyers frequent the place. Join in the conversation or sit back and listen while you enjoy a pint of Tetley's Mild and maybe a bar snack or two.

THE PERFORMING ARTS   **Leeds Town Hall,** The Headrow (☎ 0113/2477985,** or box office 0113/2476962), hosts orchestras from around the globe as part of the city's annual **International Concert Season,** and is also home to the world-famous **Leeds International Pianoforte Competition,** held every 3 years, with the next scheduled competition in 1999. Opera North offers on average three to four productions during its October-through-April seasonal run at the **Leeds Grand Theatre and Opera House,** New Briggate (☎ 0113/222622), featuring a beautifully renovated 1,500-seat auditorium behind its original 1878 Victorian facade.

Theatergoers are much impressed by the facilities at the £12 million ($19.2 million) **West Yorkshire Playhouse,** Playhouse Square, Quarry Hill (☎ 0113/2137700), home to the "national theatre of the north." Playhouse artistic director Jude Kelly started out strong in the early inaugural seasons, with 17 productions, including eight British or world premieres. There's been no slowing down since then, and you can find a dramatic offering at most any time in either The Playhouse's Quarry Auditorium, which seats 750, or The Courtyard, seating 350. The Playhouse, which is the cornerstone of a proposed £70 million ($112 million) Quarry Hill arts complex, also hosts other events throughout the year, including the annual Jazz at the Playhouse series.

The **Yorkshire Dance Centre,** St. Peters Building, York Street (☎ 0113/2439867), is home of the internationally renowned **Phoenix Dance Troupe.**

3 Bradford

212 miles N of London; 32 miles NE of Manchester; 9 miles W of Leeds

This city of nearly half a million souls retains a rich ethnic heritage from the succession of immigrants who came to work the mills beginning in the mid–19th century. Generations of Irish, German, Italian, Eastern European, and later, Asian and African Caribbean immigrants, today give this West Yorkshire town an international flavor.

Bradford boosters like to say the town is one of the best-kept secrets in the United Kingdom. High-tech firms, galleries, and museums have displaced many of the textile factories of the past. Centrally located between the Yorkshire Dales and the Pennines, Bradford provides a nice diversion and is convenient to a historic countryside where the Brontës once dwelled and armor-covered soldiers clashed in the Wars of the Roses.

ESSENTIALS

GETTING THERE   Bradford is readily reached by car via the M62 and M606.

Most rail links go through nearby Leeds (see above), but at least one direct train each day connects London's Forster Square Station with Bradford (a 3-hr. trip). Hours are Monday through Saturday from 9:30am to 5:30pm and Sunday from 1 to 5pm. Train travel from Manchester takes about 1 hour; it's 3 hours from Birmingham.

Leeds/Bradford Airport (☎ 0113/2509696) is located about 10 miles from Bradford, and a number of scheduled flights connect to London's Heathrow and Gatwick airports and most major regional U.K. airports. A taxi from the airport to town costs about £10 ($16). Bus service schedules and Day Rover discounted tickets are available through the tourist office.

VISITOR INFORMATION   The **Bradford Tourist Information Centre** is located at the National Museum of Photography, Film, and Television, Pictureville, Bradford (☎ 01274/753678). The center assists visitors in selecting accommodations or purchasing tickets, and provides public-transit timetables and city guides. Hours are Monday through Saturday from 9:30am to 5:30pm and Sunday from 1 to 5pm.

EXPLORING BRADFORD

Bradford's museums, mill shops, and restaurants provide the main attractions for tourists. The city also boasts Bradford University, one of the better regional universities in the United Kingdom.

The **Industrial Museum and Horse at Work,** Moorside Mills, Moorside Road (☎ 01274/631756), depicts mill life for worker and owner in the 1870s and offers free Shire horse rides for kids. The **Saltaire,** Salt's Mill, is the restored model factory-community developed in the mid–19th century by mill owner and philanthropist Titus Salt. The **1853 Gallery** at Saltaire (☎ 01274/531163) exhibits more than 400 works of local artist David Hockney, among other works.

Visitors can travel by steam-driven train on the **Keighley & Worth Valley Railway** (☎ 01535/647777) for a tour of Brontë Country in Haworth, through Oakworth's Edwardian station, and Damen's Station, billed as Britain's smallest rail station. A Day Rover ticket costs £5 ($8).

The **National Museum of Photography, Film, and Television,** Pictureville (☎ 01274/727488), captures the history of photography, film, and television in audiovisual presentations that span the past 150 years. The 5-story-high IMAX screen, the largest in England, explores a dazzling variety of cinematic images in a series of new and continuing exhibitions. Admission to the museum is free; the IMAX movie costs £3.90 ($6.25) and advance booking is recommended. Open Tuesday through Friday from 10:30am to 5pm, Saturday and Sunday from 10:30am to 6pm.

Bradford's textile industry is still represented in dozens of area mill shops where bargain hunters may find a great variety of mohair, pure-wool yarns, fabrics, sportswear, and other clothing and accessories. Some mill shops provide tours of factory spinning, weaving, and textile finishing.

Listers Mill Shop, Manningham Hills, Heaton Road (☎ 01274/542222), specializes in made-to-measure services for upholstered furniture, curtains, cushions, and other furnishings. **Suit Length & Fabric Centre,** Wakefield Road, Dudley Hill (☎ 01274/729103), will customize suits and garments for the individual tastes and fit of shoppers. **British Mohair Spinners,** Valley Road (☎ 01274/728456), showcases the art of spinning hair and cotton into the heavy, shiny mohair fabric.

WHERE TO STAY

Restaurant Nineteen (see "Where to Dine," below) also rents rooms.

The Guide Post Hotel. Common Rd. (3 miles from Junction 26 of M62), Low Moor, Bradford, W. Yorkshire BD12 0ST. ☎ **01274/607866.** Fax 01274/671085. 43 units. TV TEL. Mon–Thurs £65–£85 ($104–$136) double, Fri–Sat £40–£55 ($64–$88) double. AE, DC, MC, V.

Welcoming both business and leisure travelers, this is a winning little choice. Designed and created by Robert and Catherine Dey, it is expertly run and comfortable. You get a warm welcome as you're shown to your spacious, well-furnished room, each filled with all the amenities needed, including beverage-making equipment and satellite TV. The more expensive executive rooms have a spacious lounge area and include trouser-pressing facilities. The hotel is known for its Woodland Restaurant, serving a good English Anglo/Gaelic cuisine, with an affordable wine list. There's also a spacious bar area.

Victoria Hotel. Bridge St., Bradford, W. Yorkshire BD1 1JX. ☎ **01274/728706.** Fax 01274/736358. 60 units. TV TEL. £80.25–£107 ($128.40–$171.20) double; £109–£119 ($174.40–$190.40) suite. AE, DC, MC, V. From the M62, take Junction 26 to the M606, then to A6177 and A611, and exit at roundabout to Hallings; turn right at traffic light and hotel is at left.

Built in 1875, the Victoria in City Centre has been entirely restored since new owners acquired the hotel in 1995. Once the showpiece of the Lancashire and Yorkshire Railway, the hotel provides stylish accommodations at affordable rates. The well-furnished bedrooms all have stereos, VCRs, trouser presses, hair dryers, and superb bathrooms with power showers. Vic and Bert's restaurant is a modern interpretation of a Parisian brasserie (see "Where to Dine," below). Facilities include the Pie Eyed Parrot Pub, and a gym and sauna.

WHERE TO DINE

Bradford is called "the curry capital of the U.K.," boasting a vast array of Asian restaurants featuring dishes from Kashmir, Gujerat, the Punjab, and beyond.

Bombay Brasserie. Simes St. ☎ **01274/737564.** Main courses £4.75–£8.95 ($7.60–$14.30); set-price menu for 4 £13.25 ($21.20) per person. AE, MC, V. Mon–Sat noon–2pm; Sun–Thurs 6pm–midnight, Fri–Sat 6pm 1am. NORTH INDIAN/BANGLADESHI.

Here you'll find a variety of curry dishes, from mild versions such as *korma* (with nuts and cream) and *bhoona* to medium-strength curries like *dhansak* (lentil based curry) and *jal frezi* (dry curried meat cooked in onion slices). For those who like their curry hot, there's *madras* and *very* hot *phal* dishes. The restaurant also caters to vegetarian tastes.

Restaurant Nineteen. N. Park Rd., Heaton. ☎ **01274/492559.** Fax 01274/483827. Reservations recommended. Fixed-price dinner £19.95 ($31.90). AE, MC, V. Tues–Fri 7–9:30pm, Sat 7–10pm. Closed 2 weeks in Aug–Sept. ENGLISH/CONTINENTAL.

This highly rated, classic restaurant—the best in Bradford—takes up the main floor of a onetime mill-owner's Victorian mansion that overlooks Lister Park. Main course samplings include seafood bass with a potato cake, marinated venison, and rabbit with a mustard pudding. Even the soups have imagination and flair—witness the pumpkin and smoked haddock or the zucchini and sweet corn flavored with cream of coconut. The cooking is light and deft, and the service is of a high standard.

If dessert, perhaps a chocolate pot filled with frozen coffee parfait and served with a pear compote, has got you too stuffed to move, you can also stay here. It's a rather elegant B&B, renting four classy rooms, all with bathroom, shower, TV, and phone, at rates ranging from £70 to £85 ($112 to $136) for a double, including breakfast. Many English stars such as Derek Jacobi, appearing at the nearby Alhambra Theatre, often stay here.

Vic and Bert's. In the Victoria Hotel, Bridge St. ☎ **01274/728706.** Reservations recommended. Main courses £12.95–£14.95 ($20.70–$23.90); fixed-price 3-course menu £11.50–£14.50 ($18.40–$23.20). AE, DC, MC, V. Mon–Fri noon–2pm; daily 6:30–10pm. CONTINENTAL.

This elegant brasserie offers wood-grill cooking with an Oriental flavor. The clever chefs here have managed to lighten and modernize many dishes, although still showing a respect for traditional favorites. Their eclectic menu borrows liberally from around the world, and may include tuna steak marinated in Thai fish sauce and served over noodles, Japanese sushi rolls, and prawn and curried vegetables. For the heartier appetite, guests may select from courses featuring beef bourguignon, deep-fried duck pancakes, or the popular "bottomless" bowl of spaghetti.

BRADFORD AFTER DARK

The **Alhambra Theatre,** Morley Street (☎ **01274/752000**), offers a variety of presentations ranging from amateur to professional. At certain times of the year, leading actors of the English stage and screen may appear here. You can also see children's theater, ballet, and musicals. Ticket prices vary depending upon the type of performance. The theater is closed in August.

But perhaps you're just looking for a local pub. In the city center, the **Shoulder of Mutton,** 28 Kirkgate (☎ **01274/726038**), has a beer garden that comes complete with flower beds and hanging baskets. The oldest brewery in Yorkshire, it was originally Samuel Smith's Old Brewery. Lunch is available, and they also sell real ale here. As many as 200 drinkers can crowd in here on a summer night.

As an alternative choice, try the old-fashioned ale house, the **Fighting Cock,** 21–23 Preston St. (☎ **01274/726907**), with its bare floors and 12 different bitters. The best ales are Exmoor Gold, Timothy Taylors, Black Sheep, and Sam Smiths, but they also sell foreign-bottled beers and farm ciders. On nippy nights, coal fires keep the atmosphere mellow. Bar snacks are among the most reasonable in town, and the house specialty is chili (the chef guards the recipe).

4 Haworth: Home of the Brontës

45 miles SW of York; 21 miles W of Leeds

This village, on the high moor of the Pennines, is famous as the home of the Brontës, which is the most visited literary shrine in England after Stratford-upon-Avon.

ESSENTIALS

GETTING THERE   To reach Haworth by rail, take the West Yorkshire Metrotrain from Leeds City Station to Keighley (it leaves approximately every 30 min.). Change trains at Keighley and take the Keighley and Worth Valley Railway to Haworth and Oxenhope. Train services operate every weekend throughout the year, with 7 to 12 departures. From late June to the end of August, trains also run four times a day Monday through Friday. For general inquiries, call ☎ 01535/645214; for a 24-hour timetable, dial 01535/647777.

Yorkshire Rider, a private company, offers bus service between Hebden Bridge (which has rail links to Leeds and York) and Haworth. Bus no. 500 makes the trip between Hebden Bridge and Haworth from June through September only, four trips per day Sunday through Friday and one on Saturday. For information, call ☎ 01422/365985.

If you're driving from York, head west toward Leeds on A64 approaching the A6120 Ring Road to Shipley; then take A650 to Keighley, and finally link up with the B6142 south to Haworth.

VISITOR INFORMATION   The **Tourist Information Centre** is at 2–4 West Lane in Haworth (☎ 01535/642329). It's open April through October daily from 9:30am to 5:30pm; November through March daily from 9:30am to 5pm (closed December 24 to 26).

LITERARY LANDMARKS

Anne Brontë wrote two novels, *The Tenant of Wildfell Hall* and *Agnes Grey;* Charlotte wrote two masterpieces, *Jane Eyre* and *Villette,* which depicted her experiences as a teacher, as well as several other novels; and Emily is the author of *Wuthering Heights,* a novel of passion and haunting melancholy. Charlotte and Emily are buried in the family vault under the **Church of St. Michael.**

While in Haworth, you'll want to visit the **Brontë Weaving Shed,** Townend Mill (☎ 01535/646217). The shop is not far from the Brontë Parsonage, and features the famous Brontë tweed, which combines browns, greens, and oranges to evoke the look of the local countryside.

Brontë Parsonage Museum. Church St. ☎ **01535/642323.** Admission £3.80 ($6.10) adults, £1.20 ($1.90) children; free for children under 5; £8.80 ($14.10) family ticket (2 adults and 3 children). Apr–Sept daily 10am–5pm, Feb–Mar and Oct–Jan daily 11am–4:30pm. Closed mid-Jan to early Feb and at Christmastime.

The parsonage where the Brontë family lived has been preserved as this museum, which houses their furniture, personal treasures, pictures, books, and manuscripts. The stone-sided parsonage, originally built near the top of the village in 1777, was assigned for the course of his lifetime as the residence of the Brontë's father, Patrick, the Perpetual Curator of the Church of St. Michael and All Angel's Church. Regrettably, the church tended by the Brontës was demolished in 1870; it was rebuilt in its present form the same year. The parsonage contains a walled garden very similar to the one cultivated by the Brontës, five bedrooms, and a collection of family furniture (some bought with proceeds from Charlotte's literary success), as well as personal effects, pictures and paintings, and original manuscripts. It also contains the largest archive of family correspondence in the world.

The museum is maintained by a professional staff selected by the Brontë Society, an organization established in 1893 to perpetuate the memory and legacy of Britain's most famous literary family. Contributions to the society are welcomed. The museum tends to be extremely crowded in July and August.

WHERE TO STAY

Old White Lion Hotel. 6 West Lane, Haworth near Keighley, W. Yorkshire BD22 8DU. ☎ **01535/642313.** Fax 01535/616222. 14 units. TV TEL. £58–£68 ($92.80–$108.80) double. Rates include English breakfast. AE, DC, MC, V.

At the top of a cobblestone street, this hotel was built around 1700 with a solid stone roof. It's almost next door to the church where the Reverend Brontë preached, as well as the parsonage where the family lived. Paul and Christopher Bradford welcome visitors from all over the world to their warm, cheerful, and comfortable hotel. The bedrooms are attractively furnished. Although full of old-world charm, all rooms are completely up-to-date.

Meals feature fresh vegetables and are table d'hôte in the evenings. Bar snacks include the usual favorites: ploughman's lunch, hot pies, fish, and sandwiches.

WHERE TO DINE

Weaver's Restaurant. 15 West Lane. ☎ **01535/643822.** Reservations recommended. Main courses £8.95–£14.95 ($14.30–$23.90); fixed-price dinner £10.95 ($17.50) for 2 courses. AE, DC, MC, V. Tues–Sat 7–9:30pm. MODERN BRITISH.

The best restaurant in the Brontë hometown, this spot is British to the core. It not only has an inviting, informal atmosphere, but it serves excellent food made with fresh ingredients. Jane and Colin Rushworth are quite talented in the kitchen. Dinners might include such classic dishes as Yorkshire pudding with gravy. If available, try one of the Gressingham ducks, which are widely praised in the United Kingdom. For dessert, you might select a British cheese or one of the homemade delicacies. The restaurant is likely to be closed for vacation for a certain period each summer, so call in advance to check. They also rent four bedrooms of high caliber that cost £69.50 ($111.20) for a double.

5 Yorkshire's Country Houses, Castles & More

Yorkshire's battle-scarred castles, Gothic abbeys, and great country manor houses (from all periods) are unrivaled anywhere in Britain. Here are some of the highlights.

IN NORTH YORKSHIRE

Yorktour, Tower Street, York (☎ **01904/645151**), provides daily coach service to Castle Howard from June to September on Tuesday, Friday, and Sunday and to Fountains Abbey and Studley Royal on Saturday. The coaches leave in the afternoon for a half day of sightseeing.

✪ **Castle Howard.** Malton (15 miles northeast of York, 3 miles off A64). ☎ **01653/648444.** Admission £7 ($11.20) adults, £6 ($9.60) seniors and students, £4 ($6.40) children. Mid-Mar to late Oct, grounds daily 10am–5pm, house daily 11am–5pm (with last admission at 4:30pm).

In its dramatic setting of lakes, fountains, and extensive gardens, Castle Howard, the 18th-century palace designed by Sir John Vanbrugh, is undoubtedly the finest private residence in Yorkshire. The principal location for the TV miniseries *Brideshead Revisited,* this was the first major achievement of the architect who later created the lavish Blenheim Palace near Oxford. The Yorkshire palace was begun in 1699 for the third earl of Carlisle, Charles Howard.

The striking facade is topped by a painted and gilded dome, which reaches more than 80 feet into the air. The interior boasts a 192-foot-long gallery, as well as a chapel with magnificent stained-glass windows by the 19th-century artist Sir Edward Burne-Jones. Besides the collections of antique furniture, porcelains, and sculpture, the castle has many important paintings, including a portrait of Henry VIII by Holbein and works by Rubens, Reynolds, and Gainsborough.

The seemingly endless grounds around the palace also offer the visitor some memorable sights, including the domed Temple of the Four Winds, by Vanbrugh, and the richly designed family mausoleum, by Hawksmoor. There are two rose gardens, one with old-fashioned roses, the other featuring modern creations.

⚙ **Fountains Abbey & Studley Royal.** At Fountains, 4 miles southwest of Ripon off B6265. ☎ **01765/608888.** Admission £4.20 ($6.70) adults, £2 ($3.20) children, £10 ($16) family ticket. Oct–Mar daily 10am–5pm; Apr–Sept daily 10am–7pm. Closed Dec 24–25, Fri in Nov–Jan. It's best to drive, although it can be reached from York by public transportation. From York, take bus no. 143 leaving from the York Hall Station to Ripon, 23 miles to the northwest (A59, A1, and B6265 lead to Ripon). From Ripon, it will be necessary to take a taxi 4 miles to the southwest, although some prefer to take the scenic walk.

On the banks of the Silver Skell, the abbey was founded by Cistercian monks in 1132 and is the largest monastic ruin in Britain. In 1987, it was awarded World Heritage status. The ruins provide the focal point of the 18th-century landscape garden at Studley Royal, one of the few surviving examples of a Georgian green garden. It's known for its conservation work in the water gardens, ornamental temples, follies, and vistas. The garden is bounded at its northern edge by a lake and 400 acres of deer park. The Fountains Hall and Elizabethan Mansion are undergoing restoration.

IN WEST YORKSHIRE

✪ **Harewood House & Bird Garden.** At the junction of A61 and A659, midway between Leeds and Harrogate, at Harewood Village. ☎ **0113/2886331.** House, grounds, Bird Garden, and the Terrace Gallery £6.75 ($10.80) adults, £6 ($9.60) seniors, £4.50 ($7.20) children, family ticket £21 ($33.60). Grounds only, £5.50 ($8.80) adults, £4.50 ($7.20) seniors, £3 ($4.80) children 15 and under, family ticket £16.75 ($26.80). House, Bird Garden, and adventure playground Mar–Oct daily 10am–6pm. Terrace Gallery 10am–6pm. From York, head west along B1224 toward Wetherby and follow the signs to Harewood from there.

Twenty-two miles west of York, the home of the earl and countess of Harewood is one of England's great 18th-century houses. It has always been owned by the Lascelles family. The fine Adam interior has superb ceilings and plasterwork and furniture made especially for Harewood by Chippendale. There are also important collections of English and Italian paintings and Sèvres and Chinese porcelain.

The gardens, designed by Capability Brown, include terraces, lakeside and woodland walks, and a 4½-acre bird garden with exotic species from all over the world, including penguins, macaws, flamingos, and snowy owls. Other facilities include an art gallery, shops, a restaurant, and cafeteria. Parking is free, and there is a picnic area, plus an adventure playground for the children.

6 Yorkshire Dales National Park

The national park consists of some 700 square miles of water-carved country. In the dales you'll find dramatic white limestone crags, roads and fields bordered by drystone walls, fast-running rivers, isolated sheep farms, and clusters of sandstone cottages.

Malhamdale receives more visitors annually than any dale in Yorkshire. Two of the most interesting historic attractions are the 12th-century ruins of Bolton Priory and the 14th-century Castle Bolton, to the north in Wensleydale.

Richmond, the most frequently copied town name in the world, stands at the head of the dales and, like Hawes (see below), is a good center for touring the surrounding countryside.

EXPLORING THE DALES

For orientation purposes, you might head first for **Grassington,** 10 miles north of Skipton and 25 miles west of Ripon. Constructed around a cobbled marketplace, this is a stone-built village that's ideal for exploring Upper Wharfedale, one of the most scenic parts of the Dales. In fact, the Dales Way footpath passes right through the heart of the village.

Drop in to the **National Park Centre,** Colvend, Hebdon Rd. (☎ 01756/752774), which is open April through October daily from 9:30am to 5:30pm. From November through March, hours are Monday to Thursday 10am to 1pm, Friday 1 to 4:30pm, and Saturday and Sunday from 10am to 12:30pm and 1 to 4:30pm. Maps, bus schedules through the dales, and a choice of guidebooks are available here to help you navigate your way. If you'd like a more in-depth look than what you can do on your own, you can arrange for a qualified guide who knows the most beautiful places and can point out the most interesting geological and botanical features of the wilderness.

For another insight before setting out, visit the **Upper Wharfedale Folk Museum,** Market Square (no phone), which is open April through October daily from 2 to 4:30pm; Saturday and Sunday 10am to 12:30pm and 1 to 4:30pm. Admission is 50p (80¢). The museum features exhibits relating to the history and geology of the dales.

If you're in Grassington for lunch, drop in at **Old Hall Inn,** Thresfield, 1 mile west of the center (**01756/752441**). Try their local sausages with an onion confit along with their brew.

Ten miles west of Grassington (reached along the B6265), **Malham** is a great place to set out on a hike in summer. Branching out from here, you can set out to explore some of the most remarkable limestone formations in Britain. First, it's best to stop in for maps and information at the **National Park Centre** (☎ 01729/830363), which is open Easter through October daily from 9:30am to 5pm; off-season, only Saturday and Sunday from 10am to 4pm. Amazingly, this village of 200 or so souls receives a half million visitors annually. May or in September is the time to come, as the hordes descend from June through August.

The scenery in this area has been extolled by no less an authority than Wordsworth, and it's been painted by Turner. A trio of scenic destinations, **Malham Cove, Malham Tarn,** and **Gordale Scar,** can be explored on a circular walk of 8 miles that takes most hikers 5 hours. If your time (and your stamina) is more limited, you can take a circular walk from the heart of the village to Malham Cove and Gordale Scar in about two hours. At least try to walk a mile north of the village to Malham Cove, a large natural rock amphitheater. Gordale Scar is a deep natural chasm between overhanging limestone cliffs, and Malham Tarn is a lake in a desolate location.

Another interesting center, **Kettlewell,** lies 8 miles northwest of Malham and 6 miles north of Grassington. This is the main village in the Upper Wharfedale and is a good base for hiking through the local hills and valleys, which look straight out of *Wuthering Heights.* Narrow pack bridges and riverside walks characterize the region, and signs point the way to **The Dales Way** hiking path.

After Kettlewell, you can drive for four miles on B6160 to the hamlet of **Buckden,** the last village in the Upper Wharfedale. Once here, follow the sign to **Kidstone Pass,** still staying on B6160. At Aysgarth the river plummets over a series of waterfalls. This is one of the dramatic scenic highlights of the Yorkshire Dales.

HAWES: A BASE FOR EXPLORING
YORKSHIRE DALES NATIONAL PARK

About 65 miles northwest of York, on A684, Hawes is the natural center of Yorkshire Dales National Park and a good place to stay. On the Pennine Way, it's England's highest market town and the capital of Wensleydale, which is famous for its cheese. There are rail connections from York taking you to Garsdale, which is 5 miles from Hawes. From Garsdale, bus connections will take you into Hawes.

While you're there, you might want to check out the **Dales Countryside Museum,** Station Yard (the old train station; (☎ 01969/667494), which traces folk life in the

Dales, a story of 10,000 years of human history. Peat cutting and cheese making, among other occupations, are depicted. The museum is open April through October daily from 10am to 5pm. Winter opening hours vary; you'll have to check locally. Admission is £2.50 ($4) for adults and £1.75 ($2.80) for children, students, and senior citizens.

WHERE TO STAY

Cockett's Hotel & Restaurant. Market Place, Hawes, North Yorkshire DL8 3RD. ☎ **01969/667312.** Fax 01969/667162. 8 units. TV TEL. £49–£69 ($78.40–$110.40) double. Rates include English breakfast. AE, DC, MC, V.

Charming, with reminders of its age, this building has the date of its construction (1668) carved into one of its lintels. Set in the center of town, it's a 2-story, slate-roofed, stone cottage whose front yard is almost entirely covered with flagstones. Accommodations are done in an old world style with exposed wooden beams; they're snug, cozy, and well maintained.

A table d'hôte evening meal (four courses plus coffee) costs £15.95 ($25.50) per person. Lunches from £3.95 ($6.30) are served Easter through October, as well as substantial midafternoon cream teas at £2.60 ($4.15) per person.

Simonstone Hall. 1½ miles north of Hawes on the road signposted to Muker, Hawes, North Yorkshire DL8 3RD. ☎ **01969/667255.** Fax 01969/667741. 18 units. TV TEL. £70–£105 ($112–$168) per person double. Rates include half board. MC, V.

Just north of Hawes, you can stay and dine at Simonstone Hall. Constructed in 1733, this building has been restored and converted into a comfortable family run, country-house hotel. It's the former home of the earls of Wharncliffe. Not only the public rooms but the bedrooms are ideal for relaxation and comfort. Most of them are spacious, and all are furnished tastefully with antiques. The rooms are prettily decorated and kept in immaculate order by the helpful young staff.

Dining/Diversions: You can have drinks in the Tawny Owl Bar and enjoy good food in the hotel's dining room. Nonresidents can enjoy home-cooked bar meals or order a two- or four-course dinner. Dinner can be complemented with good wines from the extensive cellar.

7 North York Moors National Park

The moors, on the other side of the Vale of York, have a wild beauty all their own, quite different from that of the dales. This rather barren moorland blossoms in summer with purple heather. Bounded on the east by the North Sea, it embraces a 554-square-mile area, which has been preserved as a national park.

If you're looking for a hot, sunny beach vacation where the warm water beckons, the North Yorkshire Coast isn't for you—the climate here is cool because of the brisk waters of the North Sea. Even the summer months aren't extremely hot. Many Britons do visit North Yorkshire for beach vacations, however, so you will find a beach town atmosphere along the coast. Brightly colored stalls line the seafront and the people seem to be a bit more relaxed than their inland counterparts.

The beauty and history of the area are the real reasons to visit North Yorkshire. The national park is perfect for solitary strolls and peaceful drives. For remnants of the area's exciting days of smugglers and brave explorers, visitors can follow the Captain Cook Heritage Trail along the coast. The fishing industry is still very much alive in the area, although the whaling ships of yesteryear have been anchored and the fishmongers now concentrate on smaller trappings.

Because the park sprawls over such a large area, you can access it from five or six different gateways. Most visitors enter it from the side closest to York, by following either the A19 north via the hamlet of **Thirsk,** or by detouring to the northeast along the A64 and entering via **Scarborough.** You can also get in through **Helmsley,** where the park's administrative headquarters are located; just follow the roads from York that are signposted Helmsley. Gateways along the park's northern edges, which are less convenient to York, include the villages of **Whitby** (accessible via A171), and **Stokesley** (accessible via A19).

For information on accommodations and transportation before you go, contact **North York Moors National Park,** The Old Vicarage, Bondgate, Helmsley, York YO6 5BP (☎ 01439/770657). Advice, specialized guidebooks, maps, and information can be obtained at the **Sutton Bank Visitor Centre,** Sutton Bank, near Thirsk, North Yorkshire YO7 2EK (☎ 01845/597426). Another well-inventoried information source is **The Moors Centre,** Danby Lodge, Lodge Lane, Danby, near Whitby YO21 2NB (☎ 01287/660540).

EXPLORING THE MOORS

Bounded by the Cleveland and Hambleton hills, the moors are dotted with early burial grounds and ancient stone crosses. **Pickering** and **Northallerton,** both market towns, serve as gateways to the moors.

The North York Moors will always be associated with doomed trysts between unlucky lovers and ghosts who wander vengefully across the rugged plateaus of their lonely and windswept surfaces. Although the earth is relatively fertile in the river valleys, the thin, rocky soil of the heather-clad uplands has been scorned by local farmers as wasteland, suitable only for sheep grazing and healthy (but melancholy) rambles. During the 19th century, a handful of manor houses were built on their lonely promontories by moguls of the Industrial Revolution, but not until 1953 was the 554-square-mile district designated the North York Moors National Park.

Encompassing England's largest expanse of moorland, the park is famous for the diversity of heathers, which thrive between the sandstone outcroppings of the uplands. If you visit between October and February, you'll see smoldering fires across the landscape—deliberately controlled attempts by shepherds and farmers to burn the omnipresent heather back to stubs. Repeated in age-old cycles every 15 years, the blazes encourage the heather's renewal with new growth for the uncounted thousands of sheep that thrive in the district.

Although public bridle and footpaths take you to all corners of the moors, there are two especially noteworthy, clearly demarcated trails that comprise the most comprehensive moor walks in Europe. The shorter of the two is the **Lyle Wake Walk,** a 40-mile east-to-west trek that connects the hamlets of Osmotherly and Ravenscar. It traces the rugged path established by 18th-century coffin bearers. The longer trek (the **Cleveland Walk**) is a 110-mile circumnavigation of the national park's perimeter. A good section of it skirts the edge of the Yorkshire coastline; other stretches take climbers up and down a series of steep fells in the park's interior.

Don't even consider an ambitious moor trek without good shoes, a compass, an ordinance survey map, and a detailed park guidebook. With descriptions of geologically interesting sites, safety warnings, and listings of inns and farmhouses (haunted or otherwise) offering overnight stays, they sell for less than £4 ($6.40) each at any local tourist office.

The isolation and the beauty of the landscape attracted the founders of **three great abbeys:** Rievaulx near Helmsley, Byland Abbey near the village of Wass, and Ampleforth Abbey. Nearby is **Coxwold,** one of the most attractive villages in the moors. The Cistercian Rievaulx and Byland abbeys are in ruins, but the Benedictine Ampleforth still functions as a monastery and well-known Roman Catholic boys' school. Although many of its buildings date from the 19th and 20th centuries, they do contain earlier artifacts.

BASING YOURSELF IN THIRSK

You can drive through the moorland while based in York, but if you'd like to be closer to the moors, there are places to stay in and around the national park.

The old market town of Thirsk, in the Vale of Mowbray, 24 miles north of York on A19, is near the western fringe of the park. It has a fine parish church, but what makes it such a popular stopover is its association with the late James Herriot (1916–95), author of *All Creatures Great and Small*. Mr. Herriot used to practice veterinary medicine in Thirsk.

WHERE TO STAY

Brook House. Ingramgate, Thirsk, N. Yorkshire YO7 1DD. ☎ **01845/522240.** Fax 01845/523133. 3 units, none with bathroom. TV. £17 ($27.20) per person. Rates include English breakfast. Discount available for children. No credit cards. From Thirsk, turn left at Ingramgate, then turn left again in the driveway just before the bridge. Brook House is the 2nd house along the drive.

This large, brown-brick Victorian house, originally built in 1887, is situated on 2 acres of land and overlooks the Barbeck Brook (which flows through its front yard) and the open countryside. Despite its peace and isolation, the town's Market Square is only a 3-minute walk away. The charming and kind owner, Mrs. Margaret McLauchlan, has even been known to do a batch of washing for guests at no extra cost (but we can't promise that). She serves a good, hearty, and filling Yorkshire breakfast, plus an English tea in the afternoon. Tea-making facilities are also available for the guests, and the spacious and comfortable living room has a color TV. The house is centrally heated, and in the guests' drawing room there is an open log fire in cool weather. There is ample parking for cars. You'll enjoy the hospitality here.

The modern brick-sided bungalow set adjacent to Brook House's driveway also accepts overnight guests, but it is *not* associated in any way with the McLauchlan family or its enterprises.

✪ **Sheppard's Hotel, Restaurant & Bistro.** Front St., Sowerby, near Thirsk, N. Yorkshire YO7 1JF. ☎ **01845/523655.** Fax 01845/524720. 12 units, 10 with bathroom. TV. £40 ($64) double without bathroom, £50–£85 ($80–$136) double with bathroom; £88 ($140.80) 4-poster room. Rates include English breakfast. MC, V. Closed 1st week of Jan.

The late James Herriot treated his last horse on these premises, but now the Sheppard family has turned the complex into one of the finest lodging choices in the area. This family run concern operates out of an old stable block and granary (now restaurant and bistro, with well-furnished bedrooms overhead). A country atmosphere with pine furniture prevails, and the decor often consists of nailed horse brasses on the beams. Many guests request the "fat bedroom," so named because of its outsize double bed. All the buildings in the complex are grouped around a cobbled courtyard.

Dining: Many visitors come here just for a meal. The restaurant operates out of the old stables; a garden-room bistro was opened in the granary. Guests dine informally by candlelight in a setting of potted plants and palms. Mr. Herriot used to entertain his American publisher here. Main-course dishes, served with a choice of fresh vegetables, might include supreme of duckling lightly grilled and fanned over a kumquat glaze. Fillet of Moors lamb is oven-roasted with rosemary.

EXPLORING THE NORTH YORKSHIRE COAST

Along the eastern boundary of the park, North Yorkshire's 45-mile coastline shelters such traditional seaside resorts as Filey, Whitby, and Scarborough, the latter claiming to be the oldest seaside spa in Britain, located supposedly on the site of a Roman signaling station. The spa was founded in 1622, when mineral springs with medicinal properties were discovered. In the 19th century, its Grand Hotel, a Victorian structure, was acclaimed the best in Europe. The Norman castle on the big cliffs overlooks the twin bays.

It's easy to follow the main road from Bridlington north to Scarborough and on to Robin Hood's Bay and Whitby. As you drive up the coast, you'll see small fishing ports and wide expanses of moorland.

BRIDLINGTON

18 miles SE of Scarborough

Bridlington is a good starting point for a trip up the North Yorkshire Coast. A fishing port with an ancient harbor, the wide beach and busy seafront markets draw crowds who enjoy relaxing on the sand or browsing through the gift shops and stalls that line the streets. Flamborough Head is one of the most distinguishable features on England's east coast.

Jutting out into the North Sea, it features an 85-foot-tall lighthouse that stands atop a chalk cliff towering 170 feet above the sea. A path that winds up the cliffs ends at Bempton, site of a bird sanctuary that is one of the finest reserves on the coast. You can enjoy watching the seabirds or simply take in the view of the sea off Flamborough, the final resting place of more than a few ships. Bridlington also has many country houses that are open for tours, in addition to Pickering and Helmsley castles and the deserted village of Wharram Percy.

Where to Stay

The Manor House. Flamborough, Bridlington, E. Yorkshire, YO15 1PD. ☎ **01262/850943.** 2 units. TV. £30–£35 ($48–$56) per person double; £8 ($12.80) single supplement. Rates include English breakfast. AE, MC, V.

The current manor house of Flamborough was built around 1800. It was fully restored by local craftspeople and now boasts comfortable accommodations and a friendly atmosphere. Many visitors come to the house to browse through the variety of antiques sold in the converted stable block or to purchase a Gansey sweater. (These intricate fishermen's sweaters are handmade in the traditional way, an almost-lost process that has been revived by Lesley Berry, the house's proprietor.) For guests who choose to stay a night or two at the house, dinners can be arranged. These often feature local seafood and cost £19.50 ($31.20) per person.

SCARBOROUGH

18 miles NW of Bridlington; 34 miles NE of York; 253 miles N of London

Scarborough, one of the first seaside resorts in Britain, has been attracting visitors for more than 3 centuries. A mineral spring discovered in the early 17th century led to the establishment of a spa that lured clients with promises of its water's healing benefits. In the 18th century, swimmers were attracted to the waters off the coast—sea bathing had come in vogue, and the beaches of England swarmed with tourists taking part in the craze.

The city of Scarborough is divided into two unique districts separated by a green headland that holds the remains of Scarborough Castle, which dates from Norman times. South of the headland, the town conforms to its historical molds. High cliffs and garden walks interspersed with early Victorian residences dominate the landscape. The north side is more touristy; souvenir shops and fast-food stands line the promenade. "Rock" (brightly colored hard candy that can be etched with the saying of your choice) and cotton candy ("candy floss" to Britons) satisfy even the most die-hard sweet tooth.

For more information about what to see and do while you're in Scarborough, call or visit the **Tourist Information Centre**, St. Nicholas Cliff (☎ **01723/373333**), open daily from 9:30am to 6pm in summer; the rest of the year it's open from 10am to 4:30pm.

Trains leave London's Victoria Station approximately every hour headed for York, where you'll have to transfer to another train. The entire trip takes just under 3 hours. For more information on schedules and prices, call ☎ **0345/484950** (in the U.K. only) or 01603/764776 from the U.S. One bus a day leaves London heading for York, another will take you from York to Scarborough. If you're taking the bus, plan on spending most of a day riding. **National Express** bus service can be reached at ☎ **0990/808080**.

EXPLORING THE TOWN

The ruins of **Scarborough Castle**, Castle Road (☎ **01723/372451**), stand on the promontory near a former Viking settlement. From the castle, you can look out over the North Bay, the beaches, and the gardens along the shore. Throughout the summer, there are fairs and festivals that celebrate days of yore with mock battles, pageantry, and falconry displays. The castle is open March to September daily from 10am to 6pm; in October and November it closes at 4pm. During the winter, Scarborough Castle is open Wednesday through Sunday only from 10am to 1pm and 2pm to 4pm. Admission is £2.20 ($3.50) for adults, £1.70 ($2.70) for senior citizens and persons with disabilities, and £1.10 ($1.75) for children.

Nearby is the medieval **Church of St. Mary,** Castle Road (no phone), where Anne Brontë, the youngest of the three sisters of literary fame, was buried in 1849. She died in Scarborough after being brought from her home in Haworth in hopes that the sea air would revive her health.

Wood End Museum, The Crescent (☎ **01723/367326**), was once the vacation home of writers Edith, Osbert, and Sacheverell Sitwell. It now houses a library of their works as well as the collections of the **Museum of Natural History.** The house is open from May to September, Tuesday through Sunday from 10am to 5pm. The rest of the year it opens Friday through Sunday from 11am to 4pm. Admission is free.

Also located at The Crescent is **The Art Gallery** (☎ **01723/374753**). The gallery's permanent collection features pieces ranging from 17th-century portraits to 20th-century masterworks. Many of the works relate to the Scarborough area. Changing exhibitions by young artists and local craftspeople are also displayed. If you're interested in learning how to create your own works of art, you may want to spend a while at the **Crescent Arts Workshop,** which is located in the basement of the gallery. Local artists offer courses and demonstrations in their respective mediums. The Art Gallery is open May to September, Tuesday to Sunday from 10am to 1pm and 2pm to 5pm. The rest of the year it opens Friday through Sunday from 11am to 4pm. There is no admission charge. For information about workshop offerings, call ☎ **01723/351461.**

Local history collections as well as displays of important archaeological finds can be found at the **Rotunda Museum,** Vernon Road, just down the street from Wood End (☎ **01723/374839**). The museum is housed in a circular building originally constructed in 1829 for William Smith, the "Father of English Geology," to display his collection; it was one of the first public buildings in England to be constructed specifically for use as a museum. The Rotunda is open from May to September, Tuesday through Sunday from 10am to 5pm; October to April, Friday through Sunday from 11am to 4pm. Admission is free.

More than 70 species of sea creatures are housed at the **Sea Life Centre,** Scalby Mills, North Bay (☎ 01723/376125). An acrylic tunnel passes under the watery habitat of rays and sharks and feeding pools; hands-on displays encourage interaction with the animals. A favorite of children and adults alike is the Seal Rescue and Rehabilitation Centre, which takes in and cares for stray pups and provides a haven for resident adult gray seals. The center is open daily from 10am to 8pm in the summer and from 10am to 5pm the rest of the year. Admission is £5.50 ($8.80).

If it's a dreary day, **Kinderland,** Burniston Road, North Bay (☎ 01723/354555), is an excellent choice for entertaining the kids. The park caters to children under 14. Rides and activities, plus an array of play equipment, are sure to keep both the young and the young-at-heart occupied. Admission to the park is £4.50 ($7.20); opening times vary, so call ahead.

Of course, Scarborough still has the springs that established its popularity. **The Spa,** South Bay (☎ 01723/376774), no longer offers guests the opportunity to partake of the waters; it is now an entertainment and conference center in the midst of elegant gardens and buildings dating from several eras. In the summer months, there is a concert of some kind every day (usually classical and often held outdoors). Unless you just want to wander through the grounds, which is entertaining in itself, you may want to call ahead for concert times and prices.

Where to Stay

The Crown Hotel. Esplanade, Scarborough, N. Yorkshire YO11 2AG. ☎ 01723/373491. Fax 01723/362271. 77 units. TV TEL. £55–£65 ($88–$104) double. AE, DC, MC, V.

This hotel overlooks South Bay and the castle headland from its setting atop Scarborough's South Cliff. In recent years extensive renovations have brought everything up to date. The accommodations are comfortable and well equipped, with many rooms offering pleasant views over the sea. The bar is a popular meeting place for both guests and locals, many of whom enjoy sampling locally brewed beers. There is also a game room with a snooker table.

Palm Court Hotel. St. Nicholas Cliff, Scarborough, N. Yorkshire YO11 2ES. ☎ 01723/368161. Fax 01723/371547. 50 units. TV TEL. £54–£82 ($86.40–$131.20) double. Rates include English breakfast. AE, DC, V.

The Palm Court provides guests with modern amenities in an elegant, old-world atmosphere. Inviting common areas, such as the lounge and cocktail bar, provide ideal settings for sharing a drink with friends. Rooms are tastefully furnished and among the most comfortable at the resort. There's also a sauna and an indoor heated pool where guests can take a dip. Table d'hôte dinners are served in the dining room for £9.25 to £16.50 ($14.80 to $26.40). On Saturday nights guests can enjoy dinner and dancing as the resident band plays catchy, toe-tapping tunes in the ballroom.

Wrea Head Country House Hotel. Barmoor Lane, Scalby, Scarborough, N. Yorkshire YO13 0PB. ☎ 01723/378211. Fax 01723/371780. 21 units. TV. £90–£155 ($144–$248) double. Rates include breakfast. AE, DC, MC, V.

This Victorian country house is situated just north of Scarborough on 14 acres of beautifully kept grounds. There are several very compelling common rooms, such as a library and comfortable bar, that entice guests to sit and relax. The rooms vary in size and are individually styled with tasteful furnishings. The hotel restaurant, the Four Seasons, serves appealing meals prepared with locally grown produce. Guests often spend part of their stay strolling through the well-tended gardens or participating in a game of croquet with friends.

Where to Dine

Lanterna. 33 Queen St. ☎ **01723/363616.** Reservations recommended. Main courses £9.50–£16 ($15.20 $25.60). MC, V. Tues Sat 7–10pm. ITALIAN.

The Arecco family runs this small Italian restaurant, which is well known for its tasty, straightforward dishes featuring local seafood. Small scallops called "Queenies" are sweet tasting—perfect in the light marinara sauce served over homemade pasta. Many diners end their meal with one of the decadent desserts, such as zabaglione or baked Alaska.

Scarborough After Dark

The Talbot Inn, Queen Street (☎ 01723/364723), has shows that offer a variety of musical genres from folk to funk almost every night of the week. For jazz enthusiasts, **The Mermaid,** Foreshore Road (☎ **01723/377215**), is the place to go.

Alan Ayckbourn, a popular contemporary playwright, calls Scarborough home. **The Stephen Joseph Theatre,** Westborough, performs many of his plays as well as other favorites. Call the box office at ☎ **01723/370541** for information about shows and prices.

The Hole in the Wall, Vernon Road (☎ 01723/373746), is a well-stocked, lively pub where both locals and visitors gather to share drinks. Theakston's BB, XB, and Old Peculiar are among the ales served at the long bar, and basic meals are served at lunch.

ROBIN HOOD'S BAY

13 miles NW of Scarborough

Although Robin Hood's Bay was once a notorious port for smugglers, there is no connection with the well-known outlaw who shares the village's name. The tiny fishing port is tucked into a deep ravine; in fact, space is so limited that cars can't enter the village center. The villagers live in cottages precariously balanced on the steep cliffs, where narrow roads curve between the dwellings.

Where to Stay

Raven Hall Hotel. Ravenscar, N. Scarborough, YO13 0ET. ☎ **01723/870353.** Fax 01723/870072. 53 units. TV TEL. £104 ($166.40) double. Rates include English breakfast. AE, DC, MC, V.

Many guests never leave the grounds of the hotel for entertainment, though Raven Hall makes a good base from which to venture out into Strasbourg and nearby Robin Hood's Bay. The rooms have pleasant views of the water, the moors, or the garden, and are well equipped.

Dining: In the restaurant, diners enjoy dishes such as roast guinea fowl with red wine, bacon, and onion sauce or lamb cutlets with honey-and-rosemary glaze.

Amenities: 9-hole golf course, two tennis courts, a heated indoor pool and sauna, putting green, lawn bowling.

WHITBY

7 miles NW of Robin Hood's Bay; 350 miles NE of London

The resort town of Whitby, which lies at the mouth of the River Esk, has a rich and interesting history. It began as a religious center in the 7th century when Whitby Abbey was first founded. Later, Whitby became a prominent whaling port and eventually, like most coastal towns, it was an active participant in the smuggling trade.

Several famous explorers have pushed off from the beaches of Whitby, including Capt. James Cook. Captain Cook circumnavigated the globe twice as the king's surveyor in ships constructed by local carpenters and craftsmen; he also claimed Australia and New Zealand for Great Britain.

Literary references to Whitby add intrigue to the town. Herman Melville paid tribute to William Scoresby, captain of some of the first ships that sailed to Greenland and inventor of the crow's nest, in his novel *Moby Dick,* and Bram Stoker found his inspiration for *Dracula* in the quaint streets of Whitby.

The **Whitby Tourist Centre,** Langborne Road (☎ **01947/602674**), is open daily during the summer months from 9:30am to 6pm. The rest of the year it opens daily from 10am to 12:30pm and 1 to 4:30pm.

There is one bus a day that travels between London and Whitby. The trip takes approximately 7 hours and is a direct route. Call the **National Express** bus service at ☎ **0990/808080** for more details. To get to Whitby from London by train, you'll have to ride to Middlesborough or Scarborough then transfer to the train to Whitby. The number of trains to Whitby varies, so call ahead. The number for rail information is ☎ **0345/484950** (in the U.K. only) or 01603/764776.

Seeing the Sights

The ruins of **Whitby Abbey,** Abbey Lane (☎ **01947/603568**), lie high on the East Cliff, where they are visible from almost everywhere in town. The abbey dates from the 12th century and adjoins the site of a Saxon Monastery that was established in A.D. 657. Caedmon, the first identifiable English-language poet, was a monk here. It was on this site in A.D. 664 that the date for Easter was decided. The abbey is open Easter to September daily from 10am to 6pm; the rest of the year it closes at 4pm. Admission is £1.60 ($2.55) for adults, £1.20 ($1.90) for senior citizens, and 80p ($1.30) for children.

Another religious sight is the uniquely designed **Church of St. Mary** (no phone). Stairs leading to the church (there are 199 of them) begin at the end of Church Street. If you have the stamina to climb them, you can walk through the rather spooky churchyard; it was here that Lucy was taken as Dracula's victim in Bram Stoker's novel. The church itself is an eclectic mix of architectural styles.

The **Whitby Museum,** Pannett Park (☎ **01947/602908**), features exhibits that center around the city's history. Of course, ship models and details of Captain Cook's adventures are essential to the museum, but there are also displays about the archaeology and natural history of the area. The Pannett Art Gallery (same address and phone) has a permanent collection featuring paintings by George Weatherill. There are also constantly changing special exhibits. The museum and gallery are open from May 1 to September 30, from 9:30am to 5:30pm Monday to Saturday and from 2 to 5pm Sunday. From October 1 to April 30, they're open Monday and Tuesday from 10:30am to 1pm, Wednesday through Saturday from 10:30am to 4pm, and Sunday from 2 to 4pm. Admission to the museum is £1.50 ($2.40) for adults and £1 ($1.60) for children; there is no charge for the gallery.

The **Captain Cook Memorial Museum,** Grape Lane (☎ **01947/601900**), deals more specifically with the life and achievements of the famous explorer James Cook. It is open Monday through Friday in March from 11am to 3pm and daily from April through October from 9:45am to 5pm. Last entry is 15 minutes before closing. Admission is £2.50 ($4) for adults, £1.70 ($2.70) for senior citizens, and £1.50 ($2.40) for children.

The **Whitby Tourist Information Centre** (☎ **01947/602674**) can give anglers information about fishing along the town's coastline. Fishing is free all along the Whitby shore. If you'd rather go out to sea to reel in a big one, there are boats for hire at points throughout the city. The cost usually includes tackle and bait.

Golfers should visit the **Whitby Golf Club,** Low Straggleton (☎ **01947/602768**). The 6,134-yard course is open to visiting golfers daily. **Raven Hall Hotel Golf Course,** Ravenscar (☎ **01723/870353**), is open to nonguests all day, every day. The

9-hole course is well tended and offers panoramic views of the moors and the sea. Raven Hall is also the best place in the area for tennis.

Where to Stay

Dunsley Hall. Dunsley, Whitby, N. Yorkshire YO21 3TL. ☎ 01947/893437. Fax 01947/893505. 7 units. TV TEL. £47.50 ($76) per person double; £55 ($88) per person 4-poster room; £74.50 ($119.20) per person minisuite. Rates include breakfast. V.

Just outside of Whitby in a small hamlet, Dunsley Hall was built at the turn of the century by a Newcastle shipping magnate who lived here with his family until 1940. Some of the original carpets and furnishings remain and now add historical charm to the well-appointed hotel. There are carefully tended gardens around the house where guests can enjoy a stroll; there's also a fitness room and an indoor heated swimming pool. The rooms are all equipped with beverage-makers and hair dryers. In the Terrace Dining Room, traditional dishes are prepared with locally grown produce.

Larpool Hall. Larpool Lane, Whitby, N. Yorkshire YO22 4ND. ☎ 01947/602737. Fax 01947/820204. 20 units. TV TEL. £35 ($56) double; £50 ($80) suite. Rates include English breakfast. DC, V.

Larpool Hall is set in 10 acres of landscaped gardens with views overlooking the Esk Valley. Hospitality trays are delivered to all of the tastefully decorated rooms, some of which have exposed beams and wooden beds. The Dale Restaurant, with its bay window and 17th-century fireplace, is a lovely setting for a meal. The menu features meals that reflect Electra's interest and knowledge of cooking; you can enjoy traditional Yorkshire fare or more exotic flavors.

Stakesby Manor. Manor Close, High Stakesby, Whitby, N. Yorkshire YO21 1HL. ☎ 01947/602773. Fax 01947/602140. 8 units. TV. £69 ($110.40) double. Rate includes breakfast. AE, MC, V.

From your room at Stakesby Manor, a converted 1710 Georgian manor, you'll have a view either over the old town of Whitby or of the surrounding moorland. The guest house is located within a mile of the beach, golf course, and town center. Rod and Jill Hodgson are responsible for the day-to-day running of the hotel and are happy to arrange theater bookings or other entertainment for their guests. The Oak Room restaurant, with its wood-paneled walls, serves traditional English fare, and packed lunches are available on request.

Where to Dine

Many hotels in the area offer half-board plans (with dinner) in addition to bed-and-breakfast rates; it may save you time and money if you take advantage of these. If you don't, or if you're looking for lunch, try **Trencher's,** New Quay Road (☎ 01947/603212), for terrific fish-and-chips. Fresh fillets of haddock or cod are fried in a crispy batter and served with thick-cut fries. For good food in an even better atmosphere, stop by **White House and Griffin,** Church Street (☎ 01947/604857). While surrounded by the character of the 18th-century structure, you might enjoy panfried herring or Whitby bouillabaisse.

8 Durham

230 miles N of London; 15 miles S of Newcastle upon Tyne

This medieval city took root in 1090 after the Normans, under William the Conqueror, took over and began construction of Durham's world-renowned cathedral and castle on a peninsula surrounded by the River Wear. The cathedral, "Half Church of God, half Castle 'gainst the Scots," was built as a shrine to protect the remains of St. Cuthbert, while also providing a sturdy fortress against the warring Scots to the north.

The cathedral castle thrust Durham into its role as a protective border post for England. For centuries, Durham Castle was the seat of the prince bishops—kings of the wild northern territories in all but name—and a pilgrimage site for Christians coming to pay tribute to St. Cuthbert, a monk on Lindisfarne. His life of contemplation and prayer led to his consecration as a bishop in 685, and his sainthood after death.

Today, Durham boasts a university (built on the cornerstone of the castle), and is an excellent base for exploring this stretch of the North Sea coast, as well as the unspoiled rolling hills and waterfalls of the Durham Dales in the North Pennines.

ESSENTIALS

GETTING THERE   Trains from London's King's Cross Station arrive hourly during the day, with the trip taking about 3 hours, and trains from York leave every 2 hours, arriving approximately an hour later. Durham lies on the main London-to-Edinburgh rail line. For schedules and information, call ☎ **0345/484950** (in the U.K. only) or 01603/764776.

Contact the **Durham County travel hot line** at ☎ **0191/3833337** for more information on public transportation in the area.

Blue Line buses from London arrive twice daily, with the trip taking about 5 hours. For schedules and information, call ☎ **0990/808080.**

If you're driving from London, follow the A1/A1(M) north to Durham.

VISITOR INFORMATION   The **Durham Tourist Office** is at Market Place (☎ **0191/3843720**), and is open July and August, Monday through Saturday from 9:30am to 6pm and Sunday from 2 to 5pm; June and September, Monday through Saturday from 10am to 5:30pm; October through May, Monday through Friday from 10am to 5pm, and Saturday from 9:30am to 1pm.

SPECIAL EVENTS   At the **Durham Folk Festival,** held the last weekend in July, you can sing, clog, or just cavort to music; almost every event is free. The weekend also includes free camping along the River Wear, though you'd better arrive early on Friday if you want to get a choice spot. In mid-June, crowds swarm along the riverbank to cheer the crew racing the **Durham Regatta,** and the first weekend of September brings the sodden celebration of the nation's second-largest **beer festival.**

SEEING THE SIGHTS

✪ **Durham Cathedral.** Palace Green. ☎ **0191/3864266.** Free admission to cathedral; tower £2.50 ($4) adults, £1 ($1.60) children; treasury £1 ($1.60) adults, 20p (30¢) children; Monk's Dormitory 80p ($1.30) adults, 20p (30¢) children; audiovisual Visitors' Exhibition 50p (80¢) adults, 20p (30¢) children. Cathedral Mon–Sat 9:30am–4pm, except during services. May–Aug daily 7am–8pm; Sept–Apr daily 7:15am–6pm. Guided tours May 27–Sept 6 Mon–Fri at 10:30am. Treasury Mon–Sat 10am–4:30pm, Sun 2–4:30pm. Monk's Dormitory Apr–Oct Mon–Sat 10am–4pm, Sun 12:30–3:30pm and 4:30–6pm. Audiovisual Visitors' Exhibition Mar–Oct Mon–Sat 11am–3pm.

Under construction for more than 40 years, the cathedral was completed in 1133, and today is Britain's largest, best-preserved Norman stronghold and one of its grandest surviving Romanesque palaces. The structure is not only breathtaking to view, it is also architecturally innovative, the first English building to feature ribbed vault construction. It is also the first stone-roofed cathedral in Europe, an architectural necessity because of its role as a border fortress.

The treasury houses such relics as the original 12th-century door knocker, St. Cuthbert's coffin, ancient illuminated manuscripts, and more. You can still attend daily services in the sanctuary.

Durham Castle. Palace Green. ☎ **0191/3743800.** Admission £2.75 ($4.40) adults, £1.50 ($2.40) children, £6 ($9.60) family ticket. Guided tours Mar 22–Apr 25 and July–Sept

Mon–Sun 10am–noon and 2–4:30pm; other times of the year, Mon, Wed, and Sat 2–4:30pm. Closed during university Christmas breaks.

Adjoining the cathedral, the castle was the seat of the prince bishops of Durham for more than 800 years. In 1832, it became the first building of the fledgling local college, now Durham University, and today still houses University College. During university breaks, it offers unique bed-and-breakfast accommodations to the public.

Oriental Museum. Elvet Hill off South Rd. ☎ **0191/3747911.** Admission £1.50 ($2.40) adults, 75p ($1.20) children and seniors. Mon–Fri 9:30am–1pm and 2–5pm, Sat–Sun 2–5pm.

This is the nation's only museum devoted entirely to Eastern culture and art. It covers all major periods of art from ancient Egypt through India, as well as relics from Tibet, China, and Japan. The attractions are displayed in a way designed to make them understandable to the nonspecialist.

OUTDOOR PURSUITS

Fishing is a good sport all along the Rivers Tees and Wear, as well as in the several reservoirs and ponds scattered throughout the county. Boating is also available, and **Brown's Boat House,** Elvet Bridge (☎ **0191/3869525**), rents rowboats for pulls up or down the Wear, as well as offering short cruises from April through October, at the price of £2 ($3.20) for adults and £1 ($1.60) for children.

Hikers can either take the challenge provided by the 270 miles of trails (40 miles of which are in the county) along the **Pennine Way,** the **Weardale Way's** 78-mile course along the River Wear from Monkwearmouth in Sunderland to Cowshill in County Durham, or the **Teesdale Way,** running 90 miles from Middleton in Teesdale to Teesmouth in Cleveland. Rambles in town along public footpaths have recently been supplemented by more than 50 miles of former railway. Seven such trails make use of interlinked routes and range from the 4½-mile **Auckland Walk** to the 10½-mile **Derwent Walk.** If you don't feel like going it alone, there are also more than 200 guided walks throughout the county, providing background on the history, culture, and plant and animal life of the surrounding area; contact the tourist office (see above).

Cyclists can opt for road biking along quiet country lanes and converted railway routes, or mountain biking in **Hamsterley Forest.** The acclaimed **C2C national cycle route** passes through the Durham Dales and North Durham, along a 140-mile signposted route. Both road- and mountain-bike rentals are available at several locations, including **Dave Heron Cycles,** 29 Claypath St. (☎ **0191/3840319**), open Monday through Saturday from 9am until 6pm. A bike rental costs £15 ($24) a day, with a £30 ($48) deposit.

WHERE TO STAY

✪ **Georgian Town House.** 10 Crossgate, Durham DH1 4PS. ☎ **0191/3868070.** 6 units. TV. £55 ($88) double. Rates include breakfast. No credit cards.

This is the most desirable B&B in Durham, an unusually decorated place lying on a steep cobbled Georgian terrace street, close to everything, including the cathedral. It is a wonder of decoration, especially the reception hallway with its stenciled pillars and leaf patterns. It's almost like entering an arbor in sunny Sicily. In the lounge, "stars" twinkle on the walls. Sofas upholstered in deep stripes are placed around the fireplace where guests can mingle. Rooms, except for a cramped single, are tastefully decorated in vibrant fabrics and stencil work and are light and airy. The house has a panoramic view of the cathedral and castle. The grilled English breakfast is a hearty way to start the day.

Royal County Hotel. Old Elvet, Durham DH1 3JN. ☎ **0191/3866821.** Fax 0191/ 3860701. 150 units. MINIBAR TV TEL. £130–£143 ($208–$232) double; from £160 ($256) suite; £145 ($232) family unit. AE, DC, MC, V.

This is where we prefer to stay. Although some critics consider this an anonymous chain hotel (it's part of the Swallow chain), it has many winning features in its three Georgian buildings, plus a convenient location right in the heart of Durham. Skillfully converted from a row of riverside houses, it was once the home of the Bowes Lyon family before being turned into one of the region's premier hotels. Many of its original details have been retained, including an oak staircase that was transported here from Loch Leven in Scotland, the castle where Mary Queen of Scots was held prisoner. The bedrooms all maintain a high standard of comfort and furnishings, although they vary in size. Room features include tea- and coffeemakers, trouser press, iron and ironing board, and hair dryer.

Dining: On the premises, the County Restaurant offers traditional English dishes. The service is the most attentive in Durham, and you can enjoy piano music in the evening, while taking in the crisp linen, fresh flowers, and sparkling silver. You can also dine more informally in the Brasserie, which is open all day.

Amenities: Heated indoor swimming pool, fitness room, solarium, steam room, and sauna.

Three Tuns Hotel. New Elvet, Durham DH1 3AQ. ☎ **0191/3864326.** Fax 0191/3861406. 50 units. TV TEL. £115–£125 ($184–$200) double. Rates include breakfast. AE, DC, MC, V.

The second-best property in town was formerly a 16th-century coaching inn, housing travelers on their way north to Scotland. Almost all traces of its former role are gone today, and the property is run by the Swallow chain, which also operates the Royal County (see above). In fact, Three Tuns is only 200 yards from the Royal County and lodgers here are allowed to use the health-club facilities there. Bedrooms, done in tasteful fabrics, have been completely modernized and furnished to a high if not exciting standard. Each room has satellite TV, beverage-makers, a hair dryer, and an iron and ironing board; many also offer trouser presses and minifridges. Public rooms have more character and are roomy and inviting. Acceptable English and French meals are efficiently served in the hotel dining room.

WHERE TO DINE

Bistro 21. Aykley Heads House, Aykley Heads. ☎ **0191/3844354.** Reservations recommended. Main courses £8.50–£16 ($13.60–$25.60); fixed-price lunch £12–£14.50 ($19.20–$23.20). AE, DC, MC, V. Tues–Sat noon–2:30pm and 6–10:30pm. INTERNATIONAL.

A big hit locally, this is a bright, farm-themed bistro. Chef Adrian Watson's cuisine is precise and carefully prepared, with market-fresh ingredients that are allowed to keep their natural essence without being overly sauced or disguised. We especially recommend trying the blackboard specials. The food is full of flavor and rather forceful, borrowing from all over Europe—certainly the Mediterranean, but also offering traditional British fare at times, such as deep-fried plaice and chips. You can finish with one of the rich desserts, including double chocolate truffle cake. But if you want to be terribly old-fashioned and very English, you'll ask for the toffee pudding with butterscotch sauce. If you go in for this type of thing, it's prepared to perfection here.

DURHAM AFTER DARK

Much of Durham's nightlife revolves around its university students. When school is in session, **Brewer and Firkin,** 58 Saddler St. (☎ **0191/3864134**), is popular with a young crowd, and plays disco Friday and Saturday nights and live alternative/punk music on Sunday nights. It's open Monday through Saturday 11am to 11pm, and Sunday from noon until 10:30pm. **Coach and Eight,** Bridge House, Framwellgate Bridge (☎ **0191/3863284**), has disco Thursday through Sunday nights, and is open Monday through Saturday from 11am to 11pm, and Sunday from 11am to 10:30pm.

SIDE TRIPS TO THE DURHAM DALES, BARNARD CASTLE & BEAMISH

This densely populated county of northeast England was once pictured as a dismal, forbidding place, with coalfields, ironworks, mining towns, and shipyards. Yet the **Durham Dales,** occupying the western third of the county, is a popular panorama of rolling hills, valleys of quiet charm, and wild moors. **Teesdale** is particularly notable for its several waterfalls, including **High Force,** the largest waterfall in England, which drops a thundering 70 feet to join the River Tees. It is equally known for the rare wildflowers that grow in the sugar limestone soil of the region and have helped it earn protection as a National Nature Reserve.

Also notable is **Weardale,** once the hunting ground of Durham's prince bishops, with its idyllic brown sandstone villages. For more information on the wide range of options the area has to offer, contact the **Durham Dales Centre,** Castle Garden, Stanhope, Bishop Auckland, County Durham DL13 2SJ (☎ **01388/527650;** fax 01388/527461). Hours are November 4 through March 21, Monday through Friday from 10am to 4pm and Saturday and Sunday 11am to 4pm; and March 22 through November 3 daily from 10am to 5pm.

The 12th-century **Barnard Castle** (☎ **0183/3638212**) is an extensive Norman ruin overlooking the River Tees. It is open daily, March 27 through September 30, from 10am to 6pm; daily in October, 10am to 4pm; and Wednesday through Sunday, November 1 to March 26th, 10am to 4pm. Admission is £2 ($3.20) adults, £1 ($1.60) children under 16.

Barnard Castle is also home to the **Josephine and John Bowes Museum** (☎ **0183/3690606**), a sprawling French-style château housing one of Britain's most important collections of European art, including paintings from Goya to El Greco, plus tapestries, ceramics, costumes, musical instruments, and French and English furniture. There is also a children's gallery. The museum is open Monday through Saturday from 10am to 5:30pm and Sunday from 2 to 5pm. In March, April, and October it closes at 5pm, and November through February at 4pm. Admission is £3 ($4.80) for adults and £2 ($3.20) for children and senior citizens. Buses run from Durham several times daily.

✪ **North of England Open Air Museum.** Just off the A693 in Beamish. ☎ **0120/7231811.** Admission July 19–Aug 31 £7.99 ($12.80) adults, £4.99 ($8) children; spring and the rest of summer £6.99 ($11.20) adults, £4.99 ($8) children; winter £2.99 ($4.80) adults, £1.99 ($3.20) for children. Free for children under 5. Spring and summer daily 10am–5pm (to 6pm in July–Aug); off-season Sat–Sun and Tues–Thurs 10am–4pm. Closed Dec 15–Jan 2.

West of Chester-le-Street, 8 miles southwest of Newcastle upon Tyne, and 12 miles northwest of Durham City, this is a vivid re-creation of a turn-of-the-century village. A costumed staff goes through the motions of daily life in shops, houses, pubs, a newspaper office, garage, candy store, and candy factory, as well as a Methodist chapel, village school, home farm, and railway station. An average summer visit takes around 4 hours, and a winter visit, including the town and railway only, takes about 2 hours.

9 Hexham, Hadrian's Wall & the Pennine Way

304 miles N of London; 37 miles E of Carlisle; 21 miles W of Newcastle upon Tyne

Above the Tyne River, the historic old market town of Hexham has narrow streets, an old market square, a fine abbey church, and a moot hall. It makes a good base for exploring Hadrian's Wall and the Roman supply base of Corstopitum at

Corbridge-on-Tyne, the ancient capital of Northumberland. The tourist office has lots of information on the wall, whether you're hiking, driving, camping, or picnicking.

ESSENTIALS

GETTING THERE   Take one of the many daily trains from London's King's Cross Station to Newcastle upon Tyne. At Newcastle, change trains and take one in the direction of Carlisle. The fifth or sixth (depending on the schedule) stop after Newcastle will be Hexham. For schedules and information, call ☎ **0345/484950** (in the U.K. only) or 01603/764776.

Hexham lies 14 miles southeast of Hadrian's Wall. If you are primarily interested in the wall (rather than in Hexham), get off the Carlisle-bound train at the second stop (Bardon Mill) or at the third stop (Haltwhistle), which are 4 miles and 2½ miles, respectively, from the wall. At either of these hamlets, you can take a taxi to whichever part of the wall you care to visit. Taxis line up readily at the railway station in Hexham, but less often at the other villages. If you get off at one of the above-mentioned villages and don't see a taxi, call ☎ **01434/344272** and a local taxi will come to get you. Many visitors ask their taxi drivers to return at a prearranged time (which they gladly do) to pick them up after their excursion on the windy ridges near the wall.

National Express coaches to Newcastle and Carlisle connect with Northumbria bus service 685. Trip time to Hexham from Carlisle is about 1½ hours and from Newcastle about 1 hour. For schedules and information, call ☎ **0990/808080.** Local bus services connect Hexham with North Tynedale and the North Pennines.

If you're driving from Newcastle upon Tyne, head west on A69 until you see the cutoff south to Hexham.

VISITOR INFORMATION   The **Tourist Information Centre** at Hexham is at the Manor Office, Hallgate (☎ **01434/605225**). It's open Easter to mid-May, Monday through Saturday from 9am to 5pm and Sunday from 10am to 5pm; mid-May to October, Monday through Saturday from 9am to 6pm (9am to 5pm in October) and Sunday from 10am to 5pm; November through March, Monday through Saturday from 9am to 5pm.

HADRIAN'S WALL & ITS FORTRESSES

✪ **Hadrian's Wall,** which extends for 73 miles across the north of England, from the North Sea to the Irish Sea, is particularly interesting for a stretch of 10 miles west of Housesteads, which lies 2¾ miles northeast of Bardon Mill on B6318. Only the lower courses of the wall have been preserved intact; the rest were reconstructed in the 19th century using original stones. From the wall, there are incomparable views north to the Cheviot Hills along the Scottish border and south to the Durham moors.

The wall was built in A.D. 122 after the visit of the emperor Hadrian, who was inspecting far frontiers of the Roman Empire and wanted to construct a dramatic line between the empire and the barbarians. Legionnaires were ordered to build a wall across the width of the island of Britain, stretching 73½ miles, beginning at the North Sea and ending at the Irish Sea.

The wall is one of Europe's top Roman ruins. The western end can be reached from Carlisle, which also has an interesting museum of Roman artifacts; the eastern end can be reached from Newcastle upon Tyne (where some remains can be seen on the city outskirts; there's also a nice museum at the university).

From early May to late September, the Tynedale Council and the Northumberland National Park run a **bus service** that visits every important site along the wall, then turns around in the village of Haltwhistle and returns to Hexham. Buses depart Saturday and bank holidays from a point near the railway station in Hexham at roughly

10am, noon, 2pm, and 4pm; and Sundays at 11am and 1:30pm. From late July to late August, the tours are given daily. Call ☎ **0191/2123000** for more information. The cost is £4 ($6.40) for adults, £2 ($3.20) for children, and £10 ($16) for a family ticket. Many visitors take one bus out, then return on a subsequent bus, 2, 4, or 6 hours later. Every Sunday, a national-park warden leads a 2½ -hour walking tour of the wall, in connection with the bus service. The Hexham tourist office (see above) will provide further details.

Housesteads Fort and Museum. 3 miles northeast of Bardon Mill on B6318. ☎ **01434/ 344363.** Admission £2.50 ($4) adults, £1.90 ($3.05) seniors and students, £1.30 ($2.10) children. Apr–Sept daily 10am–6pm; Oct–Mar daily 10am–4pm. Closed Dec 24–26 and Jan 1.

Along the wall are several Roman forts, the most important of which was called *Vercovicium* by the Romans. This substantially excavated fort, on a dramatic site, contains the only visible example of a Roman hospital in Britain.

Vindolanda. Just west of Housesteads, on a minor road 1¼ miles southeast of Twice Brewed off the B6318. ☎ **01434/344277.** Admission £3.50 ($5.60) adults, £2.90 ($4.65) seniors and students, £2.50 ($4) children. Feb–Oct daily 10am–5pm (to 6:30pm in July-Aug).

This is another well-preserved fort south of the wall. There is also an excavated civilian settlement outside the fort with an interesting museum of artifacts of everyday Roman life.

Roman Army Museum. At the junction of A69 and B6318, 18 miles west of Hexham. ☎ **01697/747485.** Admission £2.80 ($4.50) adults, £2.40 ($3.85) seniors and students, £1.90 ($3.05) children. Mar–Sept daily 10am–4:30pm (to 6:30pm in July–Aug); Oct daily 10am–5pm. Closed Nov–Feb.

Near Vindolanda at the garrison fort at Carvoran, close to the village of Greenhead, the Roman Army Museum traces the growth and influence of Rome from its early beginnings to the development and expansion of the empire, with special emphasis on the role of the Roman army and the garrisons of Hadrian's Wall. A barracks room depicts basic army living conditions. Realistic life-size figures make this a strikingly visual museum experience.

Within easy walking distance of the Roman Army Museum is one of the most imposing and high-standing sections of Hadrian's Wall, **Walltown Crags,** where the height of the wall and magnificent views to the north and south are impressive.

HIKING THE PENNINE WAY
IN NORTHUMBERLAND NATIONAL PARK

Northumberland National Park, which was established in 1956, encompasses the borderlands that were a buffer zone between the warring English and Scots during the 13th and 14th centuries. Today, the park comprises almost 400 square miles of the least-populated area in England and is noted for its rugged landscape and associations with the northern frontier of the ancient Roman Empire.

Touching on the border with Scotland, the park covers some of the most tortured geology in England, the Cheviot Hills, whose surfaces have been wrinkled by volcanic pressures, inundated with sea water, scoured and gouged by glaciers, silted over by rivers, and thrust upward in a complicated series of geological events. Much of the heather-sheathed terrain here is used for sheep grazing; woolly balls of fluff adorn hillsides ravaged by high winds and frequent rain.

Northumberland Park includes the remains of Hadrian's Wall, one of the most impressive classical ruins of northern Europe. Footpaths run alongside it and there are a variety of walks in the country to the north and south of the monument. One of the most challenging hiking paths in Britain, the ✪ **Pennine Way,** snakes up the back-bone of the park. The 80 miles of the 250-mile path that are in the park are clearly marked; one of the most worthwhile (and safest) hikes is between Bellingham and the Hamlet of Riding Wood.

A map of the trails, priced at less than £1 ($1.60), can be purchased for these and other hiking trails at almost any local tourist office in the district. There are **National Park Centres** at Once Brewed (☎ **01434/344396**), Rothbury (☎ **01669/620887**), and Ingram (☎ **01665/578248**). The Head Office is at Eastburn, South Park, Hexham, Northumberland NE46 1BS (☎ **01434/605555**).

NEARBY PLACES TO STAY & DINE

Anchor Hotel. John Martin St. (on the A69, 7 miles west of Hexham), Haydon Bridge, Northumberland NE47 6AB. ☎ **01434/684227.** Fax 01434/684586. 10 units. TV TEL. £42.50 ($68) double. Rates include English breakfast. AE, DC, MC, V.

This is the social center of the village. Ideally situated for visitors to the wall and its surroundings, between Haltwhistle (9 miles away) and Hexham (7 miles), this river-side village pub was once a coaching inn on the route from Newcastle to Carlisle. The building, which was constructed in 1700 near the edge of the North Tyne River (which still flows within a few feet of its foundations), sits in the heart of the tiny vil-lage of Haydon Bridge. The cozy bar is a local hangout. In the country dining room, wholesome evening meals are served. The bedrooms are comfortably furnished.

George Hotel. Chollerford, Humshaugh, near Hexham, Northumberland NE46 4EW. ☎ **01434/681611.** Fax 01434/681727. 46 units. MINIBAR TV TEL. £110 ($176) double. Rates include English breakfast. AE, DC, MC, V. Take A6079 5 miles north of Hexham.

Standing on the banks of the Tyne, this country hotel has gardens leading to the river-bank. It's a convenient base for visiting Hadrian's Wall. The hotel dates from the 18th century, when the original structure was built of Roman stone. It has been extensively refurbished to a high standard, with conference facilities and a health club. All bed-rooms are comfortably furnished and equipped with such amenities as minibars with fresh milk daily for the beverage-maker, an iron and ironing board, and a hair dryer.

The Fisherman's Bar is where locals gather for a traditional pub welcome and bar snacks served at lunch. A fixed-price buffet luncheon is served in the Riverside Restau-rant, as is dinner.

Hadrian Hotel. Wall, near Hexham, Northumberland NE46 4EE. ☎ and fax **01434/681232.** 6 units. TEL. £49 ($78.40) double. Rates include English breakfast. DC, MC, V.

Ideal for a stopover along Hadrian's Wall, the Hadrian lies on the only street of the hamlet of Wall, 3½ miles north of Hexham. It's an ivy-covered 18th-century building erected of stones gathered long ago from the site of the ancient wall. The owners have carefully refurbished the place, which now has two Jacobean-style bars serving bar meals. There is also a restaurant, serving à la carte lunches and dinners. Each attrac-tive bedroom has a beverage-maker. The hotel has a private garden and a beer garden that serves as a warm-weather extension of its pub.

Langley Castle Hotel. Langley-on-Tyne, Hexham, Northumberland NE47 5LU. ☎ **01434/688888.** Fax 01434/684019. 21 units. TV TEL. £99 ($158.40) double; £145 ($232) suite. Rates include English breakfast. AE, DC, MC, V. From Hexham, go west on A69 to Haydon Bridge, then head south on A686 for 2 miles.

To experience a stately home, we recommend this hotel located on 10 acres of wood-land at the edge of Northumberland National Park, southwest of Haydon Bridge and about 7 miles west of Hexham. It's the only medieval fortified castle home in England that receives paying guests. The castle, built in 1350, was largely uninhabited after being damaged in 1400 during an English-Scottish war, until it was purchased in the late 19th century by Cadwallader Bates, a historian, who spent the rest of his life carefully restoring the property to its original beauty. Medieval features here include the 1350 spiral staircase, stained-glass windows, huge open fireplaces, 7-foot-thick walls, and many turrets. The luxuriously appointed bedrooms vary in size; some have whirlpools or saunas. An adjacent building has extra accommodations, including four new suites, as well as a small conference room in view of the castle.

The hotel has an elegant drawing room, with an adjoining oak-paneled bar. Local specialties are served in the intimate restaurant.

Index

FROMMER'S® COMPLETE TRAVEL GUIDES

(Comprehensive guides with selections in all price ranges—from deluxe to budget)

Alaska
Amsterdam
Arizona
Atlanta
Australia
Austria
Bahamas
Barcelona, Madrid & Seville
Belgium, Holland & Luxembourg
Bermuda
Boston
Budapest & the Best of Hungary
California
Canada
Cancún, Cozumel & the Yucatán
Cape Cod, Nantucket & Martha's Vineyard
Caribbean
Caribbean Cruises & Ports of Call
Caribbean Ports of Call
Carolinas & Georgia
Chicago
China
Colorado
Costa Rica
Denver, Boulder & Colorado Springs
England
Europe
Florida

France
Germany
Greece
Hawaii
Hong Kong
Honolulu, Waikiki & Oahu
Ireland
Israel
Italy
Jamaica & Barbados
Japan
Las Vegas
London
Los Angeles
Maryland & Delaware
Maui
Mexico
Miami & the Keys
Montana & Wyoming
Montréal & Québec City
Munich & the Bavarian Alps
Nashville & Memphis
Nepal
New England
New Mexico
New Orleans
New York City
Nova Scotia, New Brunswick & Prince Edward Island
Oregon
Paris
Philadelphia & the Amish Country

Portugal
Prague & the Best of the Czech Republic
Provence & the Riviera
Puerto Rico
Rome
San Antonio & Austin
San Diego
San Francisco
Santa Fe, Taos & Albuquerque
Scandinavia
Scotland
Seattle & Portland
Singapore & Malaysia
South Pacific
Spain
Switzerland
Thailand
Tokyo
Toronto
Tuscany & Umbria
USA
Utah
Vancouver & Victoria
Vermont, New Hampshire & Maine
Vienna & the Danube Valley
Virgin Islands
Virginia
Walt Disney World & Orlando
Washington, D.C.
Washington State

FROMMER'S® DOLLAR-A-DAY GUIDES

(The ultimate guides to comfortable low-cost travel)

Australia from $50 a Day
California from $60 a Day
Caribbean from $60 a Day
England from $60 a Day
Europe from $50 a Day
Florida from $60 a Day
Greece from $50 a Day
Hawaii from $60 a Day
Ireland from $50 a Day

Israel from $45 a Day
Italy from $50 a Day
London from $70 a Day
New York from $75 a Day
New Zealand from $50 a Day
Paris from $70 a Day
San Francisco from $60 a Day
Washington, D.C., from $60 a Day

FROMMER'S® MEMORABLE WALKS

Chicago
London

New York
Paris

San Francisco

FROMMER'S® PORTABLE GUIDES

Acapulco, Ixtapa/
   Zihuatenejo
Bahamas
California Wine
   Country
Charleston & Savannah
Chicago

Dublin
Las Vegas
London
Maine Coast
New Orleans
New York City
Paris

Puerto Vallarta, Manzanillo
   & Guadalajara
San Francisco
Sydney
Tampa Bay & St. Petersburg
Venice
Washington, D.C.

FROMMER'S® NATIONAL PARK GUIDES

Grand Canyon
National Parks of the American West
Yellowstone & Grand Teton

Yosemite & Sequoia/
   Kings Canyon
Zion & Bryce Canyon

THE COMPLETE IDIOT'S TRAVEL GUIDES

(The ultimate user-friendly trip planners)

Cruise Vacations
Planning Your Trip to Europe
Hawaii

Las Vegas
Mexico's Beach Resorts
New Orleans

New York City
San Francisco
Walt Disney World

SPECIAL-INTEREST TITLES

The Civil War Trust's Official Guide to
   the Civil War Discovery Trail
Frommer's Caribbean Hideaways
Israel Past & Present
New York City with Kids
New York Times Weekends
Outside Magazine's Adventure Guide
   to New England
Outside Magazine's Adventure Guide
   to Northern California

Outside Magazine's Adventure Guide
   to the Pacific Northwest
Outside Magazine's Guide to Family Vacations
Places Rated Almanac
Retirement Places Rated
Washington, D.C., with Kids
Wonderful Weekends from Boston
Wonderful Weekends from New York City
Wonderful Weekends from San Francisco
Wonderful Weekends from Los Angeles

THE UNOFFICIAL GUIDES®

(Get the unbiased truth from these candid, value-conscious guides)

Atlanta
Branson, Missouri
Chicago
Cruises
Disneyland

Florida with Kids
The Great Smoky
   & Blue Ridge
   Mountains
Las Vegas

Miami & the Keys
Mini-Mickey
New Orleans
New York City
San Francisco

Skiing in the West
Walt Disney World
Walt Disney World
   Companion
Washington, D.C.

FROMMER'S® IRREVERENT GUIDES

(Wickedly honest guides for sophisticated travelers)

Amsterdam
Boston
Chicago

London
Manhattan

New Orleans
Paris

San Francisco
Walt Disney World
Washington, D.C.

FROMMER'S® DRIVING TOURS

America
Britain
California

Florida
France
Germany

Ireland
Italy
New England

Scotland
Spain
Western Europe

WHEREVER YOU TRAVEL, *H*ELP IS NEVER FAR AWAY.

From planning your trip to

providing travel assistance along

the way, American Express®

Travel Service Offices are

always there to help

you do more.

American Express Travel Service
Offices are found in central locations
throughout Great Britain.

do more AMERICAN EXPRESS

Travel

www.americanexpress.com/travel